Introduction to Human-Computer Interaction

Introduction to Human-Computer Interaction

Kasper Hornbæk
University of Copenhagen

Per Ola Kristensson
University of Cambridge

Antti Oulasvirta
Aalto University

OXFORD
UNIVERSITY PRESS

OXFORD
UNIVERSITY PRESS

Great Clarendon Street, Oxford, OX2 6DP,
United Kingdom

Oxford University Press is a department of the University of Oxford.
It furthers the University's objective of excellence in research, scholarship,
and education by publishing worldwide. Oxford is a registered trade mark of
Oxford University Press in the UK and in certain other countries.

© Kasper Hornbæk, Per Ola Kristensson, and Antti Oulasvirta 2025

The moral rights of the authors have been asserted.

This is an open access publication, available online and distributed under the
terms of a Creative Commons Attribution-Non Commercial-No Derivatives 4.0
International licence (CC BY-NC-ND 4.0), a copy of which is available at
https://creativecommons.org/licenses/by-nc-nd/4.0/
Subject to this licence, all rights are reserved.

Enquiries concerning reproduction outside the scope of this licence should be sent
to the Rights Department, Oxford University Press, at the address above.

Published in the United States of America by Oxford University Press
198 Madison Avenue, New York, NY 10016, United States of America

British Library Cataloguing in Publication Data
Data available

Library of Congress Cataloging-in-Publication Data: 2025935533

ISBN 9780192864543
ISBN 9780192864550 (pbk.)

DOI: 10.1093/oso/9780192864543.001.0001

Printed and bound by
CPI Group (UK) Ltd., Croydon, CR0 4YY

The manufacturer's authorised representative in the EU for product safety is Oxford University Press España S.A., Parque Empresarial San Fernando de Henares, Avenida de Castilla, 2 – 28830 Madrid (www.oup.es/en or product.safety@oup.com). OUP España S.A. also acts as importer into Spain of products made by the manufacturer.

Links to third party websites are provided by Oxford in good faith and for information only. Oxford disclaims any responsibility for the materials contained in any third party website referenced in this work.

Contents

Part I **Overview of Human–Computer Interaction**

1 Introduction to human–computer interaction *3*

Part II **Understanding People**

2 Introduction to understanding people *27*

3 Perception *37*

4 Motor control *63*

5 Cognition *83*

6 Needs and motivations *109*

7 Experience *123*

8 Collaboration *141*

9 Communication *159*

Part III **User Research**

10 Introduction to user research *183*

11 Interviews *197*

12 Field research *215*

13 Survey research *229*

14 Unobtrusive research *249*

15 Representations of user research *259*

Part IV **Understanding Interaction**

16 Introduction to interaction *279*

17 Information and control *291*

18 Dialogue *309*

19 Tool use *325*

20 Automation *339*

21 Rationality *355*

22 Practice *375*

Part V **User Interfaces**

23 Introduction to user interfaces *389*

24 Input devices *405*

25 Displays *425*

26 Interaction techniques *445*

27 Commands and navigation *469*

28 Graphical user interfaces *485*

29 Reality-based interaction *503*

Part VI Design

30 Introduction to design *529*

31 Design cognition *543*

32 Design practice *565*

33 Design processes *585*

Part VII Engineering

34 Introduction to engineering *599*

35 Systems *607*

36 Design engineering *623*

37 Safety and risk *645*

38 Software *667*

39 Computational representations and models *681*

Part VIII Evaluation

40 Introduction to evaluation *707*

41 Analytical evaluation methods *719*

42 Think-aloud studies *741*

43 Experiments *751*

44 Field evaluations *771*

Part IX Conclusion

45 Growing into the HCI discipline *783*

46 Summary: HCI principles *793*

References *805*
Index *849*

Part I

Overview of Human–Computer Interaction

1
Introduction to human–computer interaction

From fishing nets to drilling machines, tools are vital to human ability. They enhance our physical abilities and are central to many intellectual activities, such as writing, mathematics, and accounting. It is hardly surprising that great efforts have been made throughout history to innovate and refine them. In the long history of tools, the birth of the computer marks a watershed. The invention of transistors in the twentieth century, together with the theory of computation and the architecture of the digital computer, pushed humanity to transform itself.

At the core of this revolution was the ability to flexibly define and execute *computer programs*—sequences of logical operations executed by a computer. Transistors enable energy-efficient and noise-resilient logic gates, which, in turn, enable the implementation of Boolean operations, such as nand and nor. These logic gates are organized as logic circuits to implement the necessary functions of a computer, such as arithmetic logic units and registers, all the way up to a complete microprocessor. A computing system integrates a microprocessor with the memory and peripherals necessary to execute programs. An important enabler is the operating system, a special computer program that manages the hardware and software resources of a computer, such as access to memory and displays, and allocates such resources to programs. It also provides common services to programs, such as access to networks.

Programmability lends computers their power as tools. Computer programs can decompose complex activities into sequences of much simpler operations. When input is provided to a program, it is executed according to the program. For example, the task of sending a message to a contact is broken down into subtasks, such as sensing user input, committing letters, updating the display, selecting a recipient from a menu, or sending a message over a network. Each of these subtasks is implemented via numerous simpler operations performed by a computer. Computer programs also permit computation using different formalisms, from algebra to probability theory. They can be used to flexibly represent the types of input that are important. An input can represent virtually anything that can be defined using a binary system, such as images, text, and sound. This has been central to the wider appropriation of computing as a tool. Thus, the remarkable efficiency, flexibility, and scalability of computers as tools boil down to the concept of a programmable machine capable of interpreting computer programs.

However, computers would be useless as tools if they did not offer a way for people to control them. A special part of a computing system is the *user interface*. It is the part that the user can see and utilize to control the computer. Through the user interface, users can provide input and instructions to a computer and receive feedback from it. In short, the user interface enables *interaction* with a computer. The user interface simplifies the underlying technical system for the user: It allows users to command a computer without bothering with what it does under the hood. Instead of defining a long and incomprehensible binary code that commands a microprocessor to delete a file, the command can be provided with a few mouse movements and clicks. When a user drags an icon representing a file to the trash can to delete it, this instruction is propagated through many layers of instructions, trickling down from the file system managed by the operating system to low-level disk management handled by the physical storage device. In the end, the computer updates the display to communicate to the user what it has done.

The development of technology for *interactive computing systems* has been an important driver behind the widespread adoption of computing we have witnessed in the last 50 years. Figure 1.1 shows a few snapshots of the transformation of computing from machines used exclusively by trained professionals to tools suitable for everyone. The speed of this development has been mind-boggling. The authors of this book have experienced the adoption of the personal computer, the world wide web, the mobile phone, intelligent interactive systems, and virtual and augmented reality. These and many other technologies have impacted practically all areas of life during their lifetimes. Computing has had a pervasive impact on what we do, how we think, what we value, how we play, and even how we build and maintain social relationships, including romantic relationships. Computers have shaped our economies, leisure, transportation patterns, social networks, and even elections and wars.

Although computing systems can be autonomous, most systems are intended to be used by humans, specifically to assist them. The realization that this is not a trivial task has led to the field of research called *human–computer interaction*, or HCI for short. HCI emerged gradually through early efforts in other fields, including psychology, computer science, and electrical engineering. What we now know as the field of HCI emerged in the late 1970s. The birth of the field coincided with the revolution of the personal computer, which marked the transition of computers from expensive mainframes kept in organizations to computing technology suitable for homes and workplaces. Interest in HCI was fueled by the belief that computing technology will fail unless it is designed with serious consideration for its users.

Two fundamental questions characterized early research: *How* should all this computing power be used and *for what*? Around the emergence of the personal computer in the late 1970s, it became clear that software needs to be designed for end-users and not just for specialists, such as programmers. These and other observations prompted a search for both new visions of computing and fundamental knowledge about the nature of the human use of computers. Over the years, the focus in the HCI field shifted to the question we now see driving HCI research:

> How can people with different goals and capabilities, and in different contexts, be able to use computing productively, enjoyably, and safely?

In short, the noble goal of HCI research is to help create computing that supports the betterment of humankind.

The book provides an introduction to the field of HCI. HCI is primarily a research-driven field. It focuses not only on the scientific principles underpinning human–computer interaction but also on the very concrete goal of designing better computing systems. For this reason, while the starting point in this book is theoretical research that helps us understand interaction, we also cover various aspects of design. The pragmatic aims of HCI research cannot be overstated. Accordingly, the chapters in this book acknowledge the many challenges that practitioners face, and identify the solution principles that can be used to tackle them.

Since HCI is not typically taught in basic education, most HCI researchers to date have discovered the field during university studies. Everybody has a unique story to tell about how they fell in love with the area. We, the authors of this book, discovered HCI in very different ways. Kasper found HCI via scientific curiosity. As a student of computer science, Kasper realized during his third undergraduate year that HCI, and not lambda calculus as he thought at the time, unified his

INTRODUCTION TO HUMAN–COMPUTER INTERACTION | 5

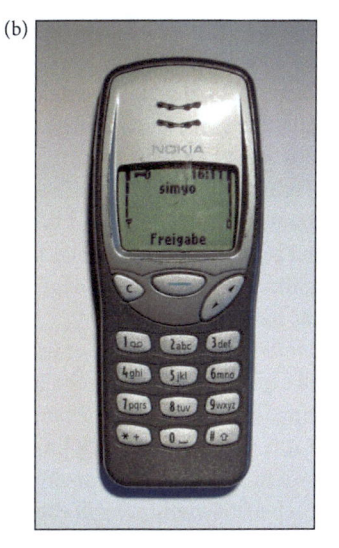

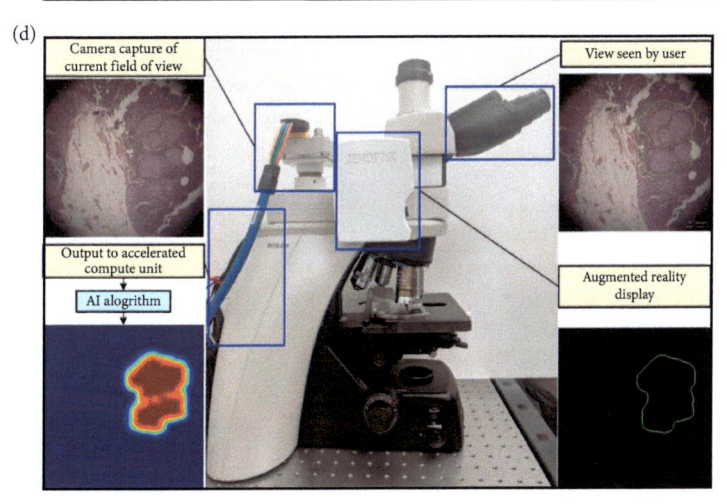

Figure 1.1 The evolution of interactive computing. The emergence of *personal computing*, exemplified by the Xerox Star from 1981 [391] (image by Leigh Klotz, reused under Creative Commons License). The emergence of *mobile computing*, exemplified by the popular Nokia 3210, around 1999 (image from Basic Master, reused under Creative Commons License). The emergence of *social computing*, exemplified by the collaborative encyclopedia Wikipedia, created in 2001 (image from archive.org). The emergence of *computing enhanced by artificial intelligence (AI)*, exemplified by an AI-assisted microscope from 2019 [146].

interests in technology, psychology, and philosophy. Another co-author, Per Ola, studied cognitive science and quickly became interested in applying it to the practical problem of how to help people enter text, a pursuit that eventually led to the invention of the gesture keyboard, a text-entry technique that is integrated into many mobile devices today. Finally, Antti was motivated by frustration while studying cognitive psychology for a master's degree. He felt that HCI is too complex for verbally expressed theories. Over the years, he has developed a view that scientific knowledge about users' behavior and thinking can be encapsulated into computational models, similar to other areas of applied science, which can then be used—with the help of algorithms—to explain and enhance interaction. We hope that this book can plant the seeds of new stories that will change the field in the future!

In the remainder of this chapter, we will expand on the defining characteristics of HCI. In particular, we will explain why HCI is a challenging field and why it needs to combine science, design, and engineering. We will also give a brief historical account of how HCI emerged as a field and became what it is now: a multidisciplinary melting pot. We strongly believe that HCI is of pivotal importance to society, which is why we will also dedicate some space to the key arguments supporting this belief. Finally, we will explain our approach to HCI and the structure of this book.

1.1 Why is HCI challenging?

What makes HCI worth studying, and why is a separate research field needed? First, humans are complex biological and social organisms. A human being is capable of complex thought and has developed language abilities, capabilities for fine motor movements, and generally excellent skills for learning to develop, use, and adapt tools to achieve goals. Several of these fundamental abilities are sufficiently well-understood to apply them in HCI, such as central aspects of human motor control. However, many open questions remain, such as those related to experience and language. Furthermore, HCI must account for individual differences. What may work for one user may be unsuitable for another. Individual differences in computer use are staggering, not only in terms of performance but also in terms of what is considered interesting or culturally appropriate. For example, an expert in HCI4D (HCI for development) described the challenges faced in non-Western contexts as follows [184, p. 2228]:

> We need to address the everyday problems of people. Most people don't know how to scroll, navigate. We need to do basic HCI work to make text larger. Also, time of day is the most prominent thing on [a phone's] screen. Let's replace that with the amount of airtime you have left. We need to improve upon what we built yesterday rather than doing novel interventions or focusing on the future.

Second, the computer is among the most complex tools humans have devised. The complexity of this tool stems from its elaborate stack, which ranges from transistors, logic gates, microcontrollers, and memory chips to operating systems, software drivers, software libraries and toolkits, applications, and user interfaces. Designing systems with this level of complexity is inherently challenging.

Third, HCI involves people interacting with computers in complex contexts where they try to accomplish a variety of goals. Thus, HCI requires some systems thinking. This means taking into account the full sociotechnical context in which specific HCI activities are situated. In HCI, even if we often focus on a subsystem (e.g., interaction with a graphical user interface), successful deployment relies on the ability to understand and relate observations to their wider, system-level context.

Fourth, design is hard. Ultimately, the purpose of HCI research is to influence the design of applications, interaction techniques, systems, or services so that users can achieve their goals in an effective, efficient, safe, and satisfactory manner. Why is doing such designing hard? One reason is that there is no perfect design. Design is about identifying and generating suitable solutions that trade off desirable characteristics, such as the user's speed for accuracy. In addition, designing requires creating new ideas. In design fixation, a designer maintains an early identified solution despite being inferior to other possible designs. It is hard to let go of old ideas and generate new ideas that are also valuable. Even experienced designers suffer from design fixation. Moreover, arriving at a design is a complex process where it is easy to introduce mistakes early in the process, such as accidentally injecting faulty user requirements based on misunderstandings, which are exceedingly difficult to correct later in the design process.

These reasons explain why HCI is hard. They indicate that HCI requires a unique combination of skills that almost no student receives from basic education. The skills cover software development, such as understanding software architectures and programming user interfaces; analytical skills, such as formal modeling of a user's performance; design practice, for example, interaction design, service design, or product design; and user research skills, such as carrying out and analyzing experiments, conducting interviews, and engaging in field studies. This book covers these basic skills.

1.2 Human–computer interaction as a field

The term *human–computer interaction* has been in use since the mid-1970s [e.g., 131]. Before then, the terms *man–computer interaction* and *man–machine interaction* had been in use since the early 1960s [e.g., 476, 588]. Until the 1970s, real-time interaction with a computer was impossible, mostly due to limited capabilities in processing power and displays. Computer requests were made in batches, sometimes in the clumsy form of punch cards. In addition, the time it took to get an answer from the computer was often in the order of hours. With the advent of interactive terminals and later graphical displays, the term *interaction* suddenly became relevant. Although computer users at that time were primarily professionals—such as managers, developers, and operators—researchers started to explore ways to provide more people with better access to computing. Consequently, the next decades saw the birth of a new scientific community with research groups, publication venues, and shared interests.

In the early 1990s, the international computer science organization—the Association for Computing Machinery (ACM)—set up a task force on education that defined HCI [339]. This has become the most widely used definition for characterizing the field. It reads as follows:

> Human–computer interaction is a discipline concerned with the design, evaluation and implementation of interactive computing systems for human use and with the study of major phenomena surrounding them.

The definition has three noteworthy parts. First, HCI is about building interactive systems. It is concerned with design and engineering, including implementation, as highlighted in the quote. Ultimately, the goal of the field is to improve the interactive systems we use and to invent new ones. For example, if you attend an academic HCI conference, one presentation may be about the construction of super-resolution touchscreens [800], a second about how to design technologies for tracking the periods of adolescents [784], and a third about how to place content in the most comfortable places in mixed reality technology [233].

Second, people are the starting point for HCI. They also define what makes interactive computing ultimately good. Therefore, researchers and practitioners study people's needs and wants in depth and evaluate how people use systems. HCI's uncompromised focus on human aspects distinguishes it from areas in computer science that mostly focus on computation and algorithms and areas in other disciplines that typically focus on technology. In such areas, it is commonplace to make assumptions about users without always grounding them in empirical observations or theory. Conversely, HCI is based on justifiable and explicit knowledge about people and their abilities, needs, and wants. HCI goes beyond wishful thinking: It is about discovering solutions that actually make computer use more effective, efficient, and safe.

Third, HCI is concerned with investigating all phenomena relevant to interaction. In other words, its focus extends beyond technology to work and leisure and, more generally, to social, organizational, psychological, and many other factors. Wright and McCarthy [915] noted that "HCI is concerned with understanding the influence technology has on how people think, value, feel, and relate" and "using this understanding to inform technology design" [p. 644]. It is not a detour to understand people when developing technology—it is necessary to create technology that brings value to the world.

1.2.1 Research in HCI

According to the definition of HCI quoted in the previous section, research problems in HCI concern the human use of computing and how we might improve it. However, what does this mean in practice? What research problems are relevant to this goal?

Three main types of research problems can be distinguished in HCI [625]:

Empirical problems: These concern developing accounts of phenomena in interaction grounded in empirical data. An empirical research problem is often motivated by a lack of understanding of some aspect of interaction. For example, empirical research might focus on understanding how people discover and learn to use features in an interface or examining the effects of social media on relationships. As mentioned earlier, empirical problems may be about "all major phenomena surrounding interaction."

Conceptual problems: These are about explaining previously unconnected phenomena occurring in interaction through reference to theoretical constructs. Conceptual problems involve hypotheses, explanations, theories, and models. For example, a conceptual problem may concern reconciling different views of what privacy is or formulating an account of what it means for users to feel immersed in virtual reality.

Constructive problems: These tackle the knowledge needed for constructing interactive systems for some stated purpose concerning the human use of computing. This understanding does not need to be expressed formally in terms of models. Constructive problems may just as well concern visions for building brain–computer interfaces or guidelines that help designers create accessible user interfaces.

These three types of research problems complement each other. Addressing empirical problems can help identify new phenomena that HCI theory will need to be able to explain. The solutions to conceptual problems may help identify ideas for how to construct interactive systems more effectively. Engaging in the construction of user interfaces may create new forms of interaction that give rise to new empirical research problems. As such, the three types of research problems go hand in hand within the HCI domain. Empirical data are linked to knowledge and knowledge is linked to design.

Throughout this book, we will provide numerous examples of classic and contemporary research in HCI, as well as many examples of contributions from such research. Good venues for finding examples of ongoing research are conferences supported by the ACM Special Interest Group on Computer-Human Interaction, such as the flagship *ACM Conference on Human Factors in Computer Systems* (CHI), and academic journals, such as *ACM Transactions on Computer-Human Interaction, Human–Computer Interaction*, and the *International Journal on Human-Computer Studies*.

1.2.2 The practice of HCI

In addition to research, HCI is also practice. Hundreds of thousands of professionals around the world engage daily in designing, implementing, and evaluating interactive systems. Many of those systems have already found real-world applications or will do so in the near future. HCI practitioners hold different and continually evolving professional titles, such as *interaction designer, usability specialist, HCI specialist, user interface engineer, user researcher, behavioral analyst*, and *user experience designer*, among others.

What practitioners actually do has been a topic of research in HCI. Multiple studies have attempted to characterize their work and their views. A key takeaway from such studies is that practitioners' work spans four main activities:

- Many HCI practitioners work to create an understanding of users and their activities. For instance, this may involve the analysis of the tasks of users or the collection of empirical data that focus on the activities and work of users [862]. To inform practical decisions, practitioners determine user requirements, benchmark solutions against competitors, and conduct task analysis and user studies in the real world [43]. User research (Part III) forms the basis of their methodology.

- Most HCI practitioners actively contribute to and often drive constructive activities. For instance, they may design and prototype interactive systems using mockups or sketches [372]. A user interface designer, for example, may use digital tools to sketch wireframes of graphical user interfaces. The design of such tools has a significant impact on their work and, thereby, the world. They may use design techniques such as wireframing, sketching, and prototyping (Part VI).

- HCI practitioners evaluate interactive systems from the user's perspective, for instance, by testing the systems with users or by doing expert reviews [43, 862]. Many of these methods have roots in the behavioral and social sciences, especially psychology and sociology. We discuss the evaluation methods in Part VIII.

- HCI practitioners engage with other professionals, for example, from marketing and software development, as well as other stakeholders, including representatives of clients and end-users [613]. Occasionally, the structure of such engagements is systematized into a process model, which we discuss in Part VI. In such engagements, success often lies outside any defined process and depends on one's ability to communicate and persuade. Such soft skills are important in influencing decision-makers and opinion leaders in organizations. They can be decisive for the success of a project.

What is the relationship between academics and practitioners? Obviously, practitioners have been trained in HCI methods and theories such as the ones covered in this book. To apply such methods effectively in a situationally appropriate manner, it is desirable to know how these methods and theories have evolved, the explanatory mechanisms they rely on, the scientific and practical assumptions they make, and their advantages and disadvantages. Together, these aspects determine their suitability for different tasks and contexts.

Nevertheless, the relationship between research and practice is complex [164]. Researchers and practitioners continually debate the relevance of research for practice and the other way around. The intertwining of research and practice in HCI has been conceptualized as a three-stage process [767]. In the first step, thousands of researchers study a phenomenon. The results are eventually packaged into guidelines, demonstrations, software tools, and much more. In the second step, millions of developers who produce HCI applications are influenced by those outcomes. In the third and final step, these applications are used by billions of people. More generally, ideas and methods propagate through undergraduate and graduate students studying and researching HCI and postdocs and academic staff actively contributing to work in industry.

This book does not cover tools and issues tailored for practitioners; for such content, we refer the reader to the fast-moving frontier of practitioner books. In this book, we focus on more enduring HCI principles and skills.

1.2.3 Relation of HCI to other fields and disciplines

HCI is a field that brings together researchers and practitioners from different disciplines. As will become evident throughout this book, HCI also draws on methods and insights from other fields, including those from psychology, sociology, cognitive science, anthropology, computer science, design, art, economics, health science, media studies, organizational studies, and many more.

Let us give a more in-depth example. Suchman [804] drew on methods from anthropology and sociology to critique early attempts to design interactive systems based on an assumption about people that was then prominent in cognitive science. They suggested that users interact based on *plans*, that is, sequences of actions they imagine before actually doing something with a computer. Her studies of photocopies showed that plans often fail and need to be changed. Users need to improvise actions and recover from errors and unplanned events. Moreover, plans are often not construed in advance. Such observations called for research on users' actual practices and a change in the way user interfaces are designed, providing more room for different structures of action and, importantly, for improvisation. Throughout the book, we will encounter many similar results from other fields.

Sometimes, other phrases are used in place of human–computer interaction. They include *usability*, which emphasizes whether users can use systems to achieve goals effectively, efficiently, and safely; *user experience*, which emphasizes the motivations and experiences of users; *interaction design*, which emphasizes the design of user interfaces and the conceptualization of novel interactions; and *human factors and ergonomics*, which emphasize human capabilities as the basis of interaction. In this book, we prefer the term HCI when describing this field.

1.3 Fundamental concepts

The book is centered on a few fundamental HCI concepts. Next, we will briefly outline them, explain why they are important, and highlight how they contribute to HCI. Figure 1.2 shows these concepts.

1.3.1 Human-centered approach

HCI focuses on people who use an interactive system or are affected by its use. This focus is often called being *user-centered* or *human-centered* to contrast it with a focus on the technology itself [423, 604]. Human-centeredness distinguishes HCI from many other technical disciplines.

Being human-centered has three immediate and important implications: (1) a requirement to understand users, including their needs and motivations; (2) a requirement to engage with people as part of research and design; and (3) a requirement to conduct an ethical evaluation of how an interactive system may directly or indirectly affect people.

First, being human-centered means that you seek to understand the people who will use the interactive system. This understanding encompasses everything that depends on computer use, from basic theories of human perception to how people organize work and communicate with each other. Part II of the book summarizes key theories for understanding people. This knowledge has implications for how we design the system to *match people* as opposed to requiring people to match the system. Being human-centered also means striving for the best possible understanding of people. In this book, we cover vastly different points of view and theories, ranging from theories on how humans process information (Chapter 5) to theories on motivation (Chapter 6) and collaboration (Chapter 8). A rich set of theories can be brought to bear on any use situation. Figure 1.3 shows an example.

Second, being human-centered means engaging with people as part of any research and design activity to understand their *specific* concerns and practices. In 1985, Gould and Lewis [285, p. 300] noted that

> designers must understand who the users will be. This understanding is reached in part by directly studying their cognitive, behavioral, anthropometric, and attitudinal characteristics, and in part by studying the nature of the work expected to be accomplished.

This is as true now as it was then. HCI researchers and practitioners aim to create interactive systems that support humans and their goals; therefore, they need to start from those goals. Part III presents methods for empirically studying users, what they want, what they do, and what they value.

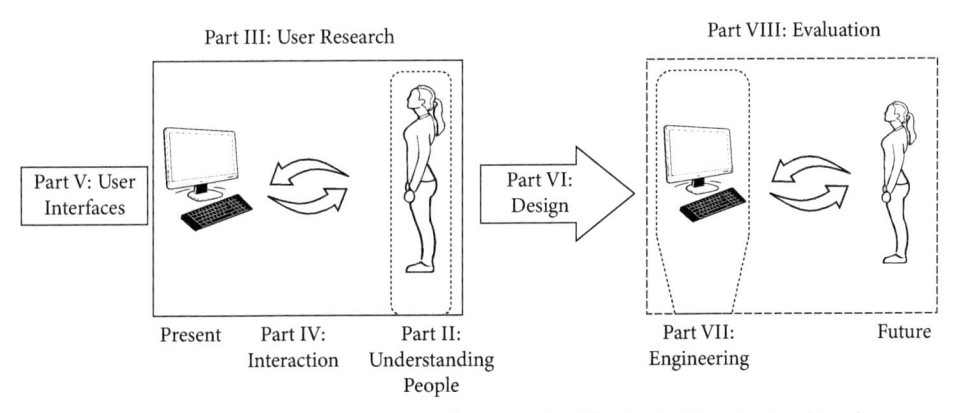

Figure 1.2 An overview of the central areas of concern in HCI. The left-hand side of the figure is about the present; the right-hand side of the figure is about the future as envisaged through design, realized through engineering, and assessed through evaluation. The dark areas indicate the corresponding parts of the book.

Visual saliency models
Visual objects that are unique in their visual primitives attract user's attention.

Task analysis
Even complex-looking activities can be decomposed into hierarchical and sequential relationships.

Information foraging theory
Users attend displays only as long as they contain valuable information.

Coordination theory
Collaborators need to continuously construct and maintain a shared understanding of a problem

Social information processing theory
Users continuously adapt their social behavior to compensate for the lack of social cues in computer-mediated communication

The pragmatic and the hedonic
Experiences with computers are both for utility (pragmatic) and for pleasure (hedonic).

Self-determination theory
Users' behavior is driven by three basic psychological needs for self-determination: autonomy, competence, and relatedness

Multiple resources theory
In multitasking, tasks compete for limited sensory, motor, and central (cognitive) capacities

Fitts' law
Users' performance in providing input to a computer is limited by a speed–accuracy trade-off

Figure 1.3 Theories of HCI shed light on what happens in interaction: how people perceive, experience, and behave. This figure indicates some of the core theories covered in this book, including the ones about perception, movement, motivation, and cognition.

Third, being human-centered implies a particular ethical stance toward people. This stance means that the primary rationale for any practical decision should be rooted in understanding the people who use or are affected by the system. There is a responsibility, even if it is not often stated aloud, to avoid harm and try to find the best possible solution for people. For instance, the ACM code of ethics states that "a computing professional should contribute to society and human well-being, acknowledging that all people are stakeholders in computing."[1] Thus, being human-centered means ensuring users' privacy, security, fair treatment, good work conditions, and much more. This is a theme we will revisit throughout this book.

1.3.2 Interaction

Interaction is a concept that is fundamental in HCI and specific to this field [357]. Intuitively, it refers to the reciprocal influence between people and an interactive system that takes place through the user interface. Interaction is, in other words, not a property of the system design or the user but something that emerges when they influence each other. Therefore, we need to understand the interaction to understand how users can be supported in their tasks. Interactive systems are tools that help users achieve their goals. Interaction also concerns how users operate or manage the user interface, how they interpret messages, and how they decide what to do next.

The interactive relationship between humans and computers can be complex because it is not singularly defined by the user or the computer. Additionally, interaction is often complex because it is also affected by specific activities and the context of use. This complexity is a key aspect of HCI that affects even the most mundane considerations. For instance, our expectations about the response time of a game may affect how we experience the game; our experience might fundamentally change when there is also a lag in the game's response time. However, our expectations concerning lag may differ depending on our location (on the move, at home). User expectations may be completely different for other applications and depend on factors such as social norms or what is considered an acceptable lag.

Finally, interaction often involves co-adaptation between people and computers [646], meaning that both the user and the system learn and adapt to each other during interactions. Such co-adaption can happen without hands-on contact, through changing work practices, or by fundamentally changing values or habits. Part IV outlines the concept of interaction and the distinct ways of thinking about computer use it affords.

1.3.3 User interface

A key technical construct in HCI is the user interface. It refers to the parts of an interactive system that the user comes into contact with or that in other ways shape the user's perception of the system. Because the behavior of the system that the user experiences is affected by the system and the interface, design is almost invariably concerned with both the user interface and the broader system. Interactive systems include digital products, online services, appliances, web sites, smartphones, and so on. These are the primary objects of design and what practitioners and researchers try to envision differently.

The user interfaces studied in HCI research are continuously changing (Figure 1.4). The 1970s and the early 1980s saw a lot of work on command-line interfaces, for example, research on the naming of commands and the syntax of command-line arguments. The 1980s saw pioneering work on the Xerox Star personal desktop computer.

---

[1] https://ethics.acm.org.

14 | OVERVIEW OF HUMAN–COMPUTER INTERACTION

(a)

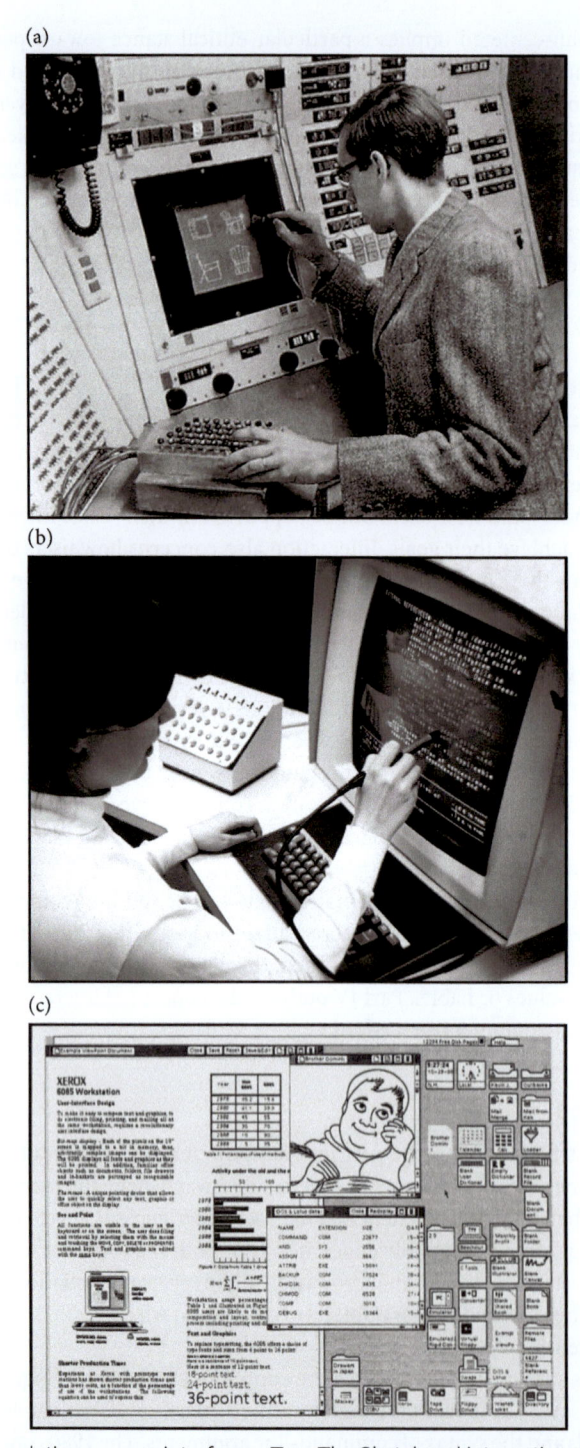

(b)

(c)

Figure 1.4 Three revolutionary user interfaces. Top: The Sketchpad interactive system was unveiled in 1964 [807]. Middle: The Hypertext Editing System, developed around 1969 [843], provided hypertext links that the user could follow by selecting them with a pen (image by Gregory Lloyd under Creative Commons License). Bottom: The Xerox Star pioneered the graphical user interface around 1981.

In addition to recent developments, research on user interfaces can draw lessons from older works. Many insights from studies on earlier systems remain relevant. For example, spoken-dialogue systems build on work on command-line interfaces, and augmented reality interfaces contain menus that are similar to those of graphical user interfaces. Part V covers a variety of user interfaces and the current understanding of what makes them work and how to design them.

1.3.4 Design

HCI aims to change the world by designing human-centered systems. Designing is the process of arriving at a plan, specification, prototype, system, or service—a *design*. In HCI, this often means designing a user interface and relevant parts of the underlying interactive system. However, it can also be about designing other elements, for example, services.

In general, design is about envisioning things as they could be. Although design processes have always been present in HCI, since the mid-1990s, they have been intensively developed and reflected upon [551, 899]. The book edited by Winograd [899], titled *Bringing Design to Software*, reflects this ethos. A key sentiment in that book is as follows.

> The education of computer professionals has often concentrated on the understanding of computational mechanisms, and on engineering methods that are intended to ensure that the mechanisms behave as the programmer intends. The focus is on the objects being designed: the hardware and software. The primary concern is to implement a specified functionality efficiently. When software engineers or programmers say that a piece of software works, they typically mean that it is robust, is reliable, and meets its functional specification. These concerns are indeed important. Any designer who ignores them does so at the risk of disaster.
>
> But this inward-looking perspective, with its focus on function and construction, is one-sided. To design software that really works, we need to move from a constructor's-eye view to a designer's-eye view, taking the system, the users, and the context all together as a starting point. When a designer says that something works (for example, a layout for a book cover or a design for a housing complex), the term reflects a broader meaning. Good design produces an object that works for people in a context of values and needs, to produce quality results and a satisfying experience.

The bottom line is that all interactive systems are designed. This gives HCI practitioners and researchers immense importance but also immense responsibility. Design is discussed in Part VI of the book.

1.3.5 Engineering and computing

Engineering refers to the use of technical principles, such as mathematics, science, and technical know-how, to realize a design that best meets a given set of expectations, which are typically captured in a requirements specification. Several emergent qualities of an implementation are important to users, including the performance, safety, robustness, and explainability of a system. When HCI researchers work on such engineering problems, they need to integrate their understanding with the theory and practice of engineering and computer science.

While there are many engineering and technical challenges in creating interactive systems, HCI focuses on the challenges that matter to people. A well-engineered interactive system is shaped and refined throughout the development process. As a consequence, HCI spills over into many areas that are not traditionally associated with it. In particular, HCI intersects many areas of computer science. For example, computer graphics considers questions on people's perception of graphical displays, scenes, and objects. Moreover, many outputs from machine learning and natural language processing research, such as speech recognition, automatic text summaries, recommendations, and search, are relevant only when implemented in interactive computers. HCI has always been central to software engineering. Early HCI research discovered that software design that assumes users will make errors tends to work more reliably [597]. This had deep implications for the design of software architectures. For example, allowing users to reverse their actions—providing an *undo* feature—can be surprisingly difficult to implement well, demonstrating that such concerns are not simply minor features to be added later on. Instead, they should be considered in the early stages of software architecture development [64, 514]. HCI is also relevant in research on computing networks and systems; for instance, researchers are making efforts to understand how people perceive network latency in networked applications, such as games [396].

In summary, HCI is not merely about the surface properties of interactive systems, but it also has deep implications for other fields regarding the development of interactive systems. Engineering is discussed in Part VII of the book.

1.3.6 Evaluation

In HCI, *evaluation* refers to the application of some systematic methodology to attribute human-related values to an artifact, prototype, system, or process. Examples of such attributes include performance, experience, safety, and ethical aspects, such as the avoidance of bias or harm. HCI research places a relatively strong emphasis on carrying out evaluations with users, which contrasts with some technically oriented disciplines that often measure technical properties without the involvement of users.

Verification, validation, and testing are variants of evaluation. *Verification* means ensuring that the design meets all the requirements and constraints imposed on the design task. For example, we review requirements specifications in Part VII. *Validation* means ensuring that the design is suitable for its intended purpose. As such, a design can succeed in verification but fail in validation, for example, if the design is used in some way that was unanticipated during the design process. In this sense, HCI is no different from other design fields. This book emphasizes the need to evaluate both assumptions and designs. Finally, *evaluation* refers to getting information about how well interactive systems fulfill their goals. For example, in usability testing (Chapter 43), the evaluation is performed by asking users to perform the tasks assigned to them. Several usability metrics are used to gauge how well they succeeded.

HCI evaluations almost always use multiple methods. In HCI, we need to arrive at robust, generalizable, and reproducible findings that practical decisions can be based on. It is often naive to expect a single or just a few evaluation methods to be sufficient; these methods, despite some overlaps, complement each other. As a result, practitioners often employ multiple evaluation methods, ranging from ethnographic studies and interviews to studying log files, conducting controlled experiments, and analyzing computational models.

In HCI practice, evaluation is closely coupled with iterative design. Most design processes incorporate evaluation as an ongoing activity throughout all design, building, and deployment activities. Early HCI pioneers [285] argued that "design must be iterative: There must be a cycle of design, test and measure, and redesign, repeated as often as necessary" [p. 300].

In Part VIII, we discuss principles and methods for evaluating user interfaces.

1.4 Why HCI matters

Understanding HCI is crucial when creating interactive systems for human use to ensure that such systems have a positive impact on their users and the world. Despite popular belief, this understanding is not trivial and cannot be achieved by amateurs; it requires knowledge and discipline. Next, we outline the main justifications for this argument. The intention is to make clear *why* research, practice, and education in HCI matter.

1.4.1 **Interactive systems are difficult to use**

HCI was born out of the realization that interactive systems are difficult to use. As interactive systems began to be used by nonexperts in computers, it became increasingly clear that many users had difficulties understanding how to provide input and how to interpret output. We have all used interactive systems that exhibit unexpected behavior and difficult-to-understand instructions, requiring us to work around stumbling blocks or give up using the system altogether. Paper Example 1.4.1 shows how even door handles can be difficult to use; throughout the book, many similar examples from papers are presented.

Paper Example 1.4.1: The design of everyday things

The Design of Everyday Things is a book written by Norman, one of the pioneers of HCI. Norman's book introduced ideas from cognitive psychology to bear on the design of everyday things and interactive systems. The book changed the general perception of why everyday things need to be designed with users in mind [600]. Consider the three doors below, in particular, how to open them.[2] The doors are difficult for most users (search the World Wide Web for "Norman doors" for similar examples).

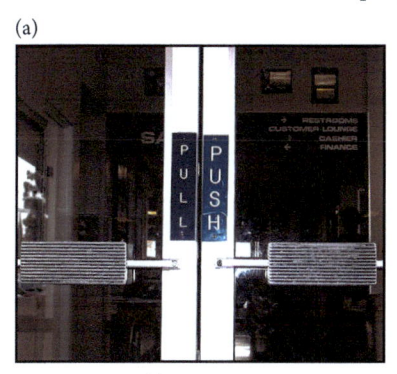

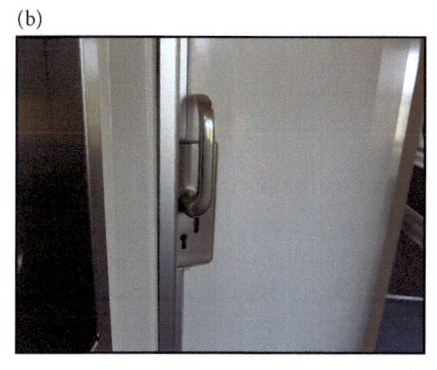

(a) (b)

(c)

continued

---

[2] Photographs from Don Norman, with permission to reprint. These were also used in Figures 1.2 and 1.3 in Norman's book [600].

> **Paper Example 1.4.1: The design of everyday things** *(continued)*
>
> The flat handlebar on the door to the left signals the door should be pushed; however, the left door needs to be pulled. The door in the middle does not offer any hint of how it can be opened. The door to the right is a sliding door, but this is so unclear to people that some friendly person has added an explanation. Whenever you see explanations or labels added to things, think: Why was this not designed to make the explanation/label unnecessary?
>
> This example makes three points. First, even simple things are hard to design right; for interactive systems, the challenge to match users' abilities is magnitudes harder. Second, all objects, including interactive systems, have been designed; sometimes, designers have not paid sufficient attention to the people who will use their designs. Third, designers have the opportunity and even a responsibility to improve the world through their designs. Does this responsibility also apply to you?

Data suggest that such frustrations are a common experience. A study found that frustrating episodes with computers occur frequently due to error messages, faulty network connections, long download times, and difficult-to-find features [141, 334]. Shockingly, about half of the time spent on a computer can be spent dealing with such incidents. These challenges may seem minor, but over time, they compound and can have unexpected and unfortunate downstream consequences. For example, consider how poorly some user interfaces support elderly users, some of whom may struggle to use computers for even basic tasks. Such struggles are known to negatively affect users' willingness to use computers and thus their ability to benefit from computers, which can have negative effects on their ability to participate in society. Therefore, as computing spreads to broader user groups and new contexts of use, HCI is needed to make interactive systems usable and useful.

1.4.2 The egocentric fallacy

People are complex beyond ordinary intuition, and not all people are alike. It is an *egocentric fallacy* to assume that others are like us—to attempt to explain other people by reference to one's own experience. You are often NOT the user [452]. As a consequence, intuition only goes so far in helping practitioners understand interaction and design interactive systems—it can even be misleading.

A good example is HCI research on mental models. A mental model captures how people understand something. For instance, people have vastly different beliefs about how calculators work [598]. These beliefs can explain the errors and the issues they face when using calculators. For instance, many people think they need to press "clear" (or the equivalent) multiple times when using a calculator. More generally, many constructs that we use in HCI help us go beyond our everyday observations and avoid the egocentric fallacy. The implication is that we must use time and energy effectively to understand users.

1.4.3 HCI is right

As we have argued above, being human-centered is a value of its own. We have a responsibility to take the needs and abilities of users seriously when designing technology. In the words of designer Rams, "Indifference towards people and the reality they live in is the one and only cardinal sin in design." HCI has the potential to have a positive impact on the world, and HCI research can cause less bias, less frustration, and greater well-being [649].

In a classic book, Landauer [454] argued that computers are difficult to use and that this is why, at the time, computers did not improve the productivity of companies that invested in them. Landauer argued that the duty of HCI was to improve computers. We find that this argument is still valid.

1.4.4 HCI pays off

HCI has financial value when done correctly, as it can help open up and conquer new markets, increase productivity, and lower the costs of completing work. Investments in HCI pay off. Research on this topic has found several-fold returns on the investments in HCI made by a company [71].

User interfaces and interaction design constitute a significant part of nearly all technology projects. In 1992, Myers and Rosson [571] found that 48% of the software code was related to the user interface. This means that getting anything related to the user interface right early is important, and that necessary fixes to the user interface that are identified after the interactive system is deployed are very costly to implement. This is because the implementation, training, and documentation for the parts that need fixing may have already been completed. In summary, instead of asking if HCI pays off, it is better to ask if one can afford to do without.

1.4.5 HCI shapes the future

HCI is well-positioned to shape the future; see Figure 1.5 for an example of how this has occurred in the past. Systems, products, and services go through constant lifecycles of introduction, growth, maturity, and decline in the market. Competition and changing demand create a need for existing systems, products, and services to evolve or be replaced with new alternatives. User interfaces

Figure 1.5 Dynabook, created in the late 1970s by Kay and Goldberg [407]. This vision predated tablets and contained many ideas for the creative and programmable use of media.

are integral parts of people's experiences when using mobile phones, apps, web sites, and so on. HCI is critical to discovering new ways to use new products, enjoy new services, and manage new systems.

Two common strategies for bringing something new to the market are *market pull* and *technology push*. Market pull refers to sensing that there is market demand for a new offering. HCI, with its rich plurality of human-centered research methods, is eminently suitable for capturing users' needs and wants and framing such findings as actionable design know-how. HCI is also exceptional at facilitating technology push. Technology push refers to the introduction of new technology into the market, which generates demand for something that was previously unavailable. Many visions and research discoveries in HCI have changed how we view computer use, such as ubiquitous computing, tangible interfaces, and virtual and augmented reality.

1.5 Our approach to HCI

The approach we follow in this book differs from those of many other textbooks. In this section, we outline the key tenets and the philosophy that have shaped the book.

1.5.1 A focus on principles

The book focuses on *elementary* HCI principles and skills. By "principle" we refer to a foundational idea or rule that explains or controls how something happens or works in HCI. For example, *direct manipulation* is a principle for organizing the interaction with graphical user interfaces (Chapter 28). The principle states that computational objects must be presented on display and acted on by the user through direct, reversible, and incremental actions with immediate feedback. There is substantive empirical evidence on the benefits of direct manipulation; hence, we find it an important principle to teach. Throughout the chapters, we introduce several principles, and we summarize them in a table in Chapter 46.

1.5.2 Pluralism in methods and theories

All methods are limited [532]. Consequently, we will cover a range of different research approaches and methodologies and carefully account for their strengths and weaknesses. We will cover the views of science, design, and engineering as ways of knowing in HCI. For example, we will explain the principles of design thinking alongside concepts of validity for experimental studies. We consider them all useful, even if they are rarely utilized together. The value of a viewpoint does not lie in the authority of who stated it but in how it helps to achieve better HCI.

At the same time, we believe that HCI phenomena can be studied at a variety of levels, all of which are relevant. This is a form of theoretical pluralism [713]. HCI phenomena span eye movements, emotional reactions, aesthetic experiences, social interactions, and organizational structures; they also span behaviors from the millisecond level to changes in the use of interactive systems over decades as well as the individual, group, and societal levels. The book covers many of these phenomena and the associated theories but makes no argument that any of them is more important than others, nor that a single theory can be used for all HCI phenomena.

1.5.3 Essential insights supported by research

This book focuses on some essential insights into HCI rather than analyzing current user interfaces or cataloging trends in contemporary HCI research. We have distilled the principled insights that we believe will hold and be valuable to academics and practitioners for decades. Therefore, while the reader (including instructors) may apply these essential insights to their HCI problems, it is hoped that the insights presented in this book will outlive particular interaction problems, fashions, and fads.

We have picked essential insights we believe are supported by evidence, including from academic areas other than HCI. We have prioritized this evidence-based approach over allegiance to any particular method, philosophical stance, or set of beliefs. To provide supporting evidence, we often cite relevant empirical studies. For example, consider the Gestalt principles of visual perception (Chapter 3), a set of ideas about how people group visual stimuli. Our reason for including them in this book is the evidence that they are useful in HCI, for instance, the study by Parush et al. [642]. Many parts of the book present empirical findings related to HCI principles, insights, and methods.

1.5.4 Optimism in solving HCI problems

Our attitude toward HCI is that many of the issues that HCI practitioners and researchers try to address are solvable. We base this attitude on the historical observation that many of the world's most successful systems are based on HCI research [e.g., 570, 767]. They include mobile devices, Wikipedia, search engines, extended realities, and computer games. Many key technologies, such as e-commerce systems, social media, augmented reality, text input technology, and editing software, have been shaped by HCI. Figure 1.6 shows an overview of computing innovations on which HCI has had a substantial, if not pivotal, impact. For us, this type of analysis shows that with the right combination of innovation, strong theories about people, and careful evaluation, HCI problems *are* solvable.

Furthermore, HCI insights are currently helping to design and improve numerous interactive systems. It does not mean that there is necessarily one complete solution for a given HCI issue, that all situations are straightforward to design for, or that HCI is easy. However, for a surprisingly large number of problems in HCI, we actually *have* suitable methods or actionable insights. As we can apply known principles and findings to solve HCI problems, the conclusion "it depends" is used less often in HCI than one might think. In this book, we emphasize that there are known answers in HCI. The reader will find that this book takes a critical position toward many popular beliefs in the field. The book emphasizes how the field has developed its capacity to solve problems. We want to give the reader actionable access to the collective insights that underpin this statement.

Do not mistake this optimism for the belief that all problems are solvable with HCI. We do not subscribe to the idea that any societal or individual problem is solvable by technology, such as by an app. We believe that in some situations, the best design decision is not to implement a system. Such decisions, just as the decision to design, should be based on a principled understanding of users and other stakeholders.

Summary

- Computing is a powerful tool; interactive systems and user interfaces help control and tame it.

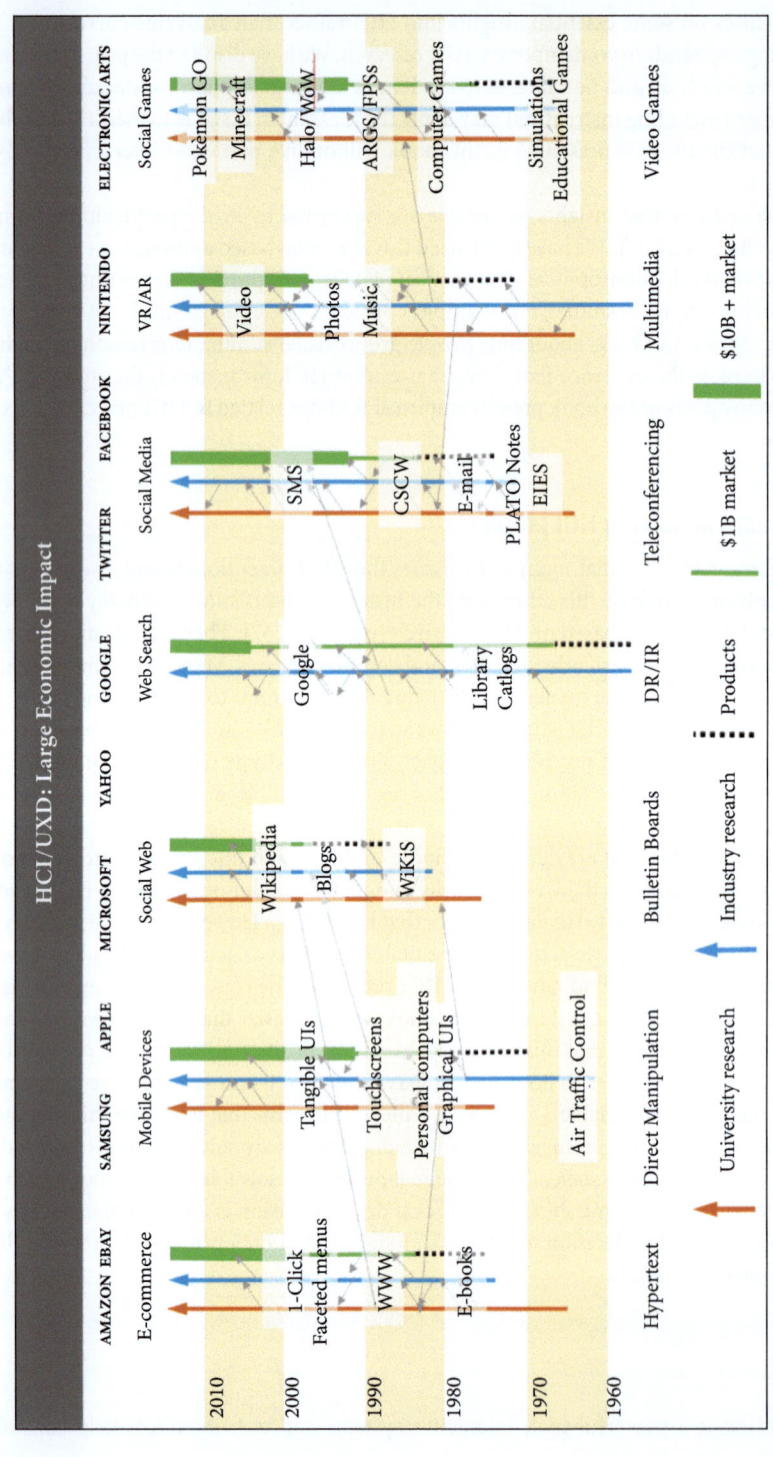

Figure 1.6 The economic impact of HCI [767]. The figure shows how well-known successes in interactive computing are related to research on HCI in academia and industry.

- HCI is concerned with people, developing technology, and understanding interaction.
- Essential activities in HCI concern understanding people, studying what users need and want, designing and engineering interactive systems, and evaluating their benefits to users.
- HCI is important because you are not the user. HCI offers a disciplined approach for tackling some of the tough problems faced in design and innovation where intuition is insufficient.

Exercises

1. Can you identify the user? Identify three relevant user groups for the following systems: (a) a mobile phone app allowing users to view timetables for buses in their city; (b) an online banking web site; (c) an educational web site that teaches children early-stage mathematics; and (d) a C++ compiler (a piece of software that translates program code into machine code).

2. Identify user-centered design (or the lack thereof) in everyday objects. As you go through your day, take note of examples of everyday things that are *not* designed well. Try to adopt the mindset that made Norman [597] see so many difficult doors; see Paper Example 1.4.1. Why are they designed or not designed well? What do you think their designers had in mind? How could they be improved?

3. Analyze the bottleneck. Think about a product or service you frequently use and consider a feature or function you find annoying or frustrating. Why do you find this feature or function annoying? What are you trying to achieve? Why is it difficult to achieve? What are the assumptions that the product or service is making that cause the bottleneck? Can you think of all the relevant factors that determine this function or feature? Can you think of an alternative design that might work better? Why do you think that your design would solve the problem? How would you test your assumptions?

4. Approaches to interactive computing. HCI is pluralistic, but what does this mean in practice? Consider being responsible for a multidisciplinary effort to improve the usefulness and usability of a social media application. Consider how the following disciplines might contribute to such effort: (a) psychology, (b) computer science, and (c) design.

5. Investigating frustrations in computer use. Choose an hour during which you will track the frustrations you encounter during computer use. Do not fuss over a definition of frustration— simply log whatever you experience as frustrating. For each frustration, write down what it was about, how frustrated you became, and how much time you lost on the episode. You can use a spreadsheet or a piece of paper. When you are done, look at your frustrations or those of fellow learners. Are they about the user interface or something else? Could they be avoided through better design? Are they frequent or rare? You can compare your findings on these frustrations to, for example, Ceaparu et al. [141] or Hertzum and Hornbæk [334].

Part II

Understanding People

2
Introduction to understanding people

Can we design for people if we do not understand them? History has shown that we cannot—user interfaces that have failed often lacked awareness of users' behaviors, feelings, needs, and wants. For example, some mobile text entry methods have failed because they did not support users in becoming better at using them [436], and some collaborative systems have failed because they did not incorporate an understanding of people's needs, motivations, and work practices [302].

In the introductory part of this book (Part I), it was noted that human-centeredness is one of the pillars of human–computer interaction (HCI) as a discipline. It requires us to take a real interest in people. It requires us to base our decisions in research and design on our understanding of people. But *how* is one human-centered—what does it mean to work in a human-centered way?

To claim that a choice is made with people in mind—that it is *human-centered*—means that the choice is justified by reference to knowledge of how people feel, think, and behave. For example, we may choose colors for a user interface based on how the human visual system works, design mechanisms in an application to motivate changes in unwanted behaviors such as smoking, or choose to develop a product concept based on ideas about what people desire. Furthermore, decisions about how to evaluate a collaborative system can be based on knowledge about how people coordinate work when aiming to achieve a shared goal.

In these and many other instances, we know things about people—from research in HCI or through other sciences—and put that knowledge to use in HCI activities. We call this knowledge and its use to improve interactive systems *understanding people*.

Understanding people is hard. Most of the factors influencing a person's observable behavior are hidden. We cannot precisely know what a person thinks, what they feel, or what drives a person's behavior. However, using scientific methods and theories, it is nonetheless possible to obtain some knowledge of these factors. Such knowledge gathering is valuable in HCI because it allows us to reason about user behavior.

To illustrate such reasoning, compare the two photos in Figure 2.1.

Perception: The two situations differ in terms of what the users can perceive. During driving, the user *shares* their visual attention between the computer and the road, where the latter is continuously changing. In many countries, using a mobile device while driving is illegal because of the effect of the device on the user's ability to perceive events on the road.

Motor control: Many games require not only fast reflexes but also the ability to intercept a fast-moving target that can be small and move erratically. Using a mobile device for non-gaming purposes mostly involves static targets selected with a very different input device, such as a touchscreen.

Thinking: The gamer must keep track of several events, such as the status of enemy players, to choose their next action effectively. By contrast, the selection of options from a mobile display is based on the recognition of icons and labels that are most likely to lead to the target state.

Figure 2.1 Chapter 2 introduces methods and theories that help understand people as users of computers. Compare the two situations in the photos: desktop gaming and driving. How do you believe they differ in terms of the users' goals, experience, thinking, and cognitive demands?

- **Needs:** What kinds of desires and risks are associated with the two situations? Do people play games for different reasons than those that drive the use of social media? Or are there a few basic psychological needs that can be met equally well through either activity?
- **Experience:** Immersion in a virtual world is a desired quality in gaming but not in mobile interaction, which places greater emphasis on instrumental experiences such as being able to complete tasks.
- **Collaboration:** In the game example, the ad hoc formation of a team of players and their mutual awareness of what is going on are essential to the team's success. Understanding how to achieve this collaborative state is an important part of developing interactive systems. Driving a car, by contrast, requires a different type of collaboration, for instance, with any other people in the car and other road users.
- **Communication:** Competitive gaming is an extreme situation in which two parties have conflicting goals. Both users must infer what the other party means or desires via the limited cues on the interface. Every so often, this requires intense communication and impromptu collaboration. Similarly, driving, in this case, co-occurs with the use of a mobile phone, which shapes what is being communicated by the multitasking user.

We write about people in other parts of the book. What is the difference between this part and the others? The defining focus of this part is the pursuit of *general* knowledge about people, for instance, as theories, models, concepts, and taxonomies. We seek to understand how people feel, think, and behave in ways that hold across different times and settings in computer use. This is a very important type of understanding because it has wide applicability. For example, the mechanisms involved in how the human visual system works are universally relevant for graphical user interfaces.

At the same time, such knowledge about people is *abstract*: It does not prescribe a *specific* user, setting, or configuration. Therefore, to be valuable for design and engineering, the understanding described in this part of the book needs to be complemented by other forms of insights about users. Table 2.1 shows an overview of the types of knowledge covered in this book. The part on user research (Part III) covers methods for gathering information on specific users, activities,

Table 2.1 Different types of knowledge about people in interaction with computing systems.

Topic	Part	Focus
Understanding people	This part	Generalizable understanding of how people think, feel, and behave
User research	Part III	Methods for obtaining insights on specific users, activities, and use contexts
Interaction	Part V	Generalizable understanding of how users interact with computer systems
Evaluation	Part VIII	Methods for assessing interaction with specific interactive systems

and contexts of use. The part on interaction (Part IV) provides HCI theories and models that explain how users interact with a variety of computer systems. Finally, the part on evaluation (Part VIII) explains how to assess HCI systems using a variety of different approaches, such as experiments and deployment studies.

Understanding people is central to HCI, and many HCI studies contribute new insights that can inform design. Next, we provide some examples.

- Borst et al. [88] proposed and evaluated a process model to predict when interruptions are disruptive to users. Their experiments support two design guidelines to minimize disruptions resulting from interruptions.
- Bachynskyi et al. [34] studied user performance and ergonomics on different touch surfaces, such as public displays, tabletops, tablets, and smartphones, thereby informing the design of user interfaces that use these surfaces for interaction.
- Lottridge et al. [495] investigated how chronic multitasking with relevant and irrelevant distractors affects the quality of writing. They found that multitaskers write better essays when provided with relevant distractors and worse essays when provided with irrelevant distractors. This tells us that while multitaskers can be negatively affected by irrelevant distractors, they are also able to integrate different sources of information when writing essays.

Next, we review the different forms of understanding we employ in HCI, the different areas of understanding, and how we use them in evaluation and design.

2.1 Types of understanding

Several types of understanding are relevant in HCI. A concept may help us to see an underlying driving factor, such as a need or motivation, behind users' behavior. A computational model enables us to predict what a user can recall. A model may help us separate the actions that a user performs when searching for information. What is common to the types of understanding covered in this part, and to those just mentioned, is that they are general, robust across time and place, and linkable to empirical phenomena. In this part, we will discuss five main types of understanding.

Theories: They consist of constructs and relations among those constructs. Theories help us understand, explain, or predict phenomena related to interactive systems. They are more general and encompassing than models. For example, in Chapter 6, we describe self-determination theory. This theory outlines the motivations of people. It describes the factors involved in intrinsic motivation and the general human tendency to engage in activities that are seen as enjoyable and interesting.

Concepts: They name particular phenomena, often with additional characteristics, such as how to identify the phenomena, information on when they usually occur, or knowledge about their underpinning mechanisms. For example, in Chapter 9, we learn about turn-taking as a concept for understanding human conversations offline and online. This concept has implications for how we support communication in interactive systems.

Taxonomies: They propose a system of elements or mechanisms of how people think, feel, or act. For example, we describe how human memory consists of several systems in Chapter 5. A simple taxonomy separates declarative and procedural memory, each broken down into further, distinct types of knowledge. This taxonomy may be used to analyze the types of knowledge that a particular interface requires.

Models: Models are formally expressed simplifications of reality. They link concepts, often in a visual form, but also mathematically or through computer code. They may be verbal or quantitative, provide numerical estimates, or allow the model to be simulated computationally. For example, Chapter 4 discusses models that predict how design affects the time it takes people to select a target, such as an icon, on a display.

Guidelines: Guidelines are practical rules of thumb or heuristics that summarize theoretical knowledge. For example, the chapter on cognition (Chapter 5) provides knowledge from which one can derive guidelines for evaluating interactive systems (Chapter 41).

These five types of understanding represent different forms of understanding people. However, such understanding cannot be static. In HCI, effective understanding has four qualities. First, researchers can and should update their understanding in light of new observations. An understanding of people that is immutable is not understanding—it is a dogma. Research progresses by advancing or rejecting previous knowledge based on new evidence.

Second, simplification is often the crux of understanding—not just in HCI but also in the social and behavioral sciences in general. Something complex, such as someone's behavior, is explained by reference to something more straightforward, such as a construct like personality, or a concept about collaboration.

Third, understanding people should be actionable to be useful in HCI. Knowledge should help practitioners make better choices. An understanding of people that only calls for more empirical research may be interesting to academic researchers looking for a new line of inquiry but ultimately has little practical value in itself. Thus, our discussions in this part of the book balance an extensive theoretical understanding of some aspects of people with simple—actionable—approximations.

Fourth, claims about people should be logically sound and empirically justifiable. Theories are subject to constant scrutiny and public criticism. A theory based on someone's opinion is not really a theory. Scrutiny can take place both in a related discipline, such as psychology, and in the field of HCI. In the construction of theories to understand users, HCI has drawn from several areas of psychology, most notably cognitive psychology, social psychology, and the psychology of motivation and needs. The application of such theories in HCI has frequently resulted in HCI research feeding information back to the original disciplines that provided the theories.

2.2 Areas of understanding

HCI is fascinating because it encompasses a wide range of human activities, from delicate adaptations of movement in virtual reality to changes in adolescents' well-being due to digital communication technologies. It includes people browsing a web page and local communities using social media to organize activities. The areas of understanding relevant to HCI therefore include *all* areas of understanding people and encompass many areas of scholarship. However, which of these areas are the most beneficial to learn about?

2.2.1 Seven areas of understanding people

In this book, we focus on seven areas that have historically been prominent in HCI research and that cover many types of understanding needed in practice. This part of the book, Part II, summarizes what each area teaches us about the individual and social factors that affect the use of computers. Table 2.2 shows an overview of these areas.

These areas allow us to understand the basic perception and motor aspects of interaction, making us aware of the limits of human performance and how design can shape such performance. The areas help us discuss people's cognition and how their needs shape people's behavior and their experiences with interactive systems. They also help us understand communication and collaboration. The areas mentioned in Table 2.2 are mainly rooted in sociology and social psychology. Knowing these areas is essential for the design of applications and services that are used by groups and organizations.

All of these areas are important and interdependent. Independently of the interactive system and the people involved, any task will involve motor control. Furthermore, all people form experiences

Table 2.2 Seven areas of understanding people that provide useful knowledge on the human use of computing.

Area	Focus	Relevance for design
Perception	How people see, feel, hear, taste, and smell	Informs the design of user interfaces
Motor control	How people plan and execute movements	Informs the design of input devices and interaction techniques
Cognition	How people remember, pay attention, and think	Informs the design of complex interactive tasks that require memory and reasoning
Needs	How needs motivate people	Tells us what is important for users in computer use and beyond
Experience	How people experience and form experiences	Tells us how users experience events involving computers
Communication	How people communicate with each other	Informs the design of services and applications for human–human communication
Collaboration	How people achieve joint goals	Informs the design of collaborative software

along the lines outlined later when they interact with systems. We, therefore, reject claims that some of these areas are of low priority for understanding people and that some of these areas have faded in importance for HCI. Nevertheless, specific projects or interactive systems may require particular attention to certain areas. For example, a study of sharing bereavement on social media may require particular attention to the areas of communication (Chapter 9) and experience (Chapter 7). If we are interested in creating a new way of working together in virtual reality, we need to know about both perception (Chapter 3) and collaboration (Chapter 8). However, focusing on specific areas does not mean the other areas are irrelevant.

2.2.2 Special application areas

Special application areas are specific areas of activity, such as work or games, whose characteristics make them unique. These areas are unique in terms of what people do, how they feel, or what they think to such a large extent that it is invaluable to study them. Research in such areas often involves both general theories and principles and specific ones that are developed especially for each area.

The special areas that HCI engages with are continuously changing. Recent examples include personal health, leisure, sustainability, technology in the developing world, creativity, games, and learning. Much can be learned about such areas through user research, following the principles outlined in Part III. The scientific literature outside HCI is likely to contain a lot of general information as well. For example, there is a lot of knowledge in the literature about why people play games. This includes theories of motivation in games, particular behaviors in games, and measures of states in games, such as immersion or flow (Chapter 7). In studies of health and well-being, we employ theories of behavior change and motivation (Chapter 6). In studies of security and privacy, we consider users' basic needs for personal safety (Chapter 6). In studies of computer-supported cooperative work, we employ an understanding of how people collaborate (Chapter 8) and communicate (Chapter 9). A proper understanding of such special application areas, regardless of how particular they are, should always include general knowledge of HCI.

2.2.3 User groups

Another area of general understanding concerns *user groups*. User groups are differentiated by their interests, capabilities, and the systems they use. They may differ in important ways across the seven areas of understanding people. Therefore, HCI studies, as well as other fields, often take into account the characteristics of user groups. One example of a user group is older adults. Much is understood about this user group in terms of sensory, motor, and cognitive capabilities, as well as disabilities. Such understanding can be critical for projects concerning older adults. Numerous other user groups have also attracted a substantial amount of research, such as design and evaluation activities involving children, users with disabilities, people in low-income countries, and families.

2.2.4 Individual differences

It is almost a cliché that everyone is different; in addition to looking at how groups of users differ, we also need to understand how users' characteristics vary. No matter how homogeneous a user sample is, significant differences between individuals are the norm, not an exception [241].

Individual differences can also be pronounced in HCI tasks. In tasks such as text editing and programming, differences between individuals can be in the order of 20:1 [195]. The scale of such differences can have great practical significance.

To go beyond merely stating that differences exist, we need to understand the mechanisms that produce them. Why is age, gender, or education an important factor? In this part of the book, we will learn about the mechanisms that underpin differences among users.

2.3 Applying our understanding of people

The HCI field values *actionable* knowledge. However, how can we apply our knowledge about people? The general answer to this question is that understanding people *helps solve problems in HCI*. Many research problems in HCI involve explaining and predicting how people use computers, considering what systems to construct, or investigating how an interactive system affects a community or organization. The theories presented in this part of the book help tackle such problems.

Work in HCI has explained how we might apply theory in this field. For instance, Bederson and Shneiderman [56] and Rogers [706] separated descriptive, explanatory, predictive, prescriptive, and generative theories in HCI. We use this categorization to identify some ways of using different understandings of people and present some examples of such uses.

First, we may use an understanding of people *to direct what to pay attention to* in a project. Understanding people in general might help direct attention in encounters with particular users. For example, research shows that motivation plays a key role in what people do and what value they derive from their actions (Chapter 6). Thus, in encounters with users in a particular project, we may want to pay attention to their motivations. We may also use such knowledge about people when we analyze and reflect on such encounters.

Second, we may use the understanding of people *to explain empirical findings*. For example, users may mention the need to stay in touch during a particular activity. This may be explained by the concept of coordination work (Chapter 8). As another example, Steinberger et al. [793] explored how to increase engagement in driving via gamification. They constructed prototypes and explained their empirical results on driving with a general model of opportunities and costs.

Third, we may use the understanding of people *to make design decisions*. These may be high-level decisions concerning the overall concept of an interactive system. For instance, we may depart from the typical biases of memory (Chapter 5) to design a photo-based memory tool [345]. As another example, Consolvo et al. [167] used theories of behavior change to build a system that encourages people to be more physically active. Theories may also inform particular design decisions. Oulasvirta et al. [629] used models of how perception is integrated across different channels (Chapter 3) to discuss the design of buttons.

Fourth, we may use an understanding of people to help *explore a design space*. That way, general understanding, in addition to direct contact with users (see the discussion on user research in Part III), serves to generate design ideas. For example, Ballendat et al. [37] used proxemics—a theory of the distances people perceive and how people use physical distance in encounters with other people—to generate design ideas. They created a suite of devices and interaction techniques based on an awareness of nearby people and other devices. In short, the theory of proxemics served an important generative role.

Fifth, we may use an understanding of people to *predict people's behavior*. Predictions may refer to expected events or processes, and they may involve numerical estimates. For example, researchers have modeled visual search patterns on web pages. Such models allow us to predict the most salient part of a web site with some probability, or predict the average time needed to find a particular link on a web page.

2.4 Is a general understanding of people possible?

We have argued that there are general understandings of people that are useful across topics in HCI. We have argued that such understandings are useful for solving practical problems in HCI, although a consequence of their generality is that they must be augmented with user research.

However, this view is not accepted by all. Some researchers argue that a general understanding of people is impossible. The argument is that general understanding is not typical of any particular situation; as such, it does not provide much, or any, benefit. Furthermore, Lincoln and Guba [483] argued that generalizations imply a belief in determinism—if the antecedent of a generalization is present, the consequent must follow—and some form of reductionism—phenomena relate only to one or a few generalizations. While we agree that it is difficult to arrive at generalized knowledge, we argue that such understandings exist in many areas and show examples of how they may be used. For example, we know things about the human visual system and collaboration that can—and indeed must—play a role in designing and evaluating interactive systems.

Another related belief is that we are all equipped with empathy—the ability to intuitively understand other people and their experiences. Why do we need theories if we have such an ability? Unlike empathy, theories can be communicated to others and subjected to scrutiny. Moreover, our empathy and intuition often fail us. The inferences we make about other people are often incorrect, especially when they involve people from different backgrounds (Chapter 5). Scientific concepts are more comprehensive, precise, and—if properly applied—appropriate for describing what happens when a user interacts with a system.

Finally, why bother to understand people in the first place? Why not just create a quick prototype of an interactive system and improve the design later on? Indeed, Petroski [652] described the evolution of everyday artifacts as occurring through trial and error. The pencil, for example, has gone through hundreds of development cycles throughout its history, some related to the manufacturing of pencils, and some to its use. In a discussion about the role of theory in HCI, Landauer [453] argued that we need to "get real" about the possible impact of cognitive psychology—a type of understanding of people—in HCI. The argument is that the real world of users is not captured well or in its entirety by cognitive psychology. Instead, empirical work and formative evaluation are suggested to be sufficient to drive the development of interactive computing systems. That is, rather than using an understanding of people, we rely on empirically testing user interfaces with people. We share this empirical orientation. However, relying exclusively on empirical data is costly and prone to failure.

In summary, we find theories about people essential. Although such theories need to be complemented by empirical research, we think that the HCI field can, and should, draw on general understandings of people. The rest of this part presents such understandings.

Summary

- A deep and scientific engagement with interactive systems and the phenomena that surround them begins with people. We call this approach human-centered.
- Being human-centered requires us to draw on theories and models of how people feel, think, and behave.
- There are seven key areas of understanding people: (1) perception, (2) motor control, (3) cognition, (4) needs, (5) experience, (6) communication, and (7) collaboration.
- These understandings of people are general, holding across many individuals, many types of user interfaces, and many use contexts.

3
Perception

Consider the situation in Figure 3.1, where you are walking down a street, look around, and have a sense of being lost. You grab your mobile device to search for directions from a navigation application. You unlock the device, launch the application, and press a button to locate yourself on the map. You may have stopped walking to read the map. Alternatively, you may have kept walking but slowed your pace to avoid bumping into other people. *Perception* is a critical capability that made all this possible. You used visual perception to locate the buttons and guide your finger to press them. If you had approached another person while walking, you may have noticed that through your peripheral vision. Beyond vision, you used your tactile sense to guide touches on the device, audition (hearing) to monitor sounds in the background, and vestibular sense to maintain balance.

Perceptual tasks that we may consider simple, like looking for a button on a display, often have plenty going on in the background. A display consists of light-emitting pixels. As you move your eyes, patterns of activations of rod and cone cells occur on the retina, feeding into a perception of regions with colors, shapes, sizes, and orientations. Over many glances (fixations) on the display, you construct a more coherent *percept* of it. This percept has structure. It is not a chaotic galore of colors: some objects are in relation to each other. For example, certain elements appear as being in front of others or belonging together. These percepts ensure that when we search for something, it happens in an orderly and efficient way. We focus our attention not on random elements but on elements that have a higher probability of being the ones we are looking for. This process is affected by both the content of the percept itself and expectations that we have unconsciously learned from previous encounters. After a few glances, you locate the button, read the label, confirm that it is what it is supposed to be, and click it.

This mundane example demonstrates why understanding human perception is fundamental to human–computer interaction (HCI): Perception is the main means of acquiring information about the state of a computer. A user interface (UI) "communicates" to users through perception. Therefore, the way people sense and perceive is essential knowledge to study and design HCI. The example also demonstrates another important property of perception. The design does not fully determine the way we look at the interface; our previous experience and strategies also play a role. To understand how to design perceptually efficient interactive systems, we need to understand how prior experience, attention, and the designed world work together.

More generally, perception is the ability to collect and organize information about the environment through physiological sensory systems. Thus, perception refers not only to the subjective sensory experience of the interface. It also refers to the processes that help us *organize* a representation of the display. Its functioning can be understood via three primary components (Figure 3.2). One component is the *sensory information* that our sensory systems produce. A sensory modality is a biologically specialized system dedicated to a type of transduction. In sensory transduction, a form of physical stimulation is transformed into neural events. For example, when light hits the back of the retina, it triggers a cascade of physiological events through the rod and cone cells, which ultimately contribute to our perceptual experience. Sensory modalities

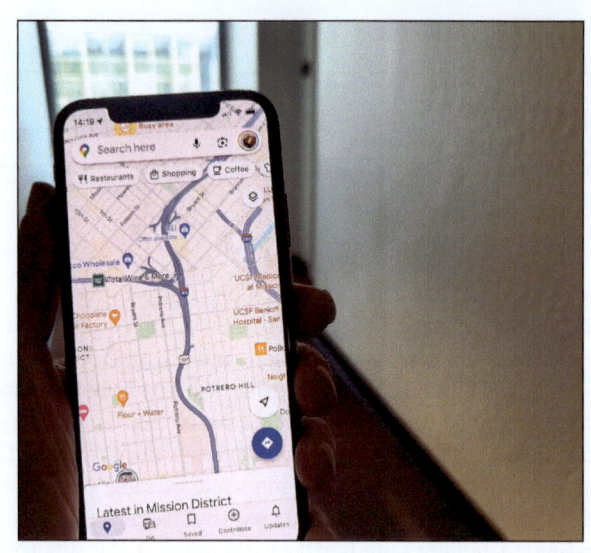

Figure 3.1 Perception serves a multitude of roles in human–computer interaction. We regulate our actions in interaction via perception. User interfaces communicate their state via perception. In this example, perception has a decisive role in helping us find elements on the display, guide fingers, maintain awareness of the background, and control gait and walking.

commonly used in HCI include vision, hearing (audition), and touch (tactition). There is also experimental research on smelling (olfaction) and tasting (gustation). Moreover, we can rely on the sense of our body, or proprioception. It refers to the knowledge of the position of our limbs in space.

The second component concerns *expectations*. Over years of interacting with the world, we have accumulated experience. Such experience enables the brain to *project* its expectations back to the world. To achieve this, perception utilizes *internal representations* to constantly make guesses on how the world *might* be. Internal representations allow us to deal with the fact that sensory stimulation is relatively poor; in other words, they help us fill in the blanks.

The third component is *attention*. Attention refers to the ability to focus our processing power on a select portion of the full perceptual scene. The decision on what to attend to is strategic: At any given moment, you could be attending to almost anything in your vicinity, but you only attend to one thing at a time. Attention strategies affect what we perceive and are as important to understand as the other two components of perception. If you were left with sensory information only, you would have no way to form a coherent organization of a UI. We need top-down processing to impose organization on sensory data, and we need attention to guide the formation of that organization.

But why is understanding perception important for HCI—is it not something that only psychologists and biologists should care about? As stated in the introduction to this part, understanding people may be put to many uses, such as explaining empirical findings and designing UIs. In the case of perception, we do this by drawing on concepts and models developed in biology, neuroscience, and cognitive sciences. This may help us do the following in HCI:

- Design display technology. A display is a device that presents computer-controlled patterns of physical stimulation to express information in a computer-controlled way (Chapter 25). The paper by Denes et al. [185] is one example of such work. Their study aims to achieve

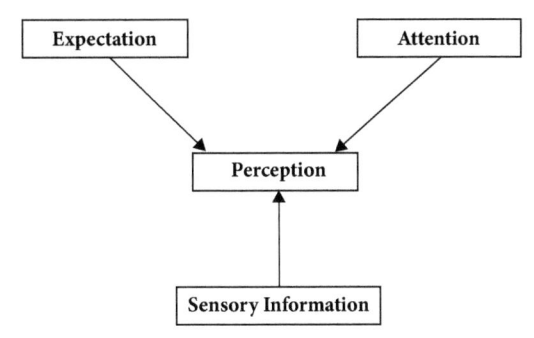

Figure 3.2 Our perceptual experience of the world may appear as veridically (truthfully) reflecting the sensory data we receive. However, it is a representation that our mind actively constructs. On the one hand, perception is affected by our expectations, which are drawn from prior experiences. On the other hand, perception is shaped by how we deploy attention to sample information.

a high number of frames on a VR headset. They do so by exploiting features of the human visual system to reduce the resolution of every other frame. In that way, they can reduce the transmitted data by about 40% with a limited cost to the perceived image quality.

- Explain why people use computers as they do. For instance, Figure 3.1 suggests that the visual search on a UI is influenced by both expectations and the visual features of the page. This is confirmed in eye-tracking studies showing a distinct pattern in search based on users' expectations from previous pages on which the most relevant information is located. We can use such patterns to place information in the most salient places [393].

- Evaluate designs. The understanding presented in this chapter directly underlies guidelines for effective design and may be used to evaluate UIs. For instance, the Gestalt laws for visual perception explain how visual stimuli are organized into unified wholes. This allows us to check if our intended organization of a page is the one that users are likely to perceive (Section 3.3).

- Inform the design of visualizations, interaction techniques, and UIs. For example, laws of contrast perception and the Gestalt laws have been used to algorithmically optimize data visualizations such as scatter plots, enabling people to see structures in complex datasets that would otherwise be difficult to see [540]. In interaction techniques (Chapter 26), we can find optimal ways of providing feedback based on human perception; occasionally, we might even exploit its limitations to make interaction techniques work.

It is hard to design a good UI without understanding the foundations of human perception. Next, we discuss commonly needed sensory modalities in interaction and the key functions of perception in interaction. We then take a closer look at the visual modality, which has a prominent role in present-day UIs. For more information on the anatomical and physiological aspects of perception, see, for instance, [876].

3.1 Sensory modalities

Sensation is a physiological process that produces information about the environment for perception. Sensation feeds perception. From a biological perspective, sensation is about *transduction*. A *sensory system* transforms energy in one form—say, light or physical contact—to electrochemical events in the brain that produce the experience of sensation. This is a complex physiological process. It is important to understand, on the one hand, how sensation is different from perception and, on the other hand, how the two are interrelated. In the rest of this section, we discuss the differences of sensory systems commonly considered in HCI, how percepts are constructed from sensory inputs, and how they are integrated for multimodal percepts.

3.1.1 Comparing modalities

Human sensory modalities are served by three basic types of transduction [778]:

Mechanosensitivity: Examples of mechanosensitivity are kinaesthesia (sense of own movement), touch, hearing, and equilibrium. Here, the energy of physical contact is transduced, for example, through hair cells in the ear.

Chemosensitivity: Examples of chemosensitivity include gustation and olfaction. Here, chemical properties are transduced, for example, by taste buds on the tongue.

Photosensitivity: Examples include the retina. Here, the stimulation by photons is transduced into electrochemical events in the rod and cone cells.

Another way to look at sensory modalities is based on *what* they sense. *Exteroceptive* modalities sense stimuli outside our body. They include vision, hearing, feeling, smelling, and tasting. *Interoceptive* modalities sense stimuli inside our bodies. They include proprioception and the vestibular sense.

These sensory modalities differ greatly with respect to the properties important for interaction. In HCI, we consider the following differences as important:

1. **Information rate:** How much information can be sensed per unit of time? This is tricky to measure, except for visual and auditory perception.
2. **Parallelism:** How much parallel processing of information can occur? For example, vision is highly parallel; audition can also do parallel processing, though to a lesser extent.
3. **Sensitivity:** The minimum intensity of physical stimulation that a receptor needs to exceed its sensation threshold. Vision has high speed and sensitivity. Such properties can be measured and modeled using psychophysics (see Section 3.2.2).
4. **Receptive field:** The size of the region that produces an integrated feature. It is a measure of the association between neurons and receptors.
5. **Adaptation:** The tuning of outputs to attenuate non-informative signals (see "habituation" below).

These differences are important to understand when considering which modalities to use in a UI. Table 3.1 summarizes three main modalities and their key properties for HCI. Vision is fast and has high bandwidth thanks to parallel processing, and it can be used to communicate information through visual (e.g., color, shape, size), spatial (e.g., layouts), and lexical (e.g., words) features. Audition (hearing) is fast but serial in presentation and can be used to present information via sound (e.g., auditory icons) and voice. Taction is fast but requires physical contact. It can be used to convey low-dimensional events and information via the amplitude and frequency of vibrations and haptic texture characteristics.

While the three sensory modalities mentioned in Table 3.1 are the most frequently considered in HCI, the human body also has other sensing mechanisms. These include thermal sensing

Table 3.1 Most common sensory modalities studied in HCI and their design implications.

Sensory modality	Key characteristics	Design considerations
Vision	Fast, high bandwidth for parallel processing with a field of view of about 190 degrees (horizontal)	Visual, spatial, and lexical aspects of graphical displays, such as contrast, acuity, use of color, visual primitives, symbols, and text
Hearing	Very fast (about 40 ms faster reaction times than vision), serial presentation, 360-degree detection area	Properties of sound and voice, such as pitch, timbre, melody, and phrasing
Tactition	Fast but limited to areas of physical contact	Properties of haptic stimulation, such as the amplitude and frequency of vibration

and pain, which have been explored as alternative sensory modalities for design. For instance, Wilson et al. [896] developed thermal icons. Like visual icons, thermal icons have a specific thermal profile associated with a meaning.

> **Paper Example 3.1.1: You have 50 milliseconds to make a good impression**
>
> When users see a web page for the first time, how quickly do they form an impression about it? Lindgaard et al. [484] asked participants to view homepages in random order for short durations. They were then asked to rate the pages on different dimensions of design. In one of the studies, the exposure time was just 50 milliseconds. The visual appeal ratings given after just 50 milliseconds were consistent with those given after 500 milliseconds, suggesting that impressions about the quality of a design form very quickly. This calls attention to visual saliency—what grabs users' attention when they first see a UI.

3.1.2 Constructing percepts from sensory information

Perception must construct an actionable percept based on the sensory data it receives. However, if the input to perception is fleeting activations of receptors (e.g., photons stimulating cells on the retina), how is it able to construct coherent, organized percepts that guide our actions? How can we perceive a button as a button and not just as the numerous sensations that are caused by its LED lights? Two processes are important here: integration and adaptation.

First, let us explain integration. A sensory system consists of receptors, for example, the mechanoreceptors on a fingertip. It also consists of a neural code and brain regions dedicated to *integrating* information over the distributed sensing inputs. Some sensory modalities, like vision, are *topographically projected* in the brain. That is, the topological structure of the receptors is retained in the corresponding receptive fields. In other words, peripheral receptors, such as those on a fingertip, are projected to central neurons in such a way that their *neighborhood relationships* are preserved. This pertains to brain regions dedicated to visual, auditory, and somatosensory modalities. They integrate information over a larger sheet of peripheral receptors. *Convolution* is a special type of topographical projection in visual perception where receptive fields of increasing size form an interconnected hierarchy. In other words, one layer of neurons is dedicated to precise local information, another layer is dedicated to a higher level of integration, and so on. One benefit of this structure is that it gives perception access to *both* larger homogeneous regions in the visual field and detail in the foveated region. This makes it possible for larger objects to pop out or appear organized. The visual system is specialized in spatiotemporal information; the auditory system integrates information across frequency and time. We exploit such integrative capabilities in UI design, for example, in graphical interface design when considering how to group graphical elements (Chapter 28).

Adaptation is another key process. Environments change, and so must percepts. Have you ever been startled, for example, when an ambient background noise that you were not paying attention to suddenly stopped? A sensory system is adapted to maximize information gain within its sensing limits. In *habituation*, a sensing threshold adapts to continued stimulation. For example, have you ever noticed that if you rest your fingers on a keyboard, you must move them slightly to "sense them again"? This is because when resting your fingers, there is no novel information to perceive. The opposite of habituation is *strategic adaptation*. Perception shows sensitivity to the statistical structure of the environment. For example, we develop attentional patterns of looking at mobile applications [472]. Early research on web pages found an F-shaped pattern for traces of gaze. However, when similar studies were done for mobile applications, a different pattern emerged. Although we tend to look at the top-left corner the most, faces and text are also likely to attract attention. This is a learned adaptive pattern.

3.1.3 Multimodal perception

In most HCI tasks, sensory modalities rarely operate on their own. Everyday interaction *requires* the integration of information not only within a modality but also across modalities. Even when you are pointing with a mouse, four modalities participate: proprioception (feeling the angles of the joints moving), taction (feeling the palm of the hand move against the surface), audition (hearing the movement), and vision (seeing the hand and the mouse cursor move).

The McGurk effect is a great example of multimodal integration [822]. It is a perceptual phenomenon in which vision *alters* speech. If you look at a face that pronounces the syllable "ga," but you hear the sound "ba," your brain might combine the two and create a perception of "da." Besides specific effects like this, discrepancies between modalities in HCI can distort integration. You may have noticed that in a videoconferencing situation where there is latency between the audio and video channels, it is difficult to follow what the other people say (Figure 3.3).

The McGurk effect is an example of *cross-modal perception*. There are a number of similar cross-modal effects. For example, the *ventriloquist effect* is something that we commonly experience when watching videos with humans speaking [14]. Due to this effect, we perceive the speech as originating from the characters we see on the display even if there is a large distance between the audio speakers and the person speaking on the display. One takeaway from studies of this effect is that vision tends to dominate other sensory modalities.

Another example is *pseudo-haptics*: the creation of a tactile sensation when there is none [683]. In a pseudo-haptic illusion called the hand-displacement illusion, the visual presentation of the user's hand is dynamically displaced, creating a sense of a force field when no such field exists. For example, if a mouse cursor is slowed down when moving up a mountain on a map, users report a sensation of a resisting force field.

It is important to note that the term *multimodal interaction* has a different meaning in HCI. It refers to the study of novel combinations of technical modalities in input and interaction techniques (Chapter 26). Many modalities can be combined for a given task, for example, speech, gesture, touch, and facial expressions. However, from a biological perspective, even a "regular"

Figure 3.3 Multimodal integration is needed when attending a videoconference. We not only listen to other speakers but also look at their lips and facial gestures when they speak. If the audio signal is delayed, for example, due to network latency, it is difficult to follow what the other person says.

workstation interaction is multimodal. Even when just using a mouse, we engage our tactile, auditory, visual, and proprioceptive sensory systems.

3.2 Elementary functions of perception in HCI

As an applied field, research on HCI pursues the *functional* understanding of perception. HCI has been less interested in the neural and physiological processes that underpin perception and more interested in the properties of perception that affect outcomes and performance in interactive tasks. From a functional perspective, perception is about obtaining the *information* that helps complete some task. Thus, the design of a UI, from a functional perspective, starts with the question: What is *required* of perception for the user to successfully achieve the set goal?

The concept of a *perceptual task* is central to the functional understanding of perception. Some sensory information is available, and the user must make a decision or act in a certain way to reach some goal. Consider the task of finding a link on a web page, keeping a finger on a particular key when playing a game and preparing to respond to an event, or detecting a beep when a new message has arrived. These are all tasks where perception is required, albeit in very different ways. In this section, we look at five elementary perceptual tasks:

Detection: The task of telling whether an event of interest occurs in the environment. For example, was there a link on a page you scrolled quickly through?

Discrimination: The task of telling whether a difference occurs in sensory stimulation. For example, is this object brighter than this other object?

Recognition: The task of categorizing a stimulus. For example, you are playing a game and see something pass your screen quickly—was it an enemy or a friend?

Estimation: The task of estimating a property of an object or event in the environment. For example, how far is an object you see in a virtual reality (VR) environment—could you reach it?

Search: The task of localizing an object of interest. For example, where on the keyboard is the key for the character ≤?

To understand how these tasks are solved by perception, we need to understand both the "hard" and "soft" sides of perception. That is, the hard-wired capabilities of perception that have evolved with us as a species and how, via lifetime learning, they are adaptively controlled and shaped. Our perceptual system has specialized capabilities to support us in tasks that are important for our success. Changes occur via two processes: phylogenetically, via evolution, and ontogenically, via learning. Some physiological enablers of perception, such as the structure of the retina, change slowly over a lifetime. However, many defining physiological characteristics have remained stable for millennia, as they have evolved for tasks important to our species such as finding food, spotting predators, and understanding the facial expressions of our companions. From an evolutionary viewpoint, the time that *Homo sapiens* has spent with computers is too short to have had an impact on phylogeny.

Learning and adaptation to perception occur as a consequence of experience. Consider, for example, learning where to look when looking for a link. We know that the first places where we look reflect the statistical distribution of elements on the screen. On a web page, we first look in the upper left corner; when using a mobile application, we tend to be drawn to faces and large logos [472]. Adaptation can be remarkably fast. For example, when looking for a link, we try to avoid looking at places we have already checked. This "inhibition of return" is important for making visual search efficient.

The rigorous definition of perceptual tasks has been instrumental in advances in understanding perception in HCI. Tasks that can be controlled in experimental settings have enabled the exposition of the underpinning phenomena and the mathematical modeling of perceptual capabilities. In such models, we see the hard limits posed by the capabilities of our sensory organs, as well as the softer, more malleable limits posed by learning.

3.2.1 Detection

In a detection task, the user must decide whether an event has occurred or not. Consider, for example, playing a game and having to decide if a shadowy dark contour in the distance is another player, or a radiologist examining a computer tomography image and having to decide whether cancer is present (Figure 3.5). The study of detection tasks in HCI originates from the study of radar operators in World War II. Radar operators had to examine grainy black-and-green displays and determine whether a blob was an enemy plane. For instance, a blob could also have been a bird or caused by interference in the radar reading. Detection models can inform the design of displays to help people better detect events.

Signal detection theory offers a theory and a model to understand detection performance. It assumes that detection is affected by two components: sensitivity and response bias. In a noisy environment, detection performance is limited by the observer's ability to discriminate the signal from noise (sensitivity). In Figure 3.4, the HCI researcher wanted to study whether a contrast enhancement algorithm improves the ability of radiologists to detect bone cancer in images. The quality of the X-ray imaging equipment affects the ability of radiologists to detect cancer. Moreover, a novice radiologist, or one with poor eyesight, may be less sensitive to differences.

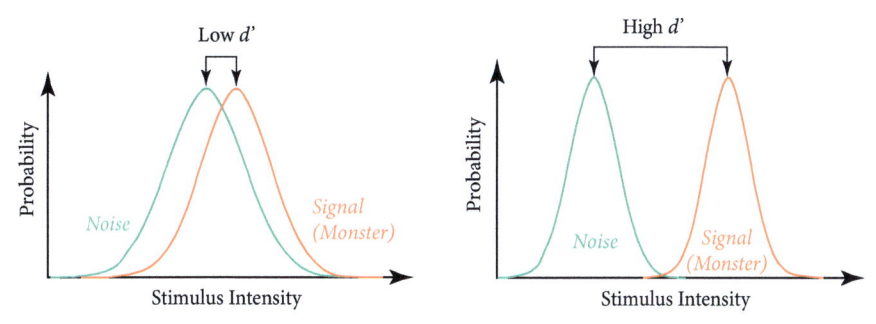

Figure 3.4 You hear a sound during your sleep: is it a monster or just noise? In a hard detection task, the distributions of the two sounds are similar; as they are hard to discriminate, many errors occur. In an easy task, the two sounds are so different that they can be easily discriminated. The d' statistic describes how far apart the two events are.

However, people may not respond simply on the basis of what they sense. They may also strategically adjust their responses, resulting in biased results. Such adjustments may reflect the expected value of failing versus succeeding in a task. For example, radar operation in World War II was not without risks. The consequences of a poor choice were potentially devastating. If an enemy went undetected, people could lose their lives; if noise was incorrectly interpreted as an enemy, time and money would be lost. In this context, the radar operator may be biased toward responding "yes" (enemy) even when somewhat unsure. Let us look at the sensitivity and response bias components more closely.

Will a user perceive something shown on display? The *sensitivity* of an observer depends on the perceived properties of the signal compared to noise. For example, how sensitive is a user to changes in the pitch of an auditory icon? Sensitivity, across modalities, can be empirically measured in a task where a participant is shown signals and non-signals (noise) and asked to report yes/no accordingly. We categorize the responses into four classes: true positive, true negative, false positive, and false negative. The sensitivity can be calculated using this response classification. It is often described using a statistic called d', which describes the difficulty of detecting a signal, in particular how difficult it is to distinguish it from noise. It can be computed from the observed hit rate (H) and the false alarm rate (FA):

$$d' = z(\text{FA}) - z(H). \tag{3.1}$$

Here, $z(\text{FA})$ and $z(H)$ give the right-tail probabilities of the rates on the normal distribution. We cast the rates to the normal distribution to ensure we can compare sensitivities across different types of tasks.

Intuitively, d' represents an index of how far apart two distributions are:

$$d' = \frac{\mu_{\text{SignalPresent}} - \mu_{\text{SignalAbsent}}}{\sigma}. \tag{3.2}$$

Figure 3.5 shows two examples: one with low and one with high d'. d' provides a way to compare the detection performance across an experimental task. The closer d' is to zero, the less discrimination is possible. When $d' = 0$, the performance is pure chance. The higher the d', the more sensitive the observer. When $d' = 4.65$, performance is already very high; for example, the hit rate is 0.99, and the false alarm rate is 0.01.

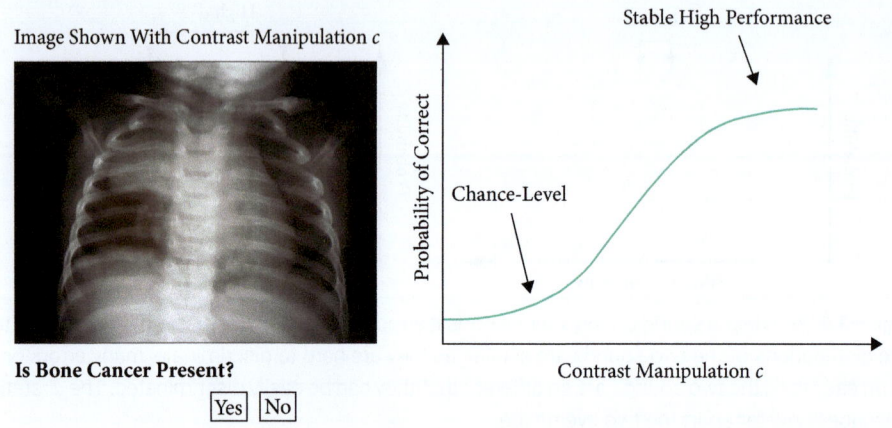

Figure 3.5 A hypothetical psychophysics experiment and a model. Here, an HCI researcher has come up with a contrast manipulation that is expensive to compute but could help radiologists detect bone cancer from images. In the study, radiologists are presented with images and must press yes/no to indicate whether an event (bone cancer) is present or not. Some proportion (e.g., 10%) of the stimuli have the event, while the rest do not. Over multiple trials where the contrast is manipulated, a psychophysical function can be built that tells the odds of detection as a function of contrast. A psychophysical function relates a physical measure to a measure of perceptual ability. Here, the graph shows that stable detection is only reached when the contrast algorithm is applied at a level of 0.8c or higher.

Response bias denotes a participant's bias (tendency) toward a particular response. For example, if an enemy in a competitive game shoots me because I failed to shoot first, this can have a high cost. However, if I erroneously shoot an important co-player in my team, this can have an even higher cost. In signal detection theory, the response criterion is denoted with β. A rational player adjusts β to favor a more reserved policy, for example, to avoid shooting co-players. This high criterion means fewer hits but also fewer false alarms. Conversely, a low criterion means more hits but also more false alarms. Response bias can also occur for other reasons. For example, if the "yes" button is easier to reach, a response bias can emerge even if it is not in favor of the player.

3.2.2 Discrimination

In a discrimination task, the user must decide whether a level of stimulation is available or if that level has *changed* due to some reference. The *discrimination threshold* defines the minimum level of stimulation required for sensing. For example, healthy young adults can hear sounds between 20 and about 20,000 Hz. With aging or hearing loss, the discrimination threshold changes. The thresholds for sensing visual contrasts also change. Such individual differences are important to note. All too often, we design interfaces with our peers in mind and forget that many (and in some cases most) users are not the same.

Psychophysics refers to the study of psychological (psycho) responses to physical (physics) events. Its core aim is to measure an observer's ability to distinguish differences in physical stimulations. In computer graphics, psychophysical models are used to optimize rendering, image processing, haptics, audio, and video. For example, many common video compression algorithms exploit discrimination thresholds. Knowing that a human cannot observe a minute change in color can be exploited in compressing images. In HCI, psychophysics laws have gained recognition among design guidelines [477] and in the design of haptic and other displays.

A psychophysics model is a systematic way to describe people's ability to discriminate stimuli. It relates mathematical physical changes to the perceiver's ability to detect those changes. To obtain data for such models, a participant in a psychophysics experiment is presented with two stimuli, for example, two auditory beeps, and asked to determine whether they are different. The researcher knows if a difference exists and how large it is and uses this information to model the participant's detection capability. By systematically controlling the properties of the baseline stimulus and its difference relative to the other stimuli, this capability can be described for a range of stimulations. In another common task type, the user is presented with a reference stimulus and has to *adjust* another source of stimulus to match it.

A well-known psychophysical model, *Weber's law*, states that equal stimulus ratios produce equal subjective ratios [794]. Weber, a German physician from the nineteenth century, provided different physical stimulations such as weights or intensities of light to people and asked them to state if a difference existed between them. He discovered that there is a relationship between the size of the stimulus and the accuracy of people in identifying differences. Specifically, Weber's law states that the *just noticeable difference* (JND) is proportional to the size of the standard stimulus:

$$JND = kS, \qquad (3.3)$$

where S is the size of the standard and k is a constant called the Weber fraction. S can represent physical quantities such as weights, intensities of light, or pressure. k describes the increase in the standard stimulus required before the observer can make a reliable discrimination. JND thresholds have been charted for perceptual events and qualities relevant to UIs: visual length and area, visual distance, visual velocity, visual flash rate, and duration [794].

One application in HCI has been *time perception*, with applications to the response times of the system and progress bars [755]. For example, the pace of change of a progress bar affects the user's perception of system speed or the perceived duration of loading.

3.2.3 Recognition

In a recognition task, a stimulus must be classified as one out of a number of classes. For example, icons, words, faces, alarm sounds, and so on need to be recognized as a *particular* member of a set. "This is the icon of Excel." All other things being equal, the larger the set, the harder the recognition task. It matters whether you have 12 or 100 icons on a display. Discrimination becomes harder as the number of candidates increases.

People are surprisingly good at recognizing faces and objects they have seen before. In controlled studies, participants can accurately recognize hundreds of objects that were presented to them previously [617]. Performance in a recognition task can be measured by precision and recall. *Precision* is the number of true positives divided by the sum of true and false positives. *Recall* is the number of true positives divided by the sum of true positives and false negatives.[1]

---

[1] Not to be confused with memory recall; see Chapter 5.

Human ability in visual recognition is leveraged in the direct manipulation paradigm of graphical user interfaces (GUIs; Chapter 28). It is important for training better machine learning algorithms. Humans are often asked to classify data that are used to train algorithms. However, people do not always agree on what the "true" classes are. Categories that show disagreement among human observers are problematic for machine learning because they add noise to the training data. HCI researchers can help build UIs that improve recognition accuracy and help annotators solve conflicts effectively.

3.2.4 Estimation

Estimation is the task of assessing a property of an object from stimulus information. Users may be estimating, for example, the size of a 3D object in a VR environment or the color of a product on an e-commerce site. Here, they need to assign the estimated value to some property. For example, they may estimate how far away another car is based on what is shown on the display of a self-driving vehicle.

According to *cue integration theory*, our prior experiences affect our estimations. Over time, users become more sensitive to how likely different properties are [231]. The theory assumes that people consider all information available to them optimally. For example, when trying to respond to a serve in a virtual tennis game, we need to estimate the ball's speed. To this end, we have two types of cues at our disposal: (1) the sound we hear when the ball was hit by the opponent and (2) the motion of the ball as we see it move on the display. The two cues provide unique and complementary information.

The theory suggests that we integrate cue-specific percepts into one estimation of the ball's velocity. The idea of optimality is that we make an optimal estimate based on the observed data (the two cues). In new tasks, where users have little exposure to the cues, they would struggle to make a good estimate. However, with more time, their performance improves and is better described by the theory. Despite the optimistic assumption of optimality, the theory has turned out to be accurate in fast-paced perceptual tasks in HCI, for example, in tasks where a moving target needs to be selected [468].

3.2.5 Search

In search tasks, the location in space of some object must be determined. For example, a user may need to localize an icon on a display or a command in a menu. In auditory search, the task is to localize the source of a given sound. We talk about visual search as a case below in Section 3.3.5.

3.3 Visual perception and attention

Visual perception refers to perception through the sensing of stimulation by light. It is a sensory modality of prime importance in HCI. Vision offers a rich and efficient way of conveying information to a user. First, visual perception is fast. Unlike olfaction, visual sensory experience is fast, formed within milliseconds from the onset of the stimulating event. However, constructing a more comprehensive percept, which requires several eye movements, can take seconds when the display is complex.

Figure 3.6 Ware's windows of visibility can be used to understand how viewing conditions affect perceptual tasks in the wild. For example, consider wanting to glance at a smartwatch while outdoors. Using the windows of visibility, assess the situation: What are the key limits to the user's visual performance? Photo used under Creative Commons Zero.

Second, it offers unparalleled parallel processing. It benefits massively from parallel processing over the entire field of perception. Unlike the sense of touch, with visual perception, no physical contact is required with the perceived objects. The human visual system is proposed to involve three neuroanatomically distinct pathways [662]:

What: The ventral pathway encodes the identity of visual objects, such as tools, faces, or animals. In the case of GUIs, it recognizes the types of elements and objects on the display.

Where and how: The dorsal pathway encodes the locations of visual objects and actions related to these objects. In the case of GUIs, it registers which elements can be clicked and tracks moving objects.

Who: A more recent discovery, the superior temporal sulcus specializes in dynamic social processing. It processes the actions of moving objects and bodies, such as their expressions, gaze, intentions, and moods. In the case of GUIs, it is employed in contexts such as VR, games, and videoconferencing.

Third, the visual system offers a hierarchical and highly interconnected structure. *Visual primitives*, such as the shape, size, orientation, color, and motion of objects, are extracted in massively parallel processing in low-level areas. The low-level areas feed into high-level areas that recognize objects and encode their identities. These, in turn, are projected back to the low-level areas. This structure realizes the top-down and bottom-up processing discussed in the previous section.

In the following section, we discuss the limits of the visual system and then cover the basics of eye movement, perceptual organization, and visual attention.

3.3.1 Limits to the human visual system

Take a look at Figure 3.6. The photo shows an example of an extreme environment encountered when using computers. Even if the face of the smartwatch may look fine when printed on the pages of this book, the real-world experience would be challenging. Before reading on, think about the following: What is it exactly that makes the case challenging for the user?

Ware [876] summarized the key limits of the visual system under the concept of *windows of visibility*. A "window" is a metaphor to describe the physiological limits posed to visual perception. Here, we describe four windows that are important in HCI: (1) the visible spectrum of light, (2) the field of view, (3) contrast, and (4) foveated vision. First, we can only perceive a limited range in the spectrum of light, from about 380 to 780 nm. Our rod and cone cells permit only three chroma of color (trichromaticity). This sets limits to the range of light that displays need to cover.

Second, our field of view is limited to about 190 degrees horizontally and 125 degrees vertically. This sets limits for how large displays can be and how and where they must be located in relation to our eyes.

Third, our perception of detail is limited. *Contrast* refers to the differences in luminance and color that make something in the field of view stand out from the rest. *Contrast sensitivity* refers to our ability to distinguish between levels of contrast. The contrast sensitivity function is a standard way of expressing this as a function of spatial cycles per degree. The function shows thresholds for contrast perception in a typical viewer. At first, contrast sensitivity is low because the information density is low. The contrast sensitivity is highest in the middle when the cycles-per-degree value matches the properties of the human visual system. As the cycles-per-degree value increases, the sensitivity decreases, as the system is not able to discriminate between cycles.

Fourth, the retinal image is limited and very non-uniform. It loses accuracy at the periphery. Vision is physiologically divided into two regions:

Foveal vision: It refers to a narrow but precise, high-fidelity perception around the point on which you fixate. This area spans only 2 degrees of angle, roughly corresponding to the size of your thumb held out at arm's length.

Peripheral vision: It refers to the rest of the field of view, which has eccentrically decreasing fidelity. The farther away from the foveal area, the lower the fidelity.

In the peripheral region, vision retains some access to visual primitives but not so much to objects. The visual primitives of human visual perception are color, shape, size, and depth. *Drop-off functions* describe how information is lost going from the foveal to the peripheral regions. An example is given in Figure 3.7.

In the case of the smartwatch (Figure 3.6), which windows are relevant? The answer is at least three of them. First, the watch may reside outside the field of view depending on the posture of the user. To view it, the smartwatch must be brought closer to where the eyes are operating. Second, even then, the smartwatch is likely to be foveally viewed because the eyes need to attend to the shoelaces. To attract the user's attention, the smartwatch would need to use highly salient visuals (e.g., salient colors, motion). Third, given that the watch face is small and far away, all its text is beyond human contrast sensitivity. Typically, users bring the watch closer to their eyes for reading.

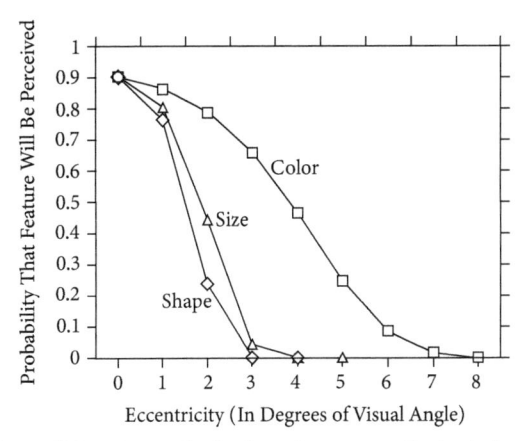

Figure 3.7 Peripheral drop-off functions. The farther a feature on display is from the foveal region (the area of high acuity), the less probable it is that it is available for perception [413]. Note that different perceptual tasks have different drop-off curves.

Visual impairments: Visual impairments that limit a person's ability to view computer displays are surprisingly prevalent. Red–green color deficiency, for example, is about 8% prevalent in European Caucasian males and 0.4% in females, and between 4% and 6.5% in Chinese and Japanese males [73]. Visual impairments include a wide range of physiological and neurological problems that cause color blindness, low-level vision, blindness, and deficiencies in controlling eye movements.

Color blindness, or color deficiency, manifests itself as difficulties in perceiving differences between colors, the brightness of colors, or different shades of colors. People with color blindness are often unable to distinguish certain colors, most commonly green–red and blue–yellow. Humans perceive color using cone cells in the retina that detect either red, green, or blue light. The outputs from these cone cells are then passed to the brain to produce the impression of a particular color. When cone cells do not function as expected, or are absent, this gives rise to color blindness. Color blindness covers a spectrum from mild color blindness that may be affected by, for example, dim lighting to severe color blindness that results in perceiving the world in shades of gray only. Color blindness is usually stable and affects both eyes. There is no treatment for people born with color blindness. However, various visual aids are available, such as apps that allow the user to take a photo and point anywhere on the photo to get the app to identify the color at that point. More generally, the effects of color blindness can be mitigated in GUI design by carefully choosing how information is encoded using colors. In Chapter 25, we talk about HCI research automating color decisions to help users with color perception deficiencies.

3.3.2 Eye movements

The human oculomotor system controls eye movements. It offers three main modes of controlling where we look:

Fixations: They encode information about the visual scene consisting of multiple micro-fixations, each lasting a few tens of milliseconds. What eye trackers do is cluster micro-fixations into fixations of 200–400 ms. The way we pick information during a fixation is task-dependent. For example, when reading text versus searching for an icon, we pick different visual information (e.g., color, text, shapes, orientations, motion).

Saccades: Saccades move the gaze point in ballistic leaps that are not perceived during the scene. They are ballistic in the sense that the target of the saccade is not changed after the onset of the movement. They are also blind in the sense that no information is sampled during a saccade.

Smooth pursuit: It is used for following moving targets, such as when following an animated character moving on the display. No saccading occurs. An example of an innovative application in HCI is shown in Paper Example 3.3.1.

The speed and accuracy of eye movements can be modeled mathematically; see Paper Example 3.3.2.

Fixations are the main means for the perceptual system to sample the visual environment. Every micro-fixation can gain progressively more information. As described above, this amount decreases *eccentrically*; that is, the farther an object is from the foveal region, the less information we gain about it in a fixation.

This process explains how eyes move when reading text. When reading, the visual system gains information about the fixated word and the following word [155]. The control of the eyes is affected by lexical processing. In turn, lexical processing is affected by three properties: the frequency, length, and contextual predictability of the word. For example, if a phrase is hard to understand, we may need to fixate on words we had already fixated on. When a phrase is easy to grasp or familiar, we may not need to look at every word and may be able to skip some words.

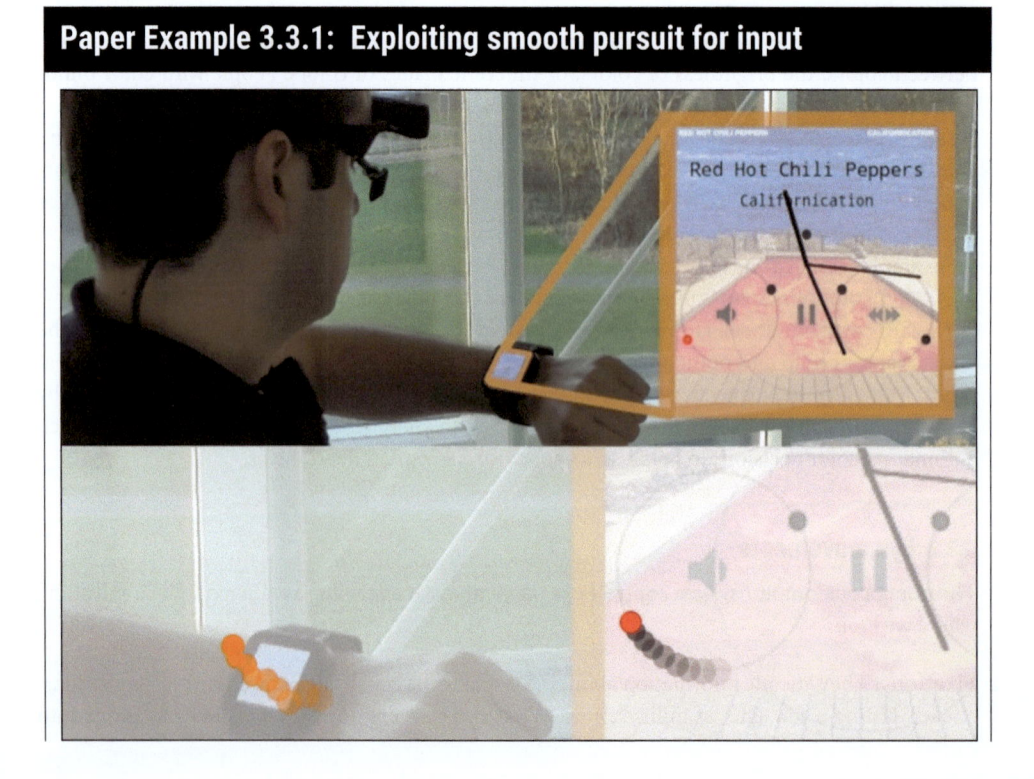

Paper Example 3.3.1: Exploiting smooth pursuit for input

Orbits is a selection technique that exploits smooth pursuit as an input modality [232]. Gaze-based selection normally uses dwell time to detect the object the user wants to select. For example, if one looks for one second at an icon, the icon is selected. The idea behind Orbits is matching. The user needs to move their eyes to match the motion or trajectory indicated by a to-be-selected widget. For example, the user can raise the volume of a player on the smartwatch by following the trajectory of a moving circle.

Paper Example 3.3.2: Speed and accuracy of discrete eye movements when viewing displays

Mathematical models of eye movements are important tools in HCI. They can be used to predict the time costs of using complex displays. Such costs depend on the layout (e.g., distances and sizes of targets) and the expertise of the user. Salvucci [724] proposed the eye movements and movement of attention (EMMA) model to better predict the performance of eye movements in HCI. It consists of equations for predicting the time spent encoding fixated objects as well as the movement time and accuracy of saccades.

First, when fixating on an object, the time needed to encode it, T_e, is a function of the amount of experience with the object. Objects we have encountered more often take less time to encode, and vice versa. This relationship is captured as follows:

$$T_e = K \cdot [-\log(f)] \cdot e^{k \cdot \epsilon}, \qquad (3.4)$$

where K and k are constants and f is the frequency of the object. ϵ is the eccentricity, measured as the distance of the target from the current eye fixation (in degrees). When the eccentricity is high, to account for its high cost, the visual system may initiate a saccade to get closer to the target. According to the EMMA model, an object (e.g., a word) can be skipped if sufficient information has been encoded during a fixation.

The duration of a saccade, T_s, depends on the distance to the object D, measured in degrees:

$$T_s = t_{\text{prep}} + t_{\text{exec}} + D \cdot t_{\text{sacc}}, \qquad (3.5)$$

where t_{prep}, t_{exec}, and t_{sacc} are constants related to the human visual system, specifically to movement preparation and movement execution.

An important property of eye movements is that they are noisy and therefore inaccurate. The actual landing point often differs from the intended landing point. This error can be modeled as signal-dependent noise. The inaccuracy follows a normal distribution with a standard deviation of σ_V times the distance D. That is, the greater the distance, the greater the noise [724].

When applying the EMMA model, the constants need to be calibrated to the particular viewing conditions. Previous applications provide indications for calibrating the constants. Note that the model does not predict the duration of fixations but the encoding time. Encoding can happen over multiple fixations.

Another feature of attention is that we do not always need to move our gaze to encode information. When the encoding time is lower than the movement preparation time, the target can be encoded without moving the eyes. These eye movements are called *covert* movements rather than *overt* movements. Covert movements explain many of the variations we see in the duration of fixation.

3.3.3 Perceptual organization

When you look at a graphical display, it nominally consists of just pixels on a two-dimensional array. How is perception able to make sense of it? Consider the example in Figure 3.8. Information appears to be organized into regions defined by the desktop, the menu bar, and the window. Some regions, like the window, are standing in front of other regions, like the wallpaper. Some elements belong together and form regions. For example, the list of recommended apps consists of a group of icons that we tend to perceive as different from other application icons.

Figure/ground perception refers to the organization of visual experience in a visuospatial hierarchy. That is, some objects belong to an object in front (a figure) while others belong to objects in the background (the ground). Graphical interfaces utilize the figure/ground perception to show a *display hierarchy*, or screen hierarchy. It defines to what element or whole another element belongs: this belongs to that, and that is different from this. We use cues such as shadows, occlusion (an object covering another), and different sizes to parse the display. When binocular stereo displays are used, stereoscopic depth cues can also help with forming the figure/ground perception.

The perception of organization decomposes a display into *regions*. For example, look at the GUI in Figure 3.8. What you most likely experience is a layout consisting of a few main regions, which in turn consist of elements with text or images. How do we achieve this? If you think about it, there are actually many ways to parse a layout into regions. Two elements A and B are associated

Figure 3.8 Perceptual organization refers to (1) the division of elements into figure versus ground and (2) their grouping into coherent regions. In this example, the application window (figure) is clearly in front of the desktop wallpaper (ground). There are also many visual groups on the display. For example, the region of recommended apps forms a distinct region from the rest of what is presented in the window. Similarly, the icons on the horizontal taskbar form a visual group.

by their similarity in color, distance, and alignment. Elements B and C have the same qualities but different values. How do we determine that two elements belong to the same group and not to some other group?

Visual grouping refers to the tendency of people looking at elements on a display to organize them in visual groups. The *Gestalt laws* originate from a German branch of psychology from the early twentieth century. The goal of Gestalt psychology was to understand what constitutes a whole. Wertheimer studied the visual factors that cause the perception of elements as belonging together on a complex display. He identified seven laws that are now called the Gestalt laws. These laws have endured well [864]. Below, we present four commonly used principles of visual grouping and a related example (Figure 3.9):

Proximity: The closer some elements are to each other and the farther they are from other elements, the stronger they are grouped together.

Common area: Elements that are located in the same closed region are grouped together.

Similarity: Elements that are similar (e.g., in color, size, or orientation) are grouped together.

Continuation: Elements that are connected by the continuation of flow are grouped together.

Brumby and Zhuang [104] found that when menu groups are marked using visual grouping cues, items are found more quickly. However, this strategy only works when there are fewer, larger groups. Having multiple small groups dilutes the facilitatory effect of visual grouping.

Although the Gestalt laws are called *laws*, they are less like scientific laws in, say, physics and more like heuristics to understand certain tendencies in how perception works. The laws are popular among designers because they offer a good way to estimate how users perceive structure in graphical interfaces and layouts. They help us understand how to present the hierarchy of a UI in a way that users find easy to match. They are also part of design education and are frequently used by interaction designers. However, they ignore the fact that perception is an active and adaptive process: Depending on the task and their beliefs, users can organize the display in different ways. We return to discussing active perception at the end of this chapter.

Ungrouped	Proximity	Common area	Similarity	Continuation
Email Word Excel Powerpoint Drive Mastodon Facebook Snap Instagram WhatsApp	Email Word Excel Powerpoint Drive Mastodon Facebook Snap Instagram WhatsApp	Email Word Excel Powerpoint Drive Mastodon Facebook Snap Instagram WhatsApp	Email Word Excel Powerpoint Drive Mastodon Facebook Snap Instagram WhatsApp	Email Word Excel Powerpoint Drive Mastodon Facebook Snap Instagram WhatsApp

Figure 3.9 Principles of visual grouping. On the left, the figure shows an ungrouped menu design. The other columns show how the principles can be utilized to visually communicate which menu items belong together.

3.3.4 Visual attention

Attention is the focusing of perceptual processing on a region or object in the perceptual field. *Visual attention* is traditionally considered to consist of three processes:

Selective attention: The ability to direct attention to a desired object or location.

Vigilance: The ability to sustain attention on something for a long period.

Divided attention: The ability to split attention between one or more objects, locations, or tasks.

Selective attention refers to the deliberate refocusing of attention to another object or region in the perceptual field. *Overt attention* refers to the movement of eyes to fixate on something. However, we can also sample information without moving our eyes. *Covert attention* is the processing of extra-foveal information without moving the eyes. When reading displays, both covert and overt attention are utilized. Eye trackers are instruments used for measuring overt attention. The limit of how long we can hold our attention on a task or object is called *vigilance*.

Divided attention refers to the division of perceptual processing between multiple objects or regions. For example, *situation awareness* is the ability to keep track of events and objects in a dynamic setting. Consider driving a car through a busy intersection, or an air traffic controller keeping track of planes in the airspace of an airport. Such tasks require us to continuously shift our attention between multiple objects and update our mental representations of their properties. For example, when walking down a busy street, our visual attention on a mobile device is fragmented; the average glance lasts just 3–4 seconds [626]. However, if we walk down a less crowded street, we can maintain our gaze on the device for longer periods.

3.3.5 Visual search

Visual search is a common task with graphical interfaces involving selective attention. The goal is to find an element on the display, for example, an icon or a label of interest. This task poses a control problem for the visual system, which must decide where to place the next fixation. How does it do this? Three things interact to guide the eyes when searching for something: (1) the visual features of the display, (2) learning, and (3) strategic decisions on *how* to search.

First, the display consists of a spatial distribution of visual features. Compare, for example, an application menu and a mobile app in terms of how colors, sizes, and shapes are distributed. Depending on what you are looking at (your current fixation), these features are differentially available to the visual system. If you look at the top-right corner of a mobile app screen, different parts of the visual feature distribution are available compared to if you were looking at the center of the screen.

In *disjunctive search*, or feature search, the visual search is based on so-called visual primitives such as color, shape, size, curvature, orientation, and motion. When the target is unique in any of these features, the search is fast (typically < 100 ms). For example, if you are looking for a green icon on a display that does not have other green elements, you can spot it almost instantaneously if it is large enough. Feature search is fast because such features can be spotted peripherally by the perceptual system. By contrast, in *conjunctive search*, the target cannot be singled out with a single feature: We need to look for a combination of features. For example, if there are multiple green elements, the only way to know which one is the icon you are looking for is to look at each icon and its label. In such cases, the search cannot be "solved" with peripheral processing: It requires fixating on candidate items to pick up the relevant information. This type of search is much slower. In the design of GUIs, elements that should be quickly found can be designed to be found via disjunctive search (Chapter 28).

The *feature integration theory* of Treisman and Gelade [829] explains why this difference emerges (Figure 3.10). The low-level visual features of a stimulus environment are directly represented in what she calls *feature maps*. Attentional spotlight, or information collected via fixations, on the other hand, is needed to find *combinations* of these features. This combined map integrates low-level features; it maps objects (and their features) to their locations. In other words, selective attention is needed to bind features to recognizable objects that can be further processed.

What this model does not account for is the fact that there is less information in the peripheral view than in the foveal view. Kieras and Hornof [413] proposed a model called *active vision*. It emphasizes that people choose where to look based on the description of the target and the visual features available via peripheral vision. However, peripheral information is compromised: The farther away eccentrically an object is from the current fixation point, the more it is compromised. The visual system has to deal with uncertainty about the regions of the display it is *not* attending to immediately; it must "gamble" with its priorities and look at those regions later. According to the theory, it does this only after checking candidate items close to the foveal region. The model is dubbed "active" because users are not passively drawn to visual features; their choice of the next fixation points depends on what they are looking for and what they presently see.

However, these models do not account for the effect of *learning*. If you have already seen an item a few times, it is easier to locate it. In menu systems, for example, a user who has experienced the design a few hundred times can fixate on it virtually immediately when looking for it [127]. The *Guided Search* model of Wolfe [910] attempts to explain this (see Figure 3.11). It proposes that decisions on where to fixate are guided by *priority maps*. A priority map combines bottom-up and top-down information to guide the user on where to look next. Depending on how strong the

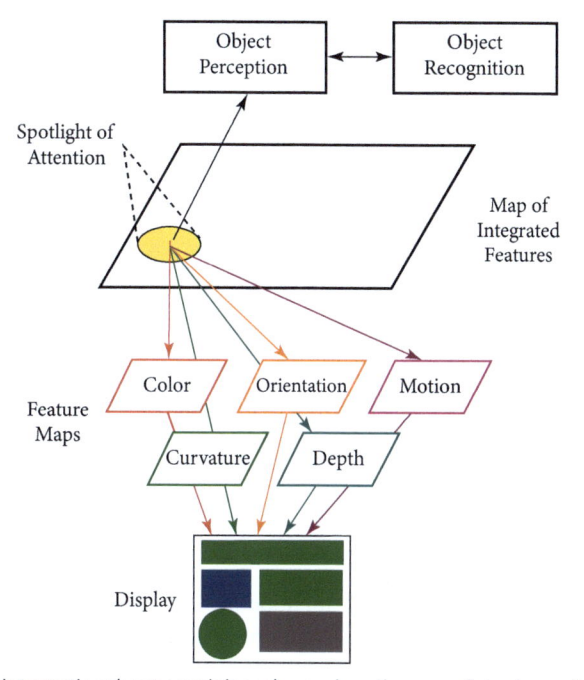

Figure 3.10 Feature integration theory explains why conjunctive search is slower than feature search. Feature search can be carried out using parallel processing of the peripheral vision, whereas conjunctive search requires users to fixate on the region. User interface designers can exploit these differences.

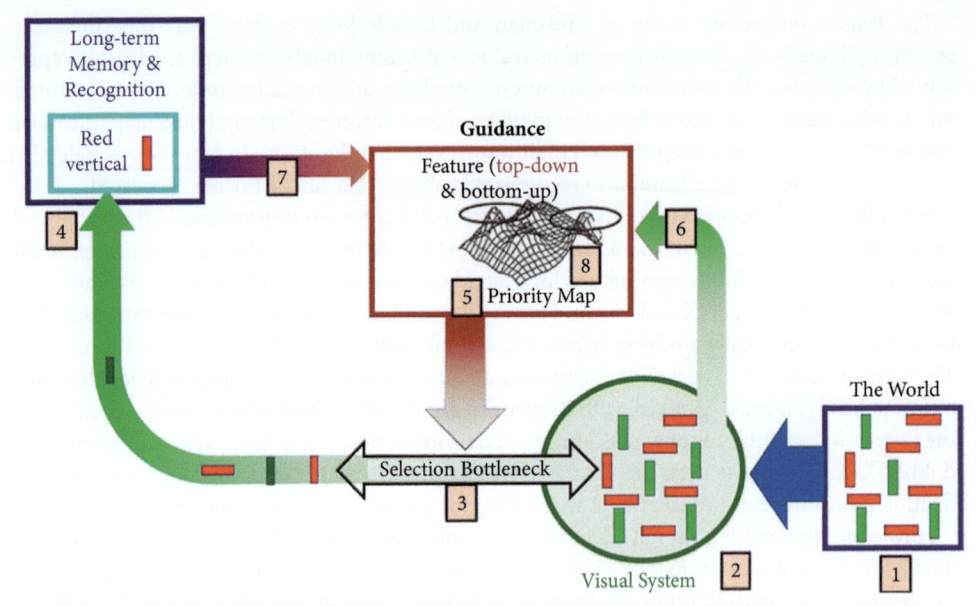

Figure 3.11 A model of visual search by Wolfe [910]. The model suggests that both the long-term memory of locations (top-down) and the perceived features (bottom-up) contribute to the selection of where to place a fixation. This takes place via what is called the *priority map* where this information is combined. This model (Guided Search 2.0) has been updated to also consider scene composition, lexical and semantic features, and task rewards.

long-term memory is, it differentially contributes to the map and therefore to guidance. Users who have seen a UI a few times have positional memory of where objects are located on it, especially those that are often searched for. With more repetition, the locations of elements will be remembered and do not need to be actively rediscovered every time. However, if the display changes, the value of long-term memory is reduced or completely lost, and the user needs to rely on bottom-up guidance again. Wolfe's model has been updated a few times. The version shown in the figure is 2.0. Since this version, the model also covers the effect of task rewards (Chapter 21) as well as scene syntax and semantics.

Users often explore displays to form an actionable priority map. For example, when seeing a new ticket vending machine, should one try to directly find the entry point to the display (exploit) or first become familiar with the overall layout of the system (explore)? We often explore briefly and then search. In such cases, we must decide whether *enough* is known about the scene to find the target of interest, or if more information needs to be collected.

3.3.6 Visual saliency

Visual saliency is an application of visual attention modeling that has become popular recently. Saliency refers to the probability with which a graphical element can attract visual attention during the first few seconds of viewing a display (Figure 3.12). Saliency depends on the visual properties of the target and those of the rest of the display. It also depends on the tendencies learned from repeated exposure.

Attention, generally, is drawn to *visually unique elements*. Through their different color and bold font, these words stand out relative to the rest of this paragraph. Generally, regions and elements

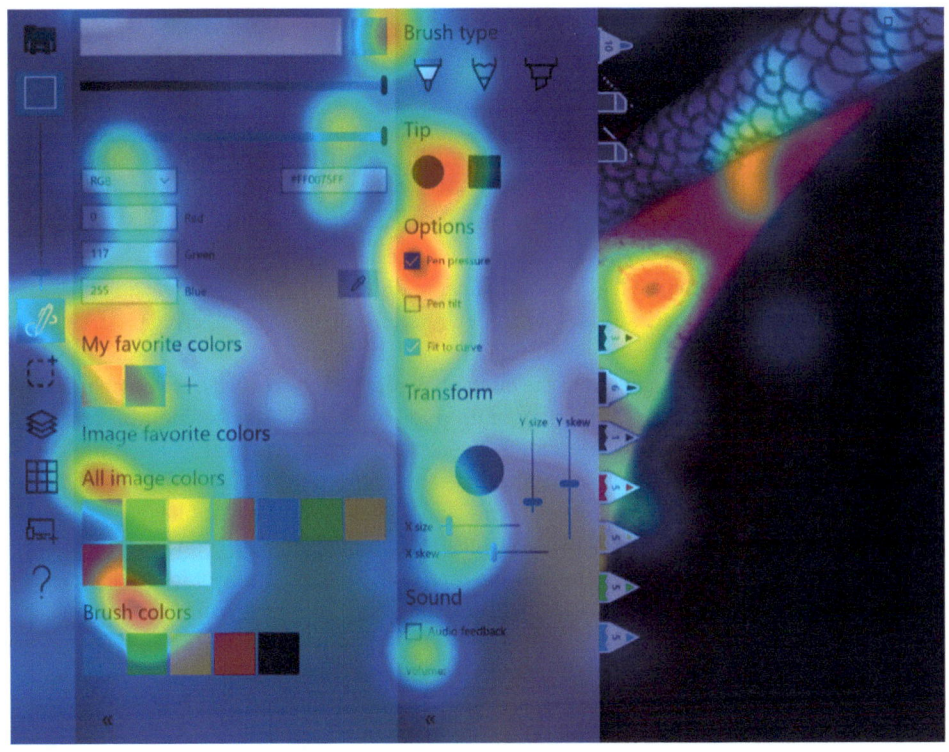

Figure 3.12 This heatmap of eye-tracking data shows what people look at when viewing a UI [385]. Visual saliency denotes the probability with which visual features attract attention when we see a UI for the first time. Saliency depends on the distribution of visual features on the UI, user expectations (including any prior experience with related designs), and the user's attentional strategy.

that are unique in terms of visual primitives, such as color, shape, size, orientation, or motion, stand out.

On the one hand, saliency emerges in the parallel processing of retinal input at lower levels in the visual cortex. On the other hand, visual saliency is also affected by top-down factors such as memory and expectations of informative locations. That is, we learn how to look. For instance, if a color such as red appears in an image full of green tones and green-filled shapes, observers tend to look at the red shape. Top-down factors include task goals and expectations based on the learned statistical distribution of features. For example, in many natural scenes that show a horizon, most of the information lies close to the horizontal medial line, which also attracts attention. When the visual task or content changes, both bottom-up and top-down factors may change in response. Therefore, an empirical effect related to the saliency reported for one context does not carry over to another trivially.

Research has found that there is something special about UIs. They differ from natural scenes (say, a forest) in several respects. With natural scenes, there is a tendency to look at the center and the horizontal line. This is understandable, as the horizontal line often provides the most information about a natural scene. However, for UIs, this is often not the case [472]. Attention tends to be drawn to the top-left quadrant of the page. In addition, color is a poorer predictor of saliency than in natural scenes. Instead, attention is drawn to large texts and images with faces.

However, despite visual saliency having emerged as one of the better-known aspects of the human visual system, designers often use rules of thumb and gut feelings instead. It can also explain what makes a display cluttered (Paper Example 3.3.3).

Paper Example 3.3.3: What makes a display cluttered?

Take a look at the desk in the picture below (picture used under Creative Commons License). Anyone can see that it is cluttered—but what does clutter mean?

Consider visual clutter as the "evil twin" of saliency. Rosenholtz et al. [712] noted that visual saliency can be used to explain and measure how cluttered something is perceived to be. *Clutter* means that *everything* is attempting to be salient.

The underpinning hypothesis is that the human visual system has evolved to detect unusual objects in scenes. A salient item is unusual in its visual context. Clutter, by contrast, refers to excess items competing for our attention. In the state of clutter, all visual features are "congested." For example, color clutter means that many colors from the visible spectrum are used in the display. Many elements are unique in this, and, therefore, nothing is salient.

Rosenholtz proposed a simple test to determine if a display is cluttered. If you wanted to place a note on the desk (e.g., a Post-it note) that the user should notice, how would the design be? Which color, size, and shape would you choose? If the desk is cluttered, it may not be possible to pick a visual feature that makes the note stand out on the display.

Clutter is detrimental to visual performance. It is empirically associated with a decrease in object recognition performance and visual search performance, as well as forgetting due to exceeding the limit of short-term memory.

3.4 Perception as an active process

One of the main takeaways from this chapter is that users are not at the mercy of their senses. They are not passive recipients of stimulation determined solely by the display design. Instead, they actively construct percepts.

Users apply their knowledge to actively decide where to focus their attention, including guessing where things are or what they are called. In addition to learning, users strategically change how they perceive things. For example, experienced users rely more on their long-term memory than novices do. The reward–cost structure of a task also affects perception. When a task structure changes, for example, to penalize mistakes and errors, users may change their strategy accordingly.

Moreover, users actively explore their environment using their bodies. They also adjust the relationship their body has with the environment. For example, if you were for some reason abruptly re-positioned one meter farther from this text, you would want to step closer to continue reading it. In short, people use their bodies to facilitate and support their perception of things. This approach is called *active perception*. Active perception refers to perception that is actively sampling, exploring, and learning to better support the organism. *Ecological perception* refers to the idea that these processes are sensitive to and adapt to the structure of the environment. For example, once we have learned to look at web pages in a particular way, we expect items to appear in specific locations that reflect the probability of those items being there. *Embodied perception* refers to a more radical view whereby perception and bodies cannot be decoupled: All perception is neurobiologically coupled to motor systems. No matter the view, it is clear that understanding embodiment is as important for understanding perception as it is for understanding its underpinning sensory modalities.

A prominent example of active perception is *perceived affordance*, a term coined by Norman in the book *The Design of Everyday Things*. Affordance is a property of an element that invites interaction. For example, a door may have an opening mechanism that invites the user to either push a plate or pull a handle to open the door. Users would, in general, know which method is suitable for the door without trying both based on the affordance of the door handle. Graphical objects can also afford interaction, for example, by signaling whether they should be clicked, dragged, or similar. However, Norman argues that the useful property for a GUI is not affordance but perceived affordance: "In similar vein, because I can click anytime I want, it is wrong to argue whether a graphical object on the screen 'affords clicking.' It does. The real question is about the perceived affordance: Does the user perceive that clicking on that location is a meaningful, useful action to perform?"[2]

Buttons, for example, can communicate affordance through shapes, colors, and shadows. However, perceived affordance is cultural. Our ability to perceive affordance in graphical objects relies on our existing knowledge and experience. For example, the blue hyperlinks that are now common did not elicit clicks from users until people learned that it was possible to click on links in the text.

---

[2] http://www.jnd.org/dn.mss/affordances_and_design.html.

Summary

- Perceptual experience is not determined by what is shown on the display alone but in conjunction with our expectations and strategies of deploying attention.
- Perception in HCI can be understood through the elementary tasks it needs to serve: discrimination, detection, recognition, estimation, and search.
- Another key role of perception is to "bring order into chaos," in other words, organize the overwhelming sensory experience into something we can act on.
- Visual saliency refers to the probability with which something on display attracts our visual attention. When the UI is cluttered, all visual primitives are "congested" and nothing can be made to stand out from the page.

Exercises

1. Analysis of a visual design. Choose a GUI you think is difficult to use. Could this be because of the organization of the display? Take a screenshot and analyze it in terms of how it uses (a) the principle of visual saliency (what attracts attention) and (b) the Gestalt laws (grouping of information).
2. Alternative modalities. Section 3.1 lists three types of sensory modalities prevalent in computer use. Consider designing a display that shows the speed of a car to the driver. What are the pros and cons of each sensory modality when used as a display in this case?
3. Perceptual tasks. This chapter has discussed five perceptual tasks in HCI: discrimination, detection, recognition, estimation, and search. Which perceptual task is the defining task in the following cases? (a) Playing a first-person shooter, you see a shadowy character move in the distance; is it a friend or a foe? (b) You arrive at the airport and look at a display of departing flights; from which gate is your flight leaving? (c) You're on the subway and feel a slight vibration in your pocket; is it your mobile device or a tremble from the subway? (d) You're wearing a VR headset and see a button close to you; is it close enough that you can press it without moving, or should you first walk closer to it? (e) You see an icon that has a circle with a cross (X) in the middle; is it a "Close window" button?
4. Using smell in UIs. Compare olfaction (smell) and vision as sensory modalities. Think about everyday HCI: Even if technology were to allow for olfactory displays, why are they unlikely to replace vision-based displays?
5. Understanding clutter. Pick a UI (e.g., a ticket vending machine) that you think looks cluttered. Why is it so? Refer to the conjunction search to identify three regions of the UI that might be hard to find. Circle and number the regions in the UI and explain why they are hard to find.
6. Visual grouping in GUIs. Take a GUI and look at it. Which elements belong together, i.e., are grouped? Which visual grouping principles are applied to achieve this?
7. Unhelpful use of color. A simple mobile device is operated by holding the device with the non-dominant hand and a plastic pen with the dominant hand. The device enables text entry through a graphical keyboard presented on a resistive screen. The system does not perform word prediction or autocorrect. A designer proposes to improve the text entry performance by changing the colors of the keys on the graphical keyboard. Based on the principles taught in this chapter, explain why this approach is fundamentally flawed.

4
Motor control

When users type on a keyboard, tap on a touchscreen, steer a car, or generally perform an action using their body, they rely on *motor control*. Human motor control refers to the regulation of all movement in a human, including the integration of relevant internal and external sensory information to determine the necessary signals to activate the right muscles. Motor control is critical for fundamental human tasks such as balancing the body, pointing at things, and grasping objects.

Motor control in human–computer interface (HCI) focuses on humans interacting with computing systems, for instance, typing on a keyboard, moving a mouse pointer toward an icon, and reacting to prompts. An in-depth understanding of motor control supports the design of user interfaces that better fit the capabilities of users. Such an understanding is often captured in the form of mathematical or computational models. For example, the average time it takes an average user to touch an app icon on a touchscreen phone can be predicted with a model if we know (1) the distance of the user from the app icon and (2) the size of the app icon. Such predictive models have many applications in HCI, including the following:

1. Graphical layouts can be personalized to better match a user's motor abilities [266]. Depending on the amount of tremor, the elements on an interface can be made bigger and the layout reorganized so that the elements can be reached more easily.
2. Target selection techniques utilize motor control models to dynamically make the objects on display easier to select. For example, they can change the selection areas to support fast selection (Chapter 26).
3. Keyboard layouts have been optimized using models of pointing. For example, letters and characters can be assigned to keys so that the average selection time for a given language is minimized. The Dvorak Simplified Keyboard is a famous early attempt to break the hegemony of the QWERTY layout. While optimized keyboard layouts demonstrate faster and less error-prone typing, this is achieved at the expense of having to learn a new layout [e.g., 70, 239].
4. The performance of input methods and devices can be compared using metrics rooted in models of motor control. For example, we can compare an in-air input method and a fingertip-based input method—two methods that involve widely different movement sizes and types—using the concept of throughput.

Motor control models can also help us understand how difficult certain tasks are for users. Figure 4.1 shows two slightly different examples. Navigating a drop-down menu is surprisingly complex, but Ahlström [12] showed how to do it with two laws that are discussed in this chapter: Fitts' law and the steering law. Before we provide a more in-depth understanding of such examples, let us look at elements of motor control tasks in HCI.

Introduction to Human-Computer Interaction. Kasper Hornbæk, Per Ola Kristensson, and Antti Oulasvirta,
Oxford University Press. © Kasper Hornbæk, Per Ola Kristensson, and Antti Oulasvirta (2025).
DOI: 10.1093/oso/9780192864543.003.0004

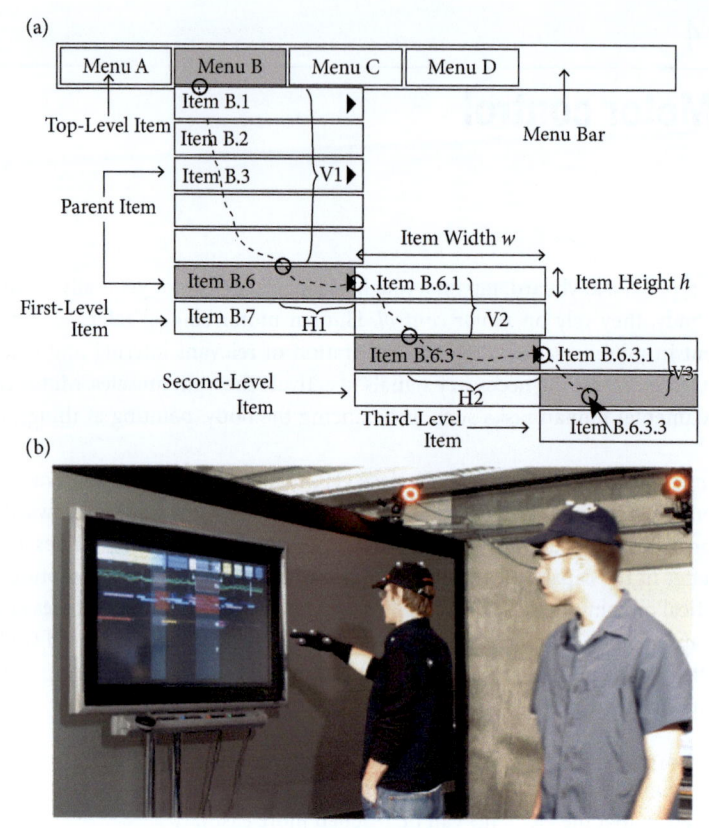

Figure 4.1 Two examples of motor control in HCI. The figure to the top shows how to select an item in a hierarchical drop-down menu. Fitts' law and the steering law can be used to predict users' performance in this task [12]. The figure to the bottom shows a system where the user can point toward a large display from a distance [859] (photo from Vogel's master thesis, p. 51).

4.1 Elements of a motor control task in HCI

Movement control concerns how our nervous system produces purposeful and coordinated movement. In HCI, movement most often occurs through our fingers, although some systems have used movements of the head, feet [29], or the entire body. Even if the movement is done by multiple body parts, in HCI, we are typically only interested in the part we use for something: the *end-effector*.

End-effectors controlled by different body parts have different *degrees of freedom*. For instance, the knee has one degree of freedom (it is basically a hinge), whereas the hip has three degrees of freedom (it can rotate around three axes). These degrees of freedom are often used to define an end-effector in 3D space and rotate it along three axes: roll, pitch, and yaw. This gives a total of six degrees of freedom.

Movement is often complicated. Joints need to work together to produce movement, the environment's effect on the body varies, and the level of muscle fatigue also varies. All of this causes variability in movement. Learning to move your body and learning to control computers through movement is about regulating that variability.

The movement of end-effectors may be coordinated in two principled ways. One is called *open loop*, referring to a system without a feedback loop influencing the movement. When you quickly press a blinking button or grab your coffee mug, you are doing open-loop control. Conversely, in a *closed loop*, feedback is received and incorporated during motion. This feedback allows you to correct your movements, making them more precise. We discuss these control principles in Chapter 17.

In HCI, we care mostly about *aimed movements*, such as the movement of a user attempting to move an end-effector (say, their finger) to a certain location (say, a button on a touchscreen). However, a large class of non-aimed movements also has applications in HCI. Gestures are one example (say, swiping); walking is another.

More formally, aimed movements are movements in which success is defined by external constraints. To elicit the right command, we need to move the body in the right way and at the right time. For example, to send character "a," a sufficiently small body part must land exactly on the cap of the button with sufficient (but not excess) force. Except for brain–computer interfaces, most UIs are operated by aimed movements. Two fundamental types of *movement constraints* can be distinguished.

Spatially constrained aimed movements: These movements are restricted at the end or during the movement to a specified region or point. *Discrete aimed movements* are movements toward spatially bounded targets. An example is moving a mouse cursor on top of a button to select it. This movement type is prevalent in HCI. It is also one of the prime paradigms used to communicate intentions and commands to a computer; consider buttons, widgets, links, icons, and so on. By contrast, *continuous aimed movements* require the user to keep the control point within a bounding box during the entire duration of the movement. For example, keeping a cursor within a tunnel when navigating a hierarchical menu requires continuous "steering" (Figure 4.1). We discuss steering and gesturing in the next two sections.

Temporally constrained aimed movements: These movements are necessary when a target must be hit within a defined period. The goal may be to hit a target during a specific interval or to hit as close to the target as possible. An example of the former is jumping over obstacles in a video game; an example of the latter is playing notes on a piano. These two types of constraints often occur together.

In an *interception* task, spatial and temporal demands co-occur. For example, we need to catch a moving object by (1) placing a selector on its future path and (2) pressing the button when the object is within the selector's effective region. Consider, for example, hitting a tennis ball served by the opponent or sniping an enemy player in a first-person shooter game.

A fundamental tendency holds for virtually all aimed movements. The *speed–accuracy trade-off* limits the motor system, which cannot be both fast and accurate at the same time. If you think about moving your hand toward a target, it is clear that you can either move your hand quickly toward the target or be precise when hitting it. While you can carry out an action that balances these two objectives, you cannot optimally achieve both objectives at the same time.

4.2 Target acquisition

Target acquisition is a discrete, spatially constrained aimed movement. *Pointing* is perhaps the most typical target acquisition task in HCI. Here, the goal is to move the control point on top of an area denoting the target. If the control point misses the area, the movement is considered to have missed the target. Typically, there are two performance objectives: (1) be as fast as possible and (2) do not miss the target, that is, keep the error rate below a set threshold.

While pointing is the most common target acquisition task in HCI, three other tasks are also widely studied in the literature:

- **Point target:** The target is defined as a point in space. The user's accuracy is measured as the Euclidean distance of the end point from the point selected by the user. This is practical for targets with diffuse shapes, such as a moving game character on a display that changes its shape.
- **Line/surface target:** The target is a line in space, and the user's goal is to move the control point to cross the line. Performance is measured in terms of movement time. When the target is a line segment (i.e., with finite length), accuracy can be measured as hit/miss. For example, we can define items in a menu as lines as opposed to regions to make them faster to select.
- **Postural/angular target:** Joints must be rotated to a particular angle. For example, in some dancing games, users need to replicate a specific posture shown on the display.

Two immediate questions in HCI are when these tasks are difficult to do and how we may design them to be simpler. Fitts' law provides answers to these questions.

4.2.1 Fitts' law

The time it takes a user to point to a *target*, for example, a 2D button, depends on how large it is and how far away it is. The average movement time in this task can be mathematically predicted using Fitts' law. Fitts' law is a mathematical model for predicting the average movement time required to hit a target along a one-dimensional path, which is assumed to be proportional to the difficulty of hitting the target. This difficulty is affected by the distance to the target and the width of the target.

Fitts' law is not a law in the sense of a natural law; it is a statistical regularity that was discovered through experimentation. Fitts [243], an American psychologist interested in human performance, used what is now known as the reciprocal task paradigm. Participants were asked to select targets of varying distances and widths by alternatively pointing to the left and to the right. Figure 4.2 illustrates this reciprocal task paradigm as it was used in the original experiment.

For such a task, Fitts' law states that the average movement time MT can be predicted by a linear relationship [505]:

$$MT = a + bID, \qquad (4.1)$$

where a and b are regression coefficients and ID is the *index of difficulty*. The ID is an encoding of how far away the target is and how large it is, and it is defined as

$$ID = \log_2\left(\frac{D}{W} + 1\right), \qquad (4.2)$$

where D is the *distance* to the target and W is the *width* of the target. The ID is easy to interpret: The closer the target is, the lower D is, and hence the lower ID is. Similarly, the larger the target is, the larger W is and thus the lower ID is. In other words, targets that are either close, large, or both have a low ID; targets that are far away, small, or both have a high ID.

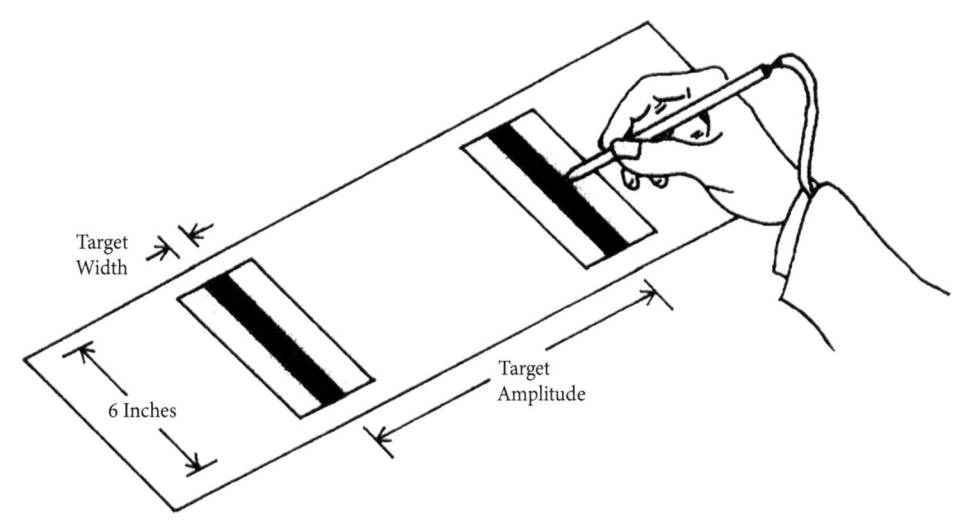

Figure 4.2 Fitts' experimental setup for manipulating movement D and target width W in a reciprocal tapping task. The two metal plates were to be hit with a stylus in an alternating sequence as fast as possible. Figure adapted from [505].

Another intuition from $\frac{D}{W} + 1$ is that it denotes how many targets of width W can fit within a distance D. In other words, *ID* denotes how many targets could have been selected, even if only one was selected in the end. We add 1 to the fraction to account for the fact that pointing aims at the center of a target, which means we have to add 0.5 W to each end of the movement. By convention, the *ID* for pointing tasks is nearly always defined in terms of logarithm base 2, which means *ID* has a unit of *bits*. The more bits that are required to express the $\frac{D}{W}$ relationship, the higher the *ID*. This intuition is discussed in more detail in Chapter 17, where we discuss the relationship between this law and information theory.

Mathematically, Equation 4.1 is identical to the equation of a straight line, *y = a + bx*, where *a* is the intercept and *b* is the slope of the line. This is because Fitts' law describes a linear relationship. The variables *a* and *b* are regression coefficients, as the intercept and slope of a line under Fitts' law are determined experimentally. By varying the distances and widths of the targets and measuring the average movement times, it is possible to infer the intercept *a* and the slope *b* of the line using a mathematical technique known as linear regression. This is what Fitts did in his 1954 paper when he discovered this regularity.

4.2.2 Using Fitts' law to assess input performance

The model has another interesting property: It can be used to compare users' performance across conditions with different target properties. Consider, for example, wanting to compare a joystick and a touchpad for target selection; how would you do that? Throughput can help us achieve this. Several definitions of throughput exist, as none is ideal. One definition of throughput is [505]

$$TP = \frac{ID_{avg}}{MT_{avg}}. \qquad (4.3)$$

The downside of Equation 4.3 is that it relies on an arbitrary average *ID*. An alternative definition of throughput is given by Zhai [921]:

$$TP = \frac{1}{b}, \qquad (4.4)$$

which relates throughput solely to the slope *b* of a line under Fitts' law. The downside of Equation 4.4 is that it ignores the effect of the intercept *a*. Using either definition of throughput, it is possible through experimentation to determine the throughput of various pointing methods. A higher throughput is better.

The parameters *a* and *b* may vary depending on the task, user group, and use context; there is a rich body of research investigating how these parameters may change. Also, several extensions to the model have been considered in the HCI literature, such as modeling 2D target selection [506] and targets that move on the screen.

4.2.3 Worked example

Let us show in more detail how to apply Fitts' law. The experimental task in Fitts' work, shown in Figure 4.2, is called a *reciprocal tapping task*. One can arrange this study protocol relatively easily to obtain a model under Fitts' law. In this task, users are asked to tap two targets of width W placed at distance D from each other.

In the original study, Fitts systematically manipulated *D* and W—the distance and width of the target, respectively. His data are reported in Table 4.1 [243], which tabulates the average *MT* as a function of *D* and W. Fitts noted that while there is no obvious relationship between *MT* and either *D* or W, they can be combined into a single term. This is the basis of Fitts' law.

Why are tasks with higher *ID* motorically harder? You can approach this question by thinking about what happens when the distance increases and when the width decreases. Both increase *ID* and therefore *MT*. In other words, all other things being equal, targets that are farther away

Table 4.1 Data from Fitts' original stylus pointing task. The predicted *MT* is 12.8 + 94.7*ID*, where $ID = \log_2(2D/W)$.

MT	D	W	ID	Predicted MT
180	2	2	1	107
212	2	1	2	202
203	4	2	2	202
281	2	0.5	3	297
260	4	1	3	297
279	8	2	3	297
392	2	0.25	4	392
372	4	0.5	4	392
357	8	1	4	392
388	16	2	4	392
484	4	0.25	5	486
469	8	0.5	5	486
481	16	1	5	486
580	8	0.25	6	581
595	16	0.5	6	581
731	16	0.25	7	676

or smaller are harder to hit, and, therefore, it takes longer to hit them. Thus, movement time is related to the inverse of spatial error. Using *ID* also makes computations with the model simpler. Instead of the nonlinear relationship, we can now deal with a simpler, linear relationship.

Fitts' model based on the obtained data is shown in Figure 4.3. Averaging the *MT* data obtained in each *ID* condition, and fitting the empirical parameters *a* and *b*, Fitts found the relationship in Equation 4.1. After computing *ID*, parameters *a* and *b* are estimated,[1] yielding in this case:

$$MT = 12.8 + 94.7 \times ID, R^2 = 0.967. \tag{4.5}$$

The fit of the model, indicated by R^2, is high. R^2 is a statistical measure that indicates how much of the variance in *MT* can be explained by the regression model. Paper Example 4.2.1 shows how to compute movement time taking into account user's precision in pointing.

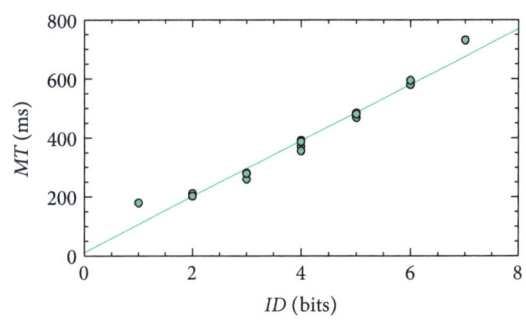

Figure 4.3 A model of stylus pointing consistent with Fitts' law. The plot shows the observed movement time *MT* versus the index of difficulty *ID*. The linear trend depicts the model $MT = 12.8 + 94.7 \times ID$. The model fit is $R^2 = 0.967$. The data are reported in Table 4.1.

Paper Example 4.2.1: Effective width

So far, we have assumed that *W* is defined by the interface or a researcher. Another way to look at it is that the user can affect it. A precise user may be more accurate than the designed target, and vice versa, and an imprecise user may be unable to reliably hit the designed target because the effective width is too large. To account for this variance, MacKenzie [505] provided a variant of the model:

$$MT = a + b \log_2\left(\frac{D}{W_e} + 1\right), \tag{4.6}$$

where W_e is the *effective width*. It refers to the empirical spread of end points around the target center. While *W* refers to the actual width of the target, W_e is the target that users *can* hit most of the time, or its *effective* width. You can consider the effective width to be the motor variability we can measure when a user is repeatedly carrying out the motor task.

The effective width can be computed if we can collect data on the end points of movements; that is, where the users' aimed movements end. When the end points are normally distributed,

continued

---

[1] Parameters *a* and *b* can be fitted to data with a statistical method called ordinary least squares, which is included in most statistical packages.

> **Paper Example 4.2.1: Effective width** (continued)
>
> the standard deviation can be used to determine W_e. The typical cut-off is $\sigma = 4.6$, which corresponds to 4% of the end points. In other words, the effective width W_e determines the width of a target that would be hit 96% of the time. The idea is shown in Figure 4.4. Because the cut-off defines the acceptable proportion of errors, it should be decided case-by-case.
>
> This formulation clarifies the relationship of the model with the speed–accuracy trade-off. If the user tries to be faster, the target width may not change, but the effective width will increase. When *ID* increases—in other words, when the task becomes harder—either the noise (effective width) increases or the user will need to be slower.
>
> **Figure 4.4** The effective width denotes the target size that the user would be able to hit X% of the time, usually set to 96%. The effective width is computed by assuming that the end points are normally distributed and setting a cut-off based on the standard deviation. Image source: Mackenzie [505].

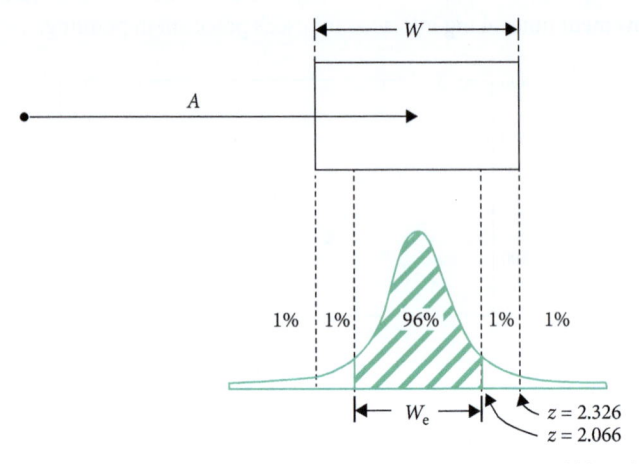

4.2.4 Applications of Fitts' law

Fitts' law is widely used in user interface design and evaluation. If the *a* and *b* parameters are known, then it is possible to calculate how average movement times will change depending on the size and distance of targets. Fitts' law and its variants are used for designing better layouts, interaction techniques, and input devices. By exposing how user performance is affected by design-relevant factors, and by offering a unified account of both speed and accuracy, Fitts' law has become the core of our understanding of aimed movements. Fitts' law also provides a basis for empirical comparisons of input devices, and it has driven innovation in interaction techniques. Good examples are the key-target-resizing technique used in virtual keyboards and the layout optimization algorithms that have challenged QWERTY as the dominant keyboard layout [70].

Fitts' law permits the rigorous empirical comparison of input methods. Consider the problem of comparing two input devices. Figure 4.5 shows a plot comparing data from MacKenzie [505]. The plot shows that the stylus is better across the *ID* range, indicating that it is the better input option. If there was a *crossover* point, it would be exposed by the model, even if there was no observation at that *ID* point.

The concept of *ID* is powerful here. It collapses two parameters that describe a motor task into a single variable that is linearly correlated with *MT*. The alternative, called the naive-but-tempting approach by Zhai [921], involves measuring speed and accuracy on a pointing task. However, the comparison would be limited to the selected observation point. Conducting a study using

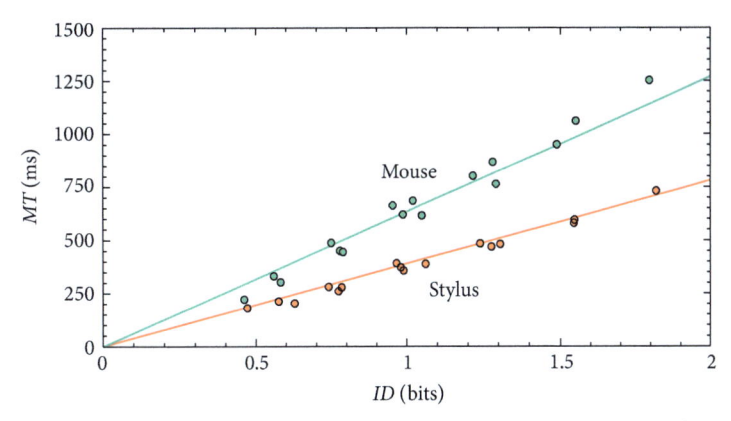

Figure 4.5 Fitts' law models allow for the comparison of user interfaces. Here, the stylus shows superior performance over the mouse. Data from Mackenzie et al. [505].

Fitts' law invites us to systematically vary D and W; the model will then provide a point of reference, the a and b parameters, for comparing the input methods across the full scope of the motor task.

Fitts' law is not limited to empirical comparisons. It can be used *analytically*—that is, prior to collecting empirical data—for the following two tasks:

- Predict the mean MT for a pointing task. However, the empirical parameters a and b must be known. They can be obtained, for example, from the literature.
- Compare pointing tasks. When a and b are equal, they can be ignored since MT will be determined by ID only.

The index of difficulty ID thus offers a handy entry point for analyzing a motor task. As we learned, increasing ID is associated with increasing MT. All other things being equal,

- an increase in D will increase MT;
- a decrease in W will increase MT;
- if D or W changes, MT can be kept constant by changing the other.

Paper Example 4.2.2: Accounting for corrective movements

Fitts' law is perhaps the most widely tested model in HCI research. It has been evaluated for many user groups, input devices, and contexts, including underwater [785]! It has weathered numerous challenges to its theoretical and mathematical assumptions. However, it says very little about what happens during movement. During pointing, we have several feedback signals available: vision, audition (the sound of movements, clicks, etc.), and proprioception. We use such signals to guide movement. Several models have been proposed that account for corrective movements.

One such variant is the *iterative corrections model* [174]. The idea is that any pointing movement consists of several *ballistic* movements with in-between corrections. A ballistic

continued

> **Paper Example 4.2.2: Accounting for corrective movements**
> *(continued)*
>
> movement cannot be modified after it is triggered; however, the next one can be planned considering sensory feedback. These redirections are corrections, hence the term "iterative corrections." Detailed recordings of how laboratory participants move showed only one or at most two corrections. Moreover, considerable variation was found in the duration of the initial submovement, violating the idea of equal durations.
>
> An extension of the model was proposed by Meyer et al. [539]. The *stochastic optimized submovement model* defines MT as a function of not only D and W but also the number of submovements n:
>
> $$MT = a + b\left(\frac{D}{W}\right)^{1/n}, \qquad (4.7)$$
>
> where n is an upper limit on submovements. The authors found empirically that $n = 2.6$ minimizes the RMSE.[2] Several extensions have also been proposed to compute end point variability, similar to the concept of effective width.
>
> The iterative corrections model and the stochastic optimized submovement model assume *intermittent feedback control*. Intermittent control means that control actions cannot be carried out at any time but only after "locked" periods. In this case, the ballistic part of a motor action cannot be altered, but there is a window of time afterward to make corrections. The two models assume that such corrections are based on the error at the start of that action. Meyer's model also assumes that the neuromotor system is noisy and that this noise increases with the velocity of the submovements. This causes the primary submovement to either undershoot or overshoot the target. One known shortcoming of the model is that the number of submovements is fixed. For some given D and W, the sequence of submovements is always the same, and it is not possible to explain why the target is missed at times.

4.2.5 Limits of Fitts' law

Fitts' law is a simplification of what happens in pointing. Because it models the average MT in ID conditions, it effectively hides *variability* other than that of the resulting performance. Variability is inherent to all motor control and is affected by factors such as the movement strategy (e.g., eye–hand coordination), feedback, and the involved muscle groups. For example, if you ask a user to carry out a pointing experiment with 5–10 cm targets, the resulting model may not generalize to a setting where the targets are 10–20 cm. The model is also brittle. Even small changes in the task, user, or conditions can require the collection of a new dataset and the adjustment of the model parameters. Numerous variants have been proposed, each accounting for a specific limitation. See Paper Example 4.2.2. for one example.

4.3 Simple reactions

A *simple reaction* is another type of fundamental motor action in HCI: Something appears on the display or in the environment and the user must respond to it as quickly as possible. Figure 4.6

---

[2] The RMSE is the root mean square error of the distance between the model's prediction and the data. It serves as an indication of a model's fit to the data.

Figure 4.6 A *simple reaction* is a motor task where the user must respond to a prompt as quickly as possible by pressing a button. *Choice reaction* generalizes this to the case where more than one response option is available. Image by Evan Amos, used with permission.

shows an example of both simple reactions and the more general case, choice reaction. *Motor response* refers to the elicitation of a motor movement appropriate to the presented event or stimulus. This happens, for instance, when:

- reacting to a flash on the display;
- blocking an enemy's move with a counter-move in a computer game;
- answering an incoming call on a mobile device;
- braking a car;
- getting rid of an annoying dialogue box asking if you want to install a new software version.

Only one response option is available in a simple reaction—this is why it is called simple. The response can be expressed by saying something aloud, pressing a button with a finger, or even by thinking the response in brain–computer interaction. A simple reaction carries a single bit of information: a response was given. Typing a phrase, for instance, is much more complex since one must consecutively choose and select the right key from a set of at least 26 different characters. We call such choices *choice reactions*.

Simple reaction tasks have among the fastest human responses in HCI. Performance in this task is measured in milliseconds as the time duration between the onset of the event and the user's response. Typical responses, depending on the input and output modalities, are in the range of 200–250 ms. However, within this rather narrow range, relatively large differences can be observed depending on the task conditions.

Simple reactions have been studied in psychology for more than a century, and the involved cognitive processes are somewhat known. Some of the earliest studies considered the vigilance of soldiers in World War II: After sleep deprivation, or in a stressful situation, how would reaction time be altered? In HCI, simple reactions can be used to understand fast reactions, such as when playing games or musical instruments on a computer. The response consists of a decision process ("I must react") and a motor response (pressing a button). Next, we present one way of understanding this process.

4.3.1 Drift diffusion model

Ratcliff and Van Dongen [690] presented an *evidence accumulation model* that predicts the distribution of reaction times as a function of what happens after the stimulus has appeared. While it has been mostly used in safety-critical reaction tasks, such as driving, it is also illuminating for HCI applications where it is important to understand what affects the reaction time.

The idea underpinning evidence accumulation models is that the perceptual evidence for and against responding accumulates until a *threshold* is met and the motor response is launched.

- **Stimulus onset:** The event that one should respond to appears. For example, a big figure suddenly appears on the screen in a first-person shooting game.
- **Perceptual encoding:** The event is encoded as a candidate event that one should respond to. For example, the visual shape and figure of the thing that has appeared are encoded.
- **Evidence accumulation:** Every fixation samples more evidence for/against the decision to respond. In the shooting game example, "Is this a friend or a foe?"
- **Decision:** When enough evidence has been accumulated to reach the decision threshold, the corresponding motor action is launched. For example, "Yes, this is an enemy!"
- **Motor action:** The user starts an overt movement response to trigger a suitable response.

In other words, between the stimulus and the observable response, many things happen. Evidence accumulation models can account for some effects of the user interface design as well as various task-related, individual, and contextual factors. They can predict the naturally occurring variations we observe in performance when a reaction task is repeated.

The model assumes that the simple reaction RT has two sources of variation: the decision time T_d and the nondecision time T_{er}. The nondecision time is further broken down into two components, x and y. The first nondecision event is the perceptual encoding of the stimulus that lasts for some duration, marked with x. After perceiving the stimulus, a stochastic decision process starts. During this period, evidence is accumulated ("diffused") in the brain regarding whether the stimulus should be responded to. This evidence accumulation phase is affected by perceptual conditions such as noise (e.g., poor resolution, poor eyesight) and the complexity of the visual scene.

Finally, after sufficient evidence has been diffused to surpass threshold a, the decision process stops and the brain continues to the motor response process with duration y. Summing up, the average reaction time is given by

$$RT = T_d + T_{er} = T_d + x + y. \qquad (4.8)$$

Figure 4.7 illustrates the model.

This model sheds light on how user interfaces can improve users' reaction time. The duration of the decision process T_d is user- and task-dependent and varies across trials. The drift rate (or the accumulation of evidence) is assumed to be normally distributed with mean v and variance η.[3] The two nondecision components x and y are summed to T_{er} and treated together in the model.

---

[3] The diffusion process is given by $dX(t) = vdt + sdW(t)$, where $dX(t)$ is the change in the accumulated evidence X for a time interval dt, v is the drift rate, and $sdW(t)$ are zero-mean random increments with infinitesimal variance $s^2 dt$.

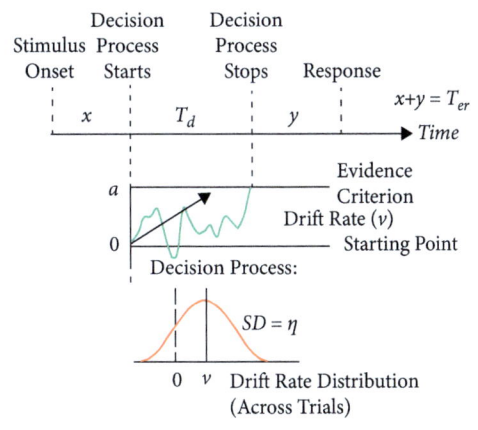

Figure 4.7 The model of Ratcliff and Van Dongen [690] defines simple reaction as consisting of a decision task and two nondecision tasks. After perceiving the prompt, a decision task starts. This is assumed to be a stochastic diffusion process where evidence accumulates toward the threshold a, at which point the response is emitted.

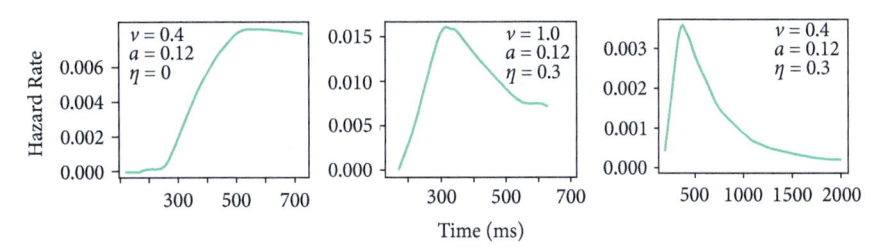

Figure 4.8 Three hazard function examples. Note the different scales of the axes. The figure is adapted from [690].

They can also change according to the user interface. For example, an auditory prompt may take longer to register than a simple visual symbol. This nondecision component is also assumed to vary across trials with standard deviation (SD) s_t.

The standard way of plotting the predictions is through the *hazard rate function*. It gives the probability that the decision process terminates in the next instant of time, given that it has survived up to that time. Formally, $h(t) = f(t)/(1 - F(t))$, where $f(t)$ is the probability density function and $F(t)$ is the cumulative density function. Figure 4.8 shows three examples that assume the same decision threshold a:

- **Slow but perfect responder:** In the top figure, the drift rate v is mediocre (0.4) with no variation ($\eta = 0$). The shape of the function is perfect in the sense that it is only achievable by a user who can decide their response to the stimulus with no hesitation.
- **Fast responder:** Here, the drift rate v is higher, but there is more variation ($\eta = 0.3$). This yields a much faster response, peaking at around 300 ms.
- **Slow responder:** Here, the drift rate v is mediocre (0.4), but there is still some variation ($\eta = 0.3$). The hazard distribution has a long tail. This kind of variation could be produced, for example, by sleep deprivation or by a noisy, hard-to-interpret display.

Consider an application for controlling an avatar in a 3D world. A user controls the avatar from an egocentric perspective and has to accelerate, decelerate, and steer the avatar. If the user is asked to speak on a phone simultaneously, their response times to abrupt events will be higher. This result can be attributed to the reduced drift rate. When speaking on the phone, their sampling rate slows down, and, therefore, they take longer to respond to events.

4.4 Choice reaction

In a *choice reaction task*, instead of having only one response option like in a simple reaction, n options are available. When a cue (stimulus) appears, the user must execute the *corresponding* response as quickly as possible by pressing the correct key. Each cue is associated with a single response; cues can appear with different probabilities. The fingers are supposed to rest on the possible keys to minimize the effect of pointing on the response. Consider this example: You are playing a racing game and your car is approaching a T-crossing at a fast pace. Which way should you turn? This is a two-alternative forced-choice (2AFC) task.

Performance in choice reaction tasks is measured by the *choice reaction time* (*CRT*). It is the time that has elapsed between the presentation of the cue and the response. Errors—choosing the wrong response or not responding—can be dealt with by insisting on a correct response or by allowing errors to happen and reporting the error rate alongside the *CRT*.

Choice reaction is a generalization of a simple reaction. When $n = 1$, we have a simple reaction. When $n = 2$, we have a 2AFC task where there are two response options and only one can be chosen. 2AFCs are common in HCI. For example, a "restart now" system prompt forces the user to pick between the options yes and no. When n increases above 2, we find an interesting and practically important relationship between n and *CRT*.

4.4.1 The Hick–Hyman law

The Hick–Hyman law is a statistical relationship between n and *CRT* that was discovered independently by Hick and Hyman [340, 369]. The law states that when the number of response options increases, the *CRT* increases. Trying to be faster than what the law suggests will lead to errors; allowing more time for responding will result in fewer errors.

Formally, given n equally probable response options, the average *CRT* follows approximately:

$$CRT = a + b \cdot \log_2(n), \tag{4.9}$$

where a and b are empirical constants determined by fitting a line to the data. In cases with uncertainty about whether to respond or not, a value of 1 can be added to n:

$$CRT = a + b \cdot \log_2(n + 1). \tag{4.10}$$

Do-not-respond is just one more option.

The parameter b controls how strongly the increase in n affects *CRT*. Figure 4.9 shows two examples.

Why is there a *binary* logarithm in the standard formulation? One interpretation is that it reflects a binary search on the part of the user. When a cue appears, the user first picks half of the options and rejects the other half, and then picks half of the remaining options, and so on, until they finally

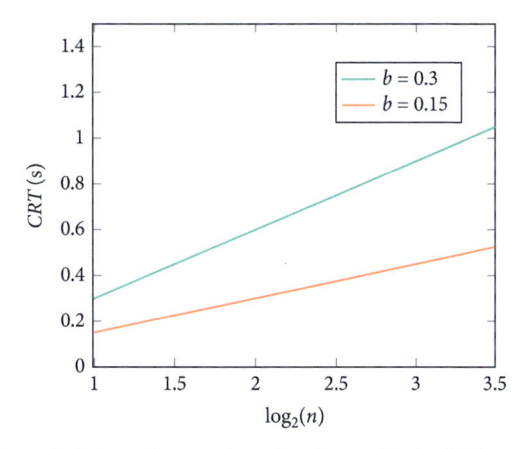

Figure 4.9 Parameter *b* controls how the number of options affects *CRT*.

identify the correct response. This process also links Hick–Hyman law to information theory [754]; see Chapter 17.

Another interpretation of the law is that it denotes the *uncertainty about the stimulus*. In the case of choices with unequal probabilities, the law can be expressed as

$$CRT = a + bH, \qquad (4.11)$$

$$H = \sum_{i}^{n} p_i \log_2(1/p_i + 1), \qquad (4.12)$$

where p_i is the probability of response option *i*. Even though there is a large number of options available, if only a small subset is considered (i.e., the sum of their probabilities is close to 1), *CRT* can be low.

4.4.2 Applications in HCI

Both the Hick–Hyman law and Fitts' law were introduced to HCI by Card et al. [129] as motor control principles for improving the usability of user interfaces. However, the Hick–Hyman law has had fewer applications than Fitts' law. Why?

To answer this question, note that the Hick–Hyman law states that less is better, which appears trivial; if you design an interface with fewer possible responses, users will be quicker in responding to it. However, if you need to decide how to show *n* elements on a display, the law predicts that there is a benefit from showing *all* the elements at once. Consider the design example in Figure 4.10. Because of the logarithmic term, the best design, contrary to our intuition, is Design (a). Hence, the design principle should be "more is better." However, when other factors are considered, the situation is not so simple. There are also benefits from pagination and hierarchy, which are not governed by the Hick–Hyman law. Information foraging theory explains that well-organized hierarchies help users save time by *skipping* whole sections of elements (Chapter 21). Visual search and pointing also take more time as the number of elements increases.

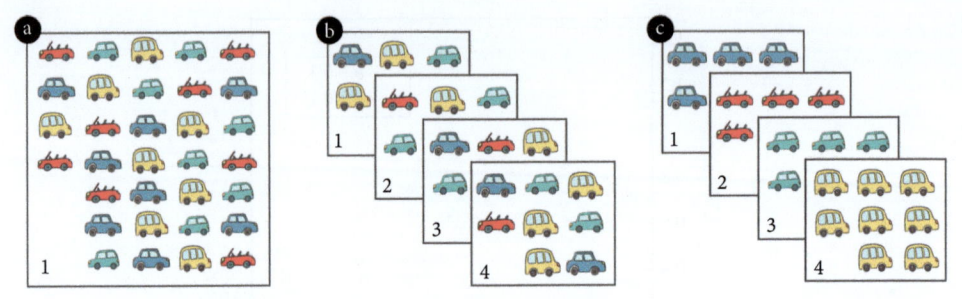

Figure 4.10 You need to show 32 items to the user. According to the Hick–Hyman law, which of the designs is the fastest to use? Figure from Liu et al. [490].

The second form of the law we discussed, which defines *CRT* as a function of entropy *H*, implies that decreasing uncertainty improves performance. How can we exploit this in practice? *Stimulus–response compatibility* has a strong effect on *CRT*. When stimuli and responses are compatible, they are ordered or otherwise structured in a consistent way. Some simple mapping exists; for example, cues have the same spatial order as responses. This means that the response should be similar to the stimulus itself, such as turning a steering wheel to turn the wheels of the car. The action the user performs is similar to the response the driver receives from the car. Liu et al. [490] showed that in HCI tasks where compatibility is high, the Hick–Hyman slope almost flattens out. It is generally desirable to find consistent mappings between stimuli and responses.

Design and training also have an effect on the slope *b* and intercept *a* of the model. The Hick–Hyman law governs the novice-to-intermediate range of performance. When the user has had extensive practice in responding to the task, the slope decreases, eventually flattening out. With thousands of practice trials on the same task, the response time can effectively be constant when *n* is lower than 10 [560].

One should be careful when applying the law to cases where $n > 10$. In its basic interpretation, the *n* end-effectors are supposed to rest on the *n* keys associated with the *n* responses. When $n > 10$, other factors come into play, such as moving fingers, finding targets visually, and reasoning.

4.5 Gesturing

Gestural interfaces use continuous shapes as input. Consider, for example, handwriting as text input: For a letter to be recognizable by the decoder, its shape must have certain segment lengths and curves.

4.5.1 Crossing

A *crossing* task is a task that relaxes the stopping constraint in Fitts' law, that is, the *D* parameter of the target [7].

Recall that Fitts' law describes a one-dimensional pointing action. Hence, when a user is attempting to hit a target, the user needs to both move the pointer toward the target *and* stop the pointer before leaving the target. By contrast, in a crossing task, the user does not need to stop at the target.

Instead, the user needs to ensure the target is crossed. In this case, the width parameter W refers to the size of the target the user is crossing.

Through experimentation, it has been established that crossing tasks follow a similar statistical relationship as Fitts' law and can be described using the equation from this law:

$$MT = a + b \log_2\left(\frac{D}{W} + 1\right). \tag{4.13}$$

Unlike pointing, crossing actions can be chained together, allowing the user to cross multiple targets in one motion. An example of a system leveraging crossing actions is CrossY [26], a drawing program that allows the user to input commands via crossing actions with a pen.

4.5.2 Steering

A *steering* task is a task where the user is moving a cursor through a form of tunnel constraint, as proposed by Accot and Zhai [6]. It has a relationship to Fitts' law (Paper Example 4.5.1).

In general, the time T it takes a user to steer a cursor through a tunnel is

$$T = a + b \int_C \frac{ds}{W(s)}, \tag{4.14}$$

where a and b are empirically determined parameters, C is the tunnel constraint parameterized by s, and $W(s)$ is the width of the tunnel at s. As with Fitts' law and the crossing law, the parameters a and b may vary depending on the user group, task, and use context.

It is possible to define an index of difficulty for steering tasks. In this case, the index of difficulty is directly related to the parameterized curve C:

$$ID_C = \int_C \frac{ds}{W(s)}. \tag{4.15}$$

By differentiating both sides of Equation 4.14 with respect to s, we obtain

$$\frac{ds}{dt} = \frac{W(s)}{b}, \tag{4.16}$$

where we observe that, as expected, the instantaneous movement speed $\frac{ds}{dt}$ at point s in the tunnel is proportional to the width $W(s)$ of the tunnel at that point.

Steering law can be used to model users moving cursors within tunnels, such as a user moving a mouse pointer along a hierarchical linear pull-down menu structure.

> **Paper Example 4.5.1: Relationship between Fitts' law and steering law**
>
> There is a mathematical relationship between steering law and Fitts' law [6]. A steering task with a single goal constraint on each end follows the same logarithmic relationship as Fitts' law:
>
> $$ID_1 = \log_2\left(\frac{D}{W} + 1\right). \tag{4.17}$$
>
> This task can be extended by adding a single further goal constraint, which yields the following relationship:
>
> $$ID_2 = 2\log_2\left(\frac{D}{2W} + 1\right). \tag{4.18}$$
>
> Note that as the number of goal constraints increases, the user has to be more careful in ensuring they pass through all the goal constraints.
>
> Then, by generalizing the number of goal constraints the user has to pass through to N, the goal constraints form a tunnel constraint:
>
> $$ID_N = N\log_2\left(\frac{D}{NW} + 1\right). \tag{4.19}$$
>
> With the limit $N \to \infty$, we obtain the following relationship:
>
> $$ID_\infty = \frac{D}{W\ln 2}. \tag{4.20}$$
>
> Note that in the limit, the index of difficulty is no longer related to $\log_2\left(\frac{D}{W}\right)$ but directly to $\frac{D}{W}$. In other words, in an N goal passing task, as N approaches infinity, the difficulty in achieving the task is no longer related to the logarithm of the distance W and the width W. This explains why the index of difficulty for a steering task in Equation 4.15 lacks a logarithmic relationship.

4.5.3 Viviani's power law of curvature

The models discussed thus far in this chapter aim to predict the task completion time. One limitation of steering law is that it does not account for complex shapes or changing shapes. Consider, for example, tracing a shape or drawing. What happens *during* the movement? If we wish to understand gestures, we need to understand where the curvature changes.

Viviani's *power law of curvature* (PLoC) is a kinematics model for smooth curved trajectories [858]. *Kinematics models* cover aspects of motion during pointing, such as position, velocity, acceleration, or jerk, without consideration of the time-varying phenomena that produce them. They predict the moment-by-moment motion or its properties, such as the radius of curvature or the tangential velocity at any point. This makes kinematics models useful for modeling gestures.

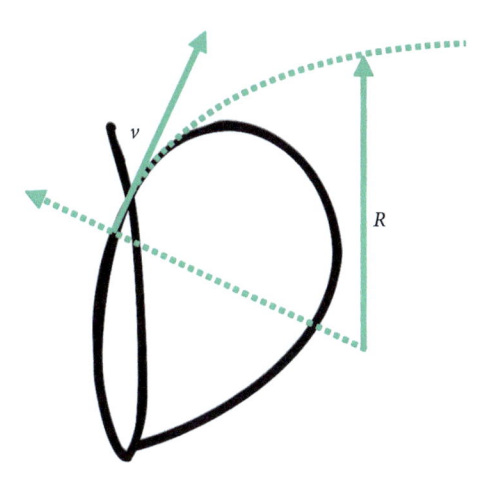

Figure 4.11 Try drawing the letter "d" with a stylus or pen. Viviani's power law of curvature predicts the momentary velocity v when drawing such smooth curved trajectories. R is the radius of the curvature.

PLoC pertains to handwriting and drawing behavior, particularly when the trajectories are smooth (i.e., without sharp corners). PLoC relates the radius of curvature $r(s)$ at any point s along the trajectory with its corresponding tangential velocity $v(s)$:

$$v(t) = kr^\beta, \qquad (4.21)$$

where k is an empirical gain factor and β is an empirical parameter. The model indicates that the larger the curvature, the slower the motion of the end-effector at that point.

Next, the total time for a full segment S, assuming a smooth curvature without corners, can be computed as

$$T = \frac{1}{k} \int_0^S r(s)^{-\beta} ds. \qquad (4.22)$$

For example, in a study using a stylus as the input device, $K = 0.0153$ and $\beta = 0.586$ [125]. The model has achieved a high fit with empirical data in drawing, with and without visual guidance.

What happens if the movement is physically larger or smaller? *Isochrony* refers to the empirical observation that the average velocity of movements increases with distance [858]. Thus, movement distance is a weak predictor of movement time in a trajectory. Users simply cover larger distances faster. Viviani's PLoC has been shown to cover isochrony. The PLoC-like pattern has been argued to be due to pattern generators in the neuromotor system that operate in an oscillatory fashion [737].

Summary

- Motor control is necessary for users to perform actions in a user interface.
- The time it takes users to perform actions can be predicted for some fundamental activities, such as pointing, crossing, steering, and reacting to stimuli.

Exercises

1. Applying Fitts' law. Given the following target widths and distances, calculate the average movement times for all combinations using Fitts' law. Comment on the validity and implications of the calculated average movement times: $D = [0.01, 0.05, 0.1, 1, 100]$ m; $W = [0.01, 0.050.1, 1, 100]$ m.

2. Keypad design. Considering Fitts' law, think about a layout of 3×3 icons, for example, a numeric keypad. What happens to the movement time when you make the icons bigger? How much faster will the interface be if you arrange the icons in a list (1×9) instead of a 3×3 layout? Could you do anything else to reduce the movement time?

3. Applying the Hick–Hyman law. Use the Hick–Hyman law to calculate the CRT for an interface with four options, where the probability of each option is 0.1, 0.1, 0.1, and 0.7, respectively. Then, recalculate the CRT assuming the probability of each option is 0.25. Compare and comment on the results.

4. Understanding menu navigation. Consider a cascading linear pull-down menu. The user wishes to select a menu item in a submenu. In one variant, the user has to steer the cursor through a top-level submenu item to trigger the submenu. When the cursor is not over the top-level submenu item, the submenu instantly disappears. This type of implementation is common in web interfaces. In another variant, the submenu triggers when the user steers the cursor to the top-level submenu item and the submenu stays in place even when the user moves the cursor away from the top-level submenu item. Comment qualitatively on the type of movement time model that is suitable for the two types of menus and which design would be preferable and why. Optionally, consider how the preferable submenu trigger could be implemented in the simplest way possible.

5. Comparing input devices. Carry out a controlled pointing study with two input devices of your choice, fit the free parameters (a, b) of Fitts' law, and plot the resulting models. To collect the data, you can use an implementation of the task on the web, such as http://simonwallner.at/ext/fitts/. Tip: Pay attention to the ranges of D and W you pick.

6. Beating Fitts' law. User interfaces make it possible to do things to targets, such as changing their size or distance, that are impossible in physical environments. Given Fitts' law, ideate interaction techniques that would facilitate pointing (i.e., decrease MT). Tip: Ravin Balakrishnan discussed relevant techniques in a classic paper titled "Beating" Fitts' law: https://www.sciencedirect.com/science/article/pii/S107158190400103X.

7. Use the drift diffusion model (code available via the book's homepage) to estimate a gamer's reaction time in two conditions: good health and after sleep deprivation. To this end, you need to think about which process in the model is affected by sleep deprivation.

5
Cognition

Have you ever stopped to think about some seemingly simple interaction, wondering how people do it? For example, consider Figure 5.1. What should the user press to be able to edit a photo? This can be solved by recalling from memory: "Hmm, does PowerPoint have image editing capabilities?" It can also be solved by means of visual attention, that is, by looking around for recognizable icons. Some reasoning may be required, for example, considering whether PowerPoint allows for importing the image type that is being used. In the end, the user may need to decide between trying to use PowerPoint, trying some other means, and giving up. Such thoughts and processing occurring in one's mind are jointly called *cognition*.

The term *cognition* comes from the Latin word "cognoscere," which means to know or learn. As a scientific term, it refers to mental activities that enable thinking and understanding. It is often taken to refer to how people process information in their mind; that is, how they perceive, learn, remember, reason about, and utilize knowledge. This view is called the *information processing view* of cognition. The study of cognition is a multidisciplinary effort spanning psychology, cognitive science, and neuroscience.

The main function of cognition in human–computer interaction (HCI) is to help the user control a computer to do what they want. Attention is needed to find elements, memory to learn and recall their properties, linguistic abilities to understand text and generate command names, and reasoning to make use of the knowledge obtained so far and deduce what happens inside the computer. Unfortunately, these cognitive capabilities have limits. People differ greatly in their cognitive abilities. Moreover, the way these abilities are used is affected by the type of task and the design of the user interface. Cognitive capabilities are used adaptively. Users learn and try to discover new possibilities and strategies; for example, they change behavior when a practice does not work. These properties of cognition make it important but also challenging to understand. There are five *elementary cognitive capabilities* that relate to our ability to interact with computers:

Cognitive control: Adaptively deciding goals (what to do), allocating cognitive resources to tasks, and changing the course of action as needed. For example, cognitive control is needed when a user decides to multitask by looking at their phone while driving [725].

Memory: Forming, maintaining, and accessing beliefs about objects that are not directly perceivable. For example, long-term memory (LTM) helps users locate previously seen icons more quickly [393].

Attention: Selectively processing part of the perceptual field, for example, by deploying visual attention on a screen or by sensing a tactile display by sweeping fingertips on it. We discuss visual attention in Chapter 3.

Reasoning: Applying transformation rules to beliefs to form *new* beliefs. For example, reasoning is needed to infer if software can do certain things when one cannot recall it doing that before [671].

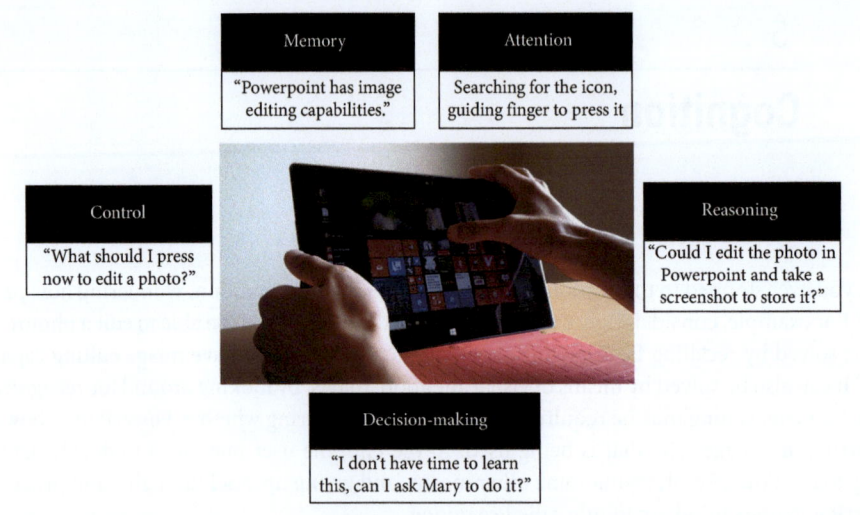

Figure 5.1 To use a computer, users need to choose actions that get the computer to do what they want. This is challenging because the computer is a non-transparent system. That is, users cannot "see" what actually happens inside the computer. The role of cognition in interaction is to help us overcome this challenge. Cognition underpins our ability to control actions, reason about the computer, learn from experience, and make decisions on what to do.

Decision-making: Interaction often requires decision-making. For example, a user might decide to install application A and not application B because A appears to have a more favorable cost and better features.

In this chapter, we discuss general findings about cognition that are relevant to HCI. This is followed by an explanation of how cognitive control allows us to direct our thinking and actions toward achieving goals. Then, we review working memory (WM), LTM, and mechanisms that assist us in learning. This leads to an examination of processes that allow us to reason and make decisions. We conclude by discussing how we can create cognitive models that allow us to simulate aspects of cognition to inform design.

5.1 General findings about cognition

Many researchers have investigated cognition. We summarize some general findings that are relevant to HCI.

Cognition helps us set goals and maintain focus on them.

Cognition helps users achieve their goals. A *goal* is some desirable state of affairs. In HCI, a goal often refers to something that people would like the computer to do for them. For example, a user's goal could be to email a message to someone or to change some privacy settings.

Goals affect how cognition processes information. Human memory is less about storing experienced events veridically (accurately) and more about offering access to memories that may be useful for a given task at hand. Goals set expectations about how the world is structured and what might happen next.

An important phenomenon related to visual attention is *inattentional blindness*. If users are given a goal related to one part of a user interface, they recall features related to that part and largely ignore the other parts. This holds even if the users did look at those other parts, as confirmed by, for example, eye-tracking data [275]. Later, when the users are asked about parts unrelated to the goal, they cannot recall the information contained in those parts.

Cognition is limited.

Human cognition is limited. For example, our WM is limited; we can only keep a few mental representations active in our minds. The typical WM capacity that can be simultaneously maintained active in our mind is thought to be two to four items [607]. Forgetting occurs in LTM. We cannot remember everything we have experienced, and as a result, we forget details of things we have attended. Visual attention is also limited. For instance, people can extract more information from the foveal region than the periphery (Figure 3.1). Finally, our capacity for abstract reasoning and planning is limited. We often resort to external aids, such as calculators and notes, to help us go beyond the limits posed by our cognition.

These limits are real and potent, although we may not be consciously aware of them. In computer use, these limits affect our ability to find items on display, make sense of the information shown to us, navigate through the information space, and remember instructions on how to use something.

Cognition is based on internal models of reality.

Cognition supports our ability to reason about things that are not directly perceivable. This ability necessitates the construction of internal models of reality that can be used to formulate goals and plans. One example of such an internal model is a *metaphor*. In HCI, metaphors help users understand what to expect from a user interface. The desktop metaphor uses spatial concepts that are rooted in our everyday experiences in the physical world. For example, folders are *on*, not under, the desktop, and they can be moved *into* the trash when they are no longer required.

Cognition is necessary for learning and adaptation.

For some time, it was believed that human action is driven by *plans and reasoning*. That is, we plan sequences of actions and execute them. Suchman [804] challenged this view in studies of repair and maintenance personnel of Xerox photocopiers. Suchman [804] found that even in a highly regulated profession, a worker's action is not heavily scripted but requires constant adaptation and planning. While planning is carried out, such plans are often noncommittal sketches that need to be revised and updated.

The present understanding is that our cognitive, motor, and perceptual processes are constantly adapting—forming beliefs, trying new tactics, and fine-tuning. This is needed to respond to the structure of the environments we experience. This need is particularly pronounced in HCI, as both the systems people use and the ways people carry out work keep changing. This results in users having to continually formulate new plans and adapt to new ways of working with computer systems.

Hence, cognition is not simply passively processing information from external environments and reacting to it. Instead, cognition takes actions to facilitate its own functioning. We use external aids, such as notes, calculators, and browsers, to augment our abilities. Over time, such dependencies affect the way we use cognition in interaction. For example, since the uptake of the GUI, which relies heavily on visual recognition, we have less need to use our LTM to store computer commands that would be typed in a command prompt.

Cognition requires energy and effort.

Mental effort refers to the use of energy for controlling thinking to achieve our goals [236]. Mental effort has two main components. *Task effort* refers to the additional energy required in response to an increase in the computational demand. This can occur when we face a novel environment, for example, when learning to use a new user interface. *State effort* refers to the energy required to protect performance from physiological fatigue, which can be caused by sleep deprivation, among other factors.

Effort may sound like a negative concept in that it is something that limits performance. However, it also has a positive function: The feeling of effort prevents us from overconsuming energy through less important activities.

5.2 Cognitive control

Cognitive control refers to our ability to direct thinking and action toward achieving some goal. When using a computer, cognition must decide between possible actions to reach a goal. It must activate the right representations for achieving that goal [671]. It may also need to share representations among multiple tasks at the same time. In dynamic task environments, it needs to learn to control action in a predictive fashion.

The basic problem of cognitive control is the following. At any given time, countless stimuli bombard our senses, and we have several options for sharing our limited resources among them. How can we ensure that the *right options* are allocated the *right resources* at the *right time*? For example, just now, you could stop reading and start watching a movie. Similarly, if a notification pops up, do you immediately attend to it or do you first complete what you were doing? If you knew there was an important message coming, such as a letter of acceptance for a job application, you may want to check it immediately, which might be a rational decision. Cognitive control is critical to performing tasks in information-rich environments. The concept has been used to derive implications for the design of multi-part tasks (e.g., the use of automatic teller machines, or ATMs) and regulations for multitasking settings such as driving (e.g., suggesting minimum limits for maintaining sufficient attention on the road).

5.2.1 Activating goals

Cognitive control is also needed to activate the right subgoals at the right time. Faced with a complex task with multiple goals, cognition breaks it down into simpler, more manageable parts. Altmann and Trafton [16] explained this with a *goal activation model*. Contextual cues *prime* subgoals. For example, when we see a familiar intersection on the way home, it subconsciously activates our next subgoal. *Priming* is about the subconscious activation of concepts by perceived cues. However, previously activated goals can *interfere* with the activation of the relevant goal. Cognitive control is required to suppress the activation of interfering goals. The model can explain *postcompletion errors*, which result from the user forgetting to carry out an action that should be taken *after* achieving a goal. For example, one may forget to take the credit card out of an ATM after receiving cash unless the ATM issues a reminder to retrieve it.

5.2.2 Activating task representations

When a task is performed, cognition needs to make relevant task representations available. Cognitive control operates through two mechanisms: the *activation* of relevant representations in memory and the *inhibition* of irrelevant representations. For example, consider the act of searching for an application icon on a desktop. Let us assume that this task is challenging and that you have already looked at several locations. Cognitive control is needed to select and plan the locations to visit next as well as to prevent you from revisiting locations you have already visited. The latter phenomenon is called *inhibition of return*. Without this ability, you would be constantly revisiting locations, which would make the search less efficient.

This kind of regulation is important in information-rich environments. Inhibitory control is needed to avoid attending to every flash or blink on an interface and maintain focus on the task at hand. In this way, cognitive control helps us balance between an internal and external locus of control. Without internal control, we would be at the mercy of our environment. Any pop-up or notification would capture our attention, and we would not be able to complete our tasks.

5.2.3 Choosing actions

Cognition is necessary to choose what to do. A central problem in computer use is that *rewards are delayed*. In other words, we cannot immediately obtain what we are interested in. Instead, we must choose one action now, then another, and so on. Cognition helps us solve sequential decision-making problems. However, how do we know which action to choose at a given moment when the goal is not immediately available but instead distal? An essential ability for effective interaction is to evaluate actions by considering their long-term rewards.

Two key mechanisms underpinning decision-making are posited by cognitive sciences [719]. First, through experience, users learn to associate an action with *recurring contextual cues*. For example, the familiar wallpaper of your mobile device is associated with certain action possibilities, such as pressing on some icons. How are such mappings established? Trying things allows users to learn *value estimates* of actions available in a particular state. The associative learning of such value estimates occurs subconsciously over time. It does not require effortful cognitive control; it is largely automatic. For example, you may notice that when you start using a new mobile device or operating system, it is hard to locate things. After a while, you start to find the items that you use frequently more quickly. However, this type of associative learning is slow to start and slow to update. If the user interface changes, users need to relearn some associations.

The other mechanism is *reasoning about and simulating possibilities in the mind*. For example, before selecting what to do, we may think about possible routes in a virtual environment. This requires cognitive control; you need to activate representations and compare your options, which requires effort.

5.2.4 Multitasking

We often need to carry out multiple tasks at the same time. Consider, for instance, driving a car. At any given time, there are numerous things you *could* do. You could be texting, attending to the road, talking to your passengers, checking the gasoline level, changing the AC settings, and so on. Cognitive control is crucial for effective *multitasking*. The problem for cognitive control in multitasking is how to allocate limited resources among the tasks we want to perform simultaneously.

Multitasking is a resource-sharing problem. The resources include those defined by attention, the motor system, and WM. Some of these resources can only be shared in an all-or-nothing fashion, whereas others can be shared in a graded manner. For example, you only have one dominant hand; in most cases, it cannot be shared in a graded manner between two tasks. However, in some cases, different tasks may be completed by different fingers. Visual attention, likewise, can only be focused on a single location in space at a time. Conversely, auditory attention can be somewhat better shared among sound sources around us, even when the sources are spatially apart.

The *multiple resource theory* (MRT) of Wickens [888] provides a rough but useful heuristic for understanding how resource conflicts arise in multitasking. The MRT cube is presented in Figure 5.2. The cube can be used to estimate whether two tasks, when carried out simultaneously, will cause conflicts in resource utilization and should therefore not be performed simultaneously. For example, consider two tasks, A and B:

- Task A is playing a video game on a console;
- Task B is following a conversation on social media via a mobile device.

The MRT cube in Figure 5.2 consists of segments divided into three axes. These segments denote limited-capacity cognitive resources. To apply MRT, you mark all the segments that the to-be-done tasks need. If two or more tasks end up occupying the same segment, conflict will emerge and negatively affect performance.

Returning to our case:

1. Both A and B rely on the visual modality, so there is resource competition in this aspect.
2. Both A and B rely on manual responding, leading to resource competition.
3. While A relies on spatial processing, B relies more on verbal processing, so there is no competition here.
4. Both A and B can involve ambient auditory and visual stimuli (e.g., notifications, sounds).

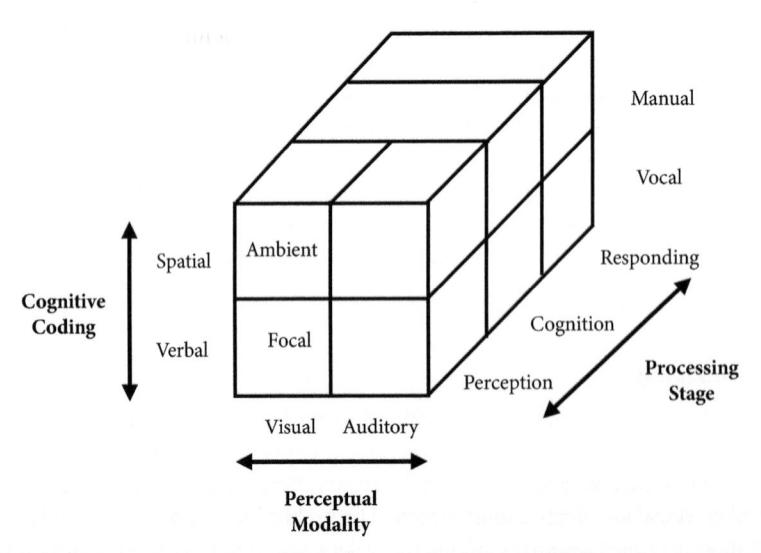

Figure 5.2 Multiple resource theory explains why certain task combinations are more prone to conflicts when multitasking than others [888]. The cube has three axes that help us understand the motor, perceptual, and cognitive demands of a task. To assess whether two tasks can lead to resource competition, you start by marking the slots in the cube that the tasks occupy. If the two tasks occupy the same slots, we can predict that there will be resource competition and thus performance degradation. Different types of resource competition occur in different cells.

MRT predicts that Tasks A and B cannot be carried out simultaneously unless Task B relies on notifications. Task A can only be carried out with visual attention, and so can Task B. This means that at any given time, the cognitive controller must decide which task gets attention. Hence, attention must be switched between the tasks. However, the tasks may not need to be processed simultaneously, as is the case with asynchronous conversation.

If notification sounds are turned on, visual attention does not need to be sustained on the social media app all the time. When a notification pops up, it must be decided whether to disconnect the video game or not. Attention can be shared momentarily to read the message while keeping the hands on the video game controller.

What happens if two tasks require the same cognitive resource at the same time? This scenario necessitates cognitive control to decide which task receives the cognitive resource at a given time. The result is interleaving: Switch to Task A for a few seconds, then switch to Task B, and so on.

This kind of interleaving is adaptive. In driving, for example, we do not switch between tasks arbitrarily. Doing so would result in a dramatic increase in accidents.

Since every task switch is somewhat costly, as you lose a few hundred milliseconds just for the switch and you may forget part of the task if you switch too abruptly, the cognitive controller must be sensitive to both the estimated gains of switching to other tasks and the benefits of carrying out the current task. For example, switching too late may result in a missed opportunity in another task. Switching to another task for too long may also incur excessive costs. This is because the longer a user is prevented from working on a task, the longer it typically takes to resume that task later on.

Empirical studies have investigated people's ability to switch between tasks and learned that our task-switching strategies are sensitive to switching costs [384]. Cognition seeks to perform switches at natural breakpoints. In other words, users prefer to avoid switching immediately and instead postpone interruptions to natural boundaries between subtasks.

Uncertainty is a prevalent characteristic in almost all multitasking environments. Many tasks we need to complete in everyday life are dynamic. This means that they change on their own, even when we do not attend to them.

One implication is that at any given time we are not attending to them, we are uncertain about their state. Furthermore, this uncertainty accumulates: The longer you leave a task unattended, the higher the uncertainty about its state.

For example, consider someone driving a car. The longer the driver attends to their smartphone, the more uncertainty the driver will have about the driving environment. Guidelines for safe driving recommend a maximum of 2.0-second shifts in attention away from the road [612].

To decide when to switch to a different task, cognitive control needs access to sufficient information to maintain estimates of subtask states and their uncertainties. It needs to track what it does *not* know about the world. When the risk of not attending to a specific task becomes too high, the cognitive controller needs to move attention to this task.

For example, when driving in the rain, glances to secondary tasks tend to be shorter than when driving on a day with better road visibility. This is because there is more uncertainty about the driving environment when visibility is poor. When cognition does not have access to sufficiently accurate estimates of the costs and rewards of a task, it may incorrectly engage with an irrelevant task.

5.2.5 Predictive control

When the task environment is dynamic, that is, changing on its own regardless of the user's actions, cognitive control needs to be *proactive*. Instead of waiting to be triggered by the right stimulus, it needs to anticipate the need for a representation even before the event occurs.

To enable this, the cognitive controller requires an *internal model* of the world. The internal model should be able to predict what *might* happen if an action were taken. However, this internal model should not determine actions, as perception is also an important determinant for choosing the correct action. Cognitive control needs to integrate all of these aspects.

One hypothesis about how we do this is called the *Bayesian brain* [424]. According to this hypothesis, the brain is a statistical estimator that assigns probabilities to hypotheses about the state of the world. As the brain receives new sensory information, it updates the probabilities of these hypotheses. This is referred to as updating the beliefs. This updating follows the rules of probability theory, including the well-known Bayes' theorem. A Bayesian brain uses past experiences to anticipate new experiences. The less expected a new experience is, the greater the surprise. A Bayesian brain attempts to optimize its knowledge about the world to minimize such uncertainty.

For example, as you interact with an AI-driven feature such as autocomplete, you may think: "What would happen if I did this, how would the feature react?" We become better at making such predictions thanks to belief updates. Even in surprising new situations, such as when typing a word borrowed from another language, we utilize such beliefs to predict how the AI might react—would it know how to complete the word?

Consider a collaborative puzzle game. Your teammate is running very fast from one side of the display to the other. How do you know when to trigger an action to throw a piece to her? A Bayes optimal perceptual system does not represent the property of an object, for example, the velocity of an object moving on the display, as a single variable. Instead, it is a conditional probability density function $p(V|I)$, where I is the available sensory information (e.g., the change in the object's location since the last observation). This specifies the conditional probability that the object is perceived to be moving at different speeds V based on the available sensory information I.

In other words, the probability that a user correctly interprets a certain velocity depends on what is shown on the display. However, an optimal observer must also take into account the relative uncertainty of each source when computing an integrated estimate. When one cue is more biased or unreliable than others, it should be given proportionately less weight. For example, when gamers estimate when to press a button to intercept an object, they give different weights to visual information, auditory information, and their own estimates of the object's movement [468]. By integrating all the evidence, they get a more reliable estimate than by considering either piece of evidence alone.

5.2.6 Cognitive workload

Maintaining cognitive control is tiresome. Do you remember the first time you learned how to program or how to use a spreadsheet application? Do you recall how taxing it felt to carry out a simple task, such as keeping track of a mouse cursor and remembering what to do, and when? Having to continuously decide what to do is mentally demanding, and doing this for an extended period of time can cause fatigue or stress. In addition to having to decide what to do, users also frequently act under uncertainty and some level of risk, both of which further increase stress.

The experience that follows from such effort and stress is called *cognitive workload*. The perceived workload can be measured with the NASA Task Load Index (NASA-TLX) questionnaire (Chapter 7). Over time, with experience, people develop *minimum effort task strategies*—routines that diminish the perceived workload. In practice, this often means requiring less executive control. This requirement also decreases with *automaticity*; that is, when users learn a skill, it consolidates and becomes more automatic. This allows users to build on previously learned skills when refining some skills or acquiring new ones.

5.3 Memory and learning

Memory is critical in computer use. Without memory, you would struggle to complete even simple tasks, such as filling out a registration form, changing settings, or navigating a page. We need memory to keep track of things, reason, recall, and recognize. However, memory does not refer only to consciously accessible memories. According to dual process memory models, there are separate neural processes for conscious and unconscious remembering [903]. What one has experienced can affect performance in an implicit way. For example, you may "just know," without explicitly recalling, where certain common commands are, such as where File is in an application menu.

Current neuroscience evidence suggests that several distinct memory systems are involved in interaction, each with different functions, purposes, and neural bases [789]. It is important to understand these systems because, in almost every interactive task, we have more than one at play. This also challenges a common lay conception of human memory. Memory is *not* like a storage house or a hard disk that lets you store items and retrieve them later.

5.3.1 Working memory

Working memory refers to the temporary maintenance and manipulation of representations in the mind that are needed for action [607]. WM is set apart from LTM due to its time- and capacity-limited nature. We can only maintain a few items at a time in our WM. The nature of this capacity has been the subject of several decades of research.

Early research suggested that our WM is limited to only two to six items at a time. This was initially known as Miller's magical number 7 ± 2 and was later revised to a more conservative 4 ± 2. According to this view, at any given time, we can only hold about two to six items in WM; trying to hold more items will result in losing some of the existing ones for two reasons. First, this would exceed the capacity limit of WM; second, the items would not be rehearsed. Active rehearsal is needed to keep items in WM. This is what makes the use of WM seem mentally taxing. Access to the items fades quickly unless it is actively maintained.

The limited capacity of WM can be demonstrated and measured with a simple task called the *n-back task*: Ask your friend to read aloud random numbers between one and nine at a constant pace. Your task is to report the *n*th item *before* the last one. To be able to do this, you must now keep active *n* items in your WM and update the memory contents upon hearing a new number. The task is much harder than it sounds and exposes the radically limited ability we have for the simultaneous maintenance of multiple ideas. It is best learned by trying it out.

Currently, it is thought that the capacity of WM is even smaller than what Miller estimated, perhaps just three to five items in young adults [170]. Moreover, WM is argued to not consist of memory "slots," and its limits emerge due to the inability to maintain several active representations in associative memory networks. In other words, items in WM are not fully "lost" when we stop rehearsing them; they just lose their active state and it becomes increasingly harder to reactivate them.

WM is needed in many interactive tasks. Consider, for example, the task of copying text from one application to another. You need to not only remember what to copy but also keep track of where you are in the to-be-copied text. Another example is interruptions. We get notifications and switch between tasks all the time. The more disruptive the interruption, the more we rely on WM at the time of the interruption. If there is a single takeaway for design from this research, it is to avoid relying on WM. This can be done in cases where representations can be encoded into the LTM.

5.3.2 Long-term memory

Fortunately, users do not have only WM to rely on. LTM refers to memory systems that are responsible for exploiting past experiences. Figure 5.3 shows a taxonomy of LTM systems. Evidence of these systems comes from brain imaging and studies of patients with abnormal brain functioning.

Declarative memory refers to long-term memories that can be consciously experienced, or *explicit memory*. By contrast, *non-declarative memory* refers to *implicit memories* that affect our behavior without conscious recollection.

For example, how do you remember your password? This is a good example of how both declarative and non-declarative memories contribute to our ability to perform interactive tasks. For one, you can recall a password by recalling the act of typing it—a memory of moving your index finger on a keypad to enter the PIN one character at a time. You just know this. However, you might also be able to recall the password as a word. When users are asked to *generate* a password, they are asked to think about its letters and words. Thus, they may remember the password using semantic associations. However, for a password that we have entered several times, we may have forgotten the semantic representation of the password and rely on our ability to "just type it." For example, you may have noticed that it is difficult to type a familiar password using an unfamiliar keyboard layout.

The declarative memory system contains the *semantic* and *episodic* subtypes. Semantic memory is responsible for propositional knowledge, for example:

- Folders contain documents.
- "Save" is related to "Open."

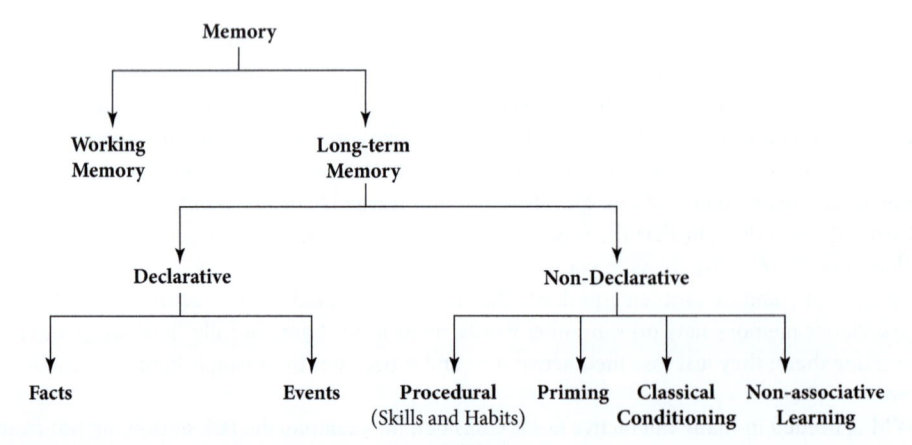

Figure 5.3 Taxonomy of human memory systems [789].

Episodic memory can be thought of as mental time travel: It allows us to re-experience past events. "What did I do last time I wanted to print in A3 size?" Programmers who scroll program code keep track of where they are using episodic memory.

Non-declarative memory systems are further divided into procedural, priming, conditioning, and non-associative learning. *Non-associative learning* refers to reflexes, such as retracting the hand from a hot stove. *Procedural memory* refers to learned sequences of actions and thoughts. Procedures are like recipes. Instead of controlling actions one by one, the user can trigger them as a sequence. After extensive repetition, actions become associated to a larger extent, which allows the user to execute them without conscious awareness. For example, you may "automatically" know the sequence in which you enter your name and password to log in.

Priming refers to the unconscious effect of previously seen stimuli on responses to subsequent stimuli. Priming has an important role in preparing us to respond in a manner appropriate to the given context. Contextual cues "prime" or make us more ready to give certain responses. For example, asking a user to press the left arrow button in a gaming context may lead to faster responses from gamers than from users with a form-filling background.

Conditioning refers to the learning of actions that are triggered (conditioned) by the environment. While only the readiness to act is affected in priming, in conditioning, the probability of action selection changes. Conditioning is an unconscious association between the environment (the cue) and the response. The strength of this association can be affected by reinforcement. *Positive reinforcement* is a reward given for successful behavior; *negative reinforcement* is a penalty or punishment for unwanted behavior. When reinforcement is removed, a specific behavior can be inhibited and eventually removed. Conditioning is one mechanism that can be used for behavior change (Chapter 6). A positive behavior, such as ceasing smoking or starting physical exercise, can be reinforced by introducing a positive reward. In gaming, a positive reward can be, for example, a loot box or a badge.

The multiplicity of memory systems provides desirable redundancy that improves robustness: If one system fails, the other can be used. Vice versa, overly relying on a single system, while beneficial when circumstances stay the same, can be detrimental to our flexibility to adapt and recover from errors.

5.3.3 A three-stage view of memory functioning

Time is a defining aspect of interaction with computers. Most things we do with computers take more than a few seconds; some activities take years. It is therefore natural to look at memory functioning from the perspective of time. Both declarative and non-declarative LTM can be understood in terms of three *stages* organized in time:

Encoding: Memory traces are formed during interaction.

Storage: The traces are retained between encoding and retrieval; some are forgotten.

Retrieval: The traces are retrieved at a later stage, for example, when using the same user interface again.

Encoding affects what we can, in principle, remember later on. The type of encoding depends on how much attention is paid and how deeply we process information. The *levels of processing (LOP) effect* refers to the association between the depth of mental operations carried out during the task and the strength of the encoded memory trace [172]. The deeper you process something that happens on the interface, the better you will remember it. Items on a user interface that are interesting are typically processed more deeply. Those that are just glanced at and rejected are encoded in a shallow way and are more quickly forgotten. For example, when some users were asked to navigate or read the content on a web page, they remembered the corresponding elements well and almost entirely forgot the others [624]. An exciting application of the LOP effect in gesture-based interaction is presented in Paper Example 5.3.1.

To retrieve a memory trace, we need some *cue*. The cue can be something you see, feel, or do. It can (or can fail to) reactivate the original trace. Depending on the type of cue available, three types of recall can occur. First, a *free recall* refers to an attempt to retrieve a trace by self-generating cues; that is, without relying on externally presented cues. For example, if you are deciding which programs can be used to complete some task, you typically do this without having those programs visible. Second, a *cued recall* refers to trace retrieval via external cues and is generally much easier than a free recall. Success, however, depends on the cues. Third, a *recognition* is an extreme version of a cued recall where the whole object is presented instead of its part. For example, when the whole app logo is presented, the user simply needs to recognize it as the one that is being searched for. You need to decide whether it corresponds to a particular class or experience you have seen before.

Our visual recognition memory is amazingly good. You can recognize hundreds of faces you have seen during a football match, or many passwords you have used during your life. However, recalling them would be very difficult. This ability is exploited by *graphical user interfaces* (GUIs; Chapter 28). When we need to recall a command, such as in *command language interfaces*, we need to use free recalling (Chapter 27). This is effortful. By contrast, with GUIs, we can rely on strong visual cues and simply recognize familiar graphical elements.

There is an interesting interplay between cues and recalls, and interface design affects this interplay. *Encoding–retrieval symmetry* refers to the similarity between the conditions in the encoding of an item and those in retrieving it. High symmetry facilitates retrieval. For example, it is harder to retrieve a password if the color of the login screen has changed.

Paper Example 5.3.1: What makes a gesture memorable?

Gesture-based input holds great promise. However, memory is a limiting factor in gesture-based interaction. Unless gestures are demonstrated to users, users must actively recall them in order to use them.

Nacenta et al. [574] wanted to understand what makes a gesture memorable. They compared three types of gestures. The first type comprised gestures specifically designed by designers for a particular application. The designers were informed about the goal of producing memorable gestures that would also be easy to perform and easily recognizable by the gesture recognizer. The second type was stock gestures, that is, generic gestures that would typically be preloaded in an application. The third type was user-defined gestures. Here, the researchers asked users to generate their own gestures.

These types of gestures were examined in three experiments. Overall, it was found that user-defined gestures result in better recall than the other types of gestures. User-defined gestures were recalled up to 44% better than others. They were also perceived to be less effortful and time-consuming. Users also rated them higher in terms of gesture preference. The authors recommend allowing for user-defined gestures when possible.

5.3.4 Forgetting

What happens between retrieval and encoding? Memories are lost. How does this happen?

According to *decay theory*, memory traces lose their activation or strength over time. Events in the recent past usually have more pronounced importance for actions in the present. The more time has elapsed since a memory was activated, the less probable it is that it can be retrieved. According to *interference theory*, memory traces get confused with each other. When we try to retrieve a memory trace, another (false) memory is activated at a similar level. Memories are not simply forgotten; they become mixed up.

Moreover, not all memories are forgotten in the same way. Our encoding and forgetting processes adapt to the statistical structures of our environments. If all previous memories were competing for attention, we would have difficulties retrieving what we need. Nevertheless, we need to forget in a way that keeps the organismically most important memories available.

With practice, computer users become better at predicting what they will need to remember later. As we discuss in Chapter 21, memory adapts to the statistical distribution of the environment. For example, to recall a password, we need to retrieve it from our LTM—but what determines how easily it can be retrieved? Ecological theory suggests that human LTM evolved to help survival by anticipating organismically important events. It is evolutionarily important to remember things that are important for survival and thriving. The expected value of remembering it in the future should gain priority in how deeply something is encoded in memory. Paper Example 5.3.2 shows an example of predicting how people forget where things are in a UI.

Paper Example 5.3.2: Modeling how users remember where things are on a user interface

Theories of human LTM can explain how we remember, and why we fail to remember, interface elements over time. Consider, for example, the icons on your smartphone. Over time, you learn to find them with increasing performance without putting conscious effort into it. How is this possible?

LTM is an associative network in which nodes that encode UI elements are associated with other nodes [22]. An item in memory has a base level of activation that determines how likely it is to be recalled. It also has associations with other items, which can help or inhibit its retrieval. These associations have different strengths.

Consider a user who occasionally taps icons. When an icon is selected, its association with its properties, such as its color and location, increases. Afterward, the association starts to decay. The farther in the past the previous accesses are, the less they contribute to the activation, accelerating the decay of the memory. This can be expressed mathematically. The base activation of the icon B_i is

$$B_i = \ln(\sum_{j=1}^{n} t_j^{-d}), \tag{5.1}$$

where t_j is the time since the jth visitation of i, and d is a decay parameter.

When retrieving the location of an item, the probability of its retrieval is related to this base level. If $B_i > \tau$, where τ is some minimum threshold for retrievability, the item is retrievable. If a cue related to the item is given, the *source activation* B_{sa} can be added to B_i. This is called

continued

> **Paper Example 5.3.2: Modeling how users remember where things are on a user interface** *(continued)*
>
> *spreading activation*, that is, the activation of whatever is in the focus of attention boosts the activation of relevant items, thereby facilitating their retrieval.
>
> Finally, the time to retrieve the location of the item, T_i, depends on its activation. This is given by
>
> $$T_i = Fe^{-fB_i}, \qquad (5.2)$$
>
> where F and f are individual-specific constants.

5.3.5 Learning over time

Every time you do something, subtle neural changes take place. These changes prepare you so that you can better tackle the task in the future when you encounter it again. Over time, the change in performance is dramatic. What used to be hard and taxing becomes more automatic, and therefore more effortless. However, *how* you practice, as well as whether you deliberately practice the task or simply execute it, affect how well you learn.

Perhaps the most dramatic improvements in performance occur early on. For example, after just a few tests with a new input device, we typically see large changes, which then become proportionately smaller with more practice. Another way to say this is that increasing practice provides *diminishing returns*.

For example, in a motor learning task, this relationship is captured in the *power law of practice*:

$$RT = aP^{-b} + c, \qquad (5.3)$$

where RT is the reaction time, P is the number of completed practices, and a, b, and c are free parameters whose values are case-specific. The law portrays a quantitative relationship between the best-effort performance and the amount of practice. It has been found to describe motor tasks, such as pointing or rolling cigars, and to some extent mental performance, such as retrieving facts or solving arithmetic tasks. The free parameters (a, b, and c) control different aspects of the slope: the intercept and the rate of change. An example is given in Figure 5.4. In the figure: Which curve shows faster learning? What do the three free parameters (a, b, and c) mean?

When performance improves, the expected reaction time is not the only factor that changes; the performance also becomes more *stable*. In other words, the variance in performance decreases. In some cases, this trend has been observed to follow the power law of practice, although with different free parameters. The point is that early on when learning a skill, we struggle to keep performance stable and see large differences across trials. Large improvements are seen during the first trials, and performance stabilizes further, albeit with diminishing returns, with more practice. Stability is important in HCI because it means the user can better predict the outcomes of interaction, is less prone to errors, and has greater self-confidence.

With extensive practice, skills transition from controlled to automatic. *Automaticity* refers to the fast and effortless performance of skills. For example, when first using the camera application on a smartphone, you probably struggled to find some settings and even basic functionalities such as

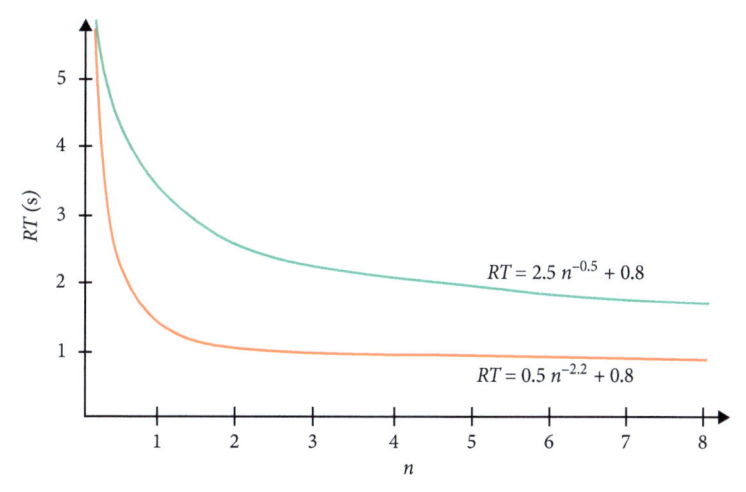

Figure 5.4 The power law of practice states a relationship between the reaction time and the number of practices: $RT = aP^{-b} + c$. Here, it is shown with two parameter sets.

video recording. However, with practice over time, you can now focus more on the object of photography than on the camera itself. The downside of automaticity is its inflexibility. Automaticity is often described as a ballistic skill: The skill is triggered by some cues and carried out to its completion with little opportunity to redirect it. This means that with increasing practice, users may become insensitive to changes in a design.

5.3.6 Designing practices

In many settings, we are not just using computers; we invest time and effort to practice their use. *How* we practice matters. The most inefficient way to learn a skill is to just mindlessly do it. Significant performance gains can be obtained by putting some thought into training.

The basic parameters of a practice regime are:

1. Scheduling of practice: When practice happens
2. Selection of practices: Which practices are done
3. Feedback: How feedback informs changes in strategy.

In the following, we discuss these one by one.

Scheduling practices: How practice trials are scheduled over time has a significant impact on learning. The worst schedule is *massed*:

| | | | | | | |

Here, all practice takes place in a compressed timeframe, which leaves very little time for the consolidation of memories in the brain. Somewhat better is *equi-spaced* training:

| | | | | | |

Here, practices take place not too long after each other but not too shortly after either. The best training schedule is *expanding practice*, represented here with an exponent of 2:

This means that practice will take much longer. However, it provides much more time for slower learning processes in the brain.

Selection of practices: Perhaps the worst way to learn a skill is to just perform the activity. *Focused practice* refers to the selection of *isolated* practices with clear objectives and corrective feedback. These practices should not be arbitrary, but focus on those aspects that show room for improvement. But how to identify such practices? This can be done by a human mentor or by tracking the user's development and comparing it against the expected level of performance at that level of training.

Feedback: Feedback is important in HCI, as it helps users set goals and correct mistakes in computer use. Consider a computer game you have recently played: What kind of feedback does it provide about your performance? For example, it may provide a numerical score or indicate which level you have mastered. It could also be more specific; for example, it could tell you how many events of a particular kind you have mastered. Feedback can be of three different kinds: (1) performance-indicating, for example, a score or words per minute in text entry, (2) performance-correcting, providing qualitative feedback to help identify problematic areas of performance, and (3) strategy-enhancing.

5.3.7 Stages of skill development

How good do you think you are at using your mobile device? It is probably hard to tell. Skill development in HCI is often described in three stages: novice, intermediate, and expert.

The novice stage is characterized by a struggle to complete tasks and high variability in performance. Performance is neither high in comparison to peers nor stable. While performance improvements can be obtained through repetition for simple tasks, for complex tasks, this may not suffice. After the initial gains from repetition, the next improvements are achievable only through changes in the *interaction strategies*. Learning is very specific to the interaction strategy. For example, if you first use a menu for selecting commands and later shift to keyboard shortcuts, there is little—if any—skill transfer from the first skill to the new one. Any change in strategy may initially reverse previous advances in performance. Users may initially perform much worse than before the shift. However, performance will improve quickly, and in some cases according to the power law of practice. The power law of practice can be used to estimate whether the new strategy will eventually allow for achieving a superior level of performance.

Most of our computer skills are self-taught. Without deliberate practice, skill development stops at the intermediate level. This level is characterized by performance that is acceptable for most regular activities. However, the acquired skill may not be robust or generalize to new tasks. For example, in a study of mobile users, the skills obtained by intermediate-level users were found to be device-specific [627]. The users mainly learned their skills via early familiarization with a device, repeated use, and problem-solving situations. While experienced users exhibited superior performance in tasks, they failed to transfer what they had learned to *other* tasks due to a lack of deeper conceptual representations of how the technology works. Instead, their performance was attributed to their being overall better at navigating interfaces and knowing where things are.

The highest level of skill, the expert level, is only achievable with years of deliberate practice. Significant practice, in the order of thousands rather than hundreds of hours, is required. The design of such practice matters and is normally done by coaches and other experts, such as in the case of video games. Practices should be isolated, focus on areas of low performance, and provide corrective feedback. Because such practice can require significant effort, the motivation for persisting is important: How to keep the user motivated, particularly when the practice is not fun?

In this regard, the role of coaches, mentors, and exemplary users is important. In *apprenticeship learning*, an expert user guides the practice. Consider, for example, a medical doctor teaching novice users how to use a new patient record system. An experienced user can be involved in the selection and scheduling of practices, the provision of feedback, and motivating others.

5.3.8 Knowledge-in-the-world, knowledge-in-the-head

Finally, users are not at the mercy of what they remember. They can flexibly *externalize* knowledge and use such externalized representations for recalling purposes. The key distinction is between *knowledge-in-the-world* and *knowledge-in-the-head* [288]. For example, to avoid disclosing our passwords to others, we would like to store and maintain them in our LTM, safe from peering eyes. This is knowledge-in-the-head. However, we often end up storing passwords on slips of paper, files on computers, and so on; in other words, knowledge-in-the-world. Our cognitive functioning may become dependent on having access to that externalized knowledge, negatively affecting knowledge-in-the-head.

People also actively manipulate the environment to change the cognitive requirements of a task. The case of Tetris players is an eye-opening one. In a study of expert Tetris players, it was found that not all of them try to mentally rotate a piece to fit it to the landscape below [417]. Instead, some players quickly flip the piece to *visually recognize* the best slot. This is beneficial because we are fast in recognizing solutions but much slower in mentally simulating events.

Distributed cognition can be very involved in complex task environments. Consider an airplane with a pilot and a co-pilot operating in the cockpit to land the plane [364]. There are numerous computer devices showing the state of the airplane. There are standard operating procedures—checklists that show what to do and in what order. Moreover, there are two pilots who communicate to establish common ground on the status of the airplane. Speech, such as telling the status of a checked meter, can provide a status update for the other pilot. Together, these devices, practices, and communications form a distributed cognition. The idea is that we cannot attribute cognition to a single brain, and its functioning is best understood by considering the joint operation of the pilots and the environment.

5.4 Reasoning and decision-making

We often face a situation in interaction where we do not have a direct solution to something that we need. We cannot see anything or recall anything that could help us proceed.

Reasoning is about thought processes that allow us to conclude something that we do not already know. Reasoning forms new beliefs from old rules via some rules or mechanisms. For example, if the browser window has not yet opened, you may reason that the application has not yet been launched, or that the tap was not registered. Another form of reasoning is *inference*, where we form a new belief based on observations. For example, we can infer that an icon in a different operating system, say macOS, will have the same function as the one we have seen in Windows.

Prediction is a special kind of reasoning that is needed to act effectively in a dynamic environment. Predictions are reasoning about the future. The challenge is to leap from observations about the present to what *will* or *might* happen in the future.

Reasoning is commonly needed when dealing with complex systems, for example:

- Reasoning about what a piece of software can do based on other knowledge about it, which may come from various sources such as advertisements, word of mouth, etc.
- Reasoning about what will happen if you issue a particular command to software you have not used before.
- Reasoning about the risks involved in a decision.

5.4.1 Mental models

Mental models are memory-based representations of interactive systems that are used for reasoning, inference, and prediction. They are representations of systems and the way users' inputs affect them. For example, a mental model of a thermostat may tell us how the temperature set by the user affects the perceived warmth in a room. By simulating a scenario in the mind using a mental model, the user can reason about the unobservable qualities of a system.

In a study of mental models, Mayer and Gallini [527] asked students to read descriptions of how a pump works. Some of these descriptions showed parts, operating steps, or both parts and steps, as shown in Figure 5.5. The parts-and-steps illustrations significantly helped the participants in both recall and problem-solving tasks. This finding indicates that mental representations of devices help users simulate what happens to the internal state of a device when a certain input is given.

The current understanding is that regular untrained users are often unable to form coherent and complete mental models of the devices they use. Mental models are rarely complete models. Instead, users' knowledge tends to be multifaceted and fragmented. For example, one may remember episodes of using a device and use this to recall how to operate it. One may also remember unrelated facts about what a device can do. In practical problem-solving situations, users are often reluctant to engage in effortful reasoning; they would rather just try out things and see what happens.

5.4.2 Decision-making

Decision-making refers to any situation in which multiple options are given and one or a subset must be chosen. Example: Your computer is infected with a virus. Which virus removal application would you pick?

- Software A: Removes the virus with 95% probability but slows down the computer significantly in 5% of cases.
- Software B: Removes the virus with 70% probability but never slows down the computer.

In the more general case, N options are given, each associated with gain g (e.g., removing the virus) that occurs with probability p and a loss (e.g., slowing down the computer) that occurs with probability $1 - p$. Note that users may not be rational and always choose the option that is best for them.

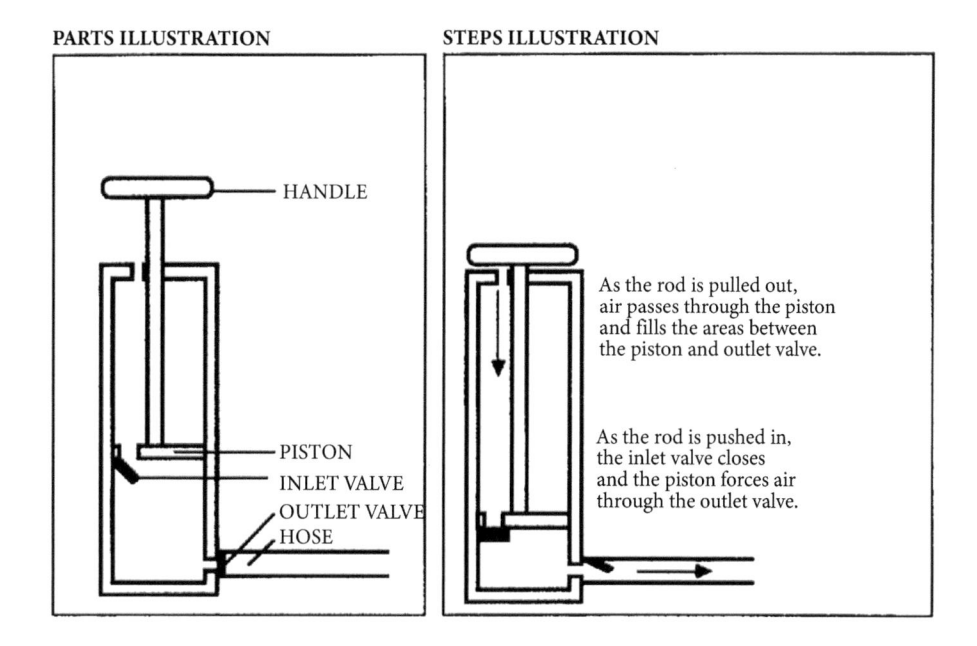

Figure 5.5 Mental models of a pump system used in the experiment of Mayer and Gallini [527].

Prospect theory posits that such choices are evaluated relative to a *reference point* [402]. For example, the status quo (the most common choice) or the most recent choice may work as a reference point. Such reference points guide how the user reasons about the gains and losses involved. The second claim from the theory is that some people are *risk-averse* about gains relative to the reference point, but risk-seeking about losses. In other words, they do not want to lose the gains provided by the reference point, but they are willing to gamble with losses. The third claim is that some people are loss-averse. In other words, losing something hurts them more than gaining the same thing. For example, loss-averse gamers prefer an option that avoids the loss of a precious game award and view this as more important than the possibility of gaining the same award.

This theory is perhaps the most successful theory of economic decision-making, applied in studies of bargaining, consumer choice, voting, and even politics. In HCI, users face such decision-making all the time: How should we choose clothes for our avatar, our privacy settings, or the length of our passwords? These decisions involve various expected gains, losses, and risks. Many decisions in HCI can be analyzed through this lens; the challenge lies in estimating the gains and losses and their probabilities.

Multi-attribute choice refers to choice in the case where the options are characterized by multiple attributes. By contrast, in the previous example, there were only two attributes to consider: the efficiency of virus removal and the effect on the speed of the computer. We can generalize to more than two attributes. For example, if you want to buy a bicycle on an e-commerce site, you need to consider multiple attributes, such as price, type, size, location, and so on. Multi-attribute problems are hard for users, especially novices [494]. Their eye movement patterns are scattered; they can spend a lot of time going back and forth inspecting options, and they may feel unsatisfied with their eventual choice. Why is multi-attribute choice hard?

Users need to move their limited visual attention between rows to examine the options available. While doing that, they need to keep in mind the attributes they have considered so far, or at least those important for making a decision. They also need to reason about what the best option is and why. Few people can do this in a single pass since keeping all these attributes in mind is hard. Rather, what users often do is "satisficing": They decide on what would be a good enough option and select it as soon as they find it. To circumvent the limits of WM, users may write down options, for example, in a spreadsheet, or seek external advice (reviews, opinions from friends). With experience, decisions become easier to make. Eye-movement strategies become less taxing and faster. Users learn to scan the options in a more systematic way and directly reject options that are irrelevant.

5.4.3 Decision heuristics

Kahneman [400] popularized the finding in neuroscience that we have two systems of decision-making. System 1 is a fast system driven by intuition, emotion, imagery, and associative memory. System 2 is a slow system that monitors System 1 and intervenes if intuition is not sufficient for the task. For example, you may feel like you want to click on a social media application to check the latest posts (System 1). However, as you start doing that, System 2 may intervene to stop that from happening, for example, because you have already checked that application recently.

In many circumstances, we do not have the possibility to evaluate all our options, and even if we did, the situation would be too complex for full analysis. In such cases, we use System 1. A *cognitive heuristic* is a rule of thumb used to identify a quick solution to a complex problem. For example:

Anchoring: It occurs when we center our choice around a known reference solution. For example, when choosing which application to use for some task, users often start with an application they already know.

Decoying: Decoying occurs when a reference point we have prevents us from seeing another one behind it. For example, a user who recalls ChatGPT as a large language model (LLM) that can answer questions may fail to remember the names of other LLMs.

Availability: Availability in heuristics refers to people's estimates of the probability of an event. Similar to its anchoring, the availability of a memory makes it more likely to be entered as a solution. PowerPoint, because of its prevalence as a slide editing software, may be the most likely option users consider even if there are many alternatives.

Status quo: Status quo bias refers to the prevailing solution, such as a famous or popular option. For example, popular products such as ChatGPT may first come to mind.

Bandwagon bias: Bandwagon bias occurs when we see our peers choosing the same option.

For example, if I ask you to name a great smartphone, you are likely to name something that comes to mind quickly, which may be the most recent smartphone model. This heuristic is called the *availability heuristic*.

The catch with heuristics is that while they allow us to generate a solution quickly, they limit the visibility of other solutions. They lead to *biases*. A bias, in this context, means a tendency to consider a skewed subsample in the space of options.

5.5 Simulating cognition in interactive tasks

Having described several aspects of cognition relevant to HCI, a natural question is how we would go about applying it to understand interactive tasks. *Cognitive models* are models that formally describe what happens in a person's mind during an interactive task. They provide an exact description of a cognitive mechanism—the way in which cognition mediates observable user behavior and the user's task.

A cognitive model receives some input that represents the task and has a mechanism to link that input to predictions about behavior. A model can be expressed in different ways:

Rule systems: Sets of rules or logical clauses that describe how information is processed in the mind. For example, mental models are described as logical statements.

Mathematical models: Statistical models that describe a relationship between factors related to the task or design, the outcomes of the interaction, and the cognitive factors that mediate the two.

Simulations: Stepwise executed computer programs. The best-known example is a class of cognitive architecture models, where different cognitive capacities, such as perception and memory, are program modules with their own inputs and outputs.

Data-driven models: Models developed using training data or via trial and error. For example, artificial neural networks can be used to understand aspects of visual saliency. Although such networks learn parameters from data, they also express architectural assumptions about the mind, such as the process of convolution.

In the early years of HCI, cognitive modeling had a central role in HCI [129]. One well-known example is Project Ernestine, which is discussed in detail in Paper Example 5.5.1. Another example is the goals, operators, methods, and selection rules (GOMS) model, an early cognitive model developed by Card et al. [129] that facilitated the development of cognitive architectures.

The development of cognitive architectures was inspired by computer architectures, which are descriptions of computer systems in terms of their underpinning components and their relationships. Cognition consists of serial and parallel information processing units. This terminology will be familiar to anyone who has studied computer science or software engineering:

Peripherals: These are sensors and actuators for interacting with the external environment. Examples include the oculomotor system, perception, and hearing.

Internal modules: Such modules may operate independently, processing inputs and sending outputs to other modules. They have capacity limitations, such as the number of items they can store or the amount of time they take to process input, and they can maintain internal states and run complex programs.

Production rules: These describe what is done and under which conditions. They are similar to computer programs that consist of a series of commands executed by modules.

Central processing unit: The central executive is limited in capacity and can only process things serially. When a program is run, it produces a *trace* of human behavior. Such a trace may contain the time needed to take an action or complete a task, the errors produced, and so on.

One of the main motivations for cognitive architectures in early HCI was that they could be used to decrease the cost of empirical evaluations with human participants. In addition, they were used to construct systems that adapt to the user, such as in cognitive tutoring, where cognitive models track a learner's cognitive development to select suitable study materials and interventions.

Why have cognitive models not been as widely adopted by practitioners as perhaps hoped at the outset of the field? First, applying a cognitive architecture model to an HCI problem requires a deep understanding of the user's task. Sometimes this understanding has to be so deep that it is easier to evaluate the design empirically than to build a model. For example, GOMS requires the researcher to specify rules that describe what the user does at the level of cognitive operations. Producing such descriptions can take weeks or even months. Approaches for lowering such barriers and helping practitioners to demonstrate tasks were not widely adopted, possibly because they still require significant work [388].

Second, cognitive models tend to work only within a narrow range of applications. A production system that has been created for one task and one particular design cannot be readily adopted for another setting—it must be updated and revised. In other words, models based on cognitive architecture have a scaling problem.

However, the topic of cognitive modeling is experiencing a revival with machine learning methods. New modeling approaches have been explored in HCI, most recently neural network models and reinforcement learning (Chapter 21). A key benefit of such approaches is that the researcher does not need to specify the production systems or policies. Instead, such models can learn them.

Paper Example 5.5.1: Project Ernestine

Project Ernestine is an example of cognitive modeling in HCI [289] that demonstrates the practical value of modeling cognition for HCI.

A telephone company was interested in improving the efficiency of their teleoperators. Teleoperators, a profession that no longer exists as switchboards are automated, were professionals who spoke with a caller and connected the call to its destination.

The company had designed a new workstation they believed would improve task performance and help the company save millions of dollars. They hired cognitive scientists to understand if the new design was better than the old one and, if so, by how much. The goal was simple: to estimate task completion times for the two workstation designs.

The researchers came back with a startling result: The new design was slower than the old one. The researchers pointed out that while the company had focused on the time that manual operations take, the new design changed the cognitive requirements, with non-obvious consequences on performance. The new design required the recall of information, which is slow, and this factor was neglected by the company.

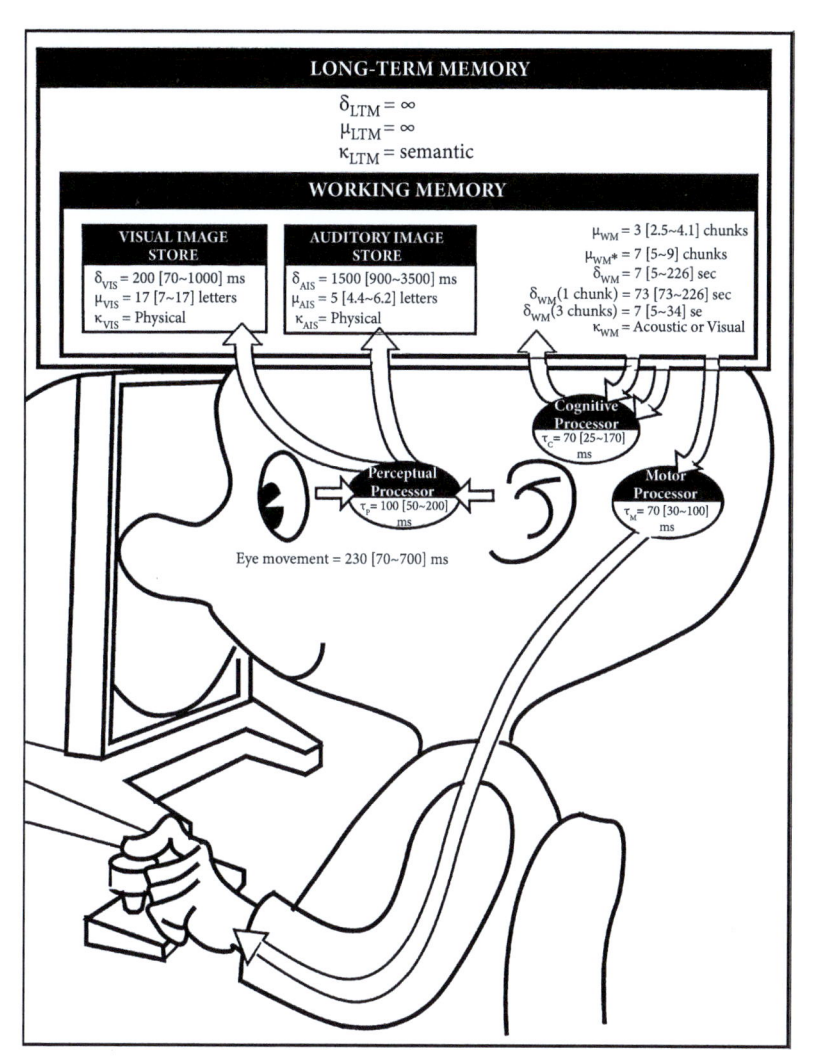

Figure 5.6 GOMS is a cognitive architecture model. It simulates the processing of information in separate modules of the mind and the flow of information between them. Modules have internal capacity limits and processing times [129].

To arrive at this conclusion, the authors used a variant of GOMS called CPM-GOMS. Figure 5.6 shows the cognitive architecture. CPM-GOMS predicted that the new workstation was 3% *slower*, not faster, than the old one. It further predicted that performance varied across categories of call-handling tasks. Thus, the researchers predicted the company would lose money if it switched to the new workstation.

continued

> **Paper Example 5.5.1: Project Ernestine** *(continued)*
>
> To ensure the results were trustworthy, the authors validated the results against empirical data they collected after the deployment of the new workstation. Comparing model predictions against real data on calls collected over four months, they learned that the average prediction error was small, varying between 11% and 12% in performance time, which corroborated their modeling approach.
>
> Project Ernestine is an example of the special character of modeling in an applied field such as HCI. Modeling in HCI is often driven by practical needs in the evaluation and design of systems as opposed to a pursuit of knowledge for rigorous theory. Cognitive modeling can sometimes be used to evaluate designs and provide insights into their cognitive requirements.

Summary

- The main function of cognition in interaction is to help users deal with complex systems and situations.
- Cognition is limited, yet learning and adaptive.
- Theories of cognition help us answer several key questions about information-rich task environments, for example, what makes multitasking situations demanding, what happens when users learn to use a user interface, why they may fail to remember something they have seen before, and how they draw conclusions based on their beliefs about systems that are opaque to them.
- Many of HCI's guidelines and evaluative models are rooted in theories of cognition.

Exercises

1. Cognitive abilities. Measure your or your friend's cognitive abilities using PsyToolkit: https://www.psytoolkit.org. Carry out tests to assess WM capacity (e.g., n-back), cognitive control (e.g., task switching), and reasoning (e.g., Hanoi tower). Repeat each test a few times to obtain reliable measurements. What are some tasks in computer use where these abilities are important?

2. Cognitive load. Cognition requires energy and effort; how does design affect these? Take a computer game that you find mentally taxing. Ask a friend to play it and administer the NASA-TLX questionnaire after each level. Take measurements a few times for more robust estimates. Plot the components of the NASA-TLX as a function of the game level. What aspects of the game made each level less/more effortful?

3. Multiple resource theory. (a) Name two common tasks in mobile interaction that, according to MRT, would interfere with each other when carried out simultaneously, and illustrate the conflict by annotating the MRT cube given in Figure 5.2. (b) Explain why interference occurs. (c) Explain how either of the two tasks from (a) might be changed to reduce interference.

4. Observational study of human error. When was the last time you forgot your PIN code, missed your turn when driving, or forgot to unmute yourself on Zoom? Observational studies

are an important part of the HCI toolbox. To prepare for this task, read more on error taxonomies based on human cognition: http://www.errordiary.org/blog/wp-content/uploads/HumanErrorSGSWMarch2013.pdf. Fully understand the notions of activation, schema, and cross-talk. Then, download the error table Word file from the homepage of the book. It contains a table with eight error types on different rows: (a) capture, (b) double capture, (c) omission, (d) loss of activation, (e) description slip, (f) associative activation slip, (g) repetition of action slip, and (h) cross-talk slip. Your task is to observe an everyday interaction taking place with technology for one hour and to systematically identify errors using this taxonomy. We recommend a public interface similar to a vending machine. Ensure that (a) you can safely observe users, for example, by standing at a distance and taking auditory or written notes, and (b) the case is interesting from an error perspective, that is, different error types might appear.

5. Cognition and design. Pick a user interface design that you think is hard to use. Take full screenshots and analyze them using the design guidelines of Jeff Johnson listed in Table 41.1.

6. Memory. Human memory is important in interaction. Think about an interactive system that goes against the characteristics of memory discussed in this chapter, for example, a system that demands too much of our short-term memory. Propose how the design could be improved.

6
Needs and motivations

From the word processor to the Internet, interactive computer systems have changed the way we work, consume, and even lead our romantic lives. However, in addition to technical limitations, are there *human-related* limits to a wider adoption of computing?

What we *need* or desire as human beings is a defining factor in technology adoption and success. Technology enters society in two ways: *market pull*, which means there is a market for a solution, and *technology push*, which means that new technology creates new needs in the market. People and their needs shape *both* pull and push factors.

The scientific study of human needs has become increasingly important in an attempt to understand the role that computing plays in our lives. In early computing research, researchers focused on what was *possible* to achieve with computers. This has now changed to identifying what is *desirable* for people. This chapter discusses human needs and motivations and how they relate to interactive technology.

Needs are generally understood as requirements to live a fulfilling and healthy life. The satisfaction of needs is linked to positive experiences with the activities that mediate them. If it is possible to satisfy a need of fundamental importance, then it is likely that there are resulting positive effects. As such, needs shape what we do and strive for, and the fulfillment of needs is our motive for engaging with technology.

These insights can be put to use in human–computer interaction (HCI). Let us consider a few examples.

- Hassenzahl et al. [323] noted that feeling related to other people, such as feeling in love, closeness, and intimacy, is important for well-being. They then identified different user interface strategies that could be used to promote feeling related to others, including giving gifts, sharing memories, and being aware of one another. All of these considerations depart from the psychological need for relatedness.
- How to motivate people through interactive systems remains a challenge. Naqshbandi et al. [575] used self-determination theory (SDT; Section 6.2.3) to increase the motivation for volunteering. In particular, they attempted to use gratitude to increase motivation.
- How can interactive systems help people become who they desire to be? This appears to be a basic need related to autonomy and meaning-making. Zimmerman [927] drew on product attachment theory to create design patterns to create such systems. For example, he created the Smart Bag to help parents transfer the responsibility of packing clothes and equipment for athletics to their children. In this way, parents are supported in increasing the autonomy of their children.

First, let us look at the basic psychological needs that psychology research has identified and what they can be used for. Then, we move on to discussing motivation, that is, what makes people act or not act. One important application of this in HCI concerns changing people's behavior, which we discuss toward the end of this chapter.

6.1 Psychological needs

A need is commonly defined as a *deficit*: People need something they do not have. According to this definition, interactive systems must strive to create conditions that satisfy unfulfilled needs. However, this reasoning is circular. We need something because we do not have it, and since we do not have it, we need it.

To make it possible to reason more usefully about needs, we need to *ground* needs into something outside the needs themselves, to factors that drive us as biological and social beings. This grounding has been a central theme in psychological science for almost a century. As a consequence, researchers have compiled and empirically verified several taxonomies of needs.

In this regard, computer use is not about satisfying deficits. However, the satisfaction of needs positively contributes to well-being and positive experiences. For example, using social media can be both disturbing to social relationships and a way to satisfy various forms of inter-relatedness. Meeting basic psychological needs is necessary for our thriving and well-being. However, as we learn in this chapter, such needs manifest in complex ways as motivations, wants, and desires.

A central finding in psychological research on human motivation is that there are *basic psychological needs*. Such needs are experienced in many forms. Some may want to talk to their grandchildren, others like to help their friends move, and others still like to leave letters of appreciation. These needs are similar in that the aim of these people is to feel *related* to other people. Thus, we say that relatedness is a psychological need that is satisfied via intentions or actions.

Perhaps the most well-known variant of this idea is Maslow's hierarchy of needs. As part of a larger humanistic psychology, Maslow posited five needs organized in the shape of a pyramid [522]. From the lowest level to the highest level:

1. Physiological needs, such as food, water, warmth, and rest
2. Safety needs, such as security
3. Belongingness and love needs, pursued via intimate relationships and friends
4. Esteem needs, pursued via prestige and a feeling of accomplishment
5. Self-actualization, pursued by achieving one's felt potential and via creative activities.

Two ideas underpin this hierarchy. First, the specifics of human needs can be grouped into these five types. Second, low-level needs must be satisfied before individuals can attend to their high-level needs.

Maslow's needs have not received much attention in HCI. Two other frameworks have been more influential: the ten psychological needs proposed by Sheldon et al. [762] and adapted to HCI by Hassenzahl et al. [322], and the three needs from SDT [183].

6.1.1 Catalog of psychological needs

Sheldon et al. [762] integrated and empirically validated a catalog of basic psychological needs. This work resulted in a list of 10 needs. In the context of HCI, Hassenzahl et al. [322] suggested that rich experiences with technology can be based on a much smaller set of universal psychological

Table 6.1 Six psychological needs that are relevant for interactive systems [322]. They were selected from 10 needs developed in earlier work [762].

Psychological need	Explanation
Relatedness	Need for social relationships
Meaning	Need for purpose and direction
Stimulation	Need for novel sensations and thoughts
Competence	Need for the ability to perform well in important activities
Popularity	Need for recognition by others
Security	Need for protection of self from harm

needs and that the satisfaction of those needs is the reason why interaction with technology is generally a positive experience. This list of six needs is reported in Table 6.1.

As an example, the need for meaning may be assessed by asking people to which extent they engaged in an experience for "becoming who I really am," to have "a sense of deeper purpose," or to obtain "a deeper understanding of myself." The degree to which a person agrees reflects the degree to which the motivation to participate in the experience was a need for meaning. One may also ask about the extent to which an experience fulfilled the need for meaning using the same questions.

6.1.2 The three needs in self-determination theory

Self-determination theory is the most prominent theory in HCI in terms of needs and motivations. It assumes three basic psychological needs:

1. **Autonomy:** The sense that actions are performed willingly, in alignment with one's self, and not directed by external forces.
2. **Competence:** The feeling of achieving mastery and controlling the outcomes of actions.
3. **Relatedness:** The sense of reciprocal belonging in relation to other humans.

A *basic psychological need* is a biologically determined driver behind a behavior. Basic needs, as opposed to learned quasi-needs and motivations, are shared by all humans across cultural, economic, and societal circumstances. Any activity that satisfies a basic need can lead to intrinsic motivation and better well-being. Optimal psychological functioning requires that all three needs be met. To this end, people need support and nurturing from society.

What is the role of basic needs in the use of technology? The most important implication of the theory is that computers *per se* are not needed. A computer is a tool—it is a means to an end and not an end in itself. However, to answer that question more deeply, we first need to understand how basic needs develop into motivations to act in a particular way.

6.1.3 Using needs in HCI

How may HCI researchers and practitioners use an understanding of psychological needs to improve HCI? Need satisfaction provides energy and leads to positive affect; need thwarting can lead to a lack of energy and negative affect.

There are two basic uses of needs in HCI research and practice. Psychological needs may be used for *analysis*. A model of needs may be used to analyze the results of user research. We discuss such research in Part III; for now, imagine interviews with or observations of users. The insights from such research may clarify which basic needs have been assessed and addressed in sufficient depth and which ones require more attention from designers. Thus, needs, as an explanatory construct, enable us to both avoid solutions that do not satisfy any needs and detect new opportunities for improving people's lives by fulfilling previously ignored needs.

As an example, Kraus et al. [434] conducted semi-structured interviews (Chapter 11) to understand users' motivations for taking actions related to privacy and security on their smartphones. The analysis revealed that multiple needs determined the users' actions. For instance, some users switched off their Wi-Fi and data connections. This was not about being secure but rather about the need for autonomy ("I want to be left alone") or saving money ("I can save some of my data contingent"). In this case, the users' actions can be understood better when considering their multiple needs rather than just the need for security.

The second use of models of psychological needs in HCI is for *inspiring design*. The idea here is that models of needs are assumed to be the source of positive experiences with technology. If this assumption is accepted, we can use models of needs to consider ways to make experiences positive. Paper Example 6.1.1 presents an example where the need for relatedness is used to drive design solutions.

Paper Example 6.1.1: How to make couples apart feel related

Due to work, pandemics, and other circumstances, partners are sometimes forced to spend long periods physically away from each other. Although couples can send each other emojis and make phone calls, many researchers have been interested in finding ways to better support people in such situations.

Hassenzahl et al. [323] focused on experiences of relatedness as a fundamental psychological need that technology may support in such situations. To this end, the authors reviewed more than 140 published designs and identified six strategies for supporting relatedness.

(a) Awareness   (b) Expressivity   (c) Physicalness   (d) Gift Giving   (e) Joint Action   (f) Memories

Each strategy is associated with examples of designs that implement the strategy and a set of supporting psychological principles.

For example, in the awareness strategy for promoting relatedness, an interactive system shares information about what one's partner is doing or feeling. This type of information sharing, while passive, nevertheless promotes relatedness. Designers could draw on several psychological processes to further increase awareness. Nevertheless, the self-disclosure through technology should be gradual. Several of the designs that Hassenzahl et al. [323] evaluated indicated that such awareness can be intrusive and strange if it happens too quickly or to a too large degree. Furthermore, awareness through technology works against an idealization of the distant partner. This happens in long-distance relationships because mundane details about the distant partner's life are not available and because partners make extra efforts when they

> are together. As such, technology that supports relatedness could help distant partners build and maintain a realistic picture of each other.
>
> Similarly, the other strategies contain details on psychological processes to create technology that can help partners meet their need for feeling related.

6.1.4 Needs and values

Some approaches to HCI focus on values rather than psychological needs. This is the case for value-sensitive design [258]. Let us outline this approach and discuss its relation to research on needs.

In value-sensitive design, the values of stakeholders are continuously taken into account over the course of a design process. Value-sensitive design identifies autonomy as a central value. Friedman [257] discussed the concrete considerations in the design of a workstation for autonomy as follows.

> The workstation was designed to support speech input and multimedia, and thus included a built-in microphone. Nothing strange here. Except that the microphone automatically recorded audio information whenever the workstation was on. Now, imagine that you are in the middle of a video-conferencing session and a visitor comes into your office, or the phone rings. The only way to ensure audio privacy is to turn off the application, which is a cumbersome solution. Alternatively, a simple solution existed in the design process (ultimately vetoed by the design team): to install a hardware on/off switch on the microphone at the cost of 25 cents.

This example shows how a focus on basic values such as autonomy can inspire design considerations.

What is the difference between the view of needs just discussed and value-sensitive design? Values, as understood in value-sensitive design, are about what is important to people in their lives, in particular regarding how they should act (i.e., morality). Such values include welfare, trust, informed consent, ownership, and many others. In this regard, values are conscious choices about how to realize our needs. While they are different concepts, values and needs may be used in similar ways in the evaluation and analysis of interactive systems.

6.2 Motivations

If behavior is driven by the same basic psychological needs, why do people have different behaviors? How we choose to behave in a particular situation is often driven by an *anticipation* of the fulfillment of such needs. The *motivation* for using particular interactive systems is related to the needs we anticipate these systems will fulfill.

Generally, *needs* are considered to be universal. By contrast, motivations are individual and contextual expressions that drive individual behavioral choices. Needs are rigid and evolve slowly; motivations are more malleable. Motivations are the cogs that link needs to actions: They define why we choose to do one thing and not another. Needs explain why people universally reject certain types of technologies—consider, for example, surveillance. Motivations explain why technology that is adopted by one user group in one context is rejected in other circumstances.

Motivations can be affected by technology. For example, it is easy for a user to become distracted by a notification or a news feed on a social media web site. However, technology can also help us, for example, stop smoking or start exercising by affecting our motivations. As we experience technology and hear others talk about it, our anticipations and motivations change. Over time, people diverge in the way they manifest their basic needs.

6.2.1 Wants and desires

Desires and *wants* are cravings for things that one may not already have. Above, we have learned that needs are basic; they may not be the same as our desires and wants. What people say they want may be very different from what they find satisfying. Awareness of this discrepancy is essential in user research. One naive approach is to simply ask people what they want. If over a decade of psychology research has taught us anything, it is that introspection does not offer special access to the causes behind behavior. In other words, asking people simply does not work.

6.2.2 Quasi-needs

We can all recognize that we have urges to do things that are not necessarily a true need. My craving to check social media, for instance, may not be beneficial for my mental health. How is this possible? The reason is that they are learned. A *reinforcer* is an event that affects the satisfaction of a need. *Primary reinforcers* are basic psychological and biological needs, such as food, drink, and sexual pleasure. Most of our reinforcers are *secondary*; that is, learned. For example, money or grades are reinforcers that do not directly satisfy a biological or psychological need. Secondary reinforcers are learned via *associative learning*. Through experience, primary reinforcers are linked to secondary reinforcers, which are individually and culturally shaped.

Because motivations are based on learned associations, they can also be "wrong"; that is, they can be detrimental to well-being. A *quasi-need* refers to a statement of need that appears like a need but is not one. For example, the urge to acquire a loot box in a computer game is not a need in a psychological sense, although it may feel very real and intense for the player. While reinforcers can be observed directly, they are not the same as motivations.

6.2.3 Motivation in self-determination theory

Proposed by psychologists Deci and Ryan, SDT is one of the most successful broad theories in psychological science [183]. It is widely used in HCI, too. Unlike Maslow's theory, which assumes that behavior is driven by the minimization of deficits, SDT starts with the idea of people as active organisms pursuing self-growth, mastery, and fulfillment. The theory considers both practical and wider cultural and political conditions that can affect motivational dynamics.

Equipped with new data and theories, psychological science has steered away from deficit needs and reinforcers and turned to *motivational dynamics* that underlie positive development, or self-growth. *Self-growth* refers to the motivational mechanisms that drive us to improve our ability to act socially and psychologically. People are seen as actively seeking new opportunities to master themselves rather than satisfy deficits. Another research direction has been linking needs to behavior. The concept of motivation and the processes shaping it are much better understood today than at the time of Maslow. These processes explain via reference to environmental and developmental differences why people end up behaving so differently around technology. SDT is currently one of the most widely studied theories in psychology; it is also gaining ground in HCI applications.

Research on motivation is concerned with what moves people to action. According to SDT, motivations are ultimately rooted in a sense of self-determination. Two types of motivations are distinguished. *Intrinsic motivation* consists of activities that a person has integrated into their sense of self. By contrast, *extrinsic motivation* refers to the external regulation of motivation. Both

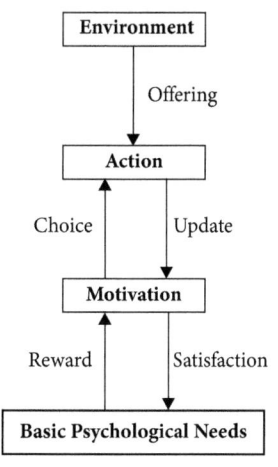

Figure 6.1 According to self-determination theory, the motivations for acting in a certain way develop over time from the interplay of environmental offerings and rewards and basic psychological needs.

controlled and autonomous motivations *energize* action, which gets people to actively pursue technology use. The opposite of motivation is *amotivation*: the lack of appeal for activity.

In the case of extrinsic motivation, it is not the self but external forces that determine the conditions for reward or punishment. An information worker may be motivated to learn to use a new information system just to avoid being punished or viewed negatively by colleagues. A computer gamer may seek approval or self-esteem by building a reputation in the game. Extrinsic motivation is thus *instrumental*, that is, aimed at outcomes distinct from the behavior itself. However, being controlled by an external entity may lead to feeling pressured to behave or think in an externally defined way. This may ultimately lead to the thwarting of an activity.

Internalization is the process of transforming an extrinsic motive into personally approved activities. When given the chance to direct their own behavior, the user's actions will reflect the underlying values of self. The theory identifies the following continuum in internalization [835]:

- External regulation
- Introjected regulation
- Identified regulation
- Integrated regulation.

In external regulation, motivating rewards are controlled by the environment. This is the least self-determined type of extrinsic motivation and is associated with negative drivers such as the avoidance of punishment. Introjected regulation is a partially internalized motivation, not yet fully integrated as one's own. This can, for example, be about the avoidance of guilt or shame. In identified motivation, the activity is consciously valued as personally important. Lastly, in integrated motivation, the activity is congruent with personally valued goals and needs that are part of the self.

6.2.4 Applications of self-determination theory in HCI

There are many uses of SDT in HCI. Considering the needs from SDT systematically allows us to identify opportunities for technological development. A generalized understanding of users' needs is a more solid foundation for innovation than observations of behaviors not underpinned by an explanation. The coupling of needs to *motivation* is a key part of SDT. As needs are what motivates us, paying attention to both needs and motivation helps us to design and evaluate interactive systems.

According to SDT, when we study user needs, we actually study users' motivations—the acquired drivers that make us pursue particular ends related to computers. For example, a programmer may have intrinsic motivation linked to the competence need; someone else may not have this, or even manifest amotivation. SDT posits that individuals are oriented toward the three basic needs to different extents. One user may be pursuing autonomy more than relatedness or competence. These orientations are relatively stable individual traits and can be found out via surveys.

We can also use SDT to develop technology that helps people achieve their goals and maintain motivation. Assisting people in such ways is a key goal in healthcare, for example, through the use of technology and models of motivation to change undesirable behaviors. Later in this chapter, we will discuss behavior change technologies, which draw on motivation theories to help people change their behavior.

As another example, Peters et al. [649] discussed how different types of motivations can affect how we adopt technology. In particular, they argued that if our motivation to pick up a technology is autonomous ("I really want to try that app because I think it will help me engage with exercise more"), it differs from situations where the adoption is externally controlled ("my boss is forcing me to download this app").

SDT also allows us to *analyze* and classify user research by using models of needs and motivations to identify patterns in user reports and the key drivers underpinning what people want and do.

Paper Example 6.2.1 describes how we may obtain information on motivations through questionnaires. In this context, SDT helps us establish measures for use in empirical studies. Another example is games, where the sense of need satisfaction has been measured using the player experience of need satisfaction (PENS) scale [389]. It consists of five subscales partially motivated by SDT: competence, autonomy, relatedness, presence/immersion, and intuitive controls. Various studies have validated this structure.

SDT has been applied in a number of domains. For example, Tyack and Mekler [835] have charted the use of SDT in the context of HCI and games. In any application, three questions stand out.

- Can the technological feature be linked to need satisfaction? Is it a potential means for meeting any of the three basic needs? If the answer is no, people may still be extrinsically motivated to use technology. However, intrinsic, integrated motivation will not appear.
- Are feedback and rewards in place to encourage behaviors that grow intrinsic motivation? Offering an extrinsic reward for an originally intrinsically motivated behavior can undermine intrinsic motivation because behavior becomes controlled by external rewards, diminishing the user's autonomy. Deadlines are a good example. Conversely, providing more options can increase intrinsic motivation, while competence can be encouraged by giving positive feedback. Unexpected positive feedback on a task has been found to increase intrinsic motivation, arguably because it is fulfilling the need for competence. Negative feedback can have the opposite effect.

- Is the user able to imagine or predict the effects of a given feature on outcomes related to motivation? If the possibilities offered by the application are not visible, they are not tried out. The better the user knows or at least can imagine the outcomes, the more likely related action is.

Paper Example 6.2.1: Questionnaire on motivations

This chapter posits that the motivations that drive us to use interactive systems—the whys of interaction—are essential for effective HCI. However, they have generally received little attention in HCI research and design. As a result, Brühlmann et al. [103] developed a questionnaire to measure such motivations.

Questionnaire development is difficult, as we discuss later in Chapter 13. The main idea underpinning their User Motivation Inventory (UMI) questionnaire was to draw on the motivation types from SDT. Six motivation types were distinguished and questionnaire items were developed from them. For instance, amotivation was gauged using statements such as "I use [X], but I question why I continue to use it" and "I use [X], but I don't see why I should keep on bothering with it." Extrinsic motivation, in the form of external regulation, was gauged through statements such as "Other people will be upset if I don't use [X]." Finally, intrinsic motivation was gauged through statements such as "I think using [X] is an interesting activity" and "Using [X] is fun."

Brühlmann et al. [103] found that these statements cluster into six groups corresponding to the six motivation types. They also showed that the type of motivation can help identify participants who had considered quitting using a technology. Finally, more self-determined types of motivation—notably intrinsic motivation—were positively associated with need satisfaction measures and, interestingly, with so-called vitality scores (e.g., "When I use [X], I feel alive and vital").

Altogether, this example shows that we can assess motivation with interactive systems. It also suggests that motivation that comes directly from users tends to be associated with positive attitudes toward technology.

6.3 Behavior change

It has long been acknowledged that artifacts in our environment, including technology, can influence our motivations. This is the case, for example, with clocks, calendars, and memorabilia. They can help us remember what to do, what we have committed to, and what sort of person we would like to be. In short, they help us align our actions with our needs and motivations.

Interactive computer systems are one of these types of artifacts. They can also help us stay motivated and remind us of goals we have set ourselves. Such interactive systems are used for *behavior change*, and a large body of literature has investigated how technology supports such changes [329, 657]. For instance, applications have been developed to help people exercise more, quit smoking, and drink more water. The rise of self-tracking is also related to behavior change. Paper Example 6.3.1 details an example of using early mobile phone displays to change one's fitness regime. However, behavior change is about more than one's health and well-being. Whenever people have the choice *not* to start using a new service or system, we face a behavioral problem. Any new system may ask users to change their practices, and they may be unwilling to do so.

One early perspective on influencing people's behavior likened it to persuasion. Following that line of thought, technology should simply mimic what we know about persuasion from other areas, and we should apply such knowledge in the design of interactive systems. This was the view adopted in early work on so-called *persuasive design*. Fogg [248] proposed an early framework for persuasive design. This framework separates three components of behavior: motivation, ability, and triggers. It posits that all three components must be present for a behavior to occur. For instance, to get a user to consider using a stronger password, there must be motivation, ability (e.g., being able to use special characters fluently when typing), and a trigger (e.g., a suggestion from a colleague). Despite the original intention of persuasive design to not include deceit [329], it might be misconstrued. Thus, this section focuses on *behavior change* in a more general way.

The fundamental challenge in behavior change is that people commit to goals that they then fail to achieve. Much work on behavior change has focused on helping people through the stages of changing their behavior and on nudging them toward their desired behavior. Next, we discuss some key principles for doing so and some ethical considerations around behavior change.

Paper Example 6.3.1: Getting healthy with a mobile phone app

UbiFit Garden is a classic example of an early mobile phone app that promotes behavior change, specifically a healthier lifestyle [166]. UbiFit Garden aimed to tackle the prevalent sedentary lifestyle and its impact on people's health and well-being.

Is it possible to use technology to encourage people to exercise more? UbiFit Garden attempted to do so via three key elements. First, a fitness element that infers fitness activities from sensor data. Second, an application that allows users to see their workouts and the associated statistics. Third, a display that shows the user's activity and recent goal attainment as butterflies and flowers (a and b; the system is shown in c). These mechanisms aimed to improve the contemplation, preparation, and action stages in the transtheoretical model (see Section 6.3.1).

A field trial showed that the system was well received and that participants found the display motivating.

Table 6.2 Overview of the stages in the transtheoretical model [676].

Stage	Explanation
Precontemplation	People are unaware of the need to change, the benefits of doing so, and the drawbacks of their current behavior
Contemplation	People are ambivalent about changing behavior but consider the pros and cons
Preparation	People are ready to change and share this information with friends and family
Action	The new behavior is trialed and evaluated
Maintenance	Circumstances are ensured for continuing the behavior in the future

6.3.1 Stages of behavior change

One of the most influential models of behavior change is the *transtheoretical model*, called so because it is supposed to integrate several previous models of behavior change [676]. Its key idea is that behavior change occurs in five phases (Table 6.2).

The model has been widely used in HCI to reason about how interfaces help users change behavior. He et al. [324] used the model to develop feedback mechanisms for energy consumption, aiming to make people's energy use more sustainable. For each of the five stages, they discussed goals, rationales, and recommendations for what information to present in tools for managing energy consumption.

For instance, in the precontemplation phase, a person is uninformed or unwilling to change behavior. The scenario presented by He et al. [324] concerns Mary, who is "36 years old, married, the mother of two school-age children (Logan and Sarah), and lives in Edsen Community." Mary is "somewhat aware of general environmental problems; she does not believe that her personal energy use (and in particular, her computer usage) has much negative effect. In general, Mary does not believe she has the time or energy to make big energy changes." Based on the model, it is recommended to give personal feedback about the "benefits and consequences of the individual's non-sustainable energy behavior" and the small things Mary could do that would positively influence the environment. Furthermore, based on the model, the authors suggested practitioners to "refer to social norms regarding sustainable energy behaviors by aligning the use of descriptive and injunctive normative messages." Similar advice is given for the other phases, providing a theory-based set of recommendations for changing behavior in a particular domain.

6.3.2 Other factors in behavior change

Several models do not segment behavior change into phases but rather in terms of what makes people act. Some determinants require people to reflect and be aware of their attitudes, the required changes, and the obstacles they face.

Notably, work on *goal setting* has been influential in behavior change research. The key idea is that setting concrete goals is instrumental to working toward those goals and ultimately changing behavior.

SDT may also be seen as a way to conceptualize behavior change. The idea is that if the needs and motivational processes outlined in Section 6.2.3 are correct, then supporting those needs and processes with technology might help bring about or maintain a certain behavior. Villalobos-Zúñiga and Cherubini [854] pursued this idea and related the features of 208 applications to SDT.

They identified five features of the apps that are related to SDT. One common application of SDT is to justify the use of *gamification*, that is, the use of game elements in user interfaces for nongaming contexts.

Another approach to behavior change has come from the field of behavioral economics, in particular the work of Thaler and Sunstein [819]. Their key idea, *nudging*, involves making subtle changes in the choices that people make to ultimately achieve surprisingly large changes in behavior. Nudging is "any aspect of the choice architecture that alters people's behavior in a predictable way without forbidding any options or significantly changing their economic incentives" [819, p. 8]. Nudging has been widely used in user interfaces [126].

Lastly, *dual-process theories* have been influential in understanding behavior change (Chapter 5). In the context of behavior change, they separate a mostly fast, automatic process of thinking about behaviors from a slow, reflective process. The former is associated with habits and holds great power in human behavior. However, tapping that process might rely on what Adams et al. [9] called mindless behavior changes. Several of these ideas have been used in HCI to understand and design technologies for behavior change. For example, Lyngs et al. [499] used dual-process theory to understand digital tools for self-control.

6.3.3 Ethics of behavior change

Changing people's behaviors is not to be taken lightly. We might lead them to believe things that are not correct or have them act in a particular way. When we change what people do, we may also cause their actions to be incongruent with their needs. Thus, influencing users' needs, wants, and motivations carries ethical implications.

Another area where ethical discussions have amassed is the role of technology design in creating addictive or otherwise problematic relations to technology. The concern here is that the profound understanding of behavior we have just discussed might be used to manipulate users rather than to help them achieve their goals and needs. A classic example is the design of gambling environments [747]. In HCI, similar concerns have been voiced for the use of social media and mobile phones in particular.

One area where ethical discussions have become prominent is the use of dark patterns in HCI. A dark pattern comprises user interface elements "that benefit an online service by coercing, steering, or deceiving users into making unintended and potentially harmful decisions" [524]. By definition, such patterns are not in the best interest of users. Yet, it remains a thorny question whether it is unethical for HCI researchers to contribute to them or for software developers to implement them. In the context of nudging, Caraban et al. [126] discussed how the *transparency* of a nudge is related to its ethics. More generally, when behavior change technologies are clear to people, they are less ethically problematic than when they are not.

6.4 Gamification

It is clear from the discussion in this chapter that intrinsic motivation can be forceful. Thus, many people have thought that we should add user interface elements to interactive systems that promote intrinsic motivation. The idea is that if we can make different aspects of computer tasks more intrinsically motivating, we could boost performance and satisfaction.

Gamification is the idea of adding game mechanics to engage users in solving a problem or performing a task. A range of gamification strategies have been considered in the past. One approach is to add reward strategies, such as awarding points or giving badges based on users' performance. A variation of this approach is to make it a competition by making rewards visible to other users through score tables or other means. Another strategy is to make the task itself feel more like a game. This can be achieved, for example, by adding storylines based on progress or direct game mechanics, such as increasing the difficulty as users become more proficient with the task.

One example of gamification in HCI concerns image labeling, which is very laborious. One way to perform such labeling at a large scale is to let users play a game that simultaneously results in images being correctly labeled by users [861]. For example, two remote players are shown an image and are instructed to provide the word that best describes the image. A player cannot see the other player's guess. Once the two players agree on a common word, the game moves on to the next image. The game has "taboo words" (very common words for images). The players cannot use taboo words to describe the images, which makes the game harder. The list of taboo words grows dynamically as the game continues. Through such games, very large sets of images (e.g., all the images indexed by Google) can be labeled relatively quickly.

Gamification is an instance of incentive-based design in which users are encouraged to perform certain functions by a system that rewards particular behaviors. Such mechanisms can be very effective, but they are also often criticized for manipulating users; if they are used, they must be used with care.

According to SDT, through cognitive evaluation, people associate *external rewards* (e.g., success in a game) with the satisfaction of basic needs. However, this external reward can undermine intrinsic motivation. For example, success in a game can transform into a negative, controlling, or amotivating experience. Thus, gamification remains a contentious strategy because it might undermine intrinsic motivation and its associated benefits.

Summary

- Self-determination theory proposes universal psychological needs that are manifested in behavior via motivations.
- Besides the identification of user needs, theories related to needs are used in behavior change applications, which is an ethically contested practice.
- The theory of motivations warns against the naive view that experiences can be designed. Because of the very complex relationship between internal and external processes in behavioral regulation, there is no deterministic relationship between design and experience. Only by thoroughly understanding both the prevailing state and the psychological processes in a particular case can one hope to positively influence the formation of experiences.

Exercises

1. Psychological needs. Pick an application you use frequently. Which of the six psychological needs of Hassenzahl (Table 6.1) are relevant and why? How about the basic needs of Deci and Ryan?
2. Do users know what they need? In a group discussion, find a technology that you all use. Could you have anticipated its usefulness before you started using it? Could the other users? Could participants in a contextual study?

3. Quasi-needs vs. needs. Which are potential needs and which are quasi-needs in the following statements by users? "I need to check email often." "I want to see if there are new messages from my son." "I must update my Facebook application." "I want to avoid anyone stealing my account."

4. Technology push vs. market pull. What makes people desire some technology according to SDT? Think about a hypothetical technological feature that uses AI. Answer the following questions: (a) Will the technological feature be linked to need satisfaction? (b) Will there be feedback and rewards in place that grow intrinsic motivation? (c) Will users be able to imagine or predict the effects of that feature on outcomes related to motivation?

5. Behavior change. Consider a hypothetical application where a large language model (e.g., ChatGPT) is used to motivate people to start using public transportation. Develop a scenario for the application and analyze it using the transtheoretical model.

7
Experience

A key part of human life and hence of interacting with computers is our experience. Consider the three examples in Figure 7.1. They include software and hardware errors, as well as carefully designed functionality. They also include people who experience despair, frustration, and anger, and users who recall interactions and associated experiences of joy and competence. All of these encounters describe people's *experience*—the topic of this chapter.

On the surface, the concept of experience seems straightforward. We all know what experience is from our wake movements. The full picture, however, is much more complex. What we all share is *experiencing*—all the time, we witness the totality of our mental life play out as pictures, emotions, internal speech, and sensations. This experience is ongoing and constantly changing. When typing on a laptop, we experience the feel of the keyboard, the background buzz from the fridge, the breeze of air from an open door, the nagging feeling of not knowing where a function is in a pull-down menu, and much more.

> **A:** When I first purchased my phone, I had problems with the use of the GPS application and Google Maps and usually had difficult in reaching a destination on time or even reaching one at all. So one day I decided that it would be in my best interest to look into the iPhone's capabilities and see if I could rectify the situation myself. I've always been sub-par with technology, and this was certainly a step up from my Blackberry that I had for a number of years. I had found out that you could pinpoint the exact location of your phone and use that as a starting point for directions. Needless to say, when I found out about this, I was ecstatic knowing that the directions I was receiving were not only accurate but also the most efficient route available. I never stopped using that feature after that day.
>
> **B:** I was on the computer with my son, who lives in Las Vegas, and we were Skyping for the first time. My granddaughter was born four days before, I wasn't able to get to Vegas to see her, so we decided this was the next best thing. We turned our Skype on and there she was ... four days old, he showed me all her toes and fingers, she was the prettiest thing I ever saw. The Skype experience was great. I would never imagine in all my years we could do this and be so far away but having the feeling that I could touch her through the computer screen. We have Skyped every day for two weeks now. I have seen my grand daughter cry, sleep, I even watched them change her diaper and take a bottle. It was like I was right there doing it myself.
>
> **C:** I had a bad experience with a presentation at my sister's wedding. I was trying to present a slides how of pictures of the bride and groom as atribute, and I had spent weeks preparing it on my computer. When the day finally came, I gave a little speech, announced my slides how, and then attempted to start it. All I got was an error message!

Figure 7.1 Examples of positive and negative experiences [831]. Some participants answered the prompt "Bring to mind a single outstanding positive experience you have had recently with interactive technology," others a similar prompt concerning a negative experience.

Introduction to Human-Computer Interaction. Kasper Hornbæk, Per Ola Kristensson, and Antti Oulasvirta, Oxford University Press. © Kasper Hornbæk, Per Ola Kristensson, and Antti Oulasvirta (2025).
DOI: 10.1093/oso/9780192864543.003.0007

By contrast, our *experience* is what we tell ourselves and others. We might feel satisfied after typing up a text, or we might say something about the hassle caused by forgetting the location of the comment feature in the menu hierarchy. However, what we remember and how we recount our experiences are only indirectly linked to our experience. They result from a context-dependent process of creating experiences. These processes and the broad categories of experience content are the topics of this chapter.

Why is understanding experience and the processes that create it important to human–computer interaction? There are at least three reasons. First, during the past 20 years, HCI has expanded from interactive systems or products to also include experiences. The area of *user experience* has developed theories and methods to help achieve this extension [42, 321, 463]. One argument in this area is that people derive more value and more positive emotions from experiences than from products. While the personal computer of the 1980s was intended for "getting things done"—ergo, usability was important—the computer of the 2020s offers many diverse opportunities to consumers, who *choose* these opportunities partly based on their experiences of using computers. The principles of how people experience help us understand the mechanisms behind their choices and the extent to which we may influence them via design.

Second, experiences matter. When we move, think, and collaborate, we do so not only as described in the respective chapters of this book; we also *experience* all this. Ethically, positive experience constitutes an objective as important in design as anything else. Thus, independently of our other understanding of people, we need to understand their experienced perspectives.

Third, experiences, despite their incomparable quality, can be categorized and measured, and obtaining such knowledge can be informative. For example, we may separate aspects of experience that are about affect, the stimulation of curiosity, novelty, or aesthetics. We can also evaluate some of these aspects empirically using appropriate methods, helping to set design goals, conducting research studies, and promoting iterative development. For example, Carroll and Thomas [133] presented an early argument about the importance of fun when engaging with interactive systems—fun being a particular type of experience that we all know. Their work inspired much subsequent work on how to design for fun and how to measure it.

Next, we discuss why experience is important, different types of experience, the processes that shape them, and how to assess experiences in HCI.

7.1 What is experience?

Think back to your last vacation or long trip. What was it like? Did you enjoy yourself? What were you expecting before going on vacation? What was the highlight of the vacation? These questions are all about experiences. In studies of people's responses to such questions, the answers can be surprising.

In a study of students' experiences before, during, and after a spring break, among other things, the researchers asked about students' overall subjective experience [901]. They asked them to rate the statement "I will be satisfied with this vacation" on a 1–5 scale with the endpoints representing disagreement and agreement, respectively.

To the surprise of the researchers, the satisfaction with the vacation was higher *after* the vacation than during the vacation. Satisfaction before the vacation influenced not only the experience during the vacation but also the experience after it. Furthermore, when the researchers asked the students if they wanted to repeat the vacation, their ratings of experience during the vacation did not influence their answers. Only the ratings submitted after the vacation influenced their desire to repeat the vacation. What is the explanation for this surprising result?

7.1.1 Experiencing and experiences

As noted at the beginning of this chapter, it is useful to distinguish between *experiencing* and *experiences*. The former refers to the ongoing, moment-to-moment experiencing, for instance, of a computer system when using it. The latter refers to aggregated accounts of an experience, for instance, as you would share them with a friend.

Each construct is associated with different methods of assessment, principles of development, and implications for design. This distinction is grounded in research on psychology, in particular the notions of experiencing and remembering one's own experiences [401]. In the vacation example, experiencing influences experiences less directly than might be expected. Furthermore, experiences seem to influence the desire to redo the vacation more directly than experiencing.

In HCI, experiencing has been defined as "momentary, mainly evaluative feeling (good–bad) while interacting with a product or service" [319, p. 12]. Thus, experiencing encompasses the totality of feelings, memories, and thoughts, as available to us through introspection. Often, we are mainly interested in the reactions to a product or service and therefore mainly focus on a simple evaluative feeling.

In HCI, experience is commonly defined as "a person's perceptions and responses that result from the use or anticipated use of a product, system or service" [376]. Thus, experiences are accounts of episodes of interaction; they are aggregates or summaries of a series of experiencing. Usually, they are constructed as wholes that can be named, and they have a beginning and an end. As seen in the vacation example, the relationship between experiences and experiencing is complex. Psychologists have detailed many surprising dynamics in how momentary experiencing is turned into experiences. Some of those relations have been given names such as sequencing effects, duration neglect, and the peak–end rule.

Sequencing effects mean that the order in which we are experiencing things is important for our experience. Whether something has happened recently or some time ago, and how distinctive an experience is, affect the way experiences are remembered.

The peak–end rule: It captures the finding that people tend to anchor their assessment of experience to ends and peaks. "Ends" are the most recent experiences, say, the last time you used a particular information system. Peak experiences, on the other hand, are the best or worst experiences associated with the system. For example, if you experienced something surprisingly delightful with a service, you are prone to rate the overall experience higher than what that singular event might warrant.

Duration neglect: It is the finding that pleasure ratings are insensitive to the duration of those sequences. Even very short experiences can have a strong influence on the stated experience.

These effects matter in HCI. For example, Figure 7.2 shows two screenshots. If experiences were just summaries of experiencing, there would be no difference between working through the top row of screens and the bottom row. However, Cockburn et al. [158] suggested that there would be a difference based on the peak–end rule. They showed that a combination of different peak-and-end workloads (here, the number of sliders to manipulate) changed which sequence the participants in their study experienced as the best, which was measured by asking the participants for their preferences.

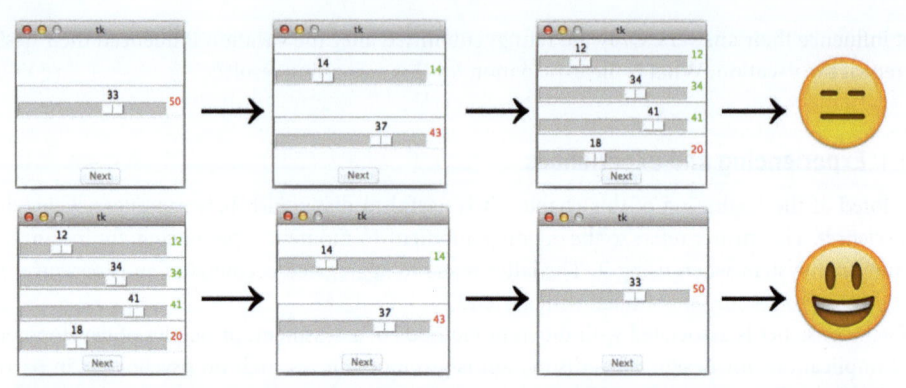

Figure 7.2 Two sequences of screenshots used in an experiment on peak–end effects [158]. Going through the three screens starting from the top row decreases satisfaction compared to starting from the bottom row.

More generally, researchers currently understand that user experiences are a result of *inference*. Experiences are created as a result of an active interpretative process that is shaped by mood, context, attention, goals, and attitudes, among other factors [202]. At any given moment, there are many facets of experience that could be used to form a view about experience. For example, you could infer it based on emotions, previous experiences, peak–end experiences, socially shared beliefs, or any combination thereof. When inferring, we form a representation of what our experience is. This inference process is largely unconscious unless we ask users to report their experiences. The inference itself can happen in at least two ways [846]. First, inference can happen as a specific-to-general inference, such as creating an overall experience from its parts. For example, users may infer how great an application is based on momentary feelings of joy or disappointment they happen to recall. Second, inference can happen via a general assessment that spills over into specific parts of an experience. For example, users can make an overall evaluation of an experience of an interactive system, which may spill over into the evaluation of its components. This is called the *halo effect*. The "halo" of the product affects the inference of its parts.

It is important to understand that this inferential process means that design does not directly determine experience. Although designers may talk about *user experience design*, experience is not literally designed. Rather, design can influence what users consider as input to this inferential process.

7.1.2 Consequences of experiences

User experiences are not without consequences. One reason is that well-being is more closely associated with experiences than with the use or ownership of products. So, rather than the interactive system itself, it is the experiences that facilitate what matters to people. For example, one study found that purchases made to provide users with an experience were valued more than those made for material possessions [841]. The researchers asked students to answer the question "How happy does thinking about it make you?" with respect to a material purchase and a life experience. Ratings were markedly different along this and other dimensions—experiences made students happier. Other papers have reported similar findings, and many researchers believe this is a key argument for why experiences are an important part of HCI [320].

Another part of the argument is that experiences are important for several high-level decisions. They include decisions to purchase a product, whether to continue using a computer system, and whether to recommend a digital service to a friend. It is not only each moment of use or the outcome that matters. Our experiences, as we summarize them to ourselves and tell them to others, are also critical. For example, Norman [603] raised an interesting riddle about the memory of things—that is, our experiences of things—instead of the actual state of the world:

> The argument starts with a simple thought experiment. Suppose in some task, using a product or getting a service from a company, you had some perfectly horrid experience along with some positive ones. Now, just suppose you had no memory of the horrid experience. Would you go back and repeat the experience? Most people would repeat something they remembered as enjoyable. Of course, the premise is suspicious: If the experience were truly that horrible, I would maintain a memory of the negative parts. Yes, but memories for bad experiences dissipate differently than those for good ones. The negative emotions associated with the bad parts fade away more quickly than the cognitive evaluation does. So although I remember the events, the emotions have dissipated. Notice the delight with which the writer of the email shared her story of the negative experience with me. Yes, the bad things were horrible. But yes, she would go back.

This is similar to the vacation example; the willingness to go back to the vacation destination is not strongly related to the actual vacation experiences. Norman's argument is that our memories and experiences are what matter in such decisions.

A third reason is that experiences provide material for sharing stories with others. Outside HCI, this aspect has been shown to be important. For example, people talk more about their experiences than their material purchases [443]. They also find more pleasure in talking about their experiences. Thus, experiences have distinct social consequences, including their potential for storytelling. This consequence is about experiences that occur to an individual. Forlizzi and Battarbee [253] suggested the term *co-experience* to capture such situations as well as situations where the experience was initially shared.

7.1.3 Processes in experience

Experiences are complex, constructed phenomena that develop over time. McCarthy and Wright [529] formulated a temporal model that combines these insights; see Table 7.1. They separated several processes that together shape experiences. The processes occur in a particular order. This account highlights that experience encompasses all parts of our mental lives. It also means that attention to experience covers moments that do not include the actual use of a system. It also covers the full spectrum of psychological phenomena around system use, including perceptions of the system, oneself, and other users.

Some processes in Table 7.1 are of particular importance. Anticipation has been shown to shape experiences, and thereby experiencing. Some researchers even defined satisfaction as the fulfillment of expectations. Most definitions in the literature emphasize that all aspects of product use are in focus, and some include the anticipated use of products and experiences based on the use situation.

As suggested by the table, experiences are also shaped well after they have happened. Reflection shapes experiences after they have happened. Isaacs et al. [374] targeted reflection head-on by developing a mobile system to support reflection by helping users capture everyday

Table 7.1 Six processes related to experiences, based on McCarthy and Wright [529].

Process	Explanation
Anticipation	Expectations for an interactive system and its use. Having an idea of how a mobile phone should feel is an example.
Connecting	The immediate response to a system, before talking about it or attempting to put it into words. The sense of spaciousness and wonder the first time one dons a virtual reality headset is an example.
Interpreting	Making sense of the experience, its structure, and valence. For instance, one might try to figure out where on a web site one has ended up.
Reflecting	This is about making judgments of the experience as a whole and figuring out why. An example is considering whether an experience has met our expectations and how that makes us feel.
Appropriating	Making an experience our own and relating it to ourselves, our history, and our planned future. For example, figuring out when and where one feels comfortable texting using a new smartwatch.
Recounting	Recalling past events for personal reminiscence or social sharing.

experiences and return to reflect on them at a later time. In a system deployment with 44 users, the researchers documented that the app supports reflection and, through that, improves psychological well-being. Finally, recounting emphasizes the role of experiences relative to other people. People share their experiences with others and derive value from that. McCarthy and Wright [529] also considered the stories we tell ourselves about interactive systems for recounting.

What might we use such a framework for? Grönvall et al. [293] were interested in how people experience a shape-changing bench. The bench was 2.5 m long with a rectangular form. It accommodates up to six people and can change shape through eight linear actuators embedded in the upholstery. The researchers wanted to use it to explore how people experience shape changes as part of their daily lives. In addition, their intention was to study how co-located strangers might interact around a shape-changing bench.

Based on the deployment of the bench in an airport, a mall, and a concert hall foyer, Grönvall et al. [293] analyzed video recordings and brief interviews with 129 users of the shape-changing bench. The results from the interviews were analyzed using the McCarthy and Wright model. Let us consider a few insights from that analysis. The anticipation process was shaped by whether the bench was viewed as an actual bench or something else. Some participants said things like "I went off right away when it began to move. I thought, oh . . . this is not for seating." Later, participants noted that as the bench moved, it impacted them not only through their senses, giving rise to "fright, to confusion, surprise, dizziness, and amusement."

Grönvall et al. [293] also found an active process that did not fit the model—*exploring*. This process consisted of trying out things to make sense of the bench. Nevertheless, the model overall helped them structure and analyze the empirical data.

7.2 Types of experience

Research on experiences in HCI started by focusing on dissatisfaction from experiences. Early work focused on avoiding errors, interface features that annoyed people, and frustrating parts of the user interface. This can be called the *deficit approach* to experiences. Conversely, later work on HCI and user experience has focused on *positive experiences*, including those of enjoyment, meaning, and stimulation.

Another feature of HCI research on experience is that experience is considered to be *multifaceted*. This means that researchers focus not only on the value of a product to accomplish tasks; they also focus on symbolic and aesthetic value. For an example of aesthetic value, see Paper Example 7.2.1.

So far, we have emphasized that experience is holistic, covering all of our momentary mental lives. How does this work with the idea that there are *types* of experience, which suggests that experiences can be reduced to a set of simpler components? We believe that it is possible and useful to distinguish types of experiences. Our rationale follows that of Göritz and colleagues [322].

> Due to experiences' highly situated, unique and inseparable character [...] they lend themselves to description, but not to any type of categorization or reduction to a set of underlying principles. [...] experiences can be described in retrospect. However, in the moment of description, they are gone and will never occur again. This actually would be the end of story for experience in HCI, because designing for bygone and unrepeatable experiences is futile. [...] although two experiences may never be alike, we may nevertheless be able to categorize them. [...] To give an example: the positive experience from arc-welding is a consequence of challenge, skills and mastery—in short: competence. This competence experience differs clearly from the experience of an "I love you" message. Here the positive experience stems from feeling related to other people and, thus, maybe thought of as relatedness experience.

Thus, experiences can be classified without disregarding or denying the fleeting and complex quality of experiencing. On this basis, a couple of classes of experiences may be distinguished. We cover those next.

Paper Example 7.2.1: Is that which is beautiful usable?

Form versus function, or beauty versus ease of use, is a classic tension in art and design. Is that which is beautiful also useful, do useful artifacts become beautiful to users, or are these concepts orthogonal? Tractinsky et al. [826] were interested in this question because it is significant for HCI—it determines which aspects of experience we should focus on.

Tractinsky and colleagues managed to turn this question into something that could be explored experimentally. They did so by creating different variations of the interface of an automatic teller machine (ATM), appearing high, medium, or low in aesthetics. Some variants of the ATM were easy to use; others were difficult to use. They expected the comparison of these variations to reveal whether form and function, or aesthetics and ease of use, are indeed unrelated. The figure below shows the ratings of perceived usability and perceived aesthetics across three levels of aesthetics and two levels of usability (square versus circle marks in the graph). Note that usability and aesthetics are both independent variables (something that is manipulated; see Chapter 43) and dependent variables (something that is measured, in this case via questionnaires).

continued

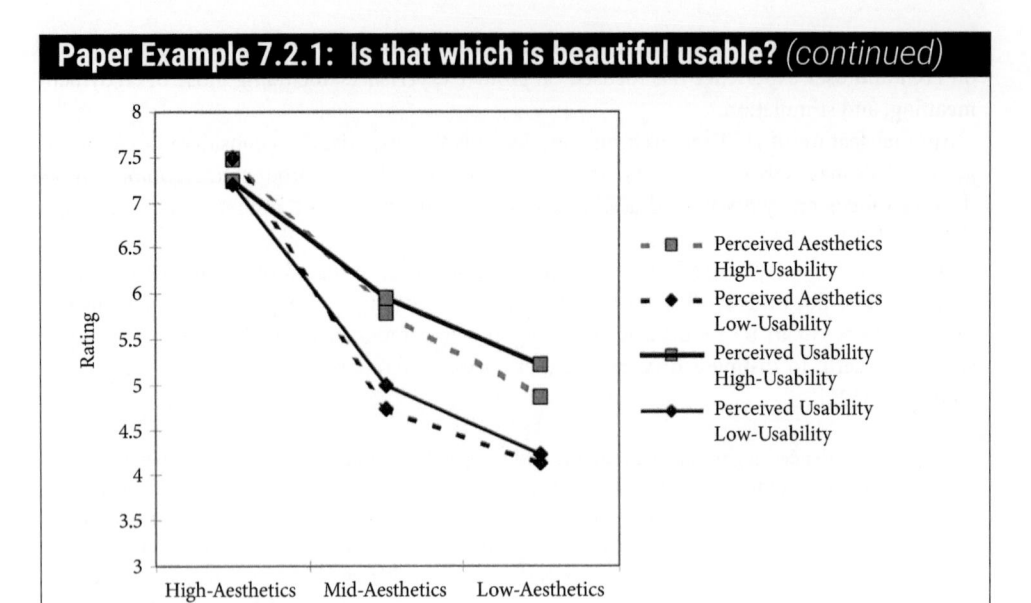

Paper Example 7.2.1: Is that which is beautiful usable? *(continued)*

[Chart showing Rating (y-axis, 3 to 8) vs. High-Aesthetics, Mid-Aesthetics, Low-Aesthetics (x-axis) with four lines: Perceived Aesthetics High-Usability, Perceived Aesthetics Low-Usability, Perceived Usability High-Usability, Perceived Usability Low-Usability]

The key insight is that while there is a difference between low and high usability (the gap between the two groups of lines), the effect of aesthetics (*x*-axis) is much larger on measures of both perceived aesthetics and perceived usability.

Initially, participants rated their perception of the aesthetics of the interface and the perceived ease of use of the ATM interface. This showed a correlation between aesthetics and ease of use. Next, participants experienced the usability of the ATM by using it to complete tasks. Surprisingly, this showed that aesthetics influenced the rating of usability *after* participants had used the system. By contrast, the actual usability of the system did not influence the ratings of usability and aesthetics. This might explain why the authors titled their paper "What is beautiful is usable." It is important to realize that this is merely a correlation, not evidence that one caused the other. Still, it indicates that some simple aspects of experience, such as the perception of aesthetics, may fundamentally impact the use of interactive computing systems.

7.2.1 The pragmatic and the hedonic

There is a saying that the journey is more important than the destination. It reflects a particular type of travel experience that emphasizes novelty, experience, and time to observe and reflect. By contrast, many trips are about getting from A to B; they are about being efficient and hassle-free. This difference is reflected in the distinction between the qualities of *pragmatic* and *hedonic*, in particular, regarding types of experience and the perception of interactive systems.

Pragmatic experiences are those that concern practical matters and the achievement of goals. When interactive systems are simple, clear, and understandable, people describe having pragmatic experiences. Such experiences are also sometimes described as utilitarian or instrumental. For most of the history of interactive systems, researchers and practitioners have considered the user's experience as a side effect of other parts of the interaction or the functionality of an interactive system. Typically, they viewed the instrumental value of the interactive system as the most important aspect, even above users' experience when using the interactive system. This is no longer the case.

a) Designer Perspective

Product Features	Intended Product Character	Consequences
Content	Pragmatic Attributes — Manipulation	Appeal
Presentation	Hedonic Attributes — Stimulation, Identification, Evocation	Pleasure
Functionality		Satisfaction
Interaction		

b) User Perspective

Product Features	Apparent Product Character	Situation / Consequences
Content	Pragmatic Attributes — Manipulation	Appeal
Presentation	Hedonic Attributes — Stimulation, Identification, Evocation	Pleasure
Functionality		Satisfaction
Interaction		

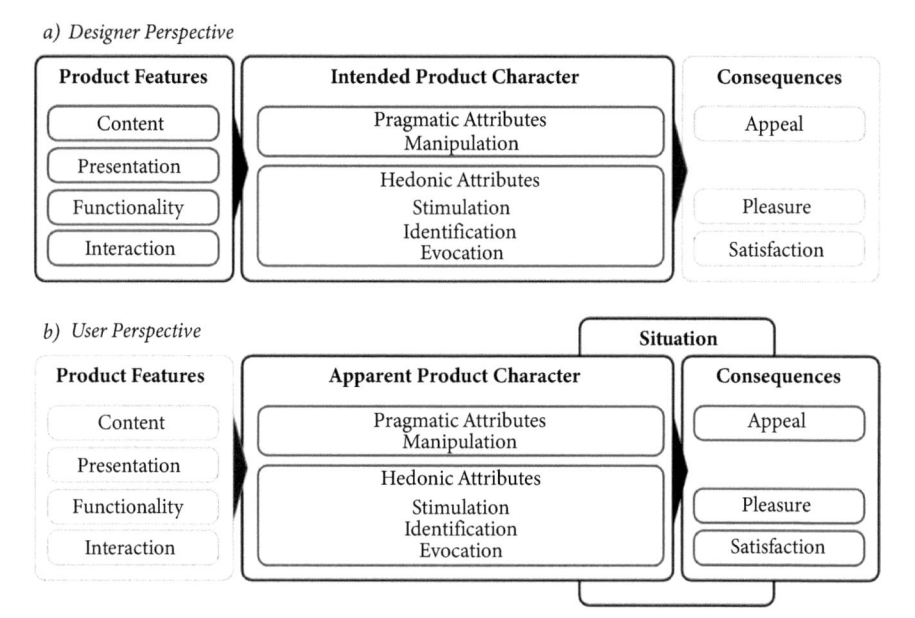

Figure 7.3 A model of user experiences by Hassenzahl [318]. The top part shows the designer's perspective: The designer controls the product features and has intentions for the product. The bottom part shows the user's perspective. The product, as it appears to the user, has certain experiential consequences when used in a particular situation.

In a general sense, the hedonic aspects of interactive systems and experiences are about stimulation, novelty, curiosity, aesthetics, and pleasure. They are not about what is being achieved, such as getting to the right destination quickly, but about the pleasure involved in getting there. In a frequently used questionnaire on the hedonic aspects of interactive systems, the AttrakDiff questionnaire, central items include stylish, professional, inventive, creative, challenging, and captivating. Examples of pragmatic qualities include simple, practical, and straightforward.

In HCI, this distinction was empirically investigated around the turn of the millennium and later turned into a model for user experience evaluation [318]. Figure 7.3 shows the model. Three key ideas emerge. First, a designer designs product features that are associated with an intended product character (top row). Whether the user sees that intended product character is another question (bottom row).

Second, among the apparent product characters, Hassenzahl separated pragmatic attributes from hedonic ones. Hedonic attributes are divided into three kinds:

- Stimulation is the extent to which interactive systems provide new impressions or opportunities, and thereby make us pay attention, feel curious, or be motivated.
- Identification is the way in which products help us express ourselves to others.
- Evocation is the extent to which a product reminds us about past events, thoughts, or relationships. Though important, this aspect has not been included in much work on the hedonic and the pragmatic.

Third, according to the model, the combined perception of hedonic and pragmatic attitudes drives the overall evaluation of a product, such as its goodness. This is a form of inference, where individuals weigh together different types of perceptions of an interactive system.

Diefenbach et al. [193] showed that across many studies that used AttrakDiff, the pragmatic and the hedonic dimensions of technology perception are correlated. They found a correlation coefficient *r* of 0.62. The coefficient quantifies the strength of the relationship between the two variables. In this case, it was unexpectedly high, suggesting that the current instruments for separating hedonic and pragmatic qualities need more work. In other words, such instruments are not discriminative enough when it comes to these qualities. Nevertheless, AttrakDiff remains a widely used instrument.

7.2.2 Pleasure

The experience of pleasure is a fundamental and positive emotion. It is related to other terms such as enjoyment, delight, and fun. For simplicity, let us consider pleasure as a sensation that is good or desirable. Although we can all name a multitude of such pleasures, would it be possible to distinguish some general types?

Jordan [395] presented an influential model of different kinds of pleasure in the context of interactive systems. He distinguished four kinds of pleasure:

- *Physio-pleasure* is the pleasure derived from the senses, such as the tactile quality of a keyboard or the smell of a car.
- *Socio-pleasure* is the pleasure that comes from our relationships with other people and groups.
- *Psycho-pleasure* is the pleasure from thinking and feeling.
- *Ideo-pleasure* is the pleasure derived from the values they embody or help us embody.

Jordan's model is handy because it lends itself to a more systematic understanding of pleasure in evaluation and design. For instance, one might design for particular types of pleasure or evaluate the pleasures an interactive system delivers by categorizing users' statements using the model above.

7.2.3 Emotions

It has been said that emotion is at the heart of any human experience [253, p. 264]. The feeling of whether something is good or bad is a fundamental evaluation that is central to our reactions to our environment, the objects in it, and the people who surround us. It is also fundamental to our experiences with interactive systems.

But what is emotion? Before answering, let us note that the study of emotion is highly complex [46]. It encompasses a host of theories that fundamentally differ in their conceptions of what emotions and related phenomena are. Some theories hold that there is a set of basic, fundamental emotions, such as anger and disgust. Other theories hold that emotions are a result of appraisal, that is, of an individual's active processing of internal and external stimuli. The mechanisms and measures of emotion that are derived from such sources differ markedly; Ekkekakis [221] provided a useful first step to understanding emotion. With that said, two approaches to understanding emotion have been prominent in HCI.

One prominent model of *core affect* separates valence and arousal [720]. The general idea of this model is that there are two fundamental dimensions:

1. Valence, which describes positive versus negative emotions. Positive emotions are energizing emotions, such as being happy or proud.
2. Arousal, which describes the level of energy involved or the degree of activation. High-arousal states are related to being alert or attentive.

These dimensions capture what is called core affect—the essence of how we feel at any moment. Core affect is not directed at anything but is a fundamental evaluative orientation. This is why the term affect, not emotion, is used in this model; emotion can be directed at something or someone. Sometimes, other dimensions are included in core affect, in particular dominance (how controlling a stimulus is).

Core affect has been used in numerous studies in HCI as a way of capturing basic aspects of emotional reactions. Gatti et al. [271] collected ratings of valence and arousal for a selection of auditory, haptic, and visual stimuli. What can such ratings be used for? One idea is to use stimuli to influence affect—for instance, we may play stimuli high in valence and arousal to influence people to feel high valence and arousal.

Another approach is to focus on changes in core affect directed toward an object or internal antecedent; somewhat confusingly, this is often referred to as an emotion. For instance, I may experience fear if a shape-changing interface moves toward me, or I may experience bliss when an odor-creating device makes me recall my childhood. Emotions in this sense are often called basic emotions; such emotions include fear, anger, surprise, disgust, happiness, and love.

Desmet [187] identified 25 positive emotions that people experience with physical and interactive products. The intention was to find emotions that are specific to such products. The emotions were identified, and it was checked whether regular users do indeed experience them with products. The list of emotions includes emotions already mentioned as well as (1) dreaminess, "To be dreamy is to enjoy a calm state of introspection and thoughtfulness," (2) pride, "The experience of an enjoyable sense of self-worth or achievement," and (3) worship, "Worship is the experience of an urge to idolize and honor someone (or something)." These emotions can, for instance, be used as design goals or to evaluate whether an interactive system supports them.

7.3 Assessing and measuring experience

Given that it is useful to know about experiences in HCI, how do we assess or measure them? When we consider our own experiences, it is immediately clear that they are highly complex and elusive; indeed, there are aspects that only we can likely ever know in their full richness. However, several methods have been developed to capture the dynamics of experience. Most methods focus on self-reports and first-person techniques. We will discuss such methods in depth in Part III; below, we just provide a sample.

We believe it is possible to capture the dimensions of experience. Being able to do so is important to develop an understanding of how people experience computers in general, as well as to evaluate the experiences with a particular interactive system (Part VIII). Thus, we also discuss commonly used measures of experience.

7.3.1 Rich reports on experiences

One method is to ask people to report their experiences. This can be through open-ended questioning, for example, in an interview session (Chapter 11). For instance, Woo and Lim [912] were interested in understanding people's experiences with using sensors and actuators to create their smart homes. To get rich accounts on this, they used semi-structured interviews.

Another approach is the *narrative method*, illustrated in the vignettes in Figure 7.1 and in Paper Example 7.3.1. Narratives are first-person accounts of events organized in the form of a story. They can describe events from a remembered perspective. As they rely on memory, narrative accounts tend to be selective and focus on the narrator's viewpoint. They can help designers empathize with another person's viewpoint. The *critical incident method* builds on narrative accounts but focuses on certain definitive types of experience. Critical incidents can be elicited by asking participants, for example, to "Bring to mind a single outstanding positive experience you have had recently with interactive technology. Please retell the experience as accurately and detailed as you remember and try to be as concrete as possible. You can use as many words as you like, so that outsiders can easily understand your experience" [831].

Finally, micro-phenomenological interviews can be used to obtain rich reports on experiences (Chapter 11). The idea is to go deep into the participants' experiences. For instance, Obrist et al. [610] were interested in understanding how particular tactile stimuli are experienced. To obtain such data, the authors first stimulated participants with different tactile stimuli and then asked them open-ended questions such as "What words would you use to describe how it felt on your hand, if at all?" This process allowed the researchers to collect rich data on the experience of the stimuli and its development over time.

Paper Example 7.3.1: The experience of a new phone

Imagine that you get a new smartphone. Obviously, you have expectations about how it will work. Once you begin using it, your view of the phone will likely develop as you discover features, bugs, and unexpected uses. What exactly do people experience with a new phone, and how do their experiences develop over time?

This is what Karapanos et al. [403] decided to study. They followed six new users of iPhones over a period of four weeks, as well as a week before the phones were purchased. After each day of use, the participants reconstructed their experiences throughout the day, writing more details about the three most impactful experiences and rating the product in general using a variant of AttrakDiff. This resulted in 482 reports on impactful experiences. For instance, one participant noted the following:

[Day 8] I had the chance to show off my iPhone to some of my colleagues. I showed them some functions that are rather difficult to operate in other phones . . . I felt good having a BETTER device. I still have some cards to show which I will in do due time to surprise them even more.

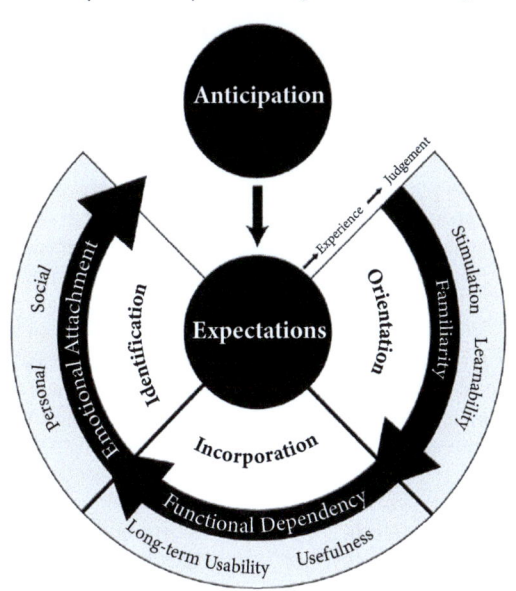

The authors used content analysis to analyze these reports and develop the model shown below.

Diagram: A circular model with "Anticipation" at top flowing down to "Expectations" in the center. Around the center are three phases — Orientation (with Stimulation, Familiarity, Learnability; and Experience → Judgement), Incorporation (with Functional Dependency, Long-term Usability, Usefulness), and Identification (with Personal, Social, Emotional Attachment).

The main point of the model is that there is a phase of orientation, where gaining familiarity is central. In that phase, the stimulation of the device as well as its learnability are central. At some point, that phase turns into a phase of incorporation into the users' lives, where they come to depend on the functionality. In turn, that develops into identification with the device, where, for instance, social aspects of the device become more important to participants.

7.3.2 Measures

An alternative way to characterize the experiences of users of interactive systems is through measures, that is, quantitative indicators of dimensions of the experience. For instance, we may measure the pragmatic aspects of a software system or the emotion toward a system. Measures of experience are important for being able to quantify and work systematically with experiences in development. They have also helped identify many of the phenomena discussed in this chapter.

These measures can be obtained in several ways. We can use rating scales that contain specific statements about experience (Chapter 13). An example related to player experiences is shown in Paper Example 7.3.2. We can also use self-reports. Following the *UX curve* method, users are given a timeline on a piece of paper (e.g., starting from day 0 when starting to use a service) and are asked to draw a curve that describes their level of experience over time. Users are then interviewed to elaborate on their experiences, the factors behind any increases or decreases, and what happened at peaks and ends [442]. This method, however, is susceptible to bias caused by the act of drawing a curve. The threat is that forcing experiences into a curve may omit and embellish memories of experiences.

Another way to obtain such measures is through repeated self-reports during use. The *experience sampling method* (ESM) originates from flow theory and is widely used in HCI. In an ESM study, users install a mobile application or use a digital beeper that notifies them when it

Table 7.2 Measures of users' experience that are often employed in HCI research and design.

Concept	Explanation	Examples of measures
Affect	Fundamental assessment of experiences in terms of their valence, arousal, and dominance.	The self-assessment mannequin requires participants to rate the valence, arousal, and dominance using drawings of themselves [92].
Enjoyment	The extent to which users experience positive emotions and pleasure.	Perceived enjoyment has been conceptualized as "the extent to which the activity of using the computer is perceived to be enjoyable in its own right, apart from any performance consequences that may be anticipated" and is measured based on this idea [181].
Aesthetics	The extent to which users experience attraction and beauty, for instance, in a user interface.	Lavie and Tractinsky [461] separated the classical aesthetics and expressive aesthetics of web sites. The former is about whether the site is clear, symmetric, and pleasant; the latter is about whether the site is creative, fascinating, and original.
Engagement	The extent to which something is attractive and draws interest.	Doherty and Doherty [203] reviewed different theories and measures for engagement.
Burden	The extent to which users experience burdens in using technology.	Suh et al. [806] developed a questionnaire that assesses users' experience of burden. The questionnaire encompasses (1) the difficulty of use, (2) physical burdens, such as physical discomfort, (3) the negative impact on time and social factors, (4) mental and emotional burdens, (5) issues about privacy, and (6) financial burdens, such as costs.

is time to provide experience reports. Such reports are most often ratings but can also be rich reports.

Table 7.2 shows a list of frequently discussed dimensions of experience and their corresponding measures synthesized from the literature [42, 653]. These dimensions show that the fun or practical aspects of experiences are not all there is. Researchers increasingly argue that the *meaning* people experience (or derive from interactive systems) is central. One way of thinking about this is ancient; it is called eudaimonia, which refers to how an experience is related to personal happiness. It is presently thought that meaning stems from events that have long-term value to the self.

Paper Example 7.3.2: Measures of the gamer experience

Computer gamers often play games for the experience of playing the games: the challenge of mastering the game, the fun of winning, the arousal of opening a loot, and so on. For the reasons discussed in this chapter, researchers studying games have been interested in asking questions about games across levels, storylines, and types of players to learn about their experiences.

Abeele et al. [2] developed and validated a method for investigating player experiences. Their idea was to discover the fundamental dimensions of such experiences and develop a questionnaire to assess them. The dimensions were discovered through discussions with experts in game user research and from evaluations of players' salient game experiences. From that work, a model comprising five functional dimensions and five psychosocial aspects was developed. These dimensions appear to be mostly unrelated, yet they are important to gaming experiences.

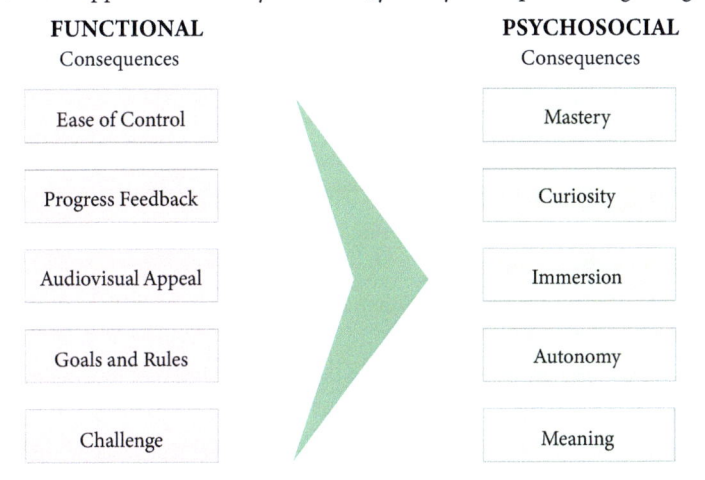

FUNCTIONAL
Consequences

- Ease of Control
- Progress Feedback
- Audiovisual Appeal
- Goals and Rules
- Challenge

PSYCHOSOCIAL
Consequences

- Mastery
- Curiosity
- Immersion
- Autonomy
- Meaning

Each dimension is assessed through three statements. For instance, for ease of control, the statements are "I thought the game was easy to control," "The actions to control the game were clear to me," and "It was easy to know how to perform actions in the game." For mastery, the statements are "I felt capable while playing the game," "I felt I was good at playing this game," and "I felt a sense of mastery playing this game."

7.4 Can experiences be designed?

Given that HCI is about developing interactive systems, you may reasonably wonder if experiences of the types we have discussed so far may be designed. For instance, would it be possible to design an interactive system that makes users feel pride? Can we design something that makes users feel happy?

One answer to this question is negative. Designers have no control over users' experiences, which are individual and idiosyncratic. In particular, for more complex experiences such as those discussed above, it is difficult to find scientific papers where such experiences are determined through changes in an interactive system. From this viewpoint, the notion of "user experience design" is a misnomer.

An alternative answer is positive. Experiences are intentionally created all the time, from dining over movies to enjoying arts. Why should HCI be different? This chapter has covered general principles and characteristics of experiences; these may be drawn upon in design. For instance, the peak–end rule suggests that we should pay particular attention to the end of experiences to achieve the impact we want. One promising direction has been to create chart designs that produce certain emotions. This helps us determine which interface design choices to make. For instance, Lim et al. [482] suggested a set of attributes to describe interactivity, one of the components of interactive systems that design can affect. The attributes included response speed (fast, slow), expectedness (expected, unexpected), and movement speed (fast, slow). In a user study, Lim et al. [482] linked such attributes to emotional qualities. For example, movements that happen sequentially, continuously, and slowly are perceived as sympathetic.

Overall, the correct answer to the question in the section heading is still being worked out. It is clear that the formation of an experience is complex and depends on the individual and what happens in interaction. While design affects that process, it does not determine it.

Summary

- Experiences are created through inference from ongoing experiencing.
- Experience is not a single monolithic thing but comprises, among other things, pragmatic and hedonic aspects.
- Affect is a special aspect of experience characterized by positive and negative dimensions—valence.
- Experiences are indirectly influenced by the designer; they cannot be directly designed.

Exercises

1. Understanding experience. Return to the three examples at the beginning of this chapter (see Figure 7.1). Pick one of the frameworks for experience types presented in this chapter (e.g., hedonic/pragmatic, core affect). Then, analyze the three narratives using that framework. What do the aspects help you notice?

2. Measuring experience. In this chapter, we discussed several ways of assessing experience through questionnaires. Find an online version of AttrakDiff, the self-assessment mannequin, the burden scale, the player experience questionnaire by Abeele et al. [2], or another one of the questionnaires. Use it to assess a user interface or web site that you use.

3. Exceptional experiences. Think about an exceptional experience you have had with computers. Try to bring to light the details of how it came about, what happened, and how it affected you later. You may write a description or narrative, in the form of a story, of the experience. Then, go through the six processes identified by McCarthy and Wright [529] and shown in Table 7.1. If nothing matches a particular process, think about why. If the processes help you think about new facets of your experience, consider why you did not initially notice those facets.

4. In 1974, the philosopher Nozick discussed the experience machine [606]. He imagined the machine to work as follows:

    > What matters other than how people's experiences feel "from the inside"? Suppose there were an experience machine that would give you any experience that you desired. Superduper neuropsychologists could stimulate your brain so that you would think and feel you were writing a great novel, or making a friend, or reading an interesting book. All the time you would be floating in a tank, with electrodes attached to your brain. Should you plug into this machine for life, preprogramming your life's experiences?

    It is possible to imagine virtual reality or brain–computer interfaces that work as described by Nozick. Answer the following questions: (a) Should we build such a machine? (b) Should we regulate the use of such a machine? (c) Would you want to plug into such a machine? (d) How does the idea of this machine relate to Norman's discussion of memory and actuality?

5. Pick a model of experience. Consider the design of a new fitness app and discuss how this model might enhance the experience of fitness. Detail at least three different ways in which the design might be shaped by the model and discuss them with others, if possible.

6. Narrative experiences. Below are a number of stories about good and bad experiences with interactive systems from Tuch et al. [831]. The participants were given the following prompt: "Bring to mind a single outstanding positive experience you have had recently with interactive technology." Your task is to sort these statements into clusters reflecting the different ways in which a system can be good. Bad systems are put in the same clusters based on what they lack or do not fulfill for the users. Name the clusters. Discuss if anything is missing. What aspects of usability and user experience are the clusters about? What aspects are not mentioned?

> When I first purchased my iPhone 4, I had problems with the use of the GPS application and Google Maps and usually had difficulty in reaching a destination on time or even reaching one at all. So one day I decided that it would be in my best interest to look into the iPhone's capabilities and see if I could rectify the situation myself. I've always been sub-par with technology and this was certainly a step up from my Blackberry that I had for a number of years. I had found out that you could pinpoint the exact location of your phone and use that as a starting point for directions. Needless to say, when I found out about this, I was ecstatic knowing that the directions I was receiving were not only accurate but also the most efficient route available. I never stopped using that feature after that day.

> I was recently able to assist a foreign student in contacting her family and boyfriend through the use of Skype on my laptop. As soon as the program was up and running, she was in touch with her family for around 30 minutes. It was very nice to know that her stay was made easier by being able to see and talk to her loved ones on Skype and it made me feel good to be able to let her do that. It was also nice to know that it didn't cost her any money. This experience made me more likely to use Skype myself, even though I don't have friends and family overseas.

> An outstanding positive experience that I had recently with my iPhone happened yesterday. My dog had a toy hanging out of his mouth and I used my camera on my iPhone to capture that image. If I had tried to grab my Nikon from the other room, I would have missed this photo. These are the types of moments that you have to capture as they happen. It's so handy to have a good camera on my phone, which is always on me.

> The specific experience I had was with Dropbox. I was working on an important document for work. And then I needed to access that document but did not have my work computer with me. But, because I had the document stored in my Dropbox, I was able to simply load Dropbox onto my home computer, have it sync, and start working on my document at home. Then, when I saved it, I didn't have to email it to myself or do anything like that—I knew that it would simply appear updated at work the next day.

> I was on the computer with my son who lives in Las Vegas, and we were Skyping for the first time. My granddaughter was born 4 days before, I wasn't able to get to Vegas to see her so we decided this was the next best thing. We turned our Skype on and there she was . . . 4 days old, he showed me all her toes and fingers, she was the prettiest thing I have ever saw. The Skype experience was great. I would never imagine in all my years we could do this and be so far away but having the feeling that I could touch her through the computer screen. We have Skyped every day for 2 weeks now. I have seen my granddaughter cry, sleep, I even watched them change her diaper and take a bottle. It was like I was right there doing it myself.

8
Collaboration

When we interact with computer systems, we frequently collaborate with other people. It is challenging to identify a complex activity that does *not*, at some point, involve other people. There are numerous systems for collaboration and communication, such as messaging services, videoconferencing, shared calendars, and so on. However, there are many challenges in designing, building, deploying, and supporting collaborative systems, and, as a consequence, many such systems have failed in the past [302]. In this chapter, we learn about what is known about people collaborating through the use of interactive technology, which is an important piece of the puzzle in realizing successful collaborative systems. It turns out that there are substantial changes in interaction depending on the particular purpose and context of a collaborative activity, as illustrated in the following three examples.

- London Underground operators have learned to collaborate without constantly announcing their actions or requesting information [326]. The practices that create this notion of shared awareness are tacit and cannot easily be taught using formal procedures and rules. Nonetheless, it is a kind of knowledge that new operators learn as apprentices in their teams.
- Workers do not "just collaborate"; they actively need to coordinate *how* they collaborate. This is called *articulation work*. Figure 8.1 shows the setup of a medical team carrying out vascular surgery. The displays are oriented so that other people in the room can see and refer to them, thus helping establish a common knowledge ground [537].
- In some computer games, such as *League of Legends*, players collaborate with strangers for less than an hour. Even in such settings, collaboration is rich and complex. For example, players exercise self-discipline to ensure that collaboration between players remains frictionless and players make conscious efforts to create a pleasant working atmosphere [431].

Collaboration is not only the act of collaborating. It also involves activities that *support* collaboration, such as planning collaborative work, being aware of other collaborators' goals and actions, and determining what to do next. These aspects give rise to an underpinning question, which we will continually investigate in this chapter: What is *special* about human–computer interaction (HCI) when it involves multiple people?

Collaboration generally involves *sharing information and objects*. For example, co-workers might need to share a document they are writing, and standard operating procedures might govern the information flows within a team. Such sharing is inevitable, particularly when work is distributed and mediated through interactive systems. Thus, understanding how such sharing takes place in collaboration and how to rethink such sharing structures to create collaborative interactive systems is central to achieving effective HCI.

Collaboration is increasingly important in modern society, and this realization has propagated to the design of interactive systems. Yet, it is only recently that computers' roles in cooperative work have been studied at a large scale. Schmidt [741] attributed the usefulness of computer systems to

Introduction to Human-Computer Interaction. Kasper Hornbæk, Per Ola Kristensson, and Antti Oulasvirta,
Oxford University Press. © Kasper Hornbæk, Per Ola Kristensson, and Antti Oulasvirta (2025).
DOI: 10.1093/oso/9780192864543.003.0008

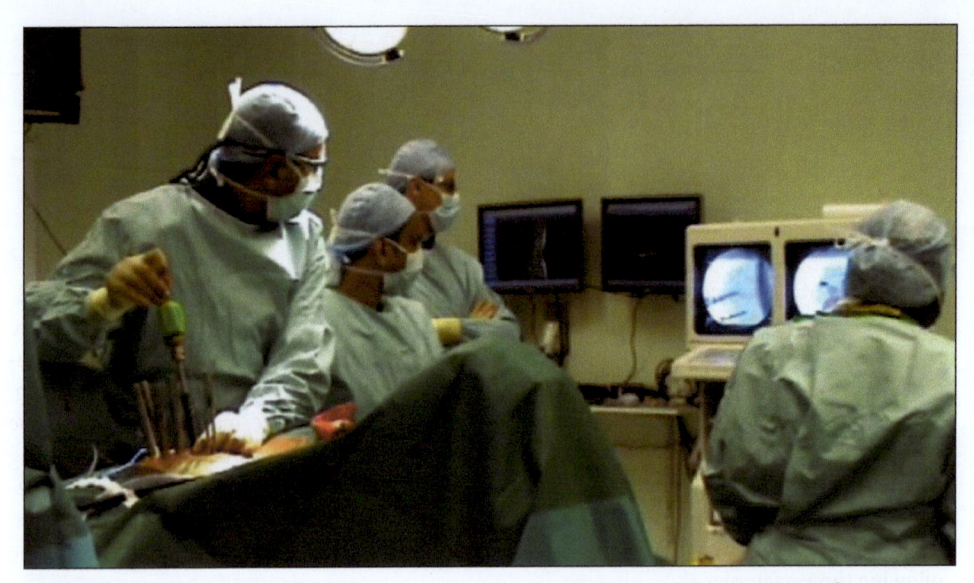

Figure 8.1 Articulation work refers to communication that helps establish conditions for collaboration. In this figure, surgeons need to ensure their displays are oriented so that others in the room can see and refer to them to maintain a common ground during the procedure [537].

their ability to allow for *horizontal coordination*. In contrast to vertical coordination, which occurs with top-down management from a higher level of an organization to a lower level, computers allow workers to coordinate work among themselves in the horizontal direction. This results in one-to-one and one-to-many communication among arbitrary subgroups within an organization.

Since collaboration is a central human activity, it is important to be aware of the many facets of collaboration and collaborative behavior to design interactive systems that allow users to collaborate to achieve their goals. Failure to do so results in systems that do not support people as they should because they induce friction when users seek natural and effective ways of collaboration. Ackerman [8, p. 179] expressed the problem of bridging this *social–technical gap* as follows:

> human activity is highly flexible, nuanced, and contextualized and that computational entities such as information sharing, roles, and social norms need to be similarly flexible, nuanced, and contextualized. However, current systems cannot fully support the social world uncovered by these findings. [...] The social–technical gap is the divide between what we know we must support socially and what we can support technically.

As a consequence, our understanding of interactive systems for collaboration has expanded and has given rise to a subfield of HCI called computer-supported cooperative work. This subfield studies "the ways in which software, developed to support groups, affects individuals and is adapted to different organizational contexts: and systems developed to support organizational goals as they act through individuals, groups, and projects" [301, p. 21]. An example of such a collaborative system is shown in Figure 8.1. In this chapter, we call such systems, and other systems that facilitate collaboration, *collaborative systems*.

Using knowledge from HCI research, it is possible to design various interactive systems that facilitate collaboration, including so-called *groupware*, which are "computer-based systems that support groups of people engaged in a common task (or goal) and that provide an interface to a shared environment" [223, p. 40].

In the rest of this chapter, we will introduce concepts and theories rooted in social sciences to understand collaboration, coordination, and common information spaces. This will serve as a knowledge foundation for building interactive systems that allow users to collaborate in desirable ways.

8.1 Understanding collaboration

As a motivation to understand the value of *some* form of collaboration, let us first consider a very simple situation that would benefit from cooperation. Game theory is a field of mathematics that studies how rational agents interact by constructing mathematical models. A well-known problem, *the prisoner's dilemma*, studies the optimal strategies of two agents, two prisoners A and B, who are investigated for a crime. Each prisoner is told that they both face two years in prison on a lesser charge unless one of them betrays their partner. The prisoner who betrays their partner receives no prison sentence, while the betrayed partner receives 10 years in prison. If both prisoners confess, they each receive five years in prison. The prisoners are held in isolation and have no means to communicate with each other or anyone else, except for the police. In addition, it is assumed the prisoners have no means of retaliation as a result of being betrayed.

In this situation, both A and B face a choice: *cooperate* with the other prisoner or *betray* them. The optimal rational choice is for each prisoner to betray their partner. This can be realized by considering the choices of prisoner A. If B cooperates, the rational choice is for A to betray B. This is because A then receives no years in prison while B receives 10 years. On the other hand, if B betrays A, the rational choice is for A to also betray B. In this case, both receive five years in prison. The alternative, to cooperate, would result in A receiving 10 years. The same reasoning holds for B.

Therefore, the rational strategy is for each prisoner to betray their partner. The dilemma is that if both prisoners cooperate, they would both receive only two years, which would be a collectively better outcome. Hence, while cooperation results in the optimal outcome for the group as a whole, this choice is irrational from the point of view of the individual prisoner. This is an example of a system that does not allow individuals to achieve the optimal outcome for the group as a whole because the system does not facilitate cooperation.

8.1.1 Collaboration and cooperation

The word *collaboration* originates from Latin: "col" means together and "laborare" means to work. Collaboration can be defined as follows [152]: "A mutually beneficial relationship between two or more parties who work toward common goals by sharing responsibility, authority, and accountability for achieving results."

By contrast, *cooperation* refers to activities where there does not need to be shared responsibility. In cooperation, a *division of labor* is in place; each person is responsible for some part of problem-solving. In cooperation, this division can be imposed onto a particular participant, so there may not be a need to negotiate or establish a division of labor during the activity. In other words, collaboration emphasizes the joint construction of goals, the development of understandings, and the division of labor.

Cooperation and collaboration often occur within the context of work. *Work* is typically cooperative—the success of work frequently depends on other people. However, work is not necessarily collaborative; in some cases, workers can be autonomous and may not need to share goals or even information. For this reason, administrators, scientists, and engineers can sometimes work relatively far from colleagues and still carry out productive work.

A defining aspect of cooperation and collaboration is the *distribution of work*. That is, different aspects of work are distributed among actors based on their contexts. The communicative actions workers take to support cooperation and collaboration in a team are jointly called articulation work. These can include anything from a digital work hour scheduling system in a hospital to materials and communicative practices.

These concepts are important because collaboration changes the focus of design. Schmidt [742, p. 4] wrote: "In order to develop computer-based system that support the articulation of cooperative work in terms of making articulation work more flexible, efficient, and effective, the very issue of how multiple users work together and coordinate and mesh their individual activities has become the focal issue."

Thus, a central question in the design of collaborative systems is how technology contributes to the organization of work.

8.1.2 Size of collaboration

There are different types of collaboration and, consequently, different collaborative systems. One key aspect of any collaboration is the size of the collaboration, which is typically divided into four different units of analysis: small groups, project organizations, organizations, and social networks.

Small groups consist of 2–20 group members. A group is a unit that perceives itself as having a shared identity, a "we." An example of small group collaboration is three people working together on a shared tabletop display. *Project organizations* can have hundreds of participants from a local or distributed group. An example is a large scientific conference, which may involve 40–80 people managing various aspects, such as paper reviewing, and a small local committee of 5–10 people who are in the same geographical location and ensure local arrangements are appropriate. *Organizations* may have tens to millions of members. Examples of such organizations are universities, government agencies, and large firms. Finally, *social networks* consist of people participating in large cooperative undertakings, such as the Wikipedia online encyclopedia project. Social networks vary in size but tend to be very large.

These units differ in the types of practices, power structures, and so on that they establish and utilize. Therefore, they tend to require different approaches, technological support, and research methods.

8.1.3 Types of collaboration

As a starting point for analysis, a model of collaborative technology is the two-axis model (see [618]), which is shown in Figure 8.2. Fundamentally, the two-axis model captures two important aspects of collaboration: *time*, that is, how people collaborate with respect to the timing of collaborative events and actions; and *space*, that is, how users are distributed in space when they collaborate.

The *synchronous–asynchronous* axis describes how close in time the collaboration is. A completely asynchronous collaborative system does not allow the sender of, say, a message to know

	Synchronous	Asynchronous
Co-located	Tabletop Group Interaction	Public Display Message Board
Remote	Videoconferencing	Email

Figure 8.2 Collaborative systems and activities can be viewed according to a two-axis model: synchronous–asynchronous and co-located–remote.

when the receiver will receive the message or whether the receiver will see the message. A completely synchronous collaborative system means that collaboration is taking place at the same time.

The *co-located–remote* axis captures where users are located with respect to each other. A collaborative system that only allows for remote collaboration means that users have to be in different locations and have no means of using local communication facilities, such as face-to-face conversations. On the other hand, a completely co-located collaborative system demands that users be present at the same location. The two-axis model is useful at a high level, as time and space considerations have a substantial impact on how people collaborate and, for example, coordinate their work. See Paper Examples 8.1.1 and 8.1.2. for examples of local collaboration. To get a feel for the two-axis model, we now discuss an example for each cell in the model.

An example of a co-located synchronous collaborative activity is a group of users collaborating by interacting via a tabletop display. Such collaboration raises unique considerations, such as how people decide to share the tabletop display among group members.

An example of an asynchronous co-located activity is a public interactive display that allows users to attach notices to other people. Another, more provocative, example is the "snatcher catcher" [498], a prototype fridge that maintains a record of which user took what food and when, thus potentially enforcing a sharing protocol among the fridge users.

A common example of a remote synchronous collaboration is videoconferencing, which enables people to have virtual meetings. However, virtual meetings and collaborative activities can also take place in a virtual world, for example, inside a game.

Finally, asynchronous remote collaboration allows people to work together from remote locations without being present at the same time. A common example is email—in fact, this is an extreme example, as the sender is not notified if and when their email is read by the recipient. Other examples are instant messaging services and chat applications, some of which inform the sender when a message is being read or has been read.

The two-axis model can be used to explore new designs. For example, Stewart et al. [795] explored single-display groupware, whereby collaboration is co-located and synchronous. The system enabled high school students to interact on the same display with multiple mice. Usability testing revealed 85% of the children felt using two mice was easier and 98% felt it was more fun. Comments revealed the children felt it enabled peer-teaching ("if [my partner was stuck and] I wanted to help there's another mouse") and increased agency ("you could do whatever you want"), as the system did not enforce collaboration.

> ### Paper Example 8.1.1: Local mobility in the workplace
>
> What do people do in the workplace? Do workers mostly sit at their desks, or do they move around? Bellotti and Bly [58] studied the movement of workers in a product design team. By observing the movement of workers, they found that they spent a considerable amount of time not at their desk, instead sharing resources, communicating, and creating possibilities for information sharing. This contributed to a greater awareness of what was going on in the organization. The schematic below shows the movement of an engineer ("Gus") in the workplace over a single four-hour morning.
>
> This distributed working style with local mobility also raised challenges. It was difficult to locate people since they kept moving around; this was especially problematic when trying to locate workers by phone. This way of working also meant that remote workers had a lack of awareness, as they were not physically present and could therefore not benefit from people walking around in the workplace. It was also observed that communication was difficult between remote workers and that most coordination activities occurred between people working near each other. Finally, coordination was in general more difficult when workers were not co-located. It was observed that while local mobility benefits local collaboration, it disadvantages remote collaboration.
>
> Based on their observations and analysis, Bellotti and Bly [58] suggested two design goals. First, replicate some of the advantages of local mobility, such as coordination and opportunities for enhancing awareness and taking part in informal communication. Second, reduce friction and make it easier for remote collaborators to communicate, coordinate, and collaborate.

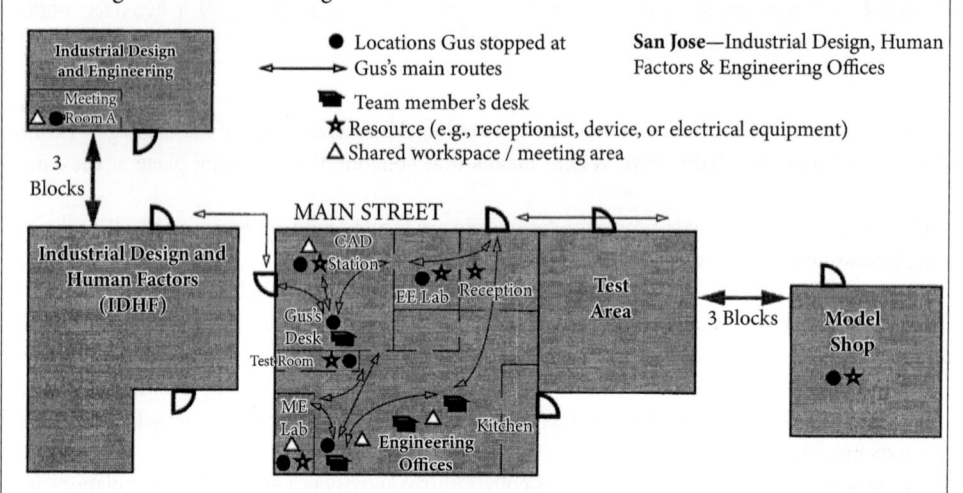

While the two-axis model is useful as a starting point, there are additional factors that govern collaborative systems. Lee and Paine [469] proposed a set of such additional factors, which we elaborate on in what follows:

Paper Example 8.1.2: Territoriality when collaborating using tabletop displays

Tabletop displays allow for new forms of collaboration. However, they also involve many design decisions, such as whether these systems should enforce ownership of digital content on the workspace or automatically reorient items, for example, by allowing users to define regions in the workspace.

Scott et al. [750] investigated users' territoriality on regular tabletops in two studies. The first study examined users who solved puzzles collaboratively in a casual setting. Among other things, the study revealed that the participants partitioned the space into three different interaction areas, which the authors called personal, group, and storage. The second study investigated users who collaborated on a furniture layout planning activity in a more controlled laboratory setting. In this study, all tabletop activity was recorded. To assist the analysis, the tabletop region was divided into 16 directional zones, as shown below in the figure to the left, and four radial zones, as illustrated to the right.

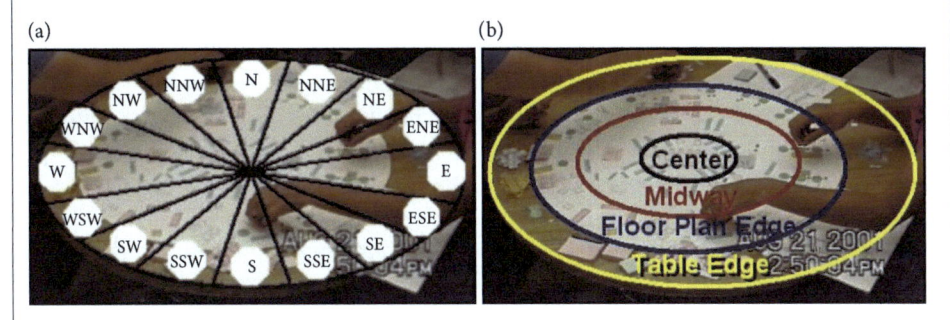

(a)　　　　　　　　　　(b)

The results indicate that users define territories on a tabletop. The personal territory enables users to reserve a certain area and a certain set of resources on a shared tabletop space for their own use. Group territories provide users with spaces to collaborate, such as solving a puzzle together. Storage territories are used to store task resources that are not currently in use, such as tools, and non-task items, such as food and drink. Knowledge of such territorial behavior facilitates the design of digital tabletops that better support users' natural collaborative instincts.

Scale: The number of participants involved in a collaboration is important: The larger the group, the more coordination is required. With up to 1,000 members in a project or organization, negotiation, grounding, and other collaborative tasks become much harder, as we will see later in this chapter. This means that different interfaces may be needed as systems suddenly have to handle more complex social arrangements and practices. What works for a small group will not necessarily work for a large organization.

Communities of practice: *Communities of practice* "are groups of people who share a concern or a passion for something they do and learn how to do it better as they interact regularly" [883]. The term refers to a concept of learning that describes how beginners learn the practices, tools, and norms of a community. A beginner assumes a role in the periphery of interaction and gradually grows increasingly competent, and thereby closer to the center of gravity in the community. Since forming a new community takes time, newcomers must be exposed to each other, taught, and mentored, which means communicative resources must be allocated for their benefit.

Nascence: The degree of coordination actions that are under development by the participants is called *nascence*. The more such actions are being discussed, the higher the nascence. Consider a bulletin board used for bureaucratically defined messages; this is a highly regulated platform with little nascence. After the initial setup of the information space, it will rarely require modifications. Now contrast this system with social media apps, which have become sites of continuous adaptation and appropriation. Their interfaces must support creative expression, different media, and other ways of matching the evolving practices of users. An important part of a designer's work becomes following such evolving practices and reacting to them by continually offering better interfaces to support them.

Planned permanence: The intended stability of a collaborative arrangement is another factor. In arrangements that are intentionally short-term, participants may be continuously negotiating collaborative practices. If they fail to establish such practices, they may struggle in their collaborative efforts. Consider a project or coursework. Because of the short-term nature of the group, the practices that are set up may fail to support healthy group functioning, say, the safe expression of differing opinions, which may hamper the group's effort.

Turnover: The stability of a group of participants is called *turnover*. For example, in events attended by a large number of people, such as a scientific conference, participants frequently enter and leave rooms, which provides a barrier to the disclosure of private information. Moreover, overhead may increase as practices need to be communicated frequently. Imagine having to manage a continuously changing crowd versus managing a stable team; the challenges would likely be very different.

8.1.4 Collaborative tasks

Just as there is no single interaction task, there is no single collaborative task. Research on collaborative systems always starts by trying to understand what is being done. In the case of collaboration, this understanding is very different from the individual-centric interaction that we have focused on so far in this book.

McGrath [531] provided a comprehensive and well-known typology for group tasks. The typology has two primary dimensions: *conflict–cooperation* and *conceptual–behavioral*. The conflict–cooperation axis distinguishes between tasks where members have conflicting interests and tasks where the interests are shared. The conceptual–behavioral dimension distinguishes between tasks where thoughts and beliefs, which are conceptual, dominate versus tasks where action dominates.

The typology is further divided into four quadrants:

Quadrant I—Generate: This quadrant contains tasks where ideas and plans are generated for cooperation.

Quadrant II—Negotiate: This is the quadrant where conflicts are resolved.

Quadrant III—Choose: This quadrant shows tasks where an option is to be chosen from a set of options.

Quadrant IV—Execute: This quadrant contains tasks related to executing tasks and resolving conflicts of power.

Creativity tasks require participants to generate novel ideas. The defining characteristics of the result are its novelty and informativeness. In this context, brainstorming is commonly studied as a collaborative activity for supporting creativity.

Planning tasks involve the formulation of a plan to reach some desired state in some environment. The goal is to produce a plan that meets the stated criteria, such as achieving the target outcomes.

Decision-making tasks involve choosing a desirable alternative among multiple options. In decision-making tasks, people may need to consider multiple attributes, uncertainty, and even conflicting interests.

Conflict resolution tasks seek acceptable compromises among members with conflicting interests. The goal is to resolve an existing policy or conflict. The former involves understanding how to act and the latter how to think.

Performance tasks are tasks carried out in light of some objective or standard. The goal here can be to meet a stated goal, excel at something, or win.

To support collaboration by design, the first challenge is to recognize the type of task at hand. The kind of support that, say, a decision-making task requires is very different from the support needed in a performance task.

8.1.5 Group interactions

The way a group functions is affected by a number of factors, some external and some internal to the group. McGrath [531] proposed a model of group interactions that outlines the main classes of factors and their interrelationships. Some of these factors are latent—they are not directly visible in apparent actions. Consider, for example, the effect of personality or power structures. Complicating this further is the fact that many factors interact with other factors. Consider, for example, the case where a group has learned a particular way of acting that does not work in a new setting.

The model by McGrath [531] outlines five main classes of factors:

Task: Group members perform together to complete something. The objectives, constraints, and other properties of the task affect the behavioral patterns and interactions that emerge. The typology of tasks introduced by the group circumplex earlier in this chapter is helpful here.

Environment: Action takes place in some context, with particular resources, constraints, and so on.

Individual attributes: The group members' individual properties, such as their personality traits, beliefs, and so on, affect the group's interactions, behavioral patterns, and structure.

Group structure and relations: This refers to facilitatory and impeding factors governing interrelationships among group members, such as affection, power, and so on.

Behavioral patterns: Constructs that shape the expected or routine way of interaction are called *behavioral patterns*. Examples of such patterns are the assumed roles and divisions of labor within a group.

Consider a hypothetical case of a distributed software team. This team is using email to decide between features for a product update. How might the factors that govern group interactions manifest in this context?

First, assuming that some options for features are already known, the task would be a decision-making task. The challenge in this type of task is to understand the value of various options and compare them in light of some set of objectives. It may be then expected that some of the group's exchanges relate to defining the objectives and what makes a feature desirable for this update. One can also expect exchanges about the options and their perceived positive and negative qualities. Second, the environment consists of the email clients, the organizational practices, and the artifacts. The environment is open-ended since anything on the Internet can be used to achieve the task. Third, the researchers would look at the individual properties of the team—introverts and extroverts, skeptics, promoters, and so on. Fourth, group relations can affect those who feel responsible for taking initiative or giving orders to others. Fifth, the group may have established patterns for how software updates are managed; for example, a particular member may initiate discussions while another member may step into a particular role.

8.1.6 Communication acts

Interactions within a team, especially when we talk about computer-mediated collaboration, are *communication acts*. They can be one-to-one, such as when member A communicates with member B. They can also be one-to-many, such as when member C communicates with members A and B.

Communications can be about tasks; for example, they can be about choices, negotiations, or preferences. However, in group interactions, task-focused messaging may be insufficient. In such cases, the group's process itself needs to be organized so that the group can function efficiently. To this end, communication acts may have *interpersonal purposes*. This means that these acts may seek to attract or convince another member about one's competence. They may also attempt to directly influence the group's process, for example, by dividing up labor or by establishing a specific process or form for collaboration.

The effective performance of a group boils down to communication acts that establish the task and the processes that the group should follow. What we observe as functional or dysfunctional group performance is the result of such efforts.

McGrath [531] identified three problems that affect a group's performance: (1) establishing a consensus on underlying values and goals; (2) ensuring or developing resources and abilities to achieve those goals; and (3) developing norms to guide the group's work.

8.2 Coordination

Coordination refers to the "construction and maintenance of a shared conception of a problem" [708]. Everybody knows mechanisms for coordination outside HCI. Sharing a project plan, glancing at what fellow puzzle players do, shouting to a biking friend to slow down—these are all examples of coordination.

However, why do we need to coordinate? One answer is due to the dependencies of different tasks we wish to carry out. A user working on one task might require the results from another task, which is being handled by another user. Another—somewhat related—answer is that these task dependencies are not static, that is, they tend to change. If a task dependency changes, the people affected by the change need to be informed in some way.

So, how do users coordinate? One answer is through artifacts [744, p. 162]:

> Artifacts have been in use for coordination purposes in cooperative settings for centuries, of course—in the form of time tables, checklists, routing schemes, catalogues, classification schemes for large repositories, and so on. Now, given the infinite versatility of computer systems, it is our contention that such artifacts in the form of computational coordination mechanisms can provide a degree of perspicuity and flexibility to artifactually supported articulation work that was unthinkable with previous technologies, typically based on inscriptions on paper or cardboard.

Another coordination mechanism is a *protocol*. Protocols define socially dictated distributions and constraints, such as a checklist that tells a pilot and a co-pilot who does what and in what order. However, these protocols are frequently not prescriptive. This means that after users have learned the protocols, they tend to deviate from them when they have reasons to do so.

8.2.1 Articulation work

An important finding in HCI is that one cannot "just" work. The concept of *articulation work* describes activities that are extraneous to the work itself. From a productivity perspective, it is *additional work*. However, this is a simplistic view.

Articulation work is about getting things done in a way that is situationally more appropriate. Its purpose is to help us define and continue the work with others. Articulation work is about deciding how tasks are carried out, for example, how tasks are scheduled, divided, managed, aligned, and organized into larger clusters.

Even a strong organizational procedure does not predetermine the way work actually happens. Work emerges through articulation work among members of a group. Articulation work is required to decide how the work is carried out. In practice, this means that articulation work refers to tasks that mediate interactions among individuals during work. It influences task allocation, task scheduling, and work practices—in essence, how the work is carried out.

As an example, Nardi et al. [578] used the term *outeraction* for instant messaging that aims to create the conditions for social exchanges with others in the workplace: "Outeraction is a set of communicative processes outside of information exchange, in which people reach out to others in patently social ways to enable information exchange" [578, p. 79]. While instant messaging is normally considered a channel for quick clarification of questions about ongoing work and a way to keep in touch with friends and colleagues, it is also used to set conditions for collaboration at work. For example, workers used it to see who is available for communication [578, p. 83]:

> First thing this morning I opened it up [the buddy list] and looked to see who was online. My boss was online and I saw that people in Commerce were online. Other designers were online and I knew that there was a certain person that I wanted to contact and she wasn't there so I knew that I could check later.

Sometimes, workers also used instant messaging to "probe" other users. For example, "Suzi?" was a message that, when answered to, almost formed an attentional contract: For some period after sending the response, the respondent would be available for messaging. Workers also used instant messaging to move some conversations to other media that might be more suitable for communication.

Articulation work is important not only in teams but also in multi-site distributed work. For example, Neang et al. [583] reported on articulation work among data scientists. They interviewed 43 ocean science researchers in 22 laboratories in three countries and discovered that open science does not simply mean that a dataset is released to others in a "dead drop." Data scientists do not only provide a dataset for others to use, waiting for others to obtain and use it. Instead, they work with other groups to define if and how other people's datasets can be transferred, and what the benefits would be. Such conversations bring together those who collect datasets and those who use them to, for example, build computational models. Researchers engage in discussions on how datasets can be used across sites using different software and following different practices.

Awareness of articulation work is important in HCI since the design of an information space for work is not only about supporting the work itself but also about enabling the articulations needed to make such work possible. HCI research can support the design of the interface required to facilitate the articulations that make work possible.

8.2.2 Awareness

A collaborator's ability to follow what others are doing, how their subtasks are progressing, and what they attend to is called *awareness*. Maintaining awareness is easy when others are co-located or next to you. However, when collaboration is distributed in time and space, maintaining such awareness is more challenging. When awareness breaks down, the coordination of work becomes hard and prone to errors, and even conflicts.

Awareness systems are interactive systems that sense and mediate *cues* about distant collaborators [211]. For example, an awareness system may show a live video stream from a remote office, or it could be implemented as a small symbol on a user interface that indicates when a particular worker is at their desk.

Awareness systems help collaborators coordinate their work. Simply knowing where a person is becomes an indication of what can be done with that person. Awareness systems, and articulation work in general, can also help psychological functions unrelated to work, such as those about friendship, emotional support, and so on. These awareness systems can have a surprisingly strong effect on the coherence and performance of a group.

8.2.3 Boundary objects

Another prominent way of understanding the sharing of information and artifacts is through the concept of *boundary objects*. A boundary object is an object that is shared among collaborators and helps them coordinate and share information. Consider, for example, a map that is shared in a dispatch center. Good boundary objects are hard to design. Star [792] wrote:

> both plastic enough to adapt to local needs and constraints of the various parties employing them, yet robust enough to maintain a common identity across sites. They are weakly structured in common use, and become strongly structured in individual site-use. Like a blackboard, a boundary object "sits in the middle" of a group of actors with divergent points of view.

8.3 Group cognition

The process of learning and negotiating a shared representation of a problem is known as *group cognition* [791]. Research on group cognition comes from studies of small-group learning and ideation. A central tenet is that shared knowledge is constructed in a process of mutual learning and negotiation. The diverse views of members are learned, and a joint understanding is established via reciprocal action. Compared to the theories discussed so far, it provides an alternative view of collaboration. It emphasizes the formation of joint beliefs, or common ground, as a central aspect for a group to function. Paper Example 8.3.1 presents an example of an online system designed to facilitate group functioning.

Group cognition emphasizes that the key is mutuality: Members construct not only their own interpretations but also interpretations of each other's beliefs. Assuming that all members engage in learning and negotiation, all members are deemed legitimate partners in the collaboration. This can improve the experience of ownership over a joint activity. Achieving group cognition may require participants with very different viewpoints to consider new understandings that challenge their beliefs. This may be difficult to support through computer-mediated activities.

Paper Example 8.3.1: Do online juries work?

A jury is a common means for making decisions in judicial systems, and many jury decisions are reached through an online jury. However, a jury must be consistent to be effective. That is, it has to make similar decisions in cases that share similar characteristics.

Hu et al. [361] studied whether online juries make repeatable, consistent decisions in an online experiment involving 1,121 workers on the online crowdsourcing platform Amazon Mechanical Turk. The research question was whether individuals or groups make consistent decisions.

The participants were presented with a case and jury instructions and asked to deliberate via an online chat system, as shown in the figure below.

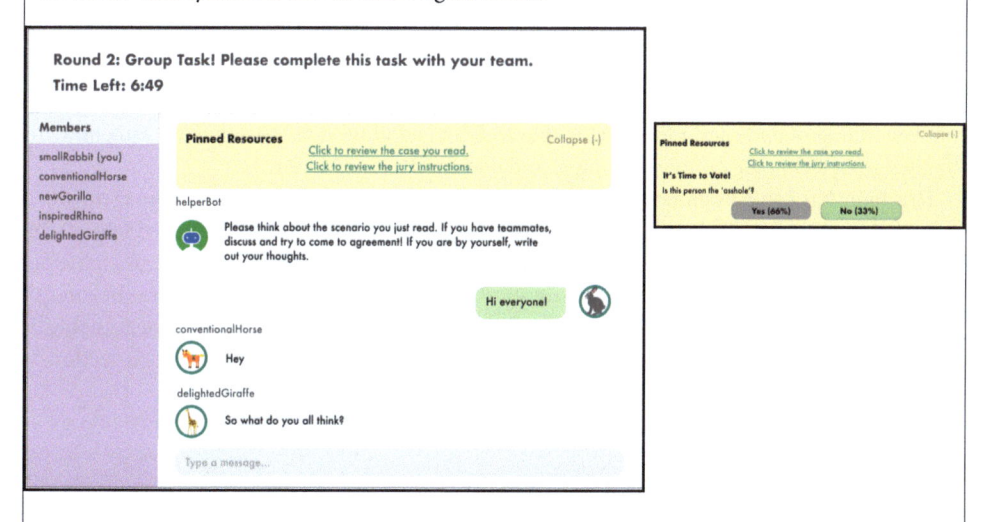

Hu et al. [361] used a within-participants design to answer their research question. Each participant participated in four jury deliberations. In the first deliberation, participants deliberated as part of a group, as shown in the figure above. Then, there were two successive deliberations where the individual juror considered a case on their own. Finally, each participant was part of

continued

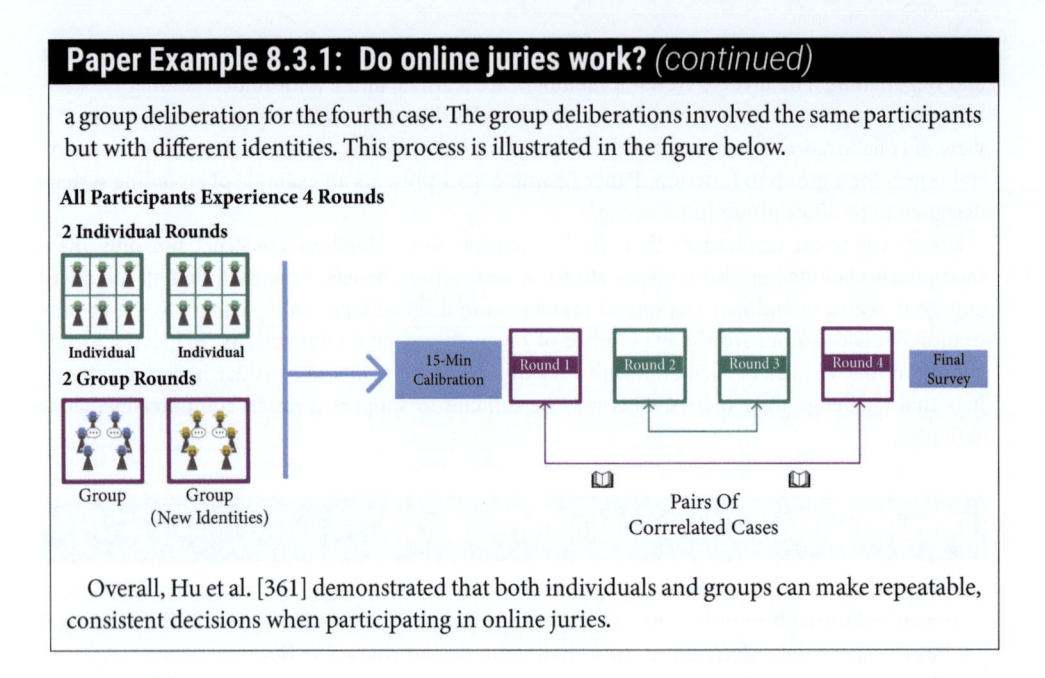

> **Paper Example 8.3.1: Do online juries work?** *(continued)*
>
> a group deliberation for the fourth case. The group deliberations involved the same participants but with different identities. This process is illustrated in the figure below.
>
> **All Participants Experience 4 Rounds**
> **2 Individual Rounds**
>
> Individual — Individual
>
> **2 Group Rounds**
>
> Group — Group (New Identities)
>
> 15-Min Calibration → Round 1 → Round 2 → Round 3 → Round 4 → Final Survey
>
> Pairs Of Corrrelated Cases
>
> Overall, Hu et al. [361] demonstrated that both individuals and groups can make repeatable, consistent decisions when participating in online juries.

8.3.1 Intersubjectivity

Consider the following situation. You and two friends are messaging about evening plans, discussing where to go. One of you suggests going "to the usual place" and the rest of you agree with thumbs up. The amazing brevity of this interaction was possible because of co-participated shared knowledge—all members of the group know what "the usual place" is and why it is a good choice.

Now, consider what would change if one of the three members of the group were an outsider. How much more effort would have been required to achieve the same outcome? This example illustrates an important point for HCI: Collaboration is impossible unless there is some shared understanding of ends and means. This shared understanding must be achieved somehow, and the design of technology provides context and constraints to achieve it.

This topic has gained significant attention in philosophy, social sciences, and management sciences, where this type of shared understanding is called *intersubjectivity*. More precisely, it refers to how two or more individuals interrelate, that is, how they understand each other with the purpose of acting together. For design, the implication is that the target of design lies beyond the interface itself. A question a designer must ask is not which features or contents are available but how those features affect the joint construction of intersubjectivity. In the rest of this section, we examine different activities involving intersubjectivity.

8.3.2 Grounding

Grounding refers to the active creation of shared knowledge related to a collaboration. Grounding is one mechanism for establishing intersubjectivity. A participant does something in order to update the knowledge of another participant. Grounding has a more prominent role in smaller collaborations. Grounding can help express, for example:

Objectives: What needs to be done

Focus of attention: What is being done

Beliefs: Beliefs about the task or the environment.

Two types of grounding can be distinguished based on modality. First, in *embodied grounding*, bodies are used for grounding. One way to achieve this is through *indexical gestures*, which are gestures that specify an object of interest for the partner. For example, pointing or looking at an object can index it. A lecturer may move the cursor on the display during a slideshow to index an object while delivering a talk. The flick of the cursor on top of an element reduces the ambiguity about what the talk refers to. Second, *linguistic grounding* achieves the same purpose through the use of language. For instance, a participant can directly state what others should think or believe.

As an example, in a study of information sharing in an emergency department [644], a registration associate (RA2) encounters two patient records for the same patient. This ambiguity must be resolved in some way. RA2 asks EM2, a member of a medical service team, for help. EM2 suggests that the patient was treated at another hospital, which RA2 then confirms using an information system [644, p. 325]:

> RA2, a registration associate, is registering a patient and finds that the patient has two different medical record numbers, one that she found in Eclipsys and the other provided by the patient. RA2 is looking in Eclipsys, trying to figure out which one is correct. The EMS member, EM2, who brought in the patient, is standing next to her. RA2 asks EM2 whether he knows why the patient has two different medical record numbers.
> EM2: "Is that because she went to [another hospital] for a while?"
> RA2 (looks through Eclipsys): "Ah, I found it. It seems she hasn't come to us in a while. What is the address you picked her up at?"
> EM2 tells her where he picked up the patient. RA uses the address information to verify that she has the correct record number and makes a note of it in Eclypsis.

So far, we have discussed grounding as a one-way activity—a kind of declaration to co-present to other members of a group. However, what if the other group members fail to notice a grounding? This can, and does, happen. It may, for example, occur due to users being unable to perceive it or due to a misunderstanding of the grounding act. This is why participants often need to verify whether the grounding was successful. This can be achieved by directly asking people. However, more frequently, there are cues such as "hmm" or nodding that help infer reception. In more experienced teams, collaborative practices have developed to offer a "receipt." In social media, this can be a thumbs-up emoji or simply a "k."

An intriguing trade-off has been noted in grounding behavior. A participant can choose to invest effort into being very clear, thereby preventing having to put effort into addressing misunderstandings. However, there is also another possibility. The participant can choose to be sloppy in the initial act and then be ready to engage in repair efforts. *Least effort* groundings are specific and simple responses; conversational agents may use such tactics to balance this trade-off. If an actor misunderstands an utterance, they may need to ask for more information to support grounding. If this happens frequently, such requests should be made as brief as possible to avoid encumbering the user.

8.3.3 Theory of mind

In the Sally–Anne experiments, a young child sees an adult insert an object into one of two drawers. After the adult leaves the room, another adult takes the object and puts it into the other drawer while the child is watching. The first adult then returns, and the child is asked which drawer they should open to retrieve the object.

The problem may appear trivial, but it is not. The ability to attribute mental states and infer their content is called *theory of mind*. It develops relatively late in humans. Knowing what the collaborator knows is important for predicting what a collaborator may do. Another aspect of the theory of mind is the awareness of one's beliefs and their relevance to the collaboration. If you know that the other partner may have a different belief than you, you may invest effort into communicating or harmonizing that understanding.

Theory of mind is also an aspect of human collaboration that computers struggle with. At times, people may expect capabilities from computers that they do not possess, especially if the computer appears human-like. Although a computer can receive an explicit command from the user, there are presently no methods that allow computers to infer what the user may be thinking or believing. This makes collaboration more effortful. In the absence of this capability, interfaces must resort to handcrafted rules to ask for confirmations, such as "Are you sure you want to do this?" If computers had a theory of mind, this might not be needed.

Some recent research on artificial intelligence has looked at the possibility of a theory of mind in computers. Researchers have found that in cases where the human's beliefs can be easily inferred, this can be exploited to improve recommendations. Interestingly, if the user knows this, this capability can be exploited. Theory of mind thus relaxes communication requirements.

8.4 Why collaborative systems fail

Understanding collaboration is important in HCI to design successful *collaborative systems*, such as messaging services, videoconferencing systems, and shared calendars. The terminology for such systems varies. In the past, such systems were often called *groupware* or *computer-supported cooperative work applications*.

Early research on collaborative systems focused on understanding *why* such systems failed. One review [302] lists eight challenges emerging from detailed investigations of failed collaborative systems:

Disparity between work and benefit: Users have their own experiences, preferences, and goals. To maximize the uptake of collaborative systems, all users should benefit from the uptake, though not necessarily to the same extent. However, collaborative systems tend to not provide the same benefits to all members of a group, nor do they tend to require the same amount of work from all members. Such disparities can limit the uptake of such systems. This is problematic, as collaborative systems tend to only be successful if a critical mass of users chooses to use them.

Critical mass and the prisoner's dilemma: For collaborative software to provide benefits to group members, it needs to be used by many, possibly all, members of a group. Moreover, some systems can induce situations where pursuing personal benefits leaves all members, and the group as a whole, worse off. This is analogous to the problem in game theory known as *the prisoner's dilemma*, which we discussed at the beginning of this chapter.

Disruption of social processes: Collaborative systems sometimes promote activities that clash with social, political, and motivational factors. Outside of collaborative systems, such factors may be implicit, changing, or depending on subtle negotiations. For example, a joint calendar system may suggest meeting times that appear to be unscheduled among participants. However, the absence of a calendar entry does not necessarily mean that the time is available. As another example, a joint decision-making system that records each user's position may be deemed politically unacceptable, as having a record of individuals' opposing opinions at a given time may be used against those users at a later time.

Exception handling: Grudin [302] noted that work processes can be thought of as being either (1) the way things are *supposed* to work or (2) the way they *do* work. In reality, users engage in a range of activities, *exception handling*, to make things work when the supposed work processes are not fit for purpose. When collaborative systems assume work is solely organized as how things should work, the systems inevitably fail to accommodate contingencies, improvisations, and odd cases that characterize established work practices. This lack of support for how work is actually carried out can lead to systems not being used.

Infrequently used features: In practice, individual work is frequent, and most organizations try to minimize communication and communication overhead to enable workers to more efficiently complete their tasks. As a consequence, collaborative systems that overemphasize collaboration frequently cause individual tasks to be harder to accomplish. Infrequently used features in collaborative systems should therefore not obstruct frequently used features that workers require to carry out their individual work effectively.

Difficulty of evaluation: Evaluating collaborative systems is more difficult than evaluating typical single-user systems. First, the benefits that a collaborative system brings are difficult to measure. Which metric can you put in place to demonstrate to managers that System A is better than System B? Second, lab studies cannot capture organizational complexities, which means collaborative systems have to be evaluated when they are deployed into organizations. Third, the evaluation of collaborative systems is likely to take time, as substantial benefits may only materialize after extensive usage. Fourth, collaborative systems typically have to be evaluated with imprecise qualitative methods that require expertise to be applied effectively. Fifth, it is difficult to generalize the results since some groups of users may find ways to use a flawed collaborative system while other groups may struggle with a poorly installed but otherwise excellent collaborative system. All these factors make it difficult for designers and researchers of collaborative systems to learn from users' experiences.

Failure of intuition: Users rarely have a full picture of the systemic effects of a collaborative system, yet they can form strong opinions based on their individual experiences and expectations. While intuition may sometimes serve as a guide in single-user applications, it fails when there is a need to anticipate the effects of extra work required by people, which will likely result in resistance and neglect.

Adoption process: Collaborative systems are complex, and when they are introduced, they require the proper training of workers and technical support to achieve widespread adoption. Furthermore, the different stakeholders affected by the collaborative system should be engaged as active stakeholders in the process of designing and installing the system to motivate workers and encourage a sense of ownership of the system.

These eight challenges make it clear that there are substantial difficulties to overcome in designing successful collaborative systems. They also highlight that the key to a successful outcome is understanding how people choose to collaborate, coordinate, and communicate as a group of users.

Summary

- Collaboration is a mutually beneficial relationship between two or more parties who work toward common goals by sharing responsibility, authority, and accountability for achieving results.
- The central challenge in supporting collaboration with interactive systems is that they are rigid, scripted, and rule-abiding while social activity is flexible, improvisational, and negotiated.
- Articulation work refers to activities that are extraneous to the work itself and are necessary to get things done in a way that is situationally appropriate.
- The process of learning and negotiating a shared representation of a problem is known as group cognition. Intersubjectivity is a shared understanding between group members. Grounding and theory of mind are two mechanisms for achieving intersubjectivity.

Exercises

1. Social gap. Ackerman [8] described the social gap as the gap between what we can support technically in current systems and what human activity requires [p. 8]. Choose a specific activity that interests you, such as participating in an online forum, playing a computer game with other people, or co-authoring using a collaborative document editor. Describe the social gap between this activity and the technology platform that you are using.
2. The matrix model of collaboration. Consider four collaborative activities in which you are participating using some form of collaborative system. Map these four activities to the synchronous–asynchronous, co-located–remote matrix model. Now, describe how the nature of these activities would change if they were moved to another location in the matrix. Would users still be able to achieve their goals? What issues would arise, and how could they be resolved?
3. Analyzing collaborations. Use the factors suggested by Lee and Paine [469] to describe the following collaborative activities: (a) volunteer editors determining editing policies for Wikipedia; (b) experienced employees and new hires in a small firm who are using a shared spreadsheet to calculate a budget for a business proposal; and (c) online learners working on a joint lab report.
4. Why collaborative systems fail. The eight challenges explaining why collaborative systems fail [302] were published in 1994. Since then, many collaborative systems have been deployed, some of which are widely used. Reflecting on the systems you use, which of the eight challenges is the most relevant? Have any of these eight challenges been fully addressed by now?

9
Communication

Communication technology is a strong candidate for the most influential technology in human history. The communication technologies that we use today started as disruptions and gradually became woven into the fabric of our daily lives. Email, social media, videoconferencing, and instant messaging have transformed the ways we work, learn, plan, stay in touch with others, and even lead our romantic lives. It is remarkable how diverse these technologies are. Instant messaging is an asynchronous one-to-one texting channel. Email is an asynchronous texting channel with a small, definite audience size. Video conferencing, by contrast, is a multimodal synchronous channel. Social media is a multimodal, many-to-many asynchronous channel. Each of these channels has numerous variants.

The field of *computer-mediated communication*, or CMC for short, employs a variety of methodologies and theories to understand what is special about communication when it is mediated by technology. CMC aims to answer the following questions: When conversation partners are unable to experience each other in the "usual" way, in person, what happens to communication and, in the longer term, to our social relationships? To answer this question, researchers use log analysis and large-scale surveys to chart what people do online and why. They interview users, record conversations, and perform controlled experiments to study how social relationships develop.

Figure 9.1 In CMC, many things are different from unmediated communication: the modalities we use for communication, how conversations are structured, the synchronicity of communication, how other people are presented, and so on. Such differences affect the content, style, and consequences of communication. Picture by Santeri Viinamäki, shared under CC BY-SA 4.0.

Introduction to Human-Computer Interaction. Kasper Hornbæk, Per Ola Kristensson, and Antti Oulasvirta,
Oxford University Press. © Kasper Hornbæk, Per Ola Kristensson, and Antti Oulasvirta (2025).
DOI: 10.1093/oso/9780192864543.003.0009

Although most of us use communication technologies, our intuitions may not reflect the general tendencies or reasons behind our behaviors. When communication acts are digital, they can be separated in time and space in surprising ways and adopt formats that would not occur in face-to-face interactions. Many things change, from how conversations are structured to how people are presented to each other (Figure 9.1). This means that lay expectations may simply not hold. Indeed, research on CMC has led to some surprising findings.

- In 1985, Kiesler et al. [414] compared how people communicate in face-to-face exchanges when they are in separate locations and when they write text to each other on a computer. They anticipated that participants in the computer-based setting would communicate more freely than those in the face-to-face setting. To investigate this hypothesis, they counted the times the participants wrote something impolite, how often they swore, and how much they flirted. The CMC channel led to more uninhibited communication. Although we now know about trolling and flaming on social media, the result was surprising in 1985 and foreshadowed the phenomena we are now familiar with.
- Bos et al. [89] studied whether the trust formed through communication with others is affected by the type of communication technology used. This was studied using a social dilemma game. Participants could invest tokens as individuals or as a group. If the players invested as a group, the reward was greater. They played the game while communicating face-to-face or via video, audio, or text. The authors found that the text chat led to the worst performance in terms of investment, while the video and audio channels were almost as good as face-to-face communication. Still, the video and audio channels took longer for full trust to build and were more vulnerable to opportunistic behavior. To explain this, we need to understand how the cues allowed by a channel affect the formation of trust.
- In virtual reality, people may experience that a virtual body feels like their own. When the virtual body moves in synchronicity with the real body, such body ownership may be felt strongly. Embodying a virtual body that speaks makes participants misattribute the speaking to themselves and, surprisingly, shifts the fundamental frequency of their voice when they subsequently speak [38]. Therefore, body ownership can fundamentally affect communication.

The results of research on CMC have helped develop new systems to facilitate communication; see Figure 9.2.

In the next section, we start our look at communication by contrasting face-to-face conversations with how we might communicate through interactive systems. The main lesson there is that CMC is fundamentally different in many aspects of communication. We then dive into the structure of conversations, which is key to understanding how to mimic or replace conversations in interactive systems. Communication may not take place only between two persons. Thus, we look at distributed groups and networks of people communicating synchronously or asynchronously, with SNSs as a prime example. Here, the focus shifts from individual acts of communication (e.g., messaging) to the formation and maintenance of social relationships. This changes communication and is related to collaboration (Chapter 8). Finally, the computer itself can be thought of as a conversation partner. Recent advances in AI have made it possible to converse with artificial agents, such as intelligent agents. We have intelligent assistants at home and in our cars with whom we can talk. The question is not whether they are special as communication partners, but in what ways.

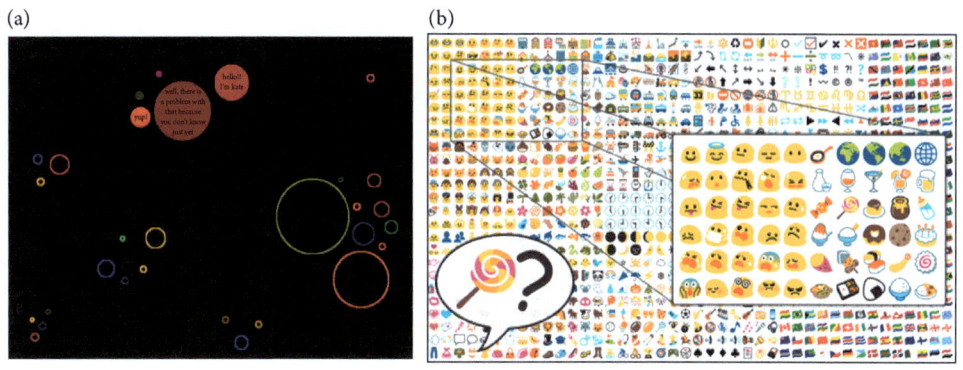

Figure 9.2 HCI studies interfaces and systems for human–human communication. The left figure shows the Chat Circles interface [852]. Rather than the typical list of messages ordered by time, users and their chat messages are shown as colored circles. The circles fade out over time and can be moved around the display, allowing the user to read them. The right figure shows an interface for picking emojis [667]. Emojis have transformed communication but are still cumbersome to input, slowing chats and limiting expressivity. Using this interface, users zoom in to select emojis, which improves communication.

9.1 Beyond face-to-face communication

Human-to-human communication is diverse and has been shaped through millennia, first through face-to-face communication and later via written communication. Although communication technology is a relatively recent phenomenon, its evolution has been fast and dramatic. Many systems that were once popular have been overtaken by others. For instance, Usenet was created around 1980. It allowed users to read, post, and reply to messages in a list of categories. This technology extended earlier bulletin board systems, and the idea of threaded messages, which was used by some clients, is still widely used today, for example by email clients. Yet, we suspect that most of our readers have never used or even heard of Usenet. Besides Usenet, many other systems have captured the interest of researchers, including Internet Relay Chat, Short Message Service (SMS), email, wikis, blogs, instant messaging, videoconferencing, and different branded social media sites. Currently, an increasing proportion of communication occurs through interactive systems (see [618]).

Little is gained by enumerating such systems; instead, we should focus on understanding the characteristics that define them as communication channels. Only then can we begin to understand how those characteristics affect the communication behaviors that emerge from their use. Unique to human–computer interaction (HCI) research on this topic is the attempt to expose the relationship between the designed features of a system and the patterns that emerge in communication.

Table 9.1 lists eight defining characteristics of communication that can be mapped onto typical face-to-face conversations. Communication technology offers different *modalities* for communication. In the context of communication, the term modality refers to the presentation method of a communication act. We presently have, among others, textual, auditory, pictorial, and video-based modalities. There is also experimental HCI research on other modalities, such as touch. For instance, Samani et al. [726] created an interface that allows people to kiss each other at a distance, transferring the kiss from a receiving device and transmitting it to a distant conversation partner.

Table 9.1 Eight characteristics of human-to-human, face-to-face communication. These characteristics are affected when we communicate through computers.

Characteristic	Human–human conversation	Computer-mediated communication
Modalities	Speech, hearing, vision, touching	Potentially any human modality
Cues	Speech, gestural, facial	Potentially anything, including speech, gestural, facial, textual, and paralinguistic
Structure	Conversation	Conversation and many other forms
Synchronicity	Synchronous	Synchronous or asynchronous
Audience	Others within a few meters	Potentially any group of people using the system anywhere
Identity	Negotiated	Designed; constrained by the system
Power	Socially defined	Socially defined but also enforced by the system
Norms	Existing norms and etiquette for conversations	Emerging and negotiated

Mediation also affects the *cues* available for communication. In everyday conversations, communication is not just about what we say. Our body language, facial gestures, prosodic features such as pauses, and direction of gaze all affect the way the other person interprets our utterances. Compare this to the following exchange with a friend:

You: Can you pick me up at 3 p.m. from school?
Friend: Fine.

What do you think the friend may feel when given this response? Is the friend positive about the favor, or does the period signify dissatisfaction? The non-availability of cues has been a major topic of research in CMC. Paper Example 9.1.1 shows how the lack of cues from the gaze of the eye can affect communication.

The *structure* of communication refers to the way in which communication acts are organized and represented in the system. CMC supports the traditional conversational structure where verbal expressions are taken in turn. Consider, for example, the way group messaging is organized in popular applications: in reverse chronological order, with the latest message at the bottom. Moreover, structural constraints are often imposed. For example, social media posts often have a character limit. Only 10 years ago, text messaging was limited to 140 characters. However, technology has also enabled radically different structures, such as computer-vision-based overlays on faces shown in video communications.

Synchronicity denotes the simultaneity of communication; see also the taxonomy presented in Chapter 8. In synchronous communication, the exchange of information occurs in near real time, such as in a face-to-face meeting. In *a*synchronous communication, the exchange of information cannot occur in near real time, for example, if the sender sends the receiver a letter by post. This seemingly small difference has significant consequences. Most importantly, it makes it possible to maintain several communications simultaneously since a message does not need to be attended to upon receiving it.

The traditional boundaries that define who we address and how are redefined in CMC. The *audience* is no longer limited to those within shouting distance; it can be anyone who has access to a particular communication system. While one-to-one communication is limited to two defined individuals, communication can also occur with arbitrarily defined, and even undefined, audiences. Consider a group messaging service where messages can only be read by named individuals, or social media applications where a post by a public profile can be read by any user of the system.

Another factor is the *power relationship* among the participants. The system can, by design, nominate a subset of participants with special access or powers. Consider, for example, discussion moderators or group owners who can decide the audience and permitted topics in a forum. Finally, *identities* can be redefined in ways allowed by the channel. Users can take up names, avatars, and even arbitrary histories available to others. This is captured in a caption from a New Yorker comic: "On the Internet, nobody knows you are a dog." Thereby, users get new opportunities for self-expression but also for subversion and exploitation. In response, *norms* place restrictions on what is socially and culturally appropriate. While norms are not a designed aspect of a channel, they influence their use so much that ignoring them would be a mistake.

This section has explored some differences between technologies. Next, we turn to how these affect what actually goes on in face-to-face conversations between people. This turns out to be complicated, yet necessary to understand.

Paper Example 9.1.1: Eye gaze in video conversations

While we have mostly discussed verbal communication, embodied cues such as gaze and gestures have a significant role, especially in video-based communication. Video is popular as a communication medium between pairs or small groups of people. Video communication typically uses a camera that is located in a different place from the representation of the person who is being talked to (e.g., on top of a laptop). As you may have noticed when using applications such as Zoom or Teams, this creates a mismatch between where a person is looking and the camera image of that person.

Studies of face-to-face communication have shown that even a slight displacement in where you are looking significantly impacts conversations. To illustrate this, during your next conversation, look about 1 cm (0.4 in) down from your conversation partner's eyes toward their nose. In videoconferences, it is hard to say whom a person is talking to, and we must use other means to infer this, which may increase the workload and make it harder to control turn-taking.

continued

> **Paper Example 9.1.1: Eye gaze in video conversations** *(continued)*
>
> Vertegaal et al. [851] studied how the movement of the camera can affect conversations. Their findings suggest that camera shifts can be distracting when they are large. In their study, changes in the visual angle above 8 degrees were found to be particularly distracting. To help create more natural videoconferencing, researchers need to figure out how to communicate eye gaze via video.

9.2 Conversations

Let us go a little deeper into conversations. Their importance is obvious: We engage in conversation to transmit knowledge, coordinate activities, form beliefs, show identities, and conduct social transactions. In other words, conversation is the main means of social interaction. Although we routinely participate in conversations, we may be blind to their underlying structures.

These structures become visible when they break down. Consider the following exchange:

A: How are you doing?
B: I love cheese.

Clearly, this is not an adequate response. It would disrupt the conversation, which would then need to be repaired or stopped. But *why* is it not an adequate response? After all, it is a linguistically correct sentence.

Conversation analysis (CA) refers to the study of how *order* is interactionally achieved in conversation. It became a popular topic in sociology after Goodwin and Heritage [284] asked a foundational question: How is social interaction possible? Their emphasis shifted from mental constructs to social and cultural constructs, especially rules, procedures, and conventions. Although these constructs are present, they are not overt in communication. Participants in a conversation have expectations of what those rules are and what they mean; in other words, how one ought to behave in a particular circumstance. These constructs can be exposed through CA.

Before Schegloff and colleagues' work, regular talk among people was seen as a degenerate form of communication. The prevailing idea was that linguists should focus on idealized sentences. Schegloff and colleagues challenged this view. They asked how *casual* conversations are organized. In their view, the answer centers on choice. When given the freedom to choose what to respond, participants choose to respond in a particular way. Why? By contrast, heavily scripted conversations, such as conversations in a courtroom, restrict the choice of the participants and therefore diminish the evidence that one can collect on the conversational practices involved.

CA subscribes to an interactional view of communication. That is, conversation is seen as a dynamic process where the outcome depends on the actions taken by both parties. What a participant intends at the outset does not predetermine the actual outcome. Instead, the outcome is shaped as the conversation unfolds. The participants, through their choices, steer and modify the conversation. Each action or utterance is understood within the context of the conversation, including its outcome.

Unique to CA is its focus on "real" or "ordinary" communication events. This makes the approach suitable for studying everyday CMC. The recording and transcribing of talk is the starting point for CA. However, CA does not stop at transcription. It offers a *transcription system* that aims to expose the techniques participants use to achieve order. The system consists of symbols that denote pauses, stress, intonation, overlap, cut-off, tempo-changes, and loudness in conversations. A list of basic symbols used in transcriptions is shown in Figure 9.3. The way communication

Symbol	Correspondance to features of talk
(.)	A dot in a bracket indicates a pause of less than two-tenths of a second
(0.2)	Numbers in brackets refer to pauses in tenths of a second
:	Colons indicate an extension of the preceeding vowel sound. The more colons there, the greater the extent of the stretching
Wh<u>a</u>t	Underlining indicates stress or emphasis in the speech
↕	Pointed arrows indicate a marked rising or falling in speech intonation
[ ]	Square brackets indicate the begining and end of overlapping talk
Well-	A dash following a word indicates a cut-off sound at the end of the talk
><	'Greater than' and 'less than' signs enclose speech which is noticeably faster than the surrounding talk. When the order is reversed (<>) this indicates slower speech
°heh°	Degree signs indicate talk that is noticeably quieter than the surrounding talk
(so)	Words in brackets indicate the transcriber's best estimate of unclear speech
CAPITALS	These indicate that the talk is noticeably louder than the surrounding talk
=	Equal signs indicate continuous talk between speakers

Figure 9.3 Conversation analysis uses several symbols to present turn-taking and the temporal structure of conversations. Based on Wiggins' work [891].

partners take turns, how they sequence and time their responses, and how they engage in guiding other partners all become visible via the system. The transcription system is generic in the sense that almost any verbal exchange among two or more participants can be transcribed with it.

The transcription system may appear rigid and heavy. While an audio tape can be transcribed at a rate of 4:1 (e.g., four hours to transcribe a one-hour recording), CA requires an order of magnitude more time. However, the advantage of CA is that it offers a rigorous and reproducible approach to understanding conversations via turn-taking. It also provides a systematic presentation of empirical evidence. The transcripts produced via CA can be examined by peers, facilitating the reproducibility of the results.

Still, why bother with pauses and "uhms"? It turns out that these "empty" actions can be an important mechanism to make conversations work. As part of the repertoire of communication acts, they contain information—not necessarily in a strict linguistic sense, but pragmatically within the conversational setting. For example, an "uhm" in the middle of another's utterance can signal a desire to speak, hesitancy, or criticism. There is also information in pauses and silences. For example, as we learn later in this chapter, smartwatch users exploit small pauses to check notifications on their watches.

After transcription, CA is carried out with a variety of analytical devices that can expose the reasoning and inference behind social interactions. Next, we look at some of these analytical devices.

9.2.1 Turn-taking

Turn-taking refers to the organization of conversations into a sequence of utterances (turns) between conversation partners. Each turn consists of an action (utterance) by one participant, the nature of which affects the turns that can follow. Turns are mostly non-overlapping, although overlapping turns can be used as a cue for changing turns.

Sacks et al. [722] proposed "simplest systematics" to explain turn-taking. In *turn construction*, a turn is put together, including signals about its start and end and opportunities for others to start talking. The way this is done defines what others can do.

The three central techniques people use for coordinating turn-taking, as described by Sacks and colleagues, are:

1. Turn constructions, which guide the possibilities for the next turn. Example: signaling with a pause that a sentence has come to a conclusion.
2. Speaker specifications, which define who is expected to take the next turn, which can also be the current speaker.
3. Rule sets for ordering options for actions.

Another insight from CA is that not all utterances are communicative. A speaker may take a *strategic* action that directs turn-taking in the conversation. Consider, for example, completing an utterance and stopping speaking, then realizing that no one is replying. What would you do—extend your original turn or select the next speaker? This example illustrates that the speaker can influence the organization of the conversation by choosing who speaks next. *Recipient design* refers to the selection of the next speaker. These designs can be subtle additions to an utterance or explicit requests made verbally or nonverbally, for example, by directing one's gaze.

Rooksby et al. [707] used the concept of turn-taking to inform the design of an activity-tracking application. In contrast to normal activity trackers, where one logs in on an individual basis, their application restricted tracking to one member. This changed the tracking practice, making users of the app communicate and interact with each other.

9.2.2 Interactional sequences

The concept of *interactional sequence* concerns how turns can be ordered. With this concept, the focal point of analysis becomes the "here and now," or the current conversational action [284].

Turn adjacency is the simplest type of interactional sequence: A turn in communication is understood as being related to the one immediately preceding it. The first part of a pair (e.g., a question) requires a suitable action (e.g., giving an answer) to provide the second part of the pair. In other words, the first part limits the options of the conversation partner. An everyday adjacency pair is the terminal exchange "Bye" and "Goodbye."

If the second part is omitted, the initiator may engage in remedial efforts such as repeating the question. If the other produces an *acknowledgment token*, such as "hmm," the response can be delayed or even avoided. If this adjacency is disrupted (adjacency disruption), other simultaneous threads interrupt it, as the following Facebook conversation shows:

```
1  Isla:   back to that profile pic haha
2          (41.0)
3  Gavin:  haha
4          (8.0)
5  Isla:   how's work going?
6          (3.0)
7  Gavin:  I change profile pics like
```

```
8       boxers
9       (3.0)
10 Gavin: not working yet
```

In this excerpt, taken from logged Facebook conversations [538], Isla mentions Gavin's profile picture. However, Gavin self-selects and ends up taking the next turn as well. This leads to several turns being taken consecutively. Such a disruption can occur deliberately or because participants do not monitor each other's turns.

The concept of turn adjacency highlights the interactive character of conversation. An appropriate conversational action is underpinned by an understanding of what precedes it. The preceding action also limits the options for the following action. In this way, conversations are seen as interactional and context-bound. As we will learn later, conversational agents struggle with adjacency and other features of interactional sequences.

9.2.3 Repair

Like everything in human behavior, conversations are prone to errors and breakdowns. *Repair* refers to mechanisms for correcting misunderstandings. A repair may be first announced to signal that it is about to start. It is often the same person who announces the repair and then performs the repair. The initial announcement also offers an opportunity for the other person to intervene and perform the repair instead. The other person may also request a repair, for example, by expressing uncertainty or asking a question. It is important for CMCs to allow for repairs. This does not necessarily mean editing or undoing messages; it could mean offering a feature that helps explain misunderstandings.

Sharples [761] studied breakdowns and repairs in a synchronous application for tutoring students. The delays in connection led the students to adopt strategies in which they waited to ensure that their tutor was still listening. Although this sometimes worked, it also led to awkward periods of silence. As in many other studies, the students and tutors developed new conventions to deal with the limitations of the application.

9.2.4 Common ground

Common ground refers to shared beliefs and goals related to a shared activity. In joint tasks, communicators must often establish common ground before talking about the subject matter. For example, consider gamers talking about which objectives are available on a map, or which roles they can take, before actually embarking on a quest together. When there is no common ground, repairs and compensations may be needed. Participants must correct misunderstandings or take time to re-establish common ground.

Sometimes, common ground can become the topic of discussion: "What are we talking about?" Users may also talk about how to achieve common ground when the channel does not support it: "How should we talk about it?"

It is interesting to note that common ground is difficult for artificial agents to achieve. When conversing with an intelligent agent, it cannot use embodied means to facilitate the communication of meaning. Moreover, while they are reasonably good at speech recognition, they have not yet mastered "the simplest systematics" of conversations. In Chapter 22, we provide an example of a communication breakdown with Alexa in a family setting [60]. Paper Example 9.2.1 contains an example where technology enters the conversation as a topic.

9.2.5 Compensation mechanisms

Although early CA work focused on face-to-face interactions, CA has been successfully applied in a variety of settings, from doctor–patient discussions to CMC. It can also be used to understand digitally mediated conversations. However, present-day communication is increasingly multimodal and requires going beyond conventional transcription-based methods.

Consider emoticons and emojis. Emoticons like :) and :(use special characters to convey facial expressions [538]. They predate emojis, which use graphical icons and offer a broader repertoire. Meredith [538] argued that these "smilies" do not only convey facial expressions; they have a conversational function. A smilie inserted at the beginning of a text can indicate irony or some other stance toward one's own turn, hinting at how it should be interpreted. Similarly, special combinations of punctuation have emerged that do not have correspondents in face-to-face communication. For example, a double question mark (??) may indicate surprise; capital letters may indicate excitement or anger.

Paper Example 9.2.1: The smartwatch in everyday social interactions

The smartwatch is not just a small smartphone for notifications and health tracking. Compared to smartphones, one difference that we rarely think about is that smartwatches are mostly not visible to others unless they are being displayed on purpose. At the same time, they make notifications and other information more readily available to the user.

To understand how this affects social interactions with others, Pizza et al. [664] provided 12 participants with a "stalk camera" (see the figure in this paper example box) and recorded them for 34 days. The authors found that the smartwatch is emerging as a complement to the smartphone, providing users with quick, unobtrusive, and less disruptive access to communications.

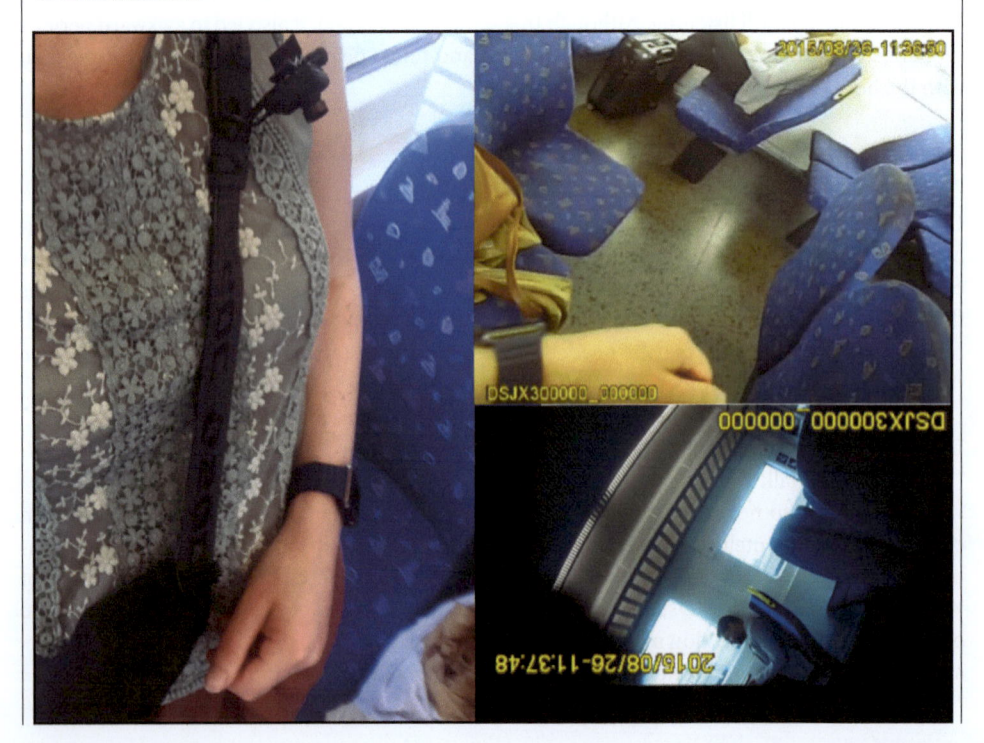

> To understand the smartwatch's effect on social interactions, the authors first investigated how its notifications may cause disruption. Interestingly, they recorded no incidents of conversations with other people being disturbed by a smartwatch. The authors then looked at whether responses to other people would be delayed, if hesitations would occur, or if repairs in conversations would occur; surprisingly, none of these things occurred.
>
> Instead, they found that smartwatch users can skillfully intertwine micro-interactions with notifications without disrupting the structures of turn-taking. One can look at a notification while talking and preparing a meal or postpone such glances until a later moment. Although notifications had no visible effect on the temporal structure of conversations, the participants were nonetheless aware of their disruptiveness [p. 5464]:
>
> "It's like, something vibrated, I know something happened. I'm curious now, but I don't want to be rude so I'm not going to look. There are two processes, trying to listen to somebody and trying to not listen to your watch."
>
> The smartwatch was thought to offer more control and much less disruption to social interactions than a smartphone. This is because the latter requires more attention and more time to pick it up and check it. In CA terms, it enables richer turn-taking strategies. For example, users sometimes check their watches while doing something else, even when their hands are under the table.
>
> The authors also found that smartwatches are not just disruptions; they can be appropriated as communicative resources. Moreover, the information that notifications bring can contribute to social interactions. The authors found that users would, for example, read aloud topics from their notifications, bringing them into a conversation.

9.3 Online behavior

Online behavior refers to the tendency of a communicator to send specific message contents. Online behavior is affected by the design of the communication channel. Consider receiving the following response to a compliment you sent to a person close to you: "Thank you." Is this message sarcastic, a retort, or a genuine expression of thankfulness? Answering this question would be much easier in face-to-face interaction, where facial and other cues are available. Indeed, the availability of cues has a large impact on the way we behave online.

According to the *cues-filtered-out hypothesis*, communication applications that do not allow for nonverbal cues can hamper social functions that involve those cues [867]. The study of this idea started in the 1970s when several experiments found that a lack of nonverbal cues limited the warmth and involvement experienced in communication. The theory suggests that in such cases, users cannot assess the characteristics of their communication partners, such as their demographic, personality, or interpersonal characteristics. Consequently, they rely on verbal persuasion. Although newer theories have superseded the cues-filtered-out theory, its core finding remains valid: Changes in cue systems affect the way social interactions, and thereby relationships, form.

9.3.1 Social presence

Virtual environments make it possible to radically change the way we present ourselves to others. In situated interactions, we rely on cues about the place, social context, and bodies when communicating; in virtual spaces, these can be practically anything.

An *avatar* is a virtual character that is used in virtual environments to represent a person. An avatar may give the impression of a real body. It has limits when compared to real bodies, but it can also have extraordinary characteristics that do not correspond to the real body. The avatar can be almost anything that can be graphically presented, from an animal to a human-like character. Users do not choose avatars arbitrarily; they tend to pick avatars that are aligned with their desired selves [830]. Users who are unhappy with themselves tend to pick avatars that are dissimilar. For instance, they may pick avatars that look more attractive or more competent.

One of the most significant findings of CMC research is that avatars have consequences. The avatar you choose affects the social interactions and relationships you form. For example, among its various roles, the physical body makes the communicator present; altering the corresponding virtual body results in the person controlling it being misrepresented. How does this affect the experience of the conversation partner?

Social presence refers to the experience of being together with another actor in a virtual world. In a landmark experiment, Nowak and Biocca [605] asked undergraduate students to get to know a partner to compete together in a competition with a USD 100 prize. The experiment varied the level of anthropomorphism of the images of the interactants—that is, how human-like they appear. In the high-anthropomorphism condition, each image was a graphical model of the face; in the low-anthropomorphism condition, it consisted of only lips and eyes. In the no-image condition, no image was shown. Moreover, the participants were told that their partner is a computer agent in half of the conditions and a real human in the other half of the conditions.

All interactions took place in a 3D environment resembling a meeting room where discussions took place via speaking. The virtual confederate was either an agent or an avatar. The virtual confederate would first introduce himself or herself, after which the participant provided introductory information. Everything was scripted; however, the virtual confederate was pre-recorded. After a trial, the participants completed the social presence questionnaire:

- To what extent did you feel able to assess your partner's reactions to what you said?—Able to assess reactions, not able to assess reactions.
- To what extent was this like a face-to-face meeting?—A lot like face to face, not like face to face at all.
- To what extent was this like you were in the same room with your partner?—A lot like being in the same room, not like being in the same room at all.
- To what extent did your partner seem "real"?—Very real, not real at all.
- How likely is it that you would choose to use this system of interaction for a meeting in which you wanted to persuade others of something?—Very likely, not likely at all.
- To what extent did you feel you could get to know someone that you met only through this system?—Very well, not at all.

The results were surprising. The images with higher anthropomorphism did not lead to a higher social presence. Having an almost cartoon-like image led to a higher felt presence. Yet, having no image at all led to the lowest felt presence. The authors hypothesize that high anthropomorphic images led to the highest expectations about the social skills of the conversant. When the partner was unable to take the next turn, it may have led to a harsher evaluation. The results show that the way a conversation partner is presented affects the user's expectations of their partner's conversational competence and behavior. When the user's expectation is not met, they feel their partner is less present in their social interaction.

In a follow-up experiment, the level of anthropomorphism was systematically manipulated at 12 levels. At one extreme, the images were photos of human faces. At the other extreme, they were cartoons. Participants were asked to engage in tasks posing social dilemmas, where success is affected by how trustworthy the interactant is perceived to be. In a social dilemma task, a user takes on the role of giving advice in a hypothetical scenario involving risk, such as in careers, relationships, or personal finance. Their advice can be risky with potentially high rewards or safe with likely low rewards. The results of the experiment suggest that, in this context, a higher level of anthropomorphism has a positive linear effect on social responses, especially trustworthiness. When the representation of a partner is more human-like, the partner is perceived as more reliable.

These results indicate that the sense of presence is more complicated as a psychological construct than initially thought. Many factors affect the experience, and the full picture is still emerging. For example, people evaluate the competence of the conversation partner based on cues such as style, attractiveness, gender, age, and race.

9.3.2 Media richness

Media richness theory is a candidate for explaining *how* social behavior adapts as a function of communication [867]. The theory has two constructs: media richness and equivocality. Media richness is defined through four dimensions: (1) the number of cue systems supported by a medium, (2) the immediacy of feedback, (3) the potential for natural expression (as opposed to formal, structured expression), and (4) the specificity of the audience. Face-to-face communication is the richest medium because it has the most cue systems and offers simultaneity, natural language, and a high level of control over the desired audience. Text messaging, by contrast, is lower in the first two dimensions. Equivocality, the second construct, is the degree to which information in a social situation is subject to multiple interpretations.

The theory states that media richness should match equivocality. When the medium is leaner than the social situation requires, communication is less effective. Such suboptimality can have negative consequences, although the theory does not specify what those consequences may be.

In one study, managers in a company were asked to rate which channels would be most suitable for different communication purposes. Their responses were taken to support the theory, as they showed sensitivity to optimality, consistent with the theory. Further studies, however, suggested that managers may not behave as they claim [867]. When they were observed in their workplaces, they would often choose a suboptimal channel and use it with no discernible consequences on communication effectiveness. Later research suggested that instead of the effectiveness of communication, media richness may affect its efficiency. That is, groups using a richer channel may be able to complete their tasks faster.

Testing the theory turned out to be difficult, as it is hard to vary the four dimensions independently. In practice, many dimensions change together. Moreover, when people are given a choice of communication medium, they do not only consider its optimality for communication. They may also consider factors such as the cost or the convenience of using a particular medium.

9.3.3 Signaling and reciprocity

The decline of trust in social media has been one of the most significant sociopolitical phenomena of recent times. Trust is a desirable factor in most social interactions. A higher level of trust can promote deeper interactions and engagements that would not happen otherwise. Why is it that establishing trust is so difficult?

Early theories suggested that trust follows from *reciprocity*. When interactants have matching levels of self-disclosure, trust follows. For example, if you disclose your age and gender but the other party does not, reciprocity is not achieved and trust will be harder to establish. How can we interpret reciprocity and trust in social media settings, where posters can be anonymous or even take up deceptive identities? Such settings are associated with increasing negative behavior, such as flaming.

Signaling theory is about text-based social media, X (formerly Twitter) being the most well-known example. According to the theory, people engage in assessing which signals from others are reliable [205]. They are active in thinking about how to best use social cues in communication. They weigh the costs of deceiving against the potential benefits. For example, in text-based discussions online, participants can easily craft any sort of self-description. In other words, the cost is low. Anyone can easily deceive others about their age: You can type "24" in your profile as easily as you can type "42." This is drastically different from face-to-face situations, where manufacturing false signals is more difficult. For example, if you intend to claim that you are wealthy but you are not, you should first acquire external signals of wealth. The signals in face-to-face communication are more reliable and, according to the theory, more trustworthy. There are ways for users to improve the reliability of their signals. For example, they can present auxiliary information as proof of authenticity or ask other contacts to comment on their credibility.

9.3.4 Social information processing

Social information processing theory differs from other theories in that it proposes that the lack of nonverbal cues does not impede social interaction [866]. Communicators are willing to develop interpersonal affinity regardless of the medium, and they try to do so by adapting their behaviors to compensate for the lack of cues. They do this by expressing more information using the medium, changing their styles, and finding alternative ways to express themselves.

Such techniques take time to develop. However, once developed, they can be culturally shared and assist users in using the medium. For example, emoticons and emojis can compensate for the lack of emotional cues in textual communication. Their evolution has taken more than a decade and is still ongoing.

The theory is not limited to emoticons. For instance, it makes a surprising prediction: Because communicating nonverbal cues verbally is inefficient, establishing sufficiently deep relationships takes more time. The slower rate of nonverbal communication means that constructing representations of the other partner takes more time. These two predictions—compensating for the lack of cues and the longer periods needed to build relationships—have been supported by evidence from experimental studies. In these studies, the cue systems are experimentally removed or added, and the effect on other cue systems and the approaches people use is recorded. It has also been found that on multimodal platforms, users select which messages to convey and in which modes. For example, profile images on social media can be designed to convey certain traits while text conveys other information.

9.3.5 Self-presentation

So far, we have discussed how users process information about each other. Given that such inferential processes happen, it is not a surprise that users may want to control how others perceive them.

Self-presentation refers to actions taken to present oneself in some fashion that is desirable to oneself. Self-presentation can occur through any communication channel: text, video and audio clips, streaming video, and so on. Some video- and photo-based SNSs have become repositories of digital self-presentations [487]. With self-presentation, users do not passively show who they are or what they do; they actively *construct* how they are seen by others. Users not only curate what they post but also stage events to create favorable posts and use technical features such as filters and settings to control who sees what. An example of online self-presentation is given in Paper Example 9.3.1.

Paper Example 9.3.1: Self-presentation in an online game

Ducheneaut et al. [215] discussed social behavior in World of Warcraft (WoW), a massive multiplayer online game. They analyzed how players' networks are structured and found that self-presentation is a key factor. They found that while WoW is a social environment, the role of others is mainly that of an audience. That is, instead of playing with others or against them, players rely on others as their audience. Gamers reported that they play the game for its social aspects, yet many gamers remain outside groups (e.g., guilds). Instead of forming groups, many players perform for themselves and for others; for example, they gather artifacts and chitchat about them with others. The authors described this as being "alone together": Gamers are surrounded by others but do not interact with them with the aim of forming relationships. Why do such behaviors emerge? The authors pointed out that WoW, like many other multiplayer games, has incentives based on reputation. An avatar showing rare items is part of the player's identity. An audience that rewards such displays rewards the underlying behavior, thereby reinforcing it. The game is addictive not because of other gamers but because of the self-image players are able to build with their help.

Another role of the other players is to provide social presence. The game offers a general communication channel that gamers can use to communicate with players who are not close by in the virtual world. These channels host constant chatter, which creates the impression of being with others, similar to being in a crowded cafeteria. This, along with other designed communication features, ensures that the players experience the feeling of being with others during a game.

Self-presentation in virtual worlds can be tricky since posts cannot be controlled after they are shared [487]: "Consider the example of Alex tagging a Facebook photo of Bill at a party. Facebook's interface provides Alex with little information about Bill's privacy settings including the visibility of tagged photos, or how many and which of Bill's Facebook friends might see the photo." The issue is that other users may not care about the original poster's self-presentation goals. Shares, likes, and comments may be seen as threats to self-presentation, even if these were not done with a malevolent intent. This issue is harder to handle for users who have diverse audience groups. The corresponding challenge in HCI research is determining how to allow for better control and visibility of the audience [487]. *Audience cues* are visualizations and controls that help posters understand who sees their posts. The dilemma is that limiting the audience more than suggested by a norm (expectation) may work against the poster, throttling dissemination or even attracting negative views about the poster.

9.4 Social networks and online communities

It is clear that CMC has changed the very way people create and maintain relationships with others. Both one-to-many and many-to-many communications have changed dramatically in the past decades. From Facebook to Tinder, social networks and online communities are not considered "virtual" and thus "less real"; they are just as important and consequential in our lives as face-to-face interactions. However, why do some social networks become unsustainable while others flourish? To design sustainable networks and communities, it is important to understand the mechanisms that underpin social relationships.

According to Boyd and Ellison [91], *social network sites* (SNSs) are "web-based services that allow individuals to (1) construct a public or semi-public profile within a bounded system, (2) articulate a list of other users with whom they share a connection, and (3) view and traverse their list of connections and those made by others within the system." LinkedIn, Facebook, and CouchSurfing are SNSs according to this definition; other services, such as WhatsApp, only include elements of a social network. For example, WhatsApp does not allow users to traverse other connections' connections, whereas Facebook does.

An *online community* is another relevant concept. It is an interest-based forum of connections and interactions, such as Stack Overflow for programming. Online communities often have some features shared with SNSs, such as the creation of profiles and networks.

When social networks started to gain popularity, they attracted lots of attention from research. Initially, it was assumed that these services would be used to create new networks and meet new people. However, this is not always the case. Studies of Facebook found that it is used primarily to maintain existing (offline) relationships and solidify offline connections rather than meeting new people [224]. It was also surprising how many social networks never attracted enough users to become sustainable and how some encouraged ill behaviors such as flaming.

One of the attractions of social networks and online communities is that they may be subjected to a host of statistical analyses. Statistical methods can precisely describe a network's structure with people as nodes and their connections as different types of links. The benefit of such analysis is that it can help illuminate large-scale patterns that would be difficult or outright impossible to detect with other methods. Analyses of social networks have revealed, among other things, that social relationships can be described in terms of the strength of the connection [286]. Weak ties are connections to strangers and ad hoc acquaintances who may be met online or in person. Strong ties are connections to relatives, friends, and other close-knit groups. One observed issue in social networks is that users would like to communicate differently with these two types of connections; this may require putting extra work into communicating, and, if that fails, it may inhibit self-presentation.

While the macro-level of social networks can be studied using such methods, to understand the role of design in the emergence of social ties, we need to understand the basic social psychological mechanisms in online relationships.

9.4.1 Online social relationships

Baym [52] pointed out SNSs as a breakthrough that led to an increase in *networked individualism*. Each user is at the center of a personal community. While online communities such as bulletin board systems existed before the now-popular SNSs (e.g., Facebook, TikTok, and Mastodon), what has changed is the ease with which users can define who they include in their personal networks. Most SNSs allow users to "follow," "invite," or otherwise define whose posts they attend to. Other users' networks can be traversed. SNSs, however, have not replaced other types of relationships.

Instead, they provide new platforms for social relationships that develop between blogs, which focus on the individual, and online communities, where the focus is on a group or community.

Design matters in the emergence of social networks. Comparing two SNSs, Baym [52] wrote:

> The two sites differ in their affordances. Neither allows much flexibility in page design, as MySpace and LiveJournal do, but Facebook allows users more breadth in shaping their profile. Facebook users can add applications (including several from Last.fm) in order to shape their self-presentation, play games with their friends, and promote causes they find important. They can maintain photo albums, import blog posts, share items and videos from elsewhere on the net. Last.fm users can do very few of these things, but they can display the music they listen to in real time, create radio streams for others to hear, tag music and to bands, author band wiki entries, and see personalized charts of their own and others' listening habits, which cannot be done on Facebook. Both sites allow users to create groups, and both recommend people with whom one might connect—Facebook by calculating the number of shared friends, Last.fm by calculating the number of shared listens. Not surprisingly, the two sites result in differing social contexts. While Facebook is seen as a space in which to socialize playfully with peers, Last.fm is all and only about music—one may socialize, but it's most likely going to be about music. Some of its users do not use its social features, friending no one, yet still have satisfying interaction with the site, a situation that would be unimaginable on Facebook.

Design affects social relationships by affecting the social psychological mechanisms underlying the formation of social relationships [52]. Social relationships need to be created; for instance, you need to add someone to your network. Social relationships also need to be maintained; via messaging, we create the content needed to maintain social relationships. Design affects how all of this happens.

Identity and authenticity: Early online interactions were often anonymous, which increased flaming. Modern SNSs, by contrast, allow users to link to organizations they belong to (e.g., companies, sports clubs). They can also share rich media such as videos and photos. These aspects are important for the authenticity of contacts. In turn, authenticity is important for reciprocity: You are more likely to share personally relevant information with a stranger whose authenticity you trust. Users are also more likely to connect with people with whom they share acquaintances. Shared connections increase trust in others' authenticity.

Audience and self-presentation: Every communication act in an SNS is visible to a specific audience. This is a critical consideration in social interactions. Who sees a message and what kind of effect will it have on them? In the case of X, the audience is anyone using X, but it is more likely to be the people who actively follow you. In the case of WhatsApp, the audience is the people who belong to the group you post in. Knowing the audience is important for self-presentation since we aim to control how we appear to others.

Affordances for communication: Some SNSs show which contacts are available and how. For example, you may see a friend appear online and start chatting with them. Visibility is important because it tells users about the types of communication available: synchronous or asynchronous. SNSs can also show other information: other people's comments on one's posts, profile images, email addresses, and so on. Such information provided by SNSs contributes different degrees of freedom that influence how the audience acts.

Privacy: The concept of an audience is bound to the concept of privacy. In SNSs, users can control *what* they disclose to others. Users can also affect what is supposed to be disclosed: They can explicitly ask for disclosures and create an expectation for reciprocity. Privacy, in other words, is *constructed* via social interactions [635].

A personalized network can become unsustainable over time. It is known that in larger networks like Facebook, pairwise interactions can be very rare [52]. However, because contacts tend to be added more often than they are removed, the audience keeps growing, making it harder to control self-presentation and privacy. Concepts like "a friend" are becoming harder to define in the era of SNSs. However, users may also utilize the *ambiguity* of such concepts in creative ways. They can situationally decide who is invited, for example, to some group or event; in such cases, the ambiguity of some relationships provides plausible deniability.

9.4.2 Online communities

Online communities are often interest-based. The motivation for joining is a shared interest in something outside the online service itself, for example, particular types of media (e.g., music, cartoons) or local groups (e.g., community shelters, sports clubs).

Unlike SNSs, which are individual-centric, online communities are group- or community-centric. This characteristic influences online communities. Unlike SNSs, online communities develop *social norms* for desirable behavior [52]. They may provide instructions on how to post and comment or information on power structures (e.g., community moderators). SNSs, by contrast, often have implicit norms—"ways of the house" that everyone knows but are not written anywhere. For example, Stack Overflow and Tinder have different norms governing posting and the use of emojis.

An important question is how to foster longevity and respectful behavior in social communities. The *silent majority* is a common phenomenon both offline and in social networks. It refers to users who mainly follow others and avoid engaging with original content. Activating such users requires the consideration of both the designed features and the *incentives* provided for participation. The techniques studied in HCI include *reputation systems*, which can, for example, inform users about who has the most followers, the most likes, and so on, thus encouraging social comparison and social motivation. A key challenge, then, is how to create growing communities based on *legitimate, peripheral participation*. That is, how to help users increase their participation from being "lurkers"[1] toward becoming active members.

Research has shown that being connected may have a dark side. Online communities and social networks suffer from harassment and trolling, and they have been misused to distribute misinformation and manipulate political opinions. Moreover, the increasing use of AI for selecting content has created *filter bubbles* (echo chambers). Because AI tends to pick posts based on predicted liking and sharing, users tend to be exposed to confirmatory content. Filter bubbles thus feed the polarization of social networks. This can reinforce biases that are inherent in a community. These issues and potential solutions are extensively researched across fields, including HCI.

9.4.3 Communication affects social relationships

So far, this chapter has reviewed social mechanisms affecting CMC. Perhaps the most obvious takeaway for HCI is this: Human–human communication poses requirements for the design of communication technology. The modalities, cues, and structures of communication, and the features offered for the specification of the audience and the negotiation of power structures, affect what kind of communication emerges. Communication services that ignore these factors are bound to see little participation and unwanted behaviors such as flaming. Yet, behind these factors is a slower dynamic process that shapes users and societies. The way people use communication

---

[1] An oft-used term we do not condone. Instead, we recommend using the term passive user.

technology affects their social relationships, well-being, and culture. For example, the mere presence of communication technology can affect the way people hold conversations and what they are ready to disclose. An early study looked at how the presence of mobile devices affects conversations between co-located people [679]. In two experiments, the authors found that in one-to-one (dyadic) communication, the presence of mobile devices changes the discussion of personally meaningful topics. The authors concluded [p. 244]: "the mere presence of mobile phones inhibited the development of interpersonal closeness and trust, and reduced the extent to which individuals felt empathy and understanding from their partners. [. . .] these effects might happen outside of conscious awareness." This effect has been replicated [218]. However, different communication media can have widely different effects, as we saw in the case of online forums [414].

While the causal mechanisms behind long-term changes are still being studied, findings like these suggest that communication technology is not an inert outlet for communication. Rather, it is shaped by and shapes the formation of social relationships. For instance, it has been found that people addicted to smartphones are more likely to "phubb" others in a social situation [151]. The term refers to the act of snubbing others by attending to one's phone. Such effects can have complex societal consequences. Research looking at population-level statistics suggests that changes in social relationships caused by the increased use of digital media may have worsened mental health issues such as depression, self-harm, and suicide among the youth [834]. These dynamic processes are still evolving; their consequences are hard to study and even harder to predict and control. More research is needed to understand the mechanisms that drive these dynamic processes.

9.5 Computers as communication partners

So far in this chapter, we have mostly discussed analytic machinery for understanding computer-mediated human–human communication. The reader may wonder if this machinery also applies to conversations with computers. Such a system could, for instance, be an animated agent that writes back when the user writes something or an intelligent agent that speaks back when the user asks something. We can use analyses of turn-taking, for example, to see how conversations are structured with intelligent agents. We can also look at the cues that are conveyed and how they contribute to efficient communication. However, there is a more fundamental question: Are computers perceived as competent social actors?

Nass et al. [580] argued that people largely treat computers as social actors, almost like they treat humans. Rather than treating computers as inanimate tools, people maintain many expectations and perceptions that they transfer from their everyday social interactions with other humans.

One representative experiment asked if people are polite to computers like they are to other humans [579]. Nass and colleagues tested this in a study where a computer tutored participants. After tutoring, the participants rated their impression of the computer tutor. This was done in three ways: on the same computer, using paper, and on another computer. Take a moment to consider which medium resulted in the best ratings.

The evaluations submitted via the same computer were better than those on paper. Nass et al. [579] interpreted this as showing that participants were more polite to the computer tutor when providing feedback directly to it. Crucially, the evaluations submitted through another computer were also less positive than those provided via the same computer. In other words, the participants seemed to apply social norms to computers. The same pattern has been shown to hold for other individual and social patterns in communication. For instance, if an interactive system is perceived to have a personality, its users respond along the lines with which they would respond to a computer.

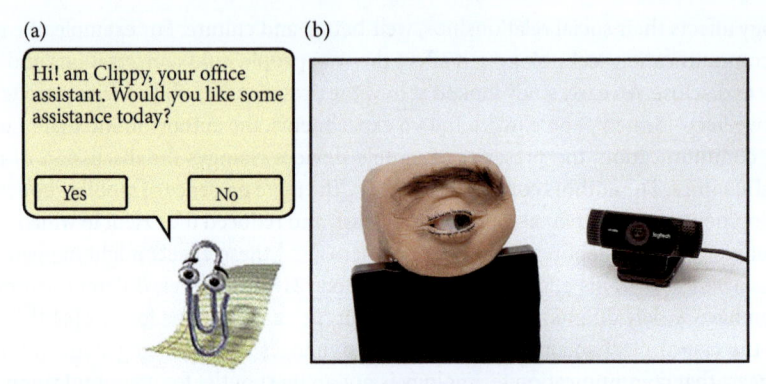

Figure 9.4 To the left, a commercial example of an early agent, Clippy. It was part of Microsoft Office for years, although it was widely criticized for providing unsuitable help at points when the user did not wish to be interrupted. To the right, a web camera designed by Teyssier et al. [818] to appear like a human eye. It even moves to follow the user (look for a video of it online; it is quite interesting).

The methodologies presented in this chapter have also been applied to study conversations [672]. For example, *anthropomorphic systems* try to make a system's looks and actions resemble those of humans. The interactive system Rea, for instance, presented the user with a humanoid real estate agent the user could interact with [140]. Figure 9.4 shows two additional examples of interactive anthropomorphic systems.

At the same time, many researchers have criticized anthropomorphic systems. The argument has been that even though people *may* treat computers as social actors, it does not mean that we *should* design computers with this goal in mind, and, in particular, it does not mean that we should make computers look and behave like people. There are three main arguments supporting this view [769]. First, new technologies are often designed to resemble older ones. This is an ineffective strategy that limits innovation. As an example, the first cars contained reins; this did not facilitate the invention of a better way of controlling cars—the steering wheel. Second, anthropomorphic systems may make users anxious and even undermine their feelings of control and responsibility. Third, anthropomorphic systems lead to a conflating of the abilities of people and machines.

Summary

- Communication mediated by interactive systems differs from face-to-face communication.
- CMC can be discussed by the features of its channels or its impact on the individual and the social functions of the communication.
- CA is used to understand the structure (turn-taking, adjacency, repairs, etc.) of both online and human-to-human communications.
- Social networks are associated with both positive (social capital) and negative (e.g., trolling, biases, polarization) phenomena.
- Design affects authenticity, audiences, privacy, serendipitous communication, and the maintenance of social networks. These, in turn, affect the type of social relationships that emerge. However, how to design mediated interactions that promote fair and unbiased participation remains an open question.

Exercises

1. Analyzing computer-medicated communication. Consider an interactive system that you use for communication. It may be a computer game where you need to coordinate with a team, an electronic whiteboard where you leave messages for others, a chat client, or something similar. Use the features in Table 9.1 to analyze the differences between the interactive system and face-to-face conversations. If you have experienced breakdowns in communication with the interactive system, select a couple of examples and analyze them using the table.

2. Self-presentation. Choose a social media application and look at its posts. What are the means of self-presentation it allows? Which audience cues does it allow?

3. Repair and compensation in conversations with artificial agents. Pick an everyday discussion topic and an interactive language model (e.g., ChatGPT). Run a few conversations on the topic with the purpose of causing some misunderstanding. (a) Which interactional sequence strategies does the agent utilize (e.g., acknowledgment tokens)? (b) When a conversation breaks down, how does the agent try to repair it? Does it notice it breaking down? How does it support you in repairing it?

4. Real versus artificial communication partners. Many interactive systems mimic conversations among people, for example, by creating the impression that you are conversing with a person. Such agents or avatars often resemble people in their physical appearance, manner of wording, or body language. Try to identify such human-like or anthropomorphic communication systems among the systems you use. According to this chapter, what might be the benefits of using such systems for communication with a computer? What are the drawbacks?

5. Designing systems for communication. Consider interactive systems for communicating with people in your neighborhood. How could one design such a system to support communication, as described by Table 9.1? How would the concepts related to online communities from this chapter help us design the system?

6. The Coordinator. Winograd and Flores [900] presented a famous view on computer-based communication rooted in the view that language is action. Building on this view, the Coordinator tool was created. Rather than just sending an unspecified message, the tool supported structured requests such as those shown in the following figure. For instance, your message could request or offer something.

```
                         C O N V E R S E

OPEN CONVERSATION FOR ACTION         REVIEW / HANDLE
    Request                              Read new mail
    Offer                                Missing my response
                                         Missing other's response
OPEN CONVERSATION FOR POSSIBILITIES
    Declare an opening                   My promises/offers
                                         My requests
ANSWER                                   Commitments due: 24-May-88

NOTES                                    Conversation records
```

Discuss how such a system might influence communication. Does it make it easier or harder to request anything? What can you do if you are not sure whether you are making a request or an offer?

Part III

User Research

10
Introduction to user research

Many products, systems, and services are ultimately unsuccessful because their designs do not meet the needs, wants, and motivations of users. This part of the book concerns how to obtain actionable knowledge about users, including their activities, needs, wants, and contexts of use. *User research* comprises the principles and methods of empirical research used to obtain, analyze, and represent this knowledge. For instance, we might observe users as they do their work (Figure 10.1) to learn what it is about and what concerns them. Alternatively, we might conduct a large-scale survey study to learn about practices and experiences related to a piece of technology that we are interested in. A key aspect of user research is the synthesis of observational data in a form that can inform design.

One of the main motivations for user research is the realization that, in general, *you are not the user*. Basing critical design decisions on our opinions is risky, as developers and designers often represent very different points of view from the users for whom they design. Moreover, neglecting end-user viewpoints can be outright unethical because it may result in systems, products, or services that cause harm or distress. Thus, the data we collect as part of user research should be

Figure 10.1 A researcher observing a user [198]. User research is about the empirical description of interaction in the present, particularly the users, their activities, the roles of any existing interactive system, and their contexts of use, including the social, organizational, and physical contexts. It also concerns the users' needs and wants. These descriptions are collected and represented to inform design and decision-making.

Introduction to Human-Computer Interaction. Kasper Hornbæk, Per Ola Kristensson, and Antti Oulasvirta, Oxford University Press. © Kasper Hornbæk, Per Ola Kristensson, and Antti Oulasvirta (2025).
DOI: 10.1093/oso/9780192864543.003.0010

about actual users engaged in specific activities with specific needs and capabilities. We should also obtain insights about other (non-using) stakeholders. For example, the parents of a child playing a mobile game are non-using stakeholders about whom researchers would aim to gather knowledge.

User research complements researchers' efforts to understand people (Part II). The theories and principles discussed in that part of the book aim to be *general*. They relate to the psychological and social factors that pertain to most, if not all, cases of human–computer interaction (HCI). However, this understanding is necessarily limited. The current theoretical view of humans is patchy. As a consequence, almost every practical HCI project will face questions that are not covered by existing theories. Any interactive system also involves *particular* users performing particular activities in particular contexts. We need to know these particulars when we do not have a general understanding that covers them or when it is not clear which general ideas from Part II apply to our case. General theories in psychology are at the population level and may not be good predictors of behavior at the individual level [241]. Therefore, the general understanding of people in Part II must be complemented by empirical insights into the particulars of each case to inform design and decision-making. For instance, the selection of icons for an interactive system depends on general features of human visual perception (Chapter 3). However, selecting the actual icons to integrate into a system requires designers to know the particulars of the users' work and which representations would best match their work.

The main aim of user research is to *obtain concrete, empirical knowledge about users*. This goal has been central to HCI since the early days of the field. Its importance is captured in slogans such as "know the user" [311], "early focus on users" [285], and "start with the needs of the user" [599]. User research is where "know the user" happens. This requires that we, as researchers and designers, be in direct contact with users rather than rely on second-hand descriptions or assumptions about them. We cannot indirectly know the particulars of users. As mentioned in Part I, this is a central tenet of being human-centered. We need concrete empirical knowledge about users to design interactive systems that match what they do and want.

A key commitment in user-centered design is to *understand first and design later*. The idea is simple: Do not jump to solutions or try to come up with interactive systems that will solve the problem that you see. Instead, try to determine what obstacles and challenges users are facing and identify their needs and wants.

User research aims to produce design-neutral descriptions. This means that we wish to understand users without tying ourselves to specific design decisions. Based on this aim, user research is rooted in social science, psychology, and other behavioral sciences. We discuss design separately in Part VI. For example, in co-design, we do not study users' activities and context to establish a basis for design. Instead, users are included in the design process to break the barrier that separates user research and design. When using design probes, we do not aim to obtain accurate descriptions of people but to generate knowledge that inspires new ideas. More generally, in many design-oriented methods, designers who immerse themselves in the world and data may not need to articulate their understandings to others. By contrast, this part of the book approaches user research as an applied empirical science where such articulation is central. This is a key difference between user research and design.

Unfortunately, obtaining knowledge about users is complicated. Many factors contribute to this complexity, and understanding those factors can help us avoid pitfalls and put the necessary care into user research. These factors include the following:

- The say–do gap. This problem comes from the frequent observation that *what users say they do* might differ from *what they actually do*. For instance, when people are asked how much they use the Internet, their self-reports tend to have a low correlation with the logged data [739]. In this case, directly asking the users is not a reliable method.

- In their activities, users rely on knowledge that is difficult to articulate [670]. Many factors driving our behavior are *latent* in such a way that they are not accessible to conscious inspection and are difficult or impossible to describe verbally. *Tacit knowledge* refers to knowledge that we are largely unaware of but can be easily put into use in the right situation. High-repetition motor skills, such as riding a bike or typing in a familiar password, are good examples of tacit knowledge. If you ask people how they ride a bike, you are unlikely to get full, precise answers.

- Users' needs may only be recognized in the future [727]. For example, no user of a batch computer system is likely to be able to articulate specific, detailed needs for a graphical user interface. This is because identifying what users need requires them to imagine the impact of new technology on their activities, which is very difficult.

- Social reasons also make it difficult to get insights into users. Suchman [803] discussed how the ways work is done are often kept secret. Making work visible is fraught with difficulties. For instance, making work practices visible can challenge the power between those doing the work and other members of an organization.

Due to these factors, user research is both required and difficult to do right, which is why we have dedicated an entire part of this book to it.

If user research is so difficult, why attempt to do it at all? Perhaps the most important reason is ethics: User research is a commitment to listening to your users and taking them seriously. Rooting decisions in empirical data can help avoid biases in decision-making. However, even the most rigorous user research is no guarantee that the result will not be harmful to end-users. Another motivation is that user research can help build better interactive systems. Gathering insights about users can inform decisions about whether and how to build an interactive system. Properly conducted, empirical research outweighs empathy and opinion. The insights from such research can help us make decisions about the desired impact of our design efforts, such as novel interactive computer systems, on future users. User research can also challenge assumptions about products. For example, Kumar and Whitney [445] conducted user research to uncover patterns of daily life in a culture, including its value systems and social structures. The results of such user research can challenge the one-design-fits-all idea. Discovering drastic differences in a user population that was thought to be homogeneous can help rescope and diversify product offerings.

Finally, user research can pay off. Most technology companies engage in some sort of user research, for example, through log data, surveys, or qualitative research. Some academics and companies have tried to gauge the value of user research. Harper [312] described several cases of user-centered design at Hewlett-Packard. The estimated return on investment (ROI) ranged from USD 6 million to USD 125 million per case. However, the ROI is difficult to estimate in such cases since the effect of design decisions on revenue is notoriously difficult to measure [71].

The rest of this chapter explains the key parts of user research; the rest of this part details methods for doing user research.

10.1 Goals of user research

The primary goal of user research is to obtain, analyze, and represent knowledge about current or prospective users. We call this goal *gathering knowledge for design*. What do we seek to gather knowledge about? In some cases, the user researcher will have a brief design, a focus, or a relatively clear idea of the scope of the interactive system under consideration or the use-related issues that need to be studied. In such cases, these early considerations will shape the user research. In other cases, the outcomes of user research will determine what the focus of the interactive system will be or whether something needs to be designed at all. In both situations, the following list of insight types may provide inspiration. They may be remembered by the acronym used by Benyon [62], PACT: people, activities, contexts, and technologies.

People: People-related insights include user skills, personalities, socioeconomic status, abilities, beliefs, habits, motivations, needs, and wants. These types of insights concern the experiences and attitudes of users and their first-person views of themselves and their activities.

Activities: The tasks users perform and the practices they engage in give us important information for design. What do users do? What do they strive to achieve, and in which contexts?

Contexts: The different contexts people find themselves in when interacting with systems are a rich source of potential insights. There are several contexts to consider. The physical context is related to the physical environment and may include weather, lighting, and the built environment. The social context covers the social environment of interaction, such as social relationships and activities with others. The organizational context relates to how interaction is situated within organizations, for example, power structures, division of labor, and formal and informal work hierarchies. The historical context may be related to previous exposure to practices and systems. Finally, the cultural context captures cultural beliefs and norms that may affect the use of a system.

Technologies: Existing interactive systems and tools with which users interact serve as another important type of insight. This may include the perceived pros and cons of a solution and opinions on alternative solutions. Nevertheless, it is important to remember that the primary focus of user research is people, not technology or imagining technological solutions.

A primary goal of user research is to *inform* design and make practical decisions, such as deciding whether to launch a product or if a product embeds biases. However, because user research is often open-ended, it may not directly lead to concrete decisions. More importantly, we face the *is–ought problem*: From descriptions of how things are (*is*), we cannot conclude how they should be (*ought*). For example, imagine that you have collected vast amounts of data on what your users do on mobile devices, say, when they are cooking. What can you say about the need for a new service? The issue is that the essential characteristics of that new service may not be present in your user data. Hence, user research results are rarely strongly prescriptive of designs alone. That said, a significant value of user research is that it can convince stakeholders about the quality of the decisions made. Compare a designer who refers to personal experience with one who presents statistics, interview data, and a model that describes users. Which one will be more persuasive?

Generating insights for design is not the only goal of user research. Another prominent goal is to *involve users* in the design of interactive systems. One motivation for this is the argument that users have a political or moral right to be part of shaping the interactive systems with which they might work in the future. This argument comes from a Scandinavian tradition of system development called *participatory design* [410]. Another motivation to involve users is pragmatic: User involvement enables the creation of better systems that users are more committed to using [325, 441]. Part VI discusses techniques for involving users not only as a source of insights into the current situation but also as co-designers of the future situation.

Another goal of user research is to *create empathy* between the user researcher (who could also be the designer) and the user. This goal transforms the activity of knowing the user into "understanding what it feels like to be that person, what their situation is like from their own perspective. In short, it involves empathy" [915]. This view permeates much work on design. Hansen [311], for instance, argued that one important function of getting to know the user is to "remind the designer that the user is a human." Rams argued that "indifference towards people and the reality in which they live is actually the one and only cardinal sin in design." Thus, direct and continuous contact between user researchers and the people they seek to understand might help establish a good connection between them. However, empathy is not a substitute for empirical inquiry. As we will discuss in Part VI, empathy tends to fail. Just as it is difficult to guess—even after years of practice—what a significant other may want, it is difficult to empathize with the lived experiences of someone else.

Finally, user research is valuable as is, even with no product in mind. User research can lead to discoveries and contribute to *basic research findings*. Many examples of such findings are provided in Part II on understanding people. This is why some HCI researchers have argued that not all papers describing studies of people should contain implications for design [210]; some papers may primarily help us understand people.

10.2 Who is the user in user research?

If you are not the user, then who is? A central step in all user research is to identify who the user is and then select which users to investigate. It is essentially a three-step process, and all three steps are crucial to successful user research.

Target audience: The first step is to specify the *target audience*, which is a set of profiles that describe the user groups that the product, system, or service is intended to reach.

Other stakeholders: The second step is to specify other people directly affected by or involved in the use of the interactive system.

Sampling: Having settled on a set of profiles that accurately describe the target audience and other stakeholders, it is now possible to select (or sample) representative users to research.

These steps are critical because failure at either step risks introducing incorrect, misleading, or low-quality input into the design process. For example, failure to describe the target audience means that there is a high risk of conducting research with users who will ultimately not be affected by or interested in the product, system, or service that will be designed. Although the findings of this user research may still be relevant by sheer luck, there is a possibility that *undetected bias* in the user research data will be incorporated into the design process. Such undetected bias is dangerous, as the designers are unaware of it and its consequences may only be discovered at deployment.

10.2.1 Target audience

The *target audience* is a description of the intended customers or users affected by your system, service, or product. This group is usually defined by constructing a set of profiles that are intended to capture various subgroups of the target audience.

There are many ways to form a profile for a target audience. One process that is frequently used in user research for product development is the following.

- First, consider the inclusion criteria for the profile. The *behavioral criterion* means including people who actually do or want to do the things you intend to enable with your product. The *technological criterion* involves considering the background and interest of people in related technology, such as how frequently they use social media or interact with a system based on spoken dialogue. Finally, the *demographical criterion* means capturing people's anticipated age, geographical location, household income, and so on.
- Second, having considered behavioral, technological, and demographical criteria, it is possible to develop an initial profile. For example, consider a hypothetical wearable health monitor coupled with a smartphone that is meant to use persuasive gamification methods to encourage a healthy lifestyle. An initial profile may then have a *Demographics* section that says the intended age range is 25–55, the occupation can be anything, and it is specifically aimed at single people who are educated at the university level and have a post-tax income of USD 60,000. A *Behaviors* section may state that this typical user walks or uses public transportation to go to work. Finally, a *Technology use and experience* section may specify that a person within the profile may use their mobile phone to browse the web and Facebook several times a day.
- Third, the initial profile is reviewed to make it suitable for user research. One trick is to try to identify additional criteria for ideal users that would provide the most valuable feedback. Several prompts can facilitate this exercise, such as considering which *segments* within your target audience you should focus on, how much experience they should have with *your product* and *competing products*, and whether there are any undesirable characteristics to avoid, for instance, fitness power users. The profile revision will then concentrate on removing factors that are not going to affect users' behaviors when interacting with your product or otherwise add information and instead focus on isolating factors that are more likely to produce an ideal target audience. For example, the *Behaviors* section from the previous step may be updated to include additional criteria, such as a person in the target audience: (1) prefers not to exercise; (2) currently does not wear a watch; and (3) talks about health issues with their friends.

In practice, the process of creating such a set of profiles will vary. For example, a company developing a new variant of a product in a market in which the company has been active for a long time will likely already have significant knowledge about its customers and other stakeholders, such as key members of the procurement teams. By contrast, early-stage research may be required to discover potential product development experiences. In turn, this may require a process of iteration in which the target audience is gradually refined until a set of users is discovered that find the new potential product appealing.

Multiple ways of thinking about users have emerged in HCI. Perhaps the most prominent is that the users we focus on in user research—encompassing various interviewing, observing, and surveying processes—should be *representative*, that is, a group of users who vary enough to be typical of the major types of users. What is representative is largely an empirical question. User research can chart both existing and potential user bases, for example, via customer surveys. However, defining a user is often a political decision. Are we designing for wealthy young professionals or managers, or are we designing while considering the real and diverse needs of all users? User-centered design should strive to cater to all audiences equally while considering their diverse needs. This means fighting the urge to design for managers or oneself and instead empirically studying who will, or might be, a user.

Another approach to selecting users is to focus on extreme or *extraordinary users* [681]. This idea originally emerged in accessibility research, where it was argued that we should focus on users whose abilities are outside of what we may consider ordinary. The point here is to learn from users at the extremes of ability distributions since they may be the ones posing the hardest requirements for design. Pullin and Newell [681] listed a number of products that originated from these user groups, including the tape recorder (developed for blind people) and large-grip kitchen products (for people with tremors).

Another way to select users is to think of users in terms of *early adopters*. The rationale here is that early adopters of technology have needs and wants that will likely apply to other users months or years later. One popular approach is *lead users*. The idea here is that some users have more experience and stronger needs with respect to an emerging technology than general users. A lead user may be a social media influencer, a journalist, or a member of a community of practice. As such, they can provide earlier and deeper information.

Another way to think about users is to deliberately look for *variety* in user groups. The underlying motivation is that we want to understand users and their activities with as much nuance, complexity, and diversity as possible because these may challenge us to create better designs. Identified groups should be different in terms of their needs, beliefs, contexts, purchasing power, and so on.

10.2.2 Other stakeholders

In addition to direct users of interactive systems, other people are often affected by the systems, indirectly involved in their use, or benefiting from them. For instance, they may be the parents of children who use a kids' web page or the co-workers of users of an accounting system. We call these people *stakeholders*. We may conduct research with stakeholders in the same way as we do with users. However, methods that focus on observing and analyzing HCI are less relevant here. As stakeholders do not directly need to interact with a given system, they may have different views and varying knowledge of the benefits, drawbacks, and activities relevant to the system. The participation of stakeholders is necessary to answer questions related to the power, interest, and relationships between users and stakeholders.

How do we identify a stakeholder? *Stakeholder analysis* refers to a systematic attempt to identify stakeholders. The goal of such analysis is to identify groups and organizations that affect or are affected by the system.

Mitchell et al. [550] proposed three relationship attributes to start defining a stakeholder group: power, legitimacy, and urgency. First, *power* refers to a relationship in which one group of users can get another group to do something. For example, election monitors may have certain powers over local organizations, which in turn may affect the layout of a voting interface, which in turn affects interaction. Management at a construction company has power over contractors, who in turn may have power over subcontractors. To the extent that a system is involved in the control of this power, such groups become stakeholders in that system. Second, *legitimacy* refers to the legal or normative basis of a stakeholder group. For example, hackers are illegitimate stakeholders in many network systems. Third, *urgency* refers to how time-sensitive a relationship is. For example, some groups may be perceived as "calling for attention," being "in need of immediate attention," or "driving" development. Urgency can also be thought about by considering criticality: What is the opportunity loss of *not* addressing this group versus the gain from addressing it? In short, urgency is about the timeliness and criticality of a group.

Stakeholder analysis is hard and has not gained as much popularity outside academia as it perhaps should have. The reason lies in the complexity of the relationships between people in a system. Some stakeholder groups are latent; they are affected not directly but through some mediating mechanisms. For example, the excessive use of gamification affects not only children playing mobile games but also their parents. Some stakeholders are dormant; they are silent most of the time and are triggered only in special circumstances. For instance, legal experts may not be stakeholders in the regular use of a system; in the case of an accident or crime, they become stakeholders. The authors also note that managers have a tendency to be biased. They focus not necessarily on those stakeholders who are the most urgent but on those who are most important to them, for example, because of commercial or political reasons. Stakeholder analysis is further complicated by the fact that some stakeholders are not humans. Animal welfare, for example, is foregrounded in attempts to design "the Internet of dogs." There is also increasing interest in including the natural environment as a stakeholder.

10.2.3 Sampling

To do user research, specific participants should be chosen. One consideration is *representativeness*: Does this user group represent the target audience or a valid segment of other stakeholders? This is an important consideration, as failing to sample representatively can produce a very skewed dataset, and this skewness may be difficult to detect.

Another consideration is the *variability in the sample*: Will we learn about the breadth and variety of the target audience's attitudes and work? In interview studies and observations, we are often interested in covering as varied situations as possible to get the full complexity of users' worlds.

Yet another consideration is *statistical power*: Will this sample size be large enough to draw reliable conclusions about it? Often, a larger sample is better—provided it is representative. In practice, however, it is often necessary to sample only as many people as needed to draw reliable conclusions. In situations where our aim is to get statistically reliable results, we can perform power analysis; see, for instance, [162].

There are a few practical considerations that are worth dwelling on. First, *access and availability*: Are these users available to study? Second, *cost efficiency*: Is this user group providing enough information for design relative to the cost of studying them? Third, *participation costs*: Does participating in the user research present any cost or danger to the participants? These considerations may lead to different choices regarding which and how many users to include in the research. The subsequent chapters provide more detailed advice.

10.3 User research methods

Research methods in user research are means to obtain empirical knowledge about users, including research-based instruments, techniques, and procedures for collecting, analyzing, and reporting

Table 10.1 Overview of popular user research methods covered in this part of the book.

Research method	Description
Interview	Ask users questions about their attitudes, experiences, and activities.
Contextual inquiry	Observe and speak to users as they do their work.
Observation	Observe users without affecting them.
Ethnography	Explore the viewpoint of the user through observations, interviews, and participation in the community being studied.
Survey	Collect a large sample of structured self-reported data.
Diary	Have users keep a diary of their use of interactive systems.
Log file analysis	Automatically analyze what users do with interactive systems.
Analysis of archival data	Analyze the activities and products users create in or with interactive systems.

insights. As in any empirical research, the goal of user research is to obtain accurate and defensible knowledge about the subject under study.

Many research methods facilitate user research. In this part of the book, we cover a number of qualitative and quantitative methods used extensively in both universities and companies for user research. Table 10.1 provides an overview of the most commonly used methods. Some methods are open-ended, that is, they make few assumptions about the categories of observations to "let the data speak." Log analyses and observations, for example, can be carried out in an open-ended way. By contrast, other methods are close-ended. They assume we know in advance what the interesting phenomena and factors are and focus on uncovering their statistical tendencies. Surveys, for example, are a close-ended method. Another aspect of user research methods is whether they provide a first-person or third-person perspective. Ethnography, for example, attempts to provide a first-person perspective of the lived, experienced world of people. By contrast, log file analysis provides more distant third-person accounts.

10.3.1 Research strategy

The *research strategy* concerns how to select one or more research methods for gathering insights about users. The selection of research methods depends on what the user researchers think is important to obtain insights about. On the one hand, the outcomes from using a particular method should be useful for the problem at hand. On the other hand, the resources needed for the method must also be considered. Yet, the choice of method is not just about cost efficiency.

McGrath [532] introduced three general principles for defining a research strategy. The first principle states that *research methods bound what we can empirically learn*. According to McGrath, "all methods have inherent flaws, although each has certain potential advantages." From this principle, it follows that there is no unique correct method; the selection of methods requires careful consideration of the specific goals of the user research to identify the most suitable method or methods. The user researcher should not assume that, for example, interviews are always the best method or that field studies are superior. Instead, the researcher should remember that each method has specific limitations and strengths.

The second principle of McGrath [532] states that the research strategy is about *trading off conflicting criteria*. The criteria are as follows, in no particular order:

Realism: It concerns how similar the situation being studied is to the situations that the researcher wants to gather insights about. Studies that look at user-initiated behavior in its naturally occurring surroundings, such as field studies, are high in realism.

Precision: It concerns how much accuracy and detail one obtains about the users' behaviors and attitudes, and how much control there is over variables and circumstances of no interest. For example, user studies that track every detail of people's hand movements with motion-tracking equipment are high in precision.

Generalizability: It refers to how well the findings generalize to other people or situations. Studies that collect input from a lot of users, such as surveys, are often high in generalizability.

Each of these criteria works against any of the others, and, in general, it is impossible to maximize all of them at the same time. For instance, let us say that we seek to maximize realism and change the situation being studied as little as possible. This has the consequence that every feature of the context, even those we are not interested in, influences our study. It also means we essentially obtain evidence for one specific situation and face challenges when we try to generalize it to others. These principles can also be used to inform the selection of users, for instance, to decide whether one should seek insights about users in general (maximizing generalizability) or particular users (maximizing realism).

The third principle of research strategy follows from the inherent limitations of methods—*triangulation*. McGrath [532] explained the idea as follows:

> "If you only use one method, there is no way to separate out the part that is the 'true' measure of the concept in question from the part that mainly reflects the method itself. If you use multiple methods, carefully selected to have different strengths and weaknesses, the methods can add strength to each other by compensating for each other's weaknesses."

The meaning of triangulation in everyday language is to establish the location of something by taking bearings from two or more positions. In research, triangulation refers to the combination of multiple research methods to study the same phenomenon. The rationale is that if all research methods are limited in different ways, then their combination should be able to mitigate some of those limitations. Thus, triangulation is a multi-method approach commonly used in user research rather than a single research method.

How is triangulation done in practice? The following checklist helps to understand the requirements for triangulation [565, p. 400]:

- The approaches chosen for the study must be able to address the same underlying question. For example, users' beliefs about interaction can be studied with interviews, surveys, and possibly observations but may not be—at least not easily—studied via log analysis.
- For each approach, the inherent biases should be analyzed and made explicit. Every method has a tendency to focus on particular facets of the world, ignoring others; hence, bias. Being aware of such observational biases, we can better select methods that complement each other.
- Mechanisms that produce bias should be understood and acknowledged. For example, researchers tend to use terminology in interviews and surveys that is more approachable to user groups that are similar to them. Each of the methods we discuss in this part is susceptible to biases that can be mitigated via careful triangulation.

- Critical shortcomings or biases should be compensated for somehow, for example, by adding a method that compensates for them. If one method is more susceptible to the researcher's own biases, this should be compensated by adding a method that is less so.
- The results from using the two methods are compared and assessed to understand how the methods affected the results. When reporting the results of a triangulated study, we should be systematically aware of the limitations of the methods that produced the observations.

In triangulation, several things can happen. The different methods may result in the same overall results, corroborating the findings and offering converging evidence. The methods can also offer complementary findings, highlighting different phenomena or relations. Finally, the methods may offer contradicting findings. Pettersson et al. [653] showed that about half of a set of user experience studies used methodology triangulation; the other half relied on just one method, which carried the risks outlined in the five bullet points.

10.4 Methodological quality

Research methods have different strengths and weaknesses. We may characterize methods in terms of their realism, generalizability, or precision. In addition, methods may be used more or less well; we call the criteria by which this is judged *methodological quality*. Next, we discuss the four dimensions of methodological quality.

Validity: Validity refers to whether the conclusions drawn from a study are justified. *Threats to validity* are anything that could go wrong and threaten the validity of the conclusions drawn. A classic taxonomy of validity covers four types [758]. *Internal validity*: Whether a variable under the control of the researcher, for example, user groups, devices, or tasks, has an effect on observations. *Construct validity*: Whether a measurement that is supposed to measure something, such as user experience, actually measures it. *Statistical conclusion validity*: Whether the conclusions drawn from the data are statistically reliable. *External validity*: Do the conclusions hold for other participants and settings?

Reliability: The reliability of user research and empirical research in general concerns whether the research gives consistent results. That is, we want our methods to produce the same results if they are applied again to the same context in the same way. McDonald et al. [530] offered guidelines on how to assess and leverage reliability in HCI research.

Transparency: The transparency of user research refers to the idea that researchers should make their design, data, analysis approach, and derivation of conclusions accessible and inspectable. Transparency is often associated with open scholarship and a desire to increase the replicability of research. To many, this ideal of research quality applies to all forms of research in HCI, including those that draw on social science methods [542]. However, current HCI research is not transparent; many studies do not share artifacts, protocols for research methods, and so on [863]. Several practices are associated with transparency, such as sharing data, planning decisions before reviewing data, conducting careful analysis and reporting, and maintaining a chain of evidence throughout the study.

Ethics: Doing user research requires the person conducting the research to carefully consider what is right and wrong in collecting, analyzing, and reporting data. Ethical concerns also encompass allegiances to various stakeholders, notably the prospective users who participate in the research and the client for whom the research is conducted, the professional standards of the field of HCI, and the researcher's responsibility toward society at large. We also discuss ethics in Chapters 43 and 45.

Validity, reliability, and transparency are key considerations in analysis; frequently, ethics become relevant in analysis as well. For instance, the transcription of interviews impacts the reliability of the analysis. If the transcription is sloppy, the resulting analysis may suffer. Similarly, the care with which we record user observations impacts the validity of our findings; if we miss writing down certain observations, our data might be invalid.

The specific techniques differ depending on the research method. They include thematic analysis, affinity diagramming, statistical analysis, and machine learning classifiers. The rest of this part will detail these techniques.

10.5 Data analysis and representation

A key challenge in user research is transforming the results obtained into a useful and actionable form. Thus, both the analysis and representation of results are important in user research. For representation, the key issue is to synthesize the results of user research in a way that is helpful for design. A representation is helpful if it brings forward critical insights from user research clearly and transparently. It may also have a positive impact on those involved in decision-making about the design.

In the rest of this part, we discuss different techniques for representing user research, including the following techniques. *Personas* are profiles of fictional characters that describe representative users within relevant segments of the target audience. *Scenarios* are narrative accounts of what happens when users try to use a system to achieve their goals. *Artifact and context models* are descriptions of key objects and their contextual relationships within a situation. *Quotes* are rich representations of users' attitudes and needs. Finally, *journey maps* are temporal accounts of users' encounters with a system. Chapter 15 discusses representation in depth.

10.6 Does user research work?

What evidence is there that user research works? This is a difficult question to answer. One answer is that user research is akin to an axiom: It is considered valuable as a basic commitment to do user-centered research. One can go as far as saying that *not* doing user research is unethical, as it may lead to outcomes that harm end-users in ways not predicted by designers. The time lost to frustrations with computers is one example. Another example, arguably more severe, is algorithmic bias—AI algorithms that discriminate against users based on race or gender. Moreover, engaging in user research often has economic benefits. As mentioned in Part I, many HCI activities have been linked to a positive ROI. Another answer is to point to the many success stories of work in HCI that have departed from users, such as the "tire track diagrams" of HCI's history discussed in the introduction to this book (Chapter 16). In the history of HCI, there are examples of discoveries made in user research that have helped shape a product.

However, the evidence is by no means unequivocally in favor of user research. Before modern user-centered design, many interactive systems were developed without involving users systematically in the development of the systems before launch. Many of the tools we use today, including musical instruments, are the result of many rounds of design iteration.

HCI pioneer Donald Norman [602] argued that human-centered design can sometimes lead to incoherent systems. Such systems may strive to fulfill user requests but end up as a jungle of disentangled and confusing functionalities. *Feature creep* is the unavoidable consequence of too closely adhering to even the weakest signal in user research. Moreover, as Norman argued, users adapt; they appear willing to adapt to systems that offer value, even if such systems are not necessarily adapted well to human abilities.

In summary, user research has not been proven to be necessary or sufficient for building interactive systems. However, one can argue that despite the lack of conclusive evidence, user research is currently the best available approach for understanding people in design and development. Its core value may lie more in informing good design than in driving radical innovations, as discussed by Norman [602].

Summary

- You are not the user: Empirical research is required to obtain knowledge on the practices and experiences of other people.
- User research uses empirical methods to understand users, their activities, the contexts in which they act, and the interactive systems they presently use, if any.
- User research aims to produce actionable knowledge about users, that is, insights that may subsequently help design an interactive system or make a decision about its use.
- All methods for user research are limited, for instance, with respect to their realism, generalizability, and precision.
- The key qualities of research methods are validity, reliability, transparency, and ethics.

11
Interviews

One way to learn about users is to speak with them. However, just talking to people is not research. From a research point of view, the *way* we talk to people in everyday encounters is fraught with problems. Everyday conversations are often not planned and, therefore, may provide a scattered view of a topic. Everyday conversations may not aim to understand the conversational partner's viewpoint. Moreover, we rarely record our conversations, and it is practically impossible to later form a systematic account of what happened.

Interviewing, in user research, concerns learning about the subjective experiences of users. The purpose is to learn how *they* view their tasks, values, experiences, and practices, and what their wishes are for interactive systems. The purpose of such learning is primarily to understand users and secondarily to inform design and decision-making related to technology. Interviews may also be used as a general research strategy in human–computer interaction (HCI), aiming to obtain insights about users rather than input for a particular design.

An *interview* is where the researcher meets the user. An interview aims to elicit first-person views on a selected topic from a particular user while avoiding omissions and biases. In interviewing, an interviewer talks with an interviewee following some planned script or schema. The session can be organized as a structured series of fixed questions or as an open-ended but thematically defined conversation. The systematic nature of interviewing distinguishes it from everyday talk.

The interview method has helped establish many important findings in HCI and is routinely used in both user research and interactive system evaluation. For example, from interviews, we have learned about the motivations behind the use of social networks (Paper Example 11.0.1). Other examples of interviews in user research include the following:

- Ljungblad et al. [491] studied human–drone interactions by interviewing professional drone pilots. Their data show how drone pilots are inventing new work and businesses enabled by drones, such as new types of photogrammetry for imaging potential rockfall areas. Pilots are particularly pleased with the improved safety level compared to earlier solutions. For example, drones reduce the risk to workers in hazardous jobs, such as inspecting power lines or in forestry work.
- Kumar et al. [444] studied the experience of 21 Uber drivers in Dhaka, Bangladesh. Their data exposed a surprising finding: The design of the ridesharing service amplified feelings of oppression. One reason for these experiences was the use of English on the map and in the application. Many drivers, some of whom were illiterate, had to rote-learn to use the application while others had to "rely on luck" when using it. The drivers had to invent creative workarounds.
- Simpson and Semaan [777] studied the impact of TikTok algorithms on LGBTQ+ communities. Their interviews revealed that TikTok's *For You Page* both supported and hindered the users' identity work. The authors also described the practices adopted by the users in response to these issues.

Introduction to Human-Computer Interaction. Kasper Hornbæk, Per Ola Kristensson, and Antti Oulasvirta,
Oxford University Press. © Kasper Hornbæk, Per Ola Kristensson, and Antti Oulasvirta (2025).
DOI: 10.1093/oso/9780192864543.003.0011

> **Paper Example 11.0.1: Why we tag**
>
> In their paper *Why We Tag: Motivations for Annotation in Mobile and Online Media*, Ames and Naaman [20] studied motivations for the use of tags, or annotation, in photo sharing. At the time when the study was conducted in 2007, photo sharing was becoming popular as a type of social media, and there was a need to understand why tagging was gaining popularity. Tags, at that time, were used in some social media services but not all, raising the question of what motivated people to use them. Why would users put effort into using tags? Ames and Naaman approached this question by interviewing 13 Flickr users.
>
> The interviews revealed a surprising diversity of motivations, which Ames and Naaman categorized using two dimensions: sociality and function. While we usually think about tagging as something we do to attract attention and do self-promotion, they showed that tags are also used to help memory and remind oneself to do things. According to the first dimension, people tag for social and self-related purposes. According to the second dimension, they tag to either organize information or communicate it. For example, Participant 2 in their study said:
>
>> If I have the time, the neighborhood, or the event, I have enough information to look at my own collection and know where this came from. I don't have the bandwidth to tag for the benefit of the Flickr system. [...] I want at least one hook of association in there that can help me reconstruct what I was thinking. I don't have time to put all the hooks in but I can put one in.
>
> This example illustrates the strength of interviews: They can help shed light on phenomena for which there is no systematic understanding yet. Interviews complement other methods by providing an open-ended, non-committal approach to data collection that does not need to commit to predefined categories of observation or assume there is a "true" or "valid" point of view. Instead, interviews help us expose individual subjective viewpoints on technology.

Interviews may be criticized as being "easy" or even not scientific. Nothing could be further from the truth. While we all know how to talk to other people, the interview method requires not only an understanding of the underlying scientific principles but also years of practice to master. Interviewing is hard, and numerous pitfalls threaten the inexperienced interviewer. Learning to ask questions and listen to answers to uncover meaningful insights is a craft. Many guidelines are available to help you organize interviews and talk to users in a valid and useful way. This chapter covers some of those guidelines and types of interviews; more details can be found in chapters and books on interviews, such as the work by Rubin and Rubin [716].

The fundamental idea behind using interviews for research is that they allow interviewers to gain an understanding of the lives of *others*—people who are very different from themselves. The strength of the interview lies in capturing the interviewee's attitudes and interpretations of the world in which *they* live and work. Interviews thus provide a unique perspective on felt experiences that are accessible exclusively through such structured approaches. To this effect, interviewers must not impose their views or beliefs on those they interview: "don't argue, never give advice" [528]. More than that, interviews can empower people by allowing them to express themselves.

It is important to understand when to use an interview and when not to. Interviews are not particularly well suited for obtaining numerical or statistical information. Instead, interviews are typically used to gain an understanding of beliefs, attitudes, and experiences. For example, it is not necessary or advisable to use interviews to figure out how often people use a particular software or if they are using a particular web site.

Many forms of interviews have been developed for a range of purposes in many research fields. At a high level, interviews can be divided into structured, semi-structured, and unstructured.

A *structured interview* has two fundamental variants: quantitative and qualitative. The purpose of a quantitative structured interview is to collect statistical survey data; accordingly, the format of the interview and the sequence of questions are predetermined. Such interviews are commonly conducted as part of demographic or market surveys. A qualitative structured interview consists of a set schedule and a set sequence of questions. Unlike in quantitative structured interviews, the main purpose is not to learn about the distribution of answers but rather their content.

An *unstructured interview*, or non-directed interview, is, as its name implies, an interview where there is no fixed schedule or sequence of questions. Questions may or may not be prepared in advance. Unstructured interviews are an important research methodology in some fields, such as sociology; however, they are not common in HCI and will not be discussed in detail in this chapter.

Researchers often compromise between these two variants and conduct *semi-structured* interviews. This variant does not impose a rigorous schedule or a fixed sequence of questions, but it is also not completely loose in its structure. Semi-structured interviews tend to follow a loose structure and are frequently referred to as *open-ended interviews* in HCI. Open-ended interviews are discussed in detail in this chapter. An example is gievn in Paper Example 11.0.2.

Paper Example 11.0.2: Death on social media

People on social media eventually pass away. Brubaker et al. [101] were interested in how their digital profiles were involved in grief and how such profiles were used after death.

The interviews were open-ended, allowing participants to guide the discussion to the topics that most interested them but with a general focus on feelings about and approaches to death, experiences with social media and other communication technologies, and interactions and experiences with death on Facebook in particular. The interviews revealed critical views of postmortem walls on Facebook:

"To be honest, I just don't think death on Facebook is ever appropriate ... I feel like all that's doing is attention calling [...] maybe you want to share that you are in pain and in grief, but you probably just want people to know that you knew somebody who died and it makes you sad [...] there's a reason people put that crap on their Facebook profile, and I don't think it's for the benefit of the dead person."

More surprising was the finding that encounters with the deceased allowed users to participate in the mourning in new ways, as illustrated by this quote:

"Maybe about a year and a half ago, he contacted me on Facebook and he wanted to know what I was up to. And we had a long conversation on instant messenger ... that's the last time I was in contact with him. [...] I went on his Facebook to wish him a happy birthday and saw that he had died. [...] It had been nine months or so ago he was in a car accident."

This example shows how the interview method can help researchers gain access to personally deep experiences that would be very hard to gauge by other means. For example, how would one form a questionnaire on mourning on social media?

11.1 Open-ended interviews

Open-ended interviews are the most common form of interviews in HCI. They are called open-ended because the questions asked during the interview are not fully planned in advance and, at least in part, they are developed and adapted based on the interviewees' answers. In this way, the interviewer can further investigate unexpected but interesting answers or adapt the questions to help the interviewees. Open-ended interviews try to minimize the influence of the person asking the questions on the interviewees' answers. Open-ended interviews are sometimes called *responsive* interviews [716] to highlight that the structure and the questions develop as the interview progresses. Nevertheless, the interviews retain a certain theme, structure, and focus.

Open-ended interviews can be thought of as a development of conversation. In an open-ended interview, a conversation takes place—typically face-to-face—between two conversational partners, the interviewer and the interviewee. The interview shares the following characteristics with a conversation:

- The interview is flexible in content and structure, just as a conversation may freely develop. The interviewer adapts their questions based on what is being said; they follow up on answers and may pursue new information with additional questions.
- The interview has a certain continuity; the conversation partners understand where the conversation is going.
- The interview is about understanding what the conversational partner says. If you do not understand what the interviewee says, you follow up and probe with additional questions. If you are not being understood, for instance, if your interview questions are unclear, you should clarify them.
- The interview needs the full attention of the interviewer and, ideally, of the interviewee. Minimize the attention paid to notes and note-taking, other people, and the environment.
- The interview requires conversational partners to treat each other with respect and protect any information that is shared in confidence.

However, not all aspects of ordinary conversations are reflected in interviews. First, the interview is initiated by the interviewer for the purpose of doing user research. Thus, there is a basic asymmetry in the conversation that needs to be carefully managed so that the interviewee feels valued and can follow the purpose and content of the conversation.

Second, even if an interview may appear as a casual conversation, the interviewer has carefully prepared, and the questions are thoughtfully designed. This is the result of preparation to identify a theme for the interview, design the interview, and carefully word the questions.

Third, during the interview, an interviewer often spends more time listening than in an average conversation; in short, "listen, don't talk" [528, p. 65]. Listening closely, noting the relation between what is being said and what is left unsaid, is a craft far beyond most of the conversations we have most of the time.

Fourth, an interview may often be recorded to be analyzed in depth later; indeed, some follow-up questions may be posed in anticipation of that later analysis.

User research with open-ended interviews typically consists of four phases: (1) developing the themes of the interview, (2) planning and wording the questions, (3) conducting the interview, and (4) analyzing the ensuing conversations. These phases are often iterative; for instance, conducting the interview and analyzing it may lead to different questions and wordings thereof. Next, we discuss these phases in detail.

11.1.1 Themes

The basis of any interview is the development of the themes of the interview. The themes refer to the topics the interviewer wants to learn about. In user research, themes may concern practices of using an existing system, patterns of collaboration in an organization, perceptions of implantable devices, or exceptionally thrilling experiences with computers. Themes can be specific or broad. They may focus on a specific system, event, or use situation—or they may be broad and cover the totality of the interviewee's life and aspirations. The former might be appropriate when trying to understand breakdowns in an existing system, whereas the latter might be appropriate to understand the implications of remote work.

Existing interview studies in HCI provide examples of the outcomes of developing themes. For instance, Grudin [303] was interested in the increasing use of multiple monitors. He discussed the literature on multiple monitors and found that a number of simple questions around this topic had not been answered, including "How do multimonitor users make use of the extra space?" and "Is the second (or third) monitor an extension of their workspace, or do they use it for different purposes?" Those themes formed the basis for designing the questions used to interview 18 multi-display users.

In addition to technology-centered themes, an interview can also be centered on research questions [716] or more closely formulated hypotheses [449]. In these cases, the themes can depart from theory, attempt to build theory, or challenge a known theory. However, when developing such themes, the intent is the same as in the general case: to spell out why the interview is done and what it should be about.

11.1.2 Questions

Given a set of themes for an interview, the next phase consists of finding effective ways to ask about those themes. In open-ended interviewing, you want to ask simple questions that allow the interviewees to give complex answers. Three types of questions may be distinguished: main questions, probes, and follow-up questions [716].

Main questions directly correspond to the themes of the interview; typically, a study has a few of these questions. Each of these questions can be asked to start a conversation. Main questions are often broad and allow the interviewee to cover the basics. For instance, Kirk et al. [415] were interested in the work that people do on their digital photos after capture but before sharing them. They argued that previous work mainly focused on sharing photos and had not investigated this aspect of digital photography. Based on an initial analysis of what such photo work might involve, they identified a series of themes and topics that were currently unclear and that could be investigated in an interview study. These themes are represented in the paper through questions such as "When and why do you delete your pictures?" "How do you file your photos away (using file structure, folder labels, and so on)?" and "When do you look at your pictures?"

A few types of main questions can be differentiated.

- In a tour question, the interviewee is asked to give a tour of the interview topic, be it a workplace, an interactive system, a work task, or a location. One may ask "walk me through what happens when X," "show me Y," or "tell me about Z." For instance, Odom et al. [611] organized their interviews with tweens and teens on virtual possessions as a tour:

> We asked participants to give us a tour of their material possessions both stored and on display in their bedroom, and to describe their relationships with these artifacts. This was typically followed by a tour of participants' virtual possessions, where we observed virtual artifacts on their personal computer, phone, media player, etc.

- In a grounded question, the interviewee is asked to give a specific example that grounds their answer. For instance, the most recent file they downloaded or the worst mistake they have made in sending out a social media message.
- In a your-experience question, the interviewee is asked to explain their beliefs or attitudes regarding a certain topic or event.
- In a key concept question, the interviewee is asked to explain a certain topic as they understand it.
- In a stage question, the interviewee is asked to account for the stages or chronology of an event.
- In a comparison question, the interviewee is asked to compare or contrast events, technologies, or anything else that is of interest to the interviewer.

Main questions in specific interviews may, of course, differ completely from these types. What is advisable is that there is a clear link from each theme to one or more main questions. Together, these questions should allow for a good exploration of the theme.

The second type of question, *probes*, is designed to make the interviewee comfortable and continue to talk. Such questions have no explicit link to the themes of a study but are simply tactics for moving the conversation forward, asking for elaboration and clarification, or returning to the indented point of a main question after a digression. For instance, the interviewer may say "mmh, then what . . ." "please go on," "what hapened next?" or "tell me more about that." Nonverbal acknowledgment, such as nodding and smiling, may work similarly. Sometimes, the interviewer may simply echo the interviewee's words to indicate that they find them interesting and worthy of further explanation. If the interviewee says "but the system does not work as intended," the interviewer may echo "does not work as intended."

The third type, *follow-up questions*, aims to extend the answer to a main question. The intent is to ensure the conversation resulting from a main question is thorough and deep and to explore new ideas and concepts that the interviewee brings up. Some follow-up questions can be prepared in advance based on likely answers. They may also be improvised during an interview when new information or interesting stories are shared. Follow-up questions can also come up during the analysis of earlier interviews, as the interviewer realizes they should have pursued certain topics further with the interviewee.

Many things can warrant follow-up questions. Next, we offer a brief list of possible lines for follow-ups.

- Clarify answers. Follow up on undefined terms or unclear explanations. For instance, "You said that the system was X; what do you mean by X?" or "What you said there seemed very important and I want to be sure that I understand it; please explain it again."

- Get concrete answers. Follow up on answers that oversimplify, lack depth, or are abstract. For instance, "Could you give me an example?"
- Compare or contrast answers. You may follow up on answers by asking the interviewee to compare or contrast them to previous answers. For instance, "Earlier you said that X; how does that situation compare to what you just told me?"
- Understand variation. Here, you follow up to understand how responses vary based on the circumstances. For instance, "Do you always do it this way?" or "How has this changed over time?"
- Ensure thoroughness. You may follow up when answers do not cover all the aspects of a main question or when you feel that information is missing. For instance, "I think we have not covered X much; please tell me about that."
- Understand personal attitude. Follow up on questions where it is unclear how the interviewee thought or felt. For instance, "Why was this important to you?" or "How did you feel about that?"

The wording of main and follow-up questions is crucial in interviews. The right wording keeps the interview on track and ensures the questions do not bias the interviewee.

The questions should be as neutral as possible. Avoid wording that could influence the answers in a particular direction, introduce bias, or give cues for answering. For instance, instead of asking "How much did you like the system?" which is highly biasing, you can ask "Can you tell me about your experiences while using the system?" Questions should be asked one at a time; avoid double-barreled questions, for example, "Let me know how you normally do the same task when at home and what kinds of features you use in your toaster." The questions should be clearly expressed. Make them short and be sure to use appropriate, jargon-free, and culturally appropriate terms; if in doubt, ask in an open-ended manner and learn the clearest terms and ways of questioning.

It is also important to avoid *leading questions*. A leading question is a question that implies there is a specific set of "right" answers to a question. Consciously or unconsciously, asking leading questions is a frequent source of error in user research. Non-directed interviewing is about setting up an interview situation that is completely focused on the interviewee; leading questions prevent this by injecting conscious or unconscious prejudices from the interviewer into the interview.

While avoiding leading questions sounds simple, it is very difficult in practice. It requires a constant awareness of the risk of suddenly injecting bias or steering the conversation in a way that influences the interviewee's thoughts. A central idea is to be a *neutral interviewer* to fully understand any positive and negative information provided and to be able to relate back what the *user*—not the interviewer—wants or needs. This requires the interviewer to try to step out of everything they know and feel about the HCI idea or system in question. Depending on the interviewer, this may be easy or difficult. Being personally invested in an HCI idea or system will make it more difficult for the interviewer to put aside all their previous work and creativity efforts. It is important to remember this and be honest with yourself about your ability to be a neutral interviewer on the subject matter. In practice, it demands self-imposed distancing from the issues being discussed, a comprehensive self-evaluation, and an introspective examination of the assumptions, values, and so on related to the interview topic.

So, how do we create non-directed questions? In general, it is best to focus each non-directed question on a single topic to avoid ambiguity. For example, a question such as "How would you use your camera on a holiday or at work?" is best broken down into two separate questions. Non-directed questions should focus on immediate experiences and impressions. People are poor at predicting the future, including their own future. Therefore, asking users whether they will use something in the future is not meaningful. A better strategy is to try to find out what they find compelling and usable in the present. Related to this, it is important to avoid having interviewees extrapolate from their own understanding of their behavior, as people's understanding of their behavior often does not correspond to their actual behavior. For instance, a question such as "Is handwriting recognition useful?" may be understood by the interviewee as a question on whether handwriting could be useful for *someone* in *some* hypothetical situation. The interviewee is unlikely to know the answer to such a question and is likely to speculate. A better way to phrase such a question is to simply ask "Is handwriting recognition useful to you right now?" Questions should also not use judgmental language; in other words, the interviewee should not get the impression that they are requested to answer a question in a specific way or that their answer to a question was wrong. For example, a question such as "Don't you think it is a great idea to enable autocorrect by default on all smartphones?" implies the interviewer holds this opinion and is looking for affirmation.

Let us provide a warning about interview questions that appear in the methodology literature [703, 716]. Questions are often of the *5W1H* form (or variants thereof): who, what, when, where, why, and how. Although the question "why?" is simple and often seems a good interview question, use it carefully. It may prompt participants to give a simplified answer or offer justifications when they cannot provide a more thorough answer. This may cause nervousness and affect the rest of the interview. As such, "why?" questions should be used sparsely and always with care.

11.1.3 Conducting interview conversations

An interview conversation consists of several parts [716]. Although these may vary depending on the theme and the circumstances of the interview, they typically include the following six parts.

Introduction: In the first phase, both the interviewer and the participant introduce themselves, and the interviewer explains the purpose of the interview. Typically, the interviewer wants to establish themselves as neutral but sympathetic. It is often a good idea to start interviews with a bit of casual chat to create a relaxed, conversational atmosphere. Show people that they are competent and noteworthy. Introduce yourself and your focus: Why do you want to speak to the interviewee?

Warm-up: In the second phase, the objective is to make the participant step away from their normal life and change their focus to consider the objective of the interview, typically a particular system, product, or service. This part typically includes some easy questions to start the conversation and make the interviewee comfortable. The questions may be about background information, for example, the theme of the interview.

General issues: In the third phase, the interview is centered around direct experiences and related attitudes and expectations with the product, system, or service in question. Asking these types of questions early in the interview prevents adverse effects from the interviewer inadvertently skewing the interviewee's perception as the interview progresses.

Deep focus: In the fourth phase, the central focus of the interview is introduced. This is the key part of the interview, where the main questions are asked, prompts are given, and follow-up questions are used to deepen the interview.

Retrospective: In the fifth phase, the interviewee has time to reflect on the broader issues of the HCI idea or system that has been discussed. This is also an opportunity for the interviewee to relate the *general issues* identified earlier with thoughts that arose in the deep focus phase. Another purpose of this part may be to minimize any intellectual or emotional tension in the interview to ensure it ends on a relaxed note.

Wrap-up: In the sixth phase, the interviewer completes the interview to avoid interviewees feeling left hanging at the end of the interview. This includes thanking the interviewee for their time and answers. Typically, the interviewer also explains what will happen next, for instance, if they expect to send the whole or parts of the interview, or the analysis of the interviewee's answers, to the interviewee for comments or approval. It may also cover other plans for staying in touch, such as sending a final report to the interviewee.

An important objective for an interviewer is to be pleasant, polite, and at least appear to be enjoying the conversation.

Interviews often last about one hour. Robson [703] offered the following advice: "Anything under half an hour is unlikely to be valuable; anything going much over an hour may be making unreasonable demands on busy interviewees, and could have the effect of reducing the number of persons willing to participate, which may in turn lead to biases in the sample that you achieve." In practice, depending on the setting and the themes of the interview, an interview on HCI can be much shorter.

Several options are available for the interviewer to record answers during an interview. If the interviewer does not take any notes, they can pay full attention to the conversation; however, later, they will not be able to analyze what the participants actually said or easily discuss the interviews with persons who were not present. As such, this approach is generally not recommended. The interviewer may record the conversation to transcribe and revisit it later. Usually, an audio-recording device is sufficient; video does not add much unless the talk is about artifacts or practices that are better explained through visual demonstrations.

Interviews are often supported by an *interview guide*. Such a guide contains the main questions and a list of anticipated prompts and follow-up questions for each of them. It can also contain a procedure for the entire interview, either outlined or written out in full. Writing it down in full is recommended for novice interviewers.

11.1.4 Analysis of open-ended interviews

The analysis of interviews transforms the interview conversation into insights. The recommendation for open-ended interviews is to do this as soon as possible after the interview. The point is to keep as much of the conversation and the accompanying hunches and associations clear when the interview is analyzed. In this way, the insights from the analysis can inform later interviews, for instance, by changing the questions, improving the follow-up questions, or improving the tone set in the introduction to the interview.

The details of how to do the analysis will be covered in Section 11.5, as they are similar for several forms of interviewing. Various ideas for constructing representations of users to aid design work are presented in Chapter 15.

11.2 Structured interviews

Structured interviews have predefined questions and structures, which makes them more rigid than open-ended interviews. Compared to open-ended interviews, such scripted interviews are easier to conduct because they require less improvisation. This structured format also simplifies analysis and helps minimize the level of overlap between interviewees. In this sense, structured interviews are relatively similar to surveys. As Paper Example 11.2.1 shows, interview methods can be combined with other data collection methods, such as questionnaires.

> **Paper Example 11.2.1: A mixed-methods study of phishing**
>
> Have you received a suspicious email asking you to fill in information on a web site that mimics a legitimate one? *Phishing* refers to fraudulent web sites or emails used to acquire personal information on users. Dhamija et al. [192] conducted structured interviews on phishing with 22 participants.
>
> Their methodology comprised structured interviews and questionnaire-based data collection. They showed some web sites to the participants and asked them to determine which ones were fraudulent: "Imagine that you receive an email message asking you to click on one of the following links. Imagine that you decide to click on the link to see if it is a legitimate website or a spoof." Their data collection process included a structured part where they asked participants to state if the shown site was legitimate or not and assess their confidence. They also asked the participants for their reasoning and to think aloud when assessing the web sites. Finally, in a debriefing session, the experimenters revealed the incorrect answers to the participants and held an open discussion about the mistakes.
>
> The study found that the participants did not look at cues such as the address bar, which would have exposed the fraudulent web sites, resulting in 40% incorrect choices. The post-session interviews shed more light on why this happened. For example, the participants did not know what the Secure Sockets Layer padlock icon meant and could not explain its presence.

Structured interviews can provide both general and specific information. For example, they can be used to ask participants to describe their experiences using adjectives or nouns. For instance, Obrist et al. [610] studied the experiences associated with the stimulation of two classes of mechanoreceptors on participants' hands. Participants were subjected to different simulations and asked detailed questions about what they felt on their hand, including "what words would you use to describe how it felt on your hand, if at all?" and "was there anything else you felt or thought or are there any sensations or pictures that come in your mind?" From the resulting descriptions, it was possible to build 14 categories of tactile experiences.

11.3 Micro-phenomenological interviews

Micro-phenomenological interviews have recently gained interest as a method for understanding the lived experiences of users. *Phenomenology* refers to the felt experience of interviewees; *micro* refers to the idea that the interview consists of sequences of small questions and responses that iteratively elaborate on the account of an experience:

> **Interviewee:** I was frustrated when installing an update to the software.
> **Interviewer:** What happened during the update?
> **Interviewee:** The screen just blanked in the middle. The computer was running but the display was blank.
> **Interviewer:** When did you see it go blank?

Interviewee: I left the computer to do the update and went to lunch. I saw it when I came back.
Interviewer: When you saw the display, what did you feel?

Three aspects are important here:

- The interview focuses on an evocative experience and keeps the focus there.
- The interviewer follows up on responses by asking the interviewee to elaborate on particular moments or facets. This allows the interviewee to iteratively elaborate on the account of the experience.
- The interviewer's questions are content-free. Here, content-free means that the interviewer asks questions that do not suggest an experience. A question should not lead the interviewee to misconstrue the experience. "Why" questions, and any other questions that may trigger reasoning as opposed to remembrance, should be avoided.

For example, Petitmengin et al. [651, p. 55] described how they applied this method to learn about people's experience of meditation:

Interviewee: When I realized that I was gone, the thought vanished.
Interviewer: How did it vanish? Was it instantaneous or gradual?
Interviewee: It was very quick, but it nevertheless took a moment.
Interviewer: And what happened during this moment?

When asking how the experience vanished, the interviewer gave a spectrum of options but invited the interviewee to describe their experience. By contrast, a leading question would have asked "Was it quick?"

Micro-phenomenological interviews are semi-structured, sitting between open-ended and structured interviews. On the one hand, the interviewer picks the themes and follow-up questions. On the other hand, the interviewee has degrees of freedom in picking aspects that are personally important. When using this interview method, it is important to give the interviewee enough time to recall and construct their experience. Hence, even if the interview consists of short back-and-forth exchanges, it should still include many pauses. Moreover, in some cases, it can be beneficial to iterate over the same experience a few times. The interviewer's task is to keep the discussion focused on the event and guide the interviewee's attention to relevant moments or aspects of their experience, slowing down the conversation as needed to create room for thinking.

Prpa et al. [677] provided a guide for utilizing this method in HCI research. After establishing a communication contract (an agreement on the content and timing of interviews), the interviewer states the theme of the interview: "I would like to go back the moment [when something was experienced] and talk about it. Take your time and tell me when you are ready." To start interviewing on an experience, the interviewer should first induce an evocative state of remembrance. The goal is to get the interviewee to relive what happened. This can be tried by first asking about the context of the experience ("Where did this take place? Who was there?") and then asking about the experience. After this, different techniques can be used to iteratively elaborate the accounts:

- Shifting the attention between what to how: "What" questions ask the interviewee to focus on what something felt like, while "how" questions unfold the dynamics of how that happened ("How did you know the installation was still running even if the display was blank?"). The authors warn against asking "why" questions, as they ask for analytical explanations and may disrupt the flow of the interview.

- Redirecting attention to the evocative experience: If the discussion departs too much from the experience, the interviewer should refocus the discussion. "Could we go back to the moment when you were seeing the blank display?"
- Asking to describe the temporal order of the event (diachronic): "What did you do then?" or "How did you start the installation?"
- Deepening to the desired level of detail: By referring to an element in the interviewee's response, the interviewer can ask the interviewee to elaborate on an aspect of interest.
- Reflecting about the experience: Asking the interviewee to come back to the present and reflect on the experience in the present moment.

Mastering these techniques in the thick of an interview requires practice.

11.4 Contextual inquiry

Contextual inquiry is a type of interview developed for HCI by Holtzblatt et al. [349]. It has been influential in HCI because of its intertwining of observing users' activities with interviewing, and it has attracted many hands-on descriptions of how to conduct such interviews; see also Holtzblatt and Beyer [348].

The key idea in a contextual inquiry is to watch users do activities that are important to them and talk to them about those activities. The activities should be ongoing work or leisure activities whenever possible, or concrete summaries thereof. The interviews should focus on understanding the activities and the reasons why users engage in them. Holtzblatt and Beyer argued that the resulting understanding of users' world and their desires forms an important basis for the design of technology. This approach to interviewing emphasizes *realism*, in that it attempts to come close to users' activities and their perceptions thereof. It emphasizes obtaining concrete data about a few users over generalizability and a full understanding of activity over precise details about a single task. A typical contextual inquiry session lasts between one-and-a-half and two hours—enough to engage deeply on a matter but not too long to disrupt the interviewee.

11.4.1 Principles of contextual inquiry

In a contextual inquiry, four principles guide the interviewer's attitude toward the interview situation and the subsequent data analysis.

Context: The first principle is called context. By being close to the activity and the interviewee's perception of it, we gain insights into all the aspects of context that shape what people do. In other words, we prefer to be with the interviewee during the activity: watching them cook, listening to them make a phone call, watching them finish their tax returns, and so on. Presence allows us to see how the activity is performed, how coordination happens, which things and devices are part of the activity, and what is important. Presence helps us notice elements of an activity that only become apparent in context; a standard interview, for instance, may miss many of these elements.

Sometimes, being present during the activity is impossible. The topic of interest may be confidential, occur very rarely, or last so long that it cannot be followed or distributed. In such cases, *retrospective interviews* may be a suitable option, although they may lack cues that are usually present in context such as particular devices, physical layouts, or colleagues.

A contextual inquiry pursues concreteness. The inquiry should be about the ongoing activity to reveal its details, including what it is about and why it matters. The role of the interviewer is to help the interviewee focus on the activity; it is important to avoid summaries, abstractions, and generalizations that may obscure the actual evidence. When interviewees use such descriptions, the interviewer should use probes to direct their attention back to the activity. This may be done in many ways, including "could you show me how?" (in response to "I typically do it some way"), "tell me about when you last did that" (after "I do this often"), and "may I see one?" (after "often people file complaints").

Partnership: The principle of partnership refers to the collaboration between the interviewer and the interviewee to understand the activity and the interviewee's perception of it. When collaborating, for example, it is best to avoid having a long list of questions.

The ideal partnership in contextual inquiry is described as one between a master and an apprentice. This has two implications. First, the user needs to do the talking. Second, the interviewer must take on the role of the apprentice, attempting to inquire about the activity and immerse themselves in it. Thus, in the words of Holtzblatt and Beyer, the interviewer needs to be "nosy."

The interviewer can support the partnership by moving between withdrawal and return. During withdrawal, the interviewer discusses the topic with the user, probing about what happened while trying to understand what the user thinks. During return, the interviewer looks, listens, and tries to learn about the activity.

Interpretation: According to the principle of interpretation, the interviewer and the interviewee attempt to create meaning together. The interviewer should be listening for "no," "but," and "maybe" regarding the activity. The interviewer should also strive to confirm views and be sensitive to cues about the interviewee being hesitant about the interpretation.

Focus: Finally, to make the most out of the interview, the interviewer should go for depth—focus. This does not mean avoiding an open, explorative mindset but rather trying to electively engage in topics that provide depth and insight into the interaction. This is the richest ground for surprises and where most of the energy and the strongest emotions can be found.

11.5 Analysis of interviews

The analysis of interviews concerns how we turn the data collected from structured or open-ended conversations into insights about people, their activities, and the contexts of use. As in other user research, the goal is to make sense of the participants' world from their perspective. Any consideration of possible technological interventions or clever designs is secondary.

One common approach to analysis comprises the following four phases.

- During *transcription*, the audio or video of the interview is typed so that text analysis may be performed. The level of detail of the transcription can vary, ranging from cursory notes to detailed annotations of rhythm, pauses, and intonations in speech. This phase includes returning to the participants to verify any open questions or tentative conclusions with them. Reliability is a key concern here.

- During *analysis*, the interviewer performs rich readings of the transcripts while trying to organize and condense the data. The focus is on the meanings the interviewees have assigned to their behaviors and the world around them.
- During *verification*, the interviewer may return to the participants for clarifications and to check if the interpretations are correct. While this is not always possible, it may provide valuable input and increase the validity of the findings from the interview.
- During *reporting*, the interviewer writes up the outcome of the interviews. This may be in the form of a research paper or representations of users, such as models of work sequences, personas, or something else; see Chapter 15 for more examples. In reporting, the focus is, or should be, on the transparency of the findings.

The rest of this chapter focuses on how an analyst creates meaning, as the other three phases are already covered in depth in guides on how to analyze interviews.

11.5.1 Expanding and condensing meaning

The analysis of interviews encompasses two processes with different intents. In the *expansion of meaning*, analysts aim to expand the interpretation and meaning found in particular parts of interviews. For beginners, this process may seem daunting. How can one sentence of an interview lead to so many interpretations and so many discussions among a team of researchers? The answer is that if one pays enough attention, a multitude of interpretations and implications can and do follow from one sentence. For example, imagine that you are doing an interview on Instagram filters and one interviewee says "I use them to liven up my feed." The question that analysts should be asking is what "liven up" means. This may be interpreted in different ways; for instance, it can mean making images more energetic or aesthetic or inviting comments via exaggeration. How can an analyst determine the best interpretation?

Interpretation demands comprehensive yet sufficiently detailed readings of relevant interview data. Such readings might be supplemented by asking further questions, comparing answers within and across participants, seeking to understand the answers relative to the themes of the interview, and comparing the answers to what is known. Different methods for analyzing interviews prescribe different techniques for expanding meanings and interpretations. Because it is difficult to identify and expand meanings in interviews, this phase is often completed in collaboration with other researchers. This approach also increases result reliability by reducing the influence of the knowledge, skills, and peculiarities of a single analyst on the final result.

The other key process in interview analysis concerns the *condensation* of insights. Rather than to expand the possible meanings and interpretations of the interview, the aim here is to reduce what is being said to patterns or concepts in an organized and manageable structure. These will then provide answers to the themes of the interview and the research questions. This process may be based on beliefs or theory (i.e., deductive or top-down condensation) or it may be guided by the data (i.e., inductive or bottom-up condensation).

The main strategy for condensation is *coding*. In coding, parts of interview transcripts are assigned one or more codes that describe important aspects (e.g., a particular activity). Such codes can be identified from the data in so-called bottom-up coding or from a set of a priori codes, for instance, from a relevant theory.

Analysis may be done at two different times: after all the interviews are done or between the interviews. Most commonly, it is done after all the interviews are completed. However, some researchers find that "analysis is not a one-time task, but an ongoing process" [716, p. 16]. Intertwining interviews and analysis brings many benefits. It allows researchers to change their questions based on insights from analysis and test early conclusions in later interviews. This approach is often combined with open-ended interviews (Section 11.1) to facilitate a series of expansions and condensations of meanings. No matter if analysis is done between or after interviews, insights about the themes and content of interviews may be obtained at any point during the research. Therefore, it is good practice to capture insights in notes (sometimes called memos, field notes, or field diaries) as they come throughout the study.

11.5.2 Affinity diagramming

Affinity diagramming is a simple technique to identify themes from interviews and other data. It was developed and called the KJ method by Kawakita [405], and it became popular in HCI through its use in contextual design [348]. The basic idea is to do a collaborative bottom-up coding of parts of interviews or other data based on any affinity (or similarity) between those parts.

Affinity diagramming can be done in many ways; here, we separate four phases based on the empirical work by Lucero [496]. These phases are typically completed by a group.

1. When *creating notes*, the interviews become manageable distinct notes. These notes may come from transcriptions, subdividing interviews into sentences, question–answer pairs, or other segments that contain an understandable point. The notes may also come from people who were present at the interviews and contain insights or interpretations of what was said in the interviews. If affinity diagramming is used on other sources of data, these are similarly segmented into small, meaningful units. Notes may be put on Post-it notes or small pieces of paper.

2. When *clustering notes*, the group doing the clustering first reads all the notes, either together or individually. Then, the group begins to form rough clusters of related notes, for instance, on a wall or table (Figure 11.1). As the clusters begin to form, the group explains the rationales for placing notes in particular clusters.

3. When *walking the wall*, the group looks over the entire organization of notes; this is called the wall because the notes may be stuck on one. Clusters may be merged or split up to better organize the notes. The group may also discuss the content of the wall and add notes, split notes that contain multiple themes, or clone notes that contain multiple ideas.

4. When *documenting* the analysis, the group transfers the organization of the wall to some digital format for future use.

11.5.3 Thematic analysis

Thematic analysis is a systematic approach to data analysis that helps identify and organize insights and meanings derived from qualitative data. The data may come from interviews, surveys, online content such as blogs or social media posts, or physical documents. The classic description of thematic analysis is provided by Braun and Clarke [94].

Figure 11.1 An example of affinity diagramming activities [496]: (a) pre-clustered notes, (b) talking through clusters and notes, (c) reclustering notes, (d) verbally explaining the reasons for moving notes between clusters, and (e) incorporating quotes from the interviews (yellow Post-it notes).

Like all other methods, thematic analysis is driven by the researchers' questions. It can be explicitly inductive, going from data to themes (like affinity diagramming), or deductive, going from theoretical constructs to themes. It can also be a combination of these two approaches. Thematic analysis may be concerned with obvious meanings in data, more latent insights, or a mix of both. As such, it provides a flexible framework for analysis.

Thematic analysis consists of six steps:

1. Familiarizing yourself with the data. Read the interview transcripts or whatever form the data are in. Form a first opinion about interesting parts of the data based on active and critical thinking about the data. What does what is said or written mean?

2. Generating initial codes. Codes are the building blocks of analysis; they label features of the data that might be important. Codes may be based on what the participants said, the researchers' conceptual framework, factual aspects of the data, or deep interpretations. Coding may happen at any level, from individual sentences or words up to long segments of an interview. Coding happens as one goes over the data. Therefore, be generous in creating codes; at any stage of reading, it is difficult to know if something is relevant. Moreover, be sure to make several passes over the data to develop your codes as you learn more about the data.

3. Searching for themes. This step requires the analyst to generate themes from the codes. A theme captures a pattern of meaning in the data that is important to the research question. According to Braun and Clarke [94], themes are generated or constructed relative to the research question; unfortunately, they cannot be just found or identified. Searching for themes is an active, interpretive process. In practice, this happens through the collapsing or clustering of codes based on similar features.

4. Reviewing themes. This step begins to consolidate and quality-check the themes relative to the entire dataset. Such checks may concern overlaps among themes, if a theme is interesting given the research question, or if a theme has sufficient and substantial data to back it up. As a result, themes may be merged, split, discarded, or developed in different ways.

5. Defining and naming themes. This step is about ensuring the themes have a clear focus and address the research question by defining and naming them. Often, participants' words and phrases are used to define and name a theme, letting the participants speak through the themes.
6. Producing a report. This step aims to combine a coherent argument with a narrative of the themes, excerpts from the data, and the existing literature. This step is about describing and staying close to participants' words and what they said. It is also about explaining how and why themes are interesting, that is, about interpreting the interviews as answers to the research question.

11.6 The say–do gap

The interview method provides a privileged position for understanding the experienced life of users. It gives us special access to the concepts and structures that people use to think about computer use. However, it is not a panacea. Its main limitation boils down to one question: Is it possible to obtain accurate information about users' practices by asking them?

The say–do gap poses a practical obstacle to this aim. This gap refers to the discrepancy between what an interviewee says and what they do. For example, when asked whether they wash their hands after using the toilet, most people answer that they do. However, according to one study that directly observed handwashing behavior [86], 15% of men and 7% of women do not wash their hands after using the toilet. In computer use, there are events that users may be embarrassed to disclose or simply do not remember.

More generally, there are many causes for the say–do gap. One cause is the inability to imagine the future. This is important in user research, as we are often tempted to ask users about alternative and possible technologies. However, as interviewees lack first-hand experience with them, how accurate can their estimates be? Even professionals struggle to predict developments in their fields. For example, most IT professionals failed to predict the pervasive impact of smartphones on our use of computers, and we are now witnessing similar failures in predictions related to emerging forms of AI. Interviews are not ideal for obtaining such insights into future technology.

Another cause of the say–do gap is that not all knowledge can be articulated; some knowledge is tacit. However, tacit knowledge can be exposed by acting it out. If you ask regular users about their use of smart features on smartphones, such as autocorrection or password managers, they may not be able to recall whether and how they use them. Using methods such as contextual inquiry, tacit behaviors can be observed, recorded, and discussed.

A third cause is social. Users may deliberately exaggerate or omit aspects of their behaviors. They may want to give a positive impression of themselves or avoid negative social consequences. Recognizing such situations is important for interviewers. For example, building trust with vulnerable groups can take months or years.

A skilled interviewer is aware of the say–do gap and its causes. Part of the expertise of interviewers is to recognize such issues, avoid misinterpreting their data, and design the study methodology accordingly.

Summary

- The interview method is an indispensable method in user research. It provides access to first-person views and helps us uncover how users experience and perceive interaction.
- Interviews can activate people, empower them, and get them to narrate their experiences.

- Interview methods are divided into structured, semi-structured, and open-ended interviews.
- Contextual inquiry is a mixed-methods approach that combines interviews with field observations.
- Methods for analyzing interview data aim to produce comprehensive overviews of the data as well as data-driven interpretations.

Exercises

1. Open-ended interview. Pick an application you do not know well but your friend (the interviewee) does. Pick a theme for an interview and design a few lead-in questions following the guidelines given in this chapter. Interview your friend (10–15 minutes) and record the interview. Listen to the interview recording. Instead of analyzing the content, focus on how you led the interview.
2. Designing an interview structure. Think about a future product, something you believe might come out in 3–4 years. Think about the potential user needs. Write an interview structure for this product. The goal is to find out early adopters' experiences with the product.
3. Analyzing transcripts. There are many datasets with interview transcripts of varying quality available online. Pick one that has more than one person's data and analyze it. (a) Identify a relevant theme for the interview. (b) Develop a code (minimum 2–3 categories) for the theme. (c) Verify your code against the transcripts; iterate if needed. (d) State your conclusion about the theme.
4. Contextual inquiry. Conduct a contextual inquiry on an everyday activity with a computer. Working with another person, plan, run, and analyze a contextual inquiry that focuses on an everyday activity, for instance, checking the latest posts on social media.
5. Micro-phenomenological interview. Following the guidance given in this chapter, design an interview structure to find out how your friend experiences awareness cues (Chapter 9) on social media. Mastering this type of interview takes practice; pay attention to how you respond and lead the discussion without biasing the interviewee.

12
Field research

One potential source of insight into users is their exhibited behavior in their natural environment while they attempt to achieve their goals. This chapter elaborates on methods that allow us to gain such insight by studying users in situ in the field.

Field research, in the context of user research, refers to the collection of data on users in their real-world contexts. In much field research, users are observed doing things that would also occur without the researcher being present and—as much as possible—with minimum bias due to the researcher being present (for more on reactivity, see Chapter 14).

Observation is a key method in field research. In observation, we pay close attention to what users do, aiming to understand what happens and make inferences about why activity unfolds as it does. Observations may be supplemented with both informal conversations and open-ended interviews. In this chapter, we focus on observation; interviews and contextual inquiries were covered in Chapter 11.

A key strength of field research is its *realism*. Field research provides insights into how users act, collaborate, and communicate in their natural environments. For this reason, it is sometimes called naturalistic research. In the array of user research methods, field research is vital for capturing aspects of use that other methods might miss. Due to its openness, it sheds light on the complexity of the social and organizational settings in which an interaction is accomplished. By making a few commitments to predefined notions of the phenomenon under study, field research can uncover factors that might not be discovered through other means. Field research also produces knowledge about the practices of stakeholders and how they understand those practices. It also teaches us about the relationship between prescribed procedures (e.g., manuals, organizational procedures) and how work actually gets carried out.

Such insights can be put to multiple uses. Field research has helped describe many important phenomena in human–computer interaction (HCI), for example, how interactive televisions are used in the home [609], how people develop romantic relationships in computer games [254], and how new information systems create unexpected *new* work for end-users [665].

Field research may also be used to inform the design of new interactive systems, serving as a way to build empathy with prospective users and gain background knowledge about them and their practices. It may also help inform decisions about whether to adopt a system or not. Paper Example 12.0.1 describes the use of field research to uncover the safety issues posed by the planned automation of a paper-based system used in air traffic control.

An example of an observation site is given in Figure 12.1. It may seem deceptively simple to observe what is happening. However, one cannot simply "go and watch" users. It is not obvious who to observe, what to look for, or how to make sense of it all. This chapter provides the foundation for addressing these considerations. A key challenge in field research is understanding *contextual contingencies of HCI*, that is, the different ways interactions are produced and shaped by users' social, physical, and technical circumstances.

Figure 12.1 Field research is uniquely positioned to understand how technology use is contingent on its context, including material (room setup), social (relations between workers), and technical (digital and other artifacts) aspects. Observing technology use in its context is not trivial; it requires planning and skills to decide what to observe and how. The figure shows an example recording from a field study of a rally control center [865].

Generally, field research should address three formative questions [493]:

1. What to focus on? In any complex real-life situation, there are several things to observe; the researcher needs to decide what to pay attention to and what to ignore.
2. How to gather data? In particular, how to plan and conduct observations. The way this is done affects everything from the recorded data to access to sites and ethics.
3. How to analyze the data? Field research often produces a substantial amount of data.

For example, fieldwork on Facebook use in rural Kenya collected "24 transcribed interviews, 174 pages of field notes, and 1,375 digital photographs" [916]. The authors aimed to answer the question "What is the Facebook experience in contexts where the social, economic, and technical contexts affecting use differ from the American college campuses where the site was first popularized?" [p. 33].

In the rest of this chapter, we discuss observation in general and then ethnography, a particular form of observation where the observer engages and participates in what is observed. The last section deals with the analysis of data from field research.

Paper Example 12.0.1: Understanding automation and work practices

Many interactive systems digitalize or automate human practices. However, such attempts may fail if the social, cognitive, and material aspects of practices are misunderstood or ignored.

On a case in point, in the late 1990s, MacKay [504] conducted a four-month ethnographic study of air traffic controllers and their use of paper. Her study was motivated by the objective of mimicking and replacing paper with digital systems. However, her research has shown the benefits of paper and its role in coordinating work flexibly.

The author observed how a team consisting of senior controllers, qualified controllers, and students worked together. Their task was to organize planes at an airport and provide instructions to pilots on safe and efficient routes. To respond to changing situations during traffic hours, the team had to collaborate.

A paper flight strip is a paper-based representation of a single flight; see the figure in this paper example box. It contains a few basic parameters of a flight in a structured format. Being in paper format, it can be easily edited with a pen. Paper strips can also be spatially organized. It may seem trivial to replace such simple representations with digital versions; after all, there is no information that could not be presented on a display or interacted with. However, Mackay's study revealed that this is not the case.

She found that an essential aspect of a controller's work routine is sequentially checking each aircraft, first on radar and then on the paper strips. She found that regardless of how many aircraft are in the air, controllers execute this cyclical checking routine because it allows them to stay vigilant and ensure a certain level of situational awareness at all times. This, some controllers said, remains important even during "boring" times.

Paper strips could be organized on a control table to provide a quick overview of a situation. This spatial organization also helped the team maintain awareness of each other's situations. The paper strips also served an anticipatory function: Mackay observed that controllers make markings "for the future." For example, a controller might insert information that would serve as a reminder to call a pilot in a few minutes. Having such information on a paper strip helps the controller "offload" information to the strip so that it does not have to be kept in memory. A computerized representation that does not facilitate free-form annotations, some controllers argued, might increase their workload.

Mackay concluded that switching to a computerized system could endanger air traffic due to unforeseeable consequences. She proposed a radical alternative: maintain the physical paper strips but turn them into an interface that links them to the computer. This, she argued, would help controllers leverage their established safe practices with paper strips. Alas, this vision was difficult to realize using the technology of that era.

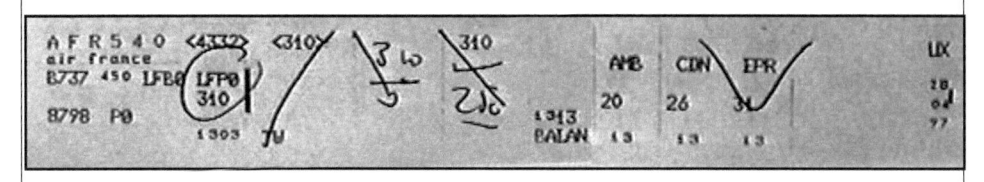

12.1 Observation

In HCI, *observation* is a method of data collection where the researcher is positioned to observe and take notes on activities related to the use of an interactive system. The goal in collecting such notes is to account for relevant types of events, their frequencies, and patterns occurring over time. This section deals with the basic idea of observation and how to use it to describe what users do.

One ideal in observation is to interfere as little as possible with what is being observed. The researcher should be positioned in such a way that there is little interference or bias due to their presence. This type of observation is sometimes called an outsider's or *etic* view. For instance, etic observation could be relevant to study the following:

- how much time people spend doing something, for instance, looking at interactive exhibits in shopping windows;
- how virtual reality users engage with strangers;
- how a team of air traffic controllers responds to unplanned events.

All of these scenarios may be observed, enumerated, and verified by a researcher describing the events from an outside point of view. By contrast, in *emic* research, which we discuss in Section 12.2, the goal is to immerse oneself into a community to describe it from an insider's perspective.

In field research, the focus of data collection reflects the goal of the observation. Gathering data is mainly about finding an appropriate site for observation and good ways of capturing data. Lastly, analysis is mainly concerned with the reliability of the collected data and the analysis of the observations, particularly their types and frequency. Next, we discuss these focusing, gathering, and analyzing activities.

12.1.1 Focus

What to look for in observation is largely prescribed by the goals of the user research. For instance, to design an interactive system for groups, it may be useful to know how it is used by single users and when users are in a group; an existing system may be observed to figure this out. What to look for in observation is also influenced by how much is already known. For instance, observation in the field may be used to confirm usage patterns identified in interviews (confirmatory observation), or it may be used to figure out the most frequent activities (exploratory or open-ended observation).

The literature provides an assortment of frameworks that offer researchers inspiration for what to focus on. Table 12.1 shows nine dimensions that may be the subject of open-ended or confirmatory observation. For instance, in observing a space, a researcher may pay particular attention to the use of space in collaboration around a shared technology. Their observations may then concern how different individuals use different parts of the space, how they place and retrieve

Table 12.1 Observations in the field can be structured. This helps the researcher focus on aspects of the field that are directly relevant to the research question. The table shows dimensions of observation adapted from Spradley [788].

Dimension	Description
Space	The physical layout and organization of the observation site
Actors	Names, roles, and other characteristics of the people at the site
Activities	The doings of the actors
Objects	The physical elements of the site
Acts	Individual things that people do and say
Events	Important things that happen
Time	The sequence of events and activities
Goals	The things actors are trying to accomplish
Feelings	Actors' emotions and moods

artifacts in that space, how they physically position themselves in the space, and so on. Observations focusing exclusively on space have been conducted in research on tabletops—large vertical displays that invite users to collaborate. Observational research on tabletops has shown that users' behaviors are shaped by a sense of territoriality [751]. Users treat different parts of the display space differently depending on whether it is a personal or shared territory.

Other frameworks highlight other dimensions that may be considered in observations. Goetz and LeCompte [278] suggested looking at who is present, what their role is, what is happening, when something happens, where it happens, why it happens, and how the happening is organized. Others suggest looking at the physical setting, the activities, the social environment, the formal interactions among people, the informal and unplanned activities, nonverbal communication, and the things that do not happen but might happen [278].

12.1.2 Gathering data

Finding a site

An early question faced by field researchers is *where* to observe users, including how to obtain access to the observation site and whether the participants should know the observations will take place. Picking the observation site relates to the purpose of the user research; the site should reflect that purpose. Different observation sites allow for different types of observations to be made; poor site selection will result in limited or skewed observations.

Another concern is the effect of the selected site on the observed individuals. *Reactivity* refers to the impact of the observer on the observed individuals. Consider, for example, having a field researcher hired by your employer to observe you; how might that affect your behavior?

The first task upon coming to a site of observation is to orient oneself. The observer should understand the structure of the site, including the positions of the individuals being observed and relevant physical and digital artifacts. The following questions should be answered:

- Who are the actors in this space and what roles do they have?
- What are the relevant material or digital artifacts in this space?
- What are some typical or probable locations or routes of the relevant actors?
- How am I and my recording instruments positioned in this space? If the use of computers needs to be recorded, is everything positioned correctly to do so?

To this effect, using an annotated floor plan can be helpful. The site of observation, including the positions of any cameras, should be noted. Figure 12.2 shows a floor plan example from the field study of a control center (Figure 12.1).

Shadowing

Rather than settling on a fixed site of observation, particular people may be followed. This is known as *shadowing*. González and Mark [283] were interested in how users switched between different activities at work. To obtain information on this, they shadowed information workers at an investment management company. The researchers "sat with the informant at her cubicle and followed her, whenever possible, to meetings or other activities" [p. 114]. Observations were recorded on an "activity tracking log where we transcribed the observation notes collected during the day." These observational data were complemented with other data, including from interviews. The observations exposed a fragmentation of work. The authors found that "people spend an

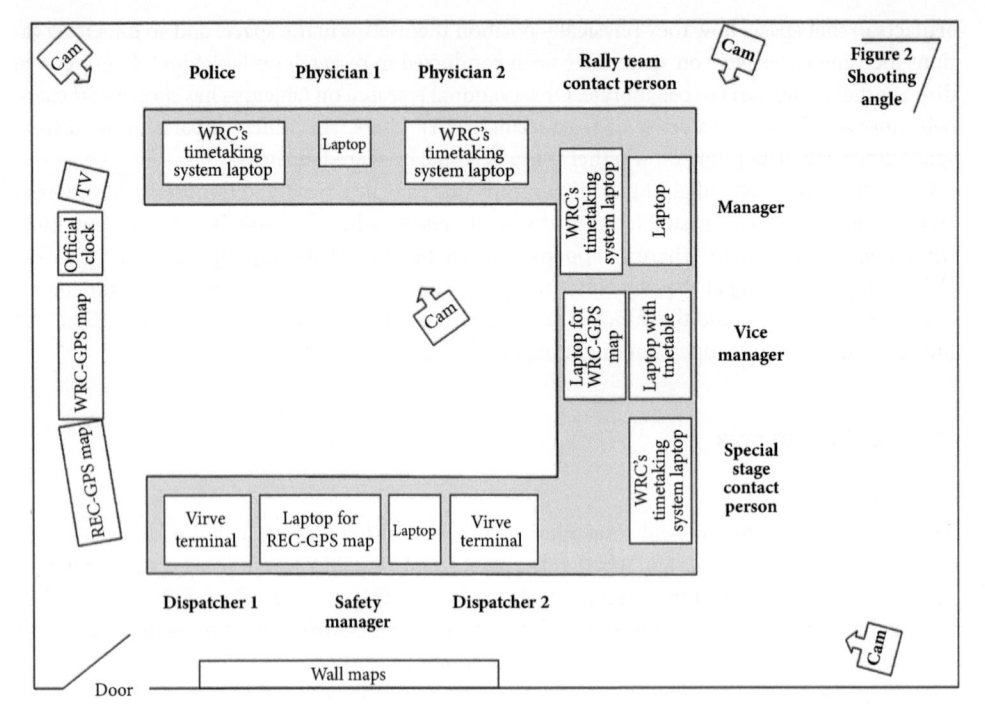

Figure 12.2 Entering a site of observation requires the researcher to orient themselves with the actors, materials, and artifacts in the setting. This floor plan example is from the study of a large-scale sports event control center [865].

average of less than two and a half minutes reading email before they switch to another event, or are interrupted" [p. 116].

Observation may also be *covert* so that users do not know they are being observed. In virtual environments, for example, covert observation is relatively easy to perform since the observer may not need to have an embodied presence in the space that is being observed. In public and semi-public spaces, video cameras may be used to collect data covertly. Researchers can also ask study participants to collect data using wearable cameras or other sensors that they carry with them [115]. However, this may alter the behavior of both the users who carry such equipment and the people around them. It is important to note that outside of institutionally cleared circumstances, covert observation can go against local, national, or international regulations. It is also ethically precarious since the individuals being observed may not have been informed about or may not have consented to the observations taking place.

Data capture and note-taking

Observations in the field should be recorded for later analysis and verification. Observations may include audio, video, photos, and textual descriptions. There are a few principled ways to do this.

Field notes are recordings of remarks made in the field; they are the raw data of field research. One method for managing field notes is to keep a *field diary*. A field diary acts as a log of observations that are typically recorded using pen and paper or digitally using a mobile device. A diary entry may relate, for example, an observation of the time of occurrence of an event. One issue with diaries is that they do not necessarily help the researcher record consistent observations over time; diary entries can be sporadic and focus on wildly different aspects.

Structured notes are field notes recorded into a previously defined observation structure [549]. Compared to the diary method, this structured method better guides observations and facilitates the discovery of patterns that occur over time. Moreover, quantitative analysis can be easier to do using structured notes. The observation structure can help the researcher focus on relevant aspects of their research, such as the chronology of events (what happened and when), artifacts, participant roles, or particular actions. Structured notes are often taken with pen and paper or using a mobile device. For example, an observer could note all the times a user sent an email and add observations on how it was done; in this case, every log entry may describe one such event.

We provide ideas on possible categories of observation in Table 12.1. Often, however, the structure evolves as the study progresses. As it is not clear during the early part of a study what will prove important, *non-structured field notes* may be recorded, which may then lead to a coding structure.

12.1.3 Analysis of observations

From video clips to diaries, field notes can take radically different forms. Nevertheless, there are a few shared principles to consider when analyzing them.

Immediate recall: When in the field and "in the thick of it," events pass quickly. A field researcher often has to choose between immersing themselves in the ongoing event and writing notes about it. Since even the most comprehensive recording offers only a glimpse into what transpired, field research almost always relies on the observer's memory. It is therefore critical to analyze observations quickly after they are recorded. Knowing when to observe, when to take notes, and what to remember from an event are some of the key skills that one develops as a field researcher.

Thick description: Important events should get more attention in analysis. To this end, a field researcher should try to recall as much as possible of an event and write it all down, answering questions such as: What was observed? What does it mean? Why does it matter? This can produce a rich account, or a *thick description*, of an event. A researcher can also jog their memory, for example, by revisiting audio or video recordings or reviewing representations of events, such as floor plans.

Coding data: Any post hoc data coding should strive to be reliable and reproducible. The categorization of observations should be based on definitions that are as unambiguous as possible. Such definitions, ideally with examples and counter-examples, should be rigorously recorded in a *coding manual*. For example: "'Map reading' This event occurs when a participant manipulates or glances a map (physical or digital) for more than 5 seconds. Keeping a map open on the side does not count as map reading." Coding manuals can be attached as appendices to field reports or scientific papers.

When statistical reliability is important, the *inter-rater reliability* should be measured and reported. This refers to statistical metrics that quantify how reliably two or more raters, working independently of each other, end up with the same coding given the same materials and the same coding manual. Since coding an entire dataset can be time-consuming, raters are usually asked to code overlapping samples to both gain coverage and be able to measure the inter-rater reliability. When the conclusions drawn from a study are quantitative, low reliability is a serious concern and calls for rethinking the coding manual.

Validation with participants: Conclusions that are drawn based on field research are statements made about users. From this point of view, users are stakeholders in field research. For them, these statements may be wrong in multiple ways: irrelevant, biased, partial, or incorrect. Even in the case of covert observation, it is their lives, opinions, and practices that are being described. Validation can help the researcher verify the conclusions drawn from the data. It can also provide some agency to users on what is being said about them, which can be particularly important for vulnerable user groups. Engaging with users may help correct misinterpretations. For example, task analysis results must be explicitly validated with stakeholders [24] (Chapter 15).

12.2 Ethnography

Ethnography is a method developed in anthropology to describe activities from the perspective of an individual or group. Although the data collection methods are similar to those used in other field research—observations, interviews, document analysis, and so on—the purpose is different. The goal of ethnography is *emic*, in other words, to describe activity from the users' point of view, often focusing on experiences or the social organization of the activity.

In HCI, ethnographic research contributes to understanding how work that involves interactive computing systems is carried out and experienced. As surprising as it may sound, emic research on computer use can provide valuable insights. Computer use often involves meanings, practices, expressions, and activities that may require an ethnographic approach to be understood. This requires the researcher to minutely observe the participants in naturally occurring settings over extended periods. As an example, Paper Example 12.2.1 describes a study of system administrators.

Ethnography requires commitment and long immersion in fieldwork. Instead of days, rigorous ethnographic research can take months or even years. As a consequence, an ethnographer may become a participant in the community they are studying. If the researcher is accepted in the community, even if only as a peripheral member, there may be a lower risk of reactivity. Individuals may be less prone to changing their behavior when the observer is familiar. In some cases, this may be a requirement to access a community as a legitimate member; think, for example, about studies of Internet criminals.

Ethnography often comprises multiple data collection methods, including observations, interviews, and the collection of artifacts. In this chapter, we focus on the high-level principles of ethnography.

Paper Example 12.2.1: An ethnography of sysadmins

Thanks to deep immersion into the experienced lives of participants, ethnographic research can illuminate technically specialized user groups. One such group is system administrators, or sysadmins—professionals who set up, maintain, and repair computer systems and infrastructure.

To understand their practices, Barrett et al. [47], then researchers at the IBM Almaden Research Center, observed web and database administrators for 25 days, obtaining over 100 hours of recorded materials. They followed a mixed-methods approach consisting of diaries, interviews, and observations. What their data uncovered would have been difficult to uncover using something other than an open-ended methodology.

In one event, a sysadmin team was creating a new web server with a tight deadline. Configuring the server produced a vague error message: "Error: Could not connect to server." The team went into intense troubleshooting mode, which included phone calls, emails, messaging, and discussions with several people in the organization. Some came to the terminal of one of the sysadmins, called George, and shared ideas on how to solve the issue:

The problem was eventually found to be a network misconfiguration. George misunderstood the meaning of a certain configuration parameter for the new web server (ambiguously labeled as "port") to be for communication from the webserver to the authentication server, when in fact it was the opposite. The former would have been permitted by the firewall, but the latter was not. George's misunderstanding affected the remote collaborators significantly throughout the troubleshooting session. We witnessed several instances in which he ignored or misinterpreted evidence of the real problem, filtering what he communicated by his incorrect understanding of the system configuration, which in turn greatly limited his collaborators' ability to understand George's error propagated to his collaborators. The solution was finally found by the one collaborator who had independent access to the systems, which meant that his view of the systems was not contaminated by George's incorrect understanding.

The paper showed that the work of system administrators includes hours of troubleshooting complex information, tools, and organizational knowledge. Yet, the existing tools that sysadmins use do a poor job of supporting them. Most importantly, they are opaque and poor at communicating their state, which means that misunderstandings can propagate even in such collaborative settings. This led the sysadmins to build their own scripts and graphical user interface tools.

12.2.1 Principles of ethnography

Ethnography is centered on three principles [80].

Members' point of view: Ethnography aims to capture a member's point of view. Instead of describing what a person does, the goal is to describe its meaning as an experience. The term "member" here refers to a member of a group or culture that is being studied. This means understanding meanings, concepts, values, and other factors that define the member's perspective. An ethnographer starts with a minimal set of assumptions. This is important when seeking to appreciate the stance of a member. Paper Example 12.2.2 provides a case example where print operators' practices were studied. Sometimes, getting the participants' viewpoint requires extensive groundwork. One first needs to gain acceptance and credibility. After sufficient levels of trust and rapport have been established, the participants may be more willing to disclose information and engage with the researcher.

The strive for a member's point of view differs from the *etic* descriptions we discussed in the previous section. Etic research routinely utilizes extraneous concepts to describe events. For example, in task analysis, we use a predefined ontology to describe an activity. By contrast, an ethnographic researcher would seek to find out the member's viewpoint.

Descriptive: Ethnographic research does not seek to impose extraneous values onto the group being studied. In other words, it describes and does not prescribe. This position can help the ethnographer approach groups that might be reluctant to value systems or concepts that they consider threatening.

Holistic: Ethnography moves away from predefined narrow categories of observation, such as those used in surveys, and instead aims to describe the totality of events. "Holistic" is often criticized as an empty, vague goal. In ethnographic research, it does not refer to the impossible feat of describing every possible detail of an event; rather, it refers to the idea of including all the factors that members consider relevant. If something is relevant to them, it should be included in the description.

> ### Paper Example 12.2.2: Print operators' practices
>
> Button and Sharrock [112] provided advice for field observations. To help gauge the participants' perspective, what people do should be described in their own terms. For example, managers and consultants may describe work in formal terms that do not match the experience of other workers. What does, for example, "business process re-engineering" mean? To a worker, it may mean very concrete changes in who sits where or what buttons need to be pressed. Ethnographers should aim to "tell it like it is," that is, describe how people do their jobs without masking the descriptions with jargon.
>
> The authors illustrate this point with a description of experienced print operators; the original study was published by Bowers et al. [90]. The company adopted a new workflow and a management system proposed by consultants who were out of touch with the operators' work on the ground. Via field observations, the researchers wanted to learn how the operators actually organize their work. One key lesson was that operators engage in a number of actions to manage contingencies in a print room and develop sensory expertise that allows them to "know" and coordinate work with others in the room. A print room, they explain, may appear cacophonic to an inexperienced bystander. However, it is experienced differently by experienced operators [p. 71]:
>
>> In addition to the resource provided by direct line of sight, operators have other ways of monitoring each other's work. First, the machines emit warning noises that alert operators to completed processes or machine problems such as paper jams or depleted paper trays. In addition to "designed-in" sounds, the machines also make regular noises when engaged in particular operations and skilled operators can monitor the printing process just by the sound that a machine is making at any one time. The neophyte to the print room encounters a cacophony of undifferentiated sounds, merged together into a booming, sometimes overwhelming noise. To experienced print workers, however, the noise can be disassembled into its component sound parts, and they can draw out a sound from the noise. Thus, what is mere noise to a neophyte is a rich resource of meaningful sounds that can be used to monitor the overall work of the print room and the state of particular machines by the experienced operator.
>
> First-person perspectives can be illuminating and offer vastly different views compared to formal descriptions of work. The authors argued that, in this case, the consultants' new management system failed to achieve its goals because it ignored the workers' practices.

12.2.2 Rapid ethnography

While these attributes necessarily make ethnographic studies longer than non-ethnographic field research, there is no intrinsic value in prolonged exposure per se. *Rapid ethnography* is the idea that immersion should only be as long as it has to be [545]. Sometimes, an actionable understanding of the subject matter may be achieved in a matter of days or even hours. In some cases, such speed may be necessary, for example, to align ethnographic work with rapid product development cycles.

Rapid ethnography involves relaxing the ideal of a holistic description and purposefully limiting the scope of the study. Several observers may be used instead of one, field data may be augmented with digital data (e.g., logs, documents), and the focus may be on a few key preselected informants. Generally, such "quick and dirty" ethnography is more feasible in the special case where the observer already shares essential aspects of the culture or where the researcher has already been approved by the community. For example, a user researcher coming from an IT company may be more easily accepted by special groups such as system administrators.

12.2.3 Ethnography in practice

In HCI, ethnography can be used for at least three main purposes. First, ethnography can be used to obtain a holistic view of how end-users view some technology. The method is indispensable when the user group in question has very different characteristics compared to the lifeworld of the researcher. Second, ethnography can be used to evaluate a technology from the perspective of the users. Third, ethnography can be used concurrently with system or service development. In this case, user researchers may need to engage with a user group for a long period, such as for several months or even years.

In practice, ethnographic studies involve four distinct phases:

Getting access and getting along: Finding and accessing informants is decisive work for the success of a study, yet rarely appreciated by outsiders. For instance, how informants were found is rarely mentioned in HCI papers reporting ethnographic studies. Approaching members with a humble, unthreatening, and polite mindset is vital for establishing trust.

Developing membership: Unlike in experimental research, where observations are supposed to be independent of each other, in ethnographic research, the observational capability of the researcher develops over time. On the one hand, this is due to epistemological development; in short, the researcher grows to understand the topic. On the other hand, it is due to their evolving membership. As the researcher becomes more familiar and trusted, they have a better chance of discovering knowledge that is inaccessible to outsiders.

Collecting data: From a methodological perspective, an ethnographer can flexibly combine data collection methods, both quantitative and qualitative. Nevertheless, two key aspects of ethnographic data collection are the ability to talk to and watch people and the ability to make recordings and take field notes. These tasks never end, as ethnographers continuously collect data. Ironically, for an outsider, an ethnographer may seem a passive researcher.

Button and Sharrock [113] outlined advice for making observations in the field. One suggestion is to follow people with open eyes and adopt the mindset of an apprentice: bear as little predisposition as possible. Another suggestion is to follow leads. The researcher should keep asking people to describe what they do as they are doing it, as such observations can provide leads on what to look at next. For example, the researcher should learn where work outputs go and how they are used by others. Throughout the study, the field researcher should make notes of everything that occurs as richly as possible. The authors also highlighted the importance of investing time into thinking about what the data mean as opposed to spending all the time just collecting data.

Analyzing data: Data analysis differs between ethnographic research and laboratory research in a few key ways. First, in lab research, extraneous variables that are not under the control of the researcher are considered a nuisance, something to get rid of. By contrast, in ethnographic research, such factors are essential for obtaining a holistic description of members' perspectives. While this may result in the appreciation of anecdotal evidence, such as the "war stories" recounted by an IT worker, these accounts are not antithetical to the aim of understanding "the big picture." Second, in laboratory research, the focus is often on understanding the causal effects of some variables on other variables. By contrast, in ethnographic research, it is assumed the world is constructed via the activities of the informant. That is, it should not be pre-fixated on some variables but "let the data speak." Third, laboratory studies often strive for statistically reliable findings; in ethnographic studies, the goal is to offer accounts that are consistent with the data obtained. The burden is on the ethnographer to show that their interpretations can be traced back to the obtained data. Fourth, while every observation is equally important in laboratory studies, ethnographic research can be selective. It can focus on events and people deemed important by some account.

12.2.4 Ethics

The deep connection that an ethnographer can achieve with the individuals under study is both an opportunity and a source of risk. On the one hand, there is the positive side: Ethnographic research is sometimes the only viable means of understanding the viewpoints of groups that are vulnerable or neglected. For example, economically or otherwise disadvantaged people's experience of computer use is completely different from that of other users. If not through ethnography, how else could one discover and report their experiences?

On the other hand, ethnographic research can be harmful. It can harm participants by releasing information about them. It can also harm them by being present in their lives. The following suggestions are essential to avoid causing harm [84, p. 176]:

1. Be extremely careful with field notes and do not leave them in a place where anyone might pick them up.
2. Do not discuss the study or any of the people in it with others outside the research group.
3. Use pseudonyms in field notes and final reports.
4. Do not report any of the uncovered information to people who might use it in ways that might embarrass or hurt the subjects.
5. Strike a clear agreement with the subjects regarding what they can expect to get out of the study and fulfill that obligation.

12.3 Can field observations inform design?

Realism is the strength of field research. Its results offer a level of fidelity and open-endedness that is out of reach for other approaches in user research. Field research conveys in detail how actions and experiences take place in context. However, there is a catch. Realism also makes it hard to draw implications for design. When every observation is detailed and contingent—tied to unique circumstances—how can one draw conclusions that are general enough to inform design decisions? One might be tempted to summarize field observations into "takeaway bullets" for design. However, this can blunt the work and discount the richness of the underlying data.

The "So what?" question riddles both academics and practitioners. In addition to the issue that the value of field research is hard to quantify, field research is costly when compared to other methods such as surveys. To make field research more cost-efficient, *rapid ethnography* has been proposed, as we discussed. Because this quick-and-dirty method involves less immersion in the domain, it may gather the information sought by designers more efficiently.

However, there is long-term value in field research; it is hard to quantify but valuable nonetheless. While field research cannot offer results that define designs, it offers knowledge of strategic value, complementing other methods. Instead of asking "Should we do field research?" one should ask "Can we succeed without it?"

There are several reasons why this is the case in HCI. First, field research is particularly strong in identifying non-obvious problems affecting computer use. While something may appear straightforward to use for a designer, many factors can hinder or impede its use in real life. Some factors are mundane (e.g., weather), while others are subtle and hard to expose (e.g., power structures). For example, field research in workplaces has revealed discrepancy problems—problems where the managers' expectations of an information system do not match what happens on the ground [665]. New practices or workflows assumed by a system may end up creating more work for the end-users, at times without the managers or developers realizing it. To draw such implications, the collected data may need to be triangulated with additional data. This can help an analyst to construe models of data—"theories" of user practices—that posit observed factors in some systematic form. We discuss methods for representing user data in Chapter 15.

Second, field research is important when changing or designing new sociotechnical practices. Many computing systems are not just adopted; they need to be domesticated and appropriated (Chapter 19). Crucially, users need to reorganize their practices, and field research excels at uncovering the fabric of such practices.

Third, sometimes field observations are instrumental to radical new concepts in design. For example, early field studies of wireless connectivity led to the concept of *seamfulness* [142]. The lack of wireless connectivity is normally seen as a disruption, something to avoid exposing users to. By contrast, the concept of seamfulness suggests that making connectivity more visible and understandable can help users better manage it in their practices. For instance, a seamful connectivity map may show where connectivity is strong versus poor.

Fourth, field research has narrative power. Well-recounted accounts of users' lived worlds are something that stakeholders can easily relate to. This can get buy-in within an organization. It can also sensitize developers by making them realize that system requirements are harder to achieve "in the wild" than they might think.

Finally, one can argue that a deep understanding of the situated use of computers is valuable on its own. If fieldwork is considered to be basic research, there is no need to justify it via its instrumental value in HCI design.

Summary

- Field research relies on observations of users in their natural contexts.
- Field observation is not just about "keeping your eyes open" but a complex task that requires the researcher to balance "being there" and taking notes.

- Observation methods can be divided into etic and emic. Ethnographic methods, which are emic, encourage long-term immersion in a culture to obtain detailed first-person accounts of practices.
- The results of field research are valuable for identifying problems, deriving models of contextual use, and sensitizing to relevant factors.

Exercises

1. Organizing field studies. Imagine that you are tasked with running a field study of a help desk in a large IT company. Following the guidance given in this chapter, how would you organize it? In your answer, consider aspects such as choosing the site of observation.
2. The value of field observations. Field research is expensive, yet there are many cases where it is more expensive not to do it. Come up with three hypothetical HCI projects where field research is necessary.
3. Membership. Why is membership in the community that is being observed important?
4. Practical observation. Choose a setting where you can observe people buying tickets. Then, determine the focus of the observation and the practicalities involved. Try to do three observations, each lasting 20 minutes. Then, analyze your observations; the concepts discussed in this chapter may guide your analysis.

13
Survey research

In *survey research*, the researcher designs a *questionnaire* and distributes it to respondents who fill it in, typically without the researcher's presence. A questionnaire consists of a series of questions presented and answered in a structured way. For example, you have probably filled in questionnaires that use the Likert scale. Here, a question is delivered in the form of a claim, and the response must be given on a symmetrical five- or seven-point ordinal scale, usually ranging from "strongly disagree" to "strongly agree":

```
I enjoy reading textbooks in an e-book format on a digital device.
1—Strongly disagree
2—Somewhat disagree
3—Neutral
4—Somewhat agree
5—Strongly agree
```

Figure 13.1 shows another example of a questionnaire used in human–computer interaction (HCI) research.

Surveys are widely used in user research. They can be used to understand users' (1) behaviors in their activities, routines, or use of interactive systems, (2) experiences, such as their positive and negative experiences during computer use, (3) needs, desires, and wants, and (4) attitudes, preferences, and beliefs. For example, surveys have given us the following insights:

- Hiniker et al. [343] used surveys to investigate how parents and children establish rules around digital technologies in their families and how effective they perceive such rules to be. Parents and children each reported two rules in free text along with ratings of the rules ranging between disagree and agree. The results suggested that rules that constrain activities (e.g., no Snapchat) are more likely to be followed than context-based rules (e.g., no phone at the dinner table).

- Ceaparu et al. [141] used surveys to study the frustrations that users experience with computer systems. They showed that users frequently experience frustration with error messages, download times, and features that are difficult to find. About half of the time spent on a computer is perceived to be lost due to such experiences. These are alarming findings.

- Vaniea and Rashidi [847] used surveys to investigate when and why users update software. They learned that users go through six distinct phases when deciding to upgrade software and that several of these pose barriers to users upgrading software, thereby potentially compromising security. Some users choose not to upgrade if the current version works fine or if the upgrade looks like it will be disruptive. Respondents frequently mentioned troubleshooting the installer and the installation process as barriers to successfully updating software.

Introduction to Human-Computer Interaction. Kasper Hornbæk, Per Ola Kristensson, and Antti Oulasvirta, Oxford University Press. © Kasper Hornbæk, Per Ola Kristensson, and Antti Oulasvirta (2025).
DOI: 10.1093/oso/9780192864543.003.0013

Surveys may also be used for understanding the psychological factors behind user behavior. Pre-validated questionnaires can be used to measure latent psychological constructs such as attitudes. To this end, several specialized questionnaires have been developed. Examples include questionnaires on the visual aesthetics of web sites [558] and the frustrations [805] and engagement [608] that people experience when using computers. Chapter 7 provides examples of questionnaires on user satisfaction and experience.

The *generalizability* of findings is a distinct benefit of survey research over other user research methods. A carefully designed survey allows the researcher to statistically estimate the distribution of phenomena in a population. This is possible thanks to two key characteristics of surveys. First, the response data are structured and defined in advance. Every respondent answers the same questions using the same response options. This reduces heterogeneity in the data and lends them to statistical analysis. Second, the sample size in survey research can be large. Assuming the surveys are distributed efficiently, the cost per respondent can be moderate or low. If the sample is representative of prospective users, the generalizability of the survey findings can be high.

However, designing a good survey is hard. A number of things can go wrong. First of all, the questions used in survey research must be understandable to the respondents. Poorly formulated questions can be interpreted by the respondents in different ways. The researcher typically cannot be present to clarify the wording of questions or quality-check the answers. Compared to the interview method, this is a significant price to pay for better generalizability. Additionally, the answer options need to be comprehensive. If an answer option is missing, or the options are biasing the respondents, the resulting data will be biased, too. Survey results are also easily misinterpreted as representing the "true" behaviors or experiences of users. However, self-reports may not be truthful. For example, if a questionnaire asked about your salary, use of pornographic web sites, or tendency to procrastinate, would you answer truthfully? Moreover, distributing questionnaires to the population of interest may be hard. Surveys often have low response rates. Moreover, some users self-select to respond, which can introduce bias into the data by over-representing those respondents who, for some reason, chose to answer the survey. We will discuss these and other biases in detail throughout the chapter. Developing a good survey is hard work that involves multiple iterations and stages.

Survey research can be carried out in many ways depending on its purpose and constraints. However, the workflow typically consists of the following steps:

1. Plan the survey research
   - Establish the research focus
   - Select the survey type
   - Decide the sampling strategy
2. Select a questionnaire
   - Use an established questionnaire or
   - Design a new questionnaire, including the questions and their types, answer options, and order
3. Piloting
4. Collect the data
5. Analyze the data
   - Process the answers, describe the answers, and carry out qualitative and statistical analyses
   - Draw conclusions and report them.

Next, we discuss these phases in detail. Further instructions can be found in textbooks on surveys [e.g., 563, 620].

Perceived Ease of Use

Learning to operate X would be easy for me

likely |extremely | quite | slightly | neither | slightly | quite | extremely| unlikely

I would find it easy to get X to do what I want to do

likely |extremely | quite | slightly | neither | slightly | quite | extremely| unlikely

My interaction with X would be clear and understandable

likely |extremely | quite | slightly | neither | slightly | quite | extremely| unlikely

I would find X to be flexible to interact with

likely |extremely | quite | slightly | neither | slightly | quite | extremely| unlikely

It would be easy for me to become skillful at using X

likely |extremely | quite | slightly | neither | slightly | quite | extremely| unlikely

I would find X easy to use

likely |extremely | quite | slightly | neither | slightly | quite | extremely| unlikely

Perceived Usefulness

Using X in my job would enable me to accomplish tasks more quickly

likely |extremely | quite | slightly | neither | slightly | quite | extremely| unlikely

Using X would improve my job performance

likely |extremely | quite | slightly | neither | slightly | quite | extremely| unlikely

Using X in my job would increase my productivity

likely |extremely | quite | slightly | neither | slightly | quite | extremely| unlikely

Using X would enhance my effectiveness on the job

likely |extremely | quite | slightly | neither | slightly | quite | extremely| unlikely

Using X would make it easier to do my job

likely |extremely | quite | slightly | neither | slightly | quite | extremely| unlikely

I found X useful in my job

likely |extremely | quite | slightly | neither | slightly | quite | extremely| unlikely

Figure 13.1 A questionnaire used to measure the extent to which people accept software (denoted by X in the table). The questionnaire is based on the technology acceptance model [180] (Chapter 19). The questionnaire contains two measurement constructs: (1) perceived ease of use and (2) perceived usefulness, each measured with six questions. These two constructs are used to predict the user acceptance of the system.

Paper Example 13.0.1: How do people use Facebook?

The uptake of social media over the past decades has been fast and widespread. Many studies have set out to describe this uptake, either as a way of understanding our use of social media or to improve social media. Lampe et al. [451] used questionnaires to study the development of Facebook use in its early stages in 2006–2008.

The study focused on three research questions: (1) How has communication with others on Facebook changed over time? (2) How has the perception of audience on Facebook changed over time? (3) How have attitudes toward Facebook changed over time? The study was *cross-sectional*, that is, the authors sent advertisements to undergraduates to fill in the questionnaire. They repeated this for three consecutive years. While this does not allow researchers to track changes in individual use, it enables them to infer it by comparing the collected data across years.

To gauge attitudes toward Facebook, the authors included statements such as "Facebook is part of my everyday activity" and "I would be sorry if Facebook shut down," which the participants rated on a five-point Likert scale. Such scales typically only have labeled endpoints (e.g., "strongly disagree" and "strongly agree"), although all the scale points can have labels (e.g., "neutral" for the middle point).

The table below from the work of Lampe et al. summarizes some of the changes detected in the study. It shows ratings of attitudes given on a five-point scale across three years. Low numbers indicate low agreement; high numbers indicate high agreement. The data were also subjected to analysis of variance, reported in the column named F. The subscript letters indicate significant post hoc tests.

Year of survey	F	2006 Mean	2006 Std. Dev.	2007 Mean	2007 Std. Dev.	2008 Mean	2008 Std. Dev.
Facebook is part of my everyday activity	36.12	3.12	1.26	3.75[1]	1.11	3.85[2]	1.12
Facebook has become part of my daily routine	35.82	2.96	1.32	3.70[1]	1.16	3.66[2]	1.19
I am proud to tell people I am on Facebook	2.90	3.24	0.89	3.40[1]	0.87	3.34	0.85
Facebook is just a fad	12.15	3.14	1.03	2.96	1.09	2.75[1,2]	1.00
I would be sorry if Facebook shut down	5.21	3.45	1.14	3.69[1]	1.19	3.72[2]	1.34
I use Facebook to get useful information	78.51	2.55	1.10	3.39[1]	1.02	3.54[2]	1.00
I use Facebook to find out about things going on at MSU	56.59	2.59	1.08	3.34[1]	1.18	3.51[2]	1.10
My Facebook use has caused me problems	22.51	1.67	0.89	2.14[1]	1.10	2.20[2]	1.12
I spend time on Facebook when I should be doing other things	9.44	3.16	1.15	3.52[1]	1.23	3.54[2]	1.18

Table 6: Ratings of attitudes towards Facebook. A mean reported with a "1" superscript indicates a significant (p<.05 or better) difference with the year before. A "2" indicates a significant difference between 2006 and 2008.

This table suggests a couple of noteworthy findings about the development of attitudes about Facebook. Over the years, the site has become increasingly part of users' daily lives, as suggested by the answers to the first two questions. This is perceived by the respondents as useful (question six), although the site also appears to increasingly cause problems for respondents.

13.1 Design of survey research

The design of survey research concerns establishing the focus of the research, selecting an appropriate type of survey, and figuring out who should receive the survey and how.

13.1.1 Research focus

The focus of the research needs to be clear and spelled out before a questionnaire is selected. Survey research is often appropriate for research goals like the ones captured in the following four bullet points. The first two items are about behaviors, also called *factual questions*; the last two items are about users' subjective experiences, also called *attitude questions*.

- Research about users' characteristics (e.g., what is often called marketing or demographics research).
- Research about users' activities, including the use of existing interactive systems and how they spend their time.
- Research about users' perceptions of their activities, the technology that surrounds them, and the context they work in.
- Research about users' attitudes toward future technology or future activities.

A second principled way to think about survey research is to consider questionnaires a *measurement tool* [620]. The idea is that well-designed questionnaires can measure behavior or attitudes precisely and at scale. For instance, we can consider questionnaires a measurement tool for assessing the loyalty of visitors to a web site. For example, the net promoter score is the percentage of web site visitors who rate the likelihood of recommending the site 9–10 (0–10 scale) minus the percentage who rate it 6 or lower [695].

A third principled way to think about survey research is that it can help collect *qualitative data at scale*.

The popularity of this purpose has increased with the use of crowdsourcing. As we will see, there are distinct limitations to the data collected in this way, although such surveys have been used to study attitudes in depth.

13.1.2 Survey types

Two main types of surveys may be distinguished: descriptive and analytic [620]. *Descriptive surveys* are known from census, election surveys, and surveys on how people spend their time. The main use of these surveys is to describe and characterize attitudes or behaviors. Such questionnaires often contain "how many" questions—for example, "How many times do you experience frustration when using a computer?"—or "what" questions—"What content do you enjoy on social media?" For example, the GVU Center at Georgia Tech began administering surveys in 1994 on people's behavior on the web, just a few years after it became publicly available [663]. The survey documented which browsers the respondents used, how much time they spent in front of their computer, and their age.

In *analytic surveys*, a deeper attempt is made to explain why a certain situation exists. This type of survey borrows some of the logic from experiments (Chapter 43) to answer "why" questions such as "Why do people like the app?" The idea is to analyze "what goes with what," that is, to see how different variables are related to each other. Compared to experiments, which can include interventions to expose causal factors, surveys are poorer at exposing causality but better at generating initial ideas about mechanisms and factors. For example, Tuch et al. [831] used surveys to collect narratives about positive and negative experiences with technology. Comparing those experiences highlighted key differences in users' experiences.

A central characteristic of analytic surveys is the attempt to relate answers to each other. Sometimes, such relationships are established by giving the same questionnaire to different people in so-called *cross-sectional designs*; see Paper Example 13.0.1. Cross-sectional designs can deal with multiple factors at the same time, which makes them similar to the factorial design for an experiment (Chapter 43). For instance, Tuch et al. [831] worked with four groups of participants obtained by crossing two factors of interest. One factor concerned the difference between positive and negative experiences with technology. The other factor concerned the difference between positive and negative wordings of questions about psychological needs. Together, these factors defined the four groups of respondents by theme: positive experience and positive wording, negative experience and positive wording, negative experience and positive wording, and negative experience and negative wording.

In *longitudinal designs*, respondents fill out the same questionnaire on multiple occasions. This may be done before and after an intervention, or it may be done to study the development of attitudes, learning, or expertise over time. For instance, Karapanos et al. [403] administered a questionnaire to six mobile phone users over four weeks. At the end of each day, the participants were required to list all the activities that had involved their phones in some way. Based on their responses and other data collected, Karapanos et al. [403] formulated a model of their user experience.

13.1.3 Sampling

We can rarely ask all users in a population of interest to fill in a questionnaire. Therefore, we need to select a subset, or *sample*, of users and base our conclusions on the insights provided by them. To ensure we can generalize our findings to the target population, the sample has to be carefully selected.

Sampling refers to decisions related to how people are approached to respond to a survey; see also the discussion on experimental studies in Chapter 43. Sampling can be done in multiple ways: via personal contact, email lists, advertisements, social networking groups, and so on.

The goal of sampling is to acquire a sample of respondents that allows the researcher to draw valid conclusions about the target population. All actual and potential users are called the *population*. We can contact a portion of the population, the *sampling frame*. We then send our questionnaire to most or some of the users in the sampling frame, who constitute the *sample* of our study. Among these users, those who choose to fill out the questionnaire are the *respondents*. Each sampling step requires care on the part of the researcher, as unintentionally excluding users can impact the validity of the results.

We can distinguish two principled ways of thinking about the sampling frame: randomization and stratification. First, sampling can be done at random from the population. This may be facilitated by panels of representative users from the population or by having your questionnaire distributed by opinion pollsters. Sampling may also be designed to ensure that certain types of users are represented equally. This is often referred to as quota sampling, cluster sampling, or stratification.

In *snowball sampling*, each respondent shares the invitation with other participants in their network or with similar characteristics; that way, the sample of respondents grows like a snowball rolling downhill. However, this may introduce unwanted (out-of-quota) characteristics. The reality of survey research in HCI is that many sampling frames are informal, being established through word-of-mouth, through one's network, or by posting on online forums. Such so-called convenience sampling does not ensure that every member of the population is equally likely to be part of a study, making it harder to draw valid inferences.

The question of which *sample size* to use in questionnaire research is difficult to answer. The practices in HCI research vary greatly. Published survey research in HCI can have as few respondents as six [403] or as many as 50,000 [230] (see Paper Example 13.3.1). A review of sample sizes concluded that the mean number of respondents in surveys in HCI papers is 371 [118].

The choice of sample size may also be informed by statistics. In descriptive surveys, the appropriate sample size depends on the *margin of error* you are willing to accept in quantitative measures. For instance, if you accept a 10% margin of error in estimates of which browser people use, you may need to ask 100 or more people; if you accept only a 1% margin of error, you need to ask many more people, for example, 700. In analytic surveys, the sample size may be determined via *power analysis*. Power analysis is a class of methods that can be used to estimate the number of respondents needed, given the analyses that will be carried out; see also Chapter 43.

13.2 Selecting a questionnaire

Survey research can be done by using existing questionnaires or developing new ones. Many questionnaires have been carefully validated and are known to be reliable. Designing a questionnaire from scratch is time-consuming and difficult, even for experienced researchers. However, much research in HCI does not use existing questionnaires. Hornbæk and Law [356] surveyed usability studies for which the full questionnaire data were available. Out of 36 studies, 16 (44%) used existing questionnaires; the other studies used custom questionnaires. Those questionnaires had, on average, lower reliability than existing ones, and six of them failed to reach commonly accepted criteria for minimum reliability (Cronbach's alpha of 0.70 or above). This survey confirms the value of using existing questionnaires.

13.2.1 Finding appropriate questionnaires

How to find existing questionnaires for user research? The key step is determining whether the constructs of interest (e.g., perceptions of privacy, feelings of satisfaction, awareness of a group) have been developed into questionnaires. Table 13.1 shows examples of existing questionnaires that are often used in HCI. Previous research on the topic of interest and HCI handbooks are also great sources for finding questionnaires. For example, Sauro and Lewis [734] listed 24 standard questionnaires for assessing the perception of usability and user experience. Outside of HCI, many questionnaires have been developed, and their reliability and validity have been assessed. Such questionnaires may be found in handbooks [e.g., 734], on dedicated search engines for questionnaires [458], and by searching scholarly databases (e.g., ERIC, Google Scholar, arXiv, PsychAbstracts) for the construct of interest.

13.3 Developing questions

Our advice is to use validated questionnaires when possible; the situations in which there is nothing available are few. Developing a questionnaire requires the careful creation, validation, and testing of the questions. This section covers some basic ideas for the cases where no existing

Table 13.1 Questionnaires that are often used in user research.

Questionnaire	Purpose
NASA Task Load Index (NASA-TLX)	Measure the experienced workload when using an interactive system using six items, including mental demand, physical demand, and effort [316].
Godspeed questionnaire	Measure five distinct components of users' perception of social robots, including their anthropomorphism, animacy, and perceived intelligence [48].
User engagement questionnaire	Assess six factors of being engaged with interactive systems, including focused attention, felt involvement, and novelty [608].
Player experience inventory	Measure the payer experience as functional consequences (e.g., audiovisual control) and psychosocial consequences (e.g., mastery) [2].
Single-item post-task usability questionnaire	A short, single-item questionnaire to assess usability after a task: "Overall this task was . . ." rated on a seven-item scale going from "very easy" to "very difficult" [732].

questionnaire is available. It also illustrates some of the reasons why developing valid and reliable questions is difficult.

Below, we distinguish two kinds of questions [738]. First, some questions are about *events and behaviors*. They concern how often something is done, which types of activities were done at some point, the frequency of use of a system, and so on. For instance, we might be interested in how frequently people use a particular web site. These questions are formulated so that they have a correct answer in principle, even if the respondent may not be able to provide it. Second, some questions are about *subjective phenomena*, including attitudes, intentions, wants, and so on. For instance, we might be interested in how somebody values virtual possessions, such as in-game possessions, relative to physical possessions.

13.3.1 Wording questions

If done sloppily, the wording of questions may lead to answers that are invalid and unreliable. For example, let us assume that we wish to design a question that probes which piece of software people use the most. Let us start by considering the question "Which software do you use and engage with the most?" What do we mean by "software"? There is software in cars, hearing aids, and washing machines—do we want answers covering all those devices? Would it be better to spell this out ("software such as apps on a phone or tablet or programs on a computer") or limit the question to a subset of devices, as in "computer (e.g., laptop, tablet, smartphone)"? If we specify "your computer," this may be limiting since a user may rarely use their personal computer yet frequently use other computers, such as their work computer or a borrowed computer. Also, what about "use"? What if respondents consider it different from "engage with"? Moreover, what about "the most"? Respondents may interpret it as "the most times" or "the longest duration," resulting in fundamentally different answers. As another example, consider the study in Paper Example 13.3.1 on asking people how often they use social media.

These examples suggest some general principles for thinking about how to craft valid and reliable questions.

Use language that respondents understand: Questions should be user-centered, that is, use terminology that users are familiar with and that they find clear and straightforward. Avoid hard-to-parse questions, including those that use difficult words (e.g., "versimulitude"), double negatives (e.g., "not uninteresting"), and excess words.

Ask one question at a time: "How satisfied are you with the system and the support for it?" This question does not work because it is possible for respondents to be simultaneously satisfied with the system but not with the support provided. Such questions are called double-barreled and should be avoided.

Ask neutral questions: Questions should be formulated so as to not impose the researcher's views or ideas about the answers on the respondents. Avoid leading questions such as "Do you agree that the web site is usable?" Instead, use something like "Do you agree or disagree that the web site is usable?" Also, avoid making assumptions about the respondents: "What is the brand of your laptop?" assumes the respondent owns a laptop, which might not be the case.

Ask specific questions: Questions should be specific so that the respondent is clear about what is being asked. For instance, "How does this product compare to others?" does not specify what aspects of the product the respondent should compare (e.g., price, functionality, usability). Specificity is particularly important for objects and events. For instance, we already saw some difficulties around the specificity of the word "computer." Specificity is also relevant with words and phrases that are assessed relative to a personal standard. For instance, "frequently," "rarely," "expensive," and so on may be assessed in different ways by different respondents. Even something like "last week" can be unclear: Is it the last seven days or the week before the current one?

Be aware of response biases: It is well known that participants may have biases when answering questions. Effective questions are worded so that they mitigate these biases as much as possible. For instance, social desirability bias may lead respondents to provide answers they believe are more socially acceptable or prestigious. We report more bias types below.

Paper Example 13.3.1: Formulating questions to learn about time usage

Designing questions that participants understand and answer validly is hard. Ernala et al. [230] wanted to find questions that would help them get valid and reliable answers on how long people spend on social media. They administered questionnaires covering 10 ways of asking about this to 50,000 respondents. For instance, one question asked: "In the past week, on average, approximately how much time have you spent actively using Facebook?" Another question asked: "How many hours a day, if any, do you typically spend using Facebook?" Additionally, the research collected data on how much time participants *actually* spent using Facebook to account for differences between recorded and actual time usage and investigate how demographics influenced these differences.

They found that the formulation with the least error was the following:

continued

> **Paper Example 13.3.1: Formulating questions to learn about time usage** (*continued*)
>
> ```
> In the past week, on average, approximately how much time PER DAY have you
> spent actively using Facebook?
> Less than 10 minutes per day
> 10--30 minutes per day
> 31--60 minutes per day
> 1--2 hours per day
> 2--3 hours per day
> More than 3 hours per day
> ```
>
> The study also showed that self-reports were only moderately correlated to the actual time people spent on Facebook.

13.3.2 Question types

Two main types of questions exist. With *closed questions*, respondents are offered a choice between different answers. Closed questions can have many different forms, including the following:

- Single-choice questions offer a list of alternatives from which one may be selected.
- Multiple-choice questions offer a list of alternatives from which one or more may be selected.
- Ranking questions allow respondents to rank alternatives.
- Rating questions offer a textual or graphical scale that the answer is given on. The scales can have different steps and anchors (i.e., descriptions of the endpoints).

One benefit of closed questions is that they are easy to analyze: Because the options for answering are restricted, statistics are straightforward to apply to the answers. The drawback is that such questions may be too crude and not capture all the relevant options for respondents. While generally recommended, including options such as "I don't know," "non-applicable," or "other" does not remove this issue. Closed questions may work if the options are derived from earlier research or pilot work; Oppenheim [620] suggested that all closed questions should start their lives as open ones.

The other main type of question is *open questions*, also called free-response questions or free-text questions. Open-ended questions are useful when it is not clear how respondents want to answer, such as in exploratory work where the closed questions are not yet known. Open questions allow respondents to answer freely and spontaneously. Often, sensitive or socially disapproved behaviors and the frequency or form of behaviors are better investigated through open questions. However, open questions are "easy to ask, difficult to answer, and still more difficult to analyse" [620, p. 113].

The decision between open and closed questions is a trade-off between the research objectives and the pros and cons of these different types of questions.

13.3.3 Question order and presentation

Traditionally, questionnaires were presented over the telephone or on paper; nowadays, most surveys are done online. Online surveys are easier to deliver to a large number of respondents. However, there are two main drawbacks. First, online surveys require a digital device. Those who do not have access to a digital device are excluded, which can lead to bias in the sample. Second, computer terminals can differ in the way they present the same survey, creating variability in the responses.

A questionnaire should start with instructions for the respondents. This should include covering the broad context of the study. It should also instruct the respondents on how to interpret and respond to the questions. Such instructions are sometimes shown one by one to ensure they are not glossed over.

The order in which the questions are presented matters. *Funneling* refers to the practice of starting with broad questions and then moving toward more specific ones. The argument is that broad questions help jog respondents' memory on the topic of the questionnaire.

Surveys must be designed for visual clarity and ease of use. The response options should be quick to choose with the terminals used by the respondents. For example, drop-down lists are time-consuming to use on touchscreen devices, and some touchscreen devices do not support sliding.

13.3.4 Question sets and scales

One key issue in survey research is reliability. Unfortunately, single-item questions can be unreliable, particularly when investigating subjective experiences. More generally, using single questions to uncover attitudes or experiences is risky, as a particular question may be vague or otherwise unclear to respondents. They may also misclick the answer option.

One solution to this issue is to use sets of questions, sometimes called scales. A scale consists of items that are about the same underlying construct (or constructs if the scale consists of multiple items). Some popular scales used in HCI research include:

- The Likert scale, which consists of a claim and a symmetric negative-to-positive range (typically 1–5, 1–7, or 1–9) with the "neutral" option in the middle.
- Semantic differentials, which provide a scale between two adjectives (e.g., "exhausting" and "effortless"). Semantic differentials are often used to measure attitudes and opinions.
- Graphical ratings, in which several options are presented in a symbolic fashion (e.g., the pain measurement scale).

13.3.5 Biases in answering questions

A question should be thought of as a measurement. It probes the respondent and records a response. The validity of this measure depends on several things we have discussed above, including biases. Many types of biases threaten validity, including the following:

Acquiescence bias: Tendency to respond in a positive manner.

Social desirability: Tendency to mirror socially desirable behaviors and views. For example, if a question asks to report if the respondent takes backups, some responses might overstate this.

Response order bias: The first and last parts of a questionnaire tend to elicit different behaviors, especially in long questionnaires, where fatigue effects may be more apparent.

Neutral item bias: Items in the middle of the scale (e.g., "neutral," "I do not know") tend to be overused. By contrast, the extrema (lowest and highest values) tend to be underused.

Demand bias: Users who know about the purpose of the study may start behaving according to their expectations regarding the study. For example, if you tell participants you are going to measure their knowledge of phishing attacks, they may pay more attention to those during the study.

There are many ways these biases can be mitigated; we look into some tactics in the exercises.

13.4 Questionnaire piloting

All questionnaires should be piloted, especially if they are modified from existing questionnaires. This includes the questions as well as the questionnaire instructions.

One overarching principle for creating good questions is to consider the experience of answering them; this principle has direct implications for the piloting of questionnaires. In Chapter 42, we discuss think-aloud studies. One adaptation of such studies is to use them to get insights into how respondents experience the questions and the questionnaire instructions. With such insights, the questionnaire may be revised to address discrepancies between the idea of the question and participants' experiences.

13.5 Data collection

The data collection in survey research is influenced by how the questionnaire is distributed to respondents and how and when the respondents complete it.

13.5.1 Distribution of surveys

Traditionally, questionnaires were distributed to respondents via paper or by telephone, with the researcher reading the questions aloud to the respondents. Presently, questionnaires are most commonly answered online using a browser or mobile app. These questionnaires are typically answered once, say, after using a new interactive system or at the time when the respondents decide to complete the survey.

HCI researchers have modified these forms to suit the purposes of their studies. Palen and Salzman [636], for instance, allowed participants to answer open-ended and structured questions via voicemail. This allowed them to collect data from participants on the go. Schwind et al. [748] investigated whether survey research is impacted by the participants answering a questionnaire in virtual reality rather than in the real world. Their data suggested it does not and that researchers can effectively administer questionnaires in virtual reality.

In the past decade, *crowdsourcing* has enabled tasks that humans are good at and computers are bad at to be distributed to people at scale [684, 418]. The idea is that tasks are broken down to be small in scale and distributed to people over the Internet. These people may do the tasks for payment. These are often small fees, so-called micropayments, because the tasks are short. Crowdsourcing has significantly impacted how survey research is conducted.

With crowdwork, including surveys, a key concern is ensuring that respondents pay attention and produce high-quality answers. If participants are just racing through a survey—sometimes called satisficing—the data may not be reliable and may dilute the quality of the full dataset. There are several ways to avoid this. Researchers have included *attention checks* in surveys, that is, questions with obvious answers—if respondents fail to answer them correctly, their data may be excluded. Similarly, in *instructional manipulation checks* [621], respondents are instructed to do something while a seemingly obvious next step is presented elsewhere (e.g., a continue button or a rating scale). The data of participants who do not follow the instructions may be excluded.

13.5.2 Compensation and treatment of participants

Like all participants in user research (Part III), survey participants must be treated ethically. Respondents should be told about the purpose of the study as well as how the data are used. All respondents should be offered a straightforward, non-punitive way to stop participating in the study if they want to stop. In cases where the respondents are compensated, the compensation should be provided in an ethical manner. This means the participants should be paid at least minimum wage for their work or be otherwise appropriately compensated for their efforts.

13.5.3 Improving the response rate

If the response rate is low, different techniques may improve it: (1) running multiple advertisement campaigns instead of just one; (2) improving the usability of the questionnaire; (3) asking a known person to approach members of the community personally; and (4) sending personal reminders.

One caveat of such techniques is that they may bias the sample away from the intended sample. This can occur in subtle ways. For example, if you call people personally to ask them to fill in your survey, this may skew the respondents pool toward those whose contact numbers you have.

13.6 Analysis

Before starting to analyze the obtained dataset, the original research questions should be revisited. They should be formulated so that they can be answered via computations done on the dataset. Then, the response data are cleaned, it is checked that they are reliable and valid, and they are analyzed statistically or qualitatively in relation to the research aims. In this book, we cover five main steps with a focus on conceptual understanding:

1. Preprocessing the dataset for subsequent computations: Cleaning, imputing missing data if needed, and recoding.
2. Assessing reliability: Computing response rates and internal validity.
3. Descriptive analysis: Describing tendencies and relations of interest among variables.
4. Explorative analysis: Exploring emergent tendencies not written up as research questions.
5. Testing hypotheses (Chapter 43).
6. Drawing valid conclusions and reporting.

13.6.1 Preprocessing

First, the response data need to be cleaned and variables need to be defined in preparation for analysis. *Cleaning* the data means removing those answers that are invalid. For example, some participants may have failed attention checks, given the same response to all questions, or produced otherwise unsuitable data such as copy-pasted data. The data of participants who are inconsistent with their answers may also be removed. When some answers are removed, the analyst faces a decision. Should one remove a participant entirely (i.e., list-wise deletion) or just the problematic answers (i.e., pair-wise deletion)? Regardless, one should be careful with data cleaning. If a large proportion of the data needs to be removed, the questionnaire is probably poorly designed. There is no clear-cut criterion for deciding what is "too large" a proportion. A good rule of thumb is that if the removed proportion is larger than 5%, cleaning may start to adversely affect the validity of conclusions.

Some data may be missing, for example, due to technical reasons (browser not storing user responses) or inattentive respondents skipping questions. Such cases may be removed; again, the proportion of removed data should not be too large. *Data imputation* refers to statistical techniques for replacing missing data with estimates computed based on the rest of the data. For example, dataset averages can be used when relatively few data are missing. Otherwise, more sophisticated statistical techniques (e.g., MICE [842]) can be used to better estimate missing values from the data available.

After cleaning and imputation, some response data may need to be *recoded*. Items of a scale may be summed to compute an index score. For example, responses to the NASA-TLX questionnaire, which consists of several components of workload, are summed to compute an aggregate index of workload. The type of recoding depends on the analyses that are done later on. However, one must remember that recoding may result in a loss of information.

Open-ended questions in questionnaires may provide extensive qualitative data. Such data can be analyzed with the same techniques that are used for interview data, such as thematic analysis (Chapter 11), and for archival data, such as content analysis (Chapter 14).

13.6.2 Assessing reliability

Response rates

In data collection, the *response rate* refers to the number of participants in our sampling frame who complete the questionnaire. It is good practice to compute the response rate when it is known how many participants have received the survey invitation. For example, if you sent an email to a list with 1,000 employees and 100 took the survey, the response rate is 10%.

In large-scale surveys, it is not uncommon for the response rate to be low. However, as pointed out by Oppenheim [620], the key issue is not the rate of responses or the proportion of non-responses but "the possibility of bias" [p. 106]. The question one should ask is: *How* do non-respondents differ from respondents? For example, the respondents can be more (or less) educated and younger (or older) than the population of interest. This will unavoidably affect the generalizability of the results. To address such concerns, it is good practice to gauge how well the respondents' characteristics match those of the population of interest. For example, one can compute the descriptive statistics (e.g., mean, median, standard deviation) of background factors such as age, education, and so on. These can then be compared to known characteristics of the target population.

Internal reliability

Testing the reliability of questionnaires is relevant for scales meant to measure some broad construct using multiple questions. For such scales, we would like the answers to vary in the same way. For example, if a user answers "low" to "Is the software useful?" they should also answer "low" to "Does the software help you do things that are important to you?" If so, we say the answers are internally reliable.

There are many ways to check the reliability of scales. One is the simple correlation coefficient between items: If the items are reliable, we expect them to correlate strongly. Another way is the commonly used Cronbach's alpha:

$$\alpha = \frac{N * \bar{c}}{\bar{v} + (N-1) * \bar{c}}, \quad (13.1)$$

where N is the number of items, $\bar{c}$ is the average inter-item covariance among items, and $\bar{v}$ is the average variance. It quantifies the internal consistency of a test on a scale from zero to one. A high Cronbach's alpha is expected for scales; one rule of thumb is that it should be at least 0.7.

Cronbach's alpha can tell us whether to trust the results of a survey. For example, when Hirzle et al. [344] explored eye strain with virtual headsets, they used several earlier questionnaires, including one on digital eye strain, comprising four subscales. They then calculated Cronbach's alpha to assess the consistency of each item. "We found acceptable values for Mall ($\alpha = 0.77$) and M_{ex} ($\alpha = 0.77$), but a slightly low value for M_{in} ($\alpha = 0.67$), and a poor value for M_{vr} ($\alpha = 0.51$). Therefore, the results for M_{vr} must be considered with caution." In other words, the items in the subscale M_{vr} did not correlate with each other as strongly as expected.

O'Brien and Toms [608] developed a new questionnaire for measuring user engagement. They initially developed 11 subscales of engagement and checked that Cronbach's alpha was satisfactory. They also used Cronbach's alpha to identify irrelevant questions, that is, questions that could be deleted without shifting alpha outside its optimal range (between 0.7 and 0.9). Another questionnaire example (QUIS) is given in Paper Example 13.6.1.

If the internal reliability is low, one can try to increase it by removing items that have low reliability. If this is not possible, the questionnaire may need to be redesigned. Note that reliability is only relevant for questions that purport to measure the same thing. If items are about different things, they should not score similarly.

Paper Example 13.6.1: Evaluating a user satisfaction questionnaire

Chin et al. [150] evaluated a questionnaire called QUIS to measure user satisfaction. The questionnaire, at the time of the evaluation in its fifth version, comprised 27 rating scales from 0 to 9. It included items such as "Overall reactions to the software" on a scale going from "terrible" (0) to "wonderful" (9) and "Learning to operate the system" on a scale going from "difficult" (0) to "easy" (9). To assess the validity of the scale, the authors asked respondents to fill in the questionnaire about a product they liked and a product they did not like. The questionnaire would be considered valid if it showed differences between the two products.

The results showed significant differences between the liked and disliked products, serving as a first rough indicator of the validity of the questionnaire. Moreover, the reliability of the

continued

> **Paper Example 13.6.1: Evaluating a user satisfaction questionnaire** *(continued)*
>
> questionnaire was found to be adequate. Cronbach's alpha was 0.94, suggesting that questions about the same aspect of satisfaction were answered in the same way.
>
> QUIS may be used by researchers who want to assess the satisfaction with a user interface.

13.6.3 Descriptive analysis

Descriptive analysis refers to the study of the distribution of variables in the dataset. This can be done using any of the widely available means in statistical tools: histograms, scatterplots, bar charts, line charts, etc. It is good practice to start by visualizing univariate distributions (i.e., how single items are responded to), for example, using histograms. This helps spot potential issues such as skewness (the tendency of a distribution to lean toward either end) and multimodality (several peaks). Another good practice is *crosstabulation*. It involves computing tables that report how two or more response variables are related. Another good practice is to add *error bars*, such as *confidence levels*, to charts. For example, the 95% confidence interval indicates the level of confidence that the true mean lies within the interval. Confidence levels indicate the degree of variability at different response levels, helping us avoid overinterpreting a plot when the underlying data are highly variable.

13.6.4 Exploratory analysis

Besides visualizing data in different ways, *factor analysis* is a form of statistical analysis that helps us uncover the underlying dimensions of a set of variables. These underlying dimensions are called factors or latent variables, as they cannot be obtained directly from respondents' answers but must be inferred from them. Factor analysis is helpful when a questionnaire has many items; in such situations, it helps determine which items are most related to each other. For instance, if the items concern how frequently you use an interactive system and how long a typical session lasts, you might expect to identify a factor related to frequency (likely composed of several items, such as questions about frequency) and one related to session duration. If factor analysis does not identify these two factors, something may not be right with our questions or the respondents' answers.

Factor analysis is mathematically complex, and several variants exist; Kline [422] provides an introduction to relevant principles, calculations, and software packages.

Factor analysis has several uses in survey research. Unlike reliability analysis, factor analysis typically concerns the relationship among all the variables of a survey. Paper Example 13.6.2 provides a detailed example of factor analysis.

> **Paper Example 13.6.2: Factor analysis in surveys**
>
> Law et al. [464] studied the game experience questionnaire (GEQ). This questionnaire is widely used in evaluating games. After a review of existing work using the GEQ, the authors conducted their own survey study using the GEQ to validate the scale.

A total of 633 participants described a recent experience. They then answered the GEQ relative to that experience, answering the 33 questions on a five-point Likert scale ranging from "not at all" (0) to "extremely" (4).

These data were subjected to confirmatory factor analysis, a variant of factor analysis. Instead of trying to find out what the factors are, the goal here is to assess how good some *given* factors are. The authors' analysis showed that two of the seven scales of the GEQ were not strong enough (i.e., alpha below 0.7). This finding means that the proposed scales of the GEQ are not independent, contrary to what was expected.

	Component	MR2	MR1	MR5	MR3	MR4	MR6	MR7	h2
15 I was good at it	Competence	-.030	.060	-.026	**.798**	-.006	-.111	.030	.739
02 I felt skillful	Competence	-.043	.058	.063	**.701**	-.019	.240	-.051	.451
17 I felt successful	Competence	-.073	.096	.035	**.604**	.102	.011	-.092	.697
21 I was fast at reaching the game's targets	Competence	.114	.042	.122	**.593**	.005	-.090	.067	.399
10 I felt competent	Competence	.016	.170	.105	**.491**	.076	-.042	.115	.650
19 I felt that I could explore things	Immersion	-.025	-.074	**.751**	.004	.030	-.065	.032	.697
03 I was interested in the game's story	Immersion	.002	.050	**.722**	-.037	-.045	-.049	-.017	.668
18 I felt imaginative	Immersion	-.037	-.027	**.680**	.023	.068	.080	-.107	.426
27 I found it impressive	Immersion	.017	.177	**.613**	.025	.015	.111	.005	.546
30 It felt like a rich experience	Immersion	.037	.152	**.489**	.070	.136	.088	.115	.518
12 It was aesthetically pleasing	Immersion	-.050	.269	**.337**	.094	.009	.018	.071	.521
31 I lost connection with the outside world	Flow	.069	.047	-.010	-.070	**.850**	-.077	-.023	.529
13 I forgot everything around me	Flow	-.086	-.128	.065	.110	**.724**	.090	-.042	.631
25 I lost track of time	Flow	.068	.086	.033	-.037	**.696**	-.023	.004	.598
05 I was fully occupied with the game	Flow	.018	.069	.101	.150	**.451**	.140	**.315**	.685
28 I was deeply concentrated in the game	Flow	-.008	.066	.159	.171	**.345**	.240	.282	.639
24 I felt irritable	Tension	**.806**	.013	-.012	-.014	.054	-.011	-.009	.595
22 I felt annoyed	Tension	**.800**	-.004	-.007	-.071	.004	.048	-.015	.693
29 I felt frustrated	Tension	**.656**	.089	-.126	-.131	.035	.275	-.013	.780
23 I felt pressured	Tension	**.393**	-.111	-.044	.104	.088	**.339**	.046	.597
32 I felt time pressure	Challenge	**.338**	-.040	-.007	.119	.000	.253	.041	.283
11 I thought it was hard	Challenge	.116	.005	.005	-.151	.001	**.679**	-.088	.583
26 I felt challenged	Challenge	-.032	.134	.049	.081	.059	**.661**	.085	.658
33 I had to put a lot of effort in to it	Challenge	.107	-.066	.137	.109	.034	**.563**	.094	.253
07 It gave me a bad mood	Negative Affect	**.782**	-.074	.009	.059	.012	-.078	.075	.470
09 I found it tiresome	Negative Affect	**.505**	-.240	.113	.063	-.043	.013	-.114	.692
16 I felt bored	Negative Affect	**.455**	-.213	.015	.089	-.043	-.208	-.212	.732
08 I thought about other things	Negative Affect	.278	.011	.102	.066	-.241	-.118	**-.327**	.467
06 I felt happy	Positive Affect	-.011	**.734**	.096	.097	.049	.049	-.184	.401
04 I thought it was fun	Positive Affect	-.041	**.703**	.111	-.006	-.012	.003	.273	.517
20 I enjoyed it	Positive Affect	-.073	**.653**	.095	.073	.020	.026	.184	.499
14 I felt good	Positive Affect	-.090	**.607**	.018	.213	.110	.049	-.097	.407
01 I felt content	Positive Affect	-.088	**.575**	.003	.217	.089	-.017	-.115	.596
After rotation Sums of Squares		3.17	3.70	3.03	2.90	2.61	2.07	1.44	
% of variance explained		9.7	11.2	9.2	8.8	7.9	6.3	4.4	

Table 5. Rotated pattern matrix of the EFA with 33 items loading on seven factors.

	ω	95% CI	Cronbach's α	AVE	MSV
Immersion	.85	[.83,.87]	.85	.48	.54
Flow	.86	[.84,.88]	.86	.54	.51
Competence	.86	[.83,.86]	.85	.54	.60
Tension	.82	[.79,.85]	.82	.55	.75
Challenge	.71	[.67,.74]	.57	.38	.42
Positive affect	.91	[.89,.92]	.91	.66	.60
Negative affect	.69	[.64,.74]	.68	.31	.75

Table 7. GEQ-33 reliability analysis. Reliability coefficient ω with bias-corrected and accelerated bootstrap (1000 iterations) 95%-confidence intervals as implemented in [35].

13.6.5 Drawing conclusions

It is easy to report plots and statistical results based on a collected dataset. It is much harder to draw solid conclusions about the population of interest. This requires consideration of different types of validity:

- *Construct validity* refers to the selection of the questionnaire: Does it capture what we intended to capture? For example, if we wanted to draw conclusions about user engagement but used a usability questionnaire, we should refrain from making conclusions about engagement.
- *Internal validity* refers to the strength of the statistical relationships between variables. Even in nominally strong relationships, there can be confounding factors we have failed to account for. For example, if one finds a relationship between the size of a mobile device and typing speed, is that because large displays are better for typing or because users who are wealthier and buy larger phones are also older and therefore more experienced?
- *Statistical conclusion validity* refers to the fact that all data come with noise and variance. One should take into account the statistical confidence with which the conclusions are drawn.
- *External validity* refers to the ability to extend conclusions from the study sample to the population of interest. If the sample poorly represents the population, external validity is compromised.

Besides statistical analysis, it is important to seek to explain the findings. What do extant theories say about them? A compelling explanation can increase confidence in the results. Results should also be compared against those from previous studies on the same topic or group: Are they similar or dissimilar? What might explain any discrepancies?

13.6.6 Reporting

Finally, the analyses that were carried out should be reported. It is important to report all analyses. They are as much a part of the survey method as the questionnaire. It is good practice to store the scripts or formulas that were used and publish them as part of the study report.

There is also an important ethical dimension to drawing and publishing conclusions. The publication of findings should not harm the respondents, for example, by disclosing information that may jeopardize their jobs or lead to discrimination.

13.7 Situating questionnaires

Survey studies are inexpensive to conduct; one only needs a computer or a paper handout and a pen. After a survey has been designed, the researcher is not needed to complete it, only to distribute it. This stands in contrast to methods that depend on the presence of the researcher throughout, such as the interview method. Moreover, the sample size tends to be much larger in survey studies than in interview studies.

However, the de-situatedness of surveys poses a challenge for user research. The moment when a respondent fills in a questionnaire is detached, in time or space (or both), from the moment or moments that these surveys are about. In such cases, respondents need to rely on memory or their imagination to close this gap. The question is: How to re-situate questionnaires?

With *diaries,* this gap can be reduced but not closed. A diary consists of questionnaires that are filled in periodically, for example, every day or week. This can be done in many ways, including on a mobile device or via phone calls. The study by Palen and Salzman [636] discussed earlier used phone diaries. They had participants call a phone service and answer structured prompts such as "Please tell us how you have used your phone service since the last time you called us, as well as any problems you have had. Also, describe any changes you may have made to your phone or service." The respondents could call whenever they wanted and they were paid per call. While diaries provide more flexibility in responding, they still depend on *when* the user chooses to add entries. Some users may want to fill them in close to the pertinent events; others may not. Therefore, the diary approach does not solve the issue of de-situatedness.

Experience sampling is an attempt to bring surveys even closer to the contexts they refer to. Experience sampling refers to the computer-controlled cueing of surveys. A notification pops up on the mobile device, or a message is sent via a messaging application. These notifications invite the respondent to fill in the survey within some time window. For example, an app can follow when the user enters the office and trigger the survey at that moment, asking the user to fill it in within, say, five minutes. These surveys, however, need to be very brief—they could consist of just one question. More details can be found in [204].

Summary

- Surveys help collect information from many respondents; their strength is generalizability.
- Since respondents cannot ask for clarifications, the survey questions need to be clear, unambiguous, and relevant.
- Questionnaires should be reliable and have a validated factor structure.
- Diaries and the experience sampling method attempt to bring surveys closer to the moments of interaction.

Exercises

1. Alternative answer options. Create answer options for the following question in four ways (single-choice, multiple-choice, rankings, and ratings): "If I suspect that an email is a phishing email, I do not even open it."
2. Learning from surveys. Go on a crowdsourcing web site such as Amazon Mechanical Turk or Prolific. Find a questionnaire and complete it. Answer the questions: (a) Does it use easily understood language? (b) Does it ask one question at a time? (c) Are the questions neutral? (d) Are the questions specific? (e) Are there potential triggers of response biases?
3. Survey as a research method. Consider the following situations. For which of them would surveys be an appropriate research method? Why? (a) Understanding how workers in a microbrewery use a mobile application for coordinating their work. (b) Charting general expectations toward augmented reality applications. (c) Charting user needs for a new version of a product.
4. Getting rid of biases. Consider the following questionnaire question: "How good is the present version of the application you use? Rate: 1—Not good at all; 2—Bad; 3—Neutral; 4—Good;

5—The best." What are some potential biases in this formulation? How would you rephrase the question and the scale to avoid them?

5. Designing a question. This exercise requires you to design one question that asks the respondent about events or behaviors in computer use. You may come up with your own target event or behavior, or you may attempt to identify how many computers a person uses—for example, imagine a context where we want to characterize how people link or do not link their different computers. Design the question. Go through it based on the design suggestions provided in this chapter. Think about sources of bias, issues of validity, and concerns about reliability.

6. Data analysis. Following the guidance given in this chapter, analyze the qualitative data from this survey: https://osf.io/m3fbk/.

14
Unobtrusive research

Typical user research affects, or changes, the activities users engage in. In other words, it *intervenes*. For example, consider carrying out user research on how people use passwords. During the course of the study, without you knowing, your participants may have changed their behavior or opinions. The fact that they selected themselves for the study, or the way they were informed about the purpose of the study, may have made them more sensitive to it. They may also want to act according to what they believe is socially desirable. To sum up, taking part in a study may affect the behavior of participants. *Reactivity*—the impact of research on what is being studied—can fundamentally change what is discovered and, therefore, potentially undermine the validity of the research.

Unobtrusive research is a form of noninterventional user research. It aims to not affect or change the activities that users engage in. Sometimes, unobtrusive research is called nonreactive [877]. This term emphasizes that the data obtained are not affected in the same manner as data from observations or interviews. In contrast to reactive methods in user research, in unobtrusive research, the data may be generated even before the research activity has begun. However, the data may still be used to characterize users, their activities, and their opinions.

Unobtrusive research uses *traces* of users' behavior or archival records to make inferences about users and their activities. In human–computer interaction (HCI), such data may come from:

- Application logs of activities in a system, such as what users click on a web site (click data). For example, Huberman et al. [362] analyzed the distributions of clicks on web sites and found statistical tendencies that were explained using information foraging theory.
- Records of posts and comments on social media. For example, Chandrasekharan et al. [143] used computational and qualitative methods to analyze posts on Reddit. They reported on norms upheld by Reddit community members. They distinguished between macro norms that are shared by most Reddit users, meso norms that are shared among some user groups, and micro norms that are specific to individual subreddits (discussion groups).
- Video recordings of a site of interest. For example, Brown and Laurier [99] analyzed publicly available YouTube videos showing incidents or near-incidents involving self-driving cars. The authors analyzed how drivers interpret the intentions of other drivers and cars.

Realism is the defining aim of unobtrusive research. It allows us to study interaction with interactive systems as it happens in the wild, without reactivity to data collection and without the sensitization of users to what they perceive to be the goal of data collection. Overall, such research helps us access people's actual behaviors rather than what they choose to report; see the say–do gap discussed in Chapter 11.

Unobtrusive research also has other benefits. It is often inexpensive, allowing researchers to collect large amounts of data with little effort. For instance, in Paper Example 14.0.1 studying web revisitation patterns, data were collected from 612,000 users [10]. Besides not affecting users' attitudes and behaviors, unobtrusive research does not disturb users or require them to take time out to attend interviews or have researchers shadow their work. For instance, Anthony et al. [25] used YouTube videos to research how people with motor impairments interact with touch-enabled mobile phones. This approach allowed them to collect substantial data spanning many more situations of use compared to previouswork.

In a classic work on unobtrusive measures, Webb et al. [877] identified four sources of nonreactive data:

Traces: Traces are obtained either via log file analysis, such as from web logs, or from instrumenting people, things, or places. Traces can be divided into two classes: direct and indirect.

Direct traces: They are recordings that result from users' actions. For example, mouse movements and clicks can be logged by an operating system and stored in a file.

Indirect traces: They result from users indirectly via some intermediary mechanism. For example, think about a numpad used to enter passwords. Wear and tear on a physical object tells us something about the users and their patterns, but they are not direct recordings of any instance of an action.

Archive data: Archive data can be of many kinds, including social media content.

Next, we discuss the analysis of unobtrusively collected data.

Paper Example 14.0.1: Revisitation patterns in web browsing

One of the most prominent applications of unobtrusive research in HCI has been using automatically logged information from computer systems to make inferences about what people do or want to do. Behavior on the web is one example of data that may be inexpensively logged at scale to allow researchers to understand how users browse the web and how to support that activity. One example of such research focused on how users return to web pages [10]. It is well known that users often return to the same pages; however, at the time when the study was done in 2008, this was mainly known from studies with few participants.

Adar et al. [10] used data from users who had opted into using a toolbar for web searches. Each toolbar was associated with a unique identifier, and all web pages visited through the toolbar were recorded for five weeks. These data were thoroughly cleaned, extreme users were removed, and the data were grouped according to the type of web page and the time between revisits. The figures in this paper example box show one insight from the study: The revisitation patterns vary between page types. The graph shows the times between revisits; shopping and reference web pages had less than an hour between visits.

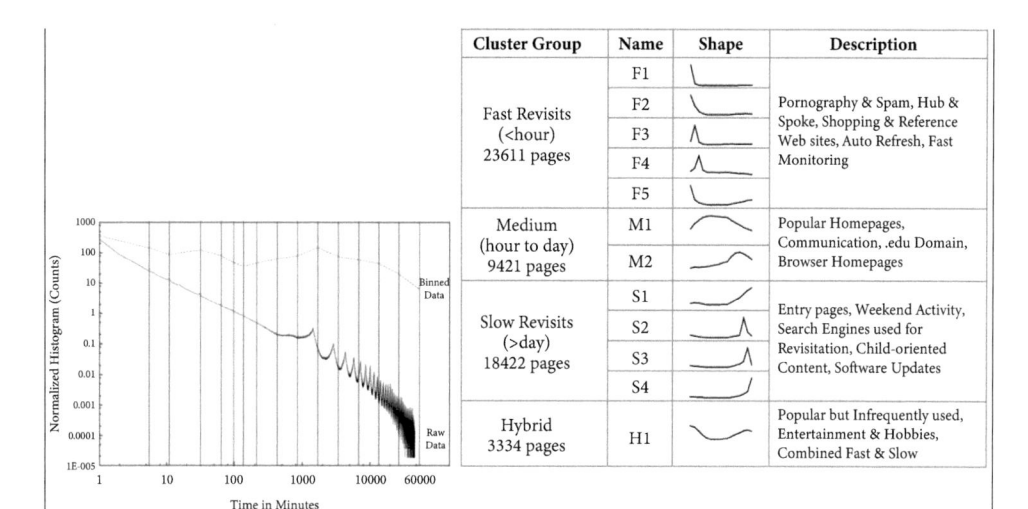

Cluster Group	Name	Shape	Description
Fast Revisits (<hour) 23611 pages	F1		Pornography & Spam, Hub & Spoke, Shopping & Reference Web sites, Auto Refresh, Fast Monitoring
	F2		
	F3		
	F4		
	F5		
Medium (hour to day) 9421 pages	M1		Popular Homepages, Communication, .edu Domain, Browser Homepages
	M2		
Slow Revisits (>day) 18422 pages	S1		Entry pages, Weekend Activity, Search Engines used for Revisitation, Child-oriented Content, Software Updates
	S2		
	S3		
	S4		
Hybrid 3334 pages	H1		Popular but Infrequently used, Entertainment & Hobbies, Combined Fast & Slow

Overall, this study provided a realistic picture of what people do on the web, reflecting one of the key strengths of unobtrusive research. It also involved data on an unprecedented scale. Adar et al. [10] faced several challenges typical of unobtrusive research. First, they had to collect additional data (survey data) to interpret the log files, which provided insufficient information by themselves to draw reliable conclusions. Second, their study raises the question of whether searches using the toolbar are indeed representative of general web searches. Finally, the researchers had to make sure that users had opted into the study and needed to anonymize their data, which often poses ethical concerns in unobtrusive research.

14.1 Log files

Log file analysis relies on the automatic capture of interactions with interactive systems in a computer file—a *log*. Logs can be obtained from a variety of systems, including program logs, logs of interactions with web pages, logs of interactions in applications, and so on. In some cases, these logs are generated automatically; in other cases, programs or servers may be modified to generate the logs.

The information of interest in log file analysis spans many time frames or levels of abstraction [341]; Figure 14.1 shows some of these. Log files contain data that are produced by people or systems; here, we only consider data that are produced as a result of interaction. Such interaction may be movement, gestures, speech, and so forth. We have access to such data through log files as long as the input devices can sense them. Often, the data may be recorded at the millisecond level (e.g., button presses) and record multiple interactions that happen synchronously; such short events are called *device events*. Longer events, perhaps spanning seconds to minutes, are called *user interface events*. They are about objects and actions in the user interface. Slightly higher in abstraction are *application* events, which are related to the functions available in the interactive system. All of these events may be logged. The event hierarchy reflects the fact that nowadays almost every aspect of hardware and software in a computing system can be instrumented to register events.

Next, we discuss how to do logging, how to clean and transform data, and how to describe what is learned from the log files. Some crucial aspects of interaction concerning people, their activities,

```
                    People, Activity, and Context ◄─────────┐
                 ┌──────────────────────────────────────┐   │
                 │         Application Events           │   │
                 │   Loading content, editing content   │   │ Inference
            Log  │         User Interface Events        │   │
            Data │ Selection, manipulating objects, shift in focus │
                 │           Device Events              │   │
                 │ Touch coordinates, button-down, hover, audio │
                 └──────────────────────────────────────┘───┘
```

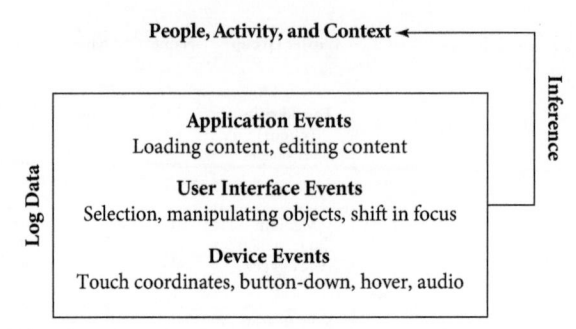

Figure 14.1 Hierarchy of log file recordings: application, UI, and device events. From these, the researcher aims to draw inferences about the people, activities, and context in which the log files were produced.

and their context may not be logged by applications. Thus, we also discuss how to use logged data to make inferences about these aspects.

With the advent of the web, toolkits were developed to help researchers and practitioners log web events. For instance, WebQuilt is a system that supports web design teams in logging interactions with web pages, analyzing the logged data, and visualizing common paths taken by users through a site [351]. Many other similar systems now exist, including Google Analytics and other software for web analytics. These may be tailored to particular interaction styles. W3touch [584], for instance, unobtrusively collects performance data related to touch interaction with web content. Among other things, W3touch allows designers to relate misclicks to the web content the users likely intended to hit.

Before analysis, log data need to be preprocessed. The data need to be cleaned and transformed into a form that is easy to describe and analyze. Such data wrangling is complicated and the focus of much research [e.g., 691]. Key challenges include dealing with missing data, wrong data, and noisy data. The cleaned data may then be segmented (i.e., divided) into categories of interest. An example is given in Paper Example 14.1.1.

Paper Example 14.1.1: Log study of real-world pointing

How well does Fitts' law apply to real-world pointing movements with a mouse? To find out, Chapuis et al. [145] logged the movement kinematics of 24 users in 36 computer configurations over several months. The data consisted of timestamped clicks and movement coordinates and velocities. To conduct a Fitts' law analysis, they first needed to decide what a movement was. At the time, most hitherto studies had taken place in laboratory settings, where the pointing task was given to users as a priority and was often their only task. As a result, there was no applicable definition of movement available.

The authors needed to decide what constitutes the beginning and end of a pointing movement. Analyzing their data, they learned that real-world pointing trajectories contain numerous *pauses*, or time segments where the velocity drops to zero. Following a closer inspection, they decided that pauses longer than 300 ms are *stops*. Any pause that occurs after a stop and before a click would be ignored. This way, they divided their data into two million pointing movements.

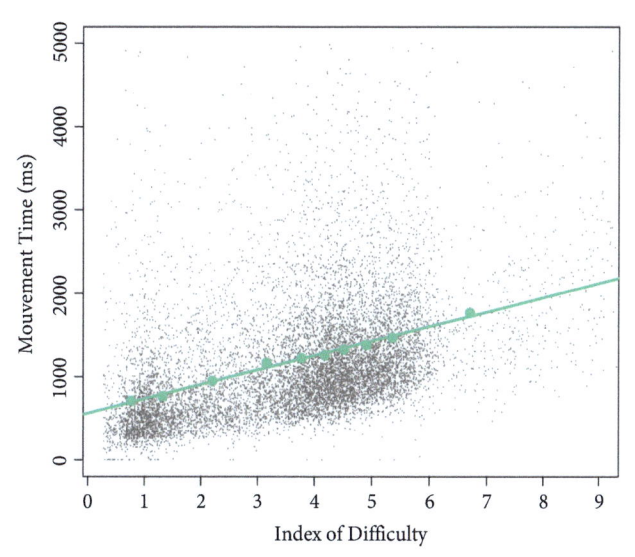

These results, are revealing. On the one hand, they show that real-world pointing movements adhere well to Fitts' law. On the other hand, there is remarkable variance in movement times unaccounted for by Fitts' law. This is highlighted by the thick gray cluster of data points enveloping the trend line. What might cause this variance? The answer is many things. For example, movements done in different regions of the display and at different distances cause variance. Moreover, users may have secondary tasks to take care of that affect their performance. Additionally, users may not care about being fast and accurate, unlike in experiments where they are paid for that.

The first thing to do with the obtained dataset is to describe and visualize it. For instance, in user research on the web, we may unobtrusively describe many aspects of the visits to a page, including the number of visits, the average duration of visits, the number of revisits, the percentage of users who leave the page within 2 s, the number of visitors who enter the site through this particular page, and many others. *Descriptive statistics* of such data can provide relevant indicators of the use of the page and its value to the users. We will discuss this in more detail later within the context of usability (Chapter 19).

After the data description, the analyst may want to *identify critical incidents* in the data, *cluster* the data, or *build a model* of the data. First, critical incidents are occurrences that are of interest for some reason. For example, a user getting lost on a web site is important for designers to know about. To recognize such incidents, one needs to develop a hypothesis on how those incidents map to the data and, based on that, write either a rule-based script or a machine-learning-based detector for those events. Second, data clustering refers to statistical methods that can describe a high-dimensional dataset using a few lower-dimensional clusters. For example, users can be clustered based on which features of a system they use [870]. Third, data models can describe the sequences followed by users when using a service [341]. Data can also be used to train a supervised-learning-based model. Supervised learning is a machine learning method where the task is to predict one label (a variable in the data, e.g., a click) given a number of other labels (the user's age, previous purchases, and so on).

Log analysis is often an inferential process. That is, the analyst needs to conclude, based on the recorded events, something about the events that produced those events. Sometimes, this inferential leap is impossible with the available data. For example, click events on a web site say very little about the emotions of the user; any attempt to infer their emotions would be tenuous. However, some usability-related events can be inferred from logs, such as *usability problems*. Such events have been extensively studied, as many aspects of usability problems can be inferred from log files [341, 377].

Undo events, for example, have been successfully used to infer usability problems. In a study of a 3D modeling application (Google Sketchup), self-reports were compared to the log-based analysis of undo actions as part of a usability test [13]. The authors found that the undo and erase actions exposed by the logs are highly predictive of usability problems rated as severe. The results from all three methods used in the study—usability testing, log-based analysis, and self-reports—coincided for events that reflected severe usability problems. When the right metric is chosen, log-based analysis offers a highly informative way to understand usability.

14.2 Instrumenting people, things, and places

Another approach to unobtrusively collecting data is to equip people, things, or places with digital recording devices to turn them into measuring instruments; in other words, *instrumenting* them.

Instrumentation has a long history in mobile computing, where sensors in mobile phones—such as accelerometers, gyroscopes, and geopositioning—have been used to understand, for example, whether people walk or stand still throughout the day [455]. Modern mobile devices have many built-in sensors, ranging from heart rate monitors to GPS. As demonstrated in Paper Example 14.2.1, the data collected by such sensors are rich and informative. For example, such data can be utilized to make deep inferences about people, such as about their emotions, with reasonable success.

Environments can be instrumented, too. Studies on ubiquitous computing have instrumented everyday environments using everything from pressure sensors to video cameras and microphones. For example, office floors can be instrumented with tiles that sense pressure to track the movements of workers. Ambient noise and light sensors can be used to identify busy areas in a building. Video cameras are already used for tracking the movement of individuals in many cities (with obvious privacy issues).

Finally, on-person measurements can be made. For example, everyday emotion sensing can be achieved by asking users to carry sensors that measure stress, or embedding such sensors in everyday objects such as the steering wheel. Such instrumentation can complement log analysis, which typically focuses on how people use an interactive system. Real-world instrumentation is weaker in terms of direct access to the interface; nevertheless, it can help researchers gain a richer understanding of interaction in its context.

Paper Example 14.2.1: EmotionSense

Modern smartphones have numerous sensors and the capability to process and communicate the collected data, which can offer valuable insights into people's everyday lives. However, how deep can such inferences go? For instance, locations and activities can be easily inferred—but what about people's emotions? To find out, Rachuri et al. [685] built *EmotionSense*, a sensing platform for social psychological studies that uses sensor data collected from mobile devices. The system makes inferences about the user's social circumstances, such as the presence of other people, their talking, and their interactions. This can aid in detecting emotions based on prosodic features in the audio data on the user's speech. Their experiments showed that, from realistic speech samples alone, 71% accuracy could be achieved with technology available in 2010.

14.3 Archival data

Unobtrusive research can also be done using material that already exists. Rather than collecting traces of use through log files or by instrumenting people, places, or things, such data can simply be gathered. We call such data *archival* because they are found in archives, such as in online archives, public repositories, or an individual's records. Archival data can teach us about users, their activities, their context, and their use of existing interactive systems.

In HCI, relevant archival data can take many forms. We already discussed the example of using YouTube videos to learn about the use of touchscreens by people with impaired motion. Other examples include the following:

- Reviews of interactive systems, for instance, from discussion forums, publications, or comments from people who have bought a system. Such reviews reflect users' attitudes toward interactive systems and may be a valuable way to learn about users.
- Reports on errors and bugs. These may be error reports from failures in medical devices, errors addressed in call centers or by support teams, or reports from formal investigations of errors in cars or planes.
- User-generated content from social media. Such content might include comments, discussions, pictures, or videos. For instance, Vieweg et al. [853] studied Twitter usage during two natural disasters. The purpose was to learn from tweets how people share information and understand the bigger picture of an emergency. They did so by obtaining about five million tweets from immediately before and after the disasters. They manually coded the tweets based on whether they were on-topic. They categorized the information being communicated.

The key benefit of using archival data for user research is that they are usually inexpensive to obtain. Moreover, archival data may be analyzed on a large scale, and multiple researchers can work with the data for as long as they like.

One challenge specific to archival data is that, in contrast to the data discussed in the two previous sections, they were often created for a purpose other than that of the user research. For instance, social media content may be uploaded with a variety of aims in mind, none of which is to create research content. Therefore, the inferential leap may be greater. Thus, archival data often need to be analyzed in more depth to be useful for user research.

14.3.1 Content analysis

Content analysis is a frequently used technique for dealing with archival data [435]. Content analysis helps the researcher reach an interpretation of the data through a systematic process that encompasses data coding, aggregation, and description. The data descriptions may focus primarily on the meaning (e.g., intention, deeper message) or the frequency (e.g., how many, how frequently) of the data. Typically, content analysis results in various content classifications and descriptions. For instance, a content analysis of complaints sent to a call center about an interactive system may attempt to describe the main types of written complaints and their causes. It may also perform a deeper analysis of the dynamics of the conversations, breakdowns in talk, and expressions of frustration.

Content analysis can be done in many ways; next, we describe one way of using archival data to answer research questions. More detailed technique descriptions can be found in [885], [61], and [435].

1. Clarify the research aim. As with all other user research, content analysis of archival data starts with a clear research question that can be answered with the selected research method. The researcher needs to determine the topic or topics of interest and the research boundaries.
2. Identify appropriate archival data. The researcher needs to determine which data will help them achieve the aim of the investigation.
3. Select the sample and unit of analysis. The appropriate archival data may be sampled in many ways. For example, samples can be selected randomly or in a stratified manner by deciding how many samples to pick for each category (e.g., education, gender). The unit of analysis refers to the smallest unit of data that is analyzed. For example, in the analysis of social media content, the unit of analysis may be a full post, a sentence, or a word.
4. Decide the depth of analysis. The analyst may deal with the archival data in one of two main ways. In manifest analysis, the research focuses on the surface properties of the archival data. In latent analysis, the researcher tries to interpret the archival data further to make inferences about the user's intention, context, and background.
5. Develop a coding scheme. Codes represent the researchers' reading of the units, captured so that they may be compared, discussed, and further analyzed in different ways. Coding is typically done by individual researchers; alternatively, it may be done automatically or in groups of researchers. Codes may be taken from earlier work, developed by coding a subset of units, or developed through a preliminary coding of the entire sample.
6. Code the units and check that relevant aspects are captured.
7. Report the findings relative to the research aims.

Three good practices in content analysis are as follows: (1) include several people representing different viewpoints as analysts to reduce biases; (2) try to contextualize the findings within assumptions made about the users and their culture; (3) document the coding units and coding schemes. Two benefits of doing all this are *transparency* and replicability [435]. For instance, it makes it easier to inspect the codes and check to which units they are applied.

Various *automated and computerized tools* can be used to facilitate content analysis, including the following:

1. Machine learning tools to transcribe spoken speech into text
2. Rapid video annotation tools to fast-forward videos and mark events using keymapping
3. Collaborative annotation tools that allow a team of annotators to work on a multimodal dataset and obtain quality indices (e.g., inter-rater reliability)

4. Tools for natural language analysis, for example, sentiment analysis methods can determine if reviews of social media events have positive or negative valence.

14.4 Why are we not doing unobtrusive research all the time?

Unobtrusive research can remove the possibly confounding effect of the research itself, thereby mitigating reactivity. Why, then, do we not always do unobtrusive research? There are three common challenges in unobtrusive research.

The first is the gap between what is logged and what needs to be known. Data are often created for other purposes than what the user research aims to study. For instance, although YouTube videos may be used to study touch-enabled mobile phones, the motivations for uploading the videos differ, and the content of the videos may not concern the topic being studied. Thus, even in the study of Anthony et al. [25], the videos available for analysis provide a limited view of all the difficulties encountered by people with motor impairments. Similarly, web logs may not contain all the actions that a researcher wants to study, and records of device errors may not contain sufficient detail.

Second, sometimes the data collected by unobtrusive research are difficult to interpret. This is often the case when the data only serve as an indicator of what we are interested in or when we aim to understand the mechanisms that produced certain data. For instance, logs of activity on web pages may produce indicators such as time-on-page. However, it is difficult to know *why* users spend a lot of time on a page—is it because the page is very interesting or because the user is forced to stay on the page? The threat is that whatever *can* be computed comes to dominate later decisions. For example, if one can compute how long users stay on a site, trying to maximize that duration might be a mistake. It might make users spend more time because they get lost on the site.

Another concern arises when we use sensor readings, such as those from mobile phones, as predictors for tasks or user characteristics. Such readings may predict the tasks that users engage in, which may be useful. However, it is often difficult to *understand* anything about the task from the sensor readings themselves. Thus, unobtrusive research often requires making difficult inferences to conclude anything about users and their activities.

Third, the ethics of unobtrusive research are challenging. Unobtrusive research is sometimes covert, meaning that to prevent reactivity, participants must not know about the data collection. In a case where it is difficult or impossible to obtain the consent of those on the record, can a study be carried out at all? What if the data were produced a long time ago, in a different place, and by unknown people? Because unobtrusive research can provide powerful predictions about users, it may be misused against them. Researchers conducting unobtrusive research need to be conscious of these ethical considerations.

Summary

- Unobtrusive research minimizes the confounding effect of reactivity, that is, the potentially biasing effect that the research can have on participants.
- Unobtrusive research methods look at traces (direct and indirect), archival records, and instrumented recordings.

- Interpreting unobtrusively collected datasets is hard because they often lack triangulating information (e.g., additional data sources).
- Content analysis can help researchers make sense of unobtrusively collected datasets.

Exercises

1. *The value of unobtrusive research.* In which of the following situations would you use unobtrusive research rather than other user research methods? Why? (a) Learning how museum visitors use audio guides. (b) Learning how museum visitors experience audio guides. (c) Learning what museum visitors need from audio guides.
2. *Inference gap.* Log data are often just a shadow of what we really want to learn about. List 10 things that user researchers may want to infer about users (e.g., needs, requirements). Then, come up with a suitable source of log or archival data for inferring each aspect.
3. *Ethics.* What are some ethical issues one must consider when carrying out unobtrusive research?

15
Representations of user research

User research aims to inform design decisions. It aims to gather knowledge about the prospective users of a system, their activities, the contexts in which they work, and the existing technologies they use. Previous chapters in this part of the book have covered the *methods* used in user research. By contrast, this chapter is about the *outcomes* of user research, in particular how we *represent* research data using diagrams, models, and text. Figure 15.1 shows a couple of examples of such representations.

The previous chapters detailed how to analyze interviews, how to do ethnography, and how to analyze surveys using statistics. Why fuss further about representations of data? The main reason is that how we represent user research matters, just as how we represent a logical puzzle or lay out a math problem impacts how easy it is to solve. Data alone do not *do* anything; a dataset is simply a collection of observations. This chapter focuses on how we can represent data to gain information, uncover insights, and help us act. In particular, we care about the following applications of user research data:

- Summarization. Representations can consolidate extensive data from user research. For instance, Tychsen and Canossa [836] used metrics collected from a computer game to create representations of how players interact with the game. Those representations pulled together many metrics on how people engage with the game and clearly captured the higher-level goals of players (e.g., play styles).
- Spelling out requirements. The identified requirements may then be used in design briefs and software production contracts; see Chapter 36.
- Inspiration. This includes finding new opportunities and concepts to drive design.
- Communicating within a development team. For example, the results of usability tests are often summarized as criticality-ranked issues, which can be shown to developers together with example data such as videos (Chapter 43).
- Checking insights with stakeholders. For example, task analyses are essentially hypotheses about how users structure their activities and should be verified with stakeholders [24].

We may use user data for all of this; the techniques described in this chapter help us do it.

User research informs design, which is the topic of Part VI. That part of the book concerns the use of insights from user research to create ideas about future interactive systems. Some of the techniques that we discuss here can also be used for creating ideas for future interactive systems. For instance, we may represent the sequence of steps to be taken in a new system in a sequence model similar to that in Figure 15.1. However, these aspects of human–computer interaction (HCI) have different aims: User research describes current affairs, while design imagines possible futures. It is important to know whether a scenario is based on interviews (user research) or reflects an imagination of how things might work (design). One of the most critical challenges in design is to go beyond the familiar and propose a change, a new way of acting in the world. This requires

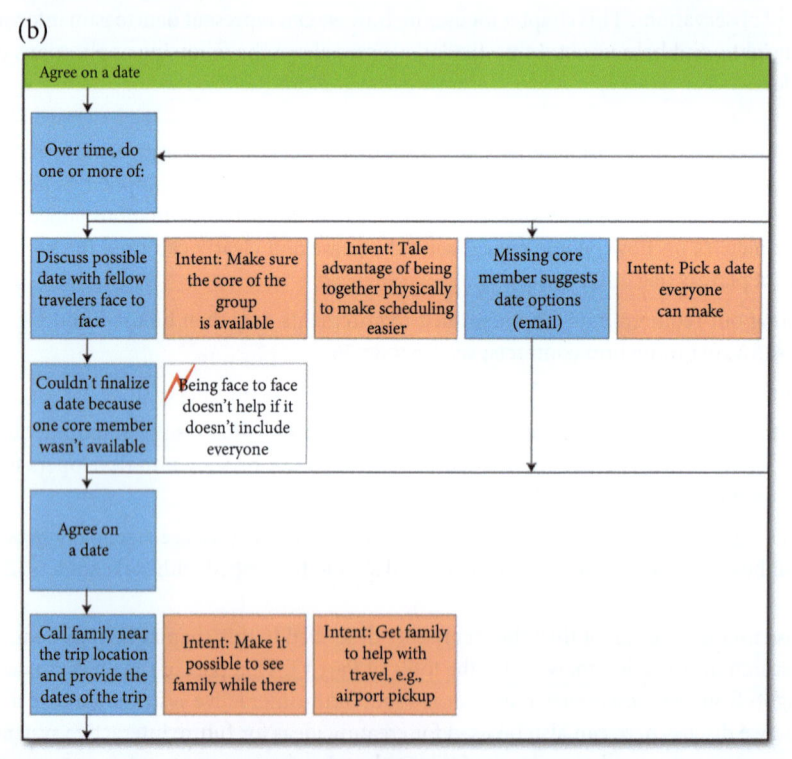

Figure 15.1 For user research to inform design and decision-making, the acquired data must be summarized in some useful way. The top panel shows a few simple personas, that is, representations of user groups as archetypes [169]; the bottom panel shows a summary of how people select a date to go traveling [348]. Both representation types help understand, apply, and communicate the findings of user research.

an understanding of the familiar, the starting point, and the constraints and expectations this challenge poses to the future.

User research also informs engineering, which we discuss in Part VII. User research obtains information on what users want, how they work, and what they value. In engineering processes, these are translated into requirements. Requirements, in turn, are used as objectives and criteria for deciding when a system is good enough. The results of user research can also be translated into algorithms, for example, as objectives and constraints in optimization and learning algorithms that drive intelligent user interfaces.

The results of user research are also part of collaborative efforts. As such, they have an important communicative purpose: They help form a shared understanding among stakeholders. To this end, user research has the obligation to be well-formed and well-communicated.

In this chapter, we discuss focal points for representing user data. We cover the following aspects: representing knowledge about users, including their needs, preferences, and capabilities; what users do and how these activities are organized; artifacts, including the influence of the physical layout of the work environment; and contexts, including understanding users' situations and use-defining factors. We also discuss user requirements for technical functionality and the performance of systems.

15.1 Representations of people

A big part of user research is understanding who the users are, what their needs are, what they try to achieve, and how technology might fit into their lives and work. At the beginning of this part (Section 10.2), we talked about establishing *who* the users are. For instance, we may define user segments based on market research, or we may spell out our initial ideas on who the users are and what their goals are. In this regard, representations of people can assist us in drawing actionable conclusions about users. Design and development teams need to be able to relate to users and make inferences about users on issues that might not have been covered by user research. The most popular tool for doing this is personas.

15.1.1 Personas

A *persona* is a description of an idealized (nonexisting) person who represents a group or type of users. The term was popularized by Cooper et al. [169] and has since been widely used in HCI. The idea is to construct archetypes of users in the form of fictional (but representative) individuals with specific characteristics. Personas are based on user research; as such, they are more a synthesis or aggregate than a fiction. Below, we report an example of two adult personas taken from Nielsen [594].

> Camilla and Jesper live on the outskirts of Copenhagen. They are 35 and 39 respectively, and they have enough on their plate with children and careers. They have lived together for the past five years. Two years ago, they had their son Storm. Jesper has two children from his previous marriage, Christian and Caroline, 11 and 8 years old. The children live with Jesper and Camilla every second week. Camilla and Jesper prefer to use self-service solutions, and they are curious about what information the public sector stores on them, and how it is stored.

Such descriptions of personas may be combined with pictures or sketches to make the personas more memorable, engaging, and concrete. Sociodemographic information can be added. Cooper suggested that the goals of the personas should also be described. Nielsen [594] further suggested that personas be combined with scenarios. Scenarios may also be used without personas, as discussed in Section 15.2.1.

Personas can summarize general tendencies in the data, acting like a mode or median member in that group. They can also be stereotypifications of that group—embellished versions that help the researcher form perspectives and ensure sufficient diversity in design.

Representing user research as personas has several purposes. The first purpose is to create specific individuals. Personas can help avoid making decisions based on idealized users who are too flexible (or "elastic"). A degree of inflexibility helps to keep design in check. It ensures that when we make design decisions, we do not distort user data to benefit the design. Second, personas help avoid self-centeredness. Technology is too often developed for developers by developers. Third, personas prioritize data. Personas require selecting which user segments are most important in design. Fourth, personas synthesize data. Raw data are often too complex to deal with in design. A few well-selected personas can efficiently distill and communicate the essence of a dataset. Fifth, personas can drive empathy. It is easier to relate to another person's (even if hypothetical) viewpoint than to quantitative summaries.

Creating personas

There are numerous methods for creating personas. Pruitt and Grudin [678] created a rich persona template for software engineering projects. The template contains slots for describing, among others, the user's basic properties—their name, age, and occupation, a day in their life, work activities, goals, fears, the market size they represent, technology attitudes, and quotes. However, long templates entail the risk of creating catalogs of information with no clear relevance to design.

We believe that personas that go beyond observable attributes ("Jane is 25, she attends a university") to capture the drivers of such behaviors ("Jane is fascinated by theoretical physics") are valuable [169]. How to obtain such characteristics without conjuring them up? One method is as follows, adapted from Cooper et al. [169]:

1. Group participants in the data by their role. Parent, student, manager, and administrator are examples of roles.
2. Identify potential drivers of behavior in the dataset. Go beyond observable behaviors and try to identify *behavioral variables* such as those describing attitudes, skills, beliefs, motivations, and aptitudes. These variables should capture aspects of why people did what they did. They may be continuous (e.g., "motivated by social connections [weak–strong]" or "excited about a new product feature [weak–strong]") or binary (e.g., "uses Windows 11 [yes/no]").
3. Map observational data about participants to behavioral variables. Take snippets of the data (e.g., interview quotes) and associate them with behavioral variables, for example, using Post-it notes.
4. Identify significant clusters forming around the behavioral variables.
5. Synthesize the characteristics of roles. Find clusters where a certain role has a particular behavioral variable strongly represented; these are candidates for the key characteristics of that role.
6. Check for completeness. Ensure that a reasonable proportion of the data belonging to a user role is covered in the clusters that reflect its characteristics.
7. Select a persona type and name it.
8. Verbally explain the key attributes and behaviors rooted in the clusters.

The method requires iteration between observational data, roles, behavioral variables, and clusters. This method ensures the personas can be rooted back to observational data; the clustering of data ensures that one can trace back what a characteristic is based on.

Drawbacks of personas

The persona method is often haphazardly applied. From a statistical perspective, a persona is a summary statistic analogous to a mean, median, or mode in some distribution. However, it is not always applied from this perspective; the questions of (1) how to cluster users and (2) how to select such persons to represent whole groups are often dismissed. The consequence is that personas can be almost anything, and the connection to the original data can be broken.

Pruitt and Grudin [678] reported issues they encountered in the use of personas at Microsoft. Their persona descriptions were not believable; the personas were "designed by committee" or lacked a link to the original data. The personas were also poorly communicated, such as via full-blown poster-sized lists, and little effort was put into understanding their main points. There was also no understanding of how to use the personas since they were not properly linked to the different stages of product development.

Personas have a relationship with user groups. *User groups* are segments of the user population. Personas are often thought to represent user groups or segments. However, defining a user group is tricky. From a statistical perspective, it is a clustering problem. Given a population of m samples (users), each depicted by a feature vector x, the goal is to assign every sample (user) to one of n groups such that the distance of two samples within a group is minimized and the distance to other groups is maximized. Unfortunately, although this is generally understood, personas and groups are often created based on intuition rather than the systematic comparison of users or statistical analysis. This has the unwanted consequence that such representations can be unconvincing to stakeholders and—worse—mislead the design process. Systematic methods like the one presented above increase the likelihood of avoiding these issues. New data-driven approaches are also emerging, as illustrated in Paper Example 15.1.1.

Paper Example 15.1.1: Automated generation of personas from log data

Generating personas has traditionally been a labor-intensive process. To form a persona, data on users must be collected, for example, via surveys or focus groups. The data then need to be labeled, clustered, and so on. Despite the high amount of effort, there is no guarantee that the personas will represent well the targeted user population. Moreover, personas can become outdated.

Automated persona generation refers to the use of online datasets to computationally generate up-to-date personas. These descriptions are automatically kept updated as changes occur in the user population.

Jung et al. [399] presented a case for automatically generating personas from data available from social media. They analyzed data from users who engage online with Al Jazeera, a popular news channel. The data came from 180,000 users in 181 countries and encompassed over 30 million interactions with Al Jazeera's YouTube channel. Such large datasets would normally be impractical for persona development.

The authors presented a statistical method for identifying user segments from such datasets. First user interaction patterns are identified from the data. These patterns indicate which

continued

> **Paper Example 15.1.1: Automated generation of personas from log data** *(continued)*
>
> products the users use and how. These clusters are then linked to demographic data, such as age distributions. Finally, persona descriptions are created around these attributes and then enriched with descriptive features, such as names and photos, obtained from generic databases (e.g., typical names of people of a certain age). An example of a resulting persona in Al Jazeera's case is as follows: "Samantha is a 25-year old female living in the US. She likes to read articles about society, environment, and racism on a computer terminal. She usually watches about 2 minutes of video." Any number of such personas can be created while ensuring they are rooted in the original data. They can be augmented by representative comments posted online by this group. The personas can also be updated on demand.

15.2 Representations of activities

In previous chapters in this part of the book, we have covered how difficult it is to obtain valid and reliable insights about the activities in which people participate. This section describes how we can represent these insights in a way that helps to clarify people's tasks.

Before we start, we need to be clear about the terminology for activities. An *activity* is the total of what a user or a group of users wishes to achieve. It is purposeful interactions among actors that develop over time. A *task* is some piece of work to be done. As an analytic tool in thinking about user research, tasks have several applications:

1. The description of a task is often about things to be done, not about how they are done. When represented like this, tasks can be compared across different interactive systems. Part IV will explain why this is a slightly simplified picture by arguing that tasks and tools are always intertwined.
2. The description of a task can be a description of how things are done. HTA, as we learn here, involves the decomposition of a task (when carried out with a particular tool).
3. The description of a task can be specific and concrete.
4. A task is a meaningful unit. That is, getting a task done is a meaningful achievement for the user, who cares about being able to complete the task.

Next, let us look at some ways to work systematically with tasks.

15.2.1 Scenarios

Scenarios are narrative accounts of an activity or task. Scenarios use storytelling to communicate relationships between users and events. They are less structured than most analytical tools, such as task analysis or user requirements. Scenarios are almost always written from the user's point of view. This facilitates empathizing with users. Scenarios are almost never prescriptive in the sense of telling how things *should* occur. As a consequence of lacking a rigid predefined structure, scenarios can be underspecified as accounts of what happened. However, a well-written narrative may help us imagine the experience of a person from their perspective. Paper Example 15.2.1 provides an example of how explainable AI was studied using scenarios.

Example scenario by Rosson and Carroll [714]:

After three years at Virginia Tech, Sharon has learned to take advantage of her free time in-between classes. In her hour between her morning classes, she stops by the computer lab to visit the science fiction club. She has been meaning to do this for a few days because she knows she'll miss the next meeting later this week. As she opens a Web browser, she realizes that this computer will not have her bookmarks stored, so she starts at the homepage of the Blacksburg Electronic Village. She sees local news and links to categories of community resources (businesses, town government, civic organizations). She selects "Organizations" and sees an alphabetical list of community groups. She is attracted by a new one, the Orchid Society, so she quickly examines their Web page before going back to select the Science Fiction Club page. When she gets to the club page, she sees that there are two new comments in the discussion on Asimov's Robots and Empire, one from Bill and one from Sara. She browses each comment in turn, then submits a reply to Bill's comment, arguing that he has the wrong date associated with discovery of the Zeroth Law.

Scenarios are written as stories. They contain the basic elements of a story: a setting, one or more actors with their goals and characteristics, and some tools and contexts that are available for that. The scenario then describes the sequence of actions and events that led to an outcome. It is important to describe the actors' thinking and experiences related to technology: how they set goals for, think about, react to, and experience it.

Paper Example 15.2.1: Scenario-based development of explainable AI

It has become almost a truism that AI systems must be designed to be trustworthy and transparent. Alas, realizing this vision has turned out to be difficult. One reason is that it is hard to explain to users the reasons behind AI's actions. Simple approaches to explaining AI, such as presenting a simplified model of the AI's reasoning to users, have failed: Users have very little interest in detailed accounts of how AI draws its conclusions. There is a need to rethink what explanations are and how they are interacted with.

Wolf [908] turned to scenario-based design to address this problem. They studied aging-in-place monitoring, that is, AI systems that help aging people maintain autonomy by monitoring their daily activities. Most of the time, these systems do not need to explain themselves; the question is when should they, and how?

The authors generated what they call explainability scenarios based on ethnographic studies of AI and machine learning professionals. In two field studies, they observed these professionals across three projects. To form the scenarios, the primary data were augmented with results reported in studies of caretakers and other stakeholders.

The following example scenario imagines the experiences of Jody and Catherine in using an aging-in-place system [p. 254]:

Jody checks the app on her phone that displays her mom's daily activity report—the outcome of in-unit monitoring that captures and analyzes her mom's activities of daily living (ADLs). Her mom, Catherine, recently moved into an aging care facility and together with Jody decided to enroll in the facility's new activity monitoring program.
[...]
The system is designed to help keep Jody aware of her mom's daily activity levels (and alerting Jody of any abnormal changes or deviances in her mom's behavior) by providing daily reports in the app. To maintain Catherine's privacy, the reports do not document each

continued

> **Paper Example 15.2.1: Scenario-based development of explainable AI** *(continued)*
>
> and every activity of the day. Instead, it classifies her activity for the day into three levels (green, yellow, red) and provides a general explanation of why the system applied that label. [...]
>
> Several days go by and Catherine's reports all turn up green. Then one day, Jody sees that her mom's been given a yellow report. "No kitchen activity recorded today." Jody calls her mom to ask how her day was and if anything was wrong. "I went for a long walk with my new neighbor, Vicki. It was nice, we have a lot in common. We ended up going out for lunch," Catherine explained. Jody was relieved to hear that "no kitchen activity recorded" wasn't anything alarming, she was actually excited to hear her mom was making friends.
>
> The scenario continues to an event where these explanations do not suffice:
>
> As Jody opens the app again she is greeted with a new message: "Your Monthly Activity Report is available." The report provides a dashboard view of Catherine's activity levels for the past month. It also provides a prediction—based on the predictive model from pilot data, the app has high confidence that seniors with activity levels similar to Catherine's will need to transition to an assisted living level of care within the next three months. Okay, Jody thinks, why would that be? She clicks on the "Tell me more" link next to the prediction, which says the top influences on the prediction are: age and frequency of ADLs. Her mom has mostly been getting "green" reports so Jody is confused why she might need escalated care. Unsure of who she is supposed to ask for help, she wonders if the app has more explanation on what to do with the Monthly Activity Reports. She looks around inside the app, and finds an FAQ list that mentions the Report. It describes the Reports contents and features a link to a demo video. She clicks on the video, but quickly recognizes it is an intro video she watched several weeks earlier when they were getting the system set up. At the bottom of the FAQ there is a "Feedback" form where she can send a message to the app developers. Unsure of what to do next, she calls Metria, the transition specialist at Catherine's facility. Metria explains that she would have to review the report with the data team to be able to answer Jody's questions. Metria says she will follow up as soon as she can.
>
> The scenario can appear messy and excessively specific. However, it is exactly these qualities of inflexibility that make it relatable. For AI designers, the main takeaway is that one broad type of explanation may not suffice: There are several layers of explanations that need to be considered when needed. Moreover, explanations are discursive. Instead of a single decision-maker seeking explanations, Jody must talk with Catherine to establish what has happened. Therefore, technical measures such as "accuracy" may not be sufficient for developing explanations that actually work.

15.2.2 Customer journeys

Customer journey mapping is an account of events where a user encounters a service or product. The map is presented in the form of a journey—a path that goes through *touchpoints*. Scenarios often focus on events during the use of technology; customer journey mapping also covers events that precede the actual use, for example, advertisements, the creation of accounts, onboarding, and so on. The term "customer" depicts this view: Touchpoints are typically depicted from the perspective of the evolving relationship between a customer and a business, where a might-be customer transforms into a loyal customer via the touchpoints. The actual use of technology may only have a minor role in this. At every touchpoint, goals, thoughts, and experiences are reported.

Rosenbaum et al. [709] described a method for creating customer journey maps. It calls for the analysis of two dimensions:

1. Touchpoints, that is, the sequence of events through which customers interact with a service
2. Strategic actions associated with the touchpoints.

Touchpoints are typically divided into three periods: pre-service, service, and post-service. The pre-service period is about the user's experience before registering or purchasing the service. For example, one may encounter advertisements for the service or hear about it from friends. The post-service period takes place after the actual service, for example, when posting on social media about the experience or complaining about the service to customer service. Strategic actions are enabling actions that different participant groups should take to make the touchpoint successful. For example, strategic actions can concern what a manager, customer-facing personnel, or designer is required to do.

15.2.3 Task analysis

Task analysis is a method for decomposing tasks and presenting them as hierarchically organized sequences of subtasks. It decomposes and exposes the *structure* of interaction [24]. Task analysis is to HCI what requirements engineering is to software engineering. Many of the analytical evaluation methods we cover later in this book (Chapter 41) build on task analysis. Task analysis can also inform design; an example is given in Paper Example 15.2.2. One reason for its popularity is its systematicity. This also means that carrying out task analysis properly, especially when it includes validating the analysis with the stakeholders, is time-consuming.

Paper Example 15.2.2 Task analysis informs layout design

Task analysis is a systematic representation of users' activities. The method is very common in the study of safety-critical systems, where it is used to identify potential errors and needs for training personnel. In user-centered design, task analysis forms the basis of several analytical evaluation methods, such as cognitive walkthrough and keystroke-level model (see Chapter 41). Task analysis can also inform low-level decisions in design.

Sears [753] presented *layout appropriateness* (LA), a metric to inform the design of widget layouts. A widget layout is a graphically laid out set of interactive widgets, such as text

continued

Paper Example 15.2.2 Task analysis informs layout design
(continued)

fields, scrollbar, toggles, buttons, and so on. To compute LA, two inputs are needed: (1) task sequences that describe users' widget-level actions and (2) estimations of their frequencies. The former can be obtained via task analysis, the latter via questionnaires, logs, or by asking designers or stakeholders to rate the priority of tasks. This knowledge is expressed in a transition graph where nodes are widgets and links transition probabilities. For example, the following graph shows an analysis of the task of opening a file in a word editor.

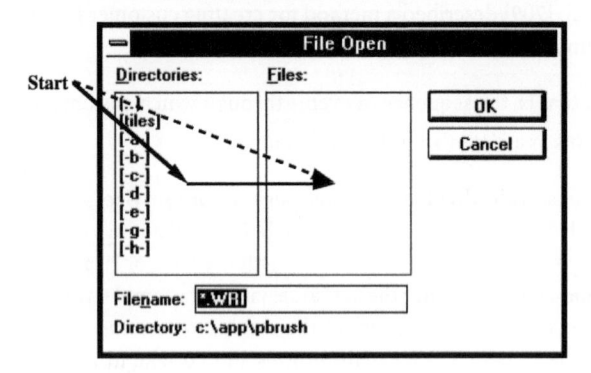

Link labels denote how probable each transition is.

Layout appropriateness can be computed by weighing the cost of each sequence by its frequency. The cost of a sequence can be estimated from the distance of mouse movements or eye movements. Layouts that favor frequent user tasks receive a better (lower) LA score. The author presented a method to optimize a given widget layout to optimize its LA score. An LA-optimal layout represents the optimal cost-minimizing widget layout for the given set of user tasks. It can be obtained using algorithmic methods of optimization (Chapter 39). For example, the following figure shows the LA-optimal widget layout for the task of opening a file:

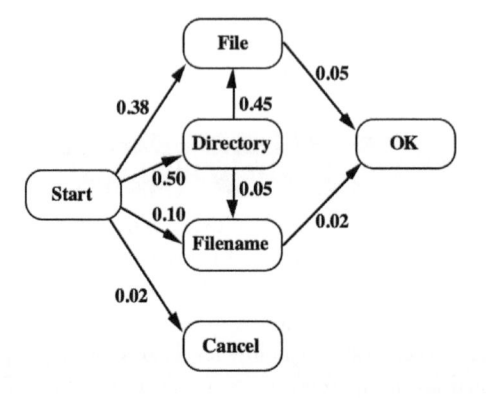

Designers can use the LA-optimal layout as a starting point for the design of a graphical interface. They can use it to assess how far their current design is from the optimal design (e.g., 95% LA-optimal).

Task analysis provides a *functional description* of behavior. It begins by outlining goals before considering actions to accomplish the task:

> Complex tasks are defined in terms of a hierarchy of goals and subgoals nested within higher order goals, each goal, and the means of achieving it being represented as an operation. The key features of an operation are the conditions under which the goal is activated and the conditions which satisfy the goal together with the various actions which may be deployed to attain the goal. These actions may themselves be defined in terms of subgoals. [24, p. 68]

The output of task analysis is a *task model*. It describes the requirements for carrying out a task successfully. It can be expressed in multiple ways: as a sequence or as a hierarchical diagram.

A *sequential task model* describes a task as a linear progression of subtasks. It is often described verbally. For example, a task model for logging into a web service could consist of the following steps:

1. Enter login name
2. Enter password
3. Click "Login."

How does one "enter" something? The first two rows can be expanded into two more subgoals, resulting in a higher-fidelity task model:

1. Click "Username" field with mouse
2. Type login name with keyboard
3. Click "Password" field with mouse
4. Type password with keyboard
5. Click "Login" with mouse.

One limitation of linear models is that the relationship between clicking and typing is not captured well. Hierarchical task analysis (HTA) can better account for this.

HTA is an established task analysis method that assumes two kinds of relationships between subtasks: (1) order, for example, task A precedes task B, and (2) part–whole relationship, for example, task B is a subtask of task A. Every subtask is thought to require operations to complete it. Operations are any actions that the user must take. An example of a simple task is given in Figure 15.2.

The core concept of task analysis is a *task*. The main task is recursively split into *subtasks*. A task (or a subtask) consists of a well-defined beginning state, goal state, and operations that transform the beginning state into the goal state. Some operations are conditional, that is, they can only be executed when some conditions apply. How many levels of subtasks one wants to use is a practical consideration.

Task analysis can be done empirically or analytically. The goal of *empirical task analysis*, which is used in user research, is to understand tasks in *unconstrained, real-world scenarios*. Typical data collection methods include interviews, the analysis of systems and their documentation (e.g., manuals), and observations in the field recorded via videos and field notes. In *analytical task analysis*, the modeling is speculative; it is carried out as part of design or evaluation. It can expose potential problems, such as complicated task structures or insufficient training. Task analysis is a modeling activity that relies on human analysts and cannot yet be adequately automated, though some attempts have been made, such as using data mining techniques on log data.

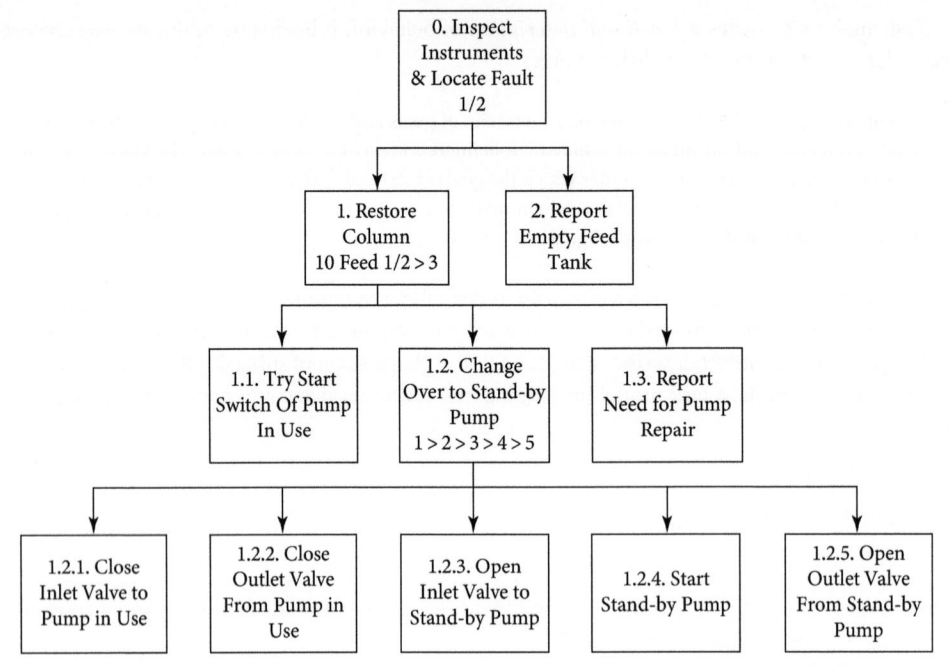

Figure 15.2 Hierarchical task analysis for the task of inspecting faults. Adapted from [24].

To conduct a HTA, one can start with a sequential model of the highest-level subtask. First, split the main task into a sequence of subtasks following each other. Consider a vending machine: You first need to decide which soda to buy, then find the corresponding button, then decide the payment method, and so on. Second, subtasks that are mutually dependent can be clustered to form a hierarchical structure.

The general steps in task analysis are [24]:

1. Decide the purpose(s) of the analysis
2. Achieve agreement between stakeholders on the definition of task goals and criterion measures
3. Identify the sources of task information and select the means of data acquisition
4. Acquire the data and draft a decomposition table or diagram
5. Check the validity of the decomposition with the stakeholders
6. Identify significant operations in light of the purpose of the analysis
7. Generate and, if possible, test hypotheses concerning the factors affecting learning and performance.

In addition to sequences and hierarchies, HTA offers notation to express *plans*, *conditions*, and *parallelisms*. Plans are routine procedures followed by people: "Do this, then this, then this . . ." Conditions are if–then rules that describe conditions for actions: "If condition X, do this." Parallelisms are subtasks that can be pursued in parallel. Moreover, stop rules can be expressed to tell a user when to stop executing a subtask. The conditions and the stop rules are annotated in the diagram.

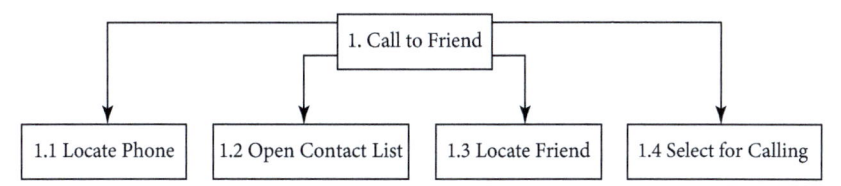

Figure 15.3 Hierarchical task analysis diagram for the task of calling a friend.

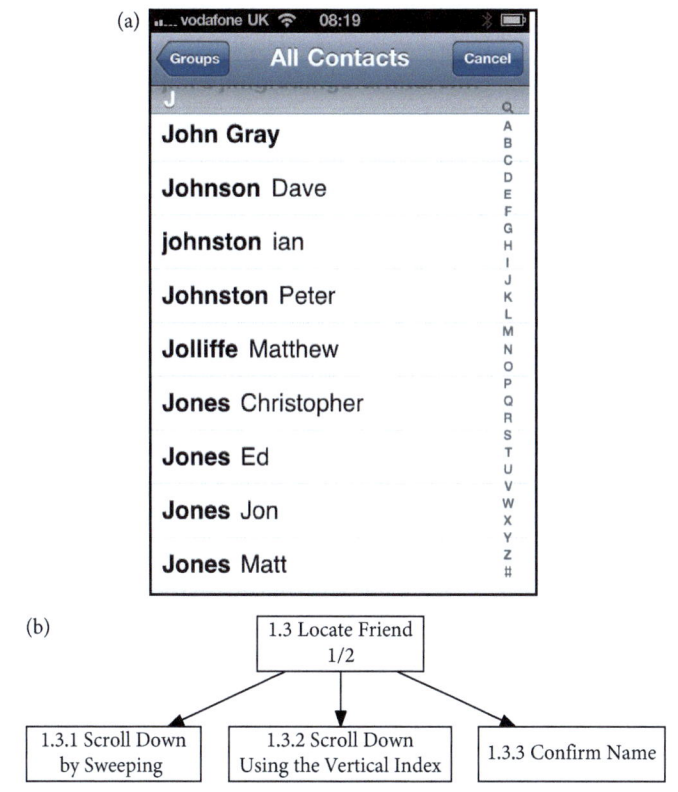

Figure 15.4 Diagram for the subtask of locating a friend in the contacts list. HTA introduces conventions to mark the order in which subtasks can be executed. Here, "1/2" means that either 1.3.1 or 1.3.2 is executed.

Example

Let us consider the task of calling a friend using a smartphone. Figure 15.3 shows a diagram with four subtasks ordered sequentially. To complete a subtask, more operations need to be carried out. For example, subtask "1.3 Locate friend" can be split as shown in Figure 15.4.

Like in Figure 15.4, one can continue splitting down the subtasks, noting their order and other important details. For example, subtask 1.3.2 involves the following steps:

1. Point at the vertical bar
2. Drag down finger
3. Confirm the right letter.

When we continue to do this for all subtasks all the way to the third level, we obtain a full HTA diagram.

15.3 Representations of context

A *contextual inquiry* (Chapter 11) offers a rich set of models to describe contexts and situations. Note that these are conceptual models, not models in the mathematical sense. They describe dependencies and causal relationships verbally or diagrammatically. A key concept is that of an *actor*. An actor can be anything—human or nonhuman, digital or physical—that participates in some active sense in the activity. A context model describes flows, sequences, artifacts, and the cultural and physical circumstances of the actors.

A *flow model* describes the main actors in the context and their relationships to the user. A flow model is drawn as a graph where actors are nodes and actions are directional arrows connecting them. The direction of an arrow indicates who takes the initiative. Arrows are annotated to describe what happens.

A *sequence model* is an ordered list of actions that need to be carried out to complete a task, that is, to get from an initial state to a goal state. The path to the goal state can have multiple subgoals. A sequence model provides a less rich representation of tasks than an HTA tree. Specifically, a sequence model provides an ordered list of subtasks equivalent to one level of depth in an HTA tree.

An *artifact model* describes interactions among artifacts in a workflow. An artifact can be a physical or digital object, such as a paper note, a social media message, a presentation template, or anything that is interacted with during work. In a contextual inquiry, such artifacts are documented, and the way they are manipulated and passed on is traced and modeled. Some artifact models are just collections of descriptions of artifacts. Sometimes, they are organized into descriptions of workflows.

A *cultural model* is an expression of the different beliefs, values, and practices of the actors. The model is typically drawn as a Venn diagram, where each circle corresponds to some designation of culture, such as data-focused, opportunity-driven, risk-averse, and so on.

A *physical model* represents the physical space and the actors' movements in the space.

15.3.1 Rich pictures

A rich picture is a way of representing the insights from user research in a diagram. It highlights the relationships between people and technologies and the richness of the use situation. Rich pictures were devised as part of the soft systems methodology and have been used in HCI by, among others, Monk and Howard [556].

Figure 15.5 shows an example of a rich picture. An effective rich picture shows some details of the structure of the situation, some of the key processes, and some of the concerns of the stakeholders. A rich picture can quote the actors or use any other means of communication. Rich pictures have no set syntax or set of notations. Rich pictures synthesize data from user research.

The process of creating a rich picture is as follows:

1. Gather people who are familiar with the research topic.
2. Outline the key stakeholders, including people and organizations, and some of the structure (e.g., geographical, physical, organizational).
3. Detail processes and concerns related to the identified stakeholders and structures.

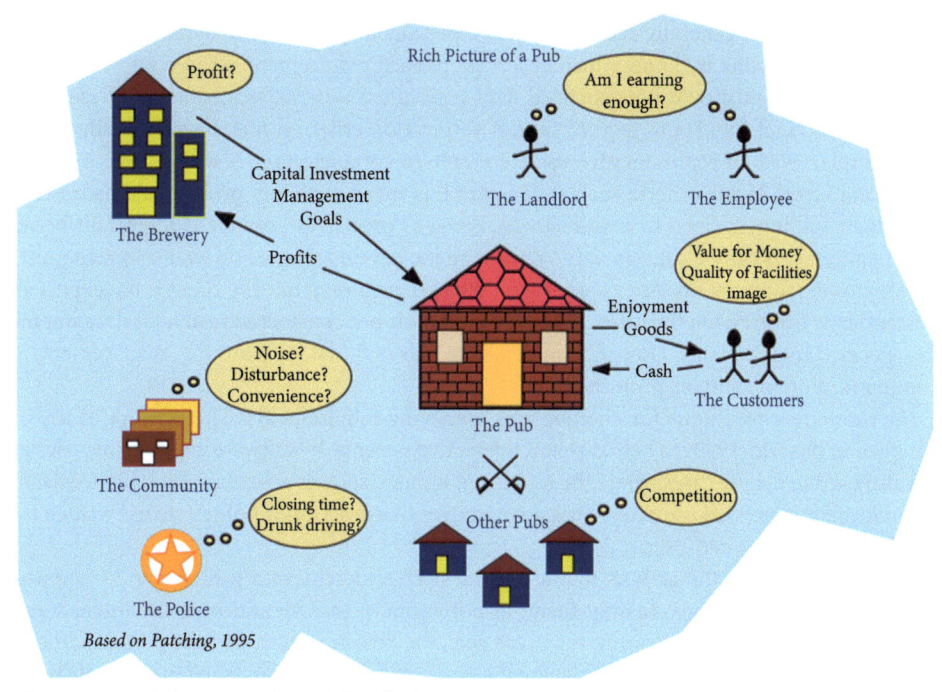

Figure 15.5 A rich picture of a pub [556]. The picture shows the main stakeholders, some of their considerations, and some links between them.

Remember that a rich picture is about capturing some of the complexity of a situation; it is not about describing a full system or the solution to a problem.

15.4 Requirements

User requirements are used in software engineering to specify users' expectations on what some software can do; see Chapter 36. Unlike system requirements, which express features with no necessary reference to users, user requirements are user-centered. They express criteria for the system's functioning from the user's perspective. For example, the requirements for a medical device might include being able to report when a sensor or the battery is not operational or allowing for quick and hygienic cleaning. Requirements can be expressed in many ways, such as non-technically for a client or technically for a developer. Normally, requirements are prioritized from both the business and end-user perspectives.

User requirements must be based on data and traceable. Triangulation is commonly recommended for identifying requirements. Different data sources provide complementary information that should be cross-checked when defining requirements. For example, a contextual inquiry may provide background information for a requirement, which is then elaborated via a focus group or interviews. In large software projects, the elicitation of requirements may involve interviews, observations, focus groups, workshops, brainstorming, and even prototyping. In some projects, requirements are gathered throughout, first during product launch and then via user feedback. In some cases, user requirements are reviewed by the users themselves. Confirming requirements with stakeholders is generally recommended, especially in professional domains. Requirement traceability means that we know which observations each requirement is based on.

Each requirement should be associated with *verification criteria*, that is, a way of identifying whether a product fulfills the requirement. A verification criterion may be empirically defined, for example, "95% of representative users are able to complete task A within time T with no significant error." Vague criteria such as "Feature F is easy to use" are problematic because they leave their fulfillment open to disagreement. Being as precise as possible is important because user requirements can be contractual: A client and the developer agree on what a system must be able to do via requirements. After agreeing on the user requirements, the client is not expected to demand new features. On the other hand, the product is not considered ready if it does not meet the specified requirements. User requirements are also essential for planning, management, and communication in complex projects.

Use cases are a technique for eliciting and specifying requirements. The concept of use case emerged in the mid-1990s to help develop interactive systems. In software engineering, use cases are also used to denote cases where the user is not human, such as an external system. *User stories* are informally expressed use cases. They are narrative-like descriptions of system use written from the perspective of an end-user.

A use case outlines the actions that a user must take to achieve a goal. Several frameworks have been proposed for expressing them; at minimum, a case should state the initial state or preconditions for the case to occur, the user's goal, the flow of events, and the post-conditions—anything that must be done after achieving the goal. *Abstract use cases* define user intents but not sequences (flows). Use cases are expressed diagrammatically in a tabular, storyboard, or verbal format. Similar to user requirements, use cases are often associated with verification criteria.

15.5 Can representations be both valid and informative?

Representations of user research data are supposed to inform practical decisions. How do personas, scenarios, task analyses, and so on actually achieve this? They achieve this through two quite different routes, the realist route and the instrumentalist route, which are challenging to balance in user research.

According to the realist view, user research produces empirically grounded statements about users. A representation of user data is essentially a proposition, a claim about users. For instance, the claim that "User Segment A has a high need for security" can be true or false. Making valid statements about users is important for design and engineering efforts. Decisions about which features to include or how to design can be thought of as hypotheses about users: When the hypotheses are wrong, the design will fail.

According to the instrumentalist view, user research has instrumental value in inspiring design. The results of user research do not need to be valid in the realist sense—whatever helps design is valuable. In creative efforts where the goal is to envision novel possibilities, it may be detrimental to be tied too tightly to reality. From this viewpoint, even exaggerations and data embellishments are fine as long as they inspire new ideas. According to this view, user research does not need to seek a firm connection between a representation and the world it represents.

In practice, user research often serves both purposes. In projects where the goal is to inform decisions, observational data are routinely selected, redescribed, and augmented with other available knowledge. For example, we saw this in how personas and scenarios are created. Data are also interpreted. An analyst may flag something as surprising or write useful notes about users. Such inferential leaps, even if small, pose a challenge. Leaps may be necessary to produce knowledge that informs practical decisions; however, such leaps may dissociate the analyst from observational data, making their conclusions less grounded. Practical decisions that are based on unsubstantiated or subjective inferences may be not only wrong but also damaging; for example, they may disregard or simplify certain user groups.

How to balance these two approaches? We hold that verifiability and traceability are important in all user research projects, even those with instrumentalist goals. *Verifiability* refers to how well a claim can be cross-checked with observations that are independent of the original dataset. For example, in task analysis, it is generally recommended to have task analysis diagrams checked by the stakeholders whose work it describes. If verification is hard or impossible, it is important to be able to trace the reasoning that led to the interpretation. *Traceability* refers to the documentation of the reasoning that led from the original data to a claim. For example, when writing up personas, one should document the data and other knowledge they were based on. Good practices like these lend credibility to user research and ensure that stakeholders pay heed to its results. Traceability is also important for accountability and the proper representation of the people involved.

Summary

- Representations capture findings and reflections in user research, aiding design.
- Representations summarize basic aspects of user data: users, events, tasks, activities, and contexts.
- Representations should be traceable and verifiable.

Exercises

1. Representation techniques. Consider a recent product launched by an IT company. Produce the following representations for the product: (a) a persona, (b) a scenario, (c) a task analysis diagram, (d) a customer journey map, and (e) a rich picture diagram.
2. The value of representations. If you have original data, why bother with second-order representations like personas and scenarios? Are we not always bound to lose information with representations? Discuss the pros and cons of using representations.
3. Large language models and user research. Large language models can be used to generate personas and scenarios. For example, you can prompt ChatGPT to generate a persona with the desired characteristics or even with real transcripts from interviews. Discuss how valid and informative such representations can be, including their pros and cons.

Part IV

Understanding Interaction

16
Introduction to interaction

By now, it should be clear that the term *interaction* covers a lot of ground in human–computer interaction (HCI). We have used it to discuss various applications, from a user typing on a smartphone to a team of information workers communicating via email. It has been used to describe individuals, groups, and communities using computers. Moreover, interaction takes place at different timescales. Pressing a button takes about a hundred milliseconds; adopting an information system in a large organization can easily take months. Interaction also occurs in different contexts, including work, leisure, and in-between contexts such as commuting. If "interaction" covers all of this, of what use is it as a construct for HCI? What *is* interaction?

To answer this fundamental question, one might turn to dictionary definitions of the term. However, as pointed out over three decades ago by Winograd [898], that may not be helpful. He noted that "Webster defines 'interaction' as 'mutual or reciprocal action or influence.' Clearly, humans act on computers and computers influence humans. But how? In what dimensions?" [pp. 444–445]. We need a more nuanced understanding of interaction, one that sheds light on phenomena occurring across timescales, units of analysis, and contexts.

Since Winograd's question, researchers have begun to articulate more specific accounts of interaction [357, 383]. This part reviews the well-known views listed in Table 16.1. They provide a *general* conceptual basis for understanding interaction. Specifically, they expound *mutual determinacy* in interaction. This focus distinguishes these theories from theories of people as users of computers, which we covered in Part II. Theories of interaction are also different from the concept of user interface. In the next part of this book (Part V), we will look at user interfaces—the *technology* through which interaction with computers takes place. That part will discuss the technology necessary for input and output in interactive systems. User interfaces are technologies that mediate interaction and are inherently part of it; they are not the same as interaction. Interaction is a dynamic phenomenon that unfolds over time as users and computers influence each other.

16.1 What is a theory of interaction?

What makes a theory *a theory of interaction*? Or more specifically, what theories of interaction could be relevant to the situation in Figure 16.1? To answer that, we first need to understand what a theory is. We then need to scope "interaction" as the subject of theory. Finally, we need to discuss what makes a good theory in HCI.

In general, a theory consists of a set of *propositions*, or statements. A proposition is a claim about the world. In the case of particle physics, the propositions that make up a theory may concern the nature and behavior of particles. HCI theories contain statements that link humans and technology and possibly some outcomes (e.g., poor usability, high user experience). Propositions characterize entities and link them to other entities, some of which are conceptual. For example, they can talk about information, difficulty, working memory, and so on.

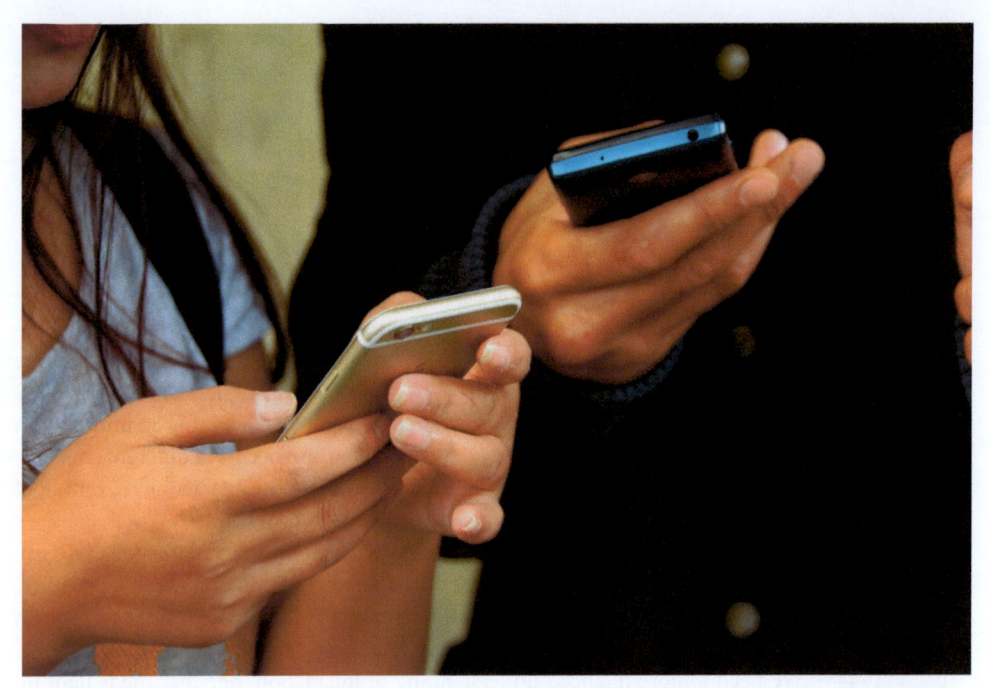

Figure 16.1 Theories of interaction illuminate interactive phenomena beyond intuition and help solve design and engineering problems in HCI. Even seemingly mundane activities such as entering text have rich structures that can be uncovered by these theories. Photo by Jonas Leupe.

In HCI, propositions come in different forms. Consider the following propositions of Fitts' law, which we discussed in Chapter 4:

1. "Human motor system is a limited capacity information channel."
2. "Attempts at reaching a target are limited by the speed and variance (accuracy) of the movement involved."
3. "If the user tries to increase speed, accuracy will be compromised, and vice versa: An increase in accuracy reduces speed."
4. "The difficulty of selecting a target is proportional to its distance and inversely proportional to its width (index of difficulty)."
5. "Average movement time can be predicted as linear regression to the index of difficulty."

Here, a progression can be observed. The theory starts with a high-level statement: The motor system is a limited-capacity channel. From there, it derives propositions about the relationship between performance and interface design through the construct of a target.

In HCI, propositions must generally link aspects of people with aspects of technology or design. In other words, they must be about mutual determinacy.

16.1.1 Mutual determinacy

The philosopher of science Bunge defined *mutual determination* as a special type of causal relationship applied in scientific explanation [110]. You may normally think of causality in terms of cause and effect. Consider pressing a button with your finger: When you press the button cap (cause), it triggers a command (effect). However, such a description does not count as a theory of interaction because it does not link the effect *back* to the cause. It is silent on how the design of the button affects its pressing. The point of mutual determination is exactly this: What happens in interaction is mutually determined by the human and the computer. In other words, what happens in interaction cannot be attributed solely to the human or the computer—the two must be considered together.

The theories we discuss in this part all commit to this idea. For example, interaction-as-tool-use focuses on this idea (Chapter 19). Tools change people and their activities; in turn, this changes the tools. This has profound effects on how we think about computer-based tools.

According to Bunge, causal determination is only one of the forms of causal relationships used in scientific theories. Bunge analyzed theories in scientific fields, from biology to physics, and developed a rich typology of mutual determination. In *mechanical determination*, an antecedent determines a consequent. The pressing of a button would count as a mechanistic determination. Here, neural events in the brain determine physiological events leading to the contraction of relevant muscles, leading to physical contact with the button that then triggers an event in the computer. In *statistical determination*, there is a stochastic relationship between the two entities. For example, statistical models, such as Fitts' law, describe a relationship that is considered a statistical determination. Here, the statistical model (regression) links the time it takes for a user to elicit a response to the design of the task environment (distance and width of buttons). However, this relationship is statistical and not definite. In *structural determination*, the end results of the interaction are jointly determined by multiple causes that make up the whole. For example, in interaction-as-rationality, courses of action emerge as a *joint* function of the user's goals and capabilities and the properties of the environment. Finally, in *quantitative determination*, interaction is described as a continuous unfolding of states. Each state dynamically leads to a new state depending on the forces involved. For example, in control-theoretical analysis, we see the interaction as dynamically changing states.

One type of determination is shared by all theories of interaction in HCI: *teleological determination*. In teleological determination, goals or purposes determine interaction in some way. In Greek, *telos* means goal or purpose. Even in interaction-as-transmission, the user has an *intended* message in mind. All theories of interaction discussed in this part assume *intentionality*: People have goals that have a (mutually) causal role in interaction. Intentionality is a litmus test for HCI theories. However, computers can also have goals or at least algorithmic objectives. This adds another level to teleological determination. An interactive AI system can possess an objective function it pursues when acting, for example, when correcting a character it flags as a typo. To conclude, Bunge's typology is useful in understanding the landscape of HCI theories. We discuss these types in the rest of this part.

16.1.2 Example: Six views of text entry

To provide an overview of theories of interaction, we view the task of text entry through the six theories discussed in this part.

First, text entry can be seen as the transmission of typed information to a computer. This concept, communication of information, is rooted in information theory (Chapter 17). Information theory provides a rigorous formalism to understand and quantify interaction via the concept of passing messages through a noisy channel. In text entry, the theory provides us with concepts and metrics that aid our understanding of typing performance. For example, the information rate of a text entry method can be quantified using the concept of throughput from information theory. As another example, text entry often relies on language models, and such modeling is based on information theory.

Table 16.1 The theories of interaction reviewed in this part can be delineated by their focus, time span, and scope.

Theory	Interaction phenomenon	Time span	Scope
Information and control	Interaction is viewed as the user and the computer sending messages across a noisy channel to communicate and control each other.	Seconds	Individual
Dialogue	Interaction is structured as communication turns between the computer and the human, with each turn changing the context of the subsequent turn.	Seconds to minutes	Individual
Tool use	Interaction involves users using computers as tools to pursue their goals in an effective, efficient, and satisfying way.	Minutes to days	Individual in context
Automation	Interaction involves users striving to achieve their goals with the assistance of an AI system that can autonomously carry out aspects of tasks, such as acquiring information, analyzing information, deciding an action, or carrying out an action.	Minutes to days	Two or more autonomous or semi-autonomous actors
Rationality	Interaction is about users choosing actions with a computer that they believe will maximize utility for them. Their success is limited by the environment (computer, context) and their abilities.	Seconds to weeks	Individual
Practice	Interactions are situated in and affected by organizational and societal contexts.	Weeks to years	Teams and organizations

Another classical view of interaction, originating in cybernetics, is to view it as a control problem (Chapter 17). Interaction is understood as actions and reactions that minimize the discrepancy between the present state and the goal state. Viewing text entry as a control problem can provide a more in-depth understanding of the human perceptual and motor control aspects of text entry, such as a user's ability to touch individual letter keys on a touchscreen keyboard or a user's ability to perform a touchscreen gesture. Moreover, control theory offers a broad view of interaction; it is not limited to input. Many things we do with computers, such as listening to music or posting messages, are about control. We want to have certain effects on the world; that is, we want to control it. For example, we may choose a song to play to regulate our emotions or influence co-present others.

Text entry can also be seen as dialogue (Chapter 18). The essence of dialogue is that communication is organized in sequences of turns. When you enter a letter (a turn), a small pop-up appears for you to confirm your press (a turn). A word prediction list may show possible completions of the word. At every press, these are updated, over time forming a graphical dialogue between the user and the system. Text entry can also be carried out via spoken dialogue. Conversational agents (e.g., ChatGPT, Siri, Alexa, Cortana) allow users to enter text messages via commands and feedback.

Text entry is also a good example of tool use (Chapter 19). A text entry method is a tool that allows the user to communicate with someone or something, typically other people or a service, using asynchronous text messages and longer documents. Thinking about text entry as tool use allows us to assess text entry in terms of its utility—how well it supports users in that pursuit—and its usability—how easy it is to enter text and learn how to enter text. Tool use also triggers the concept of accessibility. Persons with varying capabilities and backgrounds need to effectively enter text, or these systems fail as tools. For example, text entry methods such as eye typing are designed to allow nonspeaking users with motor disabilities to enter text using their eye movements only.

Text entry can also be seen as a task where different subtasks are shared between the human and the computer (Chapter 20). One example is autocorrect, which automatically corrects typing errors while the user is typing. Another example is the use of word predictions, which allow the user to select a word from a set of word suggestions instead of typing out the word in full. Such techniques provide different levels of automation. The effect of such automation critically depends on how well its design appreciates the actor's unique capabilities. For example, word prediction usage may not be beneficial if the word suggestions are poorly suited to the individual's language or if the user can type words faster than the time required to scan and select among word suggestions.

In this part, we will also look at interaction as a rational pursuit. The basic assumption underlying theories of rationality is that people choose how to act according to their benefit; in other words, they are rational. However, the design of the artifact and the user's cognitive limitations both *bound* (limit) what can be achieved in practice. In text entry, users do their best to hit the right buttons; however, because of the limits of the perceptual and motor systems, they may need to slow down to decrease the error rate. They also need to be rational in how they share their visual attention. On the one hand, visual attention is needed to check whether the typed text is right; on the other hand, it is needed to guide the fingers to the right keys. The users change their behavior to achieve optimal bounded behavior. In Chapter 21, we cover different ways to predict user behavior based on their environments and abilities.

Finally, we look at factors that affect interaction beyond the interface. A text entry method is affected by practice (Chapter 22). The practice of someone typing is shaped by norms and social factors, for example, the expected division of labor between communication partners—who is supposed to say or do what in a conversation. As another example, the use of emojis is affected by social norms that have evolved since the advent of mobile phones with text entry capability. Factors that define a practice evolve over time and may not be immediately observable; however, they heavily shape what happens and why.

16.2 Phenomena explained by HCI theories

Let us now look beyond text entry at the bigger picture of HCI theories. We look at their differing scopes and the key phenomena they explain in interaction.

16.2.1 Commanding

One goal of interaction is *communicating intentions*, for example, issuing commands to a computer, selecting graphical elements in image processing software, or entering text.

Chapter 17 presents two views of such interaction. The first view is that interaction can be seen as a communication system. This communication system is used to model the interaction as a source (e.g., the user) sending messages over a noisy channel to a receiver (e.g., a computer). Importantly, these messages can be quantified, typically by the number of bits required to encode them. This makes it possible to reason about the efficiency of interaction by defining and quantifying messages. As a consequence, this view has been used to reason about achievable limits in text entry, the time it takes a user to consider several choices, and the movement time required for a user to select a target.

The second view presented in Chapter 17 is that of interaction as control, which models interaction as a closed-loop control system. The information-centered model views the interaction as discrete bits that are transmitted over a noisy channel. By contrast, the control theory model views interaction as a user moving their body continuously in space and time to articulate their intention in such a way that it has the desired effect on the computer. A central notion in viewing interaction as control is *feedback*: The user regulates action as a response to information obtained via their senses, such as touch and vision. The control view of interaction allows for reasoning about mechanisms that underpin interaction. An example of this in Chapter 17 is the control view of modeling the movement time required for a user to select a target. Unlike the information-centered model, which merely predicts the movement time for this task, the control model can explain how actions (feedforward) and feedback together produce pointing movements moment by moment.

16.2.2 Communicating

Interaction can also be viewed as a form of communication. While Chapter 17 is concerned with interaction as sending messages or responding to feedback, Chapter 18 introduces dialogues as a way to understand interactions that go beyond a single communication act. It does so by discussing four different perspectives of a dialogue as a model of interaction. The computational perspective models dialogues as finite-state machines. This formalism allows designers to reason about emergent properties of dialogues, such as how many steps the user must take to recover from a mistake. The perspective of dialogue as a goal-directed action views interaction as a user driving a system into an intended state using a turn-based dialogue. Central to this perspective of interaction is the assumption that the main challenge for the user is understanding the system to such a degree that the user can take appropriate actions.

This perspective of interaction as goal-directed dialogue has been challenged by another perspective: dialogue as embodied action. The idea is that goal-directed dialogue reduces the users to agents who passively react to a set of options generated by the system. Dialogue as embodied action rectifies this by introducing interactive elements into goal-directed dialogue. For example, a user learns about various options by exploring the user interface. The final perspective views interaction as communication. This means accepting that human–computer dialogues are similar, yet distinct, from human–human dialogues. Similar to how we use a different language in formal settings compared to when we interact with friends, users use a different language when interacting with computers. Understanding the context of dialogue allows for the improved management of people's expectations and their preferred style of interaction.

16.2.3 Tool use

A fundamental goal of interaction is to provide users with tools that allow them to achieve goals that they would otherwise not have been able to achieve. Chapter 19 discusses the general topic of tool use and elucidates how users use the computer as a tool to accomplish a variety of tasks. This leads to a discussion around the utility, usability, fit, and accessibility of tools. Utility captures how well a tool supports users in achieving their goals. Usability refers to the ease with which a tool is operated. Accessibility is an extension of usability to ensure that as many people as possible find a tool easy to operate, regardless of individual capabilities. Understanding tool use from these aspects allows designers to ensure their user interfaces are effective, safe, and easy to learn. "Fit" refers to the match between a tool's capabilities and the user's abilities and task-related requirements.

Chapter 21 discusses the use of computers as rational acts, that is, as actions that users take for their benefit. Theories of rationality, from classical decision-making to computational rationality, offer a rich toolbox for understanding *why* users act the way they do. Underlying all of these theories are two core assumptions. The first is that a user's actions are choices from sets of options with different pros and cons for the user; the second is that actions are selected to maximize the expected utility for the user. Theories differ in terms of what kinds of limitations, or bounds, limit the user's ability to pick the best possible action.

16.2.4 Augmenting capabilities

Tools can also provide a degree of automation to augment human capabilities. Chapter 20 introduces a framework for understanding four types of automation: acquisition, analysis, decision, and action. Acquisition automation refers to the automated registration and collection of input data. Analysis automation involves performing some level of inference based on the input data, for example, extrapolating a trajectory. Decision automation refers to various degrees of automated support for deciding among several alternatives, for example, a system that automatically recommends a suitable route from point A to point B. Finally, action automation means that the system is, to some degree, automatically carrying out an action in response to a decision. For example, a photocopier can automatically sort and collate copies. These types of automation can range from fully automated, meaning the system acts autonomously, to no automation, meaning the user has to make decisions or choose actions from a set of alternatives. Designers decide the type and level of automation appropriate for a system based on a set of primary and secondary evaluation criteria.

16.2.5 Situated use

Chapter 22 discusses interaction as it happens in real life to advance users' goals, be it career goals, life goals, or something else. Importantly, interaction occurs in social contexts and physical spaces; these and other factors shape interaction in many ways. Investigating practice means understanding how people handle variations, challenges, breakdowns, and other events as part of their activities, which are governed by rules, plans, visions, and other norms. This implies that it is insufficient to understand interaction as the mediation of human activities by merely examining social structures, such as work hierarchies and delegation chains, or individual behaviors. It is necessary to look at the practice as a whole. Therefore, when we view interaction as practice, we accept that when users interact with systems, they interpret information, modify elements of systems, and work around limitations to reach their goals. In addition, viewing interaction as practice means realizing that interaction with systems is embedded in wider organizational and social settings and may involve many interactive systems that affect each other. Finally, viewing interaction as practice means studying how interaction affects people over time in different settings, such as work or leisure.

16.3 What makes a good HCI theory?

HCI theories construe interaction by reference to different mechanisms. They refer to events occurring at different timescales, at different levels of granularity, or that are mediated by different types of causal relationships. Knowing about these mechanisms is important because they help us understand and improve interaction in ways that go beyond intuition.

16.3.1 Theories should be informative

Any theory should be informative to be of relevance; in HCI, a theory should tell us something about interaction that is not obvious. The *explanatory power* of a theory refers to the empirical accuracy and coverage of the explanations offered by the theory. The more accurate and broader the coverage, the higher the explanatory power. For the sake of argument, one can compare Fitts' theory of aimed movements with Norman's theory of interaction, both of which we discuss in this part. Fitts' theory has high statistical accuracy but low coverage; Norman's theory has high coverage but low accuracy. So, how is such explanatory power achieved?

HCI theories gain their explanatory power by shedding light on *latent factors* in interaction. A latent factor is something that affects observations about interaction without being directly observable. Latent factors are the inner mechanisms of theories; they relate otherwise unrelated observations together. Famous latent factors in HCI theories include:

1. **Interaction-as-dialogue:** Norman's gulf of evaluation, or the cognitive appraisal that occurs when a computer changes its state. "Is this taking me closer to my goal?"
2. **Interaction-as-information:** The limited information capacity channel of the human motor system, which imposes a trade-off between the speed and accuracy of aimed movements in interaction.
3. **Interaction-as-control:** A controller is a latent process in the user's mind that tries to pick motor actions that minimize the distance between the present and goal states.
4. **Interaction-as-practice:** Contextual and normative factors that affect the user's choice of action.
5. **Interaction-as-bounded-rationality:** Utility or a reward that a user is trying to obtain via interaction.

Every HCI theory aims to explain how some surprising or important phenomenon *emerges* as interaction unfolds. Emergence refers to how a theory suggests that interesting high-level properties arise in interaction. In physics, the properties we attribute to water—such as its felt wetness and its properties as a fluid—emerge from low-level physical events. Many key HCI concepts emerge in interaction: usability, user experience, accessibility, fit, and so on. These constructs cannot be attributed to the interface or the human; they emerge through their interaction. Interesting theories should tell us something about their emergence. Interaction is thus more than simple cause and effect.

16.3.2 Theories should make predictions

Theories can also make predictions. In a *prediction*, a future state is estimated from a given starting condition. In HCI, we are particularly interested in predictions concerning users: their performance, errors, experiences, and so on. We need theories that link such predictions to factors we can measure or affect, such as characteristics of the task, the user interface, or the users.

Obviously, predictions are not "free." A theory needs to relate to the situation at hand and be instantiated in some way. In practice, this is often achieved via a *model*. A model is a formally expressed set of propositions that follows some axiomatic system, such as algebra, logic, or a programming language. Models contain "hard" and "soft" parts. The hard parts are mechanisms (theoretical postulates) that link observations, often via latent factors. Hard parts stay the same from one instance of a model to another; in other words, such mechanisms are invariant. The soft parts are parameters that can be changed to fit the situation at hand. Changing a parameter changes how the mechanism works but not the mechanism itself.

For example, earlier in this chapter, we noted the connection between Fitts' theory of a limited-capacity motor system and Fitts' law. Fitts' law is a model consisting of a regression equation (Chapter 4). Its hard part is the first-order regression model and the algebraic structure of the second term ($ID = \log_2(2D/W)$). Its soft part is the two coefficients *a* and *b*.

Common modeling approaches in HCI include:

- Regression models
- Probability theory
- Logic and rule-based systems
- Deep learning and other machine learning models
- Simulations.

A model stands between a theory (including its propositions) and the world:

Theory–model–data–world.

There are two possible directions in modeling: forward (from model to data) and inverse (from data to model). In forward modeling, we produce data from a model. For example, we input the starting conditions that describe a choice reaction task (Chapter 4): How many options does the user have to choose from? The model, in this case, the Hick–Hyman model, predicts the choice reaction time. In inverse modeling, we do the opposite: We fit the parameters of a model to match the data. A model's *predictive power* refers to the accuracy and precision with which it predicts events that are not in the data used to determine its parameters.

16.3.3 Theories should aid evaluation

The theories, methods, models, and even the views of interaction covered in this part of the book can be used in various ways to assist in designing and evaluating interaction.

Chapter 17 shows that it is possible to quantify aspects of interaction such as the rate of entering text, the time it takes a user to select a target, or the time it takes a user to select among multiple choices. When an interaction can be quantified, it is possible to optimize it, for example, by investigating which parameters and design choices reduce the average response time. In addition, it is possible to evaluate the interaction by observing how its metrics, such as the information rate, change as the design is modified.

To support users in exploring their options, interaction can be viewed as a dialogue (Chapter 18). Dialogue views interaction as a series of communication turns that require the user to infer what the other agent intends to communicate or how one's communication acts might influence the other agent.

Viewing interaction as the use of tools (Chapter 19) allows designers to understand the utility, usability, and accessibility of interaction. This can help designers evaluate interaction and support the design of interaction, for example, by helping designers identify and mitigate accessibility issues.

The automation framework covered in Chapter 20 allows designers to analyze each function in a design to identify suitable types and levels of automation. It can both inform design and serve as an evaluation tool.

Models of rationality (Chapter 21) can serve as tools for determining how to distribute and shape information in a user interface to allow users to maximize utility. This can be achieved, for example, by ensuring information is retrievable and presented in such a way that the cost–reward structure for the user is optimal. These models assume that users are as rational as they can be in light of the given constraints, such as the time available to make a decision or the resources available, including cognitive resources. Operating under such constraints, the user may be unable to reach the optimal solution. The term *satisficing* captures the idea that a user may settle for the first option that is deemed satisfactory given some constraints. Chapter 21 presents alternative ways to analyze interaction from this viewpoint. Such analysis can evaluate whether the cost–reward structure of the user interface allows the user to implement the optimal strategy.

Finally, Chapter 22 discusses how users personalize, tailor, and appropriate interaction as part of interacting with computer systems that are situated in larger contexts—communities, organizations, and societies. Such understanding can help designers understand design issues and requirements and assist in studying how interaction is interrelated with the use of interaction in practice. For instance, people may have many objectives in mind when trying to achieve a task; if the design of interaction does not consider this, this may lead to unexpected side effects.

16.3.4 Theories should guide measurements

Theories can help us decide what to measure. Information theory, for example, places emphasis on speed and accuracy in the entry of words. It offers precise measurements such as throughput and words per minute. Theories of practice, on the other hand, call for observations on the social processes that surround the sending and receiving of a message. Theories of tool use add to these by allowing us to measure the utility and acceptability of technology.

16.3.5 Theories should inform design

Finally, HCI theories should help us make practical decisions in design. After all, HCI as a field is concerned with design and engineering. To achieve this, theories need to offer some way of *reasoning* that links propositions to practical questions.

The logical basis of theory use in design has been traditionally attributed to *abduction*, which goes from observations to theory. For example, "Why did Aaron give up in the tenth level of the game?" Among others, this observation can be explained by reference to a motivational mechanism. Such an explanation can then be reasoned with to draw implications for the redesign of the game level.

Another form of reasoning is *deduction*. Here, we go from a theory to the world. For example, control theory suggests that feedback provided to the user should be informative; in particular, it should help the user correct their course of action. This implies that the design of feedback should aim to maximize informativeness for such corrections.

A third form of reasoning is *counterfactual reasoning*. This type of reasoning goes from a theory to a possible—but not yet existing—world. Counterfactual claims are "what might" or "what ought" claims. A counterfactual proposition can be expressed as follows:

> If design were *a*, then interaction would be *c*.

The argument has two parts, the antecedent *a* and the consequence *c*, linked by the counterfactual step. This step should be given by the theory.

For example, human performance models, cognitive models, and many other models follow a general form that maps task conditions or design (antecedents *a*) to some effect on users (consequents *c*). This counterfactual effect is marked using the symbol >:

> a (task conditions) > c (user behavior, performance, or experience).

In another variant, a feature of the design is what affects the consequent:

> a (feature of design) > c (user behavior, performance, or experience).

Theories can also inform design by simply illuminating factors that are in play in a situation. For example, the theories of practice are not expressed as models; yet, they expose critical factors that one might dismiss when thinking about the design of a user interface. A theory can also inspire and help one consider new perspectives. For example, Palen and Dourish [635] proposed a theory of privacy which countered the then-prevailing view of privacy as something determined by system design. They proposed that privacy is something we control and coordinate with other people interactively. This view inspired a new take on how to support privacy via interface mechanisms.

Summary

- Interaction is a core notion in HCI and refers to the mutual influence between people and computers.
- Phenomena in interaction are emergent, that is, they are not attributable to the user or to the computer alone.
- Theories of interaction explain the emergence of interactive behavior by referring to factors related to the user, the computer, and the environment. Some factors may be latent, that is, not directly observable.
- Theories of interaction have different theoretical commitments and they encompass different timescales and purposes.
- Theories of interaction help design and evaluate interactive systems.

17
Information and control

Interaction is a central concept in human–computer interaction (HCI); it is also relevant outside of HCI in some branches of engineering and computer science. Some of these applications in other fields are valuable and provide informative and actionable perspectives to HCI. This chapter introduces two such perspectives regarding information and control. The first is *information theory*, which views interaction as the sending of messages over a noisy channel that couples the human and the computer. The second is *control theory*, which views interaction as a feedback-guided, goal-oriented process. The objective of the user is to take actions to control a system in order to achieve the desired goal state.

Both theories are widely used in engineering and computer science. Information theory is the foundation of the mathematical modeling of communication systems such as mobile phone networks. It is also central in data compression, channel coding, and cryptography research, among other areas. Control theory forms the basis for the mathematical modeling of control in dynamic systems. For instance, it plays a pivotal role in applications involving engineering controllers that allow systems to reach stable desired values. Control theory is integral in many devices and machines we take for granted in our everyday lives. For example, a domestic thermostat controls the heating system to ensure the set temperature is reached in the home. Interestingly, although control theory is predominantly used in systems engineering, it was originally proposed in cybernetics as a general theory pertaining not only to machines but also to animals and humans [890].

Both theories have been used to develop better input methods and interaction techniques in HCI. For example:

1. Liu et al. [489] used information theory to improve navigation techniques (Chapter 26). When a user picks a navigation command, for example, to translate a map, the technique does not change the view in a deterministic way. Instead, it chooses the next view so that it maximizes information gain for the user. A high-information view tells the user a lot about the possible targets they might be navigating toward. The authors showed that this technique can reduce the number of steps required to complete a navigation task.

2. MacKenzie [505] compared input devices using the concept of throughput from information theory. Throughput allows for comparing user performance with input devices despite the fact that each device has a unique range of motion that determines what targets can be selected. In this review, the throughput was found to be 9.3–13.7 bits/s for an eye tracker, 10.6 bits/s for a hand, and 2.9 bits/s for a trackball.[1]

3. Yamagami et al. [917] used control theory to assist users with motor impairments. They modeled input action as being affected by two sources: the intended (correct) movement and error. Error is inherent to the user's motor system. Their method inferred the magnitude of error

---

[1] These studies were carried out before 1992. Because performance depends on the amount of experience, the results would likely be different if the study were repeated today.

Introduction to Human-Computer Interaction. Kasper Hornbæk, Per Ola Kristensson, and Antti Oulasvirta,
Oxford University Press. © Kasper Hornbæk, Per Ola Kristensson, and Antti Oulasvirta (2025).
DOI: 10.1093/oso/9780192864543.003.0017

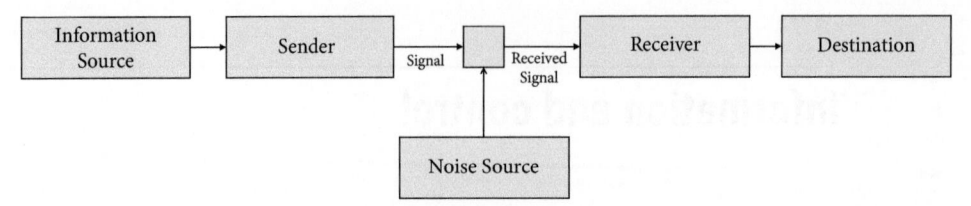

Figure 17.1 A schematic of a general communication system. An information source (e.g., user) sends a message (e.g., presses touchscreen) that is corrupted by noise before the receiver receives it. According to this view, human–computer interaction is about the transmission of messages over a noisy channel. Adapted from [760].

from observation and used this information to optimally assist users in selecting targets. They showed that muscle-controlled interfaces can be improved for motor-impaired users using this approach.

This chapter introduces central ideas of information and control and explains how the associated principles can be used to understand and model HCI.

17.1 Information

Information theory was pioneered by Shannon in his seminal article "A mathematical theory of communication" [760]. Information theory models HCI as a *communication system* (Figure 17.1). An *information source* generates a *message* that is sent to a *transmitter*. The transmitter encodes the message as a *signal*. This signal is relayed over a noisy *channel* to the *receiver*. The channel is affected by a *noise source*. The receiver decodes the signal into the original message and relays it to the sender's intended *destination*. How well the intended message is passed depends on several factors we can now analyze: the vocabulary (the set from which the message was produced), the message itself, the properties of the channel, and the properties of the receiver.

A central notion in information theory is the concept of a *message*. A message m in some message space (or vocabulary) $\mathbb{M}$ is sent from a *sender* to a *receiver*. A message is represented by a sequence of symbols, typically 0s and 1s, which is what we will use in this section. This means our messages carry information measurable in *bits*. It should be noted that information theoretical analyses are not limited to binary systems; they can be carried out for any vocabulary.

In the following section, we first introduce basic concepts of information theory and then present application examples in text entry, choice reaction, and target acquisition (Chapter 4). While the review assumes familiarity with the basics of probability theory, we explain the core ideas.

17.1.1 Self-information

A central notion in information theory is the amount of information carried by a message sent from a sender to a receiver. The amount of *self-information* I of a message m in bits is

$$\begin{aligned}I(m) &= \log_2\left(\tfrac{1}{P(m)}\right) \\ &= -\log_2(P(m)),\end{aligned} \quad (17.1)$$

where $P(m)$ is the probability of the message being chosen among all possible messages in some message space $\mathbb{M}$.

According to Equation 17.1, if the probability of the message is 1, then the amount of information is 0. Hence, if we are 100% certain we will receive a message, then that message carries *no information*: $I(m) = 0$. Less probable messages, such as messages that occur less frequently, carry more information than more probable messages—messages that occur more frequently. Two messages that are sent in succession but are otherwise independent of each other have a quantity of information that is the sum of the messages' individual quantities of information. Such messages are *mutually exclusive*.

As an example of self-information, consider flipping a fair coin. The coin has a 0.5 probability of coming up heads and a 0.5 probability of coming up tails. Flipping a coin is an example of a Bernoulli trial—a random trial with only two possible outcomes. Assume the sender flips a fair coin and wishes to communicate the outcome of this trial to a receiver via a message m. The probability of either outcome is 0.5 and the self-information of message m is then $I(m) = \log_2\left(\frac{1}{0.5}\right) = \log_2(2) = 1$ bit.

Next, consider communicating the outcome of having flipped a fair coin four times as either m_{4h} (four heads in a row) or $\overline{m_{4h}}$ (*not* observing four heads in a row). The probability $P(m_{4h})$ of observing four heads in a row is $\frac{1}{16}$, and $I(m_{4h})$ is

$$\begin{aligned} I(m_{4h}) &= -\log_2(P(m_a)) \\ &= -\log_2\left(\frac{1}{16}\right) \\ &= 4 \text{bits}. \end{aligned} \qquad (17.2)$$

To communicate the other possible outcome, $\overline{m_{4h}}$, we first find the probability $P(\overline{m_{4h}})$:

$$\begin{aligned} P(\overline{m_{4h}}) &= 1 - P(m_{4h}) \\ &= 1 - \frac{1}{16} \\ &= \frac{15}{16}. \end{aligned} \qquad (17.3)$$

Then, we calculate $I(\overline{m_{4h}})$:

$$\begin{aligned} I(\overline{m_{4h}}) &= -\log_2\left(\frac{15}{16}\right) \\ &\approx 0.093 \text{bits}. \end{aligned} \qquad (17.4)$$

In other words, the probability of observing four heads in a row $\left(\frac{1}{16}\right)$ is much smaller than the probability of *not* observing four heads in a row $\left(\frac{15}{16}\right)$. Therefore, the message that informs the receiver that the sender has observed four heads in a row has a much higher information content (4 bits vs. 0.093 bits). This is why self-information is said to measure the *surprisal* of a message. Again, note that if the outcome of the coin flips were already known to the receiver, the self-information of the message would be zero.

17.1.2 Entropy, redundancy, and perplexity

Let us first consider the case where there are only two messages and, therefore, only two probabilities:

$$H_2(p) = -p \log_2(p) - q \log_2(q), \qquad (17.5)$$

where p is the probability of the first message and $q = 1 - p$ is the probability of the second message. Equation 17.5 is referred to as the *binary entropy function*.

Note that if either $p = 1$ or $q = 1$, then $H_2(p) = 0$. For example, if p is 100% probable, then q is 0% probable; as a result, the binary entropy of p is zero. This reflects the fact that there is no *uncertainty* in the fact that the first message will be received with a probability $p = 1$. Moreover, note that the binary entropy $H_2(p)$ is maximized when $p = q = 0.5$. This reflects the fact that when

$p = q = 0.5$, the uncertainty on whether the sender will send the first or the second message is maximized when both messages are equally probable.

The average self-information of all messages in a message space is known as *entropy*. Entropy H is a measure of the uncertainty in the message space $\mathbb{M}$:

$$H(\mathbb{M}) = \sum_{m \in \mathbb{M}} P(m)I(m)$$
$$= -\sum_{m \in \mathbb{M}} P(m) \log_2 (P(m)). \qquad (17.6)$$

Entropy is the average bits required to communicate a message when using an optimal coding scheme. Entropy is also a measure of the uncertainty of the message space. An entropy of 0 means there is no uncertainty; as a consequence, every message is completely predictable, meaning it carries zero information content.

A related concept is *redundancy*. Redundancy is the difference between the average bits used for communication compared to the average bits required for communication using an optimal coding scheme. In reality, communication is nearly always redundant. For example, natural languages are highly redundant, a fact exploited by various natural language input technologies such as word prediction. Dasher (see Paper Example 17.1.1) is a text entry method that aims to reduce redundancy via adaptive word completion suggestions.

Having developed a probability model, for example, a probability model for making word predictions, the designer is often interested in understanding how well the probability model predicts the data. *Perplexity*, PP, is the weighted average number of choices a random variable has to make. It is defined as

$$\text{PP} = 2^H, \qquad (17.7)$$

where H is the entropy of the model. Perplexity is often used in statistical language modeling to help assess how well a statistical language model predicts unobserved text. Low perplexity means that the model is good at predicting the sample.

Example

As an example of the concepts of entropy, redundancy, and perplexity, consider the following source alphabet Ω (adapted from Kristensson [437]):

$$\Omega = \left\{ A = \frac{1}{2}, B = \frac{1}{4}, C = \frac{1}{8}, D = \frac{1}{8} \right\}. \qquad (17.8)$$

The source alphabet in Equation 17.8 assigns each of the symbols in the alphabet (in this case A, B, C, or D) a probability of occurrence. Note that these probabilities of occurrence sum to 1 and are not evenly distributed. For example, the symbol A is four times more likely to occur than either C or D.

The entropy H of the source alphabet is

$$\begin{aligned} H(\Omega) &= -\sum_{i=1}^{4} P_i \log_2 (P_i) \\ &= -\left(\tfrac{1}{2}(-1) + \tfrac{1}{4}(-2) + \tfrac{1}{8}(-3) + \tfrac{1}{8}(-3) \right) \\ &= 1.75 \text{bits.} \end{aligned} \qquad (17.9)$$

This entropy of $H(\Omega) = 1.75$ bits is the *lower bound* on the number of bits required to communicate using the alphabet Ω. To reach this lower bound, the coding scheme must be optimal.

Consider a naive coding scheme that is not going to be optimal. A straightforward method to implement a coding scheme for the source alphabet Ω is to assign every symbol in Ω a code of the same length. This means each code must be 2 bits long to be able to distinguish one out of four unique symbols (2^2 = 4 symbols). We can calculate the average number of bits this coding scheme will use to encode the source alphabet Ω by multiplying the bit length of each symbol by the symbol's probability of occurrence. We then find that, on average, this coding scheme will use $\frac{1}{2}2 + \frac{1}{4}2 + \frac{1}{8}2 + \frac{1}{8}2 = 2$ bits to encode Ω.

While this naive coding scheme is simple, it cannot be optimal. The reason is that we know from Equation 17.9 that the lower bound of the number of bits required to communicate the source alphabet Ω is 1.75 bits, which is 0.25 bits less than the average 2 bits required to communicate using the naive coding scheme. These additional 0.25 bits are known as the *redundancy* of the coding scheme.

Is it possible to construct an optimal coding scheme for the source alphabet Ω? In this case, this can be achieved by using variable length codes for the different symbols. For example, we can choose to assign the shortest code 0 to the most frequent symbol A, the second shortest code 10 to the second most frequent symbol B, and the longest codes 110 and 111 to the least frequent symbols C and D, respectively. These last two code assignments are interchangeable since their probabilities of occurrence are identical.

By multiplying again the bit length of each symbol with the symbol's probability of occurrence, we obtain the average number of bits when using this optimal coding scheme for encoding the source alphabet Ω: $\frac{1}{2}1 + \frac{1}{4}2 + \frac{1}{8}3 + \frac{1}{8}3 = 1 + \frac{3}{4} = 1.75$ bits. Since this is the same as the entropy of the source alphabet, this coding scheme is optimal.

The perplexity PP(Ω) of the optimal coding scheme is PP(Ω) = $2^{H(\Omega)} \approx 3.4$. By contrast, the perplexity of the naive coding scheme is 4. However, if all four symbols in Ω were equally likely, then the perplexity of the optimal coding scheme would also be 4, as the entropy of the source language would then be 2.

Paper Example 17.1.1: Dasher—Entering text via information-efficient 2D navigation

Dasher is a text entry interface that uses a language model to present word completions, which can be selected using a pointing device or gestures [874, 875]. The method was developed in the early 2000 and has had many applications in mobile devices and gaze-based interaction.

The novel method was motivated by an observation inspired by information theory: Our keyboards are highly inefficient [875]. To enter text using a regular keyboard, a user needs to select, character by character, one key from 80 keys (QWERTY). Every key press has an information capacity of $\log_2(80)$ = 6.3 bits. However, the English language has *entropy* of about 1 bit per character, meaning the keyboard is inefficient by a factor of 6.

What does this inefficiency mean in practice? It means that users can make many errors that are not linguistically valid in English. This is because users must type every character of the text they want to send, even if some characters are redundant. Consider, for example, the word "mastodon." With every character typed, there are fewer word completions that are appropriate in English. Yet, when entering the word with a regular keyboard, you would still need to enter every character by selecting it out of 80 possibilities. An efficient method would not allow non-linguistic entries.

Dasher requires a visual display and a pointing device, for example, a mouse, touchscreen, or eye tracker. Initially, the letters of the alphabet (27 in English) are shown in a column next to a space (Equation 17.1.2). The pointer is in the middle. To enter a character, say "t," the user starts moving the pointer toward that letter's rectangle. When moving toward the letter, options for the subsequent letter appear next to that letter: "th," "ta," and so on. Continuing the motion toward "th," "the" appears next to it, among other options.

continued

296 | UNDERSTANDING INTERACTION

> **Paper Example 17.1.1: Dasher—Entering text via information-efficient 2D navigation** *(continued)*
>
> A key idea of Dasher is the dynamic update of the characters on display, including their position and size. From an information-theoretic perspective, Dasher attempts to maximize the efficiency of text entry by scaling the size of the approaching letters according to their probability given what has already been typed. In controlled studies, novices could type at around 20 words per minute (wpm). With more experience, they achieved a rate of about 34 wpm.
>
> Despite initial excitement, Dasher never took off as a popular text entry method. Input rates were not as high as with conventional methods, and the method appeared effortful to use. By comparison, an average user on a smartphone types about 36 wpm, and younger users typing with two thumbs are often faster than that [637]. While Dasher utilizes language models to complete words, users still need to visually locate the right characters from a dynamically changing display. This is effortful and can be slow if you do not have an intuition of where the next option could be. Moreover, correcting mistakes takes time.
>
> You can try the method here: http://wol.ra.phy.cam.ac.uk/djw30/dasher/.

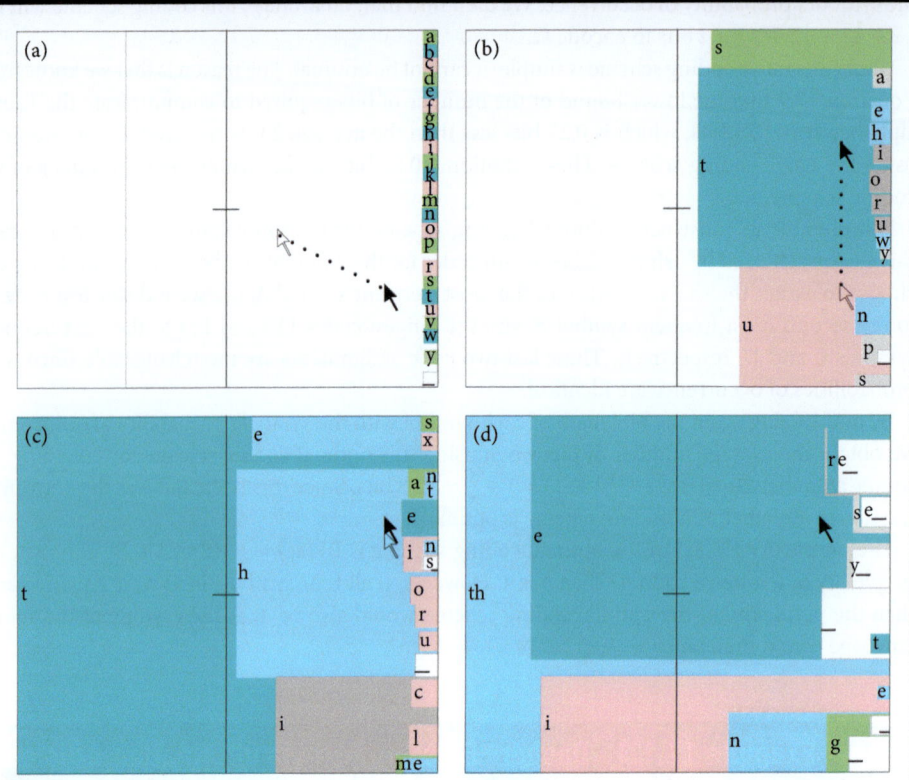

17.1.3 Rate

Information theory can be used to calculate the bitrate of a text entry method. To do this, we must first define the concept of *mutual information*. The mutual information $I(\mathbb{A}; \mathbb{B})$ of two discrete random variables $\mathbb{A}$ and $\mathbb{B}$ is

$$I(\mathbb{A}; \mathbb{B}) = \sum_{a \in \mathbb{A}} \sum_{b \in \mathbb{B}} P(a,b) \log_2 \left(\frac{P(a,b)}{P(a)P(b)} \right). \tag{17.10}$$

Mutual information expresses the number of bits of information about a random variable that can be obtained by observing another random variable. Intuitively, it captures how much knowing one random variable reduces the uncertainty of another random variable. In the extreme case where both random variables are independent, the mutual information is zero.

For example, assume a random variable $\mathbb{I}$ is a distribution over the set of words a user intends to write and the random variable $\mathbb{O}$ is a distribution over the set of words the user is writing. Using the concept of mutual information, we can arrive at a rate R in bits/s:

$$R = \frac{I(\mathbb{I}; \mathbb{O})}{t}, \qquad (17.11)$$

where $I(\mathbb{I}; \mathbb{O})$ is the mutual information of $\mathbb{I}$ and $\mathbb{O}$ and t is the average time in seconds it takes a user to write a word in $\mathbb{O}$.

We can rewrite Equation 17.11 if we introduce the concept of *conditional entropy*. Conditional entropy is the number of bits required to describe the outcome of a random variable *given* that the value of another random variable is known. The conditional entropy $H(\mathbb{B}|\mathbb{A})$ of two discrete random variables $\mathbb{A}$ and $\mathbb{B}$ is

$$\sum_{a \in \mathbb{A}, b \in \mathbb{B}} P(a,b) \log_2 \left(\frac{P(a)}{P(a,b)} \right). \qquad (17.12)$$

Since $I(\mathbb{I}; \mathbb{O}) = H(\mathbb{I}) - H(\mathbb{I}|\mathbb{O})$, where $H(\mathbb{I}|\mathbb{O})$ is the conditional entropy, the expression for the rate in Equation 17.11 can be rewritten as

$$R = \frac{H(\mathbb{I}) - H(\mathbb{I}|\mathbb{O})}{t}. \qquad (17.13)$$

If the probability of error is 0, that is, all words in $\mathbb{I}$ can always be inferred from $\mathbb{O}$, then the term for the conditional entropy $H(\mathbb{I}|\mathbb{O})$ will vanish and the rate R can be expressed as

$$R = \frac{H(\mathbb{I})}{t}. \qquad (17.14)$$

An example of information rate is given below where we discuss text entry as a case.

17.1.4 Throughput

Information theory has impacted the way we evaluate input methods. An important concept is that of *throughput* (TP). Zhai wrote [921, pp. 792–793]:

> A tempting but naive approach to measure input performance could be as follows: let users perform an input task such as pointing, under varied conditions such as different target size and distance; measure and record users' completion time; take the average of all trials for each input device as the performance metric; compare the values (e.g. 800 vs. 900 ms) between different devices; and make a conclusion based on these values (e.g. A is 10% faster than B on average). This seemingly reasonable approach unfortunately does not generalize, because such a measurement is a function of the experimental settings, in particular, the sizes and distances of the pointing targets. The conclusion based on such an approach is only valid within the set of targets tested. If the target sizes and distances were different, the same conclusion might not hold. In other words, average completion time is not only a function of the intrinsic

properties of the input devices but also a function of the experimental task parameters extrinsic to the input devices.

The quote makes an important point: An abstraction is needed to measure the performance intrinsic to an input device.

Instead of comparing raw performance scores, we should look at how many bits per second a user can express. This entails the following steps:

1. Users are asked to do pointing in varying *ID* conditions. They should point at targets as quickly as they can.
2. Movement times and accuracy are recorded and averaged per *ID* condition.
3. Fitts' law regression is fitted to the data.
4. *TP* can be computed using the formula given next.

Throughput (*TP*) is measured in bits/s and is the number of bits of information a user can communicate per second independently of the target. Different pointing devices tend to yield different throughput values.

Several definitions of throughput exist. One definition is

$$TP = \frac{ID_{avg}}{MT_{avg}}, \qquad (17.15)$$

where MT_{avg} is the average movement time measured for an average ID_{avg} range of IDs. One downside of this definition is that it depends on the arbitrary notion of an average *ID*.

An alternative definition of throughput is [921]

$$TP = \frac{1}{b}, \qquad (17.16)$$

where *b* is the regression parameter that determines the slope in Fitts' law (Equation 17.22), which we reviewed when we talked about motor control in Chapter 4. The downside of this definition is that it ignores any effect of the intercept regression parameter *a* in Fitts' law.

> **Paper Example 17.1.2: Throughput on different terminals**
>
> What does throughput tell us about our everyday input methods? Following the procedure above, Bachynskyi et al. [34] assessed several touchscreen surfaces to compare their *TP*. Their setup and results are shown in Figure 17.2. They found that the smartphone, when used with two hands, had the highest throughput, followed by the tabletop and large displays. Laptops and tablets had the lowest throughput scores. The authors used motion capture (also shown in the figure) and a biomechanical simulation to explain these results. They found that both the muscle groups and movement ranges involved matter: Using larger muscles means lower performance. Surprisingly, when given the chance to decide their posture, laptop users mainly used shoulder and arm muscles for pointing. While their posture was suitable for long-term laptop use, their pointing performance was poor. Such comparisons of input methods would be difficult without throughput or a similar construct.

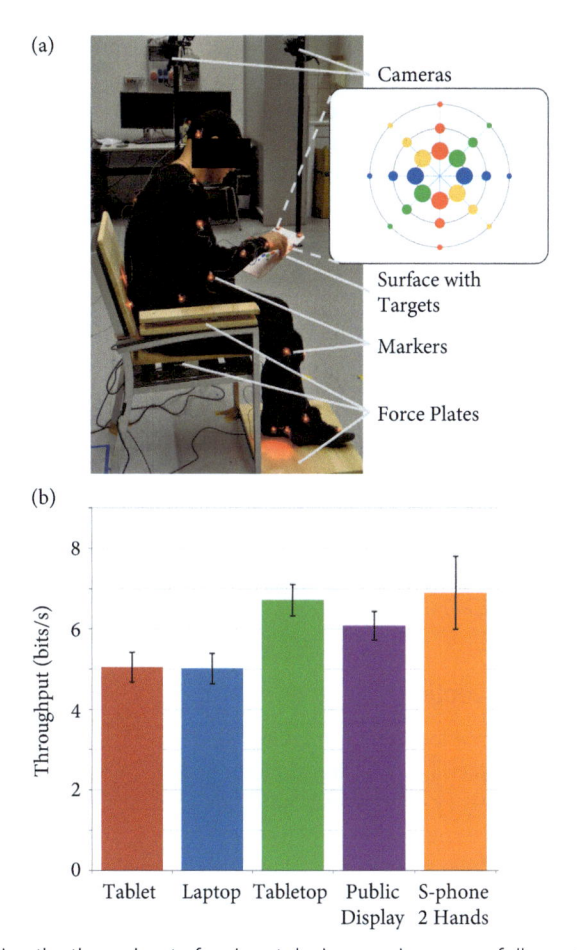

Figure 17.2 Estimating the throughput of an input device requires a carefully controlled pointing task with varying target widths and distances. In this study, touchscreen interfaces were compared via a cyclical pointing task by tracking the user's posture [34].

17.1.5 Example: Text entry

Information theory has been central to the study and development of text entry methods, including *Dasher* [502, 873, 874], which we presented in Paper Example 17.1.1. Here, we take another look at Dasher from the information-theoretic perspective.

Inverse arithmetic coding [902] is a near-optimal method of text compression based on language modeling. It inspired Dasher. Like most other gestural text entry methods, in Dasher, a user's gesture does not map to a particular letter or word. Instead, text entry in Dasher involves the continuous, visually guided, closed-loop control of gestures via, for example, a mouse or eye gaze. The user writes text by continuously navigating to a desired sequence of letters in a graphical user interface laid out according to a language model.

Dasher has an information-efficient objective in the following sense. If the user writes at a rate R_D (in bits), Dasher attempts to zoom in to the region containing the user's intended text by a factor of 2^{R_D}. If the language model generates text at an exchange rate of R_{LM}, the user will be able to reach an entry rate of R_D/R_{LM} characters per second.

Dasher can also be controlled by discrete button presses in which timing is disregarded. Assuming the button pressing is precise and therefore without errors, the capacity C of the communication channel between the user and the computer is

$$C = \frac{\log_2(n)}{t}, \quad (17.17)$$

where n is the number of buttons and t is the average time taken to switch buttons. If the process is noisy, such that the wrong button is pressed a fraction f of the time, the capacity is

$$C = \frac{\log_2(n)}{t} H_2(f), \quad (17.18)$$

where H_2 is the binary entropy function (Equation 17.5) [502]. This analysis shows that even at a rather low error rate of $f = 1/10$, the channel capacity C is scaled by approximately 0.47 and is thus reduced approximately by a factor of 2. This unintuitive result is given by the powerful analytical tools of information theory.

17.1.6 Example: Choice reaction

Another application of information theory in HCI is the Hick–Hyman model of choice reaction time [340, 490, 754]. In Chapter 4, we discussed motor control from the point of view of human performance. Information theory offers a framework for analyzing choice reactions as a form of communication. A user is presented with n choices, and there is no need for the user to linearly scan the list of choices. The latter point is important; for clarity, we refer to this task as *open-loop choice reaction time*.

The average time T it takes a user to make such a choice is

$$T = bH, \quad (17.19)$$

where b is an empirically determined regression parameter and H is the entropy in the decision:

$$H = \sum_{i=1}^{n} = p_i \log_2 \frac{1}{p_i + 1}, \quad (17.20)$$

where p_i is the probability of the ith choice.

If all choices are equally likely, Equation 17.20 reduces to what is commonly referred to as the Hick–Hyman law:

$$T = b \log_2(n+1), \quad (17.21)$$

where b is an empirically determined parameter and n is the number of choices. Consider, for example, the control of a character in a fast-paced action game. If you have more buttons to control, your reaction time will decrease, but not linearly. b, on the other hand, shows the influence of individual and design-related factors on the user's choice, such as how well the options are presented to the user.

17.1.7 Example: Target acquisition

Target acquisition is another motor control task that can be revisited in light of information theory. Specifically, the theory can help us understand the relationship between the average movement time (*MT*) and the spatial characteristics of the target, specifically its distance *D* and width *W*:

$$MT = a + bID, \qquad (17.22)$$

where *a* and *b* are empirically determined regression parameters and *ID* is the index of difficulty (in bits):

$$ID = \log_2\left(\frac{D}{W} + 1\right). \qquad (17.23)$$

Intuitively, *ID* captures the number of bits the human motor control system has to communicate to acquire a target. The more bits that are required, the higher the *ID*. This can readily be seen in Equation 17.23: A greater distance *D* to a target and/or a smaller width *W* of a target will result in a higher *ID*.

17.2 Control

Information theory views interaction as the passing of messages over a noisy channel. However, in order to send a message or even just press a key, the user needs to perceive and move. In interaction, the user's body continuously moves in space; through these movements, the user articulates intentions that are then interpreted by a computer system. The goal of the user is to *control* the system. In other words, the user wants to drive the system to a particular state corresponding to their goal. Meanwhile, the system infers the user's intentions from sensor data. The user's movements are guided by *feedback*, that is, their movements are coordinated in response to the information perceived by the user's sensory systems. The computer display is one source of such feedback; for example, it can show the position of the cursor or play a beep sound when clicking a target. *Continuous control* is a framework that can be used to model such interaction.

Figure 17.3 shows an example of a *joint* human–computer system. The system is joint in the sense that the overall function of the system depends on both the human and the computer. The user uses *effectors*, such as their fingers, hands, eyes, or mouth, to articulate intention. These articulations are sensed by the computer's *sensors* and interpreted by the machine into user intentions, which are then used to update the state of the *controlled variable* (e.g., cursor position). The user

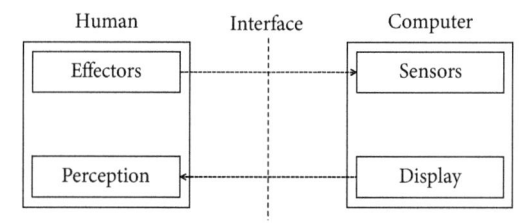

Figure 17.3 A high-level diagram of a closed-loop joint human–computer system. Humans need to control effectors (e.g., fingertips) to have an effect on sensors, which affect the internal state of the computer. The computer can then, via its displays, provide feedback so that the user can correct their course of action.

can evaluate the computer's responses by observing the computer's display, which may be a visual, auditory, or haptic display.

A system can be of two main types: *closed-loop* or *open-loop*. The system in Figure 17.3 is closed-loop because it is feedback-driven. The circuit is closed. By contrast, an open-loop system does not rely on feedback; the circuit is open. In terms of user interaction, an example of a closed-loop action is moving a mouse pointer to an icon. Such movement is guided by visual feedback. An example of an open-loop action is performing a swiping touchscreen gesture on a capacitive touchscreen to unlock a device. Closed-loop movement tends to be slower but more precise. Open-loop movement tends to be fast since it is a direct recall from motor memory; however, it is less precise. We discuss closed-loop control below.

17.2.1 Elements of a control system

The purpose of a control system is to control a variable of interest—the *controlled variable*. An example is room temperature, which is regulated by a control system sending signals to a heating and cooling system to maintain a constant temperature despite fluctuations caused by the environment. The controller aims to drive the controlled variable to a particular range or value representing the goal set by the user. This is not trivial since controlled variables are often affected by both the control system and the environment.

In HCI, an example of a controlled variable is the location of a mouse cursor. The control system consists of the user moving the mouse and perceiving the new location of the cursor and the computer interpreting the user's mouse movements and updating the cursor's location. Typically, the user aims to relocate the mouse pointer to a specific region on the screen, for example, over an icon. This can be achieved by the control system moving the mouse, thereby affecting the controlled variable.

In general, a manual control system can be described using six elements: (1) a goal selection system, (2) a controller, (3) a power source, (4) a control junction, (5) a control effector, and (6) a feedback sensor. We will now describe these in detail based on the literature on manual control [408].

Goal selection system: The *goal selection system* is typically a human, possibly assisted by a computer. For example, the user may aim to change the volume of a music player to a particular level. Generally, the objective of the goal selection system is the selection of the desired future state among a set of possible future states. The goal selection system dynamically interprets the environment, arrives at a set of possible future states, and selects the desired future state. The output of the goal selection system is transmitted to the controller.

Controller: The objective of the *controller* is to output a control signal that modulates the energy used to control the controlled variable. Several control principles exist, including the proportional integral derivative (PID), bang–bang, and model predictive control. These principles are outside the scope of this book; what matters here is that they use some principle for selecting an action (response) based on feedback and the current state. For example, the user wanting to change the volume may target a particular switch on the player with their finger.

Power source: A power source is a transfer function that amplifies or otherwise changes human input. In the case of the user changing the volume, the intended motor commands need to be transduced into muscle activations.

Control junction: A control junction sums or compares incoming inputs. For example, it can be used to compute the discrepancy between the user's intended movement and the perceived movement.

Control effector: A control effector is the last function under the user's control that can affect the controlled variable.

Feedback sensor: A feedback sensor senses the control effector and translates its signal into changes in the controlled variable. For example, the user may hear the volume change as the button is pressed.

17.2.2 Closed-loop human–computer systems

Figure 17.4 shows a diagram of a simple muscle-powered closed-loop control system. The *controlled variable*, or the *output*, is a mathematical description of the entity the user is controlling. It can, for example, be the user's fingertip location over a touchscreen or keyboard. In Figure 17.4, the user receives *feedback information* about the controlled variable, for example, a visual observation of the location of their fingertip. The user can then integrate this perceptual and feedback information and take corrective action by modulating their muscle power. This would result in the fingertip moving. Paper Example 17.2.1 shows a design concept building on closed-loop control.

Figure 17.5 shows an extension of the model in Figure 17.4 that involves the user manipulating the controlled variable indirectly using a tool. In this case, the user receives feedback information from two sources: the tool and the controlled variable. An example of such a control task is a user controlling a mouse cursor on a display by moving the mouse.

Figure 17.6 shows a further extension of Figure 17.4 where the controlled variable is indirectly controlled by a tool or device with an external power source. This means the user's muscle power is combined with an external power in order to use a tool or device to manipulate the controlled variable.

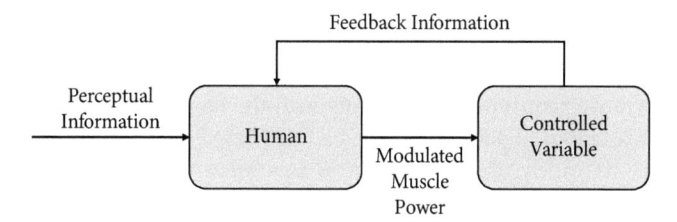

Figure 17.4 A closed-loop control system controlled by direct muscle power. Adapted from [408].

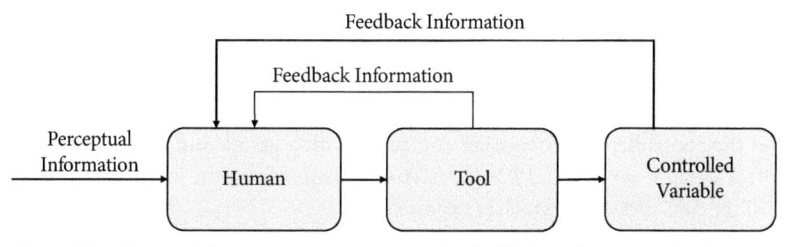

Figure 17.5 A closed-loop control system controlled indirectly using a tool. Adapted from [408].

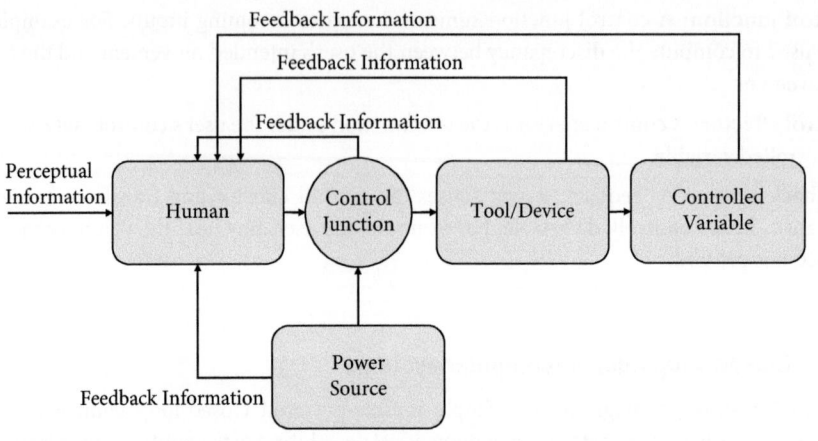

Figure 17.6 A closed-loop control system controlled indirectly by an externally powered device that is potentially regulated by automatic controllers. Adapted from [408].

17.2.3 Example: Target acquisition

An example of an application of control is *target acquisition*. The average movement time required for a user to point at a target of size W at distance (amplitude) A is predicted by Fitts' law. From Chapter 4, we recall

$$MT = a + bID, \qquad (17.24)$$

where ID is the index of difficulty:

$$ID = \log_2\left(\frac{2A}{W}\right). \qquad (17.25)$$

Equations 17.24 and 17.25 describe a linear regression model where the regression parameters a and b describe the intercept and slope, respectively. In other words, Fitts' law is a model that predicts that the movement time varies linearly with the index of difficulty. The intercept and slope of the line are empirical parameters that are fitted based on data.

While Fitts' law is widely used, the model is somewhat unsatisfying. The model predicts movement time based on empirical observations; however, it does not provide a mechanistic explanation for why its mathematical formulation accurately captures the average movement time of a user pointing at a target.

An alternative explanation can be identified by viewing target acquisition as a control problem (see Figures 17.7 and 17.8). The first step is to identify the reference variable, which we denote by r. The reference variable r corresponds to the distance (amplitude) A of the target in Fitts' law. Then, assume the change from the home position to the target position is a step change in the reference variable r.

Next, set the controller to a first-order controller with a gain k and integrator $\dot{x} = Bu$, where u is the control signal $u = r - x$, and $B = k$. A step change in r from the initial state $x = 0$ results in a response of the first-order lag, which is exponential:

$$x(t) = r\left(1 - e^{-kt}\right). \qquad (17.26)$$

Consider a target size w corresponding to the target size W in Fitts' law. The time it would take to get within $\frac{1}{2}w$ of r for a target size w centered on r is

$$\begin{aligned} x(t) &= r\left(1 - e^{-kt}\right) = r - \tfrac{1}{2}w \\ e^{-kt} &= \tfrac{w}{2r} \\ -kt &= \ln \tfrac{w}{2r} \\ t &= \tfrac{1}{k} \ln \tfrac{2r}{w}. \end{aligned} \qquad (17.27)$$

Changing the base of the logarithm in Equation 17.27 to base 2, we obtain the following expression:

$$x(t) = \frac{\ln 2}{k} \log_2 \frac{2r}{w}, \qquad (17.28)$$

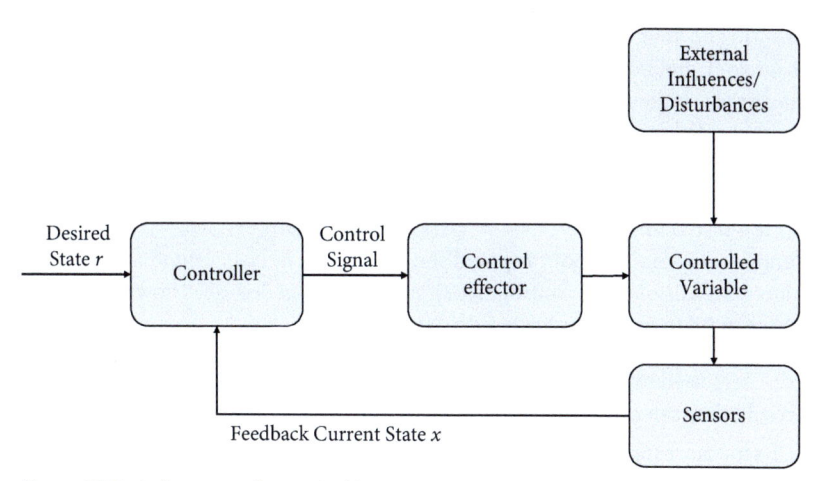

Figure 17.7 A diagram of a control loop.

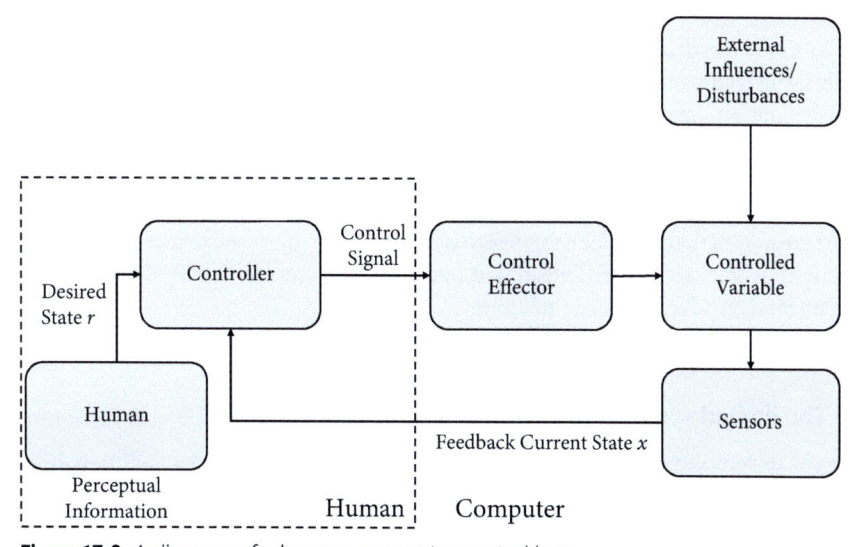

Figure 17.8 A diagram of a human–computer control loop.

which is similar to the formulation of the index of difficulty in Fitts' law (Equation 17.25):

$$ID = \log_2\left(\frac{2A}{W}\right). \qquad (17.29)$$

The gain k of the forward loop affects the speed of the target acquisition: the larger the gain, the shorter the movement time. The *time constant* is the time it takes for the system's response to reach 63% of its steady-state value from zero initial conditions. In this case, the time constant is $\frac{1}{k}$. The gain k of the forward loop is a measure of the system's sensitivity to error. A large k means the system is very sensitive to errors and quick to correct them.

> **Paper Example 17.2.1: Focused and casual interactions**
>
> Imagine sitting on your couch and watching your favorite television show when a notification appears on your mobile device. "Beep!" You would need to reach for the device, pick it up, and swipe or touch the notification to make it go away. All of this is distracting: You need to engage with the device with both your body and visual attention, which reduces your ability to focus on the TV program. Is there a better alternative? Imagine if you could casually brush the notification away, for example, with a hand gesture or by saying "Hush!" or "Go away!" This would be less distracting.
>
> Pohl and Murray-Smith [666] proposed the *focused–casual continuum* as a framework for interaction design inspired by control theory. the continuum describes how much closed-loop control users need to invest to engage with a device:
>
> **Focused:** Users need to fully engage their main senses, such as their visual and motor senses. As a result, they can express many bits per second.
>
> **Casual:** Users can express main information (e.g., "Notification, go away!") with minimal effort. Here, few bits per second are expressed.
>
> However, what determines if an engagement is focused or casual? In focused interaction, users need to sample feedback more frequently and accurately. They also need to respond more rapidly using high-bandwidth inputs (e.g., touching with fingertips on centimeter-precise targets). By contrast, casual interaction has lower control requirements. This can be achieved in a number of ways: intermittency (feedback does not need to be perceived all the time), low-bandwidth output (e.g., gross motor movements), and accepting noisy inputs from the user.
>
> The takeaway of the continuum for design is that situationally sensitive user interfaces should not only support fully focused interaction but also allow users to flexibly decide the level of engagement depending on their situations.

17.2.4 The limited scope of information and control in HCI

Despite the universality of information theory, its applications have remained limited. To apply information theory to an HCI case, we need to know the message and the character set (vocabulary) and be able to measure the speed and correctness of their communication. These requirements have limited information theory to two applications in HCI: pointing and text entry. In both, information theory has helped chart possibilities for input devices by quantifying inefficiencies, such as in the case of Dasher. It also offers the concept of throughput, which can be used to compare input methods despite large differences in the conditions in which they can be used.

Similarly, despite its rigor and power, control theory has played a relatively minor role in HCI research. The theory offers a rigorous account of interaction as goal-driven action guided by feedback. It offers precise definitions for several concepts that are central in HCI, including control, feedback, open-loop, and closed-loop. These can be used not only to talk about interaction but also to model it and make verifiable predictions. Control theory can also be used to develop computational models that can drive interactive system behavior, for example, scrollers or panners. Nonetheless, control theory applications in HCI have been limited to interaction techniques and input methods. Why is that?

One limiting factor has been the absence of adequate (computational) models of perception. Most real-world problems do not allow direct access to control or feedback variables; both humans and computers must perceive their surroundings and make inferences about each other. To model problems as control problems, we need to model both the human's and the computer's perception of the world. Another limiting factor is that the control models used in technical domains (e.g., PID) are not good models of human supervisory control. However, the most critical shortcoming may have been the inability of (regular) control models to deal with complex task structures. Most interactive tasks involve delayed gratification; in other words, several actions must be taken to reach the goal state. We return to this challenge in Chapter 21.

Summary

- Information theory provides a formal account of interaction as the passing of messages over a noisy channel. This perspective can be utilized whenever we know the alphabet (vocabulary), the intended message or its distribution, and the received message. The theory offers several metrics that are useful for characterizing and controlling input methods.
- Control theory provides a formal account of interaction as the changing of some signal toward a desired state based on feedback. It offers a way to mathematically model the complex relationships between control actions and feedback.
- Both theories have been successful in the area of input methods but have had limited uses beyond that. One main limitation has been posed by challenges in modeling control and feedback outside of simple perceptual and motor tasks.

Exercises

1. Entropy and perplexity of alphabets. Consider the source alphabet $\Omega = \{A = \frac{1}{4}, B = \frac{1}{4}, C = \frac{1}{4}, D = \frac{1}{4}\}$. Calculate the entropy and perplexity of this source alphabet. How many bits would an optimal coding scheme require on average to encode this source alphabet?
2. Throughput. Use an online application to measure your throughput in a pointing task (Google "measure Fitts' law online"). Consider how the following changes might affect your throughput: (a) limiting performance to larger targets; (b) assisting pointing with an interaction technique (Chapter 26); (c) doing the task after sleeping poorly; and (d) doing the task with your non-dominant hand.

3. Dasher. Dasher never took off despite drawing significant theoretical interest. Why?
4. Focused and casual interaction. Consider commanding your audio system to play a particular song. What might interaction look like when it is (a) focused, (b) intermediate, and (c) casual?
5. Open-loop versus closed-loop interaction. List three cases of open-loop interaction in HCI and propose ways to transform them into closed-loop interaction.

18
Dialogue

Interaction may be viewed as a dialogue, that is, a conversation that occurs between two partners in a context for some purpose. This view draws on what we know about human–human communication and, in particular, how conversations are structured; see Chapter 9 for a summary. In human–computer interaction (HCI), the communication partners are an interactive system and the user of such a system. HCI researchers have developed a rich palette of theories to understand such dialogues. These theories explain what happens in dialogue and how it shapes the relationship between the partners. These theories also have implications for how we design interaction.

The dialogue view of interaction evolved early in the history of computing. From the 1960s to the 1980s, rapid advances in computer displays made it possible to present much richer information to users. This made it possible to structure interaction in the form of a dialogue, freeing the user from having to memorize commands, as required in command-based interfaces. Initially, text consoles were used to provide access to programs running on mainframe computers. These programs had very limited means for interaction—basically, just a text display and a keyboard. Simple menu-based dialogues evolved into control programs based on some form of dialogue. Later, and before touchscreens, multifunction displays allowed for assigning physical buttons to the options presented on a graphical display. The display could show both text and graphical objects associated with each option. However, the response options were limited to a small number determined by the number of physical buttons. Nevertheless, this advancement enabled dialogue where the user would select an option by pressing the button corresponding to the desired option shown on the display. Since the 1980s, graphical displays and speech-based interfaces have made it possible to extend dialogues to offer virtually any number of options in any state. The dialogue view remains important, for instance for prompting (see Paper Example 18.0.1)

The key idea in the dialogue view of interaction is the *organization of communication as a series of turns*. Dialogue evolves through communication turns between two or more partners. In one turn, an appropriate communication act is made by one partner based on the communication context. The act aims to get the other partner to do or understand something. This understanding then forms the context within which the other partner takes their turn.

This broad definition has several immediate and important consequences for HCI. First, dialogue, as a form of interaction, is not limited to speech and language even though this is often our first interpretation of the term "dialogue." In Figure 18.1, two nominally different types of interaction are shown: speech-based and graphical. Both are forms of dialogue. This means that *the concepts of dialogue are applicable across modalities*. For instance, the seven-stage model of interaction proposed by Norman [600] applies to all modalities of interaction; Section 18.1 explains this model in detail.

Second, both dialogues in Figure 18.1 evolve in a turn-based manner. Each turn redefines the communication context. Siri's reply and the selection of "compose" would make no sense without the context provided by the preceding exchange. In other words, in dialogue, acts of communication are *conditional*: The meaning of a turn depends on the communication context. Consider the

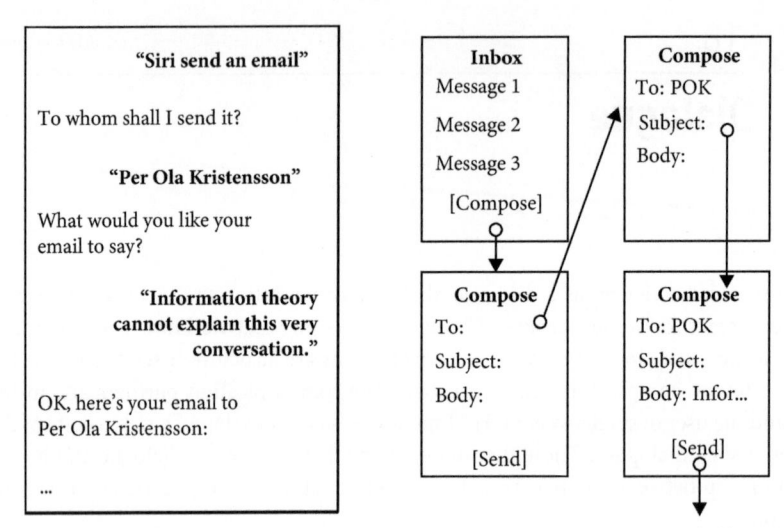

Figure 18.1 Two examples of dialogue-based interaction: speech-based dialogue (left) and graphical dialogue (right). Dialogue, as a form of interaction, is not limited to verbal communication.

dialogue to the left in Figure 18.1. The second utterance by the user (Per Ola Kristensson) would make no sense without the preceding exchange, which determined the context: sending a message and defining to whom to send it. Context, as we will see, can be understood through the concept of a *state*: The feasible communication acts and their effects are conditioned by the state of the partner. We will define the concept of state more precisely in Section 18.2.

Third, in dialogue, both the computer and the human participate in establishing a *shared* context. The computer does not simply receive a message; it also communicates the effects of that message. Therefore, the design of feedback, affordances, and cues is central to dialogue-based interaction. However, establishing and maintaining a shared context requires an intimate understanding of the situation and the contingencies that shape it. Section 18.3 outlines a view of dialogue developed by Suchman [804] that emphasizes the situated nature of dialogue.

Fourth, both the computer and the user may have *initiative*. For example, a pop-up window can be presented to confirm a risky selection. When there is a misunderstanding about the context of the dialogue, errors may happen, and the partners must recover from them. In interaction with interactive systems based on artificial intelligence, mixed-initiative dialogue is crucial. We discuss mixed-initiative interfaces in Section 18.4.

Dialogue is a particular view of interaction. It differs from the view of interaction as information and control (Chapter 17). In that view, a message is conveyed over a noisy, limited-capacity channel to the receiver. Interaction is understood as the success at the receiver's end in inferring the right symbols—the intended message. Note also that not all interaction is dialogue. For example, entering text on a physical keyboard is not considered dialogue. The symbols on the keyboard stay more or less the same throughout the task. Aside from the message to be typed, there is no need for the user to update a representation about the state of the computer. Next, we discuss the main views on dialogue in HCI.

Paper Example 18.0.1: Prompting large language models

The view of dialogue as a model of interaction, which is as old as the field of HCI, continues to be relevant. New ways of interacting that rely on dialogue keep emerging; at the time of writing this book (early 2020s), large language models such as ChatGPT and Google Bard are making the headlines daily. The interaction with such models is primarily done through text prompts to which the model replies.

Liu and Chilton [488] noted that interaction with such models faces a dilemma. While it is possible to input anything as a prompt to such models, users must "engage in brute-force trial and error with the text prompt when the result quality is poor." The challenge here is sometimes described as *prompt engineering*—the search for prompts that give the output the user finds adequate for the task. In short, it is about improving the dialogue between the user, who issues prompts, and the system that outputs results based on the prompts.

Liu and Chilton [488] studied prompt engineering for text-to-image generation; see the figure in this paper example box, which shows examples of answers to the prompt "SUBJECT in the style of STYLE." Across five studies, they generated responses to different prompts and evaluated how well the results matched the subject and style. In addition, they carefully evaluated when the prompts were particularly successful and when they failed.

The results of the studies show that a small set of responses (3–9) may be sufficient to generate an idea of what a prompt can do; the computation of more responses might just waste time. The results also show that the SUBJECT would sometimes get lost in the STYLE; some prompts inadvertently led to grotesque or inappropriate images. The studies shed light on some of the difficulties of having a dialogue with a large language model.

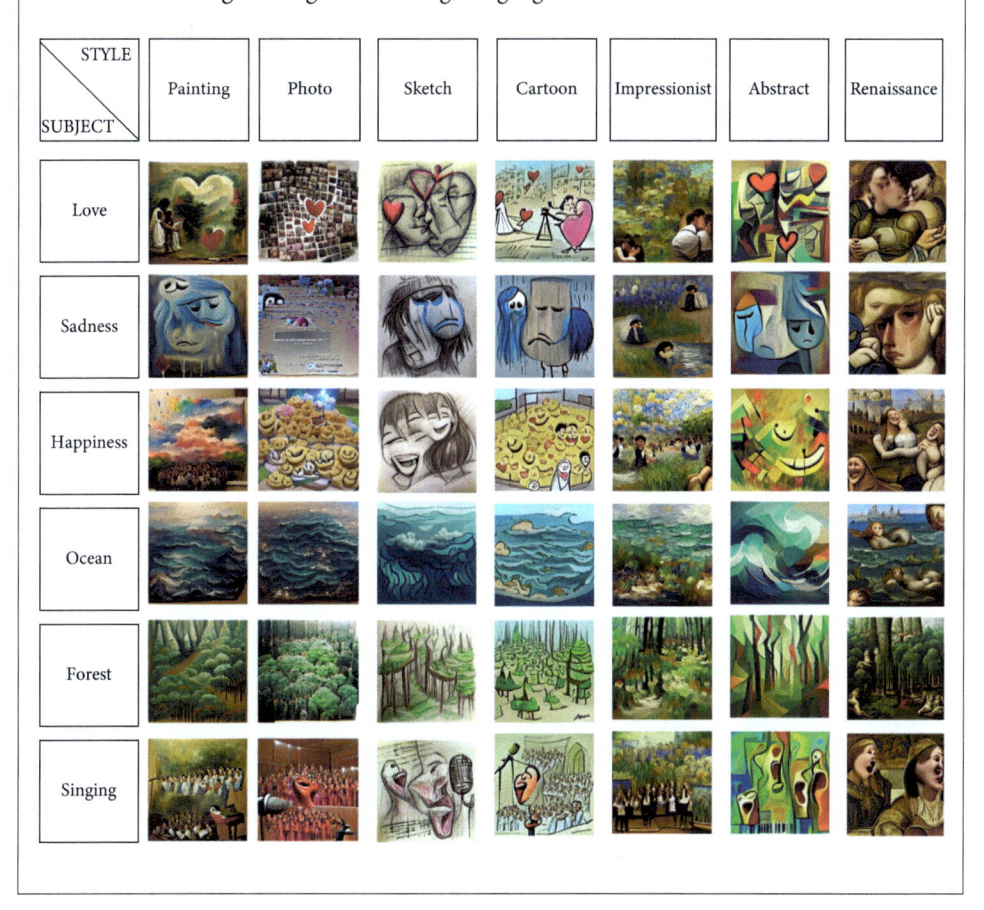

18.1 Dialogue as goal-directed action

A significant early theory of dialogue interaction is the *seven-stage model* of Norman [600]. It considers interaction as goal-directed, turn-based dialogue. The model illustrates the seven stages of a communication turn (Figure 18.2). The stages are presented linearly, with each stage's output serving as input to the next stage. In the first stage, the user formulates a goal, such as "get money from the ATM" or "put images in the presentation on a line." The next stage is planning the actions to achieve that goal, that is, forming the intention of some action. It could be "give card to ATM" or "indicate the images to be aligned." Note that the user needs to know that the action is possible with the system. Next, the user specifies what actions they want to do, for instance, "insert card into slot" or "select all images." The user then needs to execute those actions, such as inserting their card into the ATM or clicking in a particular manner to select all images.

After this stage, the user aims to determine what changes they have made to the environment, for example, whether the ATM has accepted their card or the images have been highlighted. Then, the user needs to interpret the stage, that is, they need to make sense of what they have perceived ("Why are images highlighted?"). Finally, the user needs to evaluate whether what has happened constitutes progress toward their goal, that is, whether the feedback or lack thereof has brought them closer to what they want.

The model subscribes to a theoretical assumption about dialogue: The defining cognitive challenge in dialogue is understanding the communication partner such that the appropriate next turn can be taken. In other words, the dialogue is *intentional* or goal-directed: Users aim to drive the computer to a particular desired state. However, because of known limitations of human cognition, users cannot do this perfectly. They need to engage in (1) planning (deciding what to do) and (2) inference (interpreting the computer's state).

Norman offered two central concepts to help us understand these cognitive efforts: the *gulf of execution* and the *gulf of evaluation* (Figure 18.2). These two concepts describe inferential breakpoints for users seeking to express their intentions and interpret feedback from the system, respectively.

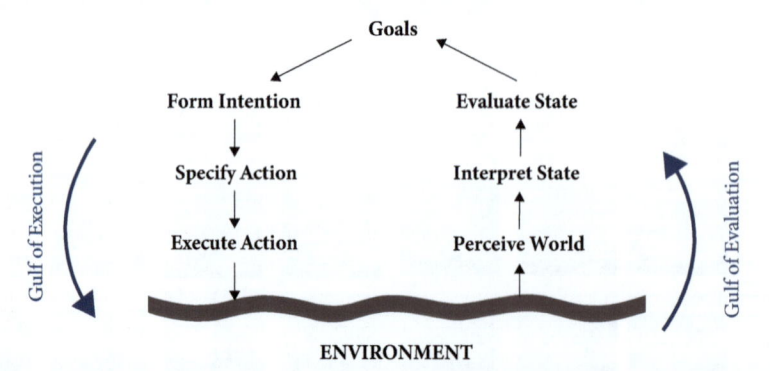

Figure 18.2 Donald Norman's seven-stage model views dialogue-based interaction through the lens of inference: The main challenge is to understand the state of the computer to plan actions to take it to the desired end state. The left-hand side of the model, from goal to environment, is called the gulf of execution. The right-hand side, from environment to goal, is called the gulf of evaluation.

Gulf of execution: This gulf is about knowing what to do to bring about a desired state change in the computer. For example, what should you do to get a piece of text copied to the clipboard and pasted in a specific location?

Gulf of evaluation: This gulf refers to knowing how a perceived change in the computer has moved it closer to the intended goal state. For example, imagine setting the temperature of an intelligent thermostat and not perceiving an immediate effect. How can you tell if your command had the desired effect on the system?

Norman's model inspired a decade of research on interface evaluation and design. In evaluation, which we discuss in Chapter 41, the model is part of the theoretical foundation that underpins the cognitive walkthrough. Norman's model stresses the need for users' acts to be understood by the computer and for users to understand the computer. Successful interfaces should also "provide a strong sense of understanding and control" [600, p. 49]. Paper example 18.1.1 contains an example of using the model.

Mapping and *feedback* are crucial concepts for understanding a computer's turn. Mapping requires the user to figure out how to accomplish a goal with an interface. It implies that "The user must translate the psychological goals and intentions into the desired system state, then determine what settings of the control mechanisms will yield that state, and then determine what physical manipulations of the mechanism are required" [600, p. 37]. Norman suggested that the ease of mapping is related to its directness, "where directness can be measured by the complexity of the relationship between representation and value, measured by the length of the description of the mapping" [600, pp. 28–29].

Affordance, which we discussed in Chapter 3, refers to how well users can interpret what actions are possible with a widget. *Visibility* is a handy related concept in design that underlies direct manipulation interfaces [416]. In direct manipulation interfaces (Chapter 28), the visual presentation of an object resembles its physical correspondent and can be directly acted on. For example, text in a text editor can be highlighted, deleted, or changed by point-and-click-style interactions. If a piece of text is selected, it is highlighted, which implies that actions can be performed on it. In this way, the user does not have to memorize the actions that are possible in a given state. Visibility can also concern the consequences of actions, such as when a progress bar shows the proportion of actions still needed to complete an installation.

The application of these and other concepts has also exposed some shortcomings in this approach to model interaction as goal-directed dialogue. The modelling subscribes to a linear account of the cognitive mechanism, going from goals to actions and back. However, according to current understanding in cognitive sciences, the picture is more complicated. One thing that is missing is an account of how beliefs about the computer are formed and updated and how they drive action specification. The current understanding is that users form internal models that predict how their actions produce perceived outputs, and they learn to minimize prediction errors. This explains why people explore interfaces (to develop better internal models) and why, eventually, they no longer need to compare outcomes against goals. Moreover, the model was initially used in a weak, heuristic sense and did not converge with efforts to implement interactive systems. This changed when formal models of dialogue were introduced, although these models do not cover all perceptual and cognitive aspects of dialogue.

> **Paper Example 18.1.1: Applying Norman's model of dialogue to the evaluation of service robots**
>
> Service robots are intended to assist or automate tasks in human activities, such as robots that serve food to customers or pick up orders in a warehouse. Designing interaction with service robots is challenging because of the limited means of communicating with a robot. Norman's model of dialogue helps to explain this. The model distinguishes between two "gulfs": the gulf of evaluation and the gulf of execution. According to Scholtz [745], the two gulfs manifest differently in the different roles a user may have when interacting with a robot:
>
> **Supervisor:** In the supervisor role, the user monitors and controls the robot. This calls for continuous evaluation of the robot—in other words, the gulf of evaluation. "What is the robot intending to do?" If the supervising user wants to intervene, the gulf of evaluation becomes relevant.
>
> **Operator:** In the operator role, the user modifies the robot's internal models to express what behavior is desirable and what behavior is not. In this role, the user must work with the gulf of execution to define which actions are suitable for the long-term goal of the robot.
>
> **Peer:** In the peer role, the user acts like a peer, demonstrating goals to the robot and only intervening if needed. "Don't do it like that, do it like this." This role is similar to the supervisor role in the sense that both gulfs are important. The user both demonstrates correct behaviors (execution) and monitors the robot (evaluation).
>
> **Bystander:** In the bystander role, the user can only intervene if the robot does something dangerous, for example, by walking in front of the robot to stop it. Here, the user deals with the gulf of evaluation: "What is the robot doing—is it potentially dangerous?"

18.2 Dialogue as state-based interaction

Dialogue can be described using models of computation from computer science. Such models include finite state machines (FSMs), pushdown automata, and Petri nets. These models can be expressed with formal languages, including context-free grammars and graphs, and they can be implemented in event handlers in user interface (UI) software. We discuss some of these applications in the chapter on software engineering for UIs (Chapter 38); here, we focus on their applications for understanding dialogue.

Formal models of computation are suitable for describing discrete, moded dialogues. A *mode* refers to the variation in the interpretation of a user's input according to an internal state. In a modeless dialogue, all inputs are possible in all states and their interpretation is always the same. To understand modes and how dialogues can be captured using such a simple concept, we look at the theory of FSMs.

An FSM is a model of discrete computation applicable to dialogues. In computer science, an FSM is a special case of a Turing machine that reads but does not write on the tape. Formally, an FSM is a tuple $(\Sigma, S, s_0, \delta, F)$, where:

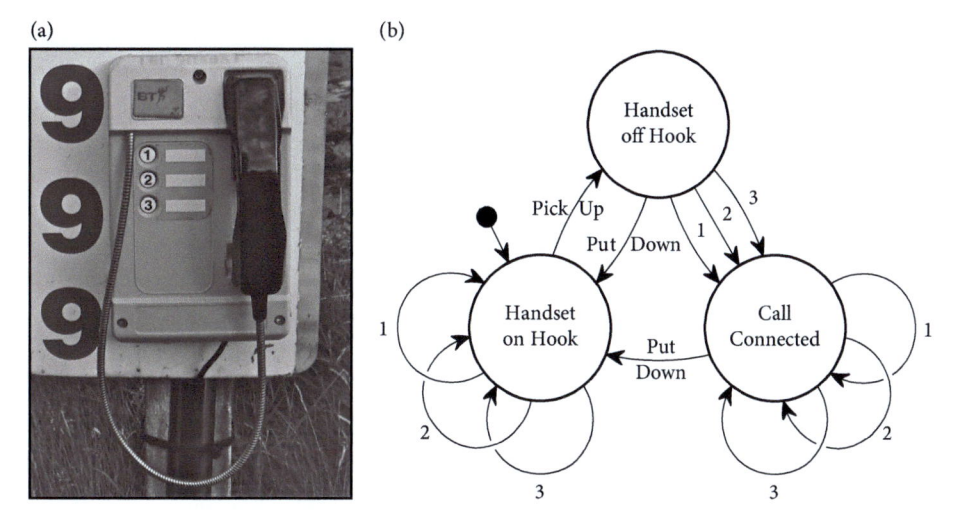

Figure 18.3 The picture on the left, (a), shows a UK coast guard phone meant for the public to make emergency calls. To make a call, there are three options: 1, 2, and 3. This is to save manufacturing costs. The diagram on the right, (b) shows the dialogue design as a FSM [120].

- Σ is the input, that is, a finite set of symbols;
- S is a finite set of states or modes;
- $s_0 \in S$ is the initial state;
- δ is the state transition function $\delta : S \times \Sigma \rightarrow S$;
- F is the set of final states, that is, a subset of S.

An FSM can be graphically presented as a graph where nodes represent states and edges represent transitions. Transitions are inputs by the user. States are modes that accept input designed by the transition function. FSMs are an effective way to describe how dialogue is structured; however, they are limited to memory-free dialogue.

A dialogue, as an FSM, is a sequence of input–state pairs from an initial state s_0 leading to a final state $f \in F$. An example is given in Figure 18.3. The figure shows a model of a telephone booth with three buttons and a handset that can be picked up and put down. This model helps us think through the states of the design. What, for example, should happen when the call is connected and the user presses a button again?

FSMs, as formal accounts of dialogue, are limited to transitions in a dialogue. They do not make assumptions about the way options or feedback are presented to the user. The same FSM could be implemented as an interface in multiple ways. FSMs do not make explicit assumptions about the user, either: FSMs are mute about how users perceive, reason, learn, and experience.

Despite their limitations, formal models offer several benefits as accounts of human–computer dialogues. One benefit is that formal descriptions of dialogues can be parsed interactively and used to operate a dialogue interface. They also aid design and engineering by highlighting desirable properties of a dialogue system [5]. For example, given a FSM, you can compute metrics for:

- **Consistency:** Are the same actions available, and do they have the same consequences across similar states? This can be computed, for example, by enumerating states that are similar and checking if available actions and their consequences are identical.
- **Dialogue length:** How many turns are needed to get from the initial state to the end state? In general, the fewer turns, the better. The duration of the dialogue is the average distance from the initial state to the final state.
- **Number of choices:** The number of options available to the user is a predictor of choice reaction time (Chapter 4). The choices are calculated by the number of edges leaving a state.
- **Error recovery cost:** If an error is made, how many turns are needed to recover from it? The fewer, the better.
- **Connectedness:** Can final states be reached from all initial states?
- **Strong connectedness:** Can final states be reached from all initial states via a particular action?
- **Reversibility:** Can the effect of a given action be reversed in one action?

Looking at Figure 18.3, we find the FSM does not have perfect consistency: Not all actions are available in all states. When the handset is on the hook, pressing any of the numbers is possible but has no effect. However, some actions are reversible: The state can be reset by hooking up the handset. Analyses like this have guided the design of dialogues for interfaces in safety-critical domains, such as the medical domain. However, analyses based on formal models such as FSMs only provide the formal structure of a dialogue, which may not be predictive of a user's typical experience. For example, whether an FSM is reversible does not determine the success or failure of a task.

18.3 Dialogue from a communication perspective

Communication between humans and computers is a long-standing topic of HCI research.[1] A cornerstone of this research is the book *Plans and Situated Action: The Problem of Human–Machine Communication* by Suchman [804].

Human–machine interaction, according to Suchman, is similar to but different from human–human dialogue. It is similar in the sense that people pursue a shared understanding: They actively work to make themselves understood. It is different in the sense that the communication abilities of computers are limited, which requires humans to adapt. Specifically, users adapt their approaches to match the capabilities of the machine rather than the other way around. For example, users may repeat utterances, increase the volume, or use simpler grammar and simpler words.

According to Suchman, robustness is a key consideration in the design of dialogue. Robustness refers to the communication partners' ability to achieve shared understanding even in light of misunderstandings and other unanticipated troubles. For example, when you visit a country whose language you do not speak, you still manage basic communication via gestures, facial expressions, and relying on context. Even if communication is less effective, it is relatively robust. Suchman argued that this is hard to achieve for computers, which rely on pattern recognition and cannot

---

[1] Not to be confused with the theory of communication proposed by Shannon, which we discuss in Chapter 17.

reframe communications as flexibly as humans. For example, when you talk with a human partner, you can always try to say the same thing using different words to correct a misunderstanding. Computer dialogues often do not offer that option.

What does the communication perspective add to our understanding of dialogue interaction? Research has drawn from linguistics, especially pragmatics, to understand how the way we talk with computers changes depending on the communication context. *Communication repair* refers to the "work of restoring shared understanding" when conversational partners misunderstand each other [60]. The partner who is talking needs to say something differently because the other partner did not understand what was said.

Code-switching refers to a switch in language to match the capabilities of the communication partner. For example, you likely use different language when talking with friends and with family. Code-switching can be analyzed linguistically from transcripts by looking at the meaning (semantics) or structure (syntax) of language. Such differences are important because depending on the communication context, people will have different expectations and styles they use in dialogue with a computer. Code-switching can be used for repair; it can also streamline communication and make it more robust.

Generally, repair strategies show sensitivity to the partner's actual or assumed communication abilities. A wealth of repair techniques has been identified, including clarification prompts such as "huh?" or "what?" In Paper Example 18.3.1, we discuss findings from a study of repair strategies with a digital home assistant.

Paper Example 18.3.1: Communication breakdowns in family conversations with Alexa

The introduction of speech-based assistance, such as Siri and Alexa, has increased expectations about the conversational capabilities of intelligent systems. However, how good are they really? A research group at the University of Washington [60] recruited 10 families and recorded their communications with Amazon Echo Dot (Alexa) for four weeks. Their focus was on *communication breakdowns*, that is, communications that failed to achieve the communicative purpose and must be recovered from in order to continue communication. The study looked at what types of communication breakdowns occurred and how communications were repaired by the families.

Their study exposed the limited nature of contemporary speech interaction from a conversational perspective. Although breakdowns were not that frequent—one occurred every four hours of use—they disrupted regular use and often required joint effort to overcome. The study found that families continuously modified their language to repair communications. For example, they changed prosody:

> Alexa ... what is ... the ... temperature? [each individual word pronounced slowly and clearly instead of in a conversational manner]

They also raised their voices, like when talking with a human partner who does not listen:

> Alexa stop.
> Alexa stop! [louder]

continued

> **Paper Example 18.3.1: Communication breakdowns in family conversations with Alexa** (continued)
>
> The families also exaggerated articulation, a phenomenon known as hyperarticulation. The paradoxical effect of hyperarticulation is that despite trying to improve understanding, it can make speech recognition worse. The families also modified their use of words and their sentence structures and even provided definitions to Alexa. Additionally, more experienced users guided less experienced users on how to speak to Alexa. In the excerpt below, a mother encourages a five-year-old to ask a question and guides them in pronouncing the word "Alexa":
>
> (MOTHER): It's A (pause) lexa. (emphasis on the last two syllables)
>
> (CHILD): Uh (slight pause) leh (pause) ska. Is it going to rain for a little bit or is it going to be sunny for a little bit (said quickly and quietly), (pause) or both. (no rising intonation at the end to indicate a question)
> (pause and no response from Alexa)
>
> (RESEARCHER): That was a good question but it might have been a little too long, too many questions I heard.
>
> (MOTHER): Let's see. (pause) Alexa, is it going to be rainy all day or sunny all day or ... (recording cut off)
> (recording resumes with child giggling)
>
> (MOTHER): Alexa, what did I ask you?
>
> (ALEXA): Sorry, I'm not sure. (everyone laughs)
>
> (MOTHER): Alexa, I asked if it was going to rain all day.
>
> (ALEXA): Probably not. Each day of the next seven days ... has at most a 30% chance of rain. (child laughs)

18.4 Mixed-initiative interaction

Mixed-initiative interaction is the idea of organizing interaction in dialogue where both the computer and the human can take initiative. Unlike in the case of an FSM, the computing system can take action without a command from the user; the initiative is mixed.

As an example of such an interface, consider an email interface that automatically analyzes incoming emails. Such a system can infer whether an email is about scheduling a meeting and suggest or automatically invoke a calendar to assist the user in achieving this goal. This is possible if the system can accurately infer the user's goal and assess the costs and benefits of providing an automated action or suggestion. Even if the system fails to trigger a calendar, the user can initiate this action at any point by clicking on the appropriate icon.

A mixed-initiative interface needs to infer the user's goals so that it can act upon them. Several machine learning techniques are potentially suitable depending on the specific AI problem. Once the system has inferred the user's goals, it needs to decide what action to take. One option is to take no action. To guide the decision on what automated action to take, the system can calculate the expected utility of each outcome for the user. Such utility can then be used as a threshold to only trigger an automated action if the estimated utility is sufficiently high. In practice, this is often hard because of the *poverty of cues* that the computer has access to. It may, for example, not have access to our gestural or facial expressions.

It is also possible to ask the user about their goal; whether to ask such a question can also be estimated by calculating its expected utility for the user. When an automated action is taken, it is important to consider the timing, as incorrectly timed automated actions can distract the user. It is sometimes possible to build models to time automated actions, for example, by estimating the time it takes a user to read an email. Generally, it is beneficial when mixed-initiative interfaces learn and adapt to individual users.

Horvitz [360] summarized the principles of mixed-initiative interfaces as follows:

Developing significant value-added automation: Only automate if a direct manipulation solution will be inferior. Identifying such opportunities may require user research and empirical evaluation.

Considering uncertainty about a user's goals: Systems should consider the uncertainty of users' actions and behaviors and incorporate such uncertainty into their automation mechanisms. For example, if the user says "home" to an intelligent assistant, does the user want to go to the home screen, view their actual home, or what? If there is ambiguity about what the user wants and wrong automation might harm the user, the system should ask for more information or not carry out the command.

Considering the status of a user's attention in the timing of services: Systems should be mindful of users' attention and the timing when invoking automated services. Systems should leverage such understanding when deciding on the costs and benefits of deferring actions to more beneficial times. This is particularly important in safety-critical domains such as driving.

Inferring ideal action in light of costs, benefits, and uncertainties: Systems should take into account the expected value of taking automated actions, given the costs, benefits, and uncertainties associated with context-specific decisions. For example, consider location-based recommendations presented to drivers. Information about a nearby cheap gas station (benefit) should be deferred until its potential effect on driving (cost) is minimal and there is little uncertainty about its value to the driver.

Employing dialogue to resolve key uncertainties: If the system is uncertain about the user's intent, the system should ask the user after having considered the cost of interrupting the user. While ambiguities can be resolved via dialogue, this principle warns against always asking the user: Every interaction bears a cost (e.g., time and effort) that should be factored in when deciding whether and when to engage in dialogue.

Allowing efficient direct invocation and termination: Since the system will be unlikely to always automate functions successfully, it is important that users can directly trigger and terminate functions. This means the status of automation should be made visible to the user. Opaque automation is stressful and prone to errors.

Minimizing the cost of poor guesses about action and timing: System-triggered alerts and suggestions should be designed such that if they are inaccurate or poorly timed, the cost of interruption of the user is minimized. This can be achieved, for example, by making suggestions less distracting, using natural timeouts if there is no user response, and supporting swift user actions to dismiss suggestions.

Scoping precision of service to match uncertainty, variation in goals: It may be beneficial to dynamically adjust the use of systems. If a system operates under a high uncertainty of the user's goals, the system should perform less automation to avoid interrupting the user with poor suggestions.

Providing mechanisms for efficient agent–user collaboration to refine results: systems should be designed to allow users to refine or complete an analysis initiated by the system. for example, if a robotic vacuum cleaner maps a room autonomously, users should be given an option to edit the map.

Employing socially appropriate behaviors for agent–user interaction: Any interruptions by a system should be compatible with the social expectations of the user being interrupted and offered automated services. For example, social media feeds may integrate AI-generated and human-generated content without disclosing the source. This may break the expectation that all content of social media feeds is generated by other (human) users.

Maintaining working memory of recent interactions: Systems should retain recent interactions and allow the user to refer to prior objects, actions, and services in their interaction with the system. This principle is important for efficient interaction and the coherence of behavior. It allows the system to avoid asking the same questions every time the user is in the same context.

Continuing to learn by observing: Systems should continuously learn and adapt their models of users' goals and needs. Because users' goals and situations change over time, the system is never "ready."

Paper Example 18.4.1: Augmentative and alternative communication for personal narratives

Augmentative and alternative communication (AAC) is a class of interactive communication applications for people with complex communication needs, such as those with little or no functional speech. For example, cerebral palsy (CP) limits the motor system and musculature, hampering articulation and gesturing with hands. Individuals with CP often have sensory and cognitive impairments that negatively affect their language development. AAC applications often use dialogue interfaces. They show graphical symbols representing words or phrases. Users can scan pages of symbols and select symbols to form sentences. Symbols are selected by pointing with a finger or an input device (e.g., a joystick). When the message is ready, the computer speaks out the composed sentence via a speech synthesizer. This process is painstakingly slow, which limits the users' ability to participate in communicative activities and lowers their quality of life.

Human–human communication is streamlined by common ground (Chapter 9); what if computers could have common ground with an AAC user?

The *How was School today. . .?* concept was developed iteratively with two children with CP and the help of school staff. This AAC system was designed to use *context* to facilitate the creation of personal narratives [75]. The authors called their approach "data-to-text": The idea was to add sensors to the environment and the wheelchair of a user. As the user traverses the environment, the locations create *events* that are made available as symbols. For example, when going around in the school, entering a room or meeting a person can create an event.

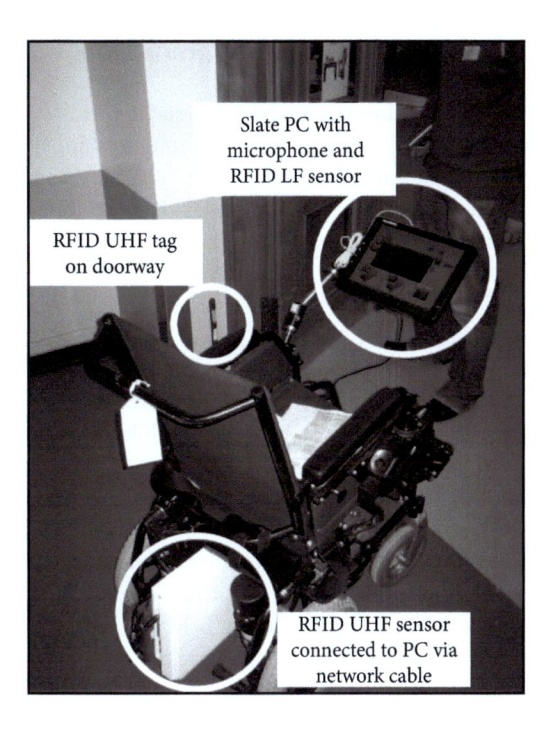

These events can be used to facilitate communication. The *event narration* UI allows the user to select and organize events that took place during the day. The event buttons allow the user to change the order of events. Users can also add annotations and invite the conversational partner to assist in composing the message. For example, if the user selects "Katie was there," the partner may respond "Do you like her?" by selecting the smiley button. The user may then respond "She is nice" or "I don't like her." Users can also express "Do not speak" to skip the discussion topic.

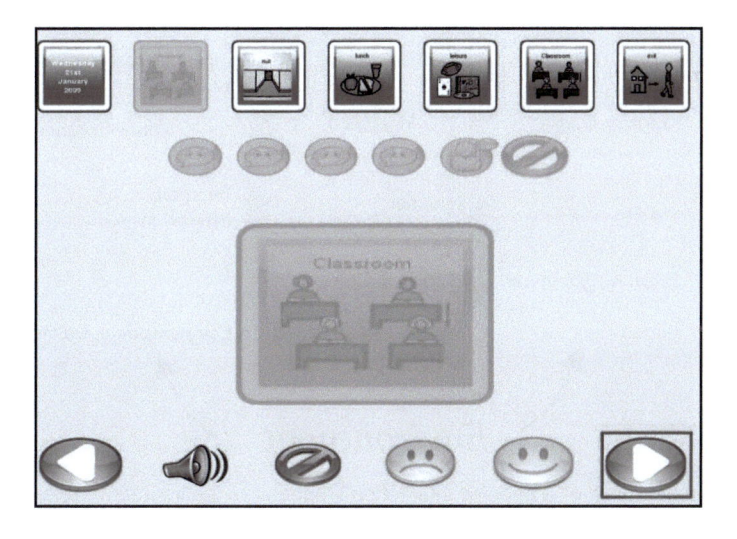

18.5 Limits of turn-taking as a model of interaction

This chapter has presented turn-taking as a model of interaction. However, it is not obvious that this is how dialogue with computers takes place. The cognitive scientist Kirsh presented a criticism of Norman's view of dialogue and developed an alternative based on the theory of embodied cognition [416]. This critique illustrates the limitations of viewing interaction as dialogue.

Kirsh points out that Norman's model makes an unrealistic assumption: The user is assumed to know the environment and its options and is merely picking an option. In practice, we do not always know what the options *mean* or even what options are available. Kirsh argued that users need to actively *explore* interfaces to become aware of the available functions and how they work. Via exploration, they also learn about their own abilities in using them. Consider the first time you launch an application; you probably try out various actions to see what happens. Kirsh argued that the *discoverability* of such options is as important as their visibility; however, discoverability is not covered well by Norman's theory.

Kirsh argued that we are not just passively reacting to computer-generated options. If we look at interaction at a higher level, beyond a single action, we see that users are also actively influencing their environments. Users are "architects" of their environments, as Kirsh put it. For example, users may change the settings to turn on or off a function or change the way it behaves. They also choose the applications they use. Such tailoring behaviors are not explained by Norman's intention–action–response–interpretation–evaluation cycle.

Building on such criticism, Kirsh proposed an alternate model, showing that every stage in Norman's model can have an interactive relationship with the environment. We learn about options by exploring the interface, discover how to specify actions by trying them out and observing the outcomes, position our bodies to better perceive environmental responses, and adjust the environment to facilitate response evaluation. This relationship of dialogue with the environment is depicted in Figure 18.4.

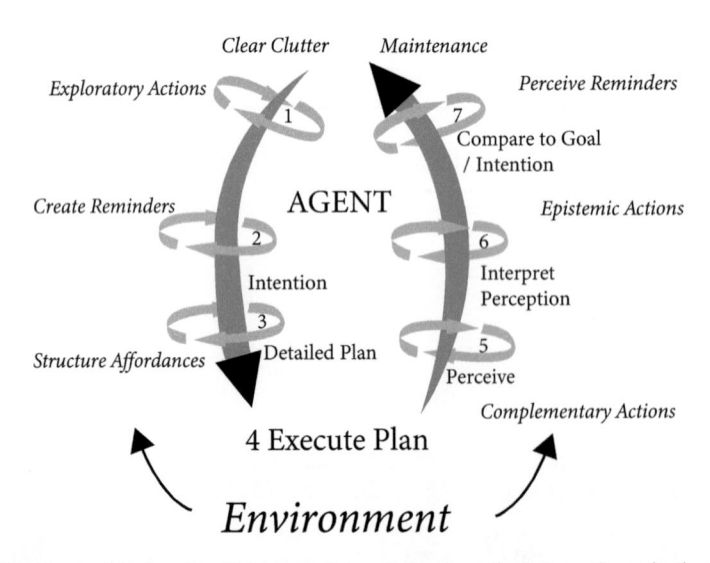

Figure 18.4 Kirsh's model of embodied interaction emphasizes the interactive role that the environment plays in action. We explore our environments to learn what is possible, change the environment to change our options, and position ourselves to better interpret and perceive relevant responses from the environment.

What does this mean for design? A good design allows users to try out options without penalizing trials. It allows them to customize and personalize the interface based on individual abilities. It presents not only options but also their consequences to the user. This serves to nuance the understanding of interaction as dialogue.

Summary

- Dialogue is about the organization of communication as a series of turns between communication partners.
- The core elements of dialogue are communication turns, the communication context, and turn interpretation.
- Dialogue interaction includes speech-based and graphical interactions.
- Dialogue can be understood as computation, goal-directed action, communication, or embodied action. Each perspective provides specific methods for the analysis and design of dialogue.

Exercises

1. **Core concepts of dialogue interaction.** Dialogue offers a rich conceptual framework for understanding interaction. First, choose an everyday interaction with which you are familiar. It can be anything from filling out a form to chatting with a chatbot. Then, choose a particular dialogue to focus on, for example, creating a user account or printing a document. Now, provide the following information for the dialogue:
   - **Communication partners**: Who are the actors in the dialogue?
   - **Communication goals**: What is the final state the computer should be in for the user to consider the task completed?
   - **Communication act**: What are the possible communication acts? In other words, what are the possible utterances or messages that can be delivered?
   - **Communication sequence**: Draw a sequence of the communication turns leading to the goal, similar to Figure 18.1.
   - **Initiative**: To which degree can each partner initiate communication on their own?
   - **Cue**: Which cues are shown to help the user understand the state of the computer?
   - **Feedback**: Which cues are shown to help the user understand the effects of their communication acts?
2. **Theories of human–computer dialogue.** Consider the following potential dialogue interfaces: (a) a user interacting with an automated chat agent from an airline to resolve a delayed flight; (b) a child uploading homework using a web interface; and (c) a user who is trying to show a picture on their mobile phone on a nearby television screen. Make any necessary assumptions about the interfaces and discuss which model of dialogue would provide the most insight for each interface: (a) FSMs, (b) dialogue as goal-directed action, (c) dialogue as embodied action, or (d) dialogue from a communication perspective.
3. **Gulfs.** Pick a graphical user interface, for example, something you use for education. Then, choose a task, for example, "sending a message to the teacher." Assess this task through the lens of Norman's two gulfs: the gulf of evaluation and the gulf of execution.

4. Mixed-initiative interfaces. Pick any AI-assisted feature that you are familiar with. Assess it against Horvitz's principles of mixed-initiative interfaces.
5. Comparing mode-based interactions. A device is designed to allow users to control the relative humidity in their house. The device has two modes. In Automatic mode, the system keeps the relative humidity in the 50%–60% range. In the Manual mode, the user can set the desired level of relative humidity and the system will attempt to maintain it. The device is a small wall-mounted unit with the following UI elements. (a) The visual display indicates the current level of relative humidity and whether the system is in Automatic or Manual mode. (b) The "–" and "+" buttons enable the user to reduce or increase the desired level of relative humidity, respectively. (c) The "Automatic" button puts the system in Automatic mode. If the user pushes the "–" or "+" button, the system switches to Manual mode and remains in that mode until the user pushes the "Automatic" button. (a) Draw a state diagram for this system. (b) By viewing interaction with this system as goal-directed action, explain the steps comprising the gulf of evaluation and the gulf of execution for this UI. (c) State the type and level of automation of this system. (d) Is this system a mixed-initiative interface? Justify your answer.

19
Tool use

Humans use tools routinely and have done so for millennia. Such tools include axes, pens, plows, and pots. What makes these objects tools is that they are not attached to the body but can be held to bring about changes in the condition of other objects [772]. By extension, the idea of *tool use* in human–computer interaction (HCI) is that a computer system is a tool for *controlling something else*. According to this view, a user using a system to accomplish a task is not markedly different from a person using a hammer to drive nails or an algebraic rule to do calculations in one's head.

The computer, when viewed as a tool, is manipulated by users. Their goal is to do something that goes beyond the interface to effect some desired change in the world. By using this tool, users extend their capabilities.

In essence, tool use is about manipulating technology to achieve some aim that goes beyond the tool itself. Some researchers have taken the view of interaction as tool use at face value. For instance, Beaudouin-Lafon [53] departed from the idea that the manipulation of physical objects with our hands can be used as the basis for designing new user interfaces. He separated domain objects that are manipulated from interaction instruments, which are computer artifacts that manipulate domain objects. For example, a scrollbar is an interaction instrument, or tool, that operates on documents. Further analysis reveals it has low integration because a 1D action is controlled by a 2D mouse, and it has low compatibility in some designs because the content moves in a different direction from the movement of the scrollbar.

More broadly, the view of interaction as a tool suggests three essential components: problems, tools, and people (Figure 19.1). Several models of tool use capture these components [e.g., 135, 448, 465, 582].

This simple view can be used to derive several principles that are central to HCI. First, understanding computers as tools emphasizes the *utility* of a tool, by which we mean how well it supports what people want to do. Second, tools may be more or less easy to manipulate when used. This is called *usability*. These three aspects are interrelated. All these models emphasize that tools influence the tasks we do and how we do them. At the same time, the tools influence us. They change how we think, what we consider easy, how we express ourselves, and how we work together. This is orthogonal to utility: A tool may be useful but difficult to operate, while another tool may offer trivial value but be easy to operate. This was captured in the 1980s by Golden [280, p. 4]: "it is perfectly possible to have a program which is structured, modular, readable, flexible, self-documenting, maintainable, which performs its specified function, and which is a source of constant frustration and irritation to its users." Tools may also be more or less *accessible* to their users. And finally, tools may be more or less acceptable to their users.

These theoretical concepts have informed some key insights in HCI research, which we review in this chapter and in the chapter on practice (Chapter 22):

1. Usability is one of the best predictors of users' willingness to adopt software. For example, the User Burden Scale is a questionnaire for measuring the felt burden in software use [806]. It consists of six subscales: difficulty of use, physical burden, time and social burden, mental

Introduction to Human-Computer Interaction. Kasper Hornbæk, Per Ola Kristensson, and Antti Oulasvirta, Oxford University Press. © Kasper Hornbæk, Per Ola Kristensson, and Antti Oulasvirta (2025).
DOI: 10.1093/oso/9780192864543.003.0019

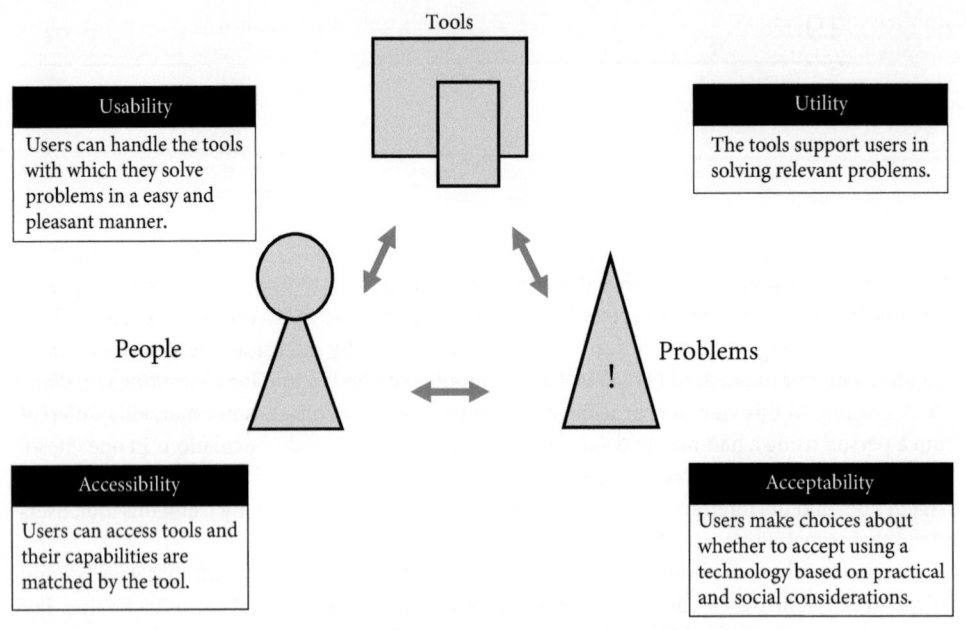

Usability
Users can handle the tools with which they solve problems in a easy and pleasant manner.

Utility
The tools support users in solving relevant problems.

Accessibility
Users can access tools and their capabilities are matched by the tool.

Acceptability
Users make choices about whether to accept using a technology based on practical and social considerations.

Figure 19.1 Three key components and four central considerations in tool use.

and emotional burden, privacy burden, and financial burden. Suh et al. [806] showed that software that is abandoned is associated with worse measures in all metrics except time and social burden. In other words, ease of use is an important consideration when people decide to abandon software.

2. Utility centers what users want from technology. For example, Koelle et al. [426] studied the adoption of data glasses (e.g., Google Glass, Meta Pro) over multiple years. They asked experts familiar with data glasses what would need to be improved to make data glasses more acceptable. Usefulness, functionality, and usability were the most important factors—more important than security, privacy, pricing, experience, and compatibility.

3. Users actively repurpose tools to make them more personally usable and relevant. Design should support such repurposing. For example, Renom et al. [696] conducted a study on text editing using a novel user interface. They found that exploration and technical reasoning facilitate creative tool use. Users who explore available commands in a tool are better at repurposing its functionality. More surprisingly, engaging in technical reasoning (reasoning about functionality and objects) supports repurposing more than procedural knowledge inherited from other software.

Next, we discuss these concepts and their associated measures and design implications.

19.1 Utility

The *utility* of an interactive system concerns its match with the tasks of users. If the match is good, the tool has high utility; if the tasks that users want to do are not supported by the tool, the tool has low utility. The tasks that users want to do using a tool may be existing tasks or some new tasks they have not yet realized. Users may realize their wants only when using a system, which makes the prediction of utility inherently hard. Moreover, even routine users of software may not be able to articulate the utility they gain from it.

Utility is about the relationship between functionality and users' needs and wants. It can be assessed in different ways. One way is through surveys of the perceived utility [180]. Such surveys may ask users whether a tool would "enable them to do their tasks more quickly" or "improve their job performance." Other researchers have developed criteria for assessing utility [386]. For them, utility can be ensured by checking that systems are "available on a wide range of devices and media along with integration of other resources" and "robust on basic functionality important functionality."

Grudin [300] noted that utility has typically been a key concern of research on information systems. For decades, systems have been developed in-house or contracted, and at the time of Grudin's analysis, their use was typically mandated. Hence, the question of utility in information system research has been prominent. However, many interactive systems depend on users experiencing them as easy to use and with few barriers. As such, there is a contrast between *getting the right design* and *getting the design right* [290]. The former is about utility; the latter is about usability. One shorthand way of expressing this is that utility is "whether the functionality of a system in principle can do what is needed" [591, p. 25]. In practice, whether people can do anything concerns—among other things—usability.

19.2 Usability

Some tools are easy to operate. It is clear what they can do, it is easy to learn to use them, and they may be safely used. For computer-based tools, these considerations are described by the term *usability*, one of the key empirically measurable constructs that the field of HCI has developed.

Usability concerns how easily computer-based tools may be operated by users trying to accomplish a task. Usability differs from utility. Usability concerns whether users can use the product in a way that makes it possible to realize its utility; utility is about whether the goal is important to the user. Ideally, the user can use the tool without unnecessary effort so that the use is direct, transparent, and unnoticeable.

Research on usability has been ongoing since the 1970s, departing from research in human factors and early notions of user-friendliness and ease of use. Since then, various ways of thinking about usability have emerged [332, 757]. The current way of defining usability is captured in the ISO 9241-11 definition, based on work by Bevan [68] and many others, which defines usability as the "extent to which a system, product or service can be used by specified users to achieve specified goals with effectiveness, efficiency and satisfaction in a specified context of use."

19.2.1 Characteristics of usability

Research on usability has uncovered several key principles and insights. One insight is that *usability is relational*; it arises as an interplay between people, tasks (problems), and interactive systems (tools); see Figure 19.1. Both the ISO definition and the introduction to this chapter make this clear: Tools are usable as a consequence of their fit to people and tasks. For this reason, usability is sometimes called *quality-of-use* to emphasize that it is a quality of interactive systems, like maintainability and reliability. However, usability emerges only when people actually use tools to achieve their goals. Because of this, it makes no sense to talk about the usability of an interactive system without considering the users and their tasks. It also does not make sense to talk about usability as a property of interactive systems. A system may be usable for some tasks and less usable for others; it may be usable for some users but not for others. In any case, usability is not a property of the interactive system.

Another key insight is that *usability is measurable*, that is, it is possible to quantify usability based on users' behaviors or opinions. We may evaluate usability as part of iterating the design of an interactive system. We may also use this insight to articulate what requirements a design should fulfill. For instance, Whiteside et al. [886] showed how to make explicit quantitative goals for usability. They provided an example of the usability of software installation. This was quantified through the time it takes to install software. This could take one hour or, in the best case, just 10 minutes. These numbers may be stated upfront and tested later on. We may also use usability measures to experimentally quantify differences between user interfaces. We may measure the time used and errors made by a user while solving a problem with different tools and then compare the results (more on experimental comparisons in Chapter 43).

Earlier work has also shown that *usability is multidimensional*. This means that in most settings, a valid characterization of usability will need to employ several dimensions and measures. This is typically found in studies where multiple aspects of usability are measured and modest correlations are found. For instance, Nielsen and Levy [592] compared users' performance and their preferences across 57 studies and found what they called a strong positive correlation. Nevertheless, they concluded that "there are still many cases in which users prefer systems that are measurably worse for them, so one should exercise caution" [p. 75]. Later studies explored this finding in different ways, generally found some correlation, and cautioned against treating usability as a one-dimensional construct [261, 356, 733]. Thus, one should typically pick multiple indicators of usability and assume that different aspects of usability (e.g., subjective and objective measures, performance, and outcomes) should be measured separately.

19.2.2 Models of usability

The characteristics described in Section 19.1.1 have led to numerous *models of usability*, dimensions of usability, and indicators or measures of those dimensions [e.g., 591, 757]. These models can help us identify some dimensions of usability that are independent. In other words, they capture different aspects of usability. These models also help us pick measures for evaluating usability and bring structure and rigor to our everyday understanding of ease of use. The quest to spell out the dimensions of usability has been going on for decades, so summarizing and integrating this work is difficult. Nevertheless, two models of usability are particularly useful.

One is the ISO 9241-11 model of usability. It defines usability as comprising effectiveness, efficiency, and satisfaction. Table 19.1 shows the definition of these dimensions as well as examples of how they may be measured. Another model for thinking about usability is that of Nielsen [591], which identifies five dimensions of usability (also in Table 19.1).

19.2.3 How to select goals for measuring usability?

Given these and other models of usability, an important question remains: How does one select or prioritize between dimensions and measures for a particular case? For instance, is the time it takes to complete a task always a good indicator of usability and one that we should seek to minimize? Is effectiveness always more important than satisfaction, or is it the other way around? In practice,

Table 19.1 Two models of usability, based on ISO 9241 and Nielsen [591], including their dimensions, definitions, and examples of how they may be measured.

Model	Dimension	Definition	Example measures
ISO	Effectiveness	The accuracy and completeness with which users achieve goals	Binary task completion, error rates, quality of outcome
	Efficiency	The resources spent by users to achieve goals	Task completion time, input rate, mental effort, learning
	Satisfaction	The users' comfort with and positive attitudes toward the use of the system	Preference, perception of ease of use, willingness to recommend to others
Nielsen	Easy to learn	The user should be able to rapidly start getting work done with the system	Self-reported learning effort, number of hours required to achieve a minimum level of proficiency
	Efficient to use	The highest level of productivity that proficient users can achieve	Task completion time and efficacy in representative tasks
	Easy to remember	Users should be able to return to a system without needing to relearn how it works	Times a manual or help is needed, change in user performance after a period of non-use
	Few errors	Users should be able to operate a system with as few errors as possible	Number of erroneous or hazardous actions
	Subjectively pleasing	Users should find the system pleasant to use	Questionnaire-based metrics (see chapters 7 and 13)

the selection of usability measures requires careful judgment—it is a matter of determining the importance and validity of parameters.

The validity of a measure concerns whether it measures what it is supposed to measure, in particular whether it is an accurate and complete indicator of the usability of an interactive system. Validity will be discussed in more detail in Chapter 43.

Newman and Taylor [587] presented a concrete approach to selecting usability measures, which they called selecting *critical parameters*, that is, "performance parameters that measure how well the system serves its purpose." The critical parameters of a system are those parameters that allow designers and evaluators to establish whether an interactive system serves its purpose and compare designs.

The categories of "satisfaction" in the ISO model and "subjectively pleasing" in Nielsen's model both refer to the experience of using a tool to accomplish a task. Rather than looking at the total experience, such as expectations, memories, and general affect, satisfaction has historically been understood as more narrowly concerned with the experience of using a tool to accomplish a task.

Numerous validated questionnaires for measuring satisfaction are available. They are typically administered to users after they have used an interactive system; the answers are summed or otherwise combined to form an indicator of satisfaction. Some questionnaires aim to measure the full satisfaction with a system. Paper Example 19.2.1 shows one of the most popular questionnaires for doing this: the System Usability Scale (SUS). It gives a satisfaction rating between one and 100 for an interactive system. Questionnaires with different levels of breadth exist for satisfaction:

- The questionnaire for user interface satisfaction [150] originally consisted of 90 questions but often only five questions are used. The items are rated on nine-point semantic differentials going from terrible to wonderful, from frustrating to satisfying, from inadequate power to adequate power, from dull to stimulating, and from rigid to flexible.
- Some questionnaires are very short to facilitate quick answers. The UMUX-Lite consists of just two items, "This system's capabilities meet my requirements" and "This system is easy to use," each answered on a seven-point scale.
- The subjective mental effort questionnaire (SMEQ) rating scale consists of just one question answered with a graphical scale.

The aforementioned questionnaires cover satisfaction in general. In addition, numerous specialized questionnaires have been developed to explore different dimensions of satisfaction. For instance, Suh and colleagues [805] developed a questionnaire for user burden.

Paper Example 19.2.1: System Usability Scale (SUS)

In the mid-1980s, the SUS was developed [97]. While other questionnaires for satisfaction were developed around the same time, SUS has become one of the most widely used scales for measuring the users' perception of usability.

SUS was developed to be relatively quick to use and freely available. Users should answer the questions reported below immediately after using the interactive system being assessed. The SUS consists of 10 questions answered on a Likert scale (from "strongly disagree" to "strongly agree," coded from 1 to 5):

1. I think that I would like to use this system frequently.
2. I found the system unnecessarily complex.
3. I thought the system was easy to use.
4. I think that I would need the support of a technical person to be able to use this system.
5. I found the various functions in this system were well integrated.
6. I thought there was too much inconsistency in this system.
7. I would imagine that most people would learn to use this system very quickly.
8. I found the system very awkward to use (changed from the original "cumbersome," as recommended by Bangor et al. [39]).
9. I felt very confident using the system.
10. I needed to learn a lot of things before I could get going with this system.

The answers to these questions are summed to calculate the overall SUS score. For odd-numbered items, subtract 1 from each score (1–5); for even-numbered items, subtract each score from 5. Then, sum these values to obtain the total SUS score. Brooke stressed to only use and interpret the summed score, not the answers to the individual questions. The summed score is indicative of the level of satisfaction with the interactive system and may be compared to the scores of other versions of the system as well as those of other systems.

Research has shown that SUS can discriminate between systems with poor and good usability, can be used with a range of technologies, correlates modestly with task performance, correlates well with other questionnaires, and has good reliability [39, 96].

19.3 Acceptability

People may choose to use a particular tool or something else to solve a task, or they may give up solving the task. These possibilities are related to the *acceptability* of the tool, that is, whether users choose to use the tool when given that option. HCI researchers have worked on understanding what factors shape acceptability; designers aim to create interfaces that users accept.

Acceptability has two main dimensions [591]. The first dimension, *practical acceptability*, includes costs, the reliability of the interactive system, and its compatibility with other systems. The perceptions of utility and usability may also influence the judgment of practical acceptability. This follows the model of inference about experiences outlined in Chapter 7.

The second dimension, *social acceptability*, concerns whether interactions map well to the social norms and roles in the settings where they occur. Koelle et al. [427] surveyed approaches to social acceptability and found indicators such as "disturbing," "inappropriate," "creepy," and "impolite." These indicators suggested that users, or indirect users such as onlookers, did not find an interaction socially appropriate. For example, social acceptability was an important consideration for early smart glasses, that is, eyewear with computational capabilities, particularly models fitted with cameras [426].

Acceptability includes the choice to *not* use a system. The studies of non-use in HCI suggest some processes and reasons why a useful, accessible, and usable interactive system may not be used by the intended user group. Such considerations include bias and accessibility.

19.3.1 Technology acceptance model

The most common way of working with acceptance is the technology acceptance model (TAM). Underlying TAM is the theory of reasoned action. Davis [180] proposed that whether an individual ends up using a system, that is, their *usage behavior*, depends on their *intention to use* the system. However, what affects the intention to use? TAM answers this question.

TAM posits that the intention to adopt a particular technology is driven by two kinds of perceptions: (1) how easy it is to use a system and (2) how useful it will be to use it [180]. Furthermore, the perceived ease of use affects the perceived usefulness: If technology is hard to use, it is less useful.

Since the 1980s, many studies have empirically validated TAM and extended it to include indicators of social norms, the availability of support, and other factors. From the HCI viewpoint, TAM has a number of strengths and limitations [355]. It says very little about interaction, which in the end is the basis of the two critical types of perception. It also has very few nontrivial

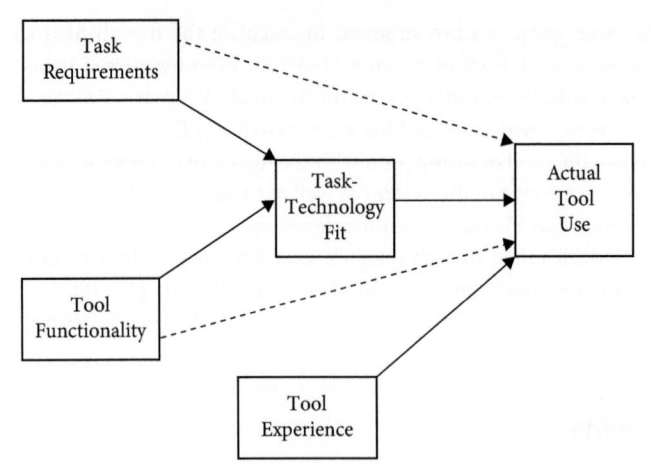

Figure 19.2 Task–technology fit refers to how well technology supports the task demands and individual capabilities of the user [197].

implications for design. While it may indicate which aspect of tool use is more important—utility or usability—it does not indicate *what* makes a system useful or usable.

19.3.2 Task–technology fit

The theory of *task–technology fit* (TTF) can illuminate what users consider useful and how this affects their decision to adopt a particular technology. TTF refers to the ability of technology to support a task [197]. The capabilities of the technology should match the demands of the task and the skills of the individual; in this case, the fit is perfect. TTF theory posits that a rational user will choose the tool with the highest fit due to its efficacy and efficiency. Conversely, a system that does not offer a good fit will not be used.

TTF has been modeled with several statistical models, including the one shown in Figure 19.2. The goal of the model is to predict a user's willingness to use a tool, which is affected by the user's experience with the tool and by the fit. The fit is affected by two key factors, task requirements and tool functionality, which must match to have a high fit. A TTF model may include a component for individual abilities, the *tool experience* component, to account for the fact that prior experience with computers can positively affect utilization.

TTF has been used to assess users' willingness to use various technologies such as email or spreadsheets. However, such models have been criticized for assuming that users are rational. Like TAM, these models tend to dismiss "irrational" factors that affect acceptance, such as one's attitude.

19.4 Accessibility

While an interactive system may offer utility and usability, it may only offer these to a limited group of people. In HCI, we typically want products to be usable by as many users and in as many diverse situations as possible; in other words, we want high *accessibility*.

One prominent definition of accessibility is given by ISO 9241-171, which defines it as "the usability of a product, service, environment or facility by people with the widest range of capabilities." Accessibility is also referred to as universal design, universal usability, or inclusive design. These terms reflect similar ambitions, insights, and methods.

In this way, accessibility concerns the match between a user's abilities and the system's required abilities. As such, it differs from usability (which is about the relationship between users, tools, and tasks) and utility (which is about whether a tool may be used to complete a task). Thus, if one wants an interactive system to be usable by all major demographic groups, one should also be concerned with accessibility rather than only usability.

There is a range of communities with accessibility issues. A comprehensive literature survey of accessibility research in HCI [500] identified the following groups: (1) blind or low-vision, (2) deaf or hard of hearing, (3) autism, (4) intellectual or development disability, (5) motor or physical impairment, (6) cognitive impairment, (7) older adult, (8) general disability or accessibility, and (9) other. However, each user manifests these factors at different degrees and in different combinations.

This is a key challenge in accessibility research: There are many disabilities, and solutions that work for one community or a particular disability may not work for others. Users may also have multiple disabilities, resulting in more or stricter design requirements. Aging is sometimes grouped with disabilities, as in the above list, even though it is not a disability. A discourse analysis of over 600 HCI research papers [856] found that aging is typically framed as a "problem" that can be managed by technology, a stance that has been framed as a form of ageism in critical gerontology.

There are many reasons for designing accessible interactive systems. Perhaps the foremost argument is that it is the right, ethical thing to do. A second reason is the large group of users affected by one or more disabilities. According to the World Health Organization, over one billion people have some form of disability.[1] A third reason is that it is a legal requirement in many jurisdictions to ensure interactive computer systems and services are accessible to a wide range of users with different disabilities. Finally, a fourth reason is that considering accessibility throughout can result in an improved design for all. The so-called curb-cut argument is an example of this. Cutting the curb and providing a ramp for approaching the pavement does not only benefit people with motor disabilities; this design benefits anyone with a situational impairment, such as a person with luggage. This thinking is sometimes referred to as "universal design" or "design for all."

19.4.1 Designing accessible interfaces

A large survey on disability research in HCI [500] identified three main strands of research: (1) increasing access to digital tools by offering users new forms of technology; (2) understanding users' needs, preferences, and abilities; and (3) increasing access to the physical world.

In practice, a significant proportion of HCI research is focused on arriving at technological solutions and designs for specific problems. Several approaches to accessibility design and research have emerged. One is ability-based design [906], which involves adopting a design stance in which a design is specifically tailored to the end-users' needs and abilities. Ability-based design thus requires a deep understanding of the target groups. Various practices, such as co-design, are often used to involve representative users of the target audience in the design process.

---

[1] https://www.who.int/en/news-room/fact-sheets/detail/disability-and-health.

Another approach is inclusive design, which is a design method for ensuring products and services are usable by a very wide spectrum of users. Inclusive design is process-oriented and adopts, modifies, and extends several product design processes originating in engineering design. It advocates the use of specific methods and toolkits to achieve inclusivity, such as the inclusive design toolkit. An important aspect of inclusive design is obtaining accurate statistics on relevant characteristics of the user population. These parameters (e.g., grasping strength) are then fed into various toolkits used by designers to ensure a wide range of users with varying abilities can be accommodated. To effectively assess the target audience, it is vital to sample representative individuals and user groups. This is challenging because it requires knowledge of which user groups must be sampled and in what proportion as well as the ability to reach user groups that may be difficult to reach.

Inclusive design is desirable because, when consistently applied, it ensures many widely used products and services can be used by as many people as possible. At the same time, there is often a limit to how broad a range of users a product or service can be designed to accommodate. For example, augmentative and alternative communication (AAC) is concerned with supporting nonspeaking individuals with motor disabilities. AAC users rely on speech-generating devices (SGDs) to communicate with other people. For example, amyotrophic lateral sclerosis and cerebral palsy patients may be AAC users.

19.4.2 Designing speech-generating devices

SGDs vary depending on the needs and wants of the user. An illiterate AAC user typically relies on a symbol- or picture-based interface. A literate AAC user enters letters, words, and sentences that are then communicated using speech synthesis. As AAC users rely on their SGDs, many aspects of this speech output are important, such as the tone and accent of the speech synthesis voice. For literate AAC users, many text entry mechanisms are available, such as physical keyboards and touchscreen keyboards. These ordinary keyboards are usually coupled with word, phrase, and sentence prediction tools intended to increase the text entry rate.

Other SGDs use interfaces based on a single switch. These interfaces may be used when a user is unable to use a physical keyboard or a touchscreen keyboard. An example of such a switch is an eyebrow switch, which activates when the user activates the muscles in the vicinity of the eyebrow. To use such a switch for typing, the SGD interface must be designed with this in mind from the beginning. The most common solution is a scanning keyboard. A scanning keyboard presents all letters in the alphabet along with some ancillary punctuation symbols, such as period and question mark, on a grid. The system begins by highlighting each row in turn. If the user activates the switch, the row is selected. The system then highlights each letter in the row. The letter that is highlighted when the user activates the switch is selected.

Activating the switch is cumbersome and error-prone. In addition, the user must wait for the desired item to be highlighted, meaning the entry rate is low. For this reason, scanning systems are often augmented with some form of word prediction system. It is also possible to optimize the scanning pattern to minimize the average waiting time for a designed selection. Regardless, false activation is a significant problem with single-switch systems.

Another SGD variant relies on eye tracking, which may be suitable for users who have no effective means of interaction beyond eye control. The typical communication solution uses a technique known as eye-typing. To communicate using eye-typing, the user moves their gaze across an onscreen keyboard. However, the system does not know whether the user wants to type a key or is merely looking at a key. This is known as the Midas touch problem. To disambiguate these two possible user intentions, eye-typing relies on a dwell timeout. If the user fixates on a key for a sufficiently long time, the system assumes the user means to type that key. Typically, this dwell timeout is shown visually to the user to both indicate the timeout and to draw the user's visual attention during the timeout.

Eye-typing is an effective means of communication; however, it is not efficient. Three fundamental problems prevent high entry rates. First, the eyes are sensory organs and not control organs. It is difficult for users to artificially maintain fixation on specific keys. Second, the dwell timeout provides a low ceiling on performance. Third, people think in terms of words, phrases, and sentences when they communicate. Eye-typing forces users to think in terms of individual letters. This has a cognitive cost and is not a fluid means of communication. Many of these considerations also apply to single-switch systems.

Eye-typing has been improved over time. Commercial eye-typing products rely on word and phrase suggestions to improve the entry rate. Another solution is to use dwell-free eye-typing, which removes dwell timeouts. To achieve this, the system uses a statistical decoder to translate observations of the user's gaze into hypotheses of what the user wishes to write. Dwell-free eye-typing has been released as part of a commercial eye-typing product but has so far not seen widespread adoption.

These examples illustrate some of the challenges that accessibility poses to design and highlight the need for thorough user research.

Paper Example 19.4.1: Generating user interfaces based on user's abilities

Supple++ [266] is a computational method developed in HCI that can improve graphical user interfaces to better fit a user's unique motor and vision abilities. In Supple++, the user is first asked to perform a series of motor tasks. This information is used to calibrate an internal computational model of the user's motor ability. Once the calibration is complete, Supple++ optimizes the user interface automatically by changing the size and location of user interface elements and the organization of the user interface, subject to constraints specified by the designer.

This constraint-based optimization allows for changing the user interface according to individual abilities without losing important qualities of a well-functioning user interface, such as consistency and clear organization. For example, a user who can make rapid but imprecise movements is provided with a user interface with large user interface elements that are farther apart. By contrast, a user who can only make slow but precise movements is provided with an interface in which user interface elements are smaller and closer together.

Figures 19.3 and 19.4 show examples of automatically generated interfaces based on individual abilities. Figure 19.3 shows an interface for a user with muscular dystrophy who relies on the mouse to make selections. Figure 19.4 shows an interface for an eye-tracker user. Note that these interfaces did not just change icon sizes and locations; they also changed the user interface organization to best accommodate their respective users.

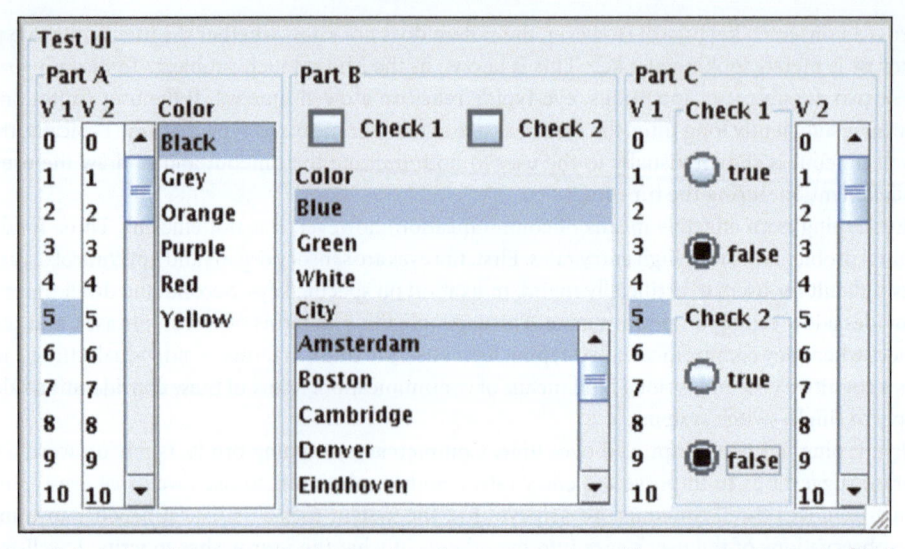

Figure 19.3 An interface generated by Supple++ for a mouse user with muscular dystrophy [266].

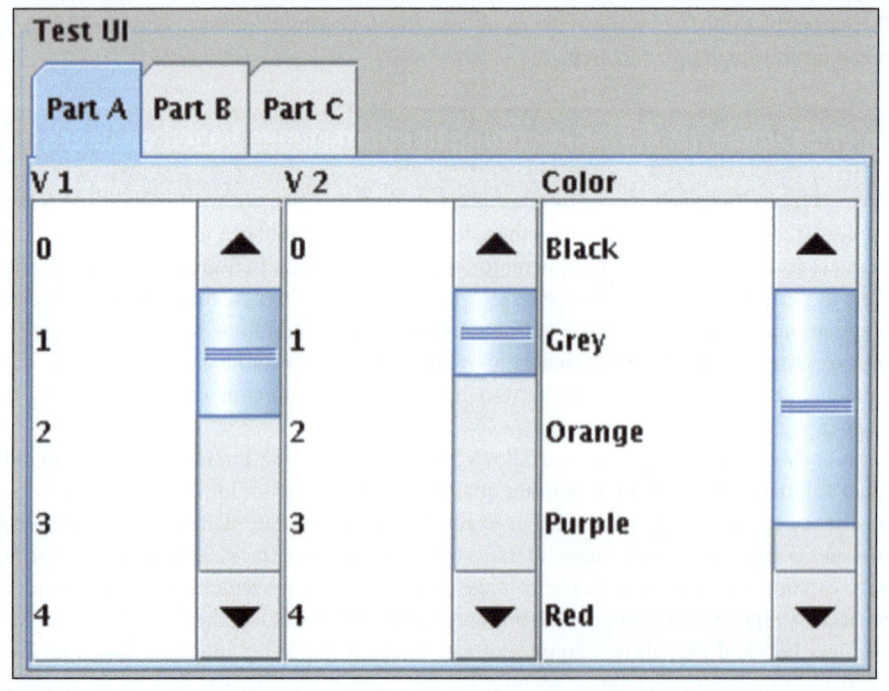

Figure 19.4 An interface generated by Supple++ for an eye-tracker user [266].

19.5 Tools change how we think and perceive

Using a tool for extended periods can fundamentally change the way a user thinks and perceives both the tool and the world. First, using a tool for an extended period can result in the *cognitive integration* of the tool. Cognitive integration means that we internalize the operation of the tool.

We not only act but also start thinking as defined by the unique constraints and mechanisms of the tool.

What is such integration based on? Tversky and Jamalian [833] proposed that embodied action is at the core of this. We move our bodies and toss, push, and pull objects. These movements can be thought about, imagined, and referred to in language. This, in turn, can change the substrate of thinking. For example, the expression "on the one hand, on the other hand" is based on our experience of hands.

Tversky and Jamalian demonstrated this claim in a clever experiment. People listened to descriptions of events in three conditions: circular gestures, linear gestures, and no gestures. Then, they were asked to draw a diagram of the event. The authors were interested in *how* they depicted the event. They found that after listening to the descriptions with linear gestures or no gestures, participants mostly drew linear diagrams, following the narrative structure of the descriptions. However, after listening to the descriptions with circular gestures, they predominantly drew cyclical diagrams. Thus, gestures affected the way participants constructed mental representations of the events.

Many tools we use, both digital and physical, are based on movement; by extension, they may change the way we think and reason. For example, the abacus is a wooden device used for teaching basic calculations. It consists of a frame with rows of wires along which beads can slide. Students who learned to do calculations with an abacus solve mathematical problems differently from others [796]. They rely more on mental imagery of the movement of beads on the abacus, which makes their mental calculations highly efficient for certain types of calculations.

The second influence from using tools, is that it may change the way *we perceive the world*. The tool itself may become "transparent" and we start perceiving "through it." In philosophy, a tool is argued to be "ready-at-hand." The tool itself is forgotten, and we construct percepts of the environment mediated by it.

Blind cane users are a good example [756]. When blind users learn to sense the environment with a cane, their perception of tactile and auditory stimuli slowly changes. Instead of sensing stimuli close to their hand, when they hold the cane, they can integrate tactile (vibration) and auditory stimuli close to the tip of the cane. They develop multimodal, integrated percepts that correspond to the tip of the cane. This was demonstrated in an experimental study where blind and sighted users were asked to react to auditory and tactile stimuli either close to their hand or farther away in the environment. Blind participants were faster in reacting to stimuli close to their hands when holding a short cane. When holding a longer cane, they were better at reacting to far sounds than to near sounds. Interestingly, when sighted users spent just 10 minutes practicing with a cane, their peripersonal space also expanded. However, when the tool was taken away, it contracted back. Learning tool-mediated multimodal integration requires time.

The cognitive integration and perceptual influence of tools are not without problems. While a tool can enhance performance in cognitively challenging tasks, its extended use may erode the cognitive capability of the user. Galletta et al. [267] warned against the effect of spell checkers on verbal ability. Having a spell checker in a word processing program may make users overly rely on the tool even if it makes several mistakes, both false positives and false negatives. The authors showed experimentally that university students who had a spell checker on during a document editing task had more errors left in the document than those who did not. Even though the spell checker only fixed the most obvious errors, having it on made users overly dependent on it.

Navigation aids are another case in point. Before mobile maps and navigation aids, we did not routinely consult maps when navigating in cities. When navigating in a city without a map, our brains actively represent and reason about our whereabouts. We use at least three kinds of neural representations: place cells, which encode locations; head-direction cells, which represent the direction of our field-of-view; and grid cells, which position the world in a coordinate-like system with the ability to compute scale and distance. In the era preceding digital navigation aids, to get from Point A to Point B, we needed to form spatial representations before the trip. These representations would get us most of the way, if not all the way. When moving around in a city, we needed to track our position on our mental map. Mobile navigation aids fundamentally changed this. Presently, we can obtain directions for navigation virtually at any time, which decreases the need for spatial cognition.

Does this mean that users who use navigational skills lose their spatial cognitive capabilities? McKinlay argued that spatial skills are "use it or lose it" [533]. However, navigation aids are only part of the picture. We still need to navigate in digital environments like games and hypertext; such activities help us retain our spatial skills. These examples show that viewing interaction as tool use reveals a surprisingly complex influence between people and interactive computing.

Summary

- The use of interactive systems can be viewed as tool use—using a system to achieve a particular objective.
- The fit of a tool describes how well its functionalities match the demands of the task and the capabilities of the user.
- Tools should be accessible to users, provide value in the world, be acceptable, and be usable.
- Tools can profoundly transform the way we act and think.

Exercises

1. Understanding tool use. This chapter has presented the view that computer use is similar to tool use. However, it is not always clear what this view encompasses. Consider whether (a) computer games, (b) visiting online virtual museums, and (c) instant messaging with friends are examples of tool use. If they are not, how should we think about these interactions? If they are, what are their outcomes and how do the principles about tools discussed in this chapter apply to the examples?
2. Concepts. Brainstorm and write down the names of two different systems, apps, web pages, or other types of computer systems. For each, identify what you deem the most important metric of success, taken from measures of usability and user experiences (Consult chapter X for a refresh). Then, consider why you find those metrics important.
3. Usability metrics. Compare the models of usability presented in this chapter: ISO 9241 and Nielsen's model. How do they overlap, and what are their non-overlapping parts?
4. System Usability Scale. Pick up the email application you use on your phone. Then, refamiliarize yourself with it. Then, fill in the SUS questionnaire and calculate the SUS score.

20
Automation

Interactive systems have evolved to increasingly automate work that people used to do. They typically do so by using some kind of AI that takes over part of a task from the user. This can take many forms. For instance, when entering text on a mobile device, language models propose completions of phrases and correct typos. Another example is the use of AI models for calculating insurance fees based on customers' health and other data. Semi-autonomous vehicles can drive parts of a route autonomously. They may need to hand over control to a human driver in parts they cannot handle. Recommender engines are used not only for movies and music but also for creative activities. For example, a recommender engine can propose possible slide layouts to an information worker or poster designs to a graphic designer. The designer can explore the recommendations, pick an interesting one, and use it as the basis for the final design. Large language models are used to summarize long texts and generate images.

An exciting and distinctive aspect of this type of interaction is that users interact with something that may have *agency*. Automation technology is capable of doing things on its own. We call such technology an *agent*, also sometimes called a software agent, intelligent agent, conversational agent, personal digital assistant, or intelligent interactive system. Interaction between users and agents opens up new ways of thinking about interaction. In some instances, an agent may only respond when the user provides input, similar to command-line interfaces and graphical user interfaces. In other scenarios, the agent may be continuously monitoring and analyzing the user's actions and proactively acting to assist the user.

The increasing autonomy of computing systems raises new challenges for human–computer interaction (HCI). The performance of the system must be reliable and controllable. Its behavior should be safe, and the way it is designed and used should be ethical [768]. Users need to trust the system's decisions and ability. It should be made clear to the user what it can and cannot do. For example, a recommender system can tell the user that the user *may* be interested in certain recommendations, thereby indicating the system is not completely certain these recommendations are relevant [19]. When the system fails, users need to be able to redirect it. To avoid biases and discrimination, some level of transparency and explainability is required.

Research in HCI has shown that interaction with partially automated systems is nontrivial (Paper Example 20.0.1 contains a more extended example of the tradeoffs in automation).

- Roy et al. [715] explored what happens when users doing a task with a simulated crane need to choose between further using automation and manually continuing the task. The authors showed that the decision of whether to use automation is affected by the users' perception of its accuracy as well as how easy it is to do the task themselves.
- Long-term engagement with automation has taken place for more than a decade in the home. Brush et al. [105] showed how lighting control, motion detectors, and multi-room audio/video systems were perceived as inflexible, difficult to manage, and difficult to set up securely.

Introduction to Human-Computer Interaction. Kasper Hornbæk, Per Ola Kristensson, and Antti Oulasvirta, Oxford University Press. © Kasper Hornbæk, Per Ola Kristensson, and Antti Oulasvirta (2025).
DOI: 10.1093/oso/9780192864543.003.0020

- Cai et al. [117] interviewed 21 pathologists who used a deep neural network to aid in the diagnosis of prostate cancer. The interviews showed that pathologists needed to learn more about the network's strengths and limitations to use it effectively. They also wanted to know the design objective of the network and the kind of data on which it was trained. This study indicates that automating tasks is only one part of what makes an interactive system work in its intended context.

This chapter discusses interaction with automation and AI. A major role of AI has been and continues to be automation, so we discuss automation first. In HCI, automation poses the foundational problem of *task allocation*: Who does which task or subtask—the system or the user? Moreover, how much should we automate? This raises the question of whether some functions that are difficult for an AI to perform should be allocated to users. However, AI is more than just automation; later in this chapter, we discuss emerging forms of interactive AI and related challenges.

Paper Example 20.0.1: Automation versus direct manipulation

The paper "Direct manipulation vs. interface agents" [770] contains a classic debate between Shneiderman and Maes on the future role of direct manipulation (a technique for graphical user interfaces discussed in Chapter 28) and "software agents"—agents that enable task delegation. The debate serves as a good introduction to some basic questions at the intersection of AI and HCI.

The expressed views and ideas, published in 1997, are still relevant today. Software agents may allow users to achieve their goals in complex environments with limited expertise. For example, a software agent may offload work from the user and offer suggestions without being prompted. Maes noted the benefits of such agents:

- A software agent knows the individual user's habits, preferences, and interests. This is important to help keep up with the increasing complexity of interactive systems and their applications.
- A software agent is proactive. It can serve as an extra pair of eyes or ears for the user, who can delegate tasks to the agent.
- A software agent can be long-lived. It can persist over sessions and systems, further aligning itself with the user's habits and interests.

However, it is still important for users to be in control. Shneiderman argued the following points supporting direct manipulation and powerful tools:

- Direct manipulation allows the user to predict what will happen, explore the system, and feel in charge.
- By showing information to users and letting them filter, select, and focus on interesting information, users get an overview of information and actively control which information to drill down on.
- Human capabilities and responsibilities should not be confused with those of machines. Direct manipulation does not anthropomorphize user interfaces or deskill users.

Later in the debate, both speakers agreed on the importance of allowing users to directly manipulate software agents. This crystallized into mixed-initiative interfaces, which are discussed in Chapter 18. More than 20 years later, a similar discussion was held [869]. This suggests that the uses and trade-offs of automation are a central problem in HCI.

20.1 Human–automation interaction

Automation refers to technology that assists users by performing a task or a subtask on their behalf. It has been defined as "a device or system that accomplishes (partially or fully) a function that was previously, or conceivably could be, carried out (partially or fully) by a human operator" [638]. Throughout the history of automation, a central challenge in HCI has been posed by the complexity of autonomous systems. Users must be able to understand and control them. They need to find and integrate information from dynamic and different sources. They need to understand how to delegate tasks, supervise their execution, and intervene if needed. Perhaps the most significant aspect for HCI is that safe and effective operation critically depends on the user and, therefore, the user interface.

The study of human–automation interaction emerged from the need to develop automation in safety-critical systems. For example, a stock analyst may be monitoring several sources of real-time information on trading algorithms. An operator of a submarine demining vehicle may need to decide whether an underwater mine is present based on noisy detection signals from sonar sensors. An air traffic control (ATC) operator may need to continuously scan several displays showing real-time ATC information and make decisions on which instructions and what information to communicate to pilots and other ATC operators. In all cases, getting the right balance between automation and human control is crucial. This depends, among other things, on how tasks are shared.

20.1.1 Task sharing

A central concern in the design of automation and AI is *task sharing*. For the sharing of tasks to occur, there have to be at least two tasks or subtasks, which can then be shared in two different ways. First, tasks can be *time-shared*, which implies that the user performs multiple tasks. In general, perfect time-sharing with no degradation in performance occurs only for tasks that are automatic, such as speaking while walking. Such tasks can reach *automaticity*. Second, tasks can be shared in terms of *control*, which means that some control over the tasks is assigned to another agent, such as another user or a machine.

There are three dominant theories of time-sharing in human cognition. The first is called the *single channel theory*, which posits that there is limited capacity in the human information processing system in a time-sharing scenario. When the channel capacity is exceeded, multiple tasks transition from parallel processing to serial processing. This theory is contradicted by empirical research showing that a multi-processor model better explains empirical data. The second theory is the *multiple resources model*, which states that resource limitation concerns the entire system rather than a channel (Chapter 5). The third theory is *information processing analysis theory*. If at least one task can be carried out automatically, the other task can be carried out with little or no impact on performance (at an appropriate time–error trade-off point). If both tasks demand controlled processing, then the strategy in processing is split into two mechanisms: facilitation and inhibition. The implementation of such a strategy requires attentional resources, which can lead to task interference when the demand exceeds the available capacity.

Successful time-sharing depends on the strategy and difficulty of the task in terms of temporal constraints—how many tasks are processed in a given interval—and task complexity—the quantity of information that needs to be processed for a given task. In a task-switching situation, the user must activate resources for the second task and inhibit resources for the first task. If the user fails to do so efficiently, performance is reduced, sometimes dramatically.

Another way to share tasks is to *share control*, which is also covered in Chapter 17. There are three principal ways of achieving this type of sharing. First, control can be shared via an *extension* that allows a machine to amplify human ability. An example of such control sharing is power steering in a car: The car provides additional work to allow the driver to turn the wheels with less effort. An HCI example is mouse acceleration, which allows a user to move the cursor on the screen farther than the physical movement of the mouse.

Second, control can be shared via *relief*, which means that the overall burden on the human is reduced by the machine. An example is automatic shift transmission, which relieves the driver of the task of changing gears in a car. An HCI example is text entry using autocomplete, which prevents the user from correcting typing mistakes as they type.

Third, control can be shared via *partitioning*. In this case, a task is decomposed into parts that can be addressed by humans and machines separately. An example of such control sharing is semi-automatic parallel parking, which provides the driver with some braking ability while the machine controls the speed and steering of the car. An HCI example is automatic spell checking, where the system detects and highlights incorrectly spelled words but does not change them. Instead, the user has to take an explicit corrective action, such as selecting a misspelled word and choosing an alternative.

Independently of the chosen strategy, some tasks are to be done by the interactive system and some by the user. The allocation of such tasks is called functional allocation.

Paper Example 20.3.1: Shared control and the H-metaphor

So far in this chapter, we have discussed the case of a single user controlling a computer. What if we have two agents both capable of controlling it? How could we *share* control between them? The question of shared control is timely; semi-autonomous vehicles are only partially autonomous. They need the human to assist them and, therefore, some way of handing control over to the human driver. They also need to have guidance from the driver, for example, on the choice of route.

Shared control is about carrying out a task together with a competent partner [1, p. 511]: "In shared control, human(s) and robot(s) are interacting congruently in a perception–action cycle to perform a dynamic task that either the human or the robot could execute individually under ideal circumstances." What does this mean?

The *H-metaphor* is a metaphor for understanding shared control [246]. Here, the "H" stands for "horse": the horse metaphor. In short, it means that shared control is like riding a horse. The metaphor makes two points about shared control. First, communication is vital for sharing control, and this can happen at different levels; second, both agents must have internal models of each other to understand what those communicative acts mean.

When riding a horse, the rider communicates high-level information (e.g., the goal) to the horse but must be ready to guide the horse at a lower level. When the horse knows what to do, for example, if the route is familiar, the rider may not need to engage in low-level control. This form of control, called *loose rein control*, is possible if the horse knows what the rider wants.

If the horse is not controlling the way the rider wants, the rider must communicate at a lower level to tell the horse what to do. In horseback riding, the subtle movements of the rider's body, such as applying pressure with the legs, guide the horse, just like voice commands ("Whoa!"). This is called *tight rein control*. The horse can also communicate with the rider at all times regardless of the type of control.

The H-metaphor is instructive: When two agents sharing control have asymmetric capabilities, both loose and tight rein control should be available. In this respect, our everyday interfaces appear clumsy when compared to the relationship that an experienced horseback rider and a horse can achieve. Control does not need to be either/or like in many semi-autonomous vehicles. Four levels of shared control can be distinguished [1]: strategic (e.g., setting a destination), tactical (e.g., doing a specific maneuver like merging into a lane), operational (e.g., maintaining a certain distance from another car), and execution (lowest-level of controlling locomotion, steering, and so on).

20.1.2 Task allocation

Task allocation is a central challenge in HCI and automation. Which system functions should be automated, and to what extent should they be automated? There are three main strategies here.

The first strategy is called *maximum automation*. Here, each task that can be automated is allocated to a machine. The aim is to increase efficiency, reduce costs, or both. This is a popular strategy for automation. However, this strategy has two implications that may cause issues. First, by automating everything that can be automated, the user is left with functions that, by definition, the designers find hard, expensive, or difficult to automate. Therefore, this automation strategy defines the roles and responsibilities of users in terms of automation instead of the other way around. The second implication is that as automation approaches its maximum, the role of the human operator becomes increasingly critical. For example, automated errors may remain unchecked until the user intervenes. This latter point, to which we will return later, is referred to as the "irony of automation" [36] in the automation literature.

The second allocation strategy is assigning each function to the most capable agent, which can be either a human or a machine. While this may sound good in theory, it is difficult to successfully implement this strategy in real-world automation problems. When functional allocation was first introduced in the literature, Fitts (whose work we also discussed in Chapter 4) made lists of what people are good at and what interactive systems are good at. These so-called Fitts' lists [242] provide a basis for functional allocation by indicating whom to assign a task (see the exercises at the end of this chapter for an example).

The third allocation strategy is to allocate each function in a way that maximizes economic efficiency. This is a very attractive strategy for many stakeholders. However, it can also be very risky since it requires accurate modeling, which is difficult to achieve in practice.

All three strategies have a common deficiency in that they may not always be able to adhere to the principle of human-centered automation, whereby a human has final control. This is also called the authority problem.

20.1.3 Types and levels of automation

This discussion highlights that simple automation strategies are unlikely to be successful. For this reason, designers can benefit from frameworks that support system design that involves automation. We now discuss one such framework: the *types and levels of automation framework* [639].

The framework uses two sets of evaluation criteria to help designers determine the appropriate type and level of automation for each application. The primary evaluation criteria concern the impact of the chosen types and levels of automation on human performance. The secondary evaluation criteria include automation reliability and the cost of decisions or outcomes.

Levels of automation: The levels of automation range from high automation to low automation. The numerical mapping of automation levels is given in Table 20.1. The table shows that the level of automation ranges from 10, where the computer system is a fully autonomous system that ignores the user, to 1, where the user is in complete control.

Types of automation: The types of automation can be understood by viewing a human operator as a simple four-stage model of human information processing:

1. Sensory processing
2. Perception and working memory
3. Decision-making
4. Response selection.

This four-stage model of human information processing is then mapped to the types of system functions that can be automated (acquisition, analysis, decision, and action), as shown in Table 20.2. In addition, adaptive automation is an emergent type of system function automation that captures a combination of these four types of automation.

Acquisition automation corresponds to the first human information processing stage, sensory processing, and it is realized by the system sensing and registering input data. An example of low-level automation is assistance in sensor adjustment, such as a system mechanically moving a radar sensor to lock on a detected target. An example of moderate automation is a system organizing information according to criteria such as a priority list or highlighting information based on static or dynamic criteria. This could be, for example, a display highlighting the rate of change in some variable of interest. This could be indicated by increasing the intensity of some pixels more rapidly than others in the display.

Table 20.1 The levels of automation and their descriptions, ranging from no automation (1) to complete automation (10) [639].

Level of automation	Description
10	The computer decides everything, acts autonomously, and ignores the human.
9	The computer informs the human only if it decides to do so.
8	The computer informs the human only if asked by the human.
7	The computer executes tasks automatically and informs the human.
6	The computer gives the human a set time to veto a decision before automatic task execution.
5	The computer performs a task automatically if the human approves it.
4	The computer suggests one alternative action.
3	The computer offers a narrowed selection of options.
2	The computer offers a complete set of options.
1	The computer offers no assistance: The human must make all the decisions.

Analysis automation refers to the automation of information analysis and involves inferential processes. It corresponds to the second human information processing state: perception/working memory. An example of low-level automation is the extrapolation or prediction of data over time, such as a system predicting a trend for the output of an industrial plant based on historical sensor data. An example of moderate- to high-level automation is a system integrating multiple sources or input variables. This could be a display with emergent perceptual features, such as an optical see-through display with a landing strip intended to assist a pilot in landing an aircraft. An example of high-level automation is a context-dependent summary of data.

Decision automation means deciding and selecting appropriate actions among alternatives. This type of automation corresponds to the third human information processing state, decision-making, which the machine is either augmenting or replacing altogether. Examples of decision automation include route planning and adaptation, such as to avoid bad weather, and systems providing medical diagnosis support. The difference between analysis automation—inference—and decision automation is that in the latter the system must make implicit or explicit assumptions about costs and values inherent in all decisions. The levels of automation reported in Table 20.1 represent the various levels of automation that can be applied to decision automation. For example, using decision automation to avoid aircraft ground collisions may be level 4 automation: A decision is recommended, but the pilot can choose to ignore it. As another example, an automated ground collision avoidance system could be levels 5–8 automation: The system can assume control if the pilot fails to act. The specific level depends on whether the system gives the pilot some time to act and the conditions for informing the pilot (Table 20.1).

Action automation means the machine is partially or fully executing an action choice. There are many levels of machine execution, such as automating human manual actuation by hand or via voice commands. A common example is automating a series of manual steps, each requiring one or more key presses, into a single key press. A photocopier is another example of action automation: It can perform various levels of action automation, from the automatic sorting of copies to the automatic collation of papers and automatic stapling. An example of very high-level action automation is modern aircraft automatic landing systems, which track user interaction and automatically execute context-specific subtasks. In the HCI domain, a common example is the automatic execution of a procedure when certain conditions are met, such as an operating system engaging in an automatic update when the update has been fully downloaded and the computer is idle.

The type and level of automation can also be allowed to vary depending on the context, giving rise to a fifth type of automation: *adaptive automation*. The type or level of automation may vary in changing situational settings, for example, when a computer display shows a sudden influx of information that the user needs to process quickly. An example of adaptive automation is aircraft

Table 20.2 The types of automation mapped to stages of human information processing.

Type of automation	Human information-processing stage
Acquisition automation	Sensory processing
Analysis automation	Perception/working memory
Decision automation	Decision-making
Action automation	Response selection
Adaptive automation	Context-dependent

navigation automation, which can be high or low depending on how quickly the joint aircraft–crew system must react to an event to avoid a catastrophic outcome. A similar mechanism can be implemented in cars: The car may engage in manual handover if the system is unable to manage an ongoing situation. A hypothetical example of adaptive automation is a system automatically correcting spelling and grammar mistakes, which may dynamically adjust the system's level of autocorrection depending on the type of text the user is writing.

20.2 What makes automation good?

User-centric evaluation criteria: The study of human–automation interaction emerged in safety-critical domains, such as driving and aviation. Besides accidents, four criteria are used to evaluate automation from the operator's perspective: mental workload, situation awareness, complacency, and skill degradation.

Automation can both reduce and increase users' *mental workload*. For example, automation can enable an organization of information that makes it easier for users to understand. Automation can also avoid searches or communication, for example, by providing pertinent context-appropriate data to the user. In addition, automation can collate relevant information sources and present them to the user. Furthermore, automation can provide predictions that may reduce the user's workload, such as predictive flight path displays in aircraft, which have been shown to reduce pilots' mental workload. All these are examples of automation reducing the user's mental workload. However, the mental workload can also increase due to systems that, for example, are difficult to initiate, understand, or engage with, or require extensive physical work to operate.

Automation can also affect users' *situational awareness*. Automation may reduce users' awareness of the system, including its dynamics and outputs. In general, humans tend to be less aware of changes in a system or environment if those changes are under the control of another agent. As such, the use of automation almost always implies some level of delegation of authority. Another concern is that automatic decision-making based on the information available may make the operator less aware of the information since the operator is not actively engaged in evaluating it as a basis for making decisions. This increases the risk that decisions are based on incorrect or low-quality information.

Another consequence of automation on human performance is *complacency* arising from overtrust or overconfidence in automation. For example, a user may fail to monitor automation or information sources if the automation is at a high level and is perceived to always be accurate. There is also a risk of errors being introduced due to users overly trusting imperfect automated information analysis, such as automated data filtering or prediction. Several well-known issues in AI systems exacerbate this risk, including the system's failure to assess the quality of the data, estimate the uncertainty in the data, and mitigate bias in the data. For example, attention-guiding systems such as automatic cueing systems can result in operators not paying attention to uncued areas. A similar effect has been observed in spell checking [267] and when indicating low-confidence words outputted by a speech recognizer [849].

The fourth consequence of automation on human performance is *skill degradation*, that is, users forgetting how to carry out functions or witnessing their skills decay due to automation.

System-level evaluation criteria: While user-centric evaluation criteria look at the system from the viewpoint of its operator, we can also look at the *joint* performance of the human–automation system. This is often done via two evaluation criteria: automation reliability and the costs of decision and action outcomes.

Automation reliability captures the extent to which the system is effective in automation. Depending on the type and level of automation, several factors may be important. One important aspect may be the *true positive rate*, also known as *sensitivity*, which is a measure of the ability of a system to correctly diagnose a condition. For example, an automated spell checker function with high sensitivity can flag the vast majority of words that are misspelled. Another important factor may be the false positive rate, also known as the *false alarm rate*. It is a measure of the system's inability to separate positive from negative cases. A high false alarm rate means the system is constantly incorrectly flagging information. An example would be a spell checker that keeps flagging words that are spelled correctly. A high false alarm rate may cause fatigue among users and may foster distrust in the system, which may well be justified.

Lower automation reliability may be acceptable in some circumstances, for example, if the users are provided with alternative means of assessing information, such as access to raw data in an easy-to-digest format. Another example is the case where users can be trained to understand not only the decision-making tasks but also the underpinning capabilities and limitations of the automation solution.

Automated systems that classify or predict events have inherent errors in their models, as such models are imperfect. Therefore, such systems should be designed to take into account the fact that automated results will inevitably be incorrect on occasion. Generally, automated systems that indicate when automation may fail or has failed are more likely to gain an appropriate level of trust from users.

The *costs of decision and action outcomes* are also important. Any potential benefit of automation has to be compared with and weighted against any possible disadvantages. Examples of such disadvantages include an increased mental workload, reduced situational awareness, higher complacency, and a higher risk of skill degradation. Therefore, it is often wise to carry out risk analysis, which is discussed in the chapter on safety and risk (Chapter 37).

Application: A workflow for determining the type and level of automation is presented in Figure 20.1. The application of this framework has six main steps:

1. Identify the types of automation that are applicable to the task.
2. Identify the levels of automation that are suitable for the task.
3. Based on the primary evaluation criteria, evaluate the consequences of automation on human performance. This may require iteration, such as revisiting the identification of types and levels of automation in light of insights from the evaluation.
4. Determine the preliminary type and level of automation of the task.
5. Apply the secondary evaluation criteria: automation reliability and the costs of decisions and outcomes. This step may also require iteration and revisiting the identification of types and levels of automation in light of insights from the evaluation.
6. Determine the final type and level of automation of the task.

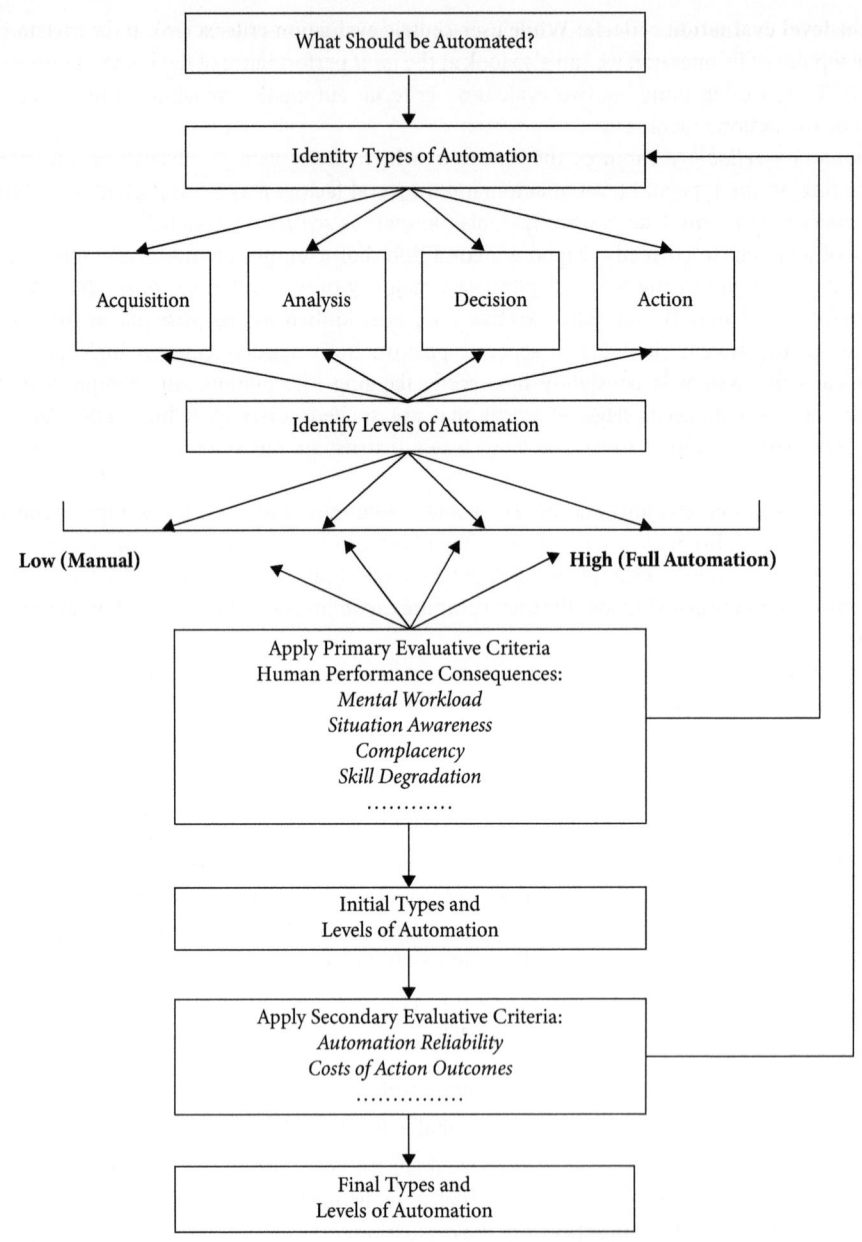

Figure 20.1 A workflow for using the types and levels of the automation framework [639].

20.3 Interactive AI

AI can be used to automate many functions. For example, Microsoft Excel can extrapolate from a user typing numbers in cells. If the user types 10 in one cell and 20 in a neighboring cell, selects the two cells, and extends the selection, the contiguous cells in the extended selection will read

40, 50, and so on. Notably, AI has brought automation to nonprofessional users. In this context, we briefly review four common applications of AI:

1. Augmentation
2. Dialogue
3. Monitoring
4. Recommendations.

First, some forms of AI provide more than just automation; they amplify users' abilities. For example, AI can allow users to type faster and sloppier on a mobile phone keyboard by autocorrecting incorrectly pressed keys. This is an example of AI using a formal model of user interaction to translate observations of user input (the touchpoints on the keyboard) into hypotheses of the user's intention (the intended text).

Second, AI can be used in dialogue interaction where a user engages in some form of conversation with an AI agent. Such a dialogue can enable user interaction with simple commands, such as the user clicking various options. Alternatively, users can use natural language as input when speech recognition is available. Spoken dialogue interfaces recently became popular (e.g., Siri and Alexa). They provide users with direct access to functions and content via spoken language. Text-based dialogue interaction is common in support functions, such as online banking and shopping. With large language models, this type of interactive AI is expected to become more popular.

Third, AI can improve engagement by monitoring the background and reacting at opportune moments. This can be achieved in two different ways, as it can be driven by user or non-user input. A simple example of a non-user input system is a thermostat-based heating system that regulates the temperature in a building or vehicle based on temperature data from a sensor. An example of a system based on user input is a 3D gesture recognition system that monitors the user's hand and finger movements using hand tracking. Such a system looks for specific gesture patterns that trigger specific commands. One commercial example of such a system is the Microsoft HoloLens 2 optical see-through head-mounted display. It uses continuous hand tracking to detect when the user is triggering one of its two recognized key gestures: a pinch, which tells the system to select something, and a bloom gesture, which tells the system to open the system menu.

Fourth, AI can make suggestions to users. Such systems use recommender systems to propose particular solutions. Examples of such systems are car navigation systems, other map-based navigation systems, and systems that provide recommendations on online shopping sites and streaming services.

As these examples demonstrate, interactive AI is already ubiquitous and available for a range of direct and indirect interactions; yet, in many ways, users do not realize this is the case. These examples of deployed interactive AI systems also show that it is possible to design, build, and release interactive AI systems that users can interact with, achieving widespread adoption and use in some cases.

Nonetheless, there are novel and partially unresolved challenges related to interactive AI systems. Some of these challenges are similar to those of non-AI interactive systems. As such, the knowledge and methods taught in this book—from understanding users, interaction, and user research to designing and evaluating a system and its risks—will still be helpful. Other challenges are unique to systems infused with AI, calling for complementary perspectives and methodologies.

20.4 Ironies of automation

In this chapter, we have learned that direct attempts to "replace" humans with automation or AI are likely to fail. Attempts to automate do not replace the human; they only change the type of engagement. Even highly automated systems require human supervision. In her 1983 paper titled "Ironies of Automation," Bainbridge summarized the negative effects of automation on human operators [36]. The irony here is that automation can have the direct opposite effect of what was intended during its design: Instead of relieving a human from chores, automation makes human contribution more crucial than before. Although she studied process control and aircraft pilots, the ironies she identified apply to modern AI, too.

The first irony concerns *deskilling*: When the level of automation goes up, the user is less engaged and may therefore lose both manual and cognitive skills over time. The operator of a chemical plant, for example, may lose the ability to understand how the automated plant works. A pilot may lose the skills needed to fly a plane without automated assistance. Similarly, users who rely on spell checkers may gradually lose their language skills [267]; users who rely on navigation aids may lose their spatial skills [533]. This means the user may not have sufficient skills to recover from a situation where automation fails. This, in turn, means that automation must now be designed in a way that does not depend on user skill, or that users' skills must be maintained by other means, for example, through training.

The second irony concerns vigilance. Vigilance refers to the user's ability to maintain attention on something over time. For example, in semi-autonomous vehicles, drivers are expected to maintain attention on the road and be ready to take over control when needed. In such cases, because the user is not continuously engaging with the task, boredom is likely to occur. Bored users will engage with secondary tasks or just get tired. The irony here is that they are *less* able to intervene than without automation.

The third irony concerns *agency*: While a system may be designed to empower the user, it may reduce the user's felt agency. When a user feels certain that an outcome is due to their action, the user is said to experience high agency. If the outcome seems less connected to the user's action, the user experiences less agency. A system that performs many functions for a user can result in less felt agency, as the user feels less in control. However, this is not always the case: A system can be designed so that users are fully aware of what is going on and can take action at any point. Vice versa, a system performing a single function may result in a low felt agency if the way it is achieved does not provide the user with a sense of ownership of their actions. An example is an auto-aim function in a first-person video game. If the auto-aim function is too generous, the player may not believe they hit the target due to their skills.

Lack of agency is detrimental to well-being in the long term because it contradicts the basic psychological needs for autonomy and competence (Chapter 6). Because of a lack of agency, a worker whose job is partially automated can easily become demotivated. This may be compounded by their professional skills being less appreciated by others. Automation is likely to decrease the perception of the profession: "Are you actually doing anything or is it the automation?" Workers may be less motivated to do their jobs, which then decreases the level of performance of the whole system. This, in turn, can lead to feelings of alienation in users. They may not feel like they have agency in their work and tasks: "It is the automation doing it, not me."

As we learned in this chapter, a central design challenge is providing users with the *right level of control*. Providing complete control may be unrealistic and even defeat the purpose of AI assisting the user to begin with. Moreover, complete control assumes the user has a thorough knowledge of the algorithmic principles that drive the AI, which is practically impossible to achieve. On the other hand, providing insufficient control may result in the user experiencing frustration when the AI requires steering or even lead to a disaster if the user and the AI work toward opposing goals. An infamous example of the latter is the Boeing 737 MAX disaster. The aircraft used a sophisticated anti-stalling control system that pilots were unaware of [827]. When the system failed due to faulty sensor readings, the pilots effectively worked against the system in trying to stabilize the aircraft.

These ironies of automation also apply to interaction with modern AI-infused systems. Moreover, research on contemporary AI-infused systems has identified one additional challenge: Generally, users and other stakeholders should be able to *understand and trust* the output of AI. Without such understanding, it may be difficult to accept the AI's recommendations or trust an AI that performs actions or makes suggestions that appear nonsensical or unintuitive to the user. The AI's output may even be unsettling: For example, users may find some accurate recommendations creepy because they are based on data harvested from them. Some AI systems may also have important consequences in real life. Consider, for example, systems that recommend insurance fees or potential love partners. A new research area has emerged at the intersection of HCI and AI research called *explainable AI*. See Paper Example 20.3.2.

Paper Example 20.3.2: Explainable AI

AI systems invariably use mathematically complex models, such as deep learning or logic models. Whenever an action or decision has consequences for the users, they may need to understand the AI's reasoning. Explainable AI refers to techniques for explaining the outputs of machine learning models. *Model visualizations* can be used to show how the internal layers of a deep neural network work, for example, which pixels in a photo contribute the most to its classification. The figure in this paper example box shows an example of saliency modeling applied to medical imaging [277]. The figure is used under Creative Commons License. *Interactive techniques* allow users to trial a model, for example, by testing it with different inputs. *Counterfactual explanations* provide "what if?" alternatives to the user. For example, when explaining an insurance decision, the user may be told how the insurance policy or fee could be changed. AI could say, for example, that "By stopping smoking, your monthly fee would go down by 20 euro."

Explainable AI is wickedly challenging to design; so far, no generic technique has been identified. This is well-reflected in clinicians' experiences with saliency-based explanations:

> The clinician cannot know if the model appropriately established that the presence of an airspace opacity was important in the decision, if the shapes of the heart border or left pulmonary artery were the deciding factor, or if the model had relied on an inhuman feature, such as a particular pixel value or texture that might have more to do with the image acquisition process than the underlying disease.

Besides the fact that these models often *do* reason in a nonhuman manner, one persistent issue is that users are not interested in investing time in reading complex explanations. Another is that those explanations may not be understandable. For example, to understand a deep learning model with a random forest model, it is first necessary to understand how random forest models work. While simplifications can aid understanding, they lower the accuracy of the explanations. This is called the explainability–accuracy trade-off.

continued

Paper Example 20.3.2: Explainable AI *(continued)*

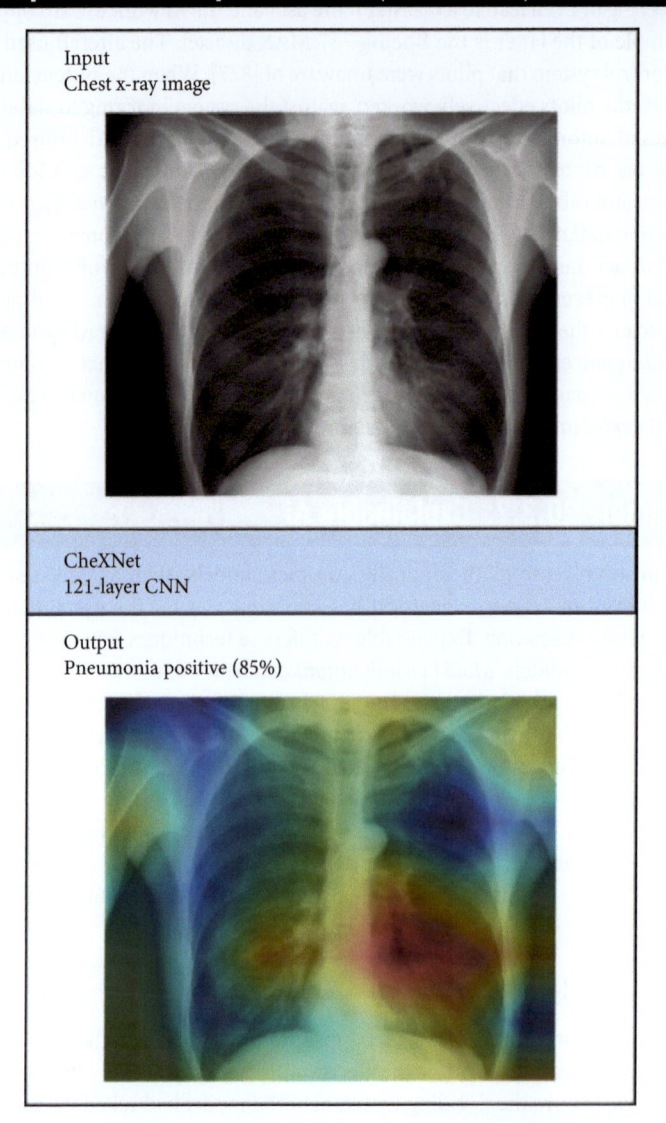

Input
Chest x-ray image

CheXNet
121-layer CNN

Output
Pneumonia positive (85%)

Wang and colleagues reviewed cognitive factors affecting people's ability to understand explanations [868]. They pointed out that explanations must be built in a way that appreciates the capabilities and limits of human cognition, which we covered in Chapter 5. They summarized five implications for design:

- Support forward reasoning: Show feature values and attributions before class attribution. This can avoid confirmation bias in users.
- Support coherent factors: Avoid showing factors in explanations that go against their typical relationships.

- Support access to source and situational data: Show the original (full) dataset and its situationally relevant subset if asked by the user.
- Show model uncertainty: Express the uncertainty to the user, for example, in the form of the posterior probability distribution of classes.
- Integrate multiple explanations: Show diverse explanations to provide users with different perspectives.

Summary

- An automation problem is a function allocation problem. It is about determining which functions should be automated and with what type and level of automation.
- Interactive AI enables users to work with AI in many different ways to complete their tasks. Such interaction can be seen as a collaborative activity between the user and an AI agent.

Exercises

1. Understanding human–automation interaction. Consider a display that is meant to assist the user in identifying targets among a set of distractors. An AI system is used to automatically detect targets and visually flag them on the display to assist the user in quickly identifying such targets.
   (a) Suggest preliminary types and levels of automation that can be used to provide such functionality.
   (b) Evaluate the preliminary types and levels of automation using the following primary evaluation criteria: (i) mental workload, (ii) situation awareness, (iii) complacency, and (iv) skill degradation.
   (c) Based on your evaluation using primary evaluation criteria, refine your selection of the types and levels of automation for this design problem.
   (d) Evaluate your updated design using the following secondary evaluation criteria: (i) automation reliability and (ii) costs of decision and action outcomes.
   (e) Consider a radical redesign in which the system is extended to use eye tracking to check whether the user has looked at all the relevant targets identified by the AI system. If the system detects that the user has not looked at all the targets, the system amplifies the saliency of unattended targets to attract the user's attention. The *irony of automation* is that increasing the level of automation may fail to solve automation problems and require even more elaborate system solutions or skilled users to cope with the effects of additional automation. Discuss the extent to which the original system and the extended system risk falling victim to the irony of automation.
2. Types of automation. State and justify the types of automation that may apply to the following functions: (a) autocomplete on a keyboard, (b) a spell checker, (c) a movie recommendation interface, and (d) a self-driving car.
3. Levels of automation. Consider a word processor that provides automated functionality for the following tasks: (a) shortening text up to a set percentage; (b) identifying spelling and

grammar errors, explaining problems, and suggesting in-depth alternative solutions; and (c) automating tasks such as finding appropriate figures and inserting them into a document. Use the types and levels of automation framework to determine the appropriate type and level of automation for each function. Discuss whether certain functions or subfunctions are more suitable for humans to execute than automation.

4. Mixed-initiative interaction. Use the principles of mixed-initiative interfaces to analyze a few representative tasks in the following interactive AI systems: (a) a spreadsheet application, (b) an email application with integrated calendar functionality, and (c) an interface to a "smart" TV. Which principles seem to be followed the most? Which are followed the least? Are there any benefits to incorporating more principles of mixed-initiative interfaces into these systems?

5. Function allocation. Fitts' lists show which things people are good at and which things interactive systems are good at. They serve as a basis for functional allocation. The following table shows such a list from Fitts' early work [242].

Humans are good at	Interactive systems are good at
Ability to detect a small amount of visual or acoustic energy	Ability to respond quickly to control signals and to apply great force smoothly and precisely
Ability to perceive patterns of light or sound	Ability to perform repetitive, routine tasks
Ability to improvise and use flexible procedures	Ability to store information briefly and then to erase it completely
Ability to store very large amounts of information for long periods and to recall relevant facts at the appropriate time	Ability to reason deductively, including computational ability
Ability to reason inductively	Ability to handle highly complex operations, i.e., to do many different things at once
	Ability to exercise judgment

Based on what you know about people and interactive systems, update the list. Also, think about whether functional allocation should be done only based on such lists.

6. Intelligent assistant. A software agent is incorporated into a spreadsheet application. The agent observes the user's work in the spreadsheet and automatically detects when data are suitable for visualization. At that point, the agent proposes the most suitable visualization method for the data. Meanwhile, the user can tell the agent to propose a visualization at any point by clicking on an icon representing the agent. If the visualization is not suitable, the user can ask the agent to generate more suggestions or show a gallery of all possibilities. Based on such interaction, the agent learns the user's preferences. (a) State the type and level of automation of this service. (b) Using the user-centric and system-centric evaluation criteria from the types and levels of automation framework, suggest three potential design issues with this system and justify your choices. (c) Determine whether the system adheres to the principles of mixed-initiative interfaces.

21
Rationality

Why do some users prefer to visually search a menu for a command while other users prefer to use keyboard shortcuts? Why do users avoid looking at advertisements on web pages but are attracted to large graphics and titles such as logos? Why do some users type with two thumbs in one context but only one finger in some other context? Why do users often reduce their walking speed when typing on a mobile device? Why do users avoid cognitively demanding tasks like generating new passwords? These questions are instances of a foundational question in human–computer interaction (HCI) research: Why does some particular behavior emerge in a given interaction setting?

This chapter introduces the notion of *rationality*. This allows us to provide explanations for interactive behavior due to users attempting to make the most out of the choices available to them.

To state that a user's choice is *rational* means that it is selected with the expectation that it yields the highest *utility* out of the available options. Thus, the notion of rationality does not only explain what a user does; it also considers what that user *could* have done but chose not to.

The concept of rationality has its roots in economics, where it was developed to study how people *should* act in economic decision-making. In such settings, the idea is that people reach their goal, such as maximizing their return, by maximizing utility. However, empirical studies demonstrated that people do not behave as such a *normative* view suggests. Instead, people constantly fail to consider all options, estimate the value of the choices provided to them, and choose the economically optimal option.

The present understanding is that users are not fully rational. The ability to make rational decisions is limited by both internal abilities, such as those posed by perception and cognition, and by the structure of the environment in which one operates. Therefore, to predict user behavior, it is insufficient to merely understand the rewards of interaction: the goals and utility. We must also understand users' limits, which are usually called *bounds* in this context.

As an example, consider the following situation: "I promise to give you money based on your preferred option. Which one would you choose?"

1. I give you £50 for sure.
2. I give you £100 with a 50% probability.

From an economic theory perspective, these two options have equal outcomes. The choice does not matter because the expected return is the same. Yet, some respondents might consistently prefer options like the first one, demonstrating *risk awareness*. By contrast, *risk-seeking* people tend to prefer the second option.

In HCI, there are many reasons for behaving in a seemingly irrational way. A user may fail to choose the (normatively) best option, for example, due to constraints such as time pressure, limited knowledge, or an incomplete set of beliefs. They may, for example, not know what the options are or what their attributes are. They may also have preferences for certain outcomes. For example, they may want to factor in the level of risk involved. They can prefer to obtain rewards quickly or be more patient and work longer for them. Thus, contrary to a common misconception, rationality does not imply the user is all-knowing, all-capable, or able to achieve what is objectively the best outcome for them. Users can only behave as well as they can.

The descriptive view of rationality explains people's actual behavior when making choices. Descriptive theories attempt to capture causes behind behavior that, from a normative perspective, may appear irrational. This view enables predictions of user behavior in real-world circumstances.

In particular, *bounded rationality* states that we are only rational to the extent allowed by the involved constraints, or bounds. The term *satisficing* is used to describe how users tend to behave when facing a complex decision-making problem. It refers to settling on a satisfactory but not optimal solution in the normative sense. Instead of searching for the very best option, users tend to search only as long as it takes them to identify a satisfactory option. Here are a few examples of satisficing in HCI:

- When looking through search results, users rarely look beyond the first page; they often settle on something that appears close to the top.
- Instead of investing effort into learning shortcut commands, such as Ctrl-C for copy, users often just look for the option in a drop-down menu.

How do users determine the satisfactory level? They use a *reference point*, for example, a previous experience. If that point is low, they may be satisfied with a much lower experience than if the point is high. Consider looking for sneakers in a web shop that offers thousands of them. After a quick scan, you bump into a pair of good-looking shoes offered for £ 40. Do you keep looking or stop now and buy the pair of shoes you just found? Your behavior would likely depend on your reference point, for example:

1. You believe that the kind of shoes you love should be available for £ 80.
2. You believe that the kind of shoes you love should be available for £ 40.

It is rational to satisfice: In most cases, good enough is good enough. Satisficing is also a good strategy for an agent with a limited time budget or an unwillingness to invest cognitive effort. For example, a user choosing a way to travel through a web service may not need to analyze all the options and fully understand their costs and benefits; they may choose the first one that is deemed good enough. In general, finding the normatively optimal solution to a *multi-attribute choice problem*, a problem where a user needs to evaluate and compare many attributes, requires extensive pairwise comparisons and retaining a lot of information in memory. We can avoid that effort if we find even just one option that is good enough. Satisficing is therefore an important concept because it factors in the amount of effort involved in finding optimal solutions.

The concept of rationality views users as agents. An *agent* is an actor with the ability to choose actions in pursuit of some goal or reward. An agent's behavior is understood in terms of the agent making a *choice*: From numerous possible ways to act, the agent chooses and carries out a specific course of action. This is a general concept in HCI since even the act of pressing a button can be understood as a choice. For example, a user pressing a button can vary the amount of force and the timing of the press in different ways. This example illustrates that for behavior to be analyzed as choice, we do not need to assume the user is consciously aware of the options available to them. It is possible to analyze even relatively low-level behavior, such as eye–hand coordination in computer use, through the lens of rationality.

To model users as agents, we need to assume they tend to choose actions that maximize their *expected utility*. In other words, users do what they believe is best for them. For an HCI researcher wanting to apply these theories, five basic concepts must be understood:

States: States describe the possible states that the user may enter.

Actions: In each state, the user can choose from several options; these options are called actions.

Rewards: The rewards represent what the user wants and are associated with different states.

Costs: Costs are negative rewards that the user incurs for transitioning between states or for being in states that are not good for them.

Environment: The space of all states, actions, and rewards is called the environment.

In any given *state* of the environment, a set of *actions* is possible. States can be specified in different ways in theories of rationality. They can be specified by the user interface, the task context, or the user's beliefs. Certain states are associated with *rewards* that are valuable for the user, such as information that is interesting or getting an email sent to a colleague. However, some states or transitions incur *costs*, such as the cost of spending time or energy. Such costs are *negative* rewards. Costs can be quantified in many ways, such as the time or effort invested.

Utility refers to the agent's consideration of positive and negative rewards when deciding how to act. Contrary to the received view from economics, in HCI, utility is often not related to money or other externally defined values. Instead, it is mostly defined by reference to *intrinsic* rewards, such as being productive, experiencing enjoyment, or being appreciated by others; see the discussion of needs and motivations in Chapter 6. Sometimes, intrinsic rewards are closely associated with extrinsic states, such as pressing a particular button to send an email or receiving a particular message.

The rest of this chapter reviews four theories of rationality relevant to HCI and illustrates them with examples. Table 21.1 compares these four theories. They share a focus on the emergence of interactive behavior; in other words, they predict how users choose to behave in certain given circumstances.

Economic models: These models predict that users choose actions by considering the costs and rewards of those actions. For example, users do not form maximally informative search queries when using search engines. Their queries' lengths can be predicted by considering

Table 21.1 Four theories of interactive behavior.

Theory	Main idea
Economic models	Users choose to interact in a way that maximizes the payoff, that is, the ratio of the benefits to the costs of actions.
Rational analysis	User behavior adapts to the ecology, that is, the experienced distribution of rewards in the environment.
Information foraging theory	Users are "informavores" who navigate information environments, such as a web site, in a way that attempts to maximize information gain while factoring in the time costs of actions.
Computational rationality	Users interact in a manner that attempts to maximize an expected future reward; however, such attempts are bounded by the capabilities of their bodies, their cognition, and the environment.

the effort and time needed to generate them (i.e., the costs) versus the additional gain from each added term [30].

Rational analysis: Such analysis is based on the assumption that the way users experience rewards being distributed in the environment shapes their behavior. This distribution is called the *ecology*. For example, when users observe an interface for the first time, they do not look at it randomly. Instead, they tend to look at those regions that they expect to contain the most information. Such gaze tendencies are an example of behavior adapted to the interface ecology.

Information foraging theory: This theory views users as "informavores" to predict how they search—*forage*—for information. It assumes that at any given time, users choose where to go next by estimating the information gain and the time cost for each option. For example, when searching for a product in a web store and looking at its menu, which link will a user click? According to this theory, the user chooses the link with the highest ratio of expected relevance—or *information scent*—to the navigation cost, such as the time spent navigating the site [661]. A study of large-scale web-clicking data employed this theory to explain why certain distributions of web page hits emerge on web sites. Huberman et al. [362] proposed a mathematical model that assumes that at any page, users decide to continue clicking as long as its information scent exceeds some threshold. This information scent can be computed using information foraging theory (IFT).

Computational rationality: This concept assumes that in computer use, we face a sequential decision-making problem: We must choose which of a set of immediate actions might eventually get us to the state we care about. To do this, we estimate the values of achievable actions. However, in doing this, we are limited by our beliefs, bodies, and cognitive capabilities. The sequential decision-making problem is computationally hard, and machine learning methods are required to predict users' actions in concrete task environments. Recent examples include generative user models for typing, multitasking, menu use, and driving tasks [632].

These four theories differ in the factors they include and how the agent's decision-making problem is formulated. As such, the theories differ in how easily they help us find a solution to the user's decision-making problem. For example, while economic models can be analyzed via pen-and-paper calculations, computational rationality requires a machine learning approach to arrive at a solution.

21.1 Economic models

Economic models examine user choices in terms of *payoffs*. A payoff refers to the benefits that are left after the costs have been subtracted. When the costs are high, the payoff may be low. When the benefits are high and the costs are low, the payoff is high. In economic models, a rational user chooses actions that maximize the payoff.

In traditional economic models, benefits and costs refer to financial variables, such as money; in HCI, they refer to subjectively relevant variables that can be positive or negative, such as the expenditure of time (a cost) and the gain of interesting information (a benefit).

Applications of economic models in HCI start by analyzing the payoffs of each option. These are described in terms of information or efficiency (the benefit) against a variable such as time (the cost). Then, a *design variable* is defined, such as the length of a query a user is typing. The payoff is then computed as a function of this design variable. The shape of this function helps us identify sweet spots—values of the design variable where the payoff is high or reaches its peak. Paper Example 21.1.1 illustrates a worked example of payoff calculations for search query lengths.

Paper Example 21.1.1: Economic modeling of query-based search

To illustrate the computation of payoffs, let us consider the example of search queries [30]. The question is how long a search query a user should type, given that entering a longer query has a higher time cost but may yield a benefit in the form of better results. We start by looking at the time cost of entering a query of varying length and then look at its effect on the quality of the information obtained from the search results. A rational user chooses the optimal query length according to the cost–benefit trade-off.

To apply the economic model to search engine use [30], we make two assumptions. First, let us assume that the time cost c of entering a query is linearly related to the number of words W:

$$c(W) = W \cdot c_w, \tag{21.1}$$

where c_w is the time spent to enter one word. Simply put: The more words you type, the longer it takes.

Second, let us assume a benefit function $b(W)$ that describes the accumulated information in search results as W increases. Let us further assume that the search results are presented in some relevance-based order. This implies that $b(W)$ yields diminishing benefit as W increases:

$$b(W) = k \cdot \log_a(W+1), \tag{21.2}$$

where k and a are empirical scaling factors. Simply put: As a increases, additional words in W contribute less to the total benefit.

To compute the payoff (also referred to as profit in the figure below) π, we need to combine these two terms as follows:

$$\pi = b(W) - c(W) = k \cdot \log_a(W+1) - W \cdot c_w. \tag{21.3}$$

To find the optimal query length W^*, Equation 21.3 is first differentiated with respect to W:

$$\frac{\partial \pi}{\partial W} = \frac{k}{\log a} \cdot \frac{1}{W+1} - c_w = 0. \tag{21.4}$$

This can be solved for W^* as follows:

$$W^* = \frac{k}{c_w \cdot \log a} - 1. \tag{21.5}$$

The figure in this paper example box shows the model with different values of the parameters a and k. For example, when $k = 10$, the profit peaks at around 1–4 words; this result corresponds well with empirical data on query lengths.

continued

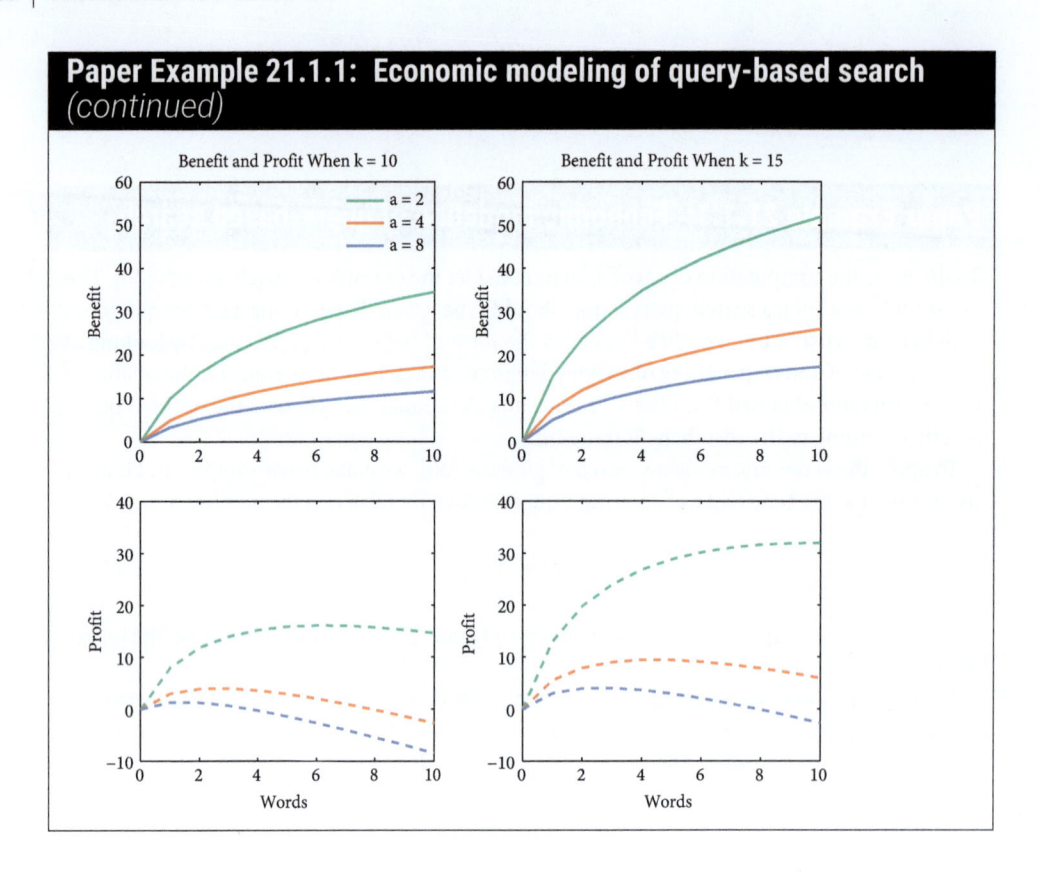

> **Paper Example 21.1.1: Economic modeling of query-based search** *(continued)*
>
> Benefit and Profit When k = 10 / Benefit and Profit When k = 15 (a = 2, a = 4, a = 8); x-axis: Words; y-axes: Benefit, Profit.

21.2 Rational analysis

Consider an ant walking on a beach. How much of the ant's route is determined by the ant and how much of it is determined by the environment? The small bumps and valleys in the sand are somewhat predictive of the ant's path.

An ant on a beach illustrates the paradox that simple organisms can produce complex behaviors. A simple control rule, when immersed in a complex environment, can produce behavior that appears complex. By implication, knowing someone's environment can be very useful for inferring their behavior.

To see the connection to HCI, instead of an ant, think about a user navigating in a graphical interface. How much is a cursor's movement controlled by the user versus the design of the layout? For example, if you move your cursor in a menu, the columns and rows of the menu are highly predictive of how your cursor will move. Moreover, the first commands of a menu are more likely to be selected than those that are hidden deeper within the menu structure. Additionally, a user's gaze and mouse cursor are less likely to dwell on areas that contain little information, such as white space. Rational analysis generalizes this observation into a principle of rational behavior.

Rational analysis is a theory of rational behavior proposed by Anderson and Schooler [21]. It examines the distribution of rewards in the environment to explain how users adapt their behavior. According to rational analysis, behavior is sensitive to the statistical distribution of rewards in the environment that a user has experienced. Users learn the way rewards are distributed through continued exposure to an environment and adapt their behavior accordingly. A user's behavior is rational because it is tuned to the distribution of rewards in the environment—the ecology.

The theory can be used to predict user behavior in cases where (1) the reward distribution can be charted and (2) when users have had enough time to adapt their behavior.

For example, consider the spatial distribution of rewards on a web page. Some elements, such as decorative elements, contain virtually no information. Other elements, such as text and titles, typically contain a lot of information. Graphics can be either informative, such as a logo, or non-informative, such as a decorative background image. When the user encounters a web page for the first time, where should they look? Rational analysis predicts that users adapt their behavior to the distribution of informative and non-informative elements. For example, the logo of the site owner is typically at the top of the web page, while a navigation menu is commonly presented either on the left or at the top of the page.

Rational analysis predicts that the probability of a user gazing at a location is proportional to the expected location of information across previously encountered user interfaces. For example, what a user initially gazes on in a mobile app depends on where the interesting elements statistically reside. If a designer wants to predict this, they simply need to know how other apps that the user might use are designed.

Visual statistical learning is a research topic in perception that studies how the statistical distribution of our environments affects the deployment of gaze. The history of interface designs encountered by users is a valuable source of information for a designer. For instance, users can find elements faster if they are placed at statistically expected locations. For example, users who look at mobile apps typically focus on the top-left quadrant (Figure 21.1). Paper Example Box 12.2.1 provides another example of rational analysis.

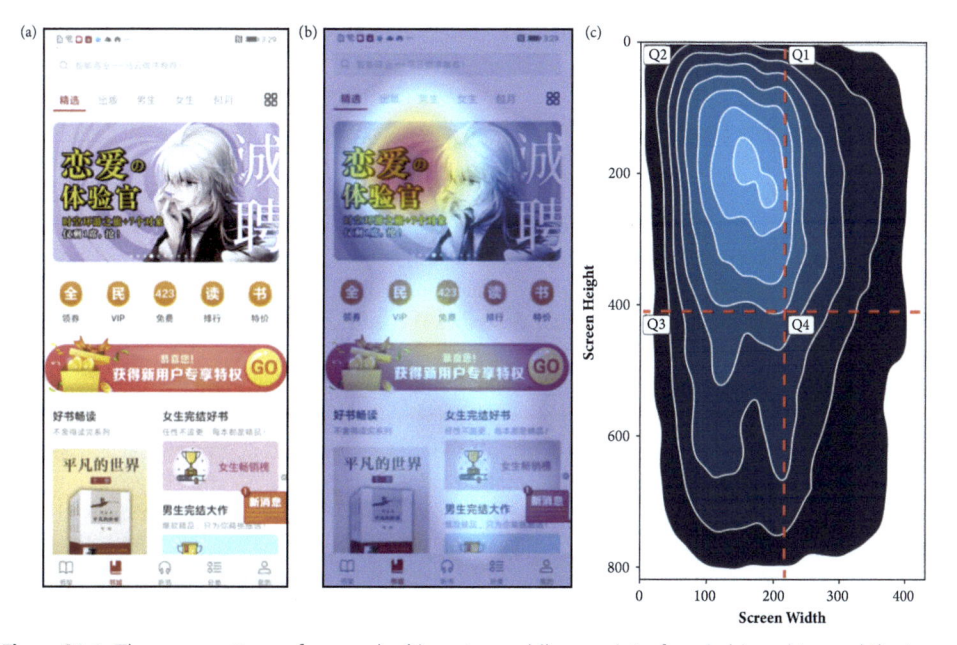

Figure 21.1 The gaze pattern of a user looking at a mobile user interface is biased toward the top-left quadrant. The figure shows (a) the original user interface, (b) the aggregated gaze pattern when viewing the content freely, and (c) the aggregated pattern over *all* mobile user interfaces in a study [472]. According to rational analysis, this phenomenon arises due to the adaptation of gaze behavior to the distribution of information in the ecology of mobile user interfaces.

> **Paper Example 21.2.1: Forgetting passwords is rational**
>
> Reusing a password is unwise and opens those accounts to attacks. As a consequence, most users have several passwords that need to be remembered for various systems in use. However, the more passwords we have, the harder it gets to create them and recall them when they are required.
>
> To recall a password, we need to retrieve it from long-term memory. However, what determines how easily it can be retrieved? Rational analysis suggests an answer to this question. It assumes that human long-term memory evolved to help survival by anticipating organismically important events. It is evolutionarily important to remember things that are important for survival. Therefore, the expected value of remembering a thing in the future should affect the probability of recalling it.
>
> Since most memory usage is not directly related to survival, Anderson and Schooler [21] proposed an adaptation of rational analysis for everyday stimuli, such as emails and news headings. This adaptation can be understood as a statistical mapping between the probability of an encounter and the probability of such an encounter being recalled at a later stage:
>
> $$\text{recall probability} \propto \text{probability of encounter}. \qquad (21.6)$$
>
> This means that the more likely a user is to need a created password in the future, the more likely they are to recall it. Vice versa, when a user does not expect to use a password, it is more likely to be forgotten. This simple principle can be used to derive a mathematical model that predicts the password retrieval probability with surprising accuracy [269].

21.3 Information foraging

Information foraging refers to information-seeking activities such as navigating, exploring, comparing, searching, or manipulating information contents in an information space. IFT attempts to explain users' choices in such activities [661]. Example applications include interaction with search engines, web sites, menus, and file systems. The roots of IFT lie in *optimal foraging theory*, originally proposed in biology, which describes the hunting and food search behaviors of animals.

IFT posits that in information-seeking tasks, users exchange their time and effort for information. If a user estimates that there is no interesting information on a web site, the user quits it and does something else to achieve a better payoff. If the user estimates that a particular link opens another web page that may have high information value, it is rational to click it, assuming that there are no better options available. However, if the time cost—the waiting time for the web page to load—associated with that link is high, the user may decide to quit.

IFT proposes that information-seeking behavior develops to maximize the rate of information gained per unit of time or effort invested. Note that the term *information* does not refer to the information-theoretic concept but to subjective interest; here, information means anything that *users* find interesting. This can be quantified in many ways, such as in terms of interest, information need, surprisal, curiosity, learning, or reduction of uncertainty.

A central problem considered by IFT is how users choose between sources of information. To answer this question, the theory introduces the concept of a *patch*. Consider a predatory animal, such as a wolf, with two alternative patches on where to forage or hunt for food. One patch is a forest while the other patch is a field. Both patches require some travel (i.e., time), although in differing amounts, and both patches offer some calories in return. The forest patch may have deer; the field patch may have rodents. According to optimal foraging theory, an animal changes the patch as soon as the gain in calories decreases to a level that makes it rational to move somewhere else.

Let us assume a wolf has nearly exhausted the food in its forest patch. What would a rational wolf do? Would it stay in the current forest patch, move to a nearby field with rodents offering a low calorie gain, or perhaps travel to another forest patch with deer, which are harder to catch but provide a higher calorie gain?

In *information* foraging, the prey are virtual contents, and the calories are their information. As in optimal foraging, the ecology is assumed to be *patchy*. This means that information is unevenly distributed across regions, or patches, with different information contents. Figure 21.2 shows a simple HCI example with two options.

Similarly, time costs are incurred when moving between patches and when extracting information from a patch. The models of information foraging operate at varying timescales. While individual cognitive actions may take place in the timescale of about 100 ms to 10 s, the adaptation of behaviors may take minutes, hours, or days.

These models have three main components:

Decision: The decision problem that is to be analyzed, such as whether to stay or explore, how long to do something, or how to divide resources among many tasks.

Currency: The dimensions that users compare to assess the choices. Examples of such dimensions include energy, information value, and time. Second, what is the goal of the user, for example, minimization, maximization, or stability?

Constraints: These are the limits of the relationship between decision and currency, such as those posed by the user, interface, or task.

Next, we focus on two well-known information foraging problems: patch departure and diet.

You are writing an essay on what is known about mycobacterial genomes. Should you try browse news articles from a research portal (Patch 1) or a Google search directly from the browser (Patch 2)?

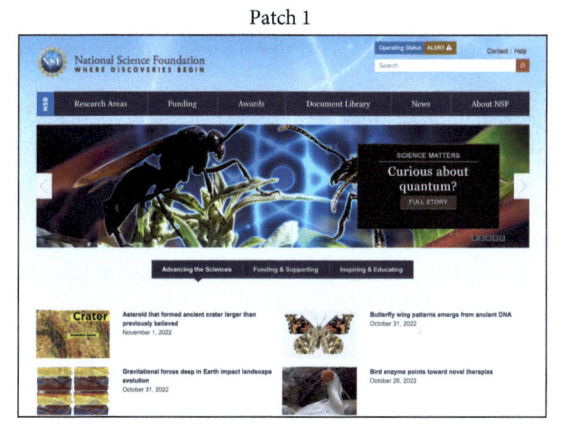

Figure 21.2 Which option should you pick if searching for information on a specialized scientific topic? While a search engine might provide results more quickly, their informational value might be lower compared to searching directly through a research portal.

21.3.1 Patch departure

Whether to enter a patch and how long to spend in it are predicted by the patch departure model. When patches are designed to have different gains in currency, gain rates, and distances between them, the situation becomes complex. The patchiness of digital information means that users must frequently decide on the best way to use their time: Should they stay here and, if not, which of the alternative patches might be the optimal option?

Let us consider a case with P patches. An example would be an interface for selecting movies. The interface shows P movies, and the user is interested in learning about the selection to pick a movie. The decision variable here is the within-patch foraging time. In other words, how long should one consider an option before moving on?

To answer this, we need to estimate the gain of information as a function of how long one stays in a patch. The patch departure model assumes a diminishing rate of information in a patch. The longer it is attended by the user, the less information the user obtains. In other words, the patch gets exhausted over time. Pirolli and Card [661] express this as follows:

$$R = \frac{G}{T_B + T_W} = \frac{G_f - C_f}{T_B + T_W}, \tag{21.7}$$

where G is the net gain, G_f is the gross amount of utility gained, C_f is the total cost of foraging, T_B is the between-patch cost (i.e., the time spent searching or moving to a patch), and T_W is the within-patch cost, that is, the time spent exploiting a patch. A higher R represents improvement.

When should one stop foraging a patch, then? To make the problem realistic, let us assume that each patch has different gain rates and a different between-patch cost. The expression $g_i(t_W)$ denotes the cumulative gain in patch i if t_W time is spent in it.

The special case of linearly increasing patch information is simple to solve. Figure 21.3 shows gain rates for different within-patch times. It illustrates when one should leave a patch.

However, the assumption of linearity is unrealistic: information is almost never extracted linearly. Rather, the relationship is nonlinear. In a well-organized interface, there is a rapid increase in g_i and a quick depletion of information. In a poorly organized interface, the increase in g would be slow at first and fast at the very end. For example, the most important information in a patch is sometimes given at the end, such as in contact forms or poorly designed link descriptions.

Cases where g_i is nonlinear can be solved by using Charnov's marginal value theorem. It states that a forager should stay in a patch as long as the slope of g_i is greater than the average gain rate R for the environment.

This nonlinear case is more challenging. Fortunately, it has a well-known solution when the diminishing returns curve is logarithmic. Figure 21.4 shows an example with two alternative ways to search for an item on a web site. To determine the optimal rates of gain $R*$ for the two cases, graphical reasoning as in Figure 21.4 can be used. A line tangent to the gain function $g_i(t_W)$ is drawn that passes through t_B to the left of the origin. The slope of this tangent is the optimal rate of gain R. More generally, when $g_i(t_W)$ and λ are known, the optimal t_W can be determined analytically. Comparing the two tangents, one concludes that patch 1 is more profitable and should be chosen.

21.3.2 Information diet

Diet models deal with environments that contain a number of potential types of food sources. The organism faces the problem of choosing a diet that optimizes its energy gain per unit cost. Pirolli raised the issue of electronic mail as an example in HCI: An email may come from a variety

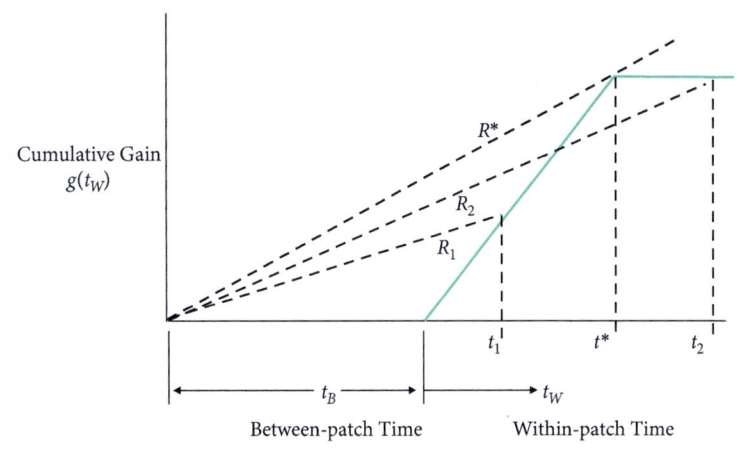

Figure 21.3 A patch with linearly increasing information gain. Here, the optimal time to stay t^* is determined by the moment all information is extracted. The gain rate is then $t^*/(t_b + t^*)$.

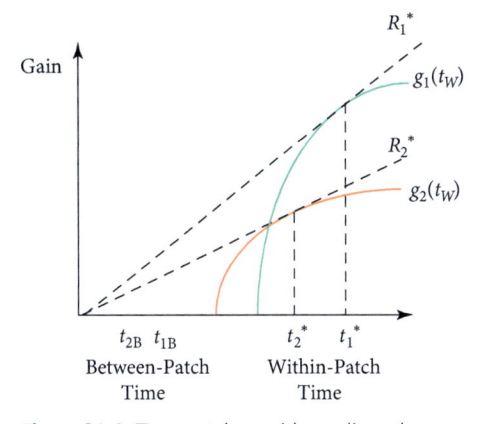

Figure 21.4 Two patches with nonlinearly changing information gains.

of sources that have different arrival rates and profitabilities. Low-profitability junk mail should be ignored if it costs the reader the opportunity to process more profitable mail. The diet of an information forager should also broaden or narrow depending on the prevalence and profitability of information sources.

The idea of the diet model is the following. Let us denote the minimum acceptable gain rate with an information threshold Φ. The diet model states that the forager should choose all patches of the diet that are above this threshold. That is, the patches in the proximal environment are ranked in decreasing order of the information gain rate, and the ones above Φ are picked.

21.3.3 Information scent

Another type of problem the theory considers is how users pick how to get to a *distal goal*. Distal goals are not immediately obtainable; they require intermediate actions. According to the theory, we need to use *proximal cues* to get to distal goals. For example, imagine you are on the landing page of a web shop. Which link should you click (proximal cue) if you want to get to a page that shows all the mustards on offer (distal goal)?

While optimal foraging theory in biology often assumes *omniscience*, or full observability of the world, Pirolli noted that we often cannot assume this in HCI. The contents of the patches are unknown to the information forager. The informavore must engage in decision-making under uncertainty. From what is locally visible, the informavore must infer what the distant environment may carry. Informavores examine proximal cues to guess what a distal state may carry for them. How do users estimate which patches to choose?

Information scent refers to a user's intuition that a cue in the interface represents the information needed (see Figure 21.5. for an example). It is an estimation of relevance based on a proximal cue. Consider, for example, the task of finding the address of a company on an unfamiliar web site. There are many ways this could be solved. One might directly start by typing "contact information" into a search field. If the first results are fruitless, the information scent is low, and one would be wise to switch to a different strategy, for example, a visual search of links. Many times when searching for links, there is no direct match, although there may be a few promising candidates. In our scenario of finding contact information, any of the following would have some "scent" but no perfect match: "Press," "Contact," or "About us."

IFT has several implications for user interface design:

1. Decreasing the between-patch transition times T_B will increase the gain rate. This can be done by decreasing the system latency or the time needed to complete the steps.
2. Decreasing between-patch times will also make users more willing to use the different options of the interface, as more patches will be above the threshold Φ.
3. Increasing gains in a patch g_i will increase the probability of users choosing the patch and spending longer in it.
4. Users can be deliberately directed to use a particular means by increasing its t_B. This "inverse usability" is used by commercial sites that want to promote certain options.
5. Gain functions that peak and asymptote quickly better support information foraging, as users can move to better patches more quickly. In other words, most information should be made quickly absorbable, for example, by using overviews or figures.

21.4 Computational rationality

In HCI, rewards are typically *sparse*; that is, several actions need to be taken to get to a rewarding state. For example, clicking a link may not take you directly to the page you want, yet the click is rational if, via that page, you get closer to your target page. Furthermore, some rewards are *very* sparse. Consider, for example, starting to use a social media app with the goal of becoming an influencer. This requires a long-term commitment to something that can go wrong in many ways and may not even pay off. In other words, in HCI, gratifications are typically delayed.

To deal with the problem of sparse rewards, we need to expand our account of rationality to cover sequential decision-making. The user starts in some state s_1 and picks an action, say a_5, which then takes the user to, say, state s_8. Here, the user picks a_9, transitioning to state s_{39}. A rational user would have chosen utility-maximizing actions. However, how would a user know which actions maximize utility?

RATIONALITY | **367**

(a)

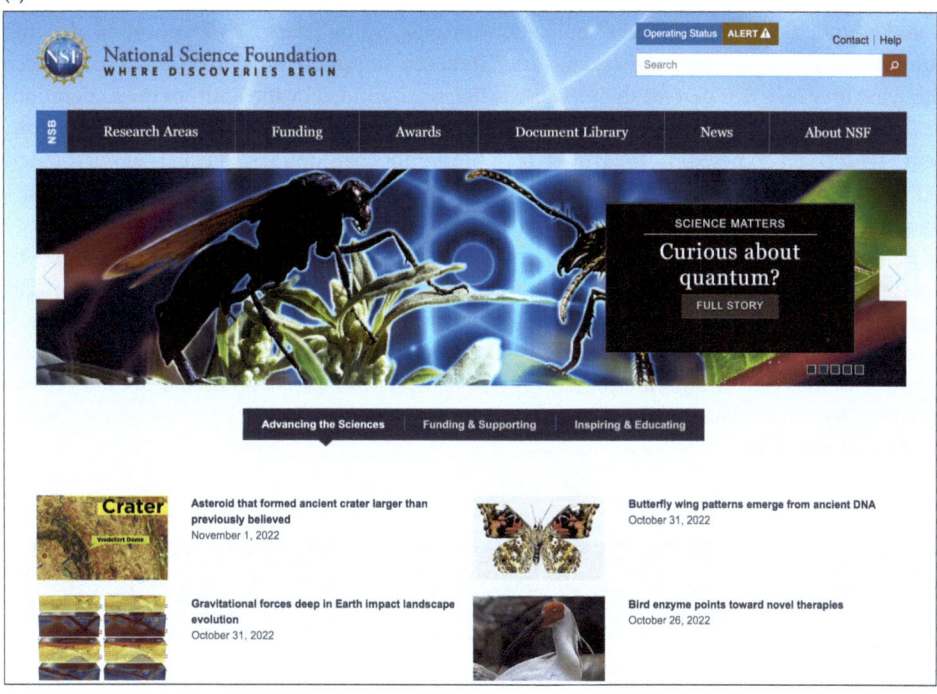

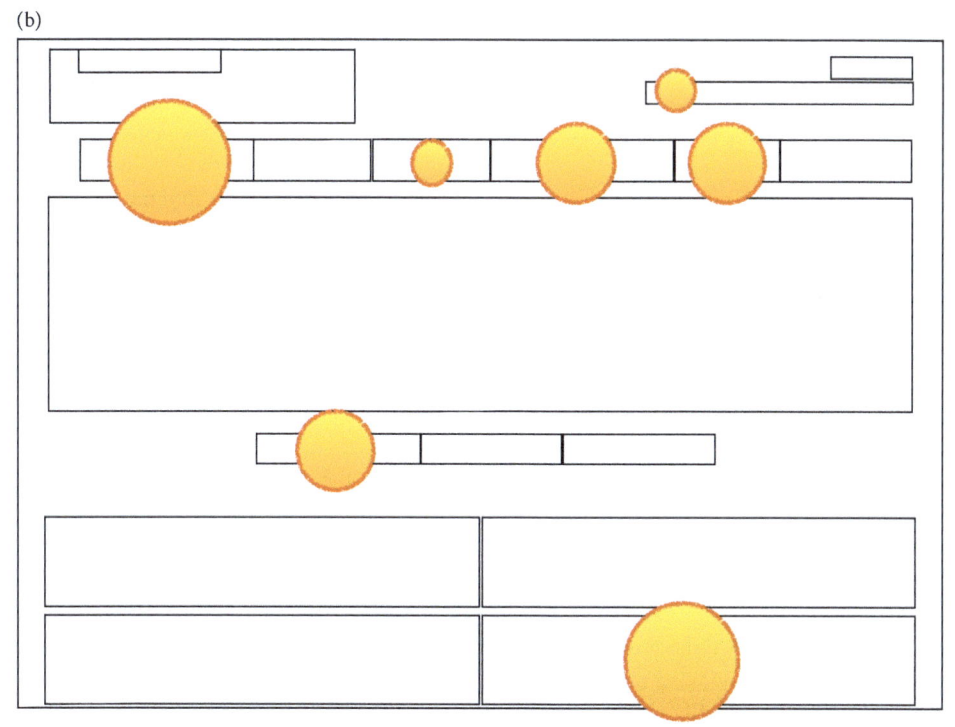

(b)

Figure 21.5 If you are looking for, say, articles on mycobacteria, certain patches have a higher information scent than others.

Computational rationality is a theory and a modeling approach rooted in bounded rationality and bounded optimality. Recent applications include typing (Figure 21.7), pointing, driving, multitasking, menu selection, and visual search. Its core assumption is that users act in accordance with what they *believe* is best for them. These beliefs are bounded by the limits of their cognition; for example, forgetting happens. They are also limited by their experience of the task environment [475]. Users do not know the true state of the world; cognition forms beliefs about it based on experience. As we learned in Chapter 5, there are many belief-forming capabilities in human cognition: perception, multiple memory systems, and the ability to reason and infer.

The theory assumes that users are "computationally rational": When picking an action—or deciding how to get from the present state to a state with positive rewards—users are as rational as their cognition allows. Users act based on their often inaccurate and partial beliefs, which they have formed via experience. Hence, unlike in IFT, in computational rationality *both* environment- and cognition-determined bounds are present. For designers, this means that design does not *determine* user behavior. It changes the external environment of the user, which the user forms beliefs about via experience.

Paper Example 21.4.1: Menu search as computationally rational behavior

To illustrate computational rationality, let us consider the task of searching for an item in a menu (Figure 21.6). For example, consider a user looking for the item "Print" in an application menu. Users often make choices on where to look and what to click quickly and without conscious deliberation. Computational rationality can explain such choices and predict the gaze and cursor patterns of users [147].

The decision-making problem the user faces is the following: At any given time, the user can perceive accurately only a part of the menu—whatever can be gathered in a fixation. Even if we think we see a menu "fully," we need to move our eyes to find the item we are looking for. After the first fixation, we have several options on where to fixate next to find the item. However, every fixation wastes time (negative reward), so the user wants to minimize the number of unnecessary fixations. When the user finds the target, a positive reward is allocated. A sequence of fixations must be chosen to land on the target, ideally wasting as little time as possible.

How does cognition solve this challenge? It can be approached in a few ways, for example, by following a simple heuristic strategy: "Start at the top and read each item one at a time." However, this strategy is inefficient: If the menu is large, a lot of time would be wasted looking at irrelevant items. Other strategies include (1) guessing where the target could be, (2) using a visual cue (e.g., a separator line) to jump to a promising area (e.g., the end of the menu), or (3) trying to recall the target's location and directly look at that location.

The optimal strategy depends on the design of the menu and how much experience the user has: If the menu is arranged randomly, guessing may be as good a strategy as any. However, if there is any structure to exploit, the theory assumes the users will pick a strategy to exploit that structure. For example, if the menu is alphabetically organized, users can jump (fixate) closer to the target and start looking at options serially there. If the menu is semantically grouped, they can try to first identify the group where the item is and then focus the search on that group. If the user is experienced with the menu, the position of the item may be recalled from long-term memory.

Still, how do users decide which strategy to follow? They make estimates on which strategy offers the best payoff. They estimate how quickly they might find the target, given what they know about it. Such decisions happen unconsciously; users "just do it." However, with eye trackers, we can expose such strategies.

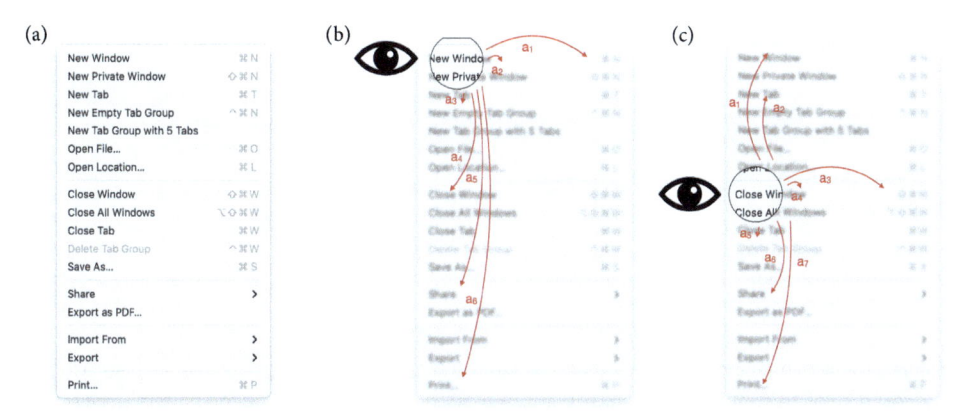

Figure 21.6 The Markov decision process is a formal description of a sequential decision-making process. An agent must sequentially decide which action to choose to maximize cumulative reward. For example, even if we think we see a menu "fully" (left), we need to move our eyes—often several times—to find the item we are looking for. After the first fixation (middle), we have several options (actions, a_x) on where to fixate next to find the item. However, every fixation wastes time (negative reward), so the agent wants to minimize the number of unnecessary fixations. When the agent finds the target, a positive reward is allocated.

21.4.1 Modeling interactions

Computational rationality allows for building computational models that generate predictions of user behavior. First, we formally define the sequential decision-making that the user is facing in interaction. The possible states are enumerated, for example, the beliefs or perceptions about the user interface. The possible actions in each state are then enumerated. They are typically commands to the motor system, such as a command to move the eyes or the hand. Then, the user's rewards—both positive and negative—are modeled.

A solution strategy—or "policy" in reinforcement learning (RL) terms—can now be approximated by using RL, a machine learning method for learning from experience. Because of the complexity of the decision-making problem, there is no analytical solution; the solution must be approximated through trial and error. In practice, this happens by allowing the RL agent to trial numerous (typically millions) possible behaviors in a simulated environment. Eventually, the RL agent learns a *policy* for which action maximizes the expected value in each state. Here, a policy is a generalization of the concept of choice we have discussed previously. In one-shot choice, we have a set of options and we can choose once; by contrast, a policy describes how a user would choose across all possible situations in a task. Technically, it is expressed as a probability function that describes how users choose *actions* in the different *states* of an environment.

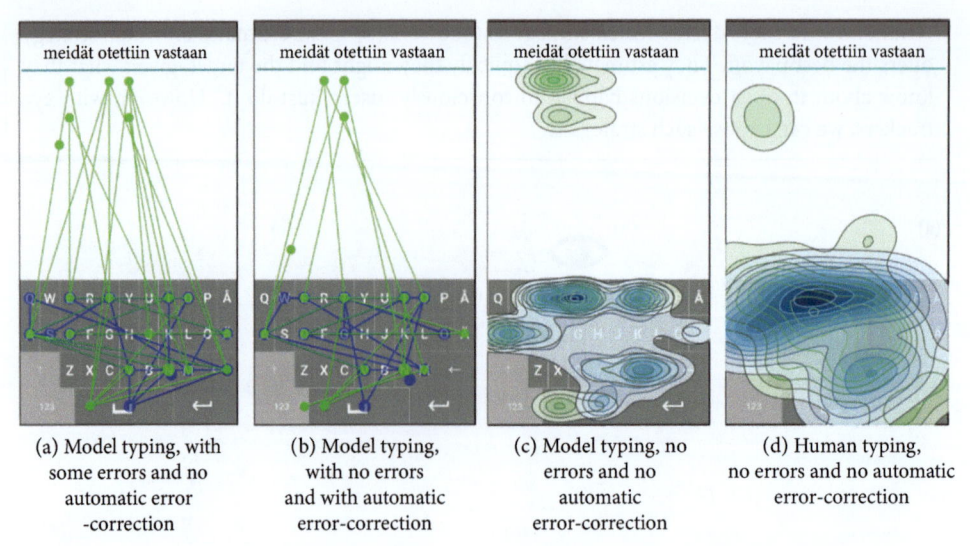

(a) Model typing, with some errors and no automatic error-correction

(b) Model typing, with no errors and with automatic error-correction

(c) Model typing, no errors and no automatic error-correction

(d) Human typing, no errors and no automatic error-correction

Figure 21.7 When typing, a user needs to decide when to look at the keyboard and when to look at the text display to spot possible typos. Visual attention is needed to guide the fingers to key locations. When it is not allocated to the fingers, uncertainty increases about their position. However, highly learned key locations can be pushed without guiding the fingers all the time. Computational rationality provides a way to model this decision-making problem and generate patterns of eye and hand movements that have a close correspondence with human data [392].

For those readers interested in machine learning, it is noteworthy that in order to enable the use of RL, the decision-making problem is first formulated as a sequential decision-making problem called the Markov decision process (MDP). MDP is a formalism that originates from studies of sequential decision-making in artificial intelligence and operations research. Instead of the choice between n actions, MDP deals with environments where rewards are delayed (or distal). This requires an ability to plan actions as part of *sequences* instead of one-shot choices. This is necessary for many applications in HCI where the environment is complex. For example, consider the task of writing an essay for homework. The rewards are mostly stacked at the end of the task, when the essay is submitted for review. Similarly, searching for a menu item has mostly a negative reward (the time cost) until the item is found and clicked (Figure 21.6).

Formally, MPD is defined as the tuple $(S, A, P(a, s, s'), R(a, s, s'), \gamma)$, where:

- S is a finite set of states and s is the current state;
- A is a finite set of actions;
- $P(a, s, s')$ defines the transition probabilities between states s and s';
- R defines the rewards obtained in each state.

The state can be changed to $s' \in S$ by an action $a \in A$. After each action, the agent receives a reward $r = R(a, s, s')$. States in MDP can also be defined in terms of *beliefs* instead of external states, forming a belief MDP. The beliefs may be about technology or the person's internal state. For example, they may include a memory of having visited a state earlier. The policy $\pi(s)$ defines which action is performed in each state.

For example, consider a linear menu with n commands. Formally, the MDP contains the following elements:

- S are fixated-upon commands in the menu;
- A are decisions that command what to fixate on next;
- $P(a, s, s')$ defines the next fixation point given the action;
- R yields a positive reward for finding the target (e.g., 100) and a negative reward for every wrong command fixated (e.g., 1).

The MDP can be solved via RL. The result is a prediction of the user's strategy for looking through the menu. The MDP predicts how the user's behavior changes depending on the given conditions. For example, when the menu is arranged randomly, systematic scanning emerges when the agent is trained with random target locations. When the menu is organized into semantic groups, the optimal policy is to inspect the first items of a group and jump to the next group if the target is not in the first group.

21.5 Are users rational?

Are people rational and maximizing utility? The answer depends on the viewpoint. Most of the time, people fail to reach the optimal choice. We procrastinate and choose shortcuts that damage our interests later on. In this sense, we are not rational. A competing explanation is that we are not rational but our behavior is driven by situations. At the opportune moment, we change our plans and goals [804]. However, rationality is not an inherent contradiction of the view of behavior as situationally shaped. In fact, that our behavior is rational is demonstrated by our ability to *adapt* to new, unforeseen circumstances.

Consider browsing a news feed polluted by numerous ads. Because of the low intrinsic value of those ads, it is rational to not attend to them ("ad blindness"). With time, we become even better at skipping ads. However, let us say we bump into one advertisement that *is* interesting. This may change our course of action from that point onward because the expected value of those ads is now higher. If our behavior were not adaptive, we would be at the mercy of convenient options in our environment.

Theories of rationality have increased our understanding of how users fail to be optimal. They fail because their beliefs are wrong. They fail because of their limited cognitive and other capabilities. They fail because they often do not have the cognitive resources or time to seek optimal solutions. We learned in Chapter 5 about multiple cognitive limits, for example, related to attention, working memory, and long-term memory. Under constrained conditions, even if users try to act rationally, they end up with choices that may seem suboptimal or lazy. However, they are still "resource-rational": We do our best, given our cognitive resources [480]. For example, while a user may *want* to find the best privacy settings for an application, time pressure, cognitive effort, or perceived incompetence (e.g., inability to comprehend the options) may limit performance.

Users also fail because the rewards are too distant in the future. If you have never completed a major project, it is easy to procrastinate. For example, the immediate reward from skimming social media feeds is higher than the reward from starting something that will take hours to complete. Theories of rationality offer us insight into this. The further in the future the state that contains the reward, the longer the chain of actions that are needed, and therefore the harder it is to identify a reasonable policy. Computational rationality explains these seemingly irrational behaviors.

To sum up, descriptive theories of rationality do not contradict the idea that users behave in a way that appears lazy or careless to an observer. For example, a user picking weak passwords simply prioritizes other goals, such as minimizing effort. What appears to be lazy behavior can be rational adaptation to achieve *other* goals.

Theories of rationality can be used to inform the design of information environments, addressing considerations such as how to distribute and shape information. The application of such theories requires careful analysis of the reward–cost structure of the interactive environment. When this structure is known, the environment can be changed to the benefit of the user in multiple ways:

1. Finding sweet spots of design parametrically, like we did for the search query length.
2. Computationally searching for the best way to structure the environment.
3. Studying how robust the environment (design) is to changes in the user's interests (rewards) or capabilities.

An open challenge for these models is how to model users' *intrinsic* motivations, such as motivations for learning or enjoyment, which are hard to observe.

Summary

- Theories of rationality do not describe what a user has done but ask what that user *could* have done. Rational behavior refers to behavior that seeks to maximize the expected utility to the user.
- Satisficing refers to boundedly rational behavior: A user picks the first satisfactory (good enough) option instead of trying to pick the best option by exhaustively assessing all options.
- Rational behavior refers to attempts to take the best course of action within the given constraints. These bounds include those of the external environment (e.g., the user interface and its structure) and those of the internal environment (e.g., cognitive limits).
- Theories of rationality can make quantitative predictions on user behavior in settings where the user's environment and goals (rewards) are well known.

Exercises

1. Optimal querying. Solve the optimal querying problem given in Paper Example 21.1.1. Plot the ratio of profit to cost as a function of query length (*x*-axis) and solve for W^*.
2. Foraging theory. Consider a card interface in an in-flight entertainment system. Each view consists of a 3 × 8 matrix of cards, each showing a movie. Let us assume that all movies contain the same amount of information and use foraging theory to estimate how long a user should skim one item. Given $a = 0.2$ and $b = 0.3$, compute t_w^* using the patch departure model.
3. Markov decision process. Define an MDP tuple for menu interaction. Assume a simple linear menu with 10 commands. The target command is in a random position. The agent starts from

the top command, and their task is to find the target. There are 11 possible actions: fixate on any of the items (1, ..., 10) or click. Moreover, there are 13 possible states, one for the item being fixated (1, ..., 10) and one for its status (unknown, not-target, target). A hefty reward is awarded for clicking the target, and a small negative penalty is administered for wasting time, that is, for every action that is not clicking the target. When this MDP is solved, what kind of policy emerges?

4. Rationality. What are some behaviors in HCI that can be argued to be (a) rational, (b) boundedly rational, and (c) irrational (i.e., not explained by theories of rationality)?

22
Practice

Interactive computing systems are astonishingly flexible. They support an innumerable variety of tasks, and any task can be done in a myriad of ways. Consider, for example, all the different ways you can send an email: all the applications you can use to do it, all the settings that can be changed, and all the messages that can be written. This overwhelming freedom raises a question: Why does the high degree of freedom *not* choke our ability to use computers? How come we are able to get our things done—at least most of the time? The answer is "practice."

The central idea of this chapter is that practice helps users achieve order in chaos. In the context of human–computer interaction (HCI), a practice is a way to regulate interaction. Practices ensure our use of computers appropriately aligns with the things we care about. In other words, an essential aspect of practices is that they are *contingent*. Practices develop in a way that enables interaction to be sensitive to the context of use, such as the activity, whether other people are present, and so on. Practices are contingent on those factors; if you change them, different behaviors emerge.

Consider typing on a keyboard to send a message to a loved one. Here, the context provides structure and meaning for the activity. The urgency with which you respond, the emojis you use, and the grammar and writing style are all contingent on the relationship that you and your loved one have formed. In turn, these factors are contingent on social norms that you have been exposed to. For instance, if you compose your message in a socially unexpected way, it might be misinterpreted by the receiver.

To sum up, practices allow for understanding factors that affect interaction but are beyond the interface itself. Interaction is not just about providing a particular input or getting a task done; it is also about advancing life, and this broader pursuit ties us to the social and material environments in which we interact.

What is practice? Dictionaries define practice as habitual or customary ways of carrying out something, yet it is more than that. It refers to the collection of habits, know-how, rules, and routines *involved* in carrying out activities. These may evolve continually as they are created and recreated to better match what is needed in the current situation. By studying the emergence of practices, we can understand how users maintain a certain level of achievement despite the highly interconnected and dynamic nature of things. This way of understanding interaction has been developed within HCI and social sciences [e.g., 447, 623, 743].

One way of understanding what is peculiar about practice is through the concept of *normatively regulated contingent activities* [743]. This concept overcomes the artificial separation of thinking and acting by looking at how people competently handle contingencies of interaction: its variations, surprises, challenges, and breakdowns. Practices are ways to respond to and regulate such contingencies. Users and communities adopt rules, routines, plans, norms, visions, and so on as part of normative regulation. This is what makes practice different from the other understandings of interaction we have discussed in this part of the book.

An important implication of this line of thinking is that practice is the smallest possible unit of analysis. Interaction is a social phenomenon; it is a normatively regulated contingent activity. This means that the analytical lens must consider more than just what happens at the interface level.

At the same time, looking at (static) social structures alone may not suffice because they do not prescribe what goes on in computer-based activities. Looking at individual actors and what they do is also insufficient because it ignores the history and social influence on their doings. Instead, the concept of practice forms the appropriate unit of analysis. It offers a compromise between high-level factors, such as social structures, and the interface.

Practices in computer use are empirically studied via a number of methods covered in this book, including interviews, observations, probes, and unobtrusive methods. However, because normative regulations are nontrivial to expose, the study of practices often requires longitudinal engagement. Practices develop over months and years, which means that a snapshot study at any given time may provide a limited view of an evolving practice [e.g., 403]. For example, many people use their mobile devices for many hours each day, and many users have stuck to the same word processor for years. Only via longer-term studies can we understand how such tools change people and how people change tools.

Understanding interaction as practice is associated with a specific set of insights and concerns. Paper Example 22.0.1 outlines one study on viewing interaction as practice. In the rest of the chapter, we will focus on three key implications of this view for HCI:

- Interaction with interactive systems involves constant tailoring and appropriation: Users interpret, modify, work around, and redesign interactive systems so that they work better for their goals. For example, Chetty et al. [148] showed that Internet users who face bandwidth caps develop practices to avoid the cap and its consequences, such as avoiding software updates. In general, it is a key challenge in HCI to understand how such appropriation and tailoring occur and how to design systems to facilitate these aspects of practice.
- Interaction with interactive systems happens in a way that is sensitive to the user's social and technical contexts. It means that the community and the organization in which the interaction is embedded are both part of and shaped by interactive systems. For example, Dix [199] studied a web store for ordering books. He found that the administrator handling customer orders needed to halt orders depending on the stock levels. However, the administrator's interface did not allow this information to be communicated to others in the chain, who simply saw the order as "uncompleted." A change was later made to the interface to allow the administrator to add notes to orders to communicate their status to others in the chain.
- Interaction with interactive systems should be understood as "historical processes and performances" and "longer-term actions which persist over time" [447, p. 3543]. The central question here is what happens in interaction over time, both in the workplace and in leisure. For example, Sas and Whittaker [729] studied what happens to shared digital possessions in social media services—like photos and videos—when couples break a romantic relationship. Such media accumulate over time and become part of the presentation of a relationship to others. The authors found that the way breaking couples treat shared digital possessions is sensitive to how they expect others in their social networks to perceive their behavior. This can lead to dilemmas, for example, when certain shared possessions are not removed even if one user would have liked to do so.

Paper Example 22.0.1: The development of a practice in groupware use

Practice is a central issue for systems that aim to intertwine with their users' work, particularly how they communicate and collaborate with the users. The positive effects expected from such systems often fail to materialize because these contingencies are neglected. Orlikowski [622] summarized an early study of a groupware system called Notes. The study pointed out that many different cognitive and organizational factors shape the effects a system may have on a particular organization in practice.

Over five months, Orlikowski [622] conducted interviews, reviewed documents, and carried out observations to study the introduction and initial use of Notes in a consulting company. The goal was to learn "how the groupware technology is adopted and used by individuals, and how work and social relations change as a consequence" [p. 363].

The results show that how individuals think about interactive systems and their work influences how they adopt systems, in this case, Notes. When individuals are confronted with new technology, they use their knowledge of earlier technology to understand the new system. This new understanding can be shaped by information about the system as well as by training. Orlikowski showed that neither of these was done extensively. Thereby, users of Notes mainly understood it as an individual technology (rather than as groupware) and had a weak understanding of what the system could do. This was not intrinsic to Notes and was developed as the system was used.

Another critical finding concerns how the organization of the company influenced how the system was used. In particular, the reward system, policies for conducting work, and work norms shaped how individuals viewed and used Notes. For instance, the company did not formulate new policies around sharing access to documents in the system or new ways of working to use Notes to its full potential.

As another example, the company's reward system shaped the use of Notes. A goal for many employees was to bill their time to clients to the greatest possible extent. This was beneficial for their careers and evaluations of their performance. This reward system worked against finding time to learn to use Notes effectively. As a consequence, people used the groupware system less than expected.

Through these findings, Orlikowski [622] offers rich theoretical perspectives for thinking about practice.

22.1 Adoption and adaption

One of the critical ideas of interaction-as-practice is that interactive systems never fully prescribe how they are used in real life. Instead, users ignore, alter, work around, or creatively modify all interactive systems as part of their practice. For instance, Gasser [270] described how people input false data to trick interactive systems into providing the desired results and keep manual or duplicate systems to work around inaccurate or wrong systems. Salovaara et al. [723] described how people used (pre-smartphone) digital cameras for a host of other tasks beyond taking pictures, including scanning documents and acting as periscopes to see better at concerts. The point here is that interaction and use are often different in practice from what is anticipated by designers.

Next, we separate three interlinked types of adaption and adoption of interactive systems: personalization, tailoring, and appropriation. These processes can affect systems, their users, and the use context to varying extents.

22.1.1 Personalization

One way users adopt and adapt information systems in practice is through the personalization of products. This is mainly an individual activity through which systems come to both reflect and help shape one's preferences and identity. Personalization is primarily about changing the appearance of interactive systems, that is, it focuses on non-functional changes. For instance, many users physically modify their mobile phones, using covers, stickers, and accessories; users also adapt the opening display of their desktop or laptop, and many people use 3D printing to personalize physical products.

Blom and Monk [79] presented a theory of why users customize their computers and personal mobile devices. This theory helps us understand what drives personalization and separates the reasons why people personalize their interactive systems from the effects of such personalization. The disposition to personalize depends on the user, the system, and the context of system use. For instance, whether one owns an interactive system and how frequently it is used influence the extent and type of adaption. For example, in the empirical studies of Blom and Monk [79], users reported personalizing their desktop because they use it frequently. Of course, users also need to know that they can personalize an interactive system and how to do it. The so-called socioemotional context of use also influences when users personalize systems. For instance, systems that involve communication with others (e.g., SMS, email) are more likely to be adapted compared to products that are mainly for oneself (e.g., a word processor).

The effects of personalization fall into three broad categories:

- *Cognitive effects* include, for instance, improved ease of use because certain parts of the system are easier to see. It may also be that the system as a whole is easier to recognize (e.g., an application with an unusual icon).
- *Social effects* include personalization that reflects one's personal identity, such as a feeling that distinguishes one user from other users of the same system. It may also show group identity, for example, allegiance to a particular brand or sports club.
- *Emotional effects* include feelings of fun and positive associations. They also include reducing boredom and an increased feeling of ownership or attachment to the interactive system.

The theory of Blom et al. applies widely to a range of information systems. From the early customization of mobile phones and information systems, similar concerns have been raised in relation to crafting, hacking, and a range of do-it-yourself activities centered on or supported by interactive systems. In all cases, these changes to interactive systems happen in practice and shape those systems as they weave into the lives of their users.

22.1.2 Tailoring

Adaption can also involve users intentionally modifying the functionality of interactive systems. This is not merely about the appearance of the system; it includes a broad range of activities from tinkering with settings and features to reprogramming parts of the system using macros, built-in programming languages, or other means to carry out modifications. Such activities are called *tailoring*.

Tailoring has been studied and supported since the 1980s. Early studies investigated tailoring work done on operating systems [503], spreadsheets [577], and computer-aided design [268]. Based on these and other studies, Mørch [557] identified three types of tailoring:

- *Customization* means that the users adapt the product by selecting attribute values from a selection. This is similar to personalization in that it often concerns appearance only but may also concern functionality. For instance, users may adapt the appearance and contents of their email replies.

- *Integration* means that the users add new functionality or features to the interactive system by linking existing components. For instance, integration may happen through macros, accelerators, or scripts.
- *Extension* means that users add new code or otherwise program the system.

The last type of tailoring has given rise to much research on *end-user programming*, particularly systems that allow users to easily change and adapt functionality.

22.1.3 Appropriation

Adaption and adoption can be complex, influencing more than just surface properties of systems or functionality. The term appropriation describes such processes [209], which may also change workflows, the division of labor, and organizational processes. Appropriation does not specifically concern modifying interactive systems; it concerns all the changes that might be associated with interaction with a system—in fact, appropriation is inherent to practice.

That systems are appropriated makes sense for several reasons. First, designers are unlikely to understand all the tasks and environments in which a product is used. This is particularly true for products that are widely used. Therefore, some degree of appropriation is necessary. Second, our needs and situations change. According to Henderson and Kyng [330], "the needs change, uses change, the users change, the organization change. Therefore the computer systems may well have to change to match the changed circumstances." For these reasons, appropriation is likely to occur often in practice.

Presently there are no models of appropriation. However, DeSanctis and Poole [186] captured some main types and proposed *appropriation moves* as an element of the social process that promotes appropriation. The following list of appropriation moves draws on their work and some of the previously mentioned empirical studies to illustrate how much practice shapes interactions:

- Actively champion the use of an interactive system.
- Substitute parts of the interactive system with other systems. This may be using a manual backup system instead of the intended system.
- Use an entirely different way of accomplishing work due to a perceived deficiency in the interactive system.
- Criticize the interactive system by comparing it to other ways of accomplishing the work.
- Interpret the interactive system, for instance, by explaining the meaning of functionality to others or prescribing how to use the system.
- Attempt to make others reject using the interactive system or otherwise actively prevent its use.
- Be slow in taking up the system or otherwise contribute to inertia in its uptake.

Some of these appropriations are faithful in that they attempt to adhere to underlying ideas and norms about work that are embedded in the system. Others are unfaithful in that they counter the system's fundamental premises. Any appropriation move may concern the interactive system in relation to other structures (e.g., tasks, organizational hierarchies) or ways of working (e.g., work routines). As appropriations are part of normatively regulated contingent activities, the list serves merely as inspiration and does not suggest any causality.

Empirical studies have highlighted how other people affect appropriation. In an ethnographic study of spreadsheet use, Nardi and Miller [577] found that most spreadsheet modifications were the work of multiple people. The modifications were also an effective way of sharing programming experience and domain knowledge. Thus, appropriating spreadsheets changes the work with respect to how people collaborate and how they learn about the domain of work; the work practice develops along with the tailoring of the spreadsheet.

The concept of appropriation implies that design is *not* finished when an interactive system is designed and implemented. Rather, design is a process: It begins in what is traditionally considered design and ends in practice, that is, during use [330]. According to this view, systems may be more or less easy to appropriate; therefore, they may be designed to make them easier to appropriate. Much work has aimed to find principles for designing systems that are easy to appropriate.

If appropriation refers to uses that a system was not designed for, how can one design for appropriation? Dix [199] claimed that this is important but not only possible. Appropriation makes the design better able to fit the task environments of the user, which are all unique. It can also increase the felt ownership of software: Something that you have invested in via appropriation is likely to feel more important. Summarizing experiences from empirical cases and prior work, Dix proposed guidelines for supporting appropriation:

Allow interpretation: Avoid fixed meanings and include elements where users can add their own meanings. For example, some email clients allow users to flag emails with colors (e.g., yellow, green, red), leaving the assignment of meaning to the user.

Provide visibility: Providing visibility of system functioning and status will help users understand how to develop appropriations. Appropriating a black box, whose internal working is unclear, is inherently hard.

Expose intentions: Tell the user what the intended use of a function is. For example, instead of simply asking a user to generate a strong password, the user can be reminded that the goal is to protect the user's data (intention). This allows cooperative users to avoid subversive appropriations.

Support not control: Some tasks can be thought of as procedures that need to be executed from the beginning to the end in a particular order. However, everyday practices may require exceptions. According to Dix, designs should not force users to do tasks in a particular way (control) but offer flexible variation (support).

Plugability and configuration: Users should be allowed to create systems on their own. This means that software should offer connections to other software and sensors, as well as clear application programming interfaces.

Encourage sharing: By allowing users to share their appropriations, they can be re-appropriated by others. If sharing is done systematically, for example, via a user community, it can facilitate wider adoption of the software.

Learn from appropriation: Observing the ways users appropriate technology can provide insights for product development. If users appropriate some functionality for a purpose it was not designed for, such functionality can be explicitly supported in the next iteration.

22.2 The context of interaction

Viewing interaction as practice means that interaction always needs to be understood as part of a larger set of activities with a history and social and organizational contexts. Earlier in this chapter, we discussed some contextual aspects of appropriation; in this section, we further discuss them and their implications for understanding interaction.

Entwistle et al. [228] presented a model with four components of practice:

- Material, which interacts with the individual component
- Individual, which interacts with the societal and material components
- Societal, which interacts with the individual and infrastructural components
- Infrastructural, which does not interact with the individual component.

This model provides a structure for the implications of considering interaction as practice. First, the model emphasizes the *social structures* surrounding interaction. Interaction is always part of a larger sociotechnical system: Norms, rules, and social organization both shape and are shaped by interaction. Therefore, we should keep in mind the sociotechnical system as well as the organization and division of labor that surround interaction (Section 22.2.1).

Second, the model emphasizes the *infrastructures* that enable and support interaction. An infrastructure is a physical or technological system that shapes or structures behavior over time in such a way that infrastructures are not at the center of our attention. Examples of infrastructure include the electricity grid, roads, and the postal system. In computer use, infrastructures include different social media channels, digital platforms, operating systems, and the Internet. In the past decade, researchers have increasingly studied such infrastructures and the work that supports them; see Section 22.2.2 for examples.

Third, the model emphasizes the *near material* surrounding the interaction. This emphasizes that interaction always happens in a particular physical setting, with other technologies and material circumstances shaping interaction. Thus, analyses of isolated interaction with one particular tool are likely to miss the influence of those other circumstances. Such limitations can be mitigated by studying the ecology of the tools used by people, which we discuss in Section 22.2.3.

Fourth, the model emphasizes the *individual*, who plays a central role in practice. The skills and knowledge required to use interactive systems need to be acquired and nurtured. This perspective is also covered in several other views of interaction. In Section 22.2.4, we highlight the influence of this perspective on identity and attachment to products. The key analytic idea of the model is that interaction is shaped by, and thus needs to be understood through, at least these four components. This idea has several implications for understanding interaction in practice. Next, we highlight four key implications.

22.2.1 Division of labor and contradictions

Activity theory is a prominent theory in HCI for understanding practices [e.g., 83, 448]. Its key idea is that activity is a minimal unit of analysis for human action—but what is an activity?

An activity involves transforming an object into an outcome using one or more tools. For instance, editing (activity) involves the user (subject) using a word processor (tool) to turn a draft into a finished paper (outcome). The individual actions with a word processor may only be understood properly by focusing on the full activity. The word processor fundamentally shapes one's editing activity through what one can do and how the activity has proceeded up to that point. An activity such as editing does not exist in a vacuum; it is simultaneously part of a web of activities involving other people. These relations form the triangle of activity between subject, object, and tool, covered in Chapter 19.

Engeström [227] extended this basic model to aid understanding of additional aspects of the context of an activity. While they are not necessarily recognized or made explicit, many contextual aspects are always present. Activity always happens as part of a *community* that shares the object with the user. In the case of an author editing a paper, the community includes the other authors of that paper. *Rules* include implicit and explicit norms and conventions within a community. In the editing example, the rules may include agreements among authors on the writing style. The *division of labor* includes implicit and explicit ways of organizing the activity of turning an object into an *outcome*. In the editing example, this may include which section is written by whom or who reviews the draft next. Spelling out the components of a system of collective activity is useful for analyzing interaction. It can help us understand the relationships between components, including any disturbances or contradictions among them, which also shape the user's practice.

22.2.2 Infrastructures

One way to understand infrastucture as outlined in the beginning of Chapter 22.2.2 is to consider a trick to make it visible. *Infrastructural inversion* is a "gestalt switch." In other words, attention is shifted from the activities invisibly supported by an infrastructure to the activities that enable the infrastructure to function and meet the needs of collaboration. We approach infrastructuring as part of the design and use of information technologies, akin to the characterization: "activities that contribute to the successful establishment of an information system usage (equivalent to a work infrastructure improvement)" [659, p. 447]. Infrastructural inversion has also been used to shift attention to mundane operational processes, that is, the silent, unnoticed work that enables infrastructures to function rather than the work that infrastructures invisibly support. Furthermore, it has been used to direct attention to "unexciting" things, such as unremarkable lists, commonplace plugs, technical specifications, standards, bureaucratic forms, and details buried in inaccessible code, as well as to hidden mechanisms subtending more visible processes.

22.2.3 Ecology of tools

In practice, interaction happens alongside a range of other technologies and artifacts that support the activity. For instance, many users own multiple devices for accessing their emails or calendars. Some users own multiple devices but use each device for a particular set of functions, for example, alternating between a work tablet and a private tablet depending on the task. Many workplaces require multiple interactive systems to be involved in routine tasks. We call this fundamental aspect of practice the *ecology of tools*. This encompasses all kinds of tools, including paper-based and digital tools.

In practice, interactive systems show a complex interplay with other tools. New systems influence why, how often, and in what way old systems are used. For instance, users transfer habits, strategies, and other ways of working from known systems to new systems. The mutual influence between interactive systems is fundamentally dynamic [116]; as a consequence, much work has focused on cross-device use and on improving the interplay between devices [102].

22.2.4 Identity and attachment

Interaction is invariably linked to social structures. In turn, this connection affects how individuals relate to their identity and the attachment they feel to interactive systems. Over time, interactive systems may become an important part of how we perceive ourselves to be and how others perceive us. This is reflected in figures of speech such as "a Mac person" or "a Wikipedian" (see Paper Example 22.2.1).

> **Paper Example 22.2.1: Becoming a Wikipedian**
>
> Bryant et al. [106] presented what is now a classic study on how interactive systems shape participation and communication among users who begin to work on Wikipedia. Wikipedia relies on unpaid volunteers who put substantial effort into writing and editing articles. However, how do users become expert Wikipedians?
>
> The authors conducted telephone interviews with nine users to understand how novice Wikipedians become experts, specifically "why the participants contributed to Wikipedia, how they had gotten started, how they perceived their role and, most importantly, how their perception of Wikipedia and their participation in it had changed over the course of their engagement with the site."
>
> The authors found that this transformative process from novice to expert is described well by the theory of legitimate peripheral participation. Initially, users are motivated by the prospect of contributing to the greater good that Wikipedia represents to them:
>
>> I really got inspired by the idea [of the Wikipedia]. I'd say a lot of what hooked me was the community aspect and knowing that I was contributing something that was going to be around for a while... at the very least, I'll have done my part to make the whole package better and more accessible and more understandable, better links, more complete, whatever I happened to accomplish. (Participant 2)
>
> Thanks to the way the community is structured, users can start contributing immediately as novices. Newcomers become members by contributing to peripheral (secondary) tasks that are simpler and less risky than those of more established editors. Through such simpler accomplishments, their movement closer to the center of the community is legitimized, and they begin to take on larger responsibilities and roles. Such accomplishments also help novices build their knowledge of the community and the technology as well as their skills and practices, including their vocabulary.
>
> It is, however, the "oldtimers" who control the movement of the newcomers toward the center. Although all editors, nominally, have access to the same editing tools, the oldtimers can lower but also raise barriers to participation. They can grant certain editing rights or provide statements to members that publicly legitimize their participation. Wikipedia has been successful partly thanks to this expert–novice relationship, which allows novices to contribute despite their limited competence.

22.3 **Putting practice into practice**

This chapter has emphasized that interaction with interactive systems reaches beyond the interface; it is a practice. Interaction shapes and is shaped by the social world. The concept of practice has three defining characteristics. First, practice is unfolding and contingent, and is best studied via field methods. Second, practice is shared and collective; it shapes and is shaped by other people. Third, while practices can develop quickly, understanding them typically requires understanding the historical and cultural contexts in which they occur.

Turning field observations into insights that can concretely inform design has turned out to be difficult, however. So far, the concept of practice has delivered less than it was hoped when its development started. The reason is that practices turned out to be difficult to identify empirically. Practices are multi-faceted, and their facets are challenging to identify. While individual practices such as appropriations can be caught via observations or interviews, group and organizational practices are harder to detect. Moreover, to understand an infrastructure, one needs to study several individuals participating in the practice, as well as their artifacts and contexts. This can require hundreds of hours of work and several site visits. Constructs such as infrastructures are outside the reach of rapid ethnographic methods and contextual inquiry.

Instead of trying to pin down practice via empirical rigor, designers have found ways to address it directly in design. Designers are often unable to run full-fledged field studies to study practice, yet they still need to know about it. To this end, they have developed methods such as technology probes [367]. A "probe" may consist of a simple artifact, for example, a digital whiteboard used by a family, whose purpose is to acquire knowledge about existing practices and inspire thinking about alternative practices that might replace the original ones. Technology probes, as a research method used by designers, are not intended to collect knowledge that is reliable or valid but rather to inspire new ideas. While technology probes do not systematically expose practices, they provide knowledge about the context *around* them, which is valuable in design.

Moreover, practice has inspired a class of design methods: participatory methods. Here, the idea is to include stakeholders in the design process (Part VI). One of the main motivations is ensuring that designers have sufficient knowledge of practices, whether they are enacted by participants or inferred from field data. Moreover, design does not need to end at product launch. There are good reasons, rooted in the concept of practice, for continuing to collaborate with users after product launch. Paper Example 22.3.1 provides an example of tailoring gone wrong; in this case, the authors argued that continuous design would have been beneficial. After launch, users may be approached via panels (selected user groups who volunteer to be available for studies), user communities (online forums for service-specific discussions), or traditional methods such as consumer surveys.

Paper Example 22.3.1: Continuing design in use

Henderson and Kyng [331] described cases where the design had failed to support tailoring, which severely hampered the fit of the technology. In one case, an information system for the payroll office of a university had been updated. Previously, a payroll officer handled employees with a particular contract type; the new system organized the employees by birth year, which led to employees having to deal with multiple contract types. While adding a feature to allow for contract-based allocations would have been technically easy, system modifications beyond bug fixing were not possible after the system's launch.

The authors made a radical proposition: If tailoring never ends, design should never end, either. They gave two reasons for supporting continuous design. First, the contexts of use change; design should respond to the users' changing needs. Second, because of the complexity of sociotechnical systems, it is practically impossible to "get it right" on the first attempt; it is much wiser to monitor use and engage in design continuously.

Summary

- Practices help users achieve order and complete goals in complex sociotechnical circumstances.
- Practices have individual, artifactual, and social facets. They call for the empirical study of not only behavior but also material and technical infrastructures.
- Despite initial excitement, it has been difficult to study practices for the purpose of informing practical decisions in design and engineering.

Exercises

1. Tailoring versus personalization. Consider your main computer or laptop. Identify elements you have tailored, for example, the desktop background or web browser plug-ins. Comment on the type of tailoring you have achieved and explain your motivations for such tailoring. Discuss whether it is tailoring or personalization.

2. Appropriation. For a few days, keep a log of how you use your mobile camera, particularly those uses it was not originally designed for. For instance, it could be used as a binocular to look at distant objects or as a mirror. What other uses did you find?

3. Appropriation moves. A large international consultancy firm is introducing a new communication tool to increase collaboration between local and remote team members engaged in consulting. The tool enables secure messaging and the sharing of documents and spreadsheets, including valuable client data. (a) Describe the difference between the personalization and tailoring of this tool. (b) Explain why, despite the system initially fulfilling the users' needs and wants, users are still likely to engage in appropriation. (c) Suggest three appropriation moves that might occur with this system and explain how guidelines for appropriation can mitigate or enhance, as appropriate, such effects.

4. Studying data practices. When commuting or traveling, sometimes we need data that are not available, for example, due to the data being stored on another device, network unavailability, or authentication errors. Users develop different practices to overcome these issues. Those who face this often develop stable routines, for example, they may always carry the same things or use cloud storage. Others plan and prepare data on a per-travel basis. Your task is to interview a friend or colleague to understand their data practices. Following the guidance given in Chapter 11, develop an interview scheme to achieve the following two goals. (a) Identify the type of travel (e.g., commuting, international work travel) where data availability has been an issue. (b) Identify the routine and preparation practices related to that type of travel.

Part V

User Interfaces

23
Introduction to user interfaces

Interactive systems are normally considered technical objects in computer science and engineering. The part of an interactive system that "faces" the user is called the user interface. The user interface is the only part of a system that is used by real people doing real tasks in real settings. Therefore, what makes an interface good is ultimately determined by humans. As a result, research on user interfaces is a cross-disciplinary effort with contributions from computer science, electrical engineering, design, and psychology.

Innovations and insights into user interfaces take many forms. Engelbart [226] suggested that interactive systems and their user interfaces should augment the human intellect. In another study, Shneiderman [764] identified direct manipulation—the idea that you can directly operate on objects in user interfaces—as the success behind GUIs. As a final example, Weiser [879] suggested that the role of user interfaces is to disappear; a good user interface does not impose itself on the user's attention.

The integrative theme in user interface design is that a user interface should *match the needs and capabilities of its users*. On the one hand, user interfaces should be designed to respect the general understanding of humans as computer users, as laid out in Part II. From this understanding follows a set of objectives that are always relevant in the design and evaluation of user interfaces. On the other hand, every user interface is unique when it comes to specific users and their contexts. Knowledge about users and their contexts usually comes from empirical research (Part III). User interfaces can also be understood more abstractly through theories and models, which are discussed in Part IV. Thus, a good user interface draws on input from both needs and capabilities, empirical studies, and theories and models of interaction.

In the rest of this chapter, we first define user interfaces and give some examples of different user interface types. These types are then discussed in depth in subsequent chapters. At the core of all work on user interfaces is a thorough understanding of what an interface is, what the key design choices are, their associated trade-offs, and how to approach open decisions systematically. The last sections of this chapter discuss these choices and trade-offs.

23.1 Definition and elements of a user interface

A user interface can be broken down into four constitutive elements according to the devices, interaction techniques, representations, and assemblies (DIRA) model [66]:

Devices: To be effective, an interactive system must allow the user to provide information and control it effectively, efficiently, and safely. Input devices allow the user to provide input to the system in a variety of ways. Examples of input devices include mice, keyboards, touchscreens, microphones, and eye trackers. In addition to the user providing information to the system, the system needs to provide information and feedback to the user. This is achieved through output devices such as laptop displays, audio, rumble, and force-feedback.

Introduction to Human-Computer Interaction. Kasper Hornbæk, Per Ola Kristensson, and Antti Oulasvirta,
Oxford University Press. © Kasper Hornbæk, Per Ola Kristensson, and Antti Oulasvirta (2025).
DOI: 10.1093/oso/9780192864543.003.0023

Interaction techniques: Input devices provide input from the user but do not necessarily interpret these inputs in a manner that helps operate an interactive system. Interaction techniques translate input from input devices and possibly context sensors into solutions to basic interactive operations, such as moving, selecting, pointing, or navigating. The gain function, which maps mouse movement to cursor movement, is an example of an interaction technique (Chapter 26).

Representations: Representations determine how data, events, objects, and actions appear to the user. Representations may be text, sounds, taste, or any other form of data in an interactive system that is shown to users through a display. Visual icons (e.g., the trash can) are an example of representations.

Assemblies: Assemblies describe the broader set of principles that organize representations. Assemblies define how the representations are organized and put together in the user interface both spatially and temporally. For instance, in a web browser, pages are linked in particular ways, pages update their representations in particular ways, and information is shown in particular ways. These ways are the essence of assemblies.

Together, these elements form a user interface. Note that this definition does not mention processing. The internal mechanisms of how the system processes information about the user are not part of the definition. Instead, the user interface is the part of the technical system that is perceivable and actionable from the user's perspective. The user interface and its broader technical operating context are jointly called an *interactive system*.

In this part, devices are discussed in the chapters on input devices (Chapter 24) and displays (Chapter 25). Chapter 26 discusses interaction techniques, and Chapter 27 discusses some central issues in representation. The question of organization for individual interface types is discussed in the respective chapters that cover those types. Below, we discuss the main types of user interfaces.

23.2 Interaction styles

User interfaces can take many styles and forms depending on the tasks they need to support users with. To understand the fundamental ideas in user interfaces, it is useful to be aware of the concept of *interaction style*. An interaction style is a particular genre of interaction that specifies how users interact with computer systems. An interaction style is a combination of particular instances of the four elements of user interfaces that recur in the literature or in practice. Each interaction style has particular characteristics, advantages, and disadvantages. Next, we briefly discuss five styles of interaction. Note that the user interface of an interactive system may mix interaction styles; for example, the combination of menus and forms is common on the web.

23.2.1 Command-line interfaces

In a command-line interface, the user enters commands and waits for the interactive system to respond. Typically, this happens in a terminal that offers nothing but a textual prompt to the user. The response from the system is also typically just text, which the user cannot interact with directly (say, by clicking on the text), except by issuing another command.

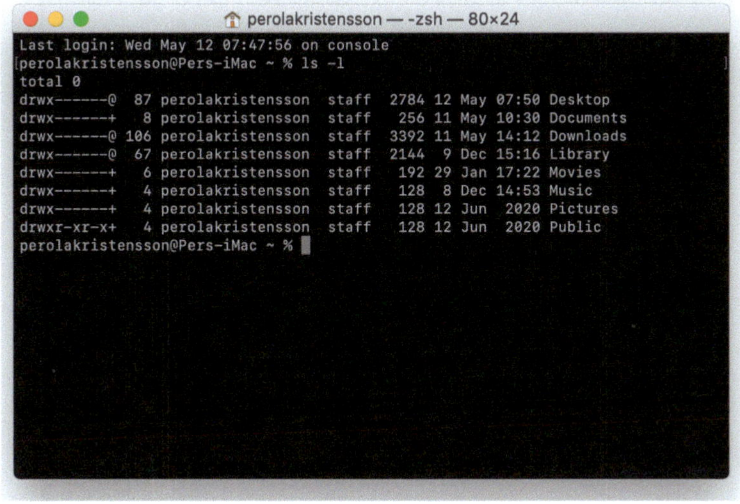

Figure 23.1 A command entry at a command prompt in a terminal window. The command ls -l lists all files and directories in the current directory.

Good examples of command-line interfaces come from the first user interfaces to computers, where commands are typed into a terminal (Figure 23.1). Nowadays, many development environments include an integrated command prompt, as do GUIs, such as the terminal in macOS and the command window in Windows.

Command-line user interfaces are now typically provided to support expert users with tasks that are impossible, difficult, or inefficient to carry out in a point-and-click interface. Such tasks are facilitated by the command-line interfaces' ability to abstract over objects (for instance, using a wildcard operator) and be customizable via multiple options and parameters. The drawback is that the user needs to recall commands. Also, command-line user interfaces allow the user to make syntactic errors (e.g., misspellings) and do not prevent meaningless operations (e.g., printing a folder).

23.2.2 Forms

Forms are another style of interaction. Forms facilitate data entry and were first used in text terminal systems. They consist of one or more widgets, such as text boxes or checkboxes, through which the user can input data. Figure 23.2 shows an example of a form. Many of the early conventions adopted for forms are still in place today, such as the use of the Tab key to move to the next field in a form.

Forms support data entry by providing a highly structured and easy-to-understand interface for collecting the required information from users. They help users understand what to input and in what order. However, forms are highly limited to data entry tasks, and even then, their efficacy and utility depend on the designer's ability to efficiently encode all data entry requirements into a form that is easy to understand and process.

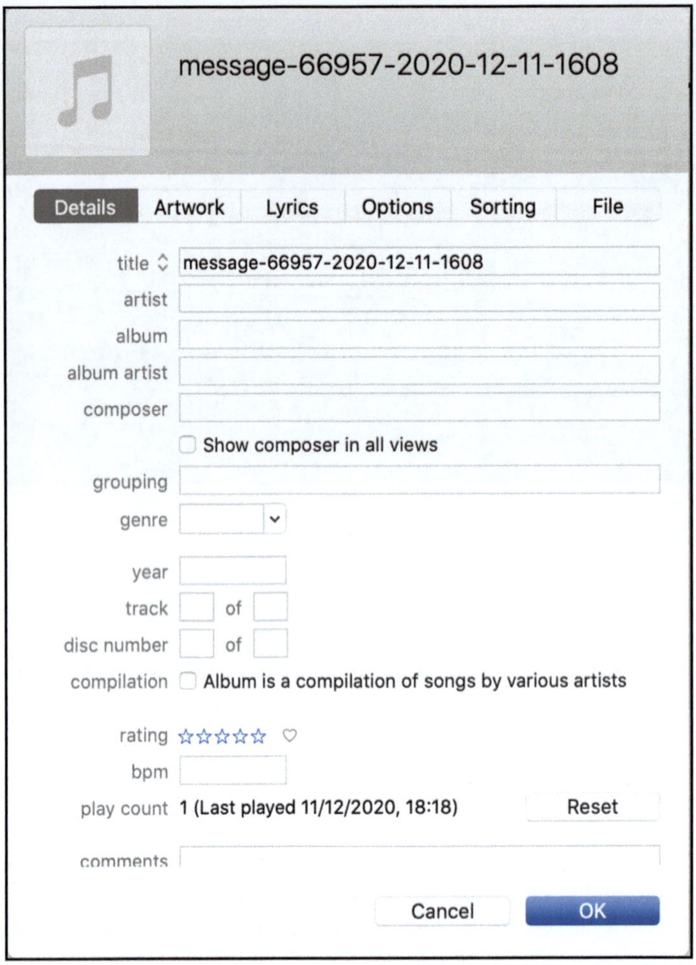

Figure 23.2 A form in a graphical user interface (GUI).

23.2.3 Menus

Another central interaction style is *menu* interaction. A menu presents the user with a set of options from which one may be selected; the selection may trigger a command or may open another part of the menu. Like forms, menus can be the only interaction style in a user interface or be combined with other interaction styles. A traditional graphical user interface (GUI) provides linear drop-down menus that let the user explore the menu hierarchy (Figure 23.3). Menus do not necessarily have a pull-down style; for example, a menu may reveal all the menu items directly.

Menus have several advantages. First, they support exploration: Unfamiliar users searching for a particular command can explore the menu structure to find it. Second, menus can help all users: novice, intermediate, and experienced. Novice users can spend time exploring the menu structure and gain familiarity with the available commands. Third, pull-down menus allow more commands to be made available compared to showing all the commands on the screen at once. Since top-level menus can be decomposed into menu items and submenus, pull-down menus also support the

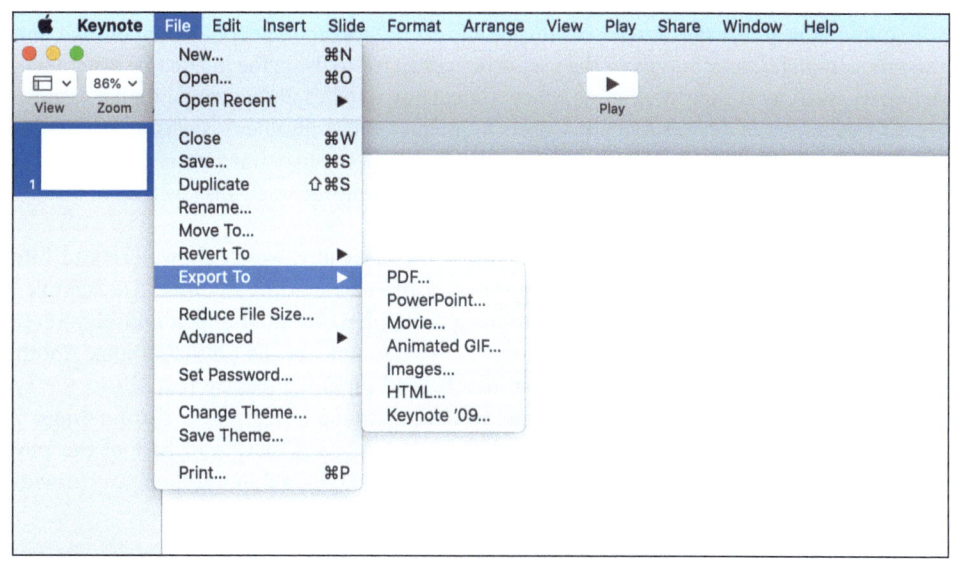

Figure 23.3 Linear pull-down menus in a presentation software GUI.

natural grouping of commands. A major disadvantage of menus is that their scalability is limited. Even though menu hierarchies can be massive in theory, in practice, they become cumbersome to navigate and difficult to explore. Moreover, frequently used commands are often easier to access for novice and intermediate users when they are readily available in a toolbar compared to opening and navigating menus.

23.2.4 Graphical user interfaces

GUIs allow users to interact directly with objects in the user interface. This ability is known as *direct manipulation*. An example of such direct manipulation is when the user deletes a file by moving the mouse cursor over the file, selecting it, and subsequently dragging it to an icon representing a trash can. The GUI has been the dominant interface paradigm since the Xerox Star was introduced in 1981 (Figure 1.1). A central idea of GUIs is direct manipulation, as discussed earlier in this chapter.

The benefits of GUIs are that they support novices in seeing the available objects and actions and that direct manipulation makes it possible to explore the user interface since the user can undo operations. The drawbacks are that it is not always effective to present objects and actions visually and that the ceiling of performance may be lower than, for instance, that of command-line interfaces. We discuss these benefits and drawbacks in more detail in Chapter 28, which is devoted to GUIs.

23.2.5 Reality-based interaction

Reality-based interaction is an umbrella term for the styles of interaction that have been developed since the GUI [381]. In reality-based interfaces, designers draw on our experience with the real world to develop new forms of user interfaces. This style covers a broad range of diverse interfaces.

To outline the advantages and disadvantages of reality-based interaction, let us consider some examples. In *mobile user interfaces*, the user is not restricted to using the interactive system while stationary, such as at their desk in an office. Calculator watches and personal digital assistants are early examples of devices that allow users to interact with computer systems off the desktop. Recent examples include touchscreen mobile phones, tablets, smartwatches, and fitness bands. Mobile user interfaces have their set of challenges, most notably the small form factor. For instance, typing on a watch-sized user interface is very difficult.

Another example of reality-based interaction is mixed reality, which allows users to interact with virtual objects registered in the physical world surrounding the user. An example of an augmented reality interface is a user moving their phone around and the display revealing virtual objects that appear located in the 3D background of the physical room. Another example is a user wearing an optical see-through head-mounted display that allows the system to display virtual objects that appear located in the user's physical surroundings. As the user moves their head around, virtual objects appear as if they were part of the physical location. More information and other styles of reality-based interaction are provided in Chapter 29.

23.3 Design objectives

Human–computer interaction (HCI) researchers and practitioners often focus on the design objectives of user interfaces. What objectives are important in designing such interfaces? If we understand those objectives, we can consider them when thinking about, designing, and evaluating user interfaces. In general, such objectives come from three sources:

- Understanding of people. User interfaces must fit the people who use them, including how they perceive, how their memory works, how they learn, and how they collaborate. We have covered these considerations in Part II. For example, the manual control of a user interface needs to be learned and remembered, which means that the learnability of an interface is important.
- Theories of interaction. User interfaces enable interaction with interactive systems. Thus, the theories of interaction presented in Part IV suggest what to aim for in a user interface. For example, the chapter on information and control (Chapter 17) discusses input rates; maximizing these is a key design objective for user interfaces.
- Attributes and structural qualities of the user interface. The objectives related to these attributes concern the structure of the user interface and the way widgets are designed. For example, consistency is often a design objective for user interfaces, as consistent user interfaces are typically easier for people to operate (but not always, as we shall discuss in Section 23.3.3).

Note that a discussion of design objectives for user interfaces brackets some issues around utility (Chapter 19) and the fit of an information system to practice (Chapter 22). This is because these issues are not primarily related to the user interface but rather to its fit to people, activities, and the context of use (for a refresher, see Part III). With this in mind, we now discuss some objectives that recur in discussions of user interfaces.

23.3.1 Supporting novice, intermediate, and expert performance

A central objective of a user interface is to allow users to learn how to use it, become proficient, and use it to achieve their goals. However, there are many aspects of learning and proficiency in a user interface. Figure 23.4 provides an overview of these aspects. First, a central concern is that user interfaces should be *easy to learn*. It needs to be easy to walk up to a system and figure out how to operate it.

Second, users should become *proficient* with the user interface. In other words, they should be able to seamlessly transition from novices to intermediate and then expert users. This requires the user interface to support users in gradually improving their performance to reach high levels of performance.

Third, user interfaces may support users in achieving *optimal performance*. This may require extensive training and practice over time. For example, studies of computer gamers show that *StarCraft 2* experts use two commands per second [918] and experts in *Tetris* can manage four pieces per second [485].

The focus on initial performance, extended learnability, and ultimate performance raises several objectives for user interfaces. These objectives have been articulated as criteria for evaluating interfaces [884], principles for designing user interfaces [593], models for transitioning novices into experts [157], and surveys of learnability [297]. Next, we review the interface *features and strategies* identified in these papers; general insights about learning are covered in Chapter 5.

Initial performance: To support initial performance, it has been suggested that user interfaces should support exploratory learning [699, 884]. In exploratory learning, users investigate the system on their own initiative, testing features and strategies to solve real tasks or to learn about the system. User interfaces can support exploratory learning in many ways.

One strategy is to allow for the reversal of actions, for example, by making the undo functionality available. This encourages exploration by providing users with an easy method to reverse any unintended changes in the state of the system.

Another strategy is to make actions and the status of the system visible, as discussed earlier in the principle of visibility. This allows users to recognize possible actions instead of having to recall command names or particular gestures. Making relevant aspects of the status of the system visible tells users that they are on the right path.

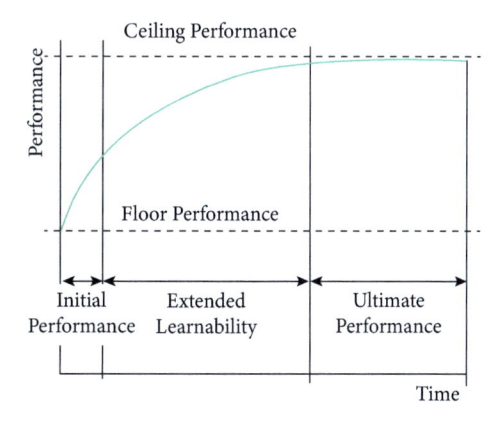

Figure 23.4 A simple model of performance with three phases of learning on the *y*-axis [157, p. 12].

A third strategy to support initial performance is to *simplify* the initial interface and gradually add new layers of functionality and complexity as the users learn to use it. Training wheels on bicycles are an everyday example of this; Paper Example 23.3.1 shows an application of this idea in HCI.

Paper Example 23.3.1: Attaching training wheels to a graphical user interface

The idea of gradually adding functionality as users become more proficient was introduced in the HCI literature as *training wheels* [132]. Through this approach, the interface identifies common errors made by novice users and prevents these errors by blocking certain states of the user interface or disallowing certain complex commands. In an experiment with a word processor, the concept of a training wheel resulted in faster and better learning of the interface.

The key challenge with simplified user interfaces is determining when and how to transition to more complex interfaces; one approach is to dynamically reveal the features of the interface. The idea is to show features when the user may need them and hide them otherwise. One commonly implemented tactic is context-dependent toolbar panels that dynamically change to show relevant commands based on the user's current selection. For example, in a word processor, a context-dependent toolbar may show commands relevant for editing a table when the user has selected a table and commands for editing a figure when the user has selected a figure.

Extended learnability: For extended learnability, other objectives are relevant. The goal here is to help users get close to their performance ceiling with the user interface. Interface features that support this goal include the following:

1. Shortcuts, also known as hotkeys. Shortcuts allow the user to access commands via keyboard combinations, such as CTRL-C, instead of having to navigate a menu structure.
2. Support for habit formation and automaticity. Raskin [688] argued that modeless interfaces support the formation of habits. In a modeless interface, all operations are available all the time; in a moded interface, part of the user interface works differently (e.g., the caps key).
3. Battling satisficing. These are ways of rehearsing and integrating extended learnability in software. For instance, the user interface ExposeHK [513] helped its users discover and rehearse keyboard shortcuts.

Paper Example 23.3.2 shows an example of how to improve the performance ceiling using an experimental interface.

Paper Example 23.3.2: Improving extended learnability with CommandMaps

User interface design often needs to consider how much information to show; Scarr et al. [736] coupled this discussion with improving intermediate learnability in a surprising way.

In a typical hierarchical structure, one needs to click icons to open a small menu with further options. By contrast, the experimental interface CommandMaps relies on the user's spatial memory to flatten the hierarchical structure (essentially a menu user interface) and improve the ceiling of performance for experts. As shown in the figure in this paper example box, CommandMaps immediately expands the hierarchy of icons. This uses a lot of space on the display but ensures that each icon appears in the same location. In theory, this should enhance learnability for all users: Experts can perform much faster and novices can still use the interface. Scarr et al. [736] tested this theory in an empirical study and found that this was indeed the case.

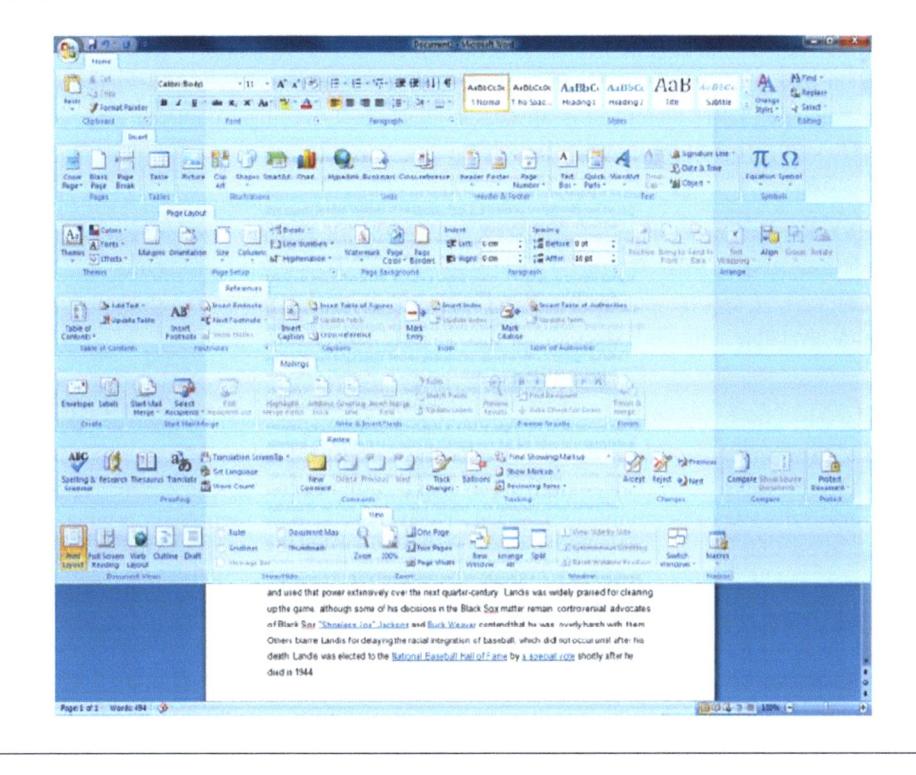

Ultimate performance: Some user interfaces may focus on the ability to achieve optimal or peak performance in the long term. What is the fastest way that can be designed to input text into a computer? This is a difficult question to answer; nevertheless, theoretical limits to performance derived from models of performance can be used to remove barriers to optimal performance.

Another way to reason about ultimate performance is to draw on models from information and control (Chapter 17). For instance, such models can help us reason about the maximal throughput of an input device. Finally, some researchers have taken inspiration from science fiction to imagine what superpowers users would want and then consider how to realize them in user interfaces [893]. For instance, we could imagine user interfaces that improve our ability to attend to information in the environment, such as being able to see things that other people miss (like Sherlock Holmes) or cannot detect at all (like Spiderman).

23.3.2 Usability and accessibility

As we discussed in the chapter on tool use (Chapter 19), a user interface is ultimately a means to an end: Users interact with user interfaces to achieve goals that are external to the interface.

Therefore, user interfaces should *help* users achieve their goals and *avoid* hindering their progress toward those goals. The concepts of usability and accessibility may work directly as design objectives for user interfaces. Recall that *usability* concerns whether users can achieve their goals effectively, efficiently, and with satisfaction. *Accessibility* refers to the goal of achieving equivalent levels of usability between user groups.

How can we turn these views of interaction into more concrete objectives for thinking about user interfaces? One option is to articulate guidelines or criteria that good interfaces should adhere to. We will discuss such guidelines in detail later within the context of evaluation (Part VIII); for now, we note that such guidelines may also be used to think about user interfaces in a general way. In heuristic evaluation [591], a method we discuss in Chapter 41, we might consider the following heuristics to ensure that a user interface is usable:

- Help users recognize, diagnose, and recover from errors. Provide error messages that are understandable by users and offer a clear solution path to rectify the problem.
- Prevent errors, for example, by displaying a warning and requiring user confirmation before a non-reversible action is triggered, such as deleting a file.

To make user interfaces efficient, we may consider the following. Note that we use the term "operation" to mean accomplishing things like selecting, navigating, entering text, and so on. This is different from "tasks" in terms of what the user might want to achieve with a system in a matter of hours or days. For operations, users generally expect to achieve their goals as quickly and accurately as possible.

Since users inevitably vary in their proficiency with a user interface, it is often desirable to provide interface features that can be tailored to suit different users. One example is providing keyboard shortcuts for menu items and toolbar buttons, providing expert users with immediate access to these functions while novice users can still locate them easily (albeit more slowly) via direct manipulation. Another strategy is to allow users to customize the user interface or have the user interface adapt to the user.

In short, we have some ideas of what a usable interface looks like, expressed in the guidelines, and we may use these ideas in the design and evaluation of user interfaces.

23.3.3 **Structure and attributes of the user interface**

User interfaces are typically evaluated at a lower level than the interactive system level. In this way, the design objectives can be much more closely related to the four elements of user interfaces than the goals discussed above. Below, we provide an overview of the three main design objectives of user interfaces.

Explorability

Explorability means that a user interface supports exploratory learning of the functionality offered [699, 884]. As discussed for initial performance, explorability is particularly important for first-time users.

Discoverability

Related to explorability, discoverability is about the effort it takes to find the possible actions in a user interface. Norman [597] considered it through the following question: "Is it possible to even figure out what actions are possible and where and how to perform them?"

One strategy is to make actions visible. This allows users to recognize possible actions rather than having to recall command names or particular gestures. In heuristic evaluation, the idea is to support discoverability through the visibility of system status. The current state of the system should be visible to the user. A simple example is a progress bar that indicates the progress of a long operation, such as downloading a large file.

Consistency

Consistency means that the representations and ways of interacting are similar across the user interface or to other (reference) interfaces. If the print command is represented with an icon showing a particular printer in one part of the interface, the same icon should be used elsewhere in the interface. The same idea applies to interaction techniques. If one has to right-click an object to invoke a particular command, one should use the same right-click action to invoke other commands. Consistency might be sought across user interfaces to achieve external consistency. The rationale is that external consistency helps users transfer their skills across interfaces.

There are several techniques to ensure consistency. Adhering to style guides—such as Apple's Human Interface Guidelines—ensures consistency across applications on a platform. Moreover, tools have been developed for checking the consistency of the bottom placement and labels [509]. However, the notion of consistency is not clear-cut. For instance, Grudin [299] provided several examples of interface design decisions where consistency was not attractive.

23.3.4 Trade-offs among objectives

Typically, there are *trade-offs* among the design objectives for user interfaces. Consistency is a classic example. It is essentially about ensuring familiarity, yet it also compromises novelty, which is a distinct design objective. Some trade-offs central to the user interface are listed in Table 23.1.

Most choices in user interface design involve trade-offs. Consider a simple binary decision, for example, whether to include a captcha on a login page. Captchas use a simple question to confirm whether the user is a human and not a bot. Including a captcha may decrease the probability of system faults due to attacks by bots; however, it lowers user performance since it takes longer to log in. By contrast, *not* including a captcha makes logging in faster; this is what users prefer. The decision to include a captcha involves balancing the trade-off between usability and vulnerability.

Trade-offs are not unique to HCI; they are inherent to all multi-objective problems in design and engineering (Chapter 39). *Pareto frontier* is a technical concept that generalizes the concept of trade-offs. It is used to describe a set of equally optimal designs. Pareto optimal designs are optimal designs that strike different compromises among the objectives. In practice, trade-offs may be solved via the consultation of design guidelines (Chapter 2), analytical methods (Chapter 41), or theories of interaction (Part IV). They may also be resolved through empirical evaluations.

Table 23.1 Common trade-offs in user interface design.

Trade-off	Explanation	Example
Speed vs. accuracy	Improvements in task completion time compromise accuracy	When we make pointing devices faster, we often affect their accuracy, and vice versa (Chapter 24)
Recognition vs. recall	Relying on recognition memory makes learning faster but curbs the maximum achievable performance; relying on recall slows learning but permits high performance over time	User interfaces such as command language interfaces vs. graphical user interfaces
Familiarity vs. novelty	Following conventions and standards improves learnability but compromises the felt novelty	Novel services often want to stand out via their user interface design, whereas users often want familiarity
Expert user vs. novice user	Trying to cater to experts may make the user interface hard to use for novices, thereby reducing user adoption	Professional photo-editing software that offers thousands of functions may be very hard to use for novices
Those who do the work vs. those who reap the benefits	User interfaces may delegate low-level tasks (e.g., information filling) to one user group, benefiting another group	User interfaces for corporate information systems may be useful for management but not for end-users

23.4 Design space analysis

User interfaces are complex. A successful user interface is a combination of input and output devices that are assembled by well-designed interaction techniques and representations that are appropriate for the tasks users are expected to carry out. Decision-making about a user interface should start by considering each decision systematically. However, how do you grasp a user interface without getting lost in the details?

Design space analysis refers to a semi-formal representation of the constituents of user interfaces [508]. Design space analysis is an essential thinking tool that helps us avoid getting lost in details by enumerating the key choices and comparing them. As such, this technique aids both problem-solving and higher-level reflection.

Table 23.2 gives an overview of three such techniques that differ in their focus and unit of analysis. *Morphological analysis* is best suited for understanding a user interface as a transducer, that is, something that transforms a user's actions into changes in the computer's state. It offers an abstraction of the user interface that is not tied to the particular technology on which the interface is implemented. *Joint system analysis* adds humans to the picture. The properties of user interfaces are described as parameters, some of which are controllable by the designer (e.g., the color of a button) while others are not (e.g., user experience). The benefit of this approach is that it can help us see the connection between technical considerations and user-related objectives. Finally, questions, options, and criteria (QOC) is an analysis method that aims not only to enumerate solutions but also to aid decision-making. Specifically, it aims to enumerate key decisions, possible alternatives (options), and criteria (what is desirable).

Table 23.2 Three forms of design space analysis that can be used to understand user interfaces.

Method	Focus	Unit of analysis
Morphological analysis	Technology	Technical variables that constitute an interface
Joint system analysis	Joint system that includes the human	Parameters that describe the properties of the joint human–computer interface
Questions, options, and criteria	Design decisions and their rationale	Questions that are mapped to design options and objectives (criteria)

Design spaces have many uses. Haeuslschmid et al. [307] developed a design space for interactive windshield displays in vehicles by drawing together and analyzing existing literature. Markussen et al. [518] were interested in developing a selection-based text entry method to be used in mid-air. They established a design space for such methods by enumerating the central design questions, the possible user interface options, and the criteria for choosing among them.

23.4.1 Morphological analysis

Morphological analysis refers to the idea of representing user interfaces as points in a parametrically described design space. The roots of this idea can be traced to Herbert Simon and Francis Zwicky. Zwicky, who worked at the Jet Propulsion Lab on rocket engineering, proposed tackling very complex engineering problems with what he dubbed morphological analysis, which entails a breakdown of decisions to form a discrete solution space. Simon proposed that many complex-looking problem-solving tasks, such as in chess, are essentially search problems in a tree: At any given moment, you have possible actions, and depending on what you choose, another state opens with another set of actions. Following these lines of thinking, user interface design is simply a set (Zwicky) or a sequence (Simon) of decisions.

Card et al. [130] introduced these ideas to HCI. For example, an input device is a transducer that associates the sensed properties of the physical world with the parameters of an application. Formally, its morphological design space is a tuple:

$$< M, In, S, R, Out, W >,$$

where:

- M is a manipulation operator (a physical action by the user that produces inputs);
- In is the input domain (the range of possible values produced by the input manipulation operator);
- S is the current state of the device;
- R is a resolution function that maps the input domain to the output domain;
- Out is the output domain;
- W is a general-purpose set of device properties that describe additional aspects of how the device works.

Most components and widgets of the user interface can be analyzed in this way. For example, consider a binary toggle that is operated by touching a finger within its bounding box on a touch-screen display. Currently, it is set to the leftmost position (off). Through morphological analysis, we get the following:

- *M* is the x and y coordinates of the touchpoint registered within the bounding box of the toggle;
- *In* is a binary event—a touch has occurred (the x and y coordinates are ignored);
- *S* is 0 (off);
- *Out* is green (on) or gray (off), making the toggle indicator change to the corresponding color.

This view is expanded in Chapter 39, where we discuss optimization as an approach to user interface engineering.

23.4.2 Joint system analysis

A user interface can also be thought of as a *joint system* that links users with computing technology. A menu interface incorporates decisions on which menu command goes where as well as the key user capabilities needed to operate the menu: perception, cognition, motor control, and so on. From this perspective, the design of a user interface involves the analysis of the controllable and uncontrollable parameters that affect the outcomes of a joint system.

A *controllable parameter* is a design parameter that the designer can directly influence, such as the color, size, animation, and behavior designed into a push button. Such parameters can be tuned by the designer or optimized for some criteria of interest, such as minimizing the task completion time or errors.

Critical distance is the minimum change in the value of a controllable parameter that causes an undesirable drop in some design objective. For example, consider a fully packed graphical layout that uses the full display space; adding just one pane to the layout might drastically reduce readability. In this case, the critical distance is 1.

An *uncontrollable parameter* is a parameter that the designer cannot directly influence but is nevertheless relevant to users achieving their goals in a user interface. An example of an uncontrollable parameter is the system delay in a web browser attempting to load information from a server, which delays the rendering of the page. Other examples include the accuracy of an autocomplete algorithm and the ability of an individual user to recall a command.

A *critical parameter* is a subtype of uncontrollable parameters. A critical parameter is an uncontrollable parameter that is considered critical to the success of a system [587]. For example, the page loading time is critical for some web applications. *Sensitivity analysis* is used to understand how robust the user interface is to variations in these design parameters.

Collectively, the controllable and uncontrollable parameters relevant to a particular user interface span a multidimensional design space. An individual user that interacts with a specific user interface design forms an *operating point* in such a design space. The ideal operating point is the one where all design parameters align to provide the optimal user interface for the user given some criteria for what an optimal user interface should provide to the user. In practice, it is almost always infeasible to set the operating point at the optimal value. First, it is not viable for designers to be aware of all the relevant design parameters. Second, many parameters are uncontrollable and therefore cannot be directly governed by the designer. Third, parameters are often conflicting for certain criteria. For example, enlarging the size of a button may make it easier for the user to click it at the expense of the button taking up more screen space. In other words, there are inevitably *trade-offs* in user interface design; an informed user interface design process involves considering these trade-offs before choosing the operating point.

This latter point motivates this part of the book. There are essentially two ways to set the operating point. First, it can be set *explicitly* by the designer. This means that the designer is aware of *most* of the relevant controllable and uncontrollable parameters of the design and, therefore, the trade-offs are carefully considered in the design process. Second, the operating point can be set *implicitly* by the design itself. This happens when the designer is unaware of critical controllable and uncontrollable parameters of the user interface. This may still result in an acceptable user interface, although it increases the risk that the user interface may not perform as well as initially hoped. In some cases, this approach can lead to dangerous user interfaces that result in financial losses, injuries, or even deaths. In reality, no designer can be aware of *all* the relevant parameters for a user interface. Therefore, it is not only unrealistic to expect optimal user interface designs—it is also unrealistic to expect fully informed ones.

A central aim of this part of the book is to examine the various components of a user interface and discuss the controllable and uncontrollable components that may affect users' ability to achieve their goals effectively, efficiently, and safely. By doing so, it is possible to develop an awareness of controllable parameters that can be set, optimized, or tuned, and uncontrollable parameters that are not directly governable but may nevertheless affect how users can interact with the user interface. Only after achieving this awareness is it possible to make informed choices about design trade-offs and ultimately design a user interface with balanced parameters that effectively support users in achieving their goals.

Table 23.3 lists examples of high-level design parameters for a physical keyboard.

23.4.3 Questions, options, and criteria

The QOC method extends design space analysis to cover the reasons for design choices [508]. It is based on the concept of *design rationale*, that is, a documented justification for the choice of design. For example: "Auditory feedback is provided for the completion of the task because it is more likely to be noticed when driving and visual attention must be allocated to the road." The

Table 23.3 Examples of high-level design parameters for a physical keyboard.

Parameter	Type
Manufacturing cost	Controllable
Sensing technology	Controllable
Layout	Controllable
Nominal key size	Controllable
Typing speed	Uncontrollable
Typing style	Uncontrollable

idea is that an artifact is defined not only by its technical nature but also by the decisions that allow one to understand how it *could* have been.

Questions structure the space of alternatives, *options* are possible alternative answers to questions, and *criteria* are used to evaluate and choose between options. For example, consider a scrollbar[1] that has several features:

1. It is normally invisible and appears only when a scrolling action is taken.
2. It is narrow.
3. It indicates the position of the view in the window.
4. It indicates the relative size of the view in the window.

Each of these features could have been formulated as a question. For example:

1. *How to display?* Permanent or appearing. *If appearing, how should it appear?* When the cursor is moved or when a scrolling action is taken.
2. *How wide?* Narrow or wide. *If wide, should it be of fixed width or relative to the size of the viewport as a proportion of the page length?*

How can one decide which option is best? According to QOR, the options should be compared with the criteria, which should also be documented. For example:

1. Screen should be compact.
2. Scrollbar should be easy to find.
3. Scrollbar should be easy to drag.
4. Scrollbar should tell intuitively how much there is to scroll still.

The options should then be assessed against all relevant criteria. This evaluation can be based on experimental studies (Chapter 43) or analytical methods (Chapter 41). Lacking such options, the evaluation can also be based on previous experience, known good design examples, or reasoning. For example, Markussen et al. [518] first argued about the design space of mid-air text entry and then empirically evaluated some candidate user interfaces that seemed promising using QOC analysis.

Summary

- User interfaces are what the user comes into contact with when using an interactive system.
- User interfaces comprise input devices, interaction techniques, representations, and assemblies.
- There are five main styles of interaction: command line, form, menu, GUI, and reality-based user interfaces.
- The design of user interfaces involves balancing trade-offs between relevant criteria.

---

[1] Based on the original example of a scrollbar given by MacLean et al. [508].

24
Input devices

This chapter reviews input devices—the elements of user interfaces that sense users and use that information to operate computers. More precisely, an *input device* is a combination of hardware and software that senses users' movements, activities, and internal states and turns them into information in the interactive system. This information can be used to trigger commands or input values, allowing users to interact with the system.

The success of an input device depends on identifying the computation that should be carried out—the goal of the input device—and then ensuring that an appropriate representation of input is obtained and can be sensed by the system. For example, a mouse is an input device that allows users to transmit their intentions about moving a mouse cursor on the screen. A mouse is a hardware device that the user can move across a desk with its movements mirrored by the mouse cursor on the screen. A software driver ensures that the computer can interpret the input signals transmitted from the hardware to the operating system.

Some input devices are familiar to us from everyday interaction; others are experimental. Paper Example 24.0.1 shows a detailed example of the latter, while the following list provides some shorter examples.

- Someone has designed the physical feel you experience when you press a button on a keyboard. Oulasvirta et al. [629] studied the relationship between the force users apply to a button and the displacement of the button and showed that this relationship greatly affects button press performance.
- In Skinput, Harrison et al. [314] used an array of vibration sensors placed on the user's arm. These sensors allowed for the sensing of contact on the skin, effectively allowing people to use their forearms as touchpads.
- Microsoft Kinect, released in 2010, used depth cameras to detect users' poses and gestures. By sensing poses and gestures, this input device allowed for a new class of games and interactions without controllers.

Recall from the introduction to this part that an input device differs from an interaction technique. Input devices sense users' movements and states; interaction techniques help users accomplish fundamental operations in the user interface using input devices and displays. Interaction techniques are discussed in Chapter 26.

Next, we discuss what it means to *sense* something with an input device. We discuss input devices that pose relatively few challenges to correct the inference of users' intentions, such as keyboards or pointing devices (e.g., a mouse). Then, we discuss a class of input devices where it is much more difficult to figure out what the user is trying to input.

> **Paper Example 24.0.1: Input in mid-air: The case of the imaginary phone**
>
> Most input devices we use rely on a surface on which something is moved. This is the case for the touchpad and the mouse. An active research area in human–computer interaction (HCI) is input devices beyond rigid surfaces. Researchers have explored letting go of the requirement for an input surface in so-called mid-air interfaces. The Imaginary Phone is a case in point. This research is based on the observation that our memory of icon positions on our phones works remarkably well (Chapter 5). For instance, you can probably point to the message application on your phone even if all the icons look the same. Gustafson et al. [305] built on this observation to remove the need for phone displays.
>
> With an Imaginary Phone, the user's hands are tracked with a wearable camera so that input can be given by moving a finger and touching skin. No display is necessary after the basic layout is memorized. For example, an alarm can be set by drawing a gesture from a center toward the desired hour, as shown in the following figure.

24.1 Principles of sensing

Every input device relies on some type of sensing. A sensor is a device that transforms physical energy into an electric signal. Input sensing means something more than "just" using sensors, however. It refers to the whole sensing pipeline, including software and hardware, that enables the computation of a command based on sensor data. An input device implements some sensing processes via hardware (e.g., sensor, microcontroller) and software (e.g., filtering, gesture recognition).

Input sensing has become a major research topic in HCI. Thanks to improvements in micromachinery and microcontrollers, we can presently augment almost any physical object with sensing capabilities. For example, existing capacitive sensing techniques enable the augmenting of plants, doorknobs, and even water with touch sensing; see Paper Example 24.3.1 for an example of augmenting plants with touch.

Despite these advances, engineering a situationally appropriate input device remains challenging. There is no universally best sensing approach. Consider an in-flight entertainment system, a crane operator's cockpit, and a GPS tracking device for boats; the user's movement capabilities and goals, the constraints and capabilities of the system, and environmental factors are vastly different among these cases. Users are good at noticing poor response characteristics, such as lag or inaccuracy. Careful engineering is needed to permit high user performance while being robust to environmental factors and cost-efficient. As a result, R&D in this area necessitates long timeframes. For instance, while the principles of computer-vision-based hand tracking were investigated in the 1990s, commercially successful solutions have only recently (2020s) started to come out in virtual reality systems.

Developing a good input device requires skills in software engineering, machine learning, systems engineering, and electrical engineering. Next, we go through the steps of the input sensing pipeline.

24.1.1 Transducing

All sensing used in HCI transforms one type of energy into an electric signal. Traditional pointing devices sense motion, position, or pressure. An isometric joystick senses pressure. The sensing principles used in HCI include mechanical (position, motion, rotation), electrical (capacitance, contact), sonic (ultrasonic, microphone, sonar), optical (proximity, light, image), radiation (radar, heat, temperature), magnetic (Hall effect), and gravitational (e.g., a pressure-sensitive floor). Chemical sensing methods are also available, for example, via moisture or implanted sensors.

Analog sensors output an analog electrical signal, typically between 0 and 5 V. This is converted by an analog-to-digital converter, which determines the resolution of the output (e.g., 10 bits). While this interface is simple, it is prone to external noise. *Digital* sensors are more robust to noise. They output a digital signal consisting of zeros and ones. To use this signal, a digital protocol is needed (e.g., UART, I2C, SPI).

For most physical events that we care about, several sensing principles are applicable. For example, touch can be sensed using a number of sensing principles, including capacitive, resistive, acoustic, infrared, vision, liquid crystals, planar scatter, and electromagnetic resonance. Popular capacitive touchscreens are based on measurements of capacitance or the energy stored in an electric field between two conductive objectives. A capacitor consists of dielectric material sandwiched between two parallel metal plates that responds to the changing distance of another dielectric object—the finger. The location can be sensed with many electrode pairs, the response characteristics of which are known. This sensing principle, unlike its predecessor (resistive sensing), allows for multi-touch sensing, although it does not support pen input without modification

24.1.2 Sensing hardware

Each sensing principle must be implemented in a *device*, consisting of at least the sensor, a microcontroller, and a rig that keeps them together. The aim is to find the optimal balance among factors such as accuracy, battery life, latency, and robustness. In the case of capacitive sensing, one needs to decide the selection and configuration of electrodes to achieve the necessary accuracy and robustness to finger moisture and different pressing angles. The touch controller, a microcontroller-based chip, must be designed to translate the measurements into a computer-readable form.

24.1.3 Transfer functions

A sensor governed by a *transfer function*. A transfer function maps a change in input energy to a change in an electrical signal (output energy). We can learn a lot about a sensor by studying the properties of its transfer function (for examples of key properties of transfer functions, see Figure 24.1; for an example of input signal, see Figure 24.2).

The analysis of an input device starts by plotting the input energy against the output energy:

$$\text{output} = f(\text{input}). \tag{24.1}$$

For example, a regular push button is based on a key switch that sends a break signal when the switch closes the circuit. From a transfer function perspective, it converts the contact force into the displacement of the keycap, whose movement is resisted, for example, by a rubber dome. The key switch then transduces the displacement into a step function—a simple on/off signal.

Next, we introduce the basic terminology needed to analyze the transfer function. The transfer function is related to a wealth of concepts that can help us understand input sensors. The *sensitivity*

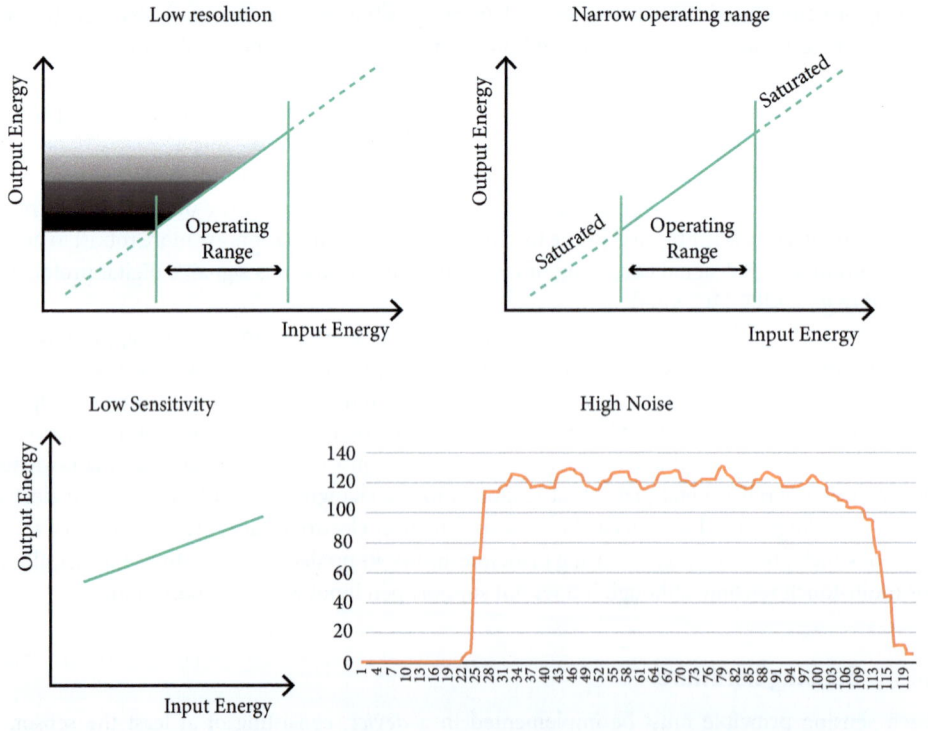

Figure 24.1 Input horror gallery: Plotting the transfer function of an input sensor can expose a number of problems that hamper user performance. From left to right, top to bottom: Inability to distinguish among levels of control; a range that is too narrow; inability to produce varied outputs; noise. Images courtesy of Sunjun Kim.

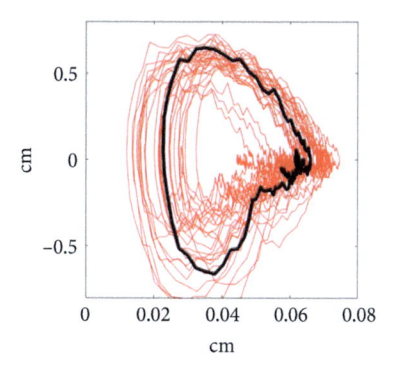

Figure 24.2 Measurements of a button press in mid-air taken with a computer-vision-based tracker showing significant noise, which can be mitigated with techniques such as filtering [630].

of a sensor refers to the mapping of the changing intensity of the input stimulation to the output signal. A sensor has low sensitivity when a wide range of input energy is mapped to only a few levels of output energy.

A sensor is said to be *linear* when this relationship is linear. The *linearity error* is the deviation of the output signal from a linear trendline $y = a + bx$, where a and b are empirically established. Some sensors have *nonlinear transfer functions*, indicating that the relationship between the input and output energy is nontrivial. Psychophysics methods can be used to find a suitable transfer function (Chapter 3).

Another relevant concept is *resolution*, which indicates how many levels of output are expressed for different levels of input. This can be measured as entropy: $H = n \log_2 S$, where n is the number of levels of input and S is the size of the set of symbols in the output. A low-resolution sensor loses information in the input signal; a high-resolution sensor is informally said to be *expressive*.

The *operating range* of a sensor refers to the minimum and maximum sensed intensity. When the input energy surpasses the upper threshold, the sensor is *saturated*. An under-saturated sensor receives input energy below its registration threshold; an over-saturated sensor receives excess input energy and may be damaged or destroyed.

Bias refers to a systematic source of error in transfer; *noise* refers to unsystematic (quasi-random) error. The difference between these two sources of error is important to understand because they are dealt with in different ways. For example, a computer-vision-based sensing solution may have a high level of noise that can be rectified by filtering. By contrast, a mechanical sensing solution may have systematic bias that can be managed by calibration.

24.1.4 Filtering

In filtering, the output signal of a sensor is suppressed in some way to get rid of noise or some other unwanted feature. Unwanted features in input sensing include noise (random variations in the measured signal due to measurement noise), dropout (loss of measurement samples), drift (growing inaccuracy over time), and glitches (random spikes or other artifacts).

A key concept in filtering is the *signal-to-noise ratio* (SNR). Intuitively, this is the proportion of noise in the power of a signal:

$$\text{SNR} = \frac{P_{\text{signal}}}{P_{\text{noise}}}. \tag{24.2}$$

The SNR is often expressed in decibels: $\text{SNR}_{\text{dB}} = 10 \log_{10} \text{SNR}$. The SNR sets a limit on how much information can be "saved" from the signal using filtering.

Frequency-based filters are the simplest filters. They suppress the signal based on a given frequency range and can be used when noise occurs on a known range of signal frequency. Low-pass filters pass only low-frequency signals; high-pass filters pass only high-frequency signals. A band-pass filter passes only a specific frequency range.

Moving averages are another simple filtering approach. Assuming that noise has a mean of zero, a *moving average filter* can estimate the true value simply by averaging over a few previous measurement samples:

$$\bar{X} = \sum_{i=t-n}^{t} X_i, \tag{24.3}$$

where $\bar{X}$ is the filtered value, X_i is the value at i, t is the current time, and n is the window size. The drawback of this approach is that if the sampling frequency of the sensor is low, its response may feel "laggy."

Single exponential smoothing, also known as first-order smoothing, is another smoothing technique:

$$\bar{X}_i = \alpha X_i + (1 - \alpha)\bar{X}_{i-1}, \tag{24.4}$$

where α is a smoothing factor $0 < \alpha < 1$. The idea is to control the contribution of older sensor readings. When the smoothing factor α increases, the filtered value is closer to the latest sensor values. When it decreases, there is more lag but less jitter. In *double exponential smoothing*, the smoothing is performed twice to handle quadratic trends in the signal.

Speed-dependent filtering dynamically changes α based on an estimation of noise and the velocity of movement. This is particularly relevant for continuous sensing, such as in position sensors like a mouse.

Paper Example 24.1.1: The €1 filter

A key issue in input is dealing with noisy signals. The noise might cause an input value, such as a (x,y) position on a touchpad, to fail to reflect the position of the user's finger. Alternatively, it may jitter, with sequential (x,y) pairs jumping unpredictably.

While we may deal with such noise, we want to do so in a way that does not decrease the responsiveness of the device. Casiez et al. [139] found an elegant solution to this problem through the €1 filter.

The idea of the €1 filter is that the alpha α gets smaller with faster cursor speed:

$$\alpha = \frac{1}{1 + \frac{\tau}{T_e}}, \tag{24.5}$$

where $\tau = 1/2\pi f_c$ and $f_c = f_{c_{\min}} + \beta|\dot{X}_i|$. The filtered value becomes

$$\bar{X}_i = \left(X_i + \frac{\tau}{T_e}\bar{X}_{i-1}\right)\alpha. \tag{24.6}$$

The intuition behind these equations is that cursor responsiveness remains high when the cursor is moved quickly, while accuracy remains high when the mouse is moved slowly.

24.1.5 Engineering challenges in sensing

Based on these considerations, three recurring issues in engineering sensing may be summarized. The first concerns *what* can be sensed. The sensing modality of input refers to the particular input stream considered, such as speech, hand movement, pen movement, handwriting, gaze, and so on. Input streams can also be multimodal, which means that multiple input streams are combined for the purpose of sensing user input. A useful input device must be robust to different interaction contexts and resilient to noise. Therefore, an input device needs a sufficiently high sensing validity to be useful in practice, where users will interact with it in a variety of settings under a variety of circumstances. The sensing interaction potential of the input device captures its expressiveness, the interaction types it supports, and at what fidelity.

The second issue concerns *resolution*. The temporal resolution of an input device is its discrete resolution of the measurement of time. For example, a mouse with high temporal resolution means that many samples of mouse movements are captured by the input device at a fixed unit of time. The spatial resolution of an input device is its discrete resolution of measurement in the spatial domain. For example, a hand-tracking input device may be able to track a user's hand with a resolution of 5 mm.

The third issue is *accuracy*. Accuracy reflects the ability of an input device to correctly sense the user's input. For example, a capacitive touchscreen will only be able to sense the location of the user's fingertip within some margin of error. Accuracy is modeled differently depending on the specific input device. For example, an input device can be thought of as a binary classifier only detecting *input* or *no input*, such as an eyebrow switch, where the data are typically classified as either true positives or true negatives. Based on this, it is possible to calculate accuracy. However, since accuracy is a composite measure, it does not reveal much useful information about the design of the input device.

In addition, as many input devices are realized in hardware, their design frequently involves considerations that are relevant to physical products: market demand, cost, development risk, certification, lifecycle analysis, and so on. While these considerations are important for designing, manufacturing, distributing, and supporting input devices, they are not central to HCI, so we do not discuss them in this book. Instead, we focus on a set of design factors that must be considered when creating a new input device in software, hardware, or a combination thereof.

24.2 Keypads and keyboards

Keypads and keyboards allow the user to input information, such as letters, symbols, numbers, and commands, into a computer. There are many ways to design them, and their construction typically depends on their use case. For example, a flat-panel membrane design is an inexpensive solution.

Keypads

A *keypad* is a set of buttons typically arranged in a matrix layout. While the layout may vary, a common layout is the alphanumeric telephone keypad layout specified by the ISO/IEC 9995-8:1994 standard.

Keypads are common in household appliances, such as microwave ovens and calculators, dial-pad phones, automated teller machines, and machines used in healthcare and manufacturing. They are suitable for extensive numeric entry and a limited amount of alphanumeric entry.

Keypads gathered considerable attention during the early stages of mobile phone development, as the majority of mobile phones predating the capacitive touchscreen era relied on a physical ISO/IEC 9995-8:1994 keypad coupled with a dot matrix display.

Keyboards

Similar to a keypad, a computer *keyboard* is a device that enables the user to input alphanumeric information into a computer system, such as text, numbers, and commands. Unlike a keypad, a keyboard typically contains all letter keys A–Z and supports a wide range of ancillary characters and functions. Most keyboards use a particular key arrangement known as the QWERTY layout, named after the first six letter keys in the top alphabet row.

24.3 Pointing devices

Keyboards allow users to enter text. Pointing devices allow users to select locations on a display for a variety of purposes, such as selecting or manipulating an object or creating a drawing. Pointing devices can be divided into two classes: directly controlled devices and indirectly controlled devices.

A directly controlled pointing device is interacted with by pointing directly at the display. This allows the user to specify the precise location of the pointing in *absolute* coordinates. For example, the user can point at the top-left corner of the display, which may be equivalent to location (1, 1) in the pixel space—the first leftmost pixel in the top row of the display.

An indirectly controlled pointing device allows the user to specify a location on the display by manipulating the pointing device. In response, the cursor on the display moves as a function of the manipulation of the pointing device. For example, the user may use a mouse to control the cursor on the display. By moving the mouse, the cursor on the display changes its location. This is an example of *relative* movement. Control is indirect: The user cannot directly select the desired location on the display by pointing at it. Instead, the user indirectly moves the cursor to the desired location by manipulating a pointing device. Relative movement can be modulated using a construct known as the control/display ratio, which is elaborated in the chapter on interaction techniques (Chapter 26).

24.3.1 Direct control

Direct control pointing devices allow the user to select absolute coordinates on a display.

Light pen

One of the earliest direct control devices is the *light pen*. A light pen is a light-sensitive rod that the user holds in their hand (Figure 24.3). Light pens were designed to be used together with cathode-ray tube (*CRT*) displays (Chapter 25). As explained in the chapter on displays (Chapter 25), a *CRT* generates a pixel image using a raster scan row by row, column by column. This means that the light-sensitive component of the light pen can be used in combination with the timing information of the raster scan to detect the location of the tip of the light pen.

As shown in Figure 24.3, a light pen allows the user to directly select a specific location on a display in absolute coordinates. In the figure, the light pen is used to select links in an early hypertext system.

Figure 24.3 A user interacting with an early hypertext system using a light pen. Image by Greg Lloyd used under Creative Commons License.

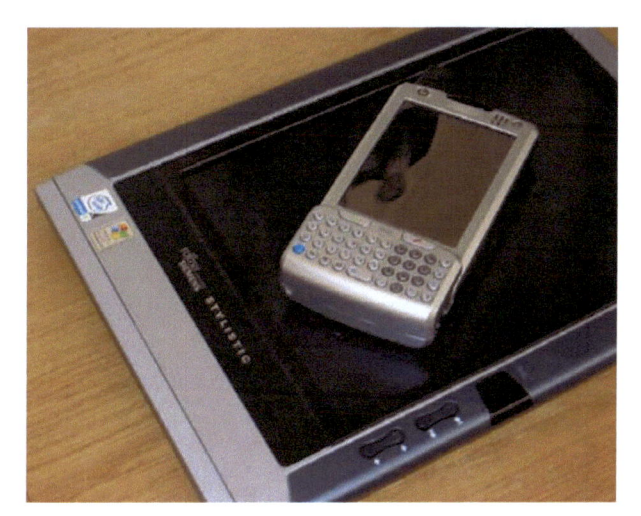

Figure 24.4 A Tablet PC with a touch display, a personal digital assistant, and a resistive screen.

Resistive touchscreen

Another method for allowing direct control is the use of a *resistive touchscreen* (Figure 24.4). At a high level, a resistive touchscreen is usually designed with two flexible sheets separated by an insulator, such as an air gap. When the two sheets are pressed together, for example, using the tip of a pen or a finger, the two sheets make contact. By ensuring the sheets have horizontal and vertical traces, it is possible to determine the touch location.

Resistive screens were popular in early mobile device design, such as personal digital assistants, Tablet PCs, and early touchscreen mobile phones. Like light pens, they provide users with the ability to precisely select a location on a display by directly selecting the desired location on the display. However, unlike light pens, resistive screens can be easily manufactured in small sizes suitable for portable electronics. Resistive screens are also inexpensive to manufacture and can be used with any implement capable of pressing the two layers together, such as a glove, which typically cannot be readily sensed by a capacitive touchscreen. A pen-operated resistive touchscreen may also provide a higher sensing resolution.

Capacitive touchscreen

The *capacitive touchscreen* is ubiquitous on mobile devices. While capacitive touchscreen technology has been available for many years, capacitive touchscreens were popularized by the introduction of the Apple iPhone in 2007.

Capacitive touchscreens can be implemented in several ways. What they have in common is that they rely on capacitive coupling between an implement, typically the user's fingertip, and the display to sense the absolute position the user touches on the display.

Advances in capacitive touchscreens have enabled users to easily select precise locations on a touchscreen by lightly touching it with their fingertips. In addition, capacitive touchscreens support multi-touch interaction, which enables a range of interaction techniques, such as pinching for zooming.

The typical trade-off between a resistive touchscreen and a capacitive touchscreen is that the latter has a faster response time but lower precision. In addition, a resistive touchscreen may have a lower visual quality due to the dual-membrane design.

Paper Example 24.3.1 Botanicus Interactus

Interaction does not need to be limited to technological objects such as computers. Present-day sensing technology creates opportunities to augment everyday environments with capabilities for input and output. An example is *Botanicus Interactus* [674], which enables interaction with living artificial plants.

Botanicus Interactus excites the plant with an electrical signal at multiple frequencies between 0.1 and 3 MHz. While regular capacitive sensing excites a surface with a single frequency, Botanicus Interactus uses multiple frequencies to account for the more complex structure of a plant. Since the electrical signal path inside the plant varies by frequency, it is possible to infer touch locations by analyzing the frequencies that have affected the signal using machine learning methods.

Paper Example 24.3.2: Frustrated total internal reflection

In the early 2000s, it was expensive and difficult to design reliable, large, multi-touch surfaces. Nevertheless, Han [310] demonstrated how to use a mechanism known as frustrated total internal reflection (FTIR) to create a low-cost and reliable multi-touch device.

Refraction refers to the phenomenon in which light changes direction, or bends, as it passes from one medium to another. Total internal reflection occurs when light passes through a medium with a lower refractive index and the angle of incidence exceeds the critical angle. By selecting the right material, the interface between the mediums can be designed to frustrate the total internal reflection, allowing light to escape through the material instead.

A multi-touch FTIR surface exploits this principle. A typical design uses an acrylic pane that is edge-lit by infrared light-emitting diodes. Due to the total internal reflection, the infrared light is trapped within the sheet. A video camera is mounted behind the sheet, capturing the resulting image. When an object, such as a user's finger, makes optical contact with the sheet, the light is frustrated, causing it to scatter through the pane toward the camera. This results in bright dots in the image, which can then be processed using relatively simple computer vision methods to determine the multi-touch locations.

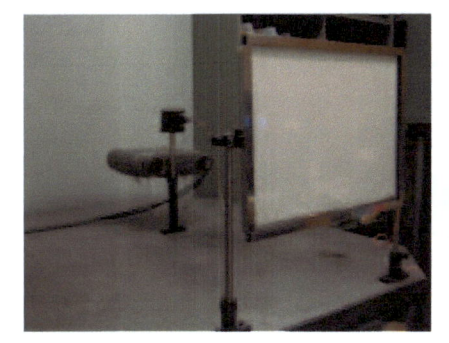

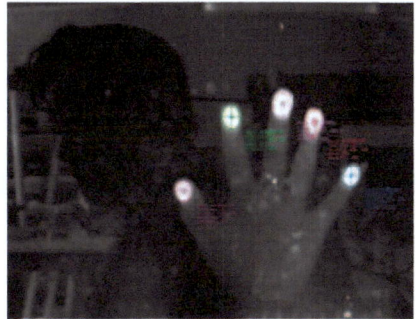

24.3.2 Indirect control

Indirect control pointing devices enable the user to control the cursor on a display by manipulating a pointing device. Thus, the cursor movements are relative to the manipulation of the pointing device.

Mouse

A *mouse* (Figure 24.5) allows the user to move the cursor by moving the mouse on a table. The physical movement of the mouse is translated into cursor movement. Several mechanisms can be used to support the functionality of a mouse. Early mice used two separate wheels below the mouse that rolled when the mouse was moved on the table. Later mice used a rolling ball design. Today, mice use optical sensors to determine relative movement without having to rely on moving parts in the electromechanical design.

Typically, a mouse includes buttons that can be used to provide further information to the system. Many mice also have a scroll wheel, which is typically used to scroll the display up or down.

Figure 24.5 A computer mouse. Image source: https://commons.wikimedia.org/wiki/File:3-Tasten-Maus_Microsoft.jpg.

In addition to moving a cursor, a mouse can be used to perform gestures. For example, a common gesture is to drag and drop an object. Mouse gestures are discussed in the chapter on interaction techniques (Chapter 26).

Touchpad

A *touchpad* is an indirect pointing device that allows the user to control the cursor on a display by moving a fingertip on a surface. The surface can be resistive or capacitive. Touchpads can be augmented with additional features, such as tactile sensation feedback and button pressing mechanisms, and they are commonly used on laptops as a replacement for a mouse.

Similar to a mouse, a touchpad can be used for purposes other than controlling a cursor, such as for articulating 2D gestures. However, unlike a mouse, a touchpad can be used in both relative and absolute coordinates. In other words, it is possible to map the input dimensions of a touchpad so that they are proportional to the display dimensions. This allows the user to, for example, select the top-left corner of the display by touching the top-left corner of the touchpad.

Paper Example 24.3.3: Touch for several people at the same time?

As touch input devices emerged, researchers began to wonder how to support touch for several people at the same time. This would require several touchpoints to be detected at the same time. It would also require each touchpoint to be attributed to the correct person. Moreover, people may put objects on the surface (e.g., a pen or a pad) that should not be detected as touch. How to achieve all this in one design?

Dietz and Leigh [194] developed the DiamondTouch table. As shown in the figure on the left, DiamondTouch uses a projector that places an image on a table between the users. The table has been prepared with a number of antennas below an insulating layer (middle). The antennas work as switches to detect when (but not where) a user touches within the area of an antenna. The DiamondTouch prototype used four antennas per square centimeter. The identification of users was accomplished by instrumenting users' chairs (right). When a user touches the table, a circuit is completed, going from the transmitter to the antenna on the table, the user and the chair, and back to the transmitter. Because each user has a unique circuit, the touchpoints can be used to identify the users.

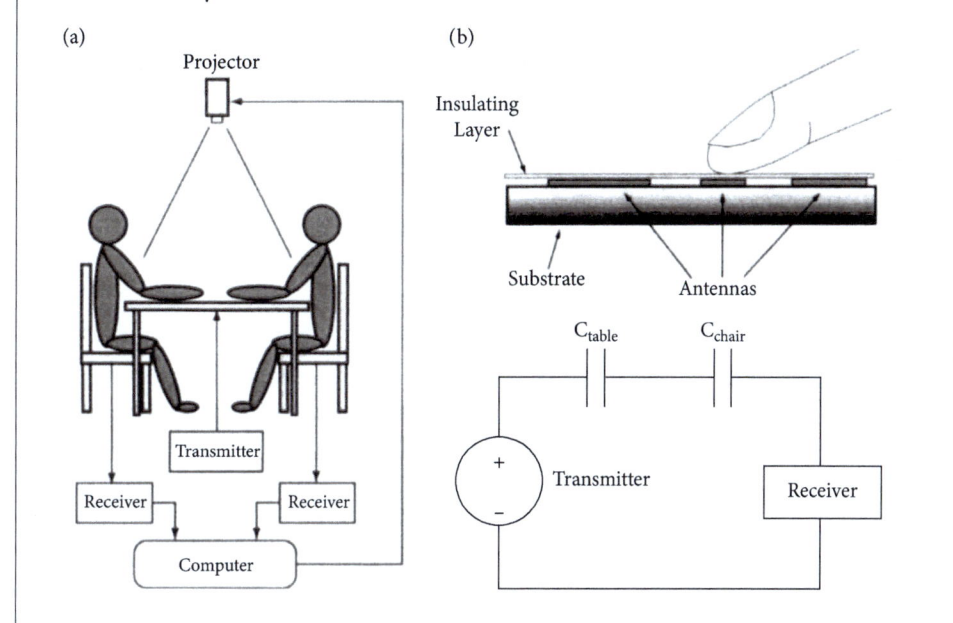

DiamondTouch was later turned into a commercial product, and it influenced the design of many subsequent tabletop interfaces.

24.4 Uncertain control

Direct and indirect control input devices can deduce users' intentions with a high degree of certainty. Here, we use the term *uncertain control* to refer to a class of input devices that must be designed to be robust in the presence of uncertainty concerning the user's intentions.

24.4.1 Switches

A simple example of uncertain control is a *switch*, such as a mechanical push button, which is perhaps the most ubiquitous input device used for binary control (on/off).

Push buttons are electromechanical devices. When the user pushes the switch, the user is forcing two electrical contacts together. The result is a path with low impedance for current flow. This flow of current tells the device that the push button has been depressed by the user. When the user lets the push button go, the contacts are separated and the current no longer flows.

This operation is subject to noise due to a phenomenon known as switch bouncing, that is, there is uncertainty around whether trailing mechanical motion has caused the switch to falsely trigger a second or third time upon activation. This is because the electrical contacts are subject to mechanical motion and will touch several times before assuming a resting position in which the contact is stable. The solution is to implement switch debouncing, which eliminates this noise. Hardware buttons have switch debouncing implemented in either hardware or software.

Another example of noise in switches is switch noise due to false activations and false detections. Some nonspeaking users with motor disabilities rely on a switch to communicate. One example is an eyebrow switch that activates when the user actuates their eyebrow. Such switches are prone to false activations due to noise and require signal processing to reach acceptable levels of performance. In practice, such switches are still error-prone and user interfaces reliant on such switches, such as specialized scanning keyboards for users with motor disabilities, have to be designed with such deficiencies in mind.

24.4.2 Accelerometers and gyroscopes

An *accelerometer* is a device that measures the rate of change in velocity, that is, the acceleration of the device. It can be used for direct control or indirectly to sense what the user is doing. At rest, the measured acceleration will carry an offset corresponding to Earth's gravity. Accelerometers are commonly integrated into mobile phones and input devices because they allow for the estimation of the orientation of the device. This information is frequently used to change the screen orientation between portrait and landscape mode depending on how the user is holding the display. Accelerometers also allow for input. For example, gamers can control a character by tilting a mobile device. Another use of accelerometers involves the use of machine learning methods to infer user activity, such as the steps a user takes over a period of time.

A *gyroscope* is a device that measures orientation and angular velocity. Input devices that use the functions provided by a gyroscope are typically implemented as micro-electro-mechanical systems. Since these devices measure device orientation and rotation, they are frequently used to estimate device movement in 3D space and enable gesture control. It is also possible to combine data from accelerometers and gyroscopes to provide more robust gesture recognition and inference of user motion. Another potential use of accelerometer and gyroscopic data is for estimating the position of a virtual reality headset.

24.4.3 Brain–computer interface

It is also possible to allow the user to communicate with a computer without actuating any muscles. This is achievable using a *brain–computer interface* (BCI). A BCI translates the electrical activity in the user's brain into signals that a computer system can understand. One of its main applications is enabling users to control robotic limbs as prosthetic devices.

BCIs can be realized using a number of methods. A common noninvasive method is electroencephalography (EEG), which uses electrodes positioned on the user's scalp. One advantage of EEG and other noninvasive methods is their practicality, as the demand on the user is low compared to more invasive methods, although there is still a considerable set-up cost. One disadvantage is that the electrodes are positioned relatively far away from the brain, so the SNR is low. As a consequence, significant effort is required to ensure robust and accurate operation when using such an input device to control a user interface. In practice, noninvasive BCI is severely limited in its use as an input device in HCI.

An alternative that achieves a much higher SNR is brain implants, although this invasive technique can have serious implications for the user. Brain implants have been used extensively to partially restore vision and movement in patients with disabilities.

24.4.4 Electromyography

An input device that is more reliable than BCI is *electromyography* (EMG), which senses the electrical activity in a user's muscles and translates it into signals that a computer system can act on. EMG devices vary in their construction; their use in HCI is based on surface EMG, which does not require inserting needles into the user.

Surface EMG input devices produce signals that can be analyzed using signal processing and machine learning algorithms to infer the user's activity. After processing, such information can be used to perform gesture recognition and, to some extent, to estimate fatigue.

24.4.5 Eye tracking

An input device based on *eye tracking* estimates the user's gaze on a display. It does this by tracking the user's rotation of the eye and mapping it to cursor control. Several methods are available, and they all require calibration.

One method is to project infrared light toward the user's eye. The anatomical parts of the eye that reflect the light efficiently generate so-called Purkinje images. These images can then be used to infer the user's gaze. High-accuracy commercial eye-tracking systems typically implement some variant of this or a similar technique.

Another method is to optically detect users' gaze via a regular camera. The gaze position is inferred using computer vision methods. These methods are very sensitive to users' head movements and thus not very practical. While all eye-tracking methods require calibration, optical methods may only require recalibration when the user moves their head significantly.

Electrooculography (EOG) can also be used. This technique involves placing electrodes above, below, to the left, or to the right of the eye. The electrodes measure the resting potential of the retina. If the eye is moved away from the center position toward an electrode, the electrode will sense this change. This information is then used to infer eye position changes. One problem with EOG is drift; another downside is the required set-up before use.

Finally, it is possible to carry out eye tracking by fitting the user with contact lenses coupled with some form of sensor, such as a magnetic field sensor. As the eye rotates, the contact lens rotates with it. This technique enables highly accurate eye movement measurements; however, it is also invasive and requires setting up.

Eye-tracking data are processed by considering saccades and fixations (Chapter 3). A *saccade* is a preplanned ballistic jump performed by the eye that can take 150–250 ms to plan and execute. A saccade is followed by a *fixation*. A fixation is the period of time after a saccade when the eye is relatively stationary. Typically, a fixation lasts between 200 and 300 ms. An example of a series of saccades and fixations is shown in Figure 24.6 for a typical reading task.

A sequence of saccades and fixations forms a *scanpath*. Scanpaths can be recorded using eye trackers capable of estimating the user's gaze location at a certain frequency, typically 30–60 Hz. Scanpaths can then be aggregated based on location and time thresholds to identify areas that attract user fixation. The assumption is that if a user has fixated on a particular area, this may

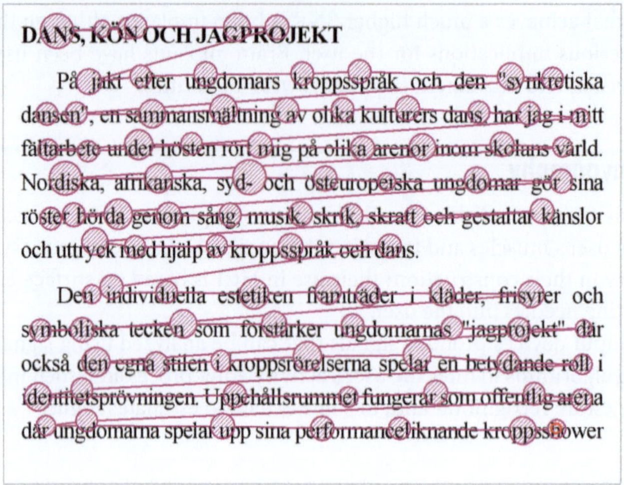

Figure 24.6 An example of saccades and fixations measured during a reading task. Image source: https://upload.wikimedia.org/wikipedia/commons/e/ef/Reading_Fixations_Saccades.jpg.

influence the user's future actions and the details registered in their memory. This assumption follows from the *eye–mind hypothesis*: What people are looking at is what they are thinking about [919]. In other words, visual attention can act as a proxy for mental attention. However, for this to occur, the user needs to be given a suitable task.

Eye tracking is used in several applications. It can be used to carry out market research and usability testing where information on what the user is looking at is valuable. Eye tracking can also be used as part of an interaction technique, for example, to enable typing via eye-typing methods (Chapter 26).

24.4.6 Hand and finger tracking

Hand and finger tracking is used to estimate the location of the user's hands and fingers in 3D space. Several technologies are available for this.

Accurate hand and finger tracking can be achieved by fitting optical markers to the user's hands and fingers. Other body parts can also be tracked using optical markers. The markers are tracked by high-resolution cameras; then, software is used to estimate the locations of the markers in 3D space. Optical marker-based systems are commonly used in HCI research that requires a high-accuracy, low-latency view of users' movements. For example, a study of 10-finger touch typing in mid-air may use an optical marker system to capture as many nuances of typing behavior as possible (Figure 24.7).

An alternative method for performing hand and finger tracking involves using a depth camera mounted on a headset paired with computer vision methods to infer the hand's skeletal structure. This approach is common in state-of-the-art virtual and augmented reality headsets. The hand skeleton serves as a low-dimensional representation of the user's fingers that can be used, for example, to aid the design of a gesture control system.

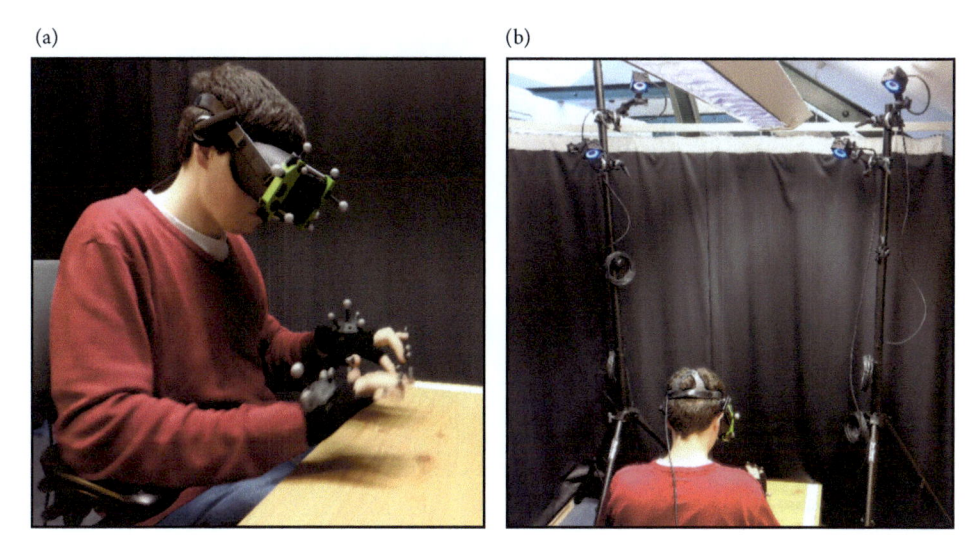

Figure 24.7 An example of using optical markers to measure users' hand movements in mid-air typing tasks [216].

24.4.7 Microphone input and speech recognition

Another type of input is the sound generated by users and their surroundings. One obvious example is voice commands, which allow the user to voice instructions directly to the computer. Sound is sensed using a transducer that converts acoustic waves into electrical signals. This type of transducer is called a microphone. Microphones can be connected to form an array, called a microphone array, to localize sound more easily. The localization of sounds opens up interaction possibilities, such as directing user feedback to a particular location.

Microphone input does not have to be the user's voice. An early commercial example of another use is the 1986 Japanese version of the adventure game *The Legend of Zelda* for the Nintendo Entertainment System (called Famicom in Japan). The Famicom featured an integrated controller that, in addition to a directional pad and some buttons, included a built-in microphone. The Famicom was too underpowered to perform speech recognition, but it could use its microphone in other ways. In The Legend of Zelda, it allowed the player to defeat enemies with particularly large ears: By making a loud noise, these enemies would disappear. This was an early demonstration of creative ways of utilizing a microphone to sense input.

Microphones can be used to perform speech recognition. Speech recognition works by turning observations of the user's utterances into hypotheses of what the user has said. Speech recognition can be based on isolated words, or it can be continuous, allowing users to speak phrases or sentences. Speech recognition is commonly used for voice control, but it can also be used as an alternative text entry method, allowing users to perform dictation.

24.5 Expanding the limits of sensing

In the early history of computing, input devices mostly comprised buttons and applied switch-based sensing. A mechanical switch affords high certainty in input; only rarely would a user accidentally activate a switch. Later, input devices began to be used to sense movement beyond

Figure 24.8 A skin-compliant input device [878].

on/off events; the mouse and the joystick are prime examples. Their input-sensing pipelines are more complex than that of a switch since they need to handle issues like noise and uncertainty; nevertheless, they are fundamentally about the sensing of movement.

Many HCI researchers have studied alternative methods for sensing movement. One research direction has been input devices that can be worn; for example, iSkin [878] is a skin-compatible tattoo (Figure 24.8). It is a thin overlay that is transparent, flexible, and made of biocompatible materials. The authors proposed methods for producing iSkins in variable sizes and shapes so that they can be worn on different locations of the body such as the finger, forearm, or ear. The sensor used in iSkin combines capacitive and resistive touch sensing. This makes it possible to sense touch even when the overlay is stretched or bent on the skin. Furthermore, iSkin supports multiple touch areas and complex widgets such as sliders.

What if one wants to go beyond sensing movement? One strand of research on input devices aims to expand *what* we can sense. For example, there has been work on sensing temperature [682], mental workload [373], and boredom [656], among other things.

Why would we want to sense such information? One reason is *adaptation*—the ability to change the user interface based on sensed information about the current state of the user. For instance, if the user's workload is high, we could simplify the user interface. Another reason is to create so-called *non-command interfaces* [590]. The idea is to infer the user's intentions through precise sensing to dispense with the need for a user to explicitly issue commands. From the perspective of Norman's seven-stage model (Chapter 18), this would dispense with the need to specify and execute actions in the user interface.

The fundamental problem in all these cases is whether the inferences on sensed phenomena or intended commands are accurate. While this has been achieved in some controlled settings, robust sensing in uncontrolled settings remains hard.

Summary

- Input devices allow users to provide information to a computer system. At a high level, this involves input computation, representation, and implementation.

- Input devices span a wide range but can be roughly divided into key-based devices, direct and indirect pointing devices, and uncertain control devices. These input devices provide different opportunities and challenges for design, as some are more suitable for a particular interaction context than others.

Exercises

1. Pointing devices. Remote pointing may be necessary when users are interacting with a large display. What types of input devices would be suitable? Consider their pros and cons.
2. Accurate input. Consider a medical device that must accurately measure the user's input, which includes numbers, words, and cursor movements on a screen. Which input devices may be suitable for which types of input? Is the choice of input device sufficient to ensure high reliability? If not, what other elements of the user interface should be considered?
3. Comparing input devices. Create a table with the following design factors as the columns: temporal resolution, spatial resolution, accuracy, sensing modality, sensing interaction potential, and sensing validity. Next, add four rows, where each row represents an input device. Score each of the following devices between 0 and 10 based on how well they meet the criteria of the design factors: (a) light pen, (b) capacitive touchscreen, (c) mouse, and (d) touchpad. Are there any trade-offs among these devices? Are the design factors included in the table sufficient to decide which input device to prefer in every conceivable use context?

25
Displays

A critical component of a user interface is the output device or display that allows the interactive system to transfer information to the user. We use the term *display* to cover visual displays (e.g., a computer screen), haptic devices (i.e., displays that you can feel), and other devices that can render information in a modality that humans can perceive. It is important to choose and design the display to match the capabilities of the user and the requirements of the task.

Displays can take many forms; consider the following examples.

1. Squeezeback [668] uses pneumatically driven compression around the arm to send notifications to people. This display can indicate different qualitative sensations that users can reliably distinguish.
2. Andrews et al. [23] explored how large displays could help intelligence analysts think about information (Figure 25.1). They found that the increased screen real estate positively influenced how analysts thought about and made sense of data.
3. SensaBubble [752] can shoot scented bubbles of particular sizes at the user. Information may be projected onto the bubbles until they burst. This allows for multimodal information display in a playful form.
4. In 1969, Bach-y Rita et al. [32] published a paper on the tongue-display unit (Figure 25.1). Because the tongue is packed with receptors, it is possible to represent visual information on it by using an array of 12 × 12 electrodes placed on the tongue.

In sum, displays are not limited to traditional displays that use light-emitting diodes (LEDs).

The defining objective of a display is to transform digital information into analog information so that people can accurately perceive it in one or more sensory modalities. To understand displays, we need to consider the human perceptual system (Chapter 3). A display needs to communicate digital information that matches what humans can perceive: There is little point in generating sound that we cannot hear or visuals with a resolution so high that our visual system cannot perceive it. Recall that our perceptual system has a range of limits. A well-functioning display ensures that the intended information, rather than a biased or incomplete version thereof, is made available to the user.

Let us give an initial example of the complexity of displays by considering the role of color in visual displays, such as a computer monitor. Let us assume that the objective is to show how charged the battery is. How would you choose the colors to show the battery level? The answer is surprisingly complex. A rainbow color scale is a poor choice. There is no natural ordering of colors from red to violet that people easily recognize. Furthermore, picking different hues (e.g., red, yellow, blue) does not work well because they do not indicate quantity; for example, it is not intuitively clear whether orange represents a 30% full battery and red a 60% full battery. The color value (i.e., the intensity of the color) is a better choice in principle. However, in practice, we cannot just halve the color encoding (say, its red–green–blue value) because humans would not perceive that value as half of the original value; in other words, the change in value is not perceived as

Introduction to Human-Computer Interaction. Kasper Hornbæk, Per Ola Kristensson, and Antti Oulasvirta,
Oxford University Press. © Kasper Hornbæk, Per Ola Kristensson, and Antti Oulasvirta (2025).
DOI: 10.1093/oso/9780192864543.003.0025

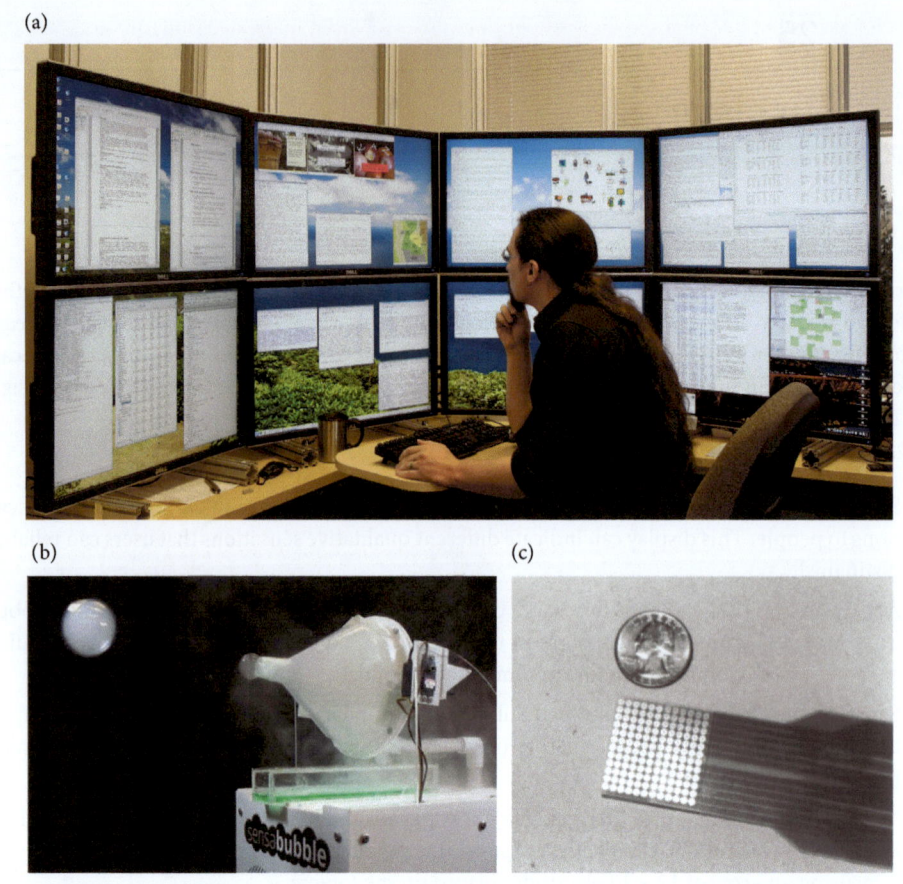

Figure 25.1 Displays are not limited to the familiar touchscreen. HCI studies different arrangements and technologies for presenting information to users. Top: A large display used for sensemaking of work and data [23]. Bottom left: A multimodal display [752]. Bottom right: An electrotactile display to be used on the tongue [32, 33].

linear. Luckily, there are tools to help us with this, such as ColorBrewer. The lesson here is that designing displays is complex.

This chapter reviews common displays. We first discuss the central issues in encoding and rendering information, which are essential processes in turning digital information into something people can perceive. Then, we discuss different devices working across different modalities, explaining their working principles and uses in human–computer interaction (HCI), and how to make informed design decisions when considering a set of output devices for a particular design problem.

25.1 Encoding and rendering

Encoding concerns the basic operation of turning digital information, be it a name or a value, into something that a display can show. Many decisions in encoding are trivial; for example, showing the digital content "v" on a screen is straightforward. However, many decisions are not, particularly when we go between modalities or when we encode something into a form that it does not naturally map to. For example, the auditory representation of a visual symbol, such as an icon, is not obvious. Brown et al. [100] created tactons, haptic versions of messages typically shown as dialog boxes or icons. This included carefully calibrating the frequency, amplitude, and duration used to encode each icon.

Rendering is the operation of transforming the encoded information into something that can be perceived by people. The issue here is that the rendering by display hardware may influence what people perceive. Early displays for virtual reality (VR), for instance, had sufficiently low refresh rates that some users experienced motion sickness from the lag between their head movement and the visual scene.

Next, let us look more closely at encoding and rendering. We start by considering what information can be rendered.

25.1.1 Types of value

A frequent point of departure for encoding is to separate different types of value. The type of value to be displayed determines the appropriate encoding method. Three types of variables can be distinguished:

- *Nominal variables* (sometimes called categorical variables). Such variables do not have an inherent ordering or mapping to numerical values. They include the names of people, zip codes, and eye colors.
- *Ordered variables*. Such variables may be ordered. They include education levels and satisfaction ratings of user interfaces.
- *Quantitative variables*. Such variables are numeric and may be subject to arithmetic. They include temperature, pulse, and rainfall.

While there are other types of variables we might want to output, the three types listed cover the most common cases.

We spend time considering what kind of value we want to display because it matters. As hinted at the beginning of this chapter, quantitative information should not be shown using changes in hue (e.g., 1, 2, 3). However, it is perfectly fine to display nominal values this way (e.g., Amsterdam, Brussels, Copenhagen). In the first case, colors should not be used because such mapping does not communicate the ordering and quantitative differences between the numbers. In the second case, color coding may be used provided that the mapping is known or available to the person viewing the display.

25.1.2 Visual encoding

Once it is known which values to show, the appropriate way to display these values can be chosen. Let us start by considering the visual modality, which is the most researched area of displays.

Visual encodings are typically separated into visual marks and visual channels [e.g., 567]. Visual marks are geometric primitives such as points, areas, and lines. Visual channels include the position of a mark, its color, and its texture. Figure 25.2 shows examples of marks and channels.

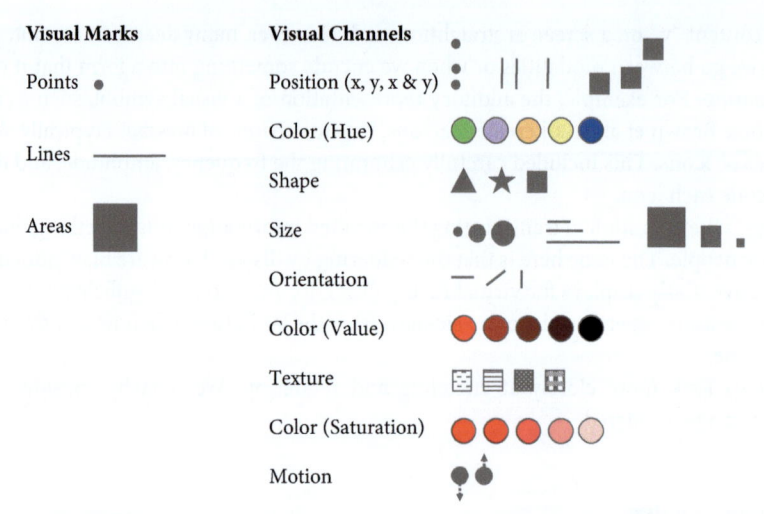

Figure 25.2 This figure shows some ways of encoding data visually, specifically visual marks (left) and visual channels (right), based on Munzner [567].

Before we discuss marks and channels in more depth, let us be more precise about color. The everyday language we use about color can be confusing. In technical terms, a color is considered to have the following three dimensions (Figure 25.2):

Hue: Hue is how we usually speak about color. We refer to hue when we say yellow or green. The RGB system for specifying colors relies on the hues red, green, and blue.

Value: It concerns the lightness or darkness of a color. It is sometimes called the luminance or brightness of the color. Value is thus the intensity of the color, going from an absence of light (dark) to the full brightness of a color.

Saturation: It concerns the depth or intensity of the color. If we set one of the values of R, G, or B to full and the rest to none in a color picker, we will have a fully saturated color. As we go toward a more even mix of R, G, and B values, the color becomes less saturated and will—when the R, G, and B values are the same—be white. Some books refer to this as intensity or chroma.

These dimensions of color work differently for encoding data, as we shall see next.

Effective channels and marks for certain variables

The area of *information visualization* is concerned with how to show marks and which channels to use. It has established which types of marks and channels may be used for which variables and, crucially, which visual variables do not work for certain variables. For example, the position channel is very well suited to show quantitative data. This is why scatter plots are commonly used for quantitative data: They encode data as coordinates. By contrast, the shape channel works poorly for encoding ordered data because they have no natural ordering. Without other information, it is hard to decide if a circle is larger or smaller than a square. However, shapes may be used effectively to encode nominal variables since our visual system can easily tell them apart.

How do we know that? Recall from Chapter 3 that psychophysics includes the study of the perception of certain physical changes. Other types of experiments (Chapter 43) have also helped empirically characterize which shapes and marks work best. An early study is shown in Paper Example 25.1.1. Numerous subsequent studies—psychophysical and experimental—have taught us more about which encodings are appropriate [327, 567]. The following results are particularly important:

- For *nominal variables*, hue is effective, as are shape and motion. Other channels, such as size and saturation, may not be appropriate to communicate a difference in quantity. We could use hue, for example, to show different cities.
- For *ordered variables*, we can use value and saturation, as well as channels such as area and volume. It should be noted that the latter two are not effective for quantitative information, as it is hard to accurately judge differences in areas and volumes.
- For *quantitative variables*, we know that position, length, and orientation are highly effective. This is why scatter plots are easy to accurately read information from, and why comparing the magnitudes of variables in a bar plot is easy. Other variables, such as curvature, volume, saturation, and value, may also work, albeit not as well as others (e.g., position).

Paper Example 25.1.1: Which visual channel works best?

Although the use of graphs and other visual displays to convey information is many centuries old, the work by Cleveland and McGill [154] is considered seminal for understanding how to accurately extract information.

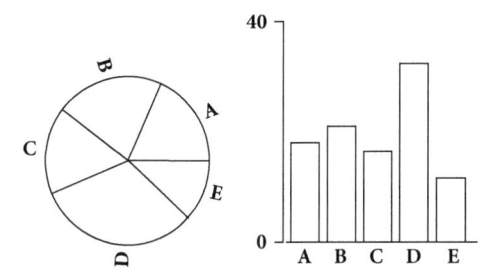

Their main contribution was to approach the use of graphs from the perspective of how accurately people read information from them rather than from the perspective of the graphs' aesthetic merits or applications in exploratory data analysis. Cleveland and McGill [154] set out to understand which elementary tasks people perform when extracting information from graphs. These tasks are similar to what we have called channels. The figure to the right shows two graphs that rely on angle (or possibly area) and position along the y-axis to encode values.

The other part of the work of Cleveland and McGill [154] consisted of several studies that assessed how accurately people perform these different elementary tasks. For instance, for the two tasks above, they collected data from an experiment where 54 participants had to state the percentage of a value relative to another value, both represented as angles or as positions. The participants' error rates (y-axis) were plotted against the actual differences (x-axis). The

continued

> **Paper Example 25.1.1: Which visual channel works best?** *(continued)*
>
> errors for the angle representations are shown to the left; those for the position representations are shown to the right. 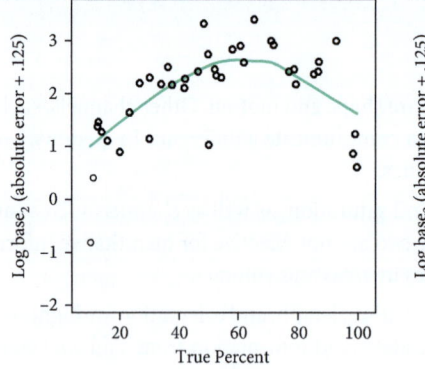
>
> The conclusion here is that angle encoding results in more errors. In fact, only very small and very large differences resulted in similar error rates. Such data are the reason why we know how to encode visual information so that people can read it accurately; they are also the reason why pie charts are considered problematic by many.

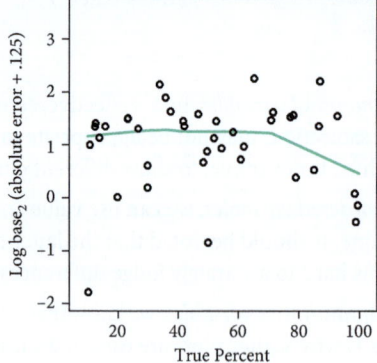

25.1.3 Encoding in other modalities

We have discussed encoding for visual displays; the considerations for encoding in other modalities are similar. First, the encoding needs to match human perception so that the intended values and nothing else are communicated. Second, the encoding should be compatible with the display so that the intended values can be rendered.

As an example, consider encoding data using vibrotactile actuators [845]. Vibrotactile rendering can only be perceived by humans if the vibrations are between 20 and 500 Hz. However, people cannot separate more than nine frequency levels, and the recommendation is that the difference between levels be at least 20%. Some devices, like pneumatic-based actuators, can typically only render lower frequencies. This limits the haptic stimuli that can be rendered.

25.1.4 Rendering

In some cases, what we want to display already exists in an appropriate modality, and there is no need to change it. For instance, we might have a 3D model that we wish to display in VR or a recording of a haptic experience to be replayed. In such cases, there is little concern about encoding and more about how accurately a display can reproduce the model for a human perceiver.

As mentioned at the beginning of the chapter, both encoding and rendering are about matching human perception. The *spatial resolution* of a display often influences human perception. In visual displays, this factor refers to the pixels per inch or similar measures; for haptic displays, it may be the number of actuators per inch (e.g., the number of pins in a pin-array display). The *temporal resolution* of a display is its refresh rate, often measured in hertz. Finally, we may also consider *particular features* of the human perceptual system. In foveated rendering, higher resolution is only offered at the spot where the user is looking, as the periphery of the human eye sees less accurately than the center.

25.2 Simple displays

An LED is a semiconductor that emits light when an electric current flows through it by releasing energy as photons. The amount of energy released determines the color of the light. LEDs are often used as indicators. For instance, in consumer electronics, a single LED is commonly used to signal that a device is turned off but connected to an electrical source, for example, the red light typically found somewhere on a television set. Computers and mobile phones with built-in cameras often include an LED in the camera circuitry that stays on while the camera is active.

LEDs can also be arranged into LED displays, where each LED represents a single picture element (pixel). Initially, such LED displays were limited in terms of color, as only red LEDs were widely available. Later developments resulted in green and blue LEDs. If red, green, and blue LEDs are arranged in a triad, they allow the user to perceive the triad as a single pixel. An LED display is a matrix of red, green, and blue LED triads.

25.2.1 *n*-segment displays

An *n*-segment display uses segments that can be turned on and off to display information, typically numbers or letters. The number of segments can vary. One design is the so-called seven-segment display (Figure 25.3), which uses seven segments to convey characters, typically numbers. These seven segments can be lit up or not. This binary segment behavior results in 7^2 = 128 possible states, although many of these states do not correspond to useful character representations. In general, an *n*-segment display can display n^2 states. Increasing the number of segments increases the number of states that can be expressed, and therefore the character set. In addition, an increase

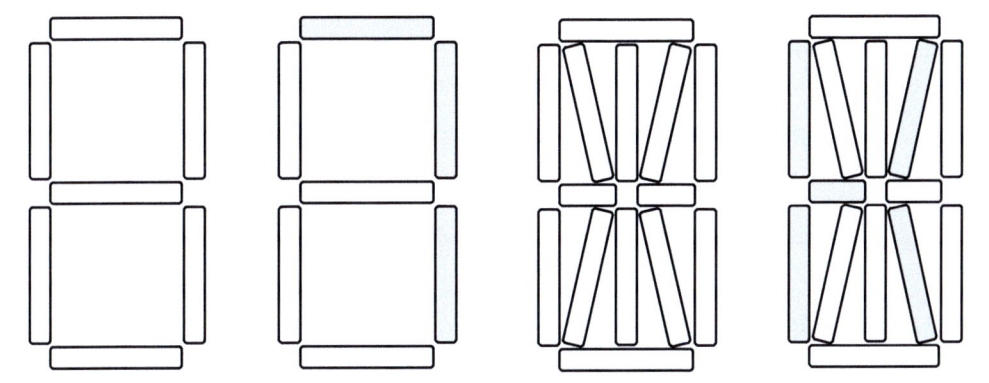

Figure 25.3 Examples of *n*-segment displays. The two displays to the left are seven-segment displays with all the segments unlit (left) and showing the number 7 (right). Since each segment can be lit or unlit, 2^7 = 128 segment combinations can be shown on a seven-segment display, although some combinations may not correspond to useful representations of characters. The two displays to the right are 14-segment displays with all the segments unlit (left) and showing the letter K (right). A 14-segment display has 2^{14} = 16,384 possible states. Placing the segments wisely can improve the representation of letters and allow for visualizing more characters.

in the number of states tends to improve the ability to accurately represent numbers, letters, and other characters. In practice, *n*-segment displays tend to be designed with a slight shear to improve readability. In addition, the base segments indicated in Figure 25.3 are often complemented with additional segments representing the period and the comma at the bottom right.

n-segment displays are very common in consumer devices and appliances, such as microwave ovens, pocket calculators, alarm clocks, and car stereos. One advantage of *n*-segment displays is their low cost of manufacture, as the number of required electrical components is small. It is also easy to create an *n*-segment display since the standardized decoder circuits for common segment display configurations, such as seven-segment and 14-segment displays, can be inexpensively procured and fitted into a device design. Well-designed *n*-segment displays can represent letters, numbers, and other characters more clearly than a low-resolution dot matrix display.

The idea of having variable segments light up to indicate information has been used since the advent of electrical light. A segment display can be realized using any combination of switchable electric light, segment arrangement, and logic mechanism. A modern segment display is typically lit using LEDs. The logic mechanism translates a predefined code for an individual character into the corresponding segments that should be lit to visualize the character. A seven-segment display with an additional segment for the period can represent all possible $2^8 = 256$ states in a byte (8 bits). A decoder circuit for a seven-segment display can then be implemented by providing eight input lines, one for each bit, and eight output lines connected to the eight individual segments (ignoring any required electrical connections to power the LEDs). In practice, 4 bits represent $2^4 = 16$ states; this is sufficient to represent the numbers 0–9 with a typical decoder circuit, such as the Texas Instrument CD4511B decoder circuit.

25.2.2 Dot matrix display

An alternative to *n*-segment displays that provides higher resolution is a *dot matrix display*. An example of a rudimentary dot matrix display is a *flip-disc display*. Such a display consists of a large number of discs with a light color on the front and a dark color on the back. A flip-disc display flips its discs to produce a dot pattern, such as a text message. They are commonly used in large outdoor signs and public transportation systems.

25.3 Visual displays

A *visual display*, such as a computer screen, allows a computer system to present information to the user. Visual displays have undergone tremendous development in the last decade.

25.3.1 Display technology

Central to a display is the mechanism used to reveal information on a screen. The traditional approach, common until the early 2000s, is color cathode-ray tubes (CRTs). It relies on three electron guns (one for each red, green, and blue color) that repeatedly scan a glass tube consisting of phosphorus dots in red, green, and blue. Each pixel position consists of three phosphor color dots, each emitting either red, green, or blue light when excited. When the phosphor dots are struck by the beam, they emit light. The electron guns scan the phosphor-coated screen in a *raster pattern*, drawing each line of the image left-to-right and top-to-bottom. The frequency of these screen updates is known as the *refresh rate*. A higher refresh rate tends to reduce the perceived screen flickering.

In a *CRT* television set, the refresh rate is determined by the color encoding system used in the region. For example, phase alternating line color encoding, common in Europe, South America, and parts of Asia, uses a 50-Hz refresh rate and 576 visible lines. National Television System Committee color encoding, common in North America and Japan, uses a 60-Hz refresh rate and 480 visible lines. The difference in refresh rate is historical: When color encodings were introduced, there was a desire to align the refresh rate on *CRT*s with the local alternating current power line frequency, which is 50 or 60 Hz depending on the region.

When the electron guns reach the end of a line, they are turned off and repositioned at the start of the next line. The delay caused by this operation is known as the *horizontal blanking interval*, often referred to as the "hblank." Similarly, when the electron guns reach the bottom of the screen, they are turned off and repositioned at the beginning of the first line at the top of the screen. This delay is called the *vertical blanking interval* ("vblank"). These intervals became very important in early video game production: Programmers aimed to update the video memory during vblank periods due to the cost of chip sets at the time. Today, a technique known as "double buffering" is used to avoid screen tearing. The central idea is that the system uses two buffers. The first buffer is used to perform graphical updates directly. Once all updates are complete, the first buffer is copied to the second buffer, which is then displayed on the screen. This prevents the user from perceiving graphical artifacts, such as screen tearing and partial graphical updates.

Since the early 2000s, improvements in flat-panel displays have phased out the use of CRTs. Common flat-panel technologies include liquid crystal displays (LCDs), LCDs backlit with light-emitting diodes (commonly called LEDs), plasma panels, organic light-emitting diode displays, and quantum dot light-emitting diode displays.

25.3.2 Head-mounted displays

A *head-mounted display* (HMD) is a wearable display that allows the user to be exposed to various degrees of virtual information. The *reality–virtuality continuum* [544] defines a spectrum of immersion for head-up displays (Chapter 29). At one extreme, the user is exposed to the real environment, and there is no exposure to virtual information. At the other extreme, the user is fully immersed in a virtual environment. This immersion can be achieved by wearing a VR headset. It is also possible to augment the real environment with virtual information, for example, by allowing the user to wear an optical see-through (OST) heads-up display that reveals virtual information mixed with the user's view of the real world. Depending on the level of immersion, the operating level moves to the left or to the right in the reality–virtuality continuum.

Virtual reality

For VR to be fully immersive, VR headsets (Figure 25.4) must produce a very large virtual world that fully occupies the user's field of view. In addition, for information—particularly text—to be legible, the resolution needs to be high. The net effect is that many pixels must have their values computed. This results in a high technical demand on the VR system to render this 3D virtual world at a high resolution at a high refresh rate. In addition, when the user moves their head, the user expects to see a new part of the virtual world. Thus, the VR system must also track the user's head movement and respond to it with low latency.

Figure 25.4 A user wearing a VR headset. Photo by Nan Palmero, used under Creative Commons License.

While a virtual world is fully immersive, a VR system is unable to offer users an experience equivalent to looking around and interacting in the real environment, resulting in a mismatch. This mismatch, exacerbated by the fatigue from wearing a headset for a long period of time, results in simulator sickness. This effect is so prevalent that most empirical VR research with users routinely test for simulator sickness. In addition to tracking the user's head movement, a VR headset can allow the user to walk around in a virtual world. This requires positional tracking of the VR headset in terms of both its Euclidean coordinates in the real environment and the direction of the headset—which way the user is looking. Several techniques have been developed to enable VR positional tracking, including active markers (e.g., Valve's Lighthouse system).

Since VR enables users to fully immerse themselves in a virtual world, VR is eminently suitable for interactive simulations. Typical simulation domains where VR usage is widespread include training activities in medicine (e.g., virtual surgery), defense, and manufacturing. In addition, VR can be used to visualize abstract information. Since VR is fully immersive, it allows complex visualizations to occupy a very vast virtual space. This may be beneficial in computer-assisted design, where users may want to analyze complex information, such as the blade geometry of an airplane engine, and at the same time see the consequences of parameter modifications (Figure 25.5).

Another example where VR may be useful is as a fully portable virtual office [298]. VR allows a user to wear a headset and consistently reconstruct an elaborate high-resolution, real-world, multi-display environment. In addition, since VR is in 3D, the additional operational space allows common productivity applications, such as spreadsheets [276] and presentation software [72], to be augmented with visualization and interaction features.

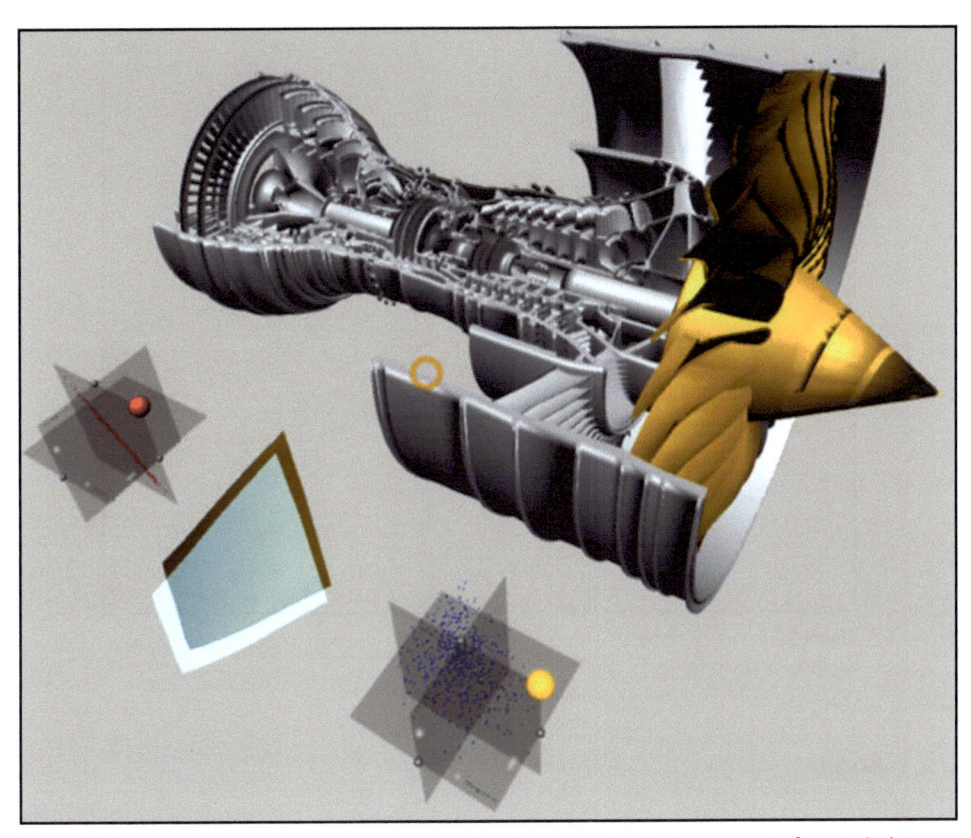

Figure 25.5 A user inspecting the implications of a change in the blade geometry for an airplane engine in VR [813].

Augmented reality

Augmented reality (AR) can be provided through a headset that allows users to view the real world by looking around and at the same time perceive virtual objects that appear to be located in the real world through a process known as registration.

AR headsets come in two common designs. The first is *video passthrough*, which means a camera is mounted at the front of the headset. The user views a video stream from this camera using displays mounted very close to the user's eyes. Virtual objects are rendered on top of this video stream. This solution is less expensive and technically difficult to realize but results in considerably lower fidelity in the user's view of the real environment. Furthermore, it is challenging to correctly register virtual objects in the video stream.

The second design, OST, allows users to perceive virtual content seamlessly blended into the physical environment. The user perceives the real world through a glass pane, and virtual objects are registered to appear in the real world using holographic technology. An example of such a headset is the Microsoft HoloLens (Figure 25.6). OST HMDs are advantageous in that the user perceives the real world through essentially a glass pane. Hence, little to no fidelity is lost. However, such displays struggle to generate accurate colors. For example, it is common to perceive rainbow bands on white panels. In addition, it is difficult to generate a wide field of view.

Figure 25.6 An example of an optical see-through head-mounted display, the Microsoft HoloLens.

25.4 Audio

Humans perceive sound as vibrations in the air. These vibrations are called acoustic waves. An acoustic wave is received by the human auditory system and perceived as sound in the brain. A human can typically perceive sound in the frequency band between 16 Hz and 16 kHz [562]; the exact range varies between individuals and is affected by factors such as age.

There is a rich design space for *auditory displays*. In an analog electrical circuit, sound is represented as an electrical signal, that is, a variation in voltage. The mathematical representation is a continuous time-varying signal; a simple example is a sinusoidal signal. In a digital circuit, sound is represented as a series of binary switching states. The mathematical representation is a series of binary digits. An analog-to-digital converter is a circuit that converts an analog signal into a digital representation. A digital-to-analog converter is a circuit that converts a digital representation into an analog signal. Several electrical circuit architectures have been proposed in academia and industry to efficiently realize this function. A speaker is a transducer that converts an electrical acoustic signal into sound pressure so that it can be perceived by humans.

Spatial sound

Humans can infer the direction and distance of the origin of a sound with some precision. Since humans typically have two ears, the sound will arrive at the individual ears with some time difference. This is known as the interaural time difference, and the human auditory system exploits it for sound localization. A monaural (mono) sound system either emits the sound signal to a single speaker or emits the same sound signal to multiple speakers. This prevents any notion of sound localization. By contrast, a stereophonic (stereo) sound system reproduces sound localization by emitting different sound signals to different speakers. A common example is a pair of headphones.

Spatial sound refers to the creation of spatial experience in listening to computer-generated sound. Consider, for example, playing a 3D video game where the sounds are heard from the directions and distances corresponding to their locations in the VR. *Sonification* uses spatial sound and other cues to cast visual or other information into sound. One could, for example, listen to a sonification of atmospheric impurities or display continuous variables in a dataset using sound.

Auditory icons and earcons

Auditory icons map an event to a sound-producing event in a computer. For example, the sound of a bell ringing may be a reminder of a calendar event. *Earcons* are auditory icons that do not resemble the event that originated the sound. They relax the requirement of mimicking the sound-originating event. This means that their meaning is learned via associative learning, which takes time. Research has looked into the design of earcons by combining them and forming hierarchies of them based on shared cues like rhythm or pitch. Earcons are commonly used to represent temporal events, such as a notification for an incoming message or an error. Brewster et al. [95] suggested the following guidelines for designing earcons:

- "Use musical instrument timbres, simple tones such as sinewaves or square waves are not effective. Where possible use timbres with multiple harmonics as this helps perception and can avoid masking."
- "If listeners are to make absolute judgements of earcons then pitch/register should not be used. A combination of register and another parameter would give better rates of recall."
- "Complex intra-earcon pitch structures are effective in differentiating earcons if used along with rhythm or another parameter."
- "Make rhythms as different as possible. Putting different numbers of notes in each rhythm is very effective."
- "Great care must be taken over the use of intensity because it is the main cause of annoyance due to sound."
- "This may be stereo position or full three-dimensions if extra spatialisation hardware is available. This is very useful for differentiating parallel earcons playing simultaneously."
- "When playing serial earcons one after another use a 0.1 second gap between them so that users can tell where one finishes and the other starts."

Recognizability poses limitations to earcons' wider use.

Speech

Speech can be synthesized by computers, which has opened the door to conversational user interfaces. Speech can be used in many contexts, including digital assistants, announcement systems, and screen readers. However, until recently, the limited accuracy of voice recognition has posed a problem. Of what use is a speech interface that one cannot talk back to? Punctuation ("Stop it!") and proper names would cause recognition issues. Moreover, a word that is recognized incorrectly requires a modality for fixing it, for example, a touchscreen. Recent advances in text-to-speech technology and language models are making it possible to use speech to command digital agents.

25.5 Haptics

Haptic technologies enable users to perceive touch or, in general, forces on their body. A traditional application of haptics is telerobotics, where the user directly controls a remote robot. Haptics are used to improve users' ability to perceive the reactions of the robot in response to control commands.

25.5.1 Vibration

A common approach for activating a sense of touch is the use of vibration. Vibration can be generated straightforwardly using a *vibrator*. An electric motor transfers torque (rotational force) through a drive shaft. If an unbalanced mass is connected to the drive shaft, the system will produce vibrations. Such a system can, for example, be used to generate the rumble sensation commonly found in video game controllers and the vibration signal in mobile phones.

25.5.2 Force feedback

A force feedback device is a system that generates a perceived force by actuation. An alternative term is force-reflecting interface [523]. One example of force feedback is a mechanical exoskeleton glove. When the user wears the glove, the system tracks the user's fingers. If the fingers are supposed to interact with a virtual object, the system uses force feedback to simulate the forces the user would experience when touching a physical object. Mechanical exoskeleton gloves have applications in telerobotics, teleoperation, and VR.

Mechanical exoskeleton gloves can be grounded. Grounding means that the system is connected to a grounding point, such as a desk or a floor. This allows the system to simulate the sensation of weight, for example, a user lifting a heavy virtual bag in VR. Another extension is to augment the gloves with additional feedback, such as vibration feedback or thermal feedback, to simulate tactile sensation or touching cold or hot surfaces.

Massie et al. [523] set out three criteria for designing effective force feedback:

Free space must feel free: The device should minimize encumberment of the user and minimize external forces when the user is moving in free space. This means the device should have low inertia and no unbalanced weight.

Solid virtual objects must feel stiff: The maximum stiffness that a virtual surface can represent determines how solid an object will be perceived by a user. In reality, there is a limit to the stiffness a system is required to simulate for users to perceive a virtual surface as solid. For example, Massie et al. [523] found that users perceive a stiffness of 20 N/cm as representing a solid immovable surface.

Virtual constraints must not be easily saturated: Virtual walls and other solid immovable surfaces should be perceived as solid and immovable. The system should support the maximum exertion force of the finger suitable for the application, which can range from a force of 10 N for precise manipulation [523] to 40 N for the maximum exertion force of a human finger [810].

The braking mechanism in a force feedback glove can be constructed using a variety of techniques. One technique involves a pulley system where each finger is connected to a cable and a motor pulls the cables to simulate force feedback [176, 523]. One advantage of this design is its relatively simple actuation principle. One disadvantage is its complicated mechanical design, which

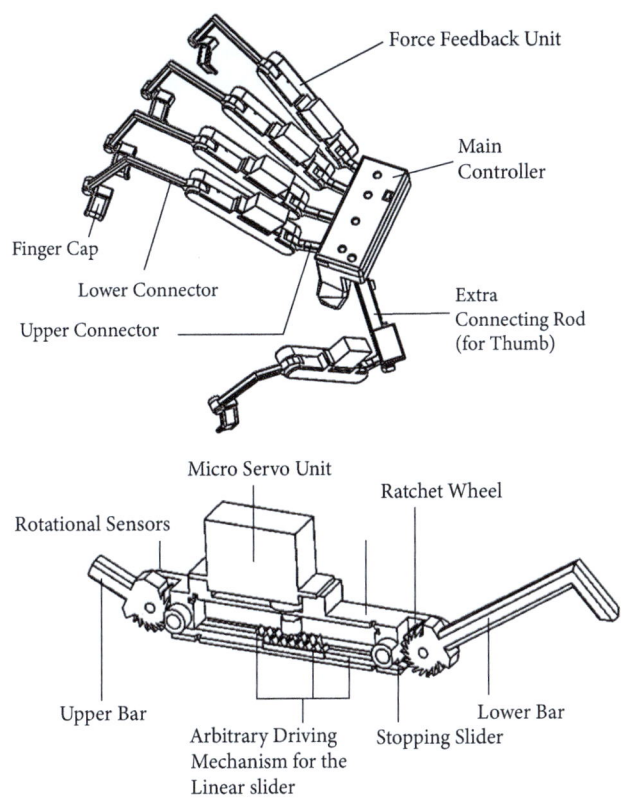

Figure 25.7 A mechanical exoskeleton for generating force feedback in VR and AR applications [304]. The design is shown to the top; the force feedback unit is shown to the bottom.

makes it expensive to build and maintain. Another disadvantage is the risk of the pulley system accidentally overextending a finger, causing injury.

Another example is a mechanism that uses a ratchet wheel to allow the mechanical exoskeleton to freely follow finger movements. When the force feedback is activated, a driving mechanism inserts a linear slider into the ratchet wheel and prevents the mechanical exoskeleton joint from moving (Figure 25.7). The result is a sensation of force feedback as the user's finger movement is stopped by the braking mechanism [304].

Paper Example 25.5.1: Haptic guidance for users suffering from vision impairments

Computer displays do not only represent digital objects; they can also represent objects in our surroundings. The augmentation of sensory capabilities is valuable for people with sensory impairments, who can be assisted in navigating environments and interacting with objects. *Sonification* encodes geographical or other information to sound, which can be used to facilitate navigation or increase situational awareness for blind users. *Vibrotactile displays* vibrate

continued

> **Paper Example 25.5.1: Haptic guidance for users suffering from vision impairments** *(continued)*
>
> based on interesting objects or events in the environment. Such displays can be placed in multiple ways and places on the user, such as around the waist, on shoes, around wrists, and so on. Each location entails different challenges for electrical engineering. Moreover, each location is different in terms of people's ability to discriminate haptic stimulations. The underlying reason is that mechanoreceptors are more densely located on certain parts of the body. In this respect, placing such displays on fingers is appealing.
>
> *FingerSight* is a haptic guidance system that helps people with vision impairments to locate and reach for objects in their peripersonal space [731]. *Peripersonal space* refers to the physical space surrounding our bodies within which we can reach for and grasp objects. For example, at the time of writing this text, one co-author had the following objects in his peripersonal space: a mobile device, a coffee mug, a water cup, a key, a plate, a knife, a laptop, a chair, a water jug, and a piece of paper. While it may appear effortless to grasp an object for a person with no visual impairment, it is effortful for blind people.
>
> FingerSight consists of a finger-worn ring that houses a camera and a haptic display. The display has four evenly spaced tactors that can stimulate the index finger; the camera tracks the distance of objects. The distance of an object is then mapped to the features of the haptic stimulation to indicate how far away the object is. As the user moves the hand closer or farther from the object, the tactors modulate their actuation frequency accordingly. An experiment showed that very little training was needed to use FingerSight: Users quickly learned to estimate distance to objects using the haptic feedback. Such feedback can help users explore nearby objects and reach for objects of interest.
>
> (a) (b)

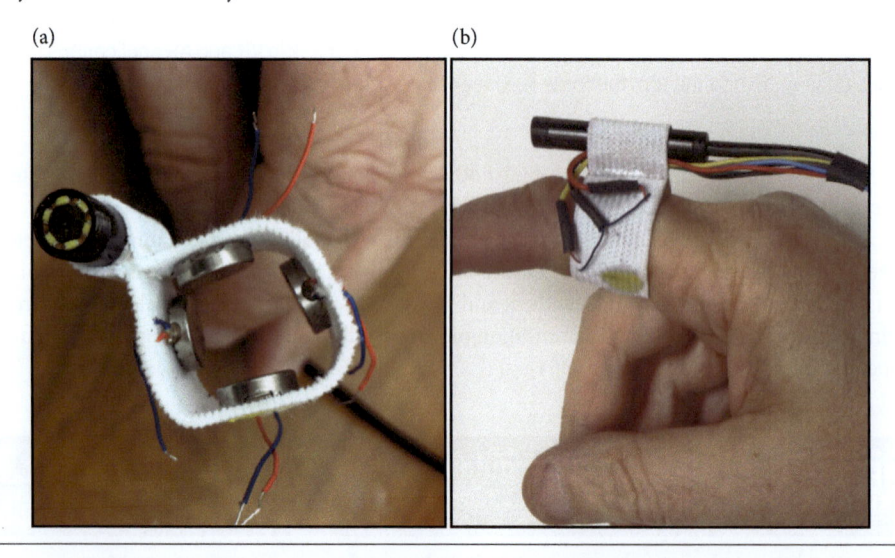

25.5.3 Haptic textures

Look at a physical surface close to you and touch it, for example, with a finger. Then, close your eyes and move your finger on the surface slowly. Can you sense the texture of the object? What if you move your finger more quickly?

Fingertips and other parts of the hand have high densities of mechanoreceptors that permit both spatial (where) and object (what) sensing. Research has found that much information can be conveyed with temporal information alone [466]. This has opened the door for conveying information via *haptic textures*: sensations of texture generated when moving a finger on a matrix of actuators.

A high-quality tactile matrix can generate haptic gradients that can closely mimic the sensation of brushing against an object. The force of each actuator is calibrated according to the real surface normal it is supposed to mimic, which allows for generating sensations of slopes and bumps. Their response can be further changed to reflect the velocity of the moving finger. With a high-resolution haptic display, global and local areas of the display can be used to convey information. For example, the whole display could resemble a "sandy" texture with local peaks and valleys that signify information.

25.6 Emerging forms of displays

This section reviews some ways in which researchers have worked toward the ultimate display, as envisioned by Sutherland et al. [809] in 1965. Sutherland speculated on what the best possible display would be. In the paper, he described the ultimate display; his final remarks read as follows:

> The ultimate display would, of course, be a room within which the computer can control the existence of matter. A chair displayed in such a room would be good enough to sit in. Handcuffs displayed in such a room would be confining, and a bullet displayed in such a room would be fatal. With appropriate programming such a display could literally be the Wonderland into which Alice walked.

Since then, HCI researchers have pursued different variants of this display. Next, we present some of these variants.

The first variant started from a simple yet profound idea: What if pixels were not limited to communication via the emission of light? Most of this chapter has focused on visual displays. By contrast, *shape-changing displays* use physical actuation to encode additional information into pixels. Users can touch, push, and explore this information with their hands.

A prominent example is *inFORM*, developed by Follmer et al. [250]. It was inspired by the concept of affordance: the perception of action potentials in an object. The system, shown in Figure 25.8, uses 30 × 30 motorized polystyrene pins arranged on a 381 × 381 mm lattice surface. The pins are attached to push–pull rods that allow the extension of a pin 100 mm from the surface. Motorized slide potentiometers are used to control the rods, producing a force up to 1.08 N. A proportional-integral-derivative controller, or PID controller, is used for real-time control of the haptic feedback upon pressing. In the prototype, a ceiling-mounted projector was used to project color on the pins.

The prototype allows for exciting new interaction techniques (Chapter 26) that are impossible with regular touch displays. *Buttons* can be formed by raising pins and responding with a button-like stiffness to pressing. *Touch tracks* are lines or curves formed by adjacent pins, which the user can touch at different locations or slide over. *Handles* are pins that can be pinched and pulled up or down. Dynamic widgets can be created that change as a response to a user's press. For example, a triangular "Play" button can change to a rectangular "Stop" button in a media player. Pins can also react to *hovering* to create affordances dynamically. With a ceiling-mounted camera for hand tracking, pins can lift up the areas of a display that are interactive. Because the pins have sensors, other objects can also be placed on the display. For example, a ball can be rolled on the display, with the display reacting to it to create a path for it. An object placed on the surface can be rotated to create a knob-like experience.

(a) (b)

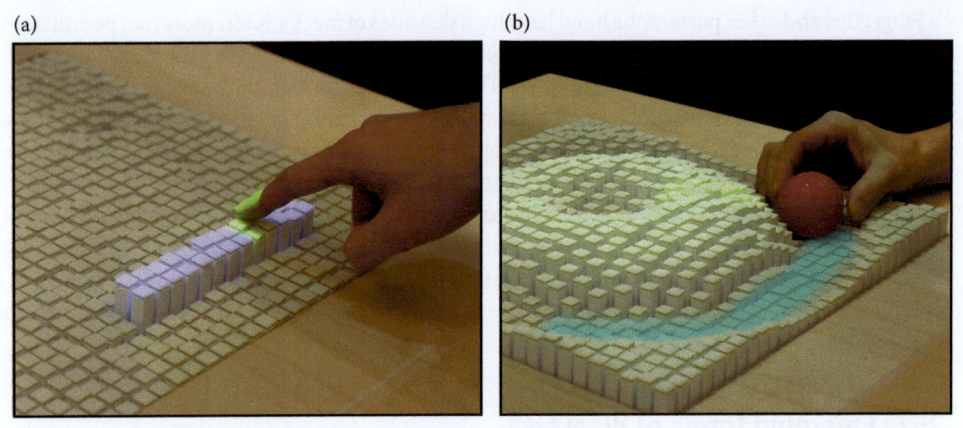

Figure 25.8 The inFORM shape-changing display enables physical affordances through the physical actuation of pixels [250]. The technique allows for the haptic perception of information encoded in a pixel. A pixel can communicate via information encoded in its (1) color, (2) height, and (3) dynamic response to pressing (e.g., stiffness).

Most typical displays have been rigid, tablet-sized, or display-sized, and made of a few specific materials (e.g., glass, plastic). Much research on displays has attempted to move beyond these sizes and materials.

Finally, *digital fabrication* concerns the computer-supported process of designing and creating physical objects. It has revolutionized many areas of manufacturing and has also been influential in the field of HCI. One reason for this influence is that it allows some parts of Sutherland's vision to be fully realized: the creation, replication, and manipulation of physical objects.

Zoran and Paradiso [930] presented early work on such digital fabrication. They aimed to create a device that bridged the gap between digital models and traditional craft. This resulted in the tool shown in Figure 25.9. The top figure (A) shows a handheld milling tool that allows the user to cut into different materials. The tool is motion-tracked so that the location of its tip is known. This means that when the user removes material from an object (B), the tool can change the spindle speed or move the shaft to alert the user if they are violating the constraints of the preselected 3D digital model. As a result (C), the user is supported in adhering to the constraints of the model while being allowed craftsmanship and freedom of expression. In this case, we consider digital fabrication a form of display or output.

Summary

- Displays turn digital information into physical phenomena that users should be able to perceive accurately.
- A key consideration is the match of a display to the human visual system. In the case of a poor match, any change in the display, visual or otherwise, may be perceived incorrectly or not perceived at all by the user.
- Displays are not limited to the visual presentation of information and can be implemented using different techniques.
- Emerging displays combine displays and sensing.

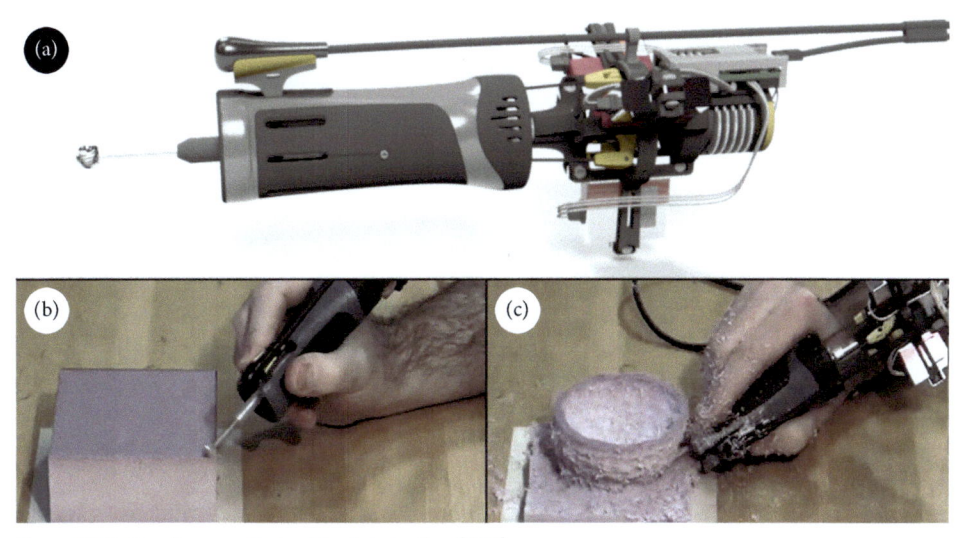

Figure 25.9 FreeD, an early tool for fabrication [930].

Exercises

1. Dot matrix displays. What can you not display with these?
2. Designing a visual display. Consider having to design a scatter plot display that is updated in real time and shows a two-dimensional dataset for a VR environment. (a) Which visual channels would you use? (b) How would you encode the variables visually? (c) What are the pros and cons of a VR display over a regular desktop monitor?
3. Haptic interfaces. Drawing from the concepts discussed in this chapter, propose how to design a haptic notification (e.g., for an incoming message).
4. Sensory modalities. Compare the auditory and tactile senses as modalities for displaying geographic data. Evaluate their advantages and disadvantages.
5. Consider small point lights (e.g., LEDs), which are used in kitchen appliances, cameras, watches, and many other interactive systems. They can vary in intensity over time. In what ways could you use such lights to encode information? What are the likely perceptual limits for people trying to decode the information? Compare your suggestions with the design possibilities provided by Harrison et al. [315].

26
Interaction techniques

Although the term may not be familiar, we use *interaction techniques* all the time. If you open an application menu on a computer, what you will see are hotkeys (shortcuts) associated with commands. In the "Edit" menu, for example, you may see "Ctrl-X" for cutting and "Ctrl-V" for copying. Alternatively, you can click on the command with the mouse. When you hover over the item in the menu, it is highlighted by changing the background color. Using hotkeys or a mouse to select a command differs in multiple ways. Using hotkeys is fast but requires learning. Selection with a pointer is slower because it requires visual search and pointing.

All basic interactive tasks that we carry out with computers are facilitated by interaction techniques such as pointing, scrolling, using menus, entering text, and navigating. Some familiar techniques that we discuss in this chapter include scrolling, word autocompletion, panning, zooming, and gain functions in pointing. At a high level, an interaction technique is *a computation that couples input and output, to support elementary interactive tasks*. Figure 26.1 shows some examples of interaction techniques; Paper Example 26.0.1 explains the Bubble Cursor, an interaction technique that expands a cursor's selection area to always hit the nearest target.

What are the elementary tasks that users need to solve? The literature cover many tasks [249]. In this chapter, we discuss the following essential tasks and techniques:

- Moving the active area or cursor in the user interface via pointing techniques.
- Selecting or manipulating objects; this includes menu techniques.
- Entering numbers and text via text entry techniques.
- Changing which part of an information space the user sees via camera control or navigation techniques.

To help users solve these elementary tasks, interaction techniques couple the input from an input device (Chapter 24) with the output shown to the user on displays (Chapter 25). Sometimes, this coupling is simple: A hotkey couples key combinations where a modifier key and a letter are pressed to execute a command, with some feedback sent to the user to notify them that the command has been invoked. Other times, the coupling is complex. For instance, most operating systems use some form of mouse acceleration, which may involve complicated mappings from the movements of a mouse to the movement of the cursor pointer [138].

Coupling distinguishes interaction techniques from other concepts discussed in this part of the book. *Input methods*, for example, primarily concern input processing, and *input devices* primarily concern the underlying hardware and software system. *User interfaces*, on the other hand, are much larger systems. They may involve multiple interaction techniques and other interactive features designed to support several user tasks. Except for simple mobile games, one interaction technique rarely suffices as the user interface for an application.

Next, let us look at what matters in interaction techniques.

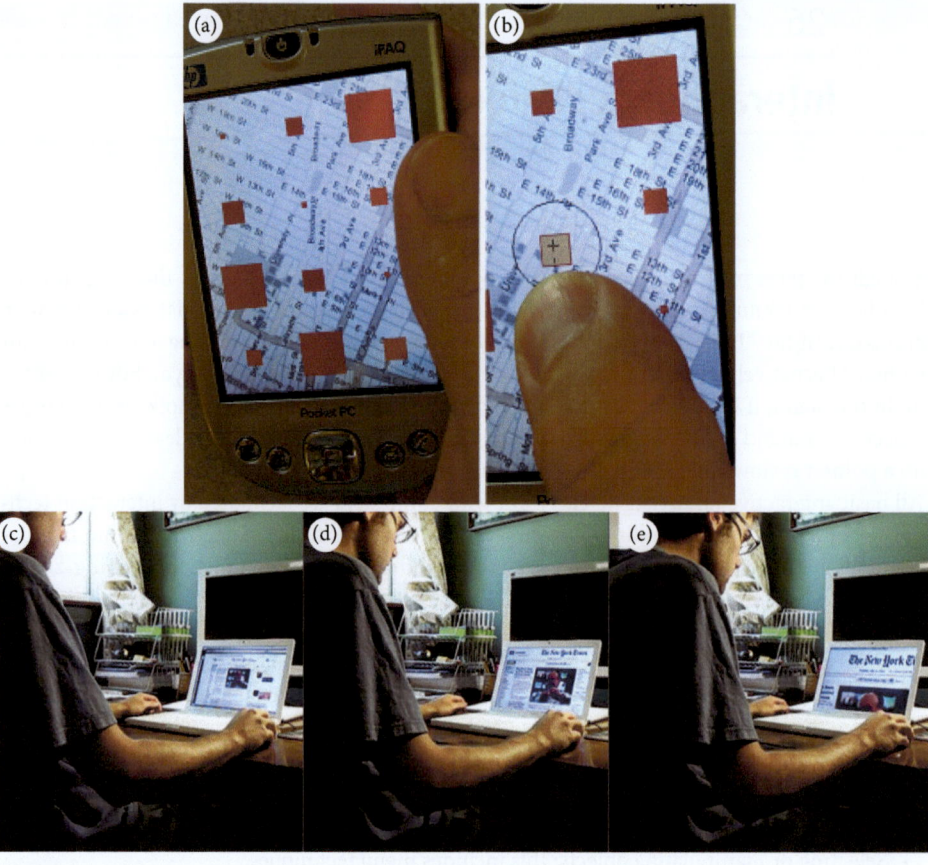

Figure 26.1 While we commonly use interaction techniques like scrolling, panning, and zooming, HCI continuously studies and develops novel designs with pros and cons compared to established designs. Top: A way of shifting icons (red squares) so that they are not obscured by a user's finger, allowing the user to see them [860]. Bottom: An interaction technique where leaning forward zooms the content on a display [313].

Paper Example 26.0.1: The end of misclicks?

Bubble Cursor is an interaction technique for selecting targets with a pointing device [294]. It facilitates the selection of targets when using an indirect pointing device, such as a mouse. The intuition is simple to grasp: Imagine pointing toward a small target. If the target has no neighboring targets, why not make the selection area much larger? This would make it easier to select the target.

Its computations consist of three steps. First, the Bubble Cursor computes a geometric shape called a Voronoi diagram for targets on the display. Given the targets, a Voronoi diagram partitions the display so that every pixel on the display is mapped to exactly one target. This defines *selection regions* for the cursor. Second, when the cursor is moving, the Bubble Cursor actively changes the selection region to whichever target the cursor is mapped to. Third, clicks are assigned to the target within the same Voronoi cell as the cursor. The figure in this paper example box shows how moving the cursor would not normally select a target (a), but when using the Bubble Cursor (b), it does. The third pane shows the corresponding Voronoi diagram.

The authors' hypothesis was that the technique facilitates the selection of smaller targets by exploiting the empty space around them. In particular, the Bubble Cursor expands the effective selection area, possibly putting an end to misclicks. This hypothesis was tested in an empirical study in which users were asked to select targets as quickly as possible. They found that the benefit is large and practically relevant: The average selection time was 1.25 s for the regular point cursor and 0.9 s for the Bubble Cursor. The downside of the technique is that it changes the familiar look and feel of pointing and may obstruct graphics or text underneath the bubble. Further, with an increasing density of distractors, the benefit vanishes. This study shows that empirical studies play a critical role in helping to identify the operating range of such techniques.

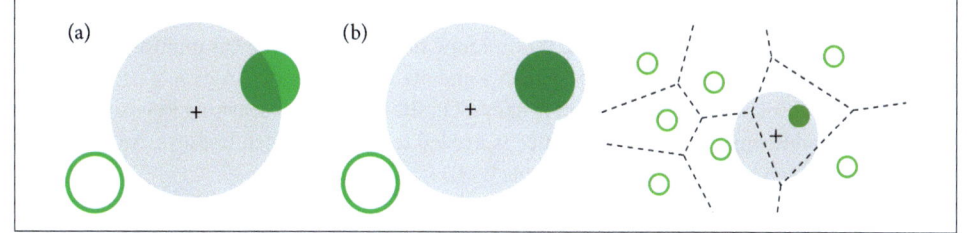

26.1 Objectives for interaction techniques

Why do we need interaction techniques? The two main purposes of interaction techniques are to improve and enable interactions. First, some interaction techniques improve user performance in some conditions of interest. The goal is to find a technique that suits the user group or the context. Gesturing—swipes and shapes drawn on a touch display—offers a faster alternative to tapping in text entry. However, like hotkeys, gestures require some time to learn. The stylus, a digital pen available for some tablets and smartphones, is another example. It offers superior tracking and drawing performance at the expense of mobility: Using a stylus requires adequate posture and support. Some design objectives commonly considered in the research of interaction techniques are given in Table 26.1.

Second, interaction techniques enable interaction in circumstances in which it would normally be challenging or even impossible. Research on enabling techniques often attempts to exploit alternative *sensory modalities*, such as gaze or haptics. In *augmentative and alternative communication*, interaction techniques are developed for people with speech and language difficulties. *Gaze-based interaction* refers to a class of interaction techniques developed primarily for users with severe motor disabilities, such as cerebral palsy. An example is *dwell-based selection*: Here, a target can be selected by fixating on it for a sufficiently long time. The downside of this technique is *the Midas effect*: Gazing at something may inadvertently select it. Hence, setting the threshold involves a trade-off between the speed of selections and false positives (Midas selections).

Interaction techniques often expose *trade-offs* in interactive tasks. In the case of hotkeys, for example, the trade-off concerns performance and learnability. Hotkeys enable an alternative

Table 26.1 Common design objectives considered for interaction techniques.

Design objective	Operationalization
Performance	Speed and accuracy in representative tasks
Experience	Self-reported experience of flow, mastery, control, or similar quality
Learnability	Rate of learning; time it takes to achieve a desired level of skill
Mobility	Suitability for conditions in which users are walking, multitasking, or otherwise encumbered
Ergonomics	Physiological and experienced comfort in representative tasks
Accessibility	Suitability for users with different abilities

modality to access commands. Instead of tapping—or point-and-click if you are using a mouse—pressing a key combination launches the desired command. On the one hand, hotkeys are quicker than pointing for accessing commands. If you know the hotkeys of the commands that you use frequently, you can be significantly faster than someone who does not. An expert user of professional photo editing software has tens of hotkeys. On the other hand, learning key combinations takes considerable time. Substantial practice is needed to adopt only ten hotkeys. An example of trade-offs in design is given in Paper Example 26.1.1.

Research on interaction techniques involves three main types of efforts: (1) innovation of novel input–output couplings, (2) engineering work to enable, implement, and optimize technical enablers of techniques, and (3) empirical research on how interaction techniques work in practice. Advances in software and hardware have opened up many opportunities for innovation. We have several new methods for sensing human movement, from eye tracking to electroencephalography. We have more responsive, higher-resolution display technology for a variety of circumstances, from cars (heads-up displays) to virtual reality. We have new and more accurate machine learning methods and compute resources, which allow us to infer, reason, and plan in real time. The abundance of possibilities has created a dilemma: Almost any interaction technique *could* be created, but which ones *should* be created? Answering this question requires a commitment to user-centric design processes.

Human–computer interaction (HCI) research is a multidisciplinary effort drawing contributions from computer science (e.g., machine learning techniques for inferring users' goals), electrical engineering (e.g., sensing methods suitable for gaze-based control), and interaction design (e.g., designing gestures for text entry on mobile devices). Design decisions can also be informed by psychology, especially research on motor control and perception. The task related to an interaction technique can be analyzed to identify the corresponding motor control task, such as pointing or steering. A suitable theory or model is then used to engineer the technique or assess potential design solutions. Techniques can also be empirically evaluated in an experimental setup where users need to perform that specific task. The performance achieved can then be compared to the *baseline design* to assess it. Baselines are often previously known state-of-the-art techniques or designs popular in everyday use. Without a baseline, it may be difficult to demonstrate that a desirable trade-off has been achieved.

In the rest of this chapter, we first review key areas of HCI research, starting with pointing techniques. Then, we look at two important perspectives on interaction techniques: control and learnability.

Paper Example 26.1.1: Trade-offs in the design of interaction techniques

The design of interaction techniques involves multiple objectives. Hotkeys are a case in point. Grossman et al. [295] compared several techniques for learning hotkeys (see the Figure in this Paper Example):

1. Traditional: The hotkey is presented next to the command label, as in desktop applications.
2. Fading-out hotkey: The hotkey label stays visible for a short time after selection and then fades out.
3. Hotkey menu replacement: The command label is replaced with the hotkey label when the user hovers over it.
4. Audio feedback: The command label and the hotkey are both read aloud by the system after selection.
5. System delay: The user is forced to look at the hotkey label of a clicked item for a few seconds.
6. Disabled menu items: Command labels are grayed out while shortcuts are more clearly visible.
7. Blinking hotkey: When the menu closes, the hotkey stays visible and blinks for a short duration.
8. Following hotkey: When an item is clicked, the menu closes but the hotkey stays visible and follows the mouse cursor for a while.
9. Visual feedback: Combines blinking, following, and replacement techniques.

This set of techniques, which may look arbitrary at first, combines three key design principles: cost, feedback, and memory. First, by manipulating the time cost associated with hotkeys, one can incentivize users to consider them (cost-based techniques). In Chapter 21, we discuss why changing costs and benefits can nudge users to adopt different sensorimotor strategies. Second, hotkeys are often not noticed; making them more prominent may promote their recognition (feedback-based techniques). In Chapter 3, we looked at visual attention and saliency. Third, using different sensory modalities can help encode and recall hotkeys better (memory-based techniques).

   A controlled, isolated task was used to compare these techniques. In the task, a command label was shown, and the user had to select it from the menu as quickly as possible. The results were surprising. Audio feedback and disabled menu techniques were the most effective, both increasing the use of hotkeys by more than 100% and reducing the task completion time—a staggering improvement! In the traditional condition, only 30% of the users used the hotkeys at all; this doubled when using the two best techniques. Users also started to use hotkeys earlier in the experiment. Despite the positive results, these techniques have caveats. Audio feedback works by continuously reminding users about hotkeys, perhaps to the point that users would rather start using the hotkeys than continue listening to feedback. Disabled menu items also force users to pay attention to the hotkeys. Visual feedback, to the surprise of the authors, did not help the users transition to hotkeys even when it was combined with other techniques.

continued

Paper Example 26.1.1: Trade-offs in the design of interaction techniques *(continued)*

The users did not appreciate it, either. The authors speculated that this was because the users had to focus on a visual task and could not divide their attention to consider cues. The delayed technique was also perceived negatively.

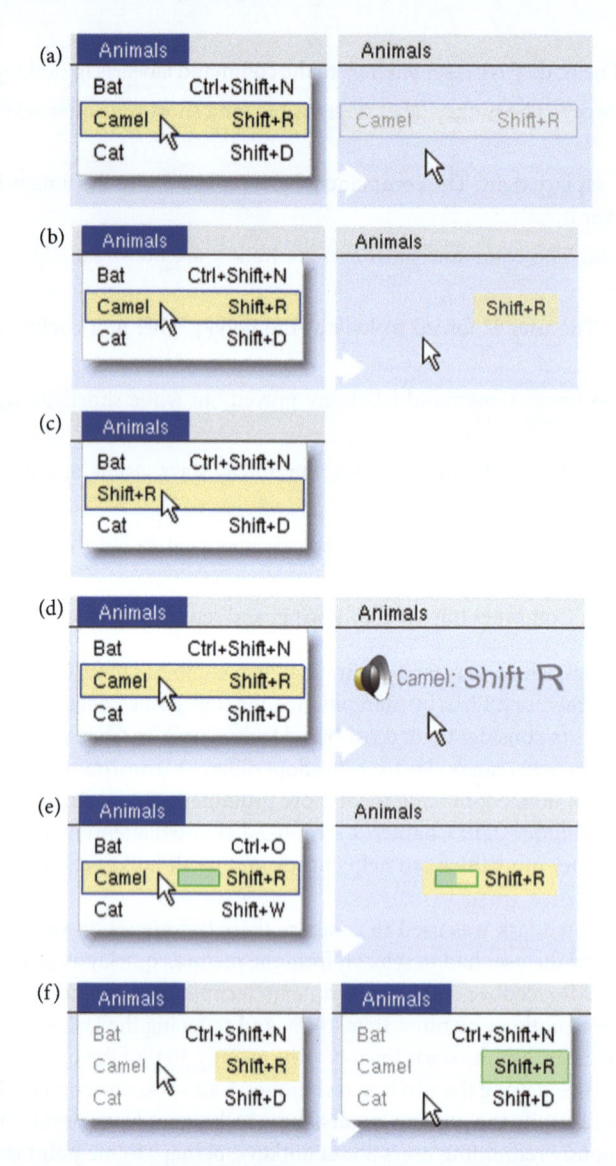

Grossman et al. [295] compared five techniques for promoting the use of hotkeys.

26.2 Pointing techniques

A *pointing facilitation technique* maps changes registered in an input device to the movement of a cursor or the presentation of potential targets on display. Two-dimensional pointing is familiar from desktop interaction (see Chapter 28). We find one-dimensional pointing in *scrolling*. Here, the end-effector must be brought on top of a region that corresponds to a page or a location in the document. Three-dimensional selection occurs in augmented and virtual reality applications.

Pointing facilitation techniques can be further distinguished into two classes:

1. **Input transfer functions:** Techniques that map changes in the input signal to cursor movements. One example is control-to-display (C/D) gain functions.
2. **Display transfer functions:** Techniques that change the presentation of potential targets to facilitate their selection. One example is Bubble Cursor, which changes the selection region of elements.

An understanding of pointing facilitation starts from an understanding of pointing. As we saw in Chapter 4, pointing is an aimed movement. An end-effector, such as a cursor, is used to refer to an object of interest. In the case of HCI, pointing often includes clicking or some other way of selecting the area under the end-effector. The understanding of this elementary interaction is based on Fitts' law, given in Chapter 4.

What does Fitts' model tell us about pointing techniques? It says that both distance and width have an effect on *movement time (MT)*. Hence, if the interaction technique can change those, it can decrease *MT*. For example, Bubble Cursor makes *width* (*W*) larger and *distance* (*D*) smaller. However, the remaining two empirical parameters in Fitts' law may hide some other effects. Some techniques adapt to the user while others change dynamically depending on, for example, the speed of motion or what is shown on the display. In other words, the empirical parameters *a* and *b* are not always constants.

26.2.1 Control-to-display functions

As a case of pointing facilitation techniques, we consider the transfer functions that map movement on a control surface to cursor motion. *C/D functions*, or gain functions, are input transfer functions used in indirect input devices such as mice, joysticks, and trackpads. They are used by almost every computer user. A C/D function maps changes in the *control space* (e.g., touchpad) to changes in the *display space* (e.g., visible cursor). Every indirect device uses some C/D function; in some cases, it is simply a linear coefficient.

Technically, a gain function computes a scalar factor (or "gain") from the instantaneous input speed (v_{in}):

$$v_{out} = f_{CD}(v_{in}) \times v_{in}. \tag{26.1}$$

A gain function can be as simple as a fixed gain: A constant ratio mediates the input and output movement velocities. However, how can we pick a good constant? Imagine that you are designing a new augmented reality technique for selecting distant targets. Local hand movements (control space) are mapped to warped hand movements shown in the distance. Casiez et al. [137] presented a principle for choosing a range of gain values. First, the minimum gain CD_{min} must allow for reaching the most distant targets without clutching (lifting the mouse or finger from the surface), and the maximum gain CD_{max} must allow for accessing an individual pixel. Setting a single value inevitably represents a compromise between these extrema.

For this reason, most commercially used gain functions are *speed-dependent*, that is, the gain changes as a function of velocity. Speed-dependent functions are better because they can respond to both fast movements, reducing the need for clutching, and slow movements, which are needed for accurate pointing. However, most functions are proprietary—their shape is not disclosed to the public.

Casiez and Roussel [136] reverse-engineered gain functions in existing operating systems and found that they share some features, namely (1) a monotonic increase at the beginning and (2) comparable maxima. They were distinguished by the minima, continuity, and the shape of the functions. The functions are shown in Figure 26.2. Speed-dependent gain functions have been shown to be up to 24% faster than a constant C/D gain in an empirical evaluation. Such differences have practical significance, given the high frequency of pointing in HCI.

Why do such differences emerge? There are four main causes. First, speed-dependent gain functions can dampen excess speeds. Since high-velocity movements cannot be controlled accurately (remember the speed–accuracy trade-off in Chapter 4), they can be made more predictable by sloping the curve to a near-constant speed at that point. Second, speed-dependent gain functions can add more granularity to high-precision movements. When the user moves the device slowly, for example with the purpose of selecting a tiny target, the cursor moves smaller distances on the display. Third, different velocity ranges are associated with different muscle groups. Consider very high-precision motions with a mouse; you probably do those with wrist and finger motions. High-speed motions, on the other hand, recruit muscles in the arm and shoulder. Fourth, they can reduce unnecessary clutching.

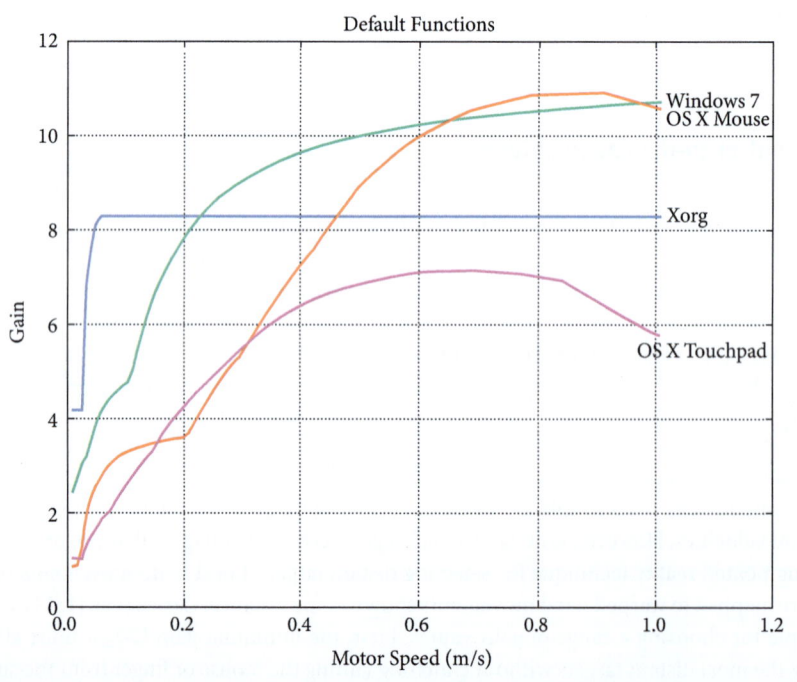

Figure 26.2 Casiez and Roussel [136] proposed a novel method to reverse-engineer C/D functions and found large and surprising differences among modern operating systems.

26.3 Selection and manipulation techniques

Selection and manipulation techniques affect an object once it has been identified, for example, by pointing. The simple case, selection, involves simply selecting an object. This might invoke a command coupled with the object or an object mark as the argument for a subsequent command. More complex selections, as in the case of menus, have enabled inventive selection techniques that help to effectively select among an array of options. Finally, objects may be manipulated in other ways—resized, moved, or rotated. Many interaction techniques have been developed for these cases. Let us look at these techniques in turn.

26.3.1 Simple selection

Usually, selection in graphical user interfaces is simple. You click the mouse over an object or tap it with your finger. However, sometimes this is difficult; recall the chapter on motor control (Chapter 4). The target might be small. Your finger may obscure the target. You may be unable to see the target. You may shake as you attempt to perform the selection. Effective interaction techniques can handle these cases.

For instance, the shifting technique shown in Figure 26.1 offsets targets so that the user can see what is below their finger [860]. Another idea is to make what is selected sticky [914]. A sticky icon reduces the cursor's gain ratio when the cursor is over the icon. This makes it easier to stop over the icon and, therefore, select it. Worden et al. [914] showed that such icons make selections faster, in particular for smaller icons, across younger participants (mean age of 23) and older participants (mean age of 70).

Another idea is to eliminate the need for clicking as we normally use it. In *crossing*, the user crosses the object with the mouse or a finger rather than clicking on it. In *dwell-time selection*, the user hovers over the object to be selected, and after a certain time (the *dwell*), the object is selected.

In this section, it is assumed that the selection is binary—either you select an object or you do not select it. However, this need not be the case. Ramos et al. [687] implemented and evaluated pressure widgets, user interface elements that allow users to select by using pressure.

These and many other works on simple selection techniques show that even for something as simple as a button click, researchers have been remarkably inventive with interaction techniques.

26.3.2 Menu selection

An *interactive menu system* organizes a collection of items on display so that the user can explore the menu and select the desired items. Graphical menu systems present the menu items visually. Menu systems often use hierarchical organization, placing items in submenus. Another defining feature is semantics. The options have labels that have semantics—they mean something. Associations between options are exploited in the organization of the menu. Items that belong together are often put into the same unit, for example, a submenu. Design can exploit this in different ways. Menus are often organized alphabetically, numerically, or semantically.

Larger menus typically utilize *transient visualizations*. That is, the menu, or a part of it, is temporarily displayed and can be dismissed. For example, when you click on the title of a menu on a workstation application, the submenu appears below; when you move the cursor away from the *activation area*, the submenu disappears. Two menu techniques—a morphing menu and a split menu—are shown in Figure 26.3.

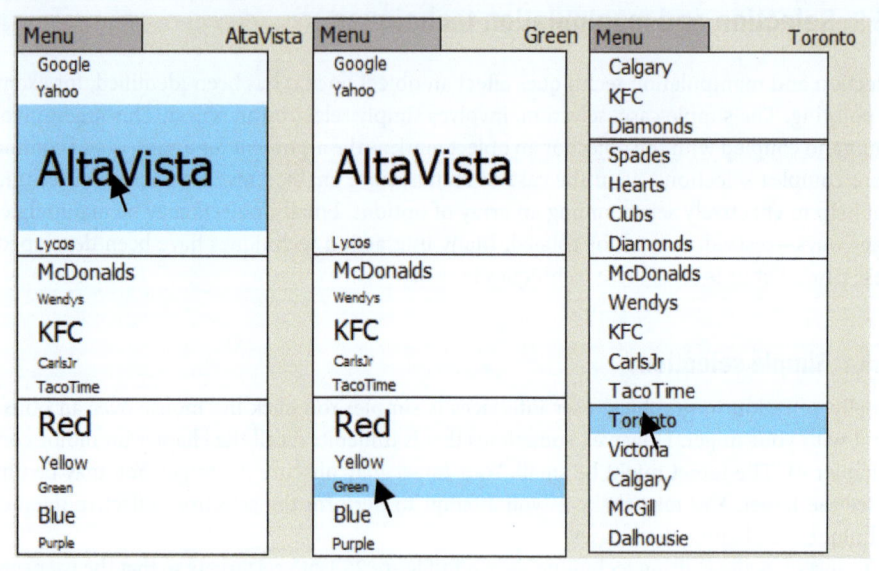

Figure 26.3 Two morphing menus and a split menu.

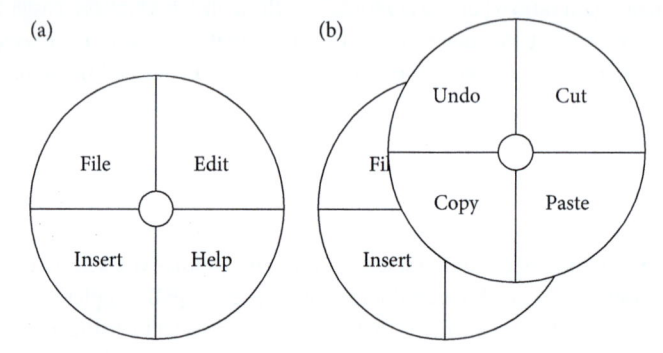

Figure 26.4 (a) An example of a first-level pie menu. (b) An example of a second-level pie menu.

Pie menus

While hierarchical linear pull-down menus dominate in most modern graphical user interfaces, they are not the only means of representing a menu structure. A *pie menu* [121] presents a menu as a circle subdivided into circular sectors associated with commands or further menu structures (Figure 26.4). The user typically triggers the pie menu using a button press, such as pressing down the left mouse button. When the pie menu is invoked, it appears in the center of the pie menu. The user can then perform a selection by sliding the cursor toward a circular sector. Upon making a selection, the circular sector is highlighted to visualize its selected state. If the user lifts the trigger button (e.g., the left mouse button), the command associated with the circular sector is issued by the system. Pie menus are not as popular as hierarchical linear pull-down menus. However, they have been used in, for example, games and computer-aided design applications.

Pie menus can be hierarchical because a circular sector can be associated with either a command or a menu structure. If the selected circular sector is associated with a menu structure, then a selection will invoke a second pie menu revealing this menu structure. In this way, pie menus allow the user to navigate a hierarchical menu structure in a manner similar to hierarchical linear pull-down menus.

An advantage of both hierarchical linear pull-down menus and hierarchical pie menus is that they are easy for a novice user to use, as they allow the user to browse all available commands in the application and select them. Assuming the menu hierarchy is reasonably logical, such navigation, while sometimes time-consuming, should limit frustration.

One disadvantage of such menus is the low performance ceiling. Since navigating pull-down menus and pie menus requires visually guided closed-loop motion, users cannot achieve high performance even when they know precisely how to navigate to a desired item. This is because visually guided closed-loop motion imposes a low performance ceiling, as discussed in Chapter 23. As an alternative, pull-down menus often use keyboard shortcuts. However, such keyboard shortcuts force a conscious shift from one mode of interaction (visually guided menu navigation) to another (direct recall by triggering a key combination).

Marking menus

A *marking menu* [446] is a refinement of a pie menu that supports a *continuous* transition from novice to expert behavior. A marking menu is an interaction technique that couples an incremental angular 2D single-stroke gesture recognizer with a pie menu (Figure 26.5).

The user triggers a marking menu similarly to a pie menu. However, unlike a pie menu, a marking menu does not reveal a pie menu immediately. Instead, there is a brief timeout period before the pie menu appears. After the timeout, the marking menu behaves like a pie menu. However, if the user performs a 2D gesture rapidly before the timeout ends, the pie menu will not be shown.

The central idea of the marking menu is to ensure that the trajectory for invoking the command, either navigating to the menu item or performing a 2D gesture, is identical. This means that during use, the user learns the motor pattern of the command by consolidating the motor memory. Importantly, this process is both continuous and unconscious. This allows marking menus to provide users with a seamless novice-to-expert transition.

Several details in the implementation of marking menus may vary depending on specific use cases or designer insights. For instance, the timeout is a controllable design parameter that can be set in various ways. If the timeout is long, users are further "pushed" to invoke commands via 2D gestures. If the timeout is short, users are encouraged to navigate to the pie menu. It is also possible to eliminate the timeout based on the user's movement dynamics. If the user's movement dynamics suggest open-loop gesturing, the system can automatically turn off the pie menu and transition to the 2D gesturing mode.

Some implementations of marking menus use a sophisticated 2D gesture recognizer that allows the user to pause the gesture to trigger the pie menu (at its current selection level) at any stage. Traditional marking menus implement this using a recognizer that analyzes movement angles. Another design consideration is the number of menu items in the pie menu. Typical choices range between four and eight menu items. The more menu items in a single pie menu, the more accurate the user has to be in selecting the desired menu item.

Marking menus have two fundamental limitations. The first is the limited number of menu items at any level of the menu. The second is the screen real estate required to support large continuous gestural motions to select menu items that are deeply nested. One solution that has been explored is to operate the marking menu using discrete single-stroke straight line segments (*simple marks*) instead of a single continuous selection across the menu hierarchy (*compound marks*). Simple

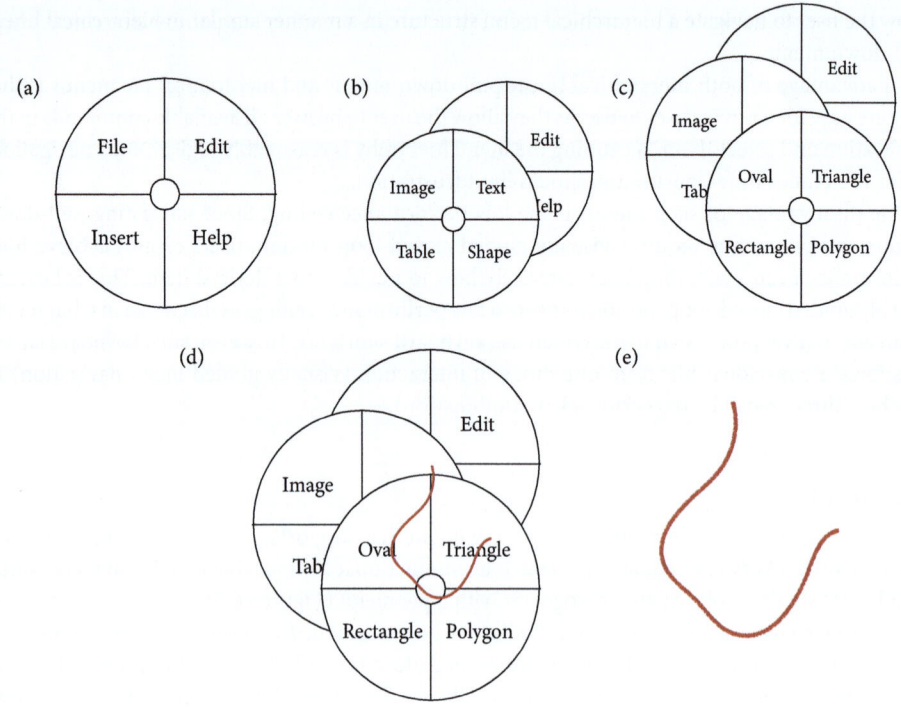

Figure 26.5 An illustration of a marking menu selection. (a) The marking menu is triggered in a similar vein to a pie menu. The user drags the cursor toward the *Insert* menu. (b) This action triggers a second-level marking menu. The user drags the cursor toward the *Shape* menu. (c) This triggers a third-level marking menu. The user triggers the *Triangle* menu item. (d) The entire selection motion for the user triggering (1) the marking menu, (2) the second-level *Insert* menu, (3) the third-level *Shape* menu, and (4) the selection of the *Triangle* menu item is illustrated as a red trace. (e) This trace forms a 2D gesture that can be directly articulated by the user without invoking the marking menu. Critically, the selection motion for *navigating* to the *Insert Triangle* command is identical to the selection motion for *gesturing* the command *Insert Triangle*. Through the repeated selection of the same command, the user gradually learns how to recall the command using a rapid gesture rather than slow visually guided menu navigation.

marks have the advantage that they use less screen real estate, meaning that they may support a higher number of menu items within the marking menu [925].

Paper Example 26.3.1: A model of user performance in menus

From a motor control perspective, menu selection is a *compound task*; that is, it consists of several subtasks. The *search–decide–point* is a mathematical model that illustrates this well [156]. The model is a linear regression model similar to the keystroke-level model (Chapter 41). It predicts the selection time in a menu as the sum of the time spent on three subtasks:

- *Search*, where the time needed to localize an item increases linearly with the number of items in the menu;

- *Decide*, which is the time needed to decide among items given the entropy determined by the frequencies of previous selections given by the Hick–Hyman law;
- *Point*, which is based on Fitts' law and predicts that items closer to the top are faster to select.

The search and decide subtasks are affected by the amount of experience that the user has with the menu, particularly the number of repeated experiences with an item. With practice, performance changes from being dominated by search (linear) to decision (logarithmic). This change is controlled by the expertise factor e.

Let us consider a linear menu. The average selection time for a menu with n items is the sum of the selection times of each item i weighted by their selection probability:

$$T = \sum_{i=1}^{n} p_i T_i, \qquad (26.2)$$

where the selection time T_i of item i is given by

$$T_i = T_{dsi} + T_{pi}. \qquad (26.3)$$

The pointing time T_{pi} is governed by Fitts' law, such that movement is assumed to start from the top of the menu. The search and decision time T_{dsi} is given by the linear interpolation between decision and visual search:

$$T_{dsi} = (1 - e_i)T_{vsi} + e_i T_{hhi}. \qquad (26.4)$$

Here, $e_i[0..1]$ is the expertise factor given as $e_i = 1 - 1/t - i$, where t_i is the number of repetitions with i. As the user becomes more experienced with a menu, there is a shift from the serial visual search T_{vsi} to the decision among competing elements T_{hhi}.

Finally, the visual search time T_{vsi} is assumed to be a linear function of the number of n:

$$T_{vsi} = b_{vs}n + a_{vs}. \qquad (26.5)$$

The Hick–Hyman decision time T_{hhi} is dependent on the *entropy* of the item $H_i = \log_2(1/p_i)$. Here, p_i is the probability of the item in the history of selections, $p_i = t_i/t_t$, where t_t is the number of total selections in the menu. Then, T_{hhi} is given by

$$T_{hhi} = b_{hh}H_i + a_{hh}, \qquad (26.6)$$

where a_{hh} and b_{hh} are empirically determined constraints.

The model has been validated for a few different types of menus, including linear, morphing, split, and rectangular menus. Figure 26.3 shows a *morphing menu* and a *split menu*. In a morphing menu, more frequently used items are enlarged. In a split menu, a special section is created at the top of the menu for recently or frequently used items. A morphing menu is modeled by changing the width of frequent targets. A split menu is modeled with two models, one for the split region and the other for the standard region. Through empirical testing, the authors confirmed the prediction that the frequency-based split menu is the fastest menu.

26.3.3 Manipulation of objects

In addition to selection, users may want to manipulate an object that has been pointed at in numerous other ways. For instance, the use of an expansion or contraction of a finger spread—a *pinch gesture*—is widely used in touch interfaces to manipulate objects, for instance, to scale them. While the pinch gesture has been known since at least the early 1990s [50], its use for scaling and zooming is surprisingly complex. One needs to consider the following questions: (1) How to detect pinching? Wilson [895] contributed an algorithm that could detect pinch gestures from a camera feed robustly. (2) How to deal with differences in hand sizes? (3) Are people equally good at rotation at different angles? Other manipulation techniques concern rotating, moving, and deleting objects.

26.4 Text entry

Entering text and data is one of the most common tasks carried out with computers. Communications and social media are predominantly text-based. Most information systems and office applications rely on the entering of text and data.

Text entry techniques use computational methods to facilitate the task of entering text. The goal is to make text entry more efficient, less effortful, or possible in circumstances in which it is not normally possible. The baseline for text entry is often physical keyboards or numeric keys. Physical keyboards allow people to enter a character at a time and typically have a large activation area. Currently, they serve only as a baseline, as much research has focused on improving text entry.

Most of the research on this topic has focused on *virtual keyboards*, especially on mobile devices, which are small and therefore more susceptible to the inherent inaccuracy and noise in human motor control. A number of reliable findings on smartphone typing motivate the need for research on intelligent support for text entry [637]:

- Young adults type at around 36 words per minute (wpm) and have an average of 2.3% uncorrected errors. This level is far off what is achievable with physical keyboards, which is around 52 wpm in a comparable sample [191].
- Typing with one finger is slower than using two fingers. On average, two-thumb typing is superior to other typing methods that use fingers.
- Errors are costly to correct in comparison to physical keyboards. Users differ in how typo-averse they are. Some users slow down to avoid having to correct errors.
- Typing is not just about motor control; users need to control how they deploy visual attention between the text display (what is typed) and the virtual keyboard.
- Typing while walking or doing other activities reduces typing performance and increases errors.
- Many aging users and users with cognitive, motor, or vision deficiencies have serious difficulties typing with standard keyboards.

Consequently, research on text entry techniques has focused on four main themes:

1. **Correcting and completing phrases:** Given the observed touchpoints and characters typed so far, the goal is to correct mistakes or complete the phrase.

2. **Offering an alternative unit of entry:** From character to syllable, word-level, and phrase-level entry.
3. **Multimodal and cross-modal entry:** Using voice, eye movements, and other such means to enter text.
4. **Editing text:** Facilitating text corrections and modifications.

26.4.1 Correcting and completing phrases

Correcting and completing phrases is an active area of research. Without an intelligent text entry method, when you touch a virtual button on the keyboard of your smartphone, the character that corresponds exactly to the touchpoint on the display is entered. However, because of the small size of the keys, the occlusion problem, and environment-caused noise, touchpoint distributions are very varied. Users often cannot reliably touch a target that is smaller than 10 mm. Unless the user slows down, many errors will occur.

Decoding-based text entry techniques use machine learning to try to infer the intended message in the presence of noise in the touchpoints. Popular applications include *autocorrection* and *word completion*. In autocorrection, a machine-learning-based decoder tries to infer the message the user intended to send based on a list of observed touchpoint coordinates. In word completion, a predictive algorithm tries to predict the next characters based on the ones typed up to that point.

26.4.2 Going beyond entering characters

The *unit* of entry can be relaxed. Instead of looking at previous characters, we can exploit information in the context of words and sentences. For example, in *gestural input*, the finger does not need to be lifted to individually tap the buttons. Instead, you can keep the finger on the display and sweep a shape that passes through the characters that form the word. Paper Example 26.4.1 presents this idea.

Research has also recently looked at *sentence-level entry*, which allows for better exploiting information about preceding words. Two downsides of this approach are the slower computation times and the higher costs of correcting errors. The user may need to re-read the whole phrase. If there is an error, it must be detected and corrected by the user.

Paper Example 26.4.1: Gesture typing with SHARK

Zhai and Kristensson [922] and Kristensson and Zhai [931] introduced gesture typing, a text entry technique that involves drawing shapes on a touchscreen keyboard. SHARK stands for shorthand aided rapid keyboarding. The method drew inspiration from handwriting, which is relatively slow at about 15 wpm. In SHARK, instead of entering a word by tapping one letter at a time, the user can draw a shape that goes through the letters that form the word. The technique is argued to support motor learning: After learning a shorthand shape (e.g., "the"), the user does not have to visually guide the movement of the finger.

continued

Paper Example 26.4.1: Gesture typing with SHARK (*continued*)

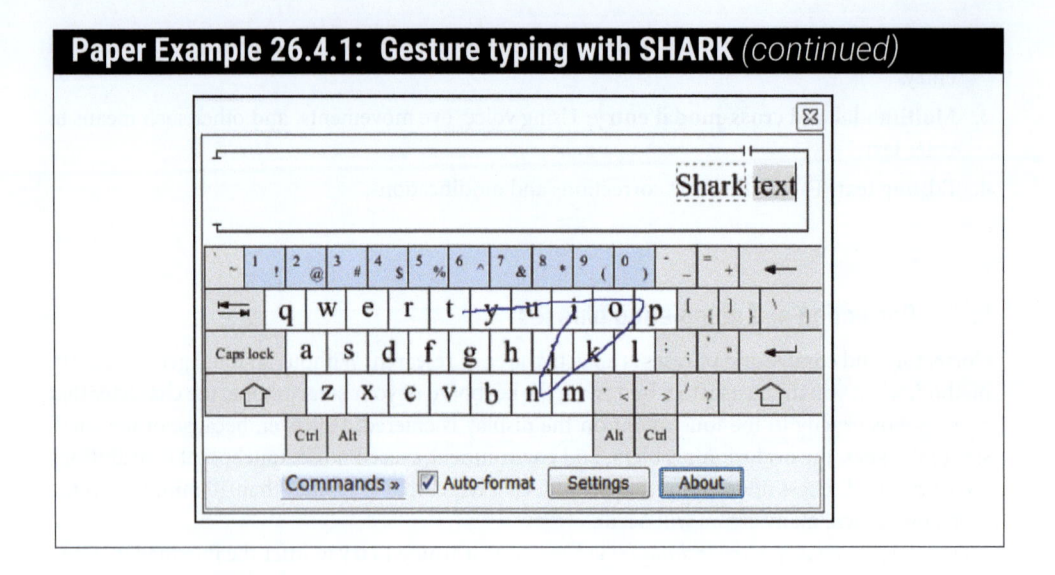

26.4.3 Other modalities for text entry

Another research area concerns alternative modalities for text entry. Alternative modalities like speech can support text entry for specific users and circumstances where it is hard to type via touch. However, speech recognition methods are error-prone, and recognition errors *cascade*. That is, an error in an earlier part of a sentence may deteriorate the inference of a word later in the sentence. The HCI challenge here is to offer efficient ways to edit and correct inferred phrases. For example, *Parakeet* is a demonstrator of continuous speech recognition supported by touch interaction [850]. The user can utter a phrase, which is then displayed on the touch display as separate words. This takes advantage of the *speech recognition hypothesis space*: There is not just one possibility but several possibilities to infer a word, and making this visible to the user can be beneficial in correcting errors. Parakeet also offers touch interactions that complete speech input. Underneath each word, there are alternative words that can be tapped to replace incorrect words in the sentence. Moreover, the user can delete sets of words by drawing through them.

26.4.4 Text editing

An additional area of research is related to *text editing*. A modern virtual keyboard must support ways to find, replace, copy, and paste text. Changes should be undoable. However, regular text editing methods are laborious. For example, to edit a character inside a word, the user may need to carefully place the cursor using an offset cursor, as their finger may occlude part of the word. This is known as the *finger occlusion problem* or the "fat finger problem." To copy a piece of text, two corners of a widget may need to be carefully dragged to the correct places. *Type, then Correct* (Figure 26.6) is an example of three editing techniques that exploit machine learning methods: Drag-n-Drop, Drag-n-Throw, and Magic Key.

To sum up, an outstanding issue with intelligent text entry is the *facilitation–correction cost trade-off*. The more we try to facilitate text entry, the higher the speed but also the higher the cost of correcting possible errors. This issue surfaces in particular when phrases contain rare words,

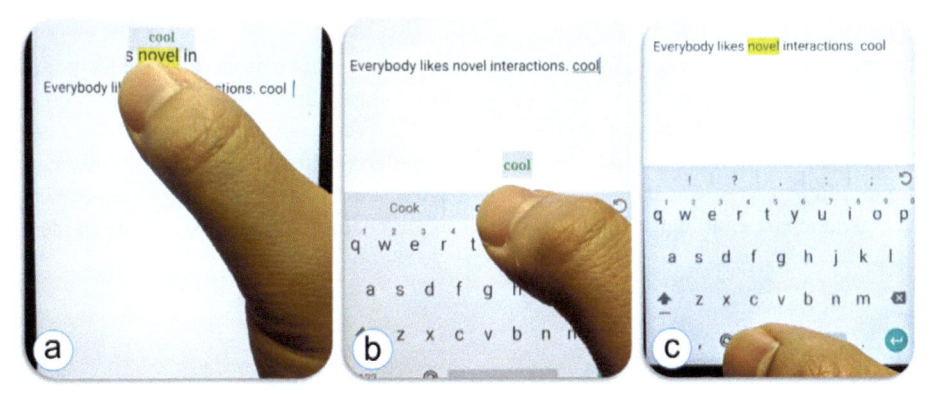

Figure 26.6 *Type, then Correct* involves three correction techniques. (a) Drag-n-Drop allows the user to drag the last word that is typed to replace an erroneous word earlier in the sentence or insert it where it was missing (omission error). (b) Drag-n-Throw allows for "flicking" a word from a word suggestion list toward the area where it should be placed. (c) Magic Key highlights possible error words after a correction that is typed; the user can then drag the magic key toward the erroneous word to correct it [924]. These techniques were shown to facilitate error correction compared to the standard cursor-and-backspace method.

such as proper nouns, or when an expression combines different languages. On the other hand, if a text entry method offers no facilitation at all, users rely on their own cognitive mechanisms to spot errors, and they are relatively good at that (i.e., the correction cost is low). Emerging large-scale studies suggest that users who use autocorrection are faster than those who do not use it, while users who use word prediction are slower but make fewer errors [637]. In this particular study, perhaps due to the speed accuracy trade-off, users using gestural entry were slower than those not using intelligent text entry.

26.5 Camera control

In user interfaces, there is often more to see than can fit on the display. For instance, a map may be so large that all its details cannot fit on a screen; an immersive 3D world may require the user to move their point of view to a different part of the scene. Techniques for camera control help to change what is shown on the display. The term comes from computer graphics, where the scene (or content) is often separated from the point of view from which the user sees it.

Before looking at some examples, it is worth noting that camera control is similar to pointing tasks (Chapter 4). When navigating an information space, positioning the camera in the right place is about pointing it to that space. Thus, the familiar term of throughput can be used for camera control tasks.

26.5.1 Panning and zooming

Two simple examples of camera control are panning and zooming. Panning moves the point of view across the space. In the 1D case, panning may involve moving a scrollbar to show a certain part of the document; in the 2D case, it may involve moving the mouse to the edge of the screen to automatically pan a map.

Zooming changes the magnification of the information shown from the current point of view. Zooming is sometimes possible with scrollbars; this changes the size of the knob (the part of the scrollbar that can be grabbed). In the 2D case, zooming is the familiar change of magnification. In *semantic zooming*, this change affects different parts of the information space in different ways. For instance, on a low-magnification map, a city might be represented with a generic circle; at high magnification, this might change to a detailed outline of the city contour.

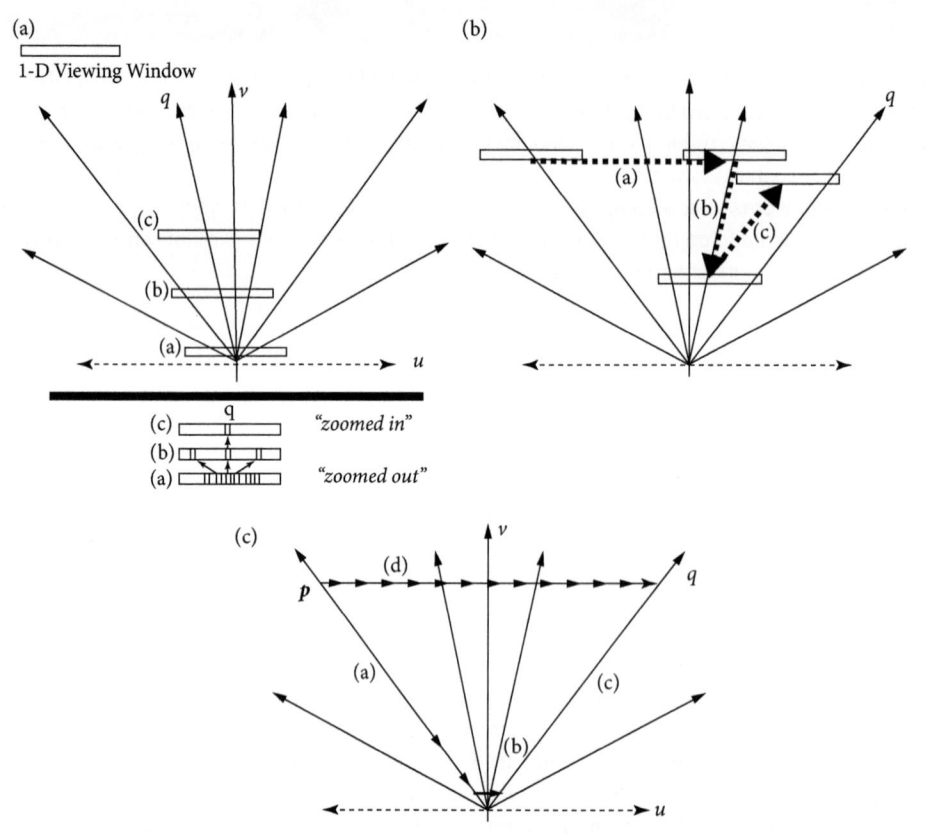

Figure 26.7 Scale-space diagrams from Furnas and Bederson [264] showing some trade-offs in zooming and panning interfaces. To the left is shown an information space with dimensions u and v (depth); the objects in the space are shown as six vectors (q). At any time, there is a viewing window into the information space, shown as a rectangle (a, b, c); at the bottom of the figure is shown which objects are visible at which magnification. In the middle are shown pure panning (a), pure zooming (b), and integral zooming and panning (c). To the right is shown how panning can be cumbersome. Navigating from p to q can be done via pure panning along the path d. It can also be done via zooming out (along a), panning (b), and zooming in (c).

INTERACTION TECHNIQUES | 463

User interfaces often offer both panning and zooming. When they can be done at the same time, we say that they are *integral*. On a map, we might be able to zoom by holding a mouse button and move the mouse as we do so. Intuitively, integral interaction techniques are more effective when the operation to be done requires simultaneous panning and zooming [380].

One elegant implementation of an integral scrollbar for zooming and panning is called Orto-Zoom. One issue in most scrollbar implementations is that if the space to scroll is large, the movement in the document coupled to the scrollbar will be coarse. Appert and Fekete [27] developed OrtoZoom, an interaction technique that combines scrolling a 1D data structure (e.g., a document) with the possibility to zoom by moving the mouse in the dimension orthogonal to the scrollbar. Assume that a document is d pixels long and the scrollbar moves up and down. If the user moves the mouse while it is on the scrollbar, each unit scrolled might correspond to $d/10$, that is, the whole scrollbar may be scrolled in 10 steps. However, if the user first moves the mouse to the left, each unit scrolled becomes smaller, potentially going all the way down to 1. This makes the scrolling more precise. A related idea is speed-dependent automatic zooming (SDAZ) [371], where the viewport is zoomed in or out when scrolling. The level of zoom depends on the information density of the document. The goal is to ensure that the user is provided with sufficient time to visually inspect the contents of the viewport.

Both OrtoZoom and SDAZ exhibit a classic trade-off in panning and zooming: If one pans at the wrong level of magnification, one either risks overshooting the target (because the pan steps are large) or having to spend a long time panning. However, changing magnification levels is tricky. Figure 26.7 shows the intuition using scale-space diagrams [264]. Much work on zooming and panning seeks to solve these problems.

A final issue in panning and zooming is ensuring that people can see the points of interest and where to go. This, too, is related to the magnification level. If you are zoomed in too much, you may see the relevant details but not all the information; if you are zoomed out, you may obtain an overview of the space but not see the details. Jul and Furnas [398] memorably talked about *desert fog*, the situation where you need to reach a target but see no navigational cues indicating where it is. If you zoom in too much, this may be the situation. Paper Example 26.5.1 shows one interaction technique that helps remedy this situation.

Paper Example 26.5.1: Visualizing off-screen targets

One problem with a small viewport is that it may not be possible to display all relevant information. For example, the figure in this paper example box to the left shows five target locations on a map. When the user zooms in, shown in the figure to the right, the target locations are no longer visible as the viewport is too small to show them.

One solution to this problem is a halo visualization [51]. The idea is to center each target location within a circle and let the circumference of the circle indicate the distance. In addition, arcs belonging to more distant target locations are shown to be more translucent, providing a secondary channel of information about the distance of an off-screen target. The halo visualization concept is illustrated in the following figure to the right.

Unlike using arrows to indicate off-screen targets, halo visualization does not require additional annotations to indicate the distance to off-screen targets.

continued

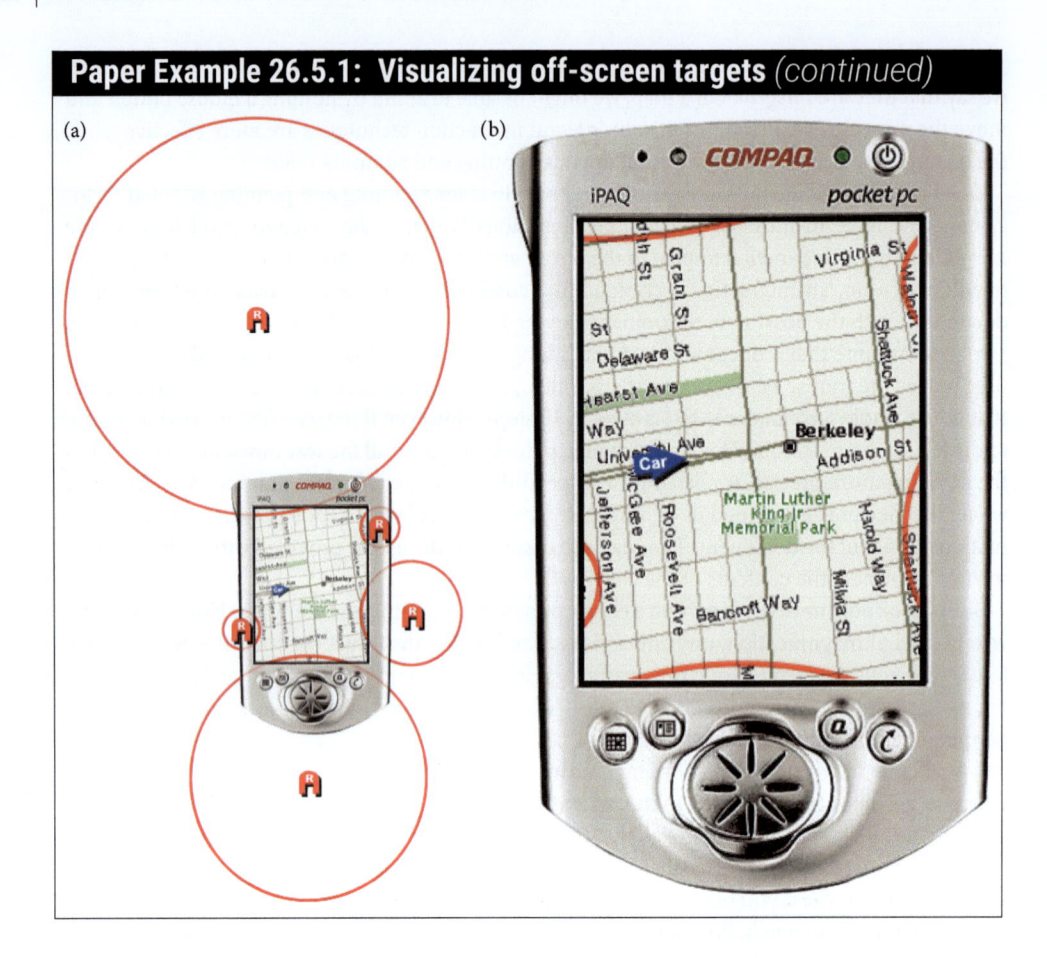

Paper Example 26.5.1: Visualizing off-screen targets (continued)

26.5.2 3D navigation

A particular challenge for camera control is the navigation of 3D space. There are two reasons behind this challenge. The first is that 3D navigation has three degrees of freedom, commonly referred to as pitch, yaw, and roll. These degrees of freedom are difficult to control for users, particularly if the input device that controls the navigation is not 3D, such as a mouse. The second reason is that as users navigate a 3D space, they build an understanding of the objects in the space. The issue is that interaction techniques affect how users build this understanding in different ways.

Another challenge in 3D navigation is that it may be quite cumbersome when large distances are to be covered. This is similar to the challenge faced by panning.

26.6 Control and learnability

Surprisingly, advanced interaction techniques are not common in the everyday use of computers. We mainly use them in a handful of tasks, such as when scrolling, selecting targets, or entering text. It has turned out to be challenging to create new interaction techniques that users would adopt. To conclude the chapter, we discuss two key challenges in their design: control and learnability.

26.6.1 Control

Control theory (Chapter 17) can illuminate the dynamic relationships between input actions and the events on display, as well as the consequent challenges for the user. A minimal analysis starts with the following elements:

- **Goal:** The user has a goal in mind, a state that the computer should be driven to, such as selecting a particular target on display.
- **Feedforward:** The user sends a control signal via the input sensor to change the state.
- **Transfer function:** A program maps changes in the feedforward signal to changes on the display.
- **Feedback:** The state change is now visible on display.
- **Comparator:** The feedback is compared against the goal state to determine the new feedforward signal.

In the control model shown in Figure 26.8a, the user chooses a feedforward signal as a linear function of how far the end-effector is from the target. In other words, the user tries to directly close the gap between where the cursor is and where it should be. Assuming that the system is noisy, this will have to be done a few times to hit the target region.

However, this analysis is overly simplistic. A user who decides to simply minimize the distance between the perceived and desired states would fail. This policy does not account for the non-linearity and dynamics that are inherent in motor control with an interactive system. Consider pointing with a mouse: The muscle control signal (feedforward) that you pick is not linearly determined by the distance of the cursor from the target (feedback). When you move your hand, the involved biomechanical events are nonlinear. Your eyes guide the hand, and several muscle groups are activated in a coordinated way.

To understand interaction techniques better, we need to understand them from the human motor control perspective. The problem it needs to solve is as follows. An interaction technique is a computer program that can do *anything* to the input signal. For the motor system, it is an opaque box. How can the motor system know *which* action to take? The *theory of internal models* in motor control can explain this [406]. Controlling an interaction technique requires *prediction*. That is, to pick a feedforward signal, the brain needs to predict what *might* happen. Its learning can be thought of as a form of *function learning*.

By interacting with the technique, the motor control system learns—implicitly and without us being consciously aware of it—a function that maps feedforward signals to the perceived state of the controlled system. The learned model then allows for predicting the consequences of actions. Alas, the predictions are never perfect. While the *prediction error* tends to decrease with practice, it is never zero; at some point, a sufficient level is reached. The more accurate the prediction, the more effective its feedforward, and the fewer iterations are needed to achieve the goal state. This model explains that we need lots of repetition to handle a new interaction technique.

26.6.2 Learning

A second hurdle concerning interaction techniques is human learning. In a nutshell, users are already familiar with some techniques and must now invest time to learn another one. Figure 26.9 illustrates this. It shows two learning curves: initial and after change. In both cases, performance develops according to the power law of learning.

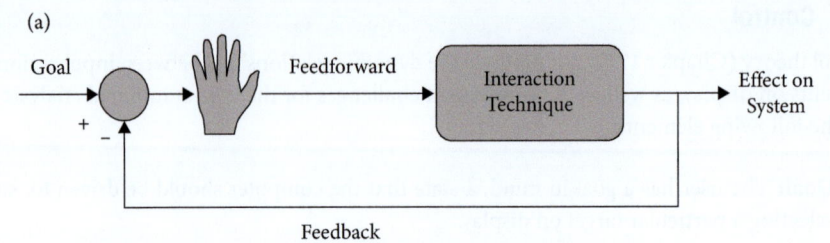

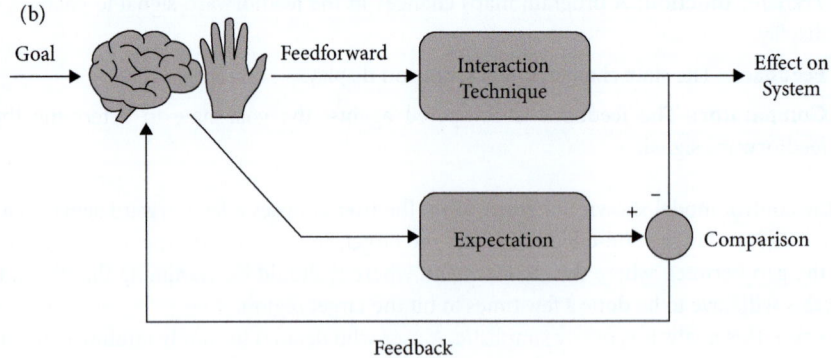

Figure 26.8 The top pane shows a simple (but wrong!) control model for interaction techniques that shows the basic components involved from a control-theoretical perspective. The bottom pane shows that to control an interaction technique, users must be able to predict the perceived consequences of their actions.

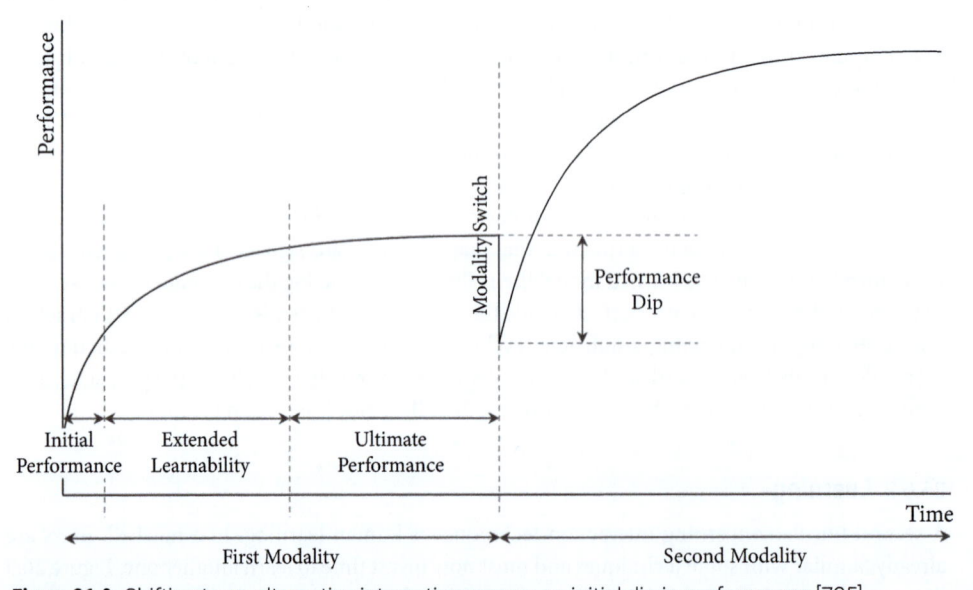

Figure 26.9 Shifting to an alternative interaction causes an initial dip in performance [735].

When a new technique is introduced, an immediate cost ensues. This is called a "performance dip." The concept is important: Changing from one technique to another has a learning cost that users may be unwilling to pay despite the long-term benefits of using the new technique. From the user's perspective, this is rational: Long-term benefits occur much later and are not guaranteed. Few users can estimate future gains, yet everybody can experience a performance dip. "Starting from scratch" hampers current performance, and there is no guarantee that there will be any benefit in the long term.

The performance dip has a non-obvious implication for design. It implies that users' initial perceptions of their performance with an interaction technique tend to be negative. Hence, one should focus not only on ultimate performance but also on incentivizing users to start and persist in learning the new technique. This could be achieved, for example, by clearly communicating what is achievable, setting performance goals, and providing feedback about their progress. Another aim of design is to minimize the immediate costs of the dip. By doing that, the long-term benefits of the technique also become more pronounced.

Summary

- An interaction technique is a computer program that couples input and output processing with the purpose of improving or enabling elementary interactive tasks.
- Many interaction techniques are about striking a desirable trade-off between learnability and performance. Consider, for example, hotkeys versus menus.
- Changing from one technique to another has a learning cost that users may be unwilling to pay despite the potential long-term benefits of the change.
- Users do not need to learn how the algorithm of the interaction technique works. Instead, they learn through experience to predict the consequences of their actions. While this learning process takes time, it can be facilitated by an appropriate feedback design.
- Design should focus not only on ultimate performance but also on incentivizing users to start and persist in learning the new technique.
- Much researched interaction techniques include the pie menu, the marking menu, speed-dependent semantic zooming, the gain function, and hypertext.
- Interaction techniques must be evaluated with realistic tasks and relevant user groups to estimate their achievable performance.

Exercises

1. Understanding an interaction technique. Scrollbars are easy to use, yet they are a technically complex user interface element. Try to identify five different types of scrollbars. Discuss them as interaction techniques: (1) How do they couple input and output? (2) What are their trade-offs in usability, discoverability, and other aspects of their value to users?
2. Trade-offs. Take two interaction techniques designed for the same purpose. Compare their pros and cons in terms of the design objectives given in Table 26.1.
3. 2D versus 3D interaction. Which ideas that you know from 2D interaction could be used for 3D interaction? For example, consider the task of navigating on a map from point A to point B.

4. Control order. Control order refers to the translation of input motion into camera or cursor motion. Zeroth-order control refers to position control, first-order control to velocity control, second-order control to acceleration control, and third-order control to the control of rate of acceleration (jerk). Your task is to implement and compare these for a panner. Which one is the best? How do you set the parameters of each control order? The code for the panner is given on the book's homepage.

5. Crossing. Why is crossing-based selection beneficial? Discuss from the motor control point of view.

6. Buttons. Clicking may be implemented in different ways. How is it done on a device you use? How may this be useful or not useful for particular users?

7. Marking menus versus pie menus. This exercise requires familiarity with motor control concepts (Chapter 4). A drawing application runs on a tablet operated with a pen. The design team wants to implement a graphical menu structure that allows users to access all commands in the software. (a) Explain the difference between closed-loop and open-loop control, including the advantages and disadvantages of each form of interaction. (b) Describe the differences between a pie menu and a marking menu. (c) Explain when interaction with a marking menu is closed-loop and when it is open-loop. (d) The design team is deciding between a hierarchical linear pull-down menu and a marking menu. Describe the primary advantages and disadvantages of the two menu options. (e) There are two ways to implement the hierarchical linear pull-down menu. In one implementation, as soon as the pen tip leaves a submenu, the submenu disappears. In the other implementation, the submenu only disappears if the pen tip enters the previous menu. Explain whether these implementations rely on crossing or steering actions.

27
Commands and navigation

The crafting of text requires the writer to find the appropriate words and bring them into an organization that conveys the intended story. Sometimes, writers make further efforts to organize their text in a specific way, for example, to help readers navigate the text and find answers to specific questions or to present a specific overview of the text. User interfaces involve similar considerations. We need to name objects and actions in the user interface: A wrong word can cause a user to pick the wrong option, and a poor organization of information can lead users to navigate to the wrong place. More than 50 years ago, the pioneering researcher in human factors, Chapanis [144], made this connection:

> The aim of this paper is to call to attention a very large and important area of human factors engineering that is almost entirely neglected. This area consists of the language and the words that are attached to the tools, machines, systems, and operations with which human factors engineers are concerned.

Thus, the words we use in menus, virtual reality, and smartphones matter. How we structure words into commands and into information structures that users engage with also matters. First, numerous papers have shown the advantage of broad over deep web page hierarchies. Jacko and Salvendy [379], for instance, showed that as the structure of a deep menu (that is, a menu with few items at each level but with many levels) became deeper, users found the menu more difficult to navigate. Second, it has been shown that providing a preview of text on a web page—often called a snippet—improves web search. Teevan et al. [816] showed that visual snippets worked better, especially for tasks where images were prominent carriers of meaning. Third, Payne and Green [645] showed that consistency in the structure of command-line arguments helps users learn how to use the commands.

This chapter introduces two styles of user interface. Both styles depart from the observation that when a user tries to find information in a user interface, they typically have an intended action or object in mind. In Norman's seven-stage model, this is called their goal (Chapter 18). In work on information search, it is called an information need, that is, an unexpressed but real need for information that will help solve some problem [815]. A user may want to locate the option to bold a word or find out how to make pasta. In such cases, what the user has in mind may only partially match what they see in an information system.

In some user interfaces, users issue *commands* to the computer system. There are many ways to issue such commands, such as using a command-line interface or navigating to a desired command using a menu structure. Search, such as on the web, may also be understood as a form of command-driven user interface. This chapter introduces the cognitive dimensions of the notation framework as a design vocabulary to help designers reason about the notation of interactive systems, including user interfaces that employ commands. The central concern about commands is the *appropriate naming of actions and objects*.

The second style of user interface is *navigation*. In navigation, users explore the user interfaces to discover commands and information. As such, navigation support is often critical to a well-functioning user interface system. This chapter will discuss common navigational techniques to

Introduction to Human-Computer Interaction. Kasper Hornbæk, Per Ola Kristensson, and Antti Oulasvirta,
Oxford University Press. © Kasper Hornbæk, Per Ola Kristensson, and Antti Oulasvirta (2025).
DOI: 10.1093/oso/9780192864543.003.0027

help users discover and issue commands and navigate hypertext. The central concern for navigation is the *appropriate organization of information*. Appropriate here means that it is recognizable by people and efficient to explore.

27.1 Naming objects and actions

Why is naming things in user interfaces challenging? Paper Example 27.1.1 explains the vocabulary problem, one difficulty in naming objects and actions in user interfaces together with the issues of polysemy (the same word means different things), the role of context in interpreting words, and many other issues. Given all these issues, it is difficult to find clear and precise descriptors for user interfaces.

> **Paper Example 27.1.1: The variability in naming objects and actions as a central user interface challenge**
>
> Imagine that you have to name a program or application that tells you about interesting things to do. What would you choose if you could only use up to 10 characters? If you were to pick alternative words for "love" or "motorcycle," what would they be? Try to write down your answers before continuing.
>
> Furnas et al. [265] considered these questions to be important to human–computer interaction (HCI). They argued that the way we name objects and actions of interest in user interfaces is important in many user interfaces. When they investigated how people named objects and actions (as you just did), they discovered something surprising. If you ask two people to spontaneously name commands, they will agree with less than 0.2 probability. Thus, only every fifth command may overlap with that of another person. They called this "the vocabulary problem." The issue is that finding a command that will work well for many users is very difficult.
>
> Furnas et al. [265] went on to consider a solution that allowed users to create unlimited aliases for particular commands. In many ways, this is similar to the way search works on many current devices. The key insight is that picking appropriate command names is extremely difficult.

Some general ideas for thinking about naming objects and actions are as follows. First, we may think about naming in terms of the information scent (Chapter 21). Recall that the information scent concerns how well a word or phrase creates associations (i.e., a scent) of what they subsume (e.g., what command they execute or what menu items they may be expanded into).

Another relevant concept for naming objects and actions is the articulatory distance. This concept quantifies the distance between the physical form of the name or command and the command that the user wants to express. In practice, we want the intended command to be as similar as possible to the user's intention.

Another relevant insight is that specific names are preferable over general names. Black and Moran [74] showed that infrequent, discriminative command names are more likely to be recalled than command names consisting of frequently used words. Thus, we should use "insert" rather than "add" as a command for placing text into a document. Recall, of course, is crucial for users who use an interface intermittently.

Furthermore, it is better to use meaningful names for objects and actions rather than purely designating a command by convention or through some symbol. Black and Moran [74] showed that non-words had higher error rates. Similarly, comparisons of the performance of keywords (e.g., "CHANGE 'KO' TO 'OK'") to symbols (e.g., "RS: |KO|, |OK|") showed that keywords are usually preferred [467].

27.1.1 Techniques for finding names

Given all this complexity, how do we find appropriate names for labels in a user interface, commands in a spoken language system, and menu items?

One approach is to pick the names that users employ in real life for objects and actions. Such names may be found during user research (Part III). This is a straightforward idea, captured in heuristics such as "speak the users' language" [593].

Another approach that is often used in HCI is *elicitation study* [905], which is also useful for figuring out command names. The basic idea in elicitation studies is to elicit from users how they would execute a particular command and study the agreement across users' commands to identify a set of commands that users will produce spontaneously with the highest likelihood. For instance, we may show users a command we would like them to execute (e.g., "make a copy of this file") and ask how they would name that action (e.g., "duplication"). We then use the most common name for that command. Elicitation studies try to find a solution to the vocabulary problem.

Paper Example 27.1.2: Programming as a naming problem

As we shall see, the concerns of naming commands have rather direct implications for interfaces that are driven by commands. However, similar concerns apply to many other areas, including programming languages. Myers and Stylos [572] looked specifically at application programming interfaces (APIs) and considered them a form of user interface.

The key idea is that APIs serve as an intermediary between the user (in this case, the programmer) and an interactive system (in this case, whatever the API provides access to). The design of the API, therefore, can be considered from the viewpoint of the programmer as an end-user.

As one example, the naming of programming constructs should make it easy to relate them to the programmer's world. Myers and Stylos [572] gave an interesting example of this:

For example, the most generic and well-known name should be used for the class programmers are supposed to actually use, but this is violated by Java in many places. There is a class in Java called File, but it is a high-level abstract class to represent file system paths, and API users must use a completely different class (such as FileOutputStream) for reading and writing.

As another example, Myers and Stylos [572] discussed consistency for the following two methods (knowledge of this particular programming language is not necessary to understand the example):

```
void writeStartElement(String namespaceURI, String localName)
void writeStartElement(String prefix, String localName, String namespaceURI)
```

continued

> **Paper Example 27.1.2: Programming as a naming problem**
> *(continued)*
>
> These two methods use a different ordering of elements, violating the principle of consistency and making the transfer of learning from one method to the other difficult. In short, the methods violate what we know about learning and consistency in user interfaces. In this case, it was also hard to recognize when an error was made because both arguments are of the type String.

27.2 Command-line interfaces

A command-line interface is a text-based user interface that enables the user to interact with the computer system by typing commands. The history of the command-line interface begins with the invention of the telegraph. Telegraph operators were tasked with transcribing Morse code into text.

A command-line interface can be decomposed into a prompt, a command, and n parameters:

```
prompt command parameter¹ parameter² ... parameterⁿ
```

Prompt: The *prompt* is a system-generated indication that the system is awaiting a command from the user. Prompts can be minimal, providing only some indication (such as a beep) that the system is awaiting a response, or they can be elaborate and provide additional information to the user, such as some aspect of the system's state.

Command: The *command* is the instruction provided by the user to the system.

Parameter list: The *parameter list*, sometimes called the *argument list*, is a set of additional command-specific instructions provided by the user to tailor the execution of the command.

A simple example of a command line is the interpreter in early adventure games, such as the early graphical adventure game *King's Quest 1* designed in 1984 by Roberta Williams. In this game, the player controls a character representing a prince who can walk around in a graphical scene. The player can interact with the environment, objects in the environment, and non-playable characters in the environment using a command-line interface. For example, if the player has moved the prince near a graphical depiction of a candle, the player can pick it up using the following command:

```
>take candle
```

Here, `>` is the prompt, `take` is the command, and `candle` is the parameter. If the candle cannot be picked up, the system responds with a message. If the prince was not close to a candle or could not pick it up for some reason, the system would respond with different messages.

This user interface is an example of a basic command-line interface. The prompt provides a minimal indication that the user is expected to type commands, and it does not change depending on the context, nor does it indicate any system state. The list of commands—the *vocabulary*—is limited to a small fixed set of commands, such as `take`, `look`, and `talk`. These commands may be executed without a parameter. For example, the user may type `look` without any parameter to obtain an overall description of the graphical scene depicted on the screen. Alternatively, the user may provide an argument such as an object, for example, `look candle`, which provides a description of a candle if such an object is present in the graphical scene.

Command-line interfaces process commands using an *interpreter*, a software component that receives text input from the user and outputs the command and the parameters typed by the user. This interpretation is frequently referred to as *parsing*; therefore, the interpreter is sometimes referred to as a *parser*. If the interpreter cannot make sense of the user's input, the system outputs an error message. Historically, these error messages have often been unclear, such as the ubiquitous "syntax error" message, which merely indicates to the user that the system failed to parse the response text. However, error messages can also be detailed and helpful, such as "Command 'save' expects a filename" (if the user forgot to indicate a filename) or "There is no command 'sve'" (if the user misspelled the "save" command).

In the case of *King's Quest 1*, the interpreter knows a specific set of commands (which are all verbs) as well as which commands accept which arguments and when. If the user types a command that is not present in the interpreter's command list, a generic response such as "I do not understand that" or "I cannot do that" is generated by the system. In this case, exploration and experimentation with commands and their parameters are part of the game design.

Nevertheless, even such a simple interpreter has a set of design issues that need to be resolved:

Availability: How does the user know which commands are available?

Naming: How does the user know the names of the commands the system understands? For example, the interpreter may understand take but not pick up.

Learning: How does the user learn the availability of the commands and their parameters?

Recall: How does the system support the user in recalling commands and their parameters?

Syntax: How does a user know which commands expect parameters and the form of these parameters?

Transparency: How does the system convey to the user the way in which it interprets commands, making it possible for the user to both understand what is achievable within the command-line interface and diagnose why a command input does not result in the intended response?

As the command-line interface becomes more complex, these design issues become more important. A common example of a command-line interface is a *command-line shell*: a piece of software that allows users to interact with the operating system and applications by typing commands. Such shells have not only many commands but also elaborate syntax, which may be difficult for users to comprehend and even more difficult to understand when the shell fails to interpret the user's commands.

Such shells may also have several categories of commands, such as:

Built-in shell commands: A shell typically provides a set of commands that are integral to the shell itself. An example of such a command in the *Bash* shell of Linux is echo, which outputs a provided parameter to the shell. For example, "echo hello" results in the shell outputting "hello" as text.

Operating system tools: In addition to built-in shell commands, most operating systems provide a range of services for connecting and disconnecting devices, managing the file system, and other services. Typically, an operating system provides command-line applications that allow the user to interact with such services. These system-specific tools are always present in a working installation. An example of such an application in Linux is cp, which allows the user to copy a file. For example, "cp file1 file2" creates a copy of file1 with the name file2.

External applications: In addition to built-in commands and operating system tools, users may also have access to additional functionality by interacting with external applications using the command line. An example in Linux is `cpp`, a compiler that can be instructed to compile code by providing it with command-line parameters.

When a command-line interface increases in complexity, the design issues—availability, naming, learning, recall, and syntax—in turn increase in significance. For example, built-in commands should use a systematic naming scheme and syntax, though this is by no means guaranteed. Ensuring consistency and standardization across commands becomes more difficult when a range of additional operating system tools are provided, some of which may be legacy tools with previously established conventions or third-party tools. External applications further exacerbate the situation. The naming conventions and syntax of external applications cannot be directly controlled by the command-line interface, and they often vary despite the availability of user interface design guidelines.

27.3 Organizing information

How to organize information has been a topic of interest for more than 100 years, starting with considerations on how to structure increasing amounts of information in books and other publications. With the invention of the Internet, these considerations have spread to the digital world, where they are often called information design or information architecture [711]. We call this concern *organizing information* and offer a high-level view of some key considerations and tools.

In general, the challenge of organizing information assumes that we have items of information (e.g., commands, menu items) that we want to organize in some way (e.g., in a list or hierarchy).

27.3.1 Ordering information

The simple case is where we have a set of items that we need to order. If you look at the items in the first menu you can find on your computer, they will have an order. How do we decide that order so that it optimizes the user interface?

The most general guideline is to *group* items that belong together. One example is grouping functionally related items (e.g., copy, cut, paste). In most empirical comparisons of ordering, grouping is the most effective ordering principle.

Another approach is to consider the *importance* of the items. One might infer the importance of options from the *frequency* with which users select them. However tempting it seems to change the order of items, for instance, based on the selection frequency, Somberg [783] showed that this strategy performed poorly. The study compared users' performance in finding an item in one of four menu orderings: alphabetic, frequency of selection, random, and positionally constant. Surprisingly, the positionally constant placement worked the best, especially as the users further practiced finding the item.

While *alphabetical* ordering is easy, it is only suitable for a few tasks. For most other tasks, there is either some way of ordering items that better matches users' typical tasks or the information can be placed into hierarchies—if you have tried searching for a country in an alphabetical list of countries, you know that hierarchies can be useful.

27.3.2 Placing information in hierarchies

Oftentimes, we have so many items to organize that placing them into a hierarchy is unavoidable. As with organization within a list, items that are semantically or functionally associated should be placed in the same panel or submenu. Place the most informative items in a group at the top of the panel; apply this principle to every level of the hierarchy.

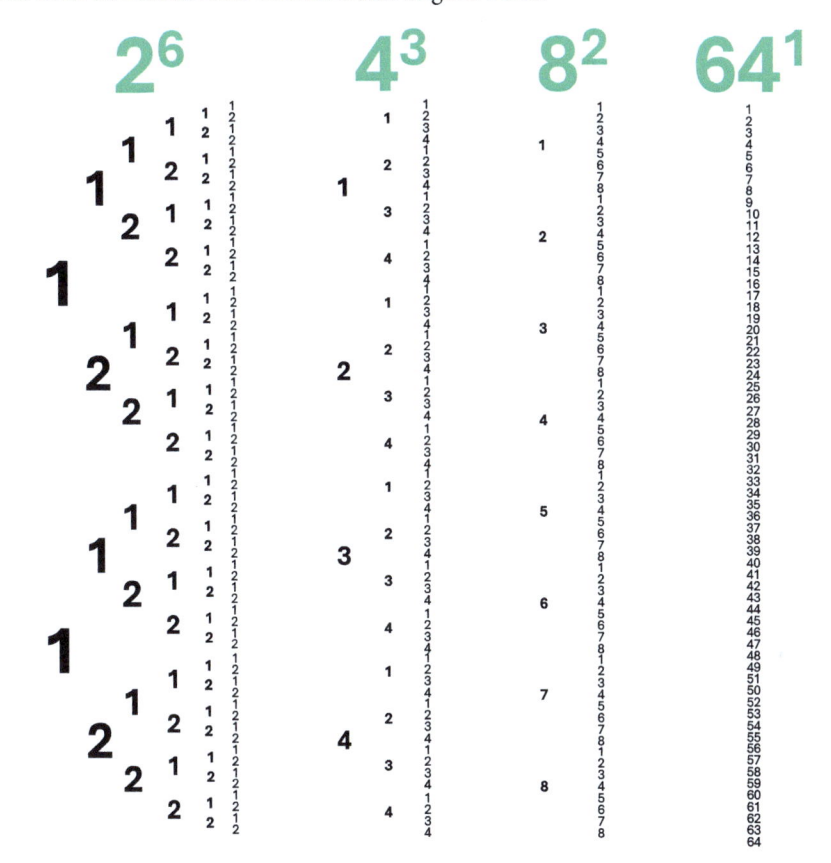

> ### Paper Example 27.3.1 Breadth–depth trade-offs in menus
>
> Miller [546] presented one of the first studies of the trade-offs between organizing hierarchies to be deep (few choices per level) or broad (many choices per level). Miller had 24 participants try one of four menus, each containing 64 items. The menu hierarchies varied between two choices at six levels, four choices at three levels, eight choices at two levels, and 64 choices at one level. The menu items were common English words.
>
> $2^6 \qquad 4^3 \qquad 8^2 \qquad 64^1$
>
> Miller [546] had the participants use one of the four menu organizations and select the 64 goals one at a time for a total of four times (so-called blocks). The purpose of these blocks was to see if the participants improved their ability to find items quickly and without errors as they gained experience with the hierarchy.
>
> The results of the study indicated a U-shaped relationship between increasing the depth of the organization and both task completion times and errors. The hierarchies with four or eight choices were optimal, leading to the conclusion that a trade-off between choices and
>
> *continued*

> **Paper Example 27.3.1 Breadth–depth trade-offs in menus** *(continued)*
>
> organization exists. In particular, showing only the leaves of the hierarchy (the 64 choices) is ineffective, as is showing a series of many choices.

Another important idea is that hierarchies should include labels or hints that allow users to quickly and without error decide whether the target they are looking for belongs to the tab or not. In foraging terms, design the information scent of the entry points of a panel. For example, when looking for "Save," if the menu label says "Window," the scent is low and the user can quickly dismiss the whole panel. If it says "General," the scent is higher and the user might look into the panel in vain.

One important decision in placing information into hierarchies, be it a menu or a web site structure, is whether the hierarchy is broad or deep. As suggested by Paper Example 27.3.1, and many other studies, broad menus are preferable in most situations. Why is that so? A broad menu structure makes it easier to compare alternatives visually, avoiding having to go down a path in the hierarchy only to discover that an alternative would have been better. A broad menu also offers fewer choice points for the user. Finally, the labels for the parts of the hierarchy are perhaps easier to make high-scent because they are fewer and therefore somewhat broader.

27.3.3 Hypertext

Text that allows the user to retrieve further information when interacted with is known as *hypertext* [585]. Hypertexts are connected using *hyperlinks*, often simply called links, which are particular elements that trigger further information retrieval. Hyperlinks consisting of text are usually denoted in some unique way to provide sufficient perceived affordance so that the user can realize a hyperlink is present.

Hypertext is ubiquitous on the World Wide Web (WWW) but is not limited to it. The traditional hyperlink on the WWW is blue and underlined to indicate its unique function in comparison to regular text, which may be selected or even edited but will not trigger the retrieval of further information if interacted with. Hyperlinks may consist of text, images, or videos. The broader term *hypermedia* is sometimes used to denote the general usage of hyperlinks.

Since hypertext documents can link to other hypertext documents, which can in turn link back to the original documents, the navigational structure of hypertext document collections can be complex. Mathematically, hypertext document collections form directed graphs. While a simple hypertext document collection may have a relatively straightforward tree structure, in practice, many hypertext documents quickly form complicated directed graphs that may be difficult for users to navigate without aid.

Originally a highly active area of research, hyperlink document navigation is now largely standardized through a set of well-known navigational structures, such as the use of a navigation bar with *forward* and *backward* buttons and an address bar. A similar structure is also used in many file browsers.

Bernstein [65] provided an overview of common navigation techniques for hypertext. The first technique is the use of presentation, layout, and links to convey information, orientation cues, and choices. The second technique is the use of maps and indexes to provide an overview of a hypertext document collection. The third technique is the use of bookmarks to allow the user to quickly retrieve a particular hypertext document. This technique allows the user to mark the parts of a hypertext document collection that are of interest. The fourth technique is the use of thumb tabs, which allow the content creator to mark parts of the hypertext document collection that may be of interest to users in general. This can be achieved, for example, by including relevant hyperlinks at the side, top, or bottom of the hypertext document. The fifth technique is the use of margin notes to allow the user to annotate hypertext documents. The sixth technique is the use of breadcrumbs, a navigational aid that reminds the user of previous locations the user has visited in the hypertext document collection. An initial "crumb" will often indicate an overall summary page or entry page, while subsequent crumbs reflect the user's navigation deeper into the structure, for example, "Animals," "Mammals," and "Cats."

27.3.4 Techniques for organizing information

One of the main techniques for discovering organizations of information that match those used by users is called *card sorting*. The basic idea in card sorting is to provide users with descriptions of the information to be organized, with each piece of information presented separately (e.g., on a card). Users are then asked to sort those into groups of similar items and possibly name each group. Across users, these groups can give a sense of how consistently users see similarities across pieces of information and what the groups of information should be called. If users are consistent, the groups may be used to organize information in a user interface.

Typically, card sorting goes as follows [633, 913]:

1. Put pieces of information on cards; the cards may be digital or physical.
2. Find users who can group the cards; any number will do, although a group of 20–30 users is generally recommended [832]. It is important that the users understand the cards.
3. Ask the users to group the cards, for example, "Please group these items as you would expect to find them on our corporate intranet" or "Group things together that seem to be similar in some way."
4. Ask the users to name the groups; those names may be used in the user interface and may explain why certain cards are grouped together.

After this, various statistical methods are available for determining the best groupings. If we have x cards with information pieces and have asked y users to group them, we obtain a matrix of $x \times x$ where each entry is the number of times between 0 and y that two items were grouped. This matrix can be used for cluster analysis, for instance, to derive a hierarchy of pieces of information or to find a set of k groups through k-means clustering [633].

It is also possible to validate the card sorting results by having users place pieces of information into existing categories (so-called closed card sorting). This may be treated as a check of the reliability of the grouping (Chapter 10).

27.4 Menu user interfaces

Command-line interfaces can be efficient if the user can take the time to learn them. As such, they are useful in many professional applications where skill development or training is expected, such

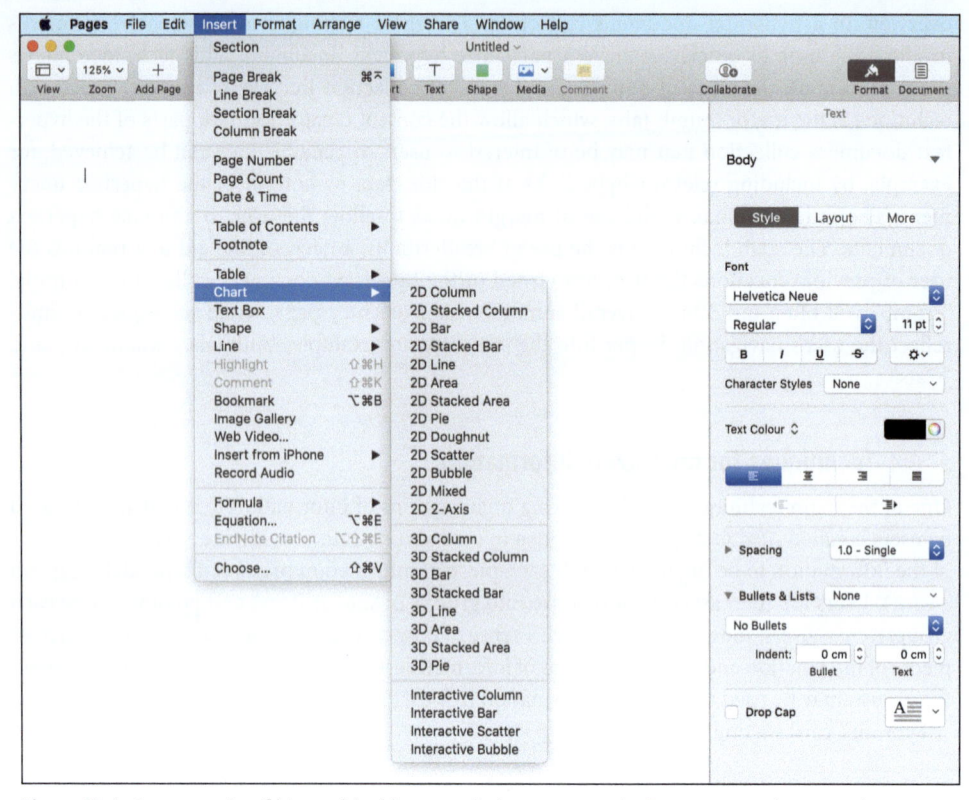

Figure 27.1 An example of hierarchical linear pull-down menus in *Pages*, a word processing application.

as system administration [47]. However, in many other cases, learnability can pose a barrier. It is time-consuming to learn command names and effortful to recall them. The principle of direct manipulation (Chapter 28) is both easier to learn and less effortful to apply; however, it does not offer as much room for improving performance. As a middle ground, interactive menu systems have evolved as a mainstream technique for command invocation in graphical user interfaces.

We are all familiar with menus. Generally, a *menu* is a set of selectable options, like a menu of desserts in a restaurant. An *interactive menu* displays its options on a computer display for selection with a pointing device [35]. While interactive menus first appeared in 1968 in AMBIT/G, a visual programming language, they were popularized much later by the Xerox Star in 1981 and the Macintosh computer in 1984 [35].

Figure 27.1 shows an example of a hierarchical linear pull-down menu, which is a common type of menu. It shows several *menu commands* organized into *menu panels*. Within each panel, there are *groups* of commands indicated by horizontal *separator lines*. The menu is linear because the commands in each panel are organized vertically. The menu is hierarchical because there are multiple panels; some panels open *submenus*. The menu is a pull-down menu because it opens in place by expanding from top to bottom.

This commercial example illustrates well the main benefit of interactive menus: They allow novice users to familiarize themselves with options by simply opening menu panels and reading the items. Items are made available via *recognition*, not *recall*, which is more effortful. There is no need to memorize command names. However, recall can be used to boost performance. *Keyboard shortcuts* (e.g., CTRL-C for copying and CTRL-V for pasting) allow users to drastically improve their performance with frequently used commands. This mode, which requires some effort to learn, is optional.

Common characteristics of interactive menus are as follows:

A finite set of options: Typically between a handful and a few hundred options, although it can go up to a few thousand in professional software.

Visual and textual presentation: Options are presented visually on display using text, icons, and interactive feedback (e.g., hover-over cues).

Interactive exposition of options: Menu options can be shown fully or be exposed interactively in response to the user's input.

Transience: Menus are often expanded in place and dismissed after use, saving screen estate.

Multimodality: Alternative ways to access the menu can be offered, such as via voice commands or keyboard shortcuts.

27.4.1 Menu techniques

In the menu design shown in Figure 27.1, submenus are opened by hovering over the parent option. This is an instance of a *menu technique*, an interaction technique for menu navigation and selection. It illustrates two principles of menu systems: interactive exposition and transience. Submenus are exposed and dismissed by bringing the cursor over a parent menu.

To issue a command, the user has to perform a series of actions: (1) trigger the menu; (2) identify the menu item with the desired command; (3) navigate to the menu item with the desired command; and (4) select the menu item. While an expert user would know where a desired menu item is located, they would still need to navigate to the item. This is inefficient compared to a direct invocation method, such as a keyboard shortcut.

Menu techniques can be divided into two main classes based on which aspect of the series of actions they support. Techniques for navigation help the user explore the menu panels. For example, keyboard navigation can be offered, or hover-over exposition like in Figure 27.2. Techniques for selection help the user select an item. In a basic form of interactive selection, shown in Figure 27.2, the item that is currently being pointed at is highlighted (activated), helping the user to keep track of the current selection. When the cursor is brought over an item, it can be interacted with.

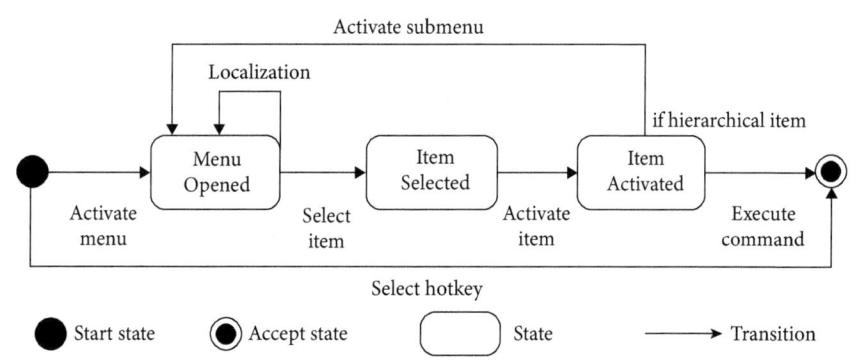

Figure 27.2 A menu interaction diagram for a user going through their options using a pointer.

The design of a menu technique should strike a suitable balance between performance and learnability. While pull-down menus can cascade indefinitely in theory, in practice they are limited in the number of commands that they can offer to the user. Moreover, careful steering of the control cursor is required to navigate a hierarchical menu structure [6], which limits performance.

27.4.2 Keyboard shortcuts

A keyboard shortcut is a keyboard combination, such as CTRL-C, that allows the user to directly invoke a command. One advantage of keyboard shortcuts is that they allow users to immediately invoke a command without having to navigate a structure. This allows expert users to achieve high performance.

The primary disadvantage of keyboard shortcuts is that the user has to consciously learn them. To aid this, keyboard shortcuts are often, but not always, shown next to a command as part of a menu item. This allows the user to learn about the keyboard shortcut at the time when they are interested in the command. On the other hand, at that point, it is easier for the user to simply select the menu item, which means that learning the command only happens due to continuous user effort.

Another disadvantage of keyboard shortcuts is that users may forget them, particularly if they are not used frequently.

27.5 Notational systems

A *notational system* is a system with graphical elements composed according to rules, sometimes referred to as a visual grammar [76]. We introduce such systems here because both commands and navigation structures may be understood and analyzed as notational systems.

An example of a notational system is a domestic heating controller. A typical heating controller consists of a set of buttons for controlling hot water and radiator heat through either direct controls or programming. The controller has buttons that allow the user to turn on the hot water, the radiators, or both systems for, say, one hour. To program the controller to turn the heating on or off at particular times during the day, the user has to move a panel and use a set of buttons to program the controller.

Such a heating controller can be analyzed in terms of its *notation*—how it allows the user to operate it, for example, to modify the times when the hot water is heated or the radiators are turned on and off. The cognitive dimensions of the notation framework [76] provide a design vocabulary for reasoning about such notational systems.

An example of how this framework can be used is captured in the following quote [76]:

> Back in the 80's one of us (TG) was shown a system that he was sure wouldn't work. Yet the received wisdom of 80's HCI seemed to have no explanation of the problems he foresaw. It was a speech-to-text dictation system for use with the Pascal programming language. The speech-recognition technology appeared to be entirely adequate for this restricted language. What problem could there be?

27.5.1 Types of notation use activities

There are many types of notation use activities, that is, ways of describing how people may interact with a notational system. In what follows, we list a few key notational activities [76].

Incrementation: Adding formulas to a spreadsheet or statements to a program.

Transcription: Copying details into a form, converting a formula into a spreadsheet, or defining a formula in terms of code.

Modification: Changing the layout of a spreadsheet, modifying a spreadsheet for a different purpose, or restructuring a program to solve a different problem.

Exploratory design: Iteratively creating incremental versions of sketches, code, or other designs in order to discover the final output, which cannot be readily realized from the onset.

Searching: Exploring a system to identify some desired piece of information or function, for example, scanning a program listing to identify a location where a function is called.

Exploratory understanding: Working with algorithms, classifications, and other structures in order to understand the underpinning mechanisms.

27.5.2 Cognitive dimensions of notation

A lack of terminology may make it difficult to reason precisely about a notational system's positive and negative qualities. The *cognitive dimensions of notation* [76] form a *design vocabulary* that can help designers and researchers to discuss, assess, and critique notational systems. The cognitive dimensions are the following [76]:

Viscosity: *Resistance to change.* Viscosity captures the extent of actions the user is required to carry out to achieve their goals in a system. *Repetition viscosity* means that a change requires many actions of the same type, such as selecting each cell in a spreadsheet individually and assigning it a color attribute. *Knock-on viscosity* means that further distinct actions are required to restore consistency following a change. The more involved and complex it is for a user to make changes in a system, the higher the viscosity.

Visibility: *Ability to view components easily.* The overall visibility provided by the system is determined by the saliency of the visual elements in the interface and the ability of the system to reveal them easily. A system that makes it difficult to view its elements has low visibility.

Premature commitment: *Constraints on the order of doing things.* This refers to the degree of flexibility a user has in carrying out operations in any order. A system requiring many operations to be carried out in a specific order exhibits a high degree of premature commitment.

Hidden dependencies: *Important links between entities are not visible.* If some elements in the system rely on other elements, such dependencies should ideally be evident to the user. A system with many hidden dependencies does not make it clear to the user that many elements rely on other elements or factors present in the system.

Role-expressiveness: *The purpose of an entity is readily inferred.* Role-expressiveness describes the ability of a user to inspect an element in the interface and understand its purpose with little or no guidance. Role-expressiveness is closely related to, but not identical to, perceived affordance. While perceived affordance relates to the immediate uses of a visual element, role-expressiveness may be provided by the system through means other than the element itself, for example, by providing a description near the element. The easier it is for a user to understand the purpose of the elements in the system, the higher the role-expressiveness.

Error-proneness: *The notation invites mistakes, and the system provides little protection.* The error-proneness of the system can manifest itself in four different ways. First, the system can be fragile and easily reach an erroneous state. Second, the system can make it easy for a user to commit an error. Third, it may be difficult for the user to realize there is an error. Fourth, there may be either no provision for rectifying an error or only a cumbersome error correction mechanism. These four error-proneness categories can interact. For example, a system may make it easy for a user to commit an error and make it difficult for the user to realize that an error has occurred. The higher the extent to which these four categories are present in a system, the higher the error-proneness.

Abstraction: *Types and availability of abstraction mechanisms.* Abstractions are definitions of underlying notations in a system. For example, a style sheet in word processing allows the user to create a new style, such as a "body text" style that encapsulates text attributes: a specific font, font size, and font style for the running text in a document. Instead of formatting the text by manually assigning these individual text attributes to each word, the user can simply assign the desired style to the whole text. As this example implies, abstraction may necessitate additional user interface components, in this case, a style sheet manager that allows the user to define and redefine styles. The more intricate the types of abstraction in the system and the more abstraction mechanisms are available to the user, the higher the abstraction provided by the system.

Secondary notation: *Extra information recorded using means other than formal syntax.* A system can provide mechanisms for users to record additional information that is unanticipated by the notation designer. For example, program code allows for the insertion of comments that are uninterpreted by the system. Such comments can then be used to record a variety of information, such as an explanation of the purpose of a variable or function. The more advanced the mechanisms available for the user to record additional information, the higher the secondary notation support provided by the system.

Closeness of mapping: *Closeness of representations to the domain.* The closeness of mapping describes how well the notation maps to the phenomena that the system is attempting to capture. The better the match between the notation and these phenomena, the higher the closeness of mapping.

Consistency: *Similar semantics are expressed in similar syntactic forms.* It is easier for the user to infer the correct application of a notation for a task if the notation of a similar task has a similar form. For example, if similar commands are named and presented in a similar manner, it is easier for the user to find them. The higher the consistency of a system, the more the system tends to express similar notation in a similar manner.

Diffuseness: *Verbosity of the language.* Notations can be redundant, resulting in overly long expressions in a text-based notation or a disproportionate use of screen real estate. The more redundant the notation, the higher the diffuseness.

Hard mental operations: *High demand on cognitive resources.* The more difficult it is for the user to conceptualize and understand tasks or components in the system, or the system as a whole, the higher the demand on the user's cognitive resources. For example, deeply nested structures, complex interrelationships between elements, and obfuscated presentation all increase the working memory demand. The more the system makes such demands, the more the system provides hard mental operations.

Provisionality: *Degree of commitment to actions or marks.* The ability of the system to allow the user to temporarily explore different solutions or designs is measured by its provisionality. The higher the provisionality, the more the system supports the user in providing noncommittal input for exploration or sketching.

Progressive evaluation: *Work-to-date can be checked at any time.* In a nontrivial system, it is beneficial for the user to receive incremental feedback on progress. For example, when writing program code in an integrated development environment, an online syntax checker can provide early feedback to the user on whether the code has syntax errors. The more a system supports providing such incremental progress feedback, the higher its progressive evaluation support.

The easiest way to understand how the cognitive dimensions of notations can be applied in practice is to use them to analyze and contrast how two different notational systems support the user in achieving a set of tasks.

27.6 Recognition versus recall

The trade-off between recognition and recall has been relevant throughout this chapter. When users *recognize*, they identify an item of relevance among a set of items based on some cue related to what they want to do. This is what we all do when we use menus. When users *recall*, they come up spontaneously with names for commands or descriptions of objects. This is what we all do when we search the web. From an HCI perspective, the difference between recognition and recall in user interfaces represents a fundamental trade-off.

The benefit of recognition follows from what we know about human cognition (Chapter 5). For most people, recognizing Ljubljana as the capital of Slovenia is easier than recalling the word and its spelling. Sometimes, recognition is referred to as "knowledge in the world"; rather than relying on memory, we rely on representations of knowledge in our external environment.

The benefit of recall is that it scales well. Independently of the number of items, recall works. The items to be recalled do not take up space on a display. Recall typically requires practice: We learn country capitals only by hearing them repeated. Recall is sometimes called "knowledge in the head"; we rely on memory rather than the external environment.

The dynamics of recall and recognition are surprisingly complex. We all know situations where we rely on knowledge in the world rather than knowledge in the head; looking up facts on your phone rather than thinking about them is one example. A study by Sparrow et al. [786] explored this phenomenon. Participants were asked to learn trivia and type them into a computer. Half were told that the computer would remember what they typed; the other half were told that what they typed would be erased. The participants who believed the information had been saved achieved *worse* performance when asked to recall the trivia. Thus, representing information externally affects how well we remember it. Gray and Fu [287] showed a fascinating effect that may appear counterintuitive. People were willing to rely on imperfect memory in interacting with a video recording machine when the cost of accessing knowledge in the world increased. Thus, we generally prefer to recall, even if recalling information leads to poorer performance.

Because of the differences in display space requirements, practice, and rational trade-offs in what we remember, it is not possible to determine the suitability of recall versus recognition as a strategy for a particular user interface in general terms. Generally, we cannot say that user interfaces that rely on commands (e.g., command-line interfaces) or navigation (e.g., menu interfaces) are better or worse. The optimal choice depends on the users, their activities, and the context in which they act.

Summary

- In user interfaces, naming objects and actions is an important activity, particularly as users are likely to call objects and actions in different ways—the so-called vocabulary problem.
- The recall of command names is facilitated by naming commands using familiar terminology and placing them in carefully thought-out hierarchies.

Exercises

1. Recall versus recognition. Come up with three cases where recall is needed in HCI. Then, think how, through user interface design, you could transform these cases to require recognition.
2. Command names. Consider the following actions and imagine that they are triggered by a single command:
   (a) Copying a photo from a mobile phone to a laptop computer.
   (b) Sorting all files in a directory in reverse alphabetical order.
   (c) Selecting all files that are image files in a directory.
   Find one other person and, working independently, propose a single command name for each action. Compare your proposed command names. How many command names are the same? Do you agree among yourselves that all proposed command names are reasonable?
3. Cognitive demands of notation systems. Choose six of the cognitive dimensions of notations and articulate some user interaction issues that are different in command-line interfaces and graphical user interfaces.
4. Notational system design. Consider the following two notational systems:
   (a) A user writing program code in an integrated development environment.
   (b) A user working with formulas in a spreadsheet.
   The task is to implement mathematical expressions where the arguments may be scalars or vectors, and the functions used are commonly used mathematical operators: addition, subtraction, multiplication, division, exponentiation, square root, absolute value, and standard deviation. Use all the cognitive dimensions of notation to analyze how these two different programming environments can support the programmer in carrying out this task.
5. Cognitive dimensions. The section on notational systems contains a quote [76]. The authors recalled an anecdote about a system using speech-to-text to support programming in Pascal (the specific programming language is unimportant). Even though the speech-to-text functionality "seemed adequate," the authors were certain that the system would have HCI problems. Use cognitive dimensions to articulate some of the problems you foresee with such a system.
6. Menu systems. Articulate the positive and negative qualities of hierarchical linear pull-down menus compared to marking menus. Are there particular use contexts where one of these menu designs is preferable? What would those use contexts be, and what factors would result in one interaction technique being preferable over the other?
7. Command discovery. A major challenge with command lines is supporting users in discovering which commands are available and their functions. Can you think of design solutions that could address this challenge? Articulate why your design solutions would improve the user experience using, for example, the cognitive dimensions of notation as the design vocabulary.

28
Graphical user interfaces

We are all familiar with *graphical user interfaces* (GUIs). GUIs are the type of user interface (UI) that dominates workstations, laptops, and touchscreen devices, including mobile phones and tablets. GUIs allow users to efficiently carry out many everyday computing tasks with ease, such as copying and pasting information, starting applications by selecting them, working in multiple windows at the same time, and using word processors and spreadsheets with easy access to hundreds of functions.

In addition to being a part of our daily lives, GUIs have been the subject of much research from the 1980s until now. Highlights of this research include the following:

- GUIs pioneered the idea that we can refer to objects by their location rather than by their name. In some circumstances, this offers powerful ways to learn and use UIs.
- The benefits of metaphors in GUIs have been much researched; examples of such metaphors are the desktop (for organizing files) and the trash can (for deleting files).
- Some studies have shown that GUIs are more useful than command-line interfaces. Rauterberg [693] compared a GUI to an interface that used menus and function keys; participants took 18%–88% less time to complete tasks when using the GUI.

GUIs evolved from command-line interfaces (Chapter 27). Although command-line interfaces are efficient for experts, they have several limitations. Users have to learn the full command set or part of it, including arguments and syntax, to instruct the computer system. They are impractical for many object manipulation techniques, such as selecting the region of an image, text in a document, or cells in a spreadsheet. They also make it hard to work on multiple tasks simultaneously since there is no easy way to switch between tasks. Moreover, the commands tend to be difficult to remember and type without errors.

Computing devices started as relatively simple calculation devices, and their input and output systems were transplanted from teleprinter devices used to relay text messages. As processing power and memory capacity increased, it became possible for computers to perform more sophisticated tasks. In parallel, new display technology and video processing enabled graphical display, while new input technology, such as light pens and computer mice, provided users with ways to make precise selections on graphical displays. However, to allow users to achieve their goals effectively, efficiently, and safely, it was recognized that there was a need to reimagine the way users interact with computer systems. As a result, several prototype systems gradually led to the refinement that is today recognized as the GUI. These technological developments converged with new human–computer interaction (HCI) to form the *direct manipulation* paradigm that we discuss in this chapter.

Introduction to Human-Computer Interaction. Kasper Hornbæk, Per Ola Kristensson, and Antti Oulasvirta,
Oxford University Press. © Kasper Hornbæk, Per Ola Kristensson, and Antti Oulasvirta (2025).
DOI: 10.1093/oso/9780192864543.003.0028

28.1 A brief history of the GUI

Limitations in command-line interfaces have long been recognized. The first prototype that resembles our modern GUI is *Sketchpad* [807], shown in Figure 28.1. Sketchpad, which was introduced in the 1960s, demonstrated a series of features associated with a modern GUI, such as the use of a pointing device (light pen) for drawing geometric shapes and the ability to create and manipulate graphical objects presented on the display. In software code, it used concepts such as "objects" and "occurrences," which predated object-oriented programming.

Around the same time, novel systems such as *PLATO* (Programmed Logic for Automatic Teaching Operations) and *HES* (Hypertext Editing System) did not provide a GUI but explored elements central to later GUI developments. PLATO allowed graphics to be shown along with text on a raster display to provide an interactive learning environment; HES allowed a user to use a light pen to navigate hypertext (Chapter 24).

In 1972, Alan Kay set out his vision and requirements for what he dubbed *Dynabook*—"a personal computer for children of all ages" [407]. Essentially, this device predicted a modern laptop or tablet along with a modern GUI, although the target audience was children.

In 1973, the *Xerox Alto* became the first computer specifically designed to support a GUI. The users could interact with a keyboard and mouse, and the GUI was shown on a black-and-white cathode-ray tube raster display. It provided a What You See Is What You Get (WYSIWYG) word

Figure 28.1 Interacting with Sketchpad [807].

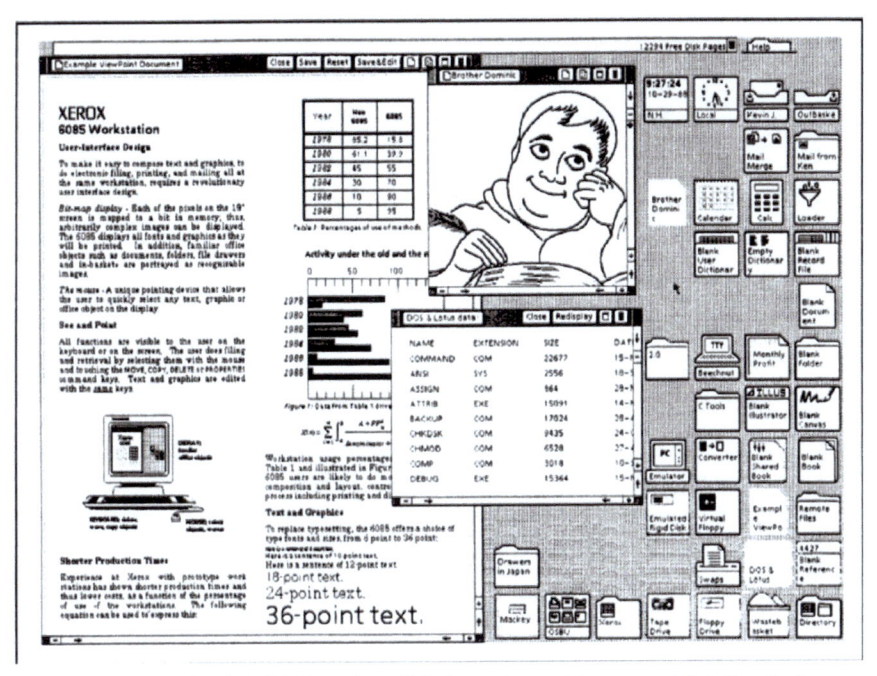

Figure 28.2 Xerox Star's WIMP interface: Windows, Icons, Menus, and Pointing devices.

processor capable of mixing several font families and font sizes, a graphics editor that allowed the user to change tools by selecting their items on a toolbar, an interactive SmallTalk environment, and a pinball game, among other applications.

This initial workstation design and its GUI concept were gradually refined (Figure 28.2), leading to the development of *personal computers*—computer systems that are suitable for individual use without having to rely on a mainframe. This led to the Apple Lisa, the IBM PC, UNIX terminals, and the Windows operating system for IBM PC-compatible computers, all of which provided a GUI for users to interact with. Since such computer systems were prohibitively expensive at the time, several personal computers targeted toward consumers, such as the Commodore C64, Amiga 500, Atari ST, and many others, were developed and commercialized in the early to mid-1980s. By the mid-1980s, the GUI was established as the de facto standard UI, typically complemented by a command-line terminal interface for tasks that could not easily be carried out using the GUI.

28.2 Design objectives

GUIs exhibit great flexibility in how they can be designed. However, this expressivity is also a challenge. Unlike, for example, a form, a GUI can have many possible design variants. To aid GUI designers, GUI software library providers make guidelines available, such as Apple's *Human Interface Guidelines*. These and other vendor-provided guidelines are specific to particular products and brands. However, there is general agreement on a core set of objectives that all GUIs should strive to meet.

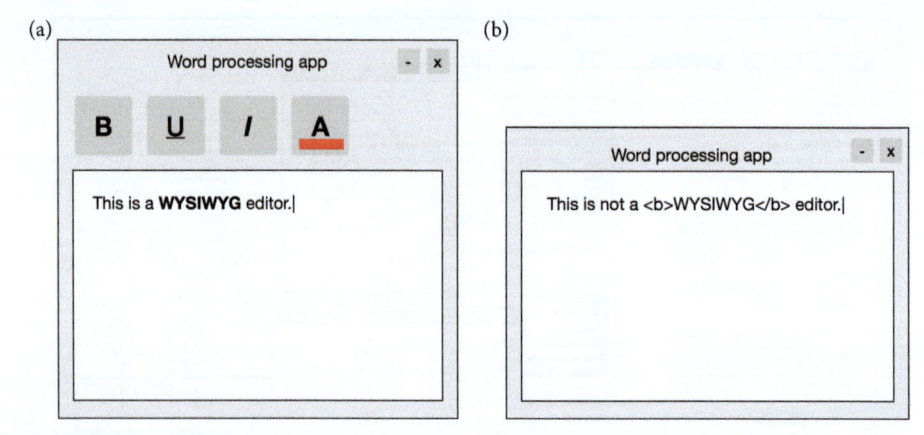

Figure 28.3 (a) A WYSIWYG interface makes the effects of choice directly visible to the user. For example, the boldface button shows the font as it will appear on the document after selection. (b) In a non-WYSIWYG editor, the effects of selections are not shown on display as they will in the final document.

28.2.1 Visibility

GUIs should strive to have high *visibility*. This means that to support users in achieving their goals, these goals and the necessary steps to achieve the goals should be visible to users.

What You See Is What You Get: One example of this principle is WYSIWYG word processors, which show the effects of choices of font families, sizes, and styles directly in the document. Figure 28.3 shows a (hypothetical) WYSIWYG word processor against a non-WYSIWYG editor. In the WYSIWYG editor, headings, body text, hyperlinks, and other formatting elements of the text are shown to the user, and the user can interact with these elements, seeing their consequences immediately. For example, if the user selects some text and changes its formatting, this change will be immediately visible in the current view of the document.

Visibility of commands: Another application of this principle is ensuring that commands are visible. For example, take a look at your word processing application. Many of them support the visibility of commands by revealing many relevant text formatting options and tools in the toolbar. The font, style, size, and color can be set directly. Common text features, such as making the text left-aligned, right-aligned, centered, or justified, are also immediately visible. If the user does not know what an element in the toolbar does, the user can hover above it with the mouse cursor to trigger a *tooltip* description.

Visibility can be supported by allowing users to browse commands using linear pull-down menus or by exploring a series of toolbars. However, visibility is about more than just making commands and other interaction possibilities obvious to the user. Visibility means designing a GUI that invites users to take action and allows them to easily interpret the possible actions and their consequences. At the same time, both screen real estate and users' visual attention are limited resources. Therefore, there is a need to strike a balance between these resources when conveying information to the UI to avoid overloading the user.

Visibility of status: Visibility of status means ensuring that the GUI shows the status of entities relevant to the user's goals. An example of visibility of status is an indicator of whether a remote user is available or busy in a communication program. Another example is the subtle padlock icon on the web address input field, which indicates that the currently visited web site uses a verified certificate.

Visibility of dependencies: The spreadsheet is an example of a well-established GUI paradigm that attempts to strike a balance between limited resources. Spreadsheets allow users to link cells together using formulas that refer to the values in other cells. Such dependencies can be difficult for the user to understand. As a result, a spreadsheet GUI provides a mechanism for visualizing such dependencies. When the user clicks a cell with a formula that refers to other cells, the dependent cells are color-coded to reflect their respective roles in the formula.

> ## Paper Example 28.2.1: A graphical user interface with physics
>
> A GUI does not have to look and feel like a traditional desktop GUI. For example, a GUI can be driven by lightweight physics and relax some of the rather rigid organizational principles applied in traditional GUIs. For instance, Agarawala and Balakrishnan [11] allowed users to organize files as piles of documents that can be quickly moved by dragging and flicking them with a pen. The resulting *BumpTop* prototype enables windows, photos, and files to be organized informally in piles.
>
> BumpTop supports a range of interaction techniques to select and browse objects. The movement of objects is physics-based and employs rigid body dynamics, friction, and collision detection, which means that when objects collide, they experience semi-realistic displacement effects.

28.2.2 Consistency

Consistency is an important design objective. As explained in the beginning of this part, it means that representations are similar across the UI.

Is striving for consistency always a good thing? There is no clear-cut answer. Grudin [299] provided several examples of interface design decisions where consistency was not attractive. Grudin pointed out that there are several considerations before employing consistency as a design guideline: (1) consistency must be defined; (2) there is a need to identify good—as opposed to poor—consistency, which means there must be a method of identifying the most suitable consistency among several competing consistencies; and (3) there must be a method of identifying when other principles are more important than consistency. Grudin argued that striving for consistency is often not useful. Instead, interface objects are better placed according to the needs associated with the user's tasks. This changes the focus from the properties of the UI to task analysis and understanding the work context.

28.2.3 Minimizing errors

Errors are outcomes in a GUI that are inaccurate or incorrect. It is important to realize that errors to some extent are unavoidable and even intrinsic in HCI. For example, the noise in the human neuromuscular system makes it exceedingly difficult for a user to move a mouse cursor to a precise pixel location on a high-resolution display. In practice, users are also bound to make mistakes due to a lack of attention, insufficient training, or misunderstandings about the UI. Furthermore, GUIs can induce errors by relying on a confusing design. It is therefore natural to introduce the objective of *minimizing errors*. A GUI should be designed to anticipate and tolerate user errors and minimize erroneous outcomes. Given the importance of eliminating as many errors as possible, UI designers commonly use several well-established tactics.

Preempting errors: GUIs should adhere to sound GUI design principles, such as those mentioned in this section. In particular, a clear, simple structure and a user interface that presents graphical elements in a consistent manner can help prevent errors from the outset.

Reversing outcomes: GUIs should allow users to reverse their actions if the results are found to be undesirable. This realization has led to the widespread implementation of *undo* and *redo*, which allow users to reverse and repeat their actions, respectively.

A simple linear undo/redo facility can be achieved by using a stack data structure: Every last executed command is put on the stack. When the user undoes, the last command on the stack is retrieved and its consequence is eliminated. For example, if the user underlined some text, the last executed command would be to underline some specific text in the document. Once the command has been executed, the command is added to the undo stack. If the user wishes to undo this action, the command is retrieved and its consequence is reversed, removing the underlining from the text. This type of undo action can be repeated by the user or reversed if the user wishes to redo the action. The size of the data structure is known as the *undo history*. An application using a linear stack-based undo model can only reverse command executions that are in its undo history. More sophisticated undo mechanisms may be required for more complex applications.

Explaining outcomes and confirming actions: An established GUI practice is to seek confirmation when the user desires to issue commands that are irreversible or may have unforeseen consequences. Such confirmation can, for example, be implemented by triggering a dialog box that explains the consequences of the action and provides the user with options, such as proceed, abort, or retrieve information about the consequences of the action. For example, such a dialog box is triggered when a user wants to overwrite a file.

28.2.4 Accessibility

Finally, GUIs should be *accessible* to all users. What this means and how it may be addressed is discussed in the chapter on tool use (Chapter 19).

Common GUI guidelines

Task support: GUIs should prioritize support for tasks that are frequent, important, or risky. Moreover, their design should offer a structure that is compatible with the task flows that users find natural. We discussed task analysis in Chapter 15.

Simplicity: "Keep it simple, stupid". Offer only those features that are needed, and nothing else. Adding functionality, graphics, descriptions, widgets, options, and colors can only increase users' workload. This increased workload, in turn, increases stress and decreases performance and satisfaction. Examine the elements of the UI and consider which ones are really needed.

Responsiveness: GUIs should be responsive. Simple interactions such as manipulations of widgets should have responses within a few tens of milliseconds. Full views should not take more than a second to load up. Most web pages take 3–4 seconds, however.

Consistency: Users are not *tabula rasa*. They approach your design with *priors*. In other words, based on prior exposure to UIs, they have formed *expectations* about your design's structure and behavior. *Consistency* refers to the perceptual similarity between a target UI and prior UIs a user has used. Consistency also pertains to interactions: Actions that have the same consequences should be presented similarly. Consistency makes it easier for users to find elements in an interface and control them. It lowers the need for learning.

Recoverability: Users make errors. Because there is a non-zero probability of an error happening, it is important that the interface minimizes the negative consequences for the user. Does your interface allow users to undo, veto, or recall their actions?

Assistance: Do not ask users to do things that can be done automatically for them. Assist them wherever possible. Information that a user has given earlier should be offered as the default option unless there is a reason why this is unlikely to be the desired option. Assistance increases efficiency.

Scaffolding: Offer support for developing skills. Starting with a new UI is often cognitively taxing and stressful. Over time, users pick up skills for performing the minimum tasks. The UI should assist novices in figuring out the interface, for example, via tips. It should not stop there, either: Intermediate users should be helped to figure out how to increase performance (e.g., via power user features like shortcuts).

Ability-based design: GUI design should support users with different motor, perceptual, and cognitive abilities.

28.3 The principle of direct manipulation

A central principle for GUIs is *direct manipulation*. The original definition of direct manipulation, provided by Shneiderman [764], states that a direct manipulation interface has the following three properties:

- Visibility of the objects and actions of interest
- Rapid, reversible, incremental actions
- Replacement of typed commands by a pointing action on the object of interest.

These properties were later refined into the following three principles [771]:

1. Continuous representations of the objects and actions of interest with meaningful visual metaphors
2. Physical actions or presses of labeled buttons, instead of complex syntax
3. Rapid, reversible, incremental actions whose effects are on the objects of interest are visible immediately.

An example of direct manipulation is the removal of a file (Figure 28.4). To delete a file from a desktop GUI, such as macOS, the user opens a file management application window. This window lists all the files in the current directory as graphical representations, such as icons coupled with filenames. The user can now move the mouse pointer over a graphical representation of a file and select it by pressing a mouse button. The graphical representation of the file changes in response to this action to indicate to the user that this file has been selected. If the user keeps the mouse button pressed, the user can drag the graphical representation of the file to a graphical representation of a delete action—the trash can icon in the lower-left corner in Figure 28.4. When the graphical representation of the file is on top of the trash can icon, the representation of the trash can changes to indicate that the graphical representation of the file is interacting with the trash can icon. If the user lifts up the mouse button, the file is moved to the trash can, which means it is considered deleted but can still be recovered if the user changes their mind. If the user continues to press the mouse button, the system will open a new file management application window.

28.3.1 Benefits and limits of direct manipulation

What makes interaction "direct"? Hutchins et al. [365] explained directness through two dimensions:

$$\text{directness} = \text{distance} + \text{engagement}.$$

Distance refers to the mental effort required to translate goals into actions and then evaluate their effects. Norman [599] named these the gulfs of execution and evaluation (Chapter 18). *Engagement* refers to the locus of control within the system. Users should feel like the agents within the system. By contrast, in command language interfaces, the user interacts with a hidden intermediary that relays the commands to a third party for execution. This interaction is like shouting a command to someone in another room and waiting for the person to respond. Direct manipulation interfaces offer a *model world*. For example, consider the desktop metaphor. It models a desktop, even some reduced form of physics. Model world interfaces allow users to act in the world in the first person rather than via an intermediary.

The low distance between the user and the system enabled by GUIs carries several cognitive benefits over command language interfaces [412]. Using direct manipulation interfaces usually involves recognition rather than recall. Visual recognition is less effortful than memorization of commands. Instead of recalling command names, objects can be searched for visually. Direct manipulation UIs also allow for concrete metaphors (e.g., the desktop metaphor) as opposed to abstract concepts. Instead of keyboard commands, a pointing device can be used.

However, whether these benefits are realized depends on a number of factors. Direct manipulation is not a panacea; a well-crafted GUI design is still required. If the metaphors or icons are poorly designed or poorly organized, visual search will become a bottleneck. Moreover, pointing can be slower than typing when the GUI is disorganized. Frohlich [260] reviewed empirical evaluations of direct manipulation interfaces and concluded that the evidence is mixed. Some studies show benefits; others do not. The interface design and the user's task together determine whether the benefits of low distance can be realized.

Kieras et al. [412] compared a keypad and a touchscreen as possible interfaces in a tactical aircraft game. Users were required to identify and act on aircraft appearing on display. They concluded that *response selection* separates direct manipulation and keypad-based interaction. When using a keypad, users must recall which key commands to use in which situation. Direct manipulation lowers this requirement. The authors noted that the touchscreen interface would have been

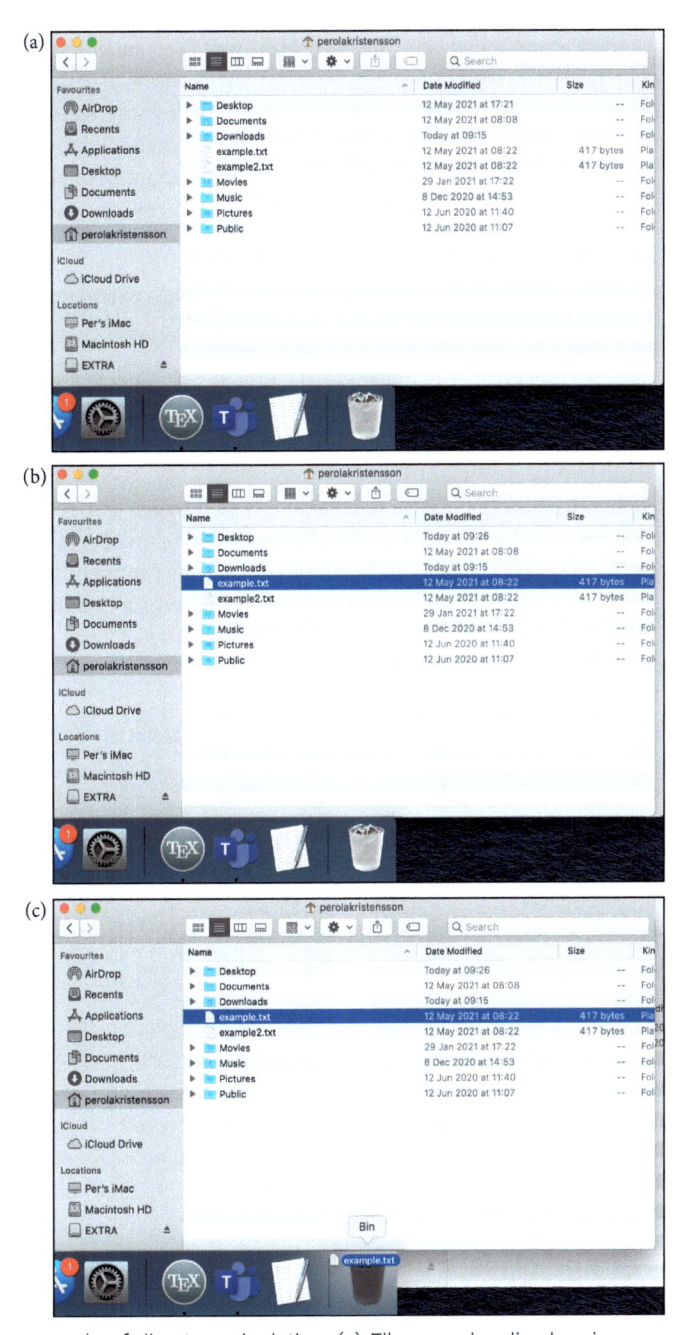

Figure 28.4 An example of direct manipulation. (a) Files are visualized as icons coupled with filenames in a file management application window. (b) The user selects a file by moving the mouse pointer over the file and pushing down a mouse button. The visual depiction of the file changes in response to this action. (c) While holding down the mouse button, the user has dragged the file to the trash can—an icon that is always shown on the desktop toolbar at the bottom of the screen. If the user lifts up the mouse button at this time, the file is moved into the trash can and is considered deleted (but recoverable) by the system.

even better if less hand movement had been involved. However, even small changes to the task or the UI could have changed this result.

Certain tasks are more difficult than others for direct manipulation interfaces [259]. It is harder to refer to previous actions, which can be alleviated with undo/redo and interaction histories. It is also difficult to perform repetitive actions, which in command language interfaces can be done with scripting. Concurrent actions are also difficult because there is only one pointer.

> **Paper Example 28.3.1: Video browsing by direct manipulation**
>
> Direct manipulation is a powerful principle for GUIs. At first sight, it may seem limited to the manipulation of icons. However, this is an underestimation of the power of direct manipulation. Let us consider, for instance, whether the browsing of a video could be done using direct manipulation. Would that be possible?
>
> Typically, video browsing is done with a slider that can be dragged across the length of the duration of a video, such as the horizontal slider in the figure below. Dragicevic et al. [213] noted that we often have an object of interest in the video, such as a car moving, a ball jumping, or our favorite actor doing a particular move. Rather than scrubbing a timeline, could we just grab and move the objects of interest? As shown in the figure, Dragicevic et al. [213] found a way to make it possible to navigate video through direct manipulation.

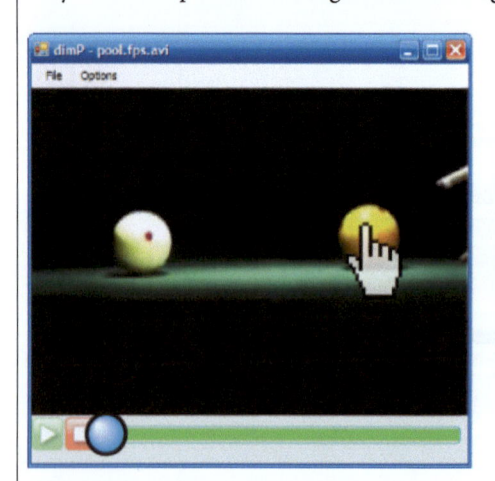

28.4 Anatomy of a graphical user interface

28.4.1 Graphical user interface elements

Windows: A *window* is a central component of a GUI. Typically, it is a rectangular panel that encapsulates an application or a task. The application windows encapsulate the primary application window. A *window manager* provided by the operating system is responsible for handling fundamental actions for windows, such as the following: (1) instructing the window to redraw its contents; (2) sending keyboard and mouse events to the window when it is in focus; (3) providing user functions for minimizing, maximizing, and closing windows;

and (4) allowing the user to drag and resize windows. Figure 28.3 shows an example of an application window.

> **Paper Example 28.4.1: Folding windows**
>
> Windows allow the user to expand documents and applications into a controllable space on a display. As an interactive widget, present-day windows are rectangles that can be moved, resized, and closed. What if the desktop metaphor were extended to windows? Dragicevic [212] presented an interaction technique for windows that allows them to fold like pieces of paper. When multiple windows are on top of each other, the user can quickly fold their corners to see what is underneath them.

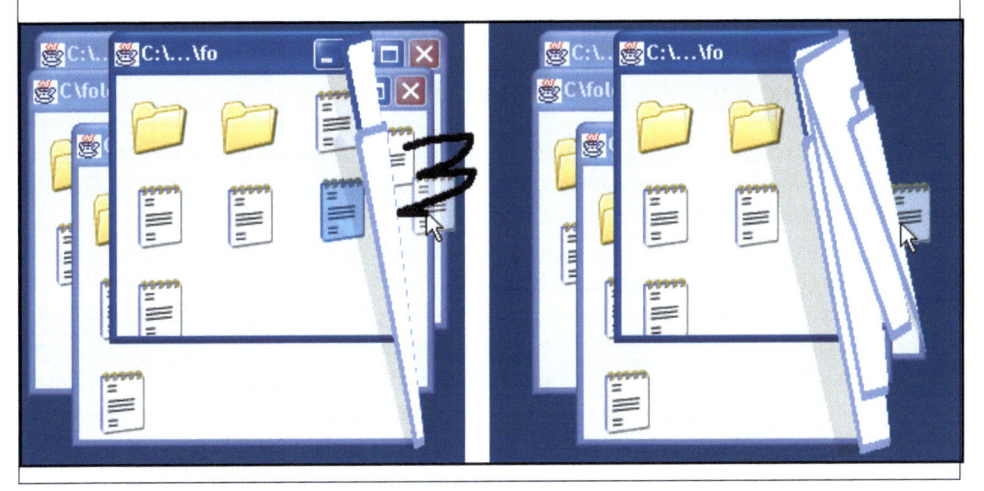

Panels: A *panel*, sometimes referred to as a *component* or *container*, is a rectangular area that can contain its own background (often simply a solid color) and a set of elements of the UI. An arrangement of panels is used to create an application GUI. For example, Figure 28.3a shows a word processing application window that consists of two panels: (1) a static toolbar panel at the top providing access to formatting commands; and (2) the main word processor panel.

Menus: Menus are widely used in GUIs. In desktop GUIs, linear pull-down menus allow the user to traverse a menu hierarchy to explore and select commands. On a mobile touch-enabled device, this menu exploration style is impractical; therefore, menus are usually shown as a series of horizontal buttons that the user can navigate. Menus are discussed in more detail in the chapter on interaction techniques (Chapter 26).

Icons: An *icon* is a graphical depiction that represents some capability of the GUI, such as the ability to launch an application or trigger a command. Icons can be generated by bitmaps or vector graphics. Depending on the context, icons can serve a number of purposes. First, an icon can be selectable by the user. For example, a group of icons representing an application or file can typically be selected in sequence. This may be done by holding down a specific keyboard key while using the mouse to click each icon. Alternatively, it is sometimes possible to use a mouse and perform a rectangular selection. This allows the user to perform an action on multiple targets simultaneously. Second, icons can be clicked. Such an action typically triggers another action, such as the launch of an application or a specific command. For example, clicking on an icon representing a pair of scissors usually triggers the command *Cut*. Third, icons can serve as targets for actions. For example, it is often possible to delete a file or application by dragging its icon to the trash can icon. Fourth, icons can reveal information. For example, the trash can icon may be represented as an empty trash can when there are no recoverable files available or as a trash can with contents when there are recoverable files. To access the recoverable files, the user can click the trash can icon, which opens a file explorer window showing the special system directory that contains deleted but still recoverable files on the system. Another example is app icons on a smartphone, which may show a number next to them to indicate the number of unseen notifications they can reveal to the user if the user triggers the app icon by touching it.

28.5 Designing a graphical user interface

GUI design is a so-called easy/hard activity. It appears easy. Anybody with moderate computer skills can just "wing it": download an interactive software development kit (SDK) and start drawing a GUI. There are plenty of examples online to learn from. However, designing an actually usable GUI is hard. You are almost certainly going to fail your users unless you follow a systematic design process or happen to be a design veteran.

The user-centered design of a GUI is not different from other areas of design, yet some unique characteristics exist. First, GUI designs are based on user research. Key decisions in GUI design—such as those concerning functionality, the UI style, and the visual design approach—require an empirical understanding of the users' practices, needs, capabilities, contexts, terminals, existing designs, and so on. Designers increasingly rely on logs from existing applications as a source of data. Second, design is iterative. Hundreds to thousands of alternatives are sketched, eventually converging toward high-fidelity prototypes worthy of evaluation. Digital sketching and wireframing tools are often used to boost productivity. A *UI kit* is a template of components that can be used in design tools such as Sketch and Figma. Several iterative cycles or sprints are carried out; these often involve some research, design, and evaluation. Third, GUI designs are evaluated with dedicated methods. Analytical evaluation methods (e.g., GUI design guidelines) are used early in the project; empirical methods such as usability testing, AB testing, and field studies are used later on. Elsewhere in this book (Chapter 41), we have discussed heuristic evaluation guidelines for GUI design. GUI designs need to be reviewed against company-specific guidelines and design systems. For example, at the time of writing, Microsoft offered *Fluent Design System* and Google *Material Design*. In a review or audit session, a design team reviews all low- and high-level details of the candidate design; changes to the UI after this point will be very expensive.

The development of GUI software still has significant costs. Although there are powerful SDKs and even sketch-to-code solutions, developing a fully functional GUI that fulfills the specifications is time-consuming. The software controlling the GUI must be interfaced with application features, business processes (e.g., payment), databases, and hardware. Software engineers must validate the software before launch. GUI design does not end at the release of the product, either; metrics and processes must be put in place to maintain and update it.

Next, we provide a primer for five elementary GUI design considerations: visual layouts, text and labels, icons, widgets, and metaphors. We review common approaches through the lens of empirical research. Nevertheless, GUI design is first and foremost a practice; the best way to learn

GUI design is to try it out. For more details, we refer the reader to dedicated practical books [771, 894].

28.5.1 Visual organization

We now look at two concepts for visual organization: hierarchy and guidance.

Visual hierarchy: Elements on a graphical layout should be organized logically—but what does this mean? Visual hierarchies use visual cues to define which elements belong together and in which order they should be looked at. Hierarchies become necessary as the number of elements grows. Instead of having N separate elements, aim for a hierarchy and use regular visual cues (e.g., rectangular boxes, colors) to indicate groups. The Gestalt laws are useful for visual grouping. Contours, regions, colors, paddings, and margins offer strong cues about which elements belong together.

A visual hierarchy ranks graphical elements and places them in groups so that high-level elements contain low-level elements. A well-designed hierarchy helps the user understand the order in which a task can be completed (i.e., the task flow). Visual cues such as proximity, common region, contiguity, and regularity in colors and style are used to communicate the hierarchy.

Grid lines are the most important organizing principle in layouts. Grid lines are horizontal or vertical lines that intersect a UI canvas. They define how the edges of UI elements can be placed. *Grid layouts* are UI layouts defined with grid lines. A grid layout is a spatial structure that places elements in a non-overlapping way on a (typically) rectangular area. A layout can be described efficiently with grid lines. One can easily define repetitive structures, such as column grids and card grids, and more complex structures. Grid layouts are used across various stages of GUI design, from sketching and wireframing to prototyping and deployment.

Grid alignment is a measure of GUI complexity [547]. It describes the minimum number of grid lines that can be used to define a layout such that all the edges of elements fall on a grid line. Empirical work on grid alignment has found it is correlated with the perceived complexity of a GUI: The smaller this number, the lower the perceived complexity of the GUI [547]. In a controlled study measuring search time and preference, Parush et al. [641] noted the importance of grid alignment and balance: "The combination of poor alignment and poor local density had the strongest adverse effect on search time. Alignment and grouping were found to have more influence on subjective preference" [p. 343]. However, the search time shortened considerably with experience, even for the worst designs.

Visual guidance: GUI design should have a *visual flow* that matches the user's *task flow*; see Chapter 15 for task analysis. Visual flow refers to the order in which users are likely to scan the regions of a UI. By contrast, *perceptual clutter* is a state where everything is competing for the user's attention and it is not clear where to start a task. Flow is affected by the use of colors, sizes, shapes, and orientations. *Negative* space—that is, white space—can also be used to guide attention. Chapter 3 covered visual saliency and clutter, which provide a systematic template for understanding what grabs a user's attention.

28.5.2 Icons

Icon design needs to take into account a number of factors. First, an icon may have many purposes at once; for instance, it can represent a digital object, an underlying action, a receivable action, or all of these. An example of such an overloaded icon is the trash can icon. It represents a status: An empty trash can communicates to the user that there are no recoverable files available, while a trash can with contents signals that there are recoverable files. Another—related—representation is the fact that if the user clicks the trash can icon, the system will open a file explorer window showing any recoverable files. Furthermore, a set of files and applications can be deleted by first selecting them and then dragging their icons to the trash can. When this happens, the representation of the trash can icon changes, for example, with a subtle change in shading, to indicate that the trash can icon has been selected. Finally, when files are deleted by dragging them to the trash can, the system plays a sound representing someone crumpling a piece of paper to indicate to the user that the action has been carried out.

Second, the design of an icon must be understandable by the user. This may involve choosing a metaphor the user is likely to understand, such as the trash can icon design. As another example, a notepad app icon may depict a notepad. Application icon design often foregoes the idea of using metaphors and instead opts for ensuring the icon represents the brand of the application in question. Application icons for Microsoft Word, Skype, and many others all reflect their respective brands.

28.5.3 Metaphors

Metaphors may be leveraged to guide interface design. The idea behind the use of metaphors is to design concepts, processes, and actions in a GUI around the user's prior knowledge. For example, digital office tasks such as file management, note-taking, and word processing may be designed around a desktop metaphor. Figure 28.5 shows an aspect of the desktop metaphor in the form of a trash can serving as a representation for discarding unwanted files and applications by throwing them in the trash can. The icon also represents the possibility of recovering discarded files and applications by picking them up from the trash can before they are thrown out with the trash (deleted permanently).

Figure 28.5 A commonplace metaphor in GUI desktops: the trash can as a representation of deleting files. This is the macOS trash can. Users can delete files by dragging them to the trash can or issuing the delete command directly. By clicking the trash can, the file management application shows previously deleted files that may be recovered by the user.

Figure 28.6 An example of a GUI making extensive use of metaphors: the Microsoft Bob product for Windows 3.1. Bob was a proposed graphical shell for inexperienced computer users. The user can start applications by clicking on their representations in the GUI. For example, the side table to the left of the armchair shows an address binder to the left and a mail tray to the right. Clicking the address binder will start the address book application; clicking the mail tray will start the email client. Image source: http://toastytech.com/guis/bob.html.

Carroll et al. [134] listed several *interface metaphors*. Word and text processing uses the metaphor of the typewriter and exploits prior knowledge about using typewriters, typing paper, and keyboards. Desktop publishing and document structures, such as headings and subheadings, use the metaphor of a physical document and exploit prior knowledge around typesetting, inserting physical figures, and the logical structure of a document. Single-user or collaborative electronic workspaces use the metaphor of a chalkboard or whiteboard and exploit prior knowledge of group interaction around a chalkboard or whiteboard and the free-form organization of text and graphics. Desktop accessories use metaphors of desktop tools and exploit prior knowledge of the use of calculators, notepads, and personal organizers. Further examples include spreadsheets exploiting prior knowledge of ledger sheets for understanding matrix-structured data organization and form-based applications exploiting prior knowledge of business forms and the codification of business processes into forms, the organization of information, and report generation.

The central idea behind interface metaphors is to support learning by analogy by exploiting users' prior knowledge in the design of a GUI. The aim is to transplant existing concepts, actions, and processes the user is already familiar with to improve users' learning and understanding of

GUIs. However, it is critical to realize that metaphors are far from perfect mappings to UIs. As noted by Carroll et al. [134], if metaphors provided a complete mapping, a word processor would fully appear and behave like an actual typewriter.

In practice, the mapping between the source of the metaphor and the target (the UI) is never one-to-one, which results in *metaphor mismatches*. For example, a form-based UI may present an electronic form similar to an existing physical business form. However, an electronic form can, and probably will, support input validation. For instance, it may provide feedback to the user on invalid input, suggest suitable inputs, and prevent the user from completing the next part of the form until the first part has been fully validated.

Furthermore, interface metaphors are often used in combination, which leads to *composite metaphors* [134]. For example, a desktop UI uses a desktop metaphor while desktop accessories use their own metaphors, such as notepads, calculators, clocks, and personal organizers. Figure 28.6 shows an alternative to the desktop metaphor.

28.6 Why do we still have GUIs?

As explained at the beginning of this chapter, research on GUIs began in the 1960s, and the first commercially successful GUIs date to the 1980s. As pointed out by Beaudouin-Lafon [55], this is curious because all other aspects of computers have improved dramatically. The Intel 8088 from 1979 ran at 5 MHz; current CPUs run at 5 GHz with multiple cores and can process about 400,000 instructions per second. How come the user interface, the GUI, has remained broadly the same?

One answer is that the GUI is a fundamentally outstanding idea. Using space to structure information helps us see what we can do and aids memory. Direct manipulation has made trial and error available to most users, allowing them to undo wrong actions. Visual representations remain compelling for many users.

Another reason is that, in reality, GUIs are being combined with all kinds of other UIs. Thus, what seems to be a dominant interface style is increasingly a mix of graphical elements, search interfaces, keyboard commands, and other interface styles. Consider, for instance, the use of speech when using mobile devices: Many users make calls or start applications in this way rather than through the GUI. Another example is the use of commands in a desktop operating system: Many users switch to a command-line interface for search, handling files, or shortcuts to applications. Thus, the GUI is increasingly combined with other forms of interfaces.

A third reason is that the alternatives to GUIs are wanting. Interfaces that are based on naming or searching for commands are sometimes hard or impossible to use for some tasks. Interfaces that automatically infer what we want, rather than take commands like the GUI, have been a vision for decades [590]. Intelligent agents and brain–computer interfaces are two examples. However, the former has been described as having "a really bad personal assistant" [497]; the latter is currently only feasible for simple tasks such as movements and simple choices. In Chapter 29, we discuss some other alternatives to GUIs that show promise.

Summary

- The GUI was invented more than 40 years ago and is still the main interaction style in many computer systems.
- Direct manipulation is a key principle for GUIs.

- GUIs exploit a number of design principles, including visual hierarchy, grid lines, and undo.

Exercises

1. Visual design principles. Analyze the visual design principles applied in the design of a GUI you are familiar with. Take a screenshot of a screen you use frequently and annotate it with principles we discussed in this chapter.
2. Direct manipulation. Consider a word processor you are familiar with. Explain how it uses direct manipulation in common tasks. Then, consider how you would redesign the word processor to *not* follow the principle of direct manipulation.
3. GUI design. Following the design principles outlined in this chapter, design a simple GUI for a note-taking app for two devices: a laptop computer and a mobile phone. Note down design challenges that differentiate the two terminals.
4. Icon design. Some icons are based on legacy technology that is not familiar to younger generations, such as the save icon (floppy disk), phone call (phone handle), folder (file cabinet), and address book (Rolodex). Following the guidance given in this chapter, design new icons (maximum size 300 × 300 pixels) for these.
5. Widget design. Consider a physical table in your environment and write down the first attributes of this table that come to mind. Then, do the following:
   (a) Ask a friend to do the same. How many attributes are similar?
   (b) Consider a typical table widget in a GUI (e.g., spreadsheet applications). How many attributes does the table widget in the GUI share with the attributes you identified?
6. Cognition and GUIs. Consider the three principles of direct manipulation. Which insights from understanding people (Part II) justify those principles? For each principle, come up with three insights.

29
Reality-based interaction

The user interfaces for computer systems have remained remarkably consistent since the emergence of the graphical user interface (GUI) in the 1980s. Processing speed has increased dramatically, storage is abundant, and network speeds are orders of magnitude higher today. Therefore, it is astonishing that we still rely on the same input methods, notably keyboards and mice, and the same user interface paradigms, including windows, icons, menus, and pointers [54].

The interaction paradigm that originates with the desktop has several limitations. First, the user is assumed to be stationary, and the physical surroundings do not change. Second, there is the assumption that only one user interacts with the interactive system at a time. Third, input, at least with desktop and laptop computers, is indirect through devices such as mice and physical keyboards. Finally, the user's surroundings have no special status in interaction. As a consequence, users do not have a natural way to interact with objects and people close to them.

To address these limitations, researchers have worked on several ways to characterize new opportunities for user interfaces. They have attempted to articulate in a principled way why and how user interfaces should be developed beyond the desktop computer model and its focus on windows, icons, menus, and pointers. These attempts have mostly been worded with negative connotations, such as "post-WIMP," "beyond the desktop," or "non-command user interfaces."

One vision stands out because it articulates the positive aims and characteristics of this type of user interface rather than simply stating that we need to go beyond GUIs. This framework is *reality-based interaction*, developed by Jacob et al. [381] (see Figure 29.1). The framework includes four goals to build interactive technology that better exploits and supports our capabilities [381, p. 222]:

- **Naive physics:** "People have common sense knowledge about the physical world." So-called tangible user interfaces move the control of computers and the display of information into the physical world (Section 29.3).
- **Body awareness and skills:** "People have an awareness of their own physical bodies and possess skills for controlling and coordinating their bodies." Interaction in mixed reality (MR) is widely based on the idea that you move your limbs as you would do outside the MR (Section 29.4).
- **Environment awareness and skills:** "People have a sense of their surroundings and possess skills for negotiating, manipulating, and navigating within their environment." Interactive systems may use the user's position to display particular information.
- **Social awareness and skills:** "People are generally aware of others in their environment and have skills to interact with them." An example of attention to such awareness and skills is the interest in video communication systems to get the gaze direction of a remote person to appear correct.

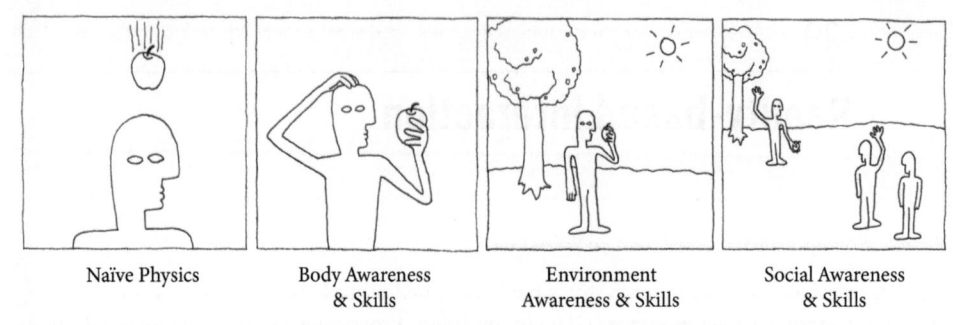

| Naïve Physics | Body Awareness & Skills | Environment Awareness & Skills | Social Awareness & Skills |

Figure 29.1 An overview of the four areas of reality-based computing [381].

In practice, this vision boils down to research on interfaces that in various ways break key assumptions about desktop-based computing. In this chapter, we will articulate four such types of interface that each break a particular key assumption:

- *Mobile interaction* breaks the assumption that interaction means a user is primarily stationary.
- *Multimodal interaction* breaks the assumption that interaction with computer systems primarily involves providing input via one modality and receiving output via another modality, such as a visual display.
- *Ubiquitous computing* breaks the assumption that users must command computers to get things done. Ubiquitous computing exploits context sensing to enhance and automate interactions for the user.
- *MR and tangible interaction* break the assumption that virtual reality (VR) and physical reality are separate.

Paper Example 29.0.1: An early vision of ubiquitous computing

Weiser presented a prominent vision of going beyond desktop computing in a paper published in *Scientific American* [879]. Weiser outlined three types of ubicomp systems that had been developed by him and his colleagues at Xerox Parc. They envisioned that computing should come in different sizes, each suitable for a particular task. Weiser noted that in any given room, there are hundreds of differently sized writing and display surfaces. He focused on three scales (viz.tabs, pads, boards) and stated: "Look around you: at the inch scale include wall notes, titles on book spines, labels on controls, thermostats and clocks, as well as small pieces of paper. Depending upon the room you may see more than a hundred tabs, ten or twenty pads, and one or two boards."

An example of a tab-sized system is ParcTab [872], shown in the following figure (left). The ParcTab had a 6 cm × 4 cm monochrome display that could be used with a pen and a dedicated input alphabet. The ParcTab could also be used with just one hand, controlled by three buttons on the side. It was made possible by innovations in low-power consumption and networking protocols. The ParcTab was used, for instance, as a remote pointer in meetings, for impromptu voting, and for paging people depending on their context.

The ParcPad is shown in the following figure to the right (photo used with permission from PARC, part of SRI International). This device was connected to other devices via a radio network and had a stylus with multiple buttons. In contrast to today's tablets, the vision of the ParcPad was to be a scrap computer that could be picked up and used when needed. Just as few people carry loose, partially used pieces of paper, the ParcTab was intended to lie around and be grabbed when needed.

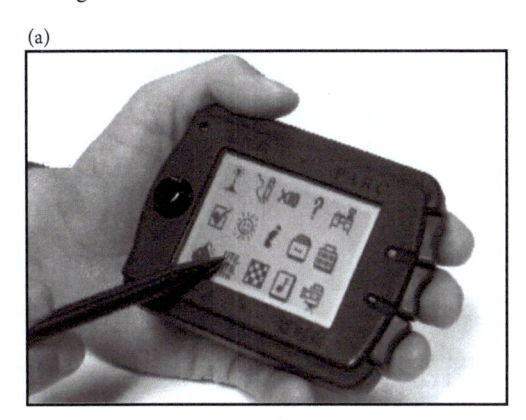

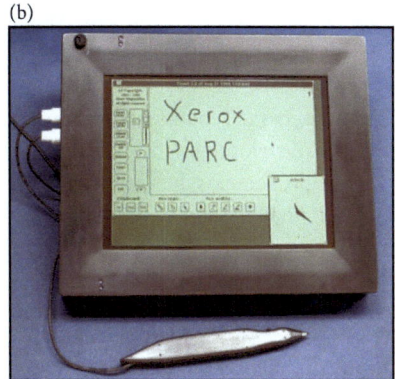

(a) (b)

An example of a board-based vision is LiveBoard [225]. LiveBoard supported wireless pen input and a back-projected screen of about 120 cm × 80 cm. The Tivoli application [647] shown in the following figure supported informal meetings around the LiveBoard (photo from [548]. Tivoli supported issuing commands with gestures and allowed multiple users to interact at once. In addition, Tivoli allowed the simultaneous sharing of content with other Tivoli applications in other places.

These three systems were influential not only in human–computer interaction (HCI) research but in computer science in general, as they were backed by a vision that was technically advanced at the time and were extensively used by the researchers themselves.

29.1 Mobile user interfaces

Smartphones, interactive mobile computers, made their explosive entry into the consumer market almost two decades ago. What few know, however, is that HCI research on the topic was ahead of this development by two decades. The topic was brought to the attention of the research community ahead of the curve at the beginning of the 1980s. In 1983, when the personal computer was making its way into the consumer market, Norman anticipated the development of computers with a lower form factor. He extrapolated a trajectory of improvements in computing power and discussed the implications for trade-offs in interaction that designers must face. His keynote at the ACM Conference on Human Factors in Computing, CHI, in 1983 [597, p. 9] ended with an insightful speculation about its consequences:

> New developments in technology are moving computer systems in several conflicting directions simultaneously. Workstations are getting more powerful, with large memories, large, high resolution screens, and with very high communication bandwidths. These developments move us toward the ability to present as much information as is needed by the user with little penalty in time, workspace, or even memory space. At the same time, some machines are getting smaller, providing us with briefcase sized and handheld computers. These machines have great virtue because of their portability, but severe limitations in communications speed, memory capacity, and amount of display screen or workspace.

Norman outlined challenges to user interfaces due to the radically different form factor and computational capabilities of the mobile computer:

> Just as workstations are starting to move toward displays capable of 1000 line resolution, showing several entire pages of text, handheld computers move us back toward only a few short lines—perhaps 8 lines of 40 characters each—and communication rates of 30 eps (300 baud). The major differences between workstations and handheld computers relevant to the tradeoffs discussion are in the amount of memory, processor speed and power, communication abilities, availability of extra peripherals, and screen size: in all cases, the handheld machine has sacrificed power for portability. Because the same people may wish to use both handheld machines and workstations (one while at home or travelling, the other at work), the person may wish the same programs to operate on the two machines. However, the interface design must be different, as the tradeoff analyses of this paper show.

Norman made an important observation about the changing form factor. A small size accentuates the trade-off he saw in desktop computing between the available workspace and the menu size. Consider, for example, a social media application that you use. How much of the screen estate is dedicated to general menu options (e.g., "Camera," "Post") compared to the space dedicated to reading and editing posts? If you were to add one general menu option, where would you add it? The larger the menu needed to navigate an application, the less workspace is left for the actual application. Any designer who designs for mobile use must figure out how to share the display space between dynamically changing and static elements.

The first technical innovations in this space occurred in 1969, when E. A. Johnson introduced the patented capacitive screen. This patent laid the foundation for the touchscreen we use on smartphones today. In 1972, Kay released a concept design of a mobile computer called the Dynabook (Figure 1.5) [45]. One can appreciate Dynabook by considering how computers were used then: via textual terminals that accessed a mainframe. By contrast, Dynabook was a media-rich networked computer that one could carry. It had a GUI and multimedia capabilities. Although the concept inspired laptop computers, the first working prototype of Dynabook—as it was envisioned—was presented almost 20 years later, largely because the concept was significantly ahead of the technology of its time. GRiD Compass, a laptop computer presented by Moggridge, was one of the first portable computers.

29.1.1 Characteristics of the mobile user interface

Compared to the desktop computer, the most radical feature of the mobile computer is its size. While anyone can see this difference, its effect on interaction is subtle and far from trivial. Size affects almost all elements of interaction, from the way we select objects to the contexts of use, with significant implications for design.

Size affects the types of input and output that are offered. Commercially available smartphones utilize touchscreens, speech, and physical buttons for input. However, the market has seen a very rich palette of alternatives, many of which have been investigated in HCI research, including radar-based sensing (e.g., Google Soli), computer vision (e.g., eye tracking via a front-facing camera), and the stylus. Output devices are not limited to touchscreens. Mobile computers can use mobile projectors, and they can connect to head-mounted displays (HMDs) and glasses, on-body haptic actuators, and even other nearby pervasive displays. The modern smartphone also features a wide variety of sensors. These allow inferences to be made about the user's context and to take information into account in interaction. Commonly used sensing includes location sensing (e.g., GPS, wireless radio-based methods), gesture and motion sensing (e.g., accelerometer and gyroscope), audio and speech sensing (microphone), and light sensing (e.g., to detect if the phone is held against the ear). More exotic sensors are also available; some devices even offer thermal imaging.

The mobile computer takes advantage of the familiar GUI we find on desktop computers, although its design generally strives toward having fewer items. Design for mobile interfaces emphasizes *visual hierarchy*: using saliency and containment to communicate the most important areas, as discussed in Chapter 28.

Because the viewport is small, it requires specific interaction techniques (Chapter 26) to support elementary interactions, such as translation for scrolling and pagination for changing pages. Collapsible menus—such as hamburger menus, which open side menus when the user clicks designated icons—and widgets are common, whereas drop-down menus are rare. To save screen real estate for the workspace, text entry is only available in a specific mode. Certain interactions, like hover-overs, are not available. Spreadsheets, which require both workspace and data entry, are typically avoided on mobiles.

The most distinct characteristic of the mobile device is its portability. Mobile interaction often takes place while users are in transition: walking, commuting, or multitasking. This poses large and nontrivial challenges to both design and empirical research. The challenge for design is to make interactions usable across the various situations the user may encounter. In simple terms, the more situations a design can support, the more mobile it is. "Mobile first" refers to the design idea that a user interface that works well in mobile contexts will also work well in desktop settings, and design should therefore start from the mobile device.

29.1.2 Small-screen interaction

The small size of the computer poses nontrivial challenges in interaction. One challenge is the limited viewport size of the display. Consider navigating a map: The map is larger than what the display can present at any given time (viewport). It needs to offer a way to translate the viewport. Zooming in and out helps the user orient to the map and plan routes.

Another challenge is that fingers occlude the display. If you press a touchscreen with your fingertip, no matter how gently you try to do that, the area of contact is much larger than a single pixel. So, which pixel did you *intend* to select? Holz and Baudisch [350] asked participants to press a crosshair presented to them. They looked at which mental representation of the fingertip best predicted the recorded touchpoint. They found that the perceived features of the finger—especially its outline and the nail—predict where users intend to touch. Users perceive these features not from their viewpoint but from a hypothesized top-down perspective, like looking down from a 90-degree angle. This is shown in Figure 29.2. This leads to systematic biases in where the finger is pressing. However, because the bias is partially systematic, it can be captured in a model that can then be used to improve the precision of touchscreen sensing on the software side.

The problem of occlusion by fingers has been a continuous topic of research in the area of interaction techniques. Many techniques studied in the HCI literature are in use in commercial products. *Touch offset* warps the selection point from the inferred touchpoint to make it easier to select a small target. In text entry, the *caret* marks the location where characters will be inserted. *Caret offset* is the offset to the touch location in pixels. The *magnifying glass* is a mode in which the region of the display under the finger is zoomed in in a warped area of the display.

While the mobile interface may appear easy to use to many readers of this book, it is imperative to remember that its small physical size can pose serious accessibility issues. Interacting with small screens is often challenging for aging users and users with impairments. Aging is associated with impairments, such as those related to motor control, strength, and visual acuity. Arthritis and other physiological impairments may cause physical pain in fingers and wrists, making it difficult to operate a mobile device. Loss of visual acuity makes small text illegible. What may appear as a completely clear button to you can be illegible to others. Given the growing digitalization of services, the ability to operate small screens may accentuate differences between those who can and those who cannot participate in society. Interaction techniques that reduce these differences are an open topic in HCI research.

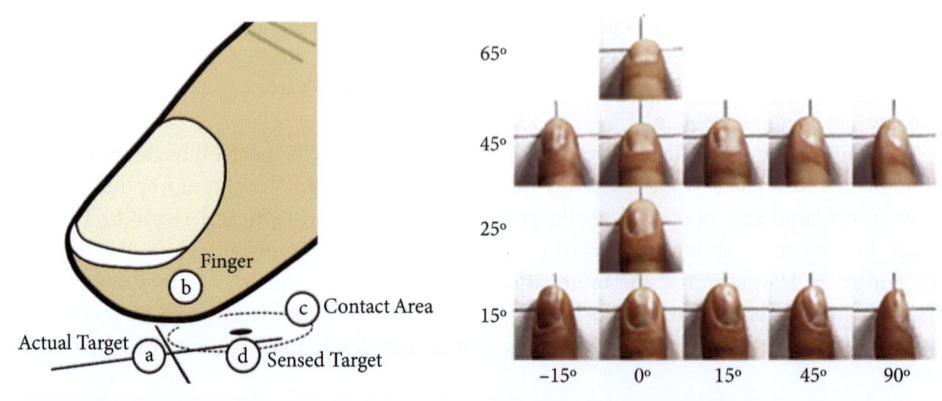

Figure 29.2 This study found that users use the perceived features of the finger—especially its outline and the nail—to touch a target, here marked with a crosshair. Users align the perceived features from a hypothesized top-down perspective. This leads to systematic biases that can be corrected in software using a proper model [350].

29.1.3 Mobility

Having a computer in your pocket enables new uses for computing that are not constrained physically in the way that desktop interaction is. *Mobility* is a fundamental modern phenomenon that presents opportunities for novel interactions. Supporting *mobile interaction* means supporting interaction that takes place while in physical transition between places.

The implications of mobility have been a topic of HCI research for two decades. *Mobile context* refers to relevant factors in a situation that may affect interaction with the computer. A defining aspect of mobility is *locomotion*, which refers to walking or movement by other means. Walking requires visual attention, which now needs to be shared between the mobile device and the environment. *Navigation* refers to finding one's way in an environment. This requires not only the ability to localize oneself but also the ability to choose where to go next.

While moving in an environment, users' capability to interact is degraded. *Environmental noise* refers to physical perturbations (e.g., tremble in a metro), visual noise (e.g., blinking lights), and auditory noise. Such factors can degrade a user's sensorimotor performance. *Multitasking* is a prevalent characteristic of mobile interaction. Users are always doing multiple things simultaneously. As we learned in Chapter 5, multitasking requires users to strategically allocate limited cognitive resources among tasks. Multitasking while mobile can be easily understood from the same perspective. We share our visual attention among events in the environment while using mobile devices. We plan and reason about routes when walking, which may disrupt our operation of a mobile device. Mobile contexts are also *social*. When mobile, we are constantly positioning ourselves physically and socially among people. Consider the way we queue, take lanes, or sit: There is an invisible order that we observe and affects the way we use our devices. All of these factors make mobile interaction *resource poor*: When designing an interface, we cannot expect visual attention and other resources to be fully deployed to the interface.

Just how resource poor is mobile interaction, and what does this mean in practice? In a study called "Interaction in 4-second bursts" [626], Oulasvirta and colleagues asked smartphone users to do information retrieval tasks while going through a route in Helsinki. The participants were asked to do regular tasks such as ordering coffee, taking the subway, and walking through busy streets. The authors set up a wearable minicamera system and recorded how their eyes moved using several camera views: one attached to their device, one attached to their chest, and one carried by the experimenter who shadowed them. Their striking finding was that users focused on mobile devices for short bursts of a few seconds at a time. The average glance duration across contexts was large, ranging from about 4 s when walking on a busy street to over 10 s when seated. Locomotion and social, dynamic environments were concluded to compete for the user's visual attention.

29.1.4 Habit formation and addiction

Are mobile computers addictive? Consider having two options right now: One option offers almost instant stimulation and requires almost no effort; the other requires effort and offers delayed gratification. Which option would you pick? This thought experiment demonstrates why mobile devices have the potential to form habits. Mobile devices offer us instant gratification at a very low cost. Right here, right now, it is rational to pick up the device and use it. However, the more you use the device, the less likely you are to find anything new in the news and social media feeds. In other words, mobile device use often has diminishing returns: The more you use it, the less you gain from it. It is the lure of immediate reward that causes addiction. The problematic use of smartphones has steadily increased in recent years. In part, this is thanks to the increasing availability of stimulating content, notably games and social media.

However, the full picture is more nuanced. Statistical methods such as structural equation modeling have been used to shed light on factors affecting compulsive smartphone users. In a questionnaire-based study of 325 individuals, Lee et al. [471] found that the compulsive usage of smartphones is affected by psychological traits. Users who experience high locus of control, anxiety about social interactions, materialism, and the need for touch were more prone to engaging in compulsive smartphone use. Recent research has also looked into "detoxification" applications and theory-based intervention programs to help users overcome problematic smartphone use.

29.1.5 Discussion

A significant change in empirical HCI methodology took place around the 2000s when the research focus shifted to mobile interaction: a change from laboratory conditions and controlled experiments to field studies [420]. Although obstacle courses and treadmills can be used to simulate mobility in the lab, field studies are argued to offer a more generalizable view of interaction, in particular by allowing everyday events to be included in observations. Mobility and its many different contexts entail a plethora of events and circumstances that are practically impossible to stage in laboratory conditions.

Field studies of mobile use have exposed two major phenomena associated with mobile devices. First, multitasking is a defining characteristic of mobile interaction. Users who multitask while driving are a safety risk; for instance, mobile devices are associated with 25% of collisions in the United States [28]. Second, the constant availability of mobile devices affects our life patterns; for example, it is associated with disturbances in sleeping habits and gaming addiction.

29.2 Ubiquitous computing

The term *ubiquitous computing*, or ubicomp, was coined by Weiser [879] to identify the emergence of a new form of computing. Paper Example 29.0.1 describes some of the early systems developed by Weiser and his colleagues in more detail. Weiser defined ubicomp as follows:

> Ubiquitous computing names the third wave in computing, just now beginning. First were mainframes, each shared by lots of people. Now we are in the personal computing era, person and machine staring uneasily at each other across the desktop. Next comes ubiquitous computing, or the age of calm technology, when technology recedes into the background of our lives.

Two parts of this definition are important. The first part suggests that computing needs to scale differently from mainframes and desktop computers. Rather than catering to one device, ubicomp assumes and designs for many interconnected devices. Rather than a system for one user, it assumes the system is for many users. Finally, rather than being limited to the desktop, it spreads to encompass larger environments (e.g., rooms, homes, cities).

The other key part of the definition of ubicomp proposes that technology needs to recede into the background of our lives; in other words, technology should be calm. Similarly, other researchers have talked about technology that is unremarkable [824], invisible [601], or disappearing [799]. The idea is that computing becomes physically integrated with our surroundings in addition to becoming cognitively less prominent. Information should be delivered to the right place and at the appropriate time.

Ubicomp has been enabled by advances in computing, particularly networking, miniaturization, and energy-efficient sensors and processors. Fulfilling the vision of ubicomp continues to raise challenges for research and development in computing. Nevertheless, the focal point of this section is how ubiquitous computing has affected user interfaces.

Four principled differences stand out when comparing ubiquitous computing to desktop computing. First, input and output become *embedded* in the environment. Second, *context awareness* emerges: Sensor data may be used for recognizing what users are doing or in which context the interaction takes place. Third, interaction becomes partially *implicit*, aiming to draw on users' natural ways of engaging with each other and the world. In other words, users may not need to give explicit commands to a computer, which, thanks to context awareness, may trigger actions on its own. Fourth, the substrates of the user interface change from the desktop and its well-known organization to objects, homes, classrooms, and the world. In short, computing becomes *smart*. The following sections outline these different ways of thinking about user interfaces and summarize their benefits and drawbacks.

29.2.1 Embedded input and output

Ubicomp extends the types of input used for user interfaces significantly beyond those used for desktop computers. As computing multiplies and is merged with the environment, we get an increasingly varied and fine-grained set of inputs related to users. These inputs may come from sensors embedded in objects, sensors distributed in the environment, or devices carried by users.

For example, consider the ActiveBadge system [871]. This early ubicomp system was produced at a time when wireless networks did not exist, telephones were rarely portable, and a common way of contacting people was to use a pager, a device that simply made a sound and showed a number when somebody wanted to chat with you. By contrast, ActiveBadge transmitted a brief, unique infrared signal every 15 seconds. This could be picked up by a sensor network and be used to locate an individual wearing the badge in a particular room within a building.

Many other types of input have been proposed since the 1980s. Similar to research on mobile computing, this has concerned the location of devices or the user. For instance, Marquardt et al. [519] captured the proximity of users to devices. They showed how to capture and use a person's distance from a display to modify the contents of the display. Cohn et al. [163] sensed electromagnetic noise using the human body as a receiving antenna to recognize body gestures as input.

It is not only input that may be embedded in the environment; *output devices* may also be embedded in the environment. The key idea here is to design hardware that allows information to be displayed to the user in a calm manner. Such output has been called ambient media [375] or peripheral displays [525]. Typically, there is no interaction possible with such displays; they merely present information.

An early example of using embedding output in the world was Jeremijenko's Dangling String, described by Weiser and Brown [880]. This is a 2.5-m art piece made of plastic that hangs from an electric motor mounted on a ceiling. The motor moves the plastic based on the amount of data being transmitted over the network: "A very busy network causes a madly whirling string with a characteristic noise; a quiet network causes only a small twitch every few seconds."

Another example is AmbientRoom [375]. AmbientRoom uses light, shadow, sound, and airflow to present information in the periphery of users' attention. For instance, one may be interested in monitoring a product that has just been launched on a web site. Each view of the product's web page may be presented as the sound of raindrops. If the soundscape changes from no rain to heavy rain, one may wish to investigate this change.

29.2.2 Context awareness

One of the main innovations in HCI developed through ubicomp research is techniques for *context awareness*. A computer system is context-aware "if it uses context to provide relevant information and/or services to the user, where relevancy depends on the user's task" [190, p. 5]. Desktop computers have little sense of context, but with new sensors and new modalities, we can characterize users, their activities, and their tasks.

Some contexts may be defined in a straightforward manner. For example, the geographical location of a user can make it clear whether the user is at home or at work. However, many other types of context are difficult or impossible to define. Schmidt et al. [740] identified two types of context. *Human factors* concern (1) information about the user, such as their emotional state or their habits, (2) the social environment of the user, such as the collocation of other people, and (3) the user's task. Information on the *physical environment* includes (1) the aforementioned location, (2) infrastructure, such as nearby resources for computation or communication, and (3) the physical conditions, such as noise and light. Each of these may be sensed and used in context-aware applications. Human factors are often hard to infer from sensor data, as they constitute latent (unobservable) mental events. Hence, interactions should be designed in such a way that the system's actions can be configured and corrected by the user.

In other cases, we need to conduct a sophisticated analysis of input to infer the context. A large portion of this work concerns *activity recognition*, that is, inferring the activities of people based on input data. For example, Fogarty et al. [247] wanted to recognize activities in the home without the cost of instrumenting all the rooms in a house. They deployed low-cost microphones on the cold and warm water pipes and on the drains. From the microphones, the authors trained classifiers that could predict which appliances were used, which parts of the bathrooms were used, and when something was being done in the kitchen. Sometimes, activity recognition concerns mental phenomena such as "being busy" or "being stressed." Other examples of activity recognition include detecting when smartphone users are bored [655] or lying [559].

Acting on context can be done in at least three ways [190, 740]:

- Services may run automatically or proactively based on users' context. For example, home lighting can be changed based on whether the user is working or cooking.
- Depending on the context, different information or services may be offered to the user. The ActiveBadge system mentioned earlier [871] used context to change when and how calls were put through: "Most people would prefer not to take unexpected telephone calls when they have just been called into their boss's office; others might not want to receive calls if they are in the lunch room between 12 and 1pm."
- Context may be tagged so that it can be acted upon by the user. In the Classroom 2000 system, for example, university lectures were recorded alongside whiteboard markings [3]. This integrated resource capturing and tagging produced a rich set of lecture notes. Later work has focused on so-called life logging, that is, the integrated capturing and tagging of everything an individual experiences. For instance, the *Forget-me-not* system

Table 29.1 Sample questions for adapted from [59, p. 417].

Question	Challenge	Possible problems
How do I address one or more of many possible devices?	How to disambiguate signal-to-noise? How to disambiguate the intended target system? How to not address the system?	No response, unwanted response
How do I know the system is ready and attending to my actions?	How to embody appropriate feedback so that the user can be aware of the system's attention; how to direct feedback to the zone of user attention?	Wasted effort, unintended actions, privacy and security concerns
How do I know the system is doing or has done the right thing?	How to select objects? How to show the system state? How to bind actions to objects?	Few operations possible, failure to do actions, unintended actions
How do I avoid mistakes?	How to control or cancel actions? How to intervene when users make obvious errors?	Unintended actions, unintended results, inability to recover state

shows the user daily information on whom they met, which documents they printed, and which calls they made.

29.2.3 Natural and implicit interaction

A main point of departure for many ubicomp systems is that interaction should be *natural* in its context. Thus, much work on input using gestures, movement, and speech has been carried out. One characteristic of interaction styles in ubicomp is that they become *implicit*. In GUIs, users give explicit commands; by contrast, in ubicomp, much interaction is command-free, using sensed input. As such, most concerns around interaction techniques for ubicomp revolve around whether users feel like the agents behind interactions and whether it is clear to them that they are indeed interactions. For instance, many people struggle with automated lighting, waving their arms to make the light go on and wondering why the light gets switched off while they are still in a room. Bellotti et al. [59] offered a set of questions about implicit interaction in ubicomp systems (Table 29.1).

29.2.4 Is implicit interaction realistic?

Although ubicomp has been researched since the 1990s, it is still an active area of research. The main benefit from HCI's point of view is that computers can be used in everyday contexts as opposed to dedicated workspaces. While Weiser's tabs, pads, and boards are already a reality, the stronger vision—implicit interaction—has proven difficult to realize. Recognizing from sensor data what a user does or wants has turned out to be very hard. Whenever a prediction fails, the user must have a way to correct or disable the system. Moreover, all sensing systems can also be used for commercial and even adversarial purposes, such as monitoring users. The user pays the price for failure, be that in terms of wasted effort or loss of privacy. If a system's benefits do not justify its costs, users may be reluctant to use it. Such concerns have led researchers to look at the *intellegibility*, *controllability*, and *personalizability* of ubicomp systems. However, despite some successful cases, no general solution has been found to these challenges.

> **Paper Example 29.2.1: The challenge of sensing complex states**
>
> One goal of ubicomp has been sensing, including the internal states of people. The research area of affective computing has focused on sensing human affect and adapting interactive systems based on the sensed information. If you recall the chapter on emotion (Chapter 7), you will remember that theories of human emotion are complex. Moreover, correctly sensing aspects of emotion (e.g., core affect) requires significant effort.
>
> Picard et al. [654] explored how to decode physiological signals from a user into predictions of the user's affective state. The authors were particularly interested in exploring the robustness and variability of the sensing methods. To that end, they collected about a month of data from a person who tried to experience particular emotions. The person was asked to go through eight emotions in turn, including anger, hate, grief, and joy.
>
> While the person tried to experience the emotions, four measures were collected: (1) facial muscle activity, (2) blood pressure, (3) skin conductance, which increases with sweat (e.g., on parts of the hands), and (4) respiration rate. Based on these measures, the authors developed a variety of models for accurately predicting emotions, mitigating the variation in emotions across days. Although affective computing is still difficult, this study was an early demonstration that some variation in measures can be dealt with.
>
> Note that Picard et al. [654] used a single participant, which highlights that HCI research does not require many participants. In this case, the strength of the data is that it spans many weeks.

29.3 Tangible user interfaces

Desktop user interfaces, in particular the GUI, use a generic input device (often a mouse), have a single user controlling that mouse, and employ a digital representation of the content that is interacted with. During the late 1980s and early 1990s, an increasing number of researchers found this form of user interface fundamentally limited. Wellner et al. [882, p. 24] expressed the limitation as follows:

> We live in a complex world, filled with myriad objects, tools, toys, and people. Our lives are spent in diverse interaction with this environment. Yet, for the most part, our computing takes place sitting in front of, and staring at, a single glowing screen attached to an array of buttons and a mouse. Our different tasks are assigned to homogeneous overlapping windows. From the isolation of our workstations we try to interact with our surrounding environment, but the two worlds have little in common. How can we escape from the computer screen and bring these two worlds together?

Tangible user interfaces were developed in response to this question. The ambition was to make the interaction with computers more physical in both input and output. The Bricks system supported input through physical manipulation and output projected on a desk [244]. This system supported what the authors called graspable interaction; later, the predominant way of talking about such interfaces became tangible user interfaces. In the system, virtual objects (e.g., a window) could be selected and subsequently moved using a physical handle (called a brick). The authors described a drawing application, GraspDraw, with two active bricks connected to a computer with cables. Those bricks can be used for drawing, making the control of GraspDraw more physical and allowing for two-handed interaction.

Compared to desktop computing, this system transforms drawing into a physical two-handed activity. It was one of a series of systems that showed that the vision outlined in the quote was within reach. Another well-known example is Durrell Bishop's concept of a marble answering machine. It represented voice messages on a phone as marbles, physically illustrating the number of incoming messages and allowing the user to manipulate each message physically.

29.3.1 Elements of tangible user interfaces

Tangible user interfaces change most components of the user interface (e.g., devices, interaction techniques, representations, and substrates). Input devices are typically physical objects that are sensed to use their position and orientation as input. This may involve using radio frequency identification tags that are embedded in objects, tracking recognizable visual markers (so-called fiducials, for instance, tracked from beneath a surface), or sensing from inside an object (for instance, based on the proximity to other objects). For example, reacTable allows physical objects that represent samples and filters to be placed and tracked on a tabletop display using a marker under the object [394]. Common output devices include projectors, which show digital content amid physical objects, and horizontal displays, on which physical objects may be placed (e.g., reacTable). Output may also be realized through the actuation of real-world objects. Greenberg and Kuzuoka [291] placed small figurines on top of a servo motor; the way the figurines were facing reflected the presence or absence of remote co-workers. In Madgets, output from the computer may be sent to physical widgets that can be electromagnetically moved around on a tabletop [881]. In these cases, the physical widgets enable the user to control the virtual content *and* the virtual content may control the positioning of the widgets, thereby combining input and output.

A key goal of interaction techniques for tangible user interfaces is to mimic interactions with physical objects. Fishkin referred to this as a metaphor of action. For instance, rotating a scan of the brain on a display may be accomplished by rotating a fist-sized model of a head [342]s. The IO brush allows users to pick up visuals from their surroundings using a brush-like device with an embedded camera [721]. Users may then use those visuals to draw. Interaction techniques may also use constraints imposed by the physical world to steer interaction. In the marble answering machine, a small dent in the machine indicates and constrains where marbles may be placed. In Pico, actuated objects could be constrained in where they could move by the user's hands and physical props such as elastic bands between objects or physical barriers [643]. Finally, some interaction techniques have been modeled over combinations of physical objects. For instance, objects may be placed on top of each other, next to each other, or assembled as an interaction. Topobo allowed users to snap together physical objects to create new forms and record the movement of those forms for later playback [686]. Such constructive assembly is a widely used interaction style in tangible user interfaces to support learning. Interaction styles may couple input and output more or less tightly; Fishkin called this the degree of embodiment. For instance, the model of the head previously mentioned is coupled to output on a display (distant embodiment), whereas IlluminatingClay uses clay as both input and output (full embodiment) [660]. In the latter case, interaction techniques ensure that physical objects simultaneously act as representations and as controls [837].

The representation of information in tangible user interfaces is shaped by it being bound to physical spaces and objects. The physical objects may be generic, such as the marbles in the marble answering machine. In Fishkin's terminology, this is a question about the metaphor of the noun or the shape of the object; bricks use no metaphor and depend on convention or learning. Generic objects allow the user to couple physical objects to interface objects or actions; Holmquist et al.

[347] called such objects containers since they may represent any kind of information. Generic objects may be augmented or annotated with information to help distinguish them from each other. The physical objects may also be non-generic; Holmquist et al. [347] called such objects tokens. For instance, in the urban planning system Urp, users provide input by moving physical architectural models on a table surface [840]. The models and their movements help calculate the shadows for arbitrary times of day, and the output is given by projecting them back over the models. Physical objects may also represent actions. The bricks serve as generic representations of actions such as move and rotate.

Perhaps the most prominent characteristic of tangible user interfaces is that the substrate of the interface is the physical world. Hornecker and Buur [359] argued that "tangible interaction is embedded in real space and interaction therefore occurs by movement in space" [p. 439]. Thereby, computing is moved out of the computer, and the social and spatial aspects of the world become key parts of the interaction. In many projects, the real-world substrate has been tabletops, such as in Urp and graspable user interfaces. Many visions of tangible computing suggest using the real world to embed information. Ishii and Ullmer [375] listed as a characteristic of tangible user interfaces the "use of ambient media such as sound, light, airflow, and water movement for background interfaces with cyberspace at the periphery of human perception" [p. 235]. While this idea has been widely explored, it does not mean that any part of an interface can be physically manipulated.

29.3.2 Models of tangible user interfaces

Figure 29.3 shows a simple model of tangible user interfaces [837]. This model was formulated in opposition to a prominent model used in GUIs called model-view-controller (MVC); see Chapter 38 for details. In MVC, the model is independent of the user interface and manages the data and logic of the system. The view makes information accessible to the user, typically in a visual form in GUIs. The controller takes the input from the user and uses it to affect the model or the view. Thus, views and controls are logically separated.

Another model is MCRpd, which stands for model-control-representation (physical and digital). Compared to MVC, this model plays a similar role concerning the digital content of the system; however, the view component is replaced by representations. These may be physical (e.g., bricks) or digital (e.g., video, audio). Unlike in MVC, the representations are always in the physical domain. Finally, the control component of the interface is always fully physical. Physical representations serve both to reflect the state of the digital model and as mechanisms for interactive control.

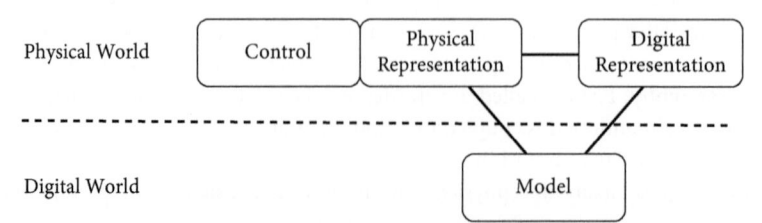

Figure 29.3 A model of tangible user interfaces by Ullmer and Ishii [837]. The physical world reflects the digital model as both digital and physical representations. The physical representations serve as controls for the digital model.

29.3.3 Pros and cons of tangible user interfaces

Tangible user interfaces have many benefits over other types of user interfaces; see [759] for an extensive review.

Tangible user interfaces leverage fundamental human skills of using our hands and bodies for thinking and acting. For instance, early experiments with the Bricks interface showed that participants were faster with the tangible user interface, had fewer difficulties in switching between tools because the tools were physically represented, and could work in parallel by relying on hand–eye coordination and proprioception. This is also evident in the many tangible projects that explore learning. Tobopo, for instance, leveraged manual skills in assembly to facilitate interaction. Tangible user interfaces leverage our understanding of physics and our body awareness and skills [381], enhancing learnability and immediate usability.

Tangible user interfaces offer multiple devices for input. This enables the simultaneous use of multiple devices, either via two-handed interaction or by multiple people. On a desktop computer, people would have to take turns (or time-multiplex); in tangible user interfaces, they can act simultaneously (or space-multiplex). For instance, reacTable allows multiple users to simultaneously manipulate sound effects and samples thanks to its round shape and multiple tokens [394]. This improves social awareness and skills [381].

Tangible user interfaces use specific physical objects rather than generic input devices. In that way, what the objects do and how to use them are more readily apparent to users. This means that actions are easily discoverable and that the gulf of execution is lessened by the specificity of the physical objects.

Tangible user interfaces integrate control and representation. Thus, the control always reflects the digital model. Thereby, feedback is integrated and direct. In tangible user interfaces, there are rarely mapping issues thanks to this direct integration.

Tangible user interfaces also have limitations. They come with the limitations of being tied to physical objects: There may be only one instance of an object, they may be lost, and they may take up all the workspace or otherwise result in clutter. While these sound like practical concerns, the specificity of physical representations imposes severe restrictions on how well tangible user interfaces work for actual tasks.

Moreover, tangible user interfaces do not support abstraction well. Most operations occur via direct manipulation and share the limitations of that style of interaction, such as not allowing abstract operators (e.g., wildcards) or syntax-based manipulations. This limits their expressivity, that is, how much may be expressed in a command, as well as their scalability, that is, how many objects they can work with. Perhaps this is the reason why ultimate performance with tangible user interfaces remains low.

A third issue is that tangible interfaces need to fully align virtual and physical models. The issue here is to make physical models accurately and quickly reflect changes in physical models, for instance, with respect to the position of an object. This issue is also related to retaining the properties of physical objects while using them to control digital models.

The development and evaluation of tangible user interfaces are active research fields, and there is strong community involvement in advancing the vision described at the beginning of this section. For some recent examples, see the papers and prototypes published at the annual Conference on Tangible Embedded and Embodied Interaction.

29.4 Mixed reality

Mixed reality refers to user interface technology that mixes virtual and real content to create a new, augmented experience that is interactive and appears authentic to the user. The two defining aspects of MR are (1) a programmatic association between virtual content and the real world and (2) an interactive display of that association.

Figure 29.4 shows the first VR system built by Sutherland and Sproull. The system, called the Sword of Damocles, as it hung over the head of the user, was built in 1968 and was an inspiration for all future MR applications based on HMDs. Sutherland described his vision as follows:

> Don't think of that thing as a screen, think of it as a window, a window through which one looks into a virtual world. The challenge to computer graphics is to make that virtual world look real, sound real, move and respond to interaction in real time, and even feel real.

The developed system consisted of a headband with cathode-ray tubes used to project to two lenses. The glasses showed vector graphics, such as a molecule or a virtual room, and the camera view was updated when the user moved. The key innovation was that the head position of the user was tracked and linked to the position of the camera in the virtual world. The authors argued that rapid response to the movement of the head is a more important requirement for creating the illusion of three-dimensionality than having authentic stereoscopic cues [808, p. 757]:

> The image presented by the three-dimensional display must change in exactly the way that the image of a real object would change for similar motions of the user's head. Psychologists have long known that

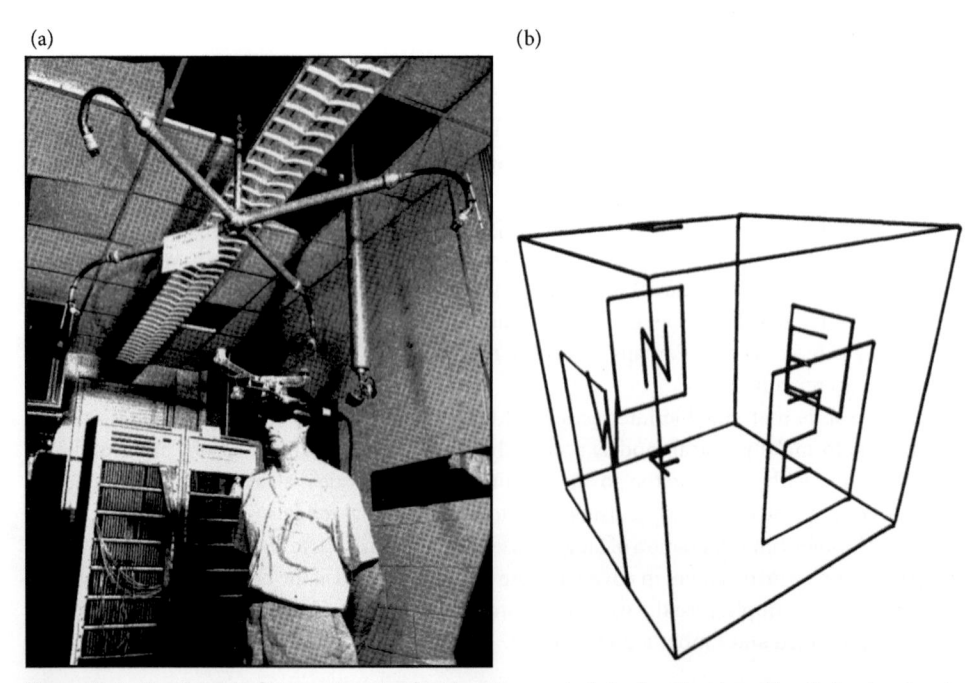

Figure 29.4 The Sword of Damocles, the first head-mounted display developed by Sutherland and Sproull in 1968.

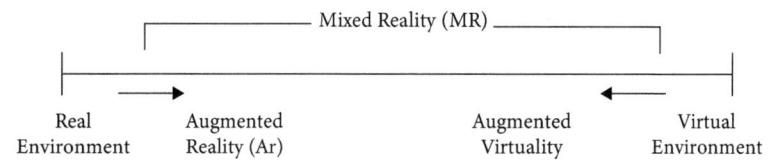

Figure 29.5 The reality continuum by Milgram and Kishino [543].

moving perspective images appear strikingly three-dimensional even without stereo presentation; the three-dimensional display described in this paper depends heavily on this "kinetic depth effect."

Presenting stereoscopic depth with glasses only became possible much later. Beyond the prototype was a bigger vision of a computer display as a window to a virtual world. As the virtual world was responsive and presented in an immersive way, it felt real.

In MR, the relationship between the virtual and the physical is understood as a graded one; it is not an all-or-none choice. The *mixed reality continuum* of Milgram and Kishino was an attempt to define this relationship more precisely:

> Our objective is to formulate a taxonomy of the various ways in which the "virtual" and "real" aspects of MR environments can be realised. The perceived need to do this arises out of our own experiences with this class of environments, with respect to which parallel problems of inexact terminologies and unclear conceptual boundaries appear to exist among researchers in the field.

The continuum is presented in Figure 29.5. At one extreme is the real environment; at the other is the virtual environment. The zone between them is called mixed reality, which is further divided into two subregions: augmented reality (AR) and augmented virtuality.

According to Milgram and Kishino, the user interface, especially the way it couples display and the tracking of the user's motion, has a decisive role in the experience of virtual environments. Accordingly, they divided interface technology into six classes:

1. **Class 1:** Monitor-based, non-immersive displays, "windows on the world." Consider, for example, a "magic lens" or a see-through view on a mobile device that overlays virtual information on a camera viewfinder.
2. **Class 2:** Video displays as in Class 1 but implemented using immersive HMDs rather than monitors.
3. **Class 3:** HMDs with optically implemented see-through capability. Graphics are superimposed on see-through glasses.
4. **Class 4:** Same as Class 3 but with a video-based see-through.
5. **Class 5:** Completely graphic environments to which video "reality" is added.
6. **Class 6:** Completely graphic environments in which are embedded physical objects from the user's environment.

The continuum was instrumental to the establishment of AR and VR as active research topics. It helped us understand the design space as well as the associated engineering challenges. For example, in Classes 2–4, *motion tracking* and *registration* are challenging. In The Sword of Damocles, both the head and hands were tracked. Sutherland stated that it would be important for the virtual environment to not only support passive viewing but also allow users to manipulate virtual objects directly with their hands. In some of their prototypes, hand positions were tracked with fishing lines connected to reels. While this solution appears crude, the technical problem of hand and finger tracking remains unresolved. The issue is that any inaccuracy in the *world coordinates* offsets the way the physical and virtual environments are registered. Consider, for example, petting a dog in VR with hands tracked by computer vision. If the tracker is several inches off, the hands as you feel them via proprioception will not feel like the ones that are shown on the display.

The continuum puts excess emphasis on the visual experience. Although MR is often about visual content, content may also be delivered through sound or haptics. For example, a virtual orchestra can be projected auditorily into a physical space; a haptic device on the finger can mimic virtual surfaces when touching them with the finger.

The interactive relationship between the real and the virtual can be more complex than that portrayed by the six classes. For example, *substitutional reality* refers to a relationship where an object in the physical reality is replaced or covered with a virtual one [774]. For example, a living room can be substituted with the command deck of a spaceship, or the couch can be overlayed with a virtual bench.

29.4.1 Virtual reality

Virtual reality refers to an interactive environment that responds to the user's actions, for example, via locomotion or camera control. A reality is more than just virtual content; it is usually understood as a space that binds content together. As a term, virtual reality is surprisingly old, from the 1980s. It is credited to Jaron Lanier, a computer scientist and an artist who worked at Atari Inc. with the team that invented the data glove. The first VR system, even if it was not called by that term, is attributed to Morton Heilig. His Sensorama was a multimodal simulator [328]. A user (or rather, a viewer) would sit down and put their head inside a large box that showed a 3D motion picture with smell, stereo sound, seat vibrations, and wind blowing in the air.

VR is a multidisciplinary topic drawing from computer science, electrical engineering, and psychology in addition to HCI. VR systems typically have some sensors (e.g., to track motion), effectors (e.g., displays), and a reality simulation (e.g., a world model in Unity). More precisely, a *VR system* is defined by seven features:

1. Blocking out sensory impressions generated by the real world (e.g., VR HMDs)
2. Continuously updated computer graphics creating a sense of immersion
3. Tracking of the user's position and orientation
4. Software for modeling the relationship between the virtual and the real
5. Synthesized sound and possibly haptic sensations (e.g., vibrating steering wheels for car games)
6. Input devices that enable interactions with virtual objects
7. Interaction techniques that substitute real interactions (e.g., hand movements).

Paper Example 29.4.1: Interacting with objects at a distance

A problem in VR and AR is that objects can be farther away than the user can reach. An early solution to tackle this problem was the *Go-Go* interaction technique [673].

The metaphor underpinning the technique is that the user's arm grows nonlinearly in VR when the user reaches out to touch, grasp, or otherwise interact with a virtual object that is out of the user's reach. When the user interacts within a set threshold, the virtual hand and the user's real hand are mapped to the same place. When the user extends their arm beyond the set threshold, their virtual arm starts to grow nonlinearly, allowing the user to reach virtual objects that are farther away than the user would be able to reach in reality.

The user's real hand position, mapped by the vector R_r in the diagram below, is mapped to a virtual hand position parameterized by R_v. Thus, R_r is the length of the user's real arm and the length of the vector R_r. The vector R_r points from the origin of the user's hand. R_v is the length of the user's virtual arm and the length of the vector R_v.

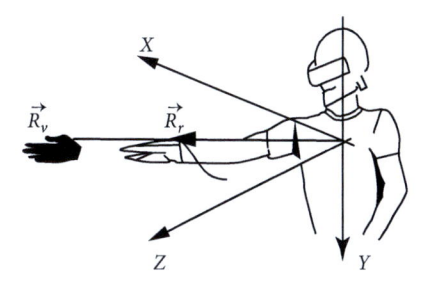

When the user moves their hand, the virtual hand is mapped differently depending on where the user's real hand is located in space. This mapping is governed by computing the length of the user's virtual arm (R_v) as a function F of the user's real arm (R_r), as described in Equation 29.1:

$$R_v = F(R_r) = \begin{cases} R_r & \text{if } R_r < D \\ R_r + k(R_r - D)^2 & \text{otherwise} \end{cases}. \quad (29.1)$$

There are two parameters in Equation 29.1. The first is k, which is a coefficient between zero and the unity controlling the nonlinear rate of expansion of the virtual arm. The second parameter, D, is the length that the user's real arm should be extended to for the virtual arm to start extending nonlinearly. This means the parameter D is a threshold. In the original paper, D is set to 2/3 of the user's real arm length. After the user extends the arm farther, the virtual arm starts to grow nonlinearly. This mapping between the placement of the virtual hand and the user's real hand is illustrated in the curve shown in the following diagram. Note that when R_r is below D, the mapping between R_r and R_v is linear; when R_r exceeds D, the mapping smoothly transitions from linear to nonlinear.

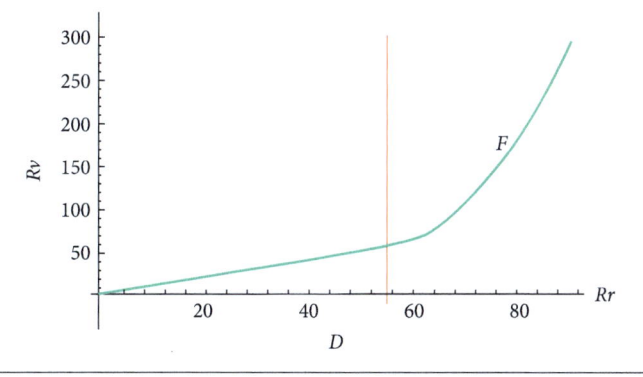

As for all interaction techniques, HCI research aims to innovate and study techniques that are performative, intuitive, and ergonomic. VR and AR pose an interesting opportunity: augmenting human capabilities to operate with objects in a way that might not be physically possible. Consider, for example, flying: MR makes it possible to transcend the limitations of the physical body. The related research topics are *camera control* and the *control of locomotion*. Several techniques have been proposed that take inspiration from the real world. In *egocentric motion*, the user's avatar is controlled by moving it in egocentric directions. In *warping*, the user moves by warping the body to a location by touching the destination. In *point-of-interest* control, the user selects an object (e.g., by tapping it) and the camera moves to the object.

Another challenge concerns manipulating and touching virtual objects that are beyond the physical reach of the user. For example, the *Go-Go* technique uses a dynamic control-to-display gain approach (see Paper Example 29.4.1). It applies a linear or nonlinear mapping that effectively warps the hand to a distant location. Moving the physical hand extends it to different locations depending on how far it is from the physical body. Nevertheless, it is an open problem how to manipulate distant objects efficiently. The issue is that the farther the object is from the viewpoint, the less perceptual information there is about it. Hence, the manipulation of distal objects requires some way of coupling camera control with interaction.

Applied psychology, particularly media psychology, has taken an interest in VR, proposing scientific constructs to measure how real it feels. *Presence* refers to the feeling of "being there" in the virtual world as opposed to being present in the real world. The formation of this experience is understood to consist of two steps. First, the virtual space must be mentally construed from perceivable cues, similar to how physical realities are construed. Second, the user must suspend disbelief—their disbelief about *not* being there in the virtual space—and experience being located in the virtual space.

Presence as a construct has become widely used in studies of VR systems, mostly as an index of how "good" the VR interface is. However, how to measure presence? The obvious idea is to let users self-report presence. However, such reports can be "colored" (biased) by confounds, such as the novelty effect or trying to please the experimenter. Therefore, self-reports should be accompanied by behavioral or physiological measures. For example, body convection can be used. Have you ever felt like actually falling in a VR game when getting to the edge of a cliff? In the cliff scenario, leaning back can be used as an index of how believable the VR world is.

A related research question in psychological research is that of *simulator sickness*, or the feeling of nausea during the use of VR applications. Simulator sickness is more prevalent among users who report being female [564]. According to one theory, sickness is caused by a mismatch between expected sensations and felt sensations [462]. Consider, for example, sitting in a virtual car when it accelerates. Your brain might expect you to experience a force on your body due to the acceleration, a change in the pressure felt against your back, and various interoceptive sensations such as feeling the acceleration "in your guts." However, the real-world sensations would be mismatched or missing. Reducing simulator sickness to a more universally acceptable level remains an open challenge.

29.4.2 Augmented reality

Augmented reality adds real-world content to a virtual environment (augmented virtuality) or virtual content to a real-world experience. Technically, this requires some tracking of the user's position in the world and the registration of virtual objects in real-world coordinates. An AR system, then, requires sensors that can help position (align) the user in the physical world. In addition, it requires computations to overlay (or augment) virtual information on a view of the physical world. The resulting augmented view can be presented via different media, such as HMDs, projection mapping (using a video projector to project graphics on real-world objects), handheld devices, and even contact lenses.

Creating the perception of touching an object is an open problem in AR systems. AR interactions require inferring the user's intentions; for example, which object does the user point at or touch? Moreover, a corresponding sensation must be created, for example, via haptic stimulation. Hand-worn systems such as gloves and exoskeletons are considered unhygienic and restricting. External systems, such as systems providing air-based or sound-based stimulation, are usually too weak to generate compelling sensations.

29.4.3 Pros and cons of mixed reality

The promise of VR is compelling and as timely as ever. It promises the possibility of being "virtually there" [457]. It is already substituting our real-world experiences of leisure and business. MR, on the other hand, promises to add virtuality to the real world around us, offering capabilities that are not physically possible.

MR has been developed over the past 50 years, alternating between periods of optimism due to novel hardware that made MR widely available and periods of pessimism about the fundamental limitations of this form of interaction. The pros and cons of MR are discussed extensively in the literature, which is overall optimistic for the following reasons:

- MR has revolutionized access to information. It can embed information in the real world in a useful form and precisely where and when it is needed.
- MR augments people. It allows us to do impossible things such as seeing through objects, breaking the limits of physical distance, and creating new means of social interaction that are not limited by physical space.
- MR enables new applications in education, medicine, and science for practice, training, and learning.
- MR changes perceptions. It allows us to take new perspectives on the world and learn about our environments and ourselves.

Are we far away from realizing these dreams? MR still faces a number of fundamental limitations. Current motion tracking technology is limited. One either has to accept a highly instrumented environment or inaccuracies that hamper the experience. Any offset, spatial or temporal, between the user's motion and the virtual character's motion will degrade performance and experience and may contribute to simulator sickness. Such offsets can also be caused by limitations of computer networks, whose performance affects the temporal discrepancy between the physical and the virtual.

For HCI research, there is a need to develop interaction techniques that are performative in 3D interactions, learnable, and ergonomic. Users get tired when lifting their arms a lot; in the worst case, they may become fatigued after only a few minutes of use.

29.5 Should we imitate reality or go beyond it?

In a classic paper, Hollan and Stornetta [346] raised an important question about communication systems. They were concerned that most work on such systems was based on a "belief in the efficacy of imitating face-to-face communication" [p. 199]. This belief could, for instance, be based on the idea that the richer the reproduction of the cues in proximate communication, the better the communication and the better the user interface; see media richness theory (Chapter 9).

The research reviewed in this chapter is to some extent based on the idea that we should imitate what people do without the involvement of interactive systems. For instance, the intent of reality-based computing to draw on environmental awareness and skills has led to strong systems. Natural interaction is also based on the idea that we should draw on what people find intuitive and immediate when designing user interfaces.

Hollan and Stornetta [346] pondered the limitations of this approach. In particular, they discussed whether communication technologies could ever bring us close to the feeling of being physically together. In doing so, they drew an analogy intended to show a way to think differently about the design of user interfaces:

> It is customary for a person with a broken leg to use crutches, but how odd it would be if they continued to use the crutches after their leg was restored to its natural condition. In contrast, one wears shoes because they provide certain advantages over our natural barefoot condition. Special purpose shoes, such as running shoes, are designed to enhance our best performance. Now crutches and shoes are both tools of a sort, but there is a difference. The crutch is designed specifically to make the best of a bad situation—to let someone hobble around until they are back in shape. On the other hand, shoes are to correct some of the problems of our natural condition, and, in the case of athletic shoes, to enhance our performance.

In that way, enhancing, compensating, and augmenting would be alternative ways to think about the role of user interfaces in relation to their users.

Much research has attempted to devise and implement user interfaces that do not imitate the real but attempt to move beyond it. Willett et al. [892] described how to use the idea of superpowers from science fiction to improve our perception, the bandwidth and acuity of our attention, and our ability to predict things. The idea is to leap beyond the natural abilities of people through interactive systems; mimicking reality is not the aim. Won et al. [911] allowed participants to control a third arm in VR by rotating their arm; participants learned to control the third arm effectively within five minutes.

In sum, mimicking reality is useful for technology development, including in HCI. Reality-based interaction provides a strong framework for thinking about such interactions. However, as a general strategy, the approach of mimicking reality is limiting; the argument of Hollan and Stornetta [346] is a strong reminder of why this is the case.

Summary

- In reality-based interaction, users' physical surroundings contribute to interaction either explicitly (by being represented in the interface) or implicitly (by affecting it via other factors). While mimicking reality is a great starting point, it also has limitations.
- In mobile interaction, physical surroundings not only cause perturbations and noise but also encourage users to multitask, which limits the attention they give to the device.

- In ubiquitous computing, sensor data are used to infer the user's context or goal with the aim of better embedding computers into everyday situations.
- In tangible interfaces, computations are associated with physical manipulations of physical objects.
- In MR interfaces, virtual content becomes associated with physical reality or vice versa, allowing for the "mixing" of content in novel ways.

Exercises

1. Understanding sensing systems. Pick a sensing system that you use regularly. Use the questions by Bellotti et al. in Table 29.1 to diagnose potential issues. Then, figure out how to improve the system.
2. Ubicomp. Choose a room and count the devices in it. Chart their interrelations. Has Weiser's dream, of the computer becoming ubiquitous, come true?
3. Natural interaction. Is mobile interaction natural? How about tangible interaction? What makes something "natural" to use?
4. Tangible interfaces. Tangible interfaces were touted as a breakthrough similar to direct manipulation and GUIs. However, tangible UIs have not found their way into everyday computing. Why?
5. Think about the last message you sent using your phone. Were you actually mobile at the time before, during, and after messaging? Which aspects of mobility are on or off?

Part VI

Design

30
Introduction to design

Look around you and choose an artifact. For example, grab your smartphone and unlock it. Everything you see—graphics, functions, applications, icons, content, widgets, and so on—has been designed. Someone has made an active decision about what functions to include and how they should look and feel. When "just" using something, we easily miss the fact that a considerable number of decisions have been made to define its look and feel. Every aspect, from high-level concepts to the smallest details, is the outcome of a series of design decisions.

Design matters to people. Yet, daily computer use is all too often cumbersome, unpleasant, or simply impossible for some of us. As we learned in the book part on understanding users (Part II), design affects the way we perceive, experience, remember, decide, and form habits. Design can be decisive for someone's ability to use something, and even small improvements in design can have a significant cumulative impact.

Design also matters for innovation and business. The most innovative companies produce a major part of the revenue from services and products that did not exist five years ago [828]. Design is also a central driver of the renewal of societies and economies. The design of services that are more lucrative, accessible, efficient, and fair is a key consideration in both industry and the wider society.

Based on these perspectives, the practice and processes of design in human–computer interaction (HCI) have developed to help pursue a variety of exploratory, critical, and artistic goals. Design is more than just designing visually appealing icons for software. The following examples and Figure 30.1 illustrate the breadth of design challenges in HCI.

- The development of design tools for users who lack the economic power and ability to influence the information systems they use [450]. These could, for instance, be low-cost ways to prototype future work situations.
- The design of a device that suggests topics for prayers to cloistered nuns [274]. This design raised questions about how to support spirituality and how to create a system that is sufficiently open to interpretation to meet the needs of the nuns.
- The design of media facades for buildings [179] with which people near the building can interact.
- The design of "ridiculous software," that is, software intended to get users to reflect on their relationship with software [773]. For example, the ATTN (for "attention") mobile app shows an empty screen that slowly dims to remind users of the scarcity of their attention.

For each of these situations, we know how to understand people in general (Part II) and assess their needs and wants (Part III). We might also know which interactions and user interfaces are suitable (Parts IV and V). In these situations, the challenge is to use our knowledge and appropriate methods to design new interactive systems; such design work is the focus of this part of the book.

Introduction to Human-Computer Interaction. Kasper Hornbæk, Per Ola Kristensson, and Antti Oulasvirta,
Oxford University Press. © Kasper Hornbæk, Per Ola Kristensson, and Antti Oulasvirta (2025).
DOI: 10.1093/oso/9780192864543.003.0030

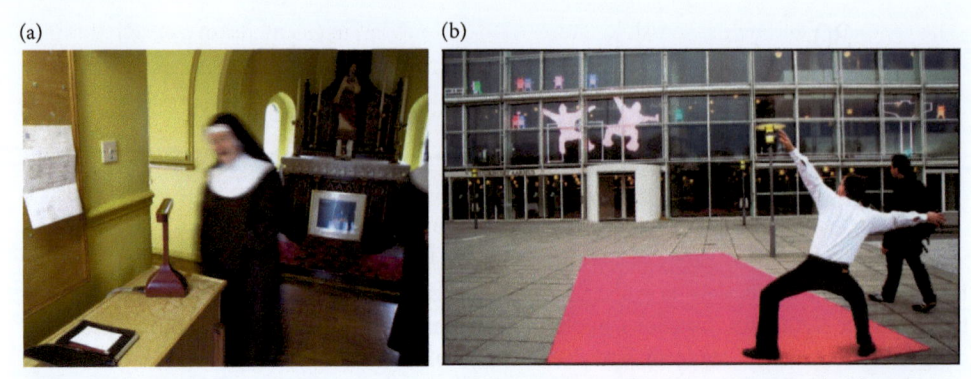

Figure 30.1 Some examples of design outcomes in the form of a prayer companion [274] and a media facade [179]. Behind these designs are specific design processes and different intentions.

Next, we discuss what design is and outline three central concerns in design: how to get ideas (Section 30.2), how to do design (Section 30.4), and how to think about design processes (Section 30.3). Each concern is discussed in further detail in the rest of this part of the book.

30.1 What is design?

What *is* design? In this section, we first discuss four common views of design and then discuss the idea that we can design interactions.

30.1.1 Four views of design

Design can mean many things. Here, we separate four meanings that are all important yet differ markedly.

First, design, as a noun, describes some artifact or plan that is the outcome of a design activity. We refer to this as *design as product*. At the end of a design project, designers arrive at some *ultimate particular*: a concept, plan, artifact, or something that realizes the idea in some form that can be tested [797]. This is what we consider when we think about the noun "design." The designer's imagination is materialized so that it can be assessed and considered. Such materializations, for instance, sketches on paper or wireframed graphical user interfaces in a design tool, also help designers think and are therefore essential aspects of design work. These materializations do not need to be actual products or services; there is a deeper, philosophical aspect to creation.

According to Gaver, ultimate particulars are about *possible worlds* [273]. To understand this concept, it is helpful to draw a contrast to the natural sciences: "The natural sciences are concerned with how things are. Design, on the other hand, is concerned with how things ought to be" [776, p. 5]. While we live in the present world, design can create an alternative reality. HCI aims to change the world through design. Since, in principle, anyone can come up with design ideas, design is not a privilege of professional designers. Simon noted the following [775, p. 67]:

> Everyone designs who devise courses of action aimed at changing existing situations into preferred ones. The intellectual activity that produces material artifacts is no different fundamentally from one that prescribes remedies for a sick patient or the one that devises a new sales plan for a company or a social welfare policy for a state.

The generation of oughts—possible futures—singles out design as an area of research. In other words, developing an idea of "the ought" is at the heart of design.

Second, design, as a verb, refers to the activity of designing. We refer to this as *design as process*. Cognitively, solving problems is a central challenge in design in addition to the creation of new ideas. Design requires decisions and plans. Designing an interactive system requires figuring out what the user interface should look like, how the user journey is structured, and so on. Each of these areas involves hundreds, if not thousands, of interconnected decisions. In other words, designers need to "get the design right." Designers' problem-solving is often characterized by extensive iteration, trial and error, and searching among possible solutions to problems. Sometimes, problem-solving can be tricky. For instance, Kyng [450] did early work on how to involve users who lack economic power and the ability to influence the information systems they use. This involves low-cost prototyping; Chapter 22 describes such prototyping activities in depth.

Third, the generation of possible worlds produces new knowledge. *Research through design* challenges the idea that design is just about creating artifacts or solving problems. Design can produce new and valuable knowledge [928]. This knowledge may be a novel perspective on a problematic situation, alternative futures, implications, or new insights about empirical phenomena. Such insights can not only trigger further empirical or theoretical research but also challenge previously held assumptions in the community. It is important to note that knowledge produced in research through design may not always take the shape we recognize and expect when approaching research from a "traditional" scientific angle. Paper Example 30.1.1 presents a research project that involved a particular method for design (design probes) and the creation of knowledge about the design for a complex phenomenon (the experience of menstruation).

Paper Example 30.1.1: Design probes

Curious Cycles is a research-through-design project that aims to encourage people to experience their menstruating bodies in new ways [122]. While the menstrual cycle can have dramatic effects on a person's well-being, people can be stigmatized when talking about it, leading to people concealing their struggles. If you wanted to transform the experience of menstruation through design, how would you do it?

The Curious Cycles kit, shown in the figure in this paper example box, is a *probe*. A design probe is a design method that involves sending a kit out in the wild to users and allowing them to engage with it without the presence of the researcher.

A kit invites participants to provoke, experience, and explore things in new ways in their lives as opposed to carrying out such activities in artificial circumstances created by a third party, typically the researcher. Some probes involve the collection of materials or memorabilia for further discussion with the researcher.

As a method, design probes purposefully exploit ambiguity, as participants have the freedom to interpret their experiences that emerge through use with the probes. Design probes seem particularly suitable for this research because they give the participants full control over what to try and what to share.

The kit was sent to five women. The purpose of the kit was to prompt participants to touch and explore their changing bodies during the cycle [122]. The kit consisted of a poster with a calendar for ovulation, the blood bank (a collection of menstruation samples collected on glass slides), the curious eye (a microscope), the reflection (a drawing kit for reflecting on the

continued

> **Paper Example 30.1.1: Design probes** (continued)
>
> vulva), the heat pad (a heating pad for exploring new sensations), and an account for sharing a (private) diary about the experience.
>
> The participants reported that they learned how to explore menstruation through touch. An unexpected finding was that some participants shared their materials with other participants, which triggered further understanding and improved self-knowledge [p. 344]:
>
>> Hannah's picture depicting a bloodstain on her underwear helped Emma feel more comfortable with her own experiences: "The first time I posted a picture of my blood I felt weird, but then I thought, oh why am I feeling this, it's just blood. [. . .] One girl posted bloody underwear and I was like what! that's so cool!"

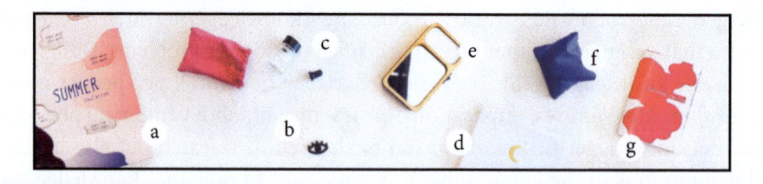

Fourth, design has transformative potential. We refer to this as *design as change*. Design is not only about producing tangible objects that you can touch and hold in your hand. Design can shake the world and get people to think and do things in new, better ways. Buchanan [108] viewed design as a means of *changing* culture and human experience. Design is not merely an application of existing principles but a continuous search for new meanings and values in human life. Designers are not just translators of wishes into artifacts; they are facilitators that catalyze changes in the world with technology.

This means that instead of aiming to fix problems, sometimes referred to as *solutionism*, design should aim to create new, *transformative possibilities*. Design can help challenge and rethink structures that limit us as humans. To achieve this, designers create narratives and interpretations of what something is or could be. For example, the Nintendo Wii was an entertainment gadget that transformed the concept of a video console to stimulate physical activity. The ridiculous software mentioned at the beginning of this chapter is another example, as it helps us reflect on and criticize the state of the art in mobile applications.

The bigger picture is that designers' thinking becomes political, as they need to take a valued position on what is desirable in life and what is not. According to this view, the most revolutionary possibilities in design may not be found through empirical observation since new possibilities are needed to shake the existing state of affairs and create a more desirable state of affairs.

30.1.2 Interaction design

Design has grown to become a large research area that includes design engineering, mechanical design, product design, industrial design, interior design, architecture, graphical design, service design, and interaction design. Within this space, HCI has two distinct characteristics: its focus on interactive technology and human-centeredness.

First, in HCI, design focuses on interactive technology. The area closest to HCI is called *interaction design*. The engineering of a network protocol for secure payment transactions is not an HCI topic, while the design of a user interface for those transactions is. Interaction design specializes in digital products, applications, and services but still shares the principles of design discussed in this part of the book.

Second, HCI is human-centered, which is not a primary concern in all areas of design or computer science. Being human-centered means that the primary success criteria in design must relate to the people who will use the artifact, and the choices made must be ethically sound and defensible. Fundamentally, design decisions should be based on an understanding of the users. User research, which we discussed in Part III, helps designers understand existing situations. It can generate knowledge about individuals and the broader sociotechnical context. However, design can also inform user research. By revealing new possibilities and questions, it can tell us what needs to be studied. In this sense, human-centered design is the meeting point of knowledge produced through user research, ideation, prototyping, and empirical evaluations with users.

To sum up, a central goal in interaction design is to create new *potential* for computing. To achieve that, designers need to create new relationships between artifacts, users, and contexts. This idea is illustrated in Figure 30.2. A designer produces an artifact based on design knowledge, including knowledge of the user and the context of use. However, the artifact only gains its meaning in the context in which it is actually used; this is when the potential of the artifact is realized. Thus, while design is about creating the concrete artifact, it is also about its potential, which creates interactions that can lead to desirable outcomes.

Elaborating on this view, Simon [775] distinguished the inner environment of the artifact, such as the parameters that define how an artifact behaves, and the outer environment, in which the artifact is used. When designing an interactive system, we can only design the inner environment, which should interact with the outer environment in some desirable way. The final artifact is, in some sense, a hypothesis about this interplay. This is a crucial point about design—no matter how well the artifact is controlled by the designer, there is always uncertainty about its potential when it is exposed to its context of use. Only evaluation (Part VIII) and, ultimately, deployment allow such uncertainty to be substantially reduced.

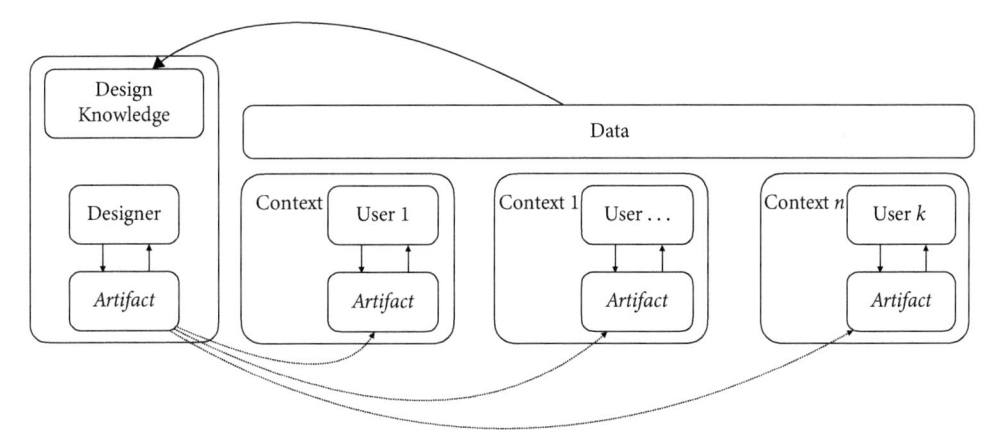

Figure 30.2 A simplified view of design is that the designer arrives at an artifact using their design knowledge and direct experiences with artifacts. Their design knowledge is captured as data informing the designer about possible contexts of use for particular users. The artifact can then be used in many contexts by many users. Some of these contexts, users, and uses are anticipated by the designer; others are not. Regardless, the potential of the design is realized in these contexts and by these users. There is fundamental uncertainty about such potential since the designer cannot anticipate all the contexts, users, and forms of use of the artifact.

Finding a role for design has been a central topic throughout the history of HCI as a field. The present understanding, mostly discussed in the area of interaction design, can be summarized into four rationales:

Improving: Design can improve the usability, accessibility, and experience of computing systems.

Creating: Design can create entirely new opportunities for people to use computing systems in contexts and ways previously not possible.

Informing: Design is the study of what is possible. By showing alternatives to the status quo, design informs decisions and creates the need for change.

Producing knowledge: Design not only applies HCI knowledge but is also necessary to evolve such knowledge. Knowledge about interaction can be advanced by testing ideas through interactive prototypes and designs.

It is also important to understand how design in HCI differs from engineering. Two aspects distinguish interaction design from engineering (Part VII). First, while problem-solving and creative ideation have a role in both, the emphasis in interaction design is on understanding problems and creating new ideas and artifacts. Colloquially, the focal point of interaction design is *knowing what to design* while engineering is more concerned with *knowing how to design*. Engineering aims to produce deployable artifacts that, demonstrably, have certain properties and qualities during use. In the next part, we learn about design engineering (Chapter 36), where the goal is to build an integrated system that embodies a design and can be deployed.

Second, interaction design can, but does not need to, commit to the use of the best methods available. Some designers consider themselves engineers, but they may also identify with creative professions and art. In design, theories and scientific methods are often perceived as primarily instrumental: They may provide inspiration and useful ideas, but they do not provide any attributable value beyond that. This is further discussed in the chapter on design practice (Chapter 32).

30.1.3 User-centered design

Human-centeredness is the idea that the primary motivation and aim in design is to improve human conduct. Artifacts are not produced for profit, algorithmic efficiency, or artistic pleasure, but with the goal of making a difference in the lives of people.

User-centeredness is human-centeredness in the particular context of computer use: "The purpose of the [designed] system is to serve the user, not to use a specific technology, not to be an elegant piece of programming. The needs of the users should dominate the design of the interface" [604].

Over the last four decades, the concept of user-centeredness has evolved and become more nuanced. It may be distilled into a few accepted principles [285, 604]:

User focus: Understanding and serving the user's goals, tasks, and needs is the primary goal of design. When solutions are presented to users, they must be easily understandable by users and avoid technical jargon when possible. This distinguishes user-centered design from many other processes in engineering and business.

User involvement: Representative users are actively engaged throughout. The different processes discussed in this chapter differ in how they can be carried out.

Iterative and incremental development: Iteration is necessary because it is practically impossible to know the specifics of what needs to be designed from the outset.

Prototyping: Early and continuous prototyping helps evaluate ideas before converging to a particular solution.

Evaluation in context: Prototypes should be evaluated with real users in real contexts whenever possible.

Holistic design: Understanding that all designed aspects of a product, from its advertisements to its social media presence and manuals, affect its use.

Process customization: Avoiding a rigid process and ensuring continuous reflection and evolution of the process.

The rest of this chapter elaborates three *conceptions of design*—different ways to think about what design is and what its goals are.

30.2 Generating creative ideas

Design is hard because producing *creative ideas* is hard. For an idea to be good, it is not enough for it to be novel; it must also meet objectives. Some of the most important goals relate to human considerations, such as usefulness, usability, efficiency, satisfaction, and so on. However, from a purely combinatorial perspective, the number of options to consider is often prohibitively large. In other words, the design space is huge. One might even ask how it is possible to arrive at *any* good design.

In addition, the tasks given to designers are often poorly—if at all—defined. Imagine being given the task of "designing the next, better version" of some product. What does "better" even mean—better for whom, and better in what sense? Much of what designers do is develop and clarify the understanding of a problem. After thinking about the problem, designers must generate new ideas. To understand how they do this, we need to understand what creativity is.

30.2.1 Problem-solving

Problem-solving refers to attempts to create "a course of action aimed at changing existing situations into preferred ones" [776]. Designers seek solutions that transform a state of affairs in desirable ways. However, in any real-world design problem, there are numerous design options that may or may not be interrelated in complex ways. Consider the problem of selecting functionality for an application. For n functions, there are $2^n - 1$ ways to combine them in an application; for just 50 functions, this means 1,125,899,906,842,623 possibilities. Furthermore, assuming that 50 functions have been selected, they can be organized into a hierarchical menu in $100! \approx 10^{158}$ ways. Now, note that this is just a minor aspect in the gamut of decisions behind an application.

Problem-solving is about identifying alternative solutions to a problem and translating those solutions into reality. To do this, designers need to be able to decompose the problem, for example, by enumerating the available options or imposing some form of structure on them.

To explore options, designers need various forms of judgment. Judgment is needed to evaluate options and decide which options to explore. Designers also use their memory and experience; for example, they may use failed or successful past designs to inform their judgment. They may have sudden flashes of intuition that provide an immediate answer to the problem at hand, but they may also use models and simulations to evaluate potential solutions. Representing problems and solutions is an essential part of design. In particular, efficient representation enables efficient problem-solving.

Viewing design as being solely about problem-solving has been criticized as solutionist. This view assumes that it is possible to first define a desired state of affairs [920] and then simply search for the best option. While problem-solving is an essential aspect of design, it is not the sole purpose of design. As discussed in the chapter on design cognition (Chapter 31), designers often learn about the objectives and the design space at the same time. This means designers tend to develop solutions and address problems in tandem. For example, underdefined problems can motivate an inquiry that leads to a new design and a new design situation with a better-understood problem.

30.2.2 Creative ideation

Design is a creative activity whose objective is to produce a novel and relevant artifact or service. Boden defined three types of creative thinking [82]:

Combinatorial creativity: Identifying a combination of decisions within a given conceptual space when it was previously believed that such a solution would be unlikely. For example, the design of the Dvorak Simplified Keyboard, which was revolutionary at its time, sought to optimize the assignment of letters for typing performance and ergonomics.

Exploratory creativity: Finding a new conceptual approach that helps identify an idea that was earlier considered impossible or not considered at all. For example, the idea of ubiquitous computing is that computer technology is seamlessly integrated into our environment rather than being confined to a workstation on our desks.

Transformative creativity: Transforming or replacing a conceptual space, thus allowing for an entirely new perspective to think about a problem space. For example, the desktop metaphor enabled a new way to interact with functionality in a computer by using a metaphor of a typical office desk and ancillary furniture, such as the file cabinet and the trash can, as a model for interaction with the operating system's file system.

30.2.3 Design thinking

Design thinking has become a popular term that is used worldwide in educational programs and firms to define their view of what constitutes design. Instead of relying on a creative individual, a "design hero," the key message in design thinking is emancipatory: Creativity is something that *anyone* can develop and foster.

Design thinking offers methods for *convergent* and *divergent* thinking (Chapter 5). In divergent thinking, the goal is to chart the options that are available; in convergent thinking, the goal is to narrow down the options to the most promising one.

Design thinking emphasizes two types of knowledge-creation activities: creative activities (knowing what to design) and problem-solving activities (knowing how to design it). This view of design is based on the observation that knowing what to design is perhaps even more important than knowing how to design. The *knowing what* part is inherently ill-defined, which forces the designer to assert a view on the problem; design thinking is about the practices for achieving that. In this part, we learn about design cognition (Chapter 31) and processes in design (Chapter 33) that underpin this idea.

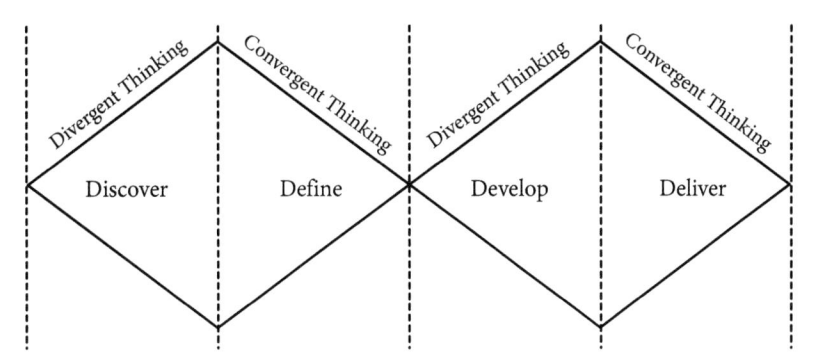

Figure 30.3 The double diamond model of design thinking by the Design Council, reused under Creative Commons License.

The double diamond model[1] is an integrative conceptual model of design that recognizes both divergent and convergent thinking in design (Figure 30.3). The first diamond is about understanding the problem. Rather than assuming what it is, designers should carry out user research to discover and define the problem. The second diamond is about developing answers to the defined problem. As in usability engineering (Chapter 33), the model encourages co-designing with other people, testing out solutions at a small scale, and quickly rejecting ideas that do not work.

The model also promotes four design principles. The first is to put people first: Design starts and ends with people, with a focus on their needs, capabilities, and goals. The second is to communicate visually and inclusively to help stakeholders gain a shared understanding of the ideas. The third is to collaborate and co-create—in other words, to work together. The fourth is iteration. These principles partially overlap with the golden rules and heuristics that underpin usability engineering (Chapter 33). The difference is that in the former, communication and collaboration are prioritized above empirical testing.

The model also outlines supportive factors for organizations, notably a culture and leadership that support design, a methodology toolbox, and engagement with stakeholders. Organizations should invest in innovation, building skills, and providing room for experimentation and learning. Finally, constant reflection is a key feature that can help organizations continually renew their design thinking.

30.3 Practicing design

Creativity is rarely something that happens spontaneously. Instead, it occurs as a result of the deliberate application of techniques and practices. *Design techniques* are defined ways of performing design tasks according to a particular structure. A good design technique fits the context in which it is executed and produces good results. *Design practices* are the actual ways in which designers think and work, as opposed to what normative accounts such as process models may dictate. Practices are not just about taking shortcuts or knowing which tool to use and how to use it; they also reflect the maturing of a designer.

---

[1] https://www.designcouncil.org.uk/our-work/skills-learning/tools-frameworks/framework-for-innovation-design-councils-evolved-double-diamond/.

30.3.1 The reflective practitioner

While design is popularly considered the act of creating, the resulting artifact is only the visible part of the outcome of design. Schön [746] argued that designers develop vastly different ways of knowing and doing via practice. Professional designers *reflect* on their creations and study others. This kind of reflection is critical to the designer's ability to understand the broader context of design. Real-world design problems may lack the well-defined goals and constraints that we see in engineering, for example. Design is messy, and it is through learning and reflection that we can find direction. The skills the designer develops are not prescriptive methods or processes, nor are they mysterious; rather, they are the product of years of training and practice.

Buchanan [108] stated that an important part of reflection for designers is trying to *contextualize* their work. That is, they deliberately or intuitively try to shape design situations, identify different perspectives, rethink issues, and develop hypotheses for exploration and development. These *placements* occur in cycles that eventually allow designers to make sense of design—taking a stance on what the design is *for*.

The accepted view is that these two ways of thinking, reflection and placements, can be developed in parallel. They are meta-cognitive activities, and these activities—not talent or one's DNA—underpin creativity in design. An essence of design is constantly striving to improve one's knowledge and capabilities.

Reflection is also needed to attack *wicked problems* [108]. A wicked problem is a hopelessly constrained or underdefined problem. Imagine you are tasked with "innovating something for an automobile company" or "improving its management practices"; how would you go about doing that? Wicked problems have no stopping rule or clear goal. They stifle creativity with impossible constraints. For example, budgetary, technological, or branding constraints can narrow the design space to the point where no outcome can meet the stated goals. It can get even worse. Some wicked problems have *indeterminacy*, that is, no definitive conditions or boundaries for design. Through repeated reflection and contextual placement, a designer can attempt to iteratively crack wicked problems.

30.3.2 Practices of participation

Participatory design is a term used for design processes that involve stakeholders, especially end-users, not only via user research and evaluation but also at the heart of the process in the generation of design ideas. The method originated in Scandinavia, where it was developed in the 1970s to increase productivity and democratize design in workplaces and industry. Workshops are commonly used as a way to facilitate involvement.

The most radical change from other design processes is that the role of the researcher changes from translator to facilitator. Researchers and designers collaborate and facilitate the work of expert and non-expert users in design. Many positive values are sought through participation. Involving users not as objects of design but as actors improves their ownership of the outcome. By designing with a user rather than for a user, it is possible to make better decisions. Instead of collecting information about people, why not engage with them as legitimate co-creators in design, giving them a voice in defining what the relevant problems and solutions are?

Co-design is a development of participatory design. Instead of just involving stakeholders as participants in design, the entire process is rethought. In co-design, design is a collective process. Trained designers and researchers work with untrained stakeholders who represent or are the end-users. In other words, more authorship is given to user communities and stakeholder groups: Design decisions and creativity are not attributed to the designer but to the stakeholders collectively. Moreover, traditional roles in design continue to change. Designers are not simply facilitating experts; they are collaborators. The expert may be both the source of design ideas and responsible for collecting or interpreting data about the user community. The Internet has enabled a wealth of new opportunities for co-design, including computer-mediated arrangements between designers and non-designers and projects involving user communities, such as large open software projects.

While participatory design changes the relationship between the designer and the user, their roles, from both an institutional and social perspective, remain the same. The user is typically a professional and an expert in their work domain, while the designer is a professional and an expert in design.

Action research challenges this role-based stance by proposing a change-oriented approach to research [811]. It transcends the traditional role assumed by designers and posits that to impact the world, the designer must become part of it. At one extreme, the designer becomes a member of the stakeholder group. This method follows the traditional design process only implicitly or interprets it as loose guidance.

Action research challenges the relationship between the designer and the community. In regular research, the researcher may want to distance themselves from the study subject; in action research, their relationship with the study subject is not only accepted but also actively created and developed during a project. Critical design is the idea that design can expose hidden agendas and make people more aware of the ethical structures in the world [41].

Action research can be summarized into five principles [811]:

Researcher–client agreement: This is the basis for mutual commitment and role expectations.

Cyclical process model: This involves diagnosing, action planning, action taking, evaluating, and specifying learning.

Theory: Theory must play a central role in action research.

Change through action: Action and change are indivisible research elements related to interventions focused on producing change.

Learning through reflection: Reflection and learning allow the researcher to make both practical and theoretical contributions.

Action research can have both research and action outcomes. It produces knowledge about the world the design is impacting. This requires the research process to be a deliberate part of the design process. It also demands public accountability and critical self-evaluation to avoid causing harm.

Paper Example 30.3.1: Value-sensitive design of AI algorithms

Intelligent systems are often developed in an algorithm-centric manner. The team acquires a dataset and then trains a machine learning algorithm on the dataset. Finally, the team quantitatively assesses the results obtained with the system. There is rarely a consideration of the broader context, such as where and how the algorithms are used. This broader context can be complex. It encompasses some particular groups of users using a particular user interface,

continued

> **Paper Example 30.3.1: Value-sensitive design of AI algorithms** *(continued)*
>
> accessing the algorithm fed with particular inputs in some particular locales. For instance, consider algorithms that decide insurance policies, detect tumors, filter job resumes, or propose medical treatments. To prevent possibly catastrophic consequences for the end-users, such systems require a user-centric design process.
>
> *Value-sensitive design* is a method for designing systems that adhere to users' values. Here, *values* are principles that users consider important in their lives. This method was developed over almost two decades of research [258]. A central aspect of the design process is involving relevant stakeholders early on. Their values and knowledge are translated into representations that can both inform and set objectives for central decisions in design.
>
> Zhu et al. [926] applied this approach to the design of intelligent systems to develop algorithms in a human-centric manner. They investigated a socialization algorithm for WikiProjects, which is part of Wikipedia. In WikiProjects, members can seek and help collaborators, organize joint activities, and manage social interactions to collectively decide edits to Wikipedia. However, these communities were suffering from unwarranted reverts and "edit wars." To improve the system, the authors investigated whether value-sensitive design could be used to design helpful algorithms and user interfaces for the editors and their projects.
>
> The authors propose five steps to this approach:
>
> **Understand the people involved:** Identify who will be using the system and, importantly, be affected by its outcomes. Investigate their values, the goals they wish to achieve, and their motivations.
>
> **Create prototypes:** Having understood who the stakeholders are and gained an understanding of their values, needs, wants, motivations, and goals, and so on, it is now possible to identify algorithmic approaches and build prototype systems.
>
> **Elaborate on the methods for working with users:** Define and create methods for recruiting representative users, deploying prototype systems, and collecting user feedback.
>
> **Learn from deployment:** Build prototype systems, deploy them, and study them by collecting feedback from the people involved. Use the feedback to iteratively improve the design.
>
> **Assess the outcomes:** Evaluate the algorithms' acceptance, accuracy, and impacts on the stakeholders and their practice.
>
> The study recruited specific users from each stakeholder group and worked with them to evaluate the different algorithmic prototypes both qualitatively and quantitatively using ratings.
>
> The study exemplifies how value-sensitive design calls for situating an algorithm as part of a *system* rather than merely in relation to data like in traditional machine learning research.

30.4 Managing design projects

Where do creative ideas come from? According to the *structural* view of creativity, creativity is essentially a rational activity that can be supported by management [17]. *Design processes* are procedural prescriptions for organizing design efforts in collaborative settings, such as firms. An appropriate process guides designers to gather data, take perspectives, seek inspiration, study standards and checklists, and so on.

There are many important features of design processes in HCI. First, explicit statements are made about what the user-related goals of the system are based on evidence that anyone can verify. Second, users are not "objects of study" but are engaged as stakeholders in a longitudinal, participatory process. Third, and perhaps most important, the criteria for accepting or rejecting a design are based on empirical data from these stakeholders, who are thereby given agency in the process. We discuss design processes in Chapter 33.

By contrast, according to the *situational* view, creativity is something situated, an emergent and stochastic process that can be nurtured but not managed. A designer's material, social, and mental contexts, as well as their life history, all influence the ideas that they generate and the techniques and practices that they develop. We discuss this view in Chapter 32.

Reality is probably somewhere between these views. A process that is too rigid will stifle creativity; on the other hand, an unregulated process may fail to create circumstances that facilitate creative thinking. An appropriate process supports the development of skills that help designers solve complex problems, obtain the right knowledge, feel motivated, and seek collaboration with others.

Although we often incorrectly attribute a great design to a famous designer, design is a *collective* creative effort. It is a complex socio-technical-economic undertaking; it is rarely about a "hero designer." It is not uncommon for design units in larger corporations to include tens or even hundreds of designers. In a typical project, designers need to work not only with other designers but also with other stakeholder groups, ranging from developers to managers and clients. Their work needs to adhere to a plethora of tools, guidelines, and practices. When working under time pressure, designers must ensure that their outputs are not only of high quality but also compatible with various technical, social, and political requirements. Carrying out design in such settings without some sort of systematic approach will almost certainly fail.

30.5 What should be designed?

A key question in human-centered design is not what can be designed but what should be designed. The purpose of a user-centric design process is to produce knowledge and artifacts that improve computing for people. The outcomes of design must be demonstrably beneficial for users in ways that they approve of.

Value-sensitive design is a design method that aims to build designs rooted in principles that users find important [258]. A *value* is any principle that users consider to be important in their lives. Making this the explicit goal of design is important, as it can help fight false human-centricity driven by economic or political needs. This means that, for accountability, value-based designs should be based on empirical data. In this sense, it is a design method firmly rooted in empirical user research. A central aspect of this approach is involving users from early-stage research (user research) to late-stage research (evaluation).

Human-centricity has a startling implication for designers: The designer should be ready to *not* design when the data suggest negative outcomes for the users. *Critical design* is the idea of recognizing ethical issues in design related to society and using these as the basis for emancipatory activities. For example, Kyng [450] ran participatory design workshops with resource-poor communities to help design digital tools to assist their work. In Chapter 32, we discuss judgment and critique in design.

Summary

- Design reaches beyond the user interface to encompass graphics, concepts, services, and so on.
- Design is about changing users' practices and experiences via novel artifacts. By contrast, natural sciences seek to obtain knowledge about the world but do not intend to change it.
- Designers' work is organized into processes that involve design techniques and practices. These aim to ensure high quality and a high likelihood of success without compromising creativity.
- Design is the nexus of human-centered design where user research, evaluation, and engineering come together. It is not just about the creation of ideas and artifacts; it produces knowledge about possibilities for innovation and research.

31
Design cognition

Is it easy to create design ideas? Let's try it out. Think about a remote controller you have used and how it is designed. Now, imagine that you were given the following design brief: "Your task is to design an alternative user interface for the remote controller, something that achieves the same purpose but is organized and looks better." Take a pen, pieces of paper, and a stopwatch. Then, spend 10 minutes sketching as many alternative interfaces as you can. After the time is up, look at the outcomes. How many ideas were you able to generate? Of those, count (1) how many are substantially different from the original design and (2) how many are possibly better. While generating ideas, did you get stuck? Was it difficult to get past the original design and think about something else?

Research on *design cognition* focuses on designers' thinking when creating new ideas and solving problems. It focuses on factors affecting this ability, challenges that designers face (e.g., design fixation, biases in thinking), and practices that support this ability. For example:

- Crilly [173] found that professional designers can recognize when they fixate or get stuck when generating ideas. They reflect on such moments to develop themselves as creative practitioners. They try to recognize such moments as a way to guard against fixation.
- Analogy is a good way to get ideas and break design fixations. Kittur et al. [419] investigated whether analogies could be identified through crowdsourcing and AI. They illustrated how multiple individuals could help identify schemas of a problem (i.e., an abstract property that captures one aspect of a problem), find analogies, and generate solutions. In some cases, AI could support finding schemas or analogies by searching in repositories like patent databases.
- Lockton et al. [492] presented a card deck for ideating metaphors to reframe problems. This can help designers get an entirely new perspective on problems when facing an impasse. The cards combine two things, a metaphor and a target: "How could [something] be a metaphor for [something else]?" For example, how could "waves" be a metaphor for "urban change"? You can try these reframings here: http://imaginari.es/new-metaphors/.

Research on design cognition draws on methods from cognitive psychology, such as think-aloud protocols (Chapter 42), and theories, such as theories of heuristic reasoning and biases. In a prototypical *design study*, design professionals—or sometimes design students—are asked to produce sketches that answer a given design brief. They are often given a *brief* with objectives and background and are asked to produce designs (or sketches) that best meet those objectives. Experimental interventions, think-aloud protocols, or interviews are used to understand their thinking. To assess how good their results are, researchers often ask an external panel of experts to evaluate them, for example, using rating-based questionnaires.

In this chapter, we review how such studies have shed light on the role of cognition in design. We consider the good and bad aspects of how people think about creating a future situation that involves a new interactive system. We also discuss the main principles underpinning how designers get ideas, converge on solutions, and rethink the problems they are working on. These fundamental aspects of design cognition will be the basis of subsequent considerations about design practice (Chapter 32) and the idea that creative design can be managed and facilitated through design processes (Chapter 33).

31.1 Cognitive processes in design

Design cognition involves four thought processes, as shown in Figure 31.1. These processes have been repeatedly observed in good designers. They have different goals, and different techniques support each of them. Being able to tell them apart is central to thinking as a designer. The processes are as follows.

Divergent thinking: Attempts to identify distant—novel—solutions by deviating from the current solution. This includes activities such as finding inspiration from related materials. It may also involve looking at art or nature. Metaphors and analogies can be sought from unrelated domains that have similar problems. Moreover, it can involve collaborative methods such as brainstorming. Sketching can also be used as a divergent thinking method.

Convergent thinking: Attempts to improve existing solutions iteratively by making local adjustments rather than considering radical new solutions. This is about getting the design right, prioritizing which features to include, and clarifying the details of the design.

Reconceptualizing problems: Rethinking the defining elements of a design problem: What are the relevant goals, constraints, viewpoints, and so on? This can be done through analogies, metaphors, and reframing. Designers are always questioning whether they are solving the right problem.

Reorganizing design situations: Designers also facilitate cognition by organizing their external circumstances. This can involve externalizing thoughts, for example, through sketching, collaborative tools, and design portfolios.

Let us briefly review the double diamond model presented in Section 30.2.3 in terms of these four processes. The model encompasses convergent and divergent thinking; these processes are reflected in the sides of each diamond. The model also involves reconceptualizing problems, which is reflected in the first part of the diamond.

This model is based on studies of designers. Such studies have found a close link between problems and solutions in designers' thinking. Designers rarely consider a solution without considering the problem; they rarely, if ever, simply "solve a problem." Instead, designers alternate between defining problems and generating solutions. They "crack the problem" using various methods until they find convergence between the problem definition and candidate solutions. This is the point when designers "make sense" of the situation: The problem is understood in terms of the solutions as well as in terms of the problem.

How do designers know when to switch between divergent and convergent thinking? In short, they are aware of the exploration–exploitation challenge. When they feel "stuck" with a design, designers use a variety of creative thinking methods to explore radically new ideas. Reorganizing the design situation in some other way can also be a useful response to being stuck. When a candidate with promising features has been found, designers "drill down" by creating explorations and variations of it (exploiting). At some point in a project, designers face a strategic decision: They

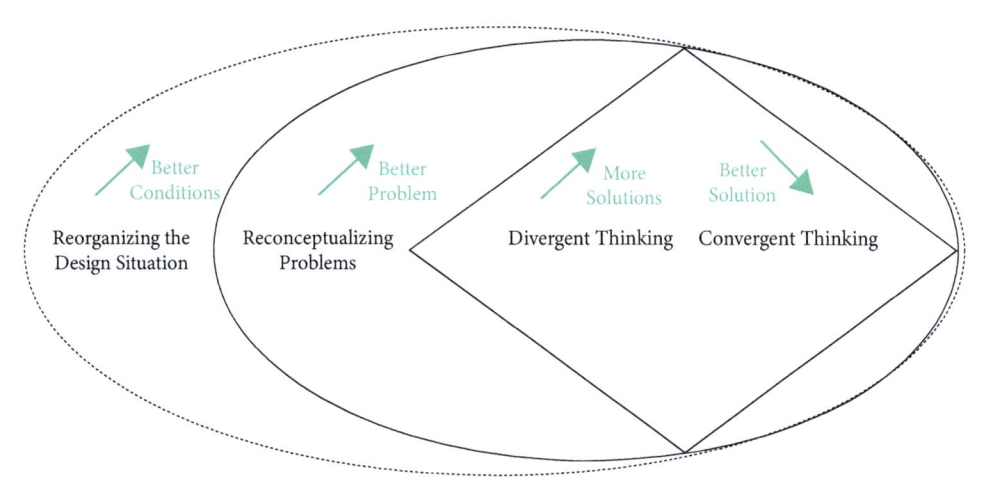

Figure 31.1 Four cognitive processes relevant in design. Designers do not only need to solve problems; they also need to generate ideas and reconceptualize problems. They also think about how to set the stage for their thinking.

must decide when to stop diverging (exploring) and shift to converging (exploiting). Shifting to exploitation too early may result in missing some superior solutions; shifting to exploitation too late means that insufficient time is left to finalize the winning ideas. Exploration–exploitation decisions are challenging because they are made under uncertainty.

Iteration is perhaps the most pervasive facet of designers' thinking. Design problems can rarely be "reasoned through." At any given time, a designer may have a clear understanding of one aspect of a design while the rest is still vague. By iteration, known solutions and new ideas are combined into several protosolutions (e.g., sketches) that can then be evaluated in some way. Iteration captures the reconceptualization of problems as well as the new solution ideas.

Finally, designers' *experience* matters. Being an expert in design does not trivially mean that you can generate more ideas. The "paradox" of expertise is that, although generating more ideas is beneficial to creativity, experts often generate fewer ideas. However, their ideas tend to be better than those generated by novices. One reason is that experts tend to focus more on redefining the problem. Once a satisfactory definition has been found, setting the stage for creative thinking, experts may generate a few good ideas. They are also better than novices at strategizing when to explore and when to exploit.

31.1.1 Cognitive heuristics and biases

The characteristics we just discussed have evolved according to how novice designers think when dealing with design challenges; that is, they help to prevent cognitive heuristics and biases. However, what are the things that designers need protection against?

First, let us do a warm-up exercise: How would you generate solutions to a simple design problem? This is a follow-up to the prior remote control exercise. Here, you are asked to design a menu interface for a desktop application with 30 functions. You must decide on the labels and shortcuts and organize the menu so that it is easy and quick to use. Take a pen and write down the approaches and activities you would take to come up with a good solution if you were given this task, without actually sketching anything.

Students with no prior exposure to design research often suggest copying existing designs. This is tempting and a reasonable first step. However, there is a significant drawback to this approach. Starting with an existing design creates a reference that may bias the other ideas you generate. If the existing solution is inappropriate for your case, what would you do? What kinds of activities might help you generate different *novel* solutions?

Another common suggestion from students is to follow an ad hoc design heuristic, such as "I'll put frequently used menu commands closer to the top" or "I'll group related commands into subgroups and then organize the groups." Unfortunately, very few real-world design problems can be solved using heuristics. At best, you will get a partial design, but you will still need to suggest how to address the rest of the design problem.

The purpose of this exercise was to demonstrate that generating good solutions is by no means trivial. It is much easier to use a good user interface as a basis than to design a new one. Caution is required, as we are easily tempted by approaches that can lock us into an inferior solution.

The problems that designers face in design are complex. In most circumstances, a designer simply cannot provide an exhaustive or conclusive solution. Designers often need to find satisfactory solutions in a short time.

A *cognitive heuristic* is a rule of thumb used to identify a quick solution to a complex problem. For example, if someone asks you to name a great design, you are more likely to name something that comes to mind quickly, such as a design you have experienced recently. This particular heuristic is called the *availability heuristic*. The catch with heuristics is that while they allow us to generate a solution quickly, they limit the visibility of other solutions. This phenomenon, known as bias, can be detrimental in design, where new ideas should be produced.

Empirical research has exposed a number of biases caused by cognitive heuristics. In general, a *bias* is the assignment of an undue weight to a particular idea or object. In the context of design, bias is a tendency to give a skewed subsample in a design space undue attention and significance. For example, the availability heuristic is a bias because ideas that are readily available to the designer are given undue weight compared to ideas that the designer needs to explore to discover.

Another bias is known as *anchoring*. It occurs when we center our design solution around a known reference solution. The bias prevents the exploration of ideas that may produce a better solution to the problem. A common example is the desire to merely update an existing design, say, last year's software, by making minor modifications, as opposed to reconsidering the fundamental design problem and discovering much more promising designs.

Another bias is *decoying*. This happens when we have a reference point that prevents us from seeing another solution behind it. For example, a wearable device designer may consider the design problem of minimizing the probability of elderly people falling in a hospital. Since the problem is considered by a wearable device designer, their solution will likely involve some form of wearable device that predicts falls and alerts the user. An alternative solution would be to redesign the hospital environment to prevent falls to begin with. This can be achieved by, for example, issuing guidelines that thresholds should be removed, door openings and corridors should be wider, and so on.

Status quo bias refers to the tendency to give undue weight to a prevailing or well-known solution, such as a famous or popular design. Status quo bias is so frequent that we often do not even reflect on it as end-users. Can you think of any good examples of status quo bias in any user interfaces you have recently experienced?

Finally, *bandwagon bias* occurs when we observe our peers choosing a particular solution and feel the urge to follow a similar solution path. This also results in us giving undue weight to a particular solution and failing to explore alternatives.

In general, adherence to past ideas helps us produce ideas quickly but limits creativity in the design process. Bias affects the quality of outcomes in design because large parts of the design space end up not being explored.

31.1.2 Design fixation

Fixation is a concept in psychology that means obsession with an idea or person. In design, *design fixation* means being mentally locked into a particular solution and being unable to generate alternatives. Compared to bias, which is an undue tendency toward a particular subspace in the design space, fixation is stronger and more constraining: It is an inability to release the idea of a particular solution. Fixation limits our ability to explore the design space in a broader way.

Design fixations are difficult to break. After investing effort into producing a particular solution, alternatives can be perceived as riskier, less desirable, or involving too much effort. We tend to stick to conveniently available solutions that we are familiar with. Furthermore, designers may not even be aware of their design fixations. Even expert designers, educated about design fixation, exhibit fixation in controlled design studies, although they are generally more aware of fixation than novices [173].

So, can one break fixation? Successful designers actively create new reference points. For example, observing design examples can help, assuming they are not too divergent. Designers are known to collect and curate example designs for this purpose [425]. They look at magazines and browse the Internet for ideas, which they collect in folders or clipbooks. We will later discuss *inspiration cards* as a systematic way to explore well-known directions in a design space. Designers also seek ideas from *metaphors* and *analogies* through solutions that exist in other domains but share isomorphic, similar, or transferable features with the task at hand. Sometimes, taking a creative break helps to "incubate" ideas. Designers also seek inspiration from art and nature. Recently, computational methods have also been introduced that can explore design spaces prompted by a given design example. However, these methods are limited to problems that can be defined sufficiently well to enable algorithmic solutions.

31.2 Generating solutions

Problem-solving is a general concept that was popular in the early years of design research for understanding how designers generate and refine solutions [586]. Problem-solving refers to the process of generating candidate solutions to meet the objectives and constraints stated in a brief. For example, in the warm-up exercise earlier in this chapter, you listed approaches to generating solutions to the given menu design task.

To generate a solution, one first needs to define what it is a solution to. A *well-defined design task* has the following constituents:

Design decisions: The open decisions that must be decided toward a design.

Design space: The set of all designs to be considered, as implied by any currently open design decisions.

Objectives: Properties that an acceptable design must possess, such as those related to ease of use, cognitive workload, or manufacturing costs.

Constraints: Hard limitations and requirements on the design. For example, in the menu design task, we can insist that all commands must be placed within the menu. Budget and software typically pose constraints in interaction design.

Optimization provides an idealized account of problem-solving (Chapter 39). When all constituents of a design task can be precisely defined, the solution generation process is reduced to a systematic search of the design space using some rule or method.

However, it has been found that design is rarely like optimization. When searching for solutions, the designer must not only overcome bias and fixation to explore the design space broadly; they must also overcome the exploration–exploitation dilemma. The designer must decide how to divide their time between (1) refining a known and promising solution (convergent thinking) and (2) exploring novel options (divergent thinking).

31.2.1 Generating creative ideas

A key challenge in design is the creation of a creative idea. *Creativity* in general refers to the ability to produce ideas or artifacts that are both novel and valuable [82]. A creative idea should contain an element of surprise. Creative ideas can be unconventional and challenge existing solutions; they may even involve a novel, insightful formulation of the problem itself.

Unfortunately, generating creative ideas is hard. Fixation and bias are the constant enemies of creativity, as we discussed earlier. It is difficult to let go of a known solution and consider something different.

Moreover, novelty alone is insufficient, as the outcome of creative thinking must also be valuable. Complicating this further is the fact that what counts as valuable often depends on the point of view. These two requirements, novelty and value, put the creative practitioner in a difficult position. On the one hand, the designer must create surprises; on the other hand, the designer must take into consideration what is considered valuable by relevant stakeholders, as informed, for example, by results from user research. Radically novel ideas may not be appreciated as valuable by others. Thus, designers need a synthetic form of creativity that allows them to come up with novel ideas while keeping in mind the context, such as market needs and technology capability.

How do designers achieve this? Besides some methods we will review in this chapter, there is a generally agreed quality of creative thinking: Quantity drives quality. In practice, designers alternate between generation, evaluation, and reflection:

1. Generate as many low-fidelity candidates as possible, even up to 100 sketches per hour. Suspend criticism to a later stage.
2. Select candidates by evaluating them against defined objectives.
3. Reflect on progress and try to find alternative approaches.
4. If needed, refine the problem description.
5. Iterate until satisfied.

This structure is clearly visible in real-world design projects. An example is shown in Figure 31.2. The number of designs at the different stages of the project went from 50 (preliminary) down to 25 (intermediate) and eventually down to two (final). Some iterations involved the use of 3D printing, preceded by computer-aided design modeling. During this process, thinking about the project matured, and as a result, many of the wilder ideas from the preliminary stage were discarded. This is visible in Figure 31.2, where there is very little resemblance between the outputs of the preliminary stage and the final design.

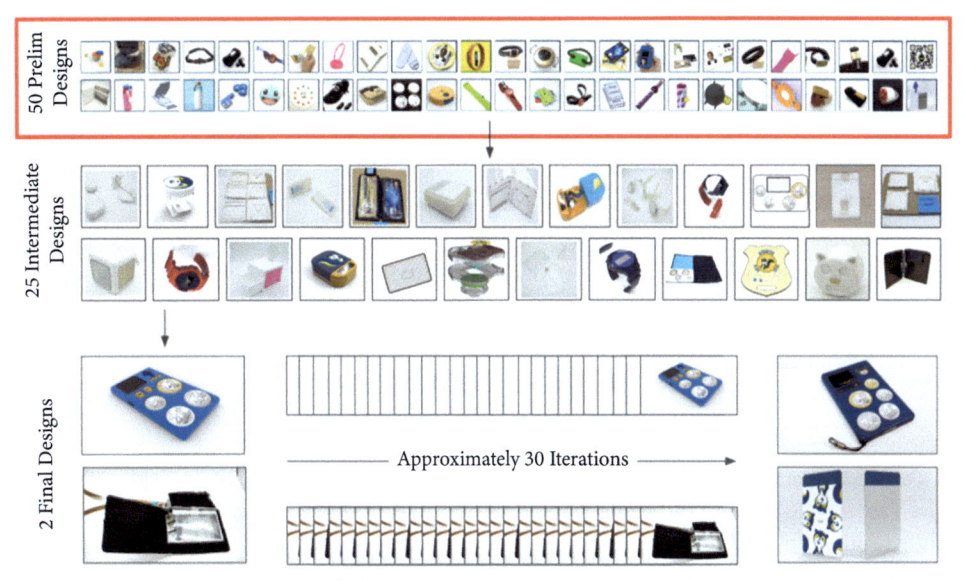

Figure 31.2 Generating a wealth of ideas is important in creative activities. Design projects often progress in iterative turns of generation, selection, and refinement. This figure shows the designs produced in a project exploring the concept of a cashless society as part of Singapore's Smart Nation project [823].

31.2.2 Ideation methods

Creative ideation requires producing alternative ideas that are of high quality. A survey of idea-generation practices found that brainstorming, function (or morphological) analysis, scenarios, conceptual maps, checklists, analogies, metaphors, and storyboards are the eight most commonly used ideation methods among professional designers [282]. Across these methods, idea generation follows the quantity-drives-quality principle of expansion followed by selection.

In the *expansion* phase, designers seek to generate several alternatives. This is achieved through generative ideation techniques such as sketching and brainstorming. Suspending criticism at this stage and focusing on producing a high number of alternatives can prevent design fixation.

In the convergent phase, the *selection* phase, designers criticize, evaluate, elaborate, and discuss ideas for further selection. They distill, combine, and elaborate the most promising alternatives to end up with a smaller set of alternatives. In many real-world projects, these two phases alternate.

Idea-generation methods can be divided according to three primary considerations:

1. How far associations are sought. All other things being equal, the further the associations, the more novel ideas can be generated. However, the proportion of valuable ideas decreases the more distant the ideas are from known solutions.
2. How other people are involved. Having more people generating ideas does not automatically translate into more or better ideas. Many collaborative methods include assigning a moderator or facilitator.
3. How different representations are used. Sketching typically involves visuospatial representations; brainstorming mostly involves verbal representations.

Brainstorming: Brainstorming is one of the most widely used idea-generation methods among creative professionals. It is easy to learn and apply either individually or in teams. Most brainstorming variations subscribe to a few shared principles:

- Postpone criticism: By withholding criticism, the team can avoid throttling the generative process.
- Divergence: Encourage wild, diverse ideas.
- Quantity: Try to produce as many ideas as possible.
- Accumulation of knowledge: It is acceptable and encouraged to build on proposed ideas and known solutions.
- Equal significance: Every participant and every idea is equally valuable.

Paper Example 31.2.1 presents a more elaborate process for brainstorming.

To avoid becoming biased by others' ideas when brainstorming in a team, individuals are often given some time alone to think about solutions. Another practice is to name a facilitator who is tasked with keeping time and assisting the team in sticking to agreed-upon principles.

Inspiration card workshops: They are collaborative ideation and design events mediated by physical cards that are used to trigger discussion among designers and users [308]. The idea of this method is to invite metaphorical and analogical thinking while keeping the evolved ideas technically realistic.

An inspiration card workshop consists of three phases: introduction, combinations, and presentations. In a session, designers and end-users together try to come up with new design concepts. The method relies on two types of cards: technology cards and domain cards. A technology card describes a technical opportunity or threat, while a domain card describes an experience or development related to end-users. For example, a technology card could describe smart home speakers using a distributed operating system, and a domain card might describe a family dinner. Cards are drawn at random and used as seeds for the ideation of possibilities.

Paper Example 31.2.1: How to organize a brainstorming session

The purpose of a brainstorming session is to generate many ideas quickly. There are many recommendations and ideas for how to do brainstorming. Kelley [409] summarized one set of recommendations for brainstorms that have become popular in human–computer interaction (HCI) as follows:

1. Sharpen the focus. Make the purpose of the problem clear; it is better to be too clear than too vague. The focus of the brainstorm session should be open in the sense that it should not limit possible solutions. Kelley also recommended focusing outward on user needs or service innovations rather than inward on organizational goals.
2. Playful rules. The goal of brainstorming is to generate many wild ideas; as such, the rules of brainstorming are to do that and to avoid criticizing ideas or debating the focus of the brainstorm.
3. Number your ideas. Assign a number to each proposed idea and keep track of the number of ideas generated. The latter allows a facilitator to ask participants to speed up the generation of ideas; Kelley suggested 100 ideas per hour as a reasonable goal.
4. Build and jump. In successful brainstorms, participants build on each other's ideas. Steal and combine ideas; the facilitator can ask how other participants' ideas may be changed or

developed. A jump suggestion is appropriate when the rate of ideas goes down. It asks participants to pull out of the part of the problem they are focusing on or the type of solutions they are considering.

5. The space remembers. The space in which brainstorming takes place is important. Spatially arranging ideas on tables, walls, or whiteboards can help a brainstorming group generate ideas and build on the work of others.

6. Stretch your mental muscle. Sometimes, it pays to warm up brainstormers, especially if they do not know each other or have not brainstormed much before. Kelley suggested a quick word game or comparing different physical designs to clear the mind.

7. Get physical. Kelley suggested bringing things to the brainstorming session, such as physical products or competitors' solutions. He also suggested having materials for physical sketching, such as blocks, foam, and other physical materials. Finally, you can stand up and act out or bodystorm ideas and solutions.

A brainstorming session should take about an hour, although it may take longer on some occasions. Kelley also warned against a number of common actions that can kill a brainstorm. These include letting the most senior person speak first (or most), insisting on experience, and not being playful.

Lateral thinking: The term refers to a set of creativity techniques [182]. The goal in lateral thinking is to identify radically new ideas. An example of a lateral thinking method is to use randomly chosen words as a starting point for idea generation. Another example is to use provocation, such as a scenario where a user's data have been hacked and the hacker is asking for ransom for the data. A facilitator might start by asking a series of *why* questions that may expose tenuous presumptions that serve as starting points for ideation.

While lateral thinking is recognized in design research, the merits of lateral thinking are unclear in the scientific literature, as there is a lack of solid evidence of the efficacy of such methods. As a consequence, lateral thinking techniques are controversial.

In addition to these methods, there are many other approaches, such as checklists, that can be used to generate ideas. However, idea-generation methods are not a panacea to creativity. Methods forcing idea generation may fail to produce creative ideas. While it is easy to generate wild ideas, it is difficult to create wild ideas that are also valuable. Ideas that are forcefully produced are often simple variations of existing solutions. For idea-generation methods to be truly effective, designers need to develop practices that help them, in their working contexts, make the most out of these methods. There is also increasing interest in computational support for creative thinking in HCI; see Paper Example 31.2.2.

Paper Example 31.2.2: How could computers support creativity?

Shneiderman [765] proposed eight tasks that may improve creativity and that could potentially be supported by interactive systems:

Searching: Allowing users to search resources, such as text, image, audio, or video collections.

Visualizing: Enabling users to view data, processes, objects, and concepts to identify, for example, new patterns and relationships.

Relating: Supporting means of clarifying requests between participants.

continued

> **Paper Example 31.2.2: How could computers support creativity?**
> *(continued)*
>
> **Thinking:** Amplifying people's problem-solving abilities when designing.
>
> **Exploring:** Enabling the consideration of implications of potential design decisions.
>
> **Composing:** Allowing people to create solutions.
>
> **Reviewing:** Providing the ability to store, review, save, and edit activities.
>
> **Disseminating:** Ensuring there are ways of distributing solutions and acknowledging people who were influential in the process.
>
> How are existing systems actually supporting these? Frich et al. [256] reviewed research on creativity support tools and identified six categories based on the stage of creative processes being facilitated: (1) preideation or background search, (2) idea generation or ideation, (3) evaluation or critique, (4) implementation, (5) iteration, and (6) meta or project management.

31.2.3 Sketching

Sketching is an idea-generation method that has assumed a special role in interaction design. Sketching uses visual representations, which are natural across many areas of interaction design (for an example, see Figure 31.3). However, it shares many characteristics with brainstorming. Like in brainstorming, ideation in sketching should be done quickly, focusing on quantity over quality. Sketches should be inexpensive and disposable, yet documented so that they can be returned to if needed. Sketching should also use clear vocabulary, including visual conventions such as techniques for drawing user interface elements, and established terminology. A sketch should not be of higher resolution than required for the intended purpose.

Designers sketch numerous (up to hundreds) sketches in a project. They keep working on several ideas in parallel, going back and forth between different levels of detail. In this sense, sketching resembles brainstorming. Sketching can also help preserve design ideas for review later in the process.

Visuospatial presentation is natural for user interface design. Designers typically prefer to work with visuospatial media when generating ideas over, for example, textual representations [282]. Pen and paper or digital sketching tools are often preferred over using code.

It is important to note that sketching is not simply about drawing an idea that is already in the mind. Sketching is a creative cognitive activity—a way to explore ideas and their relationships. It can not only help identify a solution but also create original new ideas and provide an in-depth understanding of a problem [281]. It has a dual role as a method supporting *both* divergent and convergent thinking.

The potential of sketching for exploration lies in how producing a sketch simultaneously supports evaluation, the formation of associations, and refinement: "The linked acts of drawing and looking invite designers to recognize new interpretations of the alternatives they propose. By drawing and looking, designers find visual analogies, remember relevant examples, and discover new shapes based on previously unrecognized geometric configurations in their sketches" [201, p. 1].

Sketching assists creative imagination. Sketching means changing perspectives, speculating, and taking stances. In the early phase of sketching, a designer asks what-if type questions such as

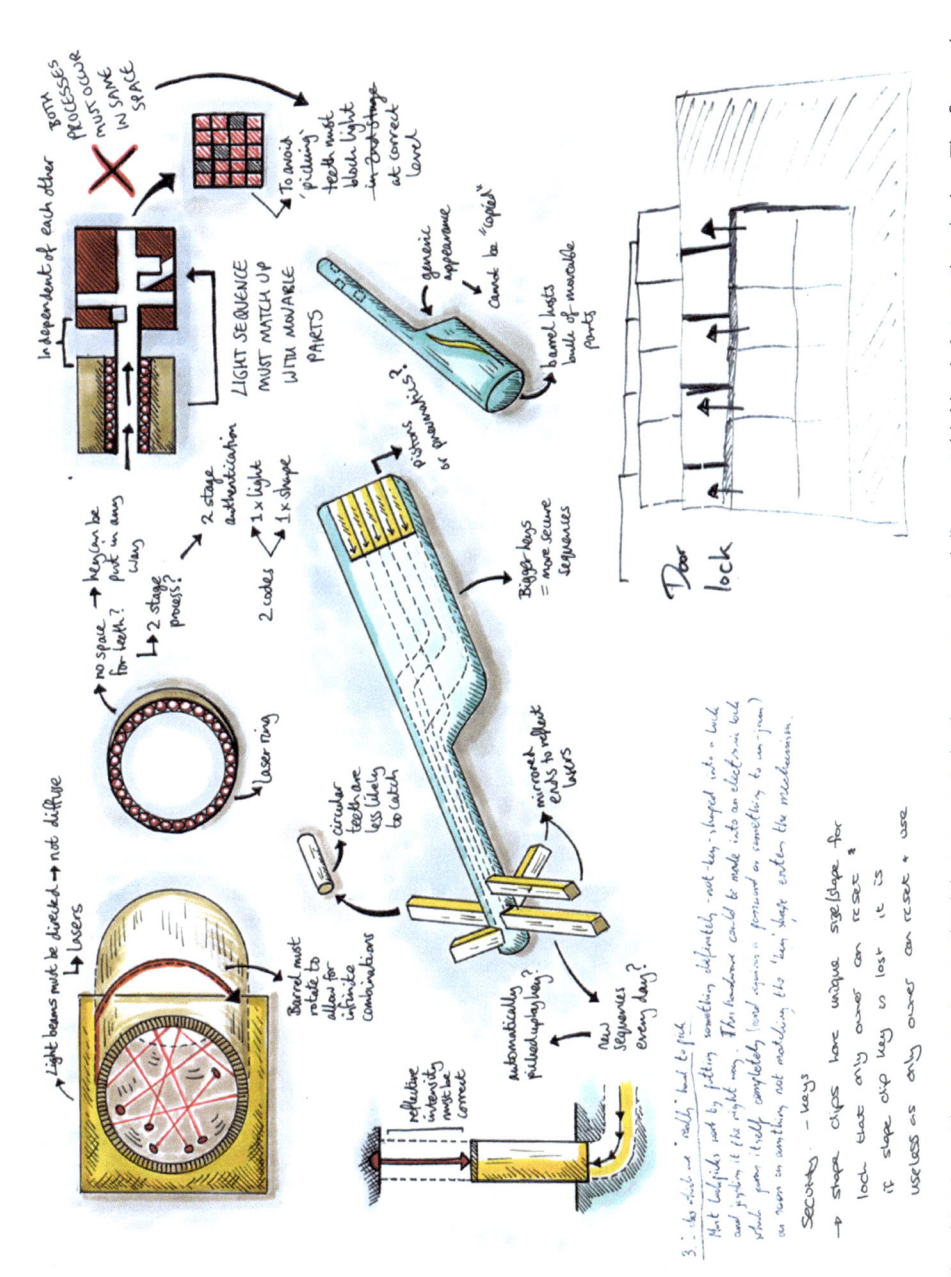

Figure 31.3 Sketching is an idea-generation method that supports both convergent and divergent thinking in interaction design. The figure shows sketches of shape-changing keys [801]; image courtesy of Miriam Sturdee. The sketches explore different ways of constructing a key with the desired properties while avoiding it becoming too bulky or requiring charging.

"What if this metaphor was followed?" and "What if the information flow was like this?" From the perspective of design as problem-solving, sketching is a valuable tool for exploring the design space.

Sketching can also help designers avoid becoming fixated on a suboptimal idea early in the process. In a provocative HCI paper titled "Usability evaluation considered harmful (some of the time)," Greenberg and Buxton [290] argued that usability evaluation can fixate designers to one or few solutions prematurely while dismissing alternative designs. The practice of sketching, which the usability engineering process does not emphasize, can alleviate this problem.

Sketching progresses from vague ideas toward concrete concepts. Drawing a sketch forces the designer to make key decisions that underpin the design. By fixing one aspect, the degrees of freedom are reduced for the remaining decisions. Observing a sketch that originated from a partial solution can help evaluate the original, frequently vague, idea.

Observing a sketch of an idea can also assist in the identification of references and *analogues*. An analogue is a concept that is similar to another concept. For example, an analogue of a button could be a mechanical toggle or a lever. The act of observing a sketch can trigger an association that leads to a reconceptualization of a design solution.

Thanks to all its properties, sketching has become a key creative method in modern interaction design practice. Several sketching techniques have been proposed. Moggridge and Buxton [551] popularized sketching techniques in interaction design. The fundamental idea is to alternate between two modes of sketching: divergent and convergent. In the divergent mode, the designer sketches as much as possible while suspending critique and disbelief. In the convergent mode, the designer refines ideas.

These modes can be alternated in different ways, for instance:

1. **Divergent sketching:** Generate as many ideas as you can within a time limit. Suspend criticism and avoid focusing on details.
2. **Selection:** Assess the designs and select a handful for further elaboration. Ensure the selected designs are different.
3. **Convergent sketching:** Create higher-fidelity versions of each selected design.
4. **Divergent sketching:** Try to generate more novel sketches, even if they are related to the previous ones.
5. **Selection:** Select the best designs out of all the ideas generated so far.
6. **Convergent sketching:** Create higher-fidelity versions of the selected designs.
7. Repeat the process until you have just a few (2–3) designs that you are happy with.

Experienced designers and novices differ in several respects in how they exploit sketching [404]. Expert designers engage in more sketching, producing more ideas per unit of time, which on average are of higher quality. In some studies, the number of sketches has been associated with the quality of the final outcomes [206].

More importantly, experts use sketching as a tool to explore design spaces systematically. Some studies have suggested that experts follow a structured, tree-like representation of the design space [404]. Choosing which sketch to tackle is important. When a super-structure, such as a tree structure, can be imposed, the designer can more efficiently focus on potentially fruitful ideas. Novices may engage in concurrent actions like experts; however, the absence of a structure makes such explorations less efficient. Experts also engage in restructuring and combining activities during design [848]. However, compared to novices, experts are not necessarily better at drawing per se.

31.3 Converging in design

Based on experience, converging is much easier than diverging in design. This is because convergence happens from a new set of ideas, whereas designers seeking divergence need to create those ideas.

Nevertheless, as discussed earlier in this chapter, designers' thinking is influenced by many types of cognitive biases and heuristics. This is why structured approaches are often used to make decisions and refine ideas. One approach is *design space analysis*, which is discussed in Chapter 23. Recall that the idea is to establish a set of criteria or parameters to evaluate design options. Each option can then be assessed against these criteria, enumerating how well it performs or is expected to perform.

Another approach is to *evaluate* the set of solutions generated. Such an evaluation may be done formally, as will be discussed in Part VIII. For instance, user feedback may be generated by comparing existing ideas against checklists of good designs, which may help to identify good aspects of a solution. In evaluations, an intermediate step is often taken in which designers critique existing ideas in an attempt to converge on a solution. Chapter 32 will describe this practice in detail.

A third approach is to flesh out design ideas to give them concrete form. This is known as prototyping. For instance, one might create paper prototypes of several imagined designs and, through the process of making the designs concrete, learn about their relative advantages and disadvantages.

A final approach is affinity diagramming, which we discussed in Section 11.5.2 in the context of the analysis of qualitative data. As a means to converge on design ideas, affinity diagramming works by having designers identify commonalities (or affinities) among design ideas. In that way, they can work on these commonalities and converge on which interactive systems to create.

The intention in mentioning these approaches is to show that we have ways of tackling the biases and heuristics that sometimes shape design thinking in less than optimal ways. Later chapters on design processes and design thinking will detail these approaches.

31.4 Reconceptualizing problems

A common challenge designers face is that the design briefs they are given are ambiguous and do not specify the elements of the task. For example, imagine that you are asked to "innovate a new style for interacting with a particular web page." What exactly is the meaning of "new" or "style" here? It makes no sense to talk about problem-solving if the design task is not properly defined.

An *ill-defined problem* has no clear objectives, or it has too many constraints that may be mutually dependent in some complex or unknown manner. Ill-defined problems may also fail to capture example solutions, resulting in the unavailability of a default design at the outset. An extreme version of an ill-defined problem is a *wicked problem*, where such unfavorable properties are extreme to the extent that the problem–solution alignment is not a useful aspect to consider.

To avoid ill-defined problems, designers must focus on properly defined objectives and constraints. This can be achieved through an iterative process called *goal refinement*. Unlike what we did for the warm-up example of the chapter, designers rarely treat the design brief as a given or invariant.

Instead, designers take perspectives to redefine the problem and reinterpret it in light of a potential solution under consideration. This may involve relaxing assumptions or refining them based on new knowledge and insights about a potential solution. Furthermore, designers study technical and organizational materials to understand the constraints and discuss them with relevant stakeholders.

Ensuring objectives and constraints are defined to an appropriate degree is an important challenge in design. Poor work in this regard will affect not only the quality of the outcome but also the designer's ability to communicate the purpose of the design, convince stakeholders, and present their rationale and evidence. The lack of clear, agreed-on objectives implies that there is also no stopping rule. That is, there is no way of knowing when to stop the design process.

Besides generating ideas, designers find new ways to conceptualize problems and situations.

The *metaphor* is perhaps the most well-known of these techniques. It is a way to understand something unfamiliar in terms of something familiar. More precisely, a metaphor is a conceptual mapping between a vehicle concept and a topic concept, where the properties of the vehicle are mapped to the topic. For example, the desktop metaphor maps physical properties of a desktop (vehicle) to interactions with a file system (topic). Document icons can be dragged and dropped to folder icons such that corresponding moves are implemented in the file system. In user interface design, metaphors can sometimes be useful in introducing complex system functioning to users in a familiar way. As we have previously seen, in creative ideation, metaphors can be used to find new conceptualizations of a problem.

Another technique is *thinking through analogies*. This refers to conceptual transfer: Something is *like* something else. Knowledge from one field (base) is mapped to another (target). For example, Marc Weiser used "the woodwork of everyday life" to describe how ubiquitous computing should work: embedded and without disrupting the user [880]. We discussed ubiquitous computing in depth in Chapter 29.

Conceptual blending is the idea of creating new concepts by combining known concepts. For example, operating systems do not only rely on the desktop metaphor but also on the window metaphor. A window, just like a physical window, offers a limited viewport to the computing environment.

Reframings are concepts or mindsets that are used to rethink a design problem, enabling people to see it in a new way. For example, ubiquitous computing was considered exciting because it challenged the idea that computers must be tied to a physical form comprising a display, a box, and a keyboard.

Finally, *concept maps* are graphical tools for organizing knowledge in a domain [429]. An example of a concept map for a toothbrush is given in Figure 31.4. Concept maps can help designers identify opportunities for reconceptualization.

31.4.1 Reframing problems

Besides evolving problems and solutions, designers try to find completely new conceptualizations of design situations.

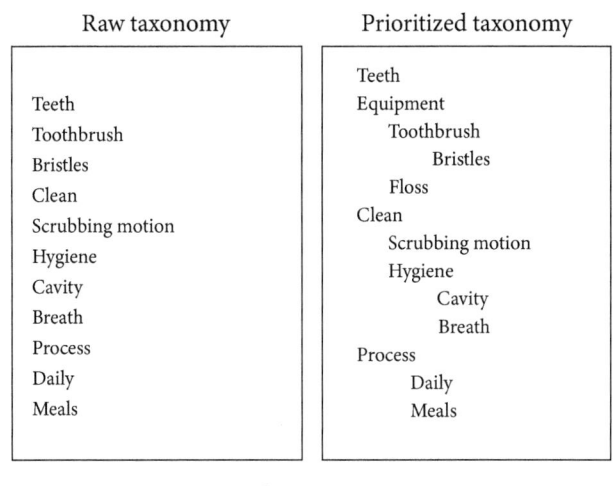

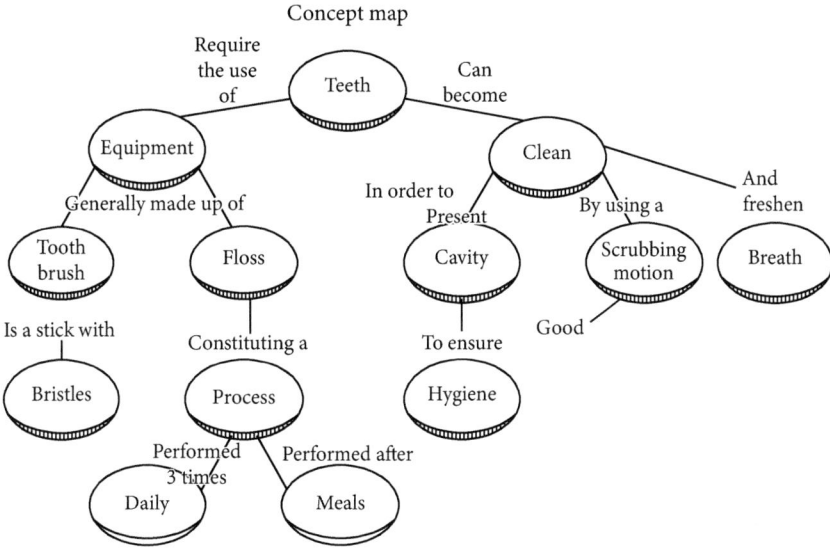

Figure 31.4 In concept mapping, a taxonomy of a domain is created, prioritized, and then mapped associatively [429]. Figure © 2009 by the Massachusetts Institute of Technology.

Framing refers to the conceptual reorganization of a situation. In the studies of Dorst and Cross [208], verbal protocols revealed that designers search through given information by asking a quasi-standard set of questions, such as "Is this ergonomic?" or "Can the company do this?" Designers simulate possibilities in their minds or seek information to answer such questions. These efforts help designers gain an overview of the project, which can be used to form the default solution. It can also lead to a collection of interesting points, for example, challenges, surprises, or opportunities, that can be revisited later to seek alternative designs. Such points can lead to reframing the problem; sometimes, the entire problem needs to be turned upside-down.

Dorst [207] proposed *frame generation* as a key activity in the early stages of a project where designers want to understand the problem. Dorst's example is illuminating. Consider the challenge that a city council in Europe may face: rowdy pub-goers disturbing the peace in the city center. A traditional solution would be to consider means of law enforcement, such as patrolling, curfews, or tightening regulations. The paradox is that such control only creates side effects, which may be more detrimental than the original situation. However, there is an alternative. What if we reframed the problem from one of control to one of support? In other words, how do we support pub-goers in making less noise? This consideration yields the following breakdown of the problem:

1. **Problem:** Pub-goers in the city disturb the peace at 2 a.m.
2. **Paradox:** The city increases law enforcement, but the problem gets increasingly worse.
3. **Themes:** Young people go to pubs to have fun, be social, and relax.
4. **Frame generation:** Instead of seeing this as a law enforcement problem, reframe it as if planning for a music festival, that is, try to help rather than control the visitors.
5. **Solution creation:** Better transit, signage, restrooms, places to "sleep it off," and so on.
6. **Pattern retention:** Rebranding and sustained marketing of the new concept.

31.4.2 Co-evolving problems and solutions

Another key finding about designers' work is that designers engage in the simultaneous consideration of the problem and the solution. The problem becomes understood and redefined via solution examples. A solution, on the other hand, is not achieved without rethinking the problem.

Empirical research has shed light on how this happens in practice [208]; see Paper Example 31.4.1. First, when designers familiarize themselves with a design brief, available loose information is collected and linked to a simplified view of the design problem. This then helps them generate a *default solution idea*.

This can be a naive or obvious design. While this is not intended to be the final design, it still plays an important role, as it helps to gain the first insight into the solution space.

Dorst and Cross [208] described the identification of this default view as an emotional event, an *a-ha* moment where the designer grasps the problem behind the assignment. From there on, any partial solution is assessed against the default solution and can be rejected as a result. This assessment can also lead to a refinement of the problem space.

This type of recursive evolution of problems is known as the *co-evolution model of problem and solution spaces* [511], see Figure 31.5. Similar to the natural world, where evolution drives surprising changes to a phenotype, designers start with a default design that they seek surprising changes to via the co-evolution of the problem and the solution. Creative bursts in design can be attributed to moments when the default design is challenged. According to the co-evolution view, this occurs not only via the solution space but also via the problem space.

Paper Example 31.4.1: Designer study exposes co-evolution of solutions and problems

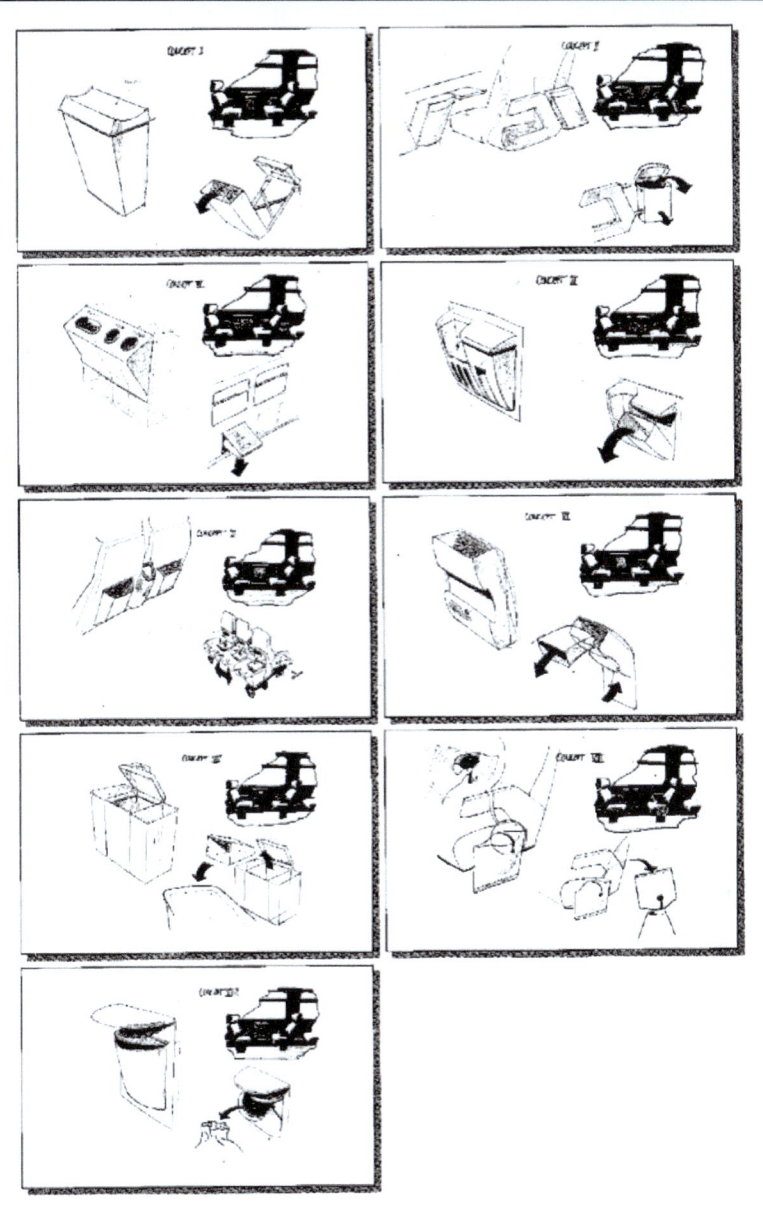

When asked to design a waste basket for newspapers on trains, designers reinterpreted the design brief differently and ended up with different solutions [208].

continued

> **Paper Example 31.4.1: Designer study exposes co-evolution of solutions and problems** *(continued)*
>
> A verbal protocol study—see Chapter 42 for details on this method—of designers has illustrated the co-evolution view of creative design of Maher [511]. Dorst and Cross [208] asked designers to propose a wastebasket design for newspapers on trains in the Netherlands. The designers had five or more years of experience. The brief included information on the materials and production techniques and survey results of train passengers. Moreover, the experimenter, sitting with the designers, served as a client representative and could answer questions. The designers were asked to think aloud and were reminded to do so if they were silent for more than 30 seconds.
>
> A panel of outsiders consisting of experienced designers was asked to rate the solutions based on five aspects: ergonomics, technical aspects, business aspects, aesthetics, and creativity. Ergonomics was found to contribute the most to the rated quality of the design. However, the most striking finding was something else.
>
> The authors found that during the 2.5 hours dedicated to the task, the designers spent considerable time evolving the problem itself. Instead of creating solutions, they went back and forth between the design brief and the solution candidates, resulting in varying solutions. For example, one designer whose outcome was rated as creative was described as follows:
>
>> In the 26th minute, the designer has the idea of doing away with the litter bins all together, and just make a hole in the floor of the train. He then asks whether or not such an idea would be outside the scope of the assignment, saying he likes to manipulate assignments, because they are often too narrow. Then he realises that there is already a litter system in a train, namely the toilets. He asks for some information about that, and is genuinely shocked to hear that they are just a hole in the train floor, which opens onto the rails. He finds this an ugly, primitive, and very backward solution, and adopts a new goal, namely to change this also. He starts designing a special litter container, which sucks in all the litter and compresses it. After some sketching he asks to confer with the Dutch Railways about his interpretation of the design assignment.
>
> The verbal protocols also exposed that designers often had a default solution in mind, which they then challenged via alternative, more surprising ideas. What was considered surprising or original was viewed from the perspective of deviation from the default solution.
>
> In summary, rather than just incrementally improving a design, designers change the problem definition, defining and redefining objectives and constraints.

31.5 Does design happen in the mind?

There are two fundamental views on creative thinking. The romantic view—also called the hero designer view—suggests that creativity is innate and thus without any obvious way to influence it or control it; one either has it or not. The non-romantic view of creativity holds that it can be fostered and improved; that is, creativity is a skill.

Over the last 30 years, design research has expanded our understanding of what the non-romantic view entails. Research has identified a number of ideation methods and practices that skilled, successful designers have. While doing that, the field has moved on from the position that the seat of creativity is the designer's mind. Instead, it has started to look at creative processes as an interplay between cognition and its environment, including social and material factors.

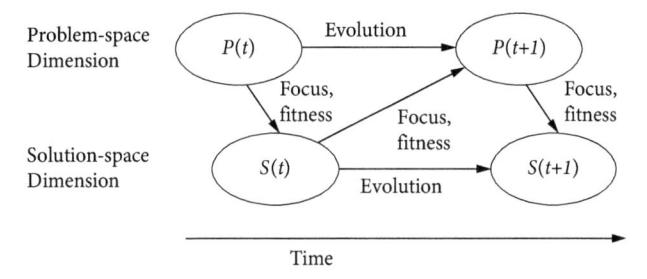

Figure 31.5 The co-evolution of creative design suggests that designers not only solve problems but also define problems [208, 511]. A solution candidate at time $t(S(t))$ may lead to a discovery in the characterization of the problem $(P(t + 1))$, which then leads to entirely different solutions.

A thought experiment demonstrates this well: If you tie a designer to a chair and ask them to solve a problem, the designer will probably not produce a very good solution. Design cognition is not simply about thinking hard; it is also about establishing the design situation—the right conditions for thinking. Designers habitually think about their practices, material surroundings, and digital tools, which they reorganize to facilitate their work.

The theory of *distributed cognition* (Chapter 5) explains this well. It points out that designers' thinking relies on interactions with the material and social environments. Designers utilize their environments to support their cognition, for example, to generate ideas, refine problems, and find inspiration. Another relevant theory, the theory of the *reflective practitioner* (Chapter 30), suggests that designers develop meta-cognitive skills and reflect on their practices. They try to improve their ability to organize their design situations, which can facilitate design cognition. We learn about these practices in the next chapter, which focuses on design practice.

Summary

- Problem-solving is central to understanding design work.
- Bias and design fixation limit the exploration of new ideas, thereby reducing the quality of the design process.
- Problems need to be well-defined. Goal refinement is the process of ensuring the design tasks address the relevant design decisions, design space, objectives, and constraints.
- Creativity can be facilitated via the systematic use of creative methods; in turn, this can assist in generating ideas. Many different creative methods exist for this purpose.

Exercises

1. Problem statements. Consider the problem of providing users with an easy way to control heating and cooling in the home. Write down a problem statement. Is this a well-defined or ill-defined problem? Use goal refinement to refine your initial problem statement into a well-defined design task.

2. Obstacles to ideation. Consider the problem of providing small groups of people with a means of collaborating using text messages. Spend 10 minutes ideating possible solutions. Then, reflect on whether you experienced design fixation or any biases, such as anchoring, decoying, status quo, or bandwagon. If you did, how would you change your process to avoid such pitfalls in the future?

3. Sketching. Use sketching to explore an initial design concept consisting of wearable rings that allow the ring bearers to communicate and receive affection. In the first phase (expansion), reserve 30 minutes for rapid sketching. Sketch at least 10 different ideas. In the second phase (convergence), pick 2–3 ideas for further elaboration and spend 30 minutes drawing higher-fidelity versions of them. Finally, reflect how the early sketches affected the later sketches.

4. Brainstorming following Kelley's method (Paper Example 31.2.1). Imagine you have a pressure-sensitive keyboard where each key press reports the character typed and the pressing force, that is, how hard a person pressed the key. What could you do with this keyboard? Generate different ideas of what you could do. It could be something useful or playful. Then, choose one or two ideas and create 10 variations or refinements of each idea.

5. Morphological charts. Design fixation can be tackled in multiple ways. One of them is to try to chart the space of decisions systematically. Morphological charts were introduced in Chapter 23. Take the designs you produced in the sketching exercise above and draw a morphological chart of them. Are there empty cells in the chart that would be worth exploring more?

6. Frame generation. Use frame generation to gain further understanding of the following problem. Users at a large corporation are experiencing a high degree of stress from managing the expectation that they should promptly respond to requests across a wide range of communication channels, including face-to-face, email, phone, text message, and an online text-based collaboration platform.

7. Creativity methods. Consider the four creative approaches introduced in this chapter: brainstorming, sketching, inspiration card workshops, and lateral thinking methods. Analyze their positive and negative qualities in terms of resource requirements, effort of participants, ability to generate many ideas, and ability to generate high-quality ideas.

8. Asking users. Why not just ask users to sketch the designs they want? Discuss.

9. Convergence and divergence. Discuss the difference between the two concepts in design. What do these terms mean? Which methods can be used for which concept? What is difficult about each concept?

10. Wicked problems. The book *Evicted: Poverty and Profit in the American City* [188] reports a longitudinal fieldwork study that followed eight low-income families in Milwaukee, Wisconsin, USA. A central conclusion is that many low-income families are evicted because they spend too much of their income on rent, approximately 70%, which is significantly above the recommended limit of 30% of income. The resulting lack of financial resilience causes unexpected setbacks and a failure to pay rent, ultimately leading to eviction. At the same time, such families have limited rental options, which forces them to rent low-quality yet expensive accommodation.
    (a) Explain why homelessness is considered a wicked design problem.
    (b) One finding is that low-income families frequently move and, as a result, they fail to receive notices from the government that are sent to their previous home address. Failing

to adhere to these notices results in cuts to benefits and evictions. Use goal refinement to establish a well-defined design task for this problem.

(c) Another finding is that the landlords renting out accommodation to low-income families profit from renting out many low-quality accommodation solutions to low-income families that have little choice. In particular, working single mothers with small children requiring expensive daycare are vulnerable. The fathers tend to not pay alimony, and the benefit system is slow and bureaucratic with many rules that make it easy to experience a sudden cut to benefits, resulting in eviction. Draw a rich picture of this design context.

(d) The study relied on fieldwork. Discuss the advantages and disadvantages of using the fieldwork method for researching the issues with homelessness identified here.

(e) Suggest a user research method for validating the findings of the study discussed here and briefly motivate your choice.

32
Design practice

This book covers many of the methods used in interaction design: sketching, personas, interviews, affinity diagrams, and heuristic evaluation, among others. We also cover various processes used in design projects. You may be wondering whether all these methods are just an academic pastime—do professional designers actually use them in their day-to-day work, and if so, how? While much of this book is about exploring principles and methods, this chapter is about something else. It is about how designers work and think, how they grow as designers, and how they develop creative cultures that support their work.

Design practice refers to the way design is *actually* done in real-world design projects, rather than how design is prescribed in sources such as textbooks and process descriptions. The concept of practice encompasses everything that characterizes the way designers do their work, including their methods, techniques, thinking tools, styles, materials, and habits. It includes intangible factors that influence design, such as values, beliefs, and preferences. It includes the craft of design: a designer's skills. It also includes the way designers collaborate with their teams and with the broader design community. In short, design practice is about describing how designers "get their work done." This chapter complements the discussion on practice in Chapter 22. There, we focused on users' practice; here, we focus on designers' practice. In the following sections, when we talk about designers, we refer to anyone who practices interaction design, regardless of whether they have received formal training.

Design-as-practice offers a radically different view of design than that of design-as-process (Chapter 33). Methods and processes *prescribe* how design should ideally be done; practices *describe* what designers actually do. There is often a gap between the prescriptive and the descriptive, which is why design practice is primarily an empirical research topic. Researchers interested in design practice study designers' work, thinking, and impact in situ. They primarily use unobtrusive methods such as interviews, ethnography, and contextual inquiry, but they may also use surveys. Case studies provide a rich and in-depth picture of practices in their organizational contexts. One challenge with such studies is that much of a designer's knowledge is tacit, which makes it difficult to express or extract. Designers, even the best ones, may not be able to fully explain why they act in a certain way. Researchers therefore need to *triangulate* or use multiple data sources to develop and test hypotheses about practices (Chapter 10).

Another motivation to study design practice is innovation. If we want to improve interactions with computers, we need to support the designers who design those interactions. Such innovations must be grounded in a proper understanding of design practice. This understanding can dispel naive or even harmful conceptions about design, such as the idea that AI can "automate design" or "replace designers." More importantly, it can help us understand the sources of variability in design. For example, two designers working on the same problem in the same organization would, most of the time, end up following different practices and obtaining different results. To understand the outcomes of design, we must first understand the sources of such variability.

So, *why* do designers not simply follow methods and processes as they are prescribed? The root cause for the development of design practices is *complexity*. Practices help designers manage the inherent complexity of design [797]. Six common causes of design practice are as follows:

1. Designers need to renew themselves to be creative.
2. Design has multiple objectives and constraints.
3. Design choices are made under uncertainty.
4. Design is affected by many contextual factors.
5. Design projects consist of many stakeholders, materials, and documents to consider.
6. Design is a multidisciplinary, collaborative effort.

First, designers need to be *creative*. Design is a creative profession seeking novelty and surprise. A designer that simply repeats age-honed methods and patterns will become obsolete. An essential part of being a designer—a "designerly" being—is thinking in new ways, and design practices help designers renew themselves. This is challenging because the designer must not only create new ideas but also reinvent the practices used to create new ideas.

Second, the artifacts that designers produce need to meet *multiple objectives and constraints*. In this book, we have discussed objectives such as usability, user experience, and ergonomics. Designers often divide such objectives into two categories: form and function. Designs need to look and feel good—*form*. They also need to help users achieve their tasks—*function*. Designers develop practices that help them find solutions to complex challenges in design, such as balancing form and function objectives.

The third reason is epistemic—knowledge-related. Real-world design problems are messy and ill-defined. There is *uncertainty*. In particular, in the "fuzzy front end of design"—at the beginning of a project—designers must manage many unknowns. Moreover, even after gaining some clarity on the objectives of the design, there may be no straightforward solution available. As Stolterman noted, "dealing with such messy and 'wicked' situations constitutes the normal and everyday context of any design practice" [797, p. 55]. Design practices help designers work under uncertainty. They allow designers to consider alternative perspectives, reflect, and find inspiration from outside the usual methods.

Fourth, design occurs in context and is thus affected by many *contextual factors*. Here, *context* refers to more than the place where designers work. It encompasses the broader technical, social, economic, and cultural systems that designers need to pay attention to, including tangible things such as manuals, guidelines, and tools and intangible things such as organizational expectations, trends, and cultural norms. Consequently, designers develop practices for making sense of design projects and communicating these understandings to others, trying to establish common ground on what is being done.

Fifth, industrial projects are *organizationally complex* endeavors. They involve multiple stakeholders who join the project with their own beliefs and agendas. Real-world projects also tend to involve tight constraints, such as those related to human resources, time, or development efforts. Often, the methods and theories developed in research are too difficult to apply within the time and resource constraints imposed on a project [705]. Designers need to find a compromise between the ideal way of doing things and simply getting the job done. Practices help designers balance such demands and find suitable compromises.

Sixth, modern design is a *collaborative effort*. Designers spend a significant amount of their time communicating with stakeholders, organizing workshops, brainstorming, sketching, and building consensus on a given project [704]. They need to take different roles and, at times, politicize to ensure that sufficient resources are allocated to design.

> ### Paper Example 32.0.1: Practices of user involvement
>
> Principles that one may think are straightforward to apply can be complicated to put into practice. Designers continuously need to balance conflicting demands, find resources and workarounds, and politicize. For example, it is commonly agreed that early focus on users is important—but how is this achieved in practice?
>
> To learn about the practices of user involvement, Wilson and colleagues [897] carried out a mixed-methods study of a small department in a UK organization. The department consisted of several internal sections, each with its own responsibilities, practices, and tools. At the time of the study, the department was in the middle of a design project aiming to produce an application for handling customer queries. The new system should integrate the functionality of existing systems and add new features desired by users, such as tracking the amount of time spent working. For eight weeks, the researchers interviewed employees involved in the project, studied organizational documents, and videotaped design meetings.
>
> The results are illuminating in that they expose the kinds of challenges that design practices can help tackle. To ensure user involvement, the design team had to:
>
> - Convince not only managers but all stakeholders that user involvement is beneficial. This involved meeting stakeholders and convincing them with arguments that bear on their own interests. Obtaining the support of managers was a strategic priority.
> - Define "representative user." Designers had two obstacles to overcome. First, convince others that the most representative users are not the ones who know most about the existing system. Second, the designers themselves seemed to not have fully understood the organizational context of the project.
> - Nominate a champion of user involvement whose task was to influence the design process, motivate people, and organize design activities.
> - Contact and keep selected users engaged, informed, and educated about the process.
> - Manage expectations by ensuring that the people involved understand that users are not treated as designers.
>
> The key takeaway of this study is that being user-centered is much harder than it sounds.

In this chapter, we review design practice in human–computer interaction (HCI) as expanding spheres of interaction (Figure 32.1) with three key components:

- The individual designer's practices in experimenting and growing as a designer via reflection and critique.
- Participatory practices, particularly those involving users.
- Collaboration with peers and communities of practice.

We focus on practice related to the design of interaction and interactive technology; for a broader review, see Micheli et al. [541]. While the challenges that interaction designers face are shared by

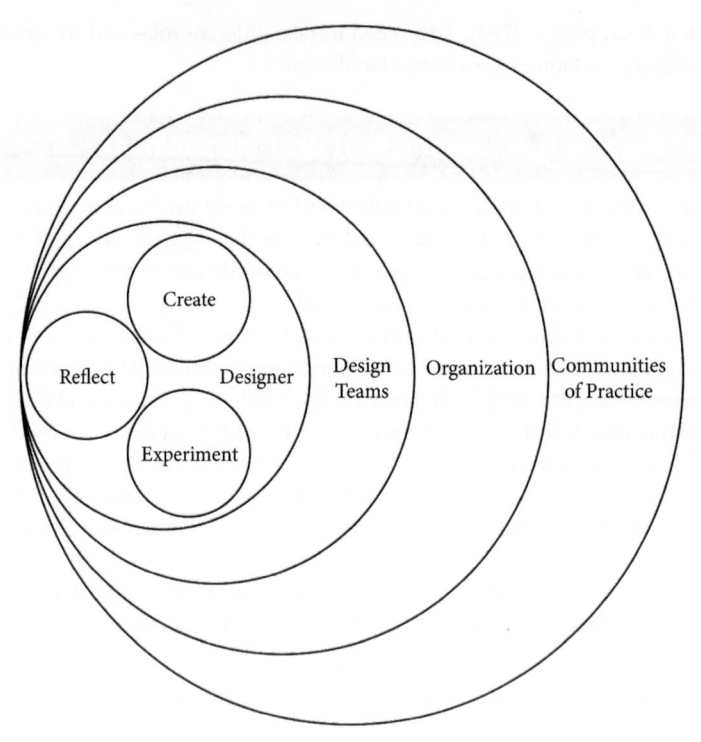

Figure 32.1 Design practice consists of individual practices that interact with those of the team, the organization, and communities of practice.

other subdisciplines of design, what sets interaction apart from other areas of design is its use of technology. When designing an interactive system, much of the design itself is carried out using software, such as integrated development environments and software tools for sketching, wireframing, and prototyping.

32.1 Experimentation

Although many formal methods are used in design practice, there is also a sense that design is a craft. While interaction designers do not tinker with chisels and saws like carpenters, they tinker with digital tools, pen and paper, and various other tools and materials. Creating a thing, be that digital or physical, is a cognitive activity. Designers create concrete realizations of their ideas to study them. The goal may not be to produce something but to learn from it. In this way, creating things is a knowledge-producing activity.

32.1.1 Prototyping

To *prototype* means to produce an instance of an idea that serves as a model that can be assessed. The term *proto* implies a sense of incompleteness: When a prototype is created, it is accepted that it is not final. It may be missing functionality or entire components compared to a complete product. Prototyping is a common practice in interaction design, in particular during the early and middle stages of a project. However, why bother creating something that is understood from the beginning to not represent the final version of a design?

Prototypes are used in HCI for two main purposes:

- Studying the feasibility of an idea by creating it. Creating a prototype requires designers to take a stance on key decisions, something that may still be avoided while ideating or sketching.
- Presenting an idea in a concrete form to others, such as users and colleagues, to experience and test it.

To serve these purposes, a prototype does not need to contain any code. In fact, in the early stages of prototyping, it may be unwise to expend effort on code.

Design research distinguishes a continuum of prototyping fidelity levels:

1. Low-fidelity prototypes, such as paper prototypes or prototypes made using rapid prototyping tools.
2. Medium-fidelity prototypes include more details about each element, such as their type, color, and position.
3. High-fidelity prototypes are high-effort simulacra of the final product and cover key details that affect interaction in selected prime scenarios.

Higher-fidelity prototypes are more expensive and therefore more difficult to dispose of. This is why designers should strive to test ideas at the low-fidelity and medium-fidelity levels before putting more effort into prototyping. Prototypes in all forms can be subjected to heuristic evaluation, walkthroughs, and, partially, empirical testing (Part VIII).

Interactive prototypes can be used in usability tests to evaluate design ideas with users. Paper prototypes, for example, are paper-made prototypes that present graphical wireframes and make certain key aspects interactive [782]. For example, slides, toggles, and screen changes can be simulated using paper prototypes.

Prototyping is not limited to computer applications. During the past 10 years, we have seen a radical increase in technical capabilities for prototyping. Some examples are provided in Figure 32.2. Modern prototyping tools include electronic prototypes, 3D printing, and conductive ink. Combined with metalworking, woodworking, and soft materials such as cardboard and textiles, new opportunities are emerging to build prototypes that are more tangible and can be integrated into everyday interactions in novel ways that are currently out of reach for mainstream computing. Moreover, in recent years, rich Internet-based maker cultures have built a bridge between academics and hobbyists. These communities are based on open science, and they share model designs, for example, for 3D printing designs, best practices, and code.

While prototyping helps designers understand problems more deeply, it is often difficult to justify its value to others. From an organizational point of view, prototyping is time- and resource-intensive. To address this challenge of prototyping in larger projects, here are a few suggested practices [823]:

1. Test core concepts quickly with low-fidelity prototypes, but try to increase the fidelity of prototypes. Do not leave prototyping at the low-fidelity level, as this could result in missing the opportunity to learn more deeply about function.

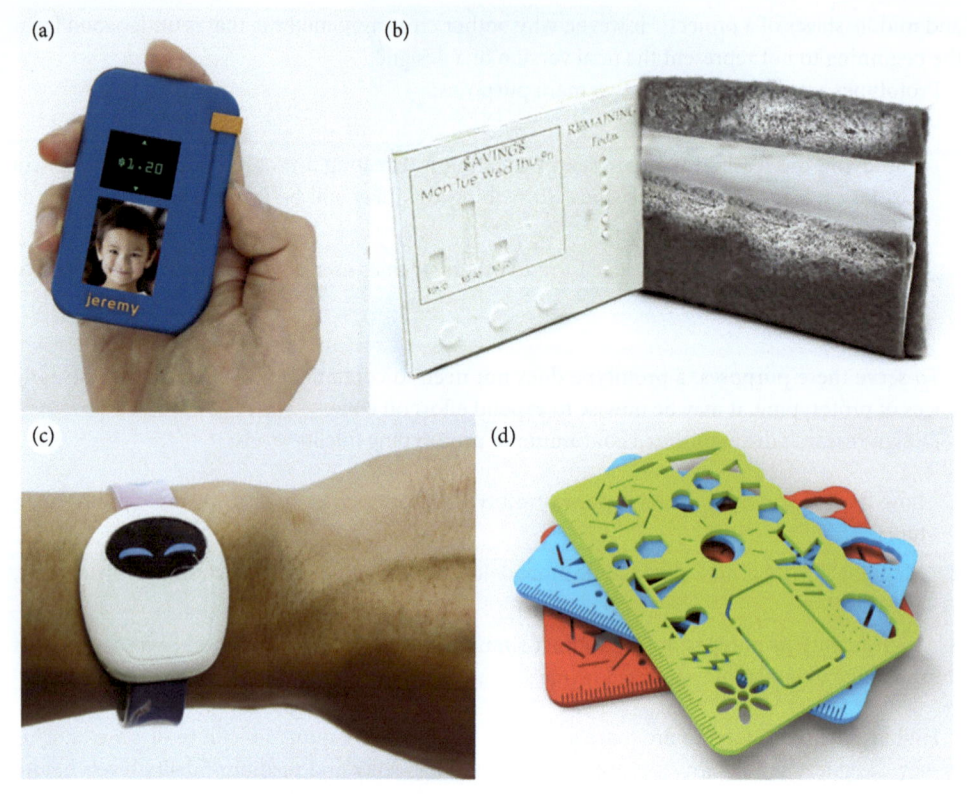

Figure 32.2 Prototypes are used to experiment with ideas, including testing their feasibility and obtaining evaluative feedback. The figure shows prototypes developed to explore how children could make electronic payments [823].

2. Use maker tools and do-it-yourself design to produce prototypes within the team as opposed to outsourcing prototyping.
3. Augment non-prototypable functions with videos and other types of media to help communicate the point. A prototype is not limited to a single object; it can include supplementary materials.
4. Use higher-fidelity prototypes to conduct systems testing through simple tests. Spotting possible issues at this early point can produce savings downstream in the project.
5. Use real-world data if possible when simulating how the system works with the prototype.

Paper Example 32.1.1 Designing for a dollar a day

When we think about prototyping, what comes to mind are technically sophisticated artifacts. Prototypes shown to the clients of academics are often the result of months of work to integrate software, hardware, and fabrication. A prototype presented at a scientific conference in HCI can easily have a price tag of tens of thousands of dollars, even discounting salaries. Building a good prototype takes considerable wealth and knowledge. This means that prototypes are mostly accessible to actors in advantaged positions. To democratize prototyping, we need to think about ways to make prototyping available for all.

In the paper "Designing for a dollar a day," Morten Kyng looked at inexpensive prototyping in 1988 [450]. Rather than just decreasing the costs of prototyping, Kyng called for methods that empower "resource weak" communities to imagine better technologies. While his research looked at professional unions, like workers at a shipyard, practically anyone outside of the field of information technology is "resource weak." These groups often have real needs for interactive technology but no technical competence or the resources to design them, which puts them in a disadvantaged position.

Kyng noted that even if prototypes can be inexpensive, designing and deploying them is a lot of work. One first needs to establish a culture and practice of thinking about redesign. Kyng approached local unions, visited their workplaces, joined their professional courses, and discussed the workers' experiences and needs. In those discussions, he established the concept of a *True Story*. A True Story is a narrative experience that recounts how someone started to study some technical opportunity and assessed some existing solution. Kyng described a case where they visited another shipyard and learned how a system had failed there, which later became a True Story of an undesirable future. This was referred to when discussing the same system in the other shipyard.

After some sessions like this, Kyng got relevant contributors to contribute to a *Future Workshop*. Here, the goal was to come up with ways to improve technology. To achieve this goal, Kyng led discussions on three themes:

1. Analysis: Discussing the current situation, including its positive and negative elements.
2. Goals: Identifying goals that are agreed to be positive versus negative for the participants.
3. Actions: Courses of action that can be taken.

In Future Workshops, Kyng arranged ways to create situations where no logical arguments would be needed to ideate technology.

In *Mock-up Simulations*, Kyng would bring inexpensive prototypes to demonstrate how the envisioned technology could work. These prototypes could be built from plywood, cardboard, and other readily available materials. Participants would be told about an imaginary work situation and asked to try to work with the prototypes, enacting activities step by step. Kyng would make changes to the prototype during a session to accommodate issues and seize new opportunities. The participants' feedback and experiences were then collected. Kyng noted how this supported empathy among co-workers: Seeing others carry out tasks with a prototype helped the participants appreciate other people's perspectives.

32.1.2 Design tools

Digital design tools have become the staple of design practice. They allow for the quick realization of a digital version of a sketch. Tools provide a diverse range of benefits to the designer:

- They catalyze interactions among teams, creating a language to communicate ideas.
- They externalize insights and facilitate their evaluation.
- They allow designers to reuse ideas from past iterations.

- They can automate parts of problem-solving, thus freeing up time and mental resources for more demanding aspects.

An essential aspect of design tools is *thinking through making* [650]. The tools invite designers to play with combinations of materials and ideas and start dialogues with peers. This is particularly valuable when the ideas are hard to articulate. They can also help designers start exploring ideas before they have a concrete understanding of what they are going to do. However, design tools also have drawbacks. They can constrain creativity and, by offering specific functionality, restrict thinking to a limited space of options.

To understand the practices surrounding design tool use, Stolterman and Pierce [798] interviewed professional interaction designers. They identified five main reasons for selecting a specific tool: (1) speeding up the design process, (2) its ease of use, (3) increasing flexibility and the degrees of freedom in design, (4) enhancing teamwork and collaboration, and (5) its availability and accessibility.

A key takeaway from the study was the observation that designers prefer tools that are not overly prescriptive. That is, design tools should not constrain thinking. For example, many user interface design tools offer grid lines to organize elements. This facilitates the design of grid layouts, for example, by enabling interactive features such as grid snapping. However, it also locks the designer into grid-adhering designs. A designer should know when to not use a tool and strive for an out-of-the-box solution.

32.2 Reflection and critique

Reflective practice is about developing and transforming one's ways of thinking and doing things [746]. However, what is reflection? In a study of design students, reported reflective practices were divided according to two dimensions [175]:

In-action versus out-action: Reflection that occurs *in* designing versus reflection that occurs *out* of design.

Remembering versus gathering: Reflection that focuses on the past versus the collection of new materials.

Some practices aim to understand the past. Examining old sketches, doodles, or notebooks can help identify connections. Later in this section, we will talk about design samples and portfolios. However, some reflective practices decidedly steer away from design. For example, the students reported napping, jogging, or walking to distance themselves from design. Taking breaks from a creative activity can help to incubate ideas and view problems in new ways. Reflection can also be social in nature. For example, conversations with colleagues, friends, or even family members at the dinner table can help to bounce ideas and generate new ones.

The main takeaway from the study is that designers develop their own ways of reflecting on ideas, and many of these involve distancing themselves from work. Reflection can also involve taking new perspectives. For example, designers may think about some aspect of a problem and try to challenge the underlying assumptions. They may try to turn constraints into opportunities, challenge norms, or reframe known problems. In the design of creative environments and organizations, it is important to make room for both in-action and out-action reflections.

Design samples are commonly used for reflection. Designers regularly collect and share design samples they consider interesting. Design samples can come from different media, for example, from magazines or the web. They serve many purposes, including supporting reminiscence, providing inspiration, and helping designers find partial solutions to problems. The Internet has strongly affected this practice. Interaction design communities, for example, share samples via web services such as Behance, Dribbble, or Pinterest. Such unmoderated samples, however, lack authority and context, making it hard to assess them and justify their use to others. To use them in a project, designers need to recontextualize them by engaging in sensemaking. Such curated folders of samples help designers reflect on and develop their practices.

32.2.1 Interpretative activities

Sensemaking is an activity in design driven by the need to find connections among disconnected facets. Designers engage in finding as well as creating representations of a problem domain; in complex problem domains, this can involve a large variety of documents. A key goal in sensemaking is to find alternative views to a problem. For example, why does a user not like a particular service? To answer this question, a designer might need to peruse user data, speculate, talk with colleagues, and possibly engage in a discussion with the user.

Abductive thinking is a form of reasoning used for sensemaking that involves generating explanations from observations. It is an alternative to deductive and inductive reasoning [429]. As a reasoning process, it yields an explanation of circumstances. In practice, one imagines what something might be rather than reasoning about what it is to gain new knowledge. As a tool for design thinking, abductive thinking offers a way to rethink and challenge existing solutions.

Designers also generate *interpretations* of their designs. By coming up with interpretations of designs and trying them out via prototypes and sketches, designers learn what their designs mean. Such interpretations typically evolve over the course of a design project.

Design interpretations can be made explicit. A *design rationale* is a statement about the reasons why a particular decision was made in design. It can explicate reasons for rejecting other choices. For example: "We chose red color for a call-to-action button ("Register"), because on that screen it attracts attention. Green and blue would be confused with the other colors on that display."

The benefit of design rationale is that it can make the chain of thought visible, exposing shaky assumptions that need more work. However, design rationale has not been adopted in design organizations, perhaps because of the amount of extra work it creates for designers.

In a retrospective assessment of IBM's social computing projects, Wolf et al. [909] noted an important role of what they called *design judgment*. This is a less formalized form of the activity of interpreting and making sense of designs. Design judgment, they wrote, "means the ability to assess, appreciate, and make appropriate decisions regarding the object and its context. In this context, the judgment does not provide a criticism that blocks further inquiry, but rather is a vehicle to inspire an informed decision" [p. 525].

They further distinguished six types of design judgments:

Appearance judgments: Judgments regarding aesthetic and experiential qualities, such as the style of design.

Compositional judgments: Judgments regarding the composition of elements or functionalities, such as how a layout is structured or how a task is organized.

Framing judgments: Judgments regarding what is included and what is beyond consideration.

Service judgments: Judgments concerning for whom the design is meant.

Deliberated off-hand judgments: Foundational decisions that were introduced early and evolved with further experience.

Navigation judgments: Judgments regarding the politics of a design, such as its position in an organization, society, or economy.

32.2.2 Design critique

Design critique is a practice of reflection, evaluation, knowledge sharing, and accountability [909]. *Crits* are sessions where designers meet to review designs. A design is presented, for example, wireframe designs of a graphical user interface, and explanations are provided for design choices. These choices are then discussed with peers. Alternatively, crits can consist of a panel that includes representatives of stakeholder groups. Crit sessions are important for the growth of competence and the formation of a design identity ("This is how we design") within an organization.

32.2.3 Design fiction

Thought experiments are experiments that are done in imagery, on paper, or in a computer simulation but not in real life. Such experiments are done across all creative professions, from civil engineering to interior design. For example, an engineer might think about what would happen if the maximum tolerances of a bridge were exceeded. An interaction designer might go through scenarios where users do not follow instructions or read manuals. The purpose of such experiments is to test ideas by pushing them to the extreme to see if they fail or succeed. Thought experiments are important for learning about ideas that emerge in design. However, they offer only a very thin, fragmented understanding of a possible future.

Design fiction is a thought experiment in narrative form [81]. A design fiction is speculative: It depicts a possible future involving a hypothetical or real artifact. Design fiction can be disruptive and subversive. As with science fiction, it asks the audience to suspend disbelief. It may also use literary means such as irony, metaphors, or hyperboles. However, design fiction is not science fiction, as design fictions are not as dramatic a departure from reality. Instead, they confine ideas within plausible futures to describe events that might happen.

Perhaps the most famous design fiction is the narrative account of Sal given by Marc Weiser in 1991 [81] to describe his idea of ubiquitous computing (Chapter 29):

> She is described waking up, having breakfast and going to work and at each point she is aided by a range of technologies that did not exist at the time. She looks out of her windows and sees "electronic trails that have been kept for her of neighbours coming and going". These smart windows tell her that her kids are up. At breakfast she circles a newspaper article she is reading and the pen sends it to her office. Driving to work she looks through a "foreview" window that lets her know that the traffic on her planned route is slow. Once at work she collaborates on a shared document with a colleague on screen. The notes on previous meetings feature biographical details about all attendees in a searchable form.

This narrative gives a more concrete form to Weiser's view that ubiquitous computing should fade into the "woodwork" of everyday life.

Design fiction is attractive because of its narrative form. Fiction offers a temporally consistent and comprehensive treatment of a possible future. A well-narrated story can provide a holistic understanding of how interaction might unfold. Moreover, unlike computational simulations, stories allow for leaving certain aspects ambiguous, which can invite further thought. For example, the way the pen works in Weiser's fiction is not described. Sometimes, fictions may go as far as creating fictional findings from user studies. Narration can express rich imaginations that can inspire new ideas, identify opportunities, invite others to study the consequences of choices, and help position researchers within a project. For example, a fictional account of PERMA-Care, a scenario where models of well-being from research were applied to residential care, describes the consequences for researchers [81]:

> This paper describes the application of Martin Seligman's PERMA model of well-being to a design for care home residents. The model includes Positive affect, Engagement, Relationships, Meaning and Achievement. In order to support these aspects of well-being a system was designed to create an online "Delphi Counsel" where retired academics in residential care could take part in question and answer sessions for geographically remote young academics. It was hoped that younger researchers would benefit from the previous generation's knowledge and that the dialogue would be engaging and meaningful for the retirees. A system was developed to allow residents in a communal room to make and upload recordings of group discussions about online academic queries. Although the residents were initially enthusiastic about contributing to the system, squabbling and bickering broke out with increasing rapidity as the study progressed. Retired ethnomethodologists, hostile to other forms of social inquiry insisted on dismissing any approach but their own. Although there were problems with conflict management many residents found the engagement meaningful and engaging, suggesting that there may be potential in further applications of the PERMA model to designs for older people.

The narrative brings a fictitious but realistic tension to the fore. Such accounts can drive a more thorough appraisal of design ideas.

When discussed in a broader setting, design fictions can form *discursive spaces* that can help teams and communities make sense of design. Thanks to the narrative format, fictions can also be communicated to a wide audience. Fiction is also easy to relate to, which can facilitate the assessment of ideas. As a result, fiction has found its place in *critical design*, which considers sociotechnical factors to expose ethically harmful developments.

32.3 Participatory practices

Design is about collaboration, both among designers and between users, designers, and other stakeholders. Many practices have evolved to support such collaboration. These practices differ in terms of who leads them (users or designers) and the role of users in the practice (active or passive) [728]. Many practices originate in the field of *participatory design*, which is broadly concerned with "the direct involvement of people in the co-design of tools, products, environments, businesses, and social institutions to ensure these work in ways that are more responsive to human needs" [702]. Next, we describe some of these practices.

32.3.1 Workshops

One straightforward yet powerful way of co-creating the design of interactive systems is through workshops between users and designers. The intended outcome is the creation of a vision of a desirable future as well as some concrete steps toward achieving that future.

How do you run a workshop? One template comes from the idea of future workshops [411]. The idea here is that users and designers come together to design the future of a particular area or problematic situation, for example, their work. Typically, several designers or researchers facilitate the workshop, and up to 20 prospective users or stakeholders may take part. Early experiences with workshops that mixed users and management suggest that keeping such groups separate may sometimes be valuable to help users speak freely.

A future workshop consists of three phases. In the *critique phase*, participants focus on critiquing the current situation. They might take turns so that everybody gets to voice a concern. The critiques may be grouped before moving on to the next phase.

In the *fantasy phase*, critical issues are turned into positives as a way to start brainstorming about how to change the current situation (answering *what-if* probes). The ideas for change may be prioritized and grouped into nuggets of utopia that may serve as points of departure for the next phase.

In the *implementation phase*, participants plan how to realize the future imagined in the fantasy phase. Workshop participants also rate how likely it is that different ideas may be realized and then sort them accordingly.

32.3.2 Co-designing visions

Another strand of participatory design practices has designers and prospective users work together on representations of visions of the future. Such representations can use many different forms, including those outlined in Chapter 15. Instead of representing the current state of users and their activities, the representations are created to represent a future state that is being imagined.

One key consideration in co-designing visions is that they should be concrete [410]. The key issue is that users may not understand abstract descriptions of a vision for an interactive system—they need hands-on experience with concrete workflows or representations of designs. This is why early participatory design researchers were excited by low-fidelity prototyping.

Another consideration in co-designing visions is to make the participation of users full and equal to that of designers [728]. This is essential to ensure that users' views are heard and to make them feel included in the design process.

Finally, the role of the researcher or designer is different in creating visions of the future than in some other design activities. Rather than serving as a translator of user research into designs, the researcher or designer supports users in creating designs and reflecting on them.

Paper Example 32.3.1: Co-design with children during a pandemic

Throughout the history of HCI, participatory design and co-design have been carried out with a variety of user groups, including people with dementia, homeless persons, and people who are vulnerable in some way [855]. Participatory design and co-design might also be done in social and organizational setups where some context-specific assumptions cannot be honored. In such cases, participatory practices need some degree of adaptation; let us look at one such adaptation.

Lee et al. [470] were interested in doing co-design with children during the COVID-19 pandemic. The children were aged between seven and 11 years, which, together with having to do co-design sessions synchronously online, added complexity and uncertainty to the process. Lee et al. [470] conducted 10 sessions of co-design with children. The figure below shows one example of a comic board, which was used to get the children to fill out images 4 and 5 with ideas.

Based on the sessions, the authors highlighted the role of the researcher as an improviser. For instance, the authors described how location (e.g., being in a moving car) and technological infrastructure (e.g., low broadband rates) influenced the co-design sessions. In these cases, the facilitator needed to improvise to reduce the tensions created.

In addition, given their young age, the children were rarely alone. The resulting interdependencies also influenced the co-design sessions and required adaptation and improvisation from the authors. We provide one example from the paper; the ^{C} in Jack^C indicates that Jack is a child.

In Session 6, the facilitator of the session gave instructions for the children to draw their ideas for two minutes. While the children were all engaged in drawing, Jack^C stated it would be better for them to just go in the breakout room. In the background, we heard Jack^C's mother correcting him saying that he should be drawing right now. In his interview, Jack^C reflected on how it was difficult to be himself with the disturbance of his parents and siblings in the room commenting on his engagement in co-design. He tried to find a closed space to have privacy. Jack^C's mom sometimes answered the question for him, and was part of the session.

32.3.3 Playing and acting

Another technique used in participatory practices is to have users and designers play or act out situations of future use. The key idea here is that play and playfulness are central to design; by playing with users, designers may break fixations and explore a broader space of ideas. Another central idea is that acting can be effective for understanding a particular design. Here, acting is meant literally—users and designers play out a particular scenario from a first-person perspective and learn from the experience.

For example, Iacucci et al. [370] developed two participatory techniques that have users and designers play or enact future scenarios of the use of mobile devices. One technique involved role-playing games where the players would imagine new devices or services and act out how they would use them. In one variation, the players used a map of locations and a toy character and were asked to play themselves in an initial scenario. They could change location by moving their character, and events and incidents could be initiated by the leader of the game, allowing the authors to explore some reactions and ideas for future mobile services.

The other technique used by Iacucci et al. [370] is called Situated and Participative Enactment of Scenarios. Its idea is to provide users with a simple mock-up device. The users then use that device in their everyday lives while being observed by the designer. Users can use the mock-ups to imagine features on the device and act out scenarios with the device as interesting situations arise.

Earlier and later work on participatory design has explored other forms of games as a technique for the design of interactive systems; see Brandt et al. [93] for further examples.

32.4 Collaboration

Design is almost always teamwork. A designer needs to work not only with other designers but also with a number of other professionals from other fields, including scientists and engineers. A typical project team in information technology consists of 10–20 members, of which two to three are tasked with focusing on user-centered design [862].

Multidisciplinarity is at the heart of present-day design teams. The distinction between "pure" and "applied" work is less than what it used to be. Shneiderman [766] noted that "applied and basic must be combined" to define products that combine meaning and function. Consequently, modern teams in research and development involve diverse partnerships, rapid electronic communication, and the sharing of data and resources. To enable multidisciplinary collaboration, team members need to *empathize* with different viewpoints, develop a joint *language* for communicating ideas, and take on different *roles* flexibly.

Sometimes, organizational settings drive designers to work with strict constraints that contrast with their aim to produce high-quality outcomes. The pressure to deliver results may drive designers to forgo healthy criticism. In a study of how designers use think-aloud protocols, Norgaard and Hornbaek [595] found that evaluators preferred to confirm problems that they already knew about over challenging them. When interviewing users in a usability test, they would rather ask about their expectations and hypothesized situations than about the users' experienced problems. Organizational practices for quality management can help mitigate such issues.

Paper Example 32.4.1 Design thinking can reduce bias in management and improve the quality of outcomes

Design practice is not something that only designers do. *Design thinking*, in the broad sense of the term, refers to applying designers' approaches to problem-solving beyond traditional design contexts. This includes methods such as observations, collaboration, rapid prototyping, and the visualization of ideas. It can be viewed as an attempt to change the way managers, developers, and entire organizations approach innovation. Design thinking offers an integrative framework for both creative and analytic modes of reasoning in design together with a process and a set of tools and methods. Its four key assumptions are: (1) defining a problem is often more valuable for innovation than seeking a solution; (2) a focus on users early on decreases the risk of innovation failure; (3) understanding must be translated into criteria to guide design and evaluation; and (4) iteration is necessary for success.

Engaging in design thinking can help managers reduce bias [481]. That is, instead of simply being a process for innovation, design thinking can transform the way managers approach opportunities in business. In particular, design thinking can:

1. Mitigate egocentric bias—the tendency of managers to focus on familiar values and experiences—by collecting data on users that help them consider different perspectives. Ethnographic data can play an important role here.
2. Mitigate confirmatory bias—the tendency of managers to look at opportunities they already know are valuable—by revealing results of real experiments and user studies.
3. Mitigate availability bias—the tendency to prefer ideas that quickly come to mind—by showing the diversity of options concretely via user data.

32.4.1 Coordinating practices in a team

Coordinating design often involves deciding which methods to use. The challenge is that for any given topic in design, several methods are available; which method should one use? Vredenburg and colleagues [862] surveyed design practitioners about the methods they use. The most frequently used methods were field studies, user requirement analyses, iterative design, usability evaluation, task analysis, and focus groups.

More interesting are their findings illuminating *why* a certain method was used. The study found a total of 18 considerations categorized into three groups based on their underlying rationale: resources, processes, and outcomes. For example, speed was both a perceived benefit of heuristic reviews and a weakness of iterative design. Speed, low cost, and the validity or quality of results were among the highest-ranked factors. However, practitioners also demonstrated high variability in their appraisal of methods. High variability poses a problem to practitioners. When the results are not predictable or reproducible, it becomes difficult to justify user-centered approaches to others.

To ensure sufficient resources for design work, designers may need to work strategically within companies to be more promotive of design. They need to advocate and champion user-centered design within the organization. They need to ensure the right stakeholders are involved. They need to advocate iteration and a focus on users. They need to convince decision-makers in the organization to secure resources for user research. All of this requires skills in persuasion, communication, and even navigating politics. A skilled designer who lacks these so-called soft skills may obtain worse outcomes than a mediocre designer with great soft skills. Nevertheless, looking at the big picture, companies should establish a culture and a set of processes that promote user-centered design; designers should help companies develop such processes. In this regard, *design maturity models* can help organizations become user-centered and take design to their core business practices. They help encode design practices into business processes and communicate their value throughout the organization.

32.4.2 Communities of practice

Communities of practice are groups of people who share an interest and interact regularly to become better at it [460]. *Design communities* are local organizations or Internet-mediated collectives focused on different topics in design. They share experiences, samples, patterns, code, and so on. For practitioners, design communities offer a channel to find guidance on design problems, share experiences, and develop professionally.

Communities of practice in design can take different forms. *Design forums* are online discussion forums that support asking questions, learning from others, and contributing to the community. *Design systems* are organizationally developed coherent systems for producing high-quality designs in an area. They contain values ("philosophies"), rules, and samples. They may also contain software elements that can be used for sketching and prototyping. Many large design teams develop their own systems collectively.

Design patterns are solution patterns that have been observed to work in several successful designs. A design pattern is more than a design guideline; it is an attempt to prescribe a structure for successful solutions in a given context. A pattern relates three elements: an application context, a problem, and a solution. The proposed solution should be argued or demonstrated to be a good solution. Tidwell defined patterns in HCI as consisting of a name, examples, a context (where a design is applied), forces (what triggers its use), a solution, diagrams (if needed), the resulting context, and notes [821].

For example, Borchers described design patterns for interactive kiosks at exhibitions. These kiosks need to be usable by multiple people at the same time with varying abilities [85]. One of the patterns is called FLAT AND NARROW TREE. The context, in this case, is navigation in a kiosk. The problem is how to organize the functionalities of a kiosk in such a way that users find them quickly and do not get lost in the structure. The FLAT AND NARROW TREE pattern is defined as follows [85, p. 125]: "Use a tree-like hierarchy to organize the content of your exhibit. Make the tree no more than 5 levels deep and put no more than 7 branches into any node." This pattern is justified by reference to the limits of human working memory. The broader point of design patterns is that by collecting and naming patterns, a community can start collecting practices that work and start talking about otherwise "invisible" high-quality designs.

Design portfolios are collections of samples that represent a designer's profile and thinking. They serve an archival role as well as communicate the character of a designer to others. *Annotated portfolios* are portfolios that show designs with annotations—usually textual descriptions. Figure 32.3 shows the PhotoStroller design with annotations. Annotations can concern anything that is distinctive about a design or that might not be obvious just by looking at it: its functionality, aesthetics, the way it was produced, what motivated it, its users, or its "politics." For the

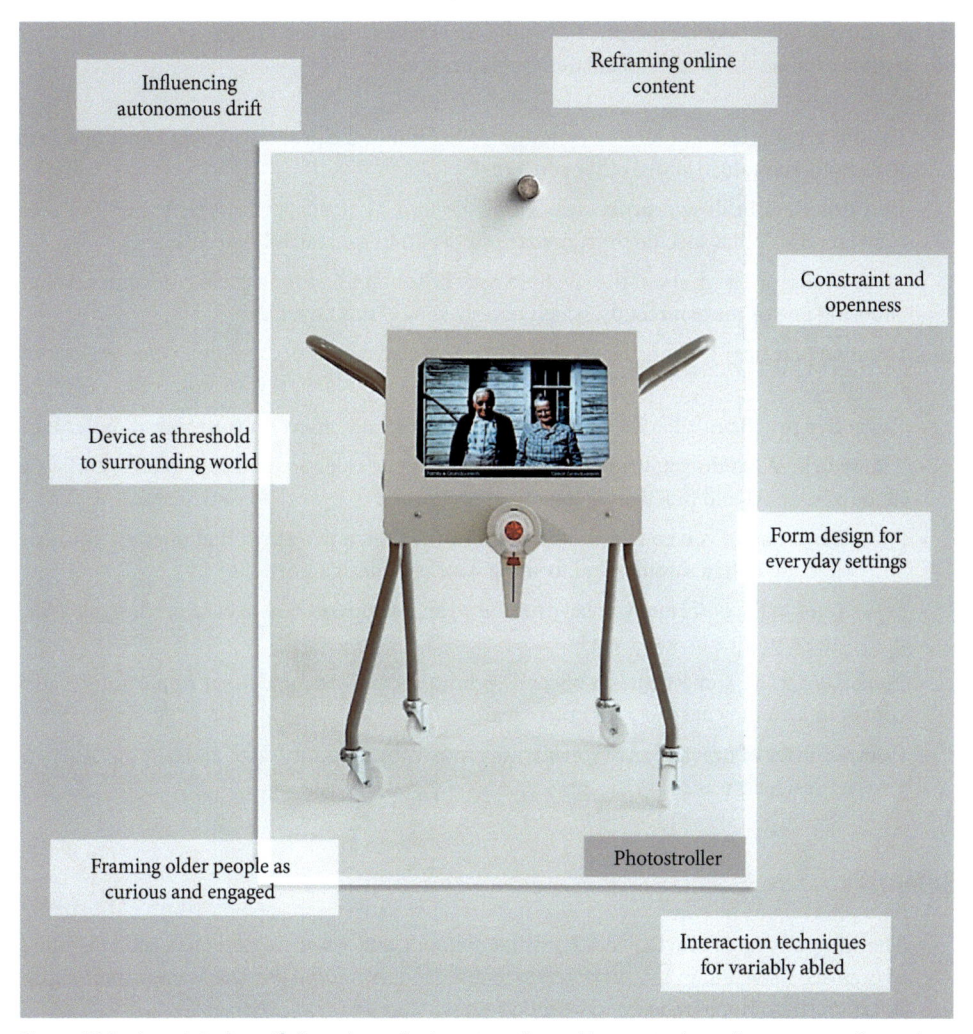

Figure 32.3 Annotated portfolios show designs together with annotations that communicate the meaning of a design and its relation to other designs [272].

designer, annotating a design can help make sense of what the design is about. For others, it helps understand the designer and the design beyond what is obvious about it. An annotated portfolio covering several designs in an area can help systematize a body of work.

32.5 **Growing as a designer**

Nobody is an expert designer straight out of school. Besides the trivial (and unhelpful) advice that design can be learned by doing, what can one do to grow as a designer? The topics we have covered in this chapter provide hints.

The suggestion is that the key is to develop one's design practice so that it suits the unique contexts, capabilities, and resources in place. Being articulate and reflective about design practice can pay off. You can talk about design practice with others and scrutinize it, thereby evolving it. One way to get started on this path is to answer these questions:

- **Values:** What is "sacred" for you in design? What is it in the process and outcomes of design that should be valued above other concerns?
- **Best practices in design processes:** Think about a particular process that you have used (Chapter 33). What specific practices are important in successfully executing it?
- **Methodology:** Think about the last time you chose a method for a project or course. When choosing one or more methods, which criteria should one consider?
- **Creative practice:** What helps you break fixation and what works for you when generating new ideas?
- **Reflective practice:** What do you do to get feedback and reflect on your way of designing?
- **Teamwork:** What do you bring to a design team, what roles are you able to take, and what kinds of support and practices do you work well with?
- **Samples:** What do you consider good examples of design in an area that interests you? Are you collecting design samples and forming your own design portfolio?
- **Style:** Look at the outcomes you have produced and compare them to baseline designs. What makes them unique or stand out?
- **Tools:** What are some digital tools and techniques you use, and what opportunities and constraints do they pose to your outcomes?
- **Communities of practice:** Are you learning from others doing design and helping others to grow as designers?

Summary

- The study of design practice looks at what methods and practices designers actually follow as opposed to what they are supposed to follow. Understanding practice is important for the development of tools and services for designers.
- Designers not only solve problems but also make sense of materials to refine them. They reflect on their practices to improve them and their position as designers.
- Designers experiment with ideas by creating sketches and prototypes at different levels of fidelity.
- Design fiction helps designers take distance from the present and develop possible futures centered on a design idea.

Exercises

1. Brainsketching. Ask a friend to spend 30 minutes sketching with you. Sit down at a table together with pen and paper. Set a timer for five minutes and ask your friend to draw a sketch for the following problem: Allowing children to negotiate screen time with remote parents. You should also sketch an idea for this. After five minutes, swap the sketches and continue sketching over each other's starting point. During sketching, you are not allowed to talk. After

five minutes, pick new pieces of paper and start from scratch, then swap the new sketches after five minutes, and so on. Assess the final results: What ideas did you take from each other?

2. Pictorials. Sometimes, design ideas are best explained visually via pictures and diagrams as opposed to the conventional textual format. Pictorials are rich visual explorations of design ideas (see https://idc.acm.org/2023/pictorials/). They may be annotated by text or accompanied by narrative accounts that frame the idea. Sketch a few design ideas for the following problem and then present the best idea as a pictorial: Helping patrons of pubs to find public transportation to get back home.

3. Imaginary abstracts. Blythe [81] proposed imaginary abstracts as a way to explore design ideas in academic contexts. Imaginary abstracts describe prototypes and findings related to them as if they were the results of an academic project. They allow for exploring the positive and negative consequences of possible futures. Write an imaginary abstract for one of the following cases: (a) using conversational AI to help aging adults use their mobile devices; (b) interactive robots taking care of infants when parents are not home; (c) communicating emotions with significant others via thermal pads placed under clothes.

4. User involvement. Ideate three different ways to involve users for the following project: improving the accessibility of electronic voting machines. Discuss the pros and cons of each method.

33
Design processes

A *design process* defines a structure and practices for carrying out design projects in an organization. It lays out activities, methods, and best practices for a project in an organized way. The typical process description consists of a sequence of activities and some conditions for progressing from one activity to another.

Activities in a design process typically consist of methods we have learned about in this book: methods for user research, idea creation, prototyping, and evaluation. In addition, it can cover management-related activities, such as how to document steps or communicate within a team. Process models also often define practices—"the ways of the house." The main purpose of a process is to ensure a certain level of quality in the way a project is carried out and in the outcomes it produces. To this end, processes can set *criteria* that define acceptable levels of quality for execution, outcomes, or both.

Design processes are the workhorse of organizations that design. For as long as there has been complex technology to design, there has been a need for processes. A design process defines which methods are chosen, how they are executed, criteria for their execution, the allocation of resources, and the way the project is communicated and documented. They do not only ensure quality—they also regulate, direct efforts, educate, communicate, and help designers form a shared identity.

The classical process model for software projects is the *waterfall model*. A waterfall model consists of a sequence of stages. After completing one stage and meeting a predefined set of requirements ("a door"), the team progresses to the next stage. The model starts with user research, which leads to requirements specification, and then continues with design, evaluation, and ultimately release.

Despite being logical, the model has been criticized as parochial and even damaging. One recognized flaw is that it does not cope well with changes and discoveries made during a project. In practice, changes are frequent in design processes, for example, in the form of revised design requirements. The model also has high *sunk costs*, as whatever is decided early in the process is difficult to change later. Furthermore, from a human–computer interaction (HCI) perspective, evaluation is carried out too late. If evaluation is not carried out iteratively, it cannot inform critical decisions made during design and implementation.

Based on such observations, process models in HCI have evolved in different directions. A core insight about HCI process models is that having a design process does not need to be antithetical to creativity. A process can be set to make room for and facilitate creativity. In other words, a creative process can be managed just like a development process in engineering can be managed.

In addition, HCI process models have three other shared aspects:

User focus: The success criteria and goals of a project are defined in terms of the user as opposed to, for example, purely economic or technical terms.

Iteration: Recognizing that perfect solutions are practically impossible to come up with in a single shot, HCI process models integrate iterative design at their heart.

Introduction to Human-Computer Interaction. Kasper Hornbæk, Per Ola Kristensson, and Antti Oulasvirta,
Oxford University Press. © Kasper Hornbæk, Per Ola Kristensson, and Antti Oulasvirta (2025).
DOI: 10.1093/oso/9780192864543.003.0033

Evaluation with users: The goodness of a design is demonstrated by reference to empirical or other evaluations that involve users.

This chapter will now introduce four major types of design processes that are applied in the design of interactive technology. These four types emphasize different aspects in design. The first type emphasizes user-centricity. If putting the user first is to be taken seriously, HCI needs process models that ensure end-users' requirements have a prime position. The second type emphasizes quality assurance while realizing the importance of iteration. Usability engineering and its variations seek to ensure that certain criteria are met before moving on while allowing for iteration. The third type, agile development, emphasizes the ability to react to discoveries made during design and development. Agile development calls for frequent re-evaluation of the purposes and constraints of a project. The fourth type focuses on risk management. Human factors engineering is a process followed in safety-critical areas, for example, in organizations like NASA.

33.1 User-centered design processes

While specific design processes differ, most user-centered or human-centered design processes share four core *phases*:

1. User research
2. Formation of design goals (requirements)
3. Generation of design ideas (design)
4. Evaluation.

In human-centered design processes, a design process is not just an account of the order in which methods are to be applied. A design process can define and communicate what is valuable in design, for example, what an organization stands for. Human-centered processes (HCPs) define how to set and reach goals for activities in design, how to talk about design, how to streamline activities for greater efficiency and compatibility, how to put safeguards in place to minimize risks, and generally how to guide and manage a project while keeping the end-user in mind.

There are numerous user- and human-centered design process models. They can be distinguished according to eight dimensions:

Application area: Different design processes are suitable for different application areas. For example, human factors engineering processes are applied in safety-critical areas; design thinking is applied in creative areas. Usability engineering, which encompasses product design and product updates, has been mainly used for software user interfaces.

Constructs and measurements: Constructs differ depending on the design process. For example, human factors engineering covers constructs related to ergonomics, breaking them into three groups with dedicated measurements: physical ergonomics, cognitive ergonomics, and social ergonomics. By contrast, usability standards do not commit to a particular construct or measurement and emphasize the user's point of view as a guiding principle for evaluation.

Methods: The specific approaches, techniques, and methods vary depending on the design process. For example, human factors engineering emphasizes analysis and modeling, while usability engineering emphasizes empirical testing (usability tests).

Phases and conditions for advancing: This refers to the phases in a process and the conditions for progressing from one phase to the next. Phases do not need to be organized in a linear manner; parallel activities can happen, and failure in one phase can lead to the resumption of an earlier phase. Processes differ vastly in these respects. Standards, such as ISO 9241, set strict advancement criteria for each phase, whereas agile development emphasizes group-level discussions when contemplating such decisions.

Inclusion: Which stakeholders are included in which phase? For example, in participatory design, end-users are involved in the process of design.

Tools and documents: Software and other tools used in the process, as well as documents, such as guidelines and checklists, vary depending on the design process. A *design system* may incorporate all of these.

Communication: The strategies, media, and tools for communicating may be different across design processes. This includes means and tools for both internal and external communication.

Management: The monitoring of progress, contingency measures, and risk management strategies, and their relative importance and implementation in the design process.

Having a design process can be a goal in itself. *Normative* design processes entail an agreed-on procedure that must be followed for economic or ethical reasons. The ISO 9241 standard is a good example: A company that complies with the standard can be perceived to be more reliable and trustworthy by a client. *Suggestive* design processes propose an idealized procedure, a set of desired characteristics. However, the details of execution are left to be decided on a case-by-case basis. Agile development, at its extreme, puts emphasis on continuous reflection over direction, which gives more responsibility to the people executing the process. However, most processes fall somewhere in between: They set certain desirable qualities and leave other parts open for the practitioner to decide.

Process models are necessarily idealizations. That is, a project rarely advances in the strictly linear manner suggested by a model. As mentioned in the chapter on design practice (Chapter 32), real-world projects are "messy." For instance, different methods are executed in parallel by different people. It is possible to go back and forth between phases and skip one or more phases. The reason for this is that design is hard: Many objectives and constraints must be met under uncertainty. Iteration and reiteration are thus necessary to reduce uncertainty. This is true even in axiomatic sciences, such as mathematics. A mathematician does not derive a proof in one giant step but instead arrives at it in an iterative fashion.

Having established fundamental traits of user-centered design processes for HCI, we now review some major representative process models.

33.2 Usability engineering

The *usability engineering lifecycle* is perhaps the most successful user-centric process model in software engineering [589, 591]. The model is an evolution of process models used in software engineering. It was introduced by Nielsen in the early 1990s as an attempt to increase the usability of information technology. Around that time, the personal computer was adopted in workplaces and homes, and its increasing complexity resulted in pressure to develop easy-to-use software. Heuristics and guidelines (Chapter 41) were insufficient: They were often based on little more than intuition and offered no help for solving trade-offs among design decisions. The usability engineering model extended other emerging models of the time, most notably the "golden rules" [285]: early focus on users, user participation during design, consistency as a goal for user interface design, empirical user testing, and iterative designs informed by test results.

The model was conceived as a *lifecycle model* to help developers not only launch products but also keep them updated. This required considering how skills acquired from previous versions affected the future versions. The model has 10 phases:

1. **Know thy user:** Usability engineering rests on user research, the goal of which is to chart user characteristics, understand tasks and needs for system functionalities, and track the evolution of skills and needs of the user over time. Contrary to how the method is now deployed, Nielsen originally proposed using task analysis to understand the structure of activities.

2. **Competitive analysis:** Analyze existing products to understand their design. This offers insights in many ways. Analyzing the design solutions of products can help develop guidelines and heuristics. Comparing products empirically can help determine minimum thresholds for usability; it is useful to define the usability of the new product with reference to the change in usability compared to competitors' products.

3. **Setting usability goals:** Concrete measurable goals are set for the design based on Phases 1 and 2. Nielsen proposed five general types of goals: learnability, efficiency, re-learnability (the ability of infrequent users to return to using the system without having to learn it all over), user errors, and subjective user satisfaction. These goals need to be prioritized to help resolve trade-offs between conflicting design objectives. This is the phase that distinguishes usability engineering from its predecessors. By setting measurable usability goals, the designer needs to provide clear evidence of the viability of the design.

4. **Design stage:** The main objective here is to produce a usable implementation that can be tested and, if successful in meeting its goals, deployed. Nielsen emphasized participatory design: "Instead of guessing, designers should have access to a pool of representative users after the start of the design phase" [589, p. 15]. Users "should be involved in the design process through regular meetings."

5. **Coordinated design:** Nielsen believed that the consistency of the interface with other products and versions was key to achieving high learnability. Therefore, in the fifth phase, a process is put in place to ensure coordination with different designs. Nielsen proposed several methods for this, including a centralized coordinator or committee, code-sharing and meetings, and company-wide documents on design patterns.

6. **Guidelines and heuristics:** Heuristic evaluation refers to the use of rules of thumb to assess a design. Nielsen recognized the need for not only general guidelines but also category-specific (e.g., video recorders) and product-specific guidelines. These different levels of specificity help designers ensure a minimum level of quality and assist them in pursuing consistency within the broader category of a design.

7. **Prototyping:** In the seventh phase, prototypes are developed for empirical testing. Nielsen warned against going directly for a fully functional version and instead suggested using primitive prototypes in the beginning, even paper mock-ups, and only increasing the level of fidelity after an appropriate level of certainty has been reached about core design decisions.

8. **Empirical user testing:** After a promising prototype has been reached, it should be tested empirically against the set usability goals. Such testing can take on many different forms. Within usability engineering, testing usually involves a controlled usability test (Chapter 43). To inform the development of a better prototype, it is important to collect a list of usability

problems, as well as hints for features that could assist users. These usability problems and hints for features should be prioritized based on empirical data and the priority of the problem.
9. **Iterative design:** A key tenet of usability engineering is to iteratively improve the prototype until it meets the stated goals. Since designs are complex, a threat is to end up going in circles, or repeating design ideas without exploring new ones. Moreover, without documenting *why* a design decision was taken, designers may easily lose sight of empirical data. Nielsen proposed using *design rationale*, that is, documenting the rationale behind decisions.
10. **Collecting feedback from the field:** Usability engineering does not end with the release of the product. Log data, customer reviews, and so on should be collected to continuously track usability as the users and the market evolve. The goal is to collect information to inform the design of the next product.

While usability engineering is one of the most widely used process models, it has attracted serious criticism for two primary reasons. The first reason is its limited support for design as a creative activity. Little help is provided on *how* to produce design ideas [290]. While many apply variants of usability engineering that put more emphasis on iteration and sketching, agile development methods address this limitation head-on.

The second reason is that usability engineering can be viewed as glorified trial and error. The method does not embrace theoretical knowledge in any significant form. The theoryless stance of usability engineering was motivated by the limited nature of some theories in the early 1990s. However, it risks creating a form of user-centered design that is detached from research in HCI.

33.2.1 A standard for human-centered design

A process model similar to the usability engineering lifecycle has been developed into a standard offered by the International Organization for Standardization (ISO). The ISO 9241-220:2019 standard defines a process model for human-centered design. The earlier versions of the standard focused on usability, defined in terms of effectiveness, efficiency, and satisfaction in a particular context of use. The latest version from 2019 also includes accessibility, user experience, and avoiding harm as stated goals for design. The standard emphasizes that usability and other variables are an outcome of interaction—they are not properties of a product. Usability or experience cannot merely be inserted into a product, system, or service. The standard defines activities, documents, criteria, and checks needed to ensure high usability can be achieved.

The standard is a document of almost 100 pages, consisting of definitions, checklists, and guidance. It recognizes that user-centered design is not merely about the generation of great design ideas; it requires the entire organization, including its management, to commit to it. This is an important message: Sufficient support and resources from management are necessary for realizing user-centricity. The standard is divided into four HCPs:

- HCP.1: Processes to ensure enterprise-level focus on users.
- HCP.2: Processes to enable human-centered design across projects and systems.
- HCP.3: Processes to execute human-centered design within a project.
- HCP.4: Processes to introduce, operate, and end a system.

HCP.3 focuses on project-level activities and has similarities to usability engineering: Both process models start with planning (HCP3.1), continue with the definition of context and requirements gathering, and end with design and evaluation. What the standard adds is a set of specific decisions, checks, and documents.

The identification of requirements plays a central role in the standard. Requirements (Chapter 36) are the goal of user research, and they are selectively used as criteria in evaluation. What do they look like? The standard distinguishes requirements for general use and requirements for interaction. Here are some examples of requirements for immigration at an airport:

1. The average time that air passengers entering the United States take to pass through immigration (during specified hours) shall be no more than half the average time taken currently, while maintaining currently specified levels of security and safety in screening arrivals.
2. 80% of all potential users of the ticket machine shall prefer the use of the ticket machine to the use of the ticket counter.
3. With the ticket machine, 95% of users shall be able to buy the cheapest ticket to a location within 30 s.
4. The percentage of use errors made by users that can cause harm (under specified conditions) shall not be greater than 1%.
5. The mean rating given by user group X for the company's reputation as the market leader for quality and innovation does not decrease after the users read advertising material for the new product.

Why bother with a standard? Following a standard can be useful in many ways for an organization. A standard can help designers develop competencies in a technically challenging area, ensure the quality of processes and products, and communicate product capabilities to customers and stakeholders. A standard can also help ensure a minimum level of quality, especially in large organizations with employees from different backgrounds. At the same time, standards are thwarted by some creative professionals who feel that they stifle creativity.

33.2.2 A standard for ethical system design

There is an increasing need to ensure that technology utilizing AI works in an ethically acceptable way. However, this is very difficult to address in complex real-world projects. Different stakeholders have different values, and a system's effect on them may not be obvious.

The IEEE Standard 7000 is a process model for addressing ethical concerns during system design and minimizing potential harm to users [812]. It builds on *value-sensitive design*, which we discussed in Chapter 30. While the standard does not guarantee ethicality, it helps ensure that relevant stakeholders and their concerns are systematically considered in design.

The standard starts by warning that addressing ethical concerns is not a simple process; it requires rigorous work and commitment from all stakeholders: manufacturers, engineers, consumers, and users. To set up a project, the specific domain of application should be named, for example, nursing homes, language education, medical advice, or music recommendations. A team is then recruited with a named champion and relevant domain and process competencies in place. The rest of the standard covers the four main steps shown in Figure 33.1.

```
                    Setting up a Project
                            │
                            ▼
              ┌───────────────────────────┐  ┐
              │ Concept of Operations and │  │
              │    Context Exploration    │  │
              └───────────────────────────┘  │
                            │                │  Concept exploration
                            ▼                │       stage
              ┌───────────────────────────┐  │
              │   Value Elicitation and   │  │
              │      Prioritization       │  │
              └───────────────────────────┘  ┘
                            │
                            ▼
              ┌───────────────────────────┐  ┐
              │ Ethical Requirements Definition │  │
              └───────────────────────────┘  │
                            │                │  Development stage
                            ▼                │
              ┌───────────────────────────┐  │
              │  Ethical Risk-based Design │  │
              └───────────────────────────┘  ┘
                            │
                            ▼
                  Transparency Management
```

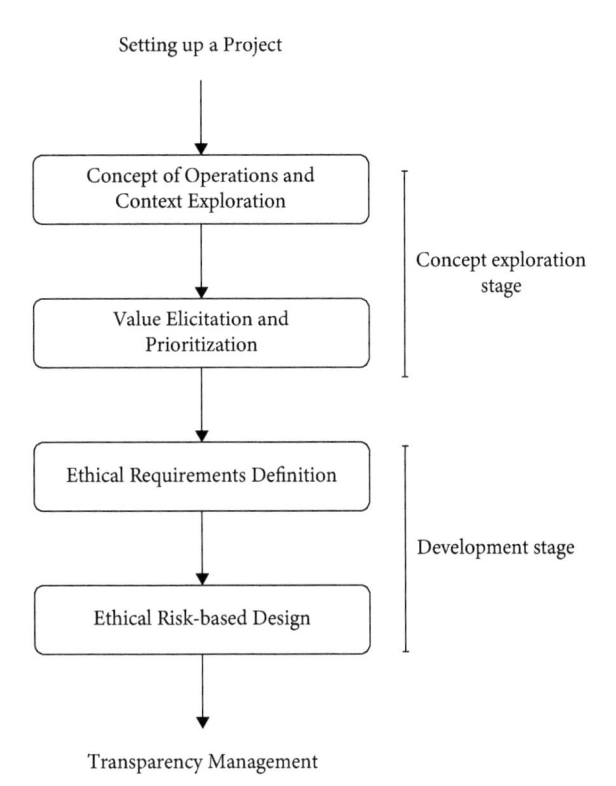

Figure 33.1 An overview of the IEEE Standard 7000 for addressing ethical concerns in system design.

Concept of operations and context exploration: The goal is to establish an understanding of the system's intended contexts of use and then identify the involved stakeholders who might be affected by the system.

Value elicitation and prioritization: Relevant stakeholders are selected for value identification. Their values are recorded, including a detailed analysis of the benefits and harms from a utilitarian perspective. While the standard gives advice for general types of values (e.g., security, safety, health, aesthetics, trust, respect, privacy, openness, autonomy, care, control, fairness, and inclusiveness), it is the stakeholders who define their values. A key question to ask is: "What benefits or harms would arise if the system was deployed in the way we envision it?" This analysis is utilitarian; in other words, it concerns the consequences of possible events.

Stakeholders are then interviewed for virtue-ethical concerns and ethical duties. In other words, it is studied how the system might change the character of the stakeholders by threatening things they regard as virtues, or how it might challenge ethical rules or maxims they hold important. The values regarded as important in the stakeholders' cultures are analyzed in a similar way.

These values are then prioritized. The standard provides some guidance for prioritization. For example, the existence of a positive value is itself a positive value, while the existence of a negative value is itself a negative value. Importantly, the ranked list of values is validated by the stakeholders. Having ranked the values, the organization's buy-in for the prioritization is sought, for example, by liaising with management.

Ethical requirements definition: Ethical value requirements (EVRs) can be expressed in many ways: as formal requirement statements, use cases, user stories, or scenarios. They should indicate how the system can threaten or promote core values. EVRs are validated with stakeholders and adjusted.

Ethical risk-based design: Design methods and activities are selected to maximize the chance of achieving EVRs. Stakeholders are consulted before implementing the plan, with explicit discussion about the probability of harm occurring.

The work does not end after implementing the design. In *transparency management*, ethical issues are tracked and shared with stakeholders for discussion.

> **Paper Example 33.2.1: Ethical risk-based design of a body scanner**
>
> The IEEE Standard 7000 [812] was applied to the design of a full-body scanner for airports. People had complained about and refused to use a previous imaging technology that used X-rays and had exposed high-quality images of naked bodies to security officers. The core value identified for the passengers concerned privacy: The scanner should avoid the exposure of passengers' figures, genitals, and confidential data. While privacy was a high-ranked EVR, the highest-ranked EVR concerned air safety: No dangerous articles should be carried onboard. Efficiency was ranked lower than these two EVRs. Based on further analyses, the privacy-related EVR that emerged were formulated both negatively (what should not be shown) and positively (what can be shown).

33.3 Agile development

Agile development processes arose as a response to the felt shortcomings of traditional software engineering process models. Agile methods are based on the idea that design is an *empirical* activity; that is, it is a process of learning from trials. The idea of agility is this: If you discover a new idea or problem during a project, it would be unwise not to consider changing direction. Consequently, agile methods put the emphasis on design sprints over requirements-based engineering.

Because the design space tends to be large, agile processes focus on rapid iteration. The faster a bad idea can be rejected, the better. The more ideas one can explore, the better. Consequently, agile development processes are organized around *design sprints*. Unlike traditional waterfall-based projects, where a single project might trial only a single design, tens or even hundreds of sprints can take place during an agile project. A design sprint may take a week—or only one day at its extreme—from beginning to end.

Scrum is one of the most popular agile development methods that emerged during the last decade. Central to Scrum and other agile development processes is the attention to constraints and objectives that set the stage for the design sprints. This includes vision and requirements from clients and competition, as in all processes. In addition, Scrum pays attention to time pressures and other resource-related constraints. The other aspects of a project evolve during the project: The product, and even the schedule of the project, can be defined while the project is ongoing. Scrum emphasizes flexibility in allocating time and people into sprints, and sensitivity in using learning from prior sprints to define the next ones.

HCI methods play a central role in many agile projects. A survey of 92 developers using agile methods found that HCI methods are integrated into their processes [363]. The most commonly used methods are those that can be used quickly during a sprint, such as low-fidelity prototyping, concept designs, rapid observational studies, and heuristic evaluations.

33.4 Human factors engineering

Human factors engineering—sometimes called cognitive engineering—refers to the design and construction of safe and reliable technological systems. At the surface, design processes in human factors engineering appear like any other user-centric process. However, they put more emphasis on safety. In safety-critical areas, human life is a major consideration. Therefore, these process models put more emphasis on the identification and mitigation of human error in design.

Medical device design is a good example [692]. In the United States alone, tens of thousands of deaths occur annually that can be attributed to medical errors. Human factors processes aim to minimize the risk of such errors through design. While human error can never be fully eliminated, good design goes a long way toward decreasing the risk of such errors occurring. For instance, regulators such as the Food and Drug Administration in the United States recommend following a human factors process consisting of five stages, each with its own methods and focus on user-centricity:

Ideation: This involves using methods such as use cases and personas to ideate cases for new features or devices. User-centricity is important to avoid biasing design toward a particular stakeholder group.

Requirements: In this key stage, human factors processes utilize empirical methods (e.g., field studies) and analytical tools (e.g., task analysis) to analyze use environments and work practice.

Design: Human factors processes utilize similar methods to other processes, such as sketching and prototyping. However, they also emphasize theories from cognitive psychology as additional justification for design decisions. For example, design decisions that aim to minimize the cognitive load may refer to theories of multitasking, cognitive load, and attention. These methods ensure that a design is safe across a wide variety of circumstances.

Testing: Making use of usability tests, heuristic analyses, cognitive walkthroughs, and other methods. Human factors processes pay special attention to evaluations that directly assess a design against its original requirements.

Maintenance: Reviewing and reacting to adverse event reports, for example, accident reports.

The process is iterated until the stated requirements are met. A focus on users, the application of theories from cognitive sciences, and ecological validity are important considerations.

The human factors engineering model differs from other process models in one defining aspect: Design is about affecting *psychological variables* [599]. By affecting such variables, for example, a person's workload, feeling of trust, or perception, design can selectively reduce the possibility of error.

Such variables can be related to physiological constructs, such as fatigue or stress, which can be analyzed using biomechanical models and questionnaires. They can also be related to cognitive factors, for example, factors related to perception (e.g., visibility), attention (e.g., situation awareness), or mental demand (e.g., cognitive workload). They also cover aspects of human reliability and error, such as reasoning errors, motor slips, and disregard of safety regulations.

The focus on psychological variables is based on the idea that cognition is the key to safe and reliable systems. Consider, for example, designing a control panel for an emergency dispatch officer. One goal for a human factors engineer would be to minimize the workload and errors. These are psychological constructs that can be empirically measured. Consequently, much of the work in the process focuses on the definition of proper measurements and experiments (operationalization).

Human factors engineering also puts emphasis on analytical methods, such as task analysis and performance modeling (Chapter 41). Simulation models of the human body are used to understand stress in harsh working environments, and cognitive models are used to predict the effects of user interface design on the mental workload of a user.

However, outside of safety-critical domains in consumer products, the analytical and formal methods of human factors engineering are often too costly to develop and require expertise that is out of reach for regular practitioners. This motivated the development of "theory-free" engineering methods, such as usability engineering, which have taken precedence in non-safety-critical areas.

33.5 Following a process is better than ad hoc practices

Design processes commit to the idea of the rational designer: One always has a good reason for a decision. As we have learned, designers do not work like that—they struggle with fixation, biases, and ill-defined problems. Does this not call into question the very possibility of a design process? In other words, if processes are idealizations that can never be attained, why bother "faking" them?

Parnas and Clements [640] made the case for sticking to design processes despite their flawed assumptions about design. Design processes guide designers. When facing a very hard challenge, they offer suggestions for how to progress. Design processes also harmonize practices in a company, thus facilitating collaboration across teams and departments. Moreover, design processes help us measure progress: When we know what designers are supposed to be doing, we can better manage the process and develop it over time. Thus, by "faking" the ideal process, one nonetheless moves closer to it. Generally, it is better to be led by an idealistic process than to be left at the mercy of ad hoc practices.

Following a design process is essential for projects that claim to be user-centric. By requiring user researchers to define design requirements, the base of a design is made explicit. For example, is a design targeting the actual end-users—or the company's boss? By requiring designers to explain how their decisions address the design requirements, the requirements can be better traced, challenged, and reasoned about. Why is this feature here—in what way is it important for end-users? Finally, requiring developers to document code makes the software easier to maintain in the future. As Parnas and Clements [640] noted, "It is very hard to be a rational designer; even faking that process is quite difficult. However, the result is a product that can be understood, maintained, and reused" [p. 256]. Thus, instead of asking if design processes are worth the effort, the question is whether one can afford not to follow one.

Summary

- Design processes define the order and manner in which design methods and techniques should be applied in a project. They are normative accounts of design that describe how it is supposed to be done.
- Most process models are iterative and have four stages: user research, requirements specification, design generation, and evaluation.

- Agile methods emphasize fast iteration and reactiveness over long-term planning.
- Usability engineering is a widely adopted process model for ensuring interactive systems have high usability. It has been criticized as being glorified trial and error and for lacking connections to theory.
- Even though processes are normative and based on an idealized assumption of design, following a process offers many advantages over ad hoc practices.

Exercises

1. Pros and cons of user-centeredness. Discuss why an organization developing a product for a consumer market may *not* employ a user-centered design process.
2. Process models. Propose and motivate a process model for the following design tasks. (a) The design of a magnetic resonance imaging visualization tool for medical practitioners. (b) A smart wristband that collects biophysical measurements from the user and provides exercise and lifestyle advice. (c) A shopping web site for clothes that allows users to "try out" clothes in virtual reality. (d) A mobile phone app that teaches children multiplication tables.
3. Choosing process models. What would you recommend as a process model for each of the following situations? (a) Developing a medical device for nurses to monitor the health of a patient. (b) Providing an innovative way for teenagers to buy clothes. (c) Updating a university's online learning system to improve its usability. (d) Launching a new social media application for road cycling enthusiasts.

Part VII

Engineering

34
Introduction to engineering

In human–computer interaction (HCI), engineering refers to the application of principles and methods from engineering research to build interactive systems. We need engineering because building interactive systems is hard. A wide range of technical functions must be realized in software or hardware while simultaneously addressing a broad set of human-related requirements. Engineering methods systematically tackle this challenge and ensure that the resulting system can be used efficiently and safely, manufactured at a low cost and high quality, and supported after launch, including during its eventual disposal.

One area of HCI research is concerned with understanding how engineering methods can be used more effectively and efficiently for developing new methods, tools, and systems. The following are two representative examples:

- Optical see-through augmented reality (AR) enables users to wear AR glasses and interact by articulating gestures using their fingers and hands in 3D space. A difficult problem in realizing such a system is *key gesture spotting*, that is, identifying gestures within a stream of unrelated movements. If the system does not work well, it results in user frustration as intended gestures are not recognized correctly while unintended gestures give rise to commands in the system. *Gesture Spotter* [763] is a rapid prototyping software tool (Chapter 38) that allows developers to easily add their own gestures and have them reliably recognized among a continuous stream of hand and finger movements. The tool includes a graphical user interface that supports the rapid design iteration of different gesture sets and an application programming interface for deploying apps with integrated gesture recognition. Evaluations with developers demonstrated that both were effective in enabling non-experts to support key gesture spotting in AR glasses applications.

- Safety-critical user interfaces can give rise to potentially disastrous human errors (Chapter 37). As a result, formal methods such as rigorously defined mathematical models are used when designing such user interfaces (Chapter 38). Formal methods allow user interfaces to be verified and corrected against a specification. Several tools are available for HCI designers and developers to use formal methods to verify whether user interfaces behave correctly. However, these tools have been developed to examine specific issues in user interface design, and it is unclear how such tools can be fruitfully used as part of a user-centered design process (Chapter 33). Campos et al. [123] investigated three such tools to understand how each of them would fit in a user-centered design process. One finding is that these three tools are largely complementary, each addressing different aspects of a user-centered design process. For example, one tool was more suitable for rapid prototyping while another tool was advantageous when addressing general usability concerns. The paper provides 22 criteria for evaluation to help developers select suitable tools.

Engineering is tightly interwoven with design, which we discussed in Part VI. A system cannot be "just built" its construction needs to be designed. Therefore, problem-solving and exploring and evaluating options are also central to engineering. In this sense, an engineer is also a designer, designing bridges, motors, circuit boards, mechanical structures, software, systems, and so on.

In this book, we do not attempt to strictly differentiate between design and engineering. Rather, in engineering, we shift the focus on what is required for *building* a system that has desirable properties. The system cannot just be a plan or a prototype; it must actually work and be effective, efficient, safe, and fulfill users' needs and wants. To realize this, we must design the technology itself—identify a functional architecture for the system, translate given functions into "function carriers," ensure the requirements are correct and have been met, and so on.

This part of the book introduces perspectives, ideas, principles, and processes from engineering and explains how they can be used in the context of interactive system design.

34.1 Structure of this part

The design of interactive systems is a *systems engineering* problem where a key challenge is to understand the *system* we are trying to build and its relation to other systems. Systems are pervasive; we are surrounded by them. We live in an ecosystem and may take part in economic and political systems. We are typically part of some form of organization, such as a university, and we work using computer systems that are interconnected through the Internet. Systems are reliant on other systems to function. For instance, our computers are reliant on the electrical grid. Furthermore, systems are embedded within other systems: A laptop is reliant on a display, a central processing unit, memory circuits, input and output devices, and so on. Similarly, the human body consists of several subsystems, such as the circulatory and digestive systems.

Chapter 35 introduces *systems thinking*, a perspective in engineering that allows us to reason about the complexity of systems and principles that help us design, build, and support systems. In addition, it is important to be able to understand systems. This can be done by mapping out systems from various perspectives, for example, from the perspective of the flow of documents and information in a large organization. Chapter 35 introduces several system mapping techniques that can be used to gain a holistic understanding of the internal mechanisms driving a system and its relationships with other systems.

Another key facet of engineering is conceiving, understanding, and managing appropriate processes that allow us to systematically arrive at interactive systems with the desired qualities. We will therefore introduce *design engineering* as an approach to engineering HCI systems (Chapter 36). Design engineering, or engineering design, is an engineering discipline concerned with processes that support the systematic creation of products, systems, and services. We believe design engineering is very useful in guiding the design of interactive systems, which typically exhibit a high degree of complexity and are often required to interface with many different types of end-users in many use contexts.

Design engineering overlaps with the design processes we discussed in the chapter on design practice (Chapter 32). The distinction we make in this book is that design engineering focuses on arriving at a *system solution* for a solution-neutral problem statement that is specified in such detail that it can be built, verified, and validated. As such, the chapter on design engineering provides practical guidance to the reader on how to realize a system. The other chapters in this part of the book provide additional perspectives and techniques for realizing systems.

A third key facet of engineering is *safety and risk*. A system must be safe to use; therefore, it is vital to understand how to design an interactive system that does not intentionally or unintentionally harm users. To this end, Chapter 37 introduces methods that can be used to ensure interactive systems are safe. We will explain what is meant by *human error*, such as taxonomies for human error and how human errors are analyzed. We will also define risk and reason about how we can assess and manage risks. Chapter 37 presents several *risk management* strategies that can be used to achieve this for interactive systems. Finally, another important aspect of safety and risk in an interactive system is the concept of a *failure*—an unintended outcome of a system. We will explain how *reliability engineering* allows us to statistically model probabilities of failure, thereby providing us with a mathematical method for estimating the reliability of various system structures.

Interactive systems rely on complex *software*. Chapter 38 introduces principles and approaches in *software design and architecture* that support the construction of interactive user interfaces. It then explains how *toolkits* can be designed to assist developers in implementing interactive systems software. The chapter also discusses how to enable end-users to program computer systems, which is known as *end-user development*. There are several approaches for designing such systems, such as programming by example. Finally, to ensure our interactive systems work correctly in software, we can construct a formal model of interaction that allows us to reason about the properties of interaction. For example, we can represent interaction as a finite-state machine and use techniques from computer science to reason about whether a user can reach all states in the system. We can also use a formal representation to represent a system function, such as *undo*, and test various properties of such a system.

Finally, engineering is also about using computation to tackle challenging tasks in interaction. Chapter 39 presents *computational methods* for interactive systems. The central notion in this chapter is the existence of a model that allows for algorithmic or mathematical reasoning about some aspect of interaction. The chapter begins by explaining how such models may be created and how they can be used to analyze an interactive system at an early stage of the design. We will discover that such models can capture controllable and uncontrollable parameters of a system. Uncontrollable parameters are parameters that affect the system's outcomes but are outside the control of the designer, for example, the user's level of motor control, cognition, or experience with a particular system. Controllable parameters are parameters we can tune to improve outcomes. Thus, they allow us to perform *optimization*. In this regard, we can do more than reason about potential outcomes and optimize controllable parameters. For instance, we can build a system that infers or predicts users' actions or makes decisions in collaboration with or on behalf of users. Techniques from *pattern recognition and machine learning* allow designers to model tasks as inference problems that the computer can address. For example, a system may recognize users' 3D gesture articulation from observations from a depth sensor. Chapter 39 outlines which types of tasks such approaches can support and some key design issues to consider when using such methods in interactive system design.

34.2 Engineering perspectives in HCI

It is natural to ask what engineering can bring to HCI that is not already there. After all, HCI already has multiple principles, approaches, and methods at its disposal for designing interactive systems. In what follows, we set out to answer this question by explaining how engineering can serve as a *complementary* approach to established design practice in HCI.

34.2.1 Building the right thing

One fundamental aspect of engineering is understanding what to do and how to do it. This is called *task clarification*. An easy—but critical—mistake to make is to design a solution for the wrong problem, or to create a solution that does not solve any problem users are facing—a "solution in search of a problem." This can be prevented by understanding how to arrive at a valid *problem statement* that is relevant to the users and their goals.

Arriving at a valid problem statement can be more difficult than it sounds. It requires a deep understanding of the nature of the problem, which often necessitates knowing about the relevant aspects of the problem context, users' needs and wants, and the system in which the interactive system or service will be embedded.

Crucially, it is insufficient to merely arrive at a problem statement. This is due to a design pitfall known as *design fixation*, which in essence amounts to immediately settling on the first obvious solution that comes to mind (Chapter 31). This "engineer's disease" prevents the designer, or the design team, from fully exploring a larger set of possible solutions and artificially constrains the design space. As a result, it frequently leads to less creative and less optimal design solutions. This may sound trivial, but it is a very real design problem with potentially a very high cost. Failing to be creative about how to do things—or even about how to *not* do things—can lead to noncompetitive products or services. For example, failing to be creative about how to test a product may lead to a failure to detect a product flaw, which later triggers an expensive product recall.

One technique to avoid design fixation in engineering is to transform a problem statement into a *solution-neutral problem statement*, which describes the problem at a suitable level of abstraction without making any direct references to solutions. For example, instead of starting out with a problem statement such as "Build a physical thumb keyboard that uses the QWERTY layout for a mobile device," the design team may consider the solution-neutral variant "Devise a method that allows a user to enter text on a mobile device" or the even more abstract variant "Devise a method that allows a user to transmit information in a mobile setting." Raising the abstraction level increases the search space.

Another technique in engineering to avoid design fixation is to first design a product or service at the *functional level*, which only considers the relationships between *functions*. For example, a keyboard may have an overall designated function `Enter Text` that can be decomposed into its key subfunctions, such as `Type Key`, `Provide Word Prediction`, and so on. Importantly, none of these functions references a *solution*. For example, the function `Type Key` can be realized using hard keys, chiclet keys, membrane keys, or touchscreen keys. These are all examples of *function carriers*. That is, they are designated solutions that carry a function. Then, we can systematically explore *combinations* of solutions that may lead to promising designs. This is known as concept generation and evaluation.

34.2.2 Building the thing right

Having understood what to build, we need to ensure we build it correctly. To do this, we need to understand the *requirements* involved in building the interactive system. There are many variants of requirements, such as user requirements, business requirements, and technical requirements; typically, it helps greatly to have an accurate understanding of all of the relevant requirements early in the design process. The tasks of eliciting and managing requirements throughout a design process are known as *requirements engineering*.

Requirements are important because they tell us how to "build the thing right" a product or service that meets its requirements specification will pass verification. Thus, managing requirements and verification are tightly interwoven processes in practice.

Since requirements are so important to arrive at a successful interactive system, they also carry a lot of risk. It is very easy to fail to capture accurate requirements. This can happen, for example, if there is a process error when eliciting requirements from users that leads to an incorrect understanding of users' needs and wants. One common source of error is undetected bias. This can easily happen, for instance, when using a survey that only a particular segment of the target audience responds to (e.g., people who do not have to work during the day). Another failure that can have disastrous consequences is failing to set up a necessary requirement to begin with, which then has to be introduced late in the design process. Managing changes in requirements throughout the design process is a very important aspect of project management known as *change management*. As a general rule, the later a requirement has to be changed, the more expensive and difficult it will be to implement that change. Therefore, requirements engineering is a very important aspect of project management.

Once requirements are in place, principles of software engineering are used to implement systems that fulfill those requirements. They inform the design of software architectures that can help manage the high complexity of interactive systems. A key aspect in software architecture is achieving *abstraction*, which means hiding implementation details at a lower level to enable designers to focus on essential design tasks.

34.2.3 Verification and validation

Having built a system, we need to ensure it works as intended and solves the problems of users. The former, known as *verification*, is the process of systematically checking that the system meets all the requirements in its specification. The latter, known as *validation*, is the process of ensuring that the deployed system fulfills its purpose for users.

Verification is, by its very nature, tightly coupled with the management of requirements since only testable requirements can be verified. Furthermore, the successful verification of a requirement demands a clear specification of a verification procedure, verification environment, and success criteria, all of which rely on the context giving rise to the requirement in the first place.

Successful verification means that a system fulfills all its requirements as specified in the requirements specification. However, successful verification does not mean the system is fit for purpose, as there may be errors in the requirements specification. In practice, inaccurate or missing requirements are common. Furthermore, circumstances may have changed, or new factors may have been introduced, which were unknown when the requirements were defined. Therefore, it is also critical to validate a system, which means ensuring that the system achieves its overall intended function in actual use contexts.

While HCI is to a large extent concerned with *evaluation* (Part VIII), verification and validation in engineering bring their own perspectives on how to ensure an interactive system is built correctly and fulfills its purpose.

34.2.4 Systems thinking

Another perspective that engineering brings to HCI is *systems thinking* (Chapter 35). User interfaces are interactive systems that are both embedded within other systems and related to other systems. They can also consist of subsystems that must work together to form a coherent whole.

Furthermore, users and other stakeholders are often relevant parts of the wider systems in which interactive systems find themselves embedded. For example, a pen injector for injecting a medical drug may have to interact with an app that calculates the correct dosage. This system may then be embedded within a complex healthcare system involving a nurse administering the dose and a patient receiving the treatment. Such *joint* systems that involve both users and user interfaces require designers to have a deeper understanding of the systems within which an interactive system will be used.

Engineering provides a toolbox to assist with such an understanding of systems in the form of *system mapping* methods. These methods allow designers to create elaborate maps of how systems are composed and how, for example, people relate to each other or how information flows within an organization.

Systems thinking requires some similar skills to design practice (Chapter 32). Paper Example 34.2.1 presents a related case.

Paper Example 34.2.1: Engineering requires getting the problem right

Engineers need not only to find the best system-level solutions but also to agree on what they are designing for. Bucciarelli and Bucciarelli [107] reported studies of practicing engineers. The authors were motivated by the observation that engineering is often presented as an instrumental process and not as a situated social process where much work is needed to negotiate and define projects with others. Their book *Designing Engineers* describes three projects: an X-ray inspection system for airports, a photoprint machine, and a residential photovoltaic energy system. What sets their studies apart is that they observed engineers working on these projects during their meetings and at their desks. The authors concluded that engineering design is a social process. It involves multiple parties beyond engineers: marketing people, researchers, accountants, and customers. A critical part of all three projects was defining what was to be done.

34.2.5 Understanding risk and keeping people safe

We increasingly rely on interactive systems for critical tasks where the consequences can be extremely serious if users are unable to reliably carry out their tasks. Engineering provides methods for understanding and minimizing human error and systematically analyzing systems to ensure their safety.

One aspect related to safety is *risk*, which refers to the possibility of a system giving rise to undesired behavior. Such behavior is called a *hazard*. The exposure of a hazard is the degree to which a hazard is able to result in undesirable consequences. The impact of a hazard is a measurement of how serious the consequences are if the system is subjected to the hazard. Risk is the combination of exposure, likelihood, and impact. For something to be high-risk, there needs to be both exposure to a hazard and a high impact and likelihood. Some hazards can have very serious consequences, including the death of a user. However, if the exposure is very low, the risk may still be low.

Risks are ubiquitous in societies and the wider systems they work within, and since user interfaces are embedded within these systems, they also involve risks. Engineering provides a rich set of *risk management* methods for assessing, mitigating, monitoring, and managing risks.

> ### Paper Example 34.2.2: Designing better warnings to keep web users safe
>
> *Phishing* is a scamming technique used to collect users' personal information by exposing users to fake web sites that mimic legitimate ones. To keep users safe, web sites try to warn users about potential phishing web sites. Egelman et al. [220] examined the effectiveness of such warnings in a laboratory study. They simulated a phishing attack and found that 97% of their participants fell for at least one of the attacks they used in the study. They noted that active warnings were more effective than passive warnings. With an active warning, the user is required to read the warning and click an acknowledgment of the threat in order to continue. With a passive warning, a recommendation is provided, but there is no need to acknowledge it—it can be simply dismissed.
>
> The authors discussed this finding in terms of a model of warnings by Wogalter [907]. The model consists of a communication flow between a source (delivering a warning), a channel, and a receiver. However, the receiver is receiving the warning with other stimulation (distractions) that may hinder the processing of the warning. Egelman et al. [220] proposed seven questions to help design safer, more effective warnings:
>
> 1. Do users notice the indicator that a warning has appeared?
> 2. Do users know what the indicators mean?
> 3. Do users know what they are supposed to do with the indicators?
> 4. Do they believe the indicators to be correct?
> 5. Are they motivated to do the correct actions?
> 6. Will they actually perform those actions?
> 7. Will the indicators interact with other environmental stimuli?
>
> This model can be used as a walkthrough to design better warnings.

34.2.6 Managing the process

An interactive system is a complex system by its very nature, as it relies on user interaction and user behavior can rarely be precisely or accurately modeled. This complexity is exacerbated by interactive systems tending to increase in complexity as software and hardware become more sophisticated and allow designers to incorporate more functions in response to users' needs and wants. In addition, interactive systems are increasingly becoming embedded in wider systems, such as manufacturing, smart homes, education, government, and healthcare systems, which necessitates understanding the wider implications of embedding an interactive system within a wider system.

To handle such a design, it is useful to systematically manage the process by using, or at least being aware of, design engineering approaches that have been conceived to support diverse design teams. Such approaches help designers systematically explore conceptual, embodied, and detailed designs all the way to deployment while managing requirements, risks, and other critical considerations such as safety and usability.

34.2.7 Systematic approaches to HCI problems

Finally, engineering allows us to view certain design problems in HCI as problems that can be attacked computationally. We can represent aspects of interaction formally and consequently apply a corresponding systematic approach, such as solving an equation, systematically searching for an approximate or exact solution, or simulating system behavior.

Computational methods are used in HCI to model an aspect of HCI as some formalism, such as a regression model or neural network, and then reason about that aspect, for example, to make inferences about users, predict their behavior, or find designs that best suit them. Computational methods are widely used in HCI, including to optimize input methods and ensure that systems used in healthcare settings can be used safely.

One powerful way engineering enhances design in HCI is through optimization. Certain design problems, such as menu structures, the organization of keys on keyboards, and haptic design parameters, can be systematically optimized to achieve as good a user performance as possible within the assumptions that have been made. Various ways to optimize a design have been proposed in the engineering literature, and many of these approaches are useful for design problems in HCI too. An awareness of such methods may allow for better designs than what may be achieved through traditional design iteration.

Computational approaches also allow us to build systems that can infer or predict users' intentions. Such systems rely on pattern recognition and machine learning to achieve their tasks. Such *inference* brings its own challenges in terms of ensuring interactive systems have high performance, are resilient to noise and changing use contexts, have access to representative training data, and allow humans to interpret their machine learning models and results. Engineering provides methods for systematically tackling such challenges, although several of these methods are currently work-in-progress methods subject to active research.

In summary, systems thinking and computational principles help designers articulate detailed rationales for design decisions and solve design problems with the help of algorithms, allowing them to produce effective, efficient, and safe interactive systems that satisfy users' needs and wants. In other words, these techniques allow designers to both build the right thing and build the thing right.

Summary

- Engineering is about using systematic principles and methods to build systems.
- Systems thinking is paramount when building interactive systems. All interactive systems rely on other systems and are embedded within several other systems.
- To build systems, we need to ensure we build the right thing and that we build the thing right. Design engineering is a design process that focuses on translating a solution-neutral problem statement into a deployed system that can be verified and validated.
- Safety and risk are central notions when engineering interactive systems. Risk is pervasive; it is impossible to design a risk-free system. Risk must be assessed and managed using systematic approaches. We can only design safe systems if we understand how to manage risk.
- Engineering methods and principles and techniques from software development allow us to systematically build interactive systems. Relevant approaches include engineering models, optimization, formal methods, pattern recognition, and machine learning; relevant principles include those from software design and software architecture.

35
Systems

Systems are pervasive in our lives. When you open a door by pulling down the handle and pulling the door open, you are interacting with a system. The door handle is a system that consists of fittings, screws, a plate, and a handle, and it interacts with another system—the door. In turn, the door interacts with the wall through its hinges, and the door frame might even be load-bearing. Furthermore, a user opening the door is attempting to reach a goal state—the door being open—and does so through planned movements executed by the user's human motor control system. The event of the door opening is monitored by the user's visual and auditory systems. At the cellular level, neurons and synapses form complex systems carrying signals through the human body to enable perception and action. Even the door's screws are part of an intricate design, manufacturing, and logistics system that includes designing the screws and efficiently producing, packaging, and distributing them. Finally, doors are subject to regulations, notably building control regulations, which specify several requirements, including acceptable door width dimensions for accessibility.

This system breakdown exercise can be repeated for just about any everyday interaction, from seemingly trivial interactions to highly complex ones. The very fact you are alive when reading these words is a testament to the functioning of a vast array of systems within your body. Your need for shelter, food, electricity, and so on is reliant on several complex systems, including a political system, an economic system, a food production system, a transportation system, and an electricity grid. Systems are truly pervasive, and our lives depend on them.

We can learn a lot from a simple exercise such as analyzing a door system. First, *systems are complex*—they have many dependencies with other systems and entities. Attaining a complete understanding of a system is therefore likely to be challenging; for example, we still do not fully understand how the human brain works. A successful human–computer interaction (HCI) system is likely to be complex in its design and implementation. However, it is also required to interact with other complex systems, including humans, and other technological systems, such as databases, sensors, and machine learning systems.

Second, *systems operate at multiple levels*, ranging from a very low level, such as a nanoscale motor protein, to a very high level, such as the exascale star cluster Omega Centauri. In HCI, we frequently need to work with systems at multiple levels. A computer is an elegant example of systems working at multiple levels in both its software and hardware organizations, ranging from different types of transistors (e.g., NMOS and PMOS) giving rise to CMOS chips at the hardware level to various software libraries and toolkits providing support for drawing primitive graphics, managing user interface elements, and so on. An app on a mobile phone frequently needs to interface with both the graphical user interface toolkit and the many sensor systems available on the phone, such as the camera, gyroscope, accelerometer, and so on.

Third, *systems are coupled*, that is, they depend and rely on each other in various ways. For example, the movement of a mouse on a desk is reflected in the movement of a pointer on a display. This is a form of coupling. In this case, the coupling is mediated by software that manipulates the ratio of pointer movement to mouse movement. Manipulating this ratio enables features such as

Introduction to Human-Computer Interaction. Kasper Hornbæk, Per Ola Kristensson, and Antti Oulasvirta, Oxford University Press. © Kasper Hornbæk, Per Ola Kristensson, and Antti Oulasvirta (2025).
DOI: 10.1093/oso/9780192864543.003.0035

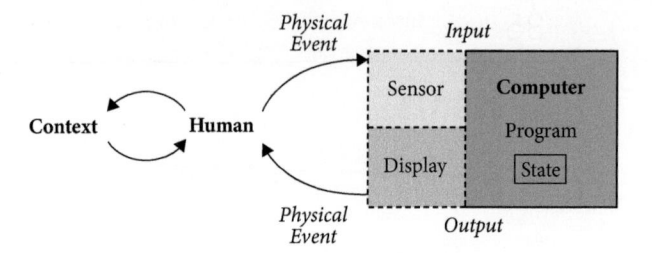

Figure 35.1 A diagram of a simple interactive system.

mouse acceleration. In general, a computer decouples hardware from applications by using an operating system. The more tightly coupled systems are, the more difficult it is to make changes to one system without affecting the other.

Fourth, *systems have emergent properties*. Systems give rise to effects that are more than the sum of their parts. The parts, modules, functions, and subsystems within a system all work together to generate properties, qualities, and outputs that the individual parts cannot provide unless they are arranged together within the system.

Based on these insights about systems, how do we think about them in HCI? Let us consider an *interactive system*, which is a central concept in HCI. From social media applications to intelligent keyboards on mobiles, we use interactive systems all the time. Formally, an interactive system is able to (1) receive and respond to input events via its sensors, (2) perform computations, (3) maintain and update its state, and (4) display its output. This definition exposes challenges that characterize interactive systems engineering.

Figure 35.1 shows an overview of a simple interactive system. The figure makes it clear that this interactive system is a coupled system connecting a user with a computer. It is also embedded within a wider system providing a context for interaction. Furthermore, the technology within the interactive system is reliant on several subsystems, including sensor and display systems, as well as means of performing computations.

The simple diagram in Figure 35.1 indicates that even rudimentary interactive systems rely on several systems to some degree. HCI research frequently needs to consider even wider systems, as illustrated in the following three examples.

- O'Hara et al. [616] reported on how to use depth sensors to enable surgeons to interact with image data in sterile environments using gestures. The research problem builds on prior research on understanding the systems surgeons operate with and within. A key takeaway is that for such a system to be successful, it has to go beyond the idea of touchless interaction in sterile environments and consider the sociotechnical aspects that affect surgeons interacting with technology. This includes taking into account the collaborative aspects of surgery, the fact that surgeons are not always in front of a display when they desire data, the risk that gestures are mistakenly recognized when a surgeon is merely moving their hands, and so on.
- Su and Liu [802] introduced a mobile application for nurses that enables the hospital to move away from paper forms and at the same time provide nurses with additional functionality. The work involved understanding existing nursing processes and forms, the needs and wants of nurses and the hospital, and the type and flow of information.
- Pu et al. [680] introduced a gesture recognition system for an entire home by analyzing wireless signals, such as Wi-Fi. Wireless signals do not suffer from line-of-sight problems, such

as walls blocking infrared light; therefore, they may be used to sense gestures regardless of where the user is in the home. The technique detects the Doppler shift that is induced by a user moving closer or farther from a transmitter. This information is then fed into a gesture recognizer. To avoid false activations, the user carries out a distinct "preamble" gesture to signal the start of a gesture. This is an example of an interactive system providing benefits for a wider system—the house—by exploiting an existing subsystem, the house's Wi-Fi network.

The rest of this chapter is dedicated to the purpose of understanding systems. The next section begins by introducing systems thinking, a holistic approach to thinking about systems. Systems thinking does not indicate how to build a system. Instead, systems thinking suggests how to holistically consider the important aspects of a system. While systems thinking can be useful, we also need means of understanding systems. Thus, this chapter also explains how system mapping can be used to describe a system to reveal how users, tasks, information, and processes link together to form a working system. Such understanding can then be used to carry out design activities (Chapter 33) or risk assessments (Chapter 37).

35.1 Systems thinking

Engineering is the practice of using systematic principles to design and construct machines, structures, and other systems, including interactive systems.

We live in a complex world where we are immersed in and surrounded by systems that we often take for granted. For example, people typically live in societies, and such societies are arranged in various governing structures, such as local governments and national governments. In addition, international agreements and frameworks across countries govern many defense, trade, finance, and climate change concerns. Societies are also embedded on planet Earth and interface with a variety of natural systems, such as our ecosystem. In addition, modern civilization is supported by a range of man-made systems governing the production and delivery of food, energy, and healthcare, as well as systems for controlling banking, insurance, finance, manufacturing, defense, and many other vital aspects. A typical house is a complex system relying on subsystems such as electrical wiring, plumbing, and telecommunications to allow people to live in homes that are heated and provide us with the everyday facilities we take for granted. These include facilities to clean our clothes using a washing machine, heat food using a microwave oven, and access the Internet using a laptop or mobile phone. Every human and animal residing in such a house is a system consisting of, for example, the musculoskeletal, circulatory, respiratory, digestive, reproductive, and neural subsystems.

To understand a system, we often first identify its subsystems. For example, the electrical wiring in a house is reliant on protective systems, such as fuses and residual current devices (RCDs) to protect against faults. Fuses and RCDs are systems that are designed to interface with electrical systems. A typical touchscreen mobile phone consists of several subsystems such as the screen, the logic board, the central processing unit, and memory circuits. The phone's software is driven by an operating system that manages drivers, processes, and security and ensures that apps can run and access all required functionality. Apps rely on software libraries to display user interface elements and to receive notifications of the user's actions.

As is evident in the above description, systems are pervasive in our environments and they are complex and difficult to understand, design, build, and maintain. *Systems thinking* [222] is an approach that allows designers to reason about systems. The terminology arose in engineering as a result of a recognized need to approach system design as a holistic cross-disciplinary team activity that considers system design across the entire lifecycle of the system. This includes the system's design, integration, management, maintenance, and eventual disposal. It also includes considerations of the system's role in its operating environment, which may in turn be a larger system, and any necessary interaction between several systems or subsystems.

A systems thinking perspective is helpful in HCI for several reasons. First, many HCI artifacts provide critical capabilities by being embedded within larger systems. For example, an interactive wearable patient monitoring device is embedded within a hospital environment, which is a system with flows of patients, doctors, medication, equipment, and information, as well as organizational hierarchies of departments and worker roles. In addition, activities in a hospital have to follow both internal rules and professional and government regulations. For a wearable patient monitoring device embedded in such an environment to be successful, the designers must be aware of the complex operational system in which the device operates.

Second, HCI artifacts are systems in their own right. For example, a mobile phone app is a system that fulfills a certain purpose by exposing the user to the necessary functionality. As HCI progresses, many HCI artifacts find themselves relying on hardware, such as sensors, or necessitating novel hardware input or output solutions. Typically, an HCI system is now a combined hardware and software system. To build one, expertise across the domains of electrical engineering, computer science, design, and psychology may be required.

A *system* is here defined as a set of parts or modules that in combination provide emergent qualities that are not present in the individual parts or modules. Synthetic systems are designed by people with the objective of providing capability. It is the desire for capability that leads to the creation of a system. Users rarely care about the creation of a system for its own sake. Instead, systems emerge to fulfill needs by providing the desired capability.

A simple hierarchy of system complexity can be decomposed into three levels (adapted from [222]):

Level 1: A subsystem that is managed primarily within one technical discipline and organization. Examples include a logic board, an app, and a wearable health monitor device.

Level 2: A system that involves two or more technical disciplines or two or more organizations. The design of a car's core functionality is one example, as it primarily involves mechanical and electrical engineering. A mobile phone and its operating system is another example involving electrical engineering and computer science. Another example is a national electronic medical records management software that is designed to work with a variety of hospitals and other health providers.

Level 3: A system that involves many technical disciplines and is impacted by wide-reaching social, economic, political, or environmental factors. Typical examples are major infrastructure, such as power grids, air traffic control, and military command and control.

An individual HCI system is situated within one level of the above hierarchy but is nearly always set to operate within another system, which may be at a different level in the hierarchy. For example, an electronic voting user interface is embedded within at least two systems. First, the voting machine design itself, which consists of electronic components providing the user with a means of inputting information and receiving confirmation. Second, the voting machine provides a critical function to society and thus operates in a highly regulative and political system

[57]. In HCI, successful design necessitates being sensitive to such wider systems, including understanding the target audience, for example, users with disabilities.

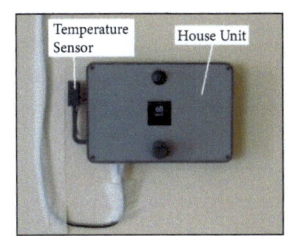

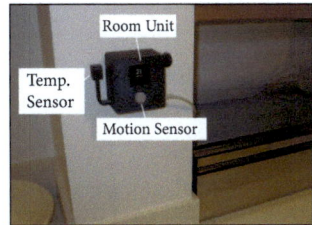

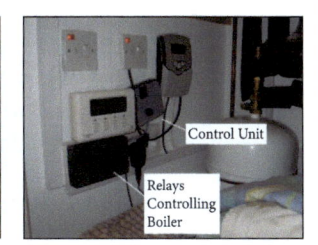

> **Paper Example 35.1.1: Heating homes more efficiently by sensing and predicting room usage**
>
> *PreHeat* [749] is a system intended to heat homes more efficiently by sensing and predicting people's room usage. It involves several subsystems, such as motion sensors, temperature units, and control units, as it has to interface with the existing heating system in the house. The figure in this paper example box shows some of these systems in one installation.
>
> PreHeat uses sensor data to estimate people's room usage needs and a prediction algorithm to estimate when individual rooms should be heated up.
>
> PreHeat was deployed to five homes and was shown to heat the homes more efficiently compared to users programming thermostat schedules.

There are several accounts of systems thinking and no de facto process to adopt it. However, a simple way to adopt systems thinking is to adopt the following six principles [222]:

Debate, define, revise, and pursue the purpose: Refine the problem and define three key parameters in system design: cost, performance, and timescale. Do not neglect the fourth parameter, risk, which needs to be understood for each of the three prior parameters. No system is optimal, which implies there are trade-offs in the system. These trade-offs must be understood. Moreover, requirements constrain the design space and make system designs tractable. However, for nontrivial systems, it is nearly impossible to arrive at the correct set of requirements early in the project. The requirements evolve with the system design.

Think holistic: Systems have boundaries; without boundaries, we do not have definitions of systems. Systems are embedded within other systems. Integrated systems need to be considered in terms of the whole system, taking into account all system components across the lifespan of the system. The components of the system and the environment in which the system operates are necessary to understand the system. The processes, tools, and people required for design, build, deployment, maintenance, and support are all part of the system.

Follow a systematic procedure: Systems are planned, designed, and built. It is necessary to identify and manage uncertainty throughout a project and use a robust design process that supports iteration, working with stakeholders, and the management of risk, changes, and rework.

Be creative: Use both innovative and conventional thinking to understand, together with stakeholders, what the system must achieve, to create the system architecture, and to guide every stage throughout the life of the system, from design and build to the support and dismantle stages.

Take account of people: People are part of systems, and they are critical for the success of systems. People build, install, use, and support systems. They may also have to defend, challenge, or tolerate systems. People's motivation, competence, attitude, and capability to deliver quality matter for the success of a system. Ergonomics, ethics, and trust, among other factors, are also critical.

Manage the project and the relationships: Complex systems involve complex projects to build them. They require many stakeholders who are scattered across different organizations and have many different roles. Just like systems are designed, projects to build, deploy, maintain, and support systems also need to be designed to take all relevant factors into consideration.

A weakness of systems thinking is that while it prescribes an approach, it does not specify methods or procedures that enable systems thinking. Nonetheless, a lack of systems thinking can often be linked to system failures. For example, an analysis of 12 problems in systems linked them to four categories of systems thinking failures [555]:

- A failure to consider the environment in which the system operated. For example, wind conditions.
- A failure to understand that non-technical factors, such as organizational, political, economic, or environmental factors, were necessary to understand and take into account in order to solve the system problem.
- A failure to correctly address planned and unplanned interactions between components within the system and interactions with the system's environment.
- A failure to take into account that many products are part of a wider user experience system and that the product can therefore only thrive if such a user experience system exists and provides adequate services.

35.2 System mapping

To understand a system, we need to describe it. *System mapping* refers to a set of techniques for achieving this. System mapping allows us to describe a system in terms of its processes, people, and flows of information.

The first step in system mapping is to establish the *system boundary*. Such boundary setting clarifies the scope of the system. Determining a system boundary is particularly important for risk assessment; we discuss this step in more detail in the chapter on safety and risk (Chapter 37).

The purpose of system mapping is to ensure there is a clear understanding of the system. System mapping is carried out by describing the structure and behavior of the system. Any technique that is suitable for this purpose can in principle be used. Here, we review a set of common system mapping techniques.

35.2.1 Task diagram

A task diagram is a hierarchical representation of tasks and the necessary conditions for carrying out the tasks. A task diagram represents tasks as nodes and relationships between tasks as links. Since task diagrams are hierarchical, they can be as detailed as required. They are often used to describe complete processes, the organization of work, and user interface workflows.

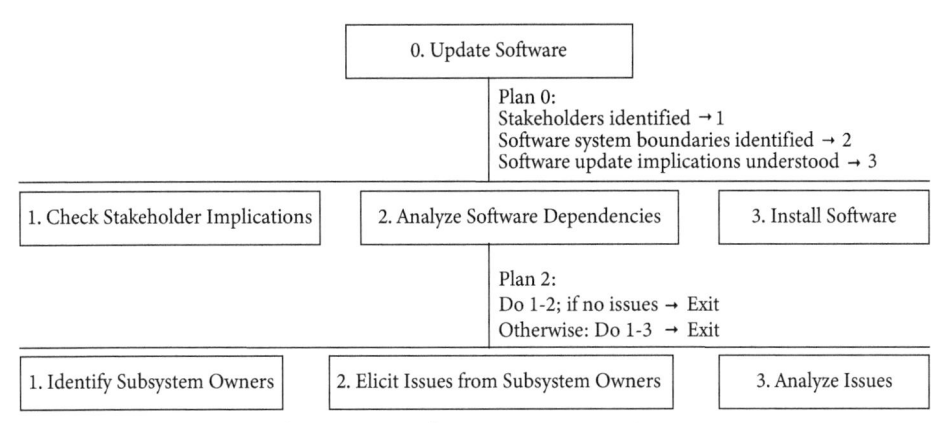

```
                    ┌─────────────────────┐
                    │  0. Update Software │
                    └─────────────────────┘
                              Plan 0:
                              Stakeholders identified → 1
                              Software system boundaries identified → 2
                              Software update implications understood → 3
```

| 1. Check Stakeholder Implications | 2. Analyze Software Dependencies | 3. Install Software |

Plan 2:
Do 1-2; if no issues → Exit
Otherwise: Do 1-3 → Exit

| 1. Identify Subsystem Owners | 2. Elicit Issues from Subsystem Owners | 3. Analyze Issues |

Figure 35.2 A task diagram for updating software in an organization.

Task diagrams focus on processes and procedures, user behavior, and HCI. Task diagrams are frequently used to describe HCI systems but can also be used to explain the wider system that an HCI system is embedded within. For example, a medical app used by a nurse may be embedded within a hospital environment, which prescribes a set of processes for the nurse to carry out a task. Task diagrams allow such processes, which may involve steps *outside* the app, to be mapped out and understood by the design team.

Figure 35.2 shows an example of a task diagram for an organization that needs to update software. Only some tasks are shown in the figure. Each task can be augmented with a plan that elaborates on the task's steps and its relationship with other tasks.

35.2.2 Information diagram

An information diagram is a hierarchical representation of documentation. An information diagram represents documents as nodes and the relationship between documents as links.

Information diagrams are used to gain an understanding of the documentation structures within an organization, such as the degree of standardization of documents and the way documents relate to each other. As documentation can be both electronic and on paper, information diagrams can capture both types of documents and link their dependencies and usages.

Figure 35.3 shows an example of an information diagram for an organization that needs to update software. Only a part of the information hierarchy is shown in the figure. The software update policy, for example, can be further decomposed into information about rules and processes around software updating in the organization. The stakeholders might be more usefully mapped using another diagram, such as an organizational diagram, which we describe next.

35.2.3 Organizational diagram

An organizational diagram is a hierarchical representation of people and their roles in an organization. It represents teams, individuals, departments, and so on as nodes and their relationships as links.

Organizational diagrams make it possible to identify users and their roles. In particular, they allow for the identification of stakeholders in an organization or wider system. This can guide further system mapping and data collection via an investigation of stakeholders that initially did not seem central to the problems considered.

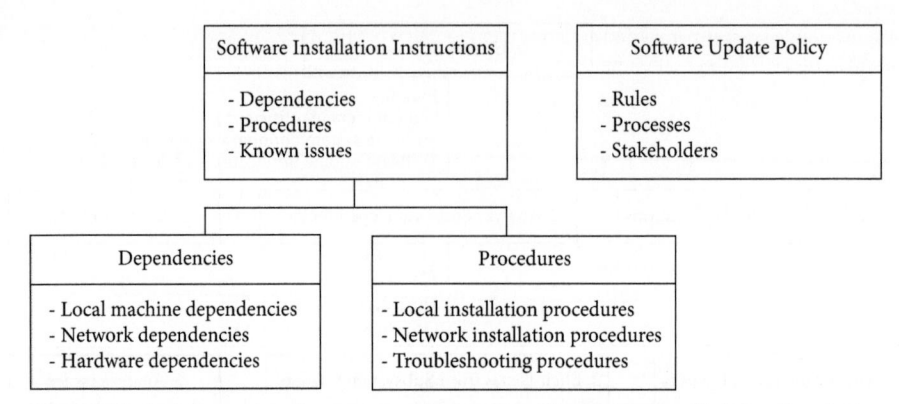

Figure 35.3 An information diagram showing a part of the hierarchy of information that a system administrator would require to update software in an organization.

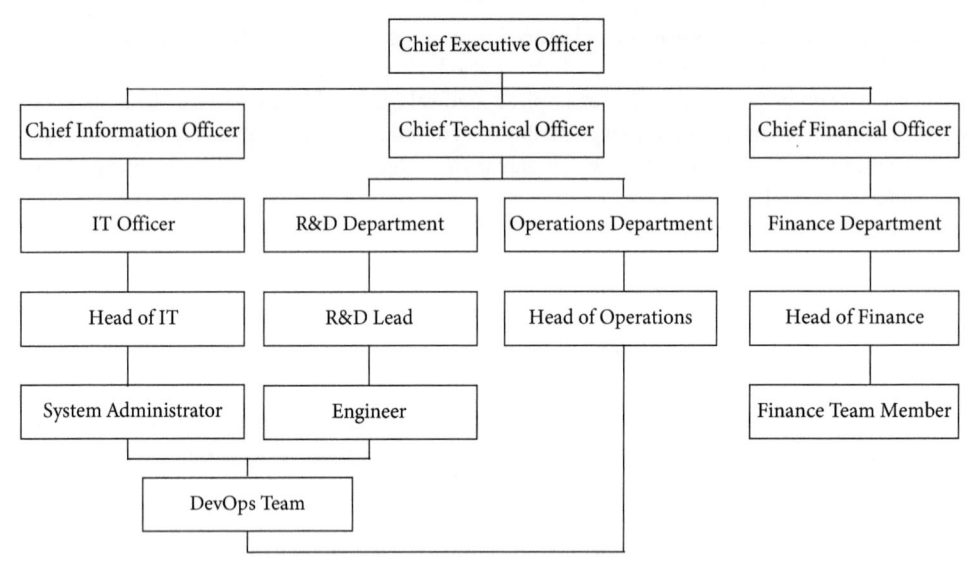

Figure 35.4 An organizational diagram for an organization subject to a software update. DevOps stands for development operations. The DevOps team combines the roles of software development and IT operations into one function.

Figure 35.4 shows an example of an organizational diagram for an organization. In the diagram, it is clear that system administrators, part of the IT office, and engineers, who are part of the R&D department, form a cross-disciplinary DevOps team managed by the head of operations.

35.2.4 System diagram

A system diagram is used to understand how data are transformed through processes and activities in the system. System diagrams show where data are stored and how data activities and processes are sequenced to allow for data transformations.

System diagrams allow for mapping out processes, in particular how users interact with systems to achieve tasks. They show data-driven processes and activities. As such, system diagrams allow for the analysis of data flows, functions, and states in a system. For example, system diagrams can be used to identify possible risks in a people-centric process by allowing designers to analyze possible failure modes in such a process.

A system diagram consists of two parts. The first is activities that indicate the flow of data between activities. The second is states and state transitions that indicate the state conditions for a transition and the actions arising from a transition.

Figure 35.5 shows an example of a system diagram for an organization. The top part shows activities as circles that a system administrator ("sysadmin") has to engage with to update software. The generated data that give rise to data flows are indicated below the activities. The flows of data are indicated by arrows. The bottom part shows the states and state transitions in this process. Transition conditions such as "Corrections required" are indicated next to each arrow (transition). Transition actions, where applicable, are indicated next to arrows and preceded by a hyphen ("-") to disambiguate between transition conditions and actions.

35.2.5 Process diagram

A process diagram shows how serial and parallel processes and activities are structured as a series of steps. A very common instance of a process diagram is a flow chart, though other forms of process diagrams also exist. The nodes in process diagrams represent the steps in a process and the links represent the conditions for transitioning from one step to another. Process diagrams show the ordering of steps within activities if the activities are serial.

A flow chart is a form of process diagram. Flow charts can be annotated to include additional information. For example, a flow chart can be linked to an organizational diagram to make it clear which stakeholders are involved in an activity. Process diagrams can thereby help understand a process in a system by linking relevant stakeholders, documents, and tasks.

Figure 35.6 shows an example of a process diagram in the form of a swim lane diagram. The lanes, indicated with dashed lines, delineate roles in the process, such as sysadmin, subsystem owner, engineer, and so on. The flow chart begins and ends with rounded rectangles indicating the start and end of the process. The thick horizontal bars represent forks and joins in activities. The rectangles indicate activities, and the diamonds indicate decisions. The arrows show process flows.

35.2.6 Communication diagram

Users who interact through a common process share information. A communication diagram is a way to represent such flows of information between users. The nodes represent users or entities representing user groups; the links represent the flow of information.

Communication diagrams are used to show the flow of information between people in the same team, in different teams, or even in different organizations. Communication diagrams can also be used to depict flows of information across different entities, such as different departments in a company.

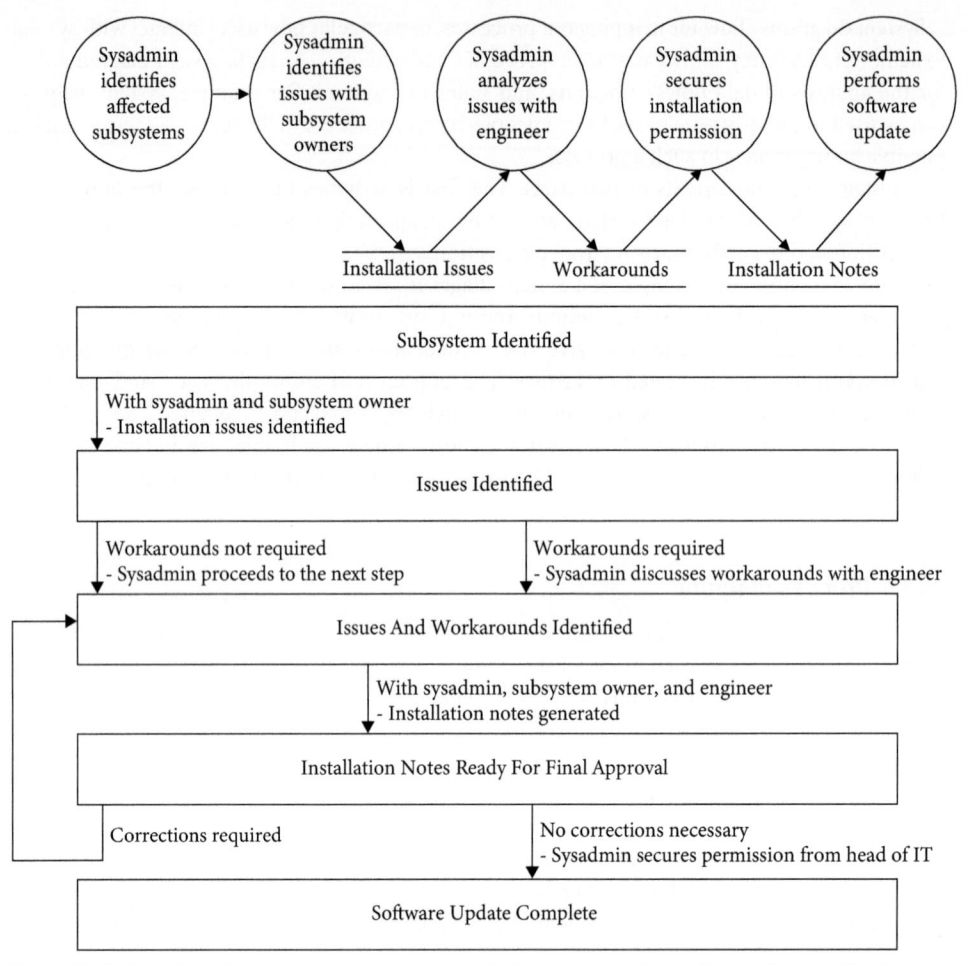

Figure 35.5 A system diagram for an organization in the process of updating software. The top part shows the flow of data between activities. These activities give rise to data that link some of the activities. The bottom part shows states as boxes and transitions between states as arrows. The conditions for a transition are indicated next to each arrow as a textual description, and the actions are indicated as a textual description preceded by a hyphen ("-").

Figure 35.7 shows a communication diagram that indicates the flow of information between the system administrator, subsystem owner, engineer, and head of IT that is required to decide whether to approve a software update.

35.3 Principles for legal and ethical systems

Systems thinking invites designers to think about and analyze systems beyond technology. In particular, systems that are deployed must meet regulatory requirements—they have to be lawful. In addition, systems should not have adverse effects, whether intentionally or accidentally, on their users or other people affected by the technology.

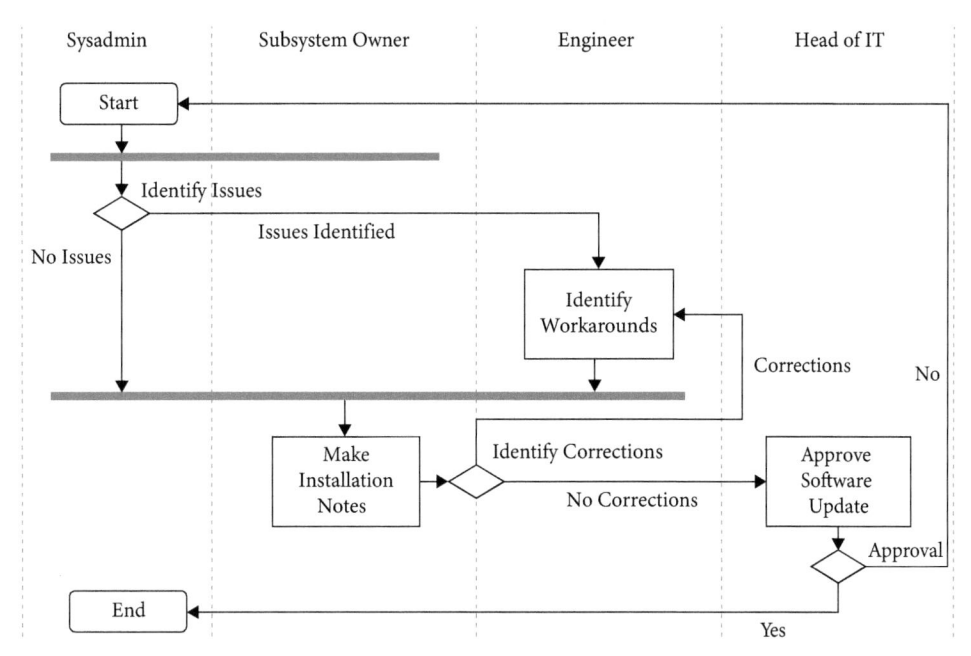

Figure 35.6 A process diagram for an organization making a decision on whether it is ready to update software.

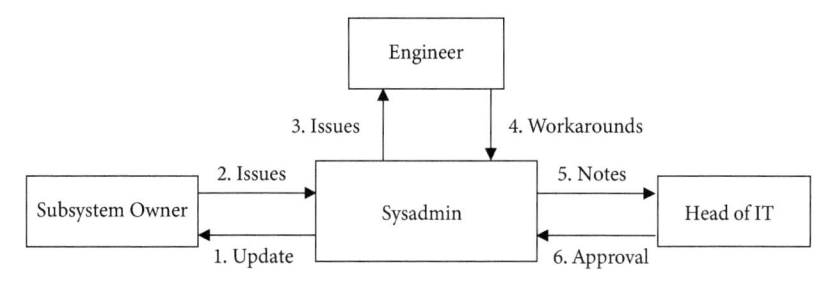

Figure 35.7 A communication diagram for an organization making a decision on whether it is ready to update software.

There is an important distinction between *legal* and *ethical* concerns. Legal system issues refer to systems that are in some ways unlawful. For example, medical devices and consumer electronics are regulated by national and international laws. Systems that break such laws can lead to prosecutions. By contrast, ethical issues do not necessarily refer to particular laws that are broken but rather to technology outcomes that are undesirable according to norms. Several communities, such as the Association for Computing Machinery, encode norms as codes of ethics and professional conduct.

Systems using AI are the latest frontier of ethical and legal debate for the simple reason that they touch an increasing number of everyday decisions. Interactive systems rely on AI to carry out parts of their functions, which affect users and other stakeholders in various ways socially and financially. Multiple guidelines have been proposed for governing and evaluating systems. Fjeld et al. [245] presented a comprehensive summary of such principles based on eight core themes: privacy, accountability, safety and security, transparency and explainability, fairness and non-discrimination, human control of technology, professional responsibility, and promotion of human values.

Privacy: Data should not be used without a person's knowledge. Furthermore, users should have control over their data and the ability to restrict the processing of their data. Users should also have the right to correct and remove data. In general, privacy concerns should be integrated into the AI design process. There is also wide recognition that privacy issues in AI systems require new regulatory frameworks from governments.

Accountability: For systems to be accountable, it is important that they produce verifiable, replicable results and that they can be examined in sufficient detail to validate their operations and mechanisms. The impact of systems must be assessed via impact assessments. Such assessments can be related to impacts on human rights or more generally study the negative impacts of systems. One example is ecological impact assessment, which highlights the need for environmental responsibility. To enable accountability, it is also important to build systems that can be audited and feed the findings of such audits back into the system. It may be necessary to create a monitoring body, such as an internal review board, to ensure best practices during design, development, and deployment. If a system is automatic and makes decisions involving humans, there needs to be an appeal function in place to challenge such decisions. Moreover, once a system's decision has been rectified, there needs to be a mechanism to remedy the consequences of system decisions. In general, liability and legal responsibility for system actions must be clearly defined. As a consequence, many design guides recommend considering new regulations to ensure systems are accountable.

Safety and security: Safety means ensuring the internal functions of the system work as expected and prevent unintended consequences that may lead to harm. Risk management best practices can be used to assess and manage safety. Risk management is discussed in Chapter 37. Security is the need to address external threats to the system. There is a need to ensure systems are resilient. A principle known as security-by-design should be applied to ensure abstract ideas about security are translated into working principles in implementation by establishing a link throughout the design, implementation, and deployment process. Finally, systems should be predictable to ensure it is possible to recognize if they have been compromised.

Transparency and explainability: Systems should be transparent, which in this context means they should be designed, implemented, and deployed in such a way that it is possible to oversee their internal operations. Explainability concerns the need for systems to be able to generate outputs that are intelligible and comprehensive and thus suitable for evaluation by humans.

This is particularly important for systems with a high potential to cause harm, such as the use of AI in healthcare. One way to improve transparency and explainability is to ensure the data and algorithms used to drive system decisions are available to the public. Governments also need to be open about their procurement and use of technology. Importantly, people have a right to information about their interaction with AI and the mechanisms used to form decisions about individuals. Related to this, individuals should be notified when decisions are made by AI and when they interact with AI. In general, regular reporting can enhance transparency and explainability in AI systems, for example, by routinely logging data such as AI decisions and the factors that led to such decisions.

Fairness and non-discrimination: Bias means a particular option has a disproportionate weight. Algorithmic bias is the phenomenon of bias being introduced in AI systems in various ways, including the particular algorithms used, the training data, or the way AI is used. Therefore, it is important to work toward non-discrimination and prevent bias in AI systems. Representative and high-quality data are thus essential. Another important principle is fairness, the idea that AI systems treat individuals fairly and the design of such systems makes an effort to avoid bias and other factors that may lead to unfair outcomes for individuals. A related principle is equity: People should have the same opportunities and protection from AI systems regardless of whether they are all similarly situated. It is also important to ensure the positive impacts of AI are inclusive and reach as many people as possible. Finally, AI systems should be inclusive in their design; thus, diverse participants should be involved in the design, development, and deployment processes.

Human control of technology: People should be able to review and opt out of automated decisions. Another important aspect is allowing humans to intervene in a system.

Professional responsibility: The people involved in designing, implementing, and deploying systems have responsibilities. One responsibility is to ensure systems are accurate, that is, they mostly arrive at correct decisions. As it is nearly always impossible to ensure perfect accuracy, this principle is sometimes phrased as a goal rather than a requirement. Related to this, developers need to be careful and thoughtful. This includes considering the long-term impacts and effects of their systems. Another concern is the need to consult the multiple stakeholder groups that may be affected by a system. Finally, systems should be built by people with scientific integrity and guided by established professional values and standards.

Promotion of human values: Systems should protect human values and ensure humans can flourish. Thus, access to technology is a critical concern in the context of avoiding systems that increase inequality. The positive impacts of systems should be felt relatively evenly across societies, and people should have access to education so that they can benefit from it as much as possible. Another relevant factor is how access to technology can provide people with disabilities with more opportunities, for example, by providing automatic closed captions for online videos. A final principle is the idea that systems should be leveraged to benefit society, that is, systems should contribute to human well-being, the environment, and a more sustainable society.

35.4 Is systems thinking actionable?

Systems thinking sounds promising in theory, and many failed designs have been linked to a *lack* of systems thinking. However, there is no concrete framework, toolkit, or procedure that can be used to ensure systems thinking is embodied in a design.

The six principles of systems thinking we introduced earlier in this chapter are high-level principles, such as "think holistic" and "follow a systematic procedure." However, *how* do I, as a designer, know that I am aware of all the relevant components, subsystems, extended systems, people, and other concerns so that I can set the correct system boundary? Furthermore, if I want to follow a "systematic procedure," *which* systematic procedure should I follow? There are many design approaches, techniques, methods, and toolkits. Even for a niche area such as user interface verification, there are several sophisticated formal tools available, and it is not obvious which tool is the most suitable for a user-centered design process [123]. Furthermore, work is required to provide HCI designers with sufficiently robust systems thinking frameworks that can be integrated into user-centered design processes.

In addition to a lack of concrete guidance, an overemphasis on analysis can lead to *analysis paralysis*—a state where decision-making is halted or very slow due to the fear of making an error or missing out on a superior solution. An overemphasis on systems thinking may induce this state by having designers despair in the face of an incredibly large number of options. It may also give rise to a sensation of hopelessness when designers realize that the systems they are working with are incredibly complex and nobody truly understands them. Finally, it may result in the design team spending too much time trying to define a complete and correct requirements specification, thereby never reaching a state where they can iterate implementation and evaluation. This may occur as a result of assuming that there is a perfect system, which is exceedingly unlikely in reality due to various trade-offs that are intrinsic to a system trying to achieve a task.

In practice, design needs to balance overall rigor against the time and cost required to arrive at a working system. This trade-off can be readily seen in the small uptake of formal methods, such as system verification, except for safety-critical user interfaces where potential errors can be catastrophic.

Summary

- Systems are pervasive, and interactive systems are typically embedded within other systems with which they interact.
- Systems thinking is an approach for reasoning about systems, including how they are embedded within other systems, how they work over time, and how subsystems and other parts of a system contribute to the wider system.
- System mapping is a set of techniques for describing systems in terms of their processes, people, and flows of information, among other things. Several system mapping techniques, such as task and organization diagrams, have been developed to depict particular aspects of systems.
- Principles can assist designers in ensuring HCI systems are ethical and legal.

Exercises

1. System as a concept. Consider the following systems: (a) a fall detector device for elderly patients in a hospital, (b) a streaming music service app, (c) a virtual reality head-mounted display, and (d) a spreadsheet used by a university professor to record exam marks and grades. Which systems are they embedded within, and which systems do they interact with?
2. Systems thinking and system failure. Read up on the initial motivation and fate of the following products: (a) 3DO Interactive Multiplayer, (b) Apple Newton, and (c) Microsoft Zune. Can systems thinking explain why these products failed? Which of the six systems thinking principles might have been useful to avoid these failures?
3. System mapping. You are tasked with developing an app that helps seven-year-old children learn multiplication tables. The app is to run on a tablet and to provide a scoreboard so that children can compare their results via anonymous aliases. Teachers and parents must have access to the results to monitor the progress of individual children. Use system mapping techniques to describe the system.

4. AI ethics. Consider how the legal and ethical principles of systems would apply to the following AI systems: (a) a sentence-generating function that allows nonspeaking individuals with motor disabilities to communicate faster by allowing them to directly select entire sentences when they type; (b) a magnetic resonance imaging (MRI) scanner interface that takes the output from an MRI machine after a patient's scan, sends the data to an offsite location, uses AI to perform image enhancements, and sends the AI-processed data back to the doctor in the hospital for analysis; and (c) an automated dialogue agent for handling customer complaints in a bank.

5. Safety engineering. (This exercise requires familiarity with methods introduced in the other chapters in this part.) A design team is creating a helmet that enables rapid triage for people near blast explosions in a war zone. The idea is that the sensors in the helmet can sense the risk of brain injury due to an explosion and communicate this information using a visual display.
   (a) Derive a solution-neutral problem statement for this problem (see Chapter 36 for details).
   (b) Suggest a suitable sensor for the helmet.
   (c) Propose a system boundary. Briefly motivate your choice of boundary.
   (d) Draw a system diagram for the system.
   (e) Create a morphological chart for the key functions you have identified.
   (f) Generate a suitable concept through concept evaluation and provide a brief narrative motivating the chosen concept. Provide justifications for all criteria, weightings, and scores.
   (g) Carry out a failure mode and effects analysis (Chapter 37) within the system boundary you identified.

6. A patient-controlled analgesia (PCA) pump enables a patient to self-administer pain relief medicine. A PCA pump, including the medication dosage and schedule, is typically set up by a nurse and subsequently used by the patient. A support engineer is responsible for ensuring the software is up to date and that the settings are cleared between each patient. Research has shown that a frequent source of patient injury or death is the user interface being difficult to use. Thus, the United States Food and Drug Administration (FDA) has specified a set of requirements for PCA pump user interfaces. A design team is tasked with creating a user interface for a PCA pump.
   (a) Derive a solution-neutral problem statement for this design problem.
   (b) Identify a system boundary for this design problem and motivate your choice.
   The following additional tasks can be done if the relevant chapters have been covered during class.
   (c) Suggest a user-centered design process suitable for this design problem. Motivate the choice of design process with reference to other user-centered design processes that are less suitable.
   (d) Propose a risk management strategy for assessing, monitoring, and communicating risk for the new PCA pump user interface design.
   (e) One FDA requirement is the following: "Clearing of the pump settings and resetting of the pump shall require confirmation." Explain why this requirement is ambiguous and raises questions about the user interface design for a PCA pump.

36
Design engineering

This chapter introduces a *design engineering* perspective to human–computer interaction (HCI) system design. As we have discussed in this part of the book, the word *system* has many meanings in HCI. In the context of this chapter, the term means a set of interconnected components that give rise to emergent properties that are not attributable to the individual components alone. As the number of components and the interactions among components increase, a system becomes more complex. *Integrated system design* is the challenge of designing an integrated system that meets the stated objectives.

Here are three examples of successful design engineering from the HCI literature.

- The data glove [929] is an instrumented glove-based system that allows a computer system to sense the position and orientation of a user's hand and fingers. By tracking the user's hand and fingers, the computer system allows the user to complete actions such as picking up virtual objects and rotating them. It also provides tactile sensation feedback below each finger. The system is a combined hardware system covering all the aspects required to allow a user to perform gestures and receive tactile feedback, including manual and automatic calibration procedures.
- *KinectFusion* [378] is a real-time 3D reconstruction and interaction system that is based on a moving depth camera. Using a custom pipeline, KinectFusion supports various actions and features that require a commodity depth camera and a graphics card. Example applications include low-cost 3D scanning and augmented reality that is aware of the physical surroundings. The system also supports the tracking of a user's fingers; thus, any physical surface can be reappropriated as a multi-touch surface with passive haptic feedback.
- *Dexmo* [304] is a force feedback glove intended for virtual reality applications. Dexmo simulates forces using a mechanical exoskeleton. The Dexmo system tracks user motion, and when it detects the user grasping a virtual object, it uses a passive haptic mechanical approach to block the user's finger movements. Thus, unlike tactile feedback, the user experiences a real force. Dexmo is lightweight and inexpensive to manufacture, and a later commercialized version introduced variable force feedback.

Here, we introduce a method for integrated system design in HCI, which is adapted from design engineering [255, 634, 839].[1] The previous part on design (Part VI) explained methods for creating ideas and prototypes. This chapter elaborates on how to transform *problem statements* into products and services using a systematic approach. In other words, the focus here is on arriving at a system that fulfills a set of *requirements* enabling it to be readily realized.

[1] Design engineering is sometimes referred to as engineering design.

Introduction to Human-Computer Interaction. Kasper Hornbæk, Per Ola Kristensson, and Antti Oulasvirta, Oxford University Press. © Kasper Hornbæk, Per Ola Kristensson, and Antti Oulasvirta (2025). DOI: 10.1093/oso/9780192864543.003.0036

We will focus on specific parts of the typical design engineering process that are relevant to designing, implementing, and evaluating interactive systems: task clarification, conceptual design, and verification. Other parts of design engineering, such as embodiment design and detailed design, tackle the specifics of constructing electromechanical systems and are thus not covered. Likewise, we do not cover specific project management techniques, such as change management. Risk management is an important aspect of all system design; we touch on this in Chapter 37.

In addition to explaining how engineers are typically taught to design systems, this chapter introduces versatile methods and addresses some challenges that are often encountered in the design process.

One such challenge is *design fixation*, the risk of committing to one particular idea too early and not considering others (Chapter 31). Another is the inability to keep in mind all the objectives and constraints that are relevant in design. Designers also often exhibit implicit or explicit bias, which can lead to short-circuiting the design exploration stage. When we fail to fully explore design options, we often do not end up identifying the best solution. A systematic design process reduces this risk by enforcing a consistent process for exploring alternatives.

Another design process challenge is making *informed trade-off decisions*. An integrated system design is rarely, if ever, optimal in all possible aspects, typically due to many design factors having a negative correlation with each other. A simple example is the trade-off between the security and usability of a system: By improving security, for example, via stricter authentication methods, one often compromises usability. These trade-offs are often not obvious, and there is a risk that trade-off decisions are implicitly dictated by the design. This can lead to suboptimal designs that are only revealed as such when the system is deployed and the net effect of all those trade-off decisions suddenly becomes apparent. A systematic design process reduces this risk by considering the translation of the set of functions in the design into a set of *function carriers* in a system as a search problem with multiple solutions. By making the advantages and disadvantages of each solution explicit, implicit trade-offs are made explicit.

A third challenge is *communication*. In practice, the integrated design of an HCI system requires the coordination of multiple people or even teams that are often distributed across geographical locations, companies, and company divisions. By documenting the key steps in a decision process, they are made scrutinizable by other people.

A fourth challenge is the *integration* of multiple technical disciplines, design knowledge, people, business, and regulatory concerns into a functioning system. Examples of difficult integrations in HCI systems include: (1) systems that rely on software, electronics, and mechanical behavior, for instance, wearable devices, medical devices, and 3D printers; (2) AI-infused systems that rely on subsystems inferring or predicting users' intention or dynamically adapt based on user behavior; and (3) human-in-the-loop systems that rely on real-time human behavior for successful system operation. An example of a system integration challenge is given in Paper Example 36.0.1, which discusses the engineering of *VuMan*, an early wearable computer.

A fifth challenge is carrying out an appropriate risk assessment and consequently implementing a suitable *risk management* strategy for an HCI system. To carry out a risk assessment, it is critical to understand the technical boundary of the system and the system architecture. Only then is it possible to perform risk assessment at the relevant level for the system. This is essential, especially for safety-critical systems. Due to the complexities and nuances of risk in design, risk management is covered in a dedicated chapter (Chapter 37).

> **Paper Example 36.0.1: Designing a wearable computer**
>
> *VuMan* is a wearable computer that can assist humans in navigation tasks in the real world, such as providing information about moving around in a museum or campus [49]. Developed in the early 1990s, VuMan consists of a handheld controller and a wearable display called Private Eye. By rotating the dial and clicking the buttons, the user can move a cursor and interact with a map (e.g., the blueprint of a house) shown on the wearable display.
>
> Three versions of VuMan were developed over several years in a multidisciplinary project. A key challenge for the team was integrated system engineering—how to engineer a wearable computer that meets several requirements for use in the wild, such as handling different temperatures, dirt, water, shocks, and so on. The project started with requirements elicitation and later centered on the development of the dial. Over several iterations of user studies and hardware and software engineering, the design became lighter in weight, smaller, more robust, more energy-efficient, quicker for users to use, and cheaper to manufacture.

36.1 Design process

The design engineering process can be decomposed into six intertwined activities:

1. Identifying the purpose of the HCI system
2. Creating a requirements specification
3. Arriving at a conceptual design
4. Translating the conceptual design into an embodiment design
5. Implementing the embodiment design into a detailed design, which is either ready for manufacturing or deployable as a purely digital product
6. Verifying that the system fulfills the requirements and validating that the system is usable for its purpose.

While the process appears linear, it is important to note that this process is rarely linear in practice. Moreover, in parallel with the above design process, *risk management* is carried out to reduce both the project risk and emergent risks of the deployed system.

36.2 Identifying the purpose

One of the important tasks when designing a system is to identify its overall *purpose*. It may seem obvious; however, it is often surprisingly difficult for a design team and different stakeholders to come to an agreement on the overall purpose of a proposed system. Writing down a technical description of the purpose of a system helps ensure the entire design team and all stakeholders have a common understanding of the overall objective. A useful technique for systematically arriving at such a purpose is to produce a *solution-neutral problem statement*.

A solution-neutral problem statement expresses the overall objective as a problem statement that avoids framing the problem in solution-dependent terms. This eliminates premature commitments to apparent but irrelevant constraints. It thereby helps to avoid initial design fixation on a prescribed solution, which may otherwise result in a suboptimal, over-constrained design space that prevents sufficient exploration of alternative designs.

The process of formulating a solution-neutral problem statement is straightforward in theory. The first step is to arrive at an initial problem statement and reflect on this problem statement. Does it clearly express a problem worth solving? Is anything critical missing in this statement? Having critically challenged the initial problem statement, the next step is to progressively raise the level of abstraction of the problem statement up to a level that is appropriate for the problem context.

The main idea in raising the level of abstraction of the problem statement is to progressively reformulate it using solution-neutral terms. This is achieved in two steps. The first step is to remove requirements and constraints that have no direct relevance to addressing the problem statement. The second step is to transform quantitative statements into qualitative statements.

Through this two-step process, the search space of possible solutions increases as the problem statement is progressively decoupled from solution-dependent terms. In practice, a solution-neutral problem statement is in a continuum between the two extremes of being completely solution-dependent or completely solution-independent. Context and professional judgment determine the appropriate abstraction level.

As an example, consider the following initial problem statement: "Design an updated form-filling warehouse inventory management interface based on last year's version of a mobile app running on capacitive touchscreen-enabled phone, consisting of five forms on five separate pages, each with a Submit and a Cancel button." It can be turned into a solution-neutral problem statement as follows:

- Design a form-filling warehouse inventory management interface for a capacitive touchscreen-enabled device, consisting of five forms on five separate pages, each with a Submit and a Cancel button.
- Design a form-filling warehouse inventory management interface for a mobile device.
- Devise a means for inputting structured information for warehouse inventory management.
- Devise a means for managing warehouse inventory.
- Devise a means for managing information.

The above example illustrates that there is a range of increasingly more solution-neutral problem statements for any initial solution-dependent problem statement. However, at some point, the level of abstraction is so high that the statement provides little to no guidance. In practice, careful judgment is required to set the solution-neutral problem statement at the correct abstraction level.

Once a solution-neutral problem statement has been produced, it can be used to denote the overall function of the system. As we shall see when performing conceptual design, the overall function is a good starting point for decomposing the function structure of a system.

Running example: A device for affection across distance

As an example of a hypothetical design, consider a wearable device that couples affection between two individuals separated in space. For example, such a device could take the form of two electronic rings connected via the Internet that will glow when one of the ring users is rubbing or turning the ring a certain way. The overall function of such a system could be described as "Couple Affection," and a solution-neutral problem statement may take the following form: "Design a wearable device that couples affection between two individuals that may be present in separate locations."

36.3 Specifying requirements

Having identified the overall purpose of the system, it is now possible to identify more clearly the objectives and constraints of the system. These are imposed in the form of *requirements* on system behavior and qualities that are either intrinsic or emergent from the system.

A *requirements specification* is a document that specifies the characteristics of a system. It is determined at the beginning of the design process. Ideally, a requirements specification is perfect in its first instantiation and remains unchanged throughout the design process; in practice, this is very unlikely to happen. A requirements specification is often referred to as a *live document* that is updated as new information alters the design specifications.

As a requirements specification is referred to frequently in the design process, it is vital that it be correct. The process of arriving at a requirements specification is often prescribed and field- or organization-specific, and requirements specifications are often reviewed. The process of arriving at a correct requirements specification is known as *requirements engineering* [430] and it is an active area of research [669].

The importance of a correct requirements specification increases with the complexity of the system. Unfortunately, it is notoriously difficult to arrive at a correct requirements specification in practice, as this demands a complete understanding of every relevant facet of the design. For example, requirements relating to users' needs or wants are difficult to elicit and unlikely to be complete or fully representative of the needs and wants of a diverse target audience. This is due to a number of factors, including sampling errors, the robustness of the methodology, and the difficulty of users to fully anticipate their own future needs and wants. This is one reason why requirements specifications are live documents.

A good requirements specification provides an in-depth understanding of the problem and covers all relevant aspects of the system design. It is also clearly written and thus facilitates communication between different team members. As a consequence, a well-written requirements specification tends to reduce time and cost in the design process and is more likely to give rise to a high-quality system.

While requirements cover all aspects of system design, they can generally be divided into four categories:

Technical requirements: They cover functional and performance characteristics of the system, such as latency and recognition accuracy.
Business requirements: They cover costs, scheduling, and other management-related aspects of the system and the design of the system.
Regulatory requirements: Regulatory requirements cover governing laws, industrial standards, and product regulations.
User-elicited requirements: User-elicited requirements cover the needs and wants of users.

A useful requirement has the following properties:

Table 36.1 Example requirements for an affective wearable device.

ID	Requirement	Source
1	Device must indicate its power on status	Technical team
2	Device must be comfortable to wear	Market research
3	Device must be able to sense at least five levels of communicated affection from the user	Focus group research and literature review
4	Device must be able to wirelessly receive an affective signal from a remote paired user	Focus group and market research
5	Device must communicate affection from a paired remote user in five discernible levels	Experimental research

Solution-independent: Normally, a requirement should not prescribe a specific predetermined solution. A requirement should specify what needs to be done, not how it is done.

Clear: A requirement should be unambiguous and understandable by all members of the design team that need to be aware of it.

Concise: The wording of a requirement should be succinct.

Testable: A requirement should be testable to ensure it is possible to later verify that the requirement has been met. In many cases, testability is ensured by introducing quantitative target values, limits, tolerances, or ranges. In other cases, testability can be ensured by prescribing acceptance criteria.

Traceable: A requirement should be traceable to its source. If the need ever arises to modify the original requirement, it is important to understand why the requirement was specified in a particular way in the first place.

In addition, the requirements specification as a whole should be complete and include all areas of concern throughout all phases of the system, which may include system support, reuse, and disposal. It is difficult and error-prone to write a complete requirements specification without reference to complete system functionality. Therefore, requirements specifications are often written while designing the function structure of the system, which is addressed in the next section.

Table 36.1 shows some example requirements for a hypothetical wearable device for coupling affection between two individuals separated in space.

36.4 Conceptual design

Having identified the overall function of a system, the *conceptual design* phase is concerned with two main tasks. The first is to elaborate on the specific functions that the system will be required to carry. Such *functional modeling* allows the design team to reason about required functionality without premature commitment to specific *solution principles* that dictate a specific method to carry out a function.

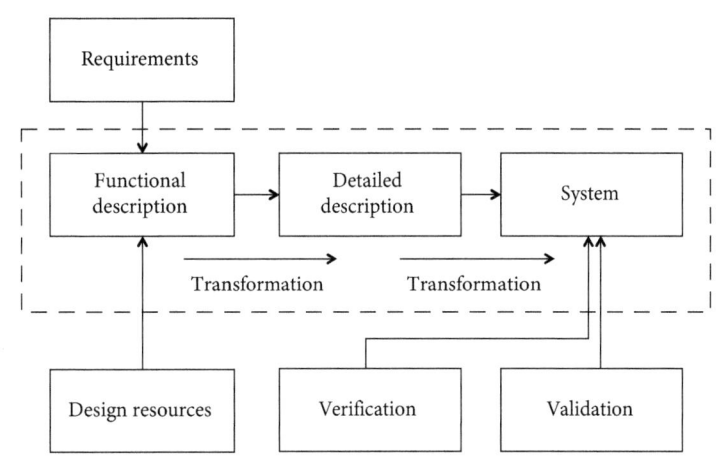

Figure 36.1 Design engineering as an information processing activity [438].

Figure 36.1 illustrates the conceptual design process as an information processing activity. A technical description, such as an initial requirements specification, and design resources, including design knowledge, feed into a transformation process that turns a functional description into a detailed description. A common mistake is to prematurely commit to a detailed description without a complete understanding of the functional description. One way to think about it is to consider the functional description the *what*—what should we build?—and the detailed description the *how*—how should we build it?

Also shown in Figure 36.1 is the transformation process from a detailed description to a working system. Once a working system has been constructed, it is possible to undertake verification and validation to ensure that all requirements have been met and that the deployed system successfully addresses the solution-neutral problem statement.

36.4.1 Function modeling

Two simple, useful modeling abstractions are *function structures* and *FAST diagrams*. FAST stands for function analysis system technique. In both methods, a *function* is described as an active verb followed by a noun: "push button," "select shape," "start motor," and so on.

A function structure is derived by first identifying the overall function. It is possible, and often necessary, to repeat the process for several overall functions of the design. Having identified an overall function, its interaction with the environment is modeled as flows of energy, materials, and signals that give rise to an overall function with inputs and outputs of energy, materials, and signals (Figure 36.2).

The rounded rectangle in Figure 36.2 is the *technical boundary of the system*. Anything that is outside it is not modeled, except for inflows and outflows of energy, materials, and signals. The technical boundary of the system is important and must be set with care. For example, in some cases, users are included within the technical boundary of the system because they carry out functions that are necessary for the overall function.

Function structures can be nested, which makes it possible to increase the granularity of the functional description. Figure 36.3 illustrates this idea by breaking down the overall function in Figure 36.2. Figure 36.3 shows an internal decomposition of the overall function split into four

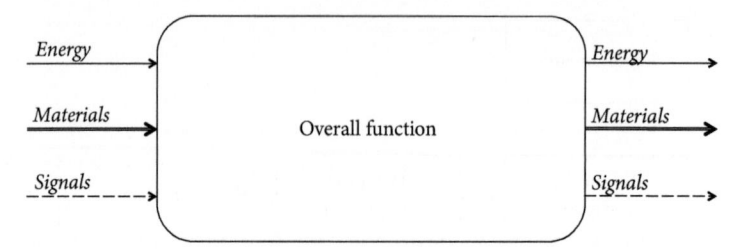

Figure 36.2 A function structure of the overall function of a system, showing the flows of energy, materials, and signals. The rounded rectangle around the overall function represents the technical boundary of the system.

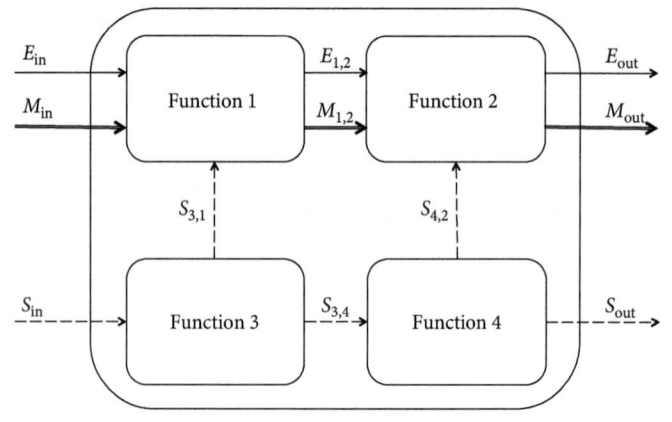

Figure 36.3 A breakdown of the overall function structure in Figure 36.2 revealing four main functions and the flows of energy, materials, and signals between them.

main functions. Functions 1 and 2 use energy to process materials, suggesting they are *process functions*. Functions 3 and 4 manage the flow of signals, which suggests they are *control* signals. Further decomposition of, for example, Function 2 could reveal subfunctions detailing various control and process aspects.

In the case of the wearable device coupling affection between two individuals, the overall function is *Couple Affection*. While simple, the function structure has already recorded one of the most vital pieces of information of any design: the overall function. To fulfill its purpose, the design needs to manage flows of energy and signals.

The overall function *Couple Affection* can then be decomposed into a number of key subfunctions as shown in Figure 36.4. The incoming signals to the overall function have now been detailed as *User Affection*, sensed locally by the wearable device, and *Remote Affection*, transmitted from a remote device. The function structure identifies a functional need to Supply Energy to sense, modulate, and send locally sensed affection to a remote device and to be able to receive and display remote affection provided from a remote device. Crucially, the function structure is focused on revealing critical functions and their dependencies; it does not prescribe any specific solution or function carrier to carry out any of the functions.

FAST diagrams are another function model design tool that can replace or complement function structures. The fundamental idea behind FAST diagrams is to gradually decompose higher-order

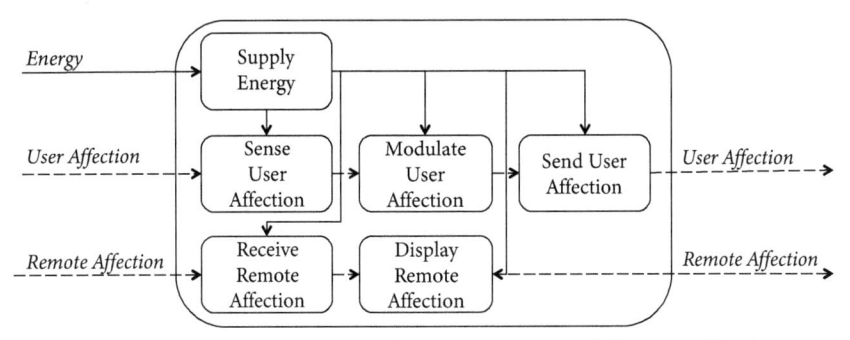

Figure 36.4 A decomposition of the overall function structure of the wearable device coupling affection, revealing the main functions and the flows of energy and signals between them.

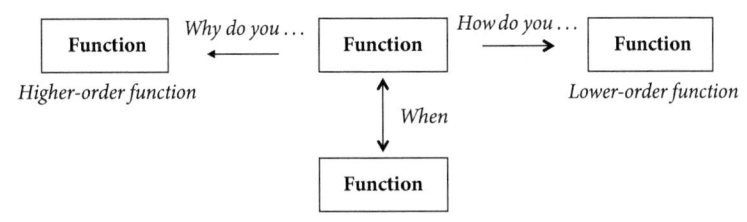

Figure 36.5 A diagrammatic representation of the grammar of a FAST diagram. The horizontal axis represents abstraction—functions at a higher abstraction level are to the left of functions at a lower abstraction level. The vertical axis represents time or the sequential ordering of functions.

functions at a higher abstraction level into one or several lower-order functions at a lower abstraction level. Figure 36.5 illustrates this idea diagrammatically. The horizontal axis is the level of *abstraction*, ranging from high abstraction to the left to low abstraction to the right. In other words, the further a function is to the right, the more concrete it is. The vertical axis is *time*, in other words, *when* a function is carried out. A function to the left of a function answers the question "*Why* do you carry out this function?" while a function to the right answers the question "*How* do you carry out this function?"

Figure 36.6 shows an example of a partial FAST diagram for the wearable device coupling affection. The overall function is *Couple Affection*. To *Couple Affection*, the device has to be able to *Communicate Affection* and *Perceive Affection*. To *Communicate Affection*, the device has to *Sense User Action*, *Module Signal*, and *Transmit Signal*. The FAST diagram can also be read the other way around. Why does the design require a *Sense User Action*? This is because it needs to *Communicate Affection*. Why does it need to *Communicate Affection*? This is because it needs to *Couple Affection*.

Several controllable and uncontrollable parameters can be attached to any of these functions as part of an early analysis of the required function characteristics. In turn, this analysis can drive another iteration of the requirements specification.

For instance, consider the function *Sense User Affection* in Figure 36.6. A signal corresponding to a proxy of a user's affection can be transmitted from the user to the wearable device in a number of ways, for example, by touch, by rubbing the device, or by applying pressure. Another possible solution is to allow the user to communicate affection through the duration of the interaction, such as the length of time they touch the device or apply pressure against it. In such a case, *duration* is a controllable parameter of the function because it can be controlled by the device

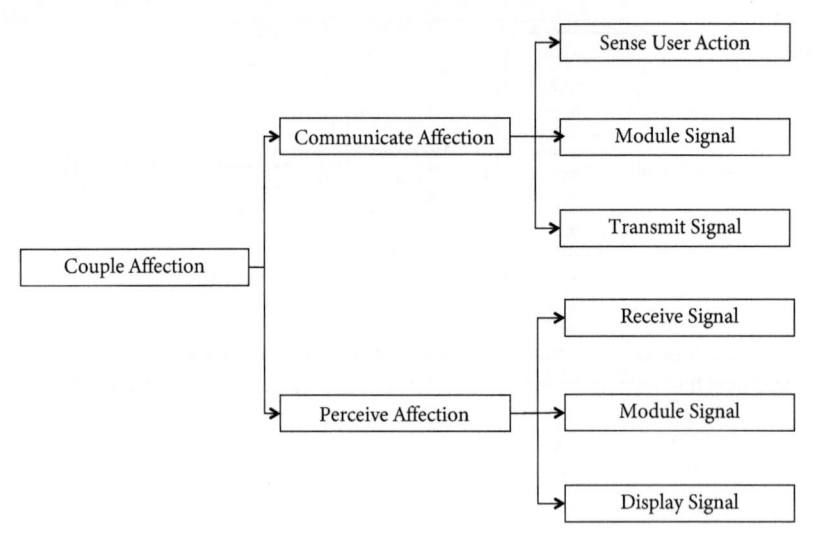

Figure 36.6 A high-level FAST diagram for a wearable device coupling affection between two individuals.

designer. An example of an uncontrollable parameter is the certainty of whether an affective signal was intended to be communicated by the user, and if so, the magnitude of affection that was intended. It is not possible to be completely sure about the user's intention in this regard, even if the system detected some form of user interaction with the device. A misdetection can happen for many reasons, including sensor error, human motor control noise, and cognitive error, such as misunderstanding how affection is meant to be communicated via the wearable device.

Another example of parameterized function is the function *Display Signal* in Figure 36.6. This function also depends on a number of parameters. The controllable parameters include concerns such as whether the device displays affection as a continuous or discrete signal, the display resolution (e.g., three discrete levels of affection), the media used (e.g., light, sound, vibration), and the governing parameters around the chosen media. As is evident, the degree of parameterization depends to some extent on how solution-dependent the FAST diagram is. An example of an uncontrollable parameter is the environment in which the device and the user operate, which will affect how well a function such as *Display Signal* can operate. Another example of an uncontrollable parameter is the context of use, including the specific situations in which the device is used. For example, a user may be alone and standing still, walking in a crowded room, or driving a car. While uncontrollable parameters cannot be explicitly controlled by the design, their effect on the design can still be analyzed and taken into account. For example, the effect of different room illumination on the display of an affective signal conveyed using a light-emitting diode (LED) array can be analyzed via experimentation.

To create a FAST diagram, it is often best to start with general functions ("Which functions must be carried out?") and then progressively develop a more specific function structure. In the example of a wearable device that couples affection, the two key functions are *Communicate Affection* and *Perceive Affection*. Each function should be described as simply as possible, ideally with just a verb and a noun. Then, chronologically trace through each function that must be realized for the

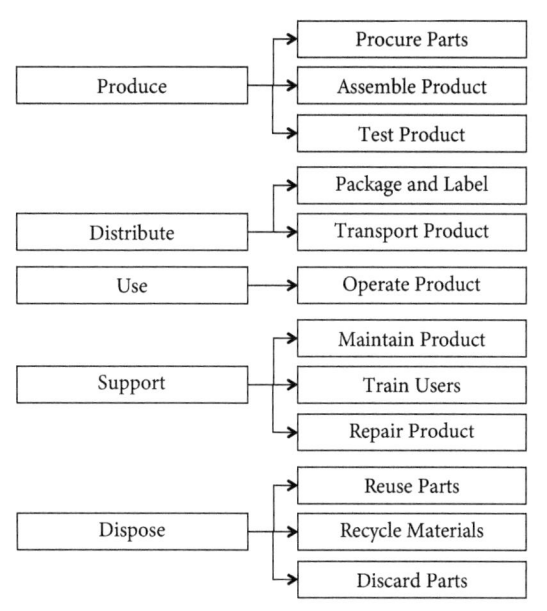

```
                              ┌──→  Procure Parts
              Produce  ────────┼──→  Assemble Product
                              └──→  Test Product

                              ┌──→  Package and Label
              Distribute ─────┴──→  Transport Product

              Use       ──────────→  Operate Product

                              ┌──→  Maintain Product
              Support   ──────┼──→  Train Users
                              └──→  Repair Product

                              ┌──→  Reuse Parts
              Dispose   ──────┼──→  Recycle Materials
                              └──→  Discard Parts
```

Figure 36.7 A FAST diagram presenting an overview of the main functions across the lifecycle of a generic product.

design to work. In practice, this often requires both careful self-reflection and consultation with other members of the design team or stakeholders to ensure all necessary functions are included. It is important to remember to include all special modes of the design, such as system standby, start-up, and restart. The focus should be on system behavior—avoid descriptions of the embodiment of the design, particularly specifying the shape, form, or structure of specific solutions. Finally, it is possible to customize the FAST diagram by annotating it to indicate critical functions, key parameters that determine function performance, and so on.

FAST diagrams are often used by engineers and designers to ensure all relevant functionality is captured in the requirements specification. The decomposition process forces everyone in the design team to be clear about which functions must be carried out to realize an overall function. Another use of FAST diagrams is lifecycle analysis. Figure 36.7 illustrates how each lifecycle phase of a product can be decomposed into sets of FAST diagrams. Functional modeling of a product's lifecycle can inform the requirements capture process by identifying all necessary functionality across all product phases, including assembly, distribution, support, and eventual reuse or disposal.

36.4.2 Translating functions into function carriers

Having identified the functions that must be realized by the system, the next step is to understand how to best implement these functions. In other words, the objective is now to consider the best alternatives for translating the functions into *function carriers*. A starting point for this design process is the construction of a *morphological chart*.

	1	2	3
Supply Energy	Human	Battery	Solar
Sense User Affection	Touch	Rub	Rotate
Display Remote Affection	LCD	LEDs	Vibrations

Combination 1

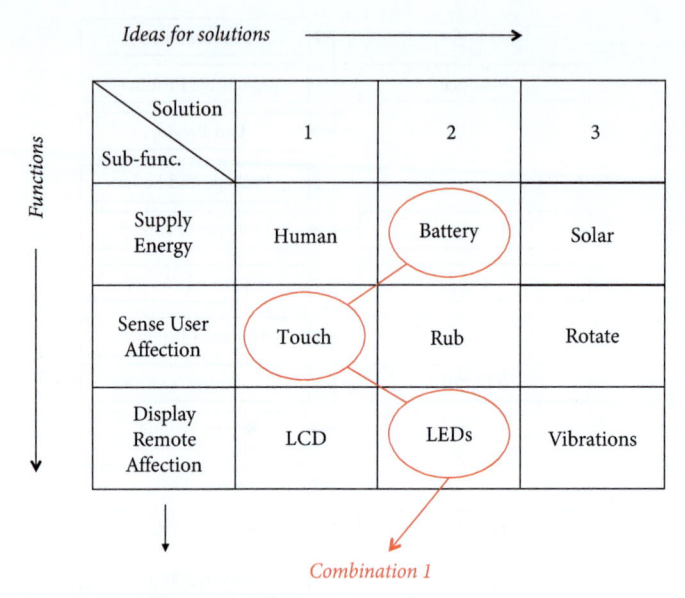

Figure 36.8 A morphological chart illustrating a set of alternative solutions for a subset of functions for a device for affection across distance.

A morphological chart is a table in which every row maps a specific *function* to a set of candidate *function carriers*, often referred to as *solutions* and sometimes as *solution principles*. This chapter uses the terms function carrier and solution interchangeably.

Figure 36.8 illustrates this idea for three functions of a wearable device for coupling affection between two individuals. The function *Supply Energy* can, for example, be mapped to three different solutions: (1) the device can harvest some of the human user's energy; (2) the device can use a battery; or (3) the device can use solar energy. The function *Sense User Affection* may be realized by (1) touch, (2) a rubbing motion, or (3) a rotating motion. Finally, the function *Display Remote Affection* may be realized using (1) a liquid-crystal display, (2) an LED array, or (3) by communicating tactile vibrations to the user's skin in preset patterns, for instance, using separate codes for three levels of affection.

All these solutions can be further detailed in a second iteration of a morphological chart following the initial selection of a preferred solution. For instance, an energy source such as a battery can be further explored in terms of the kind of battery, whether it should be replaceable, whether it should be rechargeable, and so on.

Having constructed the morphological chart, the idea is now to generate combinations of function carriers by going through each function in the morphological chart and selecting a set of corresponding solutions that realize all the functions required to carry out the overall function. For example, in the morphological chart in Figure 36.8, Combination 1 has been generated by selecting a partial design for a wearable device based on using a battery as the energy source, sensing the user's affection using touch, and displaying remote affection using an LED array.

Theoretically, assuming each function maps to exactly k solutions, there are nk combinations for n functions. This means that the morphological chart in Figure 36.8 can generate nine unique theoretical combinations. As both the number of functions and the number of solutions tend to be large in practice, it is not meaningful to exhaustively generate all or a large set of combinations.

Instead, the design team uses professional judgment, the requirements, and any other sources of design insight to generate a subset of promising combinations.

36.4.3 Concept selection

Having arrived at a set of combinations, the next step is to rank these combinations and arrive at a final recommendation. As a starting point, conceptual designs (combinations of solutions) can be scored against relevant criteria. For example, Figure 36.9 scores two concepts so that they can be compared numerically.

The scoring works as follows. First, each criterion is assigned a weighting in a nominal range between 1 and 5. Then, each concept is scored against each criterion. This results in another value in a nominal range between 1 and 5. This value is then scaled by the weighting for that feature. For example, in Figure 36.9, the value of Concept 1 for the criterion Weight is 2. Since the weighting for the criterion Weight is 3, the weighted value is 6.

The final score of a concept is a linear combination of the form $c_1 v_1 + c_2 v_2 + \cdots + c_n v_n$, where c_i and v_i are the ith criterion and corresponding value, respectively. By calculating the linear combination scores of the concepts, the scoring mechanism provides an overall score. For example, for Concept 1 in Figure 36.9, the combined score is calculated as $2 \cdot 3 + 2 \cdot 3 + 2 \cdot 2 + 3 \cdot 4 = 6 + 6 + 4 + 12 = 28$. For Concept 2, the calculation is $4 \cdot 3 + 4 \cdot 3 + 4 \cdot 2 + 1 \cdot 4 = 12 + 12 + 8 + 4 = 36$.

It is often useful to include a point of comparison that calibrates the quantification. One option is to introduce an ideal concept that attains the maximum weighted value for each criterion. Figure 36.9 shows the scoring for a hypothetical ideal concept.

Another possibility is to compare against a *datum*, for example, an existing design based on an older product or a competitor's product. In the latter case, the scoring can be used as part of a *competitive analysis* to better understand which criteria a new design could realistically excel at compared to an existing or hypothetical competitor's product.

To calculate the weighted value, two quantities are required: (1) the weighting for the criteria and (2) a function that converts a quantity (e.g., battery life, weight, height, accuracy) into a nominal value. Weightings can arise from many sources, for example, organizational knowledge of the priority of criteria based on available sales and support data. They can also arise from

| | | Concept 1 || Concept 2 || Ideal |
Criteria	Weighting	Value	Wt val	Value	Wt val	Wt val
Weight	3	2	6	4	12	15
Appearance	3	2	6	4	12	15
Power	2	2	4	4	8	10
Accuracy	4	3	12	1	4	20
			28		36	60

Figure 36.9 A comparison of two conceptual designs scored across a set of features against a theoretical ideal concept that scores perfectly in every category.

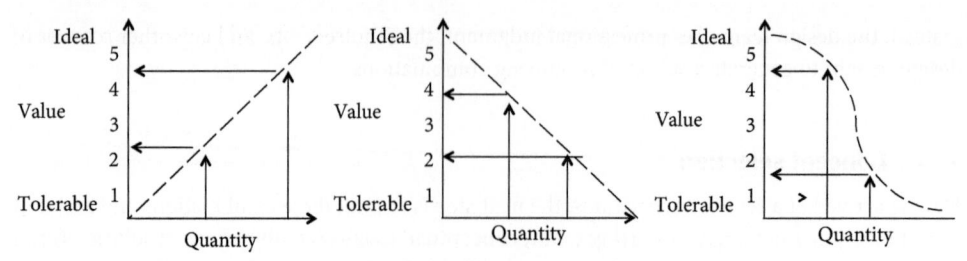

Figure 36.10 An illustration of three different functions for translating a quantity (battery life, weight, accuracy in sensing, etc.) into a value that can be used to score concepts.

market research based on focus groups asking existing or potential customers to rank product qualities. Weightings may also arise from domain knowledge, business concerns, or regulatory requirements.

There are also many methods for converting a quantity into a nominal value. The simplest method is to use a zero-intercept linear function over the effective quantity range to linearly map a quantity to a nominal value, as shown in Figure 36.10 (left). An example of a quantity is battery life. For a hypothetical wearable device worn around the wrist, the viable battery range may be determined by the designers to reside between eight hours and 24 hours. Battery life is then mapped with eight hours corresponding to a nominal value of one and 24 hours corresponding to a nominal value of 5. The battery life between eight and 24 hours is then linearly interpolated to obtain the corresponding nominal values.

For some criteria, such as weight, it is more natural to map the values in reverse order, as illustrated in Figure 36.10 (middle). For example, if a design team has determined that the weight of a wearable device must reside in the range between 100 and 250 g, then 100 g is mapped to a nominal value of 5, 250 g is mapped to a nominal value of 1, and any weight in between is linearly interpolated.

The function used to calculate a nominal value does not need to be linear. Figure 36.10 (right) illustrates a nonlinear mapping between a quantity and a nominal value. The function can also be discrete, for example, mapping a wide range of quantities to the same nominal value.

As the scoring method is merely calculating linear combinations, it is very simple, which makes it easy to understand and apply. Another advantage is that the scoring method maps directly to criteria and thus helps to ensure the conceptual design addresses the criteria articulated in the requirements specification. It may also make the design team more aware of the significance of certain criteria and question whether all relevant criteria have been fairly represented and are fully reflected in the requirements specification. Moreover, the analysis elucidates intrinsic trade-offs that emerge in any nontrivial design, such as the inherent conflict between device size and battery life, and forces the design team to carefully consider how to balance them.

The simplicity of scoring concepts as linear combinations comes at the cost of reduced accuracy and increased uncertainty. It is important to be aware of the limitations of design scoring in conceptual design selection.

First, the method assumes all relevant criteria have been represented, which is hopefully true but often difficult to ensure in practice. Second, the method assumes weightings and concept values are error-free point estimates when, in reality, they are uncertain. Third, the method assumes all criteria can be related mathematically as a linear combination.

For these reasons, concept scoring is error-prone, and the results should be used with caution. Concept selection should not be made with sole reference to how well a concept scores, particularly when using the aggregated score, which is more suitable for the initial ranking of concepts than for the final selection. A decision to select a particular concept should be complemented with a written narrative that explains the reasons for selecting a concept with reference to the criteria, weightings, and other concepts, as well as any considered datum, competitor product, or ideal concept.

As an example of the danger of relying solely on concept scores, consider the two concepts for a affective ring design in Figure 36.9. Concept 2 has a higher aggregate score (36) than Concept 1 (28). At first glance, Concept 2 appears superior. However, Concept 2 has scored only 1 for accuracy compared to 3 for Concept 1, and accuracy is the criterion with the highest weighting. Therefore, despite other drawbacks, it may be wiser to proceed with Concept 1 instead of Concept 2 and investigate whether the drawbacks of Concept 1, such as its higher weight, worse appearance, and poorer power solution, can be mitigated. Alternatively, further research may be conducted to investigate whether the accuracy can be improved for Concept 2. In this way, concept scoring is used to drive further design exploration rather than as a clear-cut method for identifying the best concept.

36.4.4 Product architecture

Having arrived at a functional model, it is possible to consider the allocation of *functions* to *modules* and how such modules should interact. A product architecture is in a continuum between *integral* and *modular*. In a fully integrated architecture, every function maps to a single module. In a fully modularized architecture, every function maps to its own module.

Product architecture was originally proposed by Ulrich [838] for the design of physical products. Here, a module can be seen as a physical component. In a more modular architecture, interfaces and interactions between modules are more decoupled. This means that changes in individual modules do not necessarily imply any changes in other modules, a reasoning similar to the encapsulation principle in object-oriented programming. Because of this, it may be possible to design individual modules separately. In theory, everything else being equal, this allows for the reuse of existing modules across products, which can reduce the design cost and allow for a variety of different products. An example is a modular video camera with a separate tripod, battery, carrying bag, lens system, and so on. By contrast, in a more integral architecture, boundaries and interactions between modules are coupled, and modifications to one part of the system are likely to affect other parts. This means that modules must be designed in collaboration and that it is difficult to allow for variety or change. In other words, such integration may enable optimization at the cost of flexibility.

A modular architecture implies some form of interface mechanism between modules. Ulrich [838] proposed three archetypal modular architectures:

Slot modularity: Slot modularity means that modules are connected using a range of standard interfaces. An example of this is a TV with a high-definition multimedia interface connector, an antenna connector, and so on.

Bus modularity: Bus modularity means that modules are connected using a single standard interface, such as the Universal Serial Bus (USB).

Sectional modularity: Sectional modularity means that there is no standard interface and no main module. An example is pipework.

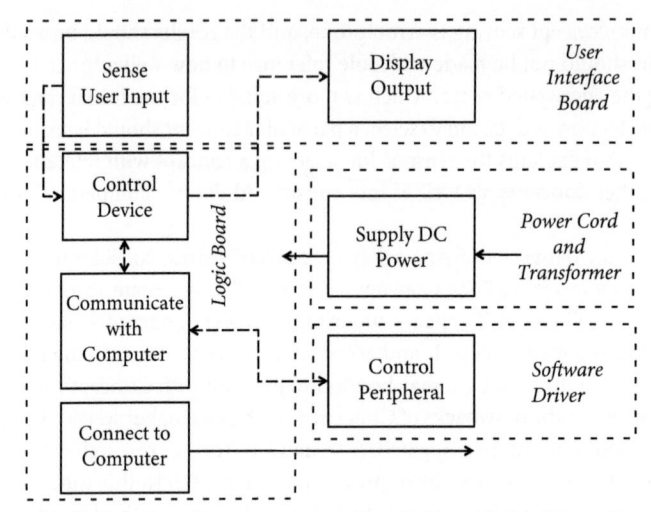

Figure 36.11 A function structure of a computer peripheral indicating the flows of energy and signals. If this peripheral were a laser printer, there would also be flows of materials (paper and toner). The function structure has been modularized into four modules based on functional affinity: (1) user interface board, (2) logic board, (3) cord and alternating current (AC) transformer, and (4) software driver.

Product architecture choices matter throughout the lifecycle of the product or system. At the design phase, how to realize functions, split design tasks, and potentially reuse existing designs depend on the architecture. At the manufacturing phase of a physical system, the architecture affects assembly sequences, tooling, reuse, and the equipment involved. At the production phase, the architecture helps determine the unit cost, the ability to reuse standard parts or modules, the viability of late customization, and the ability to offer product variety. During usage, the architecture will determine whether the product is optimized for performance (which usually involves a high degree of integration), generalizability, or flexibility. Other factors that may be affected during usage include the ability to adapt and maintain the system during use. Post-production, the architecture affects service and maintenance, such as the ease of replacing physical parts and the ability to upgrade individual software modules. The ability to change the product or system at a much later stage in the overall process is also partly determined by the level of modularity.

The starting point for creating a modular product architecture is a schematic overview of the product, for example, a function structure model of the product's underpinning system. Then, select the desired level of product variety depending on factors such as the level of reuse, the ability to change the product, and the variety of product offerings. Finally, create modules by clustering functions in the schematic overview. An example of this process is shown in Figure 36.11, which shows a function structure model of a computer peripheral and the flows of energy and signals between the functional elements. This schematic can be clustered into four modules based on functional affinity: (1) a user interface board handling user input and output, (2) a logic board controlling the device and communicating and connecting to the computer, (3) a power cord and transformer, and (4) a software driver. This ability to easily modularize a system early in the design is another advantage of function structure models.

It is also possible to design a computer peripheral using a more integral architecture, for example, by integrating the user interface board, logic board, and power into a single unit. This may be achieved by allowing the peripheral to draw power from a USB connection, thus eliminating the need for a power cord and transformer. This latter architecture can make sense if the computer peripheral is an integrated handheld unit, such as a handheld scanner. By contrast, the architecture illustrated in Figure 36.11 can serve as a blueprint for a heavy-duty computer peripheral that requires external power. Examples of such peripherals include laser printers, virtual reality headsets, and 3D printers.

36.4.5 Embodiment and detailed design

Once a concept has been agreed upon, the next two phases are *embodiment design* and *detailed design*. Embodiment design is the phase in the design process that follows the identification of a conceptual design. The embodiment phase results in design sketches, prototypes, layouts of mechanical components, the identification of critical software modules and electronic components, and so on.

Detailed design is the phase in the design where the system is ready to be distributed in the form of software or sent to manufacturing in the form of manufacturing instructions. For example, for a software-only system, the detailed design phase would involve designing the software architecture, class descriptions, and so on.

36.5 Verification and validation

Two fundamental activities in design engineering are verification and validation. *Verification* means systematically checking that all requirements have been met. In other words, verification is a process for ensuring a built system meets its specification. *Validation* is the process of ensuring a system fulfills its intended purpose. There is therefore a clear distinction between verification, ensuring the system is built correctly according to its specification, and validation, ensuring the system is capable of assisting end-users in solving their problems. Due to the separation between verification and validation, it is possible to succeed in one and not the other. For example, it is possible to pass verification by building a system that fully meets its requirements but then fail in validation because the system is incapable of carrying out its intended function or fulfilling its purpose. It is also possible to fail in verification and succeed in validation; a system can be usable for its intended purpose even if it does not meet all its requirements. A common problem is a system succeeding in verification and failing in validation. This problem arises due to the high likelihood of a misalignment between the requirements of a system and the qualities required for the system to be usable in practice.

36.5.1 Verification

Verification is the process of ensuring requirements have been met. To succeed in verification, it often helps to structure the verification process into a *verification cross-reference matrix* (VCRM). A VCRM is a row-by-row specification for how to verify individual requirements. There are many ways to set up a VCRM; however, they usually contain the following columns:

Requirement ID: An identifier that matches the identifier of a requirement in the specification.
Requirement: The requirement addressed by the verification method.
Verification method: A specification that details how verification is to be carried out.

Table 36.2 Example requirements for an affective wearable device.

ID	Requirement	Verification method	Allocation	Success criteria
1	Device must indicate its power on status	Inspection	User interface	Visible and legible power on status
2	Device must be comfortable to wear	Test	Device case	Median ratings above 4 on a 5-point Likert scale by representative user sample from target audience ($n > 24$)
3	Device must be able to sense at least five levels of communicated affection from the user	Test	User interface	Consistent ability (> 95%) by representative user sample from target audience to communicate five different levels of intended affection ($n > 24$)
4	Device must be able to wirelessly receive an affective signal from a remote paired user	Demonstration	Wireless stack	Ability to receive and respond to test signal
5	Device must communicate affection from a paired remote user in five discernible levels	Test	User interface	Consistent ability (> 95%) by representative user sample from target audience to detect five distinct levels of intended affection ($n > 24$)

Allocation: A list of components, parts, subsystems, and so on that are affected by this verification.

Success criteria: A free-text clear description of what constitutes success. This may be qualitative, quantitative, or a combination of both.

When considering a verification method, it is useful to consider a few fundamental higher-level verification approaches.

Inspection, sometimes referred to as *examination*, means using one or several of the five senses to non-destructively ensure a system possesses a certain quality. For example, the requirement to paint a door blue can be inspected by visually checking the color of the door.

Demonstration refers to ensuring that manipulating the system according to its intended use results in expected outcomes. For example, checking that a registered user's finger touch unlocks a fingerprint lock.

Test refers to checking that feeding predefined inputs yields expected outputs. For example, calling a software function with set input values and then programmatically checking that the output values of the function are correct.

Analysis means carrying out verification using calculations, models, or testing equipment to predict system characteristics based on, for example, a sampled subset of components or samples of test data.

Table 36.2 shows an example of a partial VCRM for a wearable device coupling affection between two individuals.

It is useful to develop a VCRM in conjunction with the requirements specification since a VCRM forces the designers to explicitly consider viable verification methods and success criteria early in the decision process. Such design activities can also trigger the need to construct prototypes or perform system simulations to assess the viability of adhering to requirements at an early stage. For example, the VCRM in Table 36.2 specifies five distinct levels of affective signals to be sensed by the user. This may require early prototyping and experimentation to be confident that any intended hardware or software solution is capable of satisfying such a requirement.

Paper Example 36.5.1 Designing a life-logging device

SenseCam [345] is a life-logging device in the form of a wearable camera that is worn around the neck by the user, as shown in the following figure. SenseCam takes photos periodically based on a timer or sensed events, such as a significant change in the light level of the camera image. It also allows the user to trigger image capture.

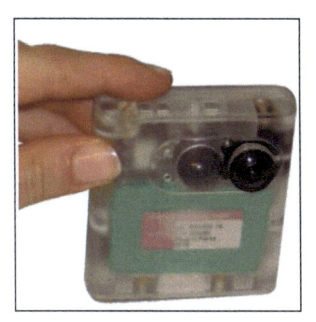

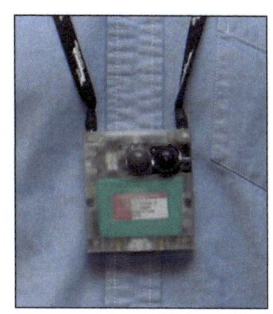

The SenseCam system was developed as a wearable retrospective memory aid. Its design process began with a requirements specification that identified important design requirements, such as the form factor, battery life, storage capacity, and ease of use. This specification was then translated into a software–hardware system that realized the system functions, such as LEDs displaying the system status, buttons for triggering user functions, an image sensor, and so on. The hardware design is shown in the following figure.

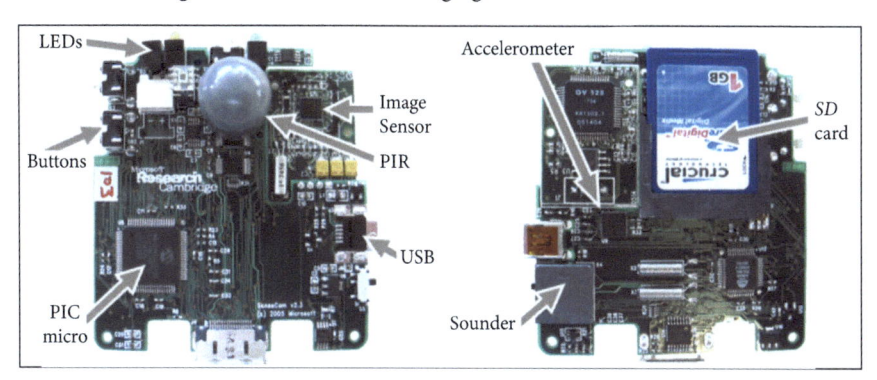

An important design parameter of SenseCam is the battery life. The analysis in the following figure (left) shows that taking images consumes the most power. The plot in the following figure (right) shows the continuous operation of SenseCam in hours as a function of the period between image captures in seconds. The chosen operating point was a period between image

continued

> **Paper Example 36.5.1 Designing a life-logging device** (continued)
>
> captures of 30 seconds, which, according to the plot, results in the SenseCam being able to operate continuously for approximately 24 hours before it has to be recharged.
>
> | Mode | Description | Power consumption |
> |---|---|---|
> | Standby | Waiting for USB connection or power on, RTC running | 152uA |
> | Running | Microcontroller active but no sensing or logging | 20.5mA |
> | Sensor capture | Sensors being read and logged | 35.0mA |
> | Image capture | Image (or audio) being transferred to *SD* card | 104mA |
>
> SenseCam has been validated over a 12-month period with one user with amnesia. The validation results show that the user was able to recall events that were previously impossible to recall. In the final test, the user was able to recall 76% of events with the aid of SenseCam images, which is considered exceptional for a user with amnesia.

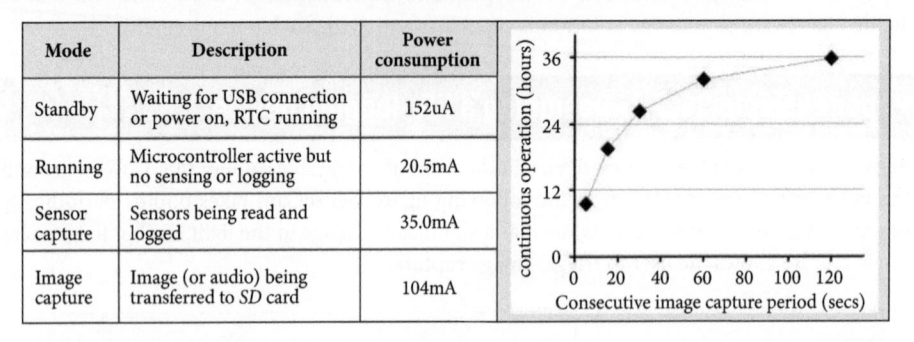

36.5.2 Validation

Validation is the process of ensuring the system is fulfilling its purpose for the intended users. As such, validation is intrinsically dependent on the particular system that has been created. See Part VIII for a detailed description of a variety of empirical methodologies that can be used to assess whether users are able to use a system for its intended purpose.

36.6 Design engineering and user-centered design

This chapter has introduced design engineering as a process that addresses the entire design spectrum, from the specification of a solution-neutral problem statement to the implementation, verification, and validation of an interactive system.

While there are several overlaps between design engineering and the user-centered design processes we discussed in Chapter 33, there are three distinct aspects of design engineering that, in our experience, can assist HCI system designers.

The first is the explicit separation of *functions*—the *what*—from *function carriers*—the *how*. This allows HCI system designers to explore *function models* that can relate functions in various ways, for example, the flow of information between functions using function structures or the level of abstraction between functions using FAST diagrams. This enables the exploration of solutions *before* considering any concrete design solutions.

The second aspect is the systematic exploration of the mapping between functions and function carriers using, for example, morphological charts. Such exploration can be aided by scoring the suitability of different function carriers using estimates of their suitability as functions of some known quantity, such as the suitability of a battery given the battery life. This allows for the *informed* exploration of a wide spectrum of possible solutions as well as the construction of a narrative that clearly explains a chosen concept with reference to a set of criteria.

The third aspect is the idea that function models and conceptual designs can be parameterized. We can use parameterization to determine the optimal values of controllable parameters—parameters the designer can influence—and understand how the system behaves in relation to uncontrollable parameters—parameters that are outside the designer's control. This allows us to carry out analyses before deciding on specific implementation strategies and before carrying out in-depth user studies.

In addition, when building a working interactive system, the management of project risk is essential. Changing requirements late in a project may be very expensive or even impossible. By taking function models and conceptual design seriously, it is possible to rectify many design mistakes and discover many unknowns early in the design process.

Thus, while design engineering shares many traits with user-centered design, the emphasis on integrated system design amplifies aspects of implementation that sometimes must be considered early in the design process. For example, for the life-logger SenseCam [345] to be effective, it was necessary to understand how the period between image captures related to the battery life. This type of analysis can be fruitfully carried out *before* building a device and engaging in user studies, particularly when the studies involve users with disabilities.

Summary

- Systematic design processes minimize risk and improve the quality of system design.
- Design engineering can be broken down into the following activities: arriving at a solution-neutral problem statement, elaborating a requirements specification, conceptual design, embodiment design, detailed design, verification, and validation.
- A function model allows a designer to specify the interrelations of functions in a system without considering how these functions should be carried out, thereby encouraging and facilitating exploration.

Exercises

1. Concepts. Explain the difference between verification and validation.
2. Problem statements. Derive solution-neutral problem statements, ranging from low abstraction to high abstraction, for the following design tasks: (1) an updated model of a coffee maker for domestic use; (2) a mechanism for detecting falls among patients in a hospital environment; and (3) a wearable device that measures the user's pulse and communicates the readings to the user.
3. Application case. An existing simple printer design allows the user to print by connecting the printer to a computer via a USB port. The printer draws power from an AC mains electrical socket. The printer has a manual paper feed, status LED indicators, and buttons for turning it on and off and for printing a test page.
   (a) Provide a solution-neutral problem statement for the design of the printer.
   (b) Identify the overall function structures, including their functional elements and the flows of energy, materials, and signals.
   (c) Distill a modular product architecture for the printer by modularizing the function structures identified in (b).

(d) A competitor has introduced a new printer that supports wireless connection to the computer and contains a paper magazine, allowing the printer to print multiple pages without the need for manual loading. Create a morphological chart to carry out a competitive analysis against this printer and identify solution principles and conceptual designs that can help ensure a printer redesign results in a competitive product.

37
Safety and risk

An interactive system should be safe; that is, it should not harm its users or people who depend on it. What we mean by safety depends on the application domain. In human factors and human–computer interaction (HCI) research, safety can mean:

- Safety from death. For example, human error in the operation of a medical device that administers medicine to a patient. Medical error is a leading cause of death [512], and it is commonly associated with errors in the user interface.
- Safety from physical harm. For example, physical injuries caused by machinery in factories are often associated with errors resulting from inattention, fatigue, or multitasking during operation.
- Safety from economic or social harm. For example, personal data should not be inadvertently released to outsiders.

Safety is a challenging engineering objective. This is due to many factors; perhaps most importantly, understanding rare events that can cause harm requires a thorough understanding of users, users' tasks and workflows, the operating environment, and the systems themselves. Safety is a complex *systems problem* that requires a systems approach (Chapter 35).

In this chapter, we discuss the concept of safety and methods for ensuring a system is safe to use. An important realization is that to ensure a system is safe, we first need to agree on the acceptable *level of safety*, as no system can be proven to be completely safe. In broad terms, the level of safety depends on the frequency and severity of an incident. Then, we need to gauge factors that affect the level of safety. What is the frequency of occurrence of possibly adverse events? Does it range from improbable to daily? Also, what is the severity—does it range from minor injury to death? Depending on the system, it may be impossible to entirely eliminate harm or even death at some probable level of occurrence.

To answer the above questions, we need to understand the "human factor" in systems safety. Cook [168] summarized important aspects of systems safety in his book *How Complex Systems Fail*. First, *all* interesting systems are complex because they need to handle different contingencies associated with things that people value. This pertains to systems related to physical safety, such as those in healthcare, transportation, and manufacturing. It also pertains to systems in finance (e.g., banking), politics (e.g., voting machines), personal data (e.g., tax data), and even entertainment (e.g., gaming avatars). Second, complex systems are heavily defended against failure. For an accident to happen, multiple failures must take place. Third, human users have a critical role in building those defenses via their actions. They adopt safety procedures, undertake training and safety courses, and so on. Humans are not passive actors in complex systems and, therefore, in their safety. Fourth, because of the complexity of systems, practitioners' actions are gambles. That is, all actions are taken under uncertainty. A driver turning on an automated lane-keeping feature in a car takes a risk; there is no guarantee that the car will operate correctly under all circumstances.

Introduction to Human-Computer Interaction. Kasper Hornbæk, Per Ola Kristensson, and Antti Oulasvirta,
Oxford University Press. © Kasper Hornbæk, Per Ola Kristensson, and Antti Oulasvirta (2025).
DOI: 10.1093/oso/9780192864543.003.0037

Fifth, because of all this, attributing causes in accidents is hard. Human error is rarely the sole culprit; it is just one cause in a complex network of factors including organizational, managerial, and design-related factors.

Questions of safety are serious and deeply ethical. Taken to one extreme, safety engineering needs to determine which factors are associated with death. When designing systems that are inherently dangerous, such as training facilities for firefighters, how often are people "allowed" to die?

Safety thereby becomes a management problem: the management of risk. At a high level, the strategies for managing risk are to transfer the risk somewhere else, avoid the risk altogether, reduce the negative effect of the risk, or accept some or all the consequences of a risk. Inevitably, safety becomes an ethical question in risk management: What is the acceptability of harm, to whom, and how much is one willing to invest to prevent it? While the methods presented in this chapter do not directly answer this ethical question, they can help us gain the necessary information to answer it.

A central concept when reasoning about safety and risk is the *system boundary*. The system boundary defines the system that is to be considered. In nearly every case in HCI, the system boundary extends *beyond* a user interface or interactive device. At the very least, the system boundary will include the user; frequently, it also includes additional elements such as the operating environment, any training facilities provided for the user, any other people the user will need to interact with, and so on.

As we will see, the setting of a system boundary is fundamental in risk assessment, as it defines which risks will be assessed—anything outside the system boundary will not be considered. This makes risk assessment both tractable and inclusive of any relevant elements within the boundary that can affect the risk of the system.

For example, an infusion pump is a medical device that delivers a fluid into a patient's body. Infusion pumps have settings that control the dosage. A nurse may use a calculator to calculate the correct dosage, for example, a calculator app on the nurse's mobile phone. The interface of the calculator app can now be said to be part of the infusion pump system. Then, for a risk assessment of the infusion pump, we will need to include the app, the mobile phone, the nurse, the patient, the infusion pump, and possibly the hospital context, for example, whether the environment provides distractions that may overload the nurse while carrying out calculations.

Risks are pervasive in complex systems. They emerge from uncertainty in, for example, project management, financial markets, legal liabilities, regulations, design, unexpected usage patterns of a product or system, or deliberate attacks. It follows that, in addition to physical risk, there are many other types of risk, such as performance risks, management risks, development risks, commercial risks, service risks, and external risks, for instance, new regulations or unexpected market competitors.

The term *risk* has many definitions. Here, we view risk from the point of view of expected system behavior. A system has a certain purpose, such as allowing users to quickly and accurately enter text, manage their information, or stay in touch with their relatives. The possibility that the system does *not* behave as expected can give rise to *undesired behavior*. The risk of an incident that results in undesired behavior of the system can then be viewed as the expected value of the undesired system behavior:

$$risk = likelihood \cdot impact, \tag{37.1}$$

where the *likelihood* is the probability of a specific incident and the *impact* is the expected loss due to this incident. This definition restricts incidents to be binary—they either happen or do not happen.

In this chapter, we discuss how to manage risks using a variety of techniques that allow us to first identify and assess risks and then minimize, monitor, and control the probabilities of undesired events.

> ### Paper Example 37.0.1: Usability-related risks in electronic voting
>
> Usability can be associated with risk. For example, electronic voting systems must be usable by all citizens eligible to vote regardless of their age, disability, level of education, poverty status, and so on. The design of voting technology can influence election outcomes and people's willingness to accept election results.
>
> Bederson et al. [57] discovered a range of usability issues with electronic voting systems that use touchscreens. The authors compared electronic voting systems including the one used in the controversial 2000 presidential election in the United States.
>
> The paper illustrates two important issues that highlight how concepts from the safety and risk literature can improve system analysis. The first is the importance of setting the system boundary of the voting system, which does not only include the voting machine but also the voter, the voting environment, and the system in place to ensure voting integrity. For example, voters are exposed to an unfamiliar system in an intimidating setting where other voters impatiently wait for their turn to vote. Thus, the system boundary needs to capture the voting environment to enable the assessment of the risk of the user failing to achieve their goal—voting for their preferred choice.
>
> The second issue is that such systems are inherently complex; as a result, it is unsurprising that they exhibit a large number of usability problems. Given its critical importance in society, voting technology should be systematically risk assessed to minimize the probability that a voter is unable to vote for their preferred choice.

A *hazard* is the possibility of an object, situation, information, or energy source to cause an adverse effect. For example, a wearable device with a sharp edge may cut the user; a confusingly labeled button may cause users to accidentally delete data.

Exposure is the likely extent to which the user (or another adversely affected agent in the system) is exposed to, or can be influenced by, a hazard. For example, if the sharp edge of a wearable device is covered by a rubber coating, there may be no exposure of the user to the hazard. If the user has limited access to a confusingly labeled button that can cause accidental data deletion, the user has limited exposure to this hazard.

For a risk to exist, there must be *both* a hazard *and* exposure to the hazard. A hazard without any exposed users is not a risk. A risk is the product of the likelihood of an incident and the impact of the incident. A risk can therefore take on a range of values, although it is always preconditioned on the presence of a hazard.

Sometimes, it is exceedingly difficult to anticipate the consequences of future systems, as such systems may give rise to unanticipated outcomes. Consider, for example, a popular social network that uses machine learning algorithms to recommend news stories to its users for discussion with their friends. Such a system can easily reinforce what are called "filter bubbles." Filter bubbles may amplify a group's perception, which can lead to users accepting conspiracy theories or becoming otherwise radicalized. The *precautionary principle* states that there is a social responsibility to protect users from significant harm if there is a risk of such harm happening.

The rest of this chapter will explain approaches and methods for both understanding safety and risk and mitigating risk. We begin by examining the nature of human error and reflecting on the problem of attributing cause or fault when accidents happen. We then introduce risk management, which encompasses analyzing, monitoring, and controlling risk. There are many risk assessment methods that have been developed for specific purposes; here, we review a selection of methods that are useful for analyzing interactive systems from different perspectives, particularly in terms of identifying, communicating, and assessing risks. We also cover a few tactics for thinking about risk in design. Then, we treat possible failures of components and systems statistically using a framework known as reliability engineering. Lastly, we consider simple series and parallel systems, noting that if we have data on failures, we can calculate the reliability of a system, subsystem, or component, which can both inform design decisions and help with assessing risks in a system.

37.1 Human error

Why do users make errors? Norman [596] argued that many human errors occur in tasks that rely on short-term memory, such as entering numerical values into a device after having been told the values by another person. He presented an early account of human error analysis based on four limitations of human short-term memory (see Chapter 5 for a detailed account of human memory): (1) the capacity of short-term memory is limited, typically between five and 10 items; (2) the rate of information search in short-term memory is limited, approximately 100 ms per item; (3) there are only a few main types of encoding—verbal, motor, pictorial, and spatial—and they engage separate short-term memory functions; and (4) rehearsal is needed to retain information in short-term memory, and other activities can interfere with rehearsal. Another cognitive cause of human error is poor attention: We are not able to share attention or focus as much as we would like to.

However, human error is neither sufficient nor necessary for accidents [596]. Accidents can happen without errors, and many errors do not lead to accidents. Furthermore, when errors do lead to accidents, such accidents are usually caused by multiple factors that are difficult or impossible to untangle. However, the errors themselves can still be analyzed. In addition to system-induced errors, Norman [596] identified two types of human error.

The first type of human error is *mistakes*. Mistakes are related to the formation of an intention. That is, the user ends up in a situation, performs a situational analysis, and decides to take some form of action. The second type of human error is *slips*. Once the user has formed an intention, the user needs to execute this intention, that is, take an action. Slips are errors in the execution of an intention.

If the user has a lack of knowledge, for instance, due to having little or no experience with a system, or a lack of training with the system, this can give rise to both mistakes and slips. Mistakes can happen because the inexperienced user forms the wrong intentions due to a lack of knowledge of the interactive system. Slips may happen due to the inexperienced user being unable to correctly carry out actions after having formed the correct intention. Such mistakes and slips can, in theory, be mitigated by training users. However, even an expert user can have a lack of knowledge; for example, they may have incomplete knowledge of a situation because there are errors in the system or because the user is overloaded. Such errors are typically mistakes and can, in principle, be mitigated via system redesign.

Even when the user has full knowledge of a system, mistakes and slips happen. For example, a user may fail to correctly identify the situation they are finding themselves in, or they may simply make incorrect decisions. Such errors can be induced by the system the user is working with, or within, which places demands on the user such as task demands or environmental demands.

It is also possible that users have the correct intentions but fail to carry them out correctly, resulting in slips.

Norman [596] noted that there is a fundamental problem in the attribution of a single, definitive cause or fault to an accident. In practice, accidents typically occur because multiple factors interact, such as social factors, environmental factors, or factors related to human aspects of the system, the environment, and the users' tasks.

37.1.1 Skills, rules, and knowledge

In a highly influential paper titled "Skills, Rules, and Knowledge; Signals, Signs, and Symbols, and Other Distinctions in Human Performance Models," Rasmussen [689] presented a framework for understanding the performance of skilled users.

Rasmussen [689] stated that there are three levels of control involved in the operation of complex systems: skill-based, rule-based, and knowledge-based. A simplified model of the interrelations among these levels is shown in Figure 37.1.

Skill-based behavior emerges from a user having an intention. Such behavior has high automaticity and happens without conscious control. Only occasionally does skill-based behavior rely on feedback control, and in such cases, the feedback is simple, such as a tracking task; see Chapter 4 for an in-depth discussion on motor control. Automaticity allows users to free up cognitive resources to focus on higher-level aspects of the task at hand.

At the next level, rule-based behavior is characterized by the user employing stored procedures or rules of the type "if X then Y." Such rules can be learned or acquired through experience.

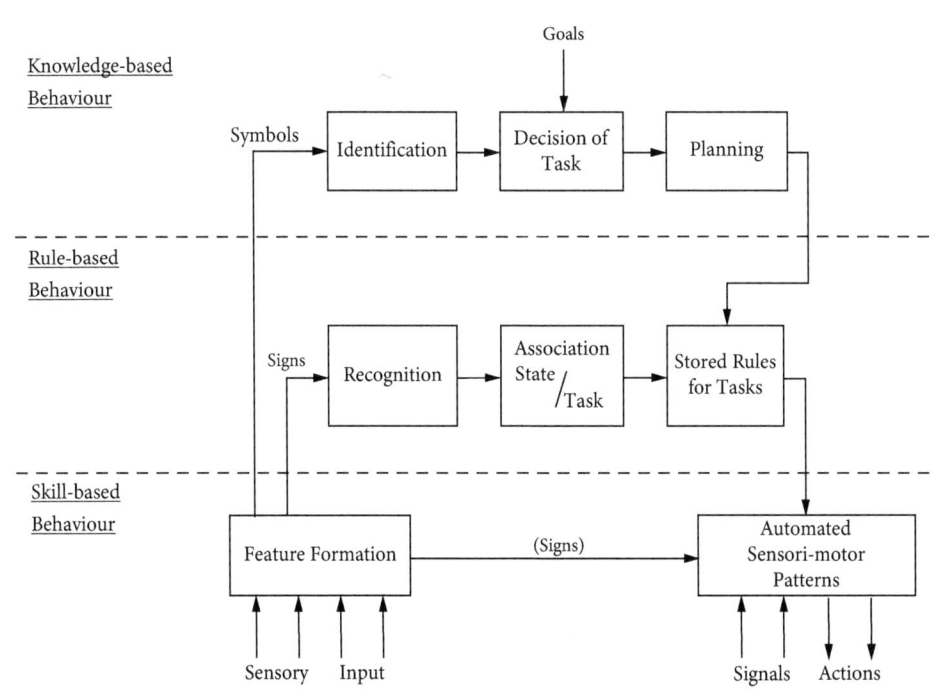

Figure 37.1 Skill-, rule-, and knowledge-based control involved in the operation of complex systems [689]. The model can be used to explain how human operators succeed and why they fail.

Performance is goal-oriented and determined by the execution of a stored rule or procedure. The user's selection of which rules to apply is governed by the previous successful application of rules in similar situations. If correction based on feedback is required, the user needs to functionally analyze the situation, which may require knowledge-based control.

The highest level of control, knowledge-based control, is needed when the user faces an unfamiliar situation and does not have any rules or knowledge that may help them control the system. In such situations, the user explicitly formulates a goal and develops a plan to achieve this goal, which may be evolved and carried out in a trial-and-error fashion or by contemplating the consequences of various actions.

Rasmussen [689] also made a distinction between signals, signs, and symbols. Signals are low-level continuous control signals that affect skill-based behavior. Such signals have no intrinsic meaning; they are merely control signals. Signs represent perceived information that guides the user's activation of predetermined actions or manipulations of the system. In other words, signs guide the selection or modification of rules for the sequence of actions necessary to carry out a skilled procedure. However, signs do not have any functional meaning; therefore, they cannot be used to generate new rules or reason about responses in an unfamiliar situation. Finally, symbols relate concepts to functional properties of the system or environment; as a result, they can be used to reason, for instance, to conceive a plan for achieving a goal. While signs are part of the external world outside the user's brain, symbols are representations of the external world inside the user's brain.

37.1.2 Taxonomies for understanding error

Reason [694] contributed an influential classification of human error. He classified error types based on their behavioral, contextual, and conceptual levels: skill-based slips, rule-based mistakes, and knowledge-based mistakes. The three error types correspond to Rasmussen's three levels of performance [689].

Reason [694] separated slips and lapses, which are due to a failure to execute a particular plan, from mistakes, which are due to the plan itself being inadequate to achieve a goal. In other words, errors can be intentional or unintentional. Intentional errors occur when the user sets out to carry out the wrong action, such as inputting an incorrect parameter into a system. A mistake occurs when the user correctly carries out an incorrect action, such as when the user believes pressing the Escape key will exit an application.

Unintentional errors can be divided into slips and lapses. Slips are incorrect operations, such as mistakenly hitting a neighboring key on a keyboard. Lapses occur when the user omits a particular action that is necessary to achieve their goal.

There is a large body of literature on human error. Given the importance of reducing human error, several design processes have been developed for this explicit purpose, most notably human factors engineering, which is discussed in Chapter 33.

37.1.3 Analysis of human error

There are in-depth analysis techniques for understanding the underlying causes of accidents, such as *root cause analysis*. At a high level, root cause analysis consists of four steps: (1) arriving at an identification and description of the problem; (2) establishing a sequence of events relating contributory factors, the root cause, and the investigated problem; (3) distinguishing between root causes, causal factors, and non-causal factors; and (4) establishing a path diagram linking the root cause to the problem through a sequence of events.

Next, we discuss design methods that can be used to manage safety and risk.

Paper Example 37.1.1: Ensuring infusion pumps have safe user interfaces

One way to help ensure a user interface is safe is to link the safety requirements of the user interface to the verification of correct operation using a formal model. Masci et al. [521] showed how to fruitfully use this approach in the medical device domain. A patient-controlled analgesia infusion pump is a pain relief device that allows the user to self-administer a drug. An example of the user interface of such a device is shown in the following figure.

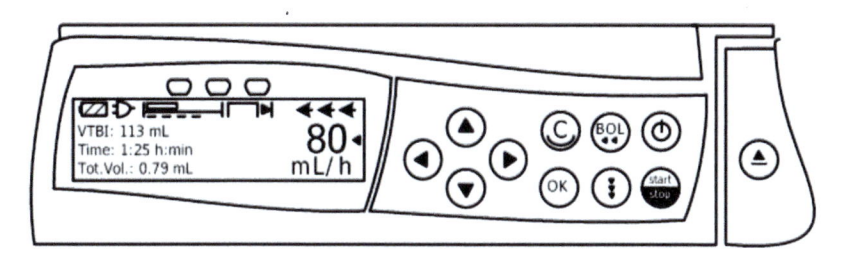

First, the paper formalizes the United States Food and Drug Administration requirements for infusion pumps, revealing ambiguities in the requirements. Then, the paper reverse-engineers a formal model of an infusion pump user interface.

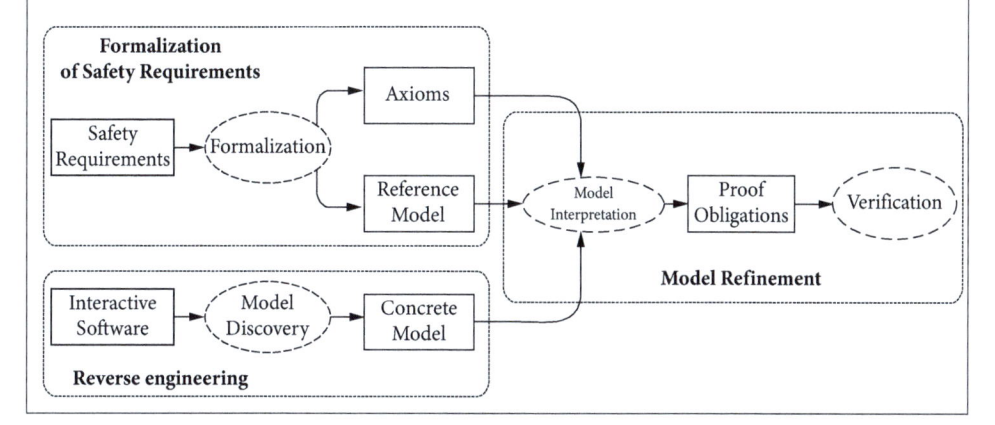

37.2 Risk management

To minimize human error, it is important to identify and minimize risks. At its core, *risk management* is about identifying and assessing risks and minimizing, monitoring, and controlling the probabilities of undesired events. There are many approaches to managing risk, and the precise risk management strategy will depend on the nature of the particular interactive system. At a high level, risk management is a process with five steps:

1. **Hazard identification:** Identify unintended system behavior that can cause unwanted outcomes.
2. **Risk estimation:** Quantify a risk by assessing the likelihood and severity of each hazard.
3. **Risk evaluation:** Decide whether risks are acceptable.
4. **Risk control:** Reduce unacceptable risks to acceptable levels.
5. **Risk monitoring:** Implement a process that ensures acceptable risk levels are maintained throughout the system's lifetime.

Risk analysis is hazard identification and risk estimation. It involves identifying the intended purpose and use of the system, identifying possible hazards, and estimating the risk of these hazards.

Risk evaluation is about risk acceptability, that is, deciding the level of risk that is acceptable for the system.

Risk analysis and risk evaluation jointly form the part of risk management known as *risk assessment*. Many risk assessment methods exist for a variety of purposes. This chapter reviews some of the more prominent methods that may be suitable for assessing risk in interactive systems.

Risk control is about analyzing options to reduce risk, such as changing the way a function is carried out, eliminating a function, increasing system redundancy, and so on. Then, it is necessary to implement suitable changes and carry out a residual risk evaluation to determine the level of risk left in the system. Finally, it is important to decide the overall level of risk designers are willing to accept for the system.

Risk monitoring is about continuously assessing the implemented system and its level of risk, taking appropriate actions as necessary. This step may also include reviews of outcomes, the experience of stakeholders, and reflections on the risk management process as a whole.

To assist risk assessment, it is often helpful to perform *system mapping*. As its name suggests, system mapping is about creating maps of the system to understand its architecture, organization, the role of people and functions, and the flows of various signals and materials, such as paper forms in a hospital and emails in an office.

One very important aspect of risk assessment is defining the system boundary. This boundary helps everybody involved to understand the scope of risk assessment. To set a boundary, it is usually necessary to first describe a broader system that encompasses the system being studied. Then, based on an understanding of this extended system, the boundary can be set. Anything outside the boundary will not be considered in risk assessment; anything inside the boundary *will* be considered. It is therefore very important to set the system boundary in such a way that factors that are likely to affect risk are captured. Failing to do so means there are unassessed risks in the system, which can be very dangerous and give rise to catastrophic failures when the system is deployed.

System mapping is frequently carried out using various diagrammatic methods, such as task diagrams, system diagrams, or communication diagrams. We discuss various system mapping techniques in the chapter on systems (Chapter 35).

37.2.1 Risk assessment

Having identified the purpose of the system and its intended use, set the system boundary, and mapped out the system, we can now carry out risk assessment.

Many risk assessment methods have been developed for various applications, including medical devices, chemical process systems, aerospace systems, and healthcare solutions. At a high level, they can be considered along two variables. First, how in-depth they are, which affects the resources required to use them. Second, where they put their focus on. Common areas include (1) identifying risks, (2) communicating risks, and (3) assessing risks.

Structured what-if technique

The structured what-if technique (SWIFT) is a team-based risk assessment method that prompts the team with *what-if* questions to stimulate thinking and identify risks and hazards in a system. SWIFT allows the design team to explore different scenarios and contexts and their causes, consequences, and impacts. Based on such discussions, it is possible to arrive at hazards and assess risks and ultimately risk controls.

SWIFT is based on a vocabulary that provides the basis for prompts. The words in the vocabulary are used by a facilitator to discuss possible scenarios, issues, operating environment conditions, and other factors that may give rise to hazards and risks. The words used as prompts typically focus on deviations, such as "failure to detect," "wrong message," "wrong time," "wrong delay," and so on.

In practice, a SWIFT analysis is carried out by filling out a table where each row has a set of columns. The precise set of columns can differ depending on the application of SWIFT. Here is one example.

Identifier: An identifier for the particular issue discussed.

What-if questions: Questions triggering an assessment, such as "how much," "how many," and so on.

Hazards and risks: Any hazards and associated risks that may occur.

Relevant controls: The controls that are in place or need to be in place to mitigate the risk.

Risk ranking: The ranking of this risk relative to other risks identified in the exercise.

Action notes: Next steps to be taken.

SWIFT can be fast and efficient with an experienced team and a good facilitator. It focuses on solutions, not just the consequences of failure. At the same time, SWIFT is highly dependent on the experience of the team and the facilitator since the results entirely depend on the knowledge of the team. SWIFT produces mostly qualitative results, and the results are difficult to audit since there is no formal benchmark for evaluating them.

Compared to a method such as failure mode and effects analysis (FMEA), which we describe next, SWIFT is a relatively lightweight method.

Failure mode and effects analysis

Similar to SWIFT, FMEA is a team-based risk assessment technique. It can be used to analyze human error at the individual and team levels. In general, FMEA analyzes component failures in the system. We will see how to model the failure of components mathematically later in this chapter where we discuss reliability.

FMEA considers each component's *failure modes* and assesses possible causes for failures, their likelihood and severity, the recovery steps available, and actions for eliminating or mitigating the consequences of the failure mode.

There are multiple ways of carrying out FMEA. Here, we provide an example of the columns that an FMEA may include.

Identifier: An identifier for the particular issue.

Component: The component assessed.

Failure mode: The specific failure mode of the component.

Causes: The possible causes of the failure mode.

Probability: The likelihood of the failure mode. This is an estimate. It may be an actual probability if the failure rate for the component is available. Otherwise, it may be a rating, for example, between 1 (extremely unlikely) and 5 (almost inevitable).

Severity: The impact of the failure mode.

Risk: The risk of the failure mode, in other words, the product of its likelihood and impact.

Recovery: Steps to mitigate the failure mode, which may include requirements for recovery and mitigation.

Action notes: Next steps to be taken, for instance, further investigation or changes to components.

An FMEA may include quantitative estimates of probability if, for example, actual failure rates of components are available. The outcome of an FMEA is a list of actions or required changes in design to mitigate risks.

Fault tree

A fault tree is a diagrammatic method for identifying and analyzing factors that contribute to a fault—unintended behavior. Fault trees are, as their name indicates, tree diagrams that link factors to a fault using logical relationships such as *and* and *or*.

A fault tree is created by starting with the fault as the top-level event and then progressively analyzing the factors that may contribute to the fault. Figure 37.2 is a schematic illustration of a fault tree.

Fault trees can be used to analyze the causes of human error. They highlight interrelationships between components, which may be system components or users.

Risk matrix

A risk matrix (Figure 37.3) is a simple visualization technique for communicating risk. A risk matrix has two axes: impact and likelihood. Risks are indicated in the matrix accordingly.

A risk matrix makes it easy for a team to visualize important risks. In general, risks in the top-right corner are more severe, having both a high impact and a high likelihood. Risk matrices are typically used in conjunction with other risk assessment methods to assist with ranking and prioritizing risks.

37.3 Reliability

Reliability is the quality of a system to *not fail*. An unreliable system gives rise to a high risk of failures, some of which can have catastrophic consequences.

Reliability engineering is a discipline that assesses the reliability of components and systems. A component, subsystem, or system can refer to a machine, an algorithm, a user interface element,

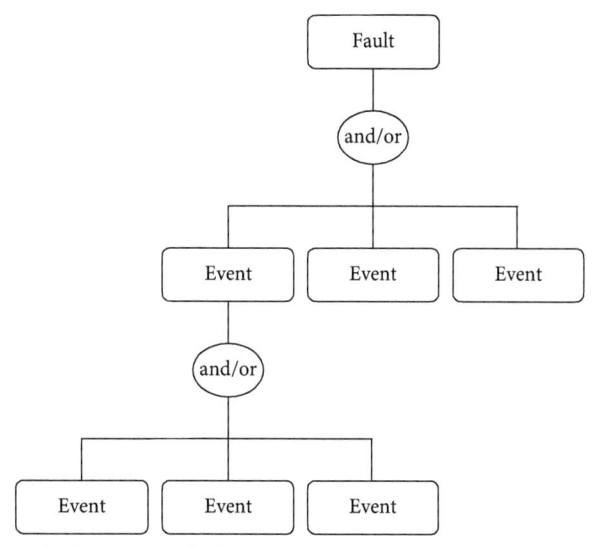

Figure 37.2 A schematic illustration of a fault tree. The fault is decomposed into a series of events that may lead up to the fault. The events are connected by logical relationships such as *and* and *or*.

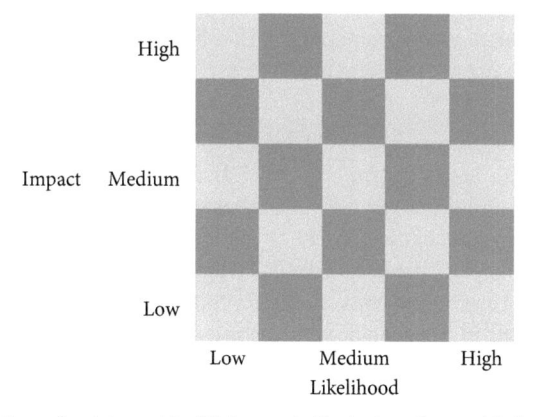

Figure 37.3 An illustration of a risk matrix. Risks are indicated on the matrix in terms of their impact and likelihood. Progress in risk management can be visualized by observing risks move from the top-right corner to the bottom-left corner.

a physical control, a user, and so on. Any component is bound to fail eventually; therefore, it is important to estimate the probability of a component or system failure as a function of time. This is a statistical problem that, at its core, requires estimating the *reliability function* that models the probability of experiencing no failure as a function of time.

37.3.1 Series and parallel systems

To understand the reliability of any system, including an interactive system, we need to understand the topology of the system. That is, how the components in the system depend on each other to carry out the overall function.

Figure 37.4 A series system with *n* components. All components need to function for the system to be able to carry out its overall function.

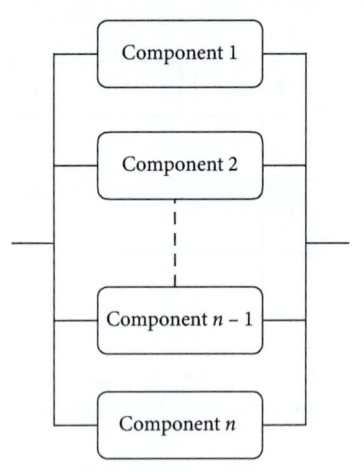

Figure 37.5 A parallel system with *n* components. One functioning component is enough for the system to be able to carry out its overall function.

The simplest system is a series system (Figure 37.4). For a series system to work, *all* components need to work. The traditional example of a series system is a decorative lights system wired in series. If a single light bulb burns out, current can no longer flow through the wire as the burned-out light bulb becomes an open circuit. As a result, all light bulbs in the light system stop working. In HCI, many systems are series systems, as system functions are frequently achieved by components carrying out tasks in a sequence, with each step relying on the correct execution of the previous step. An example of a series system in HCI is a wizard dialog that guides the user through a series of steps to assist the user in achieving their goal, such as installing an application. If such a wizard dialog is purely sequential and any step fails, the user will be unable to achieve their goal. To avoid such an outcome, the wizard must allow for some form of redundancy, such as providing an alternative means of progressing if any step in the sequence fails.

The opposite of a series system is a parallel system (Figure 37.5), which works as long as one component is working. Consider a graphical indicator that monitors some system function, such as a printer having sufficient paper loaded. If the indicator relies on a single sensor and this sensor fails, the system will fail to warn the user if the printer has insufficient paper loaded to print. If the printer uses two sensors, the system exhibits parallel redundancy—both sensors must fail for the system to fail. This example also hints at why parallel systems are not as common as they perhaps should be: Installing two sensors increases the complexity and the manufacturing cost of the printer. In HCI, a simple example of a parallel system is the way a user can delete a file on the desktop. The user may drag the file to the trash can or right-click the file and select Delete. If the user does not know how to carry out one method, the other method typically suffices for this simple human–computer system to carry out its function of deleting a file. Again, the cost of parallel redundancy is that the system must support multiple means of achieving the same goal.

Next, let us consider series and parallel systems mathematically. Consider a series system with n components C_i. Assume each component C_i has a certain probability of failure P_i and a corresponding *reliability* $R_i = 1 - P_i$.

A *series* topology means that *all* components must work satisfactorily for the system to work correctly. The reliability R_{series} of a series topology is therefore n independent events of non-failure:

$$R_{\text{series}} = R_1 R_2, \ldots, R_{n-1}, R_n. \tag{37.2}$$

A *parallel* topology means that *all* components must fail for the system to fail. The probability of all n components failing is the product of the individual failure probabilities P_i: $P_1 P_2, \ldots, P_{n-1}, P_n = (1 - R_1)(1 - R_2), \ldots, (1 - R_{n-1}), (1 - R_n)$. Therefore, the reliability R_{parallel} of a parallel topology is

$$R_{\text{parallel}} = 1 - (1 - R_1)(1 - R_2), \ldots, (1 - R_{n-1}), (1 - R_n). \tag{37.3}$$

Using the expressions for R_{series} and R_{parallel}, we can compare these two topologies for a simple case. Consider a rudimentary system with two components C_1 and C_2 with corresponding probabilities of failure $P_1 = P_2 = 0.1$. That is, each component has a 10% probability of failure in some chosen time interval. In a series topology, the reliability is $R_{\text{series}} = R_1 R_2 = (1 - P_1)(1 - P_2) = 0.9 \cdot 0.9 = 0.81$. In a parallel topology, the reliability is $R_{\text{parallel}} = 1 - (1 - R_1)(1 - R_2) = 1 - P_1 P_2 = 1 - 0.1 \cdot 0.1 = 0.99$. In other words, within the time interval, the probability is 99% that the system will succeed in carrying out its overall function if the components are in parallel. If the components are in series, the probability of success within the time period is reduced to 81%. This difference between the two systems increases if we increase the number of components. Assuming each component still has a $P_i = 0.1$ probability of failure, a series system with five components has a reliability of 59.049%, while a parallel system has a reliability of 99.999%.

It is also possible to create systems in-between all-series and all-parallel systems. For example, a *k-out-of-n* system is a system where n components will function if at least k components function. For example, a two-out-of-three system for a sensor array may take sensor readings from three different sensors. If two out of three sensors agree, then the system uses the sensor readings from the two sensors that agree and possibly triggers an alert that one sensor might be faulty. A series system is the special case where $k = n$, and a parallel system is the special case where $k = 1$. Figure 37.6 shows an example of a system where $k = 2$ and $n = 3$.

Paper Example 37.3.1: The Boeing 737 MAX disaster

The Boeing 737 MAX is an aircraft model that experienced catastrophic failures. An analysis of the failings of this model [827] explains both why it is dangerous to fully automate a function while leaving the user completely out of the loop and why parallel redundancy, in the form of a user working alongside a machine, can be of utmost importance in safety-critical systems.

Boeing management wanted to increase the number of passenger seats, which meant increasing the size of the engines. To avoid the engines touching the ground, their shape needed to be changed as well. This led to a change in the engine's centerline toward the plane's nose, which

continued

Paper Example 37.3.1: The Boeing 737 MAX disaster *(continued)*

then led to the plane pitching up and raising its nose under thrust. In turn, this led to the possibility of the plane stalling in circumstances in which the previous Boeing 737 model would not stall.

Instead of rethinking the engine design, which is expensive, Boeing engineers added a software-side solution, which is inexpensive. This ensured that the 737 MAX could be branded and sold as "just another 737" with just one added feature. This entailed significant savings, as pilots required minimal retraining.

The software solution involved a system called the Maneuvering Characteristics Augmentation System (MCAS), which "pushes the nose of the plane down when the system thinks the plane might exceed its angle-of-attack limits; it does so to avoid an aerodynamic stall." The pilot controls (pushes or pulls) something called control columns, essentially a joystick, to raise or lower the aircraft's nose. When the MCAS believes a stall is occurring, it autonomously instructs the aircraft to push the pilot's control columns forward, and the pilot will not be able to regain control by pulling back. This was an explicit design decision. This decision was taken despite the fact that

> "a human pilot could just look out the windshield to confirm visually and directly that, no, the aircraft is not pitched up dangerously. That's the ultimate check and should go directly to the pilot's ultimate sovereignty. Unfortunately, the current implementation of MCAS denies that sovereignty. It denies the pilots the ability to respond to what's before their own eyes."

If a sensor reading was incorrect, the MCAS would still take over, and the results would be catastrophic since the pilot was left with no means to recover. There was no parallel redundancy in the form of a pilot being able to override the MCAS.

Automated systems that are designed to increase safety can easily backfire. Failures are bound to happen in any complex system; as such, failures should be considered normal, and there should be systems and procedures in place to allow for recovery.

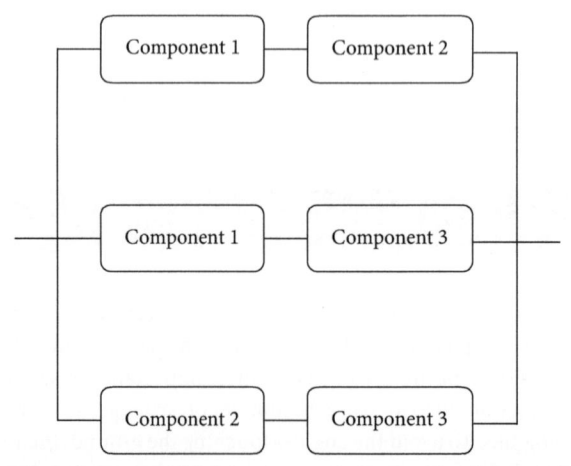

Figure 37.6 An illustration of a two-out-of-three system. Note that the diagram describes the function but not the implementation of such a system.

37.3.2 Reliability and failure rate

By tracking failures, it is possible to construct a histogram of failures as a function of the lifetime of a component or system. We can fit a probability density function $f(t)$ to this histogram. Next, we introduce a random variable T denoting the waiting time until failure.

We can find the cumulative distribution function $F(t)$ by integrating $f(t)$. $F(t) = \Pr\{T < t\}$ models the probability of failure at time t.

We can now find the *reliability function* $R(t) = 1 - F(t)$. $R(t) = \Pr\{T \geq t\}$ models the probability of non-failure at time t.

In general, *reliability* is defined as $1 - p$, where p is the probability of failure. Reliability is the probability that a product, system, or service will carry out its intended function without failure at time t. The *reliability function* $R(t)$ models the probability of no failure occurring before time t.

The failure rate is the frequency of failure of a product, system, or service in terms of failures per time unit. It is often denoted as λ. Failure rates are often modeled as constant. This makes sense because of a phenomenon known as the bathtub curve (Figure 37.7). Many systems experience an initial phase with early failures. This may be due to hardware manufacturing errors, installation problems, and inexperienced users, among other reasons. Toward the end of the lifespan of the system, late failures start to increase as the system ages and experiences fatigue, critical software components become obsolete, new working practices mean that users use old systems incorrectly, and so on. Throughout its lifespan, the system experiences random failures due to slips, arbitrary component failures, users dropping the device, and so on. The net effect of these failure rates is an observed failure rate that resembles a bathtub. Many different systems, particularly electronic devices, tend to follow this bathtub curve. It is important to note that the bathtub curve does not model an individual system's observed failure rate. Rather, it models the observed failure rate of a population of systems.

Assuming the failure rate is constant, then a useful and very common metric is the mean time between failures (MTBF), which is defined as $1/\lambda$. This provides a consistent metric for specifying the expected mean time duration between random failures during the majority of the lifespan of the product, after the initial phase of early failures and before the final phase of late failures.

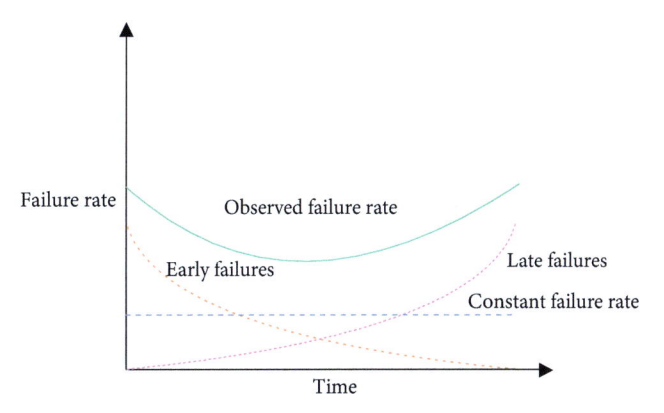

Figure 37.7 An illustration of the phenomenon known as the bathtub curve. Many systems experience an initial phase of early failures and a final phase of late failures. During the lifespan of the system, random failures give rise to a constant failure rate. The observed failure rate resulting from these three failure rates resembles a bathtub.

37.3.3 Hazard function

The hazard function $h(t)$, sometimes written as $\lambda(t)$ and called the failure rate function, is the failure rate of a component in the next instant *given* that the component has not failed up to time t. It is a conditional probability density function:

$$h(t) = \frac{\Pr\{t \leq T < t + dt | T \geq t\}}{dt}$$

$$\Rightarrow h(t)dt = f(t)dt/R(t) \qquad (37.4)$$

$$\Rightarrow h(t) = f(t)/R(t).$$

It is a hazard function because of two reasons. First, $f(t)dt$ is the joint probability of T in the interval $t \leq T < t + dt$ and at the same time $T \geq t$, which is the same as being in the interval. Second, $R(t)$ is the marginal probability that $T \geq t$.

A particularly interesting and important case arises when the time t until a failure is exponentially distributed. The probability density function of failure is then of an exponential distribution:

$$f(t) = \lambda e^{-\lambda t}. \qquad (37.5)$$

The cumulative distribution function of an exponential distribution is $F(t) = 1 - e^{-\lambda t}$. The reliability function is then

$$R(t) = 1 - F(t) = 1 - (1 - e^{-\lambda t}) = e^{-\lambda t}. \qquad (37.6)$$

Hence, the hazard function is

$$h(t) = \frac{f(t)}{R(t)} = \frac{\lambda e^{-\lambda t}}{e^{-\lambda t}} = \lambda. \qquad (37.7)$$

In other words, the hazard function is constant, and the rate parameter λ of the exponential probability distribution completely determines the hazard function. This follows from the *memoryless* property of the exponential distribution: The remaining time until failure, given no failure at time t, does not depend on t. This models a constant failure rate in the bathtub curve.

The constant failure rate is commonly used in practice, as it often suffices to model random failures due to accidents, mistakes, sudden component failures such as a loose wire due to a user dropping a device, or other unforeseen events. For example, the probability that a bicycle tire will experience a puncture due to hitting a nail on the road can be modeled using a constant failure rate. For this reason, many systems are analyzed under the assumption of a constant hazard function. This simplifies calculations; however, it is important to understand that complex systems have interdependencies that may give rise to hazard functions that are not constant.

37.4 Security

Another important aspect related to safety and risk is *security*. Security is about ensuring systems are resilient to harm from people. As such, security is closely related to risk management, as it can be viewed as an aspect of risk. Examples of physical security include fences, security guards, cameras, and so on. Examples of security involving computer systems are antivirus, cryptography, password systems, spam filters, anti-phishing mechanisms built into web browsers, as well as physical security, such as restricted access to machines.

Usable security is a discipline at the intersection of HCI and security that focuses on ensuring computer security is usable by end-users. After all, a security system can only be as strong as its users. If users do not understand how to use security mechanisms, such as passwords or encryption, then there is effectively no security at all.

Whitten and Tygar [887] provided a definition of usable security.

Security software is usable if the people who are expected to use it:

1. are reliably made aware of the security tasks they need to perform;
2. are able to figure out how to successfully perform those tasks;
3. don't make dangerous errors; and
4. are sufficiently comfortable with the interface to continue using it.

Paper Example 37.4.1: Why Alice and Bob cannot encrypt

The availability of security technology does not guarantee that security is established. For this to happen, users have to be able to achieve their goal of security, which is only possible if the interfaces that they interact with are usable. In the classic 1999 paper "Why Johnny Can't Encrypt: A Usability Evaluation of PGP 5.0," Whitten and Tygar [887] explored the reasons why end-users are unable to use the graphical user interface of the encryption program Pretty Good Privacy (PGP) 5.0. PGP enables users to encrypt and decrypt text as a means of secure communication, for instance, by email.

The paper identifies five intrinsic properties of security that give rise to usability problems:

Unmotivated users: Users are usually not interested in security because their goal in using a system is something else, such as sending an email or browsing the web.

Abstraction: Security is implemented by enforcing security policies that consist of abstract rules that end-users may find difficult to understand.

Lack of feedback: It is difficult for security software to provide meaningful feedback to the user since (1) security configurations are complex and (2) checking whether a security configuration is accurate is only possible if users know what they want.

Irreversibility: When security fails, it is typically not possible to take corrective action and return to the previous protected state. For example, if a secret is unprotected, then there is no way to know whether that secret is now in the hands of individuals external to the organization.

Weakest link: A security system is only as strong as its weakest link. This means users cannot explore a security system using trial and error but instead must be carefully guided to ensure security is maintained at every step.

The paper examines the usability of PGP through a cognitive walkthrough and a usability study. These methods are discussed in detail in the chapters on analytical evaluation methods (Chapter 41) and experiments (Chapter 43).

continued

> **Paper Example 37.4.1: Why Alice and Bob cannot encrypt** *(continued)*
>
> The cognitive walkthrough revealed that PGP failed to satisfy many of the properties in a usability standard for PGP established in the paper. Examples of problems were the use of visual metaphors and the handling of irreversible actions.
>
> The user study asked 12 educated participants experienced with email to use PGP to send secure email; only one-third of the participants correctly signed and encrypted an email. Moreover, a quarter of the participants exposed the secret key by inadvertently sending it in an unprotected email they believed had been correctly encrypted.
>
> The paper concludes that while PGP uses a graphical user interface that is thoughtful in its design, it is ultimately only usable by people who understand public key cryptography and digital signatures. In other words, following basic user interface design principles is insufficient to ensure usable security.

A central concept in security is that of a *threat model*. Threat models are systematic analyses of the mechanisms of a security threat. A threat model answers a series of questions, such as: What kinds of agents might be interested in attacking the system? What is the flow of data in the system? Which parts of the flow could an agent attack and how? What is the likelihood of such an attack succeeding? What would be the impact of such an attack? How could the system be safeguarded against the attack? Human factors related to security (e.g., phishing) can be analyzed using threat models.

37.5 Are there risk-free systems?

When discussing safety and risk, it may be natural for designers and stakeholders to envision a system that is completely safe, posing no risk of any adverse consequence to any user or other person directly or indirectly affected by it. However, such a stance is incorrect and not helpful. Any meaningful system will entail a level of risk. This is the reason why designers must determine the level of acceptable risk in a system. Accidents and threats are inevitable in a system—they are normal [648]. Therefore, it is better to design proactively to prevent them rather than address them after the fact.

Summary

- Protecting people from harm and ensuring interactive systems are safe to use are central principles and core values in HCI.
- It is not possible to eliminate all risks in a system. Instead, designers must aim to design a system with an acceptable level of risk.
- Human error is typically just one of many factors involved in an accident.
- Risk management is a continuous activity that does not only involve assessing risks but also monitoring and controlling risks throughout the lifespan of a system.
- Reliability is a statistical property of a system. It depends on the system's topology and the probability of failure of individual components.

- Security is about ensuring that systems are resilient to harm from people. For security measures to be effective, they need to be usable.

Exercises

1. Methods. Determine the system boundary for the following cases: (a) an autocorrect algorithm for a touchscreen keyboard; (b) a 3D printer; (c) an app that allows children to share videos online with their friends; and (d) a smartwatch app that allows app users to wirelessly transfer small amounts of money between them by holding two smartwatches close together. Which risk assessment methods would be useful for which case? Motivate your answer.

2. Human error. You have been asked to design a numeric keypad for a machine that delivers medicine to a patient. The numeric keypad allows nurses to input the exact doses of medicine to be administered. The keypad must provide the following 13 keys: 0-9, `Set Dose`, `Administer Dose`, and `Reset`. To provide a dose to a patient, the nurse is meant to first input `Set Dose` and then use the number keys 0-9 to input a number in the range [1, 999]. The nurse can then administer the dose by inputting `Administer Dose`. If the nurse makes an input mistake, the nurse can reset the process by inputting `Reset`, which allows the nurse to start over by first inputting `Set Dose` again.
   (a) Identify the overall function of the system and the system boundary. Briefly explain the choice of system boundary.
   (b) Identify three sources of human error permitted by the system. What types of human errors are they?
   (c) Briefly discuss how the system can be augmented to mitigate these sources of human error.

3. Fault trees. A user is typing on a mobile phone using a touchscreen keyboard with autocorrect and word prediction. Draw a fault tree for the event in which the user types a different set of characters for a word than the intended set.

4. Failures. Consider a system with three components where each component has a constant failure rate. The probability P_i of a failure of an individual component i is independent of the other components, and $P_1 = P_2 = P_3$. The MTBF for an individual component is 100,000 hours. Calculate the probability of the system failing within a five-year period when (a) all three components are wired in series and (b) all three components are wired in parallel. You should find that the parallel system has substantially higher reliability. Given this, why is not every interactive system, or any system in general, a parallel system?

5. An interactive hardware prototype has a subsystem that consists of n identical components configured for parallel redundancy.
   (a) Give a definition of the hazard function and explain why it is a conditional failure rate.
   (b) Assume each component is governed by the hazard function $h(t) = \lambda$, where λ is the failure rate. Derive an expression for the probability of a system failure at time t.
   (c) Show that the hazard function $h(t)$ can be expressed as $h(t) = -\frac{d}{dt} \ln R(t)$, where $R(t)$ is the reliability function.
   (d) Assume n components of the system are changed to a different set of n identical components where each component has an identical hazard function that varies linearly with time with an intercept of zero. Derive an expression for the probability of a system failure at time t.

6 Case study. Consider a wearable ring device prototype that can be interacted with using a small analog pointing stick.
   (a) Testing reveals that the probability density that the pointing stick fails to function at time t during its useful lifespan is

   $$f(t) = (a + bt)\exp\left(-at - \frac{b}{2}t^2\right), \tag{37.8}$$

   where a and b are parameters. Derive the hazard function of this distribution.
   (b) Does the hazard function found in (a) seem reasonable? Explain your reasoning, including any assumptions of parameter values.
   (c) Further testing reveals that a subset of pointing sticks exhibit a uniform probability density of failure at time t during their useful lifespans. Derive the hazard function for this distribution.
   (d) Briefly discuss the reliability implications of the hazard function in (b) compared to the hazard function in (c), including any assumptions of parameter values.
   (e) A user wears the ring device and interacts with it using the pointing stick. Derive an expression for the probability of failure of the pointing stick at time t due to the user dropping the ring on a hard surface. Explain your reasoning.

7. The book *Normal Accidents: Living With High-Risk Technologies* by Perrow [648] reports on a series of sociological analyses of accidents in tightly coupled systems with high complexity. The central thesis in the book is that accidents are normal in the sense that they are inevitable in highly coupled complex systems. This does not mean that normal accidents are frequent: Just as a human is expected to die at some point, a normal accident is considered a normal, albeit infrequent, event.
   (a) Explain why a tightly coupled complex system cannot be risk-free.
   (b) Two operators are tasked with monitoring a nuclear power plant. One operator is incapacitated due to tripping over a raised threshold and burning themselves with hot coffee in the process. The second operator is busy calling for medical assistance. At this time, the automated system has detected a deviating sensor reading indicating a reactor fault. This sensor reading is due to a faulty sensor and not due to any reactor fault. Nonetheless, since the two operators are either incapacitated or busy, they do not take the actions dictated by the protocol for this particular sensor reading. As a result, the automated system issues an alert. As a fail-safe measure, if the alert is not attended to by either of the two operators, it is propagated to a third operator in a different location who cannot assess whether the sensor reading is accurate. As a consequence, the third operator takes action according to the protocol, resulting in a nuclear meltdown. State all hazards in this description and draw a fault tree that explains the sources leading to the catastrophic outcome.

8. The following two subtasks continue from the previous exercise. Solving them requires familiarity with Chapter 20:
   (a) Consider the user interface design of a nuclear power plant. To avoid accidents, the user interface will incorporate redundancy in the form of an automated system that checks that the operators have followed the correct protocol and taken the correct actions given the sensor readings indicated through the user interface. If the automated system detects that

the protocol has not been followed, the automated system seizes control and proceeds to follow the protocol. What is the type and level of automation in this system?

(b) It is discovered that a sensor fault can lead to the automated system incorrectly seizing control and applying an incorrect protocol. The system is subsequently modified to merely alert operators of an incorrect action and suggest corrective steps to ensure the appropriate protocol is followed. Suggest three principles from mixed-initiative interfaces that are particularly important for this task and explain how they apply to this particular design problem.

38
Software

Interactive systems rely on *software*. Software is what enables a design to be translated into an implementation. To ensure we implement software that fulfills the requirements set for it, we need to apply *software engineering* principles.

Implementing software that is both correct and enables all desired interactions is challenging due to the many concerns involved (e.g., handling events), the need to interface with external entities (e.g., network connections), and the requirement to maintain responsiveness and robust functioning during interaction. The book *The Mythical Man-Month* [98] famously pointed out that managing software development is inherently difficult and that, counterintuitively, adding more developers to a project can delay it rather than speed it up.

Software engineering is about working with systems from a few critical viewpoints. As we have seen in the chapter on systems (Chapter 35), systems frequently consist of subsystems, and one way to manage system complexity is by *abstraction*. This is the fundamental approach taken in user interface software. The developer works at different high-abstraction levels instead of writing low-level interface code to read and work with digitized analog signals and low-level code that specifies the pixel contents and locations on a graphical display. This is achieved through *software design* and *software architecture*, which allow developers to benefit from established programming paradigms (e.g., event-driven programming) and design patterns (e.g., model-view-controller (MVC)). Furthermore, common functionality for realizing user interface software is provided through *software libraries* and *toolkits* that enable developers to directly create sophisticated user interface elements (e.g., scrollpanes) and provide support for advanced actions such as gesture recognition.

Human–computer interaction (HCI) research has tackled many of these aspects, for example:

- The *Amulet Environment* [573] is an early example of a user interface developer environment supporting cross-platform deployment across multiple operating systems. Amulet is a toolkit that provides support for building sophisticated user interfaces through constructs such as graphical objects, interactors, command objects, constraints, gesture recognition, and animation. This allows a developer to build, for example, a graphical interactive circuit designer tool in fewer lines of code compared to using standard software libraries.
- *KidSim* [781] is an end-user programming environment that allows children to create computer programs. It presents children with a graphical environment where they can provide rules controlling the behavior of software agents, which are represented graphically in the environment.
- The ability to allow users to *undo* their prior actions in a user interface is important to encourage exploration and bestow users with control. Abowd and Dix [4] systematically investigated the nature of undo and how to implement it using a combination of formal methods and an analysis of how users understand undo. One result is the principle of intent: Undo is the user's intention, rather than just a system function.

38.1 Software design and architecture

User interfaces need to be programmed. However, programming one from the ground up is difficult. There are many factors that must be taken into account. For example, managing user interface components such as buttons, scrollbars, pull-down menus, and so on means the programmer has to be able to both draw these elements correctly on the screen and detect and react to user input. This programming challenge is further exacerbated by the need to support many different possible designs, which may also rapidly change in light of additional user insight or design ideas.

To assist programmers in creating compelling user interfaces, several ideas, principles, design patterns, and tools have gradually emerged as user interfaces have become increasingly sophisticated over time. Here, we provide a high-level exposition of some of the key ideas in the area of user interface software that have achieved wide adoption.

Software design is a broad term that captures the entire software development process, including all relevant concerns related to the software, such as the levels of modularization and abstraction. The structure of the software, referred to as *software architecture*, is a component of software design. HCI-based user interfaces rely on established software design practices and architectures for their operation.

A user interface reacts and responds to user input. As technology has evolved, such user interfaces have evolved from simple command-line interfaces into sophisticated graphical user interfaces (GUIs) with various graphical elements users can interact with: windows, panels, pull-down menus, buttons, tables, plots, and other user interface components.

A modern GUI consists of certain expected elements: windows, panels, pull-down menus, buttons, and other user interface controls. A GUI relies on rules implemented in software to manage its elements in such a way that the GUI behaves as expected. A GUI toolkit is a set of software routines that allows a software developer to easily construct and manage a GUI.

A key concept related to GUIs is *representation*: how user interface elements are represented as a model accessible to the programmer. The typical method is to represent a user interface component as an *object*. In object-oriented programming, an object maintains its state and behavior. The state of an object represents the data it holds, and the behavior of an object is represented by code. For example, a button can have data indicating its size and location on the screen, its outline color, fill color, text color, text font, text size, and the text itself. The code associated with a button can consist of code detecting when the button is pressed, code changing the appearance of the button when it is pressed, and code notifying the rest of the program that a user has pushed the button.

38.1.1 Layout

The *layout* is a set of rules that determine where user interface components are displayed in relation to each other. The simplest set of layout rules is to have none, in which case the programmer has to specify the exact pixel coordinates of each user interface component. For example, if a user interface designer wants a button to be placed at the top-left corner of a panel, the programmer would set the button to be displayed with its top-left corner in the origin of the coordinate system, that is, (0, 0) (Figure 38.1).

Such *absolute* positioning makes it possible to specify the precise location and size of each user interface component. This allows a programmer to implement a highly specific layout that can be very close to an intended design. However, this expressiveness comes at a cost. When the panel is

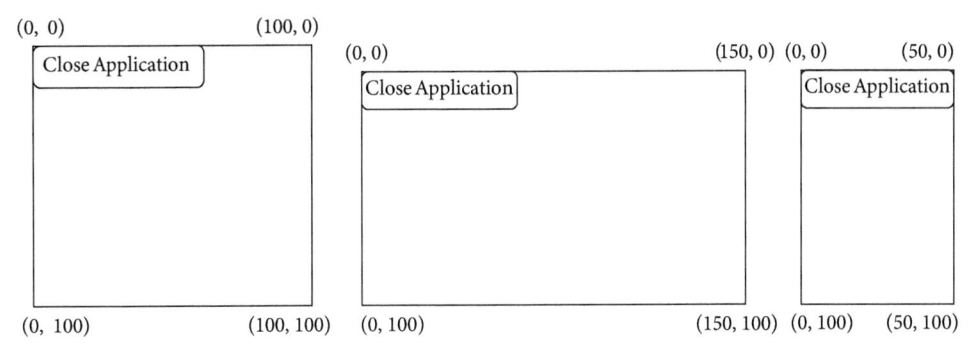

Figure 38.1 An example of using no layout and instead setting the pixel coordinates of each user interface component, in this case a `Close Application` button with its top-left corner at (0,0), relative to the panel containing the button. When the panel is resized, the button maintains its fixed location and size.

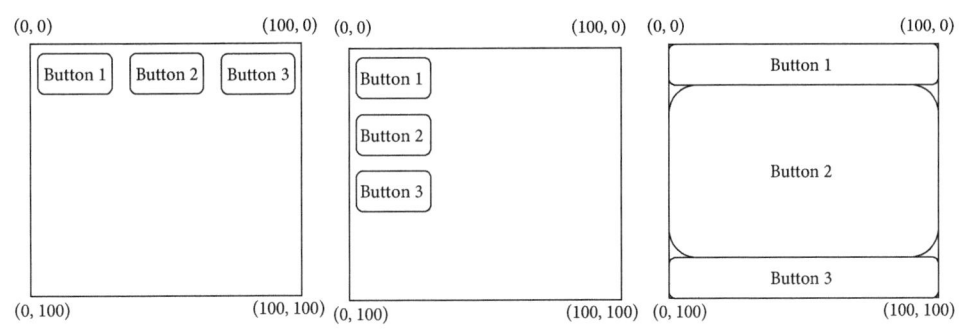

Figure 38.2 Three buttons laid out in three separate ways depending on their layout. The leftmost figure shows three buttons laid out using a horizontal layout rule. The spacing between the buttons is a fixed distance configured by the programmer. The width and height of each button are parameters unique to each button and set by the programmer. In the figure, the width and height of each button have been set to identical values. The layout rule respects these width and height parameters and renders each button according to its parameters. The middle figure shows the same layout rule applied vertically instead of horizontally. The rightmost figure shows a layout using compass rules. This layout splits the parent component into five regions: north, south, west, east, and center.

resized, for example, because the user has resized the application window, the absolute positioning of all user interface components remains fixed, preventing them from adjusting their positions according to the new size. Figure 38.1 shows how the location and size of the button are unchanged despite the panel changing size. As a result, the button can get clipped, or the panel can contain an excessive amount of unused space.

To solve such problems, various layout rules have been introduced. One layout policy is to split the panel into five sections: north, south, west, east, and center. This layout is known as the "border layout" in the Java Swing GUI library. Figure 38.2 shows different variants building on this approach.

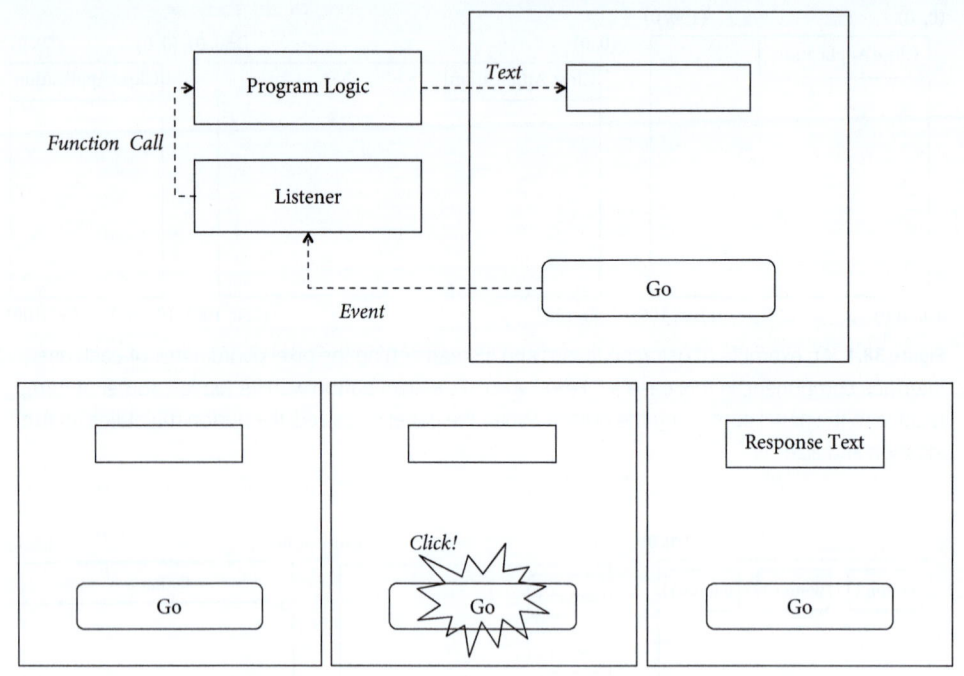

Figure 38.3 An example of event-driven programming. The button `Go` is monitored by a `Listener`. When the user triggers the button, this event is captured by the `Listener`, which makes a function call to code represented by `Program Logic`. In this example, the text "Response" is displayed inside the initially empty label.

38.1.2 Event handling

Most of the time, a user interface is doing nothing more than waiting for the user to interact with it. This has led to the concept of *event-driven programming*. In event-driven programming, the program flow is driven by events. The overall program logic takes no action until an event triggers an action. Examples of such events include the user triggering a user interface control by pushing a button and a timer being triggered after a preset period. Figure 38.3 presents an example of a *Listener* listening to a button and its programmed response logic.

38.1.3 Model-view-controller and other design patterns

Software *design patterns* are reusable strategies or solutions to common programming problems. Several design patterns have been conceived in response to difficulties in writing scalable and correct code for managing complex user interfaces. The most well-known design pattern, which we use here to illustrate this concept, is probably MVC.

MVC addresses the problem of decoupling three functional concerns of a typical GUI [433]. The first concern is the *model* representing the data the user is manipulating. The data may be text, a list of numbers or other objects, or a time series, such as $(0, 2), (1, 4), (2, 6), (2, 8)$. The second concern is the *view*, that is, what is presented to the user. The third concern is the controller.

MVC consists of three fundamental components:

Model: The model contains the data.

View: The view presents the data to the user. Note that there can be more than one view of the same model.

Controller: The controller manages user interaction by accepting user input to manipulate the model and presenting model output to the user using one or several views.

38.2 Toolkits

Another design strategy is to use an existing codebase at a high level of abstraction that is designed specifically for user interface development. A *toolkit* is a software library that defines commonly used widgets like menus, buttons, scrollbars, and so on [569].

A toolkit can be called by an application. One advantage of using toolkits is consistency: All UIs developed using a toolkit will have a similar look and feel. Moreover, developers do not need to rewrite standard widgets. However, toolkits may not be easily extended. This can limit their usefulness in practice as applications may desire variations of functionality that cannot be easily supported. In such a case, the developer has to either modify the toolkit, create their own functionality, or change their specification so that it is compatible with the functionality the toolkit currently provides.

38.3 End-user development

Software agents have the potential to assist users in achieving their goals. However, individual users may have individual goals. How should a user instruct a software agent in order for it to be able to carry out the user's goal? This question gives rise to the *end-user programming problem* [781]: How can end-users, who are typically not programmers, tell a computer system what to do?

38.3.1 Macros

One approach is using *macros*. A macro is a collection of user actions that are grouped together into a program. A macro is recorded by the system following some form of trigger, such as a user action, that causes the system to monitor and store the user's actions in a list. This list of actions is then turned into a program. The user can now rerun this program when desired. A system may also allow the user to inspect the macro and make changes to individual user actions.

A macro allows a user to group a set of repetitive actions into a single action, potentially saving time and frustration in repeating mundane tasks. Macros are relatively easy for users to understand. The user merely has to trigger the system to record actions and then trigger the system to run the macro when desired.

However, macros also have disadvantages [177]. First, they only record low-level events, such as key presses, mouse clicks, or specific pointer locations. Second, macros do not *generalize*. A macro does not have a notion of semantics that matches user intent. For example, a macro may record the precise pixel location where a user clicks an icon and can thus trigger a subsequent action when the macro is run. However, if the icon is moved to another location on the display or into a folder, the macro will fail [177]. As another example, if a user selects the words following a prefix such as "Dear," such as selecting "Professor Oulasvirta" from "Dear Professor Oulasvirta" or "Professor Antti Oulasvirta" from "Dear Professor Antti Oulasvirta," the macro cannot select "Professor Kasper Hornbæk" from "Dear Professor Kasper Hornbæk" since it cannot generalize to select all the words after "Dear" [177].

These limitations of macros have led to the development of systems that can infer users' intended programs by *demonstration*, which is usually referred to as programming by example. It is worth noting that some interactive systems now provide system functions called macros that do not behave as "pure" macros and allow for some generalization.

38.3.2 **Programming by example**

The limitations of macros led to the idea of programming the computer by providing examples. This is generally known as *programming by example*. An early system is Pygmalion [779] from 1975, which allows a user to create sketches of programs using icons as representations of internal program mechanisms, such as variables, data structures, and program flows. The system does not infer a program; instead, it allows a programmer to sketch the program interactively and have the system remember the actions, thus gradually generating program code. When the system has incomplete information on the program, it halts execution and prompts the programmer for more information. An example of a partial program for computing a factorial is shown in Figure 38.4. It is difficult to succinctly explain how a programmer can use Pygmalion to sketch and execute a program. For a complete worked example of sketching the function of a factorial, we refer the reader to Smith's work [780].

A later example is *Tinker* [478], a learning environment that allows novice programmers to teach a software agent how to program. The novice programmer provides illustrative examples, and, in response, the system generates code that manages generalizations of the examples. The system relies on the user to provide additional information to do this. For example, if the user specifies more than one example for a function, the system asks the user to specify a test that it can use to distinguish the examples.

Unlike the prior examples of programming by demonstration, which were aimed at programmers, *Metamouse* [526] is a software agent called Basil that assists end-users with their tasks through direct manipulation. The system monitors user activity in a drawing program. The software agent observes the user's task, occasionally interrupts the user to ask for clarification, and eventually takes over the task. Figure 38.5 shows a complete example.

The Metamouse system induces a program by observing repetitive user behavior in a drawing program. An important design insight is that any software agent inducing a program for a repetitive task is going to be sensitive to user variation—a user doing the same thing in a variety of ways. The Metamouse system uses interactivity to reduce such variation by alternating between executing the induced program and building it. When the user rejects the next step in the program or no step is available in the program, the system interrupts the user to ask for the next operation. In this sense, the Metamouse behaves as an "eager apprentice" [526].

Eager [177] is a software agent that automatically monitors user actions in a GUI and checks for iterations. When an iteration is detected, the system suggests the next action to the user. When Eager has suggested a sufficient number of correctly predicted actions, the user can feel confident that Eager can automate the task; by pressing the Eager button, the system automates the task for the user. Figure 38.6 shows a complete example. Unlike Metamouse, Eager cannot infer conditionals. On the other hand, it relieves the user of several burdens. Eager does not require the user to (1) indicate the start of an example, (2) answer questions about the generalization of the induced program, and (3) approve or reject each proposed actions.

```
Menu
  icons
    create
    change
    delete
    copy
    refresh
    show
    name
    value
    shape
    body
  opcodes
    +
    -
    *
    /
    =
    <
    >
    and
    or
    not
  control
    ?
    call
    return
    repeat
    done
    eval
  others
    remember
    constant
    define
    display
    draw
    text
    break
    plot
    exit
```

[Diagram showing boxes: "6" with a droplet icon; "?" arrow to "true"; "?" arrow to "false"; two empty boxes joined by "="]

Mouse value: 'If'

remembered

small talk

Mouse

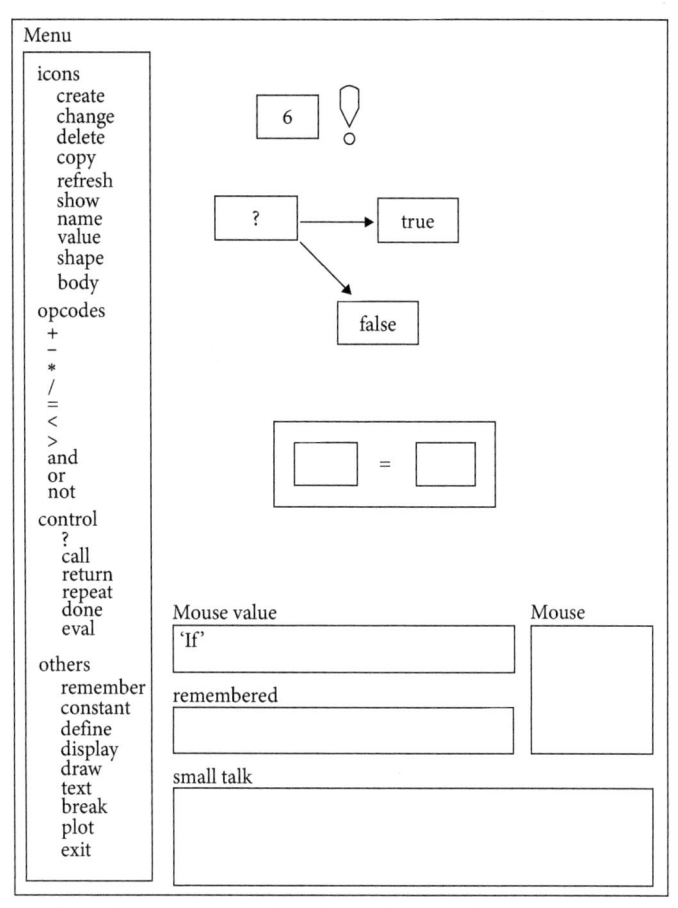

Figure 38.4 A snapshot of a programmer sketching a function for computing 6! in Pygmalion [779]. The boxes on the top-right represent icons, which represent aspects of the program. For example, the equality is represented as an icon containing two subicons. When the programmer drags a value, such as 6, to either subicon of this equality icon, the programmer is gradually completing the program. When both subicons have values assigned to them, the equality icon can evaluate the equality, giving rise to a True or False value. This value can in turn be dragged to the conditional icon—the icon with the question mark. Depending on the result of the conditional, either the icon marked *true* or the icon marked *false* will execute. Pygmalion attempts to execute code as soon as possible. However, whenever more information is required, the system halts execution and asks the programmer for additional information. In this way, Pygmalion allows the programmer to sketch out code that is then recorded by the system. However, the system does not actively infer any program from user behavior.

The design philosophy in Eager is to not burden the user by requiring confirmation of each automation step. Instead, Eager learns when its prediction is incorrect by observing the user taking a different action than the action highlighted by Eager. As such, Eager is an example of a mixed-initiative interface. The user takes the initiative by using direct manipulation to execute a program, thereby commencing automation. The software agent takes the initiative by building a program

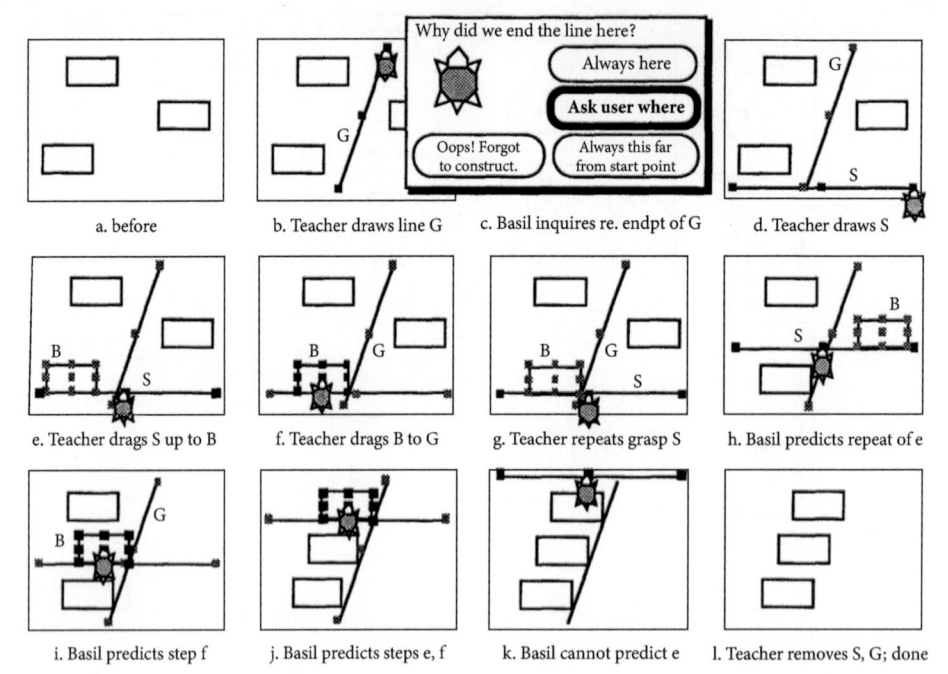

Figure 38.5 An example of the Metamouse system's software agent, called Basil and depicted as a turtle, learning to move rectangles within predefined constraints as taught by the user [526]. The user (teacher) begins by drawing a reference line G. Since the endpoints of the line do not make contact with any shape, the software agent asks the user if these locations are fixed or can change during runtime. The user indicates that they can change during runtime. The user then draws a second reference line S and moves the line so that it touches the bottom of rectangle B. The user then moves rectangle B to reference line G. When the user repeats the selection of reference line S, Basil detects a loop and predicts that the user wants to move reference line S to the bottom of a new rectangle. The user accepts this suggestion. Basil subsequently wants to move the middle box to the left of reference line G, inferring this action by ranking the constraints and ignoring the weakest constraint—in this case, the direction constraint. Subsequently, Basil can automate the remaining alignment tasks until the reference line S ends up beyond the final box. Having no new information, Basil terminates.

in the background and communicating its progress by highlighting the next element in the GUI during interaction. Importantly, the user is not required to take any action should the user not desire any automation.

38.3.3 Visual programming languages

Another way to allow end-users to develop software is to change the medium of programming from a textual list of instructions to a graphical environment. *Visual programming languages* provide users with a graphical interface that allows users to create and modify programs by representing programs graphically, thereby enabling users to manipulate software instructions for the program in a graphical environment.

Such a graphical environment can be designed in a variety of ways. For example, an interactive flow chart editor is an example of a graphical environment that allows editing programs

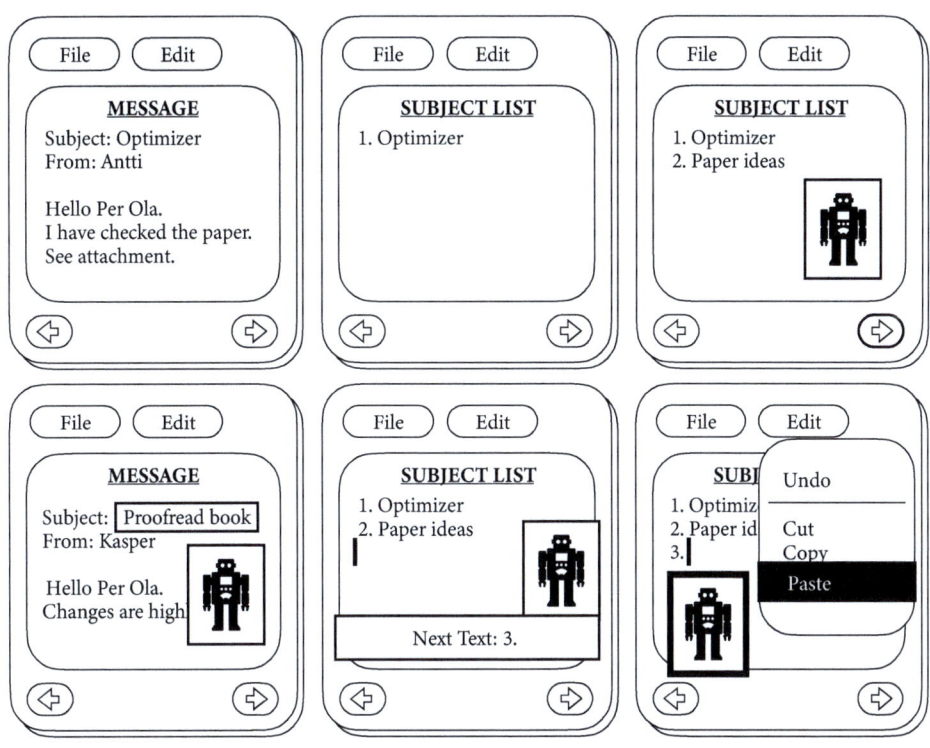

Figure 38.6 An example of a programming-by-example system using the software agent *Eager* [177]. The user wishes to make a "Subject List" by repeatedly opening message cards, selecting the subject text in the message, and pasting the subject text into the subject list. Once the user has completed this operation twice, the Eager icon pops up (top-right). Eager has detected a pattern of user behavior and highlights the right-arrow button, which Eager predicts is going to be the user's next action. When the user opens the next message card by clicking the right-arrow button, Eager predicts the user will copy the subject text (bottom-left). When the user returns to the subject list, Eager predicts the user will want to write the text "3." Finally, when the user opens the *Edit* menu, Eager predicts the user is going to paste the text from the clipboard. At this stage, the user can feel confident that Eager understands the task. If the user clicks the Eager button, the software agent will automatically go through all remaining message cards and assemble the complete subject list.

represented as flow charts. Spreadsheet applications is an example of a graphical environment that allows users to edit formulas and data flows using a graphical representation of the program that relies on the spreadsheet metaphor.

Visual programming languages have a long history. For example, Smith [779] reviewed examples that were known in 1975, including a visual language based on a circuit metaphor by W. R. Sutherland that allows the user to use a light pen to draw logic circuits.

Visual programming languages rely on a graphical representation of a program that allows users to edit programs by directly manipulating it using some form of GUI. As such, different graphical representations of programs give rise to a wide array of visual programming languages. Paper Example 38.3.1 shows an early example of a graphical representation of programs in the form of diagrams, known as Nassi–Shneiderman diagrams.

> **Paper Example 38.3.1: Nassi–Shneiderman diagrams**
>
> Visual programming languages rely on some form of graphical representation of a program. A Nassi–Shneiderman diagram [581] is a form of structured diagram designed to visualize the high-level decomposition of a program. While they tend not to be used in visual programming languages, they are sometimes used as an information visualization technique for visualizing algorithms or high-level processes for teaching purposes.
>
> The figure illustrates a Nassi–Shneiderman diagram for a conditional statement in a process for unlocking a phone. The diagram depicts this process through a branching block that specifies that the action to take, either to unlock the phone or to deny access, is dependent on a precondition, the fingerprint of the user being detected.
>
> ```
> ┌─────────────────────────────────┐
> │         Unlock Phone            │
> ├─────────────────────────────────┤
> │      \  Fingerprint Detected? / │
> │   Yes  \                     / No│
> ├─────────────────┬───────────────┤
> │ Phone Unlocked  │ Access Denied │
> └─────────────────┴───────────────┘
> ```
>
> Nassi–Shneiderman diagrams define such block structure for a wide range of programming constructs, including branching blocks with more than two outcomes, loops, parallel processes, and so on.

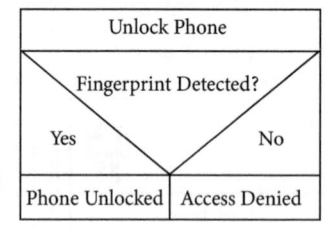

Visual programming languages can be combined with programming by demonstration. *KidSim* [781] introduced a GUI that acts as a simulation environment to enable children to construct programs graphically. The system uses so-called graphical rewrite rules [263], also called before-and-after rules, to enable the user to specify behavior.

38.4 Formal methods

We have already concluded that software systems supporting interaction are inherently complex. So, how do we know they behave correctly? This is a fundamental problem in computer science. For HCI, a way to demonstrate the correctness of models is to use *formal methods*. This term refers to a set of methods that use rigorous mathematical models to specify, develop, and verify a system.

38.4.1 Finite-state machines

One example of a formal method that can be used in HCI is modeling using finite-state machines, sometimes called finite-state automata. Finite-state machines can be used for a variety of applications. In HCI, they can be used to provide a design vocabulary for input devices. Buxton [114] presented a set of state diagrams modeling input (Figure 38.7).

Figure 38.7(a) shows a state diagram for mouse operation. The input device is in State 1, *Tracking*, when it is tracking, that is, when the user is moving the mouse and thus the mouse cursor on

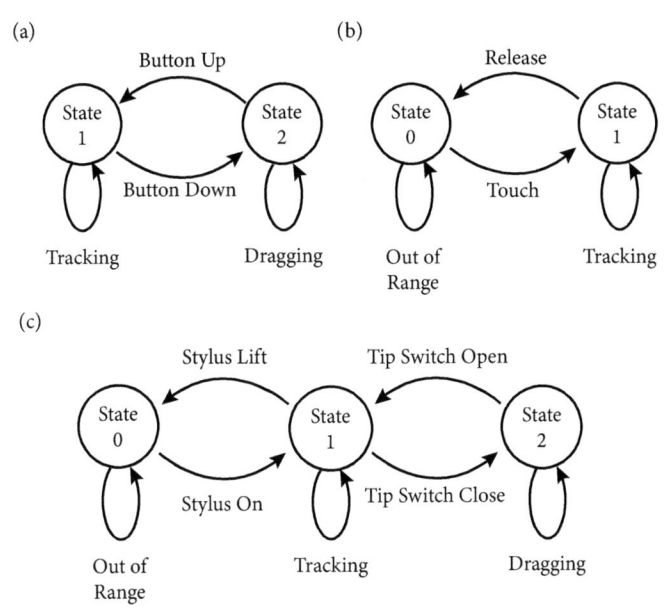

Figure 38.7 Three state diagrams modeling input [439].

the display. When the user pushes a button on the mouse, this results in a state transition that puts the input device in its *Dragging* state. The input device will remain in this state until the button is released and the input device returns to its *Tracking* state.

Figure 38.7(b) shows a different state diagram for a touchscreen. Here, State 0 denotes *Out of Range*. When the user's finger is outside the range of the touchscreen, the device has no notion of it. However, when the user is within the range, this is registered as a touch: The touchscreen transitions from State 0 to State 1 and is now in its *Tracking* state. That is, moving the finger within the range of the touchscreen results in the tracking cursor following the user's finger.

While Figure 38.7(a) and (b) look very similar, they capture different state transitions. There is a difference between State 0 (*Out of Range*), State 1 (*Tracking*), and State 2 (*Dragging*). The mouse does not have a State 0, as there is no notion of a mouse being out of range in this sense. Vice versa, the touchscreen does not have a notion of State 2, as it is modeled to only support two states: registered finger touch (State 1) and no registered finger touch (State 0).

The models in Figure 38.7(a) and (b) capture different kinds of interaction for different types of input devices. Can we have an input device that supports all three states—out of range, tracking, and dragging? Figure 38.7(c) shows one such example. It is a stylus that is operated in conjunction with a graphical tablet. The stylus can be moved above the tablet by the user. However, if the stylus is out of range (State 0), the system is unaware of such movement. A state transition occurs when the stylus is registered by the tablet and the system enters State 1 (*Tracking*). Moving the stylus can now result in, for example, cursor movement being displayed on the tablet. If the user applies additional pressure on the screen through the stylus, it may be possible to sense this using a switch in the tip of the pen. This can then lead to a state transition from State 1 to State 2. From a state perspective, the stylus and the graphical tablet offer higher interaction potential than the mouse or the touchscreen by supporting three rather than just two states.

This is an example of using state diagrams to form a design vocabulary. It allows us to discuss the expressiveness of, in this case, input devices, to compare them, and to consider whether we can add states. For example, is it possible to add a State 2 (*Dragging*) to a touchscreen, and if so, how?

> **Paper Example 38.4.1 Designing safe number entry systems**
>
> Data entry is pervasive and used in many critical environments, including healthcare, aviation, and finance. An analysis of number entry interfaces [820] found that such interfaces often contain design problems that give rise to errors.
>
> The figure in this paper example box shows a typical number interface from [820] (used under Creative Commons License). As the paper points out, the layout does not specify any interaction decisions. For instance, does the button C serve to make a correction, or does it cancel the values?
>
> Thimbleby [820] identified several design problems in number entry interfaces, including unclear and unstated design requirements, unclear record-keeping protocols for interaction steps, problems with interacting with negative numbers, and problems with timeouts. In total, the paper identifies 16 common design defects in numeric keypads.
>
> Thimbleby [820] argued that user testing is insufficient to address such defects, as user testing cannot guarantee that all defects will be identified. Instead, a formal approach is necessary. Thimbleby [820] demonstrated that it is possible to design formal rules for interaction with numeric keypads using Hoare logic. An important insight is that many years of user-centered research have failed to identify design defects that can be easily rectified. Thus, user-centered design for critical user interfaces should be complemented by formal approaches that can help detect such design defects.

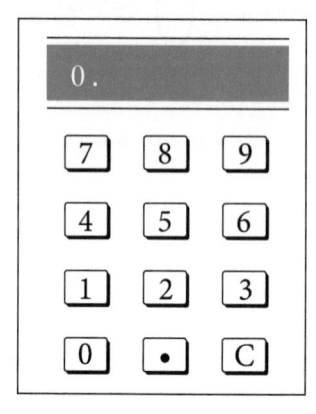

38.4.2 Formal modeling of undo

Other formal methods besides state diagrams are available, and sometimes more fruitful. As an example, let us consider the *undo* function that is present in many interactive systems. Undo allows users to revert the system state to a previous state, for instance, if the user has made an error or changed their mind.

The undo function is surprisingly complex. First, there are several ways of supporting undo in a system. The simplest model, called *flip undo*, supports a single level of undo and redo. In such a system, only the effect of the last command in a sequence of user commands can be removed by invoking undo and re-added by invoking redo [200].

A more common implementation of undo, called *backtrack undo*, involves the system maintaining a record of every command that has been invoked. When the user invokes undo, the last command (excluding meta-commands, such as undo) is removed. When the user invokes undo again, the previous command is removed, and so on [200].

A variant of backtrack undo called *stack-based undo/redo* allows the user to *redo*, that is, to undo the effect of an undo. Such a system typically maintains a separate list of undone commands. When a redo is invoked, the previously undone commands in this list are invoked again. This effectively allows a user to move back and forth in the state history of the system by repeatedly invoking undo and redo. When the user invokes an ordinary command, the list of undone commands is reset [200].

As you may now realize, implementing a correct undo policy is not as easy as it may initially seem. A straightforward definition of undo is that if we invoke *undo* following a command c, the system should return to a state as if the command c never occurred. We can write this in a formal way as follows:

$$c \frown undo \sim null. \qquad (38.1)$$

This notation specifies that the system state of a command c followed by ($\frown$) *undo* should be equivalent to ($\sim$) the system state of invoking a *null* command, that is, a command that does nothing. If we exclude *undo* from any valid command c (treating undo as a meta-command), this property is called the *strong-cu* property.

We can also introduce a similar notion for undo commands, called the *strong-uu* property. That is, an *undo* followed by an *undo* should result in the same system state as invoking a *null* command:

$$undo \frown undo \sim null. \qquad (38.2)$$

The combination of the strong-cu and strong-uu properties seems appealing. However, they have been shown to be inconsistent. In fact, it can be proven that no undo system with more than two internal states can support both of these properties simultaneously.

This can be understood by reasoning about the state transitions. In this case, we have three states, our initial state s_0 and states s_a and s_b, which arise after the user has invoked commands a and b, respectively. The user can go back from state s_a or s_b to the initial state s_0 by invoking undo. In other words, $a \frown undo \sim null$, and $b \frown undo \sim null$. This follows from the strong-cu property that a command followed by undo results in the system state equivalent to invoking the null command. That is, if undo follows a command, we are back at our initial system state. However, what happens if the user invokes undo again? According to the strong-uu property, this should result in the same system state as if we had originally invoked the null command. In other words, $undo \frown undo \sim null$. However, an undo followed by an undo is inherently ambiguous. According to the strong-uu property, we may end up in state s_a or state s_b. In other words, $s_a = s_b$. Next, consider that a and b are arbitrarily chosen commands. This means that *any* command will result in the same effect in state s_0, which, for any real system, is obviously not the case. Hence, undo cannot be treated as an ordinary command; it must be seen as a meta-command with special properties [200].

38.5 How do we know if systems and toolkits are useful?

There are many HCI systems, toolkits, visual languages, and formal approaches to HCI available in the literature. However, they tend to be difficult to evaluate in terms of their efficacy and efficiency.

Lau [459] discusses the challenges in evaluating such systems contributions in terms of their scientific merits. It is proposed that systems contributions should have clear and compelling descriptions of the problems that they solve and their impact. They should also be sufficiently replicable, that is, described in such detail that other researchers can recreate similar systems. In addition, they should discuss alternative approaches to build the system, elaborating on the particular design decisions that led to a specific system being built, instead of another viable alternative. Further, systems should demonstrate value by providing evidence they are effective and efficient for the users and scenarios that they are designed for. This may involve user studies but may also include other evaluation activities, for example, studying how such systems address users' goals in deployment. Finally, systems contributions should discuss the barriers they overcome and their limitations.

It is evident that it is highly challenging to evaluate systems contributions, even in terms of their research merits. Developing methods that allow us to understand how to efficiently and meaningfully evaluate such systems is a fundamental challenge in the HCI systems research field. It is critical, as evidence-based meaningful feedback is required for learning how to design more successful systems, toolkits, end-user programming interfaces, and formal approaches to HCI.

Summary

- Software design and architecture enable user interfaces to be efficiently and effectively developed. A prominent design pattern for user interfaces is called model-view-controller.
- End-user development refers to techniques, approaches, and systems that allow end-users to design and build executable programs.
- Formal methods enable designers to specify, develop, and verify user interfaces. Formal methods have wide uses, for instance, in modeling undo functionality, but are most frequently used in critical applications.

Exercises

1. Modeling interaction with state diagrams. Consider a virtual reality drawing application where the user's hands in 3D space are tracked by the headset. The user's hands are represented in virtual reality using virtual representations of the user's hands. To enable the user to draw, the system provides the user with a 2D virtual canvas floating in front of them. The user can then draw by ensuring their virtual fingertip makes contact with the virtual 2D canvas. Draw a state diagram for this interaction. A major limitation with this type of interaction is that the user's virtual fingertip can easily lose contact of the 2D drawing canvas, frustrating the user by causing parts of their articulated drawing motion to get lost. A common solution is therefore to not present the user with a 2D plane but with a 2D prism with a preset thickness. As long as the user's virtual fingertip is on or within the prism, the system is in its drawing state. This makes it less likely that the user will accidentally lose contact with the canvas. Draw a state diagram for this type of interaction as well.

2. Formal methods. Draw a state diagram that illustrates the proof sketched in the chapter for why undo cannot be an ordinary command and has to be treated as a meta-command with special properties.

39
Computational representations and models

Previously in this book, we have explored a number of methods to design and engineer interaction. These approaches apply knowledge from user research, theories, technical and business requirements, designers' know-how, and so on, to create a system. In these processes, the available data influence the final design *through the designer*. It is the designer who interprets the data and creates solutions based on their understanding.

In this chapter, we consider a complementary perspective that facilitates computing appropriate solutions to well-defined problems in interaction. We *represent* key features of interaction computationally, integrate these features into a *model*, and then *compute* based on this model.

Computational methods can be used to optimize interfaces, adapt them, make inferences about users, and learn from interaction. Examples include the following:

- Nonspeaking individuals with motor disabilities frequently rely on augmentative and alternative communication devices to communicate. Such devices provide users with a means to enter text that can then be read out to the speaking partner through a speech synthesizer. A common problem in this area is low communication rates. As a consequence, researchers have been investigating techniques to improve communication rates, including the use of word prediction, sentence retrieval, and sentence generation techniques that adapt to the user's vocabulary over time. By creating a computational model of interaction, it is possible to predict the performance of such systems before testing them in deployment studies spanning weeks or even months [932].

- Augmented reality glasses allow users to interact with digital information registered in the physical world. However, for such virtual content to be effective, the user interface (UI) that is used to manipulate them has to be salient to users (Chapter 3). By creating a model of visual saliency for such UIs, it is possible to optimize the presentation to make it maximally visible to users [234].

- Graphical user interface design is hard. Designers need to coordinate decisions across multiple levels, from pixel-level decisions about padding between buttons to high-level decisions about functionality. Computational methods can assist designers by generating design ideas. These are often of two types: explorative ideas or ideas that refine an existing design. Under the hood, these methods model key features of the existing design and link them to variables of interest, such as those related to visual appeal or usability. They can algorithmically search for alternatives, thus complementing designers' creative efforts [933].

What these examples have in common is that they need to *represent* interaction to create a *computational model*. Once such a model has been obtained, it is possible to *compute* with it.

Models are at the center of computational methods. Models are simplified representations of interactive systems that capture essential aspects in some formalism to allow for reasoning about it.

Mathematics and computer science offer us a rich toolbox of formalisms to this end, each with different properties. In this book, we have covered a number of models, such as saliency models using deep nets, motor control laws based on regression equations, and models of human cognition.

When we have a model, we can *predict* the performance of a system before engaging in empirical user testing. For example, models of visual discrimination ability (Chapter 3) are used for engineering the quality of displays. A model can also be used to *simulate* outcomes. Simulations allow us to learn about system behavior. We can detect risks and analyze the underlying causes. For example, models of pointing are used to analyze intelligent text entry methods. They can simulate how users type, including their errors, which then helps test methods such as autocorrection. We can also use models to study the limits of behavior. Models allow us to chart the *operating envelopes* of UIs—the upper and lower bounds of performance with different (extreme but realistic) assumptions. In *sensitivity analysis*, we do this systematically by varying the inputs to a model and studying the effect on the outcomes at the system level. "What would happen to the performance of a search engine if the queries were formulated by a non-native speaker with spelling mistakes?" Such analyses can guide us by highlighting which conditions are likely to hurt system performance. In this chapter, we will discuss the nature of models and explore how we can use such models to analyze system outcomes.

We can also use models to improve designs algorithmically. For instance, *optimization* involves engaging in a systematic search to obtain parameter values that produce desirable system outcomes. For example, a keyboard can be optimized by positioning the keys on the keyboard in a way that minimizes the average predicted time it takes a user to press the next key. Optimization can algorithmically generate a keyboard layout that maximizes the entry rate. In this chapter, we will explore the concept of optimization and demonstrate it using the case of keyboards.

Models can also be incorporated *into* interactive systems. Models can help us infer user intent, make recommendations, and carry out actions automatically. Various *machine learning* and *pattern recognition* methods can be used to create a model of interaction. Such a model can enable new forms of interaction and enhance existing ones. For example, a speech recognition system may receive data on the user's speech as audio signals and use a machine learning model to translate these observations into hypotheses about what the user wants to communicate.

In this chapter, we will discuss how to create models that allow us to perform prediction, envelope analysis, optimization, and inference. To do so, we must first understand how to represent interaction in a format that enables us to create a model that can be subsequently used for computations.

39.1 Representations and models

A *computational model* allows the computer, or us as designers, to perform computations relevant to interaction. For example, a computational model of visual saliency for a UI may allow us to maximize visual saliency, as captured by the model, by finding the parameter settings that result in the model predicting maximum saliency. The "as captured by the model" detail is important, as the model predictions are only as good as the model is at accurately representing the relevant elements of interaction.

This leads us to *representations*. A key part in arriving at a good computational model of interaction is to identify a suitable *representation*. A representation here means a way to describe relevant elements of interaction. A representation can be simple or incredibly complex depending on the purpose of the modeling effort. In general, a computational representation is about identifying the most important *features* of interaction, and a computational model is about describing how these features interact to give rise to outcomes relevant to interaction.

Any computational model in human–computer interaction (HCI) can be analyzed from this perspective. An example of a simple but popular model is Fitts' law, which we discussed in detail in Chapter 4:

$$MT = a + b \log_2 \left(\frac{D}{W} + 1\right). \tag{39.1}$$

Briefly, Fitts' law predicts that the average movement time *MT* is a function of the distance *D* to a target and the width *W* of the target. In other words, the interaction we are studying is the average time it takes a user to press a button, select an icon, and so on.

Fitts' law *represents* interaction through three constructs: movement time, which is what we wish to calculate, and two *features* of interaction, the distance to a target and the target's width. Note that other features might be relevant, such as the color of the target. However, according to the model, such additional features are not informative.

Having arrived at a representation, we can now build a *model*. The model in Fitts' law has two components. The first is the *index of difficulty* (*ID*), which is usually defined as follows:

$$ID = \log_2 \left(\frac{D}{W} + 1\right). \tag{39.2}$$

This construct captures the so-called difficulty required to select a target at a nominal distance *D* with nominal width *W*. Since the base of the logarithm is 2, the units are in bits. This implies causality—the experimenter is meant to manipulate *D* and *W* to obtain a distinct value of *ID* to influence the average movement time. A higher difficulty implies an increased average movement time. The second component in the model underpinning Fitts' law is that the movement time *MT* varies linearly with the index of difficulty. This linear relationship can be written as

$$MT = \alpha + \beta \, ID. \tag{39.3}$$

Here, the parameters α and β determine the intercept and the slope, respectively. The linear relationship is shown in Figure 39.1.

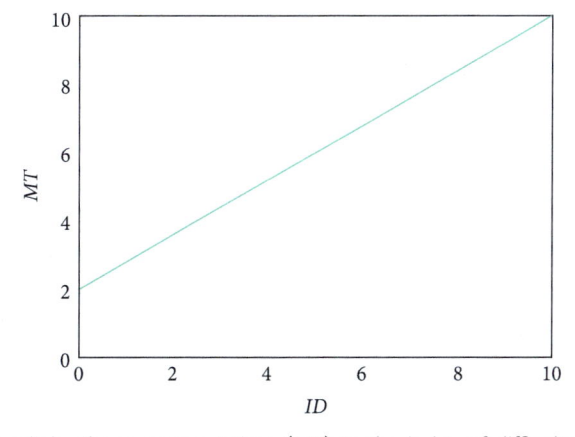

Figure 39.1 Fitts' law links the movement time (*MT*) to the index of difficulty (*ID*). The equation underpinning the model is $MT = \alpha + \beta \, ID$.

Assuming α and β are controllable, that is, we can set them to what we want, we can optimize the movement time by setting a and b to values that minimize MT. In practice, these parameters are task- and device-dependent, and therefore not generally controllable—we cannot just set them to arbitrary values. Instead, we can minimize the average movement time by minimizing D, that is, bringing together targets that the user is likely to hit in succession, and by maximizing W, that is, making the targets the user likely wants to hit as large as possible. In this way, Fitts' law can serve as a building tool in the optimization process, allowing the designer to explore different UI configurations to minimize the average movement time.

In summary, Fitts' law is a model that relies on a representation of interaction. It represents the act of hitting a target as involving two fundamental controllable parameters: the distance to the target and the width of the target. It does not involve additional elements, such as the color of the target, in its representation, as such a representation is irrelevant for determining the movement time. Much research is about understanding how to represent things, and interaction is no different. If we want to infer users' actions or optimize an interface in a systematic way, we need a model to represent what we mean by those actions. Furthermore, this model needs to be described in such a way that we can encode it into a format a computer can understand so that we can build systems that can use such models.

39.1.1 Feature engineering

The first step to arrive at a computational model is to determine a suitable representation. Only when we know how to represent interaction are we able to model it. Fitts' law represents the act of a user pointing at a target by considering its width and distance to determine the average movement time required to hit the target. As another example, if we wanted to come up with a model for human speech, we would need a representation that is informative for that domain. In such a case, an expert might represent a waveform of human speech as Mel-frequency cepstral coefficients, a computational representation of human speech that models the human auditory system's response. In general, we want to identify the qualities or features of interaction that are useful for building a model of interaction.

A *feature* is a quality of interest to our representation. One way to determine which features are important is a process called *feature selection*, sometimes referred to as *feature engineering*. Feature selection has gained a lot of attention in machine learning and pattern recognition, and several procedures exist for finding the most effective features in those domains.

Consider the problem of allowing users to issue commands via touchscreen gestures. Such a gesture recognition system translates a series of touchpoint observations into hypotheses about which gesture class the user intended to articulate. This is a *classification problem*. We have a set of labeled gestures in the system and we wish to assign a label to an unknown gesture articulation provided by the user.

One way to achieve this is to use the Rubine recognizer [718]. This linear classifier treats a user's articulation of a gesture as a *feature vector* consisting of 11 features that represent the properties of a 2D single-stroke gesture trace: the initial angle of the gesture, the length of the gesture, and so on. The Rubine recognizer can be trained by showing it example gestures for each gesture class. For example, a gesture class that is meant to resemble a rectangle can be trained by showing the system a set of gesture articulations that represent this gesture. This step allows the Rubine recognizer to determine weights for each feature in the feature vector for each gesture class. At classification time, the recognizer extracts the same 11-dimensional feature vector from the user's gesture articulation and identifies the gesture class that is the closest to the feature vector. The Rubine recognizer is reliant on its representation of a gesture as an 11-dimensional feature vector. Because of the number of dimensions, it is hard to visualize the features. For this reason, 2D and 3D visualizations are often used to understand how such features work in practice.

Generally, features that are helpful for creating representations may have one or more of the following properties:

Observable: For a feature to be effective, there must be a means to capture the feature. A directly observable feature is a feature that can be measured through a sensor or direct observation. An indirectly observable feature is a feature that we can only capture through a proxy measurement. For example, a touchpoint on a capacitive touchscreen is a directly observable feature, whereas a user's emotive state is only indirectly observable.

Informative: A feature should provide useful information about the interaction that is represented. For example, if the goal is to identify a computational representation of usable scatter plots, a useful feature may tell us something about the visual saliency of scatter plots.

Distinct: A feature should provide complementary information in relation to other features. Features that have a very high correlation provide redundant information. For example, if the goal is to identify a computational representation of a user pressing hard on a touchscreen, a feature such as the force of the press is likely highly correlated with the measured area of the fingertip.

Computable: For a feature to be effective, it must be possible to arrive at the feature through some systematic procedure. This means it must be possible to, for example, calculate or estimate a feature's value. Furthermore, even if a feature is computable, it may still not be practical to use the feature if the computation takes a long time, is unreliable, or requires significant resources. For example, while it may be informative to have a feature representing users' energy expenditure when they perform fine-grained finger movements, such a feature is very difficult to measure and hence compute.

Comprehensive: Collectively, a set of features should be as complete as possible in forming a computational representation of the interaction of interest. That is, all relevant features that can be captured and complement each other should be part of the feature set. For example, a model of pointing is not comprehensive if it considers the distance from the target but not the target's width.

39.1.2 Modeling

Having arrived at a representation, it is possible to develop a *computational model*. Such models utilize representations to capture and compute relevant qualities of interaction that can subsequently be used to inform design decisions.

To provide the intuition behind models, let us consider two variables, x and y. A very simple model, called an identity, is

$$y = x. \tag{39.4}$$

This model is shown in Figure 39.2. This model claims that the dependent variable y takes on the same value as the independent variable x. However, what if y is not related to x?

Consider the following model:

$$y = c, \tag{39.5}$$

where c is a constant. Here, y represents the *dependent* variable, the effect, and c is a parameter that can be set to any value, such as $c = 2$. This model is shown in Figure 39.3.

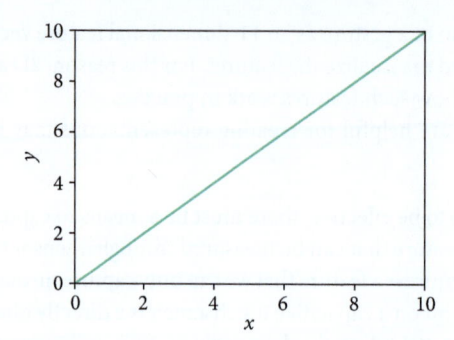

Figure 39.2 The dependent variable y varies linearly with the independent variable x. The equation underpinning the model is $y = x$.

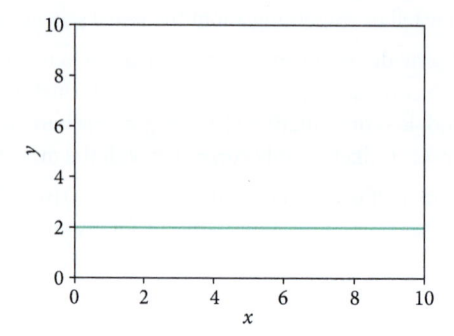

Figure 39.3 The dependent variable y is invariant of the independent variable x. The equation underpinning the model is $y = c$, where c is a constant and $c = 2$.

This model claims that the dependent variable y is unchanged as a function of the independent variable x. That is, the model claims that y is invariant, or independent, of any value of x.

Usually, models predict that y varies as a function of x based on a particular relationship between the two variables. For instance, Fitts' law posits that the movement time MT varies linearly with the index of difficulty ID for hitting a target. We can replace the movement time MT, our dependent variable, with y, and the index of difficulty ID, our independent variable, with x. We then arrive at the following expression:

$$y = \alpha + \beta x. \tag{39.6}$$

This model, shown in Figure 39.4, predicts that y varies linearly with x. If it is a model of interaction, then there is usually implied causality: We cannot directly control y, but we can change x. For example, in Fitts' law, we cannot directly control the average movement time. However, we can directly control how large the targets are and where they are located on a visual display.

We have a model of interaction with three parameters: α, β, and x. The independent variable x is a variable we control, perhaps by changing some quality in the UI. The parameter α is the intercept: It specifies the value of the dependent variable y when $x = 0$. In interaction, it is often thought of as some form of offset. For example, if x represents the task time, $x = 0$ is the point when the user has not yet begun the task. The parameter β describes the slope of the line in Figure 39.4. This parameter frequently describes a *rate*; here, it tells us how much y changes when we change x. For example, if y represents the search time and x represents a measure of visual display clutter, β tells us how much the search time increases when the measure of visual display clutter increases. The intercept,

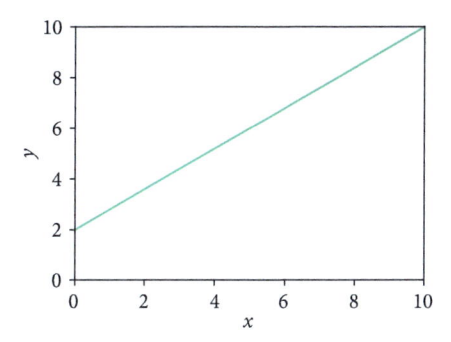

Figure 39.4 The dependent variable *y* varies linearly with the independent variable *x*. The intercept is $\alpha = 2$ and the slope is $\beta = 1.25$. The equation underpinning the model is $y = \alpha + \beta x$.

in this instance, provides us with an offset or baseline, as it tells us what the predicted search time is when the measure of visual display clutter is zero.

More generally, models are functions—expressed as equations or computer programs—that produce an output given an input. They contain two types of mathematical constructs: parameters and mechanisms that link parameters together.

To build a model, we require some formal mechanism that mediates inputs and outputs. Such a mechanism can be, for example, a regression equation, a deep neural network, a decision tree, a physical simulation, or something else.

These mechanisms work with variables that are typically referred to as *parameters*. Parameters express the values of events or states. These parameters are often updated via different inputs. For example, a visual saliency model has millions of neural network parameters that are trained using eye-tracking data (Chapter 3). When the model is fed an image that a user might see (input), these parameters gain values, allowing the model to predict which regions of the image the user might attend to (output). A different image gives rise to a different neural activation.

Problems in HCI can be modeled in different ways. Figure 39.5 illustrates this. It shows three different models for a toy task. We have a single parameter, the complexity of a web site, which we define as the number of links on the page. We also have a single outcome, the search time, which we define as the time it takes a user to find the link they are looking for.

The first model in Figure 39.5 uses a tree structure to model a binary outcome based on a threshold. If the complexity is above the threshold, the outcome is predicted to be either below or above the predefined value. This model is simple to understand, but it is also very limited. First, the model is based on a threshold that needs to be set somehow. Second, the outcome is binary and lacks resolution.

The second model in Figure 39.5 is a linear model. It predicts the outcome as a function of the parameter value. As a model, this is more informative. The slope of the line tells us how the model predicts the search time will increase as the complexity increases. The intercept encodes a fixed cost in the search time; it tells us that no matter the complexity, the model predicts there will be an initial cost in the search time. Unlike the tree-based model, this model predicts a range of values in the outcome and does not rely on a threshold to make such predictions.

The third model in Figure 39.5 is a nonlinear model. It is similar to the linear model, except that the outcome values are not predicted to vary linearly with the values of the parameter. This property allows the nonlinear model to make richer predictions. For example, unlike the linear model, this model predicts that in a certain range of complexity, the search time will rapidly increase.

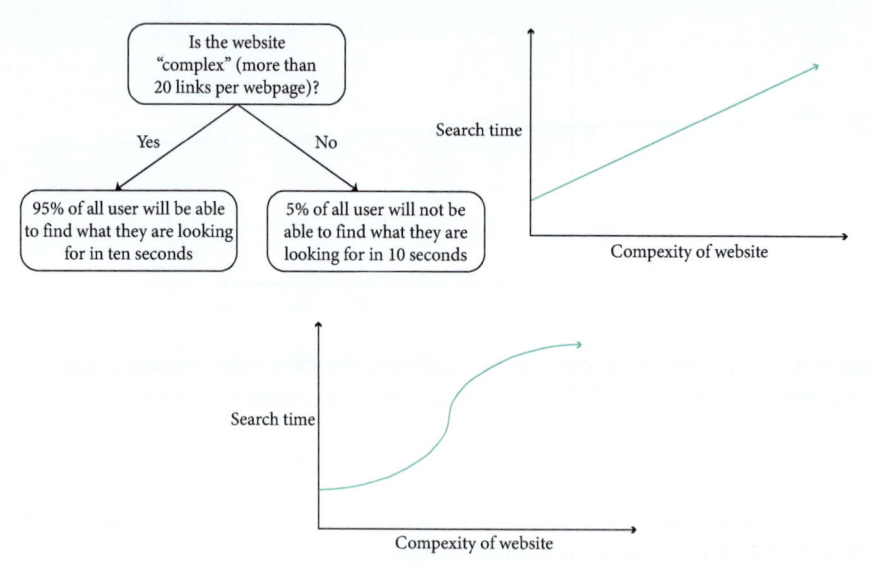

Figure 39.5 Three examples of simple models: a decision tree, a linear model, and a nonlinear model.

The three models are simplistic. First, it is unlikely that a single parameter, such as complexity, can fully determine the search time. A useful model would at the very least need to capture complexity through several parameters, such as the number of links on the page, the number of additional elements, their organization, and so on. Second, the user's strategy in engaging with the system may also affect the outcome. A complete model would therefore account for not only the parameters of the system but also the parameters governing the user's actions. While the three models may not be the most valid models, there are still cases in which they could be useful. In engineering applications, accuracy and practicality are both important.

By using more sophisticated models, we can perform *simulations* of UI outcomes. A simulation refers to the operation of a model: "The intention is to draw conclusions, qualitative or quantitative, about the behaviour or properties of a real-world process or system over time" [568]. In practice, simulations are executions of a computational model to approximate the behavior of an interactive system or part of it. Simulations allow for studying different conditions in HCI, including extreme and risky conditions. For example, we can simulate handover situations in a semi-autonomous vehicle without risking anyone getting hurt.

39.2 Envelope analysis

Models allow us to gain an understanding of the effect of parameter values on outcomes. As an example, suppose we wish to provide users with a touchscreen interface that allows them to correct speech recognition mistakes using a touch modality instead of a speech modality. Here, we use an example of such a design problem from the literature [850]. This study tackles this problem by providing the user with two methods to correct speech recognition utterances (Figure 39.6).

The speech recognizer generates a search lattice to identify the user's utterance. The system processes this speech lattice into a word confusion network, which is a time-ordered series of clusters of candidate words along with their posterior probabilities. This network is shown in Figure 39.6. Every column consists of the following elements: (1) the current output word, which may be changed by the user; (2) the first-best hypothesis, that is, the speech recognizer's best guess of the user's intended word; (3) a series of alternative words ordered by their posterior probabilities from the cluster in the word confusion network at this location; and (4) a delete button that deletes the word.

The system supports the following actions:

Substituting words: The user can substitute a word by touching an alternative word in the word confusion network. The user can also substitute multiple contiguous words by crossing them.

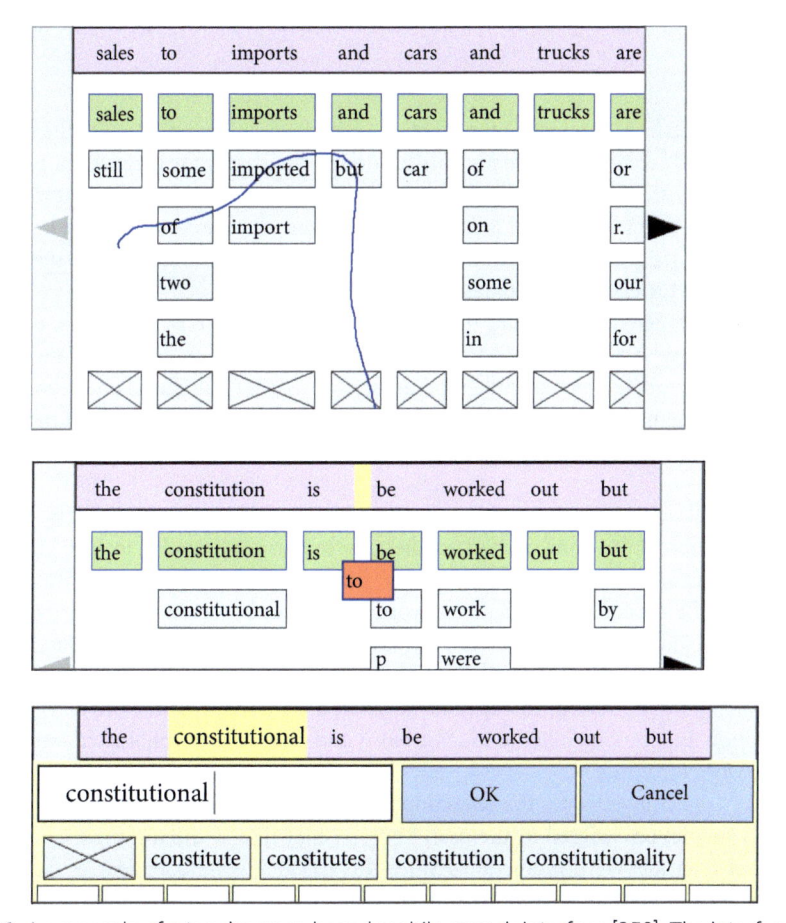

Figure 39.6 An example of a touchscreen-based mobile speech interface [850]. The interface allows the user to correct recognized utterances (shown at the top) by either direct manipulation of the word confusion network or by engaging with a keyboard that provides word prediction and a choice of morphological variants of words.

The user can also touch a word to open up a keyboard interface. In this interface, the system shows morphological variants of the word; for example, morphological variants of the word "constitutional" in Figure 39.6 include "constitute," "constitutes," and "constitution."

Editing words: The user can edit words by touching them in the top row or by double-tapping any other word. This opens up a keyboard interface that allows the user to either edit the word or type a new word.

Deleting words: The user can delete words by touching the "X" buttons in the bottom row. The user can also slide their finger and delete a sequence of words at the same time.

Inserting words: The user can insert a word using three methods. First, the user can touch a word in the word confusion network and drag it to the top location. This is useful if the intended word is on the display but is not present in the correct column. Second, the user can touch the space between two words at the top, which opens up a keyboard interface, allowing the user to type in a new word to occupy the space between the two surrounding words. Third, the user can select a preceding word, which opens up the keyboard interface, and then type a space followed by a new word.

The different interfaces supporting these actions are shown in Figure 39.6. On the surface, this system appears fairly complex with many possible design choices for the parameters. For example, how many clusters should the system display? If the system displays too few, there is a higher probability the user's intended word is not present and the user has to rely on the keyboard. On the other hand, if we show too many, the buttons will be small and difficult to select. Can we somehow quantify the effect of this parameter on the outcome?

Vertanen and Kristensson [850] did this by means of simulation. By essentially playing back recorded audio, they were able to construct word confusion networks from the resulting speech lattices and then simulate different system parameters to assess their effects on the outcome. The outcome of interest, in this case, was the word error rate—a lower word error rate is better. To simulate user behavior, they used an oracle, which is an assumed expert user that performs optimally in the interface.

Figure 39.7 (left) shows the result of one analysis. The word error rate achieved by the oracle is shown as a function of the number of word alternatives that are provided in each column (cluster). The four performance curves represent four different user configurations. We can observe that increasing the cluster size reduces the word error rate; however, the majority of the gain is realized by providing the first 3–4 word suggestions for a recognized word. This informs the trade-off design decision on the balance between providing more word suggestions and the cost of using smaller buttons. Adding the capability to delete a word reduces the word error rate; adding the copy option and the capability to touch a word and choose a morphological variant further reduces the word error rate.

Figure 39.7 (right) investigates the reduction in the word error rate as a function of the number of word predictions offered to the user. The constant line at the top represents a baseline that does not offer any word predictions. Since this baseline is independent of the number of word predictions offered, it is constant. We can observe that reductions in the word error rate are obtainable using a variety of word prediction methods. The highest reduction in the word error rate is achieved by using an acoustic model that predicts words that sound acoustically similar to the word. However, such acoustic predictions are difficult for a user to understand; for example, "aback" is acoustically similar to "attack" [850]. Similar reductions in the word error rate are obtainable using statistical language models that take the preceding or following words

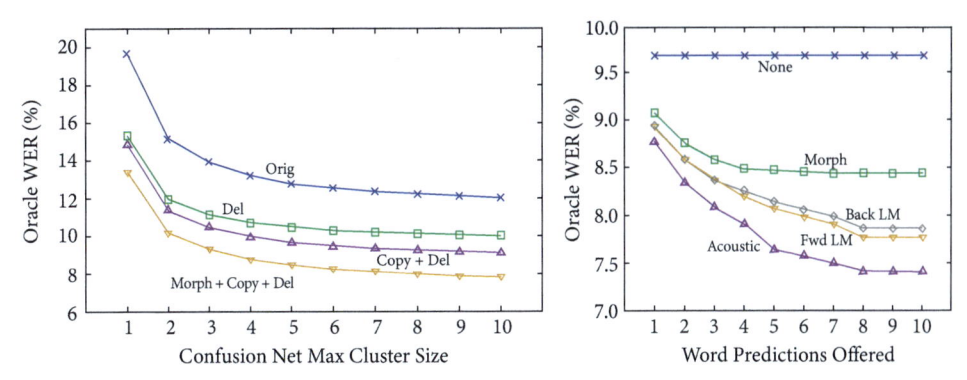

Figure 39.7 Analysis of the speech recognition interface shown in Figure 39.6, generated by playing back recorded audio and then simulating a perfect user. This has resulted in the ability to plot the *oracle* word error rate as a function of a design parameter for several different interaction methods.

into account. However, such predictions depend on the surrounding words and may be difficult for a user to understand. Finally, the lowest word error rate reduction is realized by using morphological variants. In the paper, the designers chose this option because although it did not achieve the highest word error rate reduction, these predictions are easier for users to understand [850], demonstrating that such analyses provide design guidance rather than strict design directives.

39.2.1 Conducting envelope analysis

As the previous example shows, simulating outcomes and analyzing their effect can be a very useful complementary method for understanding HCI systems. There is no formal term for this type of analysis; here, we call it *envelope analysis* (cf. flight envelope and back-of-the-envelope analysis). The idea is to extract design parameters from the functional description of the system and simulate system performance by investigating a range of parameter choices.

We first have to consider the function parameters. Having identified a functional model, it is possible to parameterize it. There are fundamentally two classes of parameters:

Controllable parameters: Controllable parameters govern function execution and can be set by the designer. These parameters are of great interest as they enable *optimization* toward design objectives.

Uncontrollable parameters: Uncontrollable parameters govern function execution and cannot be explicitly set by the designer. *Sensitivity analysis* allows us to understand the sensitivity of the outcomes to variations in these parameters.

It is also worth noting that the effects of these parameters can be investigated in various ways besides envelope analysis, including through experiments with users, prototyping, and measurements. Three common strategies to carry out envelope analysis are (1) keystroke-level modeling and similar approaches, (2) Wizard of Oz methods, and (3) computational experiments.

The first method, *keystroke-level modeling*, assumes error-free expert behavior and that reliable fixed-time estimates are available for all operators. This method and its variants are described in

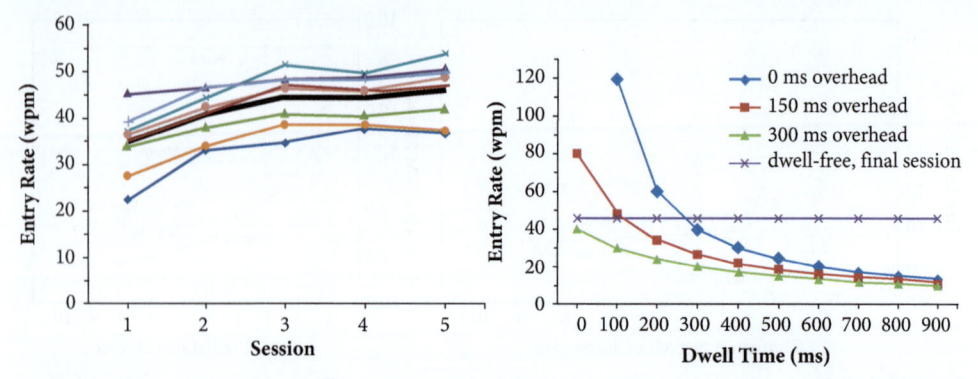

Figure 39.8 The first plot shows the measured entry rate as a function of dwell-free eye typing using a simulated recognizer. The second plot shows different operating points of dwell-free eye typing. The entry rate varies as a function of two parameters: the uncontrollable parameter overhead and the controllable parameter dwell time. For any realistic operating point involving these two parameters, dwell-free eye typing is faster [439].

detail in the chapter on analytic evaluation methods (Chapter 41). The second method relies on the *Wizard of Oz* approach [178]. The basic idea is simple: a human operator simulates responses of a complicated (typically AI) system. The peculiar name of this approach is due to inspiration from the book (and subsequent film) *The Wonderful Wizard of Oz* (1900), which has a scene where the protagonists encounter a very large screen with imposing effects purported to be due to a powerful wizard. However, when the screen is accidentally tipped over, it is revealed that the wizard is just an ordinary person using an elaborate apparatus to give the impression of being a wizard.

Another method is using *computational experiments* that generate system outcomes through a model, thus allowing designers to study the impact of parameters on performance. This is the approach taken for the mobile speech interface we discussed earlier in this section. Another example is shown in Figure 39.8. For such experiments, it is often useful to represent an expert user. An oracle can be created to perform optimally or imperfectly; the latter is sometimes called a *stochastic oracle* [438]. Oracle simulation is a very useful way to carry out rudimentary envelope analysis to tease out trade-offs and to help prioritize relevant features.

Paper Example 39.2.1: Understanding why word prediction may not be beneficial

Word prediction is a common functionality on mobile touchscreen keyboards. However, large-scale empirical research has suggested that word predictions may not be that useful [637]. What is the *mechanism* explaining this observation? Using envelope analysis, it is possible to gain an understanding of the factors contributing to this empirical observation [438].

A high-level function structure (Chapter 36) of a word prediction system is shown in the following figure.

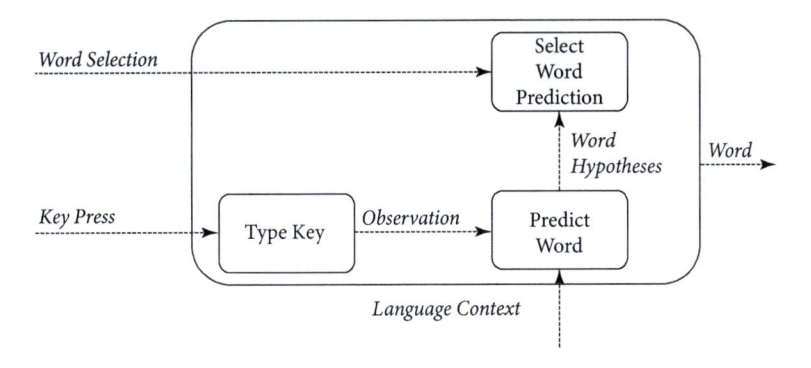

COMPUTATIONAL REPRESENTATIONS AND MODELS | 693

From this functional model, we observe that we have two input signals, and they can be parameterized as follows:

- T_{key}: the time it takes the user to hit a key;
- T_{react}: the time it takes a user to react to a word prediction suggestion.

A latent set of parameters, *strategy*, governs the interaction between the design parameters:

- L_{min}: restrict word prediction usage to words of a minimum length;
- k_{look}: type k keys, then look;
- p_{max}: only attempt to check word predictions up to p_{max} keystrokes per word.

Note that all these parameters are uncontrollable. Other strategies are of course possible, and in reality, a user is likely to use a mix of strategies. These parameters can be investigated by using them to simulate a user typing text and interfacing with word predictions. The result is a set of envelopes of performance; one of them is shown in the following figure.

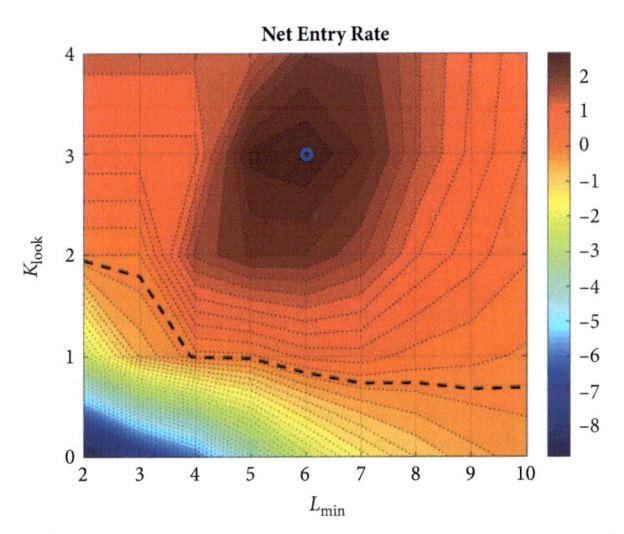

The plot shows the net entry rate as a function of two strategy parameters, k_{look} and L_{min}. The other parameters are fixed in this analysis. We note that under these assumptions, performance

continued

> **Paper Example 39.2.1: Understanding why word prediction may not be beneficial** *(continued)*
>
> is strongly tied to the choice of typing strategy. The black dotted line is the zero-crossing and marks the boundary between performance gain and performance loss due to the predictions.
>
> Any strategy that looks at word predictions without typing at least one letter is shown to slow the user down. Performance gains are only realized if the user types at least the first two letters of each word before looking at predictions. The reliability of predictions increases with the number of letters typed. The net entry rate ranges from −8.8 to +2.9 words per minute solely as a result of the choice of typing strategy. The highest point identifies the optimal typing strategy: $L_{\min} = 6$ and $k_{\text{look}} = 3$. In other words, word predictions are unlikely to provide the average user with any noticeable gain and may very well slow them down.
>
> This is an example of an analysis that would be difficult to carry out in an experiment (Chapter 43) since there are so many parameters that need to be controlled. Furthermore, it is questionable whether it is even possible to reliably control study participants' strategies in an experiment.

39.3 Optimization

Optimization refers to the algorithmic search for solutions that best meet the stated objectives. In HCI, optimization serves as a computational method for the design and adaptation of UIs [631]. It has been applied to the computational design of keyboards, menus, information displays, information visualizations, and interaction techniques. In adaptive UIs, it has been applied to enhance distributed UIs, cross-reality displays, and web layouts. The method can be beneficial in conditions in which obtaining a good design is hard, for example, because of a large number of decisions, constraints, or objectives. It can also be applied in cases where design choices must be automated, for example, when adapting or personalizing a UI. The main benefit of the method is the exploitation of powerful search algorithms (solvers). The main drawback is that the optimization task must be precisely defined for the outcomes to be relevant.

Optimization is a *constructive method*: It can not only evaluate solutions but also generate them. It can propose values of *decision variables* such that the solution they jointly describe achieves the minimum or maximum of some stated objective. These variables could govern the representations we have discussed earlier. For example, to decide the position of a button on a display, one would need to decide its x and y coordinates—two variables. To determine its size, one would need to decide the (x, y) coordinates of both the top-left and bottom-right corners—four variables.

An *objective function* assigns each candidate solution a score that indicates how good that solution is. For example, we could use Fitts' law to assess how quick to use some button designs are. An objective function can be about anything that is regarded desirable: surface features of the interface (e.g., minimal white space), the expected performance of users (e.g., "task A should be completed as quickly as possible"), and so on. In HCI, the quality of an interface is primarily determined with reference to end-users, for example, user performance and experiences. Several objective functions have been proposed in the literature, ranging from performance to ergonomics, learnability, and aesthetics [631]. There are many principled (and unprincipled) ways to obtain objective functions: (1) literature reviews, such as adopting a model or theory from prior work; (2) data-driven approaches, such as determining a function from human data; (3) standards, such as complying with W3C accessibility requirements; and (4) utilizing design heuristics.

After a problem has been formulated, numerous efficient algorithmic methods (solvers) are available to solve it. Solvers can assess a large number of possible solutions to a problem. The solution that best meets the objectives is called the *optimal design*. The process of solving can be intuitively understood as the search for the highest peaks (when maximizing) or lowest valleys (when minimizing) in a vast landscape of solutions.

Optimization offers a rigorous and actionable formal definition of what design *is*. A *design task* is an optimization task that consists of three elements:

Design space: Also called search space or candidate space, it is a defined set of alternative designs to be considered. The design space is defined by a set of *decision variables* (e.g., the *x* coordinate of the "Cancel" button) with limited ranges.

Objective function: This defines what a "good" or "desirable" design is. In practice, it maps a design candidate from the design space to an *objective score* that quantifies its goodness.

Task instance: This defines task-specific variables (e.g., which menu commands must be included in a menu system).

Formally, optimization in HCI can be defined as the search for a design vector in a design space that maximizes the objective function:

$$\text{Find } \boldsymbol{x} = \begin{pmatrix} x_1 \\ x_2 \\ \vdots \\ x_n \end{pmatrix} \in \boldsymbol{X}, \text{which maximizes } f_\theta(\boldsymbol{x}),$$

where:

- $\boldsymbol{x}$ is an *n*-dimensional *design vector* with each dimension describing a *design variable*;
- $\boldsymbol{X}$ is the set of *candidate designs*;
- f is the *objective function*;
- $\boldsymbol{\theta}$ is a set of parameters defining the *task instance*.

The first benefit of this approach for engineering is that defining a design space in this way allows for examining its size and structure. When we do this for design problems in HCI, we quickly realize that HCI design problems can be very large. For example, for *n* functions, there are $2^n - 1$ ways to combine them in an application; for only 50 functions, this means 1, 125, 899, 906, 842, 623 possibilities. Combinatorics can be used to analyze the size of problems.

Another benefit is that optimization provides methods to quantify how certain we are that our design is good. In optimization, a design is considered the *global optimum* when it achieves the highest possible objective score in the whole design space. This can be guaranteed by methods such as exhaustive search and so-called exact methods (e.g., integer programming). When we cannot use those methods, for example, because of the complexity of the objective function, we may relax global optimality. A design is *approximately optimum* when its objective value is within some margin of the optimal design or when there is a good chance that only marginally better designs exist. Most of the methods we use in HCI can only offer approximately optimum solutions. To sum up, to say that a design is optimal is to say that in the defined set of candidate designs, there is no better design; the global optimum has been identified. In practice, the term "optimal" is overused and misused. To claim that a design is optimal, one must answer the following questions: (1) The best out of which options? (design space) (2) The best for what? (design objectives and task instance) (3) The best with what guarantees? (search method)

In comparison to formal methods in HCI such as logic or state machines, optimization offers an effective yet flexible way of expressing design knowledge and objectives in a computationally approachable manner. Compared to data-driven approaches such as artificial neural networks, optimization retains direct control of the assumptions in design, in particular via the definition of the design objectives. Furthermore, optimization does not depend on one's ability to obtain a large training set, although its input parameters can be learned from datasets using machine learning methods if needed. On the negative side, formalizing an optimization task requires careful analysis of the main factors in play in a domain.

One outstanding problem with optimization is how to allow designers to apply it in their practice. The main issue is that designers are rarely able to express their problem at the level of precision required to define an optimization task. The "one-shot" paradigm of optimization is often impractical. In design practice, problems are ill-defined and designers continuously learn and update the problem definition and the design space (Chapter 32). Optimizer-in-the-loop methods can help designers address this problem. For instance, using interactive design tools, designers may explore designs, compare them, and find rationales for them.

39.3.1 **Example: The assignment problem**

The assignment problem is the most widely studied class of optimization problems in HCI research. The task is to find a one-to-one correspondence between n items (e.g., letters) and n locations (e.g., key slots) such that the total cost of the assignment is minimized. A valid assignment x can be defined formally such that each item is assigned to exactly one location and each location has exactly one item.

In the linear variant of the assignment problem, the objective function is a linear function:

$$\sum_{i,k} c_{ik} x_{ik}. \tag{39.7}$$

Here, x_{ik} represents the assignment of letter i to slot k, and c_{ik} is the cost of the assignment.

Modern solvers can find the optimum solution efficiently. However, in many HCI applications of the assignment problem, we need to account for interactions among items and locations. These require adding a quadratic term of the form

$$\sum_{i,j,k,\ell} c_{ijk\ell} x_{ik} x_{j\ell} \tag{39.8}$$

to the objective function. Here, we need to consider all pairwise assignments x_{ik} and $x_{j\ell}$. For example, the cost can be the time cost of moving the finger from one key to another key when typing typical bigrams or phrases in a language. In this case, c is the probability of that transition in language multiplied by the time cost. In Chapter 4, we provided several motor control models, such as Fitts' law, which can predict this time as a function of the movement distance and target size.

This quadratic formulation is flexible. More objectives can be combined into the cost term c, and they can be individually weighted against each other. For example, Feit et al. [239] used this formulation to help design the AZERTY French keyboard standard (Figure 39.9). They optimized the assignment of special characters against four objectives related to performance, intuitiveness,

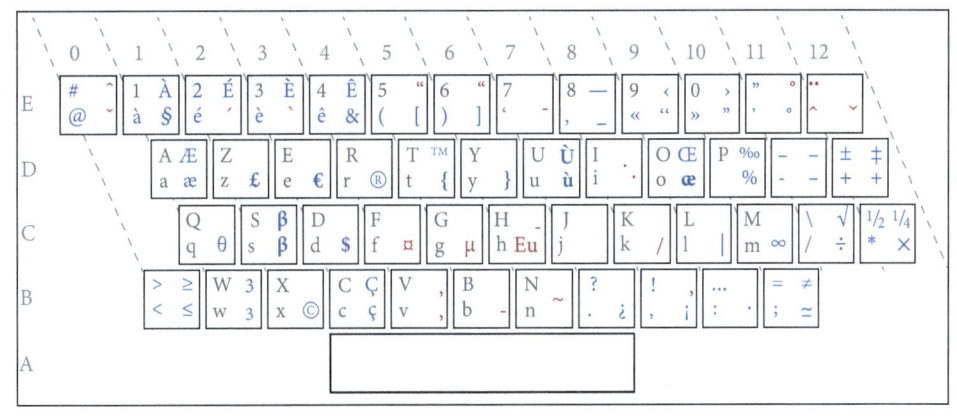

Figure 39.9 The new AZERTY standard was designed with the help of multi-objective optimization [239].

learnability, and ergonomics. The objectives were based on HCI research and models of data collected specifically for this study.

Examples of assignment problems beyond keyboards are the linear and grid menu problems. Given a set of commands and positions, the goal is to assign the commands to positions in the menu. An example application is given in Paper Example 39.3.1.

Paper Example 39.3.1: Adapting mixed reality display locations with optimization

In mixed reality interaction, information displays need to be placed such that they are reachable and visible to the user. Moreover, they should not obstruct virtual or physical objects of interest. How do we achieve this without writing a handcrafted rule set?

Belo and colleagues [234] presented an optimization-based approach to adapting information displays while considering the geometric relationship between the user and the environment. They defined an optimization task with weights for user-defined objectives. In this case, the objective function is a weighted sum of several objective terms, including reachability, visibility, and occlusion. These objectives control where in the 3D space a display is positioned in relation to the user's current position, as shown in the following figure.

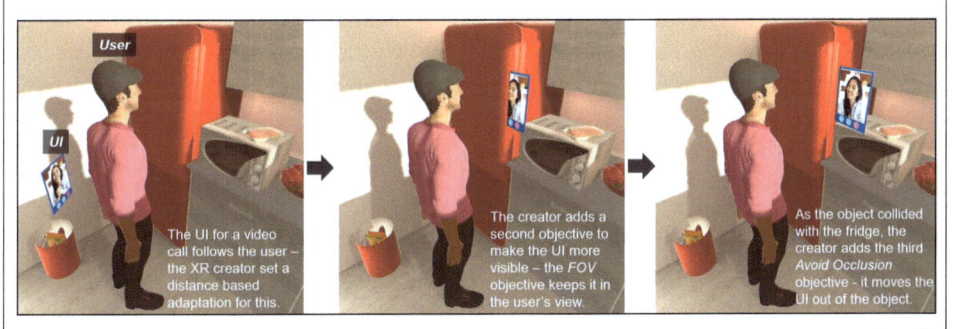

continued

> **Paper Example 39.3.1: Adapting mixed reality display locations with optimization** (continued)
>
> Moreover, end-users and developers can determine the applied weights.
>
> Here, the task instance is defined by the current positions of the display and the user in the environment. Simulated annealing was used to solve the resulting optimization problem in real time.

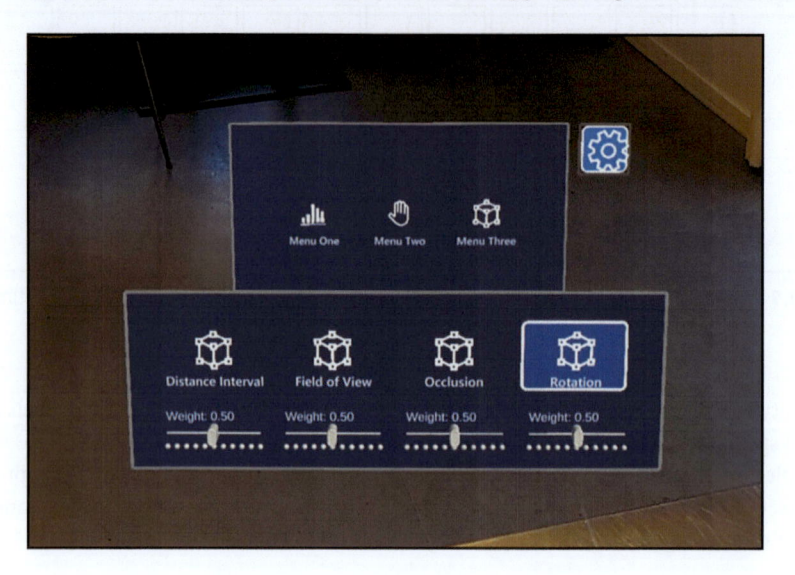

39.4 Machine learning and pattern recognition

Machine learning is fundamentally about computer programs that do not need to be fully prespecified and that learn from data. That is, a programmer does not need to code the precise behavior of the system, which learns how to make decisions, for example, by observing training data.

In general, a machine learning system extracts *features* from domain objects, that is, the objects we wish to process, such as photographs we wish to classify. These features are then fed into a *model* trained by a *learning algorithm*. The *model* provides some output. In other words, machine learning involves the model taking data as input and providing output in the form of, for example, classification decisions. The *learning problem* is to come up with a learning algorithm that can take training data as input and provide a model as output. Machine learning tasks are solved by using the right features to build the right models. Learning problems are solved by learning algorithms that produce models.

Machine learning can be used for several tasks:

Classification: This means learning a classifier that can assign a label to data points, called feature vectors, that it has not seen before. A special case is *binary classification*, where we only consider two classes, such as classifying something as either true or false.

Regression: This means learning a real-valued function from training examples labeled with the true function values. An example of a regression model is linear regression.

Clustering: This means grouping data without having prior knowledge about the groups.

In addition to these tasks, there are two fundamental classes of machine learning approaches. First, we can learn from labeled training data, such as photographs that are labeled with salient keywords describing the key objects in the photographs. This is called *supervised learning*. Second, we can learn from unlabeled data. This is called *unsupervised learning*. In general, unsupervised learning is a more challenging machine learning problem. However, it can be useful, as it may be difficult to collect a large amount of representative labeled training data.

An important aspect when using machine learning in interactive systems is validation—how do we evaluate machine learning algorithms? Unlike many other technical problems, machine learning problems usually do not have a correct answer. The data are nearly always noisy. For example, training data points can be mislabeled and features can contain errors, which means it does not make sense to perfectly predict the training data, as this would lead to overfitting and a poor ability to generalize.

We therefore need to evaluate machine learning algorithms based on their ability to perform classification, regression, and other tasks. For example, if we count the number of correctly predicted data points and divide it by the total number of data points tested, we obtain a proportion known as *accuracy*.

To avoid overfitting on the training data, and thus a reduced ability to generalize, it is important to split the data into *training* and *test* sets. To improve the robustness of the algorithm, we typically apply the train–test split repeatedly in a process called *cross-validation*. We split the data randomly into k parts of equal size and then use $k - 1$ parts for training and the remaining part for testing. We do this k times (k folds) and use the average test performance, along with other measures of uncertainty such as standard deviation, as an indicator of performance.

Machine learning is a research field in its own right that offers a wide array of approaches. Here, we describe a few fundamental machine learning algorithms to provide an overview of how such models operate.

39.4.1 An example of machine learning: Linear machines

As an example of what machine learning is about, let us consider what is known as a *linear classifier*. This class of machine learning algorithms is also referred to as *linear machines*. We consider what is called *binary classification*, which attempts to classify unknown data points as belonging to one out of two predefined classes.

Linear discriminant functions: If there exists a linear decision boundary separating two classes, the two classes are said to be linearly separable, and we can form a linear decision boundary. This is defined by the equation $\mathbf{w} \cdot \mathbf{x} = t$, where $\mathbf{w}$ is a vector perpendicular to the decision boundary, $\mathbf{x}$ points to an arbitrary point on the decision boundary, and t is the decision threshold.

The vector $\mathbf{w}$ points from the center of mass of the negative examples $\mathbf{n}$ to the center of mass of the positive examples $\mathbf{p}$. Therefore, $\mathbf{w}$ is proportional to $\mathbf{p} - \mathbf{n}$.

By setting the decision threshold appropriately, we can intersect the line from $\mathbf{n}$ to $\mathbf{p}$ at its midpoint. This line is called a *linear discriminant function* in machine learning, and $\mathbf{w}$ is a linear combination of the examples. Figure 39.10 illustrates this idea.

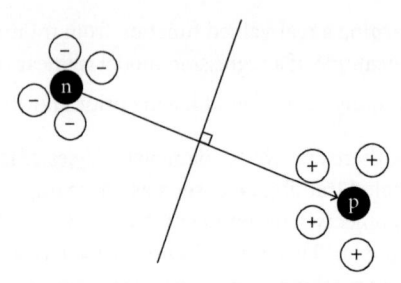

Figure 39.10 An illustration of a linear decision boundary separating positive and negative examples.

Any unknown data point will be classified as a positive example if it is to the right of the line in Figure 39.10 and as a negative example otherwise. This example uses binary classification since it is straightforward to visualize. However, linear discriminant functions can also be used to perform multi-class classification.

A linear classifier based on a linear discriminant function is a simple model that is optimal under certain specific assumptions. When these assumptions do not hold, which is frequently the case, this method performs poorly. An example of its use in HCI is as a machine learning method for allowing a designer to specify pen gestures that can subsequently be classified by the system [718].

Support vector machines: For high-dimensional data, the data space is vast; as a consequence, the examples tend to be much further apart. As linearly separable data do not uniquely indicate a decision boundary in such cases, we face a problem: Which decision boundary should we choose?

The *margin* of a linear classifier is the distance between the decision boundary and the closest instance. The classifier with the largest margin is often preferred. A particularly well-known example of a learning algorithm that attempts to identify such "maximum margins" is the *support vector machine* (SVM). This classification method is popular in HCI applications that require the classification of, for example, sensor data, as an SVM is more robust to noise than a linear discriminant function.

Assume we have some form of distance or scoring function that defines a decision boundary: $\mathbf{w} \cdot \mathbf{x} - t$. Then, a true positive example data point $\mathbf{x}_i$ has the following margin:

$$\mathbf{w} \cdot \mathbf{x}_i - t > 0. \tag{39.9}$$

Moreover, a true negative example data point $\mathbf{x}_j$ has the following margin:

$$-(\mathbf{w} \cdot \mathbf{x}_j) - t < 0. \tag{39.10}$$

For a given training set and decision boundary, let m^+ be the smallest margin of any positive example data point and let m^- be the smallest margin of any negative example data point. Then, the sum of m^+ and m^- is maximized for the maximum margin. Furthermore, since this sum is independent of the decision threshold t, we can adjust t so that m^+ and m^- are equal. Figure 39.11 illustrates a SVM with a decision boundary and a margin separating positive and negative data points.

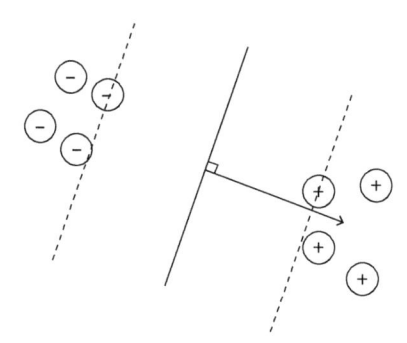

Figure 39.11 An illustration of a support vector machine separating positive and negative examples with a decision boundary (solid line) and a margin (dashed lines).

If the data are not linearly separable, we need to modify our SVM. We can do this by relaxing the constraints when identifying the support vectors by allowing some of the examples to be inside or on the wrong side of the margin. This results in a *soft margin SVM*. The degree to which the margin is allowed to be influenced by this relaxation is controlled by a *complexity parameter*, typically denoted as C, which controls the optimization.

SVMs can generalize beyond linear decision boundaries. This is because SVMs represent a notion of distance between data points, and this distance is represented by a *kernel*. While the default kernel is linear, several other kernels exist. Changing the kernel allows a SVM to find nonlinear decision boundaries in the data space. It is also possible to convert the distance between a data point and the decision boundary to a probability through a process known as calibration.

Paper Example 39.4.1: Interactive machine learning

Interaction with AI can benefit AI system developers as well as end-users. Interactive machine learning [235] is the idea to assist the machine learning algorithm by allowing the designer to rapidly provide the training data to correct errors made by the learning algorithm.

The idea is exemplified by a system that lets designers quickly build a pixel-based image classifier, allowing them to focus on classification problems rather than image processing, algorithm selection, or parameter tuning.

The image in this paper example box illustrates this concept. The user imports images into the system and then performs manual classification. This provides the system with labeled images. The system uses this dataset to train a classifier and provides visual feedback on classification accuracy. The designer can now refine the classifier by providing manual classifications. In the figure, this is illustrated by the system's increasing ability to detect the hand in the image following additional classifications provided by the designer.

continued

Paper Example 39.4.1: Interactive machine learning *(continued)*

39.5 Limits of a model and its applications

The success of a computational method critically rests on a central element—the information contained in its model. However, many situations in HCI can be represented in various ways. Consider the creation of an algorithm that generates a visualization for a provided dataset. This visualization should allow users to quickly understand the key facts in the dataset. To be useful, such a model needs to cover the key factors about the user's task, the dataset, and possibly information about human perception and decision-making. Such information can be represented in many ways—as rules, mathematical models, and neural networks, among many other potential representations. However, how do we know if the *right* information is there? To answer this question, we need to consider the ways in which the model can fail to represent the world.

One way a model can fail is if it does not represent real-world tendencies. For example, the model could fail to represent the way in which the color blue is hard to discern against a dark or red background. A common reason for such failures is that there is simply too much variation in the data. This results in the algorithm being unable to pick up the underlying trends in the data. The term *aleatoric uncertainty* refers to such uncertainty caused by stochasticity.

Another way a model can fail is by lacking knowledge of a relevant factor. This is a much more challenging problem. For example, a visualization algorithm might lack information about the limits of visual attention. Without such knowledge, there is no reason why the algorithm should not attempt to pack all the information in a dataset into a single graph, which would be impossible for a user to comprehend. The model underpinning the algorithm could also fail to contain information about the situations in which its outputs are used. A mobile user, for example, can only distill the gist of a complex dataset due to the small size of the display. Without such knowledge, the algorithm will generate charts that are unusable by a mobile user. The term *epistemic uncertainty* refers to uncertainty caused by a lack of knowledge.

Models can also be biased in the way they capture certain factors. There are two common interpretations of *bias*, statistical bias and ethical bias, which are often confused. *Statistical bias* refers to the misrepresentation of a distribution. For example, the visualization algorithm might favor certain plot types, such as line charts, over others, with no basis in the data. The much harder type of bias to catch is *ethical bias*, which refers to ethically questionable applications of a model's results. For example, our visualization algorithm could, without it "knowing," use labeling or color combinations that some users might find offensive.

HCI research plays a critical—and often underappreciated—role in identifying and rectifying inadequacies of models. For instance, user research can expose requirements that make us realize we need to include additional factors in models. Furthermore, evaluations help us expose biases and uncertainties in models. Such shortcomings may not be visible when examining the algorithmic accuracy alone. Nevertheless, at the end of the day, observations must be applied to the model, either through revised modeling assumptions or by using different datasets. Here, HCI researchers play a critical role in ensuring that the representation is the right one, meaning it represents what it is supposed to represent without bias.

Summary

- Computational methods rely on models that represent aspects of interaction for computation.
- In envelope analysis, we chart the range of behaviors of an interactive system in different conditions.

- In optimization, we search for the best solution to a well-stated design problem.
- In learning, we build a model from data to solve a learning problem, such as a classification problem.

Exercises

1. Feature engineering. Consider an accelerometer as a sensor. You are given the task of designing an input technique using the sensor. When the sensor is lifted quickly, it should trigger an event. What kinds of features would be informative for detecting this action?

2. Optimization. Consider deciding the size of a button using Fitts' law. According to this model, if you minimize the selection time, what happens to the size of the button? Next, consider the more interesting case where you have a screen with two buttons next to each other. The screen has a limited size w_s. You need to optimize the sizes of the two buttons to minimize the expected selection time. What happens to the sizes of the buttons? Next, let us assume that buttons 1 and 2 are accessed with probabilities p_1 and $1 - p_1$, respectively. What happens to the sizes of the buttons?

3. Envelope analysis. This task continues from the previous one. Consider (1) the button size to be a controllable parameter, limited in the way described previously, and (2) the parameter b to be an uncontrollable parameter describing the users. Carry out envelope analysis for the button size, that is, plot the envelope of the button size as a function of b.

4. Computational design. Consider a linear menu with n items. Assume you are given a distribution that tells you the frequency with which the items are selected by users. Formulate the task of ordering the items in the menu. To solve this exercise, we recommend first verbally defining the task and then defining the variables that need to be decided, the objective function, and possible constraints. Hint: This can be formulated as an assignment problem.

5. Developing a gesture recognizer. This task is for students familiar with neural networks. The web page of the book offers a dataset of gestures recorded using a computer vision sensor and a skeleton for a Pytorch-based recognizer. Define the classification problem, a neural network structure, and the loss function. Then, train the network. What would be a sufficient level of accuracy for a real-world application?

Part VIII

Evaluation

40
Introduction to evaluation

Human–computer interaction (HCI) is human-centered. In other words, it takes an interest in the people who use computers. A key challenge is assessing whether an interactive system is or will be "good" for people, work as intended, and not have adverse effects. We must ensure that systems are practical, usable, and accessible and that they can deliver the value envisioned by the designers to the users. In HCI, such assessments are called evaluations. This part of the book describes how to conduct evaluations of interactive systems.

In general, *evaluation* refers to the attribution of value. An evaluation determines whether something is good or bad, or if it fails or is acceptable. To arrive at such a judgment for an interactive system, one must assess a design against *evaluation criteria*—some yardsticks. Evaluation criteria allow us to conclude in some definite way how good a system is.

In the evaluation of a system, the introspective opinions of the developer do not suffice because they are typically not valid estimates of the value offered to end-users. It is unwise, and often ethically untenable, to base an evaluation on self-reflection, as such information is inherently biased and unrepresentative. Evaluations should be systematic so that their results can be trusted, replicated, and scrutinized by others.

Evaluations have played a central role in HCI throughout its history, shedding light on which design solutions work and which ones do not, as illustrated by the following examples:

- Consolvo et al. [165] developed a mobile system to encourage physical activity and discourage a primarily sedentary lifestyle. They evaluated how 12 people used the system in their daily lives for three weeks. This evaluation revealed what physical activities the participants performed and what activities the system could and could not infer.
- Amershi et al. [18] collected 18 guidelines for a successful collaboration between humans and artificial intelligence. They showed how practitioners can use the guidelines to evaluate systems that rely on AI. For instance, the item "Make clear why the system did what it did" helped practitioners identify many cases where systems violated rules.
- Egan et al. [219] used experiments and quantitative measures of usability to improve a system called SuperBook over several iterations. This evaluation helped improve SuperBook from being a reasonable manual to being better than paper manuals. This classic HCI evaluation is detailed in Paper Example 40.0.1.

Evaluation is related to but nevertheless distinct from several concepts we have covered in other parts of this book. User research (Part III) focuses on obtaining concrete insights about *particular* users, their activities, their needs and wants, and the context of use. These insights are not evaluative and are typically collected before anything is designed. By contrast, evaluation is about determining the value of an interactive system for end-users. It is done after at least some degree of implementation of an interactive system has been achieved. In other words, evaluation is about how good an interactive system is, whereas user research is about determining what a good system might be. Somewhat confusingly, some empirical methods can be used for both purposes. Interviews (Chapter 11) may be used to understand users' activities and to evaluate a system; a think-aloud study (Chapter 42) may be used to learn about a user's work and to identify problems with usability. What differs is the *intention* of the researcher in applying the method. Evaluation is also an integral part of several engineering methods that are used in HCI. For instance, Part VII discusses two specific types of evaluation in engineering: verification and validation.

It is worth being clear on *why* we evaluate systems. Evaluation has become part of most models of human-centered system development for several reasons, including the following:

- It is nearly impossible to build optimal systems on the first attempt. Gould and Lewis [285] pointed out that everyone builds a prototype; some evaluate it one or more times, while others simply deliver it to the customer or the marketplace.
- Evaluation is profitable. The literature on the return on investment of evaluations is unequivocal. When money is spent on an evaluation, it is returned many times over [71].
- Evaluation can involve and engage users. Involving stakeholders in the design and evaluation of interactive systems leads to better adoption of the systems and helps maintain a "continuous focus on users and their tasks" [285].
- Early evaluation helps prevent poorly thought-out or developed ideas from being designed and introduced to people. This also saves resources. Computer scientists and engineers often check that the systems store data reliably, do not crash, and give accurate results; however, they rarely consider the user perspective. Early evaluation of usability may, similarly, help prevent failures and disappointments.
- A lack of evaluation can negatively reflect on designers and their organizations. The Association of Computing Machinery's code of ethics states that a computing professional should "strive to achieve high quality in both the processes and products of professional work."[1]

Next, we first discuss in more depth the objectives of evaluation and then turn to the yardsticks that may be used as standards for evaluation. Based on this, we give an overview of evaluation methods and discuss their key characteristics.

---

[1] https://www.acm.org/code-of-ethics.

INTRODUCTION TO EVALUATION | 709

> ### Paper Example 40.0.1: Can computers support reading better than paper?
>
> Throughout the history of HCI, researchers have tried to understand why paper, as a material, is so good for reading and how to create interactive systems that perform better than paper. The work on SuperBook by Egan et al. [219] is an example of an iterative evaluation of a system. SuperBook, a version of which is shown on the left, is a hypertext browsing system that provides access to content about statistics. 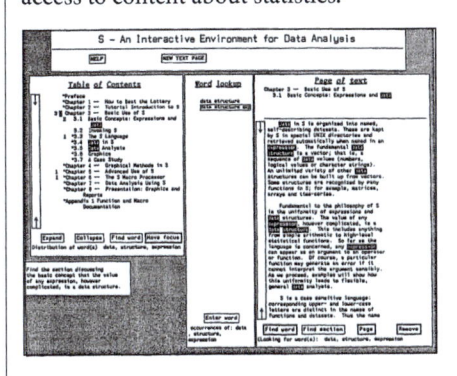 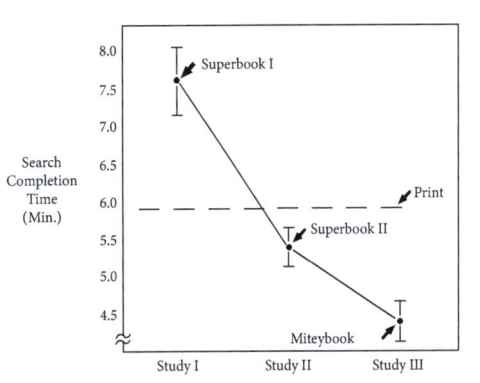
>
> The evaluation of SuperBook consisted of three rounds of iterative software development and evaluation. The evaluations compared searches conducted in SuperBook with those in printed manuals containing the same information for answering a question and writing an essay.
>
> The evaluations revealed three important results. First, as shown in the figure to the right, the first version of SuperBook performed worse on question-answering than the printed manual. People use paper flexibly, and even some of the brightest minds in the HCI field could not make a system that, in one iteration, performed better than the paper baseline. Second, through iterations, careful observations of interaction patterns and usability problems helped to improve the SuperBook system. Third, evaluations can include tasks that challenge users. In one test, participants wrote essays using either the SuperBook or the printed manual. An essay could, for instance, be about comparing three different functions of the statistics system described. Among others, an expert in statistics assessed the essays. This example shows that an evaluation can assess even complex tasks. One benefit of challenging tasks is that they may be effective at teasing out differences among systems.

40.1 Goals of evaluation

Evaluations may be performed for a variety of reasons. In general, those reasons shape what is done in an evaluation, how it is carried out, and how it is interpreted and reported. Therefore, being upfront about the goals of an evaluation helps to make the appropriate choices and plan the evaluation in the best possible way—starting with the *why*.

Table 40.1 How good is system A? How much better is it than system B? This table lists three examples of quantitative goals of a summative usability evaluation adapted from Whiteside et al. [886, p. 799].

Attribute	Measuring concept	Measuring method	Worst case	Planned level	Best case
Initial use	Conferencing task	Number of successful interactions in 30 min	1–2	3–4	8–10
Infrequent use	Task after 1–2 weeks of disuse	% of errors	Equal to product B	50% better	0 errors
Preference over product B	Questionnaire score	Ratio of scores	Same as B		None prefer B

A primary reason for performing an evaluation is to *improve an interactive system*. This is a frequent activity in the practical development of interactive systems. Most software companies have people trained to conduct human-centered evaluations of their software. These evaluations may identify features of the system that unexpectedly do not work well for a particular group of users, a particular task, or a particular use situation. We may then change those features in a future version of the system. Evaluations made for this purpose are called formative because they help shape a system. Formative evaluation is essential in the iterative development of a system because it provides information on what to improve in the upcoming iterations. As an example of improving a system through evaluation, the icons of the Xerox Star computer (early 1980s) were extensively evaluated [69]. Among other things, the evaluation investigated whether users could precisely associate a name with an icon and to what extent they found an icon easy or difficult to "pick out of a crowd." This evaluation helped to choose the set of icons used for the Star.

The other main reason for conducting evaluations is to discover *how well an interactive system performs given some objective*. The goal here is not to inform the design but to ensure the system satisfies the objectives. The objectives may be part of a requirements specification, be included in a contract, or be used to select a system for procurement or establish a superior design. This use of evaluation is often called summative. As an example, Whiteside et al. [888] proposed the establishment of quantitative objectives for different aspects of an interactive system. Table 40.1 shows three examples of such objectives for a conference system. The methods used to investigate the objectives may be of any kind.

Another important goal of evaluation is to *identify system features that work well*. This goal complements the two main evaluation goals discussed previously and can help us confirm whether our expectations of a particular design have been fulfilled. Moreover, pointing out the positive features of a design has been found to be a good way to make stakeholders, such as developers of interactive systems, appreciate the evaluation. As a result, usability reports often list positive findings and whether any non-functional objectives—such as those in Table 40.1—have been met. Evaluations can also teach us about factors outside the evaluation criteria. They may teach us about users and their tasks. For instance, a user in a think-aloud study may react to a task by saying "We do not usually do it that way," which can be important information. In other words, evaluations can provide information that we would normally obtain through user research. An example of a discovery made in an evaluative study is given in Paper Example 40.1.1.

Paper Example 40.1.1: Discovery of cascading error patterns in speech input

Evaluative studies sometimes lead to discoveries. A study is run and an anomaly—some pattern that goes against expectations—is found. Further analysis of process data—measurements of what happened during interactions—may then expose potential causes.

For example, the discovery of cascading errors in speech input was motivated for years by a finding made in 1998. Halverson et al. [309] studied three commercial automatic speech recognition systems from the late 1990s. Although the recognition accuracy was not high at the time, the error type that the authors found remains relevant.

The authors found that the input of speech was not at the level of efficiency of keyboards; even after extensive practice, the user performance was inferior by a large margin. This finding went against the prevailing idea that speech input is "natural" for users. However, speaking to a computer is very different from speaking to another human. In particular, users make very different types of errors.

Investigating this phenomenon, the authors discovered a prevalent type of error: the cascading error. When a speech recognition error occurs, the user tries to fix the error by indicating which word needs to be fixed and then re-dictating the word. However, since the word was incorrectly recognized the first time, it still has a higher-than-average chance of being incorrectly recognized. Moreover, voice commands, such as UNDO to delete a word, can also be misrecognized. Such shortcomings can lead to frustrating episodes where a user tries to fix the same word over and over again in different ways. Even a single episode like this can significantly impact a user's average performance in an evaluative study. The discovery of cascading errors motivated several interaction techniques and speech recognition approaches for addressing this problem.

40.2 Yardsticks of evaluation

Evaluations strive to *attribute value* to an interactive system. Such attribution requires some way of measuring value for end-users. However, to state that something is good in the case of interaction is challenging. What is "good"? If a system is very responsive, does it mean it is usable? It depends. If a user is skilled at using a poorly designed system, does it mean the system is usable for that person? Again, it depends. A defining characteristic of evaluation in HCI is that neither people nor technology can determine the outcome of an evaluation alone, as what is valuable emerges through interactions between people and technology.

The basic question in evaluation, then, is how to set our "yardsticks" against which we evaluate systems. Such yardsticks are typically derived from our view of what a good interaction is (Part V) or from the design objectives of user interfaces (Part V). For instance, an interactive system is only useful if it is usable. Thus, we may use a particular task as a yardstick and assess a system as good if a large percentage of users (say, 80%) can complete the task.

Table 40.2 reports some yardsticks that interactive systems may be evaluated against. Some of these are absolute. For instance, we may assess an interactive system on user satisfaction and use a questionnaire for which we have a standard. Some ways of measuring user satisfaction provide reference values; for example, the System Usability Scale ranges between 0 and 100, with systems

Table 40.2 Examples of yardsticks against which to evaluate interactive systems.

Yardstick	Definition	Example method
No (critical) usability problems	The system does not make the user err, confused, or give up a task	Think-aloud study
Don't make the user think	The system should not "make me think" unnecessarily [440]	Think-aloud study
Comply with guidelines	The system should comply with known characteristics of good systems as captured in the guidelines	Heuristic evaluation
Meet usability goals	The system should meet specified, quantitative goals for non-functional requirements	Summative usability test
Compare favorably to X	The system should be better than some baseline system X on some measure of usability, accessibility, or similar	Experiment
Compatibility with user practices	The system can be adopted, appropriated, and accepted into the everyday life of users	Field study
Reduce cost of maintaining system	Reduce calls to the support center	Deployment study
Safety	The system does not subject anyone to an unacceptable level of risk	Multiple
Meet user requirements	Requirements specified based on user research are met	Multiple

typically scoring around 70 [39]. We may also set a goal for a system so that it is learnable over a certain period of time. Absolute yardsticks may be applied to a single system. Other yardsticks are relative. That is, an interactive system can only be considered valuable in comparison to another system, be it a competitor system, an earlier version of the system, or an alternative user interface. Comparisons are often done via experiments.

To use a yardstick for evaluation, it should be *operationalized*. That means that general constructs (e.g., "no usability problems") need to be turned into a procedure that allows us to measure a system against the yardstick. For example, *usability* is often operationalized as a usability test where selected tasks are given to invited participants and their task completion time, errors, and satisfaction are measured. Error can be measured in many ways, such as inaccurate presses, misconceptions, or entering faulty states in the system. Paper Example 40.2.1 gives an example of operationalizing and evaluating sustainability.

Finally, we need to make *conclusions* based on the data obtained. If a user fails three times out of 10 in completing a task, can the system be considered usable? Many constructs are about good interaction: usability, accessibility, autonomy, awareness, memory load, and many more. We have covered several of these constructs in earlier parts of the book, specifically in Part V.

Note that merely describing a person's interaction with a system does not constitute an evaluation. We may describe which commands people use to interact with a system, in which posture they interact, or with what type of content they engage. However, none of these gives us information about whether the interaction is good or bad. Even something as straightforward as time requires standards. For instance, low time usage may be interpreted as low engagement or as high efficiency [353]. The valuation you make depends on your evaluation standard. However, descriptions may be useful. They may be used to explain and thereby complement evaluative conclusions.

> **Paper Example 40.2.1: Evaluating sustainability**
>
> Yardsticks for evaluation can be complicated to articulate and operationalize. This is because the evaluation may concern any aspect of an interaction. To illustrate this complexity, let us consider how to evaluate whether a system is sustainable.
>
> Sustainability emerged as a topic of interest in HCI around 2007 [78] and it can act as a yardstick for evaluating systems. One such evaluation was done by Preist et al. [675], who were interested in how digital service providers might accurately assess the greenhouse gas emissions associated with particular services. In particular, they were interested in quantifying the amount of greenhouse gas emissions resulting from a year of YouTube use. The evaluation showed that YouTube use in 2016 created greenhouse gas emissions similar to those of Frankfurt or Providence.
>
> Annual Total Energy Consumption (2016-01-01 – 2017-01-01)
>
> [Bar chart showing GWh/a by process: YouTube Servers (~200), Core and Metro Network (~1900), Access Network (~4300), User Devices (~6000), Cellular Mobile Network (~8200)]
>
> People often use YouTube only for audio. In the case where half of the music streaming on YouTube is audio only, it is possible to directly save 6% of the total greenhouse gas emissions. Moreover, the evaluation showed that the infrastructure for streaming content, in particular users' devices and mobile networks, contributed the most to emissions. According to Preist et al. [675], these network costs should be part of the sustainability evaluation of a system.

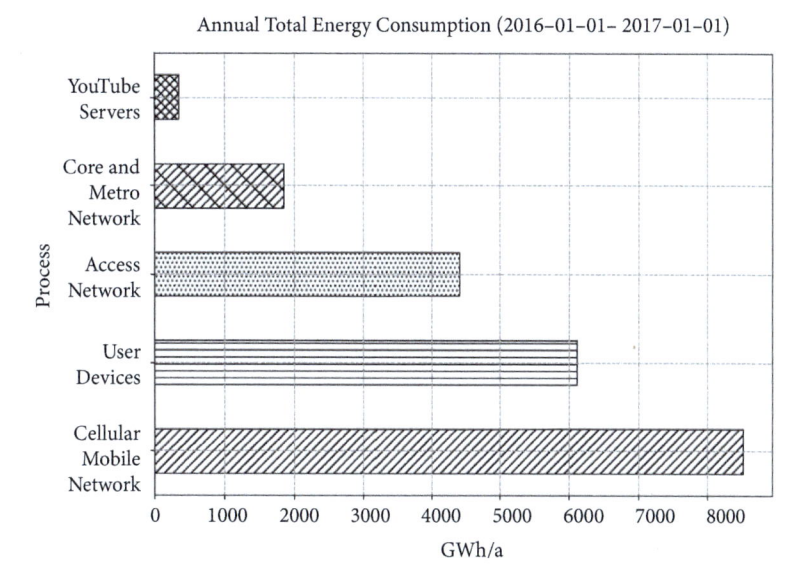

40.3 Evaluation methods

Evaluations are done following established systematic procedures called *evaluation methods*. Evaluation methods contain at least some yardstick for evaluation, a process for performing the evaluation, tools to support the evaluation, and a standardized way of reporting the evaluation. Considerable research has gone into establishing good ways of evaluating systems to provide input for the design of interactive systems that are valid, reliable, and useful.

Table 40.3 Key evaluation methods and their pros and cons.

Method	Definition	Pros	Cons
Heuristic evaluation	An analytic evaluation method in which evaluators go through an interface using a list of features of good user interfaces	Inexpensive, can be used on all representations of a system	False positives
Think-aloud test	Users verbalize what they think about while they solve tasks with an interactive system; the thinking aloud is analyzed to find usability problems	Inexpensive, convincing	Short-term use, difficult to identify and define some problems
Usability test	An evaluation of the usability of an interactive system with representative users doing representative tasks	Direct assessment of usability	Miss the broader context of use
Experiment	An experimental comparison of the usability of at least two user interfaces	High precision, clean comparisons	Limited realism
Deployment study	Measurement of evaluation criteria after deployment with real users	Problems are real	Expensive, may disrupt work

Table 40.3 provides an overview of some key evaluation methods that will be covered in detail in subsequent chapters. These methods differ in a few key ways. In *analytical evaluation methods*, an evaluator compares an interface to guidelines, principles, or theories of good interaction. The assessment of the interface does not involve users. By contrast, in *empirical evaluation methods*, users' interactions with the interactive system form the basis for evaluation.

Another distinction between these methods is whether they are performed in a *laboratory* or in the *field*. Laboratory evaluations are done in vitro, away from the users' context of use. They may therefore be done on interactive systems that are incomplete. The laboratory also allows for experimental control. By contrast, field evaluations are carried out during the actual use of a system. They offer fewer options for control and emphasize realism [532]. Neither approach is superior to the other; each approach simply has different benefits and limitations. For a recap of realism, generalizability, and precision, as well as McGrath's arguments about the fallibility of all methods, see Part III.

Evaluation methods also differ with respect to what *representations of systems* they may be based on. Early representations of systems, including use cases, scenarios, and storyboards, can be evaluated. Paper prototypes, high-fidelity prototypes, and interactive systems that have been used for years may also be evaluated using some methods. Evaluation methods are available for all types of system representations.

40.3.1 Tailoring evaluation methods

Evaluation methods are not generic to all people, activities, technologies, and contexts. They may be tailored to particular instances of those, just as understanding people may provide insights about a specific group of people or a certain domain. For instance, Druin [214] discussed the strengths and challenges of involving 100 children in the testing of interactive systems. She argued that children can offer suggestions on tests that are surprising to adults. However, children must be handled differently from adults during tests. The literature also contains adaptations of evaluation methods for elderly users and people with disabilities [844].

Similarly, we may adopt evaluation approaches that are tailored to specific technologies. Researchers have developed guidelines that fit a range of technologies, including artificial intelligence [18], displays that are distributed in the environment [515], and groupware applications [658].

Evaluation methods can also be tailored to particular activities. For example, the evaluation of games has seen the development of particular heuristics [825] and methods [535]; the evaluation of mobile computing has seen the extensive use of treadmills as a way to emulate the effects of walking on input [63].

While evaluation methods can be tailored for specific users, activities, contexts, or technologies, little is known about how these customized methods perform compared to generic ones.

40.3.2 Choosing an evaluation method

By now, the reader might wonder: Which of all these methods should we use in a given project? Due to the diversity in interactive systems, user goals, and use contexts, there is no silver bullet method. Professional evaluators master a toolbox of methods and tailor them for specific cases. Some of their considerations revolve around the goals of the evaluation relative to the pros and cons of each method. For instance, analytical methods work best for relatively simple designs and assume that experienced evaluators are available. Due to their high false negative rate, they should not be trusted for complex or safety-critical systems. For the novice evaluator, think-aloud testing is often a good choice.

40.3.3 Validity, reliability, and impact

As with user research methods (Part III), evaluation methods raise several fundamental questions about the quality of their output. The *validity* of an evaluation is about whether the evaluation result reflects the real value of the system. For instance, the usability problems predicted by an evaluation should be the real problems of real users doing real tasks; otherwise, the evaluation is invalid.

In general, the results on the validity of different validation methods are mixed. However, a couple of findings stand out. First, analytic evaluation can detect problems that cannot be detected in think-aloud studies. Second, the usability problems found in think-aloud tests might not be severe if the users experiencing them in a test find a workaround that they can apply every time they subsequently face the problem.

The *reliability* of an evaluation refers to whether the evaluation findings would be different if the evaluation were repeated or involved different evaluators. In that case, the trustworthiness of the findings is reduced, and it is unclear if action should be taken on the problems, as they might disappear upon repeating the evaluation. Reliability has been the topic of much work on evaluation methods [e.g., 382, 553]. The Comparative Usability Evaluation studies, for instance, have repeatedly compared the performance of different evaluators or teams of evaluators on the same evaluations and found markedly different usability problems.[2]

---

[2] See more at https://www.dialogdesign.dk/cue-studies/.

Impact is about ensuring that the evaluation results can be used for their purpose, in particular, with regard to formative evaluation. Impactful results will help change systems for the better by being convincing and offering concrete input or ideas on how to solve problems. John and Marks [387] compared the so-called persuasive power of usability evaluation methods. This refers to whether a developer, upon reading a description of a usability problem, actually changes the interactive system. For example, one advantage of usability tests is that they help convince developers that problems are significant. By seeing videos of users struggling, developers might be more easily persuaded that they must fix usability issues within a system.

40.4 Is evaluation needed?

Evaluation requires choosing appropriate yardsticks that best appraise a system against its intended effects. Such yardsticks vary greatly but may include benchmarking against other systems, avoiding usability problems, or increasing subjective satisfaction.

The assumption here is that evaluation, in particular empirical evaluation, is indispensable in HCI research and practice. Several researchers have tried to refine this view. It is worth noting that these voices primarily concern HCI research and not HCI practice.

One example is an essay written for *CHI Fringe*[3] in 2003 titled "The Tyranny of Evaluation" [479]. The essay does not say that evaluation is useless but laments the perceived sentiment (at the time) of top HCI publication venues being reluctant to accept HCI research papers that proposed new ideas and systems without evaluation. The essay argues that it is frequently not possible to carry out sufficiently controlled experiments for the results to be reliable. Therefore, caution is advised, and it is necessary to accept a plurality of ways of appreciating HCI research.

Five years later, a paper by Greenberg and Buxton [290] titled "Usability Evaluation Considered Harmful (Some of the Time)" expanded on the essay. The argument in this paper is that usability evaluations are often carried out without much thought and merely because they are required or because of the idea that evaluation is indispensable in HCI. However, thoughtless evaluations can harm scientific and practical progress. For example, evaluation does not help idea generation; on the contrary, it may undermine it. Evaluation does not help anticipate how people will adopt and adapt technology. Furthermore, visions of future interfaces often necessitate a gradual evolution of imperfect prototypes. Such prototypes, particularly in the early stages of design, are unlikely to perform well in initial "thoughtless" summative evaluations.

Another counterargument to the need for evaluation is the view that interactive systems are objects of design or art [352]. Their value is derived from the artist's or designer's vision and intuition; therefore, it is unnecessary to evaluate them using the traditional means. This view essentially means that the designer gives up on being human-centered.

In summary, interactive systems are complex, and simply assuming that they work as intended by their design is naive. Evaluation is about appraising whether a design meets its objectives. Evaluation is essential for the development of human-centered technology and indispensable for HCI research. There are cases where HCI-focused evaluation is not possible or

---

[3] CHI Fringe was a special ad hoc track at the largest HCI conference, CHI 2003. The first year, the track was rather informal, and contributions were simply made available on individual authors' web sites. Later, CHI Fringe became a formal track at CHI referred to as alt.chi.

needed. Nevertheless, the evidence provided should be proportional to the claims made. Whenever our design intends to have an effect on users, we should try to validate its effects via evaluation.

Empirical evaluation is one way to do that, but, as we learn in this part, it is not the only way. However, if the objectives are not human-centered but rather centered on technology or economic considerations, the methods covered in this part may not be relevant. For example, if your work focuses on reducing the rendering latency on a virtual reality headset, technical measurements may suffice, provided that other aspects affecting the user experience are not changed. Yet, we believe that the difficulty and fallibility of evaluation should not discourage one from pursuing it.

Summary

- Evaluation is necessary because systems are never perfect and because of the complexity of people, their activities, and the physical, social, and organizational contexts of use.
- Evaluation methods have different strengths and weaknesses, and they may be tailored to specific technologies and user groups.
- Validity, reliability, and impact are key concerns in evaluation.

41
Analytical evaluation methods

Most evaluation methods we will discuss in this part are *empirical*; that is, their primary sources of data are measurements and observations of real people. Although empirical methods offer the gold standard for evaluation, they are labor-intensive, costly, and at times ethically problematic. Evaluators therefore started to wonder if it would be possible to evaluate a design pre-empirically, that is, without involving users.

Analytic evaluation methods in human–computer interaction (HCI) are a class of evaluation methods that do not require the collection of data on (real) users. Their purpose is to assess the usability of a design and expose probable errors based on good questions, rules of thumb, or models of performance prediction with a user interface (UI). Generally, analytical methods consist of (1) a process for performing the evaluation and (2) a set of resources to be used in the process. The resources help the evaluator predict what problems a user might encounter when using an interactive system, which parts of a UI to focus on, or what the users' performance with the system might be. Importantly, some of these resources serve as a yardstick against which to compare a UI or a design.

The main idea of an analytic method is simple to demonstrate. Consider the task of sending a message using your messaging app. First, take your mobile phone and open the messaging application. Choose a recipient and the message you would like to send. Then, execute this task. As you do this, write down on paper all the steps you needed to take: clicking, touching, scrolling, searching, deciding, and so on. Now, repeat the sequence, but this time *purposefully introduce one error* somewhere in the sequence. For example, you could press the wrong button when you are supposed to send the message. What happened? Did the interface try to prevent you from making an error, for example, by disabling that button? Did it inform you that there is an error? Did you easily recognize that you had made a mistake? If so, did the design help you recover from that error? These considerations exemplify the *heuristic evaluation guideline* called "Help users recognize, diagnose, and recover from errors"; see Section 41.1 for a comprehensive set of heuristics. Heuristic evaluation is one of the lightest-weight analytic methods, meaning that it is inexpensive and can be applied at all times throughout development.

Heuristics are *rules of thumb* that are often expressed as guidelines. They are imperatives that instruct how to design and how not to design, for example, *strive for consistency* [771]. HCI has a long history with guidelines, which have been developed for almost every interface technology, from computer terminals in the 1970s to AI systems in the 2020s. All major organizations have their design guidelines and associated design systems.

But where do guidelines come from? Guidelines, as all analytical methods discussed in this chapter, are inspired by either the experience of professionals working in the field or theories of cognition. Most design guidelines are based on expert experience. They summarize what works and what does not. Johnson [390] is a recent example of attempts to rethink guidelines from the cognition point of view. Johnson argued that proper rationale should be given for the guidelines.

Table 41.1 Practical design guidelines rooted in human cognition. Adapted from Johnson [390].

Guideline	Cognitive factor	Example
Design for a biased perception	Perception is biased by experience and goals	Placing the "OK" button in an unfamiliar place may make users not see it
Design for figure/ground perception	Perception evolved to see structure in environment	Structure information into wholes using visual cues such as proximity, closure, and common area
Design for easy scanning of text	A visual hierarchy (e.g., headings, bulleted lists, tables) helps form structure	Instead of writing out a paragraph of text, show it as a heading and a bulleted list of steps or points
Design for limited memory	Human working memory is limited and easily distracted	Avoid moded designs where the effects of input depend on the state of the interface, as the mode can be forgotten by the user
Design for goal-driven attention	Attention is biased toward goal-relevant items in an interface	Present task-relevant information in a way and position that align with the user's ongoing task
Design for recognition, avoid insisting on recall	Recognizing stimuli is faster and less error-prone than actively recalling facts	Show options from which users can choose (e.g., icons, images) rather than requiring them to recall names (e.g., login names, passwords)
Design for goal-driven attention	Attention is biased toward goal-relevant items in an interface	Present task-relevant information in a way and position that align with the user's ongoing task
Design for the right level of skill	Frequency, regularity, and the type of practice affect the level of skill that can be expected from the user	Use consistent terminology and labels throughout the user interface
Design for slips	A wrong routine can be incorrectly executed if the visual environment bears similarity with the right one	If a rare interaction has risks, make it visually dissimilar from routine ones

Many of them are directly rooted in an understanding of human cognition. Table 41.1 lists some guidelines based on Johnson's book *Designing with the Mind in Mind*.

Analytical evaluation methods are commonly used for three purposes [31]:

1. In design, they are used to identify potential usability problems so that they can be rectified in design before deployment; this is a form of formative evaluation. For example, Langevin et al. [456] developed a heuristic evaluation method for conversational agents. The method can be used to identify potential usability problems of a prototype design. The heuristic set expands that of Nielsen and Molich [593], which has been popular in the evaluation of graphical user interfaces (GUIs); see Section 41.1.

2. In evaluation, they are used to assess usability against a baseline design or assess how ready a design is for deployment; these may be formative or summative evaluations. For example, a cognitive walkthrough can be used to assess whether users face problems in learning to use

a new system. Information systems for nurses, for example, often need to work intuitively. In an empirical study [238], five expert assessors evaluated a nursing information system. They identified 24 unique usability problems. The authors argued that by fixing some of the most critical issues, the learning time and cognitive load experienced by nurses could be reduced.

3. In accident investigation, they are used to identify factors that can increase the likelihood of accidents. Human error analysis, for example, is used in accident analysis in aviation [889].

Analytic methods are appealing because of their cost-efficiency: The savings can be remarkable compared to an empirical study. Unlike other forms of evaluation, such as think-aloud studies (Chapter 42), analytic evaluations are relatively quick to perform. The cost of an analytical evaluation primarily consists of the evaluators' salaries since not anyone can perform such evaluations. For high-quality evaluations, evaluators need to be trained in the methods. The higher the expertise, the better the results. Analytic methods can also be used on all types of representations of designs, from a system in use to an early mock-up of a design idea. Finally, analytic evaluation methods can help identify solutions to a problem. If a heuristic such as "Help users recognize, diagnose, and recover from errors" is breached, it may trigger ideas on how to fix the situation.

However, analytical evaluation methods are not a replacement for empirical studies. Compared to empirical studies, analytic methods tend to have high rates of false positives and false negatives. Cockton and Woolrych [160] found that 65% of the predictions from a heuristic evaluation were incorrect; Hvannberg et al. [368] found that 62% of the problems could not be detected in a usability test.

A common cause for the low hit rate is that their successful application heavily depends on the skill of the evaluator. If two evaluators were to perform the same analysis for the same case, their results might be different. In other words, *inter-evaluator agreement* tends to be low, leaving analytic evaluation methods vulnerable to the evaluator effect (Chapter 42). The limited scope of analytic methods is another threat to validity. Analytic methods pertain to a few predefined aspects of usability. Analytic evaluation methods do not reliably capture phenomena within their scope, and they never capture those outside their scope. For these reasons, analytical methods are not a replacement for empirical evaluations. They are best seen as complementary. When applied correctly, analytic methods decrease the cost of iterative design and increase its chances of success.

In the rest of this chapter, we look at five different approaches to analytic evaluation:

1. Heuristic evaluations, which capture theories and practitioners' experiences of what causes problems in interaction
2. HEI method, which is used to identify the potential for human error
3. Cognitive walkthrough, which builds on a theory of human cognition to propose how to evaluate the learnability of a design
4. Keystroke-level modeling (KLM), which is a simple mathematical model of experienced users' performance that predicts users' task completion time
5. Automated usability evaluation, where a yardstick for UIs is applied automatically to interactive systems.

> **Paper Example 41.0.1: Analytic evaluation for inclusiveness**
>
> Analytic methods are cost-efficient methods often considered to be limited to usability. However, plenty of methods have been developed for other factors that are important in HCI, including inclusiveness. How could one evaluate if a design is inclusive?
>
> GenderMag, which is short for Gender Inclusiveness Magnifier [111], is an evaluation method created to investigate the inclusiveness of an interactive system. The idea is to combine personas (Chapter 15) with walkthroughs, which we discuss later in this chapter.
>
> The method includes three customizable personas: Abi, Patricia/Patrick, and Tim. While Abi and Tim represent deliberately gendered personalities, Patricia/Patrick is decidedly neutral in those aspects and stronger in other facets (e.g., learning style). All three personas have five facets describing them in more detail: motivation, computing self-efficacy, risk attitude, information processing style, and learning. Self-efficacy here refers to beliefs about one's ability to complete computing tasks successfully. The evaluator starts by filling in these characteristics in light of user research data. They also walk through likely actions and relate them to the personas. In all steps, the evaluator can identify problems with the interactive systems.
>
> An evaluative study of GenderMag reported a high positive rate in predicting a software's inclusiveness.
>
> InclusiveMag is a generalization of GenderMag that considers not only gender but also eight diversity dimensions [536].

41.1 Heuristic evaluation

The term *heuristic* refers to a loosely defined rule, such as a rule of thumb. For example, if you love cooking, you may know a heuristic for checking whether an egg is fresh. If you place an egg in water and it floats instead of sinking to the bottom, it is likely to be old. In computer science, heuristics are rules for solving computational problems. For example, a useful heuristic in computer science is the following. A list of numbers can be sorted in increasing order by following this rule: "Pick any item: If it is smaller than the one before it, swap the two." If you continue applying this rule, eventually the whole list will be sorted. In HCI, heuristics refer to the best practices identified by practitioners working in the field. They are typically expressed as "dos and don'ts." Applied to a design, they can highlight potential problems in usability.

A *usability evaluation heuristic* is a rule for evaluating a UI. Such heuristics are used to detect probable *usability problems*. In a heuristic analysis of an interface, an *evaluator* is provided with a *set of heuristics* and the interface. A task is used to detect *breaches* of the heuristics; in this case, the heuristics serve as the yardstick for the evaluation. In case of breaches, the inference is that users will experience usability problems in using the system or that the usability of the system will be negatively affected.

Numerous heuristics have been presented for different platforms and uses, from GUIs for games to web pages [710]. The most popular heuristic evaluation method is attributed to work by Molich and Nielsen in the 1990s [554, 593]. They identified that a small set of guidelines covered much ground. The Molich and Nielsen heuristics are as follows.

Visibility of system status: The current state of the system should be visible to the user. A simple example is a progress bar that indicates the progress of a long-term operation (e.g., downloading a large file).

Match between system and the real world: The UI should follow the language and any relevant conventions users are already aware of. If a user has to look up a term to understand it, then usability is reduced.

User control and freedom: Users should be encouraged to explore different ways of achieving their goals in the UI. To allow this, it is important that users can reverse their actions. The ubiquitous *Undo* and *Redo* functions are examples of interface features introduced to support this heuristic.

Consistency and standards: First, UIs should follow standard platform, system, and industry conventions. This is sometimes known as maintaining external consistency. Second, similar interface features should be consistently labeled and visualized throughout the application or system. This is known as internal consistency.

Error prevention: The UI should be designed to prevent errors, for example, by displaying a warning and requiring user confirmation before a non-reversible action is triggered, such as deleting a file.

Recognition rather than recall: It is more difficult for users to recall from memory how to trigger an action than it is to recognize a mechanism for triggering the action shown on the display. Therefore, any information required to trigger common actions, such as labels, buttons, and menu items, should be either immediately visible or easily retrievable.

Flexibility and efficiency of use: Since users inevitably vary in their proficiency with a UI, it is often effective to provide interface features that can be tailored to different users. A simple example is providing keyboard shortcuts for menu items and toolbar buttons that offer an expert user immediate access to these functions, while a novice user can still use direct manipulation to easily locate them (albeit at a slower pace). Another strategy is to allow users to customize the UI or have the UI adapt to the user.

Aesthetic and minimalist design: Ensure that the UI focuses on content and information essential for allowing users to achieve their primary goals. Avoid providing information that is rarely relevant and avoid introducing UI elements that may distract users.

Help users recognize, diagnose, and recover from errors Provide error messages that are understandable by users and offer a clear solution path to rectify the problem.

Help and documentation: If documentation is required, ensure that it is focused on aiding users in their tasks and is easy to search. If possible, present documentation within the context it is required, such as a step requiring the user to make a decision. Any help is best provided by listing the concrete steps necessary for the user to carry out the task.

41.1.1 How to do a heuristic evaluation?

How to do a heuristic evaluation is best learned through an exercise. Take your laptop and open the settings panel of your operating system. Decide on a setting you want to change, such as the way your mouse cursor behaves (its transfer function), and the particular value you want to set it to. Now, go to the starting view, execute the required (i.e., correct) actions to change the setting, and write down all your steps on paper. Then, go through each step and compare it against each heuristic of Molich and Nielsen given previously. What to do with the result? First, count the number of heuristic violations. Is this an acceptable number? Note that counting violations does not tell us much about their real-world relevance. Second, think about the users of the system: What is important to them, and which violations would be harmful to them? Next, classify the violations into three classes of severity: (1) minor, (2) critical, and (3) catastrophic. If you have a single critical violation, you can consider the design to have failed.

Slightly more formally, the resources and methods that evaluators use in a heuristic evaluation are (1) the choice of heuristics and associated training materials, (2) a way of going through parts of the interactive system that is being evaluated, (3) a process for evaluation, and (4) analysis and reporting of the problems identified.

Choice of heuristics

The most common heuristics are the Molich and Nielsen heuristics described in the beginning of this section, which are deemed a safe option. Typically, each of these heuristics is associated with a more extensive explanation or teaching material. For example, the visibility of the system status concerns whether the user knows what an interactive system is currently doing and what it is possible to do with it. For instance, if the CAPS lock key is active, its status can be indicated by a light on it or a "CAPS LOCK ON" text field on a display. A full tutorial for the heuristics is available in Nielsen [591].

Heuristics that are *customized* for a particular use situation or user group can have better hit rates—but how to construct an effective heuristic set? Some heuristic sets are based on an authoritative expert's view: "This works but this doesn't." This is fair—provided the heuristics are empirically validated and their scope is well known, it does not matter where they come from. However, to develop a set of heuristics that better captures consensus in a specific application area, several experts must be involved. This can be done pre hoc with several experts jointly developing heuristics or post hoc by clustering heuristics that experts have already developed. Specialized examples include heuristics for evaluating displays that are distributed in the environment [516], mobile computing [67], and the playability of games [189]. A longer worked example of heuristics developed for interactive AI is given in Paper Example 41.1.1.

Choice of system parts for evaluation

The original instructions for heuristic evaluation were unclear as to which parts of a system to evaluate and how to go through them [161]. As a result, several different approaches have emerged. The evaluator may follow a system scanning approach, that is, the evaluator scans the system, looking for a breach of heuristics. This approach helps cover most of the features of a system. Alternatively, the evaluator may use a set of tasks that are representative of what users may like to do with the interactive system. This helps to keep the evaluation focused on what users likely want to do and uncover dependencies and inconsistencies in a large task. While the choice is up to the evaluator, the task approach is often preferred because it helps keep false positives somewhat better in check.

Which heuristic to consider and when? Some guidelines recommend focusing on one heuristic at a time, as it is relatively easy to scan a system or go through a task while keeping just one heuristic in mind. An alternative is to consider all heuristics at each step of a task or for each feature. Again, the choice is up to the evaluator. The former option has a higher risk of false positives, for example, an evaluator might report a breach of a heuristic because they are focusing on that heuristic; the latter option is harder for the evaluator, who may forget some heuristics.

Process of evaluation

A heuristic evaluation is typically a stand-alone process. It is preferable to use several evaluators who first work individually and then combine and discuss their results together. One reason for this is attention to reliability: As individual evaluators may not spot the same problems, it is useful to combine the work of several evaluators. This is a general approach to improving reliability and is the reason why, for example, a questionnaire may include multiple questions about the same construct (Chapter 13). Another reason is that if the evaluators worked together from the start, they might bias each other to see the same usability problems.

Paper Example 41.1.1: Heuristic evaluation of interactive AI

Heuristic sets can be developed for a given class of technologies. As discussed in the book, this can be done through expert panels and empirical studies. A timely example is heuristics for evaluating systems that use interactive AI. Amershi et al. [19] proposed a list of 18 heuristics:

1. Make clear what the AI system can do
2. Make clear how well it can do what it does
3. Time services based on context
4. Show contextually relevant information
5. Match relevant social norms
6. Mitigate social biases
7. Support efficient invocation
8. Support efficient dismissal
9. Support efficient correction
10. Scope services when in doubt
11. Make clear why the system did what it did
12. Remember recent interactions
13. Learn from user behavior
14. Update and adapt cautiously
15. Encourage granular feedback
16. Convey the consequences of user actions
17. Provide global controls
18. Notify users about changes.

An example is given in the Paper Example figure.

Heuristic evaluation of an autocomplete feature

phone|	
phone **number**	**Violations of Amershi et al.'s AI evaluation heuristics**
phone **number lookup**	Show contextually relevant information
phone	• Suggestions can be irrelevant to task
phone **cases**	Mitigate social biases
phone **repair**	• Suggestions can be inappropriate
phone **lookup**	Support efficient dismissal
phone **number for verizon**	• Must go to settings to turn off
phone**tic alphabet**	Support efficient correction
phone **repair near me**	• No way to correct or edit suggestions
phone **number for comcast**	Make clear why system did what it did
	• Unclear where the suggestions come from

Heuristic evaluation of an autocomplete feature in text entry. Adapted from Amershi et al. [19].

Analysis and reporting of usability problems

Based on the heuristics and the choice of the system, an evaluator makes a list of notes on the problems. The actual work of using the heuristics to identify problems is often called analysis.

Analysis is often underappreciated in usability evaluation [251]. However, because heuristics are just resources that an evaluator judiciously applies, considering and analyzing the potential problems are important steps. Does it seem plausible that a particular potential problem is *actually* a problem? What is the cause of the problem? What could be done, if anything, to resolve the problem? A couple of resources and concepts can help in the analysis of problems.

- Frequency. It is useful for an evaluator to assess how often a problem would occur for prospective users. One commonly used scale separates problems into three categories: rare, occasional, and frequent.
- Severity rating. This expresses, according to the evaluator, how serious a problem is for users. One commonly used rating scale is as follows. (1) Minor: The user is temporarily delayed. (2) Serious: The user is delayed significantly but can eventually complete the task. (3) Catastrophic: Prevents the user from completing a task.
- Persistence. This assessment concerns whether the problem is a one-off occurrence that users will learn to work around or something that will bother them repeatedly.
- Cause. What is the cause or reason for the problem? Even if an issue is pointed out by a heuristic, it may not be clear what in the interactive system is behind the problem. This is an even bigger problem in empirical evaluation (Chapter 42), where mapping users' expressed frustration to issues in the system may be very difficult.
- Redesign suggestion. This asks the evaluator to consider how the interactive system might be redesigned to avoid the problem. Redesigns can help evaluators avoid reporting problems that have no solution. This task also impacts the clarity and usefulness of the problem to other people [354].

The reporting of problems has been shown to be an important step in the analysis of problems. The above items, for instance, can be simultaneously addressed using a structured reporting format, such as that shown in Table 41.2.

41.1.2 Reliability of heuristic evaluation

Heuristic evaluation has a role in the quick assessment of designs; however, it is not a panacea or a replacement for empirical studies. The known benefits and drawbacks of heuristic evaluation include:

- **High efficiency:** Some usability problems can be spotted with little effort and experience.
- **Limited scope:** Heuristics are limited to aspects of usability that can be attributed to visible parts of the UI.
- **High false positive and false negative rates:** Many important problems are not found, and some identified problems are not problems.
- **No guarantees:** The results cannot be trusted to be comprehensive, reliable (due to the large variability), or generalizable (except for obvious usability problems).
- **High variability:** Evaluators, even experienced ones, have drastically varying hit rates.

Table 41.2 Example of a usability problem reporting format.

Description	Difficulty for user	Cause	Frequency	Severity	Solution
"Open report" is hidden	The user needs to search the entire page to find the link	The link is located in a spot that the user might not notice	Frequent: The user will experience this difficulty every time they log in	Serious: The user may struggle to find the link for a while	Move the link "Open report" to the upper-left corner

One core reason for these issues, particularly high variability, is that evaluators are imperfect as "signal detectors." Every time an evaluator inspects some facet of a design, with some probability, some problem is found. However, this can be a false positive or a false negative. In other words, the evaluator may have found an error where there isn't one, or they may have missed an actual error. The more complex the system and the more problems, even obvious ones, the more the evaluators will miss. A statistical analysis illuminates this phenomenon.

From a statistics perspective, an attempt to use a heuristic to detect a violation can be thought of as an *experiment*. It is a trial with two possible outcomes: success or failure. You can think of it as analogous to the tossing of a *biased coin*: A usability problem is either detected (success) or not (failure). In statistics, experiments with two outcomes are called Bernoulli trials. We use Bernoulli trials here to answer a central question in heuristic evaluation: What is the proportion of problems that we expect k evaluators to be able to find?

Number of evaluators

We start with the case of a single usability problem and ask how the number of evaluators k affects the probability of its detection. Let us assume that our k evaluators are imperfect. They can spot a real usability problem with probability $0 \leq p_{DETECT} \leq 1$. We further assume that *if* an evaluator detects a problem, the problem exists. In other words, for simplicity, there are no false positives in this model.

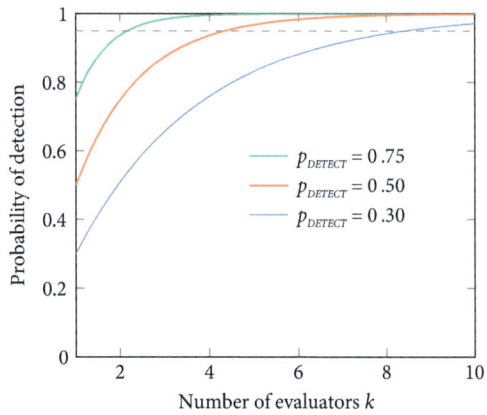

Now, let the random variable **X** denote the number of evaluators needed such that *at least one* detects the usability problem. This follows the Bernoulli distribution $\mathbf{X} \sim B(p)$. In a Bernoulli process, a Bernoulli trial is repeated k times. In this case, we are interested in the occurrence of *any* true positive within that sequence, which is given as $p(\mathbf{X} > 0) = 1.0 - p_{DETECT}^{k}$.

The plot shows that we only need two expert evaluators (red line) to detect a usability problem with high probability (≥ 0.95), increasing to four or more when the evaluators are intermediately skilled (blue). Note that for a novice, such as a computer science student, the detection probability ranges between 7% and 75% [593] and is often around 30%. The black line shows that seven or more novices would be required for reliable detection. In summary, the skill of the evaluator matters.

Coverage of problems

We can now look at the case where we have several usability problems. Let us assume that a system has n usability problems. We ask a group of equally skilled evaluators to evaluate it and assume their individual detection probability is p_{DETECT}.

Let the random variable **X** denote the number of usability problems observed by the evaluators together. The number of problems found in n trials with detection probability p_{DETECT} follows a *binomial distribution*: $\mathbf{X} \sim B(n, p_{DETECT})$. Then, the number of usability problems found is np_{DETECT}.

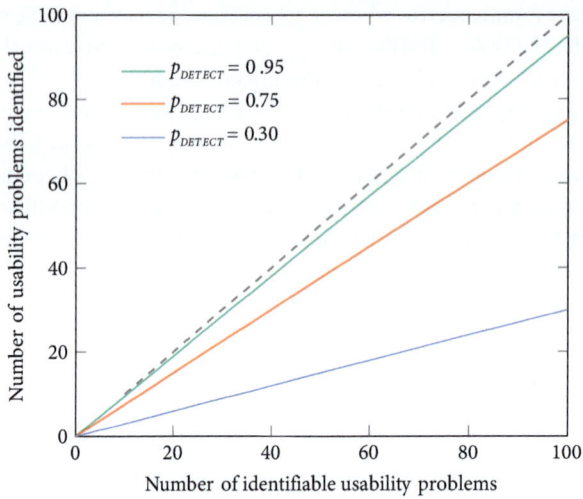

Putting the first and second results together, we learn the following:

1. High coverage of real problems is hard to achieve without experts (red). Only experts provide a high probability of detection.
2. Evaluations by a single evaluator are inherently unreliable. Even an expert evaluator will miss an unacceptably large proportion of "obvious" usability problems (blue).
3. Even a novice evaluator will find *some* usability problems.

These analyses show that heuristic evaluation is not a silver bullet, nor does it replace empirical evaluations. While well-trained experts can detect a nontrivial proportion of true problems, the analyses suggest exercising caution when applying heuristic methods and emphasize the need for rigorous evaluation of the results.

41.2 Identification of human error potential

Human error identification (HEI) is a class of analytic evaluation methods for identifying the possibilities of human error in interaction (see Figure 41.1). Although HEI techniques were originally developed for safety-critical applications, the main idea generalizes to most state-based UIs. It can be used to identify interactions where users might be confused or make a mistake.

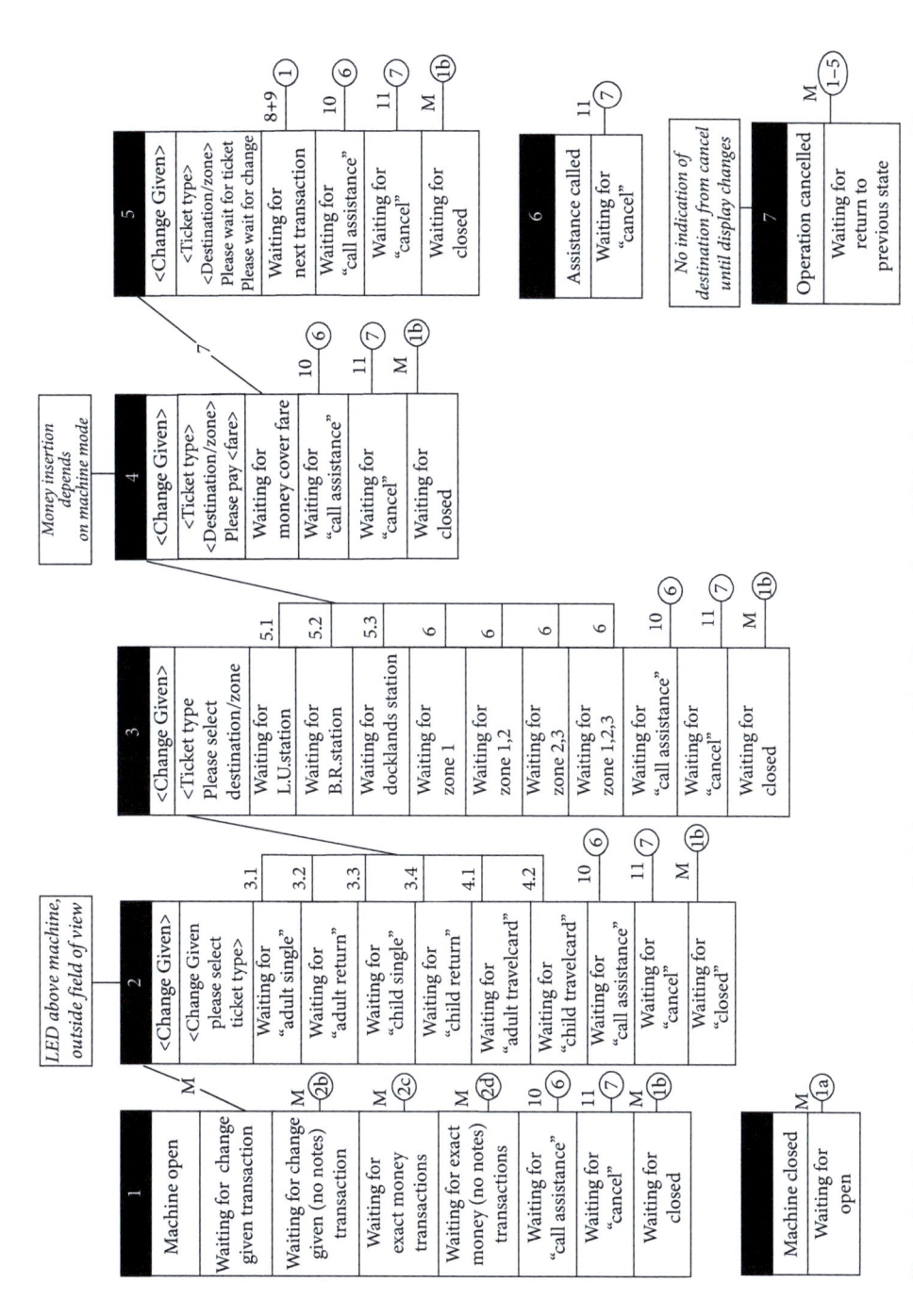

Figure 41.1 Human error identification methods focus on the identification of possibilities for transitioning to wrong states. The diagram shows the possibilities of taking a wrong step in a vending machine operation [31].

One key difference from heuristic evaluation is that HEI is preceded by task analysis (Chapter 15). In practice, this means that the states and goals of an interface are first identified. A user is then "simulated" going through the states toward a goal to investigate what kinds of errors might happen.

Consider a vending machine and the task of buying a soda can. This task is actually quite complex. It consists of several steps, such as finding the desired soda on the list, pressing the button, finding the wallet, finding the credit card, inserting it, entering the PIN, waiting for the soda, and picking it up. The basic idea of HEI is to look at the *transitions* between steps. What can go wrong when moving from one step to another? For example, why would a user not find the credit card or insert it into the wrong place? HEI can reveal possibilities for taking wrong steps.

A central concept in HEI is *state*. At any given time, the interface can be in one state where it is ready to receive input from the user. Some actions are available; others are not. The system communicates its state and possible next actions on its display, for example, via text or graphics.

To utilize HEI, we first enumerate the states of the UI. We then form a matrix showing possible transitions between states. We label each cell to show whether a transition is available: (1) legal, (−1) illegal (erroneous; should not be done by user), and (0) not available.

This state matrix is used as the basis for simulating users. Take a user persona and a particular task for that persona. Then, starting from the state in which the user would encounter the device, enumerate the reasons why the user might take a *wrong action* in that state. HEI suggests three main types of errors, but in principle any cause of error is valid:

1. User confuses the correct action with something else
2. User confuses the state of the machine
3. User selects erroneously.

For each illegal (wrong) action, assess the consequences of that error. What would happen, and how high would the cost be?

Can HEI techniques actually predict errors? To answer this question, Baber and Stanton observed public vending machine use for 24 hours, totaling 300 observations of transactions [31]. They categorized and tabulated the found usability problems; the most common problems concerned money insertion (27%), zone or destination selection (22%), and ticket type or travel card selection (21%). This formed their ground-truth dataset. Independently of these observations, they carried out HEI. Their task analysis diagram identified 11 subtasks, sometimes reaching a depth of three levels of task, reflecting the nontriviality of the machine. Error analysis was performed by taking a state and enumerating all available actions. The transitions caused by these actions were then mapped to other states, forming a matrix. The matrix marks legal (1), illegal (−1), and not available (0) transitions.

Their analysis exposed the following problems with a vending machine, which may be familiar to many of us:

1. Not understanding what to do
2. Selecting wrong ticket
3. Selecting wrong station
4. Selecting wrong zone
5. Problems in inserting money
6. Confusing mode

7. Pressing wrong buttons
8. Using a machine that is closed
9. Confusing return from cancel
10. Use a machine that is waiting.

Comparing these findings with the ground-truth dataset, the authors concluded that one evaluator using the method could identify more than 80% of the real usability problems. This analysis took about 3.5 hours per evaluator, representing significant time savings compared to conducting real-world observations.

41.3 Cognitive walkthrough

Cognitive walkthrough is an analytical evaluation method based on the mental simulation of the way users think (see Figure 41.2). It is an instance of a broader class of *walkthrough methods* used across technical disciplines, for example, architectural walkthroughs in architecture and code walkthroughs in software engineering.

In a cognitive walkthrough, an artifact is inspected systematically and evaluated against some criteria. In this sense, it is similar to HEI. What makes cognitive walkthrough special is that the evaluation criteria are related to thinking and cognition. The method relies on the evaluator *simulating* the interaction *in their mind* to determine whether a user *might* succeed or fail. The user is simulated as guessing and exploring how to use an interface. However, walkthroughs are not just any form of imagery; they follow systematic procedures and conceptual apparatuses.

The goal of a cognitive walkthrough is to expose possible problems impairing the *ease of use and learnability* of a system. The method is recommended for understanding how novice users may learn to use a system. Its scope is different from that of other methods discussed in this chapter, which focus on user performance, errors, and usability problems.

A cognitive walkthrough is straightforward but substantially more laborious than a heuristic evaluation. The inputs to the method are (1) the UI, (2) a task scenario that defines what the users are supposed to accomplish, (3) assumptions about the users and the contexts of use, and (4) a sequence of actions for completing the tasks. Task analysis is needed to prepare point (4). In most cases, the analysis of subtask *sequences* is sufficient.

There is good evidence that cognitive walkthroughs can predict a significant part of learnability-related problems. In the comparative study by Lewis et al. [474], cognitive walkthrough detected 50% of problems exposed in an empirical user study.

41.3.1 How to do a cognitive walkthrough?

In a walkthrough session, tasks are demonstrated to a team in a step-by-step manner, attempting to explain, plausibly, how the user might tackle four issues related to use:

1. Will the user try to achieve the right effect?
2. Will the user notice the availability of the correct action?
3. Will the user associate the correct action with the intended effect?
4. If the correct action is performed, will the user be aware that the task is progressing as intended?

Task: Find hotels in Helsinki

Walkthrough questions
1. Will the user try to achieve the right effect?
2. Will the user notice the availabilty of the correct action?
3. Will the user associate the correct action with the intended effect?
4. If the correct action is carried out, will the user be aware that the task is progressing as intented?

Report
1. Yes, assuming familiarity with the concept of a search box
2. Yes, assuming that the icon is large enough
3. Yes, assuming familiarity with search boxes
4. Yes, the changing of the display will be clear

Figure 41.2 Cognitive walkthrough: Simulating a user solving a task step-by-step.

If a plausible explanation cannot be given, this is recorded as a critical issue. These critical issues are reviewed together with the design team to identify design gaps and set goals for the next design iteration.

41.3.2 A theory of how people learn via exploration

Cognitive walkthrough is rooted in a theory of how people learn interfaces. Informally, it could be called a theory of how people *guess* what to do next. The theory of *cognitive exploration* was proposed by Polson and Lewis [671]. The crux of the theory is this: To complete a task, the user must set a goal relevant to the task and achieve its subgoals by taking the necessary actions. For each subgoal, the user must *select* the right action, *execute* it correctly, and *confirm* that the interaction is progressing as desired.

To solve this, two gulfs must be crossed: the *gulf of evaluation*, or determining the right action for the goal, and the *gulf of execution*, or successfully executing the action and confirming that it was a success (Chapter 18).

According to Polson and Lewis [671], people first establish the *goal structure*, which associates subgoals to the top-level goal. For example, when cooking a pasta dish, the subgoals are related to the acquisition of ingredients, the preparation of the cooking space, familiarization with the recipe, and so on. However, the goal structure may be incomplete. Missing subgoals must be figured out on the go, which puts further emphasis on how well the UI can guide the user.

A key part of the theory concerns the representation of a subgoal. A subgoal is a representation associated with (1) other subgoals, (2) actions, and (3) perceptual cues. Consider the subgoal of turning on a stove. This subgoal is associated with the top-level goal of making tea as well as the previous and following subgoals (e.g., putting the kettle on the stove). It is associated with actions that are needed to accomplish the goal, such as turning a knob. It is also associated with perceptions or cues, such as those of the knob, the stove, and the kettle. According to the theory, these cues activate the representation of the associated goals and actions: Seeing the knob is sufficient to activate the subgoal of turning on the stove. Once the subgoal has been achieved, the representation is deactivated. Thus, a representation can be *activated* and *deactivated* (inhibited) by its associated concept. When interaction flows well, percepts activate the right subgoals, which activate the right actions. When taking the right action, the state changes such that the next subgoal is activated, and so forth. When there are no actions that are highly activated, the user must explore and try something. This inevitably leads to errors. However, the erroneous paths will then be deactivated, and a better goal structure will be learned over time.

One of the benefits of the theory is that it helps to address some issues in design prior to evaluation. Lewis et al. [474] proposed four design tactics for improving guessability:

1. Make the repertory of available actions salient
2. Provide an obvious way to undo actions
3. Offer few alternatives
4. Require as few choices as possible.

A cognitive walkthrough is more time-consuming than a heuristic evaluation, and it typically requires a trained evaluator. Deployment in software teams has been reported to face problems due to time pressure [787]. Similar to heuristic evaluation, the high rate of false negatives in cognitive walkthroughs is a recognized problem. While cognitive walkthrough complements heuristic evaluation, neither method is comprehensive. Cognitive walkthroughs are best used in early, noncritical stages and should be carried out by experienced evaluators.

Several adaptations of the method have been created for various purposes. An overview of cognitive walkthrough variants and extensions is provided by Mahatody et al. [510]. A leaner version has only two questions [787]:

1. Will the users know what to do at this step?
2. If they take the right action, will they know that they did the right thing and are making progress toward their goal?

41.4 Keystroke-level modeling

The KLM is a simple mathematical model used to assess the performance of tasks. In particular, it can predict the *task completion time* of experienced users. KLM was introduced by Card, Moran, and Newell in their 1983 book Psychology of Human–Computer Interaction as a simplified version of operators, methods, and selection rules (GOMS) [129], a more comprehensive model based on a cognitive architecture (Chapter 5).

KLM deals with tasks that have sequential substructures, such as form-filling, text editing, data entry, or setting manipulation. KLM is limited to sequential tasks with clear task boundaries, no parallelisms (e.g., multitasking), and few dependencies between subtasks. By assuming that performance in each subtask is independent of performance in the others, the task completion time can be modeled as the sum of the time spent on the subtasks.

KLM is keystroke-level in the sense that it assumes nothing about higher-order control nor does it assume subtasks influence each other. In other words, behavior is deterministic, going from one subtask to another, and the task completion time is the sum of the time spent on "atomic" responses and actions. There is no learning or memory assumed in the user. Every atomic response takes place regardless of what happened in the past. Although KLM was derived from GOMS, it is not a cognitive model but a performance evaluation model. It does not say anything deep about how the mind works in interaction. Despite being simple, the model works well for UIs that are sequential in nature.

41.4.1 How to do a KLM analysis?

KLM starts with the analysis of the user's task to find the most likely way (or ways) of accomplishing it. This task performance is broken down according to three categories of *operations*: physical, mental, and system. Physical operations refer to actual actions and movements of the user, say, pressing a key or clicking a mouse. Mental operations refer to events such as recalling a command name or verifying that an answer is correct. One system operation is the system response time—the time spent waiting. These operations are counted, and the time spent on each is estimated using guidelines and look-up tables. The task completion time (T) is their linear sum:

$$\begin{aligned} T &= t_K \quad \text{keystroking} \\ &+ t_P \quad \text{pointing} \\ &+ t_H \quad \text{homing} \\ &+ t_D \quad \text{drawing} \\ &+ t_M \quad \text{mental operation} \\ &+ t_R \quad \text{system response.} \end{aligned} \qquad (41.1)$$

These values have been empirically estimated [127]. *Keystroking* is 0.12–1.2 s, 0.28 s for most users, and is affected by the level of expertise. An expert typist has an average keystroke time of 0.12 s, whereas someone with less exposure to keyboards has 1.2 s. *Clicking* a mouse button takes 0.20 s. *Pointing* averages at 1.1 s, although with varying movement distances, should be determined using Fitts' law. *Homing* is the act of moving the hands between the mouse and the keyboard. It takes about 0.4 s. *Mental operations* are in the range of 0.6–1.35 s; the recommended value is 1.2 s. Mental operations are required when initiating a task, making a strategy decision, recalling something from memory (e.g., password), finding something on the screen, thinking about what to do, or verifying the correctness of inputs. The *system response time* varies and must be measured.

KLM includes eight steps [129]:

1. Choose one or many representative task scenarios.
2. Specify the design to the point that keystroke-level actions can be listed for the scenarios.
3. For each scenario, identify the most likely ways users will accomplish the tasks.
4. List the keystroke-level actions and the physical operators involved in doing the task.
5. If necessary, include wait operators for the time when the user is waiting for the system to respond.
6. Insert mental operators for when the user has to stop and think.
7. Look up the standard execution time of each operator.
8. Sum up the execution times of the operators. This is the estimated task completion time.

41.4.2 Worked example

Let us consider a simple example with physical, mental, and system operations. An expert user is editing a document and wants to replace all instances of the word "might" with the word "will." Table 41.3 shows a breakdown of the actions, which can be summarized as follows:

$$\begin{aligned} T &= t_K + t_P + t_H + t_M + t_R \\ &= (0.60 \text{ s} + 0.48 \text{ s} + 3 \times 0.20 \text{ s}) + (3 \times 1.10 \text{ s}) + \\ &\quad (5 \times 0.40 \text{ s}) + (3 \times 1.20 \text{ s}) + 0.50 \text{ s} \\ &= 11.08 \text{ s}. \end{aligned}$$

The analysis reveals that the user spends almost one-quarter of the time just moving the hand between the mouse and the keyboard.

41.4.3 Limits of KLM

In empirical studies, KLM has proven to be effective at predicting the task completion time within a large but acceptable limit of tolerance. In one evaluation, KLM predictions were compared against the performance of 20 expert users [397]. Across six tasks used in the evaluation and UIs, KLM predicted users' performance in four tasks. The average difference between predictions and users' performance was 5.5 s (range: 0.8–13.35 s).

The time spent on system operations can be measured, and the time spent on physical operations can be estimated from observational data. However, how to measure mental operations? Best practices in KLM suggest that it is more important to get the type and number of operations

Table 41.3 Example KLM model of a replace task in text editing.

User action	KLM event	Time (seconds)
Reach for mouse	H: mouse	0.40
Search "Replace"	M: visual search	1.20
Move pointer to "Replace" button	P: menu item	1.10
Click on "Replace" command	K: click	0.20
Home on keyboard	H: keyboard	0.40
Type word to be replaced "might"	K: type	0.60
Reach for mouse	H: mouse	0.40
Point to correct field	P: field	1.10
Click on field	K: click	0.20
Home on keyboard	H: keyboard	0.40
Recall word	M: recall	1.20
Type new word "will"	K: type	0.48
Reach for mouse	H: mouse	0.40
Move pointer on "Replace All"	P: button	1.10
Click on field	K: click	0.20
Wait	R: system	0.50
Verify	M: verify	1.20
	Total	11.08

right than to determine the order in which they occur. Moreover, very different interfaces should not be compared without first identifying suitable values for M. For instance, command-language interfaces and GUIs have different requirements for recall, so using the same constant for both will bias the estimates.

Several criticisms have been leveled at KLM, including the following [619]. First, KLM assumes expert performance—a user who is able to directly use the most efficient strategy and carries out tasks without error. In this respect, it complements cognitive walkthrough, which focuses on how people "guess" what to do. Second, KLM ignores flexibility in human activity. In Chapter 21, we learned about behavioral strategies and how they are adapted to the structure of a task. Full-fledged cognitive models are needed when behavioral adaptation is a defining part of users' performance. Third, KLM ignores the variation in performance. It is known that there are dramatic inter- and intra-individual differences even in the lowest levels of actions, such as button-pressing. KLM collapses that variability into a single-point estimate. If the statistical distributions of KLM operators were known, they could be used to sample value combinations. There have been attempts to collect such distributions for different factors, such as age [279]. Fourth, KLM assumes no parallel activities in the mind, even though multitasking is a pervasive aspect of computer use.

41.5 Automated usability evaluation

In recent decades, much research has attempted to eliminate the need for an evaluator and automate usability evaluation [377]. The core idea of automated usability evaluation is that an evaluation tool encapsulates a yardstick for good interaction. The yardstick may be that an interactive system is accessible, that it is easy to perceive the information on the display, that links are not broken, and so on.

For example, Aalto Interface Metrics [628] takes a web page as input and computes its accessibility, aesthetics, and support for accurate color perception, among other aspects. The evaluator of a web page may use these descriptors to make inferences about how well the web page supports users. As another example, the Web Accessibility Initiative maintains a list of tools that help automatically check accessibility (see https://www.w3.org/WAI/). These tools typically take a web address as input and create a list of possible or likely issues with accessibility. However, their scope is limited compared to HEI, cognitive walkthrough, and KLM.

41.5.1 Interactive modeling workbenches

Computational cognitive models simulate human cognition through the stepwise execution of a program. Generally, computational models are superior to KLM and cognitive walkthroughs due to their ability to simulate cognitive states, strategies, and motor actions. They can provide insights beyond mere task completion times, shedding light on what constitutes successful and failed task performance. Generally, these tools are best suited for modeling skilled users.

However, one obstacle to their use has been that the task procedure must be provided by the researcher. At a minimum, this involves a demonstration of a sequence of actions. Interactive modeling workbenches allow us to specify a procedure by simply demonstrating it on a UI.

For example, *CogTool* is a modeling workbench that uses a version of GOMS for predicting how attention, motor control, and memory work during interaction [279, 388]. After uploading screenshots of the UI, the evaluator can demonstrate a task sequence, which is then simulated.

Comparisons against empirical results suggest a reasonable predictive power. In a study comparing CogTool's predictions against human data in 108 web-based tasks, CogTool's predictions accounted for 63%–82% of the participants' variance in success rate, number of clicks, and error rates [817].

Distract-R is a simulation workbench for multitasking in driving [725]. It uses another model called ACT-R (Adaptive Control of Thought–Rational) with a model of multitasking called threaded cognition. Evaluators can specify a secondary UI (e.g., media player UI), some limited aspects of the driving task (e.g., speed), and user details (e.g., age). Distract-R then computes task completion and lane deviation predictions and provides a video of the simulated driving.

41.6 Which analytical evaluation method to use?

Analytic methods excel at identifying usability problems; however, no serious project should rely *just* on them, especially for critical conclusions on safety, product launch, inclusivity, or accessibility. Analytic methods should be viewed as a powerful and flexible complement to empirical methods.

Which analytic method to use, and when? To understand the relative merits of each method, Blandford et al. [77] conducted one of the most comprehensive comparisons of analytic methods so far. They compared eight methods in the case of a human–robot interaction task. They proposed a few dimensions to consider when picking an analytical method:

Scope: What kinds of usability problems should be found?
Suitability: What type of interaction and user group is in question?
Reliability: What is the minimum reliability that should be achieved?
External validity: How important is the transfer of findings to real use?
Efficiency: How much information is gained per unit of resource use?
Persuasiveness: How to communicate the results in a way that convinces the audience?

Blandford and colleagues concluded that no single analytic method offered superior coverage of problems; rather, each method conquered its own niche in the space of usability problems. Their main conclusions are as follows. First, heuristic evaluation identified a broad range of issues but was most unreliable. The interpretation of the heuristic (e.g., what is "consistent"?) is left to the evaluator, producing high inter-rater variability. On the positive side, the openness of heuristics leaves room for a more qualitative consideration of the causes and consequences of issues, which can be useful for design. Second, cognitive walkthrough complemented other methods by exposing issues related to user misconceptions, consistent with cognitive exploration theory. Surprisingly, it encourages the identification of more issues than those strictly within its scope, making it similar to heuristic evaluation, which is relatively open-ended. Third, cognitive models, especially GOMS and KLM, best support the identification of system-related problems, such as the lack of undo functionality, redundant operators, or long action sequences, as well as some problems in synchronizing users' actions with those of the system. Model-based methods tend to focus on timing information, for example, how long actions or tasks take to complete. This is due to the focus on skilled users and the limited consideration of errors, learning, and behavioral variability.

Summary

- Analytic evaluation relies on expert evaluators systematically going through a design and procedurally checking system responses against some criteria.
- Analytic methods have low reliability when applied outside their scope or by inexperienced evaluators.
- There are analytic methods for covering different aspects of usability, from performance to errors and learnability. Walkthrough methods are being developed to assess the inclusiveness of a design against persona-based criteria.
- Analytic methods are best utilized as cost-efficient complements in early design stages; they are not a replacement for empirical evaluation methods.

Exercises

1. Heuristic evaluation. Pick a simple UI, such as a travel planner, the homepage of a volunteer organization, or a magazine app. Conduct a heuristic evaluation individually and report the identified problems following the format of Table 41.2. While doing the evaluation, note down difficulties, questions, and insecurities about the method.
    Next, answer the following questions and, if possible, discuss your answers with peers who have also done an evaluation of the same interface.
    - What was hard in doing the evaluation and what was easy?
    - If other people have evaluated the same interface, do your evaluations agree? Do the three most critical problems overlap? Why or why not?
    - Given how you and your peers did the evaluation, what are the three main concerns about the validity, reliability, and impact of your evaluation?
    - An open question in research on analytic evaluation methods is whether evaluators see problems and then justify them with a heuristic or whether they use the heuristic actively to identify problems. Which description best fits your work and why?
2. Cognitive walkthrough. Do a cognitive walkthrough of the interface from the previous exercise. Then, answer the same questions as in the previous exercise.
3. KLM. Consider two designs for the same task, for example, two designs for logging into an information system. Conduct a KLM analysis of the two alternatives and compare them. What aspects that might affect task completion time are not covered by the KLM analysis?
4. Designing with analytical models. Take the UI you analyzed in the previous exercise and redesign it to improve the predicted task completion time.
5. Comparison. Consider the cognitive dimensions framework presented in Chapter 27. Is this an analytical evaluation method? Why or why not?
6. Designing with KLM. A smartphone app enables a user to achieve a task through two alternative methods. In the first method, the user must push a button on the screen, navigate to a menu with five choices, and choose the fifth choice. This brings up a Yes/No confirmation dialog box. The user must select Yes. In the second method, the user must hold a physical button down for one second until the system plays a brief audio beep and then speak a command. This results in the system playing a different audio beep to indicate it has commenced

speech recognition, and yet another different audio beep to indicate speech recognition has concluded. Assuming speech recognition has recognized the command, the system uses audio to ask the user for confirmation. Again, the user has to hold a physical button down for one second until the system plays a brief audio beep and then say "Yes."

(a) Carry out a KLM analysis to understand the time durations required to carry out the task using the two methods. Propose any operators necessary and estimate their time durations. Briefly motivate the operators, their estimated time durations, and the operator sequences involved.

(b) Explain the limitations of the KLM analysis carried out in (a) with reference to the following design issues: (i) novice versus expert performance and (ii) the uncertainties inherent in interaction when attempting to carry out the task using the two methods.

(c) An undesired event may occur when the user attempts to carry out the task. This can happen when, upon having to confirm the action, the user indicates "No." Draw a fault tree (Chapter 37) to investigate the possible causes of such an event.

42
Think-aloud studies

Imagine you are to evaluate a computer system and put a prospective user in front of the system with a task they want to accomplish—and then nothing observable happens. Although their eyes might move and their hand approaches the mouse, you can decipher next to nothing about what they are pondering or why they hesitate when interacting. As they finally begin to use the system, they swiftly complete their task in silence. You have learned nothing about what works or does not work in the user interface.

When we evaluate user interfaces, our job would be easy if we had access to what goes on in people's heads as they use the system. We would know what they think about the elements of the user interface, how they match their goals to those elements, how they interpret feedback, and what they feel. The focus of the present chapter is a method—the think-aloud study—that aims to give some form of access to what goes on in people's minds as they use computers.

The think-aloud study consists of a few core steps; depending on the purpose of the test, these may be altered. The evaluator gives the participants a set of *instructions*, typically including specifics on how to think aloud and possible tasks or activities to engage in. The participants then *verbalize* their thinking when they interact with the system under evaluation or immediately afterward. The evaluator *captures* the verbalization and other notable events and then *analyzes* these data to derive insights about the thinking of the participants.

Think-aloud studies are common among practitioners [237]. They are used to identify usability problems in applications (e.g., a user gives up on a task that can be solved and looks for a workaround to complete the task). Examples of human–computer interaction (HCI) applications include:

- Srinivasa Ragavan et al. [790] studied how users understand formulas and cells in spreadsheet applications such as Microsoft Excel. They conducted a think-aloud study of 15 professionals who read others' spreadsheets as part of their work. They found that 40% of time is spent searching for additional information needed to make sense of the spreadsheet. These situations felt overwhelming, and the users often failed. Verbal protocols exposed a pattern that the authors called "over-the-hood" comprehension and "under-the-hood" comprehension. Over-the-hood comprehension is when users examine what is visible on the spreadsheet, such as text, numbers, and charts. Most of this understanding occurred through reading labels, which took place via systematic scanning. In under-the-hood comprehension, the users wanted to understand a formula and needed to seek information about the involved variables. This is complex because variables can refer to other formulas and other cells in complex ways. Sometimes, users needed to recreate information in a spreadsheet to understand it.

- Oh et al. [614] studied AI Mirror, a user interface that tells users how aesthetic their photos are based on a deep neural network model. The mirror provides an aesthetic score between 1 and 10 based on its training data. The authors used a mixed-methods approach where think-aloud protocols were used to understand thinking and experience while using the mirror. The authors found that different users understood the AI method using their group-specific expertise. Users with machine learning expertise used technical concepts such as algorithm, model, and classification to understand the AI. For example, they speculated about the source of the dataset, trying to explain anomalies in the AI's scores. By contrast, participants with a photography background mentioned concepts such as light, composition, and aperture in understanding the scores. The third group, representing the general public, focused on their favorite objects, beautiful landmarks, and landscapes. They did not fully grasp the AI's scores or why it did not always match their views, and they provided limited explanations due to their weak conceptual background.

- Tamas et al. [814] compared residential thermostat designs in Canada to understand how their design affects usability and how that, in turn, affects energy-saving practices. They compared manual, programmable, and smart interfaces using a mixed-methods approach. This included think-aloud protocols collected during task performance. The authors concluded that smart interfaces are significantly more usable than other interfaces. Protocol analysis showed that almost a third of users were confused when attempting to program their programmable thermostats. The programmable thermostat, with its small user interface, is overly complex for residential users who rarely need to interact with it.

Nielsen called think-aloud the "single most important usability engineering method" [591]. However, many uses of think-aloud studies in HCI have nothing to do with usability. For instance, they may be about understanding how users learn an application through the analysis of their verbalization. Therefore, we prefer the more general term think-aloud study. Many more thorough introductions to think-aloud studies exist [e.g., 217, 717].

Next, we cover the basic steps in a think-aloud study, focusing on the effect of instructions, how to analyze think-aloud data, and the pros and cons of the method.

42.1 Understanding thought processes

Think-aloud is grounded in the belief that it provides access to what goes on in people's heads, that is, it helps us understand their thought processes. The key argument for this belief comes from research in psychology, notably the work by Ericsson and Simon [229] on verbal protocols. Verbal protocols refer to the outcome of think-aloud studies—the analysis of what users said based on audio recordings of their verbalizations.

Ericsson and Simon studied think-aloud as a method used across the behavioral sciences to gain insights into thought processes. They focused on *concurrent verbalization*, where thinking aloud occurs during task completion. However, for tasks that last up to 10 seconds, *retrospective verbalization* may also provide valid insights into thought processes. In retrospective verbalization, users are asked to share what they thought after they completed a task.

Ericsson and Simon also distinguished three levels of verbalization:

Level 1: The participants are told to concurrently report what they think about in the same form as their thoughts. This happens, for instance, if participants report verbal information that they are about to enter into a user interface.

Level 2: The participants may transform information that they are considering from a nonverbal form to a verbal form. This could be describing mental imagery.

Level 3: The participants are required to provide explanations, filter information, or relate to information not currently held in working memory (e.g., in retrospective reports).

In Ericsson and Simon's view, only levels 1 and 2 provide valid information about the mental processes of the user, as these levels only ask about information that is currently stored in short-term memory. Level 3 verbalizations significantly change task performance and, consequently, the degree to which such think-aloud data accurately reflect users' thinking. For instance, giving rationales for what you do might improve your performance on a task, even if thinking aloud can slow you down.

This view has limitations because people know much more than they may express in verbalization; that is, think-aloud studies do not provide a complete picture of mental processes. Further, think-aloud studies are reactive; that is, thinking aloud may help or hinder task performance. Nevertheless, think-aloud studies can provide important information on thinking. The limitations of think-aloud have led to a variety of methodological elaborations; we discuss these later in this chapter.

Think-aloud studies have been used in HCI for at least 40 years [473]. As in the broader behavioral sciences, their use in HCI has been to gain insights into what participants think during interaction. For instance, Mack et al. [501] explored how users learn to use text editors (see Paper Example 42.1.1). One widespread use of think-aloud studies in HCI has been to identify usability problems in interactive systems. In this case, participants' thinking aloud is analyzed to find evidence of errors or lack of clarity in a user interface.

Think-aloud studies have many strengths for understanding mental processes. The key strength of the think-aloud study is its *precision* [532]. It allows for a more in-depth and direct analysis of the user's thought processes. It is also a relatively inexpensive form of study because it requires little more than note-taking, recording equipment, or a video link. Although think-aloud data may be analyzed in depth, less thorough analysis can also provide useful, actionable insights from mental processes, or it may help discover usability problems in an interface. Formative think-aloud studies are commonly used in industry.

Think-aloud studies also have a range of limitations. As mentioned, thinking aloud can influence how tasks are performed, the workload experienced during the task, and how quickly tasks are completed. This is particularly the case when participants generate Level 3 verbalizations. Moreover, thinking aloud does not produce a full and complete picture of what participants think: It requires verbalization, some thoughts might be suppressed because of the think-aloud setting, and so on. Thinking aloud has also been shown to be culturally specific, which means that the information it provides might vary due to the cultural background of the participants [153].

Paper Example 42.1.1: Think-aloud and word processing software

An early think-aloud study was born out of an interest in how people learn to use text editing systems [501]. The authors were interested in both specific issues in learning to use two different word processors and general issues and mechanisms around learning to use software.

Ten participants were asked to spend four half-days learning to use either system. The researchers were with the participants during that time to "prompt them to continue verbalizing, but did so nondirectively to avoid suggesting what they should think about" [p. 255]. To aid learning, participants received a self-study manual that covered how to do things with the text editing system.

continued

> ### Paper Example 42.1.1: Think-aloud and word processing software *(continued)*
>
> Below is an example of participants' verbal protocols. One notable thing is that the experimenter (denoted E) asked very uniform and undirected questions to the participant (denoted P). Furthermore, the participant gave verbal reports that are rich and hint at a couple of important mistakes in the editing system.
>
> E: What are you thinking?
>
> P: I'm trying to figure out what [this] exercise is supposed to be [for]—for line advance? [It is] supposed to be an exercise on errors. But am I supposed to be trying to make errors and then move back?
>
> P: (Participant types two lines. At the end of the second line, she types a comma instead of a period and then presses return which positions the cursor at the beginning of an new blank line. Participant notices the typing error.)
>
> P: Oh. I see. So now . . . .
>
> E: What are you thinking?
>
> P: I made a mistake up here. Now if I want to go back, I guess I would . . . (looks in manual for information).
>
> E: What are you looking at? Page 3–4? (Participant says nothing.) What is that telling you?
>
> P: Well, I'm trying to figure out how to go back to correct that mistake. Am I supposed to correct my mistakes yet? Or am I supposed to just not worry about the mistakes? Or . . . I'm going to try to go back.
>
> P: (Participant presses backspace and incurs an error which is signaled by a beep. This is because backspace will not move the cursor beyond the left edge of the screen.)
>
> P: Woo! It didn't like that!
>
> P: (Participant presses correct key to move cursor up to line with typing mistake.)
>
> E: Okay. What did you hit?
>
> P: I pressed (identifies key).
>
> In the analysis of these data, the authors did not code for frequencies of particular problems but rather aimed to be both "clinical and inductive" [p. 258], that is, they tried to infer the causes of the observed problems and learning difficulties. Their approach is inductive in that they tried to generalize across examples. They illustrated a range of situations in which participants have difficulty learning and hence experience frustration and struggle to apply what they learn. They also showed that participants have a hard time using the help system, in part because it is not clear to them what to ask when they encounter a challenge. These observations were instrumental in helping researchers design better help systems, training materials, and user interfaces.

42.2 Instructions and tasks

The instructions for think-aloud studies, including the tasks, strongly influence the results that can be obtained. Let us outline some best practices.

42.2.1 Instructions

The instructions from Ericsson and Simon are to simply prompt users to "keep talking," typically after a fixed duration of silence (e.g., 30 s). Participants should also "think aloud as if you were alone in this room." These instructions have been used extensively in HCI, where they are often referred to as *classic thinking aloud*. These instructions are believed to have minimal influence on the participants.

Alternative instructions have been proposed. Boren and Ramey [87] proposed a variant informed by speech genres. The experimenter should follow the classic variant but also (1) explain that the participant is not the object of the test—the system is, (2) ensure that the participant is the expert and primary speaker, and (3) acknowledge thinking aloud through utterances such as "mm hmm," "yeah," and "ok."

In *relaxed thinking aloud*, more emphasis is placed on explanations and reflections. Although this is not valid according to Ericsson and Simon since it is based on Level 3 verbalizations, the additional information might be useful in HCI. Researchers might ask "What are you trying to achieve?" or "What are you thinking?" The reason is that explanations of interaction are useful, for instance, because they help diagnose usability problems, offer ideas for redesign possibilities, or help to understand the rationale behind a certain interaction.

The different types of instructions for verbalization have different consequences. Hertzum and colleagues [336] investigated the consequences of using different verbalization instructions. They found that relaxed thinking aloud affected visual search behavior, navigation behavior, and mental workload. Therefore, a seemingly minor change in think-aloud instructions can impact interaction significantly; this should be kept in mind when defining think-aloud instructions. It is also important to remember that a think-aloud study is not an interview [333]. Users' actual attempts at doing tasks are the basis for the think-aloud study; thus, the focus is on concrete behavior, and observations of that behavior are invaluable for understanding think-aloud.

Alhadreti and Mayhew [15] compared three think-aloud methods: concurrent, retrospective, and hybrid. The participants were asked to use a library while using one of the three methods. They found that the concurrent method is superior to both the retrospective and the hybrid methods. More usability problems were detected than with the retrospective method. Additionally, concurrent methods are less time-consuming for the evaluator.

42.2.2 Tasks

Tasks are the other main contributors to the validity and variability of the findings of a think-aloud study. Tasks may be selected by the evaluator or, to maximize realism, by the participant. In either case, it is important that tasks be representative of the tasks that users would do. For instance, they may be based on tasks identified in user research (Chapter 15). They may also be open-ended tasks that the users make concrete as part of the test. It is recommended to not use terms that precisely describe functionality, particular options in systems, or help participants express what they want to do in the terminology used in the system. Such practices reduce realism.

Several recommendations and good practices have been proposed to help define and check tasks in think-aloud studies, including the following:

1. The tasks, especially the first few tasks, should be easy. The idea is to help users learn to think aloud rather than struggle with the task. An easy first task also helps remove nervousness about the study situation.
2. The tasks should be central to the users' real or imagined activities.

3. The tasks should be expressed in terms of users' real or imagined activities, not in terms of the system. The latter are called "hidden help" because such tasks help users identify which system features to use to accomplish the task.
4. It should be clearly stated when the task is completed. This allows evaluators to determine if users understand that they are done. If they do not, the system may need to give better feedback.
5. Tasks can be open-ended so that they are in part specified by the user. For instance, rather than asking a user to book a one-person flight from a given city, one could ask about their travel plans and use that information (e.g., the city, the party size) as the basis of the task. This is more realistic and might reveal interesting usability problems when a user's travel requirements are not well supported.

42.3 Analysis

The analysis of think-aloud protocols has a number of steps with implications for reliability. In *preprocessing*, the experimenter cleans the verbal data, transcribes them, and segments them according to the participant, the task, and so on. The transcribed data may be combined with data from other sources, such as video, eye tracking, or logged interactions.

In the *identification* phase, important or interesting aspects of the preprocessed data are identified and possibly classified. The purpose of separating this from transcription is that the interpretation may be made by different people, allowing for the assessment of inter-rater reliability.

This is typically done in one of two ways. In bottom-up analysis, insights are grouped based on their frequency or prominence in the data. For instance, this may be done through affinity diagramming or thematic analysis (Section 11.5.3). In top-down analysis, an existing framework, classification, or set of codes is used. The classification to use is determined by the purpose of the think-aloud study. For example, the User Action Framework has been used to identify usability problems [317]. This framework separates different types of usability problems and helps diagnose the cause of the problem.

Think-aloud studies are commonly used in *usability tests*. The goal is to identify usability problems. A usability problem may be one of three main types (adapted from Jacobsen et al. [382]):

Failure to reach the goal: Examples: The user articulates a goal and cannot succeed in attaining it within three minutes; the user gives up; the user produces a result different from that expected for the task given; the system crashes or reaches a state from which the user cannot recover.

Misunderstandings about the system: Examples: The user knows what the goal is but cannot pick the right action; the user expresses surprise; the user expresses ways to improve the system.

Negative experience: Examples: The user expresses a negative feeling; the user says something is a problem; the user expresses a negative sentiment toward the system.

The focus is then on identifying such problems from the verbal data, synthesizing the types of problems across users, and developing ideas on what to do about the problems. Usability problems are often reported in usability problem lists that separate (1) the problem, (2) its causes, (3) the behavioral consequences for users, and (4) any design changes that can alleviate the problem.

In the *synthesis and implications* phase, the classified think-aloud data are used to draw implications. The implications may be about how to fix problems; while seeing problems is easy, discovering how to solve them can be difficult.

> ### Paper Example 42.3.1: The evaluator effect in think-aloud studies
>
> The *evaluator effect* is the phenomenon where different evaluators find different usability problems. This is the case for both analytic evaluation techniques and think-aloud studies aimed at identifying usability problems (Chapter 41). Fundamentally, this is related to the reliability of usability evaluation.
>
> The evaluator effect was named by Jacobsen et al. [382]. They found that the same evaluators identified markedly different problems. The evaluators were told to look for *usability problems*, defined as occurrences in video recordings with characteristics, such as the user articulates a goal that they cannot reach within three minutes, the user produces a result different from the given task, a system crash, the user mentions there is a problem, and so on.
>
> What was striking about the results by Jacobsen et al. is that the evaluators agreed to a very limited degree. The figure below shows that usability problems (unique problem tokens, or UPTs) were not found by all four evaluators of the system. Only a fifth of the problems were found by all evaluators, and about half of the problems were found by just one evaluator.
>
> | | 1 Evaluator | 2 Evaluators | 3 Evaluators | 4 Evaluators |
> |---|---|---|---|---|
> | Severe UPTs | 8 (22%) | 7 (19%) | 7 (19%) | 15 (41%) |
> | All UPTs | 43 (46%) | 19 (20%) | 12 (13%) | 19 (20%) |
>
> These results cast doubts on the *reliability* of think-aloud studies and evaluations more generally.

42.4 Variations of think-aloud studies

The HCI field has seen many variations of think-aloud studies. Here, we discuss a few variations that offer novel ways of dealing with the limitations of think-aloud.

In *collaborative think-aloud*, multiple users collaborate to use an interactive system. Rather than being instructed to think aloud "as if alone in the room," they simply talk to each other as part of interacting with the technology. Thus, thinking aloud becomes more natural for participants. Sometimes, researchers who adopt this approach use techniques for classifying and making sense of data drawn from studies of conversation. These approaches generally work well for creating unencumbered talking but face validity concerns. This is because they are about explanations and because they reintroduce the aspects of conversation that Ericsson and Simon tried to eliminate. Another variant is *remote usability studies*, where users think aloud away from the evaluator.

42.5 Verbal protocols: A forgotten secret?

Think-aloud methods were covered in virtually all HCI curricula in the 1990s and early 2000s, then they gradually fell out of fashion for an unknown reason. Nevertheless, think-aloud holds a privileged position in the toolbox of evaluators. It remains the best method for obtaining access to what users think and feel during computer use. Unlike other methods, such as questionnaires and analytic methods, it is *open-ended*: It allows users to express themselves without imposing a predefined taxonomy on them.

Fan et al. [237] conducted a survey study of usability professionals in 2020 ($n = 197$). They asked professionals about their practices of using think-aloud as a method. They made a surprising finding regarding the popularity of the method: Most professionals (86%) reported using think-aloud in their usability tests. The main motivation was either to inform design or to inform design *and* measure performance. Concurrent think-aloud was more common (61%) than retrospective think-aloud.

They also found that practices tend not to follow the best practice recommendations of Ericsson and Simon [229]. Most respondents (61%) "almost never" asked their users to practice think-aloud before entering the study. Moreover, practitioners often posed leading prompts to users, such as asking them to talk about their emotions. Improving rigor is an area where easy gains can be made. To this end, the authors concluded with recommendations for think-aloud studies:

1. Practice sessions should be conducted to "warm up" users and get them to verbalize more often.
2. Instructions on what to report should be neutral and not leading.
3. Evaluators should not interrupt the participants during verbalizations.
4. Think-aloud is not limited to lab studies; it can also be done in remote usability tests (e.g., using a remote desktop feature and video conferencing).
5. Improve the efficiency of data analysis to increase the value of think-aloud studies. This can be achieved by developing reusable coding schemes, using machine learning methods for speech recognition, and using interactive tools for labeling.

Finally, it is worth noting that recording think-aloud studies can have an impact on stakeholders. Stakeholders may relate to users when seeing a short video of a user talking aloud about their struggles with usability problems. In this regard, think-aloud studies trump most other evaluation methods.

Summary

- Think-aloud studies provide insights about users' thinking processes and may be used to infer usability problems.
- Think-aloud studies are persuasive and inexpensive, although the evaluator effect suggests their reliability may be low.
- Following best practices increases the cost-efficiency and reliability of the method.

Exercises

1. Task selection for think-aloud studies. Find a selection of tasks made for usability studies and discuss them. The Cooperative Usability Evaluation studies, available at http://www.dialogdesign.dk/CUE.html, contain many examples that are suitable for this exercise.
2. Conducting a think-aloud study. Select a web site, application, or other type of user interface that helps people plan trips. Plan a think-aloud study for the system, focusing on creating a set of suitable tasks and instructions for the participants. Then, conduct the think-aloud study. Reflect on what was hard and what was easy.

3. Comparing approaches. Molich [552] provided an overview of comparative usability studies—a series of studies that compare the results of usability evaluations (including evaluations performed by professionals using think-aloud tests). Pick one of the studies that used think-aloud and compare the variation in one aspect of the planning, running, or analysis of the study. What worked well and what did not work well? What do you think might have impacted the test?

43
Experiments

Imagine that you have developed a new version of a search feature for an operating system. Users can click a magnifying glass icon and type in a search query, and the results would be listed underneath. You are certain about the benefits of the new design; however, you need something to convince other people. What kind of test could show, convincingly, whether users actually like the new feature more than the previous version?

You could ask people to use the new feature and then ask them if they like it. However, that would not help you relate it to the previous search feature; you would not know if the new one is better. You could ask users of the old feature and users of the new feature to rate how much they liked the respective search features and compare those ratings. Yet, even if you found a difference, an inconvenient alternative explanation would be there: Perhaps the difference is due to variation between the two user groups, for example, in the users' experiences or age. You could also seek expert opinion, consulting colleagues and human–computer interaction (HCI) researchers to learn which search feature is best. However, this may be difficult to assess, even for experts. In the worst case, it might turn into a clash of opinions where everything is trumped by the HIPPO—the highest-paid person's opinion [428]. What you need is a method that allows you to firmly attribute an observed difference to the new search feature and nothing else. That method is called an experiment.

An experiment is "a study in which an intervention is introduced to observe its effects" [758, p. 12]; see also Figure 43.1. An experimenter changes something, or intervenes, while keeping everything else the same and observes the effect of the change. The experimenter imposes *a new* condition or constraint. The intervention may be of a variety of kinds; in HCI, it is often a different technology, but it could also be a different kind of training, user group, use situation, or task. An intervention is typically designated as a level of treatment (e.g., a comparison of user interface (UI) designs), a group (e.g., a comparison of two age groups), or a condition (e.g., a comparison of different instructions for users).

The design of experiments boils down to defining an intervention and what is being measured. An *experimental design* associates variables that define the intervention (independent variables) with what is being measured (dependent variables). Something that is systematically varied in an intervention is called an independent variable. Consider, for example, the color of a button or the user's age group as the independent variable. The effects of the intervention are measured using dependent variables that depend on the intervention, for example, the task completion time or the error rate. In HCI, measures are often related to usability or the experience with a technology.

If the relationship between the dependent and independent variables is fully under the experimenter's control, the observed changes in the dependent variables can be entirely attributed to the intervention. In practice, experiments with human participants need to deal with a plethora of *other* factors besides the independent variable. Image a study where users were asked to first carry out task A with a UI and then complete task B. Here, the order of the interventions influences the users' learning. Any measurements in task B would be affected by what users learned in task A. In general, such factors influence the situation under study, and thus potentially affect the dependent variables. Such factors are called *nuisance factors*, as they threaten the attribution of cause to the

Introduction to Human-Computer Interaction. Kasper Hornbæk, Per Ola Kristensson, and Antti Oulasvirta,
Oxford University Press. © Kasper Hornbæk, Per Ola Kristensson, and Antti Oulasvirta (2025).
DOI: 10.1093/oso/9780192864543.003.0043

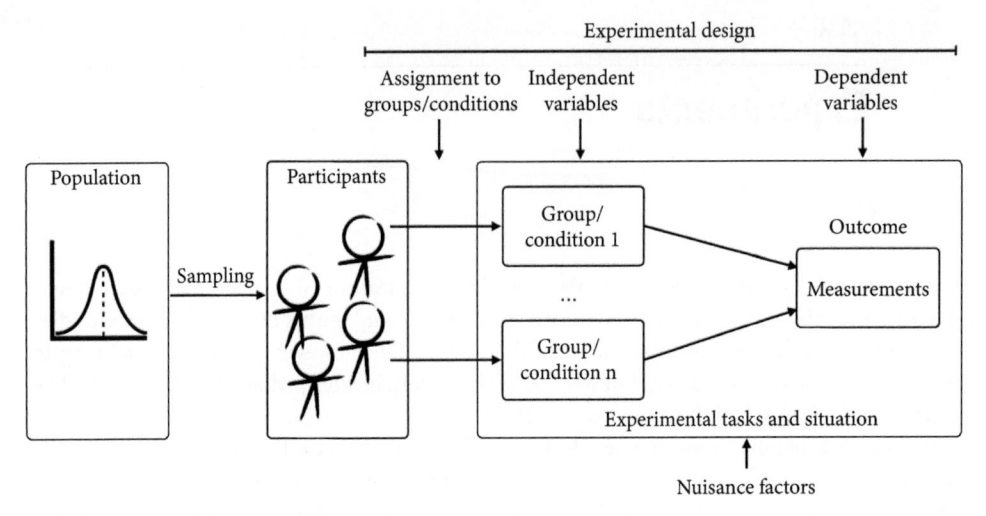

Figure 43.1 The main components of an experiment.

intervention. Was it the task or was it learning that caused the observed difference? Experimental designs have many ways to deal with nuisance factors: controlling such factors, holding them constant, or distributing them randomly across levels of the independent variable. Consider, for example, the effect of study participants having seen an old feature through their work. If we wanted to get rid of that effect, we would talk about controlling it.

Finally, the choice of interventions and measurements must not be arbitrary. *Hypotheses* are statements that connect variation in independent variables with expectations about variation in the dependent variables. Do you expect your new feature to have better usability than the baseline design, and if so, why? Explicating hypotheses is critical for high-quality evaluations. Hypotheses can help us avoid being fooled by observations subject to noise and error, being biased by our intuitions, and second-guessing ourselves.

Note that this definition of experiment excludes some common usages of this word, including "trying something new" and "an innovative act or procedure." In the context of evaluation, experiments are conducted to *establish causal conclusions about which factors influence a situation*. We conduct experiments to rule out alternative explanations besides the factors being manipulated. This chapter focuses on how to enable such conclusions to be drawn, in particular about the use of interactive computing systems. The following sections explain the components of an experiment in detail; Paper Example 43.0.1 summarizes an early and influential experiment in HCI.

Paper Example 43.0.1: Development of an experimental paradigm for evaluating input devices

In 1978, Card et al. [128] reported a now classic experiment with input devices. The study compared the efficiency of different input techniques for selecting text. At that time, such comparisons were rare; the paper was among the first in HCI to report experiments involving a mouse and Fitts' law [507] (Chapter 4).

The authors had five participants use a mouse, a rate-controlled isometric joystick, and two variants of keys; the participants used all four devices. In the experimental task, the participants had to select highlighted text at varying distances (1–16 cm) and sizes (1–10 characters). The participants used each device until their performance no longer improved. They made from 1,200 to 1,800 total selections with each device, equivalent to four to six hours of pointing.

This experimental design allowed Card and colleagues to plot the participants' development in learning to use the device. Their plot, which is shown in the following figure, illustrates the power law of practice: $T_n = T_1 \cdot n^{-a}$, where T_n is the time used at trial n and a is a constant. In a log plot, this is shown as a line whose slope indicates the learning rate.

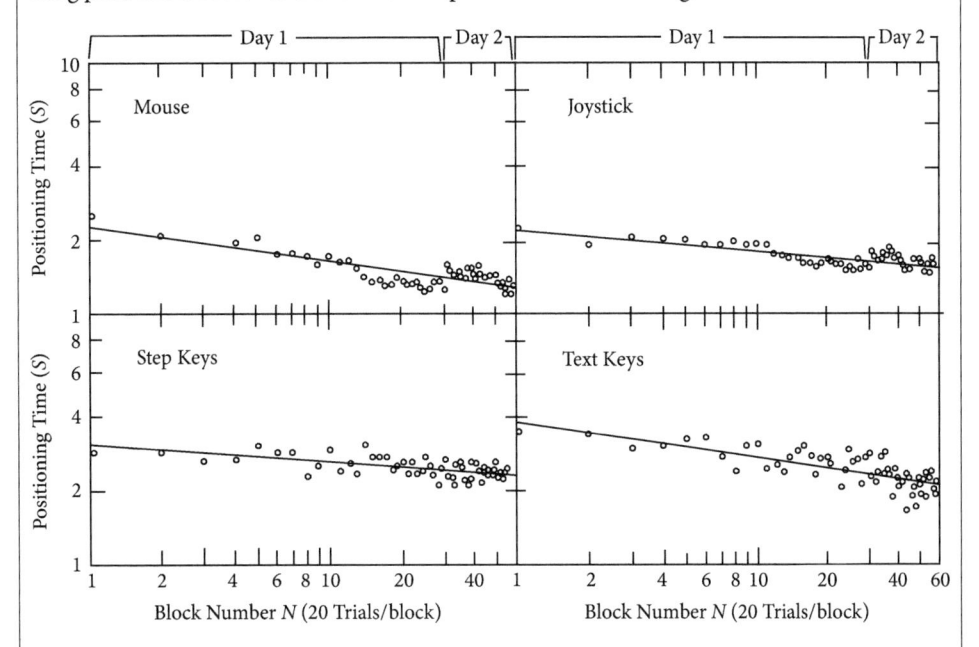

The authors also used the experiment to plot the positioning time (their main dependent variable) against the index of difficulty—a measure combining the size of targets and the distance between them (two independent variables).

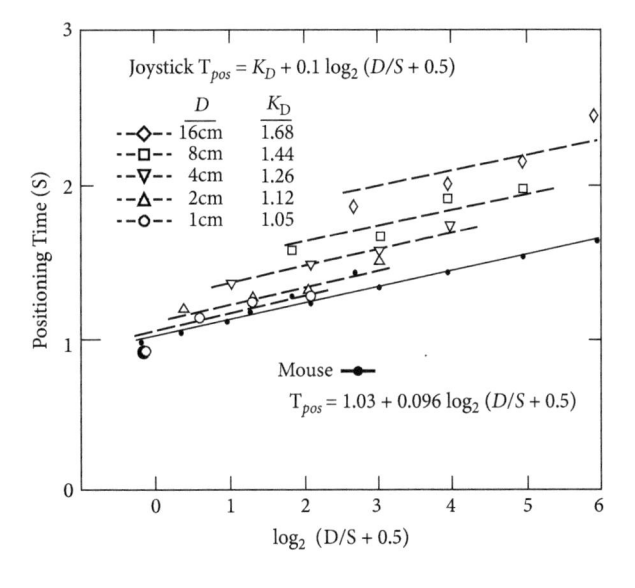

continued

> **Paper Example 43.0.1: Development of an experimental paradigm for evaluating input devices** (continued)
>
> The lesson here is that experiments can help characterize an essential aspect of input interaction. The study by Card et al. precisely characterized how users learn as well as which input device is good for selection. A carefully planned experiment can remove or minimize the effects of confounds, or alternative explanations. In this case, this allowed the authors to better understand the level of performance as a function of practice. Because of the high number of trials, the experiments by Card and colleagues also provide us with information about skilled use rather than just first impressions or initial use. The assumption here is that findings about these fundamental pointing tasks predict how well users can input data in their actual tasks.

43.1 Research questions

Planning an experiment, even for evaluative purposes, should always start from the *research questions* one wishes to address. A research question is a "stated lack of understanding about some phenomenon in human use of computing, or the stated inability to construct interactive technology to address that phenomenon for desired ends" [625]. In short, experiments are motivated by *knowledge gaps*. In the example at the beginning of this chapter, the knowledge gap concerns the effect of the new search feature on usability.

More broadly, research questions can be divided into three classes. First, empirical questions address phenomena and effects in HCI. Second, constructive questions concern the ability to construct systems and designs with desirable properties. Third, conceptual questions address relationships between theoretical constructs that represent interaction. Experimental research can address all three types of questions. In addition to empirical questions, we can conduct an experiment with the purpose of setting objectives for design (constructive) or to distinguish between competing theories (conceptual).

How to come up with a *good* research question? One can start by forming the opposite: a poor research question. Let us consider two common *criticisms* to a finished and written-up experiment: "so what" and "no surprises" [240]. The "so what" criticism suggests that the results of an experiment should be interesting and nontrivial; they should matter to theory or practice. Even if the experiment is run and analyzed as planned, will people find it interesting? Will it add to our understanding of HCI in important ways? Every so often, this criticism is voiced by reviewers as "this is not significant," meaning that while the findings are novel and valid, they do not add to the literature in a meaningful manner.

The "no surprises" criticism suggests that the results should add to or depart from what we already know; they should not be predictable given earlier studies. One should not do an experiment if the results are clear in advance. For instance, if a simple predictive model shows that a UI is superior to another or if a technology is without a doubt superior to an alternative, then the experiment cannot surprise us. Sometimes, of course, new technologies, use situations, or user groups may make it hard to know if earlier findings or theories apply. The "no surprises" criticism may be raised both because the experimental setup is biased and because the results are easily predictable from the literature; we discuss how to avoid both cases later. Most importantly, both of these criticisms should be considered *before* deciding to run an experiment.

The experimental method is only one of the many approaches available for evaluation. Following the discussion of McGrath [532] in Chapter 10, experiments maximize precision at the expense of generalizability and realism. Experiments also allow for the precise manipulation of tasks and environments, as well as detailed data collection. This allows us to understand *specific mechanisms* involved in interaction. Experiments also allow us to control external factors that may be hard to exclude by other means. For example, if you want to evaluate user performance in a mobile application, you may want to prevent notifications and multitasking during your measurements, as they would add noise to the data. Experiments also allow us to collect fine-grained data about how users behave with an interface.

Laboratory conditions permit the use of measurement devices such as eye trackers, motion trackers, and physiological sensing (e.g., electromyography), which cannot be easily deployed outside laboratory conditions. If qualities that can be measured using these devices are important for your research questions, the experimental method is appropriate. Moreover, experiments allow us to investigate research questions about the use of technology without deploying it. This is valuable when a prototype does not have all the features a finished product would need. Experiments are also time-efficient: They allow us to "compress time" and study phenomena that occur infrequently. For example, you can arrange a laboratory study that goes through 5–10 tasks within an hour, whereas in real-world use, completing those tasks might take days or weeks. Finally, in experiments, we can create conditions that allow us to study events that would otherwise be unethical due to the potential harm to participants. Research questions along these lines are suitable for experiments.

Another important reason for doing experiments is the egocentric fallacy [452]. According to this fallacy, we tend to overestimate the power of our own intuition of human behavior. Intuition is weak in discovering latent (unobservable) mechanisms behind our behavior and experience; that is, the mechanisms behind human behavior are beyond intuition. At the same time, we underestimate the extent to which we differ from other people. This is particularly problematic in HCI, where a number of technologies that we propose will have been developed and iteratively refined by ourselves or close collaborators. Experiments help overcome this fallacy.

There are also research questions for which experiments are ill-suited. Experiments rarely work well for studying how people act around technology in real-life circumstances. For more suitable methods, see the chapters on interviews (Chapter 11) and field studies (Chapter 12).

43.1.1 Research hypotheses

Research questions may be elaborated into *research hypotheses*. Hypotheses are statements that link manipulations of the independent variables to differences in the dependent variables. For example, Nass et al. [580] hypothesized that "subjects will perceive a computer with dominant characteristics as being dominant" [p. 288]. Gutwin and Greenberg [306] hypothesized that "better support for workspace awareness can improve the usability of these shared computational workspaces" [p. 511]. However, creating good hypotheses is hard.

Good hypotheses are testable, concise, and identify key constructs. The hypothesis from Nass et al. [580] given above is testable because one may compare computers with and without dominant characteristics and expect a significant difference in participants' perception of their level of dominance. That hypothesis defines the key construct of dominance as something that may be both manipulated in computer interfaces (an independent variable) and perceived by participants (a dependent variable assessed, for example, via a questionnaire).

There are many benefits of formulating research questions as hypotheses. First, hypotheses help gain clarity about what one is doing and may help refine a research question. Second, formulating hypotheses helps one think through what earlier work says about the experiment being designed. Third, hypotheses can help report an experiment. Fourth, hypotheses are tied to theory. They help one think through explanations in advance and allow for genuine surprise about the experimental results.

Not all experiments need hypotheses. There are also other types of questions that can be tackled. The questions that drive experiments fall into two broad groups, sometimes referred to as "testing theory" and "hunting phenomena" [262]. In the former group, there are clear expectations about the outcome of the experiment, typically building on predictions from earlier work. Here, the hypotheses are statements that link the levels of what is manipulated in the experiment to outcomes in the measured variables. In the latter group, the experimenter holds less clear expectations and more open-minded curiosity; these experiments are also called *explorative* experiments.

43.2 Independent variables

Independent variables refer to the types of events or factors that we want to draw causal conclusions about. Independent variables can be about anything we can systematically control. They can be about the type of users (e.g., novice, intermediate, expert), the type of UI (e.g., command line, graphical), the form of instruction (offline, online), the type of feedback, and so on.

In selecting independent variables, it is important to remember that the experiments are carried out to *gain information*. Results should not be obvious in advance, and experiments should not be set up to generate winning conditions and losing conditions.

To ensure that we do not pick arbitrary independent variables, their selection should follow from the stated research question. However, there are many challenges in bridging the gap between the research question and independent variables. Let us consider the example from the first part of this chapter [p. 856]. Recall that we wanted to compare two versions of a search function. To do so, we need to establish what is considered as belonging to the search function: Do we want to include the highlighting of search results in our study? Do we want to consider search results opening to a context menu underneath the search button, in a new window, or both? What if the new search function has a case-sensitive option whereas the old one does not? Ignoring any of these questions may invalidate the experiment.

43.2.1 Levels of independent variables

The *levels of the independent variable* are all the possible values that an independent variable can take in an experiment. For example, if your study compares three UI features, the independent variable "UI feature" would have three levels. If you compare two systems, A and B, the independent variable "system" would have two levels.

43.2.2 Eliminating confounds

One difficulty is making the levels of a variable similar in all essential aspects except for the one that is manipulated. For example, if you compare dissimilar interfaces, the effects that you study may be confounded by their dissimilar features. To establish suitable conditions, an experimenter needs to ensure the following:

- All non-essential aspects are similar. For instance, if search is supported, it should be supported across conditions. If shortcuts are available, they should be available in all conditions.
- The screen real estate is similar across interfaces.
- The users' training and skills with the interface variants are similar.
- The environments in which the interfaces are used are similar.
- Comparable information is available in the interfaces.
- Comparable hardware is used (e.g., for input and output).
- The time allocated and the criteria for success are similar across levels of the independent variable.

43.2.3 Selecting meaningful baselines

Another concern is to ensure a meaningful baseline. A "strong baseline" refers to a solution that is considered the best on the market or in the literature—the state-of-the-art alternative. This could, for instance, be an interface that implements the typical way of performing a task. Our concern here is to ensure that the baseline (or control) is as strong as possible. Munzner [566] discussed what she termed "straw man comparisons," that is, cases where authors compared their interfaces against outdated work rather than state-of-the-art alternatives. Although Munzner wrote specifically about information visualization, this phenomenon occurs in HCI in general; some HCI studies compare novel interfaces with weak or incomplete versions of the current state of the art.

43.3 Participants

The participants in the experiments are the people whose interaction with technology we want to study. They should be a representative sample of the group we want to draw conclusions about. The selection of participants impacts which conclusions can be drawn. It also shapes the practicalities of running the experiment.

The key question is *who* should participate. Representativeness is important. Recruiting a convenience sample—whoever happens to be available—should be done with caution. Barkhuus and Rode [44] found that about half of a sample of studies from a CHI conference used students. Participants are also increasingly recruited online, for instance, through Amazon Mechanical Turk. The participants shape what happens in the experiment and how well we may generalize the findings. We may choose experienced or inexperienced computer users; we may find domain experts or novices. Participants should be selected so that we can validly answer the research question we are interested in.

Another important question is *how many* should participate. Typically, the number of participants in HCI studies is around 12 [119]; in controlled experiments where participants are present in person, the number is about 20. This does not mean that 12 participants are enough for *your study*; this number is simply the average in the published literature.

One principled way of finding an appropriate number of participants is to do *power analysis* [162]. Power analysis helps estimate the probability of detecting a difference in dependent variables across the levels of the independent variable if one knows (or can reasonably estimate) the magnitude of the effect being examined. Power analyses often feel demotivating, as many participants are required to achieve a reasonable power—say, an 80% probability of finding a difference. To detect medium-sized differences between two conditions with an 80% probability, one would need 64 participants in each condition in a between-subjects experiment. Medium-sized effects found in the HCI literature include differences between broad and deep menus or between selection with mouse and keyboard. Various tools are available to help with power analysis (e.g., G∗Power).

43.3.1 Ethical treatment of participants

A key consideration in experimental research is the ethical treatment of the participants. They should in no circumstances be harmed. Participating in the study should not have negative consequences on their lives. The principles for the ethical treatment of participants in behavioral research have been established in the Helsinki Declaration on Ethical Principles for Medical Research Involving Human Subjects. Recent updates include the American Psychological Association's Ethical Principles of Psychologists and Code of Conduct (http://www.apa.org/ethics) and the code of conduct for the Association for Computing Machinery (https://www.acm.org/code-of-ethics). Research organizations have formal guidelines and requirements in place to ensure respectful, legal, and ethically defensible experiments.

Key goals for ethical experimentation include:

- Treat participants with respect; value their time, honor their opinions, and take any criticism seriously.
- Do not expose participants to dangerous or potentially harmful situations; this includes physical, mental, and emotional concerns.
- Make sure participants want to participate; get informed consent (there are templates available online and your institution might also have one).
- Make sure that any reimbursement to participants is adequate. Reimbursement should not be necessary for participants to enroll in your study, but it should still compensate participants for their time and any expenses incurred by participating (e.g., transportation costs).
- Debrief the participants; explain the purpose of the experiment and answer any questions they might have about your research.

Paper Example 43.3.1: Controversial Facebook experiments

In 2014, it was reported that a large-scale experiment had been conducted on Facebook, which attempted to manipulate the emotions of its users [432]. Close to 700,000 Facebook users had their feeds of stories manipulated so that they experienced a reduced amount of emotional content. The figure in this paper example box shows how the manipulation (negativity reduced or positivity reduced) changed the positive and negative words that users posted subsequently (the dependent variable). The figure shows a clear impact of the experimental conditions compared to the control conditions (no change in emotional content). This result is significant because it shows that emotional contagion—having your emotional state changed based on the people that surround you—can happen on social networks and without any direct interaction between people.

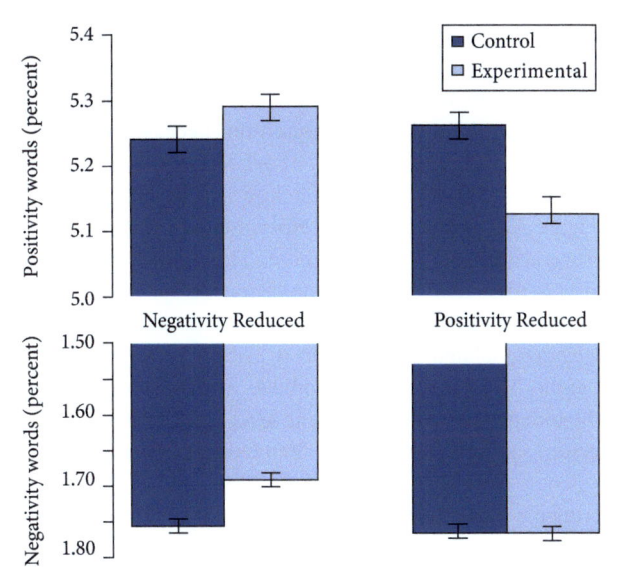

[Figure showing bar charts of Positivity words (percent) and Negativity words (percent) for Negativity Reduced and Positivity Reduced conditions, comparing Control and Experimental groups]

However, the paper was controversial. The Facebook users who were part of the study did not give informed consent as would be normally expected in research and did not, in a clear manner, give permission to have their emotions manipulated experimentally.

43.4 Experimental design

Let us consider again the search functionality example we started with. If you conducted a study where the only functionality being assessed was the new feature, you could not draw a conclusion on whether it is an improvement over the original feature. You would not have a baseline to compare against. This is an example of why we need to introduce *experimental conditions* that allow us to answer our research questions. We map experimental conditions to independent variables and allocate participants systematically or randomly to those conditions so that the observations collected in those conditions are independent of each other.

Experiments in HCI almost always involve more than one level of an independent variable, for instance, two alternative interfaces for a task, a range of different instruction materials, or different approaches for delivering notifications. The assignment of participants to the levels of the independent variable is the most important consideration in experimental design. The aim is to ensure internal validity, that is, the ability to attribute differences observed in the dependent variables to manipulations of the independent variables [758]. Furthermore, experimental design needs to consider the subsequent running and analysis of the experiments. Simple designs are easier for participants; the statistical analysis and result interpretation are easier for experimenters.

One key decision is whether participants experience all or just one level of the independent variable. The former type of design is called within-participant because the independent variable is varied for each participant; the latter type is called between-participant.

In within-participant experiments, participants serve as their own control. Even if a person varies in some trait or behavior, a so-called wild-card participant, that variation is canceled because the participant uses all levels of the independent variable. However, within-participant experiments are not without problems. For instance, they suffer from learning effects. Participants may learn about the interface or the task, which might affect their experience or performance during the experiment.

Between-participant experiments have many benefits. They are easy to analyze, and they do not suffer from the possibility of influence across conditions because participants use just one level of the independent variable. The key drawback of between-participant experiments is that they cannot control for individual differences and therefore require more participants.

As suggested in Figure 43.1, other factors in experiments may influence the experimental situation. There are several ways to deal with these. The workhorse of experimental design is *randomization*, which is often cited as a defining characteristic of experiments. Randomization means that participants are assigned to conditions at random. As a result, the influences of factors other than those being manipulated are randomly distributed over conditions. One of the authors of this book has the motto "when in doubt, randomize." Another approach is *control*, which means simply restricting the independent variable to one level. For example, one may experiment only with left-handed persons so that the influence of handedness can be ignored in the analysis of the experiment.

Sometimes, experiments have more than one independent variable, which complicates their design. For instance, an experimenter may want to study three interfaces: a command line (C), a graphical user interface (G), and a non-computer method (N). Latin squares are an easy way to combine such variation in independent variables. We could have one Latin square do C, then G, and then N. Another could do G, N, and C. Another could do N, C, and G. This organization protects against a number of issues in the experimental design by having an equal number of users use each interface first, second, and last (you can see this from the Latin squares in that the number of interfaces in each column is the same). There are also more complex ways of setting up experiments. For instance, if we want to compare the interfaces just discussed across three ways of training (hints, paper manual, and integrated manual), we can use a Greco-Latin square. It could lead to us organizing the experiment as follows:

```
              1     2     3
   User A:   C+H   G+P   N+I
   User B:   G+I   N+H   C+P
   User C:   N+P   C+I   G+H
```

Again, the sum of the types of training is the same across columns, and each combination of training and interface occurs just once. Latin and Greco-Latin square generators can be found online.

43.5 Dependent variables

In experiments, the aim is to understand how the independent variable influences the interaction. By convention, we call measures of this influence *dependent variables* because they depend on or result from our manipulations of the independent variable. Another way to think of dependent variables in HCI is that they indicate the quality of the interaction numerically, say, with the duration or accuracy of the interaction.

A crucial consideration for dependent variables is their *conceptualization* [758]. Conceptualization refers to making the meaning of concepts in an experiment's research questions clear, defining them precisely, and separating different dimensions of meaning. For instance, while the learnability of a UI appears, intuitively, easy to define, in practice it is hard. Grossman et al. [296] showed how the literature presents many interpretations of learnability. If an experiment does not clearly conceptualize learnability, the validity of any inference from that experiment is reduced since learnability can mean many different things. Similarly, the task completion time is easy to measure in many experiments, but it may not be the best conceptualization of the quality of an interface. For instance, studies vary in whether they see low task completion times as good (minimizing resource expenditure) or bad (expressing a lack of engagement); see Hornbæk et al. [358]. Therefore, measuring the task completion time aimlessly is an inadequate conceptualization of quality. Another example is the notion of user-friendliness, which has been used in HCI for decades. On the surface, it may seem like a natural ingredient of a research question and therefore a dependent variable. However, it is difficult to define, and it is hard to separate its dimensions.

To conceptualize dependent variables, one may refer to the models and concepts related to user experience, usability, performance, and collaboration presented in previous chapters. Each of these may be used to make research questions more precise. For instance, the discussion of the independent dimensions of usability suggests that we should consider whether we are thinking of effectiveness, efficiency, or satisfaction when we are experimentally trying to determine the most usable interface in a set of interfaces. Perhaps we need to consider all these factors. Alternatively, Newman and Taylor [587] proposed to think about the critical parameters of a certain situation. A critical parameter is a performance indicator that captures critical aspects of performance, is domain- or application-specific, and is stable across interface variations. Part of the challenge in applying catalogs of measures is to ensure that at least some of the chosen measures are critical in Newman and Taylor's sense (and not just generic time or error measures).

A second crucial consideration for dependent variables is *operationalization* [758]. Operationalization is about turning the concepts in our research question into something we may measure. The main consideration is the extent to which the measures collected reflect what the experimenter wishes to measure, or whether it is possible to make "inferences from sampling particulars of a study to the higher-order constructs they represent" [758, p. 65].

We may ponder the following aspects in operationalizing dependent variables. First, how we will obtain measures. Second, whether we will use validated measures and questionnaires. Third, using multiple measures of the same construct increases reliability and strengthens the validity of the claims about constructs. Using just one operationalization of the construct poses a monomethod threat to validity [758]. It means that we are more prone to not measuring what we think we are measuring if we use just one indicator for a construct.

Common measures in research studies in HCI include task completion times, accuracy or error rates, and questionnaire answers. A couple of additional types of data are worth collecting in experiments. One important type is *interaction process* data, for instance, which commands participants activate or how they move their mouse. Such data can help us understand the interaction process (rather than just the outcome) and think about why something happens in an experiment.

While dependent variables need to be numeric, many exemplary experiments also collect *qualitative data*, for instance, in the form of interviews and observations. Some experiments rely solely on qualitative data. For instance, O'Hara and Sellen [615] reported a much-cited experiment on reading from paper and from a computer. While they used an experimental setup—for instance, they randomly assigned participants to the paper or computer condition—they only reported qualitative data on reading strategies and activities that differed between paper and computer. Such data are valuable when experiments go well (as in O'Hara and Sellen's study) as well as for understanding why experiments fail.

43.6 Experimental situation

Experiments put participants in *experimental situations*: the particular circumstances in which they are asked to carry out tasks. The design of these situations matters.

One decision concerns the *activities* that participants will engage in, which are often prescribed as tasks. One may select tasks in many ways. One approach is to select tasks that are representative of what users would do outside the experiment. Munzner [566] discussed task selection in information visualization and wrote

> A study is not very interesting if it shows a nice result for a task that nobody will ever actually do, or a task much less common or important than some other task. You need to convince the reader that your tasks are a reasonable abstraction of the real-world tasks done by your target users. [p. 147]

One way of ensuring representativeness is to use tasks that users have been observed doing.

Another approach to selecting tasks is to use simple tasks that capture the essence of what is being investigated. The idea is to reduce variation and remove non-essential features of a task; this is similar to the approach for selecting independent variables based on essential features. For instance, many studies of pointing techniques use the multidirectional tapping task. This task requires participants to tap circular or square targets arranged in a circle. It does not represent pointing in the wild, but it is widely accepted as a suitable task for experiments.

Another decision about the experimental situation concerns whether the experiment takes place in the lab or in the field. In lab experiments, the environment is controlled and the effect of external influences is minimized. In field experiments, the environment is "real," although the experimental manipulations are still instigated by the experimenter. The view taken here is that neither setting is better than the other; rather, they have relative benefits and drawbacks. We discussed field experiments in Chapter 40.

43.7 Analysis and interpretation

What should one do with the collected data? The naive approach would be to take means of the data in different conditions and compare them. What could go wrong with this? If users report an experience of 3.5 in condition A and 4.2 in condition B, is this not a sufficient basis to conclude that one condition is better than the other?

Perhaps the most critical piece of knowledge in data analysis is *variance*. Every observation in an HCI experiment is susceptible to variation. Observations are affected by variations in the repeated attempts of users, our measurement instruments, and various random effects. If the variance in the two conditions A and B is large enough, it could be that the means differ because of chance. In other words, if you were to repeat the experiment, the result might change or even reverse.

Statistical analysis offers rigorous tools for understanding what we can conclude from data. Statistics is the science of drawing valid conclusions from datasets. In HCI, we use statistical analysis for different purposes, including:

- Exploring and learning about the distribution of variables or their relationships
- Describing relationships between independent and dependent variables
- Testing if relationships reliably describe differences in the population from which the sample was taken

- Identifying a factor that caused or contributed to an observed effect
- Testing if a statistical model accurately describes the dataset.

In this book, we do not offer a comprehensive overview of statistical methods for HCI. We review some of the more popular frequentist methods and the thinking behind them; for a more thorough treatment, see the book by Robertson and Kaptein [701]. Recent research has also looked at Bayesian methods for statistical testing, such as the Bayes factor. An in-depth treatment of frequentist and Bayesian statistics can be found in Cox [171]. Note that we discuss the analysis of qualitative data in Chapters 11 and 42.

Statistical analysis is divided into two main classes according to purpose:

- Descriptive statistics, where the goal is to describe relationships between variables in the dataset
- Inferential statistics, where the goal is to draw a conclusion about the population from which the sample was drawn.

It is good practice to start a statistical analysis by describing the dataset. *Descriptive statistics* refers to the use of summary statistics, such as graphs, tables, and models, to describe a set of data. For example, imagine you have collected data on the accuracy and speed of pointing with two input methods, A and B. What you should do is plot the distributions of the two dependent variables for the two methods. Are the distributions normally distributed, skewed, or do they exhibit significant variance? Based on this information, you could produce *summary statistics*, such as the mean, median, minimum, and maximum of each variable. *Graphs* can then be used to visualize such information: histograms, scatter plots, line plots, and so on. Bivariate, trivariate, and multivariate graphs show relationships between two, three, and more than three variables, respectively.

Inferential statistics refers to the attempt to generalize observations in a sample. A distinction is made between the set of observations and the population it comes from. For example, in the case of the search function considered throughout this chapter, one may be interested in estimating the task completion time for regular users (population) rather than just the ones recruited for the study (sample). Intuitively, if the sample is not *representative*, any conclusions drawn based on it can be flawed. There are many reasons why a sample may be unrepresentative. For example, we often use university students to represent regular users. However, they may differ in many respects: age, socioeconomic background, and so on. This is why it is important to sample participants and tasks so that they represent the population. There are several strategies to ensure this, including random sampling, stratified sampling, and systematic random sampling. In stratified sampling, one takes a background variable, such as age, and defines *bins* for its range (e.g., 18–25, 26–33). When recruiting participants, one tries to ensure that the sample sizes across bins are equal.

Inferential statistics may also start by plotting. *Confidence intervals* provide estimates for the range of values that we think the true population value falls in. For example, if the 95% confidence interval of the task completion time is [14.5, 17.9] seconds, we are 95% confident that the true population value is between 14.5 and 17.9 s.

Statistical testing refers to testing whether a difference exists between conditions. Since we are talking about inferential statistics, we are not interested in whether a difference exists in the dataset, as there almost always is *some* difference. Rather, we are interested in whether this difference represents a true difference in the population. Here, the research hypotheses need to be translated into statistical hypotheses, which can then be tested.

Multiple methods exist for statistical testing. They can be divided into two main groups: parametric and non-parametric. Parametric tests use parameters to describe the population. They make distributional assumptions about the population, which must be checked before proceeding with the corresponding test. The most commonly used parametric tests are the *t*-test and its generalization analysis of variance (ANOVA). *Non-parametric tests* make no assumption about the underlying distribution, which makes them more flexible as a class of tests.

Regression models help us understand the nature of the relationship among two or more variables. We use regression models to understand the relationship between *predictor* and *response* variables. Typically, predictor variables are our independent variables, and response variables are our dependent variables. Any *covariant*, or uncontrolled but recorded variable, can also be included. For example, we could use regression to find a relationship between age and task completion time. If the *p*-value of the regression is below an a priori threshold (often 0.05), we can conclude that there is a significant trend.

43.8 Hypothesis testing

A very common approach to analyzing experiments in HCI is *hypothesis testing*. In the following, we first discuss a standard way of doing statistical significance testing. We then go through an example.

43.8.1 Statistical significance testing

The high-level logic of hypothesis testing is as follows. Assume you have a sample X with n measurements, $X = \{x_1, x_2, ..., x_n\}$. We assume that this sample was drawn from a particular distribution N. We call this assumption the *null hypothesis*, which is typically denoted as H_0.

We can now ask whether our sample was indeed drawn from the distribution N by asking whether it is possible to *reject the null hypothesis*. In other words, we are asking whether we can, with some probability, state that the sample *was not drawn* from the distribution N.

While this is not a typical significance test in HCI, let us consider our distribution N to be a standard normal distribution $N(x) \sim N(0, 1)$. We can then ask whether an individual measurement x in our sample is drawn from N. In this case, this means that x should not deviate much from 0.

If a measurement x in our sample is large, say, $x = 3$, the probability that it is drawn from a standard normal distribution is very low. However, if a measure x in our sample is small, say, $x = 0.3$, the probability is quite high. This can be readily realized by considering that the range $|x| \leq 1$ occupies 68% of the probability mass of a standard normal distribution. In other words, the higher x is, the more confident we can be that x was *not* drawn from a standard normal distribution.

In hypothesis testing, we define a criterion value for determining whether the probability that x is not drawn from N justifies rejecting the null hypothesis. Common criterion values are 0.05, 0.01, and 0.001. These criterion values are called *confidence levels*. For example, if we set the confidence level to 0.046, we would reject the null hypothesis for a measurement x if x differs from the value $x = 0$ by at least 2. That is, $x \geq 2$ would give us cause to reject H_0 at a significance level of 0.046.

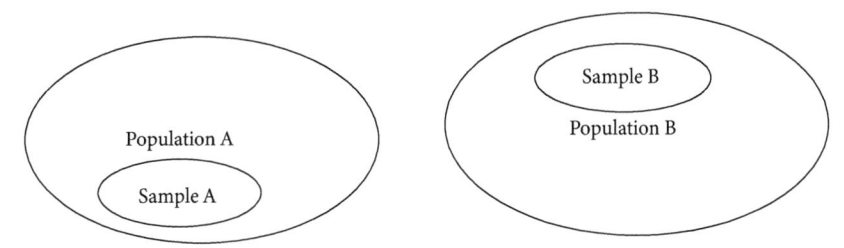

Figure 43.2 An illustration of the acquisition of two samples from two populations.

Statistical significance tests can be used to perform this type of hypothesis testing. They can also take into account additional factors, such as several measurements in the sample, and they can consider distributions other than a standard normal distribution.

43.8.2 Example: Between-participant analysis of variance

Assume there is a difference in the measurements we obtained via the dependent variables when we manipulated the independent variables. This difference can be due to two things:

1. Our manipulation of the independent variable
2. *Error*, which in this context means there is no true difference. Instead, the difference we measured was due to chance.

Significance tests help us decide whether measured differences are statistically significant, meaning that we are reasonably confident that the difference is not due to chance but due to our manipulation of the independent variables.

Assume we have sampled two groups from a user population, and we have exposed each group to a different method, say, methods A and B. Here, our independent variable *method* has two levels: method A and method B.

We believe the right way to compare these methods is to investigate if the means of the measures we have taken differ between the two groups. The null hypothesis H_0 says that for some predetermined confidence level, there is no difference between the means, and any measured difference is solely due to sampling error. If we reject H_0, we have a significant result at the predetermined confidence level.

We can demonstrate statistical significance testing by using a method called one-way ANOVA. This significance test is used to determine whether two sample means are significantly different in the statistical sense. The sample means must have been generated from a between-subject experimental design.

The statistical term *error* refers to the difference between an observation and the population mean. Typically, the population mean is *unobservable*.

The statistical term *residual* refers to the difference between an observation and the sample mean. The sample mean is *observable*.

Assume we have obtained samples from a normal distribution: $X_1, X_2, ..., X_n \sim N(\mu, \sigma^2)$. Then, the sample mean is

$$\bar{X} = \frac{X_1, X_2, ..., X_n}{n}. \tag{43.1}$$

Here, the error is $e_i = X_i - \mu$, and the residual is $r_i = X_i - \bar{X}$.

Now, *why* would there be a difference between the sample means of groups A and B (Figure 43.2)? There are two possible reasons:

1. *Because of* group membership. This means the difference is due to an effect of the independent variable on the dependent variable.
2. *Not because of* group membership. This means the difference is merely due to sampling error.

The logic of ANOVA is as follows. Two independent estimates of the population variance can be obtained: (1) a between-group estimate, which is the effect of the independent variable *and* error; and (2) a within-group estimate, which is just the error.

Our null hypothesis H_0 is that the two groups A and B have equal means:

$$H_0 : \mu_A = \mu_B. \tag{43.2}$$

Given H_0, the between-group and within-group variance estimates should be equal. This is because H_0 assumes the effect of the independent variable does not exist. Then, both variance estimates reflect error, and their ratio is 1. A ratio greater than 1 suggests an effect of the independent variable.

The *sum of squares* (SS) is the sum of the squared residuals:

$$SS = \sum_i (X_i - \bar{X})^2. \tag{43.3}$$

Now, let us consider the sources of variability in a between-subject ANOVA. The total variability *within* sample (group) A is

$$SS_A = \sum_i (X_{Ai} - \bar{X}_A)^2. \tag{43.4}$$

The total variability *within* sample (group) B is

$$SS_B = \sum_i (X_{Bi} - \bar{X}_B)^2. \tag{43.5}$$

Finally, the total variability *between* samples A and B is

$$SS_A = \sum_i (X_{Ai} - \bar{X}_{AB})^2 + SS_B = \sum_i (X_{Bi} - \bar{X}_{AB})^2. \tag{43.6}$$

We can now define the variability due to error. This is the total variability *within* samples A and B; this variability is not due to manipulation of the independent variable and is thus regarded as a source of *error*:

$$SS_{error} = SS_A + SS_B. \tag{43.7}$$

The total variability *between* samples A and B is

$$SS_{total} = SS_{A+B}. \tag{43.8}$$

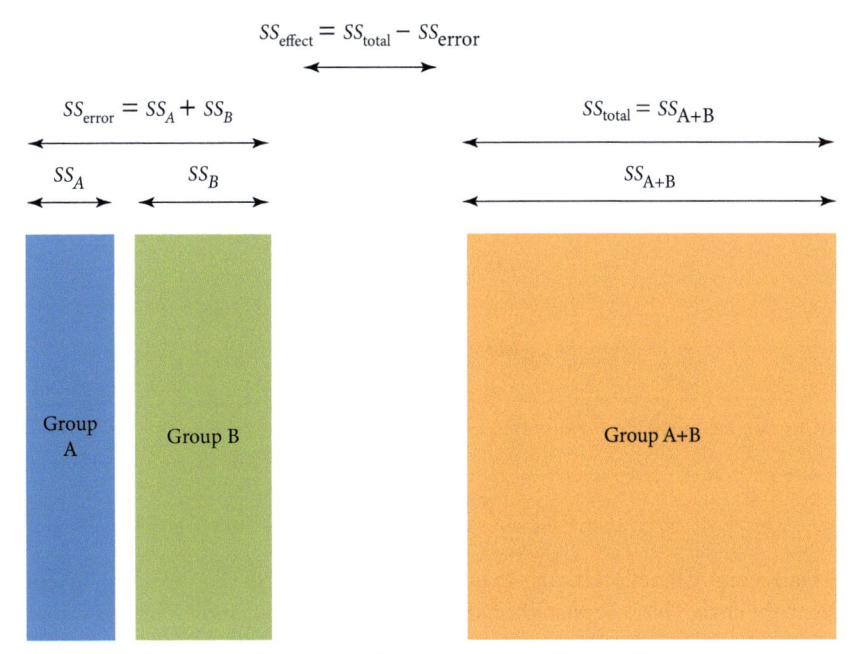

Figure 43.3 A graphical illustration of how one-way ANOVA partitions sums of squares.

Finally, the *effect* is the part of the total variability that cannot be explained by the source of error:

$$SS_{effect} = SS_{total} - SS_{error}. \tag{43.9}$$

Effectively, we have partitioned the different sources of variability in the samples: (1) the variability due to error, that is, the sum of the variability within each group; (2) the total variability across groups; and (3) the variability due to a manipulation of the independent variable—variability that cannot be explained by error. This partitioning is shown graphically in Figure 43.3.

This process allows us to separate the error from the effect in the data. We first measure the variability of the data within each group (groups A and B separately) to determine the error. Next, we measure the total variability (combining groups A and B into a single group) to obtain the effect plus the error. We can then obtain the effect by subtracting the error from the total variability.

The sums of squares provide unscaled measures of variability in the data. This can be readily observed because, as we keep adding summands, the sum becomes larger. Since sums of squares are unscaled, they need to be eventually normalized so that we can compare different sums of squares.

Scaled sums of squares are called *mean squares* (MS). Mean squares are obtained by scaling sums of squares by their degrees of freedom (df).

First, we have the degrees of freedom df$_{error}$ within group A and group B—recall that this is the error. df$_{error}$ is the number of ways you can arrange the residuals and still have them sum to zero for each group:

$$df_{error} = n - \text{participants} - m \text{ groups}. \tag{43.10}$$

Then, we have the degrees of freedom df_{effect} between groups A and B—recall that this is the effect. df_{effect} is the number of ways you can arrange their deviations away from the mean so that their average is always zero:

$$df_{effect} = m \text{ groups} - 1. \tag{43.11}$$

We now can obtain the mean squares for the error and effect:

$$MS_{error} = \frac{SS_{error}}{df_{error}}, \tag{43.12}$$

$$MS_{effect} = \frac{SS_{effect}}{df_{effect}}. \tag{43.13}$$

Finally, we can calculate the *F*-ratio, frequently referred to as the *F*-statistic:

$$F = \frac{MS_{effect}}{MS_{error}}. \tag{43.14}$$

The *F*-ratio is large if the effect is larger than the error. Vice versa, the *F*-ratio is small if the effect is smaller than the error. This is because the ratio of the between-group estimate to the within-group estimate gives rise to an *F*-distribution when H_0 is true. The *F*-distribution varies as a function of a pair of degrees of freedom, one for each of the variance estimates. The *F*-distribution is our test statistic in this case. The larger the *F*-statistic, the less likely the observed difference is due to chance. If the *F*-statistic exceeds a so-called critical value for our prespecified significance level, then we reject H_0 at that significance level.

43.9 Explaining experiments

The primary goal of evaluation is to estimate the value a design offers to users. This is typically easier to achieve if the obtained result can be explained.

A small thought experiment illustrates this. You run an evaluative study of a prototype design and find that the average task completion time is 47.5 s, the average error rate is 0.5, and the system usability scale rating is 65. What do these results tell you, and how confident can you be when taking further actions based on them?

Explanations help us understand distributions of dependent variables. Why does the task completion time have an average of 47.5 s and not, say, 14.4 s? Data collected during the experiment may offer explanations. Verbal protocols, video recordings, interviews, and so on can illuminate *explanatory mechanisms* that link independent and dependent variables. In HCI experiments, we often discover usability problems, conceptual misunderstandings, or issues in perceptual or motor performance.

Without explanations, results may be "fragile." The obtained results may not generalize. Quantitative findings may be underpinned by factors that depend on experimental conditions; if the conditions change even slightly, the results may change, too. For example, if your users are not native speakers, perhaps they failed to find an item because they missed its meaning. Deploying the same system to native speakers may produce different results.

We may also seek explanations outside of the data, for instance, from theories. Theories of cognition may help us understand why users have a hard time recalling facts or events; theories of communication may explain why users do not want to engage with user communities. For example, Cockburn et al. [159] used decision-making theories from psychology and economics to explain user behavior in using intelligent text entry systems. Because the effect of an intelligent text entry method can be fleetingly small and contingent on a number of factors, it is important to understand the mechanisms that underpin a user's decision to use a method in a particular way.

To sum up, the results of experimental research are more robust and generalizable if they can be explained.

Summary

- Experiments provide precise measurements and comparisons.
- Explicating research questions and hypotheses is an important aspect of high-quality evaluations.
- Validity and reliability are key concepts for ensuring trustworthy experiments.
- Data analysis uses methods from descriptive and inferential statistics to draw conclusions about the effects of independent variables on dependent variables.

Exercises

1. Understanding experiments. For each of the following questions, consider whether an experiment is a suitable method for evaluation.
   (a) What does it feel like to interact with a chatbot?
   (b) Why do people not upgrade software on their devices?
   (c) How quickly can people input text using a QWERTY keyboard?
   (d) How do we figure out how much people use their mobile phones?
   (e) What is the most effective way of organizing email?
2. Formulating testable hypotheses. Formulate a hypothesis for an experiment investigating the effects of embodying different avatars in a virtual reality game. Check whether you have clear dependent and independent variables. Then, try to explain the links between variables with theoretical hypotheses.
3. Experimental design. Design and run an experiment that investigates the appropriate mid-air gestures for turning on and off a television.
4. Comparative studies. You have been asked to run a study that investigates whether a mobile phone application for exercising more during the workday is better than a baseline application. Consider what "better" means and how to select dependent variables for the study. One of your collaborators suggested using the step count; what are your considerations regarding the validity of this dependent variable? Another colleague considered how to capture exercising preferences; how would you contribute to this discussion?
5. Measuring user experience. Everybody wants satisfying UIs. Imagine that you are conducting an experiment where you are interested in satisfaction. Consider how you would operationalize satisfaction in your experimental setup. What are the essential and less important aspects of satisfaction? How can you measure them?

6. Improving experimental designs. Read the paper by Card et al. [128] and suggest an improved version of the experiment.
7. Reflecting on evaluative practices. Describe how you have previously evaluated designs or software, for example, in classes or in your work. Give one concrete example and explain whether the tests were conducted from a human-centered perspective. Describe why, or why not, this was done. Next, compare this approach to the usability testing method described in this chapter. Then, answer the following questions. Is testing with people relevant? Is it your responsibility? What happens if no testing with people is done?

44
Field evaluations

The evaluation methods considered so far are similar in one important respect: They do not consider the context of use. The methods concern primarily controlled settings (e.g., think-aloud studies) or general models of human performance (e.g., keystroke-level models). These methods maximize desirable outcomes such as precision and generalizability—but what about realism? Is it not important to get as close as possible to the real contexts of use in evaluation?

Collaborative, communicative, and material practices are bound to the contexts in which they emerge. This poses a formidable challenge for evaluation. If we wish people to engage in their actual tasks, fueled by their true motivations in their real contexts, how do we carry out an evaluation? If we wish the social and organizational contexts to remain unaffected by evaluation, how do we study them without changing them? All the challenges outlined for user research in Part III seem to apply here. If we want to study an interactive system in its real setting, we need a fully developed system, and we need people and organizations willing to use the system as part of the evaluation.

This chapter focuses on evaluation using three types of field and *deployment studies*:

- *Field evaluations* of prototypes. The idea is to bring out prototypes of interactive systems in their assumed context of use—the *field*. As an example, Bardram et al. [40] conducted a 14-week field trial of a personal monitoring system for bipolar patients. The focus here was on the patients' experiences with the system as part of their lives.
- *Pilot studies*. The idea is to partially implement an interactive system and put it to use to learn about its use. Then, this learning is used to improve the design of the system and fully implement it. For example, Hertzum et al. [338] studied a pilot implementation of a system for patient transportation at a hospital. The pilot implementation revealed the potential of the system to support porters' self-organization, although that crucial functionality was missing in the system.
- Deployment studies. The idea is to gather information about a fully functional system and improve it as part of its maintenance. For example, DiMicco et al. [196] built and deployed a social networking system called BeeHive within IBM.

In this chapter, we elaborate on the advantages and disadvantages of these types of field and deployment studies, as well as their relationships with user research (Part III). Paper Example 44.0.1 provides a further example of evaluation in the field.

> **Paper Example 44.0.1: Using an app to reach AAC professionals in the field**
>
> Augmentative and alternative communication (AAC) is a field that investigates techniques and approaches for enabling nonspeaking individuals with motor disabilities to communicate. One challenge in such research is reaching users to evaluate prototypes.
>
> Fontana and colleagues [252] presented research that is based on reaching AAC professionals by releasing an app on an app market. The app presents a novel interface for AAC users who rely on symbols to communicate. The app enables the user to select a photo from a photo album. Then, the app uses a system to extract meaning from the photo and generate a set of symbols for the user to choose from. The symbols are associated with words. In addition, the system predicts phrases, consisting of sequences of symbols. Users can reorder the symbols, remove them, edit words associated with symbols, and add new words and sentences. The user can "speak" a symbol or phrase by tapping on it.
>
> To evaluate the system, the researchers released the app on an app market and, through the app, recruited AAC professionals willing to try out the app with AAC users. This enabled the researchers to carry out in-depth interviews with AAC professionals who reported on the usefulness of the app for their users in situ. It allowed the researchers to understand how this app can be used to support language learning in schools and in therapy. They discovered that having immediate access to a relevant vocabulary by tapping a photo reduces the conversational partner's workload and may help AAC users understand symbols and sentence construction. Their paper reports rich interview material from a diverse group of AAC professionals that would be difficult to source using traditional means.

44.1 Field evaluations

One major decision point for an evaluation is whether to carry it out in the laboratory or in the field. In a laboratory evaluation, the evaluator can control what happens during the evaluation: the tasks users carry out, the instructions they receive, and other factors that may affect user performance and behavior. Researchers can also ensure that observations are independent, that is, that participants do not influence each other. These practices minimize the risk of irrelevant factors compromising the validity of the conclusions drawn from a study.

Field evaluations are attractive because they tend to provide high ecological validity (sometimes also called external validity): The conditions in which the study is arranged closely resemble the real-world conditions of use of a system.

44.1.1 Degrees of a field

It is convenient to think about the field in terms of degrees. Rather than a strict distinction between lab and field settings, we can design evaluations with more or fewer features of the field. This is about realism in the sense described by McGrath [532]. Thus, an evaluation may be more field-like in terms of people, activities, contexts, and technologies (Chapter 10).

Let us give some examples. For instance, many think-aloud studies can be done in the users' workplaces, ensuring that the physical and social contexts are more similar to the imagined context of use than a usability laboratory setting. This is similar to the approach adopted by Rico and Brewster [698]. They evaluated the social acceptability of a set of gesture interactions for mobile phones on the sidewalk near a bus stop and an underground station on a busy city street. In that way, the context influenced the evaluation and increased the realism of the results. We can also vary the activities that people engage in, for instance, the tasks. In think-aloud studies (Chapter 42), tasks are sometimes supplied by the users to make them more realistic and closer to what would happen in the field (i.e., in real life). In the study by Rico and Brewster [698], although the setting was the field, the researchers gave the tasks to the participants.

To make evaluations more field-like, researchers sometimes focus on particular aspects of the lab–field continuum. In the 1980s and 1990s, many usability researchers constructed usability labs that looked like users' workplaces and experimental settings that resembled living rooms. Such attention to mundane realism is warranted but is likely less important than, for instance, ensuring that participants see the evaluation as meaningful and engaging or that the tasks given to them reflect their real-life tasks [358].

44.1.2 Evaluation methods for the field

If we wish to increase the realism of an evaluation and do it in the field, which evaluation methods can we apply? The short answer is that any empirical evaluation method may be used. Thus, we can use all the methods covered in this part of the book, including think-aloud. We can also use user research methods (Part III), including interviews (Chapter 11), observations (Chapter 12), and unobtrusive data collection (Chapter 14). Recall that the goal of an evaluation is to evaluate a system against some standard. By contrast, user research studies often focus on understanding users. In other words, the same method, say, interviews, can be used to achieve different goals in user research and evaluation.

44.1.3 Experiments in the field

One method that is extensively used in the field is experiments. Field experiments need to balance the causal logic of experiments with the realism of the field. As an example of how the deployment environment can influence results, consider a field test of two deployed mobile text entry methods: an autocorrect keyboard and a gesture keyboard [697]. This field study compared the text entry performance of both text entry methods measured in the lab with the text entry performance measured when users used the same methods on their phones in their everyday lives. Paper Example 44.1.1 describes another instance.

When thinking about experiments in the field, three core assumptions of experimental research are threatened: random assignment, control, and the independence of observations. First, we may not be able to randomly assign users to particular conditions in the field. We need to work with users who happen to use a particular user interface or need to carry out particular tasks.

Second, we cannot control events to the same extent as in a laboratory setting. Field studies are vulnerable to a surprisingly large number of unexpected events and factors that may substantially affect the outcomes. For example, while you may ask users to carry out their everyday work tasks using a prototype instead of an established user interface, something unexpected may happen, such as a crisis at work, new work rules, a new workflow, or new colleagues, which alters the way users interact with the prototype.

Third, our observations may not be independent of each other. For example, if you want to evaluate a system with a school class, the students can—or rather, will—talk about the experiment with each other, which will influence their behavior.

In the literature on experimental methods, field experiments are sometimes called quasi-experiments because they often violate assumptions of experimental research [758]. Quasi-experiments call for caution in analyzing data. We cannot rely on traditional statistical methods for drawing conclusions from data collected in field experiments.

One type of quasi-experiments is natural experiments. In such experiments, a world event works as the experimental manipulation—the influence of COVID-19 on communication is one of the most well-known natural experiments. Such events allow us to study their influence in the real world. However, these are not full experiments, as the assignment is not random and the event may be associated with many causes.

As an example, Griggio et al. [292] studied the influence of a new privacy policy for WhatsApp, in particular whether the policy made users switch to other platforms. Using surveys immediately after and some time after the policy implementation, the authors were able to conduct an experiment-like comparison by leveraging a real-world event.

Paper Example 44.1.1: Field evaluation of an interactive tutorial for Wikipedia

Sometimes, evaluation studies can only be carried out in the field. Narayan et al. [576] presented an interactive tutorial for learning Wikipedia. The goal was to encourage positive behavior and high-quality contributions. Wikipedia suffers from a high rate of change in its communities, and newcomers should quickly adapt to "the ways of the house." Wikipedia is also vulnerable to norm violations and malevolent behavior such as trolling. These issues can compound and discourage newcomers from joining communities where they might experience negative behaviors from others or low-quality contributions.

The Wikipedia Adventure (TWA) is structured in the form of a game (adventure) and uses methods from gamification research (Chapter 8). It covers critical aspects of Wikipedia contributions: wiki-markup, community policies, and communication with other editors. TWA allows for safely exploring and learning in a "sandbox" without the fear of "looking stupid" among other editors. Users go through seven "missions": "setting up their user page, communicating effectively with other users, making basic edits, maintaining a neutral point of view, evaluating content quality, understanding revisions, and using built-in tools like watchlists and history pages to see how articles can be maintained over time" [p. 1788]. Missions are themed as stories and users who complete them are rewarded with badges, a common gamification technique.

The authors hypothesized that to become a Wikipedian, a novice should be able to perceive that even small contributions are valued in the community when done according to the norms of the community. To arrange a field evaluation, the authors collaborated with the Wikimedia Foundation. First, they organized a user survey among Wikipedia editors, who were invited to comment on the tutorial. The goal was to collect *formative* feedback to evolve the design of TWA. Among the 600 respondents, 90% reported feeling more confident as an editor and feeling more informed about Wikipedia after completing the tutorial. However, the authors noted that a survey-based evaluation with experienced editors may not carry over to newcomers—their target group.

In the second phase, the authors wanted to see if completing TWA *actually* helped newcomers increase the quality of their contributions. They hypothesized that gamification might increase their confidence and self-efficacy, that is, their belief that they can master Wikipedia. To recruit participants, the authors used talk pages to invite users to play TWA. Intuitively, this limited the sample to newcomers who opted into the study. To learn about the *effect* of TWA, the authors needed to compare two types of newcomers: those using and those not using the system. Their solution was to divide the invited users according to whether they chose to use TWA or not. The opted-out users formed the control group.

> Contrary to the results from the first phase, the authors found no measurable effect of TWA on newcomer participation in the second phase. All the outcome metrics the authors used, which measured the quality of contributions 180 days after completing TWA, failed to reject the null hypothesis of no effect. The authors attributed this to the self-selection effect: Users who chose to use TWA were different from other users. The authors concluded their evaluation as follows: "In a project like Wikipedia that depends heavily on intrinsically motivated members to make contributions, a gamified tutorial may be helpful and fun to use, but ultimately unsuccessful at building long-term commitment and retention" [p. 1796].

44.2 Pilot studies

In Chapter 32, we discussed prototypes as a way to get hands-on experience with a design. Can we do the same in the field with systems that have been sufficiently developed to be used there? Such studies would allow us to evaluate systems in their intended contexts of use.

Pilot implementations have emerged for this purpose [337]. A pilot implementation is "a field test of a properly engineered, yet unfinished system in its intended environment, using real data, and aiming—through real-use experience—to explore the value of the system, improve or assess its design, and reduce implementation risk." This allows evaluators to test the entire sociotechnical system (Chapter 33) rather than just a small part of the interactive system.

A pilot implementation differs from a prototype in a few key ways. First, it is always done in the field. Second, it is "used in its intended environment for a limited period of time, with real data and special precautions against breakdowns" [337]. Third, it can be done to test the design, engineering, and implementation of a solution. Fourth, it is done for weeks to months. In these ways, a pilot implementation is a partial deployment study.

Let us consider an example of a pilot implementation. Systems in healthcare are complex, particularly in how they fit within hospital organizations that use many systems. As part of the development of an electronic patient record (EPR), a pilot EPR was implemented at a hospital [335]. For five days, the pilot implementation of the EPR replaced all paper records in the hospital. A back office was staffed for all five days to help resolve breakdowns, unavailable features, and other issues.

The *pilot implementation* showed that the EPR and the associated work procedures were successful in achieving many of the planned changes. Some unexpected consequences of the interactive system were also found, for instance [337, p. 8]:

> The nurses engaged in a process of collective reading at their handovers, during which the EPR screen was projected on the wall and thereby visible to everybody. The electronic records were inspected by the group of nurses, and they collectively participated in interpreting the status and condition of the patients, guided by the nurse team leader. The nurse team leader navigated the EPR and read selected passages aloud to draw attention to them and set a shared flow in their reading. This collective reading was a marked change in the nurses' work practice. During nursing handovers with paper records the nurse team leader provided an oral report of each patient by scanning the patient's record and reading key information out loud; patient records were seldom seen by clinicians other than the nurse team leader.

In this way, the pilot implementation helped the evaluators uncover important phenomena surrounding the use of the interactive system.

Pilot implementations can bring essential parts of an interactive system into use in the field, allowing for system evaluation. Using technology probes, researchers deploy simple and adaptable interactive systems [366] to achieve three key goals:

- Understand the real-world needs and desires of users.
- Help users and designers conceptualize new technologies.
- Field-test interactive systems.

Technology probes combine work on understanding users, designing interactive systems, and testing interactive systems in the field.

Another related concept is the *minimum viable product* [700]. The idea is to create and release a version of a new interactive system that allows its designers to collect the maximum amount of information from users with the least effort. The observed behavior with the product can then be used to improve the product and make informed business decisions about its future. Similar to a pilot implementation, a minimum viable product is a partial solution; it does not need to be fully working, and it may just be simulated via an interactive system.

44.3 Deployment studies

When a product, system, or service has been designed and built, it is ready to be *deployed* to end-users. Often ignored in research, deployment is a critical stage in the development of any product, system, or service. In deployment studies, an interactive system is fully deployed and as it is used, evaluators collect data about the success of the system.

Such evaluations are conducted for multiple reasons. First, support costs might be reduced by learning from the issues that users face with the real-life use of a product. Second, evaluators may be interested in ensuring the intended effects of a system are realized; studying the deployment of the system is a way of doing that. Fundamentally, deployment allows evaluators to determine whether a system is fulfilling its purpose of helping users achieve their goals in relevant use contexts. Third, the system may be improved through user feedback. Deployment allows for studying systems released to the intended users, who use these systems to achieve their goals in their sociotechnical contexts.

Chilana et al. [149] conducted a large-scale survey of what they called post-deployment usability. They found that only about half of the 333 surveyed human–computer interaction (HCI) professionals were involved in usability work after the deployment of a system. They also found that common activities for studying deployment include interviews, surveys, informal usability testing, analysis of customer support data, satisfaction surveys, monitoring discussion forums, and analysis of log file data.

Next, let us look at methods used in deployment studies through a few examples. We also covered many of these methods when discussing user research (Part III).

44.3.1 Analysis of user feedback

One type of deployment study involves gathering users' feedback and using that to evaluate a system. Such feedback may also be collected through questionnaires (Chapter 13) or interviews (Chapter 11). However, a prominent approach is to use feedback given by users independently of the system's formal evaluation. Users may provide such feedback through support calls, reviews of the system, or comments on community support forums. For example, Zhai et al. [923] deployed the ShapeWriter WritingPad on an app store and analyzed users' reviews of the app. All these types of feedback may be analyzed to evaluate a deployed system.

44.3.2 Log file analysis

Evaluators may use web site analytics and log file analysis to evaluate a deployed system. We discuss log analysis methods in more detail in Chapter 14.

44.3.3 App store deployment

One of the main costs in deployment studies is distributing the software to users. A popular methodology in HCI research was developed in parallel with the rise of app stores for downloading software for mobile phones and tablets [534]. The downside is that it is time-consuming to develop software that works on multiple device types. Further, acquiring licenses to release software on a platform and legal permissions to collect data take time. On the positive side, large datasets can be collected. Paper Example 44.0.1 gives another example.

44.3.4 Longitudinal studies

Longitudinal evaluations are field evaluations that track a prototype or product over a long period. Although such evaluations may be done in the lab, they often leverage the motivation inherent in field evaluations.

There is no unique definition of a longitudinal study. Such studies typically have a duration of weeks, months, or years. The duration depends on what is examined; for example, studying habits and social practices can require very long longitudinal studies.

Longitudinal studies are not only expensive to organize but also difficult to analyze. During an extended period of time, numerous events can occur that change the subject of evaluation. Users may not only develop as users but also go through significant life events, such as changing jobs, having children, and so on, that may change the way they use the system. Sometimes, we wish to carry out long evaluation studies in the field. Such studies may be organized by recruiting users or groups to adopt a prototype for some agreed-upon period of time. Modern software markets and app stores facilitate the direct deployment of prototypes to end-users.

For example, Vitale et al. [857] observed users during an operating system upgrade and followed them over four weeks afterward using a diary method. Required system updates and upgrades are often an overlooked source of frustration for end-users. Yet, the ways that updates and upgrades occur are also designed, and the effects of those designs on users may be evaluated. Their field data showed that participants had negative reactions to the upgrade process.

44.4 Is it worth the hassle?

Field studies offer the highest realism among evaluation methods in HCI; however, they are costly. Are field studies "worth the hassle"? Most of the time, researchers answer "no" [421]. At the same time, many argue that field-based evaluations are critical sources of insights even if they are costly and difficult to conduct. What insights can be obtained only in the field?

Table 44.1 An overview of the main advantages of doing evaluations in the field and in the lab. Note that these factors exist on a spectrum and allow for varying degrees of flexibility.

Type	Advantage	Explanation
Field		
	Realism	Brings evaluation to the context and activities in which the interactive system will be used
	Sociotechnical fit	Enables the discovery of the fit, or lack thereof, between social activities and structures and the system
	Flexible duration	Field evaluations typically last from a few days to a few months
Lab		
	Precision	It is easy to obtain precise measurements of system use and control for factors that are not studied
	Low cost	Requires fewer resources than a field study
	Can evaluate unusual tasks	Tasks that rarely occur "in the wild" can be arranged
	Does not require a robust system	Studies can be run with rough prototypes

Kjeldskov et al. [421] looked at the usability of a mobile medical informatics system to answer this question. To the surprise of the researchers, comparable amounts of usability problems were found in the lab and in the field. Moreover, usability problems associated with the use context were found in both settings; typically, such problems are only detected in field-based evaluations. Therefore, in this particular study, the field-based evaluation was not worth the hassle.

We find such dogmatic views problematic. Consistent with previous methodological discussions in this book, we take the view that field and deployment studies have a number of pros and cons, and neither field studies nor lab studies are inherently "good." Rather, these methods allow us to focus on different aspects of research and sources of information (Chapter 10). Table 44.1 summarizes the main advantages of field- and lab-based evaluations. Field studies offer high realism and may expose phenomena that laboratory studies cannot capture. However, they have lower precision and cost-efficiency than lab studies.

Summary

- Field and deployment studies help evaluate systems by enhancing the realism of the evaluation.
- Realism, and thus the field, is a continuum; many evaluations can be improved by increasing their degree of realism.
- Systems may be partially or fully deployed to evaluate them.

Exercises

1. Methods. Recall the field evaluation methods discussed in this chapter. Which method would you use for the following research needs: (a) learning how Facebook users use a new AI-boosted news feed; (b) learning about the usability of a tangible UI design for aging adults; (c) learning about the navigation behavior of users on a newly launched banking web site.

2. Experimental control in the field versus in the lab. Consider having to run a usability evaluation of a wearable interface that enables firefighters to communicate without a mobile device when on a mission. How would you arrange (a) a laboratory-based usability study and (b) a field-based usability study? Discuss the external validity and construct validity of each study design. Which aspects can be appropriately staged in a laboratory setting and which ones cannot?

Part IX

Conclusion

45
Growing into the HCI discipline

Congratulations on making it to the end of the book! Instead of this being the end, however, we hope that the book becomes a beginning—the beginning of a lifelong journey into studying and developing better technology. Whether your aim is to become an human–computer interaction (HCI) researcher or to apply HCI in your work, it is of paramount importance to keep developing yourself.

HCI research is a dynamic research field characterized by large volumes of results and inventions. The CHI conference alone published 15,738 full papers between 1982 and 2018 [517]. Thousands of new products and services are launched every year with the aim of improving computer use. Cao et al. [124] found that 20% of research papers in popular scientific conferences are referenced by patents; this is a much higher rate than the 1.5% of research papers in science in general. These conferences include the ACM Conference on Human Factors in Computing Systems (CHI), the ACM Conference on Computer-Supported Cooperative Work and Social Computing (CSCW), the ACM Symposium on User Interface Software and Technology (UIST), and the ACM International Joint Conference on Pervasive and Ubiquitous Computing (UbiComp). While we have covered some of what we believe are time-enduring principles of HCI, mastering the discipline is a long-term undertaking.

We now turn to some reflections on how to develop as a practitioner and research in HCI—how to *do* HCI to have a positive *impact* in academia, industry, and the world. We have collected these reflections into eight themes:

1. Learning from research
2. Choosing problems that matter
3. Turning research ideas into plans
4. Appreciating rigor (and its limitations)
5. Envisioning better interactions
6. Practicing HCI ethically
7. Contributing to research
8. Impacting the world.

45.1 Learning from research

There are two chief ways to keep up with HCI literature: technical and social. First, commonly used academic search engines are Google Scholar, SemanticScholar, the ACM Digital Library, and IEEE Xplore. They index papers from academic *journals* and *conferences.* However, if you do not know what you are searching for, you can be easily overwhelmed by the large number of papers. A better way to follow research is to attend the annual conferences and symposia in HCI, such as CHI, CSCW, UbiComp, UIST, IUI (ACM Conference on Intelligent User Interfaces), or

Introduction to Human-Computer Interaction. Kasper Hornbæk, Per Ola Kristensson, and Antti Oulasvirta,
Oxford University Press. © Kasper Hornbæk, Per Ola Kristensson, and Antti Oulasvirta (2025).
DOI: 10.1093/oso/9780192864543.003.0045

DIS (ACM Conference on Designing Interactive Systems). Most of these conferences publish their proceedings online, and there has been a push toward making these open access. The ACM Digital Library is a good starting point for browsing. There are also practitioner conferences, such as those organized by IxDA and UXPA. Such conferences allow you to see paper presentations, learn from tutorials and workshops, and network with peers around the world.

The second way to follow the HCI literature is through social media, which is generally more cost-effective. Mastodon, BlueSky, LinkedIn, X (formerly Twitter), and Facebook offer an easy way to follow recent research. Most research groups and industrial labs maintain a presence on social media. We also encourage establishing activities with peers to follow specific areas of research more actively. Academic research labs and HCI curricula often include reading groups focused on specific subjects.

When following the academic literature, it is important to engage with the plurality of the HCI community. Exciting research is published across the board in areas that may look unrelated. For example, a paper on algorithmic bias in interactive systems could be published in any of the main conferences mentioned previously. Attending these conferences will highlight the strong diversity in disciplinary backgrounds, methods, and approaches in HCI. We believe that the different parts of this book offer a launching pad to engage with the main streams of HCI research in their respective forums.

When following the literature, it is also important to actively reflect and avoid being biased by one's position and terminology. It is well known that researchers tend to cite the work of people they know or associate with, for example, other researchers from the same country or of the same gender, ethnic group, or age. This leads to not only the discrimination of disadvantaged researchers but also poorer science, as we tend to find papers that confirm our predispositions. It is a healthy practice to seek papers that present differing opinions.

When reading a paper, it is important to think critically: What are the mechanisms in play that explain the results? What alternative explanations might explain the results? What opportunities for doing both good and bad arise from the results and were not acknowledged by the authors? Only about 5% of citations in HCI papers are engaged with critically [520]; the others are not contested. Failure to engage critically with research is a threat to any field. If authors do not check facts, false claims can easily spread. For example, in HCI, we often talk about "muscle memory" even though this is not recognized in psychology. Sometimes, such claims start to live a life of their own in papers. For example, a common motivation stated in papers on affective computing is that 93% of communication is nonverbal even if this finding originated from a study with a much more limited scope [520].

How to read a paper critically? In our view, it boils down to considering five core aspects:

Argumentation: Are the conclusions drawn based on solid reasoning? Are there alternative arguments that can explain the conclusions?

Evidence: What is the evidence for the claims, and who or what is their source? How does the presented evidence compare with the evidence presented in earlier research?

Contribution: What new knowledge or competence is learned about HCI that was not known before?

Impact: Who benefits from the result, and how? What can that stakeholder group do better now? The impact can also be negative, such as harm to a group not mentioned by the authors.

Significance: Factoring in the positive and negative effects on different stakeholders, how significant is the result from a technical, economic, social, and ethical perspective?

Not by coincidence, these questions map well to the evaluation criteria used by reviewers at scientific conferences in HCI.

45.2 Choosing problems that matter

How to pick a great research problem? Research problems do not simply "pop up" in researchers' minds; they are often the result of years of development.

A great problem statement addresses a *gap* in knowledge that is important to people and can be tackled with the available resources. A *knowledge gap* is a good heuristic to think about problem statements: What do we not understand yet given our present understanding? A *capability gap* is a variant: What are we not able to do yet?

Given the applied nature of HCI, we should think about gaps that stakeholders care about. Instead of starting from a problem and then asking who cares about it, you can (and often should) start from the end: What do people need to understand or do better? Methods in user research and value-sensitive design are good candidates if you want to more seriously study what stakeholders might actually need. Great research problems are formulated with potential outcomes in mind. Imagine the future point where you have answered your research question: In what way can the answer be useful or guide future research? In the introduction of this book, we brought up the concept of *problem-solving capacity*. Good research produces results that improve stakeholders' capacity to solve important problems.

When thinking about the research gap, you will have to choose the right *level of abstraction*. A low level means high specificity, that is, you address a particular system in a particular context: "Why do aging users make errors when using Microsoft Word version 17.3 when they are sitting near a pool in Belize?" This question may be important for those involved; however, the number of people affected is likely small. Raising the level of abstraction would result in the following formulation: "What causes errors in the use of word processing software, and how do factors related to aging interact with those?" Suddenly, the research would cover millions of users rather than just tens of people. However, excessive abstraction is often not feasible or desirable. For example, you might ask: "What causes errors in human–computer interaction in aging users?" While the question is valid, it is too broad to answer in a single study.

Great problem statements should be expressed in a *solution-neutral manner*. For example, one should not ask "What does the interview method tell us about children's motivation to use tablet computers in schools?" This statement is confounded with a solution. It includes a predisposition to study the question with the interview method even though many different methods could be used: surveys, unobtrusive methods, and so on. A solution-neutral formulation would ask "What motivations do children have to use or not use tablets in schools?"

Research problems should also be formulated in a *refutable* way. A research question that presupposes its answer is probably flawed. Unfortunately, it is very easy to approach research with a predisposition; for example, one may want to prove that a (pet) theory is "right" or demonstrate that a (pet) system is "better" than some baseline. The proper way to formulate questions is to ensure they make no presumptions about the answer. Research problems should be formulated in a way that allows for more than one answer.

To develop relevant problem statements, it is vital to know what has already been done in the field of study. This avoids making naive claims about novelty. Off-hand comments about a problem being novel are almost always wrong. Most—if not all—research problems in HCI have precursors, and it is the duty of the researcher to expose their provenance.

Great research problems also demonstrate critical thinking. HCI practitioners and researchers alike tend to flock to topics that gain attention and funding; however, we should not fall prey to hype. Merely following what others do is not a proper motivation for research. It is wise to look at topics that others might *not* pick. Good research problems could come from forgotten or contested ideas, or they could focus on user groups or phenomena that are being ignored. For example, studies on accessibility and underprivileged user groups attract little industrial funding despite their importance. While we should avoid being led by hype, it is also important to be sensitive to what matters to other people. At the time of writing, key themes discussed in the context of technology include sustainability, discrimination and bias, misinformation in online networks, societal surveillance, the effects of pandemics on computer use, addiction to computers and games, and human-centric AI.

45.3 Turning research ideas into plans

Reading an academic paper on HCI, one may not fully grasp the range of challenges faced in research, from planning to execution. Papers make research look straightforward; in practice, research is messy and involves a lot of muddling in the dark. The beginning of research, when the research problem and approach are defined, is especially hard. Here, proper planning is a lifesaver.

How can one translate a research idea into a workable research plan? A good research plan should be detailed enough to guide execution. It should also prepare the researcher to handle different contingencies. Since the researcher does not control the events that happen in research, the plan should ensure that the results are valid in most realistic circumstances. For example, when planning an experiment, the sample size matters. When planning a design project, the plan must ensure sufficient resources for creative processes. When planning a technical project, the plan must ensure sufficient resources for prototyping and implementation.

Operationalization refers to the translation of an abstract research problem or hypothesis into an actionable, concrete research plan. There are multiple ways a research problem can be operationalized. For example, "What is the effect of formal education in computer science on one's ability to install software packages?" is a meaningful problem that can be studied in numerous ways. In Chapter 10, we discussed the research strategy as the exploration of different methodological options for gathering the desired insights. In other words, what is important—realism, cost-efficiency, or the level of detail or control? Depending on your answer, different research methods should be chosen. However, choosing a research method is not enough. Every method entails a number of subsequent decisions. For example, to carry out a survey study, one must develop a questionnaire, pilot it, and so on.

A *research plan* describes such decisions, possibly with a rationale justifying key choices. Empirical research can be written up following the American Psychological Association's Publication Manual, which outlines the sections that an empirical study should include.

A research plan should cover the underpinning *explanations* of a study. These explanations are the theories, concepts, and models that link the HCI setting we study with the results we obtain. Merely going and measuring things easily leads to results that cannot be properly explained; in other words, we do not understand the *conditions* in which our results hold. Thus, we need to build research plans in a way that allows us to critically entertain alternative explanations. In experimental research, significant attention is paid to identifying and attacking *confounds*. Besides that, we should seek relevant theories, models, and concepts and critically position them against our research.

Finally, research plans are boundary objects (Chapter 8). In other words, documented plans can be given to others for scrutiny. These may be people from the research community (e.g., pre-registration of studies) or representatives of stakeholder groups (e.g., participatory research). Such engagements can help you not only improve your research plan but also involve stakeholders in your research.

45.4 Appreciating rigor (and its limitations)

HCI research is not without consequences: Poor design and poor research can harm and even kill users. As practitioners and researchers of HCI, a prime consideration is that we must stand behind the conclusions we draw—in other words, we must be rigorous. *Rigor* refers to being thorough and careful in research, doing our best to ensure the high quality of both the process and outcomes of a study. What does this mean in practice?

The most important principle of rigor is that the claims we make must be commensurate with the evidence we bring to support them. For example, if you claim that the results of your evaluative study "prove" that your design is better than the baseline, how certain are you that there are no counterexamples or conditions in which your claim fails? To claim something is proven is a strong statement that requires careful consideration of all relevant circumstances. For example, your results might show that "under conditions X, design A is better in these metrics than design B." However, how certain are you that this result generalizes beyond your study?

Rigor calls for us to pay close attention to the validity and reliability of research. In HCI research, there is serious discussion about the reproducibility of findings. Ultimately, this boils down to rigor: What evidence is there that a certain finding can be generalized? However, no matter how much one emphasizes rigor, some uncertainty will remain. Rigor is also about the truthful presentation of results. We should be honest about the limits of our work. The titles and conclusions of papers should accurately express their scope and limits, avoiding overclaims.

HCI is an applied discipline concerned with the production of knowledge *and* the design of interactive systems. We often associate rigor with the former but not the latter. Yet, rigor applies to the latter as well. In that context, it means that the artifacts we present are justified, and key decisions are grounded in observations and theories about users.

Being rigorous for its own sake is dogmatic, however. There are many cases in HCI where it can be outright damaging. Notably, the call for rigor should not throttle creative acts such as experimentation and envisioning. Moreover, we should balance rigor with the needs of stakeholders. For example, releasing results that harm a vulnerable population would be rigorous but ethically unsound. A key part of growing into the HCI discipline is learning to recognize when the requirement of rigor must be relaxed.

45.5 Envisioning better interactions

The HCI literature offers many visions of how humans and computers might interact. Throughout this book, we have discussed several visions, including those of Engelbart [226], Sutherland [807], and Weiser [879]. An attractive aspect of HCI is that it is still a young field with many areas available for further exploration. Engaging in HCI research is an opportunity to widen horizons, create new subfields, discover new interaction techniques, and investigate new ways of using technology.

Much of HCI research boils down to visions of technology use. Such envisioning is occurring continuously via academic HCI conferences and different forums. For instance, there has been a discussion since 2020 about how to integrate interactive technology into the human body [561]. For instance, how to augment human senses through biosensing and actuation? Could humans have additional limbs driven by AI [730]? Visions are also increasingly explored outside of academic labs, such as in startups, incubators, hackerspaces, and do-it-yourself communities [486].

Where can one find inspiration for visions? Beyond the literature and the market, one can seek inspiration from art. Science-fiction movies and novels are full of visions of HCI. The movie *Minority Report*, for example, presented in-air gestural interaction in an illuminating manner that inspired research on the topic. Interactive exhibitions offer opportunities to experience alternative ways to interact with computers.

How to express visions? In Chapter 32, we discussed design fiction as a narrative way of exploring visions. Currently, this type of work is done too little in HCI. A key benefit of design fiction is that it offers a richer exploration of possible futures than vision statements, which tend to be short and biased toward positive outcomes. Moreover, it is important to subject visions to scrutiny by stakeholders; narratives offer a simple way to do this.

Visions can also be developed by "goofing around" with technology. Messing around with technology and asking what-if questions are important activities that can provide new knowledge. Another avenue is to build interaction techniques and systems with no clear purpose and engage in rapid design–build–evaluate cycles to shape new possible ways of interacting. Such tinkering with technology can lead to serendipitous discoveries.

Another approach is to conduct *thought experiments*, some of which suggest that HCI is at the forefront of addressing some of the definitive questions of our time. For example, what would the ultimate user interface look like? What kind of input would it allow? How would it output information? Perhaps it is more worthwhile to consider the ultimate experience machine—what would provide users with the maximum experience? What would give rise to the minimum unreality? Should we prioritize people's concerns or other concerns? Is an optimal interface even possible, considering that trade-offs are inevitable in design? Which dimensions of the ultimate interface should we optimize?

Visions should come with a healthy bit of critical thought. Consider a hypothetical, always-on, maximal social sharing system. Currently, people's presence is fragmented across various computer-mediated channels, each tailored to specific groups and types of communication. At the extreme, sharing could be always on for all groups—is this where social media development is heading? Such a system may violate the fundamental human need for privacy. Thus, this hypothetical social media system raises the need to research new ways of controlling information disclosure.

Alternatively, consider a mind-reading interface. Currently, brain–computer interfaces have very low throughput. However, let us imagine we have a brain–computer interface that achieves perfect inference of the user's thoughts and intentions. Then, the throughput will be limited by how fast you can generate your thoughts. The dilemma is that there is no longer room for private thought and planning; therefore, you still need to offer a means to correct interpretations.

Next, consider the perfect display. Currently, the level of photorealism is rapidly increasing and latency is rapidly decreasing. At the extreme, we could have displays with supra-sensory realism spanning all human senses and with the ability to perfectly represent any relevant physical phenomena. Does such a perfect display raise any dilemmas? Consider the implications of a perfect display replicating physical phenomena such as the user being shot dead, being cut into pieces, or catching a lethal disease.

As another example, consider the perfect AI partner. Currently, AI partners generate dialog, recommendations, decisions, and so on, and users can work in partnerships with AI to improve their performance, for instance, using interactive machine learning. Thus, the behavior of current AI systems is defined by people. At the extreme, an AI partner may perfectly read your mind and carry out all your tasks for you. The dilemma is that you would have no autonomy left—there would no longer be a need for humans at all.

45.6 Practicing HCI ethically

An important part of growing into HCI is developing professional integrity. At a minimum, this means adhering to relevant professional standards. As mentioned in the introduction, the Association of Computing Machinery (ACM) is a central professional organization for HCI researchers and practitioners. The ACM Code of Conduct suggests, among other things, that professionals should adhere to the following moral principles:

- Contribute to society and human well-being. Make sure that the interactive systems that we develop help people flourish.
- Avoid harm. This includes direct physical or psychological harm, as well as indirect harm through the support of harmful practices or organizations.
- Be honest and trustworthy. Make sure that you represent the potential and issues of computing correctly to clients and the public.
- Be fair and do not discriminate. Make sure that the interactive systems that we develop and evaluate are inclusive and accessible.

While these principles can be hard to apply in practice, this is not an excuse to ignore them.

Beyond written standards, HCI researchers and practitioners are ultimately responsible for the people who are affected by their results. ACM suggests that the computing professional, and by implication the HCI practitioner or researcher, has responsibilities. These include producing robust, secure interactive systems and evaluating their likely impact on users, organizations, and society at large. These principles hold universally. They apply to a developer of user interfaces, a PhD student investigating the sustainability of interfaces, a consultant conducting field studies, and a manager building collaborative systems. First and foremost, producing robust and secure systems is a moral responsibility—it transcends codes of conduct. We leave the consideration of pertinent moral principles to the reader; what matters is reflecting on ethics in everyday work.

Some readers may feel that such responsibilities do not belong to them—that they are just students, developers, employees, or subordinates and therefore need not concern themselves with these considerations. In an early paper, Bunge [109] addressed these people:

> The scientist, engineer or manager may well wash his hands but this will not free him from moral duties or social responsibilities—not only qua a human being and a citizen, but also as a professional. And this because, let us recall, they more than any other occupational group are responsible for the shape the world is in. You cannot manipulate the world as if it were a chunk of clay and at the same

time disclaim all responsibility for what you do or refuse to do, particularly since your skills are needed to repair whatever damages you may have done or at least to forestall future such damages. In short, the engineer and the manager, precisely because of the tremendous power they wield or contribute to building up, have a greater not a diminished moral and social responsibility. This being so, they had better face it.

We all need to unwaveringly discuss and argue about HCI findings and practices, using open-minded inquiry and empirical data to advance the field.

45.7 Contributing to research

Imagine that you have carried out a project and want to contribute to HCI research, for example, through a talk or a research paper. An essential part of such engagements is explicating your work's *contribution*. What does a contribution to HCI look like? This can be understood by looking at the *outcomes* of research, which shifts the focus from the research problem to the end result: What have we delivered at the end of a project?

Table 45.1 summarizes seven types of research contributions identified in a review by Wobbrock and Kientz [904]. In *empirical contributions*, new findings are presented from empirical research. The findings can be about a discovery of some new phenomenon or an elaboration of previous understanding. In *artifact contributions*, a new possibility for computing technology is presented. These are often presented in the form of demonstrations or visions. In *methodological contributions*, the goal is to help others obtain information or achieve some end in design more efficiently or effectively. In addition to empirical methods, methods in HCI include analytical methods such as task analysis, where the goal is to interpret empirical data, and constructive methods such as

Table 45.1 Types of research contributions in HCI according to Wobbrock and Kientz [904].

Contribution type	Description	Examples
Empirical	New findings based on observations and gathered data	Experiments, user tests, field observations, interviews, surveys, focus groups, diaries, ethnographies, sensors, and log files
Artifact	New possibilities, explorations, and insights that compel us to consider new possible futures	Systems, architectures, tools, toolkits, techniques, sketches, mock-ups, and visions
Methodological	Insights that influence how we do science or design	Methods that improve how we discover things, measure things, analyze things, create things, or build things
Theoretical	Testable and verifiable explanations of interaction; not simply observing *that* but explaining *why*	New or improved concepts, definitions, models, principles, or frameworks
Survey	Reviews and syntheses that expose trends and gaps	Meta-analyses and reviews
Dataset	A new and useful corpus accompanied by a description of its characteristics for the benefit of the research community	Datasets that support new or improved algorithms, analyses, systems, or methods
Opinion	Insights and views that seek to change the minds of readers through persuasion	Essays and arguments

design processes. *Theoretical contributions* are explanations and models that link propositions about interactions.

Survey-type contributions help researchers understand real-world conditions, for example, by reporting statistical distributions for variables of interest. This is important because it provides a way to gain deeper insight into expert knowledge. Surveys also help prioritize efforts based on data on how prevalent certain events are. For example, some studies of design tools present surveys of professional designers that provide their views on the problem being addressed by the tool. *Dataset contributions* are systematically collected corpora and observational data. They can serve many purposes: training algorithms, forming theories, evaluating models, or investigating empirical phenomena. Datasets support attempts to improve the reproducibility of research. When a dataset is released to the community, other research groups can try to reproduce it and build on it. For example, two published datasets on text entry [191, 637] report the typing patterns of thousands of anonymized users. Such datasets can be used for empirical research and to train better interaction techniques via machine learning. Finally, *opinion-type contributions* are essays, reviews, and other arguments. Many of these are about bridging HCI to other fields. For example, they may take a theory from another field, such as the theory of reinforcement learning (Chapter 21), and translate it to HCI. They may also present new views on core topics in HCI, such as interaction or design.

The table clearly illustrates the diversity of contributions in HCI, providing a tangible example of multidisciplinarity in practice. Perhaps not surprisingly, empirical research is at the center of HCI as a field, which distinguishes it from many other research areas in computer science. What might surprise computer science and behavioral science students, but perhaps not those hailing from design, is that artifacts, often presented in the form of demonstrations or software, can be first-class contributions to HCI research. Conversely, design students may be surprised by HCI's emphasis on theories as the basis of decision-making.

45.8 Impacting the world

Most actors in and around HCI research, especially those funded by taxpayers, have a moral obligation to contribute to the society that supports them. We need to pay back society.

The first thing to ask is who should benefit from the outcomes of research. HCI research has several stakeholder groups besides the research community: end-users of computing systems, the public sector, including governmental and nongovernmental organizations, and companies. Some of these stakeholder groups are disadvantaged. For example, people living in poverty may not have the resources to access the outcomes of research or the ability to put them into practice.

The second question is how to best impact those communities. HCI research has a rich palette of instruments at its disposal. Beyond traditional academic channels, HCI research can impact people through social media, popular media, application markets, start-ups, and consultancy work, among other channels.

Open science is a movement that aims to make scientific research accessible to the broader society. HCI has only recently started to provide open access to its scientific proceedings and journals. However, open science goes beyond merely removing paywalls—it also encompasses open data and open-source code. We should use repositories to share datasets and code while ensuring respect for the rights of the people the data are about.

The principle of openness should be extended to hardware and design. Authors who present prototypes and design artifacts in papers should help others reproduce them, for example, by sharing fabrication instructions. Open science also means open infrastructure: the opening of laboratories, including fabrication laboratories, to the public.

Open science can also mean open educational resources. For example, this book is open access, and so are the materials we developed. In turn, we hope that educators who use this book in teaching will share their experiences and developed materials.

We also have the responsibility to talk to the public about our research. This type of engagement can take a multitude of forms, from press releases to interviews, blog posts, and action research. Such engagement is important because HCI research is vulnerable to being misrepresented and overhyped. When making public statements, we should work with the media to ensure the true scope and limits of the work are disclosed. Statements should not be "colored" to attract publicity. This is detrimental not only to the HCI field but also to society at large.

Summary

- There are many principles in HCI. Understanding and applying such principles can help you engage with HCI problems effectively.
- You can learn from HCI research. It is also important to learn to critically evaluate research in terms of its contributions, validity, benefits, and significance.
- HCI shapes the world, and there are many ways to make contributions to the HCI field.

46
Summary: HCI principles

If there is one theme in this book that ties all the chapters together, it is human-centeredness. Taking human-centeredness seriously is essential for understanding and improving the use of technology in society. What does this mean in practice—how can we make this maxim actionable?

Throughout the book, we have explained what human-centered means in the various contexts of human–computer interaction (HCI). Table 46.1 provides an overview of the key principles that the chapters have covered. By *principle* we mean a statement that serves as a foundation for reasoning about problems in HCI. In this book, we have covered principles that concern how people think and collaborate, how to study the work and aspirations of prospective users, what interaction is, how user interfaces work, and how to design, engineer, and evaluate interactive systems. We sort these principles into three types:

- *Observations* reflect important and recurring aspects or factors of HCI that should be taken into consideration.
- *Models* capture formal relationships that can be exploited, for example, to explain human behavior or make decisions in design.
- *Guidance* provides concrete suggestions for approaching a problem or opportunity in HCI.

By collecting these in one place in Table 46.1, we hope it can serve as a quick and useful reference for HCI teachers and students alike.

Table 46.1 Principles of HCI elaborated in this book.

Book part	Chapter	Principle	Type
Introduction	Chapter 1	Be human centered—focus on people and their needs	Guidance
Understanding People	Chapter 2	Use the general understanding of people across perception, motor control, cognition, needs, experience, collaboration, and communication to understand users	Guidance
	Chapter 3	What we see and hear is driven both top-down by expectations and attention as well as bottom-up	Observation
	Chapter 4	Fitts' law—the movement time is related to the index of difficulty of target acquisition	Model
	Chapter 4	Hick–Hyman law—decreasing uncertainty improves the choice reaction time	Model
	Chapter 5	The difficulty of detecting a signal depends on how easy it is to discriminate the signal from noise	Observation

Continued

Introduction to Human-Computer Interaction. Kasper Hornbæk, Per Ola Kristensson, and Antti Oulasvirta, Oxford University Press. © Kasper Hornbæk, Per Ola Kristensson, and Antti Oulasvirta (2025).
DOI: 10.1093/oso/9780192864543.003.0046

Table 46.1 *Continued*

Book part	Chapter	Principle	Type
	Chapter 5	Learning can be modeled by the power law of practice	Model
	Chapter 5	Minimize the energy and effort required of human cognition; "don't make me think"	Guidance
	Chapter 6	Psychological needs drive interactive behavior, such as autonomy, competence, and relatedness	Model
	Chapter 7	Experiences are indirectly influenced by the designer—they cannot be designed directly	Observation
	Chapter 8	Support *awareness*—a collaborator's ability to follow what others do, how their subtasks are progressing, and what they attend to	Guidance
	Chapter 9	Communication mediated through an interactive system is different from face-to-face communication	Observation
	Chapter 9	Computer-mediated communication can be understood by the features of the channels, its uses, and its impact on individual and social functions of the communication	Observation
User Research	Chapter 10	You are not the user—your intuition is insufficient for design; user research is needed	Observation
	Chapter 10	All research methods are limited, for instance with respect to their realism, generalizability, and precision	Model
	Chapter 11	Interviews allow for developing an understanding of the lives of others	Observation
	Chapter 12	You can gain realism—insights into how users act, collaborate, and communicate in their natural environments—through field research	Observation
	Chapter 13	You can achieve generalizability by obtaining information from many respondents through surveys	Observation
	Chapter 14	Use unobtrusive methods, such as log analysis, to study users and their tasks without invention, that is, without affecting or changing their activities	Guidance
	Chapter 15	Data are just observations of users—to obtain insights for design, we need to arrive at representations	Observation
Interaction	Chapter 16	Interaction cannot be attributed solely to the human or the computer—the two must be considered together	Observation
	Chapter 17	Use information theory to formally view interaction as the passing of messages over a noisy channel	Guidance
	Chapter 17	Use control theory to formally view interaction as the changing of some signal toward a desired goal state based on feedback	Guidance
	Chapter 18	Interaction that is organized as a series of turns can be modeled as a dialogue	Observation
	Chapter 18	Model dialogue as computation to enable the formal analysis of several important properties of interaction, such as consistency, error recovery cost, and reversibility	Guidance

Book part	Chapter	Principle	Type
	Chapter 19	Interactive systems are tools—users use them to achieve particular objectives	Observation
	Chapter 20	View automation as a function allocation problem—deciding which functions should be automated, with what type of automation, and at what level of automation	Guidance
	Chapter 20	Use a mixed-initiative interface to allow both users and automated services to take the initiative in interaction	Guidance
	Chapter 21	Interaction emerges from users maximizing utility through their choices	Observation
	Chapter 22	For interaction to work, it needs to support practice—a way of regulating the use of computers such that it appropriately aligns with needs and contexts	Observation
	Chapter 22	Interaction is about more than providing a particular input or getting a task done—it is about advancing users' broader life and work goals	Observation
User Interfaces	Chapter 23	User interfaces comprise input devices, interaction techniques, representations, and assemblies	Model
	Chapter 23	User interfaces involve trade-offs, for instance between speed and accuracy, appropriateness for novices and experts, and between those that do the work and those who reap the benefits	Observation
	Chapter 24	Analyze an input device through three levels: computational, representational, and hardware	Guidance
	Chapter 25	A display should ensure the intended information is available to the user, avoiding transmission of biased or incomplete information	Guidance
	Chapter 26	An interaction technique should programmatically couple input and output	Guidance
	Chapter 26	Interaction techniques should balance the trade-off between learnability and performance	Guidance
	Chapter 26	Focus not only on ultimate performance but also on incentivizing users to start and persist in learning an interaction technique	Guidance
	Chapter 27	The organization of information fundamentally affects how users can access information through commands, navigation, and search	Observation
	Chapter 27	The vocabulary problem suggests that users are likely to name objects and actions in different ways, challenging interaction designers	Observation
	Chapter 28	Direct manipulation is realized through: (1) continuous representations of the objects and actions of interest; (2) physical actions or presses of labeled buttons instead of complex syntax; and (3) rapid, reversible, and	Model

Continued

Table 46.1 *Continued*

Book part	Chapter	Principle	Type
		incremental actions whose effects are visible immediately	
	Chapter 29	A reality-based interface should use the users' physical surroundings to contribute to interaction either explicitly by being represented in the interface or implicitly by affecting it via other factors	Guidance
Design	Chapter 30	Iteration is necessary for design, as it is practically impossible to know the specifics of what needs to be designed from the outset	Observation
	Chapter 30	Design is a process of divergent and convergent processes, as captured in the double diamond model of design thinking	Model
	Chapter 31	Cognitive biases lead to design fixation	Observation
	Chapter 31	Ensure the systematic use of creative methods to manage the generation of ideas in design	Guidance
	Chapter 32	Designers not only solve problems but also make sense of materials to refine them—they reflect on their practices to improve them and their positions as designers	Observation
	Chapter 32	Use design fiction to take distance from the present and develop possible futures centered on a design idea	Guidance
	Chapter 33	Reduce the risk in a project by selecting an appropriate design process and applying methods and techniques systematically	Guidance
Engineering	Chapter 34	Use systematic principles and methods from engineering to ensure interactive systems are effective, efficient, and safe	Guidance
	Chapter 35	Systems are pervasive; interactive systems are embedded within and interact with other systems	Observation
	Chapter 35	Use systems thinking to reason about systems, including how they are embedded within other systems, how they work over time, and how subsystems and other parts of a system contribute to the wider system	Guidance
	Chapter 35	Use system mapping to describe systems in terms of processes, tasks, people, information flows, and other relevant aspects	Guidance
	Chapter 36	Derive a solution-neutral problem statement to ensure you build the right thing	Guidance
	Chapter 36	Create and manage a requirements specification and use verification to ensure you build the thing right	Guidance
	Chapter 36	Design a model of a system at the functional level and then explore how to translate functions into function carriers	Guidance
	Chapter 37	Determine the acceptable level of risk of your system	Guidance

Book part	Chapter	Principle	Type
	Chapter 37	Define a suitable system boundary to ensure risk analysis is both tractable and captures all relevant aspects	Guidance
	Chapter 37	Use a hazard function to calculate the failure rate of a system or component at the next instant given that the component or system has not failed up to that point	Model
	Chapter 37	If the time to a system or component failure is exponentially distributed, the failure rate is constant	Observation
	Chapter 38	Use formal methods to specify, develop, and verify systems where correctness is vital	Guidance
	Chapter 39	Computational methods, such as envelope analysis, optimization, and learning, can be used to represent aspects of interaction	Guidance
Evaluation	Chapter 40	Evaluate systems to attribute value to them; they might not work as you expect	Guidance
	Chapter 40	Choose and tailor evaluation methods to specific tasks, technologies, and user groups, as evaluation methods have different strengths and weaknesses	Guidance
	Chapter 41	Use analytic methods to cost-efficiently evaluate systems at various stages of the design	Guidance
	Chapter 41	Analytic methods are not a replacement for empirical evaluation methods	Observation
	Chapter 41	The keystroke-level model is a linear analytic model of task completion time for sequential tasks	Model
	Chapter 42	Use think-aloud studies to gain insights about users' thinking processes and to infer usability problems	Guidance
	Chapter 42	Increase the cost-efficiency and reliability of think-aloud studies by following best practices	Guidance
	Chapter 43	Use experiments to demonstrate causal relationships between the manipulation of independent variables and measurements of dependent variables	Guidance
	Chapter 43	Use parametric models when you can assume that the data are sampled from a population that can be modeled by a probability distribution with a set of parameters	Guidance
	Chapter 43	Use non-parametric models when you cannot assume that an explicit probability distribution with a set of parameters can adequately model your data	Guidance
	Chapter 44	Use field and deployment studies to enhance the realism of evaluation	Guidance
	Chapter 44	Realism, and therefore the field, is a continuum—many evaluations can beimproved by increasing their degree of realism	Observation
Conclusion	Chapter 45	Understand HCI principles and apply them when appropriate to ensure best practices when engaging in HCI activities	Guidance

Exercises

The following exercises combine topics from across the book.

1. Bias in design. As you learned in the chapter on design cognition (Chapter 31), there are many cognitive biases that are detrimental to design. Consider the conscious and unconscious biases embedded in the design of user interfaces, such as door handles being at a certain height. Can you find user interfaces that favor some user groups at the expense of others? How should these user interfaces be redesigned to avoid biases?
2. Design and unwanted side effects. Infinite scrolling is an example of a double-edged UI innovation. On the one hand, it provides quicker access to more content. On the other hand, it can make people addicted to scrolling. In Chapter 6, we learned about factors that promote behavior change. The same factors can make someone form habits and even addictions. How could one recognize the potential for forming a habit prior to the release of a feature?
3. Principles behind UIs. Using the principles presented in the book, explain the HCI mechanisms behind the following user interfaces: (a) linear hierarchical pull-down menus, including their structures, as implemented by the operating system on your computer; (b) the keyboard interface on your mobile phone, including any gesture typing, word prediction, and autocorrect functions; (c) the interface for selecting TV shows and movies in an online streaming service; and (d) the word processor you are most familiar with.
4. Design processes. Propose and motivate a process model for the following design tasks: (a) a magnetic resonance imaging visualization tool for medical practitioners; (b) a smart wristband that collects biophysical measurements from the user and provides exercise and lifestyle advice; (c) a shopping web site for clothes that allows users to "try out" clothes in virtual reality; and (d) a mobile phone app that teaches children spelling.
5. Usability versus aesthetics. Tractinsky et al. [826] presented evidence that beautiful designs can also be usable. Read their paper and discuss potential threats to the validity of their experiment. Discuss how their hypothesis could be tested to obtain generalizable results.
6. Understanding autocorrect. A problem when using autocorrect on a smartphone keyboard is that the system may inadvertently correct text that should not be corrected. This problem has been colloquially described as the "autocorrect trap." A smartphone keyboard redesign attempts to alleviate this problem by allowing users to press harder on keys the user does not want the autocorrect algorithm to change. The harder the key press, the less likely the autocorrect algorithm changes that letter into a different letter.
    (a) Is this system open-loop or closed-loop interaction, or a combination of both? Briefly motivate your answer.
    (b) A key assumption behind this system is that users can tell beforehand whether the autocorrect algorithm is likely to autocorrect their input into the intended text. Suggest a suitable research method for validating this assumption among a large body of smartphone keyboard users. Briefly motivate your answer.
    (c) The system is implemented and evaluated in an experiment. Users are provided with sentences from a corpus and they are asked to type them as quickly and accurately as possible. The independent variable, *CorrectionMethod*, has two levels: AutoCorrect and Pressure-Sensitive-AutoCorrect. The dependent variables are the entry and error rates. Explain why a within-participants design is both suitable and practical.

(d) Discuss internal and external validity threats to the experiment outlined above.

7. Contribution types. Skim the CHI proceedings (e.g., at ACM Digital Library) and pick 10 papers you find interesting based on their abstracts. Then, classify the papers' contributions using the classification by Wobbrock and Kientz [904].

8. Identifying stakeholders. How would you go about identifying the stakeholders of a medical information system in a hospital?

9. Designing a human-centered project. Consider leading a team tasked with a human-centered engineering project: the redesign of an emergency medical dispatch workstation. Your task is to select appropriate methods for the project. For example, you may consider methods such as task analysis, usability evaluation, sketching, and rapid prototyping. Propose the main project phases (user research, evaluation, analysis, etc.) and one or more methods for each phase, justifying your choices. Your proposal should convince the customer that this is an efficient and appropriate plan for the project. The proposal should describe something that a team of five HCI researchers can achieve in six months of full-time work.

    Case brief: The goal of your hypothetical project is to propose improvements to an existing workstation for a medical dispatch operator. The proposed design should improve the productivity of the dispatcher (rate of dispatches) without compromising efficacy (accuracy of dispatches). The workstation consists of the software and hardware user interface that the dispatcher uses. (You may want to make some assumptions about which parts your project will address.) The outcome of your project should be a concept and a prototype implementation of the improved workstation. The customer also wants solid evidence for the solution, especially for its superiority over the current design. Before starting the project, read more about medical dispatch centers: https://en.wikipedia.org/wiki/Emergency_medical_dispatcher.

10. Collaborative systems. A design team is creating a collaborative information visualization interface for a team of 2–3 analysts. The visual display measures 4 × 4 m and is mounted on a wall. The positions of the individual users are tracked using an array of depth cameras mounted on top of the visual display, allowing the system to know the position of each user in relation to both the other users and the display. The information visualized changes depending on the distance between an analyst and the display: The closer the analyst is to the display, the more detailed information is provided. If two analysts stand close together, they experience the same information visualization. If two analysts stand farther apart, the display splits and shows them different visualizations that change individually depending on their respective distances from the display.

    (a) Indicate where this system is situated in the two-axis model of collaborative technology.
    (b) Explain how this system fits within the reality-based interaction framework.
    (c) Explain the difference between collaboration and cooperation.
    (d) Three analysts are to use this system to collaboratively gain insight into a complex dataset. Discuss how this system may support or impact their coordination.

11. Research strategy. A design team is tasked with creating a user interface and a workflow for a new purchasing system for a firm that makes embedded devices and has 8,000 employees distributed across the UK, United States, and Australia. The firm has an unusual set of requirements and work practices for purchases due to working in a niche area that is heavily restricted by regulations and international law. The purchasing system is to be used by engineers, engineering managers, and quality assurance testers in the UK, United States, and Australia.

(a) Propose a research strategy for carrying out user research with the stakeholders. Motivate the underlying principles with reference to the purchasing system.

(b) The design team has decided to carry out the user research by first distributing a survey to all end-users. The survey results will then be analyzed and subsequently used as a basis for contextual inquiry, which will be carried out in the UK due to the design team being based there. Discuss possible issues with the quality of this methodology.

(c) Explain how the principles of contextual inquiry could be used to gain insight into users' needs and wants based on their interactions with the existing purchasing system.

(d) Describe the say–do gap. Would the say–do gap apply to the contextual inquiry planned by the design team? Explain your reasoning.

12. Designing for children. A central task in children's education is learning multiplication tables. To support this, a design team has created a tablet app that challenges children in a class to quickly carry out a series of 10 multiplications. Depending on their speed and accuracy, each child receives points that can be used to buy equipment and clothing for a virtual rock band. This virtual rock band can be shared with other children in the class. The app is administered by the teacher, and both the teacher and the parents can observe a child's progress.

    (a) Explain how the human needs that are important according to self-determination theory support this design.

    (b) In the event that a child inputs an incorrect answer, explain the difference between a mistake and a slip. Briefly describe what a mistake or a slip may tell us about the child's learning.

    (c) Explain whether a child is exhibiting skill-, rule-, or knowledge-based behavior when using the app to answer multiplication questions.

    (d) Propose a strategy for managing the risks inherent in this system.

13. Identifying ethical problems. HCI allows you to design a wide variety of interfaces for a range of applications. For the following HCI applications, comment on whether it is possible—and if so, how—to ethically create user interfaces: (a) an instant loan mobile app; (b) an online casino; (c) a recommender-based news feed app that operates on an advertising-based business model; and (d) a mobile game that uses gamification features to keep users engaged.

14. Defining the field. Having read the book, how do you think the field should be defined? We defined HCI in the introduction (Section 1.2); this definition was published in 1992. Update it and discuss it with a group of peers.

15. Ethics of HCI publications. What kinds of HCI results cannot be published? Justify your answer.

16. Sustainability and HCI. Consider the United Nations sustainability development goals. Which ones can HCI contribute to, and how?

17. Users and stakeholders. Pick a journey planner you use as the starting point for a group discussion. Who are the direct users of the planner? Who are the indirect users of the planner? What are the ethical and political challenges in designing a journey planner?

18. User research methods. Discuss whether it is best to use questionnaires, interviews, or field studies to investigate the following aspects. Use concepts from the book to point out the advantages and disadvantages of the different methods.

    (a) To what extent and why do people feel dependent on social media?

(b) How many apps do iPhone users have on their phones?

(c) What is difficult about being an editor at Wikipedia?

(d) Why do people forget to tap their travel cards? For example, passengers in London may forget to tap their cards when getting out of the tube system.

(e) Why is a natural health record system difficult to use?

19. Accessibility. Consider designing an interface for a vending machine that is used in semi-public spaces such as hotel lobbies. The design should cater to user groups facing three types of accessibility challenges:

    (a) Neurological challenges, for example, autism

    (b) Sight limitations

    (c) Limited mobility, for example, due to cerebral palsy.

    Research basic information about these three user groups. Then, list five design considerations for each group.

20. Elicitation of user requirements and needs. Imagine that you have to develop an application that supports feelings of togetherness among geographically distributed family members during crises (e.g., the COVID-19 pandemic). First, discuss how you understand this activity, the users and stakeholders involved, and the contexts in which use could take place. Then, discuss which empirical methods you could use to identify user needs and requirements to build an application. In particular, discuss the advantages and disadvantages of contextual inquiry.

21. Human cognition and interaction design. For this long assignment, choose an interactive system that allows you to focus on a clearly defined part of the system, such as a single screen or a short interaction sequence. The system can be a web page, a console, a mobile phone, a desktop application, or something completely different. Analyze the system based on the principles of human thinking from Part II. Choose a model for analyzing the system and describe your work in a three-part report covering the following three aspects.

    (a) Describe the system you have chosen and the task you are focusing on. The description must be understandable by people who have not seen or used the system. Support your description with one or more pictures or illustrations of the system and the task.

    (b) Analyze the system using the principles of human thinking from the book. Describe two parts of the system that follow the principles and two parts that contradict them, preferably with pictures or illustrations. Ensure that your analysis is supported by references and that it is clear which parts of the system's user interface you are writing about. Referring to the book's ideas about usability, discuss the consequences for the end-users if the principles are not followed.

    (c) Report your analysis of the user experience or psychological needs. Use at least one model from the respective chapters in Part II. Discuss the system and the user's task based on the chosen model. Which aspects of user experience or needs are supported? Which ones are not supported? What changes could be made to the system to enhance the user experience or the satisfaction of their psychological needs?

22. Empirical research concepts. Discuss the concepts of generalizability, realism, and precision. What do they mean in empirical research in HCI? Identify three methods that are uniquely strong and three methods that are uniquely weak in these respects.

23. Understanding usability. Identify a system that is difficult for you to use. What is it about the tasks, the design, the context of use, or yourself that makes the system difficult to use?

Using concepts covered in this book, consider how users who are less technically able than you would cope with the system.

24. User interfaces. Think of a scenario where a user needs to interact with their surroundings.
    (a) Think about three different types of user interfaces that can be used to perform the selection task in this scenario, for example, (i) a touchscreen mobile phone, (ii) an augmented reality head-mounted display, and (ii) a speech-based user interface.
    (b) Describe the three user interfaces from each of the following perspectives: (i) sensing (sensors and signal processing), (ii) interaction techniques (compound tasks and transfer functions), and (iii) feedback (modalities and directness). Do this in a table with the three user interfaces in the columns and the three perspectives in the rows.
    (c) Then, analyze the pros and cons of the three user interfaces in the selection task. Use the table to compare the demands and possibilities of the three user interfaces from each perspective.

25. User-centered design. In this assignment, you will analyze an everyday object based on the idea of user-centered design. Analyzing an everyday item will help you notice good and bad design in simple things and put the user at the center of design. Choose something interactive—something that you can manipulate and that reacts to your manipulation. For example, it could be a stove, a lift, a camera, a washing machine, or an automated teller machine. You may not choose a computer, a phone, software, or things covered in the book. Analyze the thing based on the principles of user-centered design. The analysis must identify what users (in this case, you) experience as good and bad aspects of the design. It must also clearly relate these experiences to concepts discussed in the book. Present your analysis in a three-part report.
    (a) Describe the thing you have chosen and give at least one example of an interaction with the thing. The description must be understandable by people who have not seen or used the thing. Support your description with at least one picture or illustration of the item.
    (b) Explain what you think user-centered design means in relation to the thing you have chosen.
    (c) Exemplify how your thing is or is not user-centered. Give at least three examples of this. What are the consequences of the thing being (or not being) user-centered? At least one of the good or bad aspects of the design must relate to perception or motor control.

26. Rethinking user-centered design. In a sense, this whole book is about user-centered design. While there are definitions and processes provided for user-centered design, we encourage you to form your own view. Starting from the definitions given in Part VI, outline what user-centered means to you in your own words. Identify 1–2 examples of user-centered systems. What makes them user-centered? What consequences does this have? How do you think they were developed? Try to think of some examples of systems that are not user-centered. Do they work more or less well than user-centered systems? Why are there systems developed without a focus on the users?

27. Expert evaluation. Complete an expert evaluation of a web site of your choice. In your answer, do the following.
    (a) Choose a method for expert evaluation from Part VIII, justify your choice, and discuss the advantages and disadvantages of the chosen method compared to other evaluation methods.

(b) Describe the planning of the evaluation: how you register usability problems, which tasks you use, and how you practically carry out the evaluation.

(c) Explain three significant challenges in using the evaluation method. Compare them with the challenges described in the book.

(d) Summarize the result of the evaluation and document it in detail, including a list of the main problems. For each problem, provide a description, an analysis of its causes, and a severity rating.

28. Dark patterns. Knowledge of how people think can be used constructively in interaction design. However, it can also be used negatively in user interfaces—something called *dark patterns* in the literature. Take 15 minutes to read this article: https://uxdesign.cc/dark-patterns-in-ux-design-7009a83b233c. Then, list three dark patterns you have encountered on web sites or other interactive systems and discuss what aspects of human psychology they exploit. Additionally, discuss your responsibilities as a system developer in relation to such dark patterns.

29. Professional responsibility. Read the first part (Section 1.1) of the ACM Code of Ethics and Professional Conduct: https://ethics.acm.org. Consider a role that you may take in the future and discuss the implications of this section of the code for your future work. What are your responsibilities? What must others take care of?

References

1. D. A. Abbink, T. Carlson, M. Mulder et al. A topology of shared control systems—finding common ground in diversity. *IEEE transactions on human-machine systems*, 48(5):509–525, 2018.
2. V. V. Abeele, K. Spiel, L. Nacke, D. Johnson, and K. Gerling. Development and validation of the player experience inventory: A scale to measure player experiences at the level of functional and psychosocial consequences. *International journal of human-computer studies*, 135:102370, 2020.
3. G. D. Abowd. Classroom 2000: An experiment with the instrumentation of a living educational environment. *IBM systems journal*, 38(4):508–530, 1999.
4. G. D. Abowd and A. J. Dix. Giving undo attention. *Interacting with computers*, 4(3):317–342, 1992.
5. G. D. Abowd, H.-M. Wang, and A. F. Monk. A formal technique for automated dialogue development. In *Proceedings of the 1st conference on designing interactive systems: Processes, practices, methods, & techniques*, pages 219–226, 1995.
6. J. Accot and S. Zhai. Beyond fitts' law: models for trajectory-based hci tasks. In *Proceedings of the ACM SIGCHI conference on human factors in computing systems*, pages 295–302, 1997.
7. J. Accot and S. Zhai. More than dotting the i's—foundations for crossing-based interfaces. In *Proceedings of the SIGCHI conference on human factors in computing systems*, pages 73–80, 2002.
8. M. S. Ackerman. The intellectual challenge of cscw: The gap between social requirements and technical feasibility. *Human–computer interaction*, 15(2-3):179–203, 2000.
9. A. T. Adams, J. Costa, M. F. Jung, and T. Choudhury. Mindless computing: Designing technologies to subtly influence behavior. In *Proceedings of the 2015 ACM international joint conference on pervasive and ubiquitous computing*, pages 719–730, 2015.
10. E. Adar, J. Teevan, and S. T. Dumais. Large scale analysis of web revisitation patterns. In *Proceedings of the SIGCHI conference on human factors in computing systems*, pages 1197–1206, 2008.
11. A. Agarawala and R. Balakrishnan. Keepin'it real: Pushing the desktop metaphor with physics, piles and the pen. In *Proceedings of the SIGCHI conference on human factors in computing systems*, pages 1283–1292, 2006.
12. D. Ahlström. Modeling and improving selection in cascading pull-down menus using fitts' law, the steering law and force fields. In *Proceedings of the SIGCHI conference on human factors in computing systems*, pages 61–70, 2005.
13. D. Akers, M. Simpson, R. Jeffries, and T. Winograd. Undo and erase events as indicators of usability problems. In *Proceedings of the SIGCHI conference on human factors in computing systems*, CHI '09, page 659–668, New York, NY, USA, 2009.
14. D. Alais and D. Burr. The ventriloquist effect results from near-optimal bimodal integration. *Current biology*, 14(3):257–262, 2004.
15. O. Alhadreti and P. Mayhew. Rethinking thinking aloud: A comparison of three think-aloud protocols. In *Proceedings of the 2018 CHI conference on human factors in computing systems*, pages 1–12, 2018.
16. E. M. Altmann and J. G. Trafton. Memory for goals: An activation-based model. *Cognitive science*, 26(1):39–83, 2002.
17. T. M. Amabile. Motivating creativity in organizations: On doing what you love and loving what you do. *California management review*, 40(1):39–58, 1997.
18. S. Amershi, D. Weld, M. Vorvoreanu et al. Guidelines for human-ai interaction. In *Proceedings of the 2019 CHI conference on human factors in computing systems*, CHI '19, page 1–13, 2019.

19 S. Amershi, D. Weld, M. Vorvoreanu et al. Guidelines for human-ai interaction. In *Proceedings of the 2019 chi conference on human factors in computing systems*, pages 1–13, 2019.

20 M. Ames and M. Naaman. Why we tag: Motivations for annotation in mobile and online media. In *Proceedings of the SIGCHI conference on human factors in computing systems*, pages 971–980, 2007.

21 J. R. Anderson and L. J. Schooler. The adaptive nature of memory. In *The Oxford handbook of memory*. Oxford University Press, 2000.

22 J. R. Anderson, D. Bothell, C. Lebiere, and M. Matessa. An integrated theory of list memory. *Journal of memory and language*, 38(4):341–380, 1998.

23 C. Andrews, A. Endert, and C. North. Space to think: Large high-resolution displays for sensemaking. In *Proceedings of the SIGCHI conference on human factors in computing systems*, CHI '10, page 55–64, 2010.

24 J. Annett. Hierarchical task analysis. *Handbook of cognitive task design*, 2:17–35, 2003.

25 L. Anthony, Y. Kim, and L. Findlater. Analyzing user-generated youtube videos to understand touchscreen use by people with motor impairments. In *Proceedings of the SIGCHI conference on human factors in computing systems*, pages 1223–1232, 2013.

26 G. Apitz and F. Guimbretière. Crossy: A crossing-based drawing application. In *Proceedings of the 17th annual ACM symposium on user interface software and technology*, pages 3–12, 2004.

27 C. Appert and J.-D. Fekete. Orthozoom scroller: 1d multi-scale navigation. In *Proceedings of the SIGCHI conference on human factors in computing systems*, pages 21–30, 2006.

28 D. Ascone, T. Tonja Lindsey, and C. Varghese. An examination of driver distraction as recorded in nhtsa databases. Technical report, United States. National Highway Traffic Safety Administration, 2009.

29 T. Augsten, K. Kaefer, R. Meusel et al. Multitoe: High-precision interaction with back-projected floors based on high-resolution multi-touch input. In *Proceedings of the 23nd annual ACM symposium on user interface software and technology*, pages 209–218, 2010.

30 L. Azzopardi and G. Zuccon. Economic models of interaction. In Oulasvirta et al. *Computational interaction*, page 311, 2018.

31 C. Baber and N. A. Stanton. Human error identification techniques applied to public technology: Predictions compared with observed use. *Applied ergonomics*, 27(2):119–131, 1996.

32 P. Bach-y Rita, C. C. Collins, F. A. Saunders, B. White, and L. Scadden. Vision substitution by tactile image projection. *Nature*, 221(5184):963–964, 1969.

33 P. Bach-y Rita, M. E. Tyler, and K. A. Kaczmarek. Seeing with the brain. *International journal of human-computer interaction*, 15(2):285–295, 2003.

34 M. Bachynskyi, G. Palmas, A. Oulasvirta, J. Steimle, and T. Weinkauf. Performance and ergonomics of touch surfaces: A comparative study using biomechanical simulation. In *Proceedings of the 33rd annual ACM conference on human factors in computing systems*, pages 1817–1826, 2015.

35 G. Bailly, E. Lecolinet, and L. Nigay. Visual menu techniques. *ACM computing surveys (CSUR)*, 49(4):1–41, 2016.

36 L. Bainbridge. Ironies of automation. *Automatica*, 19(6):775–779, 1983.

37 T. Ballendat, N. Marquardt, and S. Greenberg. Proxemic interaction: Designing for a proximity and orientation-aware environment. In *ACM international conference on interactive tabletops and surfaces*, ITS '10, page 121–130, New York, NY, USA, 2010.

38 D. Banakou and M. Slater. Body ownership causes illusory self-attribution of speaking and influences subsequent real speaking. *Proceedings of the national academy of sciences*, 111(49):17678–17683, 2014.

39 A. Bangor, P. T. Kortum, and J. T. Miller. An empirical evaluation of the system usability scale. *International Journal of human–computer interaction*, 24(6):574–594, 2008.

40 J. E. Bardram, M. Frost, K. Szántó et al. Designing mobile health technology for bipolar disorder: A field trial of the monarca system. In *Proceedings of the SIGCHI conference on human factors in computing systems*, pages 2627–2636, 2013.

41 J. Bardzell and S. Bardzell. What is "critical" about critical design? In *Proceedings of the SIGCHI conference on human factors in computing systems*, pages 3297–3306, 2013.

42 J. A. Bargas-Avila and K. Hornbæk. Old wine in new bottles or novel challenges: A critical analysis of empirical studies of user experience. In *Proceedings of the SIGCHI conference on human factors in computing systems*, CHI '11, pages 2689–2698, New York, NY, USA, 2011.

43 I. Bark, A. Følstad, and J. Gulliksen. Use and usefulness of hci methods: Results from an exploratory study among nordic hci practitioners. In *People and computers XIX—The bigger picture*, pages 201–217. Springer, 2006.

44 L. Barkhuus and J. A. Rode. From mice to men-24 years of evaluation in chi. In *Proceedings of the SIGCHI conference on human factors in computing systems*, pages 1–16, 2007.

45 S. B. Barnes. Alan kay: Transforming the computer into a communication medium. *IEEE annals of the history of computing*, 29(2):18–30, 2007.

46 L. F. Barrett. *How emotions are made: The secret life of the brain*. Pan Macmillan, 2017.

47 R. Barrett, E. Kandogan, P. P. Maglio, E. M. Haber, L. A. Takayama, and M. Prabaker. Field studies of computer system administrators: Analysis of system management tools and practices. In *Proceedings of the 2004 ACM conference on Computer supported cooperative work*, pages 388–395, 2004.

48 C. Bartneck, D. Kulièc, E. Croft, and S. Zoghbi. Measurement instruments for the anthropomorphism, animacy, likeability, perceived intelligence, and perceived safety of robots. *International journal of social robotics*, 1(1):71–81, 2009.

49 L. Bass, C. Kasabach, R. Martin, D. Siewiorek, A. Smailagic, and J. Stivoric. The design of a wearable computer. In *Proceedings of the ACM SIGCHI conference on human factors in computing systems*, pages 139–146, 1997.

50 T. Baudel and M. Beaudouin-Lafon. Charade: Remote control of objects using free-hand gestures. *Communications of the ACM*, 36(7):28–35, 1993.

51 P. Baudisch and R. Rosenholtz. Halo: A technique for visualizing off-screen objects. In *Proceedings of the SIGCHI conference on human factors in computing systems*, pages 481–488, 2003.

52 N. K. Baym. Social networks 2.0. *The handbook of Internet studies*, pages 384–405, 2011.

53 M. Beaudouin-Lafon. Instrumental interaction: an interaction model for designing post-wimp user interfaces. In *Proceedings of the SIGCHI conference on human factors in computing systems*, pages 446–453, 2000.

54 M. Beaudouin-Lafon. Designing interaction, not interfaces. In *Proceedings of the working conference on advanced visual interfaces*, AVI '04, page 15–22, New York, 2004.

55 M. Beaudouin-Lafon. Designing interaction, not interfaces. In *Proceedings of the working conference on advanced visual interfaces*, pages 15–22, 2004.

56 B. B. Bederson and B. Shneiderman. *The craft of information visualization: Readings and reflections*. Morgan Kaufmann, 2003.

57 B. B. Bederson, B. Lee, R. M. Sherman, P. S. Herrnson, and R. G. Niemi. Electronic voting system usability issues. In *Proceedings of the SIGCHI conference on human factors in computing systems*, pages 145–152, 2003.

58 V. Bellotti and S. Bly. Walking away from the desktop computer: Distributed collaboration and mobility in a product design team. In *Proceedings of the 1996 ACM conference on computer supported cooperative work*, pages 209–218, 1996.

59 V. Bellotti, M. Back, W. K. Edwards, R. E. Grinter, A. Henderson, and C. Lopes. Making sense of sensing systems: Five questions for designers and researchers. In *Proceedings of the SIGCHI conference on human factors in computing systems*, pages 415–422, 2002.

60 E. Beneteau, O. K. Richards, M. Zhang, J. A. Kientz, J. Yip, and A. Hiniker. Communication breakdowns between families and alexa. In *Proceedings of the 2019 CHI conference on human factors in computing systems*, pages 1–13, 2019.

61 M. Bengtsson. How to plan and perform a qualitative study using content analysis. *NursingPlus open*, 2:8–14, 2016.

62. D. Benyon. *Designing user experience.* Pearson UK, 2019.
63. J. Bergstrom-Lehtovirta, A. Oulasvirta, and S. Brewster. The effects of walking speed on target acquisition on a touchscreen interface. In *Proceedings of the 13th international conference on human computer interaction with mobile devices and services*, pages 143–146, 2011.
64. T. Berlage. A selective undo mechanism for graphical user interfaces based on command objects. *ACM transactions on computer–human interaction (TOCHI)*, 1(3):269–294, 1994.
65. M. Bernstein. The bookmark and the compass: orientation tools for hypertext users. *ACM SIGOIS bulletin*, 9(4):34–45, 1988.
66. J. Berström and K. Hornbæk. DIRA: A Model of the User Interface. *International journal of human–computer studies*, 2025.
67. E. Bertini, S. Gabrielli, S. Kimani, T. Catarci, and G. Santucci. Appropriating and assessing heuristics for mobile computing. In *Proceedings of the working conference on advanced visual interfaces*, AVI '06, page 119–126, New York, NY, USA, 2006.
68. N. Bevan. Quality in use: Meeting user needs for quality. *Journal of systems and software*, 49(1):89–96, 1999.
69. W. L. Bewley, T. L. Roberts, D. Schroit, and W. L. Verplank. Human factors testing in the design of xerox's 8010 "star" office workstation. In *Proceedings of the SIGCHI conference on human factors in computing systems*, CHI '83, page 72–77, New York, NY, USA, 1983.
70. X. Bi, B. A. Smith, and S. Zhai. Multilingual touchscreen keyboard design and optimization. *Human–computer interaction*, 27(4):352–382, 2012.
71. R. G. Bias and D. J. Mayhew. *Cost-justifying usability: An update for the Internet age.* Elsevier, 2005.
72. V. Biener, T. Gesslein, D. Schneider et al. Povrpoint: Authoring presentations in mobile virtual reality. *IEEE transactions on visualization and computer graphics*, 28(5):2069–2079, 2022.
73. J. Birch. Worldwide prevalence of red-green color deficiency. *JOSA A*, 29(3):313–320, 2012.
74. J. B. Black and T. P. Moran. Learning and remembering command names. In *Proceedings of the 1982 conference on human factors in computing systems*, CHI '82, page 8–11, New York, NY, USA, 1982.
75. R. Black, A. Waller, R. Turner, and E. Reiter. Supporting personal narrative for children with complex communication needs. *ACM transactions on computer-human interaction (TOCHI)*, 19(2):1–35, 2012.
76. A. Blackwell and T. Green. Notational systems–the cognitive dimensions of notations framework. *HCI models, theories, and frameworks: Toward an interdisciplinary science. Morgan Kaufmann*, 2003.
77. A. E. Blandford, J. K. Hyde, I. Connell, and T. R. Green. Scoping analytical usability evaluation methods: A case study. Technical report, Working paper available from www.uclic.ucl.ac.uk/annb/CASSMpapers..., 2004.
78. E. Blevis. Sustainable interaction design: Invention & disposal, renewal & reuse. In *Proceedings of the SIGCHI conference on human factors in computing systems*, pages 503–512, 2007.
79. J. O. Blom and A. F. Monk. Theory of personalization of appearance: Why users personalize their pcs and mobile phones. *Human-computer interaction*, 18(3):193–228, 2003.
80. D. J. Blomberg and H. Karasti. Ethnography: Positioning ethnography within participatory design. In *Routledge international handbook of participatory design*, pages 106–136. Routledge, 2012.
81. M. Blythe. Research through design fiction: Narrative in real and imaginary abstracts. In *Proceedings of the SIGCHI conference on human factors in computing systems*, pages 703–712, 2014.
82. M. A. Boden. *The creative mind: Myths and mechanisms.* Routledge, 2004.
83. S. Bødker. Through the interface-a human activity approach to user interface design, 1991.
84. R. Bogdan. Teaching fieldwork to educational researchers. *Anthropology & education quarterly*, 14(3):171–178, 1983.
85. J. O. Borchers. A pattern approach to interaction design. In *Proceedings of the 3rd conference on designing interactive systems: Processes, practices, methods, and techniques*, pages 369–378, 2000.

86. C. P. Borchgrevink, J. Cha, and S. Kim. Hand washing practices in a college town environment. *Journal of environmental health*, 75(8):18–25, 2013.

87. T. Boren and J. Ramey. Thinking aloud: Reconciling theory and practice. *IEEE transactions on professional communication*, 43(3):261–278, 2000.

88. J. P. Borst, N. A. Taatgen, and H. van Rijn. What makes interruptions disruptive? a process-model account of the effects of the problem state bottleneck on task interruption and resumption. In *Proceedings of the 33rd annual ACM conference on human factors in computing systems*, pages 2971–2980, 2015.

89. N. Bos, J. Olson, D. Gergle, G. Olson, and Z. Wright. Effects of four computer-mediated communications channels on trust development. In *Proceedings of the SIGCHI conference on human factors in computing systems*, pages 135–140, 2002.

90. J. Bowers, G. Button, and W. Sharrock. Workflow from within and without: Technology and cooperative work on the print industry shopfloor. In *Proceedings of the fourth European conference on computer-supported cooperative work ECSCW'*, pages 51–66. Springer, 1995.

91. D. M. Boyd and N. B. Ellison. Social network sites: Definition, history, and scholarship. *Journal of computer-mediated communication*, 13(1):210–230, 2007.

92. M. M. Bradley and P. J. Lang. Measuring emotion: The self-assessment manikin and the semantic differential. *Journal of behavior therapy and experimental psychiatry*, 25(1):49–59, 1994.

93. E. Brandt, T. Binder, and E. B.-N. Sanders. Tools and techniques: Ways to engage telling, making and enacting. In *Routledge international handbook of participatory design*, pages 145–181. Routledge, 2012.

94. V. Braun and V. Clarke. Using thematic analysis in psychology. *Qualitative research in Psychology*, 3(2):77–101, 2006. www.tandfonline.com/doi/abs/10.1191/1478088706qp063oa.

95. S. A. Brewster, P. C. Wright, and A. D. Edwards. Experimentally derived guidelines for the creation of earcons. In *Adjunct proceedings of HCI*, volume 95, pages 155–159, 1995.

96. J. Brooke. Sus: a retrospective. *Journal of usability studies*, 8(2):29–40, 2013.

97. J. Brooke. Sus-a quick and dirty usability scale. *Usability evaluation in industry*, 189(194):4–7, 1996.

98. F. P. Brooks Jr. *The mythical man-month: Essays on software engineering*. Pearson Education, 1995.

99. B. Brown and E. Laurier. The trouble with autopilots: Assisted and autonomous driving on the social road. In *Proceedings of the 2017 CHI conference on human factors in computing systems*, pages 416–429, 2017.

100. L. M. Brown, S. A. Brewster, and H. C. Purchase. Multidimensional tactons for non-visual information presentation in mobile devices. In *Proceedings of the 8th conference on human-computer interaction with mobile devices and services*, MobileHCI '06, page 231–238, New York, NY, USA, 2006.

101. J. R. Brubaker, G. R. Hayes, and P. Dourish. Beyond the grave: Facebook as a site for the expansion of death and mourning. *The Information society*, 29(3):152–163, 2013.

102. F. Brudy, C. Holz, R. Rädle et al. Cross-device taxonomy: Survey, opportunities and challenges of interactions spanning across multiple devices. In *Proceedings of the 2019 CHI conference on human factors in computing systems*, CHI '19, page 1–28, New York, NY, USA, 2019.

103. F. Brühlmann, B. Vollenwyder, K. Opwis, and E. D. Mekler. Measuring the "why" of interaction: Development and validation of the user motivation inventory (umi). In *Proceedings of the 2018 CHI conference on human factors in computing systems*, pages 1–13, 2018.

104. D. P. Brumby and S. Zhuang. Visual grouping in menu interfaces. In *Proceedings of the 33rd annual ACM conference on human factors in computing systems*, pages 4203–4206, 2015.

105. A. B. Brush, B. Lee, R. Mahajan, S. Agarwal, S. Saroiu, and C. Dixon. Home automation in the wild: Challenges and opportunities. In *Proceedings of the SIGCHI conference on human factors in computing systems*, CHI '11, page 2115–2124, New York, NY, USA, 2011.

106. S. L. Bryant, A. Forte, and A. Bruckman. Becoming wikipedian: Transformation of participation in a collaborative online encyclopedia. In *Proceedings of the 2005 international ACM SIGGROUP conference on supporting group work*, GROUP '05, page 1–10, New York, NY, USA, 2005.
107. L. L. Bucciarelli and L. L. Bucciarelli. *Designing engineers*. MIT press, 1994.
108. R. Buchanan. Wicked problems in design thinking. *Design issues*, 8(2):5–21, 1992.
109. M. Bunge. Towards a technoethics. *The monist*, 60(1):96–107, 1977.
110. M. Bunge. *Causality and modern science*. Routledge, 2017.
111. M. Burnett, S. Stumpf, J. Macbeth et al. Gendermag: A method for evaluating software's gender inclusiveness. *Interacting with computers*, 28(6):760–787, 2016.
112. G. Button and W. Sharrock. How to conduct ethnomethodological studies of work. In *Studies of work and the workplace in HCI: Concepts and techniques*, pages 51–82. Springer, 2009.
113. G. Button and W. Sharrock. Making observations. In *Studies of work and the workplace in HCI: Concepts and techniques*, pages 83–87. Springer, 2009.
114. W. Buxton. A three-state model of graphical input. In *Human-computer interaction-INTERACT*, volume 90, pages 449–456, 1990.
115. D. Byrne, A. R. Doherty, G. J. Jones, A. F. Smeaton, S. Kumpulainen, and K. Järvelin. The sensecam as a tool for task observation. *People and computers XXII culture, creativity, interaction 22*, pages 19–22, 2008.
116. S. Bødker and C. N. Klokmose. The human–artifact model: An activity theoretical approach to artifact ecologies. *Human–computer interaction*, 26(4):315–371, 2011.
117. C. J. Cai, S. Winter, D. Steiner, L. Wilcox, and M. Terry. "Hello ai": Uncovering the onboarding needs of medical practitioners for human-ai collaborative decision-making. *Proceedings of the ACM on human-computer interaction*, 3(CSCW), 2019.
118. K. Caine. Local standards for sample size at chi. In *Proceedings of the 2016 CHI conference on human factors in computing systems*, CHI '16, page 981–992, New York, NY, USA, 2016.
119. K. Caine. Local standards for sample size at chi. In *Proceedings of the 2016 CHI conference on human factors in computing systems*, CHI '16, pages 981–992, New York, NY, USA, 2016.
120. P. Cairns and H. Thimbleby. 213From premature semantics to mature interaction programming. In *Computational interaction*. Oxford University Press, 2018.
121. J. Callahan, D. Hopkins, M. Weiser, and B. Shneiderman. An empirical comparison of pie vs. linear menus. In *Proceedings of the SIGCHI conference on human factors in computing systems*, pages 95–100, 1988.
122. N. Campo Woytuk, M. L. J. Søndergaard, M. Ciolfi Felice, and M. Balaam. Touching and being in touch with the menstruating body. In *Proceedings of the 2020 CHI conference on human factors in computing systems*, pages 1–14, 2020.
123. J. C. Campos, C. Fayollas, M. D. Harrison, C. Martinie, P. Masci, and P. Palanque. Supporting the analysis of safety critical user interfaces: An exploration of three formal tools. *ACM transactions on computer-human interaction (TOCHI)*, 27(5):1–48, 2020.
124. H. Cao, Y. Lu, Y. Deng, D. Mcfarland, and M. S. Bernstein. Breaking out of the ivory tower: A large-scale analysis of patent citations to hci research. In *Proceedings of the 2023 CHI conference on human factors in computing systems*, pages 1–24, 2023.
125. X. Cao and S. Zhai. Modeling human performance of pen stroke gestures. In *Proceedings of the SIGCHI conference on human factors in computing systems*, pages 1495–1504, 2007.
126. A. Caraban, E. Karapanos, D. Gonçalves, and P. Campos. 23 ways to nudge: A review of technology-mediated nudging in human-computer interaction. In *Proceedings of the 2019 CHI conference on human factors in computing systems*, pages 1–15, 2019.

127 S. K. Card. User perceptual mechanisms in the search of computer command menus. In *Proceedings of the 1982 conference on human factors in computing systems*, pages 190–196, 1982.

128 S. K. Card, W. K. English, and B. J. Burr. Evaluation of mouse, rate-controlled isometric joystick, step keys, and text keys for text selection on a CRT. *Ergonomics*, 21(8):601–613, 1978.

129 S. K. Card, T. P. Moran, and A. Newell. *The psychology of human-computer interaction*. Lawrence Erlbaum Associates, 1983.

130 S. K. Card, J. D. Mackinlay, and G. G. Robertson. A morphological analysis of the design space of input devices. *ACM transactions on information systems (TOIS)*, 9(2):99–122, 1991.

131 J. H. Carlisle. Evaluating the impact of office automation on top management communication. In *Proceedings of the June 7–10, 1976, national computer conference and exposition*, pages 611–616, 1976.

132 J. M. Carroll and C. Carrithers. Training wheels in a user interface. *Communications of the ACM*, 27(8):800–806, 1984.

133 J. M. Carroll and J. C. Thomas. Fun. *ACM SIGCHI bulletin*, 19(3):21–24, 1988.

134 J. M. Carroll, R. L. Mack, and W. A. Kellogg. Interface metaphors and user interface design. In *Handbook of human-computer interaction*, pages 67–85. Elsevier, 1988.

135 J. M. Carroll, W. A. Kellogg, and M. B. Rosson. The task-artifact cycle. In *Designing interaction: Psychology at the human-computer interface*, pages 74–102. Cambridge University Press, 1991.

136 G. Casiez and N. Roussel. No more bricolage! methods and tools to characterize, replicate and compare pointing transfer functions. In *Proceedings of the 24th annual ACM symposium on user interface software and technology*, pages 603–614, 2011.

137 G. Casiez, D. Vogel, R. Balakrishnan, and A. Cockburn. The impact of control-display gain on user performance in pointing tasks. *Human–computer interaction*, 23(3):215–250, 2008a.

138 G. Casiez, D. Vogel, R. Balakrishnan, and A. Cockburn. The impact of control-display gain on user performance in pointing tasks. *Human–computer interaction*, 23(3):215–250, 2008b.

139 G. Casiez, N. Roussel, and D. Vogel. 1texteuro filter: A simple speed-based low-pass filter for noisy input in interactive systems. In *Proceedings of the SIGCHI conference on human factors in computing systems*, pages 2527–2530, 2012.

140 J. Cassell, T. Bickmore, M. Billinghurst et al. Embodiment in conversational interfaces: Rea. In *Proceedings of the SIGCHI conference on human factors in computing systems*, CHI '99, page 520–527, New York, NY, USA, 1999.

141 I. Ceaparu, J. Lazar, K. Bessiere, J. Robinson, and B. Shneiderman. Determining causes and severity of end-user frustration. *International journal of human-computer interaction*, 17(3):333–356, 2004.

142 M. Chalmers, I. MacColl, and M. Bell. Seamful design: Showing the seams in wearable computing. In *2003 IEE eurowearable*, pages 11–16. IET, 2003.

143 E. Chandrasekharan, M. Samory, S. Jhaver et al. The internet's hidden rules: An empirical study of reddit norm violations at micro, meso, and macro scales. *Proceedings of the ACM on human-computer interaction*, 2(CSCW):1–25, 2018.

144 A. Chapanis. Words, words, words. *Human factors*, 7(1):1–17, 1965.

145 O. Chapuis, R. Blanch, and M. Beaudouin-Lafon. Fitts' law in the wild: A field study of aimed movements. Technical report, December 2007. https://hal.archives-ouvertes.fr/hal-00612026. LRI Technical Repport Number 1480, Université Paris-Saclay, 11 pages.

146 P.-H. C. Chen, K. Gadepalli, R. MacDonald et al. An augmented reality microscope with real-time artificial intelligence integration for cancer diagnosis. *Nature medicine*, 25(9):1453–1457, 2019.

147 X. Chen, G. Bailly, D. P. Brumby, A. Oulasvirta, and A. Howes. The emergence of interactive behavior: A model of rational menu search. In *Proceedings of the 33rd annual ACM conference on human factors in computing systems*, pages 4217–4226, 2015.

148 M. Chetty, R. Banks, A. Brush, J. Donner, and R. Grinter. You're capped: Understanding the effects of bandwidth caps on broadband use in the home. In *Proceedings of the SIGCHI conference on human factors in computing systems*, pages 3021–3030, 2012.

149 P. K. Chilana, A. J. Ko, J. O. Wobbrock, T. Grossman, and G. Fitzmaurice. Post-deployment usability: A survey of current practices. In *Proceedings of the SIGCHI conference on human factors in computing systems*, pages 2243–2246, 2011.

150 J. P. Chin, V. A. Diehl, and K. L. Norman. Development of an instrument measuring user satisfaction of the human-computer interface. In *Proceedings of the SIGCHI conference on human factors in computing systems*, pages 213–218, 1988.

151 V. Chotpitayasunondh and K. M. Douglas. How "phubbing" becomes the norm: The antecedents and consequences of snubbing via smartphone. *Computers in human behavior*, 63:9–18, 2016.

152 D. D. Chrislip and C. E. Larson. *Collaborative leadership: How citizens and civic leaders can make a difference*, volume 24. Jossey-Bass, 1994.

153 T. Clemmensen, M. Hertzum, K. Hornbæk, Q. Shi, and P. Yammiyavar. Cultural cognition in usability evaluation. *Interacting with computers*, 21(3):212–220, 2009.

154 W. S. Cleveland and R. McGill. Graphical perception: Theory, experimentation, and application to the development of graphical methods. *Journal of the American statistical association*, 79(387):531–554, 1984.

155 C. Clifton Jr, F. Ferreira, J. M. Henderson et al. Eye movements in reading and information processing: Keith rayner's 40 year legacy. *Journal of memory and language*, 86:1–19, 2016.

156 A. Cockburn, C. Gutwin, and S. Greenberg. A predictive model of menu performance. In *Proceedings of the SIGCHI conference on Human factors in computing systems*, pages 627–636, 2007.

157 A. Cockburn, C. Gutwin, J. Scarr, and S. Malacria. Supporting novice to expert transitions in user interfaces. *ACM computing surveys (CSUR)*, 47(2):1–36, 2014.

158 A. Cockburn, P. Quinn, and C. Gutwin. Examining the peak-end effects of subjective experience. In *Proceedings of the 33rd annual ACM conference on human factors in computing systems*, CHI '15, page 357–366, New York, NY, USA, 2015.

159 A. Cockburn, P. Quinn, C. Gutwin, Z. Chen, and P. Suwanaposee. Probability weighting in interactive decisions: Evidence for overuse of bad assistance, underuse of good assistance. In *CHI conference on human factors in computing systems*, pages 1–12, 2022.

160 G. Cockton and A. Woolrych. Understanding inspection methods: Lessons from an assessment of heuristic evaluation. In *People and computers XV—Interaction without frontiers*, pages 171–191. 2001.

161 G. Cockton, A. Woolrych, K. Hornbæk, and E. Frøkjær. Inspection-based evaluations. In *The human–computer interaction handbook*, pages 1279–1298. CRC Press, 2012.

162 J. Cohen. A power primer. *Psychological bulletin*, 112(1):155, 1992.

163 G. Cohn, D. Morris, S. N. Patel, and D. S. Tan. Your noise is my command: Sensing gestures using the body as an antenna. In *Proceedings of the SIGCHI conference on human factors in computing systems*, pages 791–800, 2011.

164 L. Colusso, C. L. Bennett, G. Hsieh, and S. A. Munson. Translational resources: Reducing the gap between academic research and hci practice. In *Proceedings of the 2017 conference on designing interactive systems*, pages 957–968, 2017.

165 S. Consolvo, D. W. McDonald, T. Toscos et al. Activity sensing in the wild: A field trial of ubifit garden. In *Proceedings of the SIGCHI conference on human factors in computing systems*, CHI '08, page 1797–1806, New York, NY, USA, 2008.

166 S. Consolvo, D. W. McDonald, T. Toscos et al. Activity sensing in the wild: A field trial of ubifit garden. In *Proceedings of the SIGCHI conference on human factors in computing systems*, pages 1797–1806, 2008.

167 S. Consolvo, D. W. McDonald, and J. A. Landay. Theory-driven design strategies for technologies that support behavior change in everyday life. In *Proceedings of the SIGCHI conference on human factors in computing systems*, pages 405–414, 2009.

168 R. I. Cook. How complex systems fail. *Cognitive technologies laboratory, university of Chicago. Chicago IL*, pages 64–118, 1998.

169 A. Cooper, R. Reimann, D. Cronin, and C. Noessel. *About face: The essentials of interaction design*. John Wiley & Sons, 2014.

170 N. Cowan. The magical mystery four: How is working memory capacity limited, and why? *Current directions in psychological science*, 19(1):51–57, 2010.

171 D. R. Cox. *Principles of statistical inference*. Cambridge university press, 2006.

172 F. I. Craik and R. S. Lockhart. Levels of processing: A framework for memory research. *Journal of verbal learning and verbal behavior*, 11(6):671–684, 1972.

173 N. Crilly. Fixation and creativity in concept development: The attitudes and practices of expert designers. *Design studies*, 38:54–91, 2015.

174 E. R. F. Crossman and P. Goodeve. Feedback control of hand-movement and fitts' law. *The quarterly journal of experimental psychology section A*, 35(2):251–278, 1983.

175 R. M. Currano and M. Steinert. A framework for reflective practice in innovative design. *International journal of engineering education*, 28(2):270, 2012.

176 Cyberglove Systems. Hand motion capturing and force feedback with cybergrasp, 2015. http://www.cyberglovesystems.com/.

177 A. Cypher. Eager: Programming repetitive tasks by example. In *Proceedings of the SIGCHI conference on human factors in computing systems*, pages 33–39, 1991.

178 N. Dahlbäck, A. Jönsson, and L. Ahrenberg. Wizard of oz studies—why and how. *Knowledge-based systems*, 6(4):258–266, 1993.

179 P. Dalsgaard and K. Halskov. Designing urban media façades: Cases and challenges. In *Proceedings of the SIGCHI conference on human factors in computing systems*, pages 2277–2286, 2010.

180 F. D. Davis. Perceived usefulness, perceived ease of use, and user acceptance of information technology. *MIS quarterly*, pages 319–340, 1989.

181 F. D. Davis, R. P. Bagozzi, and P. R. Warshaw. Extrinsic and intrinsic motivation to use computers in the workplace 1. *Journal of applied social psychology*, 22(14):1111–1132, 1992.

182 E. De Bono. *Lateral thinking: A textbook of creativity*. Penguin UK, 2009.

183 E. L. Deci and R. M. Ryan. Self-determination theory: A macrotheory of human motivation, development, and health. *Canadian psychology/Psychologie canadienne*, 49(3):182, 2008.

184 N. Dell and N. Kumar. The ins and outs of hci for development. In *Proceedings of the 2016 CHI conference on human factors in computing systems*, pages 2220–2232, 2016.

185 G. Denes, K. Maruszczyk, G. Ash, and R. K. Mantiuk. Temporal resolution multiplexing: Exploiting the limitations of spatio-temporal vision for more efficient vr rendering. *IEEE transactions on visualization and computer graphics*, 25(5):2072–2082, 2019.

186 G. DeSanctis and M. S. Poole. Capturing the complexity in advanced technology use: Adaptive structuration theory. *Organization science*, 5(2):121–147, 1994.

187 P. M. Desmet. Faces of product pleasure: 25 positive emotions in human-product interactions. *International journal of design*, 6(2), 2012.

188 M. Desmond. *Evicted: Poverty and profit in the American city*. Crown Publishing Group, 2016.

189 H. Desurvire, M. Caplan, and J. A. Toth. Using heuristics to evaluate the playability of games. In *CHI'04 extended abstracts on human factors in computing systems*, pages 1509–1512, 2004.

190 A. K. Dey. Understanding and using context. *Personal and ubiquitous computing*, 5(1):4–7, 2001.

191 V. Dhakal, A. M. Feit, P. O. Kristensson, and A. Oulasvirta. Observations on typing from 136 million keystrokes. In *Proceedings of the 2018 CHI conference on human factors in computing systems*, pages 1–12, 2018.

192 R. Dhamija, J. D. Tygar, and M. Hearst. Why phishing works. In *Proceedings of the SIGCHI conference on human factors in computing systems*, pages 581–590, 2006.

193 S. Diefenbach, N. Kolb, and M. Hassenzahl. The'hedonic'in human-computer interaction: history, contributions, and future research directions. In *Proceedings of the 2014 conference on designing interactive systems*, pages 305–314, 2014.

194 P. Dietz and D. Leigh. Diamondtouch: A multi-user touch technology. In *Proceedings of the 14th annual ACM symposium on User interface software and technology*, pages 219–226, 2001.

195 A. Dillon and C. Watson. User analysis in hci: The historical lesson from individual differences research. *International journal of human-computer studies*, 45(6):619–637, 1996.

196 J. DiMicco, D. R. Millen, W. Geyer et al. Motivations for social networking at work. In *Proceedings of the 2008 ACM conference on computer supported cooperative work*, CSCW '08, page 711–720, 2008.

197 M. T. Dishaw and D. M. Strong. Extending the technology acceptance model with task–technology fit constructs. *Information & management*, 36(1):9–21, 1999.

198 J. Dittrich. A beginner's guide to finding user needs, 2022. https://jdittrich.github.io/userNeedResearchBook.

199 A. Dix. Designing for appropriation. In *Proceedings of HCI 2007 The 21st British HCI group annual conference university of Lancaster, UK 21*, pages 1–4, 2007.

200 A. Dix, R. Mancini, and S. Levialdi. The cube–extending systems for undo. *School of computing, staffordshire university. UK*, 1997.

201 E. Y.-L. Do and M. D. Gross. Drawing as a means to design reasoning. In *AI and design*, 1996.

202 K. Doherty and G. Doherty. The construal of experience in hci: Understanding self-reports. *International journal of human-computer studies*, 110:63–74, 2018.

203 K. Doherty and G. Doherty. Engagement in hci: Conception, theory and measurement. *ACM computing surveys (CSUR)*, 51(5):1–39, 2018.

204 K. Doherty, A. Balaskas, and G. Doherty. The design of ecological momentary assessment technologies. *Interacting with computers*, 32(3):257–278, 08 2020.

205 J. Donath. Signals in social supernets. *Journal of computer-mediated communication*, 13(1):231–251, 2007.

206 A. Dong, A. W. Hill, and A. M. Agogino. A document analysis method for characterizing design team performance. *Journal of mechanical design*, 126(3):378–385, 2004.

207 K. Dorst. *Frame innovation: Create new thinking by design*. MIT press, 2015.

208 K. Dorst and N. Cross. Creativity in the design process: Co-evolution of problem–solution. *Design studies*, 22(5):425–437, 2001.

209 P. Dourish. The appropriation of interactive technologies: Some lessons from placeless documents. *Computer supported cooperative work (CSCW)*, 12(4):465–490, 2003.

210 P. Dourish. Implications for design. In *Proceedings of the SIGCHI conference on human factors in computing systems*, CHI '06, page 541–550, New York, 2006.

211 P. Dourish and V. Bellotti. Awareness and coordination in shared workspaces. In *Proceedings of the 1992 ACM conference on computer-supported cooperative work*, pages 107–114, 1992.

212 P. Dragicevic. Combining crossing-based and paper-based interaction paradigms for dragging and dropping between overlapping windows. In *Proceedings of the 17th annual ACM symposium on user interface software and technology*, pages 193–196, 2004.

213 P. Dragicevic, G. Ramos, J. Bibliowitcz, D. Nowrouzezahrai, R. Balakrishnan, and K. Singh. Video browsing by direct manipulation. In *Proceedings of the SIGCHI conference on human factors in computing systems*, CHI '08, page 237–246, New York, NY, USA, 2008.

214 A. Druin. The role of children in the design of new technology. *Behaviour and information technology*, 21(1):1–25, 2002.

215 N. Ducheneaut, N. Yee, E. Nickell, and R. J. Moore. Alone together? Exploring the social dynamics of massively multiplayer online games. In *Proceedings of the SIGCHI conference on human factors in computing systems*, pages 407–416, 2006.

216 J. Dudley, H. Benko, D. Wigdor, and P. O. Kristensson. Performance envelopes of virtual keyboard text input strategies in virtual reality. In *2019 IEEE international symposium on mixed and augmented reality (ISMAR)*, pages 289–300. IEEE, 2019.

217 J. S. Dumas and B. A. Loring. *Moderating usability tests: Principles and practices for interacting*. Elsevier, 2008.

218 R. J. Dwyer, K. Kushlev, and E. W. Dunn. Smartphone use undermines enjoyment of face-to-face social interactions. *Journal of experimental social psychology*, 78:233–239, 2018.

219 D. E. Egan, J. R. Remde, L. M. Gomez et al. Formative design evaluation of superbook. *ACM transactions on information systems*, 7(1):30–57, 1989.

220 S. Egelman, L. F. Cranor, and J. Hong. You've been warned: An empirical study of the effectiveness of web browser phishing warnings. In *Proceedings of the SIGCHI conference on human factors in computing systems*, pages 1065–1074, 2008.

221 P. Ekkekakis. *The measurement of affect, mood, and emotion: A guide for health-behavioral research*. Cambridge University Press, 2013.

222 C. Elliott and P. Deasley. Creating systems that work: Principles of engineering systems for the 21st century. *Royal academy of engineering*, 293074, 2007.

223 C. A. Ellis, S. J. Gibbs, and G. Rein. Groupware: Some issues and experiences. *Commun. ACM*, 34(1):39–58, January 1991.

224 N. B. Ellison, C. Steinfield, and C. Lampe. The benefits of facebook "friends:" Social capital and college students' use of online social network sites. *Journal of computer-mediated communication*, 12(4):1143–1168, 2007.

225 S. Elrod, R. Bruce, R. Gold et al. Liveboard: A large interactive display supporting group meetings, presentations, and remote collaboration. In *Proceedings of the SIGCHI conference on human factors in computing systems*, CHI '92, page 599–607, USA, 1992.

226 D. C. Engelbart. Augmenting human intellect: A conceptual framework. Menlo Park, CA, 21, 1962.

227 Y. Engeström. *Learning by expanding*. Cambridge University Press, 2015.

228 J. M. Entwistle, M. K. Rasmussen, N. Verdezoto, R. S. Brewer, and M. S. Andersen. *Beyond the individual: The contextual wheel of practice as a research framework for sustainable HCI*, page 1125–1134. Association for Computing Machinery, New York, 2015.

229 K. A. Ericsson and H. A. Simon. *Protocol Analysis. Verbal reports as data (Revised edition)*. MIT Press, 1993.

230 S. K. Ernala, M. Burke, A. Leavitt, and N. B. Ellison. How well do people report time spent on facebook? An evaluation of established survey questions with recommendations. In *Proceedings of the 2020 CHI conference on human factors in computing systems*, CHI '20, page 1–14, New York, NY, USA, 2020.

231 M. O. Ernst and M. S. Banks. Humans integrate visual and haptic information in a statistically optimal fashion. *Nature*, 415(6870):429–433, 2002.

232 A. Esteves, E. Velloso, A. Bulling, and H. Gellersen. Orbits: Gaze interaction for smart watches using smooth pursuit eye movements. In *Proceedings of the 28th annual ACM symposium on user interface software & technology*, pages 457–466, 2015.

233 J. a. M. Evangelista Belo, A. M. Feit, T. Feuchtner, and K. Grønbæk. Xrgonomics: Facilitating the creation of ergonomic 3d interfaces. In *Proceedings of the 2021 CHI conference on human factors in computing systems*, CHI '21, New York, 2021.

234 J. M. Evangelista Belo, M. N. Lystbæk, A. M. Feit et al. Auit–the adaptive user interfaces toolkit for designing xr applications. In *Proceedings of the 35th annual ACM symposium on user interface software and technology*, pages 1–16, 2022.

235 J. A. Fails and D. R. Olsen Jr. Interactive machine learning. In *Proceedings of the 8th international conference on intelligent user interfaces*, pages 39–45, 2003.

236 S. H. Fairclough and K. Houston. A metabolic measure of mental effort. *Biological psychology*, 66(2):177–190, 2004.

237 M. Fan, S. Shi, and K. N. Truong. Practices and challenges of using think-aloud protocols in industry: An international survey. *Journal of usability studies*, 15(2), 2020.

238 M. Farzandipour, E. Nabovati, H. Tadayon, and M. S. Jabali. Usability evaluation of a nursing information system by applying cognitive walkthrough method. *International journal of medical informatics*, 152:104459, 2021.

239 A. M. Feit, M. Nancel, M. John, A. Karrenbauer, D. Weir, and A. Oulasvirta. Azerty amélioré: Computational design on a national scale. *Communications of the ACM*, 64(2):48–58, 2021.

240 G. Firebaugh. *Seven rules for social research*. Princeton University Press, 2008.

241 A. J. Fisher, J. D. Medaglia, and B. F. Jeronimus. Lack of group-to-individual generalizability is a threat to human subjects research. *Proceedings of the national academy of sciences*, 115(27):E6106–E6115, 2018.

242 P. M. Fitts. Human engineering for an effective air-navigation and traffic-control system. Technical report, National Research Council, Div. of, 1951.

243 P. M. Fitts. The information capacity of the human motor system in controlling the amplitude of movement. *Journal of experimental psychology*, 47(6):381, 1954.

244 G. W. Fitzmaurice, H. Ishii, and W. A. Buxton. Bricks: Laying the foundations for graspable user interfaces. In *Proceedings of the SIGCHI conference on human factors in computing systems*, pages 442–449, 1995.

245 J. Fjeld, N. Achten, H. Hilligoss, A. Nagy, and M. Srikumar. Principled artificial intelligence: Mapping consensus in ethical and rights-based approaches to principles for ai. *Berkman Klein center research publication*, 2020.

246 F. O. Flemisch, C. A. Adams, S. R. Conway, K. H. Goodrich, M. T. Palmer, and P. C. Schutte. The h-metaphor as a guideline for vehicle automation and interaction. Technical report, Langley Research Center, 2003.

247 J. Fogarty, C. Au, and S. E. Hudson. Sensing from the basement: A feasibility study of unobtrusive and low-cost home activity recognition. In *Proceedings of the 19th annual ACM symposium on User interface software and technology*, pages 91–100, 2006.

248 B. J. Fogg. A behavior model for persuasive design. In *Proceedings of the 4th international conference on persuasive technology*, pages 1–7, 2009.

249 J. D. Foley, V. L. Wallace, and P. Chan. The human factors of computer graphics interaction techniques. *IEEE computer graphics and applications*, 4(11):13–48, 1984.

250 S. Follmer, D. Leithinger, A. Olwal, A. Hogge, and H. Ishii. Inform: Dynamic physical affordances and constraints through shape and object actuation. In *Uist*, pages 2501–988, 2013.

251 A. Følstad, E. Law, and K. Hornbæk. Analysis in practical usability evaluation: A survey study. In *Proceedings of the SIGCHI conference on human factors in computing systems*, CHI '12, page 2127–2136, New York, NY, USA, 2012.

252 M. Fontana de Vargas, J. Dai, and K. Moffatt. Aac with automated vocabulary from photographs: Insights from school and speech-language therapy settings. In *The 24th international ACM SIGACCESS conference on computers and accessibility*, pages 1–18, 2022.

253 J. Forlizzi and K. Battarbee. Understanding experience in interactive systems. In *Proceedings of the 5th conference on designing interactive systems: Processes, practices, methods, and techniques*, pages 261–268, 2004.

254 G. Freeman, J. Bardzell, and S. Bardzell. Revisiting computer-mediated intimacy: In-game marriage and dyadic gameplay in audition. In *Proceedings of the 2016 CHI conference on human factors in computing systems*, pages 4325–4336, 2016.

255 M. J. French, J. Gravdahl, and M. French. *Conceptual design for engineers*. Springer, 1985.

256 J. Frich, L. MacDonald Vermeulen, C. Remy, M. M. Biskjaer, and P. Dalsgaard. Mapping the landscape of creativity support tools in hci. In *Proceedings of the 2019 CHI conference on human factors in computing systems*, pages 1–18, 2019.

257 B. Friedman. Value-sensitive design. *interactions*, 3(6):16–23, 1996.

258 B. Friedman, D. G. Hendry, and A. Borning. A survey of value sensitive design methods. *Foundations and trends in human–computer interaction*, 11(2):63–125, 2017.

259 D. M. Frohlich. The history and future of direct manipulation. *Behaviour & information technology*, 12(6):315–329, 1993.

260 D. M. Frohlich. Direct manipulation and other lessons. In *Handbook of human-computer interaction*, pages 463–488. Elsevier, 1997.

261 E. Frøkjær, M. Hertzum, and K. Hornbæk. Measuring usability: Are effectiveness, efficiency, and satisfaction really correlated? In *Proceedings of the SIGCHI conference on human factors in computing systems*, pages 345–352, 2000.

262 H. L. Fromkin and S. Streufert. Laboratory experimentation. *Handbook of industrial and organizational psychology*, pages 415–465, 1976.

263 G. W. Furnas. New graphical reasoning models for understanding graphical interfaces. In *Proceedings of the SIGCHI conference on human factors in computing systems*, pages 71–78, 1991.

264 G. W. Furnas and B. B. Bederson. Space-scale diagrams: Understanding multiscale interfaces. In *Proceedings of the SIGCHI conference on human factors in computing systems*, pages 234–241, 1995.

265 G. W. Furnas, T. K. Landauer, L. M. Gomez, and S. T. Dumais. The vocabulary problem in human-system communication. *Communications of the ACM*, 30(11):964–971, 1987.

266 K. Z. Gajos, J. O. Wobbrock, and D. S. Weld. Automatically generating user interfaces adapted to users' motor and vision capabilities. In *Proceedings of the 20th annual ACM symposium on user interface software and technology*, UIST '07, page 231–240, 2007.

267 D. F. Galletta, A. Durcikova, A. Everard, and B. M. Jones. Does spell-checking software need a warning label? *Communications of the ACM*, 48(7):82–86, 2005.

268 M. Gantt and B. A. Nardi. Gardeners and gurus: Patterns of cooperation among cad users. In *Proceedings of the SIGCHI conference on human factors in computing systems*, CHI '92, page 107–117, 1992.

269 X. Gao, Y. Yang, C. Liu, C. Mitropoulos, J. Lindqvist, and A. Oulasvirta. Forgetting of passwords: Ecological theory and data. In *27th USENIX security symposium (USENIX Security 18)*, pages 221–238, 2018.

270 L. Gasser. The integration of computing and routine work. *ACM transactions on information systems (TOIS)*, 4(3):205–225, 1986.

271 E. Gatti, E. Calzolari, E. Maggioni, and M. Obrist. Emotional ratings and skin conductance response to visual, auditory and haptic stimuli. *Scientific data*, 5(1):1–12, 2018.

272 B. Gaver and J. Bowers. Annotated portfolios. *Interactions*, 19(4):40–49, 2012.

273 W. Gaver. What should we expect from research through design? In *Proceedings of the SIGCHI conference on human factors in computing systems*, pages 937–946, 2012.

274 W. Gaver, M. Blythe, A. Boucher, N. Jarvis, J. Bowers, and P. Wright. The prayer companion: Openness and specificity, materiality and spirituality. In *Proceedings of the SIGCHI conference on human factors in computing systems*, CHI '10, page 2055–2064, 2010.

275. H. Gelderblom and L. Menge. The invisible gorilla revisited: Using eye tracking to investigate inattentional blindness in interface design. In *Proceedings of the 2018 international conference on advanced visual interfaces*, pages 1–9, 2018.

276. T. Gesslein, V. Biener, P. Gagel et al. Pen-based interaction with spreadsheets in mobile virtual reality. In *2020 IEEE international symposium on mixed and augmented reality (ISMAR)*, pages 361–373. IEEE, 2020.

277. M. Ghassemi, L. Oakden-Rayner, and A. L. Beam. The false hope of current approaches to explainable artificial intelligence in health care. *The lancet digital health*, 3(11):e745–e750, 2021.

278. J. P. Goetz and M. D. LeCompte. Ethnographic research and the problem of data reduction 1. *Anthropology & education quarterly*, 12(1):51–70, 1981.

279. A. Goguey, G. Casiez, A. Cockburn, and C. Gutwin. Storyboard-based empirical modeling of touch interface performance. In *Proceedings of the 2018 CHI conference on human factors in computing systems*, pages 1–12, 2018.

280. D. Golden. A plea for friendly software. *ACM SIGSOFT software engineering notes*, 5(4):4–5, 1980.

281. G. Goldschmidt. The dialectics of sketching. *Creativity research journal*, 4(2):123–143, 1991.

282. M. Gonçalves, C. Cardoso, and P. Badke-Schaub. What inspires designers? Preferences on inspirational approaches during idea generation. *Design studies*, 35(1):29–53, 2014.

283. V. M. González and G. Mark. "Constant, constant, multi-tasking craziness": Managing multiple working spheres. In *Proceedings of the SIGCHI conference on human factors in computing systems*, CHI '04, page 113–120, New York, 2004.

284. C. Goodwin and J. Heritage. Conversation analysis. *Annual review of anthropology*, 19:283–307, 1990.

285. J. D. Gould and C. Lewis. Designing for usability: Key principles and what designers think. *Communications of the ACM*, 28(3):300–311, 1985.

286. M. S. Granovetter. The strength of weak ties. *American journal of sociology*, 78(6):1360–1380, 1973.

287. W. D. Gray and W.-T. Fu. Ignoring perfect knowledge in-the-world for imperfect knowledge in-the-head. In *Proceedings of the SIGCHI conference on human factors in computing systems*, pages 112–119, 2001.

288. W. D. Gray and W.-T. Fu. Soft constraints in interactive behavior: The case of ignoring perfect knowledge in-the-world for imperfect knowledge in-the-head. *Cognitive science*, 28(3):359–382, 2004.

289. W. D. Gray, B. E. John, and M. E. Atwood. Project ernestine: Validating a goms analysis for predicting and explaining real-world task performance. *Human-computer interaction*, 8(3):237–309, 1993.

290. S. Greenberg and B. Buxton. Usability evaluation considered harmful (some of the time). In *Proceedings of the SIGCHI conference on human factors in computing systems*, pages 111–120, 2008.

291. S. Greenberg and H. Kuzuoka. Using digital but physical surrogates to mediate awareness, communication and privacy in media spaces. *Personal technologies*, 3(4):182–198, 1999.

292. C. F. Griggio, M. Nouwens, and C. N. Klokmose. Caught in the network: The impact of whatsapp's 2021 privacy policy update on users' messaging app ecosystems. In *Proceedings of the 2022 CHI conference on human factors in computing systems*, CHI '22, New York, NY, USA, 2022.

293. E. Grönvall, S. Kinch, M. G. Petersen, and M. K. Rasmussen. Causing commotion with a shape-changing bench: Experiencing shape-changing interfaces in use. In *Proceedings of the SIGCHI conference on human factors in computing systems*, pages 2559–2568, 2014.

294. T. Grossman and R. Balakrishnan. The bubble cursor: Enhancing target acquisition by dynamic resizing of the cursor's activation area. In *Proceedings of the SIGCHI conference on human factors in computing systems*, pages 281–290, 2005.

295 T. Grossman, P. Dragicevic, and R. Balakrishnan. Strategies for accelerating on-line learning of hotkeys. In *Proceedings of the SIGCHI conference on human factors in computing systems*, pages 1591–1600, 2007.

296 T. Grossman, G. Fitzmaurice, and R. Attar. A survey of software learnability: Metrics, methodologies and guidelines. In *Proceedings of the SIGCHI conference on human factors in computing systems*, CHI '09, pages 649–658, New York, 2009.

297 T. Grossman, G. Fitzmaurice, and R. Attar. A survey of software learnability: Metrics, methodologies and guidelines. In *Proceedings of the SIGCHI conference on human factors in computing systems*, pages 649–658, 2009.

298 J. Grubert, E. Ofek, M. Pahud, and P. O. Kristensson. The office of the future: Virtual, portable, and global. *IEEE computer graphics and applications*, 38(6):125–133, 2018.

299 J. Grudin. The case against user interface consistency. *Communications of the ACM*, 32(10):1164–1173, 1989.

300 J. Grudin. Utility and usability: Research issues and development contexts. *Interacting with computers*, 4(2):209–217, 1992.

301 J. Grudin. Computer-supported cooperative work: History and focus. *Computer*, 27(5):19–26, 1994.

302 J. Grudin. Groupware and social dynamics: Eight challenges for developers. *Communications of the ACM*, 37(1):92–105, 1994.

303 J. Grudin. Partitioning digital worlds: Focal and peripheral awareness in multiple monitor use. In *Proceedings of the SIGCHI conference on human factors in computing systems*, CHI '01, page 458–465, New York, NY, USA, 2001.

304 X. Gu, Y. Zhang, W. Sun, Y. Bian, D. Zhou, and P. O. Kristensson. Dexmo: An inexpensive and lightweight mechanical exoskeleton for motion capture and force feedback in vr. In *Proceedings of the 2016 CHI conference on human factors in computing systems*, pages 1991–1995, 2016.

305 S. Gustafson, C. Holz, and P. Baudisch. Imaginary phone: Learning imaginary interfaces by transferring spatial memory from a familiar device. In *Proceedings of the 24th annual ACM symposium on user interface software and technology*, UIST '11, page 283–292, New York, NY, USA, 2011.

306 C. Gutwin and S. Greenberg. Effects of awareness support on groupware usability. In *Proceedings of the SIGCHI conference on human factors in computing systems*, CHI '98, pages 511–518, New York, NY, USA, 1998.

307 R. Haeuslschmid, B. Pfleging, and F. Alt. A design space to support the development of windshield applications for the car. In *Proceedings of the 2016 CHI conference on human factors in computing systems*, CHI '16, page 5076–5091, New York, NY, USA, 2016.

308 K. Halskov and P. Dalsgård. Inspiration card workshops. In *Proceedings of the 6th conference on designing interactive systems*, pages 2–11, 2006.

309 C. A. Halverson, D. B. Horn, C.-M. Karat, and J. Karat. The beauty of errors: Patterns of error correction in desktop speech systems. In *INTERACT*, pages 133–140, 1999.

310 J. Y. Han. Low-cost multi-touch sensing through frustrated total internal reflection. In *Proceedings of the 18th annual ACM symposium on User interface software and technology*, pages 115–118, 2005.

311 W. J. Hansen. User engineering principles for interactive systems. In *Proceedings of the November 16-18, 1971, fall joint computer conference*, AFIPS '71 (Fall), page 523–532, New York, NY, USA, 1972.

312 C. Harper. Overcome barriers to end to end research with demonstrated roi. *Design management review*, 30(4):8–13, 2019.

313 C. Harrison and A. K. Dey. Lean and zoom: Proximity-aware user interface and content magnification. In *Proceedings of the SIGCHI conference on human factors in computing systems*, pages 507–510, 2008.

314 C. Harrison, D. Tan, and D. Morris. Skinput: Appropriating the body as an input surface. In *Proceedings of the SIGCHI conference on human factors in computing systems*, pages 453–462, 2010.

315 C. Harrison, J. Horstman, G. Hsieh, and S. Hudson. Unlocking the expressivity of point lights. In *Proceedings of the SIGCHI conference on human factors in computing systems*, CHI '12, page 1683–1692, New York, NY, USA, 2012.

316 S. G. Hart and L. E. Staveland. Development of nasa-tlx (task load index): Results of empirical and theoretical research. In *Advances in psychology*, volume 52, pages 139–183. Elsevier, 1988.

317 H. R. Hartson, T. S. Andre, R. C. Williges, and L. van Rens. The user action framework: A theory-based foundation for inspection and classification of usability problems. *HCI (1)*, 1999:1058–1062, 1999.

318 M. Hassenzahl. The thing and i: understanding the relationship between user and product. In *Funology*, pages 31–42. Springer, 2003.

319 M. Hassenzahl. User experience (ux) towards an experiential perspective on product quality. In *Proceedings of the 20th conference on l'Interaction homme-machine*, pages 11–15, 2008.

320 M. Hassenzahl. Experience design: Technology for all the right reasons. *Synthesis lectures on human-centered informatics*, 3(1):1–95, 2010.

321 M. Hassenzahl and N. Tractinsky. User experience-a research agenda. *Behaviour & information technology*, 25(2):91–97, 2006.

322 M. Hassenzahl, S. Diefenbach, and A. Göritz. Needs, affect, and interactive products–facets of user experience. *Interacting with computers*, 22(5):353–362, 2010.

323 M. Hassenzahl, S. Heidecker, K. Eckoldt, S. Diefenbach, and U. Hillmann. All you need is love: Current strategies of mediating intimate relationships through technology. *ACM transactions on computer-human interaction (TOCHI)*, 19(4):1–19, 2012.

324 H. A. He, S. Greenberg, and E. M. Huang. One size does not fit all: Applying the transtheoretical model to energy feedback technology design. In *Proceedings of the SIGCHI conference on human factors in computing systems*, CHI '10, page 927–936, New York, NY, USA, 2010.

325 J. He and W. R. King. The role of user participation in information systems development: Implications from a meta-analysis. *Journal of management information systems*, 25(1):301–331, 2008.

326 C. Heath and P. Luff. Collaboration and control: Crisis management and multimedia technology in london underground line control rooms. *Computer supported cooperative work (CSCW)*, 1(1):69–94, 1992.

327 J. Heer and M. Bostock. Crowdsourcing graphical perception: Using mechanical turk to assess visualization design. In *Proceedings of the SIGCHI conference on human factors in computing systems*, pages 203–212, 2010.

328 M. L. Heilig. Sensorama simulator, August 28 1962. US Patent 3,050,870.

329 E. B. Hekler, P. Klasnja, J. E. Froehlich, and M. P. Buman. Mind the theoretical gap: Interpreting, using, and developing behavioral theory in hci research. In *Proceedings of the SIGCHI conference on human factors in computing systems*, CHI '13, page 3307–3316, New York, NY, USA, 2013.

330 A. Henderson and M. Kyng. *There's No Place like Home: Continuing Design in Use*, page 219–240. L. Erlbaum Associates Inc., 1992.

331 A. Henderson and M. Kyng. There's no place like home: Continuing design in use. In *Readings in human-computer interaction*, pages 793–803. Elsevier, 1995.

332 M. Hertzum. Images of usability. *International journal of human–computer interaction*, 26(6):567–600, 2010.

333 M. Hertzum. A usability test is not an interview. *Interactions*, 23(2):82–84, February 2016.

334 M. Hertzum and K. Hornbæk. Frustration: Still a common user experience. *ACM transaction on computer-human interaction*, 2023.

335 M. Hertzum and J. Simonsen. Positive effects of electronic patient records on three clinical activities. *International journal of medical informatics*, 77(12):809–817, 2008.

336 M. Hertzum, K. D. Hansen, and H. H. K. Andersen. Scrutinising usability evaluation: does thinking aloud affect behaviour and mental workload? *Behaviour & information technology*, 28(2):165–181, 2009.

337 M. Hertzum, J. P. Bansler, E. C. Havn, and J. Simonsen. Pilot implementation: Learning from field tests in is development. *Communications of the association for information systems*, 30(1):20, 2012.

338 M. Hertzum, M. I. Manikas, and A. á Torkilsheyggi. Grappling with the future: The messiness of pilot implementation in information systems design. *Health informatics journal*, 25(2):372–388, 2019.

339 T. T. Hewett, R. Baecker, S. Card et al. *ACM SIGCHI curricula for human-computer interaction*. ACM, 1992.

340 W. E. Hick. On the rate of gain of information. *Quarterly journal of experimental psychology*, 4(1):11–26, 1952.

341 D. M. Hilbert and D. F. Redmiles. Extracting usability information from user interface events. *ACM computing surveys (CSUR)*, 32(4):384–421, 2000.

342 K. Hinckley, R. Pausch, J. C. Goble, and N. F. Kassell. Passive real-world interface props for neurosurgical visualization. In *Proceedings of the SIGCHI conference on human factors in computing systems*, CHI '94, page 452–458, New York, 1994.

343 A. Hiniker, S. Y. Schoenebeck, and J. A. Kientz. Not at the dinner table: Parents' and children's perspectives on family technology rules. In *Proceedings of the 19th ACM conference on computer-supported cooperative work & social computing*, CSCW '16, page 1376–1389, New York, NY, USA, 2016.

344 T. Hirzle, F. Fischbach, J. Karlbauer et al. Understanding, addressing, and analysing digital eye strain in virtual reality head-mounted displays. *ACM transactions on computer-human interaction*, 29(4), March 2022. ISSN 1073-0516. https://doi.org/10.1145/3492802.

345 S. Hodges, L. Williams, E. Berry et al. Sensecam: A retrospective memory aid. In *International conference on ubiquitous computing*, pages 177–193. Springer, 2006.

346 J. Hollan and S. Stornetta. Beyond being there. In *Proceedings of the SIGCHI conference on human factors in computing systems*, pages 119–125, 1992.

347 L. E. Holmquist, J. Redström, and P. Ljungstrand. Token-based access to digital information. In *International symposium on handheld and ubiquitous computing*, pages 234–245. Springer, 1999.

348 K. Holtzblatt and H. Beyer. *Contextual design*. Morgan Kaufmann, second edition, 2017.

349 K. Holtzblatt, J. B. Wendell, and S. Wood. *Rapid contextual design: A how-to guide to key techniques for user-centered design*. Elsevier, 2004.

350 C. Holz and P. Baudisch. Understanding touch. In *Proceedings of the SIGCHI conference on human factors in computing systems*, pages 2501–2510, 2011.

351 J. I. Hong and J. A. Landay. Webquilt: A framework for capturing and visualizing the web experience. In *Proceedings of the 10th international conference on world wide web*, WWW '01, pages 717–724, New York, NY, USA, 2001.

352 K. Höök, P. Sengers, and G. Andersson. Sense and sensibility: Evaluation and interactive art. In *Proceedings of the SIGCHI conference on human factors in computing systems*, pages 241–248, 2003.

353 K. Hornbæk. Current practice in measuring usability: Challenges to usability studies and research. *International journal of human-computer studies*, 64(2):79–102, 2006.

354 K. Hornbæk and E. Frøkjær. Comparing usability problems and redesign proposals as input to practical systems development. In *Proceedings of the SIGCHI conference on Human factors in computing systems*, pages 391–400, 2005.

355 K. Hornbæk and M. Hertzum. Technology acceptance and user experience: A review of the experiential component in hci. *ACM transactions on computer-human interaction (TOCHI)*, 24(5):1–30, 2017.

356 K. Hornbæk and E. L.-C. Law. Meta-analysis of correlations among usability measures. In *Proceedings of the SIGCHI conference on human factors in computing systems*, pages 617–626, 2007.

357 K. Hornbæk and A. Oulasvirta. What is interaction? In *Proceedings of the 2017 CHI conference on human factors in computing systems*, CHI '17, page 5040–5052, New York, NY, USA, 2017.

358 K. Hornbæk. Some whys and hows of experiments in human–computer interaction. *Foundations and trends® in human–computer interaction*, 5(4):299–373, 2013.

359 E. Hornecker and J. Buur. Getting a grip on tangible interaction: A framework on physical space and social interaction. In *Proceedings of the SIGCHI conference on Human Factors in computing systems*, pages 437–446, 2006.

360 E. Horvitz. Principles of mixed-initiative user interfaces. In *Proceedings of the SIGCHI conference on human factors in computing systems*, pages 159–166, 1999.

361 X. E. Hu, M. E. Whiting, and M. S. Bernstein. Can online juries make consistent, repeatable decisions? In *Proceedings of the 2021 CHI conference on human factors in computing systems*, pages 1–16, 2021.

362 B. A. Huberman, P. L. Pirolli, J. E. Pitkow, and R. M. Lukose. Strong regularities in world wide web surfing. *Science*, 280(5360):95–97, 1998.

363 Z. Hussain, W. Slany, and A. Holzinger. Current state of agile user-centered design: A survey. In *Symposium of the austrian HCI and usability engineering group*, pages 416–427. Springer, 2009.

364 E. Hutchins. How a cockpit remembers its speeds. *Cognitive science*, 19(3):265–288, 1995.

365 E. L. Hutchins, J. D. Hollan, and D. A. Norman. Direct manipulation interfaces. *Human–computer interaction*, 1(4):311–338, 1985.

366 H. Hutchinson, W. Mackay, B. Westerlund et al. Technology probes: Inspiring design for and with families. In *Proceedings of the SIGCHI conference on human factors in computing systems*, CHI '03, page 17–24, New York, NY, USA, 2003.

367 H. Hutchinson, W. Mackay, B. Westerlund et al. Technology probes: Inspiring design for and with families. In *Proceedings of the SIGCHI conference on human factors in computing systems*, pages 17–24, 2003.

368 E. T. Hvannberg, E. L.-C. Law, and M. K. Lérusdóttir. Heuristic evaluation: Comparing ways of finding and reporting usability problems. *Interacting with computers*, 19(2):225–240, 2007.

369 R. Hyman. Stimulus information as a determinant of reaction time. *Journal of experimental psychology*, 45(3):188, 1953.

370 G. Iacucci, K. Kuutti, and M. Ranta. On the move with a magic thing: Role playing in concept design of mobile services and devices. In *Proceedings of the 3rd conference on designing interactive systems: processes, practices, methods, and techniques*, DIS '00, page 193–202, New York, NY, USA, 2000.

371 T. Igarashi and K. Hinckley. Speed-dependent automatic zooming for browsing large documents. In *Proceedings of the 13th annual ACM symposium on user interface software and technology*, pages 139–148, 2000.

372 Y. Inal, T. Clemmensen, D. Rajanen, N. Iivari, K. Rizvanoglu, and A. Sivaji. Positive developments but challenges still ahead: A survey study on ux professionals' work practices. *Journal of usability studies*, 15(4), 2020.

373 S. T. Iqbal, X. S. Zheng, and B. P. Bailey. Task-evoked pupillary response to mental workload in human-computer interaction. In *CHI '04 Extended abstracts on human factors in computing systems*, CHI EA '04, page 1477–1480, New York, NY, USA, 2004.

374 E. Isaacs, A. Konrad, A. Walendowski, T. Lennig, V. Hollis, and S. Whittaker. Echoes from the past: How technology mediated reflection improves well-being. In *Proceedings of the SIGCHI conference on human factors in computing systems*, CHI '13, page 1071–1080, New York, NY, USA, 2013.

375 H. Ishii and B. Ullmer. Tangible bits: Towards seamless interfaces between people, bits and atoms. In *Proceedings of the ACM SIGCHI conference on human factors in computing systems*, CHI '97, page 234–241, New York, NY, USA, 1997.

376 Iso. INTERNATIONAL ISO STANDARD 9241-210. Technical report, 2019.

377 M. Y. Ivory and M. A. Hearst. The state of the art in automating usability evaluation of user interfaces. *ACM Computing Surveys*, 33(4):470–516, December 2001.

378 S. Izadi, D. Kim, O. Hilliges et al. Kinectfusion: real-time 3d reconstruction and interaction using a moving depth camera. In *Proceedings of the 24th annual ACM symposium on user interface software and technology*, pages 559–568, 2011.

379 J. A. Jacko and G. Salvendy. Hierarchical menu design: Breadth, depth, and task complexity. *Perceptual and motor skills*, 82(3_suppl):1187–1201, 1996.

380 R. J. Jacob, L. E. Sibert, D. C. McFarlane, and M. P. Mullen Jr. Integrality and separability of input devices. *ACM transactions on computer-human interaction (TOCHI)*, 1(1):3–26, 1994.

381 R. J. Jacob, A. Girouard, L. M. Hirshfield et al. Reality-based interaction: A framework for post-wimp interfaces. In *Proceedings of the SIGCHI conference on human factors in computing systems*, pages 201–210, 2008.

382 N. E. Jacobsen, M. Hertzum, and B. E. John. The evaluator effect in usability tests. In *CHI 98 conference summary on human factors in computing systems*, pages 255–256. Citeseer, 1998.

383 L.-E. Janlert and E. Stolterman. The meaning of interactivity—some proposals for definitions and measures. *Human–computer interaction*, 32(3):103–138, 2017.

384 C. P. Janssen, D. P. Brumby, and R. Garnett. Natural break points: The influence of priorities and cognitive and motor cues on dual-task interleaving. *Journal of cognitive engineering and decision making*, 6(1):5–29, 2012.

385 Y. Jiang, L. A. Leiva, H. R. Tavakoli et al. Ueyes: Understanding visual saliency across user interface types. In *Proceedings of the 2023 CHI conference on human factors in computing systems*, CHI '23, New York, NY, USA, 2023. Association for Computing Machinery.

386 G. H. J. Johannessen and K. Hornbæk. Must evaluation methods be about usability? Devising and assessing the utility inspection method. *Behaviour & information technology*, 33(2):195–206, 2014.

387 B. E. John and S. J. Marks. Tracking the effectiveness of usability evaluation methods. *Behaviour & information technology*, 16(4-5):188–202, 1997.

388 B. E. John, K. Prevas, D. D. Salvucci, and K. Koedinger. Predictive human performance modeling made easy. In *Proceedings of the SIGCHI conference on human factors in computing systems*, pages 455–462, 2004.

389 D. Johnson, M. J. Gardner, and R. Perry. Validation of two game experience scales: the player experience of need satisfaction (pens) and game experience questionnaire (geq). *International journal of human-computer studies*, 118:38–46, 2018.

390 J. Johnson. *Designing with the mind in mind: Simple guide to understanding user interface design guidelines*. Morgan Kaufmann, 2020.

391 J. Johnson, T. L. Roberts, W. Verplank et al. The xerox star: A retrospective. *Computer*, 22(9):11–26, 1989.

392 J. Jokinen, A. Acharya, M. Uzair, X. Jiang, and A. Oulasvirta. Touchscreen typing as optimal supervisory control. In *Proceedings of the 2021 CHI conference on human factors in computing systems*, pages 1–14, 2021.

393 J. P. Jokinen, Z. Wang, S. Sarcar, A. Oulasvirta, and X. Ren. Adaptive feature guidance: Modelling visual search with graphical layouts. *International journal of human-computer studies*, 136:102376, 2020.

394 S. Jordà, G. Geiger, M. Alonso, and M. Kaltenbrunner. The reactable: Exploring the synergy between live music performance and tabletop tangible interfaces. In *Proceedings of the 1st international conference on Tangible and embedded interaction*, pages 139–146, 2007.

395 P. W. Jordan. *Designing pleasurable products: An introduction to the new human factors*. CRC press, 2000.

396 S. Jörg, A. Normoyle, and A. Safonova. How responsiveness affects players' perception in digital games. In *Proceedings of the ACM symposium on applied perception*, pages 33–38, 2012.

397 W. Jorritsma, P.-J. Haga, F. Cnossen, R. A. Dierckx, M. Oudkerk, and P. M. van Ooijen. Predicting human performance differences on multiple interface alternatives: Klm, goms and cogtool are unreliable. *Procedia manufacturing*, 3:3725–3731, 2015.

398 S. Jul and G. W. Furnas. Critical zones in desert fog: Aids to multiscale navigation. In *Proceedings of the 11th annual ACM symposium on user interface software and technology*, pages 97–106, 1998.

399 S.-G. Jung, J. An, H. Kwak, M. Ahmad, L. Nielsen, and B. J. Jansen. Persona generation from aggregated social media data. In *Proceedings of the 2017 CHI conference extended abstracts on human factors in computing systems*, pages 1748–1755, 2017.

400 D. Kahneman. *Thinking, fast and slow*. Macmillan, 2011.

401 D. Kahneman and J. Riis. Living, and thinking about it: Two perspectives on life. *The science of well-being*, 1:285–304, 2005.

402 D. Kahneman and A. Tversky. Prospect theory: An analysis of decision under risk. In *Handbook of the fundamentals of financial decision making: Part I*, pages 99–127. World Scientific, 2013.

403 E. Karapanos, J. Zimmerman, J. Forlizzi, and J.-B. Martens. User experience over time: An initial framework. In *Proceedings of the SIGCHI conference on human factors in computing systems*, CHI '09, page 729–738, New York, NY, USA, 2009.

404 M. Kavakli and J. S. Gero. Sketching as mental imagery processing. *Design studies*, 22(4):347–364, 2001.

405 J. Kawakita. The original kj method. *Tokyo: Kawakita research institute*, 5, 1991.

406 M. Kawato. Internal models for motor control and trajectory planning. *Current opinion in neurobiology*, 9(6):718–727, 1999.

407 A. Kay and A. Goldberg. Personal dynamic media. *Computer*, 10(3):31–41, 1977.

408 C. R. Kelley. Manual control: Theory and applications. Technical report, United States Office of Naval Research, 1964.

409 T. Kelley. *The art of innovation: Lessons in creativity from IDEO, America's leading design firm*, volume 10. Currency, 2001.

410 F. Kensing and J. Blomberg. Participatory design: Issues and concerns. *Computer supported cooperative work (CSCW)*, 7(3-4):167–185, 1998.

411 F. Kensing and H. Madsen. Generating visions: future workshops and metaphorical. In *Design at work*, pages 155–168. CRC Press, 2020.

412 D. Kieras, D. Meyer, and J. Ballas. Towards demystification of direct manipulation: Cognitive modeling charts the gulf of execution. In *Proceedings of the SIGCHI conference on human factors in computing systems*, pages 128–135, 2001.

413 D. E. Kieras and A. J. Hornof. Towards accurate and practical predictive models of active-vision-based visual search. In *Proceedings of the SIGCHI conference on human factors in computing systems*, pages 3875–3884, 2014.

414 S. Kiesler, D. Zubrow, A. M. Moses, and V. Geller. Affect in computer-meditated communication: An experiment in synchronous terminal-to-terminal discussion. *Human-computer interaction*, 1(1):77–104, 1985.

415 D. Kirk, A. Sellen, C. Rother, and K. Wood. Understanding photowork. In *Proceedings of the SIGCHI conference on human factors in computing systems*, CHI '06, page 761–770, New York, NY, USA, 2006.

416 D. Kirsh. Interactivity and multimedia interfaces. *Instructional science*, 25(2):79–96, 1997.

417 D. Kirsh and P. Maglio. On distinguishing epistemic from pragmatic action. *Cognitive science*, 18(4):513–549, 1994.

418 A. Kittur, E. H. Chi, and B. Suh. Crowdsourcing user studies with mechanical turk. In *Proceedings of the SIGCHI conference on human factors in computing systems*, pages 453–456, 2008.

419 A. Kittur, L. Yu, T. Hope et al. Scaling up analogical innovation with crowds and ai. *Proceedings of the national academy of sciences*, 116(6):1870–1877, 2019.

420 J. Kjeldskov and M. B. Skov. Was it worth the hassle? Ten years of mobile hci research discussions on lab and field evaluations. In *Proceedings of the 16th international conference on human-computer interaction with mobile devices & services*, pages 43–52, 2014.

421 J. Kjeldskov, M. B. Skov, B. S. Als, and R. T. Høegh. Is it worth the hassle? Exploring the added value of evaluating the usability of context-aware mobile systems in the field. In *International conference on mobile human-computer interaction*, pages 61–73. Springer, 2004.

422 P. Kline. *An easy guide to factor analysis*. Routledge, 2014.

423 R. Kling. The organizational context of user-centered software designs. *MIS quarterly*, pages 41–52, 1977.

424 D. C. Knill and A. Pouget. The bayesian brain: The role of uncertainty in neural coding and computation. *TRENDS in neurosciences*, 27(12):712–719, 2004.

425 J. Koch, M. Laszlo, A. Lucero, and A. Oulasvirta. Surfing for inspiration: Digital inspirational material in design practice. In *Design research society international conference*, pages 1247–1260. Design Research Society, 2018.

426 M. Koelle, A. El Ali, V. Cobus, W. Heuten, and S. C. Boll. All about acceptability? Identifying factors for the adoption of data glasses. In *Proceedings of the 2017 CHI conference on human factors in computing systems*, pages 295–300, 2017.

427 M. Koelle, S. Ananthanarayan, and S. Boll. Social acceptability in hci: A survey of methods, measures, and design strategies. In *Proceedings of the 2020 CHI conference on human factors in computing systems*, CHI '20, page 1–19, New York, NY, USA, 2020.

428 R. Kohavi, R. M. Henne, and D. Sommerfield. Practical guide to controlled experiments on the web: Listen to your customers not to the hippo. In *Proceedings of the 13th ACM SIGKDD international conference on knowledge discovery and data mining*, pages 959–967. ACM, 2007.

429 J. Kolko. Abductive thinking and sensemaking: The drivers of design synthesis. *Design issues*, 26(1):15–28, 2010.

430 G. Kotonya and I. Sommerville. *Requirements engineering: Processes and techniques*. Wiley Publishing, 1998.

431 Y. Kou and X. Gui. Playing with strangers: Understanding temporary teams in league of legends. In *Proceedings of the first ACM SIGCHI annual symposium on computer-human interaction in play*, pages 161–169, 2014.

432 A. D. Kramer, J. E. Guillory, and J. T. Hancock. Experimental evidence of massive-scale emotional contagion through social networks. *Proceedings of the national academy of sciences*, 111(24):8788–8790, 2014.

433 G. E. Krasner and S. T. Pope. A description of the model-view-controller user interface paradigm in the smalltalk-80 system. *Journal of object oriented programming*, 1(3):26–49, 1988.

434 L. Kraus, I. Wechsung, and S. Möller. Psychological needs as motivators for security and privacy actions on smartphones. *Journal of information security and applications*, 34:34–45, 2017.

435 K. Krippendorff. *Content analysis: An introduction to its methodology*. Sage publications, 2018.

436 P. O. Kristensson. Next-generation text entry. *Computer*, 48(07):84–87, 2015.

437 P. O. Kristensson. Statistical language processing for text entry. In A. Oulasvirta, P. O. Kristensson, X. Bi, and A. Howes, editors, *Computational interaction*, pages 41–61. Oxford University Press, Oxford, 2018.

438 P. O. Kristensson and T. Müllners. Design and analysis of intelligent text entry systems with function structure models and envelope analysis. In *Proceedings of the 2021 CHI conference on human factors in computing systems*, pages 1–12, 2021.

439 P. O. Kristensson and K. Vertanen. The potential of dwell-free eye-typing for fast assistive gaze communication. In *Proceedings of the symposium on eye tracking research and applications*, pages 241–244, 2012.

440 S. Krug. Dont make me think: A common sense approach to usability testing. *New riders, berkeley*, 2005.

441 S. Kujala. User involvement: A review of the benefits and challenges. *Behaviour & information technology*, 22(1):1–16, 2003.

442 S. Kujala, V. Roto, K. Väänänen-Vainio-Mattila, E. Karapanos, and A. Sinnelä. Ux curve: A method for evaluating long-term user experience. *Interacting with computers*, 23(5):473–483, 2011.

443 A. Kumar and T. Gilovich. Some "thing" to talk about? Differential story utility from experiential and material purchases. *Personality and social psychology bulletin*, 41(10):1320–1331, 2015.

444 N. Kumar, N. Jafarinaimi, and M. Bin Morshed. Uber in bangladesh: The tangled web of mobility and justice. *Proceedings of the ACM on human-computer interaction*, 2(CSCW):1–21, 2018.

445 V. Kumar and P. Whitney. Faster, cheaper, deeper user research. *Design management journal (former series)*, 14(2):50–57, 2003.

446 G. Kurtenbach and W. Buxton. User learning and performance with marking menus. In *Proceedings of the SIGCHI conference on human factors in computing systems*, pages 258–264, 1994.

447 K. Kuutti and L. J. Bannon. The turn to practice in hci: Towards a research agenda. In *Proceedings of the SIGCHI conference on human factors in computing systems*, pages 3543–3552, 2014.

448 K. Kuutti et al. Activity theory as a potential framework for human-computer interaction research. *Context and consciousness: Activity theory and human-computer interaction*, 1744, 1996.

449 S. Kvale. *Doing interviews*. Sage, 2008.

450 M. Kyng. Designing for a dollar a day. In *Proceedings of the 1988 ACM conference on computer-supported cooperative work*, pages 178–188, 1988.

451 C. Lampe, N. B. Ellison, and C. Steinfield. Changes in use and perception of facebook. In *Proceedings of the 2008 ACM conference on computer supported cooperative work*, CSCW '08, page 721–730, New York, NY, USA, 2008. Association for Computing Machinery. ISBN 9781605580074. https://doi.org/10.1145/1460563.1460675.

452 T. Landauer. Research methods in human-computer interaction. In *Handbook of human-computer interaction*, pages 203–227. Elsevier, second edition, 1997.

453 T. K. Landauer. Let's get real: A position paper on the role of cognitive psychology in the design of humanly useful and usable systems. In *Readings in human–computer interaction*, pages 659–665. Elsevier, 1995.

454 T. K. Landauer. *The trouble with computers: Usefulness, usability, and productivity*. MIT press, 1995.

455 N. D. Lane, E. Miluzzo, H. Lu, D. Peebles, T. Choudhury, and A. T. Campbell. A survey of mobile phone sensing. *IEEE communications magazine*, 48(9):140–150, 2010.

456 R. Langevin, R. J. Lordon, T. Avrahami, B. R. Cowan, T. Hirsch, and G. Hsieh. Heuristic evaluation of conversational agents. In *Proceedings of the 2021 CHI conference on human factors in computing systems*, pages 1–15, 2021.

457 J. Lanier. Virtually there. *Scientific American*, 284(4):66–75, 2001.

458 K. R. Larsen and C. H. Bong. A tool for addressing construct identity in literature reviews and meta-analyses. *Management information systems quarterly*, 40(3):529–551, Sept. 2016.

459 T. Lau. Rethinking the systems review process. *Communications of the ACM*, 53(11):10–11, 2010.

460 J. Lave and E. Wenger. *Situated learning: Legitimate peripheral participation*. Cambridge University Press, 1991.

461 T. Lavie and N. Tractinsky. Assessing dimensions of perceived visual aesthetics of web sites. *International journal of human-computer studies*, 60(3):269–298, 2004.

462 J. J. LaViola Jr. A discussion of cybersickness in virtual environments. *ACM SIGCHI bulletin*, 32(1):47–56, 2000.

463 E. L.-C. Law, V. Roto, M. Hassenzahl, A. P. Vermeeren, and J. Kort. Understanding, scoping and defining user experience: A survey approach. In *Proceedings of the SIGCHI conference on human factors in computing systems*, pages 719–728, 2009.

464 E. L.-C. Law, F. Brühlmann, and E. D. Mekler. Systematic review and validation of the game experience questionnaire (geq) - implications for citation and reporting practice. In *Proceedings of the 2018 annual symposium on computer-human interaction in play*, CHI PLAY '18, pages 257–270, New York, NY, USA, 2018.

465 H. J. Leavitt. *Managerial psychology*. Chicago University of Chicago Press, 1978.

466 S. J. Lederman and R. L. Klatzky. Hand movements: A window into haptic object recognition. *Cognitive psychology*, 19(3):342–368, 1987.

467 H. Ledgard, J. A. Whiteside, A. Singer, and W. Seymour. The natural language of interactive systems. *Communications of the ACM*, 23(10):556–563, 1980.

468 B. Lee, S. Kim, A. Oulasvirta, J.-I. Lee, and E. Park. Moving target selection: A cue integration model. In *Proceedings of the 2018 CHI conference on human factors in computing systems*, pages 1–12, 2018.

469 C. P. Lee and D. Paine. From the matrix to a model of coordinated action (moca) a conceptual framework of and for cscw. In *Proceedings of the 18th ACM conference on computer supported cooperative work & social computing*, pages 179–194, 2015.

470 K. J. Lee, W. Roldan, T. Q. Zhu et al. The show must go on: A conceptual model of conducting synchronous participatory design with children online. In *Proceedings of the 2021 CHI conference on human factors in computing systems*, CHI '21, New York, NY, USA, 2021.

471 Y.-K. Lee, C.-T. Chang, Y. Lin, and Z.-H. Cheng. The dark side of smartphone usage: Psychological traits, compulsive behavior and technostress. *Computers in human behavior*, 31:373–383, 2014.

472 L. A. Leiva, Y. Xue, A. Bansal et al. Understanding visual saliency in mobile user interfaces. In *22nd International conference on human-computer interaction with mobile devices and services*, pages 1–12, 2020.

473 C. Lewis. *Using the" thinking-aloud" method in cognitive interface design*. IBM TJ Watson Research Center Yorktown Heights, NY, 1982.

474 C. Lewis, P. G. Polson, C. Wharton, and J. Rieman. Testing a walkthrough methodology for theory-based design of walk-up-and-use interfaces. In *Proceedings of the SIGCHI conference on human factors in computing systems*, pages 235–242, 1990.

475 R. L. Lewis, A. Howes, and S. Singh. Computational rationality: Linking mechanism and behavior through bounded utility maximization. *Topics in cognitive science*, 6(2):279–311, 2014.

476 J. C. R. Licklider and W. E. Clark. On-line man-computer communication. In *Proceedings of the May 1-3, 1962, spring joint computer conference*, AIEE-IRE '62 (Spring), page 113–128, New York, NY, USA, 1962.

477 W. Lidwell, K. Holden, and J. Butler. *Universal principles of design, revised and updated: 125 ways to enhance usability, influence perception, increase appeal, make better design decisions, and teach through design*. Rockport Pub, 2010.

478 H. Lieberman. An example based environment for beginning programmers. *Instructional science*, 14(3):277–292, 1986.

479 H. Lieberman. The tyranny of evaluation. https://web.media.mit.edu/ lieber/Misc/Tyranny-Evaluation.html, 2003. Accessed: 2022-10-07; First made public: 2003 (CHI Fringe).

480 F. Lieder and T. L. Griffiths. Resource-rational analysis: Understanding human cognition as the optimal use of limited computational resources. *Behavioral and brain sciences*, 43, 2020.

481 J. Liedtka. Perspective: Linking design thinking with innovation outcomes through cognitive bias reduction. *Journal of product innovation management*, 32(6):925–938, 2015.

482 Y.-k. Lim, S.-S. Lee, and K.-y. Lee. Interactivity attributes: A new way of thinking and describing interactivity. In *Proceedings of the SIGCHI conference on human factors in computing systems*, pages 105–108, 2009.

483 Y. S. Lincoln and E. G. Guba. The only generalization is: There is no generalization. *Case study method: Key issues, key texts*, page 27, 2000.

484 G. Lindgaard, G. Fernandes, C. Dudek, and J. Brown. Attention web designers: You have 50 milliseconds to make a good first impression! *Behaviour & information technology*, 25(2):115–126, 2006.

485 J. K. Lindstedt and W. D. Gray. Distinguishing experts from novices by the mind's hand and mind's eye. *Cognitive psychology*, 109:1–25, 2019.

486 S. Lindtner, G. D. Hertz, and P. Dourish. Emerging sites of hci innovation: Hackerspaces, hardware startups & incubators. In *Proceedings of the SIGCHI conference on human factors in computing systems*, pages 439–448, 2014.

487. E. Litt, E. Spottswood, J. Birnholtz, J. T. Hancock, M. E. Smith, and L. Reynolds. Awkward encounters of an "other" kind: Collective self-presentation and face threat on facebook. In *Proceedings of the 17th ACM conference on computer supported cooperative work and social computing*, CSCW '14, page 449–460, New York, NY, USA, 2014.

488. V. Liu and L. B. Chilton. Design guidelines for prompt engineering text-to-image generative models. In *Proceedings of the 2022 CHI conference on human factors in computing systems*, CHI '22, New York, NY, USA, 2022.

489. W. Liu, R. L. d'Oliveira, M. Beaudouin-Lafon, and O. Rioul. Bignav: Bayesian information gain for guiding multiscale navigation. In *Proceedings of the 2017 CHI conference on human factors in computing systems*, pages 5869–5880, 2017.

490. W. Liu, J. Gori, O. Rioul, M. Beaudouin-Lafon, and Y. Guiard. How relevant is hick's law for hci? In *Proceedings of the 2020 CHI conference on human factors in computing systems*, pages 1–11, 2020.

491. S. Ljungblad, Y. Man, M. A. Baytaş, M. Gamboa, M. Obaid, and M. Fjeld. What matters in professional drone pilots' practice? An interview study to understand the complexity of their work and inform human-drone interaction research. In *Proceedings of the 2021 CHI conference on human factors in computing systems*, pages 1–16, 2021.

492. D. Lockton, D. Singh, S. Sabnis, M. Chou, S. Foley, and A. Pantoja. New metaphors: A workshop method for generating ideas and reframing problems in design and beyond. In *Proceedings of the 2019 on creativity and cognition*, pages 319–332. ACM, 2019.

493. J. Lofland and L. H. Lofland. *Analyzing social settings*. Wadsworth Pub, 1971.

494. G. L. Lohse and E. J. Johnson. A comparison of two process tracing methods for choice tasks. *Organizational behavior and human decision processes*, 68(1):28–43, 1996.

495. D. M. Lottridge, C. Rosakranse, C. S. Oh, S. J. Westwood, K. A. Baldoni, A. S. Mann, and C. I. Nass. The effects of chronic multitasking on analytical writing. In *Proceedings of the 33rd annual ACM conference on human factors in computing systems*, pages 2967–2970, 2015.

496. A. Lucero. Using affinity diagrams to evaluate interactive prototypes. In J. Abascal, S. Barbosa, M. Fetter, T. Gross, P. Palanque, and M. Winckler, editors, *Human-computer interaction – INTERACT 2015*, pages 231–248, Cham, 2015.

497. E. Luger and A. Sellen. "Like having a really bad pa": The gulf between user expectation and experience of conversational agents. In *Proceedings of the 2016 CHI conference on human factors in computing systems*, CHI '16, page 5286–5297, New York, NY, USA, 2016. Association for Computing Machinery. ISBN 9781450333627. https://doi.org/10.1145/2858036.2858288.

498. J. Lundberg, A. Ibrahim, D. Jönsson, S. Lindquist, and P. Qvarfordt. "The snatcher catcher" an interactive refrigerator. In *Proceedings of the second Nordic conference on human-computer interaction*, pages 209–212, 2002.

499. U. Lyngs, K. Lukoff, P. Slovak et al. Self-control in cyberspace: Applying dual systems theory to a review of digital self-control tools. In *Proceedings of the 2019 CHI conference on human factors in computing systems*, pages 1–18, 2019.

500. K. Mack, E. McDonnell, D. Jain, L. Lu Wang, J. E. Froehlich, and L. Findlater. What do we mean by "accessibility research"? A literature survey of accessibility papers in chi and assets from 1994 to 2019. In *Proceedings of the 2021 CHI conference on human factors in computing systems*, pages 1–18, 2021.

501. R. L. Mack, C. H. Lewis, and J. M. Carroll. Learning to use word processors: Problems and prospects. *ACM transactions on information systems*, 1(3):254–271, July 1983.

502. D. J. MacKay, C. J. Ball, and M. Donegan. Efficient communication with one or two buttons. In *AIP conference proceedings*, volume 735, pages 207–218. AIP, 2004.

503 W. E. Mackay. Triggers and barriers to customizing software. In *Proceedings of the SIGCHI conference on human factors in computing systems*, CHI '91, page 153–160, New York, NY, USA, 1991.

504 W. E. MacKay. Is paper safer? the role of paper flight strips in air traffic control. *ACM transactions on computer-human interaction (TOCHI)*, 6(4):311–340, 1999.

505 I. S. MacKenzie. Fitts' law as a research and design tool in human-computer interaction. *Human-computer interaction*, 7(1):91–139, 1992.

506 I. S. MacKenzie and W. Buxton. Extending fitts' law to two-dimensional tasks. In *Proceedings of the SIGCHI conference on human factors in computing systems*, pages 219–226, 1992.

507 I. S. MacKenzie and R. W. Soukoreff. Card, english, and burr (1978): 25 years later. In *CHI '03 Extended abstracts on human factors in computing systems*, CHI EA '03, pages 760–761, New York, NY, USA, 2003.

508 A. MacLean, R. M. Young, V. M. Bellotti, and T. P. Moran. Questions, options, and criteria: Elements of design space analysis. *Human–computer interaction*, 6(3-4):201–250, 1991.

509 R. Mahajan and B. Shneiderman. Visual and textual consistency checking tools for graphical user interfaces. *IEEE transactions on software engineering*, 23(11):722–735, 1997.

510 T. Mahatody, M. Sagar, and C. Kolski. State of the art on the cognitive walkthrough method, its variants and evolutions. *International journal of human–computer interaction*, 26(8):741–785, 2010.

511 M. L. Maher, J. Poon, and S. Boulanger. Formalising design exploration as co-evolution. In *Advances in formal design methods for CAD*, pages 3–30. Springer, 1996.

512 M. A. Makary and M. Daniel. Medical error—the third leading cause of death in the us. *Bmj*, 353, 2016.

513 S. Malacria, G. Bailly, J. Harrison, A. Cockburn, and C. Gutwin. Promoting hotkey use through rehearsal with exposehk. In *Proceedings of the SIGCHI conference on human factors in computing systems*, CHI '13, page 573–582, New York, NY, USA, 2013.

514 R. Mancini, A. Dix, and S. Levialdi. Reflections on undo. *University of Rome*, 1996.

515 J. Mankoff, A. K. Dey, G. Hsieh, J. Kientz, S. Lederer, and M. Ames. Heuristic evaluation of ambient displays. In *Proceedings of the SIGCHI conference on human factors in computing systems*, CHI '03, page 169–176, New York, NY, USA, 2003.

516 J. Mankoff, A. K. Dey, G. Hsieh, J. Kientz, S. Lederer, and M. Ames. Heuristic evaluation of ambient displays. In *Proceedings of the SIGCHI conference on human factors in computing systems*, pages 169–176, 2003.

517 A. Mannocci, F. Osborne, and E. Motta. The evolution of ijhcs and chi: A quantitative analysis. *International journal of human–computer studies*, 131:23–40, 2019.

518 A. Markussen, M. R. Jakobsen, and K. Hornbæk. Selection-based mid-air text entry on large displays. In *Human-computer interaction–INTERACT 2013: 14th IFIP TC 13 international conference, Cape Town, South Africa, September 2-6, 2013, proceedings, part I 14*, pages 401–418. Springer, 2013.

519 N. Marquardt, R. Diaz-Marino, S. Boring, and S. Greenberg. The proximity toolkit: Prototyping proxemic interactions in ubiquitous computing ecologies. In *Proceedings of the 24th annual ACM symposium on user interface software and technology*, UIST '11, page 315–326, New York, NY, USA, 2011.

520 J. Marshall, C. Linehan, J. Spence, and S. Rennick Egglestone. Throwaway citation of prior work creates risk of bad hci research. In *Proceedings of the 2017 CHI conference extended abstracts on human factors in computing systems*, pages 827–836, 2017.

521 P. Masci, A. Ayoub, P. Curzon, M. D. Harrison, I. Lee, and H. Thimbleby. Verification of interactive software for medical devices: Pca infusion pumps and fda regulation as an example. In *Proceedings of the 5th ACM SIGCHI symposium on Engineering interactive computing systems*, pages 81–90, 2013.

522 A. H. Maslow. A theory of human motivation. *Psychological review*, 50(4):370, 1943.

523 T. H. Massie and J. K. Salisbury. The phantom haptic interface: A device for probing virtual objects. In *Proceedings of the ASME winter annual meeting, symposium on haptic interfaces for virtual environment and teleoperator systems*, volume 55, pages 295–300. Chicago, IL, 1994.

524 A. Mathur, G. Acar, M. J. Friedman et al. Dark patterns at scale: Findings from a crawl of 11k shopping websites. *Proceedings of the ACM on human-computer interaction*, 3(CSCW), 2019.

525 T. Matthews, A. K. Dey, J. Mankoff, S. Carter, and T. Rattenbury. A toolkit for managing user attention in peripheral displays. In *Proceedings of the 17th annual ACM symposium on user interface software and technology*, UIST '04, page 247–256, New York, NY, USA, 2004.

526 D. L. Maulsby and I. H. Witten. Inducing programs in a direct-manipulation environment. In *Proceedings of the SIGCHI conference on human factors in computing systems*, pages 57–62, 1989.

527 R. E. Mayer and J. K. Gallini. When is an illustration worth ten thousand words? *Journal of educational psychology*, 82(4):715, 1990.

528 E. Mayo. *The human problems of an industrial civilization*. Routledge, 1933.

529 J. McCarthy and P. Wright. *Technology as experience*. MIT Press, 2004.

530 N. McDonald, S. Schoenebeck, and A. Forte. Reliability and inter-rater reliability in qualitative research: Norms and guidelines for cscw and hci practice. *Proceedings of the ACM on human-computer interaction*, 3(CSCW):1–23, 2019.

531 J. E. McGrath. *Groups: Interaction and performance*, volume 14. Prentice-Hall Englewood Cliffs, NJ, 1984.

532 J. E. McGrath. Methodology matters: Doing research in the behavioral and social sciences. In *Readings in human–computer interaction*, pages 152–169. Elsevier, 1995.

533 R. McKinlay. Technology: Use or lose our navigation skills. *Nature*, 531(7596):573–575, 2016.

534 D. McMillan, A. Morrison, O. Brown, M. Hall, and M. Chalmers. Further into the wild: Running worldwide trials of mobile systems. In *International conference on pervasive computing*, pages 210–227. Springer, 2010.

535 M. C. Medlock, D. Wixon, M. Terrano, R. Romero, and B. Fulton. Using the rite method to improve products: A definition and a case study. *Usability professionals association*, 51:1963813932–1562338474, 2002.

536 C. Mendez, L. Letaw, M. Burnett, S. Stumpf, A. Sarma, and C. Hilderbrand. From gendermag to inclusivemag: An inclusive design meta-method. In *2019 IEEE symposium on visual languages and human-centric computing (VL/HCC)*, pages 97–106. IEEE, 2019.

537 H. M. Mentis. Collocated use of imaging systems in coordinated surgical practice. *Proceedings of the ACM on human-computer interaction*, 1(CSCW):1–17, 2017.

538 J. Meredith. Conversation analysis and online interaction. *Research on language and social interaction*, 52(3):241–256, 2019.

539 D. E. Meyer, R. A. Abrams, S. Kornblum, C. E. Wright, and J. Keith Smith. Optimality in human motor performance: Ideal control of rapid aimed movements. *Psychological review*, 95(3):340, 1988.

540 L. Micallef, G. Palmas, A. Oulasvirta, and T. Weinkauf. Towards perceptual optimization of the visual design of scatterplots. *IEEE transactions on visualization and computer graphics*, 23(6):1588–1599, 2017.

541 P. Micheli, S. J. Wilner, S. H. Bhatti, M. Mura, and M. B. Beverland. Doing design thinking: Conceptual review, synthesis, and research agenda. *Journal of product innovation management*, 36(2):124–148, 2019.

542 E. Miguel, C. Camerer, K. Casey et al. Promoting transparency in social science research. *Science*, 343(6166):30–31, 2014.

543 P. Milgram and F. Kishino. A taxonomy of mixed reality visual displays. *IEICE TRANSACTIONS on information and systems*, 77(12):1321–1329, 1994.

544 P. Milgram, H. Takemura, A. Utsumi, and F. Kishino. Augmented reality: A class of displays on the reality-virtuality continuum. In *Telemanipulator and telepresence technologies*, volume 2351, pages 282–292. International Society for Optics and Photonics, 1995.

545 D. R. Millen. Rapid ethnography: time deepening strategies for hci field research. In *Proceedings of the 3rd conference on Designing interactive systems: Processes, practices, methods, and techniques*, pages 280–286, 2000.

546 D. P. Miller. The depth/breadth tradeoff in hierarchical computer menus. In *Proceedings of the human factors society annual meeting*, volume 25, pages 296–300. SAGE Publications Sage CA: Los Angeles, CA, 1981.

547 A. Miniukovich and A. De Angeli. Computation of interface aesthetics. In *Proceedings of the 33rd annual ACM conference on human factors in computing systems*, CHI '15, page 1163–1172, New York, NY, USA, 2015.

548 S. Minneman, S. Harrison, B. Janssen, G. Kurtenbach, T. Moran, I. Smith, and B. van Melle. A confederation of tools for capturing and accessing collaborative activity. In *Proceedings of the third ACM international conference on multimedia*, pages 523–534, 1995.

549 H. Mintzberg. Structured observation as a method to study managerial work. *Journal of management studies*, 7(1):87–104, 1970.

550 R. K. Mitchell, B. R. Agle, and D. J. Wood. Toward a theory of stakeholder identification and salience: Defining the principle of who and what really counts. *Academy of management review*, 22(4):853–886, 1997.

551 B. Moggridge and B. Atkinson. *Designing interactions*, volume 17. MIT press Cambridge, MA, 2007.

552 R. Molich. Are usability evaluations reproducible? *Interactions*, 25(6):82–85, October 2018.

553 R. Molich. Are usability evaluations reproducible? *Interactions*, 25(6):82–85, 2018.

554 R. Molich and J. Nielsen. Improving a human-computer dialogue. *Communications of the ACM*, 33(3):338–348, 1990.

555 J. P. Monat and T. F. Gannon. Applying systems thinking to engineering and design. *Systems*, 6(3):34, 2018.

556 A. Monk and S. Howard. Methods & tools: the rich picture: A tool for reasoning about work context. *Interactions*, 5(2):21–30, 1998.

557 A. Mørch. Three levels of end-user tailoring: Customization, integration, and extension. *Computers and design in context*, pages 51–76, 1997.

558 M. Moshagen and M. T. Thielsch. Facets of visual aesthetics. *International journal of human-computer studies*, 68(10):689–709, 2010.

559 A. Mottelson, J. Knibbe, and K. Hornbæk. Veritaps: Truth estimation from mobile interaction. In *Proceedings of the 2018 CHI conference on human factors in computing systems*, CHI '18, page 1–12, New York, NY, USA, 2018.

560 G. Mowbray and M. Rhoades. On the reduction of choice reaction times with practice. *Quarterly journal of experimental psychology*, 11(1):16–23, 1959.

561 F. F. Mueller, P. Lopes, P. Strohmeier et al. Next steps for human-computer integration. In *Proceedings of the 2020 CHI conference on human factors in computing systems*, pages 1–15, 2020.

562 G. Müller and M. Möser. *Handbook of engineering acoustics*. Springer Science & Business Media, 2012.

563 H. Müller, A. Sedley, and E. Ferrall-Nunge. Survey research in hci. In *Ways of knowing in HCI*, pages 229–266. Springer, 2014.

564 J. Munafo, M. Diedrick, and T. A. Stoffregen. The virtual reality head-mounted display oculus rift induces motion sickness and is sexist in its effects. *Experimental brain research*, 235:889–901, 2017.

565 M. R. Munafò and G. D. Smith. Robust research needs many lines of evidence, 2018.

566 T. Munzner. Process and pitfalls in writing information visualization research papers. In *Information visualization*, pages 134–153. Springer, 2008.

567 T. Munzner. *Visualization analysis and design*. CRC press, 2014.

568. R. Murray-Smith, A. Oulasvirta, A. Howes et al. What simulation can do for hci research. *Interactions*, 29(6):48–53, 2022.

569. B. A. Myers. Uimss, toolkits, interface builders. *Human computer interaction institute, Carnegie Mellon university*, 1996.

570. B. A. Myers. A brief history of human-computer interaction technology. *Interactions*, 5(2):44–54, 1998.

571. B. A. Myers and M. B. Rosson. Survey on user interface programming. In *Proceedings of the SIGCHI conference on human factors in computing systems*, pages 195–202, 1992.

572. B. A. Myers and J. Stylos. Improving api usability. *Communications of the ACM*, 59(6):62–69, 2016.

573. B. A. Myers, R. G. McDaniel, R. C. Miller et al. The amulet environment: New models for effective user interface software development. *IEEE transactions on software engineering*, 23(6):347–365, 1997.

574. M. A. Nacenta, Y. Kamber, Y. Qiang, and P. O. Kristensson. Memorability of pre-designed and user-defined gesture sets. In *Proceedings of the SIGCHI conference on human factors in computing systems*, pages 1099–1108, 2013.

575. K. Z. Naqshbandi, C. Liu, S. Taylor, R. Lim, N. Ahmadpour, and R. Calvo. "I am most grateful." Using gratitude to improve the sense of relatedness and motivation for online volunteerism. *International journal of human–computer interaction*, 36(14):1325–1341, 2020.

576. S. Narayan, J. Orlowitz, J. Morgan, B. M. Hill, and A. Shaw. The wikipedia adventure: field evaluation of an interactive tutorial for new users. In *Proceedings of the 2017 ACM conference on computer supported cooperative work and social computing*, pages 1785–1799, 2017.

577. B. A. Nardi and J. R. Miller. Twinkling lights and nested loops: Distributed problem solving and spreadsheet development. *International journal of man-machine studies*, 34(2):161–184, 1991.

578. B. A. Nardi, S. Whittaker, and E. Bradner. Interaction and outeraction: Instant messaging in action. In *Proceedings of the 2000 ACM conference on computer supported cooperative work*, pages 79–88, 2000.

579. C. Nass, J. Steuer, and E. R. Tauber. Computers are social actors. In *Proceedings of the SIGCHI conference on human factors in computing systems*, pages 72–78, 1994.

580. C. Nass, Y. Moon, B. J. Fogg, B. Reeves, and C. Dryer. Can computer personalities be human personalities? In *Conference companion on human factors in computing systems*, CHI '95, pages 228–229, New York, NY, USA, 1995.

581. I. Nassi and B. Shneiderman. Flowchart techniques for structured programming. *ACM sigplan notices*, 8(8):12–26, 1973.

582. P. Naur. *Computing: A human activity*. ACM, 1992.

583. A. B. Neang, W. Sutherland, M. W. Beach, and C. P. Lee. Data integration as coordination: The articulation of data work in an ocean science collaboration. *Proceedings of the ACM on human-computer interaction*, 4(CSCW3):1–25, 2021.

584. M. Nebeling, M. Speicher, and M. Norrie. W3touch: Metrics-based web page adaptation for touch. In *Proceedings of the SIGCHI conference on human factors in computing systems*, CHI '13, page 2311–2320, New York, NY, USA, 2013.

585. T. H. Nelson. Complex information processing: a file structure for the complex, the changing and the indeterminate. In *Proceedings of the 1965 20th national conference*, pages 84–100, 1965.

586. A. Newell, H. A. Simon, et al. *Human problem solving*. Prentice-hall Englewood Cliffs, NJ, 1972.

587. W. M. Newman and A. S. Taylor. Towards a methodology employing critical parameters to deliver performance improvements in interactive systems. In *INTERACT*, volume 99, pages 605–612. Citeseer, 1999.

588. R. S. Nickerson. Man-computer interaction: A challenge for human factors research. *Ergonomics*, 12(4):501–517, 1969. https://doi.org/10.1080/00140136908931076. PMID: 5823965.

589. J. Nielsen. The usability engineering life cycle. *Computer*, 25(3):12–22, 1992.

590 J. Nielsen. Noncommand user interfaces. *Communications of the ACM*, 36(4):83–99, 1993.

591 J. Nielsen. *Usability engineering*. Morgan Kaufmann, 1994.

592 J. Nielsen and J. Levy. Measuring usability: Preference vs. performance. *Communications of the ACM*, 37(4):66–75, 1994.

593 J. Nielsen and R. Molich. Heuristic evaluation of user interfaces. In *Proceedings of the SIGCHI conference on human factors in computing systems*, pages 249–256, 1990.

594 L. Nielsen. *Personas-user focused design*, volume 1373. Springer, 2013.

595 M. Nørgaard and K. Hornbæk. What do usability evaluators do in practice? An explorative study of think-aloud testing. In *Proceedings of the 6th conference on designing interactive systems*, pages 209–218, 2006.

596 D. A. Norman. Errors in human performance. Technical report, California Univ San Diego LA JOLLA Center For Human Information Processing, 1980.

597 D. A. Norman. Design rules based on analyses of human error. *Communications of the ACM*, 26(4):254–258, 1983.

598 D. A. Norman. Some observations on mental models. *Mental models*, 7(112):7–14, 1983.

599 D. A. Norman. Cognitive engineering. *User centered system design*, 31:61, 1986.

600 D. A. Norman. *The psychology of everyday things*. Basic books, 1988.

601 D. A. Norman. *The invisible computer: Why good products can fail, the personal computer is so complex, and information appliances are the solution*. MIT press, 1998.

602 D. A. Norman. Human-centered design considered harmful. *Interactions*, 12(4):14–19, 2005.

603 D. A. Norman. The way i see it memory is more important than actuality. *Interactions*, 16(2):24–26, 2009.

604 D. A. Norman and S. W. Draper. *User centered system design; new perspectives on human-computer interaction*. L. Erlbaum Associates Inc., 1986.

605 K. L. Nowak and F. Biocca. The effect of the agency and anthropomorphism on users' sense of telepresence, copresence, and social presence in virtual environments. *Presence: Teleoperators & virtual environments*, 12(5):481–494, 2003.

606 R. Nozick. *Anarchy, state, and utopia*, volume 5038. Basic Books, 1974.

607 K. Oberauer, S. Lewandowsky, E. Awh et al. Benchmarks for models of short-term and working memory. *Psychological bulletin*, 144(9):885, 2018.

608 H. L. O'Brien and E. G. Toms. The development and evaluation of a survey to measure user engagement. *Journal of the American society for information science and technology*, 61(1):50–69, 2010.

609 M. Obrist, R. Bernhaupt, and M. Tscheligi. Interactive tv for the home: An ethnographic study on users' requirements and experiences. *International Journal of Human–Computer Interaction*, 24(2):174–196, 2008.

610 M. Obrist, S. A. Seah, and S. Subramanian. Talking about tactile experiences. In *Proceedings of the SIGCHI conference on human factors in computing systems*, CHI '13, page 1659–1668, New York, NY, USA, 2013.

611 W. Odom, J. Zimmerman, and J. Forlizzi. Teenagers and their virtual possessions: design opportunities and issues. In *Proceedings of the SIGCHI conference on human factors in computing systems*, pages 1491–1500, 2011.

612 D. of Transportation. An examination of driver distraction as recorded in nhtsa databases. Technical report, United States. National Highway Traffic Safety Administration, 2014.

613 A. A. Ogunyemi, D. Lamas, M. K. Lárusdóttir, and F. Loizides. A systematic mapping study of hci practice research. *International journal of human–computer interaction*, 35(16):1461–1486, 2019.

614 C. Oh, S. Kim, J. Choi, J. Eun, S. Kim, J. Kim, J. Lee, and B. Suh. Understanding how people reason about aesthetic evaluations of artificial intelligence. In *Proceedings of the 2020 ACM designing interactive systems conference*, pages 1169–1181, 2020.

615 K. O'Hara and A. Sellen. A comparison of reading paper and on-line documents. In *Proceedings of the ACM SIGCHI conference on human factors in computing systems*, CHI '97, pages 335–342, New York, NY, USA, 1997.

616 K. O'Hara, G. Gonzalez, A. Sellen et al. Touchless interaction in surgery. *Communications of the ACM*, 57(1):70–77, 2014.

617 A. Oliva and A. Torralba. The role of context in object recognition. *Trends in cognitive sciences*, 11(12):520–527, 2007.

618 G. M. Olson and J. S. Olson. Distance matters. *Human–computer interaction*, 15(2-3):139–178, 2000.

619 J. R. Olson and G. M. Olson. The growth of cognitive modeling in human-computer interaction since goms. In *Readings in human–computer interaction*, pages 603–625. Elsevier, 1995.

620 A. N. Oppenheim. *Questionnaire design, interviewing and attitude measurement*. Bloomsbury Publishing, 2000.

621 D. M. Oppenheimer, T. Meyvis, and N. Davidenko. Instructional manipulation checks: Detecting satisficing to increase statistical power. *Journal of experimental social psychology*, 45(4):867–872, 2009.

622 W. J. Orlikowski. Learning from notes: Organizational issues in groupware implementation. In *Readings in human–computer interaction*, pages 197–204. Elsevier, 1995.

623 W. J. Orlikowski. Using technology and constituting structures: A practice lens for studying technology in organizations. *Organization science*, 11(4):404–428, 2000.

624 A. Oulasvirta. Task demands and memory in web interaction: A levels of processing approach. *Interacting with computers*, 16(2):217–241, 2004.

625 A. Oulasvirta and K. Hornbæk. Hci research as problem-solving. In *Proceedings of the 2016 CHI conference on human factors in computing systems*, CHI '16, pages 4956–4967, New York, NY, USA, 2016.

626 A. Oulasvirta, S. Tamminen, V. Roto, and J. Kuorelahti. Interaction in 4-second bursts: the fragmented nature of attentional resources in mobile hci. In *Proceedings of the SIGCHI conference on human factors in computing systems*, pages 919–928, 2005.

627 A. Oulasvirta, M. Wahlström, and K. A. Ericsson. What does it mean to be good at using a mobile device? an investigation of three levels of experience and skill. *International journal of human-computer studies*, 69(3):155–169, 2011.

628 A. Oulasvirta, S. De Pascale, J. Koch et al. Aalto interface metrics (aim): A service and codebase for computational gui evaluation. In *The 31st annual ACM symposium on user interface software and technology adjunct proceedings*, UIST '18 Adjunct, pages 16–19, New York, NY, USA, 2018.

629 A. Oulasvirta, S. Kim, and B. Lee. Neuromechanics of a button press. In *Proceedings of the 2018 CHI conference on human factors in computing systems*, CHI '18, page 1–13, New York, NY, USA, 2018.

630 A. Oulasvirta, S. Kim, and B. Lee. Neuromechanics of a button press. In *Proceedings of the 2018 CHI conference on human factors in computing systems*, pages 1–13, 2018.

631 A. Oulasvirta, N. R. Dayama, M. Shiripour, M. John, and A. Karrenbauer. Combinatorial optimization of graphical user interface designs. *Proceedings of the IEEE*, 108(3):434–464, 2020.

632 A. Oulasvirta, J. P. Jokinen, and A. Howes. Computational rationality as a theory of interaction. In *CHI conference on human factors in computing systems*, pages 1–14, 2022.

633 S. Paea, C. Katsanos, and G. Bulivou. Information architecture: Using best merge method, category validity, and multidimensional scaling for open card sort data analysis. *International journal of human–computer interaction*, pages 1–21, 2022.

634 G. Pahl and W. Beitz. *Engineering design: A systematic approach*. Springer Science & Business Media, 2013.

635 L. Palen and P. Dourish. Unpacking" privacy" for a networked world. In *Proceedings of the SIGCHI conference on human factors in computing systems*, pages 129–136, 2003.

636 L. Palen and M. Salzman. Voice-mail diary studies for naturalistic data capture under mobile conditions. In *Proceedings of the 2002 ACM conference on computer supported cooperative work*, CSCW '02, page 87–95, New York, NY, USA, 2002.

637 K. Palin, A. M. Feit, S. Kim, P. O. Kristensson, and A. Oulasvirta. How do people type on mobile devices? Observations from a study with 37,000 volunteers. In *Proceedings of the 21st international conference on human-computer interaction with mobile devices and services*, pages 1–12, 2019.

638 R. Parasuraman and V. Riley. Humans and automation: Use, misuse, disuse, abuse. *Human factors*, 39(2):230–253, 1997.

639 R. Parasuraman, T. B. Sheridan, and C. D. Wickens. A model for types and levels of human interaction with automation. *IEEE transactions on systems, man, and cybernetics-Part A: Systems and humans*, 30(3):286–297, 2000.

640 D. L. Parnas and P. C. Clements. A rational design process: How and why to fake it. *IEEE transactions on software engineering*, (2):251–257, 1986.

641 A. Parush, R. Nadir, and A. Shtub. Evaluating the layout of graphical user interface screens: Validation of a numerical computerized model. *International journal of human-computer interaction*, 10(4):343–360, 1998.

642 A. Parush, Y. Shwarts, A. Shtub, and M. J. Chandra. The impact of visual layout factors on performance in web pages: A cross-language study. *Human factors*, 47(1):141–157, 2005.

643 J. Patten and H. Ishii. Mechanical constraints as computational constraints in tabletop tangible interfaces. In *Proceedings of the SIGCHI conference on human factors in computing systems*, pages 809–818, 2007.

644 S. A. Paul and M. C. Reddy. Understanding together: sensemaking in collaborative information seeking. In *Proceedings of the 2010 ACM conference on computer supported cooperative work*, pages 321–330, 2010.

645 S. J. Payne and T. R. G. Green. The structure of command languages: an experiment on task-action grammar. *International journal of man-machine studies*, 30(2):213–234, 1989.

646 S. J. Payne and A. Howes. Adaptive interaction: A utility maximization approach to understanding human interaction with technology. *Synthesis lectures on human-centered informatics*, 6(1):1–111, 2013.

647 E. R. Pedersen, K. McCall, T. P. Moran, and F. G. Halasz. Tivoli: An electronic whiteboard for informal workgroup meetings. In *Readings in human–computer interaction*, pages 509–516. Elsevier, 1995.

648 C. Perrow. *Normal accidents: Living with high risk technologies*. Princeton university press, 1999.

649 D. Peters, R. A. Calvo, and R. M. Ryan. Designing for motivation, engagement and wellbeing in digital experience. *Frontiers in psychology*, 9:797, 2018.

650 D. Peters, L. Loke, and N. Ahmadpour. Toolkits, cards and games–a review of analogue tools for collaborative ideation. *CoDesign*, 17(4):410–434, 2021.

651 C. Petitmengin, M. Van Beek, M. Bitbol, J.-M. Nissou, and A. Roepstorff. Studying the experience of meditation through micro-phenomenology. *Current opinion in psychology*, 28:54–59, 2019.

652 H. Petroski. *Success through failure: The paradox of design*, volume 92. Princeton University Press, 2018.

653 I. Pettersson, F. Lachner, A.-K. Frison, A. Riener, and A. Butz. A bermuda triangle? a review of method application and triangulation in user experience evaluation. In *Proceedings of the 2018 CHI conference on human factors in computing systems*, pages 1–16, 2018.

654 R. W. Picard, E. Vyzas, and J. Healey. Toward machine emotional intelligence: Analysis of affective physiological state. *IEEE transactions on pattern analysis and machine intelligence*, 23(10):1175–1191, 2001.

655 M. Pielot, T. Dingler, J. S. Pedro, and N. Oliver. When attention is not scarce - detecting boredom from mobile phone usage. In *Proceedings of the 2015 ACM international joint conference on pervasive and ubiquitous computing*, UbiComp '15, page 825–836, New York, NY, USA, 2015.

656 M. Pielot, T. Dingler, J. S. Pedro, and N. Oliver. When attention is not scarce-detecting boredom from mobile phone usage. In *Proceedings of the 2015 ACM international joint conference on pervasive and ubiquitous computing*, pages 825–836, 2015.

657 C. Pinder, J. Vermeulen, B. R. Cowan, and R. Beale. Digital behaviour change interventions to break and form habits. *ACM transactions on computer-human interaction*, 25(3), June 2018. ISSN 1073-0516. https://doi.org/10.1145/3196830.

658 D. Pinelle and C. Gutwin. Groupware walkthrough: Adding context to groupware usability evaluation. In *Proceedings of the SIGCHI conference on human factors in computing systems*, pages 455–462, 2002.

659 V. Pipek and V. Wulf. Infrastructuring: Toward an integrated perspective on the design and use of information technology. *Journal of the association for information systems*, 10(5):1, 2009.

660 B. Piper, C. Ratti, and H. Ishii. Illuminating clay: A 3-d tangible interface for landscape analysis. In *Proceedings of the SIGCHI conference on human factors in computing systems*, CHI '02, page 355–362, New York, NY, USA, 2002.

661 P. Pirolli and S. Card. Information foraging. *Psychological review*, 106(4):643, 1999.

662 D. Pitcher and L. G. Ungerleider. Evidence for a third visual pathway specialized for social perception. *Trends in cognitive sciences*, 2020.

663 J. Pitkow and M. Recker. Results from the first world-wide web user survey. *Computer networks and ISDN systems*, 27(2):243–254, 1994.

664 S. Pizza, B. Brown, D. McMillan, and A. Lampinen. Smartwatch in vivo. In *Proceedings of the 2016 CHI conference on human factors in computing systems*, pages 5456–5469, 2016.

665 L. Plowman, Y. Rogers, and M. Ramage. What are workplace studies for? In *Proceedings of the fourth European conference on computer-supported cooperative work ECSCW'95*, pages 309–324. Springer, 1995.

666 H. Pohl and R. Murray-Smith. Focused and casual interactions: Allowing users to vary their level of engagement. In *Proceedings of the SIGCHI conference on human factors in computing systems*, pages 2223–2232, 2013.

667 H. Pohl, D. Stanke, and M. Rohs. Emojizoom: Emoji entry via large overview maps. In *Proceedings of the 18th international conference on human-computer interaction with mobile devices and services*, pages 510–517, 2016.

668 H. Pohl, P. Brandes, H. Ngo Quang, and M. Rohs. Squeezeback: Pneumatic compression for notifications. In *Proceedings of the 2017 CHI conference on human factors in computing systems*, pages 5318–5330, 2017.

669 K. Pohl. *Requirements engineering: fundamentals, principles, and techniques*. Springer Publishing Company, Incorporated, 2010.

670 M. Polanyi. *The tacit dimension*. University of Chicago press, 2009.

671 P. G. Polson and C. H. Lewis. Theory-based design for easily learned interfaces. *Human–computer interaction*, 5(2-3):191–220, 1990.

672 M. Porcheron, J. E. Fischer, S. Reeves, and S. Sharples. *Voice interfaces in everyday life*, page 1–12. Association for Computing Machinery, New York, NY, USA, 2018.

673 I. Poupyrev, M. Billinghurst, S. Weghorst, and T. Ichikawa. The go-go interaction technique: non-linear mapping for direct manipulation in vr. In *Proceedings of the 9th annual ACM symposium on user interface software and technology*, pages 79–80, 1996.

674 I. Poupyrev, P. Schoessler, J. Loh, and M. Sato. Botanicus interacticus: Interactive plants technology. In *ACM SIGGRAPH 2012 emerging technologies*, pages 1–1. ACM, 2012.

675 C. Preist, D. Schien, and P. Shabajee. Evaluating sustainable interaction design of digital services: The case of youtube. In *Proceedings of the 2019 CHI conference on human factors in computing systems*, pages 1–12, 2019.

676 J. O. Prochaska and W. F. Velicer. The transtheoretical model of health behavior change. *American journal of health promotion*, 12(1):38–48, 1997.

677 M. Prpa, S. Fdili-Alaoui, T. Schiphorst, and P. Pasquier. Articulating experience: Reflections from experts applying micro-phenomenology to design research in hci. In *Proceedings of the 2020 CHI conference on human factors in computing systems*, pages 1–14, 2020.

678 J. Pruitt and J. Grudin. Personas: practice and theory. In *Proceedings of the 2003 conference on designing for user experiences*, pages 1–15, 2003.

679 A. K. Przybylski and N. Weinstein. Can you connect with me now? How the presence of mobile communication technology influences face-to-face conversation quality. *Journal of social and personal relationships*, 30(3):237–246, 2013.

680 Q. Pu, S. Gupta, S. Gollakota, and S. Patel. Whole-home gesture recognition using wireless signals. In *Proceedings of the 19th annual international conference on Mobile computing & networking*, pages 27–38, 2013.

681 G. Pullin and A. Newell. Focussing on extra-ordinary users. In *International conference on universal access in human-computer interaction*, pages 253–262. Springer, 2007.

682 C. Puri, L. Olson, I. Pavlidis, J. Levine, and J. Starren. Stresscam: Non-contact measurement of users' emotional states through thermal imaging. In *CHI '05 extended abstracts on human factors in computing systems*, CHI EA '05, page 1725–1728, New York, NY, USA, 2005.

683 A. Pusch and A. Lécuyer. Pseudo-haptics: from the theoretical foundations to practical system design guidelines. In *Proceedings of the 13th international conference on multimodal interfaces*, pages 57–64, 2011.

684 A. J. Quinn and B. B. Bederson. Human computation: a survey and taxonomy of a growing field. In *Proceedings of the SIGCHI conference on human factors in computing systems*, pages 1403–1412, 2011.

685 K. K. Rachuri, M. Musolesi, C. Mascolo, P. J. Rentfrow, C. Longworth, and A. Aucinas. Emotionsense: A mobile phones based adaptive platform for experimental social psychology research. In *Proceedings of the 12th ACM international conference on ubiquitous computing*, pages 281–290, 2010.

686 H. S. Raffle, A. J. Parkes, and H. Ishii. Topobo: a constructive assembly system with kinetic memory. In *Proceedings of the SIGCHI conference on Human factors in computing systems*, pages 647–654, 2004.

687 G. Ramos, M. Boulos, and R. Balakrishnan. Pressure widgets. In *Proceedings of the SIGCHI conference on human factors in computing systems*, CHI '04, page 487–494, New York, NY, USA, 2004.

688 J. Raskin. *The humane interface: new directions for designing interactive systems*. Addison-Wesley Professional, 2000.

689 J. Rasmussen. Skills, rules, and knowledge; signals, signs, and symbols, and other distinctions in human performance models. *IEEE transactions on systems, man, and cybernetics*, pages 257–266, 1983.

690 R. Ratcliff and H. P. Van Dongen. Diffusion model for one-choice reaction-time tasks and the cognitive effects of sleep deprivation. *Proceedings of the national academy of sciences*, 108(27):11285–11290, 2011.

691 T. Rattenbury, J. M. Hellerstein, J. Heer, S. Kandel, and C. Carreras. *Principles of data wrangling: Practical techniques for data preparation*. "O'Reilly Media, Inc.", 2017.

692 R. Rauschenberger, C. Wood, and J. Sala. Human factors and the design of medical devices. In J. B. Reiss, editor, *Bringing your medical device to market*, pages 215–226. Food and Drug Law Institute, 01 2013.

693 M. Rauterberg. An empirical comparison of menu-selection (((cui) and desktop (gui) computer programs carried out by beginners and experts. *Behaviour & information technology*, 11(4):227–236, 1992.

694 J. Reason. *Human error*. Cambridge university press, 1990.

695 F. F. Reichheld. The one number you need to grow. *Harvard business review*, 81(12):46–55, 2003.

696 M. A. Renom, B. Caramiaux, and M. Beaudouin-Lafon. Exploring technical reasoning in digital tool use. In *CHI conference on human factors in computing systems*, pages 1–17, 2022.

697 S. Reyal, S. Zhai, and P. O. Kristensson. Performance and user experience of touchscreen and gesture keyboards in a lab setting and in the wild. In *Proceedings of the 33rd annual ACM conference on human factors in computing systems*, pages 679–688, 2015.

698 J. Rico and S. Brewster. Usable gestures for mobile interfaces: evaluating social acceptability. In *Proceedings of the SIGCHI conference on human factors in computing systems*, pages 887–896, 2010.

699 J. Rieman. A field study of exploratory learning strategies. *ACM transactions on computer-human interaction (TOCHI)*, 3(3):189–218, 1996.

700 E. Ries. *The lean startup : How constant innovation creates radically successful businesses*. Portfolio Penguin, London; New York, 2011.

701 J. Robertson and M. Kaptein. *Modern statistical methods for HCI*. Springer, 2016.

702 T. Robertson and J. Simonsen. Challenges and opportunities in contemporary participatory design. *Design issues*, 28(3):3–9, 2012.

703 C. Robson. *Real world research: A resource for social scientists and practitioner-researchers*, volume 2. Blackwell Oxford, 2002.

704 D. J. Roedl and E. Stolterman. Design research at chi and its applicability to design practice. In *Proceedings of the SIGCHI conference on human factors in computing systems*, pages 1951–1954, 2013.

705 Y. Rogers. New theoretical approaches for human-computer interaction. *Annual review of information science and technology*, 38(1):87–143, 2004.

706 Y. Rogers. Hci theory: classical, modern, and contemporary. *Synthesis lectures on human-centered informatics*, 5(2):1–129, 2012.

707 J. Rooksby, M. Rost, A. Morrison, and M. Chalmers. Pass the ball: Enforced turn-taking in activity tracking. In *Proceedings of the 33rd annual ACM conference on human factors in computing systems*, pages 2417–2426, 2015.

708 J. Roschelle and S. D. Teasley. The construction of shared knowledge in collaborative problem solving. In *Computer supported collaborative learning*, pages 69–97. Springer, 1995.

709 M. S. Rosenbaum, M. L. Otalora, and G. C. Ramírez. How to create a realistic customer journey map. *Business horizons*, 60(1):143–150, 2017.

710 S. Rosenbaum, J. A. Rohn, and J. Humburg. A toolkit for strategic usability: Results from workshops, panels, and surveys. In *Proceedings of the SIGCHI conference on human factors in computing systems*, CHI '00, page 337–344, New York, NY, USA, 2000.

711 L. Rosenfeld and P. Morville. *Information architecture for the world wide web*. "O'Reilly Media, Inc.", 2002.

712 R. Rosenholtz, A. Dorai, and R. Freeman. Do predictions of visual perception aid design? *ACM transactions on applied perception (TAP)*, 8(2):1–20, 2011.

713 R. Rosenthal and R. L. Rosnow. *Essentials of behavioral research: Methods and data analysis*. McGraw-Hill, 2008.

714 M. B. Rosson and J. M. Carroll. Scenario-based design. In *Human-computer interaction*, pages 161–180. CRC Press, 2009.

715 Q. Roy, F. Zhang, and D. Vogel. Automation accuracy is good, but high controllability may be better. In *Proceedings of the 2019 CHI conference on human factors in computing systems*, pages 1–8, 2019.

716 H. J. Rubin and I. S. Rubin. *Qualitative interviewing: The art of hearing data*. sage, 2011.

717 J. Rubin and D. Chisnell. How to plan, design, and conduct effective tests. *Handbook of usability testing*, 2008.

718 D. Rubine. Specifying gestures by example. *ACM SIGGRAPH computer graphics*, 25(4):329–337, 1991.

719 E. M. Russek, I. Momennejad, M. M. Botvinick, S. J. Gershman, and N. D. Daw. Predictive representations can link model-based reinforcement learning to model-free mechanisms. *PLoS computational biology*, 13(9):e1005768, 2017.

720 J. A. Russell. Core affect and the psychological construction of emotion. *Psychological review*, 110(1):145, 2003.

721 K. Ryokai, S. Marti, and H. Ishii. I/o brush: Drawing with everyday objects as ink. In *Proceedings of the SIGCHI conference on human factors in computing systems*, CHI '04, page 303–310, New York, NY, USA, 2004.

722 H. Sacks, E. A. Schegloff, and G. Jefferson. A simplest systematics for the organization of turn taking for conversation. In *Studies in the organization of conversational interaction*, pages 7–55. Elsevier, 1978.

723 A. Salovaara, S. Helfenstein, and A. Oulasvirta. Everyday appropriations of information technology: A study of creative uses of digital cameras. *Journal of the American society for information science and technology*, 62(12):2347–2363, 2011.

724 D. D. Salvucci. An integrated model of eye movements and visual encoding. *Cognitive systems research*, 1(4):201–220, 2001.

725 D. D. Salvucci, M. Zuber, E. Beregovaia, and D. Markley. Distract-r: Rapid prototyping and evaluation of in-vehicle interfaces. In *Proceedings of the SIGCHI conference on human factors in computing systems*, pages 581–589, 2005.

726 H. A. Samani, R. Parsani, L. T. Rodriguez, E. Saadatian, K. H. Dissanayake, and A. D. Cheok. Kissenger: Design of a kiss transmission device. In *Proceedings of the designing interactive systems conference*, DIS '12, page 48–57, New York, NY, USA, 2012. Association for Computing Machinery. ISBN 9781450312103. https://doi.org/10.1145/2317956.2317965.

727 E. B.-N. Sanders. From user-centered to participatory design approaches. In *Design and the social sciences*, pages 18–25. CRC Press, 2002.

728 E. B.-N. Sanders and P. J. Stappers. Co-creation and the new landscapes of design. *Co-design*, 4(1):5–18, 2008.

729 C. Sas and S. Whittaker. Design for forgetting: Disposing of digital possessions after a breakup. In *Proceedings of the SIGCHI conference on human factors in computing systems*, pages 1823–1832, 2013.

730 T. Sasaki, M. Y. Saraiji, C. L. Fernando, K. Minamizawa, and M. Inami. Metalimbs: multiple arms interaction metamorphism. In *ACM SIGGRAPH 2017 emerging technologies*, pages 1–2. ACM, 2017.

731 S. A. Satpute, J. R. Canady, R. L. Klatzky, and G. D. Stetten. Fingersight: A vibrotactile wearable ring for assistance with locating and reaching objects in peripersonal space. *IEEE transactions on haptics*, 13(2):325–333, 2019.

732 J. Sauro and J. S. Dumas. Comparison of three one-question, post-task usability questionnaires. In *Proceedings of the SIGCHI conference on human factors in computing systems*, pages 1599–1608, 2009.

733 J. Sauro and J. R. Lewis. Correlations among prototypical usability metrics: Evidence for the construct of usability. In *Proceedings of the SIGCHI conference on human factors in computing systems*, pages 1609–1618, 2009.

734 J. Sauro and J. R. Lewis. *Quantifying the user experience: Practical statistics for user research*. Morgan Kaufmann, 2016.

735 J. Scarr, A. Cockburn, C. Gutwin, and P. Quinn. Dips and ceilings: Understanding and supporting transitions to expertise in user interfaces. In *Proceedings of the SIGCHI conference on human factors in computing systems*, pages 2741–2750, 2011.

736 J. Scarr, A. Cockburn, C. Gutwin, and A. Bunt. Improving command selection with commandmaps. In *Proceedings of the SIGCHI conference on human factors in computing systems*, pages 257–266, 2012.

737 S. Schaal and D. Sternad. Origins and violations of the 2/3 power law in rhythmic three-dimensional arm movements. *Experimental brain research*, 136(1):60–72, 2001.

738 N. C. Schaeffer and S. Presser. The science of asking questions. *Annual review of sociology*, 29, 2003.

739 M. Scharkow. The accuracy of self-reported internet use—a validation study using client log data. *Communication methods and measures*, 10(1):13–27, 2016.

740 A. Schmidt, M. Beigl, and H.-W. Gellersen. There is more to context than location. *Computers & graphics*, 23(6):893–901, 1999.

741 K. Schmidt. Riding a tiger, or computer supported cooperative work. In *Proceedings of the second European conference on computer-supported cooperative work ECSCW'91*, pages 1–16. Springer, 1991.

742 K. Schmidt. Cooperative work and its articulation: requirements for computer support. *Le travail humain*, pages 345–366, 1994.

743 K. Schmidt. The concept of 'practice': What's the point? In *COOP 2014-Proceedings of the 11th international conference on the design of cooperative systems*, pages 427–444. 2014.

744 K. Schmidt and C. Simonee. Coordination mechanisms: Towards a conceptual foundation of cscw systems design. *Computer supported cooperative work (CSCW)*, 5(2):155–200, 1996.

745 J. Scholtz. Theory and evaluation of human robot interactions. In *36th annual Hawaii international conference on system sciences, 2003. Proceedings of the*, pages 10–pp. IEEE, 2003.

746 D. A. Schön. *The reflective practitioner: How professionals think in action*. Routledge, 2017.

747 N. D. Schüll. *Addiction by design*. Princeton University Press, 2012.

748 V. Schwind, P. Knierim, N. Haas, and N. Henze. Using presence questionnaires in virtual reality. In *Proceedings of the 2019 CHI conference on human factors in computing systems*, pages 1–12, 2019.

749 J. Scott, A. Bernheim Brush, J. Krumm et al. Preheat: controlling home heating using occupancy prediction. In *Proceedings of the 13th international conference on ubiquitous computing*, pages 281–290, 2011.

750 S. D. Scott, M. S. T. Carpendale, and K. Inkpen. Territoriality in collaborative tabletop workspaces. In *Proceedings of the 2004 ACM conference on computer supported cooperative work*, pages 294–303, 2004.

751 S. D. Scott, M. S. T. Carpendale, and K. M. Inkpen. Territoriality in collaborative tabletop workspaces. In *Proceedings of the 2004 ACM conference on computer supported cooperative work*, CSCW '04, page 294–303, New York, NY, USA, 2004. Association for Computing Machinery. ISBN 1581138105. https://doi.org/10.1145/1031607.1031655.

752 S. A. Seah, D. Martinez Plasencia, P. D. Bennett et al. Sensabubble: A chrono-sensory mid-air display of sight and smell. In *Proceedings of the SIGCHI conference on human factors in computing systems*, pages 2863–2872, 2014.

753 A. Sears. Layout appropriateness: A metric for evaluating user interface widget layout. *IEEE transactions on software engineering*, 19(7):707–719, 1993.

754 S. C. Seow. Information theoretic models of hci: A comparison of the hick-hyman law and fitts' law. *Human-computer interaction*, 20(3):315–352, 2005.

755 S. C. Seow. *Designing and engineering time: The psychology of time perception in software*. Addison-Wesley Professional, 2008.

756 A. Serino, M. Bassolino, A. Farne, and E. Ladavas. Extended multisensory space in blind cane users. *Psychological science*, 18(7):642–648, 2007.

757 B. Shackel. Usability–context, framework, definition, design and evaluation. *Interacting with computers*, 21(5-6):339–346, 2009.

758 W. R. Shadish, T. Cook, and D. Campbell. *Experimental and quasi-experimental designs for generalized causal inference*. Boston: Houghton Mifflin Company, 2002.

759 O. Shaer and E. Hornecker. *Tangible user interfaces: Past, present, and future directions*. Now Publishers Inc, 2010.

760 C. E. Shannon. A mathematical theory of communication. *The Bell system technical journal*, 27(3):379–423, 1948.

761 M. Sharples. A study of breakdowns and repairs in a computer-mediated communication system. *Interacting with computers*, 5(1):61–77, 1993.

762 K. M. Sheldon, A. J. Elliot, Y. Kim, and T. Kasser. What is satisfying about satisfying events? Testing 10 candidate psychological needs. *Journal of personality and social psychology*, 80(2):325, 2001.

763 J. Shen, J. Dudley, G. Mo, and P. O. Kristensson. Gesture spotter: A rapid prototyping tool for key gesture spotting in virtual and augmented reality applications. *IEEE transactions on visualization and computer graphics*, 28(11):3618–3628, 2022.

764 B. Shneiderman. The future of interactive systems and the emergence of direct manipulation. *Behaviour & information technology*, 1(3):237–256, 1982.

765 B. Shneiderman. Creativity support tools. *Communications of the ACM*, 45(10):116–120, 2002.

766 B. Shneiderman. *The new ABCs of research: Achieving breakthrough collaborations*. Oxford University Press, 2016.

767 B. Shneiderman. Revisiting the astonishing growth of human–computer interaction research. *IEEE Computer*, 50(10):8–11, 2017.

768 B. Shneiderman. Bridging the gap between ethics and practice: Guidelines for reliable, safe, and trustworthy human-centered ai systems. *ACM transactions on interactive intelligent systems (TiiS)*, 10(4):1–31, 2020.

769 B. Shneiderman and P. Maes. Direct manipulation vs. interface agents. *Interactions*, 4(6):42–61, November 1997.

770 B. Shneiderman and P. Maes. Direct manipulation vs. interface agents. *Interactions*, 4(6):42–61, 1997.

771 B. Shneiderman and C. Plaisant. *Designing the user interface: Strategies for effective human-computer interaction*. Pearson Education, 2010.

772 R. W. Shumaker, K. R. Walkup, and B. B. Beck. *Animal tool behavior: The use and manufacture of tools by animals*. JHU Press, 2011.

773 M. Sicart and I. Shklovski. 'pataphysical software: (ridiculous) technological solutions for imaginary problems. In *Proceedings of the 2020 ACM designing interactive systems conference*, pages 1859–1871, 2020.

774 A. L. Simeone, E. Velloso, and H. Gellersen. Substitutional reality: Using the physical environment to design virtual reality experiences. In *Proceedings of the 33rd annual ACM conference on human factors in computing systems*, pages 3307–3316, 2015.

775 H. A. Simon. The science of design: Creating the artificial. *Design issues*, pages 67–82, 1988.

776 H. A. Simon. *The sciences of the artificial*. MIT press, 2019.

777 E. Simpson and B. Semaan. For you, or for "you"? everyday lgbtq+ encounters with tiktok. *Proceedings of the ACM on human-computer interaction*, 4(CSCW3):1–34, 2021.

778 C. U. M. Smith. *Biology of sensory systems*. John Wiley & Sons, 2008.

779 D. C. Smith. *Pygmalion: a creative programming environment*. Stanford University, 1975.

780 D. C. Smith. Pygmalion: An executable electronic blackboard. In *Watch what I do: Programming by demonstration*, pages 19–48. MIT Press, 1993.

781 D. C. Smith, A. Cypher, and J. Spohrer. Kidsim: Programming agents without a programming language. *Communications of the ACM*, 37(7):54–67, 1994.

782 C. Snyder. *Paper prototyping: The fast and easy way to design and refine user interfaces*. Morgan Kaufmann, 2003.

783 B. L. Somberg. A comparison of rule-based and positionally constant arrangements of computer menu items. In *Proceedings of the SIGCHI/GI conference on human factors in computing systems and graphics interface*, CHI '87, page 255–260, New York, NY, USA, 1986.

784 M. L. J. Søndergaard, M. Ciolfi Felice, and M. Balaam. Designing menstrual technologies with adolescents. In *Proceedings of the 2021 CHI conference on human factors in computing systems*, CHI '21, New York, NY, USA, 2021.

785 R. W. Soukoreff and I. S. MacKenzie. Towards a standard for pointing device evaluation, perspectives on 27 years of fitts' law research in hci. *International journal of human-computer studies*, 61(6):751–789, 2004.

786 B. Sparrow, J. Liu, and D. M. Wegner. Google effects on memory: Cognitive consequences of having information at our fingertips. *Science*, 333(6043):776–778, 2011.

787 R. Spencer. The streamlined cognitive walkthrough method, working around social constraints encountered in a software development company. In *Proceedings of the SIGCHI conference on human factors in computing systems*, pages 353–359, 2000.

788 J. P. Spradley. *Participant observation*. Waveland Press, 2016.

789 L. R. Squire. Memory systems of the brain: A brief history and current perspective. *Neurobiology of learning and memory*, 82(3):171–177, 2004.

790 S. Srinivasa Ragavan, A. Sarkar, and A. D. Gordon. Spreadsheet comprehension: Guesswork, giving up and going back to the author. In *Proceedings of the 2021 CHI conference on human factors in computing systems*, pages 1–21, 2021.

791 G. Stahl. Group cognition, 2006.

792 S. L. Star. The structure of ill-structured solutions: Boundary objects and heterogeneous distributed problem solving. In *Distributed artificial intelligence*, pages 37–54. Elsevier, 1989.

793 F. Steinberger, R. Schroeter, M. Foth, and D. Johnson. Designing gamified applications that make safe driving more engaging. In *Proceedings of the 2017 CHI conference on human factors in computing systems*, CHI '17, page 2826–2839, New York, NY, USA, 2017.

794 S. S. Stevens. On the psychophysical law. *Psychological review*, 64(3):153, 1957.

795 J. Stewart, B. B. Bederson, and A. Druin. Single display groupware: A model for co-present collaboration. In *Proceedings of the SIGCHI conference on human factors in computing systems*, pages 286–293, 1999.

796 J. W. Stigler. "mental abacus": The effect of abacus training on chinese children's mental calculation. *Cognitive psychology*, 16(2):145–176, 1984.

797 E. Stolterman. The nature of design practice and implications for interaction design research. *International journal of design*, 2(1), 2008.

798 E. Stolterman and J. Pierce. Design tools in practice: Studying the designer-tool relationship in interaction design. In *Proceedings of the designing interactive systems conference*, pages 25–28, 2012.

799 N. Streitz and P. Nixon. The disappearing computer. *Communications-ACM*, 48(3):32–35, 2005.

800 P. Streli and C. Holz. Capcontact: Super-resolution contact areas from capacitive touchscreens. In *Proceedings of the 2021 CHI conference on human factors in computing systems*, CHI '21, New York, NY, USA, 2021.

801 M. Sturdee and J. Lindley. Sketching & drawing as future inquiry in hci. In *Proceedings of the halfway to the future symposium 2019*, pages 1–10, 2019.

802 K.-W. Su and C.-L. Liu. A mobile nursing information system based on human-computer interaction design for improving quality of nursing. *Journal of medical systems*, 36(3):1139–1153, 2012.

803 L. Suchman. Making work visible. *Communications of the ACM*, 38(9):56–64, 1995.

804 L. A. Suchman. *Plans and situated actions: The problem of human-machine communication*. Cambridge university press, 1987.

805 H. Suh, N. Shahriaree, E. B. Hekler, and J. A. Kientz. Developing and validating the user burden scale: A tool for assessing user burden in computing systems. In *Proceedings of the 2016 CHI conference on human factors in computing systems*, CHI '16, page 3988–3999, New York, NY, USA, 2016.

806 H. Suh, N. Shahriaree, E. B. Hekler, and J. A. Kientz. Developing and validating the user burden scale: A tool for assessing user burden in computing systems. In *Proceedings of the 2016 CHI conference on human factors in computing systems*, pages 3988–3999, 2016.

807 I. E. Sutherland. Sketchpad a man-machine graphical communication system. *Simulation*, 2(5):R–3, 1964.

808 I. E. Sutherland. A head-mounted three dimensional display. In *Proceedings of the December 9-11, 1968, fall joint computer conference, part I*, pages 757–764, 1968.

809 I. E. Sutherland et al. The ultimate display. In *Proceedings of the IFIP congress*, volume 2, pages 506–508. New York, 1965.

810 P. Sutter, J. Iatridis, and N. Thakor. Response to reflected-force feedback to fingers in teleoperations. In *Proceedings of the NASA conference on space telerobotics*, 1989.

811 C. Swann. Action Research and the Practice of Design. *Design issues*, 18(1):49–61, 01 2002. ISSN 0747-9360.

812 IEEE standard model process for addressing ethical concerns during system design: IEEE standard 7000-2021, 2021.

813 S. K. Tadeja, P. Seshadri, and P. O. Kristensson. Aerovr: An immersive visualisation system for aerospace design and digital twinning in virtual reality. *The aeronautical journal*, 124(1280):1615–1635, 2020.

814 R. Tamas, W. O'Brien, and M. S. Quintero. Residential thermostat usability: Comparing manual, programmable, and smart devices. *Building and environment*, 203:108104, 2021.

815 R. S. Taylor. The process of asking questions. *American documentation*, 13(4):391–396, 1962.

816 J. Teevan, E. Cutrell, D. Fisher et al. Visual snippets: summarizing web pages for search and revisitation. In *Proceedings of the SIGCHI conference on human factors in computing systems*, pages 2023–2032, 2009.

817 L.-H. Teo, B. John, and M. Blackmon. Cogtool-explorer: A model of goal-directed user exploration that considers information layout. In *Proceedings of the SIGCHI conference on human factors in computing systems*, pages 2479–2488, 2012.

818 M. Teyssier, M. Koelle, P. Strohmeier, B. Fruchard, and J. Steimle. Eyecam: Revealing relations between humans and sensing devices through an anthropomorphic webcam. In *Proceedings of the 2021 CHI conference on human factors in computing systems*, pages 1–13, 2021.

819 R. H. Thaler and C. R. Sunstein. *Nudge: Improving decisions about health, wealth, and happiness*. Penguin, 2009.

820 H. Thimbleby. Safer user interfaces: A case study in improving number entry. *IEEE transactions on software engineering*, 41(7):711–729, 2014.

821 J. Tidwell. A pattern language for human-computer interface design. *DIALOG*, 1997.

822 K. Tiippana. What is the mcgurk effect? *Frontiers in psychology*, 5:725, 2014.

823 E. Tiong, O. Seow, B. Camburn et al. The economies and dimensionality of design prototyping: Value, time, cost, and fidelity. *Journal of mechanical design*, 141(3):031105, 2019.

824 P. Tolmie, J. Pycock, T. Diggins, A. MacLean, and A. Karsenty. Unremarkable computing. In *Proceedings of the SIGCHI conference on human factors in computing systems*, pages 399–406, 2002.

825 G. F. Tondello, D. L. Kappen, E. D. Mekler, M. Ganaba, and L. E. Nacke. Heuristic evaluation for gameful design. In *Proceedings of the 2016 annual symposium on computer-human interaction in play companion extended abstracts*, CHI PLAY Companion '16, page 315–323, New York, NY, USA, 2016.

826 N. Tractinsky, A. S. Katz, and D. Ikar. What is beautiful is usable. *Interacting with computers*, 13(2):127–145, 2000.

827 G. Travis. How the boeing 737 max disaster looks to a software developer. *IEEE spectrum*, 18, 2019.

828 H. M. Treasury. Cox review of creativity in business: building on the uk's strengths. *London: HM treasury*, 2005.

829 A. M. Treisman and G. Gelade. A feature-integration theory of attention. *Cognitive psychology*, 12(1):97–136, 1980.

830 S. Trepte and L. Reinecke. Avatar creation and video game enjoyment: Effects of life-satisfaction, game competitiveness, and identification with the avatar. *Journal of media psychology: Theories, methods, and applications*, 22(4):171, 2010.

831 A. N. Tuch, R. Trusell, and K. Hornbæk. Analyzing users' narratives to understand experience with interactive products. In *Proceedings of the SIGCHI conference on human factors in computing systems*, pages 2079–2088, 2013.

832 T. Tullis and L. Wood. How many users are enough for a card-sorting study. In *Proceedings UPA*, volume 2004. Usability Professionals Association (UPA) Minneapolis (EUA), 2004.

833 B. Tversky and A. Jamalian. Thinking tools: Gestures change thought about time. *Topics in cognitive science*, 13(4):750–776, 2021.

834 J. M. Twenge. Increases in depression, self-harm, and suicide among us adolescents after 2012 and links to technology use: Possible mechanisms. *Psychiatric research and clinical practice*, 2(1):19–25, 2020.

835 A. Tyack and E. D. Mekler. Self-determination theory in hci games research: current uses and open questions. In *Proceedings of the 2020 CHI conference on human factors in computing systems*, pages 1–22, 2020.

836 A. Tychsen and A. Canossa. Defining personas in games using metrics. In *Proceedings of the 2008 conference on future play: Research, play, share*, Future Play '08, page 73–80, New York, NY, USA, 2008.

837 B. Ullmer and H. Ishii. Emerging frameworks for tangible user interfaces. *IBM systems journal*, 39(3.4):915–931, 2000.

838 K. Ulrich. The role of product architecture in the manufacturing firm. *Research policy*, 24(3):419–440, 1995.

839 K. T. Ulrich. *Product design and development*. Tata McGraw-Hill Education, 2003.

840 J. Underkoffler and H. Ishii. Urp: a luminous-tangible workbench for urban planning and design. In *Proceedings of the SIGCHI conference on human factors in computing systems*, pages 386–393, 1999.

841 L. Van Boven and T. Gilovich. To do or to have? That is the question. *Journal of personality and social psychology*, 85(6):1193, 2003.

842 S. Van Buuren and K. Groothuis-Oudshoorn. mice: Multivariate imputation by chained equations in r. *Journal of statistical software*, 45:1–67, 2011.

843 A. Van Dam. Hypertext'87: keynote address. *Communications of the ACM*, 31(7):887–895, 1988.

844 T. Van der Geest. Conducting usability studies with users who are elderly or have disabilities. *Technical communication*, 53(1):23–31, 2006.

845 J. B. Van Erp et al. Guidelines for the use of vibro-tactile displays in human computer interaction. In *Proceedings of eurohaptics*, volume 2002, pages 18–22. Citeseer, 2002.

846 P. Van Schaik, M. Hassenzahl, and J. Ling. User-experience from an inference perspective. *ACM transactions on computer-human interaction (TOCHI)*, 19(2):1–25, 2012.

847 K. Vaniea and Y. Rashidi. Tales of software updates: The process of updating software. In *Proceedings of the 2016 CHI conference on human factors in computing systems*, CHI '16, page 3215–3226, New York, NY, USA, 2016.

848 I. M. Verstijnen, C. van Leeuwen, G. Goldschmidt, R. Hamel, and J. Hennessey. Creative discovery in imagery and perception: Combining is relatively easy, restructuring takes a sketch. *Acta psychologica*, 99(2):177–200, 1998.

849 K. Vertanen and P. O. Kristensson. On the benefits of confidence visualization in speech recognition. In *Proceedings of the SIGCHI conference on human factors in computing systems*, pages 1497–1500, 2008.

850 K. Vertanen and P. O. Kristensson. Parakeet: A continuous speech recognition system for mobile touch-screen devices. In *Proceedings of the 14th international conference on intelligent user interfaces*, pages 237–246, 2009.

851 R. Vertegaal, I. Weevers, C. Sohn, and C. Cheung. Gaze-2: Conveying eye contact in group video conferencing using eye-controlled camera direction. In *Proceedings of the SIGCHI conference on human factors in computing systems*, CHI '03, page 521–528, New York, NY, USA, 2003.

852 F. B. Viegas and J. S. Donath. Chat circles. In *Proceedings of the SIGCHI conference on human factors in computing systems*, pages 9–16, 1999.

853 S. Vieweg, A. L. Hughes, K. Starbird, and L. Palen. Microblogging during two natural hazards events: What twitter may contribute to situational awareness. In *Proceedings of the SIGCHI conference on human factors in computing systems*, CHI '10, page 1079–1088, New York, NY, USA, 2010.

854 G. Villalobos-Zúñiga and M. Cherubini. Apps that motivate: A taxonomy of app features based on self-determination theory. *International journal of human-computer studies*, 140:102449, 2020.

855 J. Vines, R. McNaney, S. Lindsay, J. Wallace, and J. McCarthy. Special topic: Designing for and with vulnerable people. *Interactions*, 21(1):44–46, January 2014.

856 J. Vines, G. Pritchard, P. Wright, P. Olivier, and K. Brittain. An age-old problem: Examining the discourses of ageing in hci and strategies for future research. *ACM transactions on computer-human interaction (TOCHI)*, 22(1):1–27, 2015.

857 F. Vitale, J. McGrenere, A. Tabard, M. Beaudouin-Lafon, and W. E. Mackay. High costs and small benefits: A field study of how users experience operating system upgrades. In *Proceedings of the 2017 CHI conference on human factors in computing systems*, CHI '17, page 4242–4253, New York, NY, USA, 2017.

858 P. Viviani and T. Flash. Minimum-jerk, two-thirds power law, and isochrony: Converging approaches to movement planning. *Journal of experimental psychology: human perception and performance*, 21(1):32, 1995.

859 D. Vogel and R. Balakrishnan. Interactive public ambient displays: Transitioning from implicit to explicit, public to personal, interaction with multiple users. In *Proceedings of the 17th annual ACM symposium on user interface software and technology*, pages 137–146, 2004.

860 D. Vogel and P. Baudisch. Shift: a technique for operating pen-based interfaces using touch. In *Proceedings of the SIGCHI conference on human factors in computing systems*, pages 657–666, 2007.

861 L. Von Ahn and L. Dabbish. Labeling images with a computer game. In *Proceedings of the SIGCHI conference on human factors in computing systems*, pages 319–326, 2004.

862 K. Vredenburg, J.-Y. Mao, P. W. Smith, and T. Carey. A survey of user-centered design practice. In *Proceedings of the SIGCHI conference on human factors in computing systems*, pages 471–478, 2002.

863 C. Wacharamanotham, L. Eisenring, S. Haroz, and F. Echtler. Transparency of chi research artifacts: Results of a self-reported survey. In *Proceedings of the 2020 CHI conference on human factors in computing systems*, CHI '20, page 1–14, New York, NY, USA, 2020.

864 J. Wagemans, J. H. Elder, M. Kubovy, S. E. Palmer, M. A. Peterson, M. Singh, and R. von der Heydt. A century of gestalt psychology in visual perception: I. perceptual grouping and figure–ground organization. *Psychological bulletin*, 138(6):1172, 2012.

865 M. Wahlström, A. Salovaara, L. Salo, and A. Oulasvirta. Resolving safety-critical incidents in a rally control center. *Human–computer interaction*, 26(1-2):9–37, 2011.

866 J. B. Walther. Social information processing theory. *Engaging theories in interpersonal communication: Multiple perspectives*, 391, 2008.

867 J. B. Walther. Theories of computer-mediated communication and interpersonal relations. *The handbook of interpersonal communication*, 4:443–479, 2011.

868 D. Wang, Q. Yang, A. Abdul, and B. Y. Lim. Designing theory-driven user-centric explainable ai. In *Proceedings of the 2019 CHI conference on human factors in computing systems*, pages 1–15, 2019.

869 D. Wang, P. Maes, X. Ren, B. Shneiderman, Y. Shi, and Q. Wang. Designing ai to work with or for people? In *Extended abstracts of the 2021 CHI conference on human factors in computing systems*, CHI EA '21, New York, NY, USA, 2021.

870 G. Wang, X. Zhang, S. Tang, H. Zheng, and B. Y. Zhao. Unsupervised clickstream clustering for user behavior analysis. In *Proceedings of the 2016 CHI conference on human factors in computing systems*, pages 225–236, 2016.

871 R. Want, A. Hopper, V. Falcao, and J. Gibbons. The active badge location system. *ACM transactions on information systems (TOIS)*, 10(1):91–102, 1992.

872 R. Want, B. N. Schilit, N. I. Adams et al. The parctab ubiquitous computing experiment. In *Mobile computing*, pages 45–101. Springer, 1996.

873 D. J. Ward and D. J. MacKay. Fast hands-free writing by gaze direction. *Nature*, 418(6900):838–838, 2002.

874 D. J. Ward, A. F. Blackwell, and D. J. MacKay. Dasher—a data entry interface using continuous gestures and language models. In *Proceedings of the 13th annual ACM symposium on user interface software and technology*, pages 129–137. ACM, 2000.

875 D. J. Ward, A. F. Blackwell, and D. J. MacKay. Dasher: A gesture-driven data entry interface for mobile computing. *Human–computer interaction*, 17(2-3):199–228, 2002.

876 C. Ware. *Information visualization: Perception for design*. Morgan Kaufmann, 2019.

877 E. J. Webb, D. T. Campbell, R. D. Schwartz, and L. Sechrest. *Unobtrusive measures*, volume 2. Sage Publications, 1999.

878 M. Weigel, T. Lu, G. Bailly, A. Oulasvirta, C. Majidi, and J. Steimle. Iskin: flexible, stretchable and visually customizable on-body touch sensors for mobile computing. In *Proceedings of the 33rd annual ACM conference on human factors in computing systems*, pages 2991–3000, 2015.

879 M. Weiser. The computer of the 21st century. *Scientific American*, 265(3):94–104, 1991.

880 M. Weiser and J. S. Brown. The coming age of calm technology. In *Beyond calculation*, pages 75–85. Springer, 1997.

881 M. Weiss, F. Schwarz, S. Jakubowski, and J. Borchers. Madgets: actuating widgets on interactive tabletops. In *Proceedings of the 23nd annual ACM symposium on user interface software and technology*, pages 293–302, 2010.

882 P. Wellner, W. Mackay, and R. Gold. Back to the real world. *Communications of the ACM*, 36(7):24–26, July 1993.

883 E. Wenger. *Communities of practice: A brief introduction*. National Science Foundation (US), 2011.

884 C. Wharton, J. Rieman, C. Lewis, and P. Polson. The cognitive walkthrough method: A practitioner's guide. In *Usability inspection methods*, pages 105–140. John Wiley & Sons, 1994.

885 M. D. White and E. E. Marsh. Content analysis: A flexible methodology. *Library trends*, 55(1):22–45, 2006.

886 J. Whiteside, J. Bennett, and K. Holtzblatt. Usability engineering: Our experience and evolution. In *Handbook of human-computer interaction*, pages 791–817. Elsevier, 1988.

887 A. Whitten and J. D. Tygar. Why johnny can't encrypt: A usability evaluation of pgp 5.0. In *USENIX security symposium*, volume 348, pages 169–184, 1999.

888 C. D. Wickens. Multiple resources and performance prediction. *Theoretical issues in ergonomics science*, 3(2):159–177, 2002.

889 D. A. Wiegmann and S. A. Shappell. *A human error approach to aviation accident analysis: The human factors analysis and classification system*. Routledge, 2017.

890 N. Wiener. *Cybernetics or control and communication in the animal and the machine*. MIT press, 2019.

891 S. Wiggins. Talking about taste: Using a discursive psychological approach to examine challenges to food evaluations. *Appetite*, 43(1):29–38, 2004.

892 W. Willett, B. A. Aseniero, S. Carpendale et al. Perception! immersion! empowerment! superpowers as inspiration for visualization. *IEEE transactions on visualization and computer graphics*, 28(1):22–32, 2021.

893 W. Willett, B. A. Aseniero, S. Carpendale, P. Dragicevic, Y. Jansen, L. Oehlberg, and P. Isenberg. Superpowers as inspiration for visualization. *IEEE TVCG, 2021*, 2021.

894 R. Williams. *The non-designer's design book: Design and typographic principles for the visual novice*. Pearson Education, 2015.

895 A. D. Wilson. Robust computer vision-based detection of pinching for one and two-handed gesture input. In *Proceedings of the 19th annual ACM symposium on user interface software and technology*, pages 255–258, 2006.

896 G. Wilson, S. Brewster, M. Halvey, and S. Hughes. Thermal icons: Evaluating structured thermal feedback for mobile interaction. In *Proceedings of the 14th international conference on human-computer interaction with mobile devices and services*, MobileHCI '12, page 309–312, New York, NY, USA, 2012.

897 S. Wilson, M. Bekker, P. Johnson, and H. Johnson. Helping and hindering user involvement—a tale of everyday design. In *Proceedings of the ACM SIGCHI conference on human factors in computing systems*, pages 178–185, 1997.

898 T. Winograd. What can we teach about human-computer interaction? (plenary address). In *Proceedings of the SIGCHI conference on human factors in computing systems*, CHI '90, page 443–448, New York, NY, USA, 1990.

899 T. Winograd. *Bringing design to software*. ACM, 1996.

900 T. Winograd and F. Flores. *Understanding computers and cognition: A new foundation for design*. Intellect Books, 1986.

901 D. Wirtz, J. Kruger, C. N. Scollon, and E. Diener. What to do on spring break? The role of predicted, on-line, and remembered experience in future choice. *Psychological science*, 14(5):520–524, 2003.

902 I. H. Witten, R. M. Neal, and J. G. Cleary. Arithmetic coding for data compression. *Communications of the ACM*, 30(6):520–540, 1987.

903 J. T. Wixted and L. Mickes. A continuous dual-process model of remember/know judgments. *Psychological review*, 117(4):1025, 2010.

904 J. O. Wobbrock and J. A. Kientz. Research contributions in human-computer interaction. *Interactions*, 23(3):38–44, 2016.

905 J. O. Wobbrock, M. R. Morris, and A. D. Wilson. User-defined gestures for surface computing. In *Proceedings of the SIGCHI conference on human factors in computing systems*, pages 1083–1092, 2009.

906 J. O. Wobbrock, S. K. Kane, K. Z. Gajos, S. Harada, and J. Froehlich. Ability-based design: Concept, principles and examples. *ACM transactions on accessible computing*, 3(3), 2011.

907 M. S. Wogalter. Communication-human information processing (c-hip) model. In *Forensic human factors and ergonomics*, pages 33–49. CRC Press, 2018.

908 C. T. Wolf. Explainability scenarios: Towards scenario-based xai design. In *Proceedings of the 24th international conference on intelligent user interfaces*, pages 252–257, 2019.

909 T. V. Wolf, J. A. Rode, J. Sussman, and W. A. Kellogg. Dispelling" design" as the black art of chi. In *Proceedings of the SIGCHI conference on human factors in computing systems*, pages 521–530, 2006.

910 J. M. Wolfe. Guided search 6.0: An updated model of visual search. *Psychonomic bulletin & review*, 28(4):1060–1092, 2021.

911 A. S. Won, J. Bailenson, J. Lee, and J. Lanier. Homuncular flexibility in virtual reality. *Journal of computer-mediated communication*, 20(3):241–259, 2015.

912 J.-b. Woo and Y.-k. Lim. User experience in do-it-yourself-style smart homes. In *Proceedings of the 2015 ACM international joint conference on pervasive and ubiquitous computing*, UbiComp '15, page 779–790, New York, NY, USA, 2015.

913 J. R. Wood and L. E. Wood. Card sorting: Current practices and beyond. *Journal of usability studies*, 4(1):1–6, 2008.

914 A. Worden, N. Walker, K. Bharat, and S. Hudson. Making computers easier for older adults to use: area cursors and sticky icons. In *Proceedings of the ACM SIGCHI conference on human factors in computing systems*, pages 266–271, 1997.

915 P. Wright and J. McCarthy. Empathy and experience in hci. In *Proceedings of the SIGCHI conference on human factors in computing systems*, pages 637–646, 2008.

916. S. P. Wyche, S. Y. Schoenebeck, and A. Forte. "facebook is a luxury": An exploratory study of social media use in rural kenya. In *Proceedings of the 2013 conference on computer supported cooperative work*, CSCW '13, page 33–44, New York, NY, USA, 2013.

917. M. Yamagami, K. M. Steele, and S. A. Burden. Decoding intent with control theory: comparing muscle versus manual interface performance. In *Proceedings of the 2020 CHI conference on human factors in computing systems*, pages 1–12, 2020.

918. E. Q. Yan, J. Huang, and G. K. Cheung. Masters of control: Behavioral patterns of simultaneous unit group manipulation in starcraft 2. In *Proceedings of the 33rd annual ACM conference on human factors in computing systems*, pages 3711–3720, 2015.

919. A. L. Yarbus. *Eye movements and vision*. Springer, 2013.

920. X. You and D. Hands. A reflection upon herbert simon's vision of design in the sciences of the artificial. *The design journal*, 22(sup1):1345–1356, 2019.

921. S. Zhai. Characterizing computer input with fitts' law parameters—the information and non-information aspects of pointing. *International journal of human-computer studies*, 61(6):791–809, 2004.

922. S. Zhai and P.-O. Kristensson. Shorthand writing on stylus keyboard. In *Proceedings of the SIGCHI conference on human factors in computing systems*, pages 97–104, 2003.

923. S. Zhai, P. O. Kristensson, P. Gong, M. Greiner, S. A. Peng, L. M. Liu, and A. Dunnigan. Shapewriter on the iphone: from the laboratory to the real world. In *CHI'09 extended abstracts on human factors in computing systems*, pages 2667–2670, 2009.

924. M. R. Zhang, H. Wen, and J. O. Wobbrock. Type, then correct: intelligent text correction techniques for mobile text entry using neural networks. In *Proceedings of the 32nd annual ACM symposium on user interface software and technology*, pages 843–855, 2019.

925. S. Zhao and R. Balakrishnan. Simple vs. compound mark hierarchical marking menus. In *Proceedings of the 17th annual ACM symposium on user interface software and technology*, pages 33–42, 2004.

926. H. Zhu, B. Yu, A. Halfaker, and L. Terveen. Value-sensitive algorithm design: Method, case study, and lessons. *Proceedings of the ACM on human-computer interaction*, 2(CSCW):1–23, 2018.

927. J. Zimmerman. Designing for the self: Making products that help people become the person they desire to be. In *Proceedings of the SIGCHI conference on human factors in computing systems*, CHI '09, page 395–404, New York, NY, USA, 2009.

928. J. Zimmerman, J. Forlizzi, and S. Evenson. Research through design as a method for interaction design research in hci. In *Proceedings of the SIGCHI conference on human factors in computing systems*, pages 493–502, 2007.

929. T. G. Zimmerman, J. Lanier, C. Blanchard, S. Bryson, and Y. Harvill. A hand gesture interface device. *ACM SIGCHI bulletin*, 18(4):189–192, 1986.

930. A. Zoran and J. A. Paradiso. Freed: a freehand digital sculpting tool. In *Proceedings of the SIGCHI conference on human factors in computing systems*, pages 2613–2616, 2013.

931. P. O. Kristensson and S. Zhai. SHARK2: a large vocabulary shorthand writing system for pen-based computers. In *Proceedings of the 17th annual ACM symposium on user interface software and technology (UIST 2004)*, ACM Press: 43–52, 2004.

932. P. O. Kristensson, J. Lilley, R. Black and A. Waller. A design engineering approach for quantitatively exploring context-aware sentence retrieval for nonspeaking individuals with motor disabilities. In *Proceedings of the 38th ACM conference on human factors in computing systems (CHI 2020)*, ACM Press: Paper 398, 2020.

933. L. Chan, Y. C. Liao, G. B. Mo, J. J. Dudley, C. L. Cheng, P. O. Kristensson and A. Oulasvirta. Investigating positive and negative qualities of human-in-the-loop optimization for designing interaction techniques. In *Proceedings of the 40th ACM conference on human factors in computing systems (CHI 2022)*, ACM Press: Article No. 112, 2022.

Index

2AFC task 76
3D environments 170
abductive thinking 288, 573
ability-based design 333, 491
accelerometer 254, 418, 507, 607
Acceptability 288, 325–326, 646, 652
    practical 331
    social 331
accessibility 189, 283, 285, 288, 325–326, 332–338, 397–398, 490, 589, 607, 694, 712, 784
accountability 143, 275, 618
ACM 7, 9, 13, 506, 781
activities
    normatively regulated contingent 375
activity theory 381
adaptation 31, 40–44, 85, 147, 361–362, 377, 422, 694
adoption 4, 109, 157, 326, 377–380
affinity diagramming 211–212, 555
affordance 61, 175, 310, 313, 322, 441–442, 481
agency 146, 339, 352, 541
agent 143, 160, 170, 177–178, 282, 320, 340–345, 349, 356–357, 369–371
agile development 592–593
aging users 32, 265, 458, 508, 783
aimed movements 65–70, 286
air traffic control 216–217, 341
Amazon 22, 153, 317
Amulet environment 667
anthropomorphic systems 178
Anthropomorphism 170–171, 236
apprenticeship learning 99, 225
appropriation 379–380
archival data 255
articulation work 141, 151–152
assembly 390
ATM 86, 130
attention 38, 83
    covert 56
    divided 56
    overt 56
    selective 56
    visual 56, 102
AttrakDif 132
audio 436–437
audition 40–41
augmentation 285
augmentative and alternative communication 320–321, 334, 769–770
augmented reality 3, 5, 14, 435–436, 522–523
authenticity 175
automaticity 90, 96
automation 339–353
    types and levels of 343–345
avatar 170

awareness 152
    situational 345

bathtub curve 659
Bayesian brain 90
behavior change 117–120
behavioral patterns 149
bias
    in answering questions 239–240
    in design 545–547
body ownership 160
boundary objects 152
brain-computer interface 418–419
brainstorming 550–551
Bubble Cursor 446–447

camera control 461–464
Chat Circles 161
ChatGPT 102–103, 282
chemosensitivity 40
CHI 9
children 32, 109–110, 149, 189–190, 229, 261, 320, 486, 570, 576, 668, 714
classification 698–701
Clippy 178
clustering 699
co-adaptation 13
co-design 576–578
co-experience 127
co-located/remote collaboration 145
cognition 31, 83–107
    group 152–153
cognitive control 86
cognitive dimensions of notation 481–483
cognitive heuristic 545–546
cognitive psychology 6, 17, 30, 34, 543, 593
cognitive walkthrough 729–732
collaboration 141–158
collaborative systems 27, 141–146, 156–157, 787
color blindness 51
command-line interface 390–391, 472–474
common ground 167–168, 320
communication 28, 31, 159–179, 283–284, 292, 317
    face-to-face 160–163
communication acts 150
communication breakdown 317
communication diagram 615–617
community of practice 147, 567–568, 580–581
computational model 6, 29, 63, 335, 369, 681–694
computer-mediated communication 159–162
computer program 3
computing system 3–4
    interactive 4, 5

concept selection 635–637
conceptual design 628–637
consistency 399, 489, 491
content analysis 255–257
context awareness 512–513
contextual inquiry 208–209, 272
contrast sensitivity 50
control theory 291, 301–307, 465–466
control to display 451–452
convergent thinking 544–545
conversation analysis 164–165
convolution 41
coordination 142, 150–152
Coordinator, the 179
core affect model 133
creativity 32, 148, 536–541, 545–552, 559, 585
critical design 541–542
critical incident method 134, 253
critical parameters 329
Cronbach's alpha 243
cross-sectional studies 232
crossing task 78–79
crowdsourcing 233, 240, 247
cue integration theory 48
cues-filtered-out hypothesis 169
customer journeys 267
cybernetics 282

dark patterns 120
Dasher 296, 307
data glove 623
decay theory 95
decision-making 84, 99–100
   sequential 366
decision heuristics 102
deployment study 713, 763, 769, 774
design cognition 543–563
design critique 574
design engineering 623–644
design fiction 574–575
design fixation 547, 602, 624
design judgment 573–574
design pattern 670–671
design probe 531–532
design space 33, 400–401, 549
design thinking 20, 536–537, 579
desires 114
detailed design 639
detection task 43
device 389
   input 406–423
   pointing 412–416
Dexmo 623
dialogue 309
diary method 247
direct control 412–415
direct manipulation 20, 340–341, 389, 491–494
discoverability 322, 399
discrimination task 43, 46–47
display 3, 27, 39, 53, 425–433
   tabletop 149
   ultimate display 441

distributed cognition 99
distribution of work 144
divergent thinking 544–545
division of labor 143, 381–382
dot matrix display 432
double diamond 437
drift diffusion model 74–75
driving 27–28, 83, 89
drones 197
dual process theory 120
duration neglect 125
dwell-free eye typing 692
Dynabook 19

earcon 437
early adopters 189
ecology of tools 382
economic model 357–360
effort
   mental 86
egocentric fallacy 18, 753
Electromyography 419
Electronic Arts 22
embodied cognition 322
embodiment design 639
emic 218, 222
EMMA model 53
emojis 161
emoticons 168
emotions 123–127, 132–133, 514
EmotionSense 254–255
empathy 34, 177, 187, 262
encoding–retrieval symmetry 94
end-effector 64, 80
end-user development 671–676
entropy 293–295, 297
envelope analysis 688–694
ergonomics 11, 29
estimation task 44, 48
ethics 13, 193, 226, 756–757, 787–788
ethnography 222–226
   rapid 225, 227
etic 218, 223
eudaimonia 136
evaluation 706–717
   field 712, 769
   formative 708
   laboratory 712
   summative 709
evaluation methods 712
   analytical 712, 718–737
   empirical 712
evaluation yardstick 710
evaluator effect 746–747
event handling 670
evidence accumulation model 74
expectations 38, 59, 61, 127, 135, 273
experience 31, 123–139
   hedonic 12, 130–131
   perceptual 37–38
   pragmatic 12, 130–131
experience machine 138

experience sampling method 135–136, 247
experiment 713, 749–767
  between-participant 757, 763
  within-participant 757
explainable artificial intelligence 264–266, 349–353, 618
explorability 398
extraordinary users 189
eye gaze 163–164
eye-hand coordination 72
eye movements 51–53
eye tracking 419–420

Facebook 22, 167, 174, 188, 199, 232, 237
factor analysis 244–245
fairness 618
failure 601
FAST diagram 629–633
fault tree 654–655
feature analysis 684–685
feature creep 195
feature engineering 684–685
feature integration theory 57
feedback 313
field diary 220
field notes 220–221
field research 215–228
filter 409–410
finger tracking 420–421
finite state machine 314–316
Fitts' law 12, 64–69, 77, 252, 287, 298, 304, 686
Fitts' lists 342, 354
fixation
  in eye movements 51–53
Flickr 198
FMEA 653–654
force feedback 438–439
form 391–392
formal method 676–679
FTIR 415
function model 629–633
function structure 629–631
funneling 239

games 16, 22, 28, 32, 43, 136–137, 173
gamification 33, 120–121
gender 33, 171–172, 722
GenderMag 721
Gestalt principles 21, 39, 55
gesture typing 459–460
gesturing 78, 94, 155
GEQ 245
Go-Go technique 520–521
goal activation model 86
goal setting 119
Godspeed questionnaire 236
GOMS 103–105, 732
Google 22, 123, 252
graphical user interface 9, 14, 22, 28, 48, 51, 54, 94, 393, 485–501
grounding 154
groupware 142, 376

group tasks 147–148
guided search model 57
guidelines 10, 30, 39, 89
gulf of evaluation 312–314, 731
gulf of execution 312–314, 731

H-metaphor 349
habituation 42
halo effect 126
hand tracking 420–421
haptics 438–441
  pseudo 42
  texture 440–441
  vibration 438
hazard 604, 647
hazard function 75, 660
HCI4D 6
head-mounted display 433–436
health 32
heuristic evaluation 713, 718, 721–727
Hick–Hyman law 76, 300
human-centeredness 11, 13, 27
human error 648–651
Human Error Identification 728–729
human factors 11, 593–594
human factors engineering 593–594
hypertext 22, 476–477
hypotheses 750

IBM 222, 487, 573, 769
icon 54, 56, 497–498
  auditory 40, 45, 437
identities 163, 175
imaginary interface 406
impairments
  cognitive 320, 333
  visual 51, 439
  motor 257, 291
inattentional blindness 85
inclusion criteria 188
inclusive design 333, 334
inclusiveness 720–721
index of difficulty 66–70
indirect control 415–417
information diagram 613–614
information foraging 12, 77, 358, 362–366
information rate 40, 296–297
information scent 365–366
information theory 291–301
information throughput 67–68, 291, 297–298
infrastructure 381–382
inhibition of return 87
initiative 310
input devices 63, 291, 405–421
input methods 63, 298, 445
intentionality 281
interaction design 7, 10, 532–534
interaction style 390
interaction technique 390, 445–468
interactional sequences 166
interactive artificial intelligence 281, 348–349
interactive machine learning 701–702

interception task 65
internal representation 38
internal model 90, 104
internalization 115
intermittent feedback control 72
interview guide 205
interview method 197–214
    open-ended 199–205
    semi-structured 199
    structured 199, 205
    unstructured 199
interview themes 201
interview questions 201
iterative design 16, 585, 588–589, 721
interference theory 95
interruptions 29, 89, 91
intersubjectivity 154
is-ought problem, the 186
ISO 9241 327–329

joint system analysis 402–403
just noticeable difference 47

keyboard 412
keyboard shortcuts 480
keypad 411–412
keystroke-level model 691, 732–736
key-target resizing 70
KidSim 667
KinectFusion 623
knowledge-in-the-world, knowledge-in-the-head 99

lateral thinking 551
large language model 102, 310–311, 339, 348
layout 40, 271, 668–689
    keyboard 63, 70
    appropriateness 271
LGBTQ+ 197
League of Legends 141
learnability 466–467
    extended learnability 396
legitimate peripheral participation 383
levels of processing effect 93
lightpen 412–413
linear discriminant function 699–700
linear machine 699–701
Likert scale 229, 239
log files 251–252
London Underground 141

machine learning 48, 698–702
market pull 20, 109
marking menu 455–456
mapping 313
Maslow's hierarchy of needs 109
McGurk effect, the 42
measurement 233, 288
mechanosensitivity 40
media richness theory 171
memory 91–99
    declarative 92
    episodic 93
    long-term 58, 85, 92–93
    non-declarative 92
    short-term 60
    working 85, 91–92
mental models 18, 100–103
menu interface 392–393, 477–480
menu selection 453–457
messaging 151
metaphor 85, 498–500
micro phenomenology 206–208
microphone 421
microprocessor 3
Microsoft Office 178
Minecraft 22
mixed-initiative interaction 318–320
mixed reality 518–523, 697–698
mobile user interface 506–510
models
    cognitive 103–104
    computational 29–30
    mathematical 53, 66, 95
    predictive 63, 286
model-view-controller 670–671
morphological analysis 401–402
morphological chart 633–635
motivation 30, 32–33, 109–122, 198
motor control 6, 27, 31, 63–82
    open loop 65
mouse 415–416
MTBF 659
multi-attribute choice 102
multimodal interaction 42
multiple resources theory 12, 88, 341
multitasking 29, 87–88
mutual determinacy 279

n-segment display 431–432
narrative method 134
NASA-TLX 90, 236
Nassi-Shneiderman diagram 676
natural language processing 15
navigation 37, 291
needs 109–122
Nintendo 22
notational system 480–483

objective
    in design 394, 399–400, 487–491, 549
    in optimization 694–698
observation method 215–222
online behavior 169
online community 174, 176
online relationships 174–177
open science 789
operating system 3
optimization 694–698
optical see-through 348, 394, 435, 519–520, 599
organization diagram 613–614
Orbits 53

PACT 186
participatory design 187, 575–577
pattern recognition 698–702
peak–end rule, the 125
percept 37, 48
perception 27, 31, 37–62
   active 61
   cross-modal 42
   ecological 61
   embodied 61
   figure/ground 54
   multimodal 42
   time 47
   visual 48
perceptual organization 54
PENS scale 116
performance
   initial performance 395–396
   ultimate performance 397
personal computer 3
personality 30, 149, 169, 177
personalization 377–378
persuasive design 118
phishing 206, 605
photosensitivity 40
planning 85
player experience inventory 236
pleasure 132
pluralism 20
power analysis 235
power law of practice 96
power relationships 163
PowerPoint 83
practice 375–385
   scheduling 97
   selection 98
prompt engineering 311
perplexity 294
personas 260–263
pie menu 454–455
precautionary principle 647
precision/recall metric 47
predictive power 287
presence 522
privacy 8, 13, 32, 112–113, 175
priming 86
prisoner's dilemma 142
privacy 32, 175, 289, 618
problem-solving capacity 783
process diagram 615–617
prospect theory 100
prototyping 568–571
proxemics 33
probability theory 3
product attachment theory 109
product architecture 637–639
programmability 3
programming 33
programming by example 672–675
psychophysics 46–47

QOC 403–404
questions, options, and criteria 403–404
QUIS 243
quasi-experiment 771
QWERTY 63, 296

randomization 758
rational analysis 358, 360–362
rationality 355–372
   bounded 356
   computational 358, 366–371
reaction
   simple 72–73
   choice 73, 76–78, 300–301
reactivity 219, 249
reality-based interaction 393–394, 503–525
reasoning 87, 85, 99–100
   abductive 288
   counterfactual 289
   deductive 288
   inductive 288
recall
   cued 94
   free 94
receptive field 40–41
receptors 41
recognition task 44, 47
recommendations 16
Reddit 249
regression 699
reliability 193, 221, 235, 242, 654–660, 714, 725
   inter-rater 221
   internal 243
reliability engineering 601
reliability function 659
representation
   user interface 390
research contribution 788–789
research question 752
research strategy 191–192, 784
research through design 531
response bias 46
requirements 15, 273–274, 602–603, 627–628
requirements engineering 602–603, 627
return of investment 185
rich pictures 272–273
risk 604, 645–665
risk assessment 652–654
risk management 624, 651–654
risk matrix 654–655

search task 44, 48, 56
saccades 52–53
sample size 235
sampling 190, 234–235
   snowball 234
safety 618, 645–665
safety critical user interface 599
say–do gap, the 185, 213
scenarios 264–265
seamfulness 227
security 32, 618, 660–662

self-determination theory 12, 30, 109–115, 119–120
self-information 292–294
self-presentation 172–173
sensation 39
sensing 406–411, 421–422
   hardware 407–408
   thermal 40
sensitivity 45
sensory information 37–39
sensory modalities 37–42
sensory system 39–42
semantic differentials 239
sensemaking 573
seven-stage model 312
shadowing 219–220
signal detection theory 44
signaling theory 172
simple selection 453
simulator sickness 522
situated action 316
situated use 285
sketching 552–555
Sketchpad 14
skill development 98
skill transfer 98
skills, rules, and knowledge 649–650
smartwatch 50, 169
smooth pursuit 52
social computing 5
social gap 158
social information processing theory 12, 172
social media 21, 199, 232, 237, 249, 255
social networks 144, 173–176
social norms 177
social presence 169, 173
social psychology 30
social structure 381
social–technical gap 142
software design 667
software development 7, 9, 16, 667–680
software architecture 667
solution-neutral problem statement 602, 625–626
speech 437
speech-generating devices 334
speech recognition 15, 421, 688–691
speed–accuracy trade-off 65, 69–70
stakeholders 189–190
state diagram 676–677
statistical power 190
statistical significance testing 762–766
steering law 64, 79
stimulus–response compatibility 78
stochastic optimized submovement model 72
Supple++ 335–336
SWIFT 653
Superbook 709–710
support vector machine 700–701
surprisal 293
surveillance 254
survey research 229–248
   analytic 233
   cross-sectional 234
   longitudinal 234
sustainability 711–712
switch 417–418
synchronicity 162
system administrator 222–223
system boundary 612, 646
system diagram 614–616
system mapping 612–617
systems thinking 603–604, 607–621
System Usability Scale 330–331, 710

tacit knowledge 185
tactition 40–41
task analysis 12
task diagram 612–613
technology probes 384, 774
technology push 20
theory of interaction 279–281
TikTok 197
Twitter 22
tailoring 378–379
tangible user interface 22, 514–517
target acquisition 65, 301, 304–305
target selection 48, 63, 67–68
target audience 188
task allocation 340, 342
task analysis 267–270
   hierarchical 268–270
task model 267–268
task-technology fit 332
Technology Acceptance Model 331–332
technology push 109
territoriality 149, 219
text editing 33, 460–461
text entry 27, 90, 281–283, 299–300, 458–461
think-aloud study 713, 741–748
Tinder 174
thematic analysis 211–212
theory of mind 155–156
thick description 221
threat model 662
tool use 284, 325–338
toolkit 671
touchpad 416
touchscreen 7, 22
   resistive touchscreen 413–414
   capacitive touchscreen 414
traceability 275
transduction 37, 40, 407
transfer function 408–409, 451–452, 465
transtheoretical model 119
triangulation 192, 273
turn adjacency 166
Twitter 255

Uber 197
ubiquitous computing 504–505, 510–514
UbiFit Garden 118
uncertain control 417–421
undo 16, 678–679
unobtrusive research 249–258
usable security 661–662

usability 10, 325, 327–231, 397–398
usability engineering 587–592
usability evaluation
    Automated 735–736
usability test 713
usability problem 724
Usenet 161
use cases 274
user-centered design 534–535
user engagement questionnaire 236
User Motivation Inventory 117
user segments 188
utility 325–327
UX curve 135

variable
    dependent 749, 758–759
    independent 749, 754–755
validation 16, 222, 603, 639, 642
validity 193, 246, 329, 714
    construct 246
    ecological 770
    external 246
    internal 246
    statistical conclusion 246
value estimation 87
value-sensitive design 113, 539–541
vending machines 58
ventriloquist effect, the 42
verbal protocol 742, 747–748
verifiability 275
verification 16, 273, 275, 603, 639–642
video conferencing 163
vigilance 352

virtual reality 3, 31–32, 39, 160, 433–435, 520–522
visibility 313, 488–489
vision 41
    active 57
    peripheral 37, 50–51, 57
    foveated 50–51
visual clutter 60
visual encoding 427–430
visual field of view 50
visual grouping 55
visual illusion 42
visual primitives 49
visual programming language 674–676
visual saliency 12, 58–59
visual system 42, 49–52
Viviani's power law of curvature 80–81
VuMan 625

wants 114
Weber's law 47
WebQuilt 252
Wikipedia 21–22, 383
wireframing 9
Wizard of Oz 691–692
word prediction 692–694
workload 90, 345
World of Warcraft 173
World Wide Web 17, 22

Xerox Star 13–14

Yahoo 22
YouTube 249–250, 257, 263